McGraw-Hill's Homework Manager, the most powerful Homework Manager system available.

- **Textbook specific exercises and problems**
- **Automatically-graded assignments and analysis**
- **Immediate grading and feedback for students**
- **Algorithmic exercises and problems**
- **Instructor course management tools**

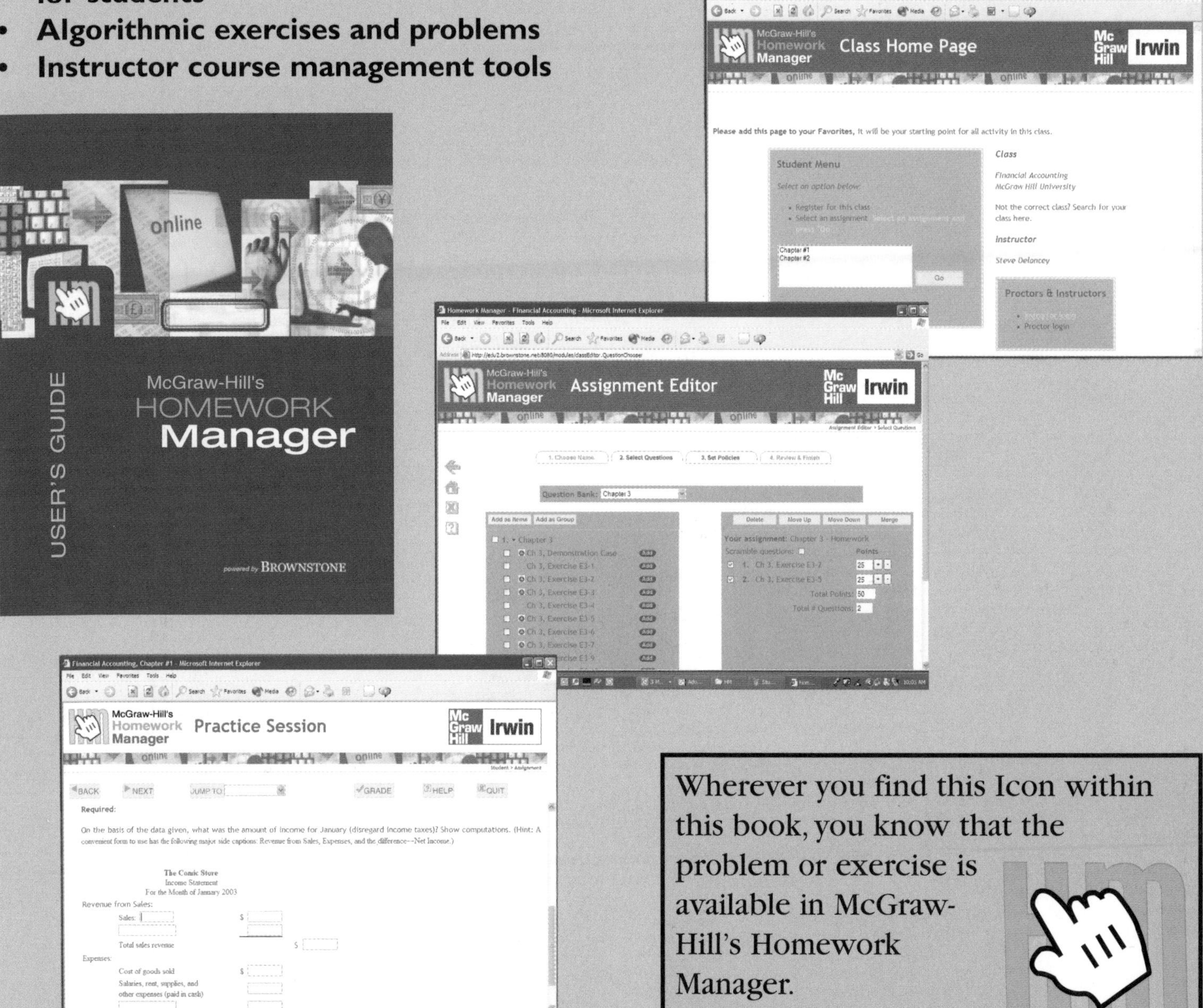

Wherever you find this Icon within this book, you know that the problem or exercise is available in McGraw-Hill's Homework Manager.

Please visit www.mhhe.com/hm, for a guided tour of Homework Manager and to experience Homework Manager content.

edition

Volume I Chapters 1–12

Fundamental Accounting Principles

Kermit D. Larson
University of Texas at Austin

John J. Wild
University of Wisconsin at Madison

Barbara Chiappetta
Nassau Community College

Boston Burr Ridge, IL Dubuque, IA Madison, WI New York
San Francisco St. Louis Bangkok Bogotá Caracas Kuala Lumpur
Lisbon London Madrid Mexico City Milan Montreal New Delhi
Santiago Seoul Singapore Sydney Taipei Toronto

To my wife **Nancy.**
To my wife **Gail** and children, **Kimberly, Jonathan, Stephanie,** and **Trevor.**
To my husband **Bob,** my sons **Michael** and **David,** and my **mother.**

FUNDAMENTAL ACCOUNTING PRINCIPLES
Published by McGraw-Hill/Irwin, a business unit of The McGraw-Hill Companies, Inc., 1221 Avenue of the Americas, New York, NY, 10020.

This book is printed on acid-free paper.

domestic 1 2 3 4 5 6 7 8 9 0 DOW/DOW 0 9 8 7 6 5 4 3
international 1 2 3 4 5 6 7 8 9 0 DOW/DOW 0 9 8 7 6 5 4 3

ISBN 0-07-251243-1 (combined edition)
ISBN 0-07-287003-6 (volume 1, chapters 1–12)
ISBN 0-07-287002-8 (volume 2, chapters 12–25)
ISBN 0-07-286993-3 (volume 1 with working papers, chapters 1–12)
ISBN 0-07-287016-8 (volume 2 with working papers, chapters 12–25)
ISBN 0-07-286999-2 (Principles of Financial Accounting, chapters 1–17)

Editorial director: *Brent Gordon*
Publisher: *Stewart Mattson*
Sponsoring editor: *Steve Schuetz*
Developmental editor I: *Kelly Odom*
Marketing manager: *Richard Kolasa*
Senior producer, Media technology: *Ed Przyzycki*
Senior project manager: *Lori Koetters*
Senior production supervisor: *Michael R. McCormick*
Lead designer: *Matthew Baldwin*
Photo research coordinator: *Judy Kausal*
Photo researcher: *Sarah Evertson*
Lead supplement producer: *Becky Szura*
Senior digital content specialist: *Brian Nacik*
Cover designer: *Matthew Baldwin*
Cover image: © *Corbis Images*
Typeface: *10.5/12 Times Roman*
Compositor: *The GTS Companies/York, PA Campus*
Printer: *R.R. Donnelley*

Library of Congress Cataloging-in-Publication Data

Larson, Kermit D.
Fundamental accounting principles / Kermit D. Larson, John J. Wild, Barbara Chiappetta.—17th ed.
p. cm.
A variety of multi-media instructional aids are available to support the text.
Includes index.
ISBN 0-07-251243-1 (alk. paper)
1. Accounting. I. Wild, John J. II. Chiappetta, Barbara. III. Title.
HF5635.P975 2005 2003061454
657—dc22

INTERNATIONAL EDITION ISBN 0-07-111123-9

www.mhhe.com

The first edition of Fundamental Accounting Principles was published fifty years ago, into a world very different from the one we live in today.

Technological tools that have reshaped the accounting profession—handheld computers, telecommunications, the Internet—could scarcely have been imagined by the men and women filling in ledgers or punching figures into adding machines. What they had were principles: tried-and-true rules and practices for collecting and interpreting information comprehensively, accurately, and responsibly.

Technology makes certain accounting functions easier, but students require a firm grounding in principles to become good business people—in any era. Teaching these principles in a way that is engaging to students while providing instructors with the support they need has been the goal of Fundamental Accounting Principles since the first copy rolled off the press.

Over the years instructors have turned to Fundamental Accounting Principles confident that they have selected the most accurate, best organized, and best written book on the market. Feedback on the book's pedagogy, real world examples, and assignment materials has always been outstanding. We've long believed in doing whatever it takes to keep students engaged, from creating interesting chapter opening vignettes to integrating leading-edge technology tools.

With fifty years of success and the expertise of our talented author team, **Fundamental Accounting Principles achieves new heights in student motivation, creative pedagogy, technology integration, and end-of-chapter material.**

Thank you for choosing Fundamental Accounting Principles. Here's to the next fifty years!

Fundamental Accounting Principles Rates #1

As with the past fifty years, we actively solicited your feedback when planning the 17th edition of Fundamental Accounting Principles (FAP). Independent research* confirmed what we already knew: **Instructors find FAP more satisfying to use than *any* other principles textbook.**

"It (FAP) is the best text I have ever used (in 15 years of teaching). It is the best resource text available for my students to keep and include in their professional library after the course."
— L. Hass, Glen Oaks Community College

Top Five Textbooks	Rated as Very Satisfied or Satisfied by Instructors	Mean Rating*
FAP, Larson/Wild/Chiappetta	100%	**4.46**
Competitor #1	75%	3.83
Competitor #2	64%	3.83
Competitor #3	60%	3.76
Competitor #4	47%	3.79

**Instructors ranked books from very dissatisfied (1) to very satisfied (5).*

The choice is clear: of the five best-selling principles books, FAP scores consistently highest in user satisfaction.

Fundamental Accounting Principles also rates #1 with instructors surveyed† in each of the following key areas:

#1 in Accuracy
#1 in Clarity
#1 in Pedagogy
#1 in Organization
#1 in Real-World Examples
#1 in Problems and Exercises
#1 in Supplements

And remember, a book that satisfies your needs is that much more likely to satisfy your students' needs as well.

"With the help of the book, my instructor, and especially the FAP CD-ROM, I am excelling in the class and like it so much I am considering becoming an Accounting major myself! Thanks and keep up the good work!"
— Aimee Liddell, Student, Liberty University

†Independent study conducted by Professional Research Group, February 2003.

Kermit D. Larson is the Arthur Andersen & Co. Alumni Professor of Accounting Emeritus at the University of Texas at Austin. He served as chairman of the University of Texas, Department of Accounting and was visiting professor at Tulane University. His scholarly articles have been published in a variety of journals, including The Accounting Review, Journal of Accountancy, and Abacus. He is the author of several books, including Financial Accounting and Fundamentals of Financial and Managerial Accounting, both published by McGraw-Hill/Irwin.

Professor Larson is a member of the American Accounting Association, the Texas Society of CPAs, and the American Institute of CPAs. His positions with the AAA have included vice president, southwest regional vice president, and chairperson of several committees, including the Committee of Concepts and Standards. He was a member of the committee that planned the first AAA doctoral consortium and served as its director.

Professor Larson served as president of the Richard D. Irwin Foundation. He also served on the Accounting Accreditation Committee and on the Accounting Standards Committee of the AACSB. He was a member of the Constitutional Drafting Committee of the Federation of Schools of Accountancy and a member of the Commission on Professional Accounting Education. He has been an expert witness on cases involving mergers, antitrust litigation, consolidation criteria, franchise taxes, and expropriation of assets by foreign governments. Professor Larson served on the Board of Directors and Executive Committee of Tekcon, Inc., and on the National Accountants Advisory Board of Safe-Guard Business Systems. In his leisure time, he enjoys skiing and is an avid sailor and golfer.

John J. Wild is a professor of accounting and the Robert and Monica Beyer Distinguished Professor at the University of Wisconsin at Madison. He previously held appointments at Michigan State University and the University of Manchester in England. He received his BBA, MS, and PhD from the University of Wisconsin.

Professor Wild teaches accounting courses at both the undergraduate and graduate levels. He has received the Mabel W. Chipman Excellence-in-Teaching Award, the departmental Excellence-in-Teaching Award, and the Teaching Excellence Award from the 2003 graduation class at the University of Wisconsin. He also received the Beta Alpha Psi and Roland F. Salmonson Excellence-in Teaching Award from Michigan State University. Professor Wild is a past KPMG Peat Marwick National Fellow and is a recipient of fellowships from the American Accounting Association and the Ernst and Young Foundation.

Professor Wild is an active member of the American Accounting Association and its sections. He has served on several committees of these organizations, including the Outstanding Accounting Educator Award, Wildman Award, National Program Advisory, Publications, and Research Committees. Professor Wild is author of Financial Accounting and Financial Statement Analysis, both published by McGraw-Hill/Irwin. His research appears in The Accounting Review, Journal of Accounting Research, Journal of Accounting and Economics, Contemporary Accounting Research, Journal of Accounting, Auditing and Finance, Journal of Accounting and Public Policy, and other business periodicals. He is past associate editor of Contemporary Accounting Research and has served on several editorial boards including The Accounting Review.

Professor Wild, his wife, and four children enjoy travel, music, sports, and community activities.

Barbara Chiappetta received her BBA in Accountancy and MS in Education from Hofstra University and is a tenured full professor at Nassau Community College. For the past 17 years, she has been an active executive board member of the Teachers of Accounting at Two-Year Colleges (TACTYC), serving 10 years as vice president and as president from 1993 through 1999. As an active member of the American Accounting Association, she has served on the Northeast Regional Steering Committee, chaired the Curriculum Revision Committee of the Two-Year Section, and participated in numerous national committees.

In 1998, Professor Chiappetta was inducted into the American Accounting Association Hall of Fame for the Northeast Region. She received the Nassau Community College dean of instruction's Faculty Distinguished Achievement Award in 1995. Professor Chiappetta was honored with the State University of New York Chancellor's Award for Teaching Excellence in 1997. As a confirmed believer in the benefits of active learning pedagogy, Professor Chiappetta has authored Student Learning Tools, an active learning workbook for a first-year accounting course, published by McGraw-Hill/Irwin.

In her leisure time, Professor Chiappetta enjoys tennis and participates on a U.S.T.A. team. She also enjoys the challenge of bridge. Her husband, Robert, is an entrepreneur in the leisure sport industry. She has two sons—Michael, a lawyer, specializing in intellectual property law in New York, and David, a composer, pursuing a career in music for film in Los Angeles.

Fundamental Accounting Principles, 17e

The principles course is crucial for accounting majors and non-majors alike. It is a student's first step into the world of accounting, one which quickly immerses them in unfamiliar and challenging new concepts.

Much of your students' future success in both accounting and business is determined in the time spent in the principles course. Will your students struggle with this new material? Or will they understand that accounting is a vital discipline relevant to any career, and use that knowledge to **achieve new heights of success** in business and throughout their lives?

Fundamental Accounting Principles has always been dedicated to presenting accounting concepts as vital tools that anyone can learn to successfully use. The 17th edition expands on this traditional strength by especially focusing on three areas: **student engagement, technology, and end-of-chapter material**.

FAP 17e portrays accounting as it truly is—a language of business communication that is vital to student success.

"FAP has good coverage for [the Principles course] and excellent exercises, problems, and end-of-chapter materials."
— S. McClure, Tri-County Tech

New heights in student engagement

Instructors repeatedly raise a common concern: the biggest hurdle they face is getting students interested and motivated in the materials. FAP provides solutions. It is more engaging and student-friendly than any competing book, from the book's eye-catching design to its comprehensive and stimulating end-of-chapter material. Each new book includes the actual shareholders' report from Krispy Kreme Doughnuts, which gets real financial data in students' hands. Moreover, engaging chapter-opening vignettes focus on small businesses and entrepreneurs to show how accounting knowledge is a springboard to success.

> "I think FAP does a better job motivating and sustaining student interest in accounting."
> **— L. Kolar, Bucks County Community College**

New heights in technology

Match our technology assets against those of any other book, and we're confident you'll agree: FAP's technology is, hands-down, the best in the market.

- **Carol Yachts General Ledger and Peachtree Complete Accounting 2004**
- **ALEKS for Financial Accounting and ALEKS for the Accounting Cycle**
- **Mcgraw-Hill's Homework Manager**
- **Topic Tackler**
- **Online Learning Center**

To learn more about these and other technology enhancements, see page xi.

New heights of end-of-chapter material

FAP's end-of-chapter content is tightly coordinated with the main body of the chapter. Icons for C.A.P. learning objectives make it easy for students to flip back in the chapter to a particular discussion, or to pick up the solution strategy for a specific assignment. In addition, FAP takes technology integration to a new level with two powerful and popular study aids, Homework Manager and Topic Tackler, both specifically written to coordinate with FAP. We also revised and expanded the two problem sets for every chapter of FAP, with a third set available on the text's Online Learning Center.

By addressing students in language that speaks to them, by providing your class with market-leading technology support, and by ensuring the textbook package is strong in the areas you rely on most, FAP helps you ***achieve new heights of success*** in the classroom—and beyond.

Decision Center

Whether we prepare, analyze, or apply accounting information, one skill remains essential: decision making. To help develop good decision-making habits *and* to illustrate the relevance of accounting, FAP uses a unique pedagogical framework called the Decision Center. This framework is comprised of a variety of approaches and subject areas, giving students insight into every aspect of business decision making. Answers to Decision Maker and Ethics boxes are at the end of each chapter.

A decision icon calls out all relevant material within chapters, whether it's a boxed item or end-of-chapter item.

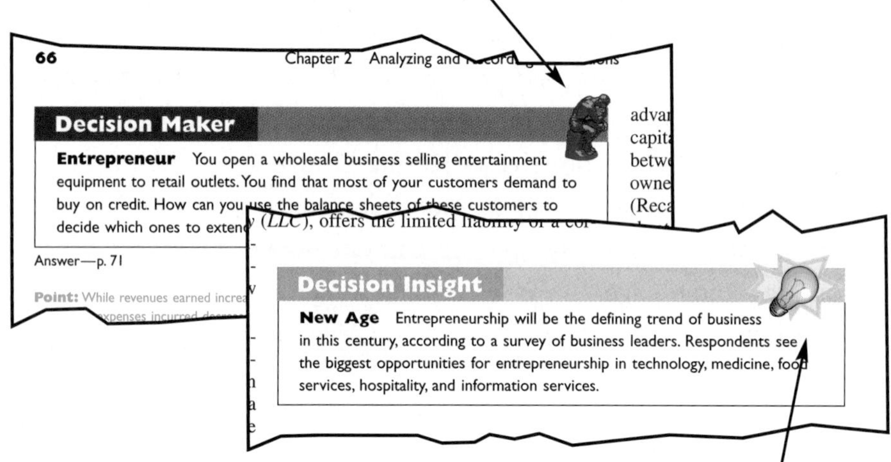
66 Chapter 2 Analyzing and Recording Transactions

Decision Maker

Entrepreneur You open a wholesale business selling entertainment equipment to retail outlets. You find that most of your customers demand to buy on credit. How can you use the balance sheets of these customers to decide which ones to exten[d]

Answer—p. 71

Point: While revenues earned increa[se] ... expenses incurred decrea[se] ...

Decision Insight

New Age Entrepreneurship will be the defining trend of business in this century, according to a survey of business leaders. Respondents see the biggest opportunities for entrepreneurship in technology, medicine, food services, hospitality, and information services.

An entrepreneurial icon calls out all relevant material within chapters, whether it's an opening vignette, box, or end-of-chapter assignment.

> "The Decision sidebars are one of the particular strengths of the text. They help the student stop and think about what he or she has read or can be used by the professor to stimulate discussion when introducing a topic. They are excellent tools!"
> **— M. Conway, Kingsborough Community College**

CAP Model

The Conceptual/Analytical/Procedural (CAP) Model allows courses to be specially designed to meet your teaching needs or those of a diverse faculty. This model identifies learning objectives, textual materials, assignments, and test items by C, A, or P, allowing different instructors to teach from the same materials, yet easily customize their courses toward a conceptual, analytical, or procedural approach (or a combination thereof) based on personal preferences.

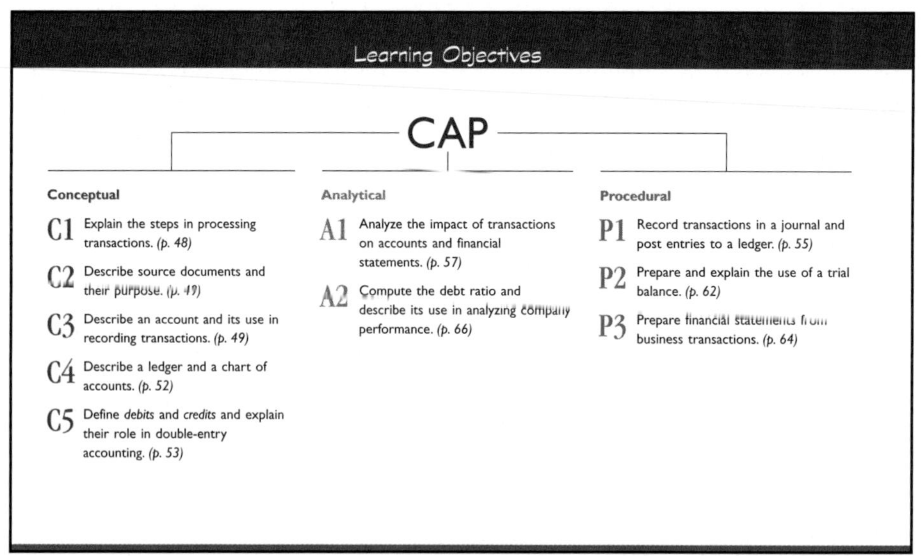
Learning Objectives

CAP

Conceptual

C1 Explain the steps in processing transactions. *(p. 48)*

C2 Describe source documents and their purpose. *(p. 49)*

C3 Describe an account and its use in recording transactions. *(p. 49)*

C4 Describe a ledger and a chart of accounts. *(p. 52)*

C5 Define *debits* and *credits* and explain their role in double-entry accounting. *(p. 53)*

Analytical

A1 Analyze the impact of transactions on accounts and financial statements. *(p. 57)*

A2 Compute the debt ratio and describe its use in analyzing company performance. *(p. 66)*

Procedural

P1 Record transactions in a journal and post entries to a ledger. *(p. 55)*

P2 Prepare and explain the use of a trial balance. *(p. 62)*

P3 Prepare financial statements from business transactions. *(p. 64)*

in Pedagogy

Chapter Preview Flow Chart

New to the 17th edition, this feature provides a handy textual/visual guide at the start of every chapter. Students can now begin their reading with a clear understanding of what they will learn and when, allowing them to stay more focused and organized along the way.

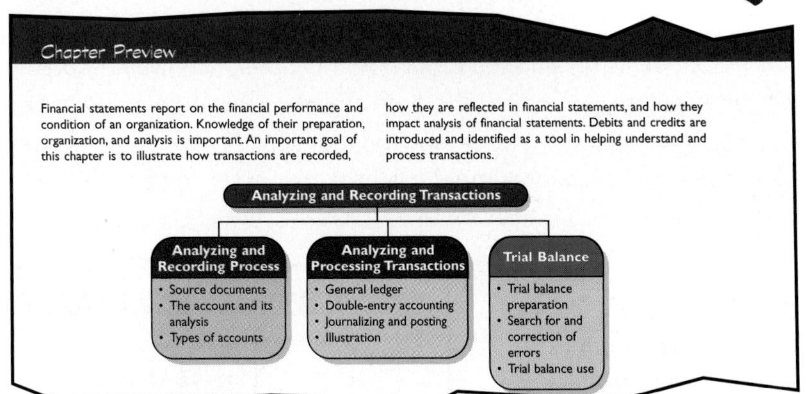

Chapter Preview

Financial statements report on the financial performance and condition of an organization. Knowledge of their preparation, organization, and analysis is important. An important goal of this chapter is to illustrate how transactions are recorded, how they are reflected in financial statements, and how they impact analysis of financial statements. Debits and credits are introduced and identified as a tool in helping understand and process transactions.

Quick Check

These short question/answer features reinforce the material immediately preceding them. They allow the reader to pause and reflect on the topics described, then receive immediate feedback before going on to new topics. Answers are provided at the end of each chapter.

Quick Check

8. What types of transactions increase equity? What types decrease equity?
9. Why are accounting systems called *double entry*?
10. For each transaction, double-entry accounting requires which of the following: (*a*) Debits to asset accounts must create credits to liability or equity accounts, (*b*) a debit to a liability account must create a credit to an asset account, or (*c*) total debits must equal total credits.
11. An owner invests $15,000 cash along with equipment having a market value of $23,000 in a proprietorship. Prepare the necessary journal entry.
12. Explain what a compound journal entry is.
13. Why are posting reference numbers entered in the journal when entries are posted to ledger accounts?

Answers—p. 73

"I think FAP does a better job with learning objectives than my book because of the CAP learning objectives organization."
— S. McClure, Tri-County Tech

FastForward

FastForward is a case that takes students through the Accounting Cycle, chapters 1-4. The FastForward icon is placed in the margin at key points when this case is discussed.

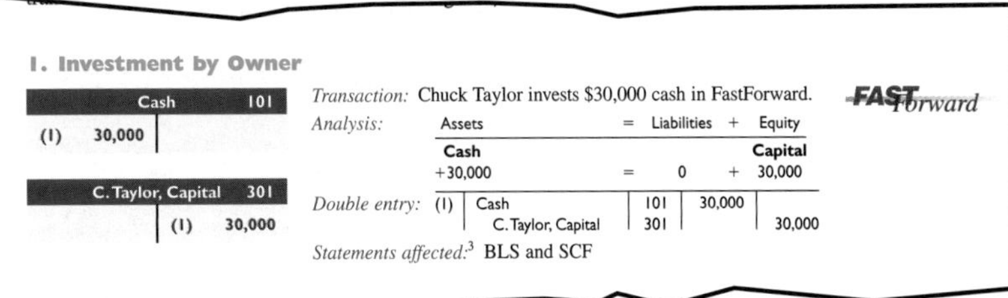

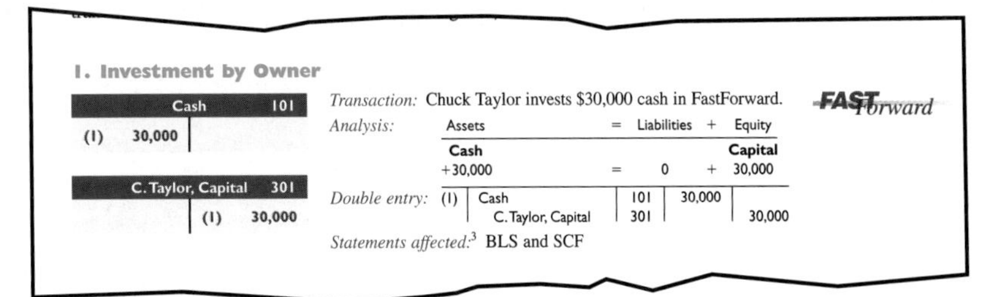

1. Investment by Owner

Cash	101
(1) 30,000	

C. Taylor, Capital	301
	(1) 30,000

Transaction: Chuck Taylor invests $30,000 cash in FastForward.

Analysis:

Assets	=	Liabilities	+	Equity
Cash				Capital
+30,000	=	0	+	30,000

Double entry:

(1)	Cash	101	30,000	
	C. Taylor, Capital	301		30,000

Statements affected:[3] BLS and SCF

Marginal Student Annotations

These annotations provide students with additional hints, tips, and examples to help them more fully understand the concepts and retain what they have learned. They also include notes on global implications of accounting and further examples.

cord for each customer, but for now, we
s and decreases in receivables in a sin-

itten promise of another entity to pay a
the holder of the note. A company hold-
s an asset that is recorded in a Note (or

are assets that represent prepayments of
expenses are later incurred, the amounts
ccounts. Common examples of prepaid

Point: A college parking fee is a prepaid account from the student's standpoint. At the beginning of the term, it represents an asset that entitles a student to park on or near campus. The benefits of the parking fee expire as the term progresses. At term-end, prepaid parking (asset) equals zero as it has been entirely recorded as parking expense.

Achieving New Heights in

Once a student has finished reading the chapter, how well he or she retains the material can depend greatly on the questions, exercises, and problems that reinforce it. FAP has consistently led the way in comprehensive, accurate end-of-chapter exercises. Independent survey research reports that instructors are more satisfied with FAP's end-of-chapter materials than any other textbook—and the 17th edition is no exception.

Demonstration Problems present both a problem and a complete solution, allowing students to review the entire problem-solving process and achieve success in the principles course.

Demonstration Problem

(*Note:* This problem extends the demonstration problem of Chapter ... ning. Sy... curred d...

a. On A...
b. On A...
c. On A...
d. On A...
e. On A... week...
f. On A...
g. On A...
h. On A...
i. Cash...
j. On A...
k. On A...

Chapter 2

Planning the Solution

- Analyze each transaction and use the debit and credit rules...
- Post each debit and each credit from journal entries to the... each amount in the posting reference (PR) columns of the...
- Calculate each account balance and list the accounts with t...
- Verify that total debits in the trial balance equal total credit...
- To prepare the income statement, identify revenues and ex... ment, compute the difference, and label the result as *net in*...
- Use information in the ledger to prepare the statement of o...
- Use information in the ledger to prepare the balance sheet.
- Calculate the debt ratio by dividing total liabilities by total...
- Analyze the future transactions to identify the accounts affe...

...transactions to identify the accounts affected and apply debit and credit...

Solution to Demonstration Problem

1. General journal entries:

GENERAL JOURNAL — Page 1

Date	Account Titles and Explanation	PR	Debit	Credit
Aug. 1	Cash	101	3,000	
	Store Equipment	165	15,000	
	S. Workman, Capital	301		18,000
	Owner's investment.			
2	Furniture	161	600	
	Cash	101		600
	Purchased furniture for cash.			
3	Rent Expense	640	500	
	Cash	101		500
	Paid rent for August.			
4	Store Equipment	165	1,200	
	Note Payable	240		1,200
	Purchased additional equipment on credit.			
15	Cash	101	825	
	Haircutting Services Re...			

Chapter Summaries provide students with a review organized by learning objectives. Chapter Summaries are a component of the CAP model (see page viii), which recaps each conceptual, analytical, and procedural objective.

Key Terms are bolded in the text and repeated at the end of the chapter with page numbers indicating their location. The 17th edition now includes a Glossary of key terms at the back of the book. Key Terms are also available as online flash cards at the book's Website.

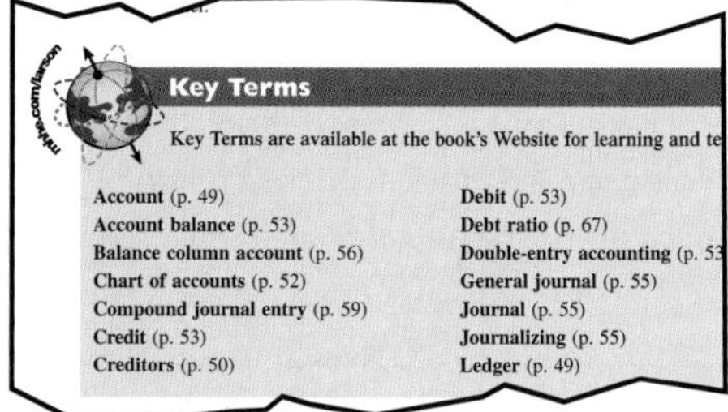

Key Terms

Key Terms are available at the book's Website for learning and te...

Account (p. 49)
Account balance (p. 53)
Balance column account (p. 56)
Chart of accounts (p. 52)
Compound journal entry (p. 59)
Credit (p. 53)
Creditors (p. 50)
Debit (p. 53)
Debt ratio (p. 67)
Double-entry accounting (p. 53...
General journal (p. 55)
Journal (p. 55)
Journalizing (p. 55)
Ledger (p. 49)

Quick Study are short exercises that often focus on one learning objective. The numerical ones are included in Homework Manager. There are usually 8-10 Quick Study assignments per chapter.

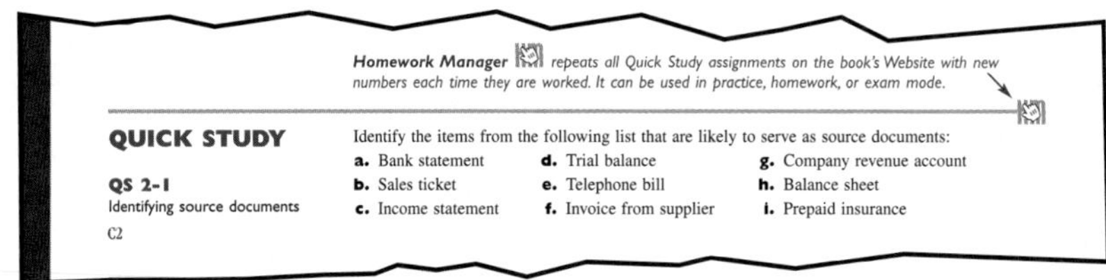

Homework Manager *repeats all Quick Study assignments on the book's Website with new numbers each time they are worked. It can be used in practice, homework, or exam mode.*

QUICK STUDY

QS 2-1
Identifying source documents
C2

Identify the items from the following list that are likely to serve as source documents:

a. Bank statement
b. Sales ticket
c. Income statement
d. Trial balance
e. Telephone bill
f. Invoice from supplier
g. Company revenue account
h. Balance sheet
i. Prepaid insurance

Exercises are one of FAP's ongoing strengths, and the 17th edition again shows its competitive advantage. There are about 10-15 per chapter and most are included in Homework Manager.

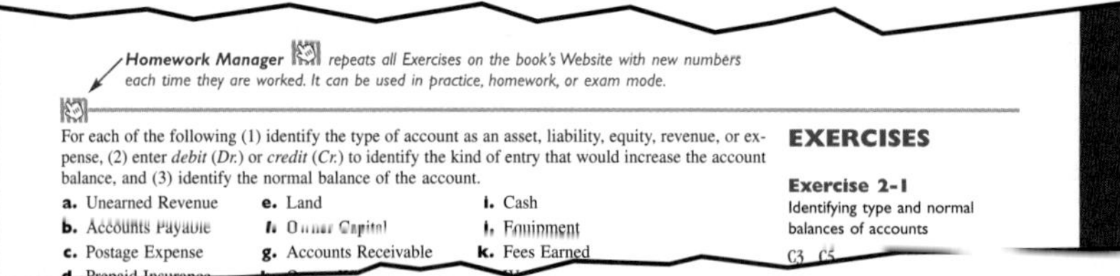

Homework Manager *repeats all Exercises on the book's Website with new numbers each time they are worked. It can be used in practice, homework, or exam mode.*

For each of the following (1) identify the type of account as an asset, liability, equity, revenue, or expense, (2) enter *debit (Dr.)* or *credit (Cr.)* to identify the kind of entry that would increase the account balance, and (3) identify the normal balance of the account.

a. Unearned Revenue
b. Accounts Payable
c. Postage Expense
e. Land
f. Owner Capital
g. Accounts Receivable
i. Cash
j. Equipment
k. Fees Earned

EXERCISES

Exercise 2-1
Identifying type and normal balances of accounts
C3 C5

Problem Sets A & B are proven problems that can be assigned as homework or for in-class projects. Problem Set C is available on the book's Website. All problems are coded according to the CAP model (see page viii), and many are included in Homework Manager.

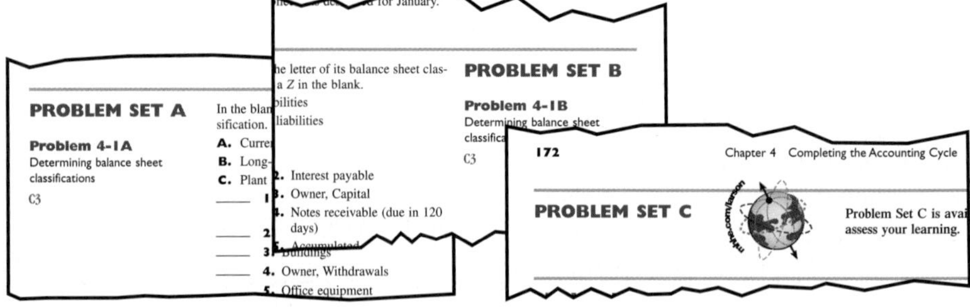

PROBLEM SET A

Problem 4-1A
Determining balance sheet classifications
C3

In the blan... sification.
A. Curre...
B. Long-...
C. Plant...

...for January.

...e letter of its balance sheet clas-... a Z in the blank.
...ilities
...liabilities

1. Interest payable
2. Owner, Capital
3. Notes receivable (due in 120 days)
4. Owner, Withdrawals
5. Office equipment

PROBLEM SET B

Problem 4-1B
Determining balance sheet classifica...
C3

172 Chapter 4 Completing the Accounting Cycle

PROBLEM SET C

Problem Set C is avai... assess your learning.

End-of-Chapter Materials

Beyond the Numbers exercises encourage your students to use the figures and understand their meaning, learning how accounting data applies to a variety of business situations. These creative and fun exercises are all new or updated, and are divided into 10 sections:

- Reporting in Action
- Comparative Analysis
- Ethics Challenge
- Communicating in Practice
- Taking It to the Net
- Teamwork in Action
- Hitting the Road—NEW
- Business Week Activity
- Entrepreneurial Decision
- Global Decision—NEW

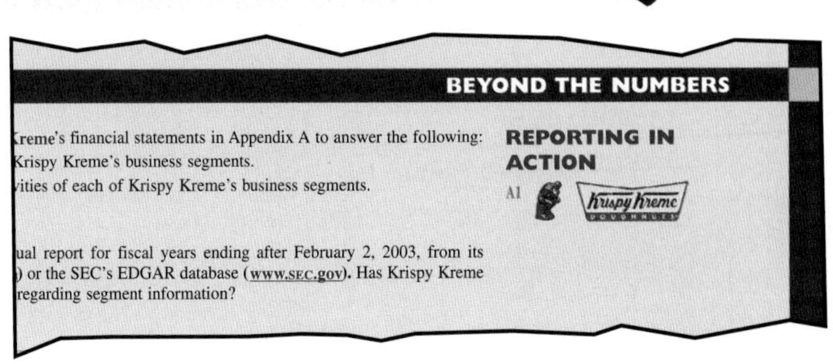

BEYOND THE NUMBERS

REPORTING IN ACTION

A1

Kreme's financial statements in Appendix A to answer the following:
Krispy Kreme's business segments.
vities of each of Krispy Kreme's business segments.

ual report for fiscal years ending after February 2, 2003, from its
) or the SEC's EDGAR database (www.sec.gov). Has Krispy Kreme
regarding segment information?

Serial Problems use a continuous running case study to illustrate chapter concepts in a familiar context. Serial Problems can be followed continuously from the first chapter or picked up at any later point in the book; enough information is provided to ensure students can get right to work.

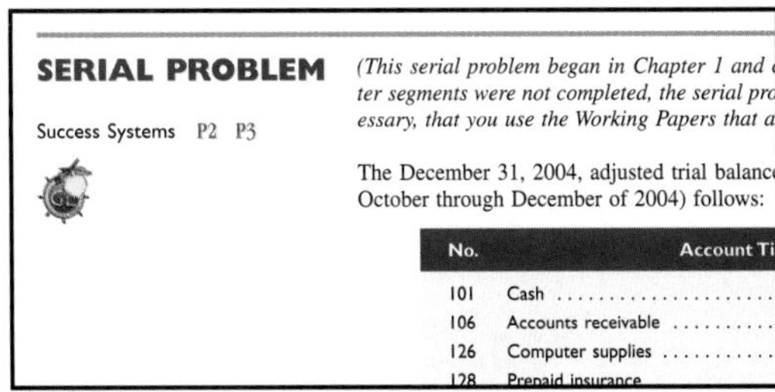

SERIAL PROBLEM

Success Systems P2 P3

(This serial problem began in Chapter 1 and c
ter segments were not completed, the serial pro
essary, that you use the Working Papers that a

The December 31, 2004, adjusted trial balanc
October through December of 2004) follows:

No.	Account Ti
101	Cash ....
106	Accounts receivable ....
126	Computer supplies ....
128	Prepaid insurance

"Some of the overall strengths of FAP include clearly stated learning objectives. Each chapter is written in a clear, concise language supported by a lot of exhibits and appropriate end-of-chapter materials to reinforce the learning process."
— **M. Bentil, Pierce College**

The End of the Chapter Is Only the Beginning

FAP's valuable and proven assignments aren't just confined to the book. From problems that require technological solutions to materials found exclusively online, FAP's end-of-chapter material is fully integrated with its technology package.

- Quick Studies, Exercises, and Problems available on Homework Manager (see page xii) are marked with an icon.

- Problems supported by the all-new General Ledger Application Software or Peachtree are marked with an icon.

- The Online Learning Center (OLC) includes more *Taking It To The Net* exercises, Personal Interactive Quizzes, more Excel template assignments, and Problem Set C.

- Problems supported with Microsoft Excel templates are marked with an icon.

- Material that receives additional coverage (slide shows, videos, audio, etc.) in Topic Tackler is marked with an icon.

Put Away Your Red Pen

We've always prided ourselves on the accuracy of FAP's assignment materials, and the market confirms this. Independent research reports that instructors pointed to the accuracy of FAP's assignment materials as a key factor in their satisfaction with the book, much more than did instructors using competing books. The 17th edition continues that tradition of accuracy.

The authors extend special thanks to accuracy checkers **Marc Giullian**, Montana State University-Bozeman; **Suzanne King**, University of Charleston; **Barbara Schnathorst**, The Write Solution, Inc.; and **Jo Lynne Koehn**, Central Missouri State University.

Achieving New Heights in

In teaching and learning from FAP, the book itself is only the beginning. Our comprehensive technology package provides ample opportunity for both assessment and reinforcement, while offering valuable practice in learning and using the digital tools that are integral to the modern accounting and business workplace.

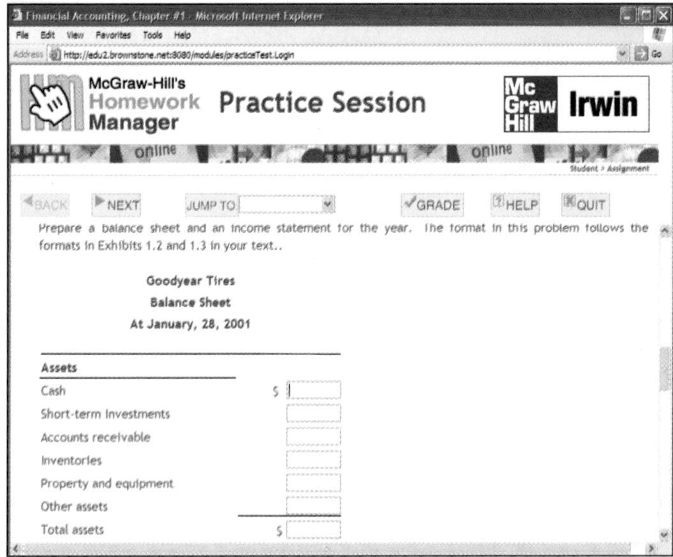

McGraw-Hill's Homework Manager

This Web-based study and review aid uses a sophisticated algorithm to generate "lookalike" versions of FAP's assignment materials. These new exercises and problems contain different values but are structured identically to those in FAP, allowing students to practice and refine their skills. The algorithm can generate infinite variations of any selected assignments, which also discourages sharing of answers.

Instructors can use Homework Manager to build custom homework assignments, tests, or quizzes that can be completed either online or with pencil and paper. Online assignments are graded automatically and the results stored in a secure online gradebook. Tests and quizzes prepared from Homework Manager overcome any inconsistencies between "test bank drawn" problems and the language and approach in the book—now there is complete consistency!

Homework Manager gives you:

- Textbook-specific quick studies, exercises, and problems
- Automatically-graded assignments and analysis for instructors
- Immediate grading and feedback for students
- Algorithmic-generated quick studies, exercises, and problems
- Instructor course management tools
- 100% consistency between test problems and the textbook

Quick Studies, Exercises, and Problems appearing in FAP that are reproduced in Homework Manager are marked with an icon.

"On the whole, in my opinion, FAP's activites are better and there are more of them."

— J. Miller, Mercer County Community College

Technology for Assessment and Learning

ALEKS®

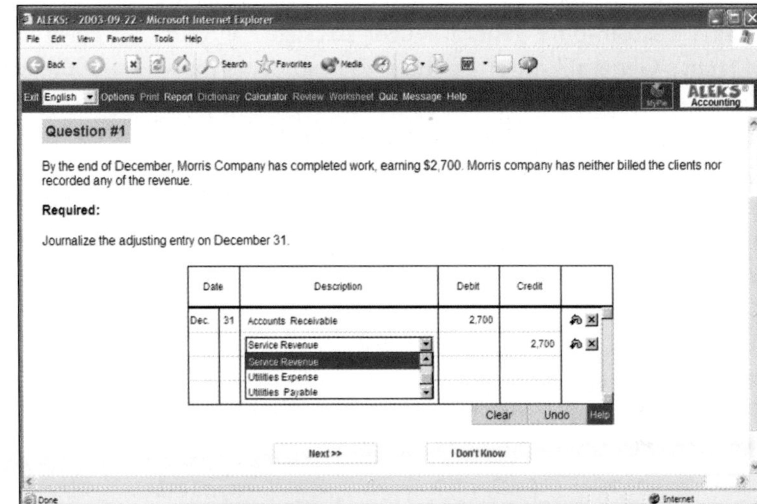

ALEKS® for the Accounting Cycle and ALEKS® for Financial Accounting

Available from McGraw-Hill over the World Wide Web, ALEKS (Assessment and LEarning in Knowledge Spaces) provides precise assessment and individualized instruction in the fundamental skills your students need to succeed in accounting.

ALEKS motivates your students because ALEKS can tell what a student knows, doesn't know, and is most ready to learn next. ALEKS does this using the ALEKS Assessment and Knowledge Space Theory as an artificial intelligence engine to exactly identify a student's knowledge of accounting. When students focus on precisely what they are ready to learn, they build the confidence and learning momentum that fuel success.

To learn more about adding ALEKS to your principles course, visit www.business.aleks.com.

GradeSummit

The online resource GradeSummit tells your students everything they need to know in order to study effectively. GradeSummit provides a series of practice tests written to coincide with FAP's coverage. Once a student has taken a particular test, GradeSummit returns a detailed results page showing exactly where the student did well and where he or she needs to improve. They can compare their results with those of their other classmates, or even with those of every other student using the text nationwide.

With that information, students can plan their studying to focus exclusively on their weak areas, without wasting effort on material they've already mastered. And they can come back to take a retest on those subjects later, comparing their new score with their previous efforts.

Carol Yacht's General Ledger and Peachtree Complete 2004 CD-ROM

Carol Yacht's General Ledger Software is McGraw-Hill/Irwin's custom-built general ledger package for FAP. Carol Yacht's General Ledger can help your students master every aspect of the general ledger, from inputting sales and cash receipts to calculating ratios for analysis or inventory valuations.

Carol Yacht's General Ledger allows students to review an entire report, and then double-click on any single transaction to review or edit it. All reports are immediately updated to reflect the revised figures. When it comes to learning how an individual transaction effects the outcome of financial reports, no other approach matches that of Carol Yacht's General Ledger.

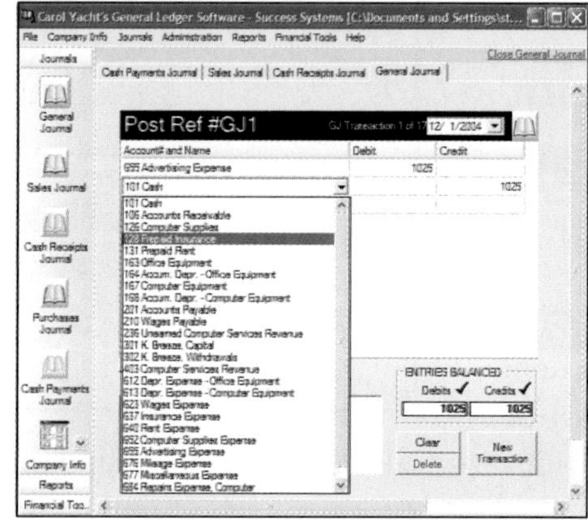

Also on Carol Yacht's General Ledger CD, students receive the educational version of Peachtree Complete 2004, along with templates containing data for many of FAP's exercises and problems. Familiarity with Peachtree Complete is essential for many students entering the job market, and Carol Yacht's Peachtree templates that accompany FAP 17e makes sure they get plenty of practice.

Students can use Carol Yacht's General Ledger to solve numerous problems from FAP; the data for these problems are already included on the Carol Yacht's General Ledger CD-ROM. You can even populate Carol Yacht's General Ledger with your own custom data.

Online Learning Center (OLC) with PowerWeb

www.mhhe.com/larson

More students are using online learning aids. That's why we offer an Online Learning Center (OLC) that follows FAP chapter by chapter. It doesn't require any building or maintenance on your part; it's ready to go the moment your students type in the address.

As your students study and learn from FAP, they can visit the OLC Website and work with a multitude of helpful tools:

- Tutorial
- Glossary
- NetTutor
- PowerWeb
- Chapter Objectives
- Chapter Overview
- Text Company Links
- Interactive Quizzes A & B
- Key Term Flashcards
- PowerPoint Presentation
- Additional appendices
- Cogg Hill Practice Set
- Updates
- Mobile Resources
- Audio Narrated PowerPoint
- Excel Template Assignments
- More *Taking It To The Net*
- Problem Set C
- Business Week Articles

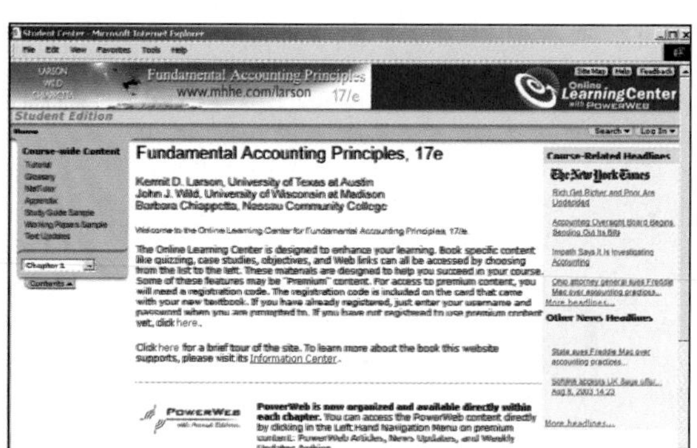

A secured Instructor Resource Center stores your essential course materials to save you prep time before class. Everything you need to run a lively classroom and an efficient course is included:

- Sample Syllabi
- Additional chapter materials
- Transition Notes
- Instructors Manual
- Solutions to Excel Template Assignments
- Cogg Hill Solutions Manual
- Updates
- Solutions Manual
- PowerPoint Presentations
- Textbook Company Links
- More *Taking It To The Net* Solutions
- Business Week Articles
- Problem Set C Solutions

Technology for Students

PowerWeb provides high quality, peer-reviewed content including up-to-date articles from leading periodicals and journals, current news, weekly updates with assessment, interactive exercises, Web research guide, study tips, and much more. PowerWeb is free with your FAP adoption.

Topic Tackler—FREE with new book

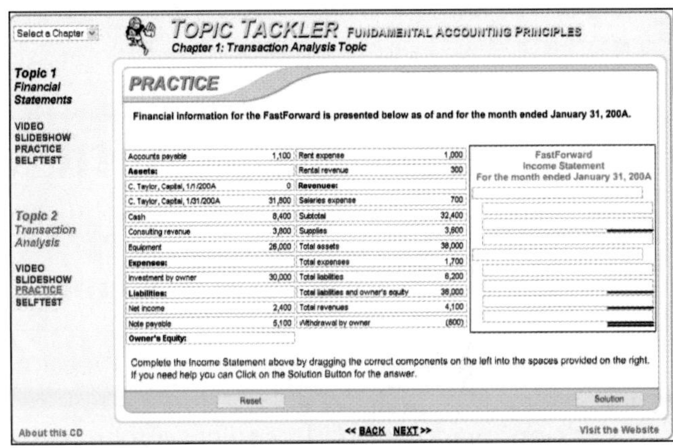

This software is a complete tutorial focusing on those areas in the principles of accounting course that give students the most trouble. Providing help on at least 2 key topics per chapter, this program delves into the material using the following learning aids:

- Video clips
- PowerPoint slide-shows (many include animations and/or audio)
- Drag-and-drop, fill-in-the-blank exercises
- Self-test quizzes

This highly engaging presentation will put your students in control of the most fundamental aspects of principles of accounting.

Concepts appearing in FAP that receive additional treatment in Topic Tackler are marked with an icon at the appropriate location in the margin of the page.

NetTutor™

NetTutor

NetTutor allows tutors and students to communicate with each other in a variety of ways:

- The Live Tutor Center via NetTutor's WWWhiteboard enables a tutor to hold an interactive on-line tutorial with several students, whose questions are placed in a queue and answered sequentially.
- The Q&A Center allows students to submit questions at any time and retrieve answers within 24 hours.
- The Archive Center allows students to browse for answers to previously asked questions. They can also search for questions pertinent to a particular topic. If they encounter an answer they do not understand, they can ask a follow-up question.

Students are issued 5 hours of free NetTutor time when they purchase a new copy of FAP. Additional time can be purchased in 5-hour increments.

In today's learning environment, a computer is as indispensible a tool as a blackboard or an overhead projector. McGraw-Hill/Irwin continues to lead in innovative classroom technology, and FAP's teaching tools put it far ahead of any other book.

Course Management

PageOut
McGraw-Hill's Course Management System

PageOut is the easiest way to create a Website for your accounting course.

There's no need for HTML coding, graphic design, or a thick how-to book. Just fill in a series of boxes with plain English and click on one of our professional designs. In no time, your course is online with a Website that contains your syllabus!

Should you need assistance in preparing your Website, we can help you. Our team of specialists is ready to take your course materials and build a custom Website to your specifications. Simply call a McGraw-Hill/Irwin PageOut specialist to start the process. (For information on how to do this, see "Superior Service" on page xvii.) Best of all, PageOut is **free** when you adopt FAP! To learn more, please visit www.pageout.net.

Third-Party Course Management Systems

For the ambitious instructor, we offer FAP content for complete online courses. To make this possible, we have joined forces with the most popular delivery platforms currently available. These platforms are designed for instructors who want complete control over course content and how it is presented to students. You can customize the FAP Online Learning Center content and author your own course materials. It's entirely up to you.

Products like WebCT, Blackboard, and eCollege all expand the reach of your course. Online discussion and message boards will now complement your office hours. Thanks to a sophisticated tracking system, you will know which students need more attention – even if they don't ask for help. That's because online testing scores are recorded and automatically placed in your grade book, and if a student is struggling with course-work, a special alert message lets you know.

Remember, FAP's content is flexible enough to use with any platform currently available. If your department or school is already using a platform, we can help. For information on McGraw-Hill/Irwin's course management supplements, including Instructor Advantage and Knowledge Gateway, see "Superior Service" on the next page.

Superior Service

No matter which online course solution you choose, you can count on the highest level of service. That's what sets McGraw-Hill apart. Once you choose FAP, our specialists offer free training and answer any question you have through the life of your adoption.

Instructor Advantage and Instructor Advantage Plus

Instructor Advantage is a special level of service McGraw-Hill offers in conjunction with WebCT and Blackboard. A team of platform specialists is always available, either by toll-free phone or e-mail, to ensure everything runs smoothly through the life of your adoption. Instructor Advantage is available free to all McGraw-Hill customers.

Instructor Advantage Plus is available to qualifying McGraw-Hill adopters (see your representative for details). **IA Plus** guarantees you a full day of on-site training by a Blackboard or WebCT specialist, for yourself and up to nine colleagues. Thereafter, you will enjoy the benefits of unlimited telephone and e-mail support throughout the life of your adoption. **IA Plus** users also have the opportunity to access the **McGraw-Hill Knowledge Gateway**.

Knowledge Gateway

Developed with the help of our partner Eduprise, the McGraw-Hill Knowledge Gateway is an all-purpose service and resource center for instructors teaching FAP online.

The First Level of **Knowledge Gateway** is available to all professors browsing the McGraw-Hill Higher Education Website, and consists of an introduction to OLC content, access to the first level of the Resource Library, technical support, and information on Instructional Design Services available through Eduprise.

The Second Level is password-protected and provides access to the expanded Resource Library, technical and pedagogical support for WebCT, Blackboard, and TopClass, the online Instructional Design helpdesk and an online discussion forum for users. The **Knowledge Gateway** provides a considerable advantage for teaching online—and it's only available through McGraw-Hill.

To see how these platforms can assist your online FAP course, visit www.mhhe.com/solutions.

Content Changes for

FAP's revisions are in response to feedback from both instructors and students. Many of these revisions are summarized below. Feedback suggests that FAP is the book instructors want to teach from and students want to learn from. Some overall revisions include:

- New chapter-opening flowchart
- Revised assignments throughout
- Updated ratio analyses
- New and revised entrepreneurial elements
- New assignments using chapter openers
- Serial problem running through nearly all chapters
- New Krispy Kreme annual report and comparisons to Tastykake, Grupo Bimbo (Mexican), and the industry
- New Harley-Davidson financial statements

Chapter 1

The Chocolate Farm NEW opener

New, early introduction to transaction analysis

Transaction analysis uses expanded accounting equation to aid student learning

Revised, early introduction to financial statements

New, early introduction to key accounting principles

Revised section on accounting and related careers

Revised table on compensation

Moved return-risk analysis and business activities to appendixes for instructor flexibility

Chapter 2

York Entertainment NEW opener

Streamlined and revised introduction to accounts

Revised discussion on analyzing and processing transactions

Revised section on preparing financial statements

Chapter 3

Mellies NEW opener

Streamlined discussion on adjusting accounts

New visual linkages from adjusting entries to the accounts

New presentation on preparing financial statements from trial balance

Chapter 4

Premier Snowskate NEW opener

Streamlined discussion of accounting work sheet

Revised Excel screen captures with acetates for work sheet

Shortened section on closing process

Reduced presentation on operating cycles

Chapter 5

Damani Dada NEW opener

New table summarizing merchandising entries

Revised description of credit terms and discounts

Revised and simplified presentation of income statement formats

Simplified descriptions of debit and credit memoranda

Chapter 6

FunKo NEW opener

New discussion on internal controls and inventory

New introduction to inventory cost flow assumptions

Added simplified journal entries to inventory computations

Revised discussion of "lower of cost or market"

Moved gross profit and retail inventory methods to appendix for instructor flexibility

Chapter 7

Rap-Up NEW opener

Revised visuals for special journals

Streamlined coverage of posting

Revised discussion of technology in accounting including ERP

Added new exercises on special journals without postings

Chapter 8

Dylan's Candy Bar NEW opener

Enhanced discussion on internal controls

New material on Internet fraud

Simplified presentation of voucher system of control

Streamlined discussion of bank reconciliation

Moved control of purchase discounts to appendix for instructor flexibility

Chapter 9

Manzi Metals NEW opener

New material on credit vs debit cards

Simplified discussion on disposing of receivables

Streamlined discussion on estimating bad debts

Deleted section on discounting notes receivable

Moved short-term investments to Chapter 15

Chapter 10

Queston Construction NEW opener

Simplified discussion of partial-year depreciation and changes in estimates

Shortened and simplified section on "Additional Expenditures"

Simplified section on exchange of similar assets

Revised discussion of intangible assets per new standards

Shortened section on goodwill and moved goodwill estimation to an appendix

Chapter 11
EEC NEW opener

Revised payroll liabilities for current tax rates

Shortened section on contingent liabilities

Removed noninterest-bearing notes from this chapter

Revised appendix on payroll records

Moved "income tax liabilities" to appendix for instructor flexibility

Chapter 12
Koch Entertainment NEW opener

Increased discussion of limited liability companies

Revised section for partner return on equity

Streamlined partnership liquidation

Chapter 13
Get Real Girl, Inc. NEW opener

Shortened introductory materials on corporations

Streamlined section on preferred stock

Shortened section on stock dividends

Streamlined reporting of discontinued operations

Simplified section on "changes in accounting principles"

Shortened sections on book value per share and dividend yield

Chapter 14
Noodles & Company NEW opener

New visual linkages from bond interest computations to amortization entries

Moved effective interest amortization to chapter appendix for instructor flexibility

Streamlined presentation on notes payable

Removed materials on noninterest-bearing notes

Chapter 15
TradeStation Group NEW opener

New, simplified organization for investments

New presentation of both short-term and long-term investments

New illustrations on adjustments for unrealized gains and losses on securities

Moved investments in international operations to appendix for instructor flexibility

Chapter 16
Atomic Toys NEW opener

Simplified preparation of statement of cash flows

New 3-stage process of analyzing investing and financing cash flows

Moved investments in international operations to appendix for instructor flexibility

Chapter 17
The Motley Fool NEW opener

Krispy Kreme vs Tastykake NEW comparative analysis

Streamlined section on common-size analysis

Chapter 18
Rap Snacks NEW opener

Streamlined flow of costs discussion with revised visuals

Expanded discussion of cost controls with service businesses

Revised presentation of manufacturing statement

Chapter 19
A. D. Morgan NEW opener

Streamlined discussion of overapplied and underapplied overhead

Expanded section on costing and pricing for service businesses

Chapter 20
All American Meats NEW opener

Simplified presentation of equivalent units of production

Streamlined discussion on costing for multiple departments

Chapter 21
Life Is Good NEW opener

Simplified discussion of activity-based costing

Streamlined section on joint costs

Chapter 22
Vosges Haut Chocolat NEW opener

Streamlined break-even point analysis

Chapter 23
Aquent NEW opener

Streamlined section on budget administration

Moved production and manufacturing budgets to appendix for instructor flexibility

Chapter 24
Technology Enabled Clothing NEW opener

Expanded discussion of service applications

Streamlined overhead cost variance analysis

Chapter 25
AnthroTronix NEW opener

Further emphasis on applied applications of managerial accounting

Expanded applications to service businesses

Instructor Supplements

Instructor's Resource CD-ROM

Volume 1: 0072869844

Volume 2: 0072870192

This is your all-in-one resource. It allows you to create custom presentations from your own materials or from FAP's text-specific materials provided in the CD's asset library:

- Solutions Manual
- Test Bank, Computerized Test Bank
- Instructor's Resource Manual
- PowerPoint® Presentations *Prepared by Jon A. Booker, Charles W. Caldwell, and Susan C. Galbreath.* Presentations illustrate crucial chapter concepts and procedures, and allow for custom-revision of lecture slides by instructors.
- Excel Templates and solutions
- Link to PageOut
- Video Clips

Solutions Manual

Volume 1: 0072869828 (Solutions Transparencies 0072869801)

Volume 2: 0072869909 (Solutions Transparencies 0072869887)

Written by John J. Wild and Jo Lynne Koehn.

Test Bank

Volume 1: 0072869798

Volume 2: 0072869895

Written by Marilyn Sagrillo and John J. Wild.

Brownstone Diploma 6.2 Computerized Test Bank

Available for Windows only, located on the Instructor's Resource CD-ROM.

Instructor's Resource Manual

Volume 1: 0072869836

Volume 2: 0072869917

Written by Barbara Chiappetta and Janice Klimek.

This manual contains (for each chapter) a Lecture Outline, a chart linking all assignment materials to Learning Objectives, a list of relevant active learning activities, and additional visuals with transparency masters. An electronic version is available on the Website and on the Instructor's Resource CD-ROM.

Financial and Managerial Accounting Video Library

Financial Videos: 0072376163

Managerial Videos: 0072376171

These short, action-oriented videos, developed by Dallas County Community College for the Accounting in Action distance-learning course, provide an impetus for lively classroom discussion. Tied closely to FAP's pedagogical framework, these videos avoid dry talking-head footage in favor of dynamic, documentary-style explorations of how businesses use accounting information.

Contributing Authors

The FAP Team wishes to thank the following contributors for their excellent work.

Jo Lynne Koehn is a professor at Central Missouri State University. She received her PhD and Master's of Accountancy from the University of Wisconsin—Madison. Her scholarly articles are published in a variety of journals including *Issues in Accounting Education, The CPA Journal, The Tax Advisor,* and *Accounting Enquiries.* Professor Koehn is a member of the American Accounting Association and the American Institute of CPAs. She also holds a Certified Financial Planning license. In her leisure time, Professor Koehn indulges her passion for golf and participates in the Executive Women's Golf Association of Kansas City. Professor Koehn also enjoys reading, traveling, and visiting bookstores.

Marilyn Sagrillo is an associate professor at the University of Wisconsin—Green Bay. She received her BA and MS from Northern Illinois University and her PhD from the University of Wisconsin—Madison. Her scholarly articles are published in *Accounting Enquiries, Journal of Accounting Case Research,* and the *Missouri Society of CPAs Casebook.* She is a member of the American Accounting Association and the Institute of Management Accountants. In 1989 she received the UWGB Founder's Association Faculty Award for Excellence in Teaching. Professor Sagrillo is an active volunteer for the Midwest Renewable Energy Association. She also enjoys reading, traveling, and hiking.

Student Supplements

Topic Tackler (free with new books)

Revised by Joan Cook and Laura Ruff.

See page xv for complete description.

Carol Yacht's General Ledger & Peachtree Complete 2004 CD-ROM

ISBN 0072870079

GL Software developed by Jack E. Terry, ComSource Associates, Inc.

Peachtree templates prepared by Carol Yacht.

The CD-ROM includes fully functioning versions of McGraw-Hill's own General Ledger Application software as well as Peachtree Complete 2004. Problem templates are included that allow you to assign FAP problems for working in either Yacht's General Ledger or Peachtree Complete 2004.

Study Guide

Volume 1: ISBN 007286981X

Volume 2: ISBN 0072869860

Chapters 1-17: ISBN 0072869968

Prepared by Barbara Chiappetta.

Covers each chapter and appendix with reviews of the learning objectives, outlines of the chapters, summaries of chapter materials, and additional problems with solutions.

Special thanks to **Joan Cook** and **Laura Ruff**, *Milwaukee Area Technical College,* for their efforts in revising the Topic Tackler CD-ROM, and to **Janice Klimek**, *Central Missouri State University,* for accuracy checking Topic Tackler.

Working Papers

Volume 1: 0072869852

Volume 2: 0072869925

Chapters 1-17: 007286995X

Written by John J. Wild.

Working Papers are available to help direct students in solving all assignments. Each chapter also contains one set of papers that can be used for either the A or B series of problems.

Excel Working Papers

Volume 1: 0072870109

Volume 2: 0072870117

Chapters 1-17: 0072870125

Written by John J. Wild.

Working Papers delivered in Excel spreadsheets. Excel Working Papers are available on CD-ROM and can be bundled with the printed Working Papers; see your representative for information.

Telecourse Guide

Volume 1: 0072869941

Volume 2: 0072869879

Prepared by the Dallas County Community College District.

Student Learning Tools

ISBN 0256255776

Prepared by Barbara Chiappetta.

This workbook helps students develop and use critical thinking and learning-to-learn skills in a collaborative team environment. It contains class activities, writing assignments, and team presentation assignments.

Achieving New Heights in

Publishing a textbook is a serious undertaking, and in creating the 17th edition of FAP we had a 50-year tradition of quality and innovation to live up to.

The process began more than two years before publication, when our editorial staff commissioned a survey of the principles market. This independent research confirmed that FAP users were more satisfied by far with their chosen textbook than users of any other book. However, that wasn't enough for us.

Early in 2003, we and our research partners surveyed 156 non-users for suggestions on how to improve FAP; at the same time we asked 35 current users what they liked about the book, and what they would change if they could. This information proved invaluable as we began the development process.

The next step was to meet face-to-face with principles instructors at 5 focus groups throughout the country. A mix of users and non-users came to meet with us in Orlando, Dallas, Chicago, Phoenix, and Los Angeles, where they were able to speak to the authors in person and talk at length about what they needed in a principles book. When the authors sat down to write, they did so having firsthand feedback and suggestions from instructors.

The book you hold in your hands is the most market-driven book available. It is the result of a lengthy dialogue between user, author, and instructor. FAP is what principles instructors all over the country are looking for: a book with solid content, engaging explanations and examples, unmatched assignment materials, and first-class technology.

We would like to acknowledge the assistance of the following colleagues for their help in making FAP the best book of its kind.

Cynthia Ash, Davenport University-South Bend
Sister Virginia Assumpta McNabb, Immaculata College
Harold Averkamp, University of Wisconsin-Whitewater
Courtney Baillie, Nebraska Wesleyan University
William Barnhart, El Centro College
Mary Barnum, Grand Rapids Community College
Sandy Barz, Rocky Mountain College
Abdul Baten, NOVA Community College-Manassas
Jim Bates, Mountain Empire Community College
Robert Bauman, Allan Hancock CommunityCollege
James Q. Beisel, Longview Community College
Irene Bembenista, Davenport University-Merrillville
Dr. Michael Bentil, Peirce College
Joseph Bentley, Bunker Hill Community College
JulieAnne Adamich, St. Petersburg College
Rayla Black, Faulkner University
Phoebe Blackburn, Bristol Community College
Linda Bolduc, Mount Wachusett Community College
Deborah Boyce-Panella, Mohawk Valley Community College
Sanithia Boyd, Arkansas State University
James Bryant, Community College of Baltimore County-Catonsville
Ronald Burnette, Macomb Community College South
Leon Button, Scottsdale Community College
Carolyn Byrd, St. Petersburg College-Clearwater
Eric Carlsen, Kean University
Robert Carpenter, Eastfield College
Lloyd Carroll, Borough of Manhattan Community College
Trudy Chiaravalli, Lansing Community College
Tom Chilcote, Messiah College
Steven Christian, Jackson Community College
Dan Chrzan, Springfield College
Anthony Cioffi, Lorain County Community College
Ron Collyer, Santa Fe Community College
Elizabeth Conner, U. of Colorado - Denver
Margaret Conway, Kingsborough Community College
James Cosby, John Tyler Community College
Ralph Cotham, University of Arkansas-Little Rock
Ken Couvillion, San Joaquin Delta College
David G. Coy, Adrian College
Louann Cummings, University of Findlay
Stanley Dabrowski, Hudson County Community College
Walter DeAguero, Saddleback College
Stanley Deal, Azusa Pacific College
David Dearman, Arkansas State University
Mary Kathryn Demarest, Carroll Community College
Louis DePaul, Ivy Tech State College
Michael Deschamps, Chaffey College
William Dillion, Carson-Newman College
Vicky Dominguez, Community College of Southern Nevada
Kevin Dooley, Kapiolani Community College
David Doyon, Southern New Hampshire University
Phyllis N. Driver, Carson-Newman College
Sam Duah, Bowie State University
Ken Duffie, Brookdale Community College
Richard Dugger, Kilgore College
Helen Edwards, College of the Redwoods
Randalei Ellis, Black Hills State University
Lori Epping, University of South Dakota
Larry Farmer, Middle Tenn. State University
Jim Ficek, Iowa Western Community College
Carolyn Fitzmorris, Hutchinson Community College
Steve Flynn, Thomas More College
James Forcier, Las Positas Community College
Kelly Ford, Dowling College
Richard Frederics, Lasell College
Benjamin Gardiner, Franklin Pierce College
Daniel Gibbons, Waubonsee Community College
Thomas J. Gilday, Thomas More College
Mike Glasscock, Amarillo College
Ellen Goldberg, Northern Virginia Community College
Jack Goodwin, Tidewater Community College - Portsmouth
Barbara Gregorio, Nassau Community College
Jennifer Gregorski, Assumption College
Steve Grice, Troy State University
Debbie Griest, Lake Tahoe Community College
Joyce Griffin, Kansas City Kansas Community College
Dennis Gutting, Orange County Community College
Amy Haas, Kingsborough Community College
Gene Hale, Iowa Wesleyan College
Mary Halford, Prince George's Community College
Patricia Halliday, Santa Monica College
Sara Harris, Arapahoe Community College
William Harvey, Henry Ford Community College
Larry Hass, Glen Oaks Community College
Robert D. Hayes, Tennessee State University
William Herd, Springfield Tech Community College
Leonard Heritage, Tacoma Community College
Jim Hoffman, Ancilla College
Merrily Hoffman, San Jacinto College
Jay Holmen, U. of Wisconsin - Eau Claire
Patricia Holmes, Des Moines Area Community College
Paul Holt, Texas A&M-Kingsville
John Horgan, Iowa Western
Kathy Horton, College of DuPage
Larry Huus, University of Minnesota
Verne Ingram, Red Rocks Community College
Tim Ireland, Columbia College of Missouri

Christine Iruno, Westfield State College

Lynn Isvik, Upper Iowa University

Mary Jackson-Heard, Norfolk State University

Lori Jacobson, North Idaho College

Catherine Jeppson, Calif.St.U.-Northridge

Peg Johnson, Omaha Metro Community College

Sharon Johnson, Kansas City Kansas Community College

Thomas Kam, Hawaii Pacific University

John Karayan, Calif. State Polytech University-Pomona

John Kim, SUNY-Hunter College

Deanna King, Ivy Tech College-Terre Haute

Deb Kiss, Davenport University

Shirly Kleiner, Johnson County Community College

Mary Kline, Black Hawk College

Dave Knight, Borough of Manhattan Community College

Sherrie Koechling-Andraes, Lincoln University

Elizabeth M. Kolar, Bucks County Community College

Leon Korte, U. of South Dakota

Terry Kubican, Old Dominion University

Phillip Landers, Pennsylvania College of Technology

Sandra Lang, McKendree College

David Lanning, SUNY-Tompkins Cortland Community College

Tom Largay, Thomas College

Brian Lazarus, Baltimore City Community College

Mike Leahy, North County C.C.

Martin Lecker, SUNY Rockland Community College

Edward LeMay, Massasoit Community College

Louieco Lewis, Stillman College

Daniel Litt, UCLA

James Lock, NOVA-Alexandria

Ronald Loesel, Davenport Univ.-Saginaw

Angelo Luciano, Columbia College-Chicago

Stephen Ludwig, NW Missouri State

Kathy Lukcso, Germanna Community College

Terri Lukshaitis, Davenport University-Gaylord

John Lynch, Ivy Tech State College

Linda Mallory, Central Virginia Community College

Jeff Mankin, Lipscomb University

Frank Marino, Assumption College

Ken Mark, Kansas City Kansas Community College

Barbara Marotta, NOVA-Woodbridge

Dr. Otto Martinson, Old Dominion University

Carol McCain, Reedley College

Cynthia McCall, Des Moines Area Community College

Susan McClure, Tri-County Technical College

Clarice McCoy, Brookhaven College

Florence McGovern, Bergen C.C.

James McKinnie, NE State Technical Community College

Shea Mears, Des Moines Area Community College

David Medved, Davenport University - Dearborn

Kenneth Meisinger, U. of Colorado-Colorado Springs

Trini Melcher, Calif. State University - San Marcos

Mary Ann Merryman, St. Mary's College

John Miller, Metropolitan Community College

Josephine Miller-Mathias, Mercer County Community College

Scott E. Miller, Gannon University

Norma R. Montague, Central Carolina Community College

Henry Moore, Florida Community College-Jacksonville

Louella Moore, Arkansas State University

Joe Moran, College of DuPage

Andrea Murowski, Brookdale Community College

Charles Murphy, Bunker Hill Community College

Dr. Ali Naggar, West Chester University

V.R. Nemani, Trinity College

Dave Nichols, University of Mississippi

Jason Nielsen, Harrisburg Area C.C.

Connie Nieser, Oklahoma City Community College

Patricia Novak, Southeast Community College

Franklin Olive, Jr., Manchester College

Liz Ott, Casper College

George Otto, Truman College

Bill Padley, Madison Area Tech College

Ronald Palma, Cape Cod Community College

Judy Parker, North Idaho College

Jeff Phillips, Clark Atlanta University

Anthony Piltz, Rocky Mountain College

Von Plessner, Northwest State Community College

Barbara Powers, Wytheville C.C.

Michael Prockton, Finger Lakes Community College

Debbie Rankin, Lincoln University

Paulette Ratliff, Arkansas State University

Clara Richardson, McMurry University

Thomas Rim, National University

Frank Rodjius, Northwestern Univ.

Donald Rogoff, Cal. State University-Northridge

Dan Roland, Hilbert College

Laura Rose, Dalton State College

Gary Ross, Harding College

David Schultz, Central Nebraska Community College

Jerry Scott, Ivy Tech State College-Sellersburg

William Shaver, J. Sargeant Reynolds Community College

Jim Shelton, Freed-Hardeman University

Leon Singleton, Santa Monica College

Brenda Skornogoski, Montana State University-Northern

Daniel Small, J. Sargeant Reynolds Community College

Warren Smock, Ivy Tech State College

Richard Snapp, Olympic College

Tom Snavely, Yavapai College

Laura Solano, Pueblo Community College

John Stancil, Florida Southern University

Undine Stinnette, Roosevelt University

Gary Stout, Cal State University-Northridge

Gina Sturgill, Concord College

Kan Sugandh, DeVry Institute of Technology-Pomona

William Sullivan, Assumption College

Ron Summers, Oklahoma City Community College

Rahmat Tavallali, Walsh University

Steve Teeter, Utah Valley State College

James Thomas, Cosumnes River College

Leslie Thysell, Richard Bland College

Christine Todd, William Woods University

Tom Turner, Des Moines Area Community College

Karen Ulbrich, Parkland College

Frank Urbancic, University of South Alabama - Mobile

Robert Urell, Irvine Valley College

John VanSantvoord, Southern New Hampshire University

Jay Wahlund, Minot State University

Pat Walczak, Lansing Community College

Scott Wallace, Blue Mountain Community College

Debra Warren, Chadron State College

Jeffrey Waybright, Spokane Community College

Christian Widmer, Tidewater Community College-VA Beach

Jack Wiehler, San Joaquin Delta College

Jo Winegar, Scott Community College

Rahnl Wood, NW Missouri State University

Joe Woods, University of Arkansas-Little Rock

Ray Wurzburger, New River Community College

Lori Zulauf, Slippery Rock University

Brief Contents

Contents

8 Cash and Internal Controls 306

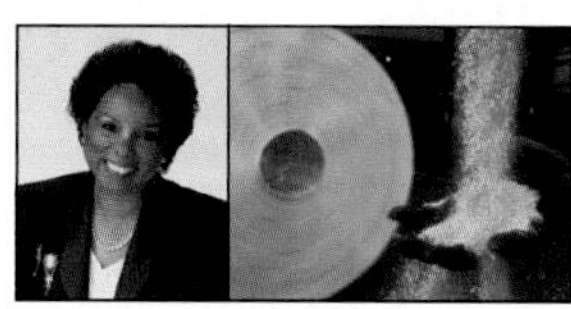

9 Accounting for Receivables 348

10 Plant Assets, Natural Resources, and Intangibles 380

11 Current Liabilities and Payroll Accounting 422

Volume 1 Chapters 1–12

Fundamental Accounting Principles

"I love chocolate, and so I'm having fun making money"—Elise Macmillan (Evan Macmillan on right)

1 Accounting in Business

A Look at This Chapter

Accounting plays a crucial role in the information age. In this chapter, we discuss the importance of accounting to different types of organizations and describe its many users and uses. We explain that ethics are crucial to accounting. We also describe business transactions and how they are reflected in financial statements.

A Look Ahead

Chapter 2 further describes and analyzes business transactions. We explain the analysis and recording of transactions, the ledger and trial balance, and the double-entry system. More generally, Chapters 2 through 4 focus on accounting and analysis, and they illustrate (via the accounting cycle) how financial statements reflect business activities.

Learning Objectives

Learning Objectives are organized by conceptual, analytical, and procedural.

CAP

Conceptual

C1 Explain the purpose and importance of accounting in the information age. *(p. 4)*

C2 Identify users and uses of accounting. *(p. 5)*

C3 Identify opportunities in accounting and related fields. *(p. 6)*

C4 Explain why ethics are crucial to accounting. *(p. 8)*

C5 Explain the meaning of generally accepted accounting principles, and define and apply several key principles of accounting. *(p. 9)*

Analytical

A1 Define and interpret the accounting equation and each of its components. *(p. 12)*

A2 Analyze business transactions using the accounting equation. *(p. 13)*

A3 Compute and interpret return on assets. *(p. 20)*

Procedural

P1 Identify and prepare basic financial statements and explain how they interrelate. *(p. 17)*

Decision Feature

Sweet Taste of Success

DENVER—Elise and Evan Macmillan—sister and brother entrepreneurs—aim to satisfy. "Our whole business is about customers," says Elise. These teenagers head **The Chocolate Farm (TheChocolateFarm.com),** which specializes in making chocolates and in helping their customers make them.

"We thought our business was going to be a one-day thing," says Elise, "but it turned into a real business." This meant Elise and Evan had to deal with issues such as organization form, accounting and information systems, transaction analysis, and financial reports. Adds Elise, "I'm kept busy with the company's future plans and new product ideas and everything else that there is to a company."

Special attention is directed at accounting information; because without income, The Chocolate Farm would be knee-deep in cocoa. Elise and Evan were able to set up a transaction-based accounting system to profitably handle customer sales and orders. They also used accounting information to make good business decisions. Relying on sales and expense information, Elise and Evan focused efforts on their best-sellers such as *Brown Cows, Mint Sheep Munch, Pecan Turtles,* and *Pigs in Mud.* Moreover, after an analysis of the accounting information, they decided to expand and now employ more than a dozen people.

Evan admits that even with the best accounting information, one must accept some risk. We "accept the fact that it's a risk," says Evan, but that's the reality of money making. Elise concurs, "I love chocolate, and so I'm having fun making money." The Farm now produces more than $1 million per year in revenues. We could all become chocolate-lovers with results like that!

[Sources: *Ernst & Young Website,* January 2004; *The Chocolate Farm Website,* January 2004; *Entrepreneur Magazine,* May 2002; *Denver Business Journal,* January 2002; *The Wall Street Journal,* March 2003.]

*A **Decision Feature** launches each chapter showing the relevance of accounting for a real entrepreneur. An **Entrepreneurial Decision** problem at the end of the assignments returns to this feature with a mini-case.*

A **Preview** opens each chapter with a summary of topics covered.

Today's world is one of information—its preparation, communication, analysis, and use. Accounting is at the heart of this information age. Knowledge of accounting gives us career opportunities and the insight to take advantage of them. By studying this book, you will learn about concepts, procedures, and analyses that will help you make better decisions throughout your life. In this chapter we describe accounting, the users and uses of accounting information, the forms and activities of organizations, and several accounting principles. We also introduce transaction analysis and financial statements.

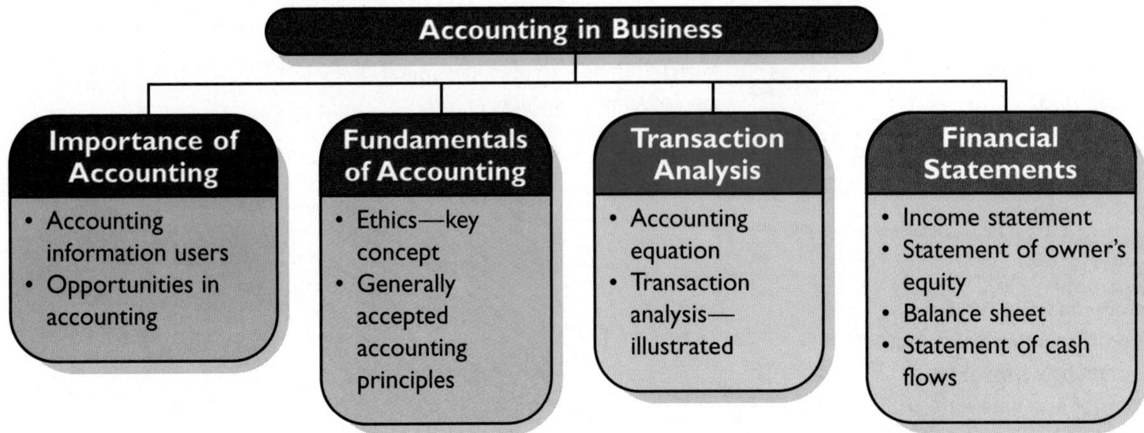

Importance of Accounting

C1 Explain the purpose and importance of accounting in the information age.

We live in an information age—a time of communication and immediate access to data, news, facts, and commentary. Information affects how we live, whom we associate with, and the opportunities we have. To fully benefit from the available information, we need knowledge of the information system. An information system involves the collecting, processing, and reporting of information to decision makers.

Providing information about what businesses own, what they owe, and how they perform is an important aim of accounting. **Accounting** is an information and measurement system that identifies, records, and communicates relevant, reliable, and comparable information about an organization's business activities. *Identifying* business activities requires selecting transactions and events relevant to an organization. Examples are the sale of vehicles by **Ford** and the receipt of ticket money by **TicketMaster**. *Recording* business activities requires keeping a chronological log of transactions and events measured in dollars and classified and summarized in a useful format. *Communicating* business activities requires preparing accounting reports such as financial statements. It also requires analyzing and interpreting such reports. (The financial statements and notes of **Krispy Kreme** are shown in Appendix A of this book. This appendix also shows the financial statements of **Tastykake** and **Harley-Davidson**.) Exhibit 1.1 summarizes accounting activities.

We must guard against a narrow view of accounting. The most common contact with accounting is through credit approvals, checking accounts, tax forms, and payroll. These

Exhibit 1.1

Accounting Activities

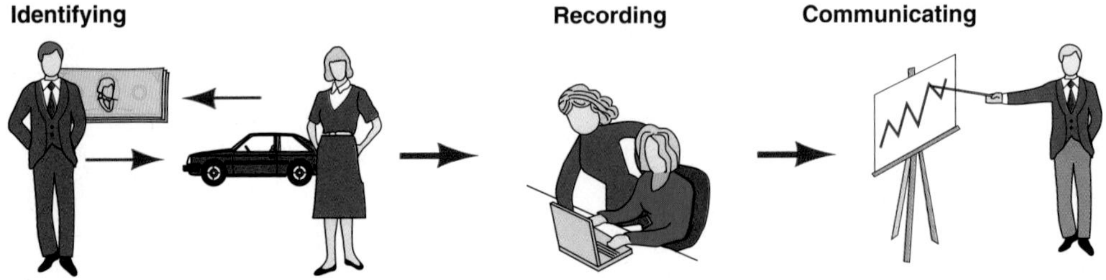

experiences are limited and tend to focus on the recordkeeping parts of accounting. **Recordkeeping,** or **bookkeeping,** is the recording of transactions and events, either manually or electronically. This is just one part of accounting. Accounting also identifies and communicates information on transactions and events, and it includes the crucial processes of analysis and interpretation.

Margin notes further enhance the textual material.

Point: Technology is only as useful as the accounting data available, and users' decisions are only as good as their understanding of accounting. The best software and recordkeeping cannot make up for lack of accounting knowledge.

Technology is a key part of modern business and plays a major role in accounting. Technology reduces the time, effort, and cost of recordkeeping while improving clerical accuracy. Some small organizations continue to perform various accounting tasks manually, but even they are impacted by information technology. As technology has changed the way we store, process, and summarize masses of data, accounting has been freed to expand. Consulting, planning, and other financial services are now closely linked to accounting. These services require sorting through data, interpreting their meaning, identifying key factors, and analyzing their implications.

Users of Accounting Information

Accounting is often called the *language of business* because all organizations set up an accounting information system to communicate data to help people make better decisions. Exhibit 1.2 shows that the accounting information system serves many kinds of users who can be divided into two groups: external users and internal users.

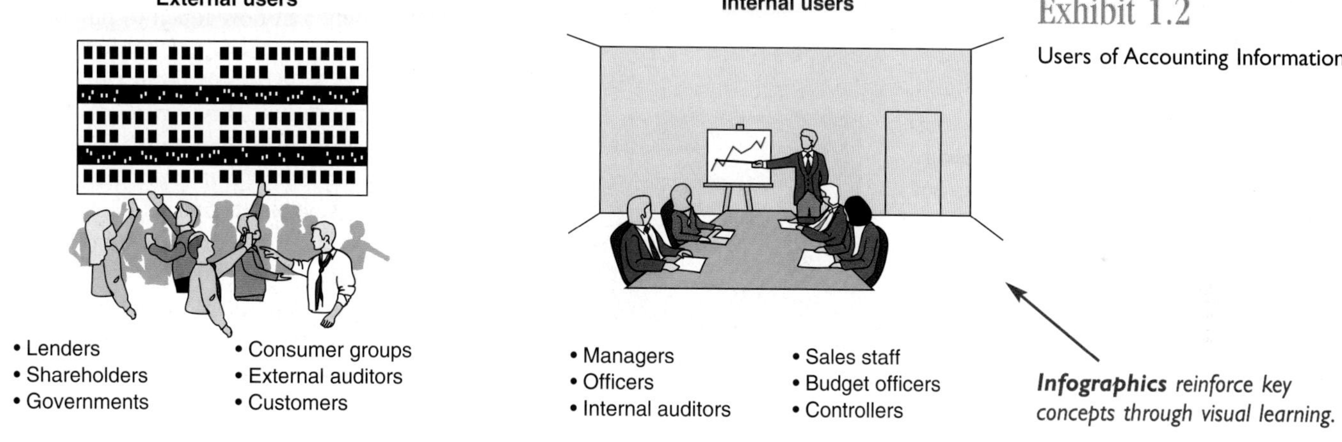

Exhibit 1.2

Users of Accounting Information

Infographics *reinforce key concepts through visual learning.*

C2 Identify users and uses of accounting.

External Information Users **External users** of accounting information are *not* directly involved in running the organization. They include shareholders (investors), lenders, directors, customers, suppliers, regulators, lawyers, brokers, and the press. External users have limited access to an organization's information. Yet many of their important decisions depend on information that is reliable, relevant, and comparable.

Financial accounting is the area of accounting aimed at serving external users by providing them with financial statements. These statements are known as *general-purpose financial statements*. The term *general-purpose* refers to the broad range of purposes for which external users rely on these statements.

Each external user has special information needs depending on the types of decisions to be made. *Lenders* (creditors) loan money or other resources to an organization. Banks, savings and loans, co-ops, and mortgage and finance companies often are lenders. Lenders look for information to help them assess whether an organization is likely to repay its loans with interest. *Shareholders* (investors) are the owners of a corporation. They use accounting reports in deciding whether to buy, hold, or sell stock. Shareholders typically elect a *board of directors* to oversee their interests in an organization. Since directors are responsible to shareholders, their information needs are similar. *External* (independent) *auditors* examine financial statements to verify that they are prepared according to generally accepted accounting principles. *Employees* and *labor unions* use financial statements to judge the fairness of

Point: World Wrestling Entertainment has more than 70 mil. shares of stock outstanding.

wages, assess future job prospects, and bargain for better wages. *Regulators* often have legal authority over certain activities of organizations. For example, the Internal Revenue Service (IRS) and other tax authorities require organizations to file accounting reports in computing taxes. Other regulators include utility boards that use accounting information to set utility rates and securities regulators that require reports for companies that sell their stock to the public.

Point: Microsoft's high income levels encouraged antitrust actions against it.

Accounting serves the needs of many other external users. *Voters, legislators,* and *government officials* use accounting information to monitor and evaluate a government's receipts and expenses. *Contributors* to nonprofit organizations use accounting information to evaluate the use and impact of their donations. *Suppliers* use accounting information to judge the soundness of a customer before making sales on credit, and *customers* use financial reports to assess the staying power of potential suppliers.

Internal Information Users **Internal users** of accounting information are those directly involved in managing and operating an organization. They use the information to help improve the efficiency and effectiveness of an organization. **Managerial accounting** is the area of accounting that serves the decision-making needs of internal users. Internal reports are not subject to the same rules as external reports and are designed with the special needs of internal users in mind.

Decision Insight boxes highlight relevant items from practice.

There are several types of internal users, and many are managers of key operating activities. *Research and development managers* need information about projected costs and revenues of proposed changes in products and services. *Purchasing managers* need to know what, when, and how much to purchase. *Human resource managers* need information about employees' payroll, benefits, performance, and compensation. *Production managers* depend on information to monitor costs and ensure quality. *Distribution managers* need reports for timely, accurate, and efficient delivery of products and services. *Marketing managers* use reports about sales and costs to target consumers, set prices, and monitor consumer needs, tastes, and price concerns. *Service managers* require information on both the costs and benefits of looking after products and services.

Decision Insight

Know-Nothing CEO The know-nothing defense of CEOs such as **Global Crossing**'s Gary Winnick and **Enron**'s Jeffrey Skilling and Kenneth Lay could soon be shattered. Through novel legal moves, prosecutors are achieving convictions provided they prove that the CEO knew the company's internal picture was different than the picture shown to outsiders.

Both internal and external users rely on internal controls to monitor and control company activities. *Internal controls* are procedures set up to protect company property and equipment, ensure reliable accounting reports, promote efficiency, and encourage adherence to company policies. Examples are good records, physical controls (locks, passwords, guards), and independent reviews.

Opportunities in Accounting

C3 Identify opportunities in accounting and related fields.

Accounting information affects many aspects of our lives. When we earn money, pay taxes, invest savings, budget earnings, and plan for the future, we are influenced by accounting. Accounting has four broad areas of opportunities: financial, managerial, taxation, and accounting-related. Exhibit 1.3 lists selected opportunities in each area.

The majority of accounting opportunities are in *private accounting,* as shown in Exhibit 1.4. *Public accounting* offers the next largest number of opportunities. Still other opportunities exist in government (and not-for-profit) agencies, including business regulation and investigation of law violations.

Point: The "top 5" greatest investors of the 20th century, as compiled in a recent survey:
1. Warren Buffett, Berkshire Hathaway
2. Peter Lynch, Fidelity Funds
3. John Templeton, Templeton Group
4. Benjamin Graham & David Dodd, professors
5. George Soros, Soros Fund

Accounting specialists are highly regarded. Their professional standing often is denoted by a certificate. Certified public accountants (CPAs) must meet education and experience requirements, pass an examination, and exhibit ethical character. Many accounting specialists hold certificates in addition to or instead of the CPA. Two of the most common are the

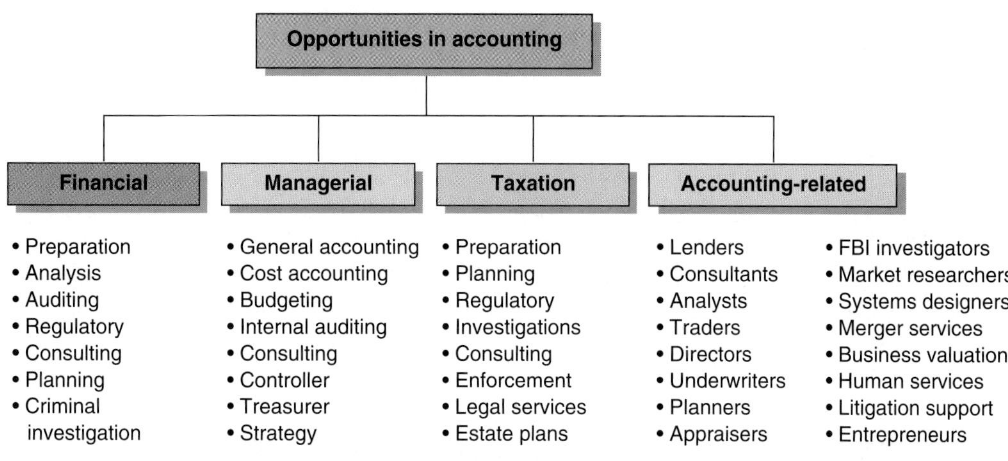

Exhibit 1.3

Accounting Opportunities

certificate in management accounting (CMA) and the certified internal auditor (CIA). Employers also look for specialists with designations such as certified bookkeeper (CB), certified payroll professional (CPP), and personal financial specialist (PFS).

Private accounting 60%

Public accounting 25%

Government, not-for-profit and education 15%

Exhibit 1.4

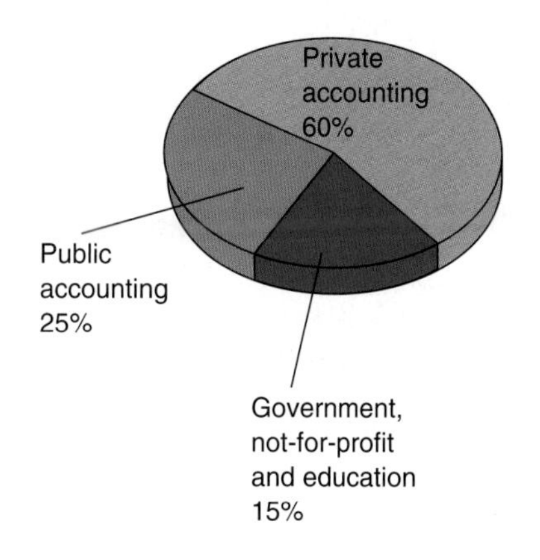

Accounting Jobs by Area

Individuals with accounting knowledge are always in demand as they can help with financial analysis, strategic planning, e-commerce, product feasibility analysis, information technology, and financial management. Benefit packages can include flexible work schedules, telecommuting options, career path alternatives, casual work environments, extended vacation time, and child and elder care.

Demand for accounting specialists is boosting salaries. Exhibit 1.5 reports average annual salaries for several accounting positions. Salary variation depends on location, company size, professional designation, experience, and other factors. For example, salaries for chief financial officers (CFO) range from under $75,000 to more than $1 million per year. Likewise, salaries for bookkeepers range from under $30,000 to more than $80,000.

Point: The firm of Ernst & Young gave its interns a vacation at Disney World.

Point: The CFOs of Cisco Systems and Qualcom received an annual salary of more than $20 mil.

Field	Title (experience)	2003 Salary	2008 Estimate*
Public Accounting:	Partner	$181,000	$231,000
	Manager (6–8 years)	89,500	114,000
	Senior (3–5 years)	68,500	87,500
	Junior (0–2 years)	49,000	62,500
Private Accounting:	CFO	221,000	282,000
	Controller/Treasurer	140,000	179,000
	Manager (6–8 years)	83,000	106,000
	Senior (3–5 years)	69,000	88,000
	Junior (0–2 years)	47,000	60,000
Recordkeeping:	Full-charge bookkeeper	55,000	70,000
	Accounts manager	48,500	62,000
	Payroll manager	52,000	66,000
	Accounting clerk (0–1 years)	30,500	39,000

* Estimates assume a 5% compounded annual increase over current levels.

Exhibit 1.5

Accounting Salaries for Selected Fields

Point: For updated salary information: www.AICPA.org Abbott-Langer.com Kforce.com

Quick Check is a chance to stop and reflect on key points.

Quick Check

1. What is the purpose of accounting?
2. What is the relation between accounting and recordkeeping?
3. Identify some advantages of technology for accounting.
4. Who are the internal and external users of accounting information?
5. Identify at least five types of managers who are internal users of accounting information.
6. What are internal controls and why are they important?

Answers—p. 26

Fundamentals of Accounting

Accounting is guided by principles, standards, concepts, and assumptions. This section describes several of these key fundamentals of accounting.

Ethics—A Key Concept

C4 Explain why ethics are crucial to accounting.

The goal of accounting is to provide useful information for decisions. For information to be useful, it must be trusted. This demands ethics in accounting. **Ethics** are beliefs that distinguish right from wrong. They are accepted standards of good and bad behavior.

Identifying the ethical path is sometimes difficult. The preferred path is a course of action that avoids casting doubt on one's decisions. For example, accounting users are less likely to trust an auditor's report if the auditor's pay depends on the success of the client. To avoid such concerns, ethics rules are often set. For example, auditors are banned from direct investment in their client and cannot accept pay that depends on figures in the client's reports. Exhibit 1.6 gives guidelines for making ethical decisions.

Exhibit 1.6

Guidelines for Ethical Decision Making

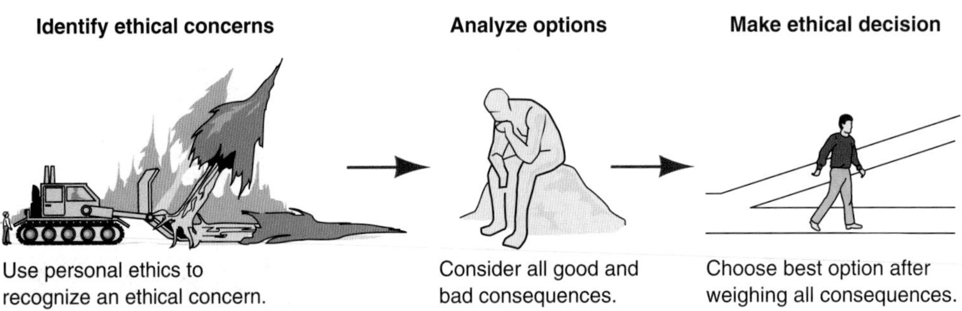

Global: Business ethics differ across countries. This is due to cultural, political, legal, economic, and other important factors.

Providers of accounting information often face ethical choices as they prepare financial reports. These choices can affect the price a buyer pays and the wages paid to workers. They can even affect the success of products and services. Misleading information can lead to a wrongful closing of a division that harms workers, customers, and suppliers. There is an old saying worth remembering: *Good ethics are good business.*

Point: A survey of executives, educators, and legislators showed that 9 of 10 participants believe organizations are troubled by ethical problems.

Point: The American Institute of Certified Public Accountants' *Code of Professional Conduct* is available at www.AICPA.org.

Some extend ethics to *social responsibility,* which refers to a concern for the impact of actions on society. An organization's social responsibility can include donations to hospitals, colleges, community programs, and law enforcement. It also can include programs to reduce pollution, increase product safety, improve worker conditions, and support continuing education. These programs are not limited to large companies. For example, many independently owned theaters and small businesses offer discounts to students and senior citizens. Still others help sponsor events such as the Special Olympics and summer reading programs.

Graphical displays are often used to illustrate key points.

Generally Accepted Accounting Principles

Financial accounting practice is governed by concepts and rules known as **generally accepted accounting principles (GAAP).** To use and interpret financial statements effectively, we need to understand these principles. A main purpose of GAAP is to make information in financial statements relevant, reliable, and comparable. *Relevant information* affects the decisions of its users. *Reliable information* is trusted by users. *Comparable information* is helpful in contrasting organizations.

Decision Insight

Virtuous Returns Virtue is not always its own reward. Compare the S&P 500 with the Domini Social Index (DSI), which covers 400 companies that have especially good records of social responsibility. Notice that returns for companies with socially responsible behavior are at least as high as those of the S&P 500.

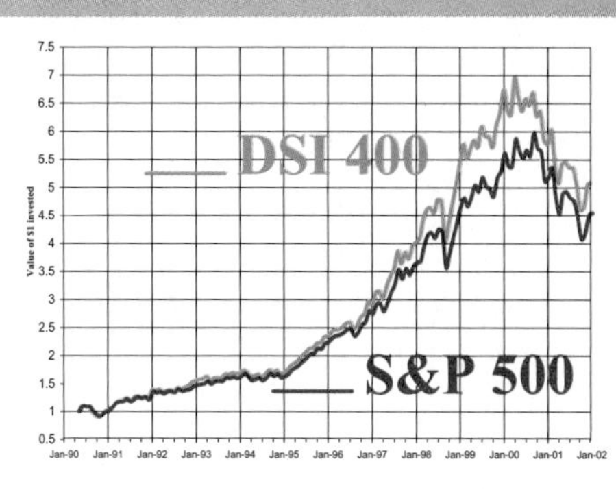

C5 Explain the meaning of generally accepted accounting principles, and define and apply several key principles of accounting.

Setting Accounting Principles Two main groups establish generally accepted accounting principles in the United States. The **Financial Accounting Standards Board (FASB)** is the private group that sets both broad and specific principles. The **Securities and Exchange Commission (SEC)** is the government group that establishes reporting requirements for companies that issue stock to the public.

In today's global economy, there is increased demand by external users for comparability in accounting reports. This often arises when companies wish to raise money from lenders and investors in different countries. To that end, the **International Accounting Standards Board (IASB)** issues *International Financial Reporting Standards* (*IFRS*) that identify preferred accounting practices. The IASB hopes to create more harmony among accounting practices of different countries. If standards are harmonized, one company can use a single set of financial statements in all financial markets. Many countries' standard setters support the IASB, and interest in moving U.S. GAAP toward the IASB's practices is growing, yet the IASB does not have the authority to impose its standards on companies.

Point: State ethics codes require CPAs who audit financial statements to disclose areas where those statements fail to comply with GAAP. If CPAs fail to report noncompliance, they can lose their licenses and be subject to criminal action and fines.

Principles of Accounting Accounting principles are of two types. *General principles* are the basic assumptions, concepts, and guidelines for preparing financial statements. *Specific principles* are detailed rules used in reporting business transactions and events. General principles stem from long-used accounting practices. Specific principles arise more often from the rulings of authoritative groups.

We need to understand both general and specific principles to effectively use accounting information. Several general principles are described in this section and several others are described in later chapters. General principles are portrayed as building blocks of GAAP in Exhibit 1.7. The specific principles are described as we encounter them.

Point: An audit examines whether financial statements are prepared using GAAP. It does *not* attest to the absolute accuracy of the statements.

Point: The largest accounting firms are Deloitte & Touche, Ernst & Young, PricewaterhouseCoopers, and KPMG.

The **objectivity principle** means that accounting information is supported by independent, unbiased evidence. It demands more than a person's opinion. Information is not reliable if it is based only on what a preparer thinks might be true. A preparer can be too optimistic or pessimistic. The objectivity principle is intended to make financial statements useful by ensuring they report reliable and verifiable information.

The **cost principle** means that accounting information is based on actual cost. Cost is measured on a cash or equal-to-cash basis. This means if cash is given for a service, its cost is measured as the amount of cash paid. If something besides cash is exchanged (such as

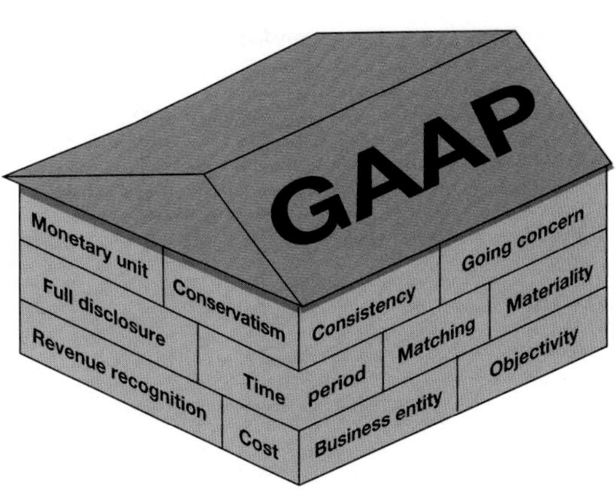

Exhibit 1.7

Building Blocks for GAAP

Decision Insight

Name that Value Abuse of the objectivity and cost principles brought down executives at **Itex Corp** who bartered assets of little or no value and then reported them at grossly inflated values—recognizing fictitious gains and assets. The deals involved difficult-to-value assets such as artwork and stamps.

a car traded for a truck), cost is measured as the cash value of what is given up or received. The cost principle emphasizes reliability, and information based on cost is considered objective. To illustrate, suppose a company pays $5,000 for equipment. The cost principle requires that this purchase be recorded at a cost of $5,000. It makes no difference if the owner thinks this equipment is worth $7,000.

The **going-concern principle** means that accounting information reflects an assumption that the business will continue operating instead of being closed or sold. This implies, for example, that property is reported at cost instead of, say, liquidation values that assume closure.

Point: The cost principle is also called the *historical cost principle.*

Point: For currency conversion: cnnfn.com/markets/currencies

The **monetary unit principle** means that we can express transactions and events in monetary, or money, units. Money is the common denominator in business. Examples of monetary units are the dollar in the United States, Canada, Australia, and Singapore; the pound sterling in the United Kingdom; and the peso in Mexico, the Philippines, and Chile. The monetary unit a company uses in its accounting reports usually depends on the country where it operates, but many companies today are expressing reports in more than one monetary unit.

Example: Cadbury Schweppes, a leading beverage and confectionery producer, recently reported sales of £5,500 million. What is the U.S.$ equivalent of these sales if the exchange rate is £1 = $1.50? *Answer:* $8,250 million (£5,500 × $1.50).

Revenue (sales) is the amount received from selling products and services. The **revenue recognition principle** provides guidance on when a company must recognize revenue. To *recognize* means to record it. If revenue is recognized too early, a company would look more profitable than it is. If revenue is recognized too late, a company would look less profitable than it is. The following three concepts are important to revenue recognition. (1) *Revenue is recognized when earned.* The earnings process is normally complete when services are rendered or a seller transfers ownership of products to the buyer. (2) *Proceeds from selling products and services need not be in cash.* A common noncash proceed received by a seller is a customer's promise to pay at a future date, called *credit sales.* (3) *Revenue is measured by the cash received plus the cash value of any other items received.*

Example: When a bookstore sells a textbook on credit is its earnings process complete? *Answer:* The bookstore can record sales for these books minus an amount expected for returns.

The **business entity principle** means that a business is accounted for separately from other business entities, including its owner. The reason for this principle is that separate information about each business is necessary for good decisions. A business entity can take one of three legal forms: *sole proprietorship, partnership,* or *corporation.*

Point: Abuse of the entity principle was a main culprit in the collapse of Enron.

1. A **sole proprietorship,** or simply **proprietorship,** is a business owned by one person. No special legal requirements must be met to start a proprietorship. It is a separate entity for accounting purposes, but it is *not* a separate legal entity from its owner. This means, for example, that a court can order an owner to sell personal belongings to pay a proprietorship's debt. This *unlimited liability* of a proprietorship is a disadvantage. However, an advantage is that a proprietorship's income is not subject to a business income tax but is instead reported and taxed on the owner's personal income tax return. Proprietorship characteristics are summarized in Exhibit 1.8.
2. A **partnership** is a business owned by two or more people, called *partners.* Like a proprietorship, no special legal requirements must be met in starting a partnership. The only requirement is an agreement between partners to run a business together. The agreement can be either oral or

Decision Insight

Revenues for the New York Yankees baseball team include ticket sales, television and cable broadcasts, radio rights, concessions, and advertising. Revenues from ticket sales are earned when the Yankees play each game. Advance ticket sales are not revenues; instead, they represent a liability until the Yankees play the game for which the ticket was sold.

Exhibit 1.8

Characteristics of Businesses

Characteristic	Proprietorship	Partnership	Corporation
Business entity	yes	yes	yes
Legal entity	no	no	yes
Limited liability	no*	no*	yes
Unlimited life	no	no	yes
Business taxed	no	no	yes
One owner allowed	yes	no	yes

* Proprietorships and partnerships that are set up as LLCs provide limited liability.

written and usually indicates how income and losses are to be shared. A partnership, like a proprietorship, is *not* legally separate from its owners. This means that each partner's share of profits is reported and taxed on that partner's tax return. It also means *unlimited liability* for its partners. However, at least three types of partnerships limit liability. A *limited partnership* (*LP*) includes a general partner(s) with unlimited liability and a limited partner(s) with liability restricted to the amount invested. A *limited liability partnership* (*LLP*) restricts partners' liabilities to their own acts and the acts of individuals under their control. This protects an innocent partner from the negligence of another partner, yet all partners remain responsible for partnership debts. A *limited liability company* (*LLC*), offers the limited liability of a corporation and the tax treatment of a partnership (or proprietorship). Most proprietorships and partnerships are now organized as an LLC.

Decision Insight

Web Info Most organizations maintain Websites that include accounting information—see **Krispy Kreme's (KrispyKreme.com)** Website as one example. The SEC keeps an online database called EDGAR **(www.sec.gov/edgar.shtml),** which has accounting information for thousands of companies that sell their stock to the public.

Lightbulb icon highlights entrepreneurial-related info.

Decision Insight

New Age Entrepreneurship will be the defining trend of business in this century, according to a survey of business leaders. Respondents see the biggest opportunities for entrepreneurship in technology, medicine, food services, hospitality, and information services.

3. A **corporation** is a business legally separate from its owners, meaning it is responsible for its own acts and its own debts. Separate legal status means that a corporation can conduct business with the rights, duties, and responsibilities of a person. A corporation acts through its managers, who are its legal agents. Separate legal status also means that its owners, who are called **shareholders** (or **stockholders**), are not personally liable for corporate acts and debts. This limited liability is its main advantage. A main disadvantage is what's called *double taxation*—meaning that (1) the corporation income is taxed and (2) any distribution of income to its owners through dividends is taxed as part of the owners' personal income (usually at the 15% rate). An exception to this is an *S corporation*, a corporation with certain characteristics that give it a tax status that removes its corporate income tax. Owners of S corporations report their share of corporate income with their personal income. (*Note:* For lower income taxpayers, the dividend tax is less than 15%, and in some cases zero.) Ownership of corporations is divided into units called **shares** or **stock.** When a corporation issues only one class of stock, we call it **common stock** (or *capital stock*).

***Decision Ethics** boxes are role-playing exercises that stress ethics in accounting and business.*

Decision Ethics

Entrepreneur You and a friend develop a new design for in-line skates that improves speed and performance by 25% to 40%. You plan to form a business to manufacture and market these skates. You and your friend want to minimize taxes, but your prime concern is potential lawsuits from individuals who might be injured on these skates. What form of organization do you set up?

Answer—p. 26

Point: Sole proprietorships and partnerships are usually managed on a regular basis by their owners. In a corporation, the owners (shareholders) elect a board of directors who appoint managers to run the business.

Quick Check

7. What three-step guidelines can help people make ethical decisions?
8. Why are ethics and social responsibility valuable to organizations?
9. Why are ethics crucial in accounting?
10. Who sets U.S. accounting rules?
11. How are U.S. companies affected by international accounting standards?
12. How are the objectivity and cost principles related?
13. Why is the business entity principle important?
14. Why is the revenue recognition principle important?
15. What are the three basic forms of business organization?
16. Identify the owners of corporations and the terminology for ownership units.

Answers—p. 26

Transaction Analysis and the Accounting Equation

A1 Define and interpret the accounting equation and each of its components.

To understand accounting information, we need to know how an accounting system captures relevant data about transactions, and classifies, records, and reports data.

Accounting Equation

The accounting system reflects two basic aspects of a company: what it owns and what it owes. **Assets** are resources with future benefits that are owned or controlled by a company. Examples are cash, supplies, equipment, and land. The claims on a company's assets—what it owes—are separated into owner and nonowner claims. **Liabilities** are what a company owes its nonowners (creditors) in future products or services. **Equity** (also called owner's equity or capital) refers to the claims of its owner(s). Together, liabilities and equity are the source of funds to acquire assets. The relation of assets, liabilities, and equity is reflected in the following **accounting equation:**

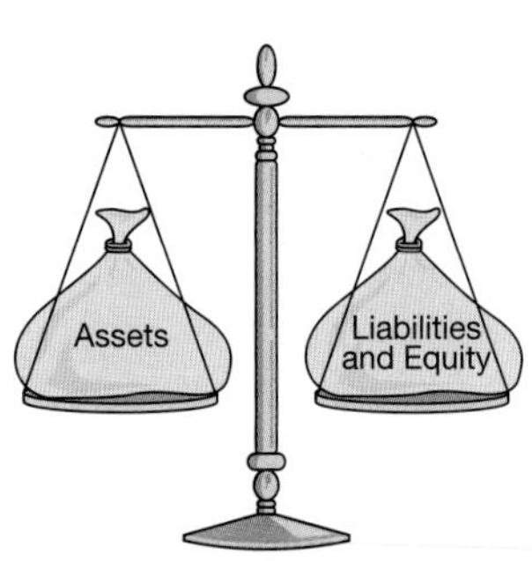

Assets = Liabilities + Equity

Liabilities are usually shown before equity in this equation because creditors' claims must be paid before the claims of owners. (The terms in this equation can be rearranged; for example, Assets − Liabilities = Equity.) The accounting equation applies to all transactions and events, to all companies and forms of organization, and to all points in time. To illustrate, **Krispy Kreme**'s assets equal $410,487, its liabilities equal $137,135, and its equity equals $273,352 ($ in thousands). Let's now look at the accounting equation in more detail.

***Real company names** are printed in bold magenta.*

Assets **Assets** are resources owned or controlled by a company. These resources are expected to yield future benefits. Examples are Web servers for an online services company, musical instruments for a rock band, and land for a vegetable grower. The term *receivable* is used to refer to an asset that promises a future inflow of resources. A company that provides a service or product on credit is said to have an account receivable from that customer.

Point: The phrase "on credit" implies that the cash payment will occur at a future date.

Liabilities **Liabilities** are creditors' claims on assets. These claims reflect obligations to provide assets, products, or services to others. The term *payable* refers to a liability that promises a future outflow of resources. Examples are wages payable to employees, accounts payable to suppliers, notes payable to banks, and taxes payable to the government.

Equity **Equity** is the owner's claim on assets. Equity is equal to assets minus liabilities. This is the reason equity is also called *net assets* or *residual equity* (*interest*).

For a proprietorship, owner investments and revenues increase equity, and owner withdrawals and expenses decrease it. **Owner investments** are the assets an owner puts into the company—included under the title **Owner, Capital. Revenues** are the gross increase in equity from a company's earnings activities. Examples are consulting services provided, sales of products, facilities rented to others, and commissions from services. **Owner withdrawals** are the assets an owner takes from the company for personal use. **Expenses** decrease equity and are the cost of assets or services used to earn revenues. Examples are costs of employee time, use of supplies, and the advertising, utilities, and insurance services from others. This breakdown of equity yields the following **expanded accounting equation:**

*Key **terms** are printed in bold and defined again in the end-of-book **glossary.***

Point: Revenues and owner investments increase equity. Expenses and owner withdrawals decrease equity.

				Equity			
Assets	=	**Liabilities**	+	**Owner Capital**	− **Owner Withdrawals**	+ **Revenues**	− **Expenses**

Net income occurs when revenues exceed expenses. Net income increases equity. A **net loss** occurs when expenses exceed revenues, which decreases equity. The accounting equation can be used to track changes in a company's assets, liabilities, and equity, which is the focus of the next section.

Transaction Analysis

A2 Analyze business transactions using the accounting equation.

Business activities can be described in terms of transactions and events. **External transactions** are exchanges of value between two entities, which yield changes in the accounting equation. **Internal transactions** are exchanges within an entity; they can also affect the accounting equation. An example is a company's use of its supplies, which are reported as expenses when used. **Events** refer to those happenings that affect an entity's accounting equation *and* can be reliably measured. They include business events such as changes in the market value of certain assets and liabilities, and natural events such as floods and fires that destroy assets and create losses. They do not include, for example, the signing of service or product contracts, which by themselves do not impact the accounting equation.

This section uses the accounting equation to analyze 11 selected transactions and events of FastForward, a start-up consulting business, in its first month of operations. Remember that each transaction and event leaves the equation in balance and that assets *always* equal the sum of liabilities and equity.

*Topic Tackler **icon** references additional help on the CD.*

Topic Tackler 1-1

Transaction 1: Investment by Owner On December 1, Chuck Taylor forms an athletic shoe consulting business, which he names FastForward. He sets it up as a proprietorship. Taylor owns and manages the business. The marketing plan for the business is to focus primarily on consulting with sports clubs, amateur athletes, and others who place orders for athletic shoes with manufacturers. Taylor personally invests $30,000 cash in the new company and deposits the cash in a bank account opened under the name of FastForward. After this transaction, the cash (an asset) and the owner's equity each equal $30,000. The source of increase in equity is the owner's investment, which is included in the column titled C. Taylor, Capital. (*Note:* Owner investments are always included under the title *"Owner name," Capital.*) The effect of this transaction on FastForward is reflected in the accounting equation as follows:

Point: There are 3 basic types of company operations: (1) **Services**—providing services for profit, (2) **Merchandisers**—buying products and selling them for profit, and (3) **Manufacturers**—creating products and selling them for profit.

	Assets	=	Liabilities	+	Equity
	Cash	=			**C. Taylor, Capital**
(1)	**+$30,000**	=			**+$30,000**

Transaction 2: Purchase Supplies for Cash FastForward uses $2,500 of its cash to buy supplies of brand name athletic shoes for testing over the next few months. This transaction is an exchange of cash, an asset, for another kind of asset, supplies. It merely changes

the form of assets from cash to supplies. The decrease in cash is exactly equal to the increase in supplies. The supplies of athletic shoes are assets because of the expected future benefits from the test results of their performance. This transaction is reflected in the accounting equation as follows:

	Assets			=	Liabilities + Equity
	Cash	**+**	**Supplies**	**=**	**C. Taylor, Capital**
Old Bal.	$30,000			=	$30,000
(2)	**−2,500**	+	**$2,500**		
New Bal.	$27,500	+	$ 2,500	=	$30,000
	$30,000				$30,000

Transaction 3: Purchase Equipment for Cash FastForward spends $26,000 to acquire equipment for testing athletic shoes. Like transaction 2, transaction 3 is an exchange of one asset, cash, for another asset, equipment. The equipment is an asset because of its expected future benefits from testing athletic shoes. This purchase changes the makeup of assets but does not change the asset total. The accounting equation remains in balance.

	Assets					=	Liabilities + Equity
	Cash	**+**	**Supplies**	**+**	**Equipment**	**=**	**C. Taylor, Capital**
Old Bal.	$27,500	+	$2,500			=	$30,000
(3)	**−26,000**			+	**$26,000**		
New Bal.	$1,500	+	$2,500	+	$ 26,000	=	$30,000
	$30,000						$30,000

Example: If FastForward pays $500 cash in transaction 4, how does this partial payment affect the liability to CalTech? What would be FastForward's cash balance? *Answers:* The liability to CalTech would be reduced to $6,600 and the cash balance would be reduced to $1,000.

Transaction 4: Purchase Supplies on Credit Taylor decides he needs more supplies of athletic shoes. These additional supplies total $7,100, but as we see from the accounting equation in transaction 3, FastForward has only $1,500 in cash. Taylor arranges to purchase them on credit from CalTech Supply Company. Thus, FastForward acquires supplies in exchange for a promise to pay for them later. This purchase increases assets by $7,100 in supplies, and liabilities (called *accounts payable* to CalTech Supply) increase by the same amount. The effects of this purchase on the accounting equation follow:

	Assets					=	Liabilities	+	Equity
	Cash	**+**	**Supplies**	**+**	**Equipment**	**=**	**Accounts Payable**	**+**	**C. Taylor, Capital**
Old Bal.	$1,500	+	$2,500	+	$26,000	=			$30,000
(4)		+	**7,100**				**+$7,100**		
New Bal.	$1,500	+	$9,600	+	$26,000	=	$ 7,100	+	$30,000
	$37,100						$37,100		

Transaction 5: Provide Services for Cash FastForward earns revenues by consulting with clients about test results on athletic shoes. It earns net income only if its revenues are greater than its expenses incurred in earning them. In one of its first jobs, FastForward provides consulting services to an athletic club and immediately collects $4,200 cash. The accounting equation reflects this increase in cash of $4,200 and in equity of $4,200. This increase in equity is identified in the far right column under Revenues because the cash is earned by providing consulting services.

	Assets					=	Liabilities	+	Equity		
	Cash	+	**Supplies**	+	**Equipment**	=	**Accounts Payable**	+	**C. Taylor, Capital**	+	**Revenues**
Old Bal.	$1,500	+	$9,600	+	$26,000	=	$7,100	+	$30,000		
(5)	**+4,200**									+	**$4,200**
New Bal.	$5,700	+	$9,600	+	$26,000	=	$7,100	+	$30,000	+	$ 4,200
			$41,300						**$41,300**		

Transactions 6 and 7: Payment of Expenses in Cash FastForward pays $1,000 rent to the landlord of the building where its store is located. Paying this amount allows FastForward to occupy the space for the month of December. The rental payment is reflected in the following accounting equation as transaction 6. FastForward also pays the biweekly $700 salary of the company's only employee. This is reflected in the accounting equation as transaction 7. Both transactions 6 and 7 are December expenses for FastForward. The costs of both rent and salary are expenses, as opposed to assets, because their benefits are used in December (they have no future benefits after December). These transactions also use up an asset (cash) in carrying out FastForward's operations. The accounting equation shows that both transactions reduce cash and equity. The far right column identifies these decreases as Expenses.

	Assets					=	Liabilities	+	Equity				
	Cash	+	**Supplies**	+	**Equipment**	=	**Accounts Payable**	+	**C. Taylor, Capital**	+	**Revenues**	−	**Expenses**
Old Bal.	$5,700	+	$9,600	+	$26,000	=	$7,100	+	$30,000	+	$4,200		
(6)	**−1,000**											−	**$1,000**
Bal.	4,700	+	9,600	+	26,000	=	7,100	+	30,000	+	4,200	−	1,000
(7)	**− 700**											−	**700**
New Bal.	$4,000	+	$9,600	+	$26,000	=	$7,100	+	$30,000	+	$4,200	−	$ 1,700
			$39,600								$39,600		

Transaction 8: Provide Services and Facilities for Credit FastForward provides consulting services of $1,600 and rents its test facilities for $300 to an amateur sports club. The rental involves allowing club members to try recommended shoes at FastForward's testing grounds. The sports club is billed for the $1,900 total. This transaction results in a new asset, called *accounts receivable,* from this client. It also yields an increase in equity from the two revenue components reflected in the Revenues column of the accounting equation:

	Assets							=	Liabilities	+	Equity				
	Cash	+	**Accounts Receivable**	+	**Supplies**	+	**Equipment**	=	**Accounts Payable**	+	**C. Taylor, Capital**	+	**Revenues**	−	**Expenses**
Old Bal.	$4,000	+		+	$9,600	+	$26,000	=	$7,100	+	$30,000	+	$4,200	−	$1,700
(8)		+	**$1,900**									+	**1,600**		
												+	**300**		
New Bal.	$4,000	+	$ 1,900	+	$9,600	+	$26,000	=	$7,100	+	$30,000	+	$6,100	−	$1,700
					$41,500								$41,500		

Transaction 9: Receipt of Cash from Accounts Receivable The client in transaction 8 (the amateur sports club) pays $1,900 to FastForward 10 days after it is billed for consulting services. This transaction 9 does not change the total amount of assets and

Point: Receipt of cash is not always a revenue.

does not affect liabilities or equity. It converts the receivable (an asset) to cash (another asset). It does not create new revenue. Revenue was recognized when FastForward rendered the services in transaction 8, not when the cash is now collected. This emphasis on the earnings process instead of cash flows is a goal of the revenue recognition principle and yields useful information to users. The new balances follow:

	Assets							= Liabilities +			Equity			
	Cash	+	Accounts Receivable	+	Supplies	+	Equipment	=	Accounts Payable	+	C. Taylor, Capital	+ Revenues	−	Expenses
Old Bal.	$4,000	+	$1,900	+	$9,600	+	$26,000	=	$7,100	+	$30,000	+ $6,100	−	$1,700
(9)	+1,900	−	1,900											
New Bal.	$5,900	+	$ 0	+	$9,600	+	$26,000	=	$7,100	+	$30,000	+ $6,100	−	$1,700
	$41,500								$41,500					

Transaction 10: Payment of Accounts Payable FastForward pays CalTech Supply $900 cash as partial payment for its earlier $7,100 purchase of supplies (transaction 4), leaving $6,200 unpaid. The accounting equation shows that this transaction decreases FastForward's cash by $900 and decreases its liability to CalTech Supply by $900. Equity does not change. This event does not create an expense even though cash flows out of FastForward (instead the expense is recorded when FastForward derives the benefits from these supplies).

	Assets							= Liabilities +			Equity			
	Cash	+	Accounts Receivable	+	Supplies	+	Equipment	=	Accounts Payable	+	C. Taylor, Capital	+ Revenues	−	Expenses
Old Bal.	$5,900	+	$ 0	+	$9,600	+	$26,000	=	$7,100	+	$30,000	+ $6,100	−	$1,700
(10)	− 900								− 900					
New Bal.	$5,000	+	$ 0	+	$9,600	+	$26,000	=	$6,200	+	$30,000	+ $6,100	−	$1,700
	$40,600								$40,600					

Transaction 11: Withdrawal of Cash by Owner The owner of FastForward withdraws $600 cash for personal use. Withdrawals (decreases in equity) are not reported as expenses because they are not part of the company's earnings process. Since withdrawals are not company expenses, they are not used in computing net income.

	Assets							= Liabilities +			Equity					
	Cash	+	Accounts Receivable	+	Supplies	+	Equipment	=	Accounts Payable	+	C. Taylor, Capital	−	C. Taylor, Withdrawals	+	Revenues	− Expenses
Old Bal.	$5,000	+	$ 0	+	$9,600	+	$26,000	=	$6,200	+	$30,000			+	$6,100	− $1,700
(11)	− 600											−	$600			
New Bal.	$4,400	+	$ 0	+	$9,600	+	$26,000	=	$6,200	+	$30,000	−	$600	+	$6,100	− $1,700
	$40,000								$40,000							

Summary of Transactions

Point: Knowing how financial statements are prepared improves our analysis of them. We develop the skills for analysis of financial statements throughout the book. Chapter 17 focuses on financial statement analysis.

We summarize in Exhibit 1.9 the effects of these 11 transactions of FastForward using the accounting equation. Two points should be noted. First, the accounting equation remains in balance after each transaction. Second, transactions can be analyzed by their effects on components of the accounting equation. For example, in transactions 2, 3, and 9, one asset increased while another decreased by equal amounts.

Exhibit 1.9

Summary of Transactions Using the Accounting Equation

	Assets					= Liabilities +	Equity			
	Cash	+ Accounts Receivable	+ Supplies	+ Equipment	=	Accounts Payable	+ C.Taylor, Capital	− C.Taylor, Withdrawals	+ Revenues	− Expenses
(1)	**$30,000**				**=**		**$30,000**			
(2)	**− 2,500**		**+ $2,500**							
Bal.	27,500		+ 2,500		=		30,000			
(3)	**−26,000**			**+ $26,000**						
Bal.	1,500		+ 2,500	+ 26,000	=		30,000			
(4)			**+ 7,100**			**+$7,100**				
Bal.	1,500		+ 9,600	+ 26,000	=	7,100	+ 30,000			
(5)	**+ 4,200**								**+ $4,200**	
Bal.	5,700		+ 9,600	+ 26,000	=	7,100	+ 30,000		+ 4,200	
(6)	**− 1,000**									**− $1,000**
Bal.	4,700		+ 9,600	+ 26,000	=	7,100	+ 30,000		+ 4,200	− 1,000
(7)	**− 700**									**− 700**
Bal.	4,000		+ 9,600	+ 26,000	=	7,100	+ 30,000		+ 4,200	− 1,700
(8)		**+ $1,900**							**+ 1,600** **+ 300**	
Bal.	4,000	+ 1,900	+ 9,600	+ 26,000	=	7,100	+ 30,000		+ 6,100	− 1,700
(9)	**+ 1,900**	**− 1,900**								
Bal.	5,900	+ 0	+ 9,600	+ 26,000	=	7,100	+ 30,000		+ 6,100	− 1,700
(10)	**− 900**					**− 900**				
Bal.	5,000	+ 0	+ 9,600	+ 26,000	=	6,200	+ 30,000		+ 6,100	− 1,700
(11)	**− 600**							**− $600**		
Bal.	$ 4,400	+ $ 0	+ $ 9,600	+ $ 26,000	=	$ 6,200	+ $ 30,000	− $ 600	+ $6,100	− $1,700

Quick Check

17. When is the accounting equation in balance, and what does that mean?

18. How can a transaction not affect any liability and equity accounts?

19. Describe a transaction increasing equity and one decreasing it.

20. Identify a transaction that decreases both assets and liabilities.

Answers—p. 26

Financial Statements

P1 Identify and prepare basic financial statements and explain how they interrelate.

This section shows how financial statements are prepared from the analysis of business transactions. The four financial statements and their purposes are:

1. ***Income statement***—describes a company's revenues and expenses along with the resulting net income or loss over a period of time due to earnings activities.
2. ***Statement of owner's equity***—explains changes in equity from net income (or loss) and from the owner investments and withdrawals over a period of time.
3. ***Balance sheet***—describes a company's financial position (types and amounts of assets, liabilities, and equity) at a point in time.
4. ***Statement of cash flows***—identifies cash inflows (receipts) and cash outflows (payments) over a period of time.

Topic Tackler 1-2

We prepare these financial statements using the 11 selected transactions of FastForward. (These statements are technically called *unadjusted*—we explain this in Chapters 2 and 3.)

Income Statement

Point: Net income is sometimes called earnings or profit.

FastForward's income statement for December is shown at the top of Exhibit 1.10. Information about revenues and expenses is conveniently taken from the Equity columns of Exhibit 1.9. Revenues are reported first on the income statement. They include consulting revenues of $5,800 from transactions 5 and 8 and rental revenue of $300 from transaction 8. Expenses are reported after revenues. (For convenience in this chapter, we list larger amounts first, but we can sort expenses in different ways.) Rent and salary expenses are from transactions 6 and 7. Expenses reflect the costs to generate the revenues reported. Net income (or loss) is reported at the bottom of the statement and is the amount earned in December. Owner's investments and withdrawals are *not* part of income.

Point: Decision makers often compare income to the operating cash flows from the statement of cash flows to help assess how much income is in the form of cash.

Statement of Owner's Equity

The statement of owner's equity reports information about how equity changes over the reporting period. This statement shows beginning capital, events that increase it (owner investments and net income), and events that decrease it (withdrawals and net loss). Ending capital is computed in this statement and is carried over and reported on the balance sheet. FastForward's statement of owner's equity is the second report in Exhibit 1.10. The beginning capital balance is measured as of the start of business on December 1. It is zero because FastForward did not exist before then. An existing business reports the beginning balance as of the end of the prior reporting period (such as from November 30). FastForward's statement shows that Taylor's initial investment created $30,000 of equity. It also shows the $4,400 of net income earned during the period. This links the income statement to the statement of owner's equity (see line ①). The statement also reports Taylor's $600 withdrawal and FastForward's $33,800 end-of-period capital balance.

Point: The statement of owner's equity is also called the *statement of changes in owner's equity.* Note: Beg. Capital + Owner Investments + Net Income − Withdrawals = End. Capital

Balance Sheet

FastForward's balance sheet is the third report in Exhibit 1.10. This statement refers to FastForward's financial condition at the close of business on December 31. The left side of the balance sheet lists FastForward's assets: cash, supplies, and equipment. The upper right side of the balance sheet shows that FastForward owes $6,200 to creditors. Any other liabilities (such as a bank loan) would be listed here. The equity (capital) balance is $33,800. Note the link between the ending balance of the statement of owner's equity and the equity balance here—see line ②. (This presentation of the balance sheet is called the *account form:* assets on the left and liabilities and equity on the right. Another presentation is the *report form:* assets on top, followed by liabilities and then equity at the bottom. Either presentation is acceptable.)

***Decision Maker** boxes are role-playing exercises that stress the relevance of accounting.*

Decision Maker

Retailer You open a wholesale business selling entertainment equipment to retail outlets. You find that most of your customers demand to buy on credit. How can you use the balance sheets of these customers to help you decide which ones to extend credit to?

Answer—p. 26

Statement of Cash Flows

FastForward's statement of cash flows is the final report in Exhibit 1.10. The first section reports cash flows from *operating activities*. It shows the $6,100 cash received from clients and the cash paid for supplies, rent, and employee salaries. Outflows are in parentheses to denote subtraction. Net cash provided by operating activities for December is $1,000. If cash paid exceeded cash received, we would call it "cash used by operating activities." The second section reports *investing activities,* which involve buying and selling assets such as land and equipment that are held for *long-term use* (typically more than one-year). The only investing activity is the $26,000 purchase of equipment. The third section shows cash flows from *financing activities,* which include the *long-term* borrowing and repaying of cash from lenders and the owner's cash investments and withdrawals. FastForward reports $30,000

Point: Statement of cash flows has three main sections: operating, investing, and financing.

Point: Payment for supplies is an operating activity because supplies are expected to be used up in short-term operations (typically less than one year).

Exhibit 1.10

Financial Statements and Their Links

FASTFORWARD
Income Statement
For Month Ended December 31, 2004

Revenues:		
Consulting revenue ($4,200 + $1,600)	$ 5,800	
Rental revenue	300	
Total revenues		$ 6,100
Expenses:		
Rent expense	1,000	
Salaries expense	700	
Total expenses		1,700
Net income		**$ 4,400**

Point: A statement's heading identifies the company, the statement title, and the date or time period.

FASTFORWARD
Statement of Owner's Equity
For Month Ended December 31, 2004

C. Taylor, Capital, December 1, 2004		$ 0
Plus: Investments by owner	$30,000	
Net income	**4,400**	34,400
		34,400
Less: Withdrawals by owner		600
C. Taylor, Capital, December 31, 2004		**$33,800**

Point: Arrow lines show how the statements are linked. (1) Net income is used to compute equity. (2) Equity is used to prepare the balance sheet. (3) Cash from the balance sheet is used to reconcile the statement of cash flows.

FASTFORWARD
Balance Sheet
December 31, 2004

Assets		Liabilities	
Cash	**$ 4,400**	Accounts payable	$ 6,200
Supplies	9,600	Total liabilities	6,200
Equipment	26,000		
		Equity	
		C. Taylor, Capital	**33,800**
Total assets	$40,000	Total liabilities and equity	$ 40,000

Point: The income statement, the statement of owner's equity, and the statement of cash flows are prepared for a *period* of time. The balance sheet is prepared as of a *point* in time.

FASTFORWARD
Statement of Cash Flows
For Month Ended December 31, 2004

Cash flows from operating activities:		
Cash received from clients ($4,200 + $1,900)	$ 6,100	
Cash paid for supplies ($2,500 + $900)	(3,400)	
Cash paid for rent	(1,000)	
Cash paid to employee	(700)	
Net cash provided by operating activities		$ 1,000
Cash flows from investing activities:		
Purchase of equipment	(26,000)	
Net cash used by investing activities		(26,000)
Cash flows from financing activities:		
Investments by owner	30,000	
Withdrawals by owner	(600)	
Net cash provided by financing activities		29,400
Net increase in cash		$ 4,400
Cash balance, December 1, 2004		0
Cash balance, December 31, 2004		**$ 4,400**

Point: A single ruled line denotes an addition or subtraction. Final totals are double underlined. Negative amounts are often in parentheses.

Point: Investing activities refer to long-term asset investments by the company, *not* to owner investments.

from the owner's initial investment and the $600 owner withdrawal. The net cash effect of all transactions is a $29,400 cash inflow. The final part of the statement shows FastForward increased its cash balance by $4,400 in December. Since it started with no cash, the ending balance is also $4,400—see line ③.

Quick Check

21. Explain the link between the income statement and the statement of owner's equity.
22. Describe the link between the balance sheet and the statement of owner's equity.
23. Discuss the three major sections of the statement of cash flows.

Answers—p. 27

***Decision Analysis** (a section at the end of each chapter) introduces and explains ratios helpful in decision making using real company data. Instructors can skip this section and cover all ratios in Chapter 17.*

Decision Analysis — Return on Assets

A *Decision Analysis* section at the end of each chapter is devoted to financial statement analysis. We organize financial statement analysis into four areas: (1) liquidity and efficiency, (2) solvency, (3) profitability, and (4) market prospects—the back inside cover has a ratio listing with definitions and grouping by area. When analyzing ratios, we need benchmarks to identify good, bad, or average levels. Common benchmarks include the company's prior levels and those of its competitors.

A3 Compute and interpret return on assets.

This chapter presents a profitability measure, that of return on assets. Return on assets is useful in evaluating management, analyzing and forecasting profits, and planning activities. **Dell Computer** has its marketing department compute return on assets for *every* mailing. *Return on assets (ROA)*, also called *return on investment (ROI)*, is defined in Exhibit 1.11.

Exhibit 1.11
Return on Assets

$$\textbf{Return on assets} = \frac{\textbf{Net income}}{\textbf{Average total assets}}$$

Net income is from the annual income statement, and average total assets is computed by adding the beginning and ending amounts for that same period and dividing by 2. To illustrate, **Nike** reports net income of $663.3 million in 2002. At the beginning of fiscal 2002, its total assets are $5,819.6 million and at the end of fiscal 2002, they total $6,443.0 million. Nike's return on assets for 2002 is:

$$\text{Return on assets} = \frac{\$663.3 \text{ mil.}}{(\$5{,}819.6 \text{ mil.} + \$6{,}443.0 \text{ mil.})/2} = 10.8\%$$

Is a 10.8% return on assets good or bad for Nike? To help answer this question, we compare (benchmark) Nike's return with its prior performance, the returns of competitors (such as **Reebok**, **Converse**, **Skechers**, and **Vans**), and the returns from alternative investments. Nike's return for each of the prior five years is in the second column of Exhibit 1.12, which ranges from 7.4% to 10.8%. These returns show an increase in its productive use of assets in recent years. We also compute Reebok's returns in the third column of Exhibit 1.12. In four of the five years, Nike's return exceeds Reebok's, and its average return is higher for this period. We also compare Nike's return to the normal return for manufacturers of athletic footwear and apparel (fourth column). Industry averages are available from services such as **Dun & Bradstreet**'s *Industry Norms and Key Ratios* and **Robert Morris Associates**' *Annual Statement Studies*. When compared to the industry, Nike performs well.

*Each **Decision Analysis** section ends with a role-playing scenario to show the usefulness of ratios.*

Decision Maker

Business Owner You own a small winter ski resort that earns a 21% return on its assets. An opportunity to purchase a winter ski equipment manufacturer is offered to you. This manufacturer earns a 19% return on its assets. The industry return for this manufacturer is 14%. Do you purchase this manufacturer?

Answer—p. 26

Nike Fiscal Year	Return on Assets		
	Nike	Reebok	Industry
2002	10.8%	6.8%	3.6%
2001	10.1	5.3	6.4
2000	10.4	0.7	5.1
1999	8.5	1.4	6.4
1998	7.4	7.7	6.1

Exhibit 1.12

Nike, Reebok, and Industry Returns

*The **Demonstration Problem** is a review of key chapter content. The* Planning the Solution *offers strategies in solving the problem.*

Demonstration Problem

After several months of planning, Sylvia Workman started a haircutting business called Expressions. The following events occurred during its first month:

a. On August 1, Workman invested $3,000 cash and $15,000 of equipment in Expressions.

b. On August 2, Expressions paid $600 cash for furniture for the shop.

c. On August 3, Expressions paid $500 cash to rent space in a strip mall for August.

d. On August 4, it purchased $1,200 of equipment on credit for the shop (using a long-term note payable).

e. On August 5, Expressions opened for business. Cash received from services provided in the first week and a half of business (ended August 15) is $825.

f. On August 15, it provided $100 of haircutting services on account.

g. On August 17, it received a $100 check for services previously rendered on account.

h. On August 17, it paid $125 cash to an assistant for working during the grand opening.

i. Cash received from services provided during the second half of August is $930.

j. On August 31, it paid a $400 installment toward principal on the note payable entered into on August 4.

k. On August 31, Workman made a $900 cash withdrawal for personal use.

Required

1. Arrange the following asset, liability, and equity titles in a table similar to the one in Exhibit 1.9: Cash; Accounts Receivable; Furniture; Store Equipment; Note Payable; S. Workman, Capital; S. Workman, Withdrawals; Revenues; and Expenses. Show the effects of each transaction using the accounting equation.
2. Prepare an income statement for August.
3. Prepare a statement of owner's equity for August.
4. Prepare a balance sheet as of August 31.
5. Prepare a statement of cash flows for August.
6. Determine the return on assets ratio for August.

Planning the Solution

- Set up a table like Exhibit 1.9 with the appropriate columns for accounts.
- Analyze each transaction and show its effects as increases or decreases in the appropriate columns. Be sure the accounting equation remains in balance after each transaction.
- Prepare the income statement, and identify revenues and expenses. List those items on the statement, compute the difference, and label the result as *net income* or *net loss*.
- Use information in the Equity columns to prepare the statement of owner's equity.
- Use information in the last row of the transactions table to prepare the balance sheet.
- Prepare the statement of cash flows; include all events listed in the Cash column of the transactions table. Classify each cash flow as operating, investing, or financing.
- Calculate return on assets by dividing net income by average assets.

Solution to Demonstration Problem

1.

	Assets							=	Liabilities +		Equity						
	Cash	+	**Accounts Receivable**	+	**Furniture**	+	**Store Equipment**	=	**Note Payable**	+	**S.Workman, Capital**	−	**S.Workman Withdrawals**	+	**Revenues**	−	**Expenses**
a.	**$3,000**						**$15,000**				**$18,000**						
b.	**− 600**			+	**$600**												
Bal.	2,400	+		+	600	+	15,000	=			18,000						
c.	**− 500**															−	**$500**
Bal.	1,900	+		+	600	+	15,000	=			18,000					−	500
d.						+	**1,200**		**+$1,200**								
Bal.	1,900	+		+	600	+	16,200	=	1,200	+	18,000					−	500
e.	**+ 825**													+	**$825**		
Bal.	2,725	+		+	600	+	16,200	=	1,200	+	18,000			+	825	−	500
f.		+	**$100**											+	**100**		
Bal.	2,725	+	100	+	600	+	16,200	=	1,200	+	18,000			+	925	−	500
g.	**+ 100**	−	**100**														
Bal.	2,825	+	0	+	600	+	16,200	=	1,200	+	18,000			+	925	−	500
h.	**− 125**															−	**125**
Bal.	2,700	+	0	+	600	+	16,200	=	1,200	+	18,000			+	925	−	625
i.	**+ 930**													+	**930**		
Bal.	3,630	+	0	+	600	+	16,200	=	1,200	+	18,000			+	1,855	−	625
j.	**− 400**								**− 400**								
Bal.	3,230	+	0	+	600	+	16,200	=	800	+	18,000			+	1,855	−	625
k.	**− 900**											−	**$900**				
Bal.	$2,330	+	0	+	$600	+	$ 16,200	=	$ 800	+	$ 18,000	−	$900	+	$1,855	−	$625

2.

EXPRESSIONS
Income Statement
For Month Ended August 31

Revenues:		
Haircutting services revenue		$1,855
Expenses:		
Rent expense	$500	
Wages expense	125	
Total expenses		625
Net Income		$1,230

3.

EXPRESSIONS
Statement of Owner's Equity
For Month Ended August 31

S. Workman, Capital, August 1*		$ 0
Plus: Investments by owner	$18,000	
Net income	1,230	19,230
		19,230
Less: Withdrawals by owner		900
S. Workman, Capital, August 31		$18,330

* If Expressions had been an existing business from a prior period, the beginning capital balance would equal the Capital account balance from the end of the prior period.

4.

EXPRESSIONS Balance Sheet August 31			
Assets		**Liabilities**	
Cash	$ 2,330	Note payable	$ 800
Furniture	600	**Equity**	
Store equipment	16,200	S. Workman, Capital	18,330
Total assets	$19,130	Total liabilities and equity	$19,130

5.

EXPRESSIONS Statement of Cash Flows For Month Ended August 31		
Cash flows from operating activities:		
Cash received from customers	$1,855	
Cash paid for rent	(500)	
Cash paid for wages	(125)	
Net cash provided by operating activities		$1,230
Cash flows from investing activities:		
Cash paid for furniture		(600)
Cash flows from financing activities:		
Cash received from owner	3,000	
Cash paid for owner withdrawal	(900)	
Partial repayment of (long-term) note payable	(400)	
Net cash provided by financing activities		1,700
Net increase in cash		$2,330
Cash balance, August 1		0
Cash balance, August 31		$2,330

6. Return on assets $= \frac{\text{Net income}}{\text{Average assets}} = \frac{\$1,230}{(\$18,000^{*} + \$19,130)/2} = \frac{\$1,230}{\$18,565} = \mathbf{6.63\%}$

* Uses the initial $18,000 investment as the begining balance for the startup period only.

APPENDIX

Return and Risk Analysis

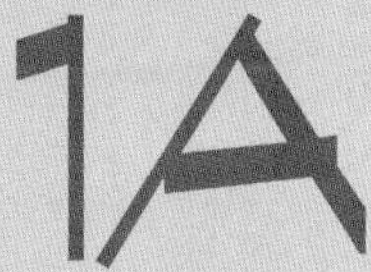

A4 Explain the relation between return and risk.

This appendix explains return and risk analysis and its role in business and accounting.

Net income is often linked to **return.** Return on assets (ROA) is stated in ratio form as income divided by assets invested. For example, banks report return from a savings account in the form of an interest return such as 4%. If we invest in a savings account or in U.S. Treasury bills, we expect a return of around 2% to 7%. We could also invest in a company's stock, or even start our own business. How do we decide among these investment options? The answer depends on our trade-off between return and risk.

Decision Insight

Celebrity Investing How do fame and fortune translate into return and risk? A poll asked people which celebrity is the best investment. Similar to business investments, many people named performers with years of earning power ahead—see results to the right.

Oprah Winfrey	27%
Steven Spielberg	19
Tiger Woods	15
Michael Jordan	14
Tom Cruise	8
Jerry Seinfeld	4
Madonna	2

Risk is the uncertainty about the return we will earn. All business investments involve risk, but some investments involve more risk than others. The lower the risk of an investment, the lower is our expected return. The reason that savings accounts pay such a low return is the low risk of not being repaid with interest (the government guarantees most savings accounts from default). If we buy a share of Nike or any other company, we might obtain a large return. However, we have no guarantee of any return; there is even the risk of loss.

The bar graph in Exhibit 1A.1 shows recent returns for bonds with different risks. *Bonds* are written promises by organizations to repay amounts loaned with interest. U.S. Treasury bonds provide a low expected return, but they also offer low risk since they are backed by the U.S. government. High-risk corporate bonds offer a much larger potential return but with much higher risk.

The trade-off between return and risk is a normal part of business. Higher risk implies higher, but riskier, expected returns. To help us make better decisions, we use accounting information to assess both return and risk.

Exhibit 1A.1

Average Returns for Bonds with Different Risks

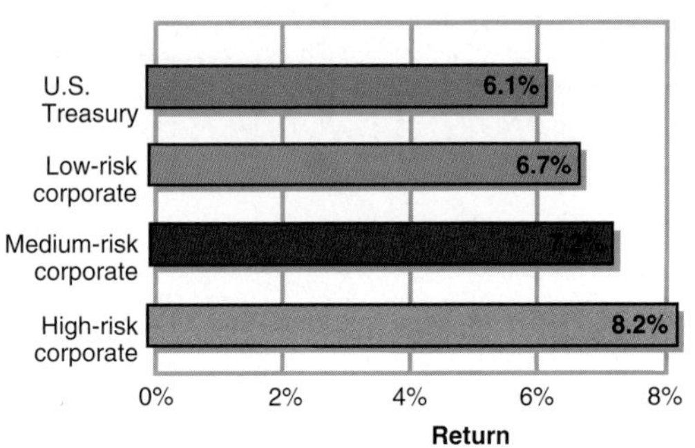

APPENDIX

1B Business Activities and the Accounting Equation

C6 Identify and describe the three major activities in organizations.

This appendix explains how the accounting equation is derived from business activities.

There are three major types of business activities: financing, investing, and operating. Each of these requires planning. *Planning* involves defining an organization's ideas, goals, and actions. Most public corporations use the *Management Discussion and Analysis* section in their annual reports to communicate plans. However, planning is not cast in stone. This adds *risk* to both setting plans and analyzing them.

Point: Management must understand accounting data to set financial goals, make financing and investing decisions, and evaluate operating performance.

Point: Investing (assets) and financing (liabilities plus equity) totals are *always* equal.

Financing *Financing activities* provide the means organizations use to pay for resources such as land, buildings, and equipment to carry out plans. Organizations are careful in acquiring and managing financing activities because they can determine success or failure. The two sources of financing are owner and nonowner. *Owner financing* refers to resources contributed by the owner along with any income the owner leaves in the organization. *Nonowner* (or *creditor*) *financing* refers to resources contributed by creditors (lenders). *Financial management* is the task of planning how to obtain these resources and to set the right mix between owner and creditor financing.

Investing *Investing activities* are the acquiring and disposing of resources (assets) that an organization uses to acquire and sell its products or services. Assets are funded by an organization's financing. Organizations differ on the amount and makeup of assets. Some require land and factories to operate. Others need only an office. Determining the amount and type of assets for operations is called *asset management*.

Invested amounts are referred to as *assets*. Financing is made up of creditor and owner financing, which hold claims on assets. Creditors' claims are called *liabilities,* and the owner's claim is called *equity.* This basic equality is called the *accounting equation* and can be written as: Assets = Liabilities + Equity.

Operating *Operating activities* involve using resources to research, develop, purchase, produce, distribute, and market products and services. Sales and revenues are the inflow of assets from selling products and services. Costs and expenses are the outflow of assets to support operating activities. *Strategic management* is the process of determining the right mix of operating activities for the type of organization, its plans, and its market.

Exhibit 1B.1 summarizes business activities. Planning is part of each activity and gives them meaning and focus. Investing (assets) and financing (liabilities and equity) are set opposite each other to stress their balance. Operating activities are below investing and financing activities to show that operating activities are the result of investing and financing.

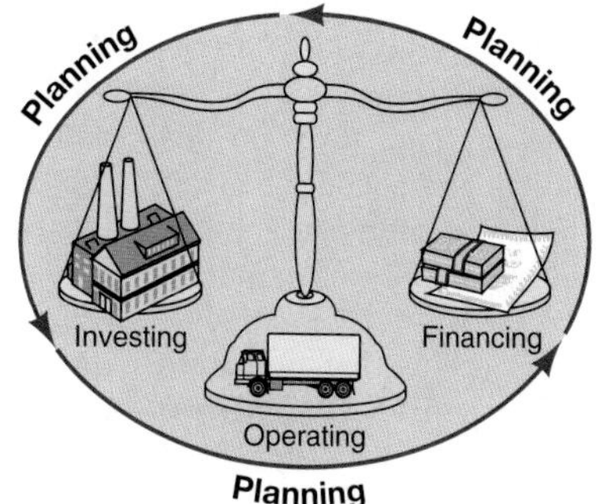

Exhibit 1B.1

Activities in Organizations

A **Summary** organized by learning objectives concludes each chapter.

Summary

C1 Explain the purpose and importance of accounting in the information age. Accounting is an information and measurement system that aims to identify, record, and communicate relevant, reliable, and comparable information about business activities. It helps assess opportunities, products, investments, and social and community responsibilities.

C2 Identify users and uses of accounting. Users of accounting are both internal and external. Some users and uses of accounting include (a) managers in controlling, monitoring, and planning; (b) lenders for measuring the risk and return of loans; (c) shareholders for assessing the return and risk of stock; (d) directors for overseeing management; and (e) employees for judging employment opportunities.

C3 Identify opportunities in accounting and related fields. Opportunities in accounting include financial, managerial, and tax accounting. They also include accounting-related fields such as lending, consulting, managing, and planning.

C4 Explain why ethics are crucial to accounting. The goal of accounting is to provide useful information for decision making. For information to be useful, it must be trusted. This demands ethical behavior in accounting.

C5 Explain the meaning of generally accepted accounting principles, and define and apply several key principles of accounting. Generally accepted accounting principles are a common set of standards applied by accountants. Accounting principles aid in producing relevant, reliable, and comparable information. The business entity principle means that a business is accounted for separately from its owner(s). The objectivity principle means independent, objective evidence supports the information. The cost principle means financial statements are based on actual costs incurred. The monetary unit principle assumes transactions can be reflected in money terms. The going-concern principle means financial statements assume the business will continue. The revenue recognition principle means revenue is recognized when earned.

C6[B] Identify and describe the three major activities in organizations. Organizations carry out three major activities: financing, investing, and operating. Financing is the means used to pay for resources such as land, buildings, and machines. Investing refers to the buying and selling of resources used in acquiring and selling products and services. Operating activities are those necessary for carrying out the organization's plans.

A1 Define and interpret the accounting equation and each of its components. The accounting equation is: Assets = Liabilities + Equity. Assets are resources owned by a company. Liabilities are creditors' claims on assets. Equity is the owner's claim on assets (*the residual*). The expanded accounting equation is: Assets = Liabilities + [Owner Capital − Owner Withdrawals + Revenues − Expenses].

A2 Analyze business transactions using the accounting equation. A *transaction* is an exchange of economic consideration between two parties. Examples include exchanges of products, services, money, and rights to collect money. Transactions always have at least two effects on one or more components of the accounting equation. This equation is always in balance.

A3 Compute and interpret return on assets. Return on assets is computed as net income divided by average assets. For example, if we have an average balance of $100 in a savings account and it earns $5 interest for the year, the return on assets is $5/$100, or 5%.

A4[A] Explain the relation between return and risk. *Return* refers to income, and *risk* is the uncertainty about the return we hope to make. All investments involve risk. The lower the risk of an investment, the lower is its expected return. Higher risk implies higher, but riskier, expected return.

P1 Identify and prepare basic financial statements and explain how they interrelate. Four financial statements report on an organization's activities: balance sheet, income statement, statement of owner's equity, and statement of cash flows.

Guidance Answers to **Decision Maker** and **Decision Ethics**

Entrepreneur (p. 11) You should probably form the business as a corporation if potential lawsuits are of prime concern. The corporate form of organization protects your personal property from lawsuits directed at the business and places only the corporation's resources at risk. A downside of the corporate form is double taxation: The corporation must pay taxes on its income, and you normally must pay taxes on any money distributed to you from the business (even though the corporation already paid taxes on this money). You should also examine the ethical and socially responsible aspects of starting a business in which you anticipate injuries to others. Formation as an LLC or S corp. should also be explored.

Retailer (p. 18) You can use the accounting equation (Assets = Liabilities + Equity) to help identify risky customers to whom you would likely not want to extend credit. A balance sheet provides amounts for each of these key components. The lower a customer's equity is relative to liabilities, the less likely you would extend credit. A low equity means the business has little value that does not already have creditor claims to it.

Business Owner (p. 20) The 19% return on assets for the manufacturer exceeds the 14% industry return (and many others). This is a positive factor for a potential purchase. Also, the purchase of this manufacturer is an opportunity to spread your risk over two businesses as opposed to one. Still, you should hesitate to purchase a business whose return of 19% is lower than your current resort's return of 21%. You are probably better off directing efforts to increase investment in your resort, assuming you can continue to earn a 21% return.

Guidance Answers to **Quick Checks**

1. Accounting is an information and measurement system that identifies, records, and communicates relevant information to help people make better decisions.

2. Recordkeeping, also called *bookkeeping,* is the recording of financial transactions and events, either manually or electronically. Recordkeeping is essential to data reliability; but accounting is this and much more. Accounting includes identifying, measuring, recording, reporting, and analyzing business events and transactions.

3. Technology offers increased accuracy, speed, efficiency, and convenience in accounting.

4. External users of accounting include lenders, shareholders, directors, customers, suppliers, regulators, lawyers, brokers, and the press. Internal users of accounting include managers, officers, and other internal decision makers involved with strategic and operating decisions.

5. Internal users (managers) include those from research and development, purchasing, human resources, production, distribution, marketing, and servicing.

6. Internal controls are procedures set up to protect assets, ensure reliable accounting reports, promote efficiency, and encourage adherence to company policies. Internal controls are crucial for relevant and reliable information.

7. Ethical guidelines are threefold: (1) identify ethical concerns using personal ethics, (2) analyze options considering all good and bad consequences, and (3) make ethical decisions after weighing all consequences.

8. Ethics and social responsibility yield good behavior, and they often result in higher income and a better working environment.

9. For accounting to provide useful information for decisions, it must be trusted. Trust requires ethics in accounting.

10. Two major participants in setting rules include the SEC and the FASB. (*Note:* Accounting rules reflect society's needs, not those of accountants or any other single constituency).

11. Most U.S. companies are not directly affected by international accounting standards. International standards are put forth as preferred accounting practices. However, stock exchanges and other parties are increasing the pressure to narrow differences in worldwide accounting practices. International accounting standards are playing an important role in that process.

12. The objectivity and cost principles are related in that most users consider information based on cost as objective. Information prepared using both principles is considered highly reliable and often relevant.

13. Users desire information about the performance of a specific entity. If information is mixed between two or more entities, its usefulness decreases.

14. The revenue recognition principle gives preparers guidelines on when to recognize (record) revenue. This is important; for example, if revenue is recognized too early, the statements report revenue sooner than it should and the business looks more profitable than it is. The reverse is also true.

15. The three basic forms of business organization are sole proprietorships, partnerships, and corporations.

16. Owners of corporations are called *shareholders* (or *stockholders*). Corporate ownership is divided into units called *shares* (or *stock*). The most basic of corporate shares is common stock (or capital stock).

17. The accounting equation is: Assets = Liabilities + Equity. This equation is always in balance, both before and after each transaction.

18. A transaction that changes the makeup of assets would not affect liability and equity accounts. FastForward's transactions 2 and 3 are examples. Each exchanges one asset for another.

19. Earning revenue by performing services, as in FastForward's transaction 5, increases equity (and assets). Incurring expenses while servicing clients, such as in transactions 6 and 7, decreases equity (and assets). Other examples include owner investments that increase equity and withdrawals that decrease equity.

20. Paying a liability with an asset reduces both asset and liability totals. One example is FastForward's transaction 10 that reduces a payable by paying cash.

21. An income statement reports a company's revenues and expenses along with the resulting net income or loss. A statement of owner's equity shows changes in equity, including that from net income or loss. Both statements report transactions occurring over a period of time.

22. The balance sheet describes a company's financial position (assets, liabilities, and equity) at a point in time. The equity account in the balance sheet is obtained from the statement of owner's equity.

23. Cash flows from operating activities report cash receipts and payments from the primary business the company engages in. Cash flows from investing activities involve cash transactions from buying and selling long-term assets. Cash flows from financing activities include long-term cash borrowings and repayments to lenders and the cash investments and withdrawals of the owner.

A list of key terms with page references concludes each chapter (a complete glossary is at the end of the book and also on the book's Website).

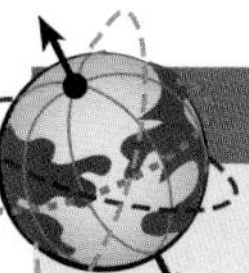

Key Terms

Key Terms are available at the book's Website for learning and testing in an online Flashcard Format.

Accounting (p. 4)
Accounting equation (p. 12)
Assets (p. 12)
Audit (p. 9)
Balance sheet (p. 17)
Bookkeeping (p. 5)
Business entity principle (p. 10)
Common stock (p. 11)
Corporation (p. 11)
Cost principle (p. 9)
Equity (p. 12)
Ethics (p. 8)
Events (p. 13)
Expanded accounting equation (p. 13)
Expenses (p. 13)
External transactions (p. 13)
External users (p. 5)
Financial accounting (p. 5)
Financial Accounting Standards Board (FASB) (p. 9)
Generally Accepted Accounting Principles (GAAP) (p. 9)
Going-concern principle (p. 10)
Income statement (p. 17)
Internal transactions (p. 13)
Internal users (p. 6)
International Accounting Standards Board (IASB) (p. 9)
Liabilities (p. 12)
Managerial accounting (p. 6)
Monetary unit principle (p. 10)
Net assets (p. 12)
Net income (p. 13)
Net loss (p. 13)
Objectivity principle (p. 9)
Owner investment (p. 13)
Owner withdrawals (p. 13)
Partnership (p. 10)
Proprietorship (p. 10)
Recordkeeping (p. 5)
Return (p. 23)
Return on assets (p. 20)
Revenues (p. 13)
Revenue recognition principle (p. 10)
Risk (p. 24)
Securities and Exchange Commission (SEC) (p. 9)
Shareholders (p. 11)
Shares (p. 11)
Sole proprietorship (p. 10)
Statement of cash flows (p. 17)
Statement of owner's equity (p. 17)
Stock (p. 11)
Stockholders (p. 11)
Withdrawals (p. 13)

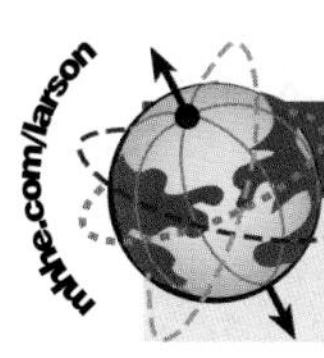

Personal Interactive Quiz

Personal Interactive Quizzes A and B are available at the book's Website to reinforce and assess your learning.

Superscript letter A (B) denotes assignments based on Appendix 1A (1B).

Discussion Questions

1. What is the purpose of accounting in society?

2. Identify three actual businesses that offer services and three actual businesses that offer products.

3. Why do organizations license and monitor accounting and accounting-related professionals?

4. Technology is increasingly used to process accounting data. Why then must we study and understand accounting?

5. Identify four kinds of external users and describe their uses of accounting information.

6. What are at least three questions business owners might be able to answer by looking at accounting information?
7. Describe the internal role of accounting for organizations.
8. What type of accounting information might be useful to those who carry out the marketing activities of a business?
9. Identify three types of services typically offered by accounting professionals.
10. Why is accounting described as a service activity?
11. Identify at least three tasks you would expect to be performed by government accounting professionals.
12. What work do tax accounting professionals perform in addition to preparing tax returns?
13. What ethical issues might accounting professionals face in dealing with confidential information?
14. Identify the two main categories of accounting principles.
15. What does the objectivity principle prescribe for information reported in financial statements? Why?
16. A business reports its own office stationery on the balance sheet at its $430 cost, although it cannot be sold for more than $10 as scrap paper. Which accounting principle(s) justifies this treatment?
17. Why is the revenue recognition principle needed? What does it prescribe?
18. Describe the three basic forms of business organization and their key characteristics.
19. Identify three types of organizations that can be formed as either profit-oriented entities or government (or non-profit) entities.
20. Define (*a*) *assets,* (*b*) *liabilities,* (*c*) *equity,* and (*d*) *net assets.*
21. What events or transactions change equity?
22. What do accountants mean by the term *revenue?*
23. Define *net income* and explain its computation.
24. Identify the four basic financial statements of a business.
25. What information is reported in an income statement?
26. Give two examples of expenses a business might incur.
27. What information is reported in a balance sheet?
28. The statement of cash flows reports on what major activities?
29. Define and explain return on assets.
30.[A] Explain return and risk. Discuss the trade-off between them.
31.[B] Describe the three major activities in organizations.
32.[B] Explain why investing (assets) and financing (liabilities and equity) totals are always equal.
33. Refer to the financial statements of **Krispy Kreme** in Appendix A. To what level of significance are dollar amounts rounded? What time period does its income statement cover?
34. Identify the dollar amounts of **Tastykake**'s 2002 assets, liabilities, and equity shown in its statements in Appendix A near the end of the book.
35. Access the SEC EDGAR database (www.SEC.gov) and retrieve **Harley-Davidson**'s 2002 10-K (filed 2003-03-28). Identify its auditor. What responsibility does its independent auditor claim regarding its financial statements?

Red numbers denote Discussion Questions that involve decision-making.

***Quick Study** exercises give readers a brief test of key elements.*

***Homework Manager** repeats all numerical Quick Study assignments on the book's Website with new numbers each time it is worked. It can be used in practice, homework, or exam mode.*

QUICK STUDY

QS 1-1
Identifying accounting users
C2

Identify the following users as either external users (E) or internal users (I).

a. Managers	**d.** FBI and CIA	**g.** Consumer group	**j.** Shareholders
b. Controllers	**e.** Sales staff	**h.** Customers	**k.** Congress
c. Business press	**f.** Brokers	**i.** Lenders	**l.** District attorney

QS 1-2
Identifying accounting terms
C1

(*a*) Identify the meaning of these accounting-related acronyms: GAAP, SEC, and FASB, and then briefly explain the importance of each to accounting. (*b*) Identify the international accounting standards setting organization, and then briefly explain its purpose.

QS 1-3
Accounting opportunities
C3

Identify at least three main areas of opportunities for accounting professionals. For each area, identify at least three job possibilities linked to accounting.

QS 1-4
Identifying ethical concerns
C4

Accounting professionals must sometimes choose between two or more acceptable methods of accounting for business transactions and events. Explain why these situations can involve difficult matters of ethical concern.

Thinker icon highlights assignments that use decision-making skills.

QS 1-5
Identifying transactions and events
A2

Accounting provides information about an organization's business transactions and events that both affect the accounting equation and can be reliably measured. Identify at least two examples of both (*a*) business transactions and (*b*) business events that meet these requirements.

QS 1-6
Explaining internal control
C1

An important responsibility of many accounting professionals is to design and implement internal control procedures for organizations. Explain the purpose of internal control procedures.

QS 1-7
Identifying accounting principles
C5 

Identify which general accounting principle best describes each of the following practices:

a. Marilyn Choi owns both Sailing Passions and Dockside Supplies. In preparing financial statements for Dockside Supplies, Choi makes sure that the expense transactions of Sailing Passions are kept separate from Dockside's statements.

b. In December 2004, A-Plus Floors received a customer's order and cash prepayment to install carpet in a new house that would not be ready for installation until March 2005. A-Plus Floors should record the revenue from the customer order in March 2005, not in December 2004.

c. If $30,000 cash is paid to buy land, the land is reported on the buyer's balance sheet at $30,000.

QS 1-8
Applying the accounting equation
A1 

a. Total assets of HLC Financial Co. equal $40,000 and its equity is $10,000. What is the amount of its liabilities?

b. Total assets of Deep Valley Co. equal $55,000 and its liabilities and equity amounts are equal. What is the amount of its liabilities? What is the amount of its equity?

QS 1-9
Applying the accounting equation
A1

Use the accounting equation to compute the missing financial statement amounts (*a*), (*b*), and (*c*).

Company	Assets	=	Liabilities	+	Equity
1	$30,000		$ (*a*)		$20,000
2	$ (*b*)		$50,000		$30,000
3	$90,000		$10,000		$ (*c*)

QS 1-10
Identifying and computing assets, liabilities, and equity
A2  **Harley-Davidson**

Use **Harley-Davidson**'s December 31, 2002, financial statements, in Appendix A near the end of the book, to answer the following:

a. Identify the dollar amounts of Harley's 2002 (1) assets, (2) liabilities, and (3) equity.

b. Using Harley's amounts from part *a*, verify that Assets = Liabilities + Equity.

QS 1-11
Classifying items by financial statements
P1

Indicate in which financial statement each item would most likely appear: income statement (I), balance sheet (B), statement of owner's equity (E), or statement of cash flows (CF).

a. Assets
b. Revenues
c. Liabilities
d. Equipment
e. Withdrawals
f. Expenses
g. Total liabilities and equity
h. Cash from operating activities
i. Net decrease (or increase) in cash

QS 1-12
Computing and interpreting return on assets
A3 

In a recent year's financial statements, **Boeing Company**, which is the largest aerospace company in the United States, reported the following. Compute and interpret Boeing's return on assets (assume competitors average a 6% return on assets).

Sales	$21,924 million
Net income	856 million
Average total assets	21,463 million

Homework Manager *repeats all numerical Exercises on the book's Website with new numbers each time they are worked. It can be used in practice, homework, or exam mode.*

EXERCISES

Exercise 1-1
Distinguishing business organizations

C5

The following describe several different business organizations. Determine whether the description refers to a sole proprietorship, partnership, or corporation.

a. Ownership of Spirit Company is divided into 1,000 shares of stock.

b. Delta is owned by Sarah Gomez, who is personally liable for the debts of the business.

c. Jo Chen and Al Fitch own Financial Services, a financial services provider. Neither Chen nor Fitch has personal responsibility for the debts of Financial Services.

d. Sung Kwon and Frank Heflin own Get-It-There, a courier service. Both are personally liable for the debts of the business.

e. XLT Services does not have separate legal existence apart from the one person who owns it.

f. BioProducts does not pay income taxes and has one owner.

g. Tampa Biz pays its own income taxes and has two owners.

Exercise 1-2
Identifying accounting principles

C5

Match each of the numbered descriptions with the principle it best reflects. Indicate your answer by writing the letter for the appropriate principle in the blank space next to each description.

A. General accounting principle
B. Cost principle
C. Business entity principle
D. Revenue recognition principle
E. Specific accounting principle
F. Objectivity principle
G. Going-concern principle

_____ **1.** Usually created by a pronouncement from an authoritative body.
_____ **2.** Financial statements reflect the assumption that the business continues operating.
_____ **3.** Derived from long-used and generally accepted accounting practices.
_____ **4.** Financial statement information is supported by evidence other than someone's opinion or belief.
_____ **5.** Every business is accounted for separately from its owner or owners.
_____ **6.** Revenue is recorded only when the earnings process is complete.
_____ **7.** Information is based on actual costs incurred in transactions.

Exercise 1-3
Describing accounting responsibilities

C2 C3

Many accounting professionals work in one of the following three areas:

A. Financial accounting **B.** Managerial accounting **C.** Tax accounting

Identify the area of accounting that is most involved in each of the following responsibilities:

_____ **1.** External auditing.
_____ **2.** Cost accounting.
_____ **3.** Budgeting.
_____ **4.** Internal auditing.
_____ **5.** Planning transactions to minimize taxes.
_____ **6.** Preparing external financial statements.
_____ **7.** Reviewing reports for SEC compliance.
_____ **8.** Investigating violations of tax laws.

Exercise 1-4
Identifying accounting users and uses

Much of accounting is directed at servicing the information needs of those users that are external to an organization. Identify at least three external users of accounting information and indicate two questions they might seek to answer through their use of accounting information.

Exercise 1-5
Identifying ethical concerns

Assume the following role and describe a situation in which ethical considerations play an important part in guiding your decisions and actions:

a. You are a student in an introductory accounting course.

b. You are a manager with responsibility for several employees.

c. You are an accounting professional preparing tax returns for clients.

d. You are an accounting professional with audit clients that are competitors in business.

Exercise 1-6
Learning the language of business
C1–C4

Match each of the numbered descriptions with the term or phrase it best reflects. Indicate your answer by writing the letter for the term or phrase in the blank provided.

A. Audit **C.** Ethics **E.** SEC **G.** Net income
B. GAAP **D.** Tax accounting **F.** Public accountants **H.** IASB

______ **1.** Amount a business earns after paying all expenses and costs associated with its sales and revenues.

______ **2.** An examination of an organization's accounting system and records that adds credibility to financial statements.

______ **3.** Principles that determine whether an action is right or wrong.

______ **4.** Accounting professionals who provide services to many clients.

______ **5.** An accounting area that includes planning future transactions to minimize taxes paid.

Exercise 1-7
Using the accounting equation
A1 A2

Answer the following questions. (*Hint:* Use the accounting equation.)

a. Fong's Medical Supplies has assets equal to $123,000 and liabilities equal to $53,000 at year-end. What is the total equity for Fong's business at year-end?

b. At the beginning of the year, Beyonce Company's assets are $200,000 and its equity is $150,000. During the year, assets increase $70,000 and liabilities increase $30,000. What is the equity at the end of the year?

c. At the beginning of the year, New Wave Company's liabilities equal $60,000. During the year, assets increase by $80,000, and at year-end assets equal $180,000. Liabilities decrease $10,000 during the year. What are the beginning and ending amounts of equity?

Check (c) Beg. equity, $40,000

Exercise 1-8
Using the accounting equation
A1

Determine the missing amount from each of the separate situations a, b, and c below.

	Assets	=	Liabilities	+	Equity
a.	?	=	$30,000	+	$65,000
b.	$ 89,000	=	$22,000	+	?
c.	$132,000	=	?	+	$20,000

Exercise 1-9
Identifying effects of transactions on the accounting equation
A1 A2

Provide an example of a transaction that creates the described effects for the separate cases *a* through *g*.

a. Decreases an asset and decreases equity.
b. Increases an asset and increases a liability.
c. Decreases a liability and increases a liability.
d. Decreases an asset and decreases a liability.
e. Increases an asset and decreases an asset.
f. Increases a liability and decreases equity.
g. Increases an asset and increases equity.

Exercise 1-10
Analysis using the accounting equation
A1 A2

Mulan began a new consulting firm on January 5. The accounting equation showed the following balances after each of the company's first five transactions. Analyze the accounting equation for each transaction and describe each of the five transactions with their amounts.

	Assets							=	Liabilities	+	Equity		
Transaction	Cash	+	Accounts Receivable	+	Office Supplies	+	Office Furniture	=	Accounts Payable	+	Mulan, Capital	+	Revenues
a.	$20,000	+	$ 0	+	$ 0	+	$ 0	=	$ 0	+	$20,000	+	$ 0
b.	19,000	+	0	+	1,500	+	0	=	500	+	20,000	+	0
c.	11,000	+	0	+	1,500	+	8,000	=	500	+	20,000	+	0
d.	11,000	+	3,000	+	1,500	+	8,000	=	500	+	20,000	+	3,000
e.	11,500	+	3,000	+	1,500	+	8,000	=	500	+	20,000	+	3,500

Exercise 1-11
Identifying effects of transactions on accounting equation
A1 A2

The following table shows the effects of five transactions (*a* through *e*) on the assets, liabilities, and equity of Bonita Boutique. Write short descriptions of the probable nature of each transaction.

	Assets				= Liabilities	+ Equity	
	Cash	+ Accounts Receivable	+ Office Supplies	+ Land	= Accounts Payable	+ Bonita, Capital	+ Revenues
	$ 10,500	+ $ 0	+ $1,500	+ $ 9,500	= $ 0	+ $21,500	+ $ 0
a.	− 2,000			+ 2,000			
b.			+ 500		+500		
c.		+ 950					+ 950
d.	− 500				−500		
e.	+ 950	− 950					
	$ 8,950	+ $ 0	+ $2,000	+ $ 11,500	= $ 0	+ $21,500	+ $950

Exercise 1-12
Identifying effects of transactions on the accounting equation and computing return on assets
A1 A2

Pamela Maben began a professional practice on June 1 and plans to prepare financial statements at the end of each month. During June, Maben (the owner) completed these transactions:

a. Owner invested $50,000 cash along with equipment that had a $10,000 market value.
b. Paid $1,600 cash for rent of office space for the month.
c. Purchased $12,000 of additional equipment on credit (due within 30 days).
d. Completed work for a client and immediately collected the $2,000 cash earned.
e. Completed work for a client and sent a bill for $7,000 to be paid within 30 days.
f. Purchased additional equipment for $8,000 cash.
g. Paid an assistant $2,400 cash as wages for the month.
h. Collected $5,000 cash on the amount owed by the client described in transaction *e*.
i. Paid $12,000 cash to settle the liability created in transaction *c*.
j. Owner withdrew $500 cash for personal use.

Required

Create a table like the one in Exhibit 1.9, using the following headings for columns: Cash; Accounts Receivable; Equipment; Accounts Payable; Maben, Capital; Maben, Withdrawals; Revenues; and Expenses. Then use additions and subtractions to show the effects of the transactions on individual items of the accounting equation. Show new balances after each transaction.

Check Net income, $5,000

Exercise 1-13
Preparing an income statement
P1

On October 1, Sasha Shandi organized Best Answers a new consulting firm. On October 31, the company's records show the following items and amounts. Use this information to prepare an October income statement for the business.

Cash	$ 2,000	Cash withdrawals by owner	$ 3,360
Accounts receivable	13,000	Consulting fees earned	15,000
Office supplies	4,250	Rent expense	2,550
Land	36,000	Salaries expense	6,000
Office equipment	28,000	Telephone expense	660
Accounts payable	7,500	Miscellaneous expenses	680
Owner investments	74,000		

Check Net income, $5,110

Exercise 1-14
Preparing a statement of owner's equity P1

Use the information in Exercise 1-13 to prepare an October statement of owner's equity for Best Answers.

Exercise 1-15
Preparing a balance sheet P1

Use the information in Exercise 1-13 (if completed, you can also use your solution to Exercise 1-14) to prepare an October 31 balance sheet for Best Answers.

Exercise 1-16
Preparing a statement of cash flows
P1

Use the information in Exercise 1-13 to prepare an October 31 statement of cash flows for Best Answers. Also assume the following:

a. The owner's initial investment consists of $38,000 cash and $36,000 in land.
b. The $28,000 equipment purchase is paid in cash.
c. The accounts payable balance of $7,500 consists of the $4,250 office supplies purchase and $3,250 in employee salaries yet to be paid.
d. The rent, telephone, and miscellaneous expenses are paid in cash.
e. Only $2,000 cash has been collected for the $15,000 consulting services provided.

Check Net increase in cash, $2,000

Exercise 1-17
Identifying sections of the statement of cash flows
P1

Indicate the section where each of the following would appear on the statement of cash flows.

A. Cash flows from operating activity
B. Cash flows from investing activity
C. Cash flows from financing activity

______ **1.** Cash paid for wages
______ **2.** Cash withdrawal by owner
______ **3.** Cash purchase of equipment
______ **4.** Cash paid for advertising
______ **5.** Cash paid on an account payable
______ **6.** Cash invested by owner
______ **7.** Cash received from clients
______ **8.** Cash paid for rent

Exercise 1-18
Analysis of return on assets
A3

Geneva Group reports net income of $20,000 for 2005. At the beginning of 2005, Geneva Group had $100,000 in assets. By the end of 2005, assets had grown to $150,000. What is Geneva Group's 2005 return on assets? How would you assess its performance if competitors average a 10% return on assets?

Exercise 1-19[B]
Identifying business activities
C6

Match each transaction or event to one of the following activities of an organization: financing activities (F), investing activities (I), or operating activities (O).

a. ______ An owner contributes resources to the business.
b. ______ An organization purchases equipment.
c. ______ An organization advertises a new product.
d. ______ The organization borrows money from a bank.
e. ______ An organization sells some of its land.

***Problem Set B** located at the end of **Problem Set A** is provided for each problem to reinforce the learning process. **Problem Set C** (with solutions for instructors) is provided on this book's Website.*

PROBLEM SET A

Problem 1-1A
Computing missing information using accounting knowledge
A1 A2

The following financial statement information is from five separate companies:

	Company A	Company B	Company C	Company D	Company E
December 31, 2004:					
Assets	$45,000	$35,000	$29,000	$80,000	$123,000
Liabilities	23,500	22,500	14,000	38,000	?
December 31, 2005:					
Assets	48,000	41,000	?	125,000	112,500
Liabilities	?	27,500	19,000	64,000	75,000
During year 2005:					
Owner investments	5,000	1,500	7,750	?	4,500
Net income	7,500	?	9,000	12,000	18,000
Owner cash withdrawals	2,500	3,000	3,875	0	9,000

Required

1. Answer the following questions about Company A:

a. What is the equity amount on December 31, 2004?

Check (1*b*) $31,500

b. What is the equity amount on December 31, 2005?

c. What is the amount of liabilities on December 31, 2005?

2. Answer the following questions about Company B:

a. What is the equity amount on December 31, 2004?

b. What is the equity amount on December 31, 2005?

(2*c*) $2,500

c. What is net income for year 2005?

(3) $46,875

3. Calculate the amount of assets for Company C on December 31, 2005.

4. Calculate the amount of owner investments for Company D during year 2005.

5. Calculate the amount of liabilities for Company E on December 31, 2004.

Problem 1-2A
Identifying effects of transactions on financial statements

A1 A2 

Identify how each of the following separate transactions affects financial statements. For the balance sheet, identify how each transaction affects total assets, total liabilities, and total equity. For the income statement, identify how each transaction affects net income. For the statement of cash flows, identify how each transaction affects cash flows from operating activities, cash flows from financing activities, and cash flows from investing activities. For increases, place a "+" in the column or columns. For decreases, place a "−" in the column or columns. If both an increase and a decrease occur, place a "+/−" in the column or columns. The first transaction is completed as an example.

		Balance Sheet			Income Statement	Statement of Cash Flows		
	Transaction	**Total Assets**	**Total Liab.**	**Total Equity**	**Net Income**	**Operating Activities**	**Financing Activities**	**Investing Activities**
1	Owner invests cash in business	+		+			+	
2	Receives cash for services provided							
3	Pays cash for employee wages							
4	Incurs legal costs on credit							
5	Borrows cash by signing long-term note payable							
6	Owner withdraws cash							
7	Buys land by signing note payable							
8	Provides services on credit							
9	Buys office equipment for cash							
10	Collects cash on receivable from (8)							

Problem 1-3A
Preparing an income statement

P1

The following is selected financial information for Valdez Energy Company for the year ended December 31, 2005: revenues, $65,000; expenses, $50,000; net income, $15,000.

Required

Prepare the 2005 calendar-year income statement for Valdez Energy Company.

Problem 1-4A
Preparing a balance sheet

P1

The following is selected financial information for Amico as of December 31, 2005: liabilities, $34,000; equity, $56,000; assets, $90,000.

Required

Prepare the balance sheet for Amico as of December 31, 2005.

Problem 1-5A

Preparing a statement of cash flows

P1

The following is selected financial information of Trimark for the year ended December 31, 2005:

Cash used by investing activities	$(3,000)
Net increase in cash	200
Cash used by financing activities	(3,800)
Cash from operating activities	7,000
Cash, December 31, 2004	3,300

Required

Prepare the 2005 calendar-year statement of cash flows for Trimark.

Problem 1-6A

Preparing a statement of owner's equity

P1

The following is selected financial information for Boardwalk for the year ended December 31, 2005:

B. Walk, Capital, Dec. 31, 2005	$15,000	B. Walk, Withdrawals	$2,000
Net income	9,000	B. Walk, Capital, Dec. 31, 2004	8,000

Required

Prepare the 2005 calendar-year statement of owner's equity for Boardwalk.

Problem 1-7A

Analyzing transactions and preparing financial statements

C5 A2 P1

mhhe.com/larson

J. D. Simpson started The Simpson Co., a new business that began operations on May 1. Simpson Co. completed the following transactions during that first month:

May 1 J. D. Simpson, the owner, invested $60,000 cash in the business.
1 Rented a furnished office and paid $3,200 cash for May's rent.
3 Purchased $1,680 of office equipment on credit.
5 Paid $800 cash for this month's cleaning services.
8 Provided consulting services for a client and immediately collected $4,600 cash.
12 Provided $3,000 of consulting services for a client on credit.
15 Paid $850 cash for an assistant's salary for the first half of this month.
20 Received $3,000 cash payment for the services provided on May 12.
22 Provided $2,800 of consulting services on credit.
25 Received $2,800 cash payment for the services provided on May 22.
26 Paid $1,680 cash for the office equipment purchased on May 3.
27 Purchased $60 of advertising in this month's (May) local paper on credit; cash payment is due June 1.
28 Paid $850 cash for an assistant's salary for the second half of this month.
30 Paid $200 cash for this month's telephone bill.
30 Paid $480 cash for this month's utilities.
31 J. D. Simpson withdrew $1,200 cash for personal use.

Required

1. Arrange the following asset, liability, and equity titles in a table like Exhibit 1.9: Cash; Accounts Receivable; Office Equipment; Accounts Payable; J. D. Simpson, Capital; J. D. Simpson, Withdrawals; Revenues; and Expenses.
2. Show effects of the transactions on the accounts of the accounting equation by recording increases and decreases in the appropriate columns. Do not determine new account balances after each transaction. Determine the final total for each account and verify that the equation is in balance.
3. Prepare an income statement for May, a statement of owner's equity for May, a May 31 balance sheet, and a statement of cash flows for May.

Check (2) Ending balances: Cash, $61,140; Expenses, $6,440

(3) Net income, $3,960; Total assets, $62,820

Problem 1-8A
Analyzing transactions and preparing financial statements

C5 A2 P1 

mhhe.com/larson

Curtis Hamilton started a new business and completed these transactions during December:

Dec. 1 Curtis Hamilton transferred $56,000 cash from a personal savings account to a checking account in the name of Hamilton Electric as its initial capital.
2 Rented office space and paid $800 cash for the December rent.
3 Purchased $14,000 of electrical equipment by paying $3,200 cash and agreeing to pay the $10,800 balance in 30 days.
5 Purchased office supplies by paying $900 cash.
6 Completed electrical work and immediately collected $1,000 cash for the work.
8 Purchased $3,800 of office equipment on credit.
15 Completed electrical work on credit in the amount of $4,000.
18 Purchased $500 of office supplies on credit.
20 Paid $3,800 cash for the office equipment purchased on December 8.
24 Billed a client $600 for electrical work completed; the balance is due in 30 days.
28 Received $4,000 cash for the work completed on December 15.
29 Paid the assistant's salary of $1,200 cash for this month.
30 Paid $440 cash for this month's utility bill.
31 C. Hamilton withdrew $700 cash for personal use.

Required

1. Arrange the following asset, liability, and equity titles in a table like Exhibit 1.9: Cash; Accounts Receivable; Office Supplies; Office Equipment; Electrical Equipment; Accounts Payable; C. Hamilton, Capital; C. Hamilton, Withdrawals; Revenues; and Expenses.
2. Use additions and subtractions to show the effects of each transaction on the accounts in the accounting equation. Show new balances after each transaction.
3. Use the increases and decreases in the columns of the table from part 2 to prepare an income statement, a statement of owner's equity, and a statement of cash flows for the month. Also prepare a balance sheet as of the end of the month.

Check (2) Ending balances: Cash, $49,960, Accounts Payable, $11,300

(3) Net income, $3,160: Total assets, $69,760

Analysis Component

4. Assume that the owner investment transaction on December 1 was $40,000 cash instead of $56,000 and that Hamilton Electric obtained the $16,000 difference by borrowing it from a bank. Explain the effect of this change on total assets, total liabilities, and total equity.

Problem 1-9A
Analyzing effects of transactions

C5 P1 A1 A2

Miranda Right started Right Consulting, a new business, and completed the following transactions during its first year of operations:

a. M. Right invests $60,000 cash and office equipment valued at $30,000 in the business.
b. Purchased a $300,000 building to use as an office. Right paid $50,000 in cash and signed a note payable promising to pay the $250,000 balance over the next ten years.
c. Purchased office equipment for $6,000 cash.
d. Purchased $4,000 of office supplies and $1,000 of office equipment on credit.
e. Paid a local newspaper $1,000 cash for printing an announcement of the office's opening.
f. Completed a financial plan for a client and billed that client $4,000 for the service.
g. Designed a financial plan for another client and immediately collected an $8,000 cash fee.
h. M. Right withdrew $1,800 cash from the company bank account for personal use.
i. Received a $3,000 partial cash payment from the client described in transaction *f*.
j. Made a $500 cash payment on the equipment purchased in transaction *d*.
k. Paid $2,500 cash for the office secretary's wages.

Required

1. Create a table like the one in Exhibit 1.9, using the following headings for the columns: Cash; Accounts Receivable; Office Supplies; Office Equipment; Building; Accounts Payable; Notes Payable; M. Right, Capital; M. Right, Withdrawals; Revenues; and Expenses.
2. Use additions and subtractions to show the effects of these transactions on individual items of the accounting equation. Show new balances after each transaction.
3. Once you have completed the table, determine the company's net income.

Check (2) Ending balances: Cash, $9,200; Expenses, $3,500

(3) Net income, $8,500

Problem 1-10A
Computing and interpreting return on assets
A3 

Coca-Cola and **PepsiCo** both produce and market beverages that are direct competitors. Key financial figures (in $ millions) for these businesses over the past year follow:

Key Figures	Coca-Cola	PepsiCo
Sales	$400	$250.0
Net income	50	37.5
Average invested (assets)	625	312.5

Required

1. Compute return on assets for (*a*) Coca-Cola and (*b*) PepsiCo.
2. Which company is more successful in its total amount of sales to consumers?
3. Which company is more successful in returning net income from its amount invested?

Check (1*a*) 8%; (1*b*) 12%

Analysis Component

4. Write a one-paragraph memorandum explaining which company you would invest your money in and why. (Limit your explanation to the information provided.)

Problem 1-11A
Determining expenses, liabilities, equity and return on assets
A1 A3 

Zia manufactures, markets, and sells cellular telephones. The average total assets for Zia is $250,000. In its most recent year, Zia reported net income of $55,000 on revenues of $455,000.

Required

1. What is Zia's return on assets?
2. Does return on assets seem satisfactory for Zia given that its competitors average a 12% return on assets?
3. What are total expenses for Zia in its most recent year?
4. What is the average total amount of liabilities plus equity for Zia?

Check (3) $400,000
(4) $250,000

Problem 1-12A[A]
Identifying risk and return
A4 

All business decisions involve aspects of risk and return.

Required

Identify both the risk and the return in each of the following activities:

1. Investing $1,000 in a 4% savings account.
2. Placing a $1,000 bet on your favorite sports team.
3. Investing $10,000 in Yahoo! stock.
4. Taking out a $10,000 college loan to earn an accounting degree.

Problem 1-13A[B]
Describing organizational activities
C6

A startup company often engages in the following transactions in its first year of operations. Classify these transactions in one of the three major categories of an organization's business activities.

A. Financing **B.** Investing **C.** Operating

_____ **1.** Owner investing land in business.
_____ **2.** Purchasing a building.
_____ **3.** Purchasing land.
_____ **4.** Borrowing cash from a bank.
_____ **5.** Purchasing equipment.
_____ **6.** Selling and distributing products.
_____ **7.** Paying for advertising.
_____ **8.** Paying employee wages.

Problem 1-14A[B]
Describing organizational activities C6

An organization undertakes various activities in pursuit of business success. Identify an organization's three major business activities, and describe each activity.

PROBLEM SET B

Problem 1-1B
Computing missing information using accounting knowledge

A1 A2

The following financial statement information is from five separate companies:

	Company V	Company W	Company X	Company Y	Company Z
December 31, 2004:					
Assets	$45,000	$70,000	$121,500	$82,500	$124,000
Liabilities	30,000	50,000	58,500	61,500	?
December 31, 2005:					
Assets	49,000	90,000	136,500	?	160,000
Liabilities	26,000	?	55,500	72,000	52,000
During year 2005:					
Owner investments	6,000	10,000	?	38,100	40,000
Net income	?	30,000	16,500	24,000	32,000
Owner cash withdrawals	4,500	2,000	0	18,000	6,000

Required

1. Answer the following questions about Company V:

a. What is the amount of equity on December 31, 2004?

b. What is the amount of equity on December 31, 2005?

c. What is net income for year 2005?

2. Answer the following questions about Company W:

a. What is the amount of equity on December 31, 2004?

b. What is the amount of equity on December 31, 2005?

c. What is the amount of liabilities on December 31, 2005?

3. Calculate the amount of owner investments for Company X during 2005.

4. Calculate the amount of assets for Company Y on December 31, 2005.

5. Calculate the amount of liabilities for Company Z on December 31, 2004.

Check (1*b*) $23,000

(2c) $32,000

(4) $137,100

Problem 1-2B
Identifying effects of transactions on financial statements

A1 A2

Identify how each of the following separate transactions affects financial statements. For the balance sheet, identify how each transaction affects total assets, total liabilities, and total equity. For the income statement, identify how each transaction affects net income. For the statement of cash flows, identify how each transaction affects cash flows from operating activities, cash flows from financing activities, and cash flows from investing activities. For increases, place a "+" in the column or columns. For decreases, place a "−" in the column or columns. If both an increase and a decrease occur, place "+/−" in the column or columns. The first transaction is completed as an example.

		Balance Sheet			Income Statement	Statement of Cash Flows		
	Transaction	Total Assets	Total Liab.	Total Equity	Net Income	Operating Activities	Financing Activities	Investing Activities
1	Owner invests cash in business	+		+			+	
2	Buys building by signing note payable							
3	Pays cash for salaries incurred							
4	Provides services for cash							
5	Pays cash for rent incurred							
6	Incurs utilities costs on credit							
7	Buys store equipment for cash							
8	Owner withdraws cash							
9	Provides services on credit							
10	Collects cash on receivable from (9)							

Problem 1-3B
Preparing an income statement
P1

Selected financial information for Online Co. for the year ended December 31, 2005, follows:

Revenues	$58,000	Expenses	$30,000	Net income	$28,000

Required

Use the information provided to prepare the 2005 calendar-year income statement for Online Co.

Problem 1-4B
Preparing a balance sheet
P1

The following is selected financial information for RWB Company as of December 31, 2005:

Liabilities	$74,000	Equity	$40,000	Assets	$114,000

Required

Use the information provided to prepare the balance sheet for RWB as of December 31, 2005.

Problem 1-5B
Preparing a statement of cash flows
P1

Selected financial information of BuyRight Co. for the year ended December 31, 2005, follows:

Cash from investing activities	$2,600
Net increase in cash	1,400
Cash from financing activities	2,800
Cash used by operating activities	(4,000)
Cash, December 31, 2004	1,300

Required

Use this information to prepare the 2005 calendar-year statement of cash flows for BuyRight.

Problem 1-6B
Preparing a statement of owner's equity
P1

The following is selected financial information of ComEx for the year ended December 31, 2005:

C. Tex, Capital, Dec. 31, 2005	$47,000	C. Tex, Withdrawals	$ 8,000
Net income	6,000	C. Tex, Capital, Dec. 31, 2004	49,000

Required

Prepare the 2005 calendar-year statement of owner's equity for ComEx.

Problem 1-7B
Analyzing transactions and preparing financial statements
C5 A2 P1

Ken Stone launched a new business, Ken's Maintenance Co., that began operations on June 1. The following transactions were completed by the company during that first month:

June 1 K. Stone invested $120,000 cash in the business.
2 Rented a furnished office and paid $4,500 cash for June's rent.
4 Purchased $2,400 of equipment on credit.
6 Paid $1,125 cash for the next week's advertising of the opening of the business.
8 Completed maintenance services for a customer and immediately collected $750 cash.
14 Completed $6,300 of maintenance services for First Union Center on credit.
16 Paid $900 cash for an assistant's salary for the first half of the month.
20 Received $6,300 cash payment for services completed for First Union Center on June 14.
21 Completed $3,500 of maintenance services for Skyway Co. on credit.
24 Completed $825 of maintenance services for Comfort Motel on credit.
25 Received $3,500 cash payment from Skyway Co. for the work completed on June 21.
26 Made payment of $2,400 cash for the equipment purchased on June 4.
28 Paid $900 cash for an assistant's salary for the second half of this month.
29 K. Stone withdrew $2,000 cash for personal use.
30 Paid $120 cash for this month's telephone bill.
30 Paid $525 cash for this month's utilities.

Required

1. Arrange the following asset, liability, and equity titles in a table like Exhibit 1.9: Cash; Accounts Receivable; Equipment; Accounts Payable; K. Stone, Capital; K. Stone, Withdrawals; Revenues; and Expenses.

Check (2) Ending balances: Cash, $118,080; Expenses, $8,070

(3) Net income, $3,305; Total assets, $121,305

2. Show the effects of the transactions on the accounts of the accounting equation by recording increases and decreases in the appropriate columns. Do not determine new account balances after each transaction. Determine the final total for each account and verify that the equation is in balance.
3. Prepare a June income statement, a June statement of owner's equity, a June 30 balance sheet, and a June statement of cash flows.

Problem 1-8B
Analyzing transactions and preparing financial statements

C5 A2 P1

Swender Excavating Co., owned by Patrick Swender, began operations in July and completed these transactions during that first month:

July	1	P. Swender invested $60,000 cash in the business as its initial capital.
	2	Rented office space and paid $500 cash for the July rent.
	3	Purchased excavating equipment for $4,000 by paying $800 cash and agreeing to pay the $3,200 balance in 30 days.
	6	Purchased office supplies for $500 cash.
	8	Completed work for a customer and immediately collected $2,200 cash for the work.
	10	Purchased $3,800 of office equipment on credit.
	15	Completed work for a customer on credit in the amount of $2,400.
	17	Purchased $1,920 of office supplies on credit.
	23	Paid $3,800 cash for the office equipment purchased on July 10.
	25	Billed a customer $5,000 for work completed; the balance is due in 30 days.
	28	Received $2,400 cash for the work completed on July 15.
	30	Paid an assistant's salary of $1,260 cash for this month.
	31	Paid $260 cash for this month's utility bill.
	31	P. Swender withdrew $1,200 cash for personal use.

Required

1. Arrange the following asset, liability, and equity titles in a table like Exhibit 1.9: Cash; Accounts Receivable; Office Supplies; Office Equipment; Excavating Equipment; Accounts Payable; P. Swender, Capital; P. Swender, Withdrawals; Revenues; and Expenses.

Check (2) Ending balances: Cash, $56,280; Accounts Payable, $5,120

(3) Net income, $7,580: Total assets, $71,500

2. Use additions and subtractions to show the effects of each transaction on the accounts in the accounting equation. Show new balances after each transaction.
3. Use the increases and decreases in the columns of the table from part 2 to prepare an income statement, a statement of owner's equity, and a statement of cash flows for the month. Also prepare a balance sheet as of the end of the month.

Analysis Component

4. Assume that Swender's $4,000 purchase of excavating equipment on July 3 was financed from an additional personal investment of another $4,000 cash in the business (instead of the purchase conditions described in the transaction). Explain the effect of this change on total assets, total liabilities, and equity.

Problem 1-9B
Analyzing effects of transactions

C5 P1 A1 A2

Tiana Moore started a new business, Tiana's Solutions, that completed the following transactions during its first year of operations:

a. T. Moore invests $95,000 cash and office equipment valued at $20,000 in the business.
b. Purchased a $120,000 building to use as an office. Moore paid $20,000 in cash and signed a note payable promising to pay the $100,000 balance over the next ten years.
c. Purchased office equipment for $20,000 cash.
d. Purchased $1,400 of office supplies and $3,000 of office equipment on credit.
e. Paid a local newspaper $400 cash for printing an announcement of the office's opening.
f. Completed a financial plan for a client and billed that client $1,800 for the service.
g. Designed a financial plan for another client and immediately collected a $2,000 cash fee.
h. T. Moore withdrew $5,000 cash from the company bank account for personal use.
i. Received $1,800 cash from the client described in transaction *f*.
j. Made a $2,000 cash payment on the equipment purchased in transaction *d*.
k. Paid $2,000 cash for the office secretary's wages.

Required

1. Create a table like the one in Exhibit 1.9, using the following headings for the columns: Cash; Accounts Receivable; Office Supplies; Office Equipment; Building; Accounts Payable; Notes Payable; T. Moore, Capital; T. Moore, Withdrawals; Revenues; and Expenses.

2. Use additions and subtractions to show the effects of these transactions on individual items of the accounting equation. Show new balances after each transaction.

3. Once you have completed the table, determine the company's net income.

Check (2) Ending balances: Cash, $49,400; Expenses, $2,400

(3) Net income, $1,400

Problem 1-10B
Computing and interpreting return on assets

A3

AT&T and **GTE** produce and market telecommunications products and are competitors. Key financial figures (in $ millions) for these businesses over the past year follow:

Key Figures	AT&T	GTE
Sales	$79,609	$19,957
Net income	139	2,538
Average invested (assets) . . .	87,261	37,019

Required

1. Compute return on assets for (*a*) AT&T and (*b*) GTE.

2. Which company is more successful in the total amount of sales to consumers?

3. Which company is more successful in returning net income from its amount invested?

Check (1*a*) 0.16%; (1*b*) 6.9%

Analysis Component

4. Write a one-paragraph memorandum explaining which company you would invest your money in and why. (Limit your explanation to the information provided.)

Problem 1-11B
Determining expenses, liabilities, equity, and return on assets

A1 A3

Aspen Company manufactures, markets, and sells snowmobile equipment. The average total assets for Aspen Company is $2,000,000. In its most recent year, Aspen reported net income of $100,000 on revenues of $1,200,000.

Required

1. What is Aspen Company's return on assets?

2. Does return on assets seem satisfactory for Aspen given that its competitors average a 9.5% return on assets?

3. What are the total expenses for Aspen Company in its most recent year?

4. What is the average total amount of liabilities plus equity for Aspen Company?

Check (3) $1,100,000

(4) $2,000,000

Problem 1-12B[A]
Identifying risk and return

A4

All business decisions involve aspects of risk and return.

Required

Identify both the risk and the return in each of the following activities:

1. Stashing $1,000 under your mattress.

2. Placing a $500 bet on a horse running in the Kentucky Derby.

3. Investing $10,000 in Nike stock.

4. Investing $10,000 in U.S. Savings Bonds.

Problem 1-13B[B]
Describing organizational activities

C6

A startup company often engages in the following activities during its first year of operations. Classify each of the following activities into one of the three major activities of an organization:

A. Financing **B.** Investing **C.** Operating

______	**1.** Providing client services.	______	**5.** Supervising workers.
______	**2.** Obtaining a bank loan.	______	**6.** Owner investing money in business.
______	**3.** Purchasing machinery.	______	**7.** Renting office space.
______	**4.** Researching products.	______	**8.** Paying utilities expenses.

Problem 1-14B[B]
Describing organizational activities C6

Identify in outline format the three major business activities of an organization. For each of these activities, identify at least two specific transactions or events normally undertaken by the business's owners or managers.

PROBLEM SET C

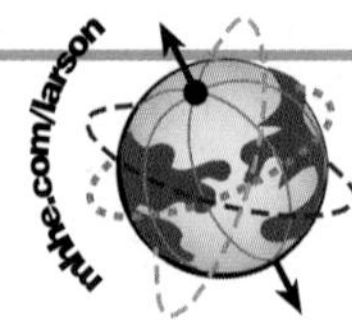

Problem Set C is available at the book's Website to further reinforce and assess your learning.

This serial problem starts in this chapter and continues throughout most chapters of the book. It is most readily solved if you use the Working Papers that accompany this book.

SERIAL PROBLEM

Success Systems

On October 1, 2004, Kay Breeze launched a computer services company, **Success Systems,** that is organized as a sole proprietorship and provides consulting services, computer system installations, and custom program development. Breeze adopts the calendar year for reporting purposes and expects to prepare the company's first set of financial statements on December 31, 2004.

Required

Create a table like the one in Exhibit 1.9 using the following headings for columns: Cash; Accounts Receivable; Computer Supplies; Office Equipment; Accounts Payable; K. Breeze, Capital; K. Breeze, Withdrawals; Revenues; and Expenses. Then use additions and subtractions to show the effects of the October transactions for Success Systems on the individual items of the accounting equation. Show new balances after each transaction.

Oct. 1 Kay Breeze invested $55,000 cash, a $20,000 computer system, and $8,000 of office equipment in the business.
3 Purchased $1,420 of computer supplies on credit from Cain Office Products.
6 Billed Easy Leasing $4,800 for services performed in installing a new Web server.
8 Paid $1,420 cash for the computer supplies purchased from Cain Office Products on October 3.
10 Hired Sherry Adams as a part-time assistant for $125 per day, as needed.
12 Billed Easy Leasing another $1,400 for services performed.
15 Received $4,800 cash from Easy Leasing on its account.
17 Paid $805 cash to repair computer equipment damaged when moving it.
20 Paid $1,940 cash for an advertisement in the local newspaper.
22 Received $1,400 cash from Easy Leasing on its account.
28 Billed Clark Company $5,208 for services performed.
31 Paid $875 cash for Sherry Adams's wages for seven days of work.
31 Breeze withdrew $3,600 cash for personal use.

Check Ending balances: Cash, $52,560; Revenues, $11,408; Expenses, $3,620

Beyond the Numbers (BTN) *is a special problem section aimed to refine communication, conceptual, analysis, and research skills. It includes many activities helpful in developing an active learning environment.*

BEYOND THE NUMBERS

REPORTING IN ACTION

A1 A3 A4

BTN 1-1 Key financial figures for **Krispy Kreme**'s fiscal year ended February 2, 2003, follow:

Key Figure	In Thousands
Liabilities + Equity	$410,487
Net income	33,478
Revenues	491,549

Required

1. What is the total amount of assets invested in Krispy Kreme?
2. What is Krispy Kreme's return on assets? Its assets at February 3, 2002, equal $255,376 (in thousands).

Check (2) 10.1%

3. How much are total expenses for Krispy Kreme?
4. Does Krispy Kreme's return on assets seem satisfactory if competitors average a 3% return?

Roll On

5. Access Krispy Kreme's financial statements (Form 10-K) for fiscal years ending after February 2, 2003, from its Website (KrispyKreme.com) or from the SEC Website (www.SEC.gov). Compute its return on assets for those fiscal years. Compare the February 2, 2003, fiscal year-end return on assets to any subsequent years' returns you are able to compute, and interpret the results.

COMPARATIVE ANALYSIS

A1 A3 A4

BTN 1-2 Key comparative figures ($ thousands) for both **Krispy Kreme** and **Tastykake** follow:

Key Figure	Krispy Kreme	Tastykake
Liabilities + Equity	$410,487	$116,560
Net income	33,478	2,000*
Revenues (sales)	491,549	162,263

* Restructuring charges are removed from income.

Required

1. What is the total amount of assets invested in (*a*) Krispy Kreme and (*b*) Tastykake?
2. What is the return on assets for (*a*) Krispy Kreme and (*b*) Tastykake? Krispy Kreme's beginning-year assets equal $255,376 (in thousands) and Tastykake's beginning-year assets equal $116,137 (in thousands).

Check (2b) 1.7%

3. How much are expenses for (*a*) Krispy Kreme and (*b*) Tastykake?
4. Is return on assets satisfactory for (*a*) Krispy Kreme and (*b*) Tastykake? (Assume competitors average a 3% return.)
5. What can you conclude about Krispy Kreme and Tastykake from these computations?

ETHICS CHALLENGE

C4 C5

BTN 1-3 Juanita Cruz works in a public accounting firm and hopes to eventually be a partner. The management of Allnet Company invites Cruz to prepare a bid to audit Allnet's financial statements. In discussing the audit fee, Allnet's management suggests a fee range in which the amount depends on the reported profit of Allnet. The higher its profit, the higher will be the audit fee paid to Cruz's firm.

Required

1. Identify the parties potentially affected by this audit and the fee plan proposed.
2. What are the ethical factors in this situation? Explain.
3. Would you recommend that Cruz accept this audit fee arrangement? Why or why not?
4. Describe some ethical considerations guiding your recommendation.

COMMUNICATING IN PRACTICE

A1 C2

BTN 1-4 Refer to this chapter's opening feature about **The Chocolate Farm**. Assume that the Macmillans wish to expand The Chocolate Farm to include a store devoted to selling food decorations related to the main business. They meet with a loan officer of a Denver bank to discuss a loan.

Required

1. Prepare a half-page report outlining the information you would request from the Macmillans if you were the loan officer.
2. Indicate whether the information you request and your loan decision are affected by the form of business organization for the proposed Chocolate Farm store.

TAKING IT TO THE NET

A3

mhhe.com/larson

BTN 1-5 Visit the EDGAR database at (www.sec.gov). Access the Form 10-K report of World Wrestling Entertainment (ticker WWE) filed on July 26, 2002.

Required

1. On page 16 of the 10-K report you will find comparative income statements of WWE for the years 1998–2002. How would you describe the revenue trend for WWE over this five-year period?
2. Has the WWE been profitable (see net income) over this five-year period?

TEAMWORK IN ACTION

C1

BTN 1-6 Teamwork is important in today's business world. Successful teams schedule convenient meetings, maintain regular communications, and cooperate with and support their members. This assignment aims to establish support/learning teams, initiate discussions, and set meeting times.

Required

1. Form teams and open a team discussion to determine a regular time and place for your team to meet between each scheduled class meeting. Notify your instructor via a memorandum or e-mail message as to when and where your team will hold regularly scheduled meetings.
2. Develop a list of telephone numbers and/or e-mail addresses of your teammates.

Book's Website provides free and easy access to all articles for every Business Week *Activity.*

BUSINESS WEEK ACTIVITY C1

mhhe.com/larson

BTN 1-7 *Business Week* publishes a ranking of the top 1,000 companies based on several performance measures. This issue is called the *Business Week Global 1000.* Obtain the July 14, 2003, publication of this issue—this book's Website maintains free access to this article.

Required

1. What are the top 10 companies on the basis of market value?
2. Are any of the top 10 companies in the same industry?
3. How many of the top 10 based on market capitalization are not U.S. companies?

ENTREPRENEURIAL DECISION

A1 A2

BTN 1-8 Refer to this chapter's opening feature about **The Chocolate Farm**. Assume the Macmillans decide to open a small retail store to supplement their chocolate operations.

Required

1. The Macmillans obtain a $50,000 bank loan and contribute $30,000 of their own assets to support the opening of the new store.
   a. What is the new store's total amount of liabilities plus equity?
   b. What is the new store's total amount of assets?
2. If the Macmillans earn $20,000 of income in the first year the retail store operates, compute the store's return on assets (assume average assets equal $80,000). Assess its performance if competitors average a 10% return.

Check (2) 25%

HITTING THE ROAD

BTN 1-9 You are to interview a local business owner. (This can be a friend or relative.) Opening lines of communication with members of the business community can provide personal benefits of business networking. If you do not know the owner, you should call ahead to introduce yourself and explain your position as a student and your assignment requirements. You should request a thirty minute appointment for a face-to-face or phone interview to discuss the form of organization and operations of the business. Be prepared to make a good impression.

Required

1. Identify and describe the main operating activities and the form of organization for this business.
2. Determine and explain why the owner(s) chose this particular form of organization.
3. Identify any special advantages and/or disadvantages the owner(s) experiences in operating with this form of business organization.

BTN 1-10 Grupo Bimbo (GrupoBimbo.com) is a leader in the baking industry and also competes with both **Krispy Kreme** and **Tastykake**. Key financial figures for Grupo Bimbo follow:

GLOBAL DECISION

A1 A3 A4 

Key Figure*	Pesos in Millions
Average assets	27,750
Net income	1,003
Revenues	41,373
Return on assets	3.6%

* Figures prepared in accordance with Generally Accepted Accounting Principles in Mexico.

Required

1. Identify any concerns you have in comparing Grupo Bimbo's income, revenue, liabilities, and equity figures to those of Krispy Kreme and Tastykake (in BTN 1-2) for purposes of making business decisions.
2. Identify any concerns you have in comparing Grupo Bimbo's return on assets ratio to those of Krispy Kreme and Tastykake (in BTN 1-2) for purposes of making business decisions.

"*I want everything done . . . like, yesterday*"—Tanya York

Analyzing and Recording Transactions

A Look Back

Chapter 1 considered the role of accounting in the information age and introduced financial statements. We described different forms of organizations and identified users and uses of accounting. We explained the accounting equation and applied it to transaction analysis.

A Look at This Chapter

This chapter focuses on the accounting process. We describe transactions and source documents as inputs for analysis. We explain the analysis and recording of transactions. The accounting equation, T-account, general ledger, trial balance, and debits and credits are shown as useful tools in the accounting process.

A Look Ahead

Chapter 3 extends our focus on processing information. We explain the importance of adjusting accounts and the procedures in preparing financial statements.

Learning Objectives

CAP

Conceptual

C1 Explain the steps in processing transactions. *(p. 48)*

C2 Describe source documents and their purpose. *(p. 49)*

C3 Describe an account and its use in recording transactions. *(p. 49)*

C4 Describe a ledger and a chart of accounts. *(p. 52)*

C5 Define *debits* and *credits* and explain their role in double-entry accounting. *(p. 53)*

Analytical

A1 Analyze the impact of transactions on accounts and financial statements. *(p. 57)*

A2 Compute the debt ratio and describe its use in analyzing company performance. *(p. 67)*

Procedural

P1 Record transactions in a journal and post entries to a ledger. *(p. 55)*

P2 Prepare and explain the use of a trial balance. *(p. 64)*

P3 Prepare financial statements from business transactions. *(p. 65)*

Decision Feature

Against Long Odds

LOS ANGELES—Tanya York produced her first film at 19. Since then she has produced hundreds of films with her company **York Entertainment (YorkEntertainment.com).** York's company has become an urban powerhouse and distributes its titles under the York Urban, York Latino, and York En Espanol labels. Says York, "I'm Jamaican myself, so I can kind of relate to being a minority in a world where so much is aimed at the majority, so, in that way I'm happy to be able to offer films with an urban appeal."

York insists that the business and accounting side of production is as important as the artistic side. "With producing you're involved in all aspects of the entertainment industry," she says, "the creative side as well as the business side." York knows that attention to financial statements and know-how of the accounting system of debits and credits is crucial to success. An understanding of the accounting details enabled York to assess and enhance her company's profitability and financial position.

York relies on the financial numbers in devising strategies to enhance income. At the same time, she does not lose sight of giving the public what they want. Adds York, "I don't see my job as changing the public [demands]." Instead she fulfills them. This includes filling her movies with stars like Ice T, Kurupt, Destiny's Child, Kool Mo Dee, and Mac 10.

York continues to grow her company. With revenues near $20 million, she shows a keen understanding of accounting information in making good business decisions. Still, she insists anyone can use such information in a business to achieve similar success. "I came to America and through hard work built a company."

Without a doubt, Tanya York has not only tasted success but is living it. Adds York, "I like to always have new challenges in front of me."

[Sources: *York Entertainment Website,* January 2004; *Cinescape,* 2002; *Rolling Out Urban Style,* January 2002; *Entrepreneur,* November 2002; *Los Angeles Daily News,* February 2003.]

Chapter Preview

Financial statements report on the financial performance and condition of an organization. Knowledge of their preparation, organization, and analysis is important. A main goal of this chapter is to illustrate how transactions are recorded, how they are reflected in financial statements, and how they impact analysis of financial statements. Debits and credits are introduced and identified as a tool in helping understand and process transactions.

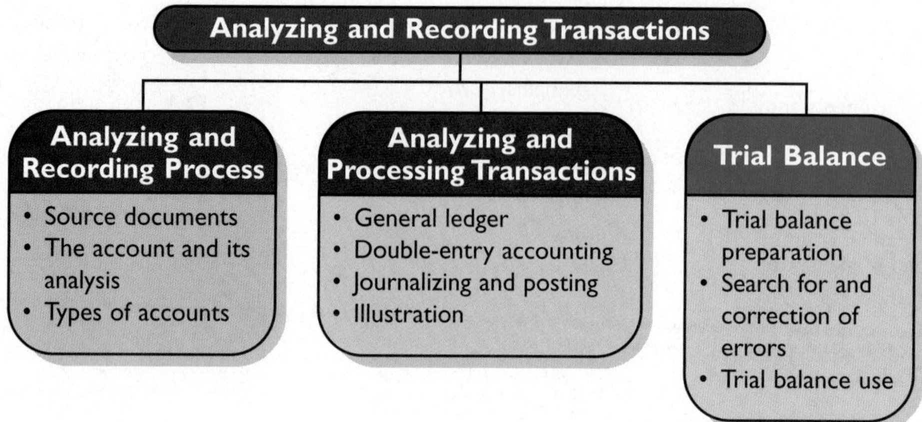

Analyzing and Recording Process

The accounting process identifies business transactions and events, analyzes and records their effects, and summarizes and presents information in reports and financial statements. These reports and statements are used for making investing, lending, and other business decisions. The steps in the accounting process that focus on *analyzing and recording* transactions and events are shown in Exhibit 2.1.

Exhibit 2.1

The Analyzing and Recording Process

Analyze each transaction and event from source documents

Record relevant transactions and events in a journal

Post journal information to ledger accounts

Prepare and analyze the trial balance

C1 Explain the steps in processing transactions.

Business transactions and events are the starting points. Relying on source documents, transactions and events are analyzed using the accounting equation to understand how they affect company performance and financial position. These effects are recorded in accounting records, informally referred to as the *accounting books,* or simply the *books*. Additional steps such as posting and then preparing a trial balance help summarize and classify the effects of transactions and events. Ultimately, the accounting process provides information in useful reports or financial statements to decision makers.

Source Documents

C2 Describe source documents and their purpose.

Source documents identify and describe transactions and events entering the accounting process. They are the sources of accounting information and can be in either hard copy or electronic form. Examples are sales tickets, checks, purchase orders, bills from suppliers, employee earnings records, and bank statements. To illustrate, when an item is purchased on credit, the seller usually prepares at least two copies of a sales invoice. One copy is given to the buyer. Another copy, often sent electronically, results in an entry in the seller's information system to record the sale. Sellers use invoices for recording sales and for control; buyers use them for recording purchases and for monitoring purchasing activity. Note that many cash registers record information for each sale on a tape or electronic file locked inside the register. This record can be used as a source document for recording sales in the accounting records. Source documents, especially if obtained from outside the organization, provide objective and reliable evidence about transactions and events and their amounts.

Point: To ensure that all sales are rung up on the register, most sellers require customers to have their receipts to exchange or return purchased items.

Decision Ethics

Cashier Your manager requires that you, as cashier, immediately enter each sale. Recently, lunch hour traffic has increased and the assistant manager asks you to avoid delays by taking customers' cash and making change without entering sales. The assistant manager says she will add up cash and enter sales after lunch. She says that, in this way, the register will always match the cash amount when the manager arrives at three o'clock. What do you do?

Answer—p. 72

The Account and Its Analysis

C3 Describe an account and its use in recording transactions.

An **account** is a record of increases and decreases in a specific asset, liability, equity, revenue, or expense item. Information from an account is analyzed, summarized, and presented in reports and financial statements. The **general ledger,** or simply **ledger,** is a record containing all accounts used by a company. The ledger is often in electronic form. While most companies' ledgers contain similar accounts, a company may use one or more unique accounts because of its type of operations. Accounts are arranged into three general categories (based on the accounting equation), as shown in Exhibit 2.2.

Exhibit 2.2

Accounts Organized by the Accounting Equation

Asset Accounts Assets are resources owned or controlled by a company and that have expected future benefits. Most accounting systems include (at a minimum) separate accounts for the assets described here.

A *Cash* account reflects a company's cash balance. All increases and decreases in cash are recorded in the Cash account. It includes money and any medium of exchange that a bank accepts for deposit (coins, checks, money orders, and checking account balances).

Accounts receivable are held by a seller and refer to promises of payment from customers to sellers. These transactions are often called *credit sales* or *sales on account* (or *on credit*). Accounts receivable are increased by credit sales and are decreased by customer payments. A company needs a separate record for each customer, but for now, we use the simpler practice of recording all increases and decreases in receivables in a single account called Accounts Receivable.

Point: Customers and others who owe a company are called its **debtors.**

A *note receivable,* or promissory note, is a written promise of another entity to pay a definite sum of money on a specified future date to the holder of the note. A company holding a promissory note signed by another entity has an asset that is recorded in a Note (or Notes) Receivable account.

Point: A college parking fee is a prepaid account from the student's standpoint. At the beginning of the term, it represents an asset that entitles a student to park on or near campus. The benefits of the parking fee expire as the term progresses. At term-end, prepaid parking (asset) equals zero as it has been entirely recorded as parking expense.

Prepaid accounts (also called *prepaid expenses*) are assets that represent prepayments of future expenses (*not* current expenses). When the expenses are later incurred, the amounts in prepaid accounts are transferred to expense accounts. Common examples of prepaid

Point: Prepaid accounts that apply to current *and* future periods are assets. These assets are adjusted at the end of each period to reflect only those amounts that have not yet expired and to record as expenses those amounts that have expired.

accounts include prepaid insurance, prepaid rent, and prepaid services (such as club memberships). Prepaid accounts expire with the passage of time (such as with rent) or through use (such as with prepaid meal tickets). When financial statements are prepared, prepaid accounts are adjusted so that (1) all expired and used prepaid accounts are recorded as regular expenses and (2) all unexpired and unused prepaid accounts are recorded as assets (reflecting future use in future periods). To illustrate, when an insurance fee, called a *premium,* is paid in advance, the cost is typically recorded in the asset account Prepaid Insurance. Over time, the expiring portion of the insurance cost is removed from this asset account and reported in expenses on the income statement. Any unexpired portion remains in Prepaid Insurance and is reported on the balance sheet as an asset. (An exception exists for prepaid accounts that will expire or be used before the end of the current accounting period when financial statements are prepared. In this case, the prepayments *can* be recorded immediately as expenses.)

Supplies are assets until they are used. When they are used up, their costs are reported as expenses. The costs of unused supplies are recorded in a Supplies asset account. Supplies are often grouped by purpose—for example office supplies and store supplies. *Office supplies* include stationery, paper, toner, and pens. *Store supplies* include packaging materials, plastic and paper bags, gift boxes and cartons, and cleaning materials. The costs of these unused supplies can be recorded in an Office Supplies or a Store Supplies asset account. When supplies are used, their costs are transferred from the asset accounts to expense accounts.

Point: Some assets are described as *intangible* because they do not have physical existence or their benefits are highly uncertain. A recent balance sheet for Coca-Cola Company shows nearly $3.5 billion in intangible assets.

Equipment is an asset. When equipment is used and gets worn down its cost is gradually reported as an expense (called depreciation). Equipment is often grouped by its purpose—for example, office equipment and store equipment. *Office equipment* includes computers, printers, desks, chairs, shelves, and other office equipment. Costs incurred for these items are recorded in an Office Equipment asset account. The Store Equipment account includes the costs of assets used in a store such as counters, showcases, ladders, hoists, and cash registers.

Buildings such as stores, offices, warehouses, and factories are assets because they provide expected future benefits to those who control or own them. Their costs are recorded in a Buildings asset account. When several buildings are owned, separate accounts are sometimes kept for each of them.

The cost of *land* owned by a business is recorded in a Land account. The cost of buildings located on the land is separately recorded in one or more building accounts.

Decision Insight

Boss-Aid Entrepreneurs were asked whom they would want—if they could have anyone—to help run their businesses for a week. Bill Gates led, with 24%, followed by Donald Trump and Warren Buffet—see selected survey results.

Bill Gates	24%
Donald Trump	6.8
Warren Buffet	5.8
Lee Iacocca	5.2
Ross Perot	3.1
Hillary Clinton	1.4

Liability Accounts Liabilities are claims (by creditors) against assets, which means they are obligations to transfer assets or provide products or services to other entities. **Creditors** are individuals and organizations that own the right to receive payments from a company. If a company fails to pay its obligations, the law gives creditors a right to force the sale of that company's assets to obtain the money to meet creditors' claims. When assets are sold under these conditions, creditors are paid first, but only up to the amount of their claims. Any remaining money, the residual, goes to the owners of the company. Creditors often use a balance sheet to help decide whether to loan money to a company. A loan is less risky if the borrower's liabilities are small in comparison to assets because there are more resources than claims on resources. The more common liability accounts are described here.

Accounts payable refer to oral or implied promises to pay later, which commonly arise from purchases of merchandise. Payables can also arise from purchases of supplies, equipment, and services. Accounting systems keep separate records about each creditor. We describe these individual records in Chapter 4.

Point: Accounts Payable are also called *Trade Payables.*

A *note payable* refers to a formal promise, usually denoted by the signing of a promissory note, to pay a future amount. It is recorded in either a Short-Term Note Payable account or a Long-Term Note Payable account, depending on when it must be repaid. We explain details of short- and long-term classification in Chapter 4.

Unearned Revenue refers to a liability that is settled in the future when a company delivers its products or services. When customers pay in advance for products or services (before revenue is earned), the revenue recognition principle requires that the seller consider this payment as unearned revenue. Examples of unearned revenue include magazine subscriptions collected in advance by a publisher, sales of gift certificates by stores, and season ticket sales by sports teams. The seller would record these in liability accounts such as Unearned Subscriptions, Unearned Store Sales, and Unearned Ticket Revenue. When products and services are later delivered, the earned portion of the unearned revenue is transferred to revenue accounts such as Subscription Fees, Store Sales, and Ticket Sales.[1]

Decision Insight

Cash Spread The **Green Bay Packers** have *Unearned Revenues* of nearly $40 million in advance ticket sales. When the team plays its regular season home games, it settles this liability to its ticket holders and transfers the amount earned to *Ticket Revenues.*

Point: If a subscription is cancelled the publisher should refund the unused portion to the subscriber.

Accrued liabilities are amounts owed that are not yet paid. Examples are wages payable, taxes payable, and interest payable. These are often recorded in separate liability accounts by the same title. If they are not large in amount, one or more ledger accounts can be added and reported as a single amount on the balance sheet. (Financial statements often have amounts reported that are a summation of several ledger accounts.)

Equity Accounts The owner's claim on a company's assets is called *equity* or *owner's equity.* Equity is the owners' *residual interest* in the assets of a business after deducting liabilities. There are four subcategories of equity: owner's capital, owner's withdrawals, revenues, and expenses. We show this visually in Exhibit 2.3 by expanding the accounting equation.

Point: Equity is also called *net assets.*

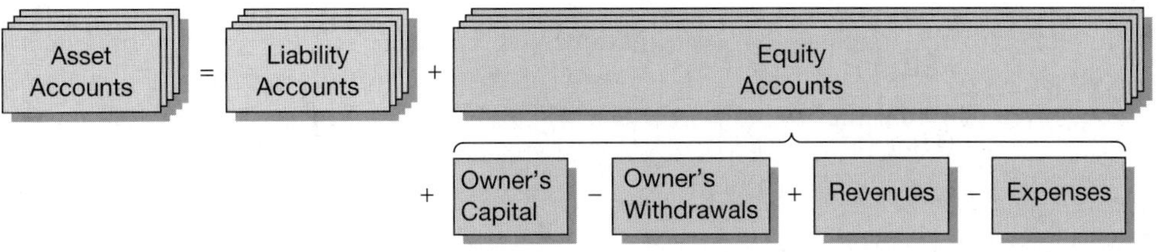

Exhibit 2.3
Expanded Accounting Equation

When an owner invests in a company, the invested amount is recorded in an account titled **Owner, Capital** (where the owner's name is inserted in place of "owner"). An account called *C. Taylor, Capital* is used for FastForward. Any further investments are recorded in this account. When the owner withdraws assets for personal use the withdrawal decreases both the company's assets and its total equity. (Owners of proprietorships cannot receive salaries because they are not legally separate from their companies and cannot enter into salary, or any other, contracts with themselves.) Withdrawals are

Point: The Owner's Withdrawals account (also called *Drawing* or *Personal* account) is sometimes referred to as a *contra equity* account because it reduces the normal balance of equity.

[1] In practice, account titles vary. As one example, Subscription Fees is sometimes called Subscription Fees Revenue, Subscription Fees Earned, or Earned Subscription Fees. As another example, Rent Earned is sometimes called Rent Revenue, Rental Revenue, or Earned Rent Revenue. We must use good judgment when reading financial statements because titles can differ even within the same industry. For example, product sales are called *revenues* at **Krispy Kreme,** but *net sales* at **Tastykake.** Generally, the term *revenues* or *fees* is more commonly used with service businesses, and *net sales* or *sales* with product businesses.

Point: The withdrawal of assets by the owners of a corporation is called a *dividend.*

not expenses of the business. They are simply the opposite of owner investments. An Owner, Withdrawals account is used in recording withdrawals by the owner. An account called *C. Taylor, Withdrawals,* is used to record Taylor's withdrawals from FastForward.

Revenues and expenses are the final two categories of equity. Examples of revenue accounts are Sales, Commissions Earned, Professional Fees Earned, Rent Earned, and Interest Revenue. *Revenues increase equity* and result from products or services provided to customers. Examples of expense accounts are Advertising Expense, Store Supplies Expense, Office Salaries Expense, Office Supplies Expense, Rent Expense, Utilities Expense, and Insurance Expense. *Expenses decrease equity* and result from assets or services used in a company's operations. The variety of revenues and expenses can be seen by looking at the *chart of accounts* that follows the index at the back of this book. (Different companies sometimes use different account titles than those in this book's chart of accounts. For example, some might use Interest Revenue instead of Interest Earned, or Rental Expense instead of Rent Expense. It is important only that an account title describe the item it represents.)

Decision Insight

Sports Accounts The **Boston Celtics** report the following major revenue and expense accounts:

Revenues	Expenses
Basketball ticket sales	Team salaries
TV & radio broadcast fees	Game costs
Advertising revenues	NBA franchise costs
Basketball playoff receipts	Promotional costs

Analyzing and Processing Transactions

This section explains several crucial tools and processes that comprise an accounting system. These include a ledger, T-accounts, debits and credits, double-entry accounting, journalizing, and posting.

Ledger and Chart of Accounts

C4 Describe a ledger and a chart of accounts.

The collection of all accounts for an information system is called a *ledger* (or *general ledger*). If accounts are in files on a hard drive, the sum of those files is the ledger. If the accounts are pages in a file, that file is the ledger. A company's size and diversity of operations affect the number of accounts needed. A small company can get by with as few as 20 or 30 accounts; a large company can require several thousand. The **chart of accounts** is a list of all accounts a company uses and includes an identification number assigned to each account. A small business might use the following numbering system for its accounts:

Decision Insight

Accoun-tech Using technology, **Sears** shrank its annual financial plan from 100 flowcharts with more than 300 steps to just *one* sheet of paper with 25 steps! Technology also allows Sears execs to analyze budgets and financial plans on their PCs. Sears says it slashed $100 million in recordkeeping costs.

101–199	Asset accounts
201–299	Liability accounts
301–399	Equity accounts
401–499	Revenue accounts
501–699	Expense accounts

These numbers provide a three-digit code that is useful in recordkeeping. In this case, the first digit assigned to asset accounts is a 1, the first digit assigned to liability accounts is a 2, and so on. The second and third digits relate to the accounts' subcategories. Exhibit 2.4 shows a partial chart of accounts for FastForward.

Account Number	Account Name	Account Number	Account Name
101	Cash	301	C. Taylor, Capital
106	Accounts receivable	302	C. Taylor, Withdrawals
126	Supplies	403	Consulting revenue
128	Prepaid insurance	406	Rental revenue
167	Equipment	622	Salaries expense
201	Accounts payable	637	Insurance expense
236	Unearned consulting revenue	640	Rent expense
		652	Supplies expense
		690	Utilities expense

Exhibit 2.4

Partial Chart of Accounts for FastForward

Debits and Credits

C5 Define *debits* and *credits* and explain their role in double-entry accounting.

A **T-account** represents a ledger account and is a tool used to understand the effects of one or more transactions. Its name comes from its shape like the letter *T.* The layout of a T-account (shown in Exhibit 2.5) is (1) the account title on top, (2) a left, or debit side, and (3) a right, or credit, side.

The left side of an account is called the **debit** side, often abbreviated *Dr.* The right side is called the **credit** side, abbreviated *Cr.*[2] To enter amounts on the left side of an account is to *debit* the account. To enter amounts on the right side is to *credit* the account. Do not make the error of thinking that the terms *debit* and *credit* mean increase or decrease. Whether a debit or a credit is an increase or decrease depends on the account. In an account where a debit is an increase, the credit is a decrease; in an account where a debit is a decrease, the credit is an increase. The difference between total debits and total credits for an account, including any beginning balance, is the **account balance.** When the sum of debits exceeds the sum of credits, the account has a *debit balance*. It has a *credit balance* when the sum of credits exceeds the sum of debits. When the sum of debits equals the sum of credits, the account has a *zero balance.*

Point: Think of *debit* and *credit* as accounting directions for left and right.

Account Title	
(Left side) ***Debit***	(Right side) ***Credit***

Exhibit 2.5

The T-Account

Double-Entry Accounting

Double-entry accounting requires that each transaction affect, and be recorded in, at least two accounts. It also means the *total amount debited must equal the total amount credited* for each transaction. Thus, the sum of the debits for all entries must equal the sum of the credits for all entries, and the sum of debit account balances in the ledger must equal the sum of credit account balances.

The system for recording debits and credits follows from the usual accounting equation—see Exhibit 2.6. Two points are important here. First, like any simple mathematical relation, net increases or decreases on one side have equal net effects on the other side. For example, a net increase in assets must be accompanied by an identical net increase on the liabilities

Assets		=	Liabilities		+	Equity	
↑ Debit for increases +	↓ Credit for decreases −		↓ Debit for decreases −	↑ Credit for increases +		↓ Debit for decreases −	↑ Credit for increases +

Exhibit 2.6

Debits and Credits in the Accounting Equation

[2] These abbreviations are remnants of 18th-century English recordkeeping practices where the terms *debitor* and *creditor* were used instead of *debit* and *credit*. The abbreviations use the first and last letters of these terms, just as we still do for Saint (St.) and Doctor (Dr.).

Point: Debits and credits do not mean favorable or unfavorable. A debit to an asset increases it, as does a debit to an expense. A credit to a liability increases it, as does a credit to a revenue.

and equity side. Recall that some transactions affect only one side of the equation, meaning that two or more accounts on one side are affected, but their net effect on this one side is zero. Second, the left side is the *normal balance* side for assets, and the right side is the *normal balance* side for liabilities and equity. This matches their layout in the accounting equation where assets are on the left side of this equation, and liabilities and equity are on the right.

Equity increases from revenues and owner investments and it decreases from expenses and owner withdrawals. These important equity relations are conveyed by expanding the accounting equation to include debits and credits in double-entry form as shown in Exhibit 2.7.

Exhibit 2.7

Debit and Credit Effects for Component Accounts

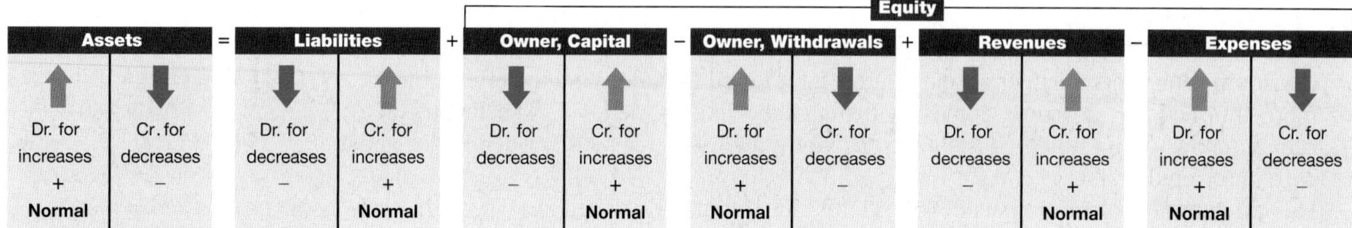

Increases (credits) to capital and revenues *increase* equity; increases (debits) to withdrawals and expenses *decrease* equity. The normal balance of each account (asset, liability, capital, withdrawals, revenue, or expense) refers to the left or right (debit or credit) side where *increases* are recorded. Understanding these diagrams and rules is required to prepare, analyze, and interpret financial statements.

The T-account for FastForward's Cash account, reflecting its first 11 transactions (from Exhibit 1.9), is shown in Exhibit 2.8. The total increases in its Cash account are $36,100, the total decreases are $31,700, and the account's debit balance is $4,400.

Exhibit 2.8

Computing the Balance for a T-Account

Cash			
Investment by owner	30,000	Purchase of supplies	2,500
Consulting services revenue earned	4,200	Purchase of equipment	26,000
Collection of account receivable	1,900	Payment of rent	1,000
		Payment of salary	700
		Payment of account payable	900
		Withdrawal by owner	600
Balance	**4,400**		

Point: The ending balance is on the side with the largest dollar amount.

Quick Check

1. Identify examples of accounting source documents.
2. Explain the importance of source documents.
3. Identify each of the following as either an asset, a liability, or equity: (*a*) Prepaid Rent, (*b*) Unearned Fees, (*c*) Building, (*d*) Wages Payable, and (*e*) Office Supplies.
4. What is an account? What is a ledger?
5. What determines the number and types of accounts a company uses?
6. Does *debit* always mean increase and *credit* always mean decrease?
7. Describe a chart of accounts.

Answers—pp. 72–73

Journalizing and Posting Transactions

P1 Record transactions in a journal and post entries to a ledger.

Processing transactions is a crucial part of accounting. The four usual steps of this process are depicted in Exhibit 2.9. Steps 1 and 2—involving transaction analysis and double-entry accounting—were introduced in prior sections. This section extends that discussion and focuses on steps 3 and 4 of the accounting process. Step 3 is to record each transaction in a journal. A **journal** gives a complete record of each transaction in one place. It also shows debits and credits for each transaction. The process of recording transactions in a journal is called **journalizing.** Step 4 is to transfer (or *post*) entries from the journal to the ledger. The process of transferring journal entry information to the ledger is called **posting.**

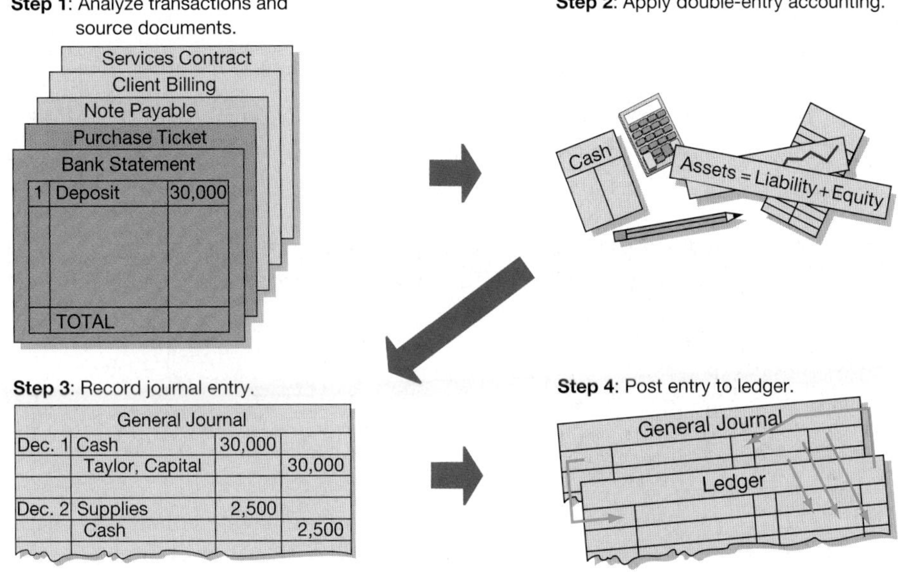

Exhibit 2.9

Steps in Processing Transactions

Journalizing Transactions The process of journalizing transactions requires an understanding of a journal. While companies can use various journals, every company uses a **general journal.** It can be used to record any transaction and includes the following information about each transaction: (1) date of transaction, (2) titles of affected accounts, (3) dollar amount of each debit and credit, and (4) explanation of the transaction. Exhibit 2.10 shows how the first two transactions of FastForward are recorded in a general journal. This process is similar for manual and computerized systems. Computerized journals are often designed to look like a manual journal page, and also include error-checking routines that ensure debits equal credits for each entry. Shortcuts allow recordkeepers to select account names and numbers from pull-down menus.

To record entries in a general journal, apply these steps; refer to the entries in Exhibit 2.10 when reviewing these steps. ① Date the transaction: Enter the year at the top of the first column and the month and day on the first line of each journal entry. ② Enter titles

Exhibit 2.10

Partial General Journal for FastForward

GENERAL JOURNAL — Page 1

Date	Account Titles and Explanation	PR	Debit	Credit
2004				
Dec. 1	Cash		30,000	
	C. Taylor, Capital			30,000
	Investment by owner.			
Dec. 2	Supplies		2,500	
	Cash			2,500
	Purchased supplies for cash.			

of accounts debited and then enter amounts in the Debit column on the same line. Account titles are taken from the chart of accounts and are aligned with the left margin of the Account Titles and Explanation column. ③ Enter titles of accounts credited and then enter amounts in the Credit column on the same line. Account titles are from the chart of accounts and are indented from the left margin of the Account Titles and Explanation column to distinguish them from debited accounts. ④ Enter a brief explanation of the transaction on the line below the entry (it often references a source document). This explanation is indented about half as far as the credited account titles to avoid confusing it with accounts, and it is italicized.

A blank line is left between each journal entry for clarity. When a transaction is first recorded, the **posting reference (PR) column** blank is left blank (in a manual system). Later, when posting entries to the ledger, the identification numbers of the individual ledger accounts are entered in the PR column.

Balance Column Account T-accounts are simple and direct means to show how the accounting process works. However, actual accounting systems need more structure and therefore use **balance column accounts,** as in Exhibit 2.11.

Exhibit 2.11

Cash Account in Balance Column Format

		Cash		Account No. 101	
Date	**Explanation**	**PR**	**Debit**	**Credit**	**Balance**
2004					
Dec. 1		*G1*	30,000		30,000
Dec. 2		*G1*		2,500	27,500
Dec. 3		*G1*		26,000	1,500
Dec. 10		*G1*	4,200		5,700

The balance column account format is similar to a T-account in having columns for debits and credits. It is different in including transaction date and explanation columns. It also has a column with the balance of the account after each entry is recorded. To illustrate, FastForward's Cash account in Exhibit 2.11 is debited on December 1 for the $30,000 owner investment, yielding a $30,000 debit balance. The account is credited on December 2 for $2,500, yielding a $27,500 debit balance. On December 3, it is credited again, this time for $26,000, and its debit balance is reduced to $1,500. The Cash account is debited for $4,200 on December 10, and its debit balance increases to $5,700; and so on.

The heading of the Balance column does not show whether it is a debit or credit balance. Instead, an account is assumed to have a *normal balance*. Unusual events can sometimes temporarily give an account an abnormal balance. An *abnormal balance* refers to a balance on the side where decreases are recorded. For example, a customer might mistakenly overpay a bill. This gives that customer's account receivable an abnormal (credit) balance. An abnormal balance is often identified by circling it or by entering it in red or some other unusual color. A zero balance for an account is usually shown by writing zeros or a dash in the Balance column to avoid confusion between a zero balance and one omitted in error.

Point: There are no exact rules for writing journal entry explanations. An explanation should be short yet describe why an entry is made.

Posting Journal Entries Step 4 of processing transactions is to post journal entries to ledger accounts (see Exhibit 2.9). To ensure that the ledger is up-to-date, entries are posted as soon as possible. This might be daily, weekly, or when time permits. All entries must be posted to the ledger before financial statements are prepared to ensure that account balances are up-to-date. When entries are posted to the ledger, the debits in journal entries are transferred into ledger accounts as debits, and credits are transferred into ledger accounts as credits. Exhibit 2.12 shows the four steps to post a journal entry. First, identify the ledger account that is debited in the entry; then, in the ledger, enter the entry date, the journal and page in its PR column, the debit amount, and the new balance of the ledger account. (The letter *G* shows it came from the General Journal. Other journals are discussed in Chapter 7.) Second, enter the ledger account number in the PR column of the journal. Steps three and four repeat the first two steps for credit entries and amounts. The posting process creates a link

Point: Computerized systems often provide a code beside a balance such as *dr.* or *cr.* to identify its balance.

Point: A journal is often referred to as the *book of original entry.* The ledger is referred to as the *book of final entry* because financial statements are prepared from it.

Point: Posting is automatic and immediate with accounting software.

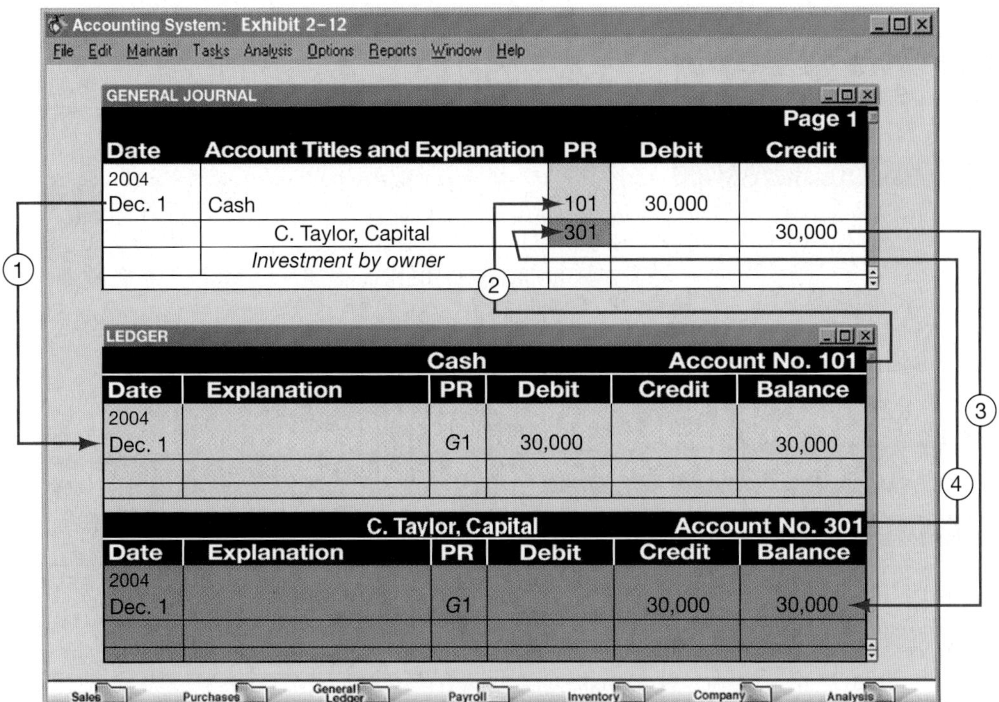

Exhibit 2.12

Posting an Entry to the Ledger

Key: (1) Identify debit account in Ledger: enter date, journal page, amount, and balance.
(2) Enter the debit account number from the Ledger in the PR column of the journal.
(3) Identify credit account in Ledger: enter date, journal page, amount, and balance.
(4) Enter the credit account number from the Ledger in the PR column of the journal.

Point: The fundamental concepts of a manual (pencil-and-paper) system are identical to those of a computerized information system.

between the ledger and the journal entry. This link is a useful cross-reference for tracing an amount from one record to another.

Point: Explanations are typically included in ledger accounts only for unusual transactions or events.

Analyzing Transactions—An Illustration

A1 Analyze the impact of transactions on accounts and financial statements.

We return to the activities of FastForward to show how double-entry accounting is useful in analyzing and processing transactions. Analysis of each transaction follows the four steps of Exhibit 2.9. First, we review the transaction and any source documents. Second, we analyze the transaction using the accounting equation. Third, we use double-entry accounting to record the transaction in journal entry form. Fourth, the entry is posted (for simplicity, we use T-accounts to represent ledger accounts). We also identify the financial statements affected by each transaction. Study each transaction thoroughly before proceeding to the next transaction. The first 11 transactions are from Chapter 1, and we analyze five additional December transactions of FastForward (numbered 12 through 16) that were omitted earlier.

Topic Tackler 2-1

1. Investment by Owner

Cash 101	
(1) 30,000	

C. Taylor, Capital 301	
	(1) 30,000

Transaction: Chuck Taylor invests $30,000 cash in FastForward.

Analysis:

Assets	=	Liabilities	+	Equity
Cash				**Capital**
+30,000	=	0	+	30,000

Double entry:

(1)	Cash	101	30,000	
	C. Taylor, Capital	301		30,000

Statements affected:[3] BLS and SCF

FASTForward

[3] We use abbreviations for the statements: income statement (IS), balance sheet (BLS), statement of cash flows (SCF), and statement of owner's equity (SOE).

2. Purchase Supplies for Cash

Supplies			126
(2)	2,500		

Cash			101
(1)	30,000	(2)	2,500

Transaction: FastForward pays $2,500 cash for supplies.

Analysis:

Assets		=	Liabilities	+	Equity
Cash	**Supplies**				
−2,500	+2,500	=	0	+	0

Changes the composition of assets but not the total.

Double entry:

(2)	Supplies	126	2,500	
	Cash	101		2,500

Statements affected: BLS and SCF

3. Purchase Equipment for Cash

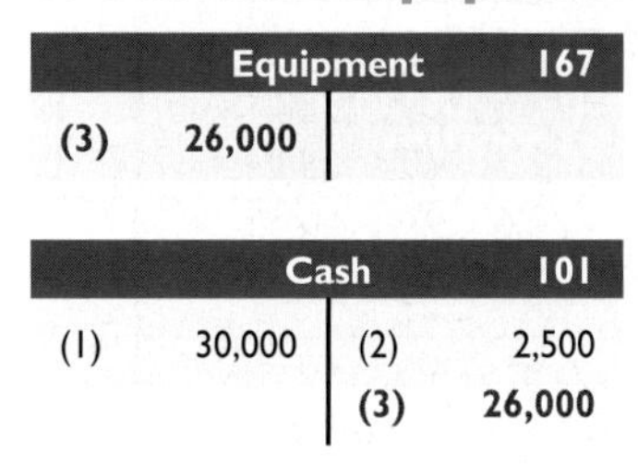

Equipment			167
(3)	26,000		

Cash			101
(1)	30,000	(2)	2,500
		(3)	26,000

Transaction: FastForward pays $26,000 cash for equipment.

Analysis:

Assets		=	Liabilities	+	Equity
Cash	**Equipment**				
−26,000	+26,000	=	0	+	0

Changes the composition of assets but not the total.

Double entry:

(3)	Equipment	167	26,000	
	Cash	101		26,000

Statements affected: BLS and SCF

4. Purchase Supplies on Credit

Supplies			126
(2)	2,500		
(4)	7,100		

Accounts Payable			201
		(4)	7,100

Transaction: FastForward purchases $7,100 of supplies on credit from a supplier.

Analysis:

Assets	=	Liabilities	+	Equity
Supplies		**Accounts Payable**		
+7,100	=	+7,100	+	0

Double entry:

(4)	Supplies	126	7,100	
	Accounts Payable	201		7,100

Statements affected: BLS

5. Provide Services for Cash

Cash			101
(1)	30,000	(2)	2,500
(5)	4,200	(3)	26,000

Consulting Revenue			403
		(5)	4,200

Transaction: FastForward provides consulting services and immediately collects $4,200 cash.

Analysis:

Assets	=	Liabilities	+	Equity
Cash				**Consulting Revenue**
+4,200	=	0		+4,200

Double entry:

(5)	Cash	101	4,200	
	Consulting Revenue	403		4,200

Statements affected: BLS, IS, SCF, and SOE

6. Payment of Expense in Cash

Rent Expense 640			
(6)	**1,000**		

Cash 101			
(1)	30,000	(2)	2,500
(5)	4,200	(3)	26,000
		(6)	**1,000**

Transaction: FastForward pays $1,000 cash for December rent.

Analysis:

Assets	=	Liabilities	+	Equity
Cash				**Rent Expense**
−1,000	=	0		−1,000

Double entry:

(6)	Rent Expense	640	1,000	
	Cash	101		1,000

Statements affected: BLS, IS, SCF, and SOE

7. Payment of Expense in Cash

Salaries Expense 622			
(7)	**700**		

Cash 101			
(1)	30,000	(2)	2,500
(5)	4,200	(3)	26,000
		(6)	1,000
		(7)	**700**

Transaction: FastForward pays $700 cash for employee salary.

Analysis:

Assets	=	Liabilities	+	Equity
Cash				**Salaries Expense**
−700	=	0		−700

Double entry:

(7)	Salaries Expense	622	700	
	Cash	101		700

Statements affected: BLS, IS, SCF, and SOE

Point: *Salary* usually refers to compensation for an employee who receives a fixed amount for a given time period, whereas *wages* usually refers to compensation based on time worked.

8. Provide Consulting and Rental Services on Credit

Accounts Receivable 106			
(8)	**1,900**		

Consulting Revenue 403			
		(5)	4,200
		(8)	**1,600**

Rental Revenue 406			
		(8)	**300**

Transaction: FastForward provides consulting services of $1,600 and rents its test facilities for $300. The customer is billed $1,900 for these services.

Analysis:

Assets	=	Liabilities	+	Equity	
Accounts Receivable				**Consulting Revenue**	**Rental Revenue**
+1,900	=	0		+1,600	+300

Double entry:

(8)	Accounts Receivable	106	1,900	
	Consulting Revenue	403		1,600
	Rental Revenue	406		300

Statements affected: BLS, IS, and SOE

Point: Transaction 8 is a **compound journal entry,** which affects three or more accounts.

9. Receipt of Cash on Account

Cash 101			
(1)	30,000	(2)	2,500
(5)	4,200	(3)	26,000
(9)	**1,900**	(6)	1,000
		(7)	700

Accounts Receivable 106			
(8)	1,900	**(9)**	**1,900**

Transaction: FastForward receives $1,900 cash from the client billed in transaction 8.

Analysis:

Assets		=	Liabilities	+	Equity
Cash	**Accounts Receivable**				
+1,900	−1,900	=	0	+	0

Double entry:

(9)	Cash	101	1,900	
	Accounts Receivable	106		1,900

Statements affected: BLS and SCF

Point: The *revenue recognition principle* requires revenue to be recognized when earned, which is when the company provides products or services to a customer. This is not necessarily the same time that the customer pays. A customer can pay before or after products or services are provided.

10. Partial Payment of Accounts Payable

Accounts Payable	201		
(10)	**900**	(4)	7,100

Cash	101		
(1)	30,000	(2)	2,500
(5)	4,200	(3)	26,000
(9)	1,900	(6)	1,000
		(7)	700
		(10)	**900**

Transaction: FastForward pays CalTech Supply $900 cash toward the payable of transaction 4.

Analysis:

Assets	=	Liabilities	+	Equity
Cash		**Accounts Payable**		
−900	=	−900	+	0

Double entry:

(10)	Accounts Payable	201	900	
	Cash	101		900

Statements affected: BLS and SCF

11. Withdrawal of Cash by Owner

C. Taylor, Withdrawals 302			
(11)	**600**		

Cash	101		
(1)	30,000	(2)	2,500
(5)	4,200	(3)	26,000
(9)	1,900	(6)	1,000
		(7)	700
		(10)	900
		(11)	**600**

Transaction: Chuck Taylor withdraws $600 cash from FastForward for personal use.

Analysis:

Assets	=	Liabilities	+	Equity
Cash				**Withdrawals**
−600	=	0		−600

Double entry:

(11)	C. Taylor, Withdrawals	302	600	
	Cash	101		600

Statements affected: BLS, SCF, and SOE

12. Receipt of Cash for Future Services

Cash	101		
(1)	30,000	(2)	2,500
(5)	4,200	(3)	26,000
(9)	1,900	(6)	1,000
(12)	**3,000**	(7)	700
		(10)	900
		(11)	600

Unearned Consulting Revenue	236		
		(12)	**3,000**

Transaction: FastForward receives $3,000 cash in advance of providing consulting services to a customer.

Analysis:

Assets	=	Liabilities	+	Equity
Cash		**Unearned Consulting Revenue**		
+3,000	=	+3,000	+	0

Accepting $3,000 cash obligates FastForward to perform future services and is a liability. No revenue is earned until services are provided.

Double entry:

(12)	Cash	101	3,000	
	Unearned Consulting Revenue	236		3,000

Statements affected: BLS and SCF

Point: Luca Pacioli is considered a pioneer in accounting and the first to devise double-entry accounting.

13. Pay Cash for Future Insurance Coverage

Prepaid Insurance	128		
(13)	**2,400**		

Cash	101		
(1)	30,000	(2)	2,500
(5)	4,200	(3)	26,000
(9)	1,900	(6)	1,000
(12)	3,000	(7)	700
		(10)	900
		(11)	600
		(13)	**2,400**

Transaction: FastForward pays $2,400 cash (insurance premium) for a 24-month insurance policy. Coverage begins on December 1.

Analysis:

Assets		=	Liabilities	+	Equity
Cash	**Prepaid Insurance**				
−2,400	+2,400	=	0	+	0

Changes the composition of assets from cash to prepaid insurance. Expense is incurred as insurance coverage expires.

Double entry:

(13)	Prepaid Insurance	128	2,400	
	Cash	101		2,400

Statements affected: BLS and SCF

14. Purchase Supplies for Cash

Supplies			126
(2)	2,500		
(4)	7,100		
(14)	**120**		

Cash			101
(1)	30,000	(2)	2,500
(5)	4,200	(3)	26,000
(9)	1,900	(6)	1,000
(12)	3,000	(7)	700
		(10)	900
		(11)	600
		(13)	2,400
		(14)	**120**

Transaction: FastForward pays $120 cash for supplies.

Analysis:

Assets		=	Liabilities	+	Equity
Cash	**Supplies**				
−120	+120	=	0	+	0

Double entry:

(14)	Supplies	126	120	
	Cash	101		120

Statements affected: BLS and SCF

15. Payment of Expense in Cash

Utilities Expense			690
(15)	**230**		

Cash			101
(1)	30,000	(2)	2,500
(5)	4,200	(3)	26,000
(9)	1,900	(6)	1,000
(12)	3,000	(7)	700
		(10)	900
		(11)	600
		(13)	2,400
		(14)	120
		(15)	**230**

Transaction: FastForward pays $230 cash for December utilities expense.

Analysis:

Assets	=	Liabilities	+	Equity
Cash				**Utilities Expense**
−230	=	0		−230

Double entry:

(15)	Utilities Expense	690	230	
	Cash	101		230

Statements affected: BLS, IS, SCF, and SOE

16. Payment of Expense in Cash

Salaries Expense			622
(7)	700		
(16)	**700**		

Cash			101
(1)	30,000	(2)	2,500
(5)	4,200	(3)	26,000
(9)	1,900	(6)	1,000
(12)	3,000	(7)	700
		(10)	900
		(11)	600
		(13)	2,400
		(14)	120
		(15)	230
		(16)	**700**

Transaction: FastForward pays $700 cash in employee salary for work performed in the latter part of December.

Analysis:

Assets	=	Liabilities	+	Equity
Cash				**Salaries Expense**
−700	=	0		−700

Double entry:

(16)	Salaries Expense	622	700	
	Cash	101		700

Statements affected: BLS, IS, SCF, and SOE

Point: We could merge transactions 15 and 16 into one *compound entry.*

Summary of debit and credit rules:

Accounts	Increase (normal bal.)	Decrease
Asset	Debit	Credit
Liability	Credit	Debit
Capital	Credit	Debit
Withdrawals	Debit	Credit
Revenue	Credit	Debit
Expense	Debit	Credit

Point: Technology does not provide the judgment required to analyze most business transactions. Analysis requires the expertise of skilled and ethical professionals.

Accounting Equation Analysis

Exhibit 2.13 shows the accounts (in T-account form) of FastForward after all 16 transactions are recorded, posted and the balances computed. The accounts are grouped into three major columns corresponding to the accounting equation: assets, liabilities, and equity. Note several important points. First, as with each transaction, the totals for the three columns must obey the accounting equation. Specifically, assets equal \$42,070 (\$3,950 + \$0 + \$9,720 + \$2,400 + \$26,000); liabilities equal \$9,200 (\$6,200 + \$3,000); and equity equals \$32,870 (\$30,000 − \$600 + \$5,800 + \$300 − \$1,400 − \$1,000 − \$230). These numbers prove the accounting equation: Assets of \$42,070 = Liabilities of \$9,200 + Equity of \$32,870. Second, the capital, withdrawals, revenue, and expense accounts reflect the transactions that change equity. Their balances underlie the statement of owner's equity. Third, the revenue and expense account balances will be summarized and reported in the income statement. Fourth, increases and decreases in the cash account make up the elements reported in the statement of cash flows.

Exhibit 2.13

Ledger for FastForward (in T-Account Form)

Assets = Liabilities + Equity

Assets

Cash			101
(1)	30,000	(2)	2,500
(5)	4,200	(3)	26,000
(9)	1,900	(6)	1,000
(12)	3,000	(7)	700
		(10)	900
		(11)	600
		(13)	2,400
		(14)	120
		(15)	230
		(16)	700
Balance	**3,950**		

Accounts Receivable			106
(8)	1,900	(9)	1,900
Balance	**0**		

Supplies			126
(2)	2,500		
(4)	7,100		
(14)	120		
Balance	**9,720**		

Prepaid Insurance			128
(13)	**2,400**		

Equipment			167
(3)	**26,000**		

Liabilities

Accounts Payable			201
(10)	900	(4)	7,100
		Balance	**6,200**

Unearned Consulting Revenue			236
		(12)	**3,000**

Equity

C. Taylor, Capital			301
		(1)	**30,000**

C. Taylor, Withdrawals			302
(11)	**600**		

Consulting Revenue			403
		(5)	4,200
		(8)	1,600
		Balance	**5,800**

Rental Revenue			406
		(8)	**300**

Salaries Expense			622
(7)	700		
(16)	700		
Balance	**1,400**		

Rent Expense			640
(6)	**1,000**		

Utilities Expense			690
(15)	**230**		

Accounts in this white area reflect those reported on the income statement.

\$42,070 = \$9,200 + \$32,870

Quick Check

8. What types of transactions increase equity? What types decrease equity?
9. Why are accounting systems called *double entry?*
10. For each transaction, double-entry accounting requires which of the following: (*a*) Debits to asset accounts must create credits to liability or equity accounts, (*b*) a debit to a liability account must create a credit to an asset account, or (*c*) total debits must equal total credits.
11. An owner invests $15,000 cash along with equipment having a market value of $23,000 in a proprietorship. Prepare the necessary journal entry.
12. Explain what a compound journal entry is.
13. Why are posting reference numbers entered in the journal when entries are posted to ledger accounts?

Answers—p. 73

Trial Balance

Double-entry accounting requires the sum of debit account balances to equal the sum of credit account balances. A trial balance is used to verify this. A **trial balance** is a list of accounts and their balances at a point in time. Account balances are reported in the appropriate debit or credit column of a trial balance. Exhibit 2.14 shows the trial balance for FastForward after its 16 entries have been posted to the ledger. (This is an *unadjusted* trial balance—Chapter 3 will explain the necessary adjustments.)

Point: Knowing how financial statements are prepared improves our analysis of them.

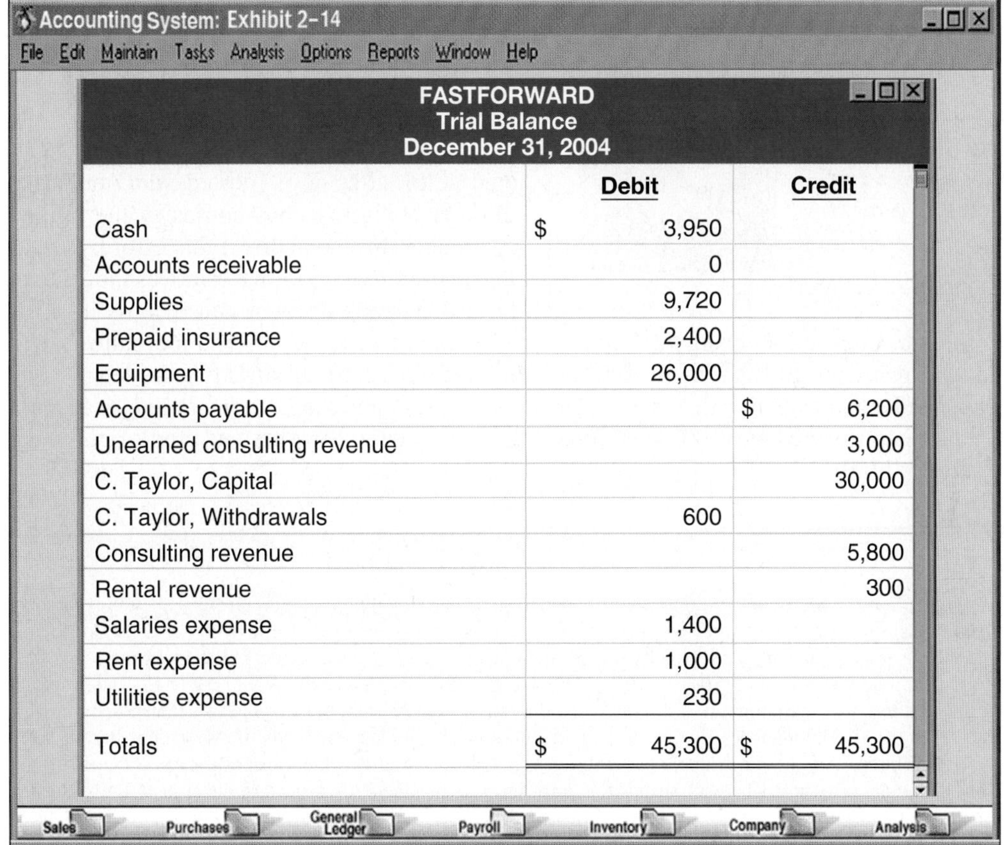

FASTFORWARD
Trial Balance
December 31, 2004

	Debit	Credit
Cash	$ 3,950	
Accounts receivable	0	
Supplies	9,720	
Prepaid insurance	2,400	
Equipment	26,000	
Accounts payable		$ 6,200
Unearned consulting revenue		3,000
C. Taylor, Capital		30,000
C. Taylor, Withdrawals	600	
Consulting revenue		5,800
Rental revenue		300
Salaries expense	1,400	
Rent expense	1,000	
Utilities expense	230	
Totals	$ 45,300	$ 45,300

Exhibit 2.14

Trial Balance (unadjusted)

Preparing a Trial Balance

P2 Prepare and explain the use of a trial balance.

Preparing a trial balance involves three steps:

1. List each account title and its amount (from ledger) in the trial balance. If an account has a zero balance, list it with a zero in its normal balance column (or omit it entirely).
2. Compute the total of debit balances and the total of credit balances.
3. Verify (*prove*) total debit balances equal total credit balances.

Point: The ordering of accounts in a trial balance typically follows their identification number from the chart of accounts.

Point: A trial balance is *not* a financial statement but a mechanism for checking equality of debits and credits in the ledger. Financial statements do not have debit and credit columns.

The total of debit balances equals the total of credit balances for the trial balance in Exhibit 2.14. Note that equality of these two totals does not guarantee that no errors were made. For example, the column totals still will be equal when a debit or credit of a correct amount is made to a wrong account. Another error that does not cause unequal column totals is when equal debits and credits of an incorrect amount are entered.

Example: If a credit to Unearned Revenue were incorrectly posted from the journal as a credit to the Revenue ledger account, would the ledger still balance? Would the financial statements be correct? *Answers:* The ledger would balance, but liabilities would be understated, equity would be overstated, and income would be overstated (all because of overstated revenues).

Searching for and Correcting Errors If the trial balance does not balance (when its columns are not equal), the error (or errors) must be found and corrected. An efficient way to search for an error is to check the journalizing, posting, and trial balance preparation in *reverse order.* Step 1 is to verify that the trial balance columns are correctly added. If step 1 fails to find the error, step 2 is to verify that account balances are accurately entered from the ledger. Step 3 is to see whether a debit (or credit) balance is mistakenly listed in the trial balance as a credit (or debit). A clue to this error is when the difference between total debits and total credits equals twice the amount of the incorrect account balance. If the error is still undiscovered, Step 4 is to recompute each account balance in the ledger. Step 5 is to verify that each journal entry is properly posted. Step 6 is to verify that the original journal entry has equal debits and credits. At this point, any errors should be uncovered.[4]

If an error in a journal entry is discovered before the error is posted, it can be corrected in a manual system by drawing a line through the incorrect information. The correct information is written above it to create a record of change for the auditor. Many computerized systems allow the operator to replace the incorrect information directly.

If an error in a journal entry is not discovered until after it is posted, do not strike through both erroneous entries in the journal and ledger. Instead, correct this error by creating a *correcting entry* that removes the amount from the wrong account and records it to the correct account. As an example, suppose a $100 purchase of supplies is journalized with an incorrect debit to Equipment, and then this incorrect entry is posted to the ledger. The Supplies ledger account balance is understated by $100, and the Equipment ledger account balance is overstated by $100. The correcting entry is: debit Supplies and credit Equipment (both for $100).

Decision Insight

Gorge'em *Disgorgement* is one of the government's strongest weapons for going after shady executives. When the SEC wins a court order or settles a case against executives, it can require them to give back their salaries, including stock gains.

Point: The IRS requires companies to keep records that can be audited.

[4] *Transposition* occurs when two digits are switched, or transposed, within a number. If transposition is the only error, it yields a difference between the two trial balance totals that is evenly divisible by 9. For example, assume that a $691 debit in an entry is incorrectly posted to the ledger as $619. Total credits in the trial balance are then larger than total debits by $72 ($691 − $619). The $72 error is *evenly* divisible by 9 (72/9 = 8). The first digit of the quotient (in our example it is 8) equals the difference between the digits of the two transposed numbers (the 9 and the 1). The number of digits in the quotient also tells the location of the transposition, starting from the right. The quotient in our example had only one digit (8), so it tells us the transposition is in the first digit. Consider another example where a transposition error involves posting $961 instead of the correct $691. The difference in these numbers is $270, and its quotient is 30 (270/9). The quotient has two digits, so it tells us to check the second digit from the right for a transposition of two numbers that have a difference of 3.

Using a Trial Balance to Prepare Financial Statements

P3 Prepare financial statements from business transactions.

This section shows how to prepare *financial statements* from the trial balance in Exhibit 2.14 and information on the December transactions of FastForward. The statements differ from those in Chapter 1 because of several additional transactions. These statements are also more precisely called *unadjusted statements* because we need to make some further accounting adjustments (described in Chapter 3).

How financial statements are linked in time is illustrated in Exhibit 2.15. A balance sheet reports on an organization's financial position at a *point in time*. The income statement, statement of owner's equity, and statement of cash flows report on financial performance over a *period of time*. The three statements in the middle column of Exhibit 2.15 link balance sheets from the beginning to the end of a reporting period. They explain how financial position changes from one point to another.

Exhibit 2.15

Links between Financial Statements Across Time

Income statement
Beginning balance sheet
Statement of owner's equity
Ending balance sheet
Statement of cash flows
Point in time
Period of time
Point in time

Preparers and users (including regulatory agencies) determine the length of the reporting period. A one-year, or annual, reporting period is common, as are semiannual, quarterly, and monthly periods. The one-year reporting period is known as the *accounting*, or *fiscal, year*. Businesses whose accounting year begins on January 1 and ends on December 31 are known as *calendar-year* companies. Many companies choose a fiscal year ending on a date other than December 31. **Krispy Kreme** is a *noncalendar-year* company as reflected in the headings of its February 2 year-end financial statements in Appendix A near the end of the book.

Topic Tackler 2-2

Point: A statement's heading lists the 3 W's: **Who**—name of organization, **What**—name of statement, **When**—statement's point in time or period of time.

Income Statement An income statement reports the revenues earned less the expenses incurred by a business over a period of time. FastForward's income statement for December is shown at the top of Exhibit 2.16. Information about revenues and expenses is conveniently taken from the trial balance in Exhibit 2.14. Net income of $3,470 is reported at the bottom of the statement. Owner investments and withdrawals are *not* part of income.

"I'LL TELL YOU, HARRIS, THEY DON'T MAKE ACCOUNTANTS LIKE THEY USED TO. THOSE I HAD IN THE '90'S, NEVER BROUGHT ME FIGURES LIKE THESE."

Statement of Owner's Equity The statement of owner's equity reports information about how equity changes over the reporting period. FastForward's statement of owner's equity is the second report in Exhibit 2.16. It shows the $30,000 owner investment plus the $3,470 of net income earned during the month. It also reports the $600 withdrawal and the $32,870 end-of-month equity (capital) balance. (The beginning capital balance in the statement of owner's equity is rarely zero. An exception is for the first period of a company's operations. The beginning capital balance in January 2005 is $32,870, which is December's ending balance.)

Balance Sheet The balance sheet reports the financial position of a company at a point in time, usually at the end of a month, quarter, or year. FastForward's balance sheet is the third report in Exhibit 2.16. This statement refers to FastForward's financial condition at the close of business on December 31. The left side of the balance sheet lists its assets: cash, supplies, prepaid insurance, and equipment. The upper right side of the balance sheet shows that it owes $6,200 to creditors and $3,000 in services to customers who paid in advance.

Point: An income statement is also called an *earnings statement, a statement of operations*, or a *P&L* (profit and loss) *statement*. A balance sheet is also called a *statement of financial position*.

Decision Maker

Entrepreneur You open a wholesale business selling entertainment equipment to retail outlets. You find that most of your customers demand to buy on credit. How can you use the balance sheets of these customers to decide which ones to extend credit to?

Answer—p. 72

The equity section shows an ending capital balance of $32,870. Note the link between the ending balance of the statement of owner's equity and the capital balance here. (Recall that this presentation of the balance sheet is called the *account form:* assets on the left and liabilities and equity on the right. Another presentation is the *report form:* assets on top, followed by liabilities and then equity. Either presentation is acceptable.)

Point: While revenues increase equity and expenses decrease equity, the amounts are not reported in detail in the statement of owner's equity. Instead, their effects are reflected through net income.

Presentation Issues Dollar signs are not used in journals and ledgers. They do appear in financial statements and other reports such as trial balances. The usual practice is to put dollar signs beside only the first and last numbers in a column. **Krispy Kreme**'s

Exhibit 2.16

Financial Statements and Their Links

FASTFORWARD
Income Statement
For Month Ended December 31, 2004

Revenues		
Consulting revenue ($4,200 + $1,600)	$ 5,800	
Rental revenue	300	
Total revenues		$ 6,100
Expenses		
Rent expense	1,000	
Salaries expense	1,400	
Utilities expense	230	
Total expenses		2,630
Net income		$ 3,470

Point: Arrow lines show how the statements are linked.

FASTFORWARD
Statement of Owner's Equity
For Month Ended December 31, 2004

C. Taylor, Capital, December 1, 2004		$ 0
Plus: Investments by owner	$30,000	
Net income	3,470	33,470
		33,470
Less: Withdrawals by owner		600
C. Taylor, Capital, December 31, 2004		$32,870

FASTFORWARD
Balance Sheet
December 31, 2004

Assets		Liabilities	
Cash	$ 3,950	Accounts payable	$ 6,200
Supplies	9,720	Unearned revenue	3,000
Prepaid insurance	2,400	Total liabilities	9,200
Equipment	26,000		
		Equity	
		C. Taylor, Capital	32,870
Total assets	$42,070	Total liabilities and equity	$ 42,070

Point: To *foot* a column of numbers is to add them.

financial statements in Appendix A show this. When amounts are entered in a journal, ledger, or trial balance, commas are optional to indicate thousands, millions, and so forth. However, commas are always used in financial statements. Companies also commonly round amounts in reports to the nearest dollar, or even to a higher level. Krispy Kreme is typical of many companies in that it rounds its financial statement amounts to the nearest thousand. This decision is based on the perceived impact of rounding for users' business decisions.

Example: How would the balance sheet in Exhibit 2.16 change if FastForward pays $2,000 of its payable on December 31 using its Cash account? What would be the new amount of total assets? Would the balance sheet still balance? *Answers:* Cash would be $1,950, accounts payable would be $4,200, total assets (and liabilities plus equity) would be $40,070, and the balance sheet would still balance.

Quick Check

14. Where are dollar signs typically entered in financial statements?

15. If a $4,000 debit to Equipment in a journal entry is incorrectly posted to the ledger as a $4,000 credit, and the ledger account has a resulting debit balance of $20,000, what is the effect of this error on the Trial Balance column totals?

16. Describe the link between the income statement and the statement of owner's equity.

17. Explain the link between the balance sheet and the statement of owner's equity.

18. Define and describe revenues and expenses.

19. Define and describe assets, liabilities, and equity.

Answers—p. 73

Debt Ratio

Decision Analysis

A2 Compute the debt ratio and describe its use in analyzing company performance.

An important business objective is gathering information to help assess a company's risk of failing to pay its debts. Companies finance their assets with either liabilities or equity. A company that finances a relatively large portion of its assets with liabilities is said to have a high degree of *financial leverage*. Higher financial leverage involves greater risk because liabilities must be repaid and often require regular interest payments (equity financing does not). The risk that a company might not be able to meet such required payments is higher if it has more liabilities (is more highly leveraged). One way to assess the risk associated with a company's use of liabilities is to compute the **debt ratio** as in Exhibit 2.17.

$$\textbf{Debt ratio} = \frac{\textbf{Total liabilities}}{\textbf{Total assets}}$$

Exhibit 2.17

Debt Ratio

To see how to apply the debt ratio, let's look at **Stride Rite**'s liabilities and assets. Stride Rite makes Keds, Pro-Keds, and other footwear. Exhibit 2.18 computes and reports its debt ratio at the end of each year from 1998 to 2002.

Stride Rite's debt ratio ranges from a low of 0.24 to a high of 0.31. Its ratio is low compared with the industry ratio. Stride Rite reports that it carries no long-term debt, which is unusual. This analysis implies a low risk from its financial leverage. Is this good or bad? To answer that question we

Point: Compare the equity amount to the liability amount to assess the extent of owner versus nonowner financing.

	2002	2001	2000	1999	1998
Total liabilities (in mil.)	$ 82	$100	$110	$101	$102
Total assets (in mil.)	$335	$362	$359	$351	$347
Debt ratio	**0.24**	**0.28**	**0.31**	**0.29**	**0.29**
Industry debt ratio	0.45	0.49	0.48	0.46	0.52

Exhibit 2.18

Computation and Analysis of Debt Ratio

Decision Maker

Investor You consider buying stock in **Converse**. As part of your analysis, you compute its debt ratio for 2001, 2002, and 2003 as: 0.35, 0.74, and 0.94, respectively. Based on the debt ratio, is Converse a low-risk investment? Has the risk of buying Converse stock changed over this period? (*Note:* The industry ratio averages 0.40.)

Answer—p. 72

need to compare the company's return on the borrowed money to the rate it is paying creditors. If the company's return is higher, it is successfully borrowing money to make more money. Be aware that a company's success with making money from borrowed money can quickly turn unprofitable if its own return drops below the rate it is paying creditors.

Demonstration Problem

(*Note:* This problem extends the demonstration problem of Chapter 1.) After several months of planning, Sylvia Workman started a haircutting business called Expressions. The following events occurred during its first month:

a. On August 1, Workman invested $3,000 cash and $15,000 of equipment in Expressions.
b. On August 2, Expressions paid $600 cash for furniture for the shop.
c. On August 3, Expressions paid $500 cash to rent space in a strip mall for August.
d. On August 4, it purchased $1,200 of equipment on credit for the shop (using a long-term note payable).
e. On August 5, Expressions opened for business. Cash received from services provided in the first week and a half of business (ended August 15) is $825.
f. On August 15, it provided $100 of haircutting services on account.
g. On August 17, it received a $100 check for services previously rendered on account.
h. On August 17, it paid $125 to an assistant for working during the grand opening.
i. Cash received from services provided during the second half of August is $930.
j. On August 31, it paid a $400 installment toward principal on the note payable entered into on August 4.
k. On August 31, Workman made a $900 cash withdrawal for personal use.

Required

1. Open the following ledger accounts in balance column format (account numbers are in parentheses): Cash (101); Accounts Receivable (102); Furniture (161); Store Equipment (165); Note Payable (240); S. Workman, Capital (301); S. Workman, Withdrawals (302); Haircutting Services Revenue (403); Wages Expense (623); and Rent Expense (640). Prepare general journal entries for the transactions.
2. Post the journal entries from (1) to the ledger accounts.
3. Prepare a trial balance as of August 31.
4. Prepare an income statement for August.
5. Prepare a statement of owner's equity for August.
6. Prepare a balance sheet as of August 31.
7. Determine the debt ratio as of August 31.

Extended Analysis

8. In the coming months, Expressions will experience a greater variety of business transactions. Identify which accounts are debited and which are credited for the following transactions. (*Hint:* You need to use some accounts not opened in part 1.)
   a. Purchase supplies with cash.
   b. Pay cash for future insurance coverage.
   c. Receive cash for services to be provided in the future.
   d. Purchase supplies on account.

Planning the Solution

- Analyze each transaction and use the debit and credit rules to prepare a journal entry for each.
- Post each debit and each credit from journal entries to their ledger accounts and cross-reference each amount in the posting reference (PR) columns of the journal and ledger.
- Calculate each account balance and list the accounts with their balances on a trial balance.
- Verify that total debits in the trial balance equal total credits.
- To prepare the income statement, identify revenues and expenses. List those items on the statement, compute the difference, and label the result as *net income* or *net loss*.
- Use information in the ledger to prepare the statement of owner's equity.
- Use information in the ledger to prepare the balance sheet.
- Calculate the debt ratio by dividing total liabilities by total assets.
- Analyze the future transactions to identify the accounts affected and apply debit and credit rules.

Solution to Demonstration Problem

1. General journal entries:

GENERAL JOURNAL — Page 1

Date	Account Titles and Explanation	PR	Debit	Credit
Aug. 1	Cash	101	3,000	
	Store Equipment	165	15,000	
	S. Workman, Capital	301		18,000
	Owner's investment.			
2	Furniture	161	600	
	Cash	101		600
	Purchased furniture for cash.			
3	Rent Expense	640	500	
	Cash	101		500
	Paid rent for August.			
4	Store Equipment	165	1,200	
	Note Payable	240		1,200
	Purchased additional equipment on credit.			
15	Cash	101	825	
	Haircutting Services Revenue	403		825
	Cash receipts from 10 days of operations.			
15	Accounts Receivable	102	100	
	Haircutting Services Revenue	403		100
	To record revenue for services provided on account.			
17	Cash	101	100	
	Accounts Receivable	102		100
	To record cash received as payment on account.			
17	Wages Expense	623	125	
	Cash	101		125
	Paid wages to assistant.			
31	Cash	101	930	
	Haircutting Services Revenue	403		930
	Cash receipts from second half of August.			
31	Note Payable	240	400	
	Cash	101		400
	Paid an installment on the note payable.			
31	S. Workman, Withdrawals	302	900	
	Cash	101		900
	Cash withdrawal by owner.			

2. Post journal entries from (part 1) to the ledger accounts:

General Ledger

Cash — **Account No. 101**

Date	PR	Debit	Credit	Balance
Aug. 1	G1	3,000		3,000
2	G1		600	2,400
3	G1		500	1,900
15	G1	825		2,725
17	G1	100		2,825
17	G1		125	2,700
31	G1	930		3,630
31	G1		400	3,230
31	G1		900	2,330

Accounts Receivable — **Account No. 102**

Date	PR	Debit	Credit	Balance
Aug. 15	G1	100		100
17	G1		100	0

Furniture — **Account No. 161**

Date	PR	Debit	Credit	Balance
Aug. 2	G1	600		600

Store Equipment — **Account No. 165**

Date	PR	Debit	Credit	Balance
Aug. 1	G1	15,000		15,000
4	G1	1,200		16,200

Note Payable — **Account No. 240**

Date	PR	Debit	Credit	Balance
Aug. 4	G1		1,200	1,200
31	G1	400		800

S. Workman, Capital — **Account No. 301**

Date	PR	Debit	Credit	Balance
Aug. 1	G1		18,000	18,000

S. Workman, Withdrawals — **Account No. 302**

Date	PR	Debit	Credit	Balance
Aug. 31	G1	900		900

Haircutting Services Revenue — **Account No. 403**

Date	PR	Debit	Credit	Balance
Aug. 15	G1		825	825
15	G1		100	925
31	G1		930	1,855

Wages Expense — **Account No. 623**

Date	PR	Debit	Credit	Balance
Aug. 17	G1	125		125

Rent Expense — **Account No. 640**

Date	PR	Debit	Credit	Balance
Aug. 3	G1	500		500

3. Prepare a trial balance from the ledger:

EXPRESSIONS
Trial Balance
August 31

	Debit	Credit
Cash	$ 2,330	
Accounts receivable	0	
Furniture	600	
Store equipment	16,200	
Note payable		$ 800
S. Workman, Capital		18,000
S. Workman, Withdrawals	900	
Haircutting services revenue		1,855
Wages expense	125	
Rent expense	500	
Totals	$20,655	$20,655

4.

EXPRESSIONS Income Statement For Month Ended August 31		
Revenues		
Haircutting services revenue		$1,855
Operating expenses		
Rent expense	$500	
Wages expense	125	
Total operating expenses		625
Net Income		$1,230

5.

EXPRESSIONS Statement of Owner's Equity For Month Ended August 31		
S. Workman, Capital, August 1		$ 0
Plus: Investments by owner	$18,000	
Net income	1,230	19,230
		19,230
Less: Withdrawals by owner		900
S. Workman, Capital, August 31		$18,330

6.

EXPRESSIONS Balance Sheet August 31			
Assets		**Liabilities**	
Cash	$ 2,330	Note payable	$ 800
Furniture	600	**Equity**	
Store equipment	16,200	S. Workman, Capital	18,330
Total assets	$19,130	Total liabilities and equity	$19,130

7. Debt ratio $= \dfrac{\text{Total liabilities}}{\text{Total assets}} = \dfrac{\$800}{\$19,130} = \mathbf{4.18\%}$

8a. Supplies *debited*
Cash *credited*

8b. Prepaid Insurance *debited*
Cash *credited*

8c. Cash *debited*
Unearned Services Revenue *credited*

8d. Supplies *debited*
Accounts Payable *credited*

Summary

C1 Explain the steps in processing transactions. The accounting process identifies business transactions and events, analyzes and records their effects, and summarizes and prepares information useful in making decisions. Transactions and events are the starting points in the accounting process. Source documents help in their analysis. The effects of transactions and events are recorded in journals. Posting along with a trial balance helps summarize and classify these effects.

C2 Describe source documents and their purpose. Source documents identify and describe transactions and events. Examples are sales tickets, checks, purchase orders, bills, and bank statements. Source documents provide objective and reliable evidence, making information more useful.

C3 Describe an account and its use in recording transactions. An account is a detailed record of increases and decreases in a specific asset, liability, equity, revenue, or expense. Information from accounts is analyzed, summarized, and presented in reports and financial statements for decision makers.

C4 Describe a ledger and a chart of accounts. The ledger (or general ledger) is a record containing all accounts used by a company and their balances. It is referred to as the *books*. The chart of accounts is a list of all accounts and usually includes an identification number assigned to each account.

C5 Define *debits* and *credits* and explain their role in double-entry accounting. *Debit* refers to left, and *credit* refers to right. Debits increase assets, expenses, and withdrawals while credits decrease them. Credits increase liabilities, owner capital, and revenues; debits decrease them. Double-entry accounting means each transaction affects at least two accounts and has at least one debit and one credit. The system for recording debits and credits follows from the accounting equation. The left side of an account is the normal balance for assets, withdrawals, and expenses, and the right side is the normal balance for liabilities, capital, and revenues.

A1 Analyze the impact of transactions on accounts and financial statements. We analyze transactions using concepts of double-entry accounting. This analysis is performed by determining a transaction's effects on accounts. These effects are recorded in journals and posted to ledgers.

A2 Compute the debt ratio and describe its use in analyzing company performance. A company's debt ratio is computed as total liabilities divided by total assets. It reveals how much of the assets are financed by creditor (nonowner) financing. The higher this ratio, the more risk a company faces because liabilities must be repaid at specific dates.

P1 Record transactions in a journal and post entries to a ledger. Transactions are recorded in a journal. Each entry in a journal is posted to the accounts in the ledger. This provides information that is used to produce financial statements. Balance column accounts are widely used and include columns for debits, credits, and the account balance.

P2 Prepare and explain the use of a trial balance. A trial balance is a list of accounts from the ledger showing their debit or credit balances in separate columns. The trial balance is a summary of the ledger's contents and is useful in preparing financial statements and in revealing recordkeeping errors.

P3 Prepare financial statements from business transactions. The balance sheet, the statement of owner's equity, the income statement, and the statement of cash flows use data from the trial balance (and other financial statements) for their preparation.

Guidance Answers to **Decision Maker** and **Decision Ethics**

Cashier The advantages to the process proposed by the assistant manager include improved customer service, fewer delays, and less work for you. However, you should have serious concerns about internal control and the potential for fraud. In particular, the assistant manager could steal cash and simply enter fewer sales to match the remaining cash. You should reject her suggestion without the manager's approval. Moreover, you should have an ethical concern about the assistant manager's suggestion to ignore store policy.

Entrepreneur We can use the accounting equation (Assets = Liabilities + Equity) to help us identify risky customers to whom we would likely not want to extend credit. A balance sheet provides amounts for each of these key components. The lower a customer's equity is relative to liabilities, the less likely you would extend credit. A low equity means the business has little value that does not already have creditor claims to it.

Investor The debt ratio suggests the stock of Converse is of higher risk than normal and that this risk is rising. The average industry ratio of 0.40 further supports this conclusion. The 2003 debt ratio for Converse is twice the industry norm. Also, a debt ratio approaching 1.0 indicates little to no equity.

Guidance Answers to **Quick Checks**

1. Examples of source documents are sales tickets, checks, purchase orders, charges to customers, bills from suppliers, employee earnings records, and bank statements.
2. Source documents serve many purposes, including recordkeeping and internal control. Source documents, especially if obtained from outside the organization, provide objective and reliable evidence about transactions and their amounts.
3.

Assets	Liabilities	Equity
a,c,e	b,d	—

4. An account is a record in an accounting system that records and stores the increases and decreases in a specific asset, liability, equity, revenue, or expense. The ledger is a collection of all the accounts of a company.

5. A company's size and diversity affect the number of accounts in its accounting system. The types of accounts depend on information the company needs to both effectively operate and report its activities in financial statements.

6. No. Debit and credit both can mean increase or decrease. The particular meaning in a circumstance depends on the *type of account*. For example, a debit increases the balance of asset, withdrawals, and expense accounts, but it decreases the balance of liability, capital, and revenue accounts.

7. A chart of accounts is a list of all of a company's accounts and their identification numbers.

8. Equity is increased by revenues and by owner investments. Equity is decreased by expenses and owner withdrawals.

9. The name *double entry* is used because all transactions affect at least two accounts. There must be at least one debit in one account and at least one credit in another account.

10. Answer is (*c*).

11.

Cash	15,000	
Equipment	23,000	
Owner, Capital		38,000
Investment by owner of cash and equipment.		

12. A compound journal entry affects three or more accounts.

13. Posting reference numbers are entered in the journal when posting to the ledger as a cross-reference that allows the record-keeper or auditor to trace debits and credits from one record to another.

14. At a minimum, dollar signs are placed beside the first and last numbers in a column. It is also common to place dollar signs beside any amount that appears after a ruled line to indicate that an addition or subtraction has occurred.

15. The Equipment account balance is incorrectly reported at \$20,000—it should be \$28,000. The effect of this error understates the trial balance's Debit column total by \$8,000. This results in an \$8,000 difference between the column totals.

16. An income statement reports a company's revenues and expenses along with the resulting net income or loss. A statement of owner's equity reports changes in equity, including that from net income or loss. Both statements report transactions occurring over a period of time.

17. The balance sheet describes a company's financial position (assets, liabilities, and equity) at a point in time. The capital account in the balance sheet is obtained from the statement of owner's equity.

18. Revenues are inflows of assets in exchange for products or services provided to customers as part of the main operations of a business. Expenses are outflows or the using up of assets that result from providing products or services to customers.

19. Assets are the resources a business owns or controls that carry expected future benefits. Liabilities are the obligations of a business, representing the claims of others against the assets of a business. Equity reflects the owner's claims on the assets of the business after deducting liabilities.

Key Terms

Key Terms are available at the book's Website for learning and testing in an online Flashcard Format.

Account (p. 49)
Account balance (p. 53)
Balance column account (p. 56)
Chart of accounts (p. 52)
Compound journal entry (p. 59)
Credit (p. 53)
Creditors (p. 50)
Debit (p. 53)
Debt ratio (p. 67)
Double-entry accounting (p. 53)
General journal (p. 55)
Journal (p. 55)
Journalizing (p. 55)
Ledger (p. 49)
Owner, capital (p. 51)
Posting (p. 55)
Posting reference (PR) column (p. 56)
Source documents (p. 49)
T-account (p. 53)
Trial balance (p. 63)
Unearned revenue (p. 51)

Personal Interactive Quiz

Personal Interactive Quizzes A and B are available at the book's Website to reinforce and assess your learning.

Discussion Questions

1. Provide the names of two (*a*) asset accounts, (*b*) liability accounts, and (*c*) equity accounts.
2. What is the difference between a note payable and an account payable?
3. Discuss the steps in processing business transactions.
4. What kinds of transactions can be recorded in a general journal?
5. Are debits or credits typically listed first in general journal entries? Are the debits or the credits indented?

6. If assets are valuable resources and asset accounts have debit balances, why do expense accounts have debit balances?
7. Should a transaction be recorded first in a journal or the ledger? Why?
8. Why does the recordkeeper prepare a trial balance?
9. If a wrong amount is journalized and posted to the accounts, how should the error be corrected?
10. Identify the four financial statements of a business.
11. What information is reported in an income statement?
12. Why does the user of an income statement need to know the time period that it covers?
13. What information is reported in a balance sheet?
14. Define (*a*) *assets,* (*b*) *liabilities,* (*c*) *equity,* and (*d*) *net assets.*
15. Which financial statement is sometimes called the *statement of financial position?*
16. Review the **Krispy Kreme** balance sheet in Appendix A. Identify three accounts on its balance sheet that carry debit balances and three accounts on its balance sheet that carry credit balances.
17. Review the **Tastykake** balance sheet in Appendix A. Identify two different liability accounts that include the word *payable* in the account title.
18. Locate **Harley-Davidson**'s income statement in Appendix A. What is the title of its revenue account?

Red numbers denote Discussion Questions that involve decision-making.

***Homework Manager** repeats all Quick Study assignments on the book's Website with new numbers each time they are worked. It can be used in practice, homework, or exam mode.*

QUICK STUDY

QS 2-1
Identifying source documents
C2

Identify the items from the following list that are likely to serve as source documents:

a. Bank statement
b. Sales ticket
c. Income statement
d. Trial balance
e. Telephone bill
f. Invoice from supplier
g. Company revenue account
h. Balance sheet
i. Prepaid insurance

QS 2-2
Identifying financial statement items
C3 P3

Identify the financial statement(s) where each of the following items appears. Use I for income statement, E for statement of owner's equity, and B for balance sheet:

a. Service fees earned
b. Owner cash withdrawal
c. Office equipment
d. Accounts payable
e. Cash
f. Utilities expenses
g. Office supplies
h. Prepaid rent
i. Unearned fees

QS 2-3
Linking debit or credit with normal balance
C5

Indicate whether a debit or credit *decreases* the normal balance of each of the following accounts:

a. Office Supplies
b. Repair Services Revenue
c. Interest Payable
d. Accounts Receivable
e. Salaries Expense
f. Owner Capital
g. Prepaid Insurance
h. Buildings
i. Interest Revenue
j. Owner Withdrawals
k. Unearned Revenue
l. Accounts Payable

QS 2-4
Analyzing debit or credit by account
C5 A1 

Identify whether a debit or credit yields the indicated change for each of the following accounts:

a. To increase Store Equipment
b. To increase Owner Withdrawals
c. To decrease Cash
d. To increase Utilities Expense
e. To increase Fees Earned
f. To decrease Unearned Revenue
g. To decrease Prepaid Insurance
h. To increase Notes Payable
i. To decrease Accounts Receivable
j. To increase Owner Capital

QS 2-5
Identifying normal balance
C5

Identify whether the normal balances (in parentheses) assigned to the following accounts are correct or incorrect.

a. Office supplies (Debit)
b. Owner Withdrawals (Credit)
c. Fees Earned (Debit)
d. Wages Expense (Credit)
e. Cash (Debit)
f. Prepaid Insurance (Credit)
g. Wages Payable (Credit)
h. Building (Debit)

QS 2-6
Preparing journal entries
P1

Prepare journal entries for each of the following selected transactions:

a. On January 13, Chico Chavez opens a landscaping business called Showcase Yards by investing $70,000 cash along with equipment having a $30,000 value.

b. On January 21, Showcase Yards purchases office supplies on credit for $280.

c. On January 29, Showcase Yards receives $7,800 cash for performing landscaping services.

d. On January 30, Showcase Yards receives $1,000 cash in advance of providing landscaping services to a customer.

QS 2-7
Identifying a posting error
P2 

A trial balance has total debits of $20,000 and total credits of $24,500. Which one of the following errors would create this imbalance? Explain.

a. A $2,250 debit to Rent Expense in a journal entry is incorrectly posted to the ledger as a $2,250 credit, leaving the Rent Expense account with a $3,000 debit balance.

b. A $4,500 debit to Salaries Expense in a journal entry is incorrectly posted to the ledger as a $4,500 credit, leaving the Salaries Expense account with a $750 debit balance.

c. A $2,250 credit to Consulting Fees Earned in a journal entry is incorrectly posted to the ledger as a $2,250 debit, leaving the Consulting Fees Earned account with a $6,300 credit balance.

QS 2-8
Classifying accounts in financial statements
P3

Indicate the financial statement on which each of the following items appears. Use I for income statement, E for statement of owner's equity, and B for balance sheet:

a. Office Supplies
b. Services Revenue
c. Interest Payable
d. Accounts Receivable
e. Salaries Expense
f. Equipment
g. Prepaid Insurance
h. Buildings
i. Interest Revenue
j. Withdrawals

Homework Manager *repeats all Exercises on the book's Website with new numbers each time they are worked. It can be used in practice, homework, or exam mode.*

EXERCISES

Exercise 2-1
Identifying type and normal balances of accounts
C3 C5

For each of the following (1) identify the type of account as an asset, liability, equity, revenue, or expense, (2) enter *debit* (*Dr.*) or *credit* (*Cr.*) to identify the kind of entry that would increase the account balance, and (3) identify the normal balance of the account.

a. Unearned Revenue
b. Accounts Payable
c. Postage Expense
d. Prepaid Insurance
e. Land
f. Owner Capital
g. Accounts Receivable
h. Owner Withdrawals
i. Cash
j. Equipment
k. Fees Earned
l. Wages Expense

Exercise 2-2
Analyzing effects of transactions on accounts
A1 

Tavon Co. recently notified a client that it must pay a $48,000 fee for services provided. Tavon agreed to accept the following three items in full payment: (1) $7,500 cash, (2) computer equipment worth $75,000, and (3) assume responsibility for a $34,500 note payable related to the computer equipment. The entry Tavon makes to record this transaction includes which one or more of the following?

a. $34,500 increase in a liability account
b. $7,500 increase in the Cash account
c. $7,500 increase in a revenue account
d. $48,000 increase in an asset account
e. $48,000 increase in a revenue account

Exercise 2-3
Analyzing account entries and balances
A1  

Use the information in each of the following separate cases to calculate the unknown amount:

a. During October, Shandra Company had $97,500 of cash receipts and $101,250 of cash disbursements. The October 31 Cash balance was $16,800. Determine how much cash the company had at the close of business on September 30.

b. On September 30, Li Ming Co. had a $97,500 balance in Accounts Receivable. During October, the company collected $88,950 from its credit customers. The October 31 balance in Accounts Receivable was $100,500. Determine the amount of sales on account that occurred in October.

c. Nasser Co. had $147,000 of accounts payable on September 30 and $136,500 on October 31. Total purchases on account during October were $270,000. Determine how much cash was paid on accounts payable during October.

Exercise 2-4
Preparing general journal entries
A1 P1

Prepare general journal entries for the following transactions of a new business called Pose for Pics.

Aug.	1	Hashim Paris, the owner, invested $7,500 cash and $32,500 of photography equipment in the business.
	1	Paid $3,000 cash for an insurance policy covering the next 24 months.
	5	Purchased office supplies for $1,400 cash.
	20	Received $2,650 cash in photography fees earned.
	31	Paid $875 cash for August utilities.

Exercise 2-5
Preparing T-accounts and a trial balance
C3 P2

Use the information in Exercise 2-4 to prepare an August 31 trial balance for Pose-for-Pics. Open these T-accounts: Cash; Office Supplies; Prepaid Insurance; Photography Equipment; H. Paris, Capital; Photography Fees Earned; and Utilities Expense. Post the general journal entries to these T-accounts (which will serve as the ledger), and prepare a trial balance.

Exercise 2-6
Recording effects of transactions in T-accounts
C5 A1

Record the transactions below for Dejonge Company by recording the debit and credit entries directly in the following T-accounts: Cash; Accounts Receivable; Office Supplies; Office Equipment; Accounts Payable; Dejonge, Capital; Dejonge, Withdrawals; Fees Earned; and Rent Expense. Use the letters beside each transaction to identify entries. Determine the ending balance of each T-account.

a. Robert Dejonge invested $12,750 cash in the business.

b. Purchased office supplies for $375 cash.

c. Purchased $7,050 of office equipment on credit.

d. Received $1,500 cash as fees for services provided to a customer.

e. Paid $7,050 cash to settle the payable for the office equipment purchased in transaction *c*.

f. Billed a customer $2,700 as fees for services provided.

g. Paid the monthly rent with $525 cash.

h. Collected $1,125 cash toward the account receivable created in transaction *f*.

i. Dejonge withdrew $1,000 cash for personal use.

Check Cash ending balance, $6,425

Exercise 2-7
Preparing a trial balance P2

After recording the transactions of Exercise 2-6 in T-accounts and calculating the balance of each account, prepare a trial balance. Use May 31, 2005, as its report date.

Exercise 2-8
Analyzing and journalizing revenue transactions
A1 P1

Examine the following transactions and identify those that create revenues for Jade Services, a company owned by Mia Jade. Prepare general journal entries to record those transactions and explain why the other transactions did not create revenues.

a. Mia Jade invests $38,250 cash in the business.
b. Provided $1,350 of services on credit.
c. Provided services to a client and received $1,575 cash.
d. Received $9,150 cash from a client in payment for services to be provided next year.
e. Received $4,500 cash from a client in partial payment of an account receivable.
f. Borrowed $150,000 cash from the bank by signing a promissory note.

Exercise 2-9
Analyzing and journalizing expense transactions
A1 P1

Examine the following transactions and identify those that create expenses for Jade Services. Prepare general journal entries to record those transactions and explain why the other transactions did not create expenses.

a. Paid $14,100 cash for office supplies that were purchased more than 1 year ago.
b. Paid $1,125 cash for the two-week salary of the receptionist.
c. Paid $45,000 cash for equipment.
d. Paid $930 cash for monthly utilities.
e. Owner withdrew $5,000 cash for personal use.

Exercise 2-10
Preparing an income statement
C4 P3

On October 1, Ming Lue organized a new consulting firm called Tech Today. On October 31, the company's records show the following items and amounts. Use this information to prepare an October income statement for the business.

Cash	$ 8,360	M. Lue, Withdrawals	$ 3,000
Accounts receivable	17,000	Consulting fees earned	17,000
Office supplies	3,250	Rent expense	4,550
Patents	46,000	Salaries expense	8,000
Office equipment	18,000	Telephone expense	560
Accounts payable	8,000	Miscellaneous expenses	280
M. Lue, Capital	84,000		

Check Net income, $3,610

Exercise 2-11
Preparing a statement of owner's equity P3

Use the information in Exercise 2-10 to prepare an October statement of owner's equity for Tech Today.

Exercise 2-12
Preparing a balance sheet P3

Use the information in Exercise 2-10 (if completed, you can also use your solution to Exercise 2-11) to prepare an October 31 balance sheet for Tech Today.

Exercise 2-13
Computing net income
A1 P3

A sole proprietorship had the following assets and liabilities at the beginning and end of a recent year:

	Assets	Liabilities
Beginning of the year	$ 70,000	$30,000
End of the year	115,000	46,000

Determine the net income earned or net loss incurred by the business during the year for each of the following *separate* cases:

a. Owner made no investments in the business and withdrew no assets during the year.
b. Owner made no investments in the business but withdrew $1,250 per month for personal use.
c. Owner withdrew no assets during the year but invested an additional $45,000 cash.
d. Owner withdrew $1,250 per month for personal use and invested an additional $25,000 cash.

Exercise 2-14
Analyzing changes in a company's equity
C5 P3

Compute the missing amount in each of the following separate companies *a* through *d*:

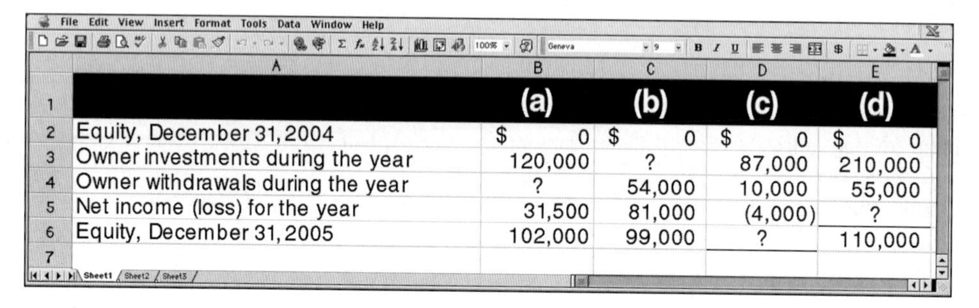

	A	B	C	D	E
1		(a)	(b)	(c)	(d)
2	Equity, December 31, 2004	$ 0	$ 0	$ 0	$ 0
3	Owner investments during the year	120,000	?	87,000	210,000
4	Owner withdrawals during the year	?	54,000	10,000	55,000
5	Net income (loss) for the year	31,500	81,000	(4,000)	?
6	Equity, December 31, 2005	102,000	99,000	?	110,000
7					

Exercise 2-15
Interpreting and describing transactions from T-accounts
C1 A1

Assume the following T-accounts reflect Joy Co.'s general ledger and that seven transactions *a* through *g* are posted to them. Provide a short description of each transaction. Include the amounts in your descriptions.

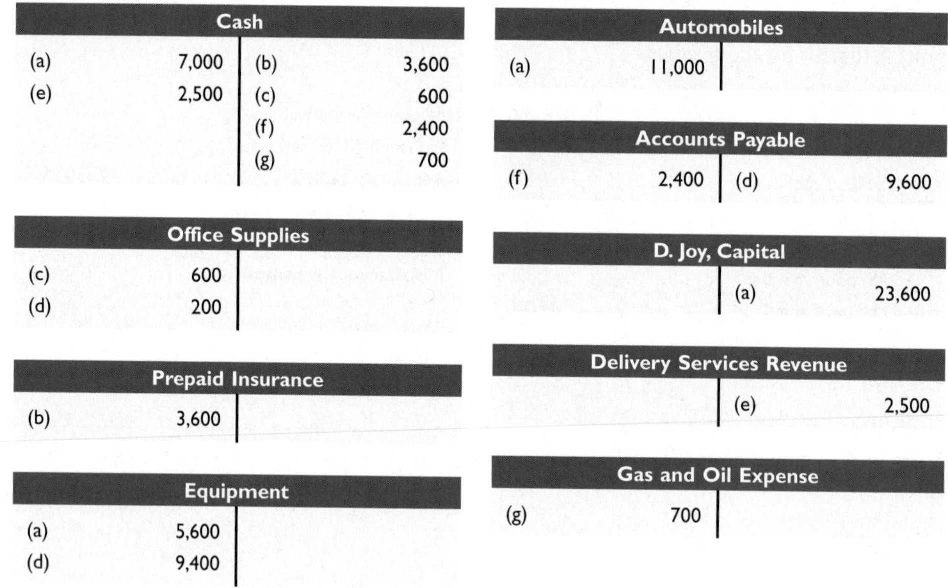

Cash

	Debit		Credit
(a)	7,000	(b)	3,600
(e)	2,500	(c)	600
		(f)	2,400
		(g)	700

Automobiles

	Debit		Credit
(a)	11,000		

Accounts Payable

	Debit		Credit
(f)	2,400	(d)	9,600

Office Supplies

	Debit		Credit
(c)	600		
(d)	200		

D. Joy, Capital

	Debit		Credit
		(a)	23,600

Prepaid Insurance

	Debit		Credit
(b)	3,600		

Delivery Services Revenue

	Debit		Credit
		(e)	2,500

Equipment

	Debit		Credit
(a)	5,600		
(d)	9,400		

Gas and Oil Expense

	Debit		Credit
(g)	700		

Exercise 2-16
Preparing general journal entries A1 P1

Use information from the T-accounts in Exercise 2-15 to prepare general journal entries for each of the seven transaction *a* through *g*.

Exercise 2-17
Identifying effects of posting errors on the trial balance A1 P2

Posting errors are identified in the following table. In column (1), enter the amount of the difference between the two (debit and credit) trial balance columns due to the error. In column (2), identify the trial balance column (debit or credit) with the larger amount if they are not equal. In column (3), identify the account(s) affected by the error. In column (4), indicate the amount by which the account(s) in column (3) is (are) under- or overstated. Answers for the first error are given.

	Description of Posting Error	(1) Difference between Debit and Credit Columns	(2) Column with the Larger Total	(3) Identify Account(s) Incorrectly Stated	(4) Amount that Account(s) is Over- or Understated
a.	$2,400 debit to Rent Expense is posted as a $1,590 debit.	$810	Credit	Rent Expense	Rent Expense understated $810
b.	$4,050 credit to Cash is posted twice as two credits to Cash.				
c.	$9,900 debit to the owner's withdrawals account is debited to owner's capital.				
d.	$2,250 debit to Prepaid Insurance is posted as a debit to Insurance Expense.				
e.	$42,000 debit to Machinery is posted as a debit to Accounts Payable.				
f.	$4,950 credit to Services Revenue is posted as a $495 credit.				
g.	$1,440 debit to Store Supplies is not posted.				

Exercise 2-18
Analyzing a trial balance error
A1 P2

You are told the column totals in a trial balance are not equal. After careful analysis, you discover only one error. Specifically, a correctly journalized credit purchase of a computer for $16,950 is posted from the journal to the ledger with a $16,950 debit to Office Equipment and another $16,950 debit to Accounts Payable. The balance of the Office Equipment account has a debit balance of $40,100 on the trial balance. Answer each of the following questions and compute the dollar amount of any misstatement:

a. Is the debit column total of the trial balance overstated, understated, or correctly stated?

b. Is the credit column total of the trial balance overstated, understated, or correctly stated?

c. Is the balance of the Office Equipment account overstated, understated, or correctly stated in the trial balance?

d. Is the balance of the Accounts Payable account overstated, understated, or correctly stated in the trial balance?

e. If the debit column total of the trial balance is $360,000 before correcting the error, what is the total of the credit column before correction?

Exercise 2-19
Interpreting the debt ratio and return on assets
A2  

a. Calculate the debt ratio and the return on assets using the year-end information for each of the following six separate companies ($ in thousands):

Case	Assets	Liabilities	Average Assets	Net Income
Company 1	$ 90,500	$ 12,000	$ 100,000	$ 20,000
Company 2	64,000	47,000	40,000	3,800
Company 3	32,500	26,500	50,000	660
Company 4	147,000	56,000	200,000	21,000
Company 5	92,000	31,000	40,000	7,500
Company 6	104,500	51,500	70,000	12,000

b. Of the six companies, which business relies most heavily on creditor financing?

c. Of the six companies, which business relies most heavily on equity financing?

d. Which two companies indicate the greatest risk?

e. Which two companies earn the highest return on assets?

f. Which one company would investors likely prefer based on the risk-return relation?

PROBLEM SET A

Problem 2-1A

Preparing and posting general journal entries; preparing a trial balance

C4 C5 A1 P1 P2

Roberto Ricci opens a computer consulting business called Viva Consultants and completes the following transactions in its first month of operations:

April 1 Ricci invests $100,000 cash along with office equipment valued at $24,000 in the business.
2 Prepaid $7,200 cash for twelve months' rent for office space. (*Hint:* Debit Prepaid Rent for $7,200.)
3 Made credit purchases for $12,000 in office equipment and $2,400 in office supplies. Payment is due within 10 days.
6 Completed services for a client and immediately received $2,000 cash.
9 Completed an $8,000 project for a client, who must pay within 30 days.
13 Paid $14,400 cash to settle the account payable created on April 3.
19 Paid $6,000 cash for the premium on a 12-month insurance policy. (*Hint:* Debit Prepaid Insurance for $6,000.)
22 Received $6,400 cash as partial payment for the work completed on April 9.
25 Completed work for another client for $2,640 on credit.
28 Ricci withdrew $6,200 cash for personal use.
29 Purchased $800 of additional office supplies on credit.
30 Paid $700 cash for this month's utility bill.

Required

1. Prepare general journal entries to record these transactions (use account titles listed in part 2).

2. Open the following ledger accounts—their account numbers are in parentheses (use the balance column format): Cash (101); Accounts Receivable (106); Office Supplies (124); Prepaid Insurance (128); Prepaid Rent (131); Office Equipment (163); Accounts Payable (201); R. Ricci, Capital (301); R. Ricci, Withdrawals (302); Services Revenue (403); and Utilities Expense (690). Post journal entries from part 1 to the ledger accounts and enter the balance after each posting.

3. Prepare a trial balance as of the end of this month's operations.

Check (2) Ending balances: Cash, $73,900; Accounts Receivable, $4,240; Accounts Payable, $800

(3) Total debits, $137,440

Problem 2-2A

Preparing and posting journal entries; preparing a trial balance

C4 C5 A1 P1 P2

Shelton Engineering completed the following transactions in the month of June.

a. Shania Shelton, the owner, invested $105,000 cash, office equipment with a value of $6,000, and $45,000 of drafting equipment to launch the business.

b. Purchased land worth $54,000 for an office by paying $5,400 cash and signing a long-term note payable for $48,600.

c. Purchased a portable building with $75,000 cash and moved it onto the land acquired in *b*.

d. Paid $6,000 cash for the premium on an 18-month insurance policy.

e. Completed and delivered a set of plans for a client and collected $5,700 cash.

f. Purchased $22,500 of additional drafting equipment by paying $10,500 cash and signing a long-term note payable for $12,000.

g. Completed $12,000 of engineering services for a client. This amount is to be received in 30 days.

h. Purchased $2,250 of additional office equipment on credit.

i. Completed engineering services for $18,000 on credit.

j. Received a bill for rent of equipment that was used on a recently completed job. The $1,200 rent must be paid within 30 days.

k. Collected $7,200 cash in partial payment from the client described in transaction *g*.

l. Paid $1,500 cash for wages to a drafting assistant.

m. Paid $2,250 cash to settle the account payable created in transaction *h*.

n. Paid $675 cash for minor repairs to the drafting equipment.

o. Shelton withdrew $9,360 cash for personal use.

p. Paid $1,500 cash for wages to a drafting assistant.

q. Paid $3,000 cash for advertisements in the local newspaper during June.

Required

1. Prepare general journal entries to record these transactions (use the account titles listed in part 2).

2. Open the following accounts—their account numbers are in parentheses (use the balance column format): Cash (101); Accounts Receivable (106); Prepaid Insurance (108); Office Equipment (163); Drafting Equipment (164); Building (170); Land (172); Accounts Payable (201); Notes Payable (250); S. Shelton, Capital (301); S. Shelton, Withdrawals (302); Engineering Fees Earned (402); Wages Expense (601); Equipment Rental Expense (602); Advertising Expense (603); and Repairs Expense (604). Post the journal entries from part 1 to the accounts and enter the balance after each posting.

3. Prepare a trial balance as of the end of this month's operations.

Check (2) Ending balances: Cash, $2,715; Accounts Receivable, $22,800; Accounts Payable, $1,200

(3) Trial balance totals, $253,500

Problem 2-3A

Preparing and posting general journal entries; preparing a trial balance

C4 C5 A1 P1 P2

mhhe.com/larson

Santo Birch opens a Web consulting business called Show-Me-the-Money Consultants and completes the following transactions in March:

March 1 Birch invested $150,000 cash along with $22,000 of office equipment in the business.
2 Prepaid $6,000 cash for six months' rent for an office. (*Hint:* Debit Prepaid Rent for $6,000.)
3 Made credit purchases of office equipment for $3,000 and office supplies for $1,200. Payment is due within 10 days.
6 Completed services for a client and immediately received $4,000 cash.
9 Completed a $7,500 project for a client, who must pay within 30 days.
10 Paid $4,200 cash to settle the account payable created on March 3.
19 Paid $5,000 cash for the premium on a 12-month insurance policy.
22 Received $3,500 cash as partial payment for the work completed on March 9.
25 Completed work for another client for $3,820 on credit.
29 Birch withdrew $5,100 cash for personal use.
30 Purchased $600 of additional office supplies on credit.
31 Paid $200 cash for this month's utility bill.

Required

1. Prepare general journal entries to record these transactions (use the account titles listed in part 2).

2. Open the following accounts—their account numbers are in parentheses (use the balance column format): Cash (101); Accounts Receivable (106); Office Supplies (124); Prepaid Insurance (128); Prepaid Rent (131); Office Equipment (163); Accounts Payable (201); S. Birch, Capital (301); S. Birch, Withdrawals (302); Services Revenue (403); and Utilities Expense (690). Post the journal entries from part 1 to the accounts and enter the balance after each posting.

3. Prepare a trial balance as of the end of this month's operations.

Check (2) Ending balances: Cash, $137,000; Accounts Receivable, $7,820; Accounts Payable, $600

(3) Total debits, $187,920

Problem 2-4A

Computing net income from equity analysis, preparing a balance sheet, and calculating the debt ratio

C3 A1 A2 P3

mhhe.com/larson

The accounting records of Crist Crate Services show the following assets and liabilities as of December 31, 2004, and 2005:

	December 31	
	2004	2005
Cash	$ 52,500	$ 18,750
Accounts receivable	28,500	22,350
Office supplies	4,500	3,300
Office equipment	138,000	147,000
Trucks	54,000	54,000
Building	0	180,000
Land	0	45,000
Accounts payable	7,500	37,500
Note payable	0	105,000

Late in December 2005, the business purchased a small office building and land for $225,000. The business paid $120,000 cash toward the purchase and a $105,000 note payable was signed for the balance. Crist had to invest $35,000 cash in the business to enable it to pay the $120,000 cash. Crist also withdraws $3,000 cash per month from the business for personal use.

Required

1. Prepare balance sheets for the business as of December 31, 2004, and 2005. (Remember that total equity equals the difference between assets and liabilities.)
2. By comparing equity amounts from the balance sheets and using the additional information presented in this problem, prepare a calculation to show how much net income was earned by the business during 2005.
3. Compute the 2005 year-end debt ratio for the business.

Check (2) Net income, $58,900

(3) Debt ratio, 30.29%

Problem 2-5A
Analyzing account balances and reconstructing transactions

C1 C4 A1 P2 

Carlos Beltran started an engineering firm called Beltran Engineering. He began operations and completed seven transactions in May, which included his initial investment of $17,000 cash. After these transactions, the ledger included the following accounts with normal balances:

Cash	$26,660
Office supplies	660
Prepaid insurance	3,200
Office equipment	16,500
Accounts payable	16,500
C. Beltran, Capital	17,000
C. Beltran, Withdrawals	3,740
Engineering fees earned	24,000
Rent expense	6,740

Required

1. Prepare a trial balance for this business at the end of May.

Analysis Components

2. Analyze the accounts and their balances and prepare a list that describes each of the seven most likely transactions and their amounts.
3. Prepare a report of cash received and cash paid showing how the seven transactions in part 2 yield the $26,660 ending Cash balance.

Check (1) Trial balance totals, $57,500

(3) Cash paid, $14,340

Problem 2-6A
Recording transactions; posting to ledger; preparing a trial balance

C4 A1 P1 P2

Business transactions completed by Eric Piburn during the month of September are as follows:

- **a.** Piburn invested $23,000 cash along with office equipment valued at $12,000 in a new sole proprietorship named EP Consulting.
- **b.** Purchased land valued at $8,000 and a building valued at $33,000. The purchase is paid with $15,000 cash and a long-term note payable for $26,000.
- **c.** Purchased $600 of office supplies on credit.
- **d.** Piburn invested his personal automobile in the business. The automobile has a value of $7,000 and is to be used exclusively in the business.
- **e.** Purchased $1,100 of additional office equipment on credit.
- **f.** Paid $800 cash salary to an assistant.
- **g.** Provided services to a client and collected $2,700 cash.
- **h.** Paid $430 cash for this month's utilities.
- **i.** Paid $600 cash to settle the account payable created in transaction *c*.
- **j.** Purchased $4,000 of new office equipment by paying $2,400 cash and trading in old equipment with a recorded net cost and value of $1,600. (*Hint:* Credit Office Equipment (old) for $1,600.)

k. Completed $2,400 of services for a client, who must pay within 30 days.
l. Paid $800 cash salary to an assistant.
m. Received $1,000 cash on the receivable created in transaction *k*.
n. Piburn withdrew $1,050 cash from the business for personal use.

Required

1. Prepare general journal entries to record these transactions (use the account titles listed in part 2).

2. Open the following accounts—their account numbers are in parentheses (use the balance column format): Cash (101); Accounts Receivable (106); Office Supplies (108); Office Equipment (163); Automobiles (164); Building (170); Land (172); Accounts Payable (201); Notes Payable (250); E. Piburn, Capital (301); E. Piburn, Withdrawals (302); Fees Earned (402); Salaries Expense (601); and Utilities Expense (602). Post the journal entries from part 1 to the accounts and enter the balance after each posting.

3. Prepare a trial balance as of the end of this month's operations.

Check (2) Ending balances: Cash, $5,620; Office Equipment, $15,500

(3) Trial balance totals, $74,200

PROBLEM SET B

Problem 2-1B
Preparing and posting general journal entries; preparing a trial balance

C4 C5 A1 P1 P2

Lummus Management Services opens for business and completes these transactions in September:

Sept. 1 Rhonda Lummus, the owner, invests $28,000 cash along with office equipment valued at $25,000 in the business.
2 Prepaid $10,500 cash for twelve months' rent for office space. (*Hint:* Debit Prepaid Rent for $10,500.)
4 Made credit purchases for $9,000 in office equipment and $1,200 in office supplies. Payment is due within 10 days.
8 Completed work for a client and immediately received $2,600 cash.
12 Completed a $13,400 project for a client, who must pay within 20 days.
13 Paid $10,200 cash to settle the account payable created on September 4.
19 Paid $5,200 cash for the premium on an 18-month insurance policy. (*Hint:* Debit Prepaid Insurance for $5,200.)
22 Received $7,800 cash as partial payment for the work completed on September 12.
24 Completed work for another client for $1,900 on credit.
28 Lummus withdrew $5,300 cash for personal use.
29 Purchased $1,700 of additional office supplies on credit.
30 Paid $460 cash for this month's utility bill.

Required

1. Prepare general journal entries to record these transactions (use account titles listed in part 2).

2. Open the following ledger accounts—their account numbers are in parentheses (use the balance column format): Cash (101); Accounts Receivable (106); Office Supplies (124); Prepaid Insurance (128); Prepaid Rent (131); Office Equipment (163); Accounts Payable (201); R. Lummus, Capital (301); R. Lummus, Withdrawals (302); Service Fees Earned (401); and Utilities Expense (690). Post journal entries from part 1 to the ledger accounts and enter the balance after each posting.

3. Prepare a trial balance as of the end of this month's operations.

Check (2) Ending balances: Cash, $6,740; Accounts Receivable, $7,500; Accounts Payable, $1,700

(3) Total debits, $72,600

Problem 2-2B
Preparing and posting journal entries; preparing a trial balance

C4 C5 A1 P1 P2 

At the beginning of April, Brooke Grechus launched a custom computer programming company called Softways. The company had the following transactions during April:

a. Brooke Grechus invested $45,000 cash, office equipment with a value of $4,500, and $28,000 of computer equipment in the company.
b. Purchased land worth $24,000 for an office by paying $4,800 cash and signing a long-term note payable for $19,200.
c. Purchased a portable building with $21,000 cash and moved it onto the land acquired in *b*.

d. Paid $6,600 cash for the premium on a two-year insurance policy.
e. Provided services to a client and collected $3,200 cash.
f. Purchased $3,500 of additional computer equipment by paying $700 cash and signing a long-term note payable for $2,800.
g. Completed $3,750 of services for a client. This amount is to be received within 30 days.
h. Purchased $750 of additional office equipment on credit.
i. Completed client services for $9,200 on credit.
j. Received a bill for rent of a computer testing device that was used on a recently completed job. The $320 rent must be paid within 30 days.
k. Collected $4,600 cash from the client described in transaction *i*.
l. Paid $1,600 cash for wages to an assistant.
m. Paid $750 cash to settle the account payable created in transaction *h*.
n. Paid $425 cash for minor repairs to the computer equipment.
o. Grechus withdrew $3,875 cash for personal use.
p. Paid $1,600 cash for wages to an assistant.
q. Paid $800 cash for advertisements in the local newspaper during April.

Required

1. Prepare general journal entries to record these transactions (use the account titles listed in part 2).

Check (2) Ending balances: Cash, $10,650; Accounts Receivable, $8,350; Accounts Payable, $320

2. Open the following accounts—their account numbers are in parentheses (use the balance column format): Cash (101); Accounts Receivable (106); Prepaid Insurance (108); Office Equipment (163); Computer Equipment (164); Building (170); Land (172); Accounts Payable (201); Notes Payable (250); B. Grechus, Capital (301); B. Grechus, Withdrawals (302); Fees Earned (402); Wages Expense (601); Computer Rental Expense (602); Advertising Expense (603); and Repairs Expense (604). Post the journal entries from part 1 to the accounts and enter the balance after each posting.

(3) Trial balance totals, $115,970

3. Prepare a trial balance as of the end of this month's operations.

Problem 2-3B
Preparing and posting general journal entries; preparing a trial balance

C4 C5 A1 P1 P2

Shaw Management Services opens for business and completes these transactions in November:

Nov. 1 Kita Shaw, the owner, invested $30,000 cash along with $15,000 of office equipment in the business.
2 Prepaid $4,500 cash for six months' rent for an office. (*Hint:* Debit Prepaid Rent for $4,500.)
4 Made credit purchases of office equipment for $2,500 and of office supplies for $600. Payment is due within 10 days.
8 Completed work for a client and immediately received $3,400 cash.
12 Completed a $10,200 project for a client, who must pay within 30 days.
13 Paid $3,100 cash to settle the account payable created on November 4.
19 Paid $1,800 cash for the premium on a 24-month insurance policy.
22 Received $5,200 cash as partial payment for the work completed on November 12.
24 Completed work for another client for $1,750 on credit.
28 Shaw withdrew $5,300 cash for personal use.
29 Purchased $249 of additional office supplies on credit.
30 Paid $531 cash for this month's utility bill.

Required

1. Prepare general journal entries to record these transactions (use account titles listed in part 2).

Check (2) Ending balances: Cash, $23,369; Accounts Receivable, $6,750; Accounts Payable, $249

2. Open the following accounts—their account numbers are in parentheses (use the balance column format): Cash (101); Accounts Receivable (106); Office Supplies (124); Prepaid Insurance (128); Prepaid Rent (131); Office Equipment (163); Accounts Payable (201); K. Shaw, Capital (301); K. Shaw, Withdrawals (302); Services Revenue (403); and Utilities Expense (690). Post the journal entries from part 1 to the accounts and enter the balance after each posting.

(3) Total debits, $60,599

3. Prepare a trial balance as of the end of this month's operations.

Problem 2-4B
Computing net income from equity analysis, preparing a balance sheet, and computing the debt ratio

C3 A1 A2 P3

The accounting records of Schmit Co. show the following assets and liabilities as of December 31, 2004, and 2005:

	December 31	
	2004	**2005**
Cash	$14,000	$ 10,000
Accounts receivable	25,000	30,000
Office supplies	10,000	12,500
Office equipment	60,000	60,000
Machinery	30,500	30,500
Building	0	260,000
Land	0	65,000
Accounts payable	5,000	15,000
Note payable	0	260,000

Late in December 2005, the business purchased a small office building and land for $325,000. The business paid $65,000 cash toward the purchase and a $260,000 note payable was signed for the balance. Schmit had to invest an additional $25,000 cash to enable it to pay the $65,000 cash. Schmit also withdraws $1,000 cash per month from the business for personal use.

Required

1. Prepare balance sheets for the business as of December 31, 2004, and 2005. (Remember that total equity equals the difference between assets and liabilities.)
2. By comparing equity amounts from the balance sheets and using the additional information presented in the problem, prepare a calculation to show how much net income was earned by the business during 2005.
3. Calculate the December 31, 2005, debt ratio for the business.

Check (2) Net income, $45,500

(3) Debt ratio, 58.76%

Problem 2-5B
Analyzing account balances and reconstructing transactions

C1 C4 A1 P2

Miguel Gould started a Web consulting firm called Gould Solutions. He began operations and completed seven transactions in April that resulted in the following accounts, which all have normal balances:

Cash	$12,485
Office supplies	560
Prepaid rent	1,500
Office equipment	11,450
Accounts payable	11,450
M. Gould, Capital	10,000
M. Gould, Withdrawals	6,200
Consulting fees earned	16,400
Operating expenses	5,655

Required

1. Prepare a trial balance for this business at the end of April.

Check (1) Trial balance total, $37,850

Analysis Component

2. Analyze the accounts and their balances and prepare a list that describes each of the seven most likely transactions and their amounts.
3. Present a report that shows how the seven transactions in part 2 yield the $12,485 Cash balance.

(3) Cash paid, $13,915

Problem 2-6B
Recording transactions; posting to ledger; preparing a trial balance

C4 A1 P1 P2

Czekai Consulting completed the following transactions during June:

a. Chris Czekai, the sole proprietor, invested $80,000 cash along with office equipment valued at $30,000 in the new business.

b. Purchased land valued at $30,000 and a building valued at $170,000. The purchase is paid with $40,000 cash and a long-term note payable for $160,000.

c. Purchased $2,400 of office supplies on credit.

d. Czekai invested her personal automobile in the business. The automobile has a value of $18,000 and is to be used exclusively in the business.

e. Purchased $6,000 of additional office equipment on credit.

f. Paid $1,500 cash salary to an assistant.

g. Provided services to a client and collected $6,000 cash.

h. Paid $800 cash for this month's utilities.

i. Paid $2,400 cash to settle the account payable created in transaction *c*.

j. Purchased $20,000 of new office equipment by paying $18,600 cash and trading in old equipment with a recorded net cost and value of $1,400. (*Hint:* Credit Office Equipment (old) for $1,400.)

k. Completed $5,200 of services for a client, who must pay within 30 days.

l. Paid $1,500 cash salary to an assistant.

m. Received $3,800 cash on the receivable created in transaction *k*.

n. Czekai withdrew $6,400 cash from the business for personal use.

Required

1. Prepare general journal entries to record these transactions (use the account titles listed in part 2).

Check (2) Ending balances: Cash, $18,600; Office Equipment, $54,600

2. Open the following accounts—their account numbers are in parentheses (use the balance column format): Cash (101); Accounts Receivable (106); Office Supplies (108); Office Equipment (163); Automobiles (164); Building (170); Land (172); Accounts Payable (201); Notes Payable (250); C. Czekai, Capital (301); C. Czekai, Withdrawals (302); Fees Earned (402); Salaries Expense (601); and Utilities Expense (602). Post the journal entries from part 1 to the accounts and enter the balance after each posting.

(3) Trial balance totals, $305,200

3. Prepare a trial balance as of the end of this month's operations.

PROBLEM SET C

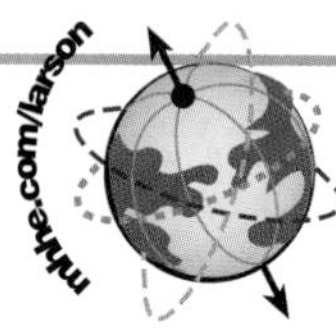

Problem Set C is available at the book's Website to further reinforce and assess your learning.

SERIAL PROBLEM

Success Systems

(This serial problem started in Chapter 1 and continues through most of the book. If the Chapter 1 segment was not completed, the problem can begin at this point. It is helpful, but not necessary, to use the Working Papers that accompany this book.)

On October 1, 2004, Kay Breeze launched a computer services company called Success Systems, which is organized as a sole proprietorship and provides consulting services, computer system installations, and custom program development. Breeze adopts the calendar year for reporting purposes and expects to prepare the company's first set of financial statements on December 31, 2004. The company's initial chart of accounts follows:

Account	No.	Account	No.
Cash	101	K. Breeze, Capital	301
Accounts Receivable	106	K. Breeze, Withdrawals	302
Computer Supplies	126	Computer Services Revenue	403
Prepaid Insurance	128	Wages Expense	623
Prepaid Rent	131	Advertising Expense	655
Office Equipment	163	Mileage Expense	676
Computer Equipment	167	Miscellaneous Expenses	677
Accounts Payable	201	Repairs Expense—Computer	684

Required

1. Prepare journal entries to record each of the following transactions for Success Systems.

Oct. 1 Breeze invested $55,000 cash, a $20,000 computer system, and $8,000 of office equipment in the business.
2 Paid $3,300 cash for four months' rent. (*Hint:* Debit Prepaid Rent for $3,300.)
3 Purchased $1,420 of computer supplies on credit from Cain Office Products.
5 Paid $2,220 cash for one year's premium on a property and liability insurance policy. (*Hint:* Debit Prepaid Insurance for $2,220.)
6 Billed Easy Leasing $4,800 for services performed in installing a new Web server.
8 Paid $1,420 cash for the computer supplies purchased from Cain Office Products on October 3.
10 Hired Sherry Adams as a part-time assistant for $125 per day, as needed.
12 Billed Easy Leasing another $1,400 for services performed.
15 Received $4,800 cash from Easy Leasing on its account.
17 Paid $805 cash to repair computer equipment damaged when moving it.
20 Paid $1,940 cash for an advertisement in the local newspaper.
22 Received $1,400 cash from Easy Leasing on its account.
28 Billed Clark Company $5,208 for services performed.
31 Paid $875 cash for Sherry Adams's wages for seven days' work.
31 Breeze withdrew $3,600 cash for personal use.
Nov. 1 Reimbursed Breeze in cash for business automobile mileage allowance (Breeze logged 1,000 miles at $0.32 per mile).
2 Received $4,633 cash from Chang Corporation for computer services performed.
5 Purchased computer supplies for $1,125 cash from Cain Office Products.
8 Billed Gomez Co. $5,668 for services performed.
13 Received notification from Alex's Engineering Co. that Success Systems' bid of $3,950 for an upcoming project is accepted.
18 Received $2,208 cash from Clark Company as partial payment of the October 28 bill.
22 Donated $250 cash to the United Way in the company's name.
24 Completed work for Alex's Engineering Co. and sent it a bill for $3,950.
25 Sent another bill to Clark Company for the past-due amount of $3,000.
28 Reimbursed Breeze in cash for business automobile mileage (1,200 miles at $0.32 per mile).
30 Paid $1,750 cash for Sherry Adams's wages for 14 days' work.
30 Breeze withdrew $2,000 cash for personal use.

2. Open ledger accounts (in balance column format) and post the journal entries from part 1 to them.

3. Prepare a trial balance as of the end of November.

BEYOND THE NUMBERS

REPORTING IN ACTION

A1 A2

BTN 2-1 Refer to **Krispy Kreme**'s financial statements in Appendix A for the following questions.

Required

1. What amount of total liabilities does it report for each of the fiscal years ended 2002 and 2003?

2. What amount of total assets does it report for each of the fiscal years ended 2002 and 2003?

3. Calculate its debt ratio for each of the fiscal years ended 2002 and 2003.

4. In which fiscal year did it employ more financial leverage (2002 or 2003)? Explain.

Roll On

5. Access its financial statements (10-K report) for a fiscal year ending after February 2, 2003, from its Website (**KrispyKreme.com**) or the SEC's EDGAR database (**www.SEC.gov**). Recompute its debt ratio for any subsequent year's data and compare it with the February 2, 2003, debt ratio.

COMPARATIVE ANALYSIS

A1 A2 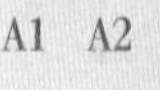

BTN 2-2 Key comparative figures ($ thousands) for both **Krispy Kreme** and **Tastykake** follow:

	Krispy Kreme		Tastykake	
Key Figures	Current Year	Prior Year	Current Year	Prior Year
Total liabilities	$131,942	$ 65,218	$ 69,035	$ 61,072
Total assets	410,487	255,376	116,560	116,137

1. What is the debt ratio for Krispy Kreme in the current year and the prior year?
2. What is the debt ratio for Tastykake in the current year and the prior year?
3. Which of the two companies has a higher degree of financial leverage? What does this imply?

ETHICS CHALLENGE

C1 C2 

BTN 2-3 Review the *Decision Ethics* case from the first part of this chapter involving the cashier. The guidance answer suggests that you should not comply with the assistant manager's request.

Required

Propose and evaluate two other courses of action you might consider, and explain why.

COMMUNICATING IN PRACTICE

C1 C3 A1 P3 

BTN 2-4 Amy Renkmeyer is an aspiring entrepreneur and your friend. She is having difficulty understanding the purposes of financial statements and how they fit together across time.

Required

Write a one-page memorandum to Renkmeyer explaining the purposes of the four financial statements and how they are linked across time.

TAKING IT TO THE NET

A1 

mhhe.com/larson

BTN 2-5 Access EDGAR online (www.SEC.gov) and locate the 10-K report of **Amazon.com** (ticker AMZN) filed on January 24, 2002. Review its financial statements reported for fiscal years ended 1999, 2000, and 2001 to answer the following questions:

Required

1. What are the amounts of its net losses reported for each of these three years?
2. Does Amazon's operations provide cash or use cash for each of these three years?
3. If Amazon has a 2000 net loss and a net use of cash in operations in 2000, how is it possible that its cash balance at December 31, 2000, shows an increase relative to its balance at January 1, 2000?

TEAMWORK IN ACTION

C1 C3 C5 A1

BTN 2-6 The expanded accounting equation consists of assets, liabilities, capital, withdrawals, revenues, and expenses. It can be used to reveal insights into changes in a company's financial position.

Required

1. Form *learning teams* of six (or more) members. Each team member must select one of the six components and each team must have at least one expert on each component: (*a*) assets, (*b*) liabilities, (*c*) capital, (*d*) withdrawals, (*e*) revenues, and (*f*) expenses.
2. Form *expert teams* of individuals who selected the same component in part 1. Expert teams are to draft a report that each expert will present to his or her learning team addressing the following:
   a. Identify for its component the (i) increase and decrease side of the account and (ii) normal balance side of the account.
   b. Describe a transaction, with amounts, that increases its component.

c. Using the transaction and amounts in (*b*), verify the equality of the accounting equation and then explain any effects on the income statement and statement of cash flows.

d. Describe a transaction, with amounts, that decreases its component.

e. Using the transaction and amounts in (*d*), verify the equality of the accounting equation and then explain any effects on the income statement and statement of cash flows.

3. Each expert should return to his/her learning team. In rotation, each member presents his/her expert team's report to the learning team. Team discussion is encouraged.

BUSINESS WEEK ACTIVITY

A2  

mhhe.com/larson

BTN 2-7 Read the article "Leveraged for Success" in the April 18, 2002, issue of ***Business Week***.

Required

1. Explain why debt financing can be a less expensive alternative than equity financing.

2. What can happen if a company takes on too much debt?

3. Name five companies cited by the article that are using a high degree of leverage but still maintaining top credit ratings.

ENTREPRENEURIAL DECISION

A1 A2 P3  

BTN 2-8 Liang Lu is a young entrepreneur who operates Lu Music Services, offering singing lessons and instruction on musical instruments. Lu wishes to expand but needs a loan. The bank requests Lu to prepare a balance sheet and key financial ratios. Lu has not kept formal records but is able to provide the following accounts and their amounts as of December 31, 2005:

Cash	$ 1,800	Accounts Receivable	$4,800	Prepaid Insurance	$ 750
Prepaid Rent	4,700	Store Supplies	3,300	Equipment	25,000
Accounts Payable	1,100	Unearned Lesson Fees	7,800	Total Equity*	31,450
Annual net income	20,000				

* The total equity amount reflects all owner investments, owner withdrawals, revenues, and expenses as of December 31, 2005.

Required

1. Prepare a balance sheet as of December 31, 2005, for Lu Music Services.

2. Compute Lu's debt ratio and its return on assets (from Chapter 1). Assume average assets equal its ending balance.

3. Do you think the prospects of a $15,000 bank loan are good? Why or why not?

A1 A2 P3  

BTN 2-9 Assume that Tanya York of **York Entertainment** wants to grow company revenues by 10% each year for the next five years. York has determined that achieving that revenue growth will require additional financing. Accordingly, the company has sought and been offered a $5 million line of credit by a Los Angeles bank to help fund current operations and new movie projects. York is not required to use the line of credit, but it does have preapproval to use the line of credit as needed. If the line of credit is used, an annual interest rate of 8% will be charged on the money borrowed.

Required

1. What will York's annual revenues be in five years if the revenue growth target rate is achieved?

2. If York decides to borrow against the line of credit, what must it do to successfully employ financial leverage?

HITTING THE ROAD

C1

BTN 2-10 Obtain a recent copy of the most prominent newspaper distributed in your area. Research the classified section and prepare a report answering the following questions (attach relevant classified clippings to your report). Alternatively, you may want to search the Web for the required information. One suitable Website is **America's Job Bank (www.AJB.org).** For documentation, you should print copies of Websites accessed.

1. Identify the number of listings for accounting positions and the various accounting job titles.
2. Identify the number of listings for other job titles, with examples, that require or prefer accounting knowledge/experience but are not specifically accounting positions.
3. Specify the salary range for the accounting and accounting-related positions if provided.
4. Indicate the job that appeals to you, the reason for its appeal, and its requirements.

GLOBAL DECISION

A2 

BTN 2-11 **Grupo Bimbo** (GrupoBimbo.com) competes with several companies, including **Krispy Kreme** and **Tastykake**. Key financial ratios for the current fiscal year follow:

Key Figure	Grupo Bimbo	Krispy Kreme	Tastykake
Return on assets	3.6%	10.1%	1.7%
Debt ratio	56.0%	32.1%	59.2%

Required

1. Which company is most profitable according to return on assets?
2. Which company is most risky according to the debt ratio?
3. Which company deserves increased investment based on a joint analysis of return on assets and the debt ratio?

"Stay focused and keep doing what you believe in"—Melody Kulp (second from left; David Reinstein is on the far left)

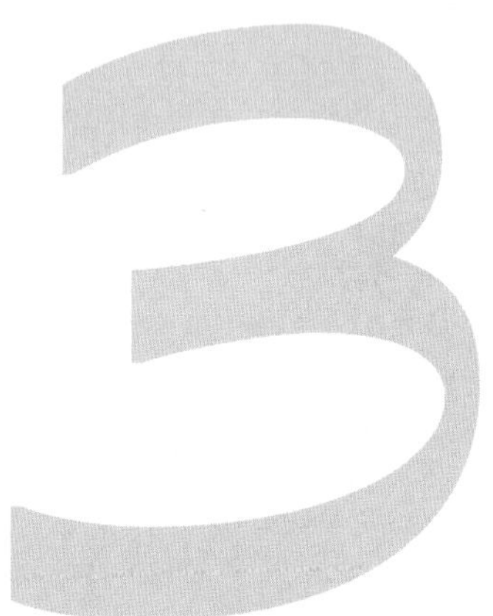

Adjusting Accounts and Preparing Financial Statements

A Look Back

Chapter 2 explained the analysis and recording of transactions. We showed how to apply and interpret company accounts, T-accounts, double-entry accounting, ledgers, postings, and trial balances.

A Look at This Chapter

This chapter explains the timing of reports and the need to adjust accounts. Adjusting accounts is important for recognizing revenues and expenses in the proper period. We describe the adjusted trial balance and how it is used to prepare financial statements.

A Look Ahead

Chapter 4 highlights the completion of the accounting cycle. We explain the important final steps in the accounting process. These include closing procedures, the post-closing trial balance, and reversing entries.

Learning Objectives

CAP

Conceptual

C1 Explain the importance of periodic reporting and the time period principle. *(p. 94)*

C2 Explain accrual accounting and how it makes financial statements more useful. *(p. 95)*

C3 Identify the types of adjustments and their purpose. *(p. 97)*

Analytical

A1 Explain how accounting adjustments link to financial statements. *(p. 104)*

A2 Compute profit margin and describe its use in analyzing company performance. *(p. 108)*

Procedural

P1 Prepare and explain adjusting entries. *(p. 97)*

P2 Explain and prepare an adjusted trial balance. *(p. 105)*

P3 Prepare financial statements from an adjusted trial balance. *(p. 106)*

Decision Feature

Sparkling Financials

EL SEGUNDO, CA—One afternoon 23-year-old Melody Kulp was playing outside with the young cousin of a friend when she placed yard-picked flowers in the girl's hair and thought how much prettier they looked than headbands or hair clips. The next day, with some silk flowers and Velcro she purchased, Kulp made similar hair accessories, called them *Sparkles,* and began wearing them.

When a friend wore one to work at Fred Segal's, the shop's buyer asked to meet with Kulp about putting together a product line. Kulp quickly organized a business—dubbed **Mellies (Mellies.com)**—and then converted a 10′ × 10′ room in her house into a minifactory. The rest is the stuff of Hollywood movies.

After only three years, Mellies is a $40 million accessories company. With her 25-year-old partner David Reinstein, Melody Kulp now manages 15 employees and plans to launch a cosmetics line. The young entrepreneurs learned a lot in a hurry. She had to meet creditors and bankers, set up a reliable accounting system, draw up financial statements, and analyze and interpret financial data. It was at times overwhelming, says Kulp, but "the key is to stay focused and keep doing what you believe in."

Kulp knows how important a timely and reliable accounting system is for Mellies' continued success. Historical and projected financial statements have enabled her company to obtain the necessary financing to propel it to new heights.

This chapter focuses on the accounting system underlying financial statements. Says Kulp, "We've got the system set up where we can look ahead, rather than live day to day." That look ahead reveals sparkling financials.

[Sources: Mellies Website, January 2004; *Success Publishing,* 2000; *Entrepreneur,* November 2000.]

Financial statements reflect revenues when earned and expenses when incurred. This is known as *accrual accounting*. Accrual accounting requires several steps. We described many of these steps in Chapter 2. We showed how companies use accounting systems to collect information about *external* transactions and events. We also explained how journals, ledgers, and other tools are useful in preparing financial statements. This chapter describes the accounting process for producing useful information involving *internal* transactions and events. An important part of this process is adjusting the account balances so that financial statements at the end of a reporting period reflect the effects of all transactions. We then explain the important steps in preparing financial statements.

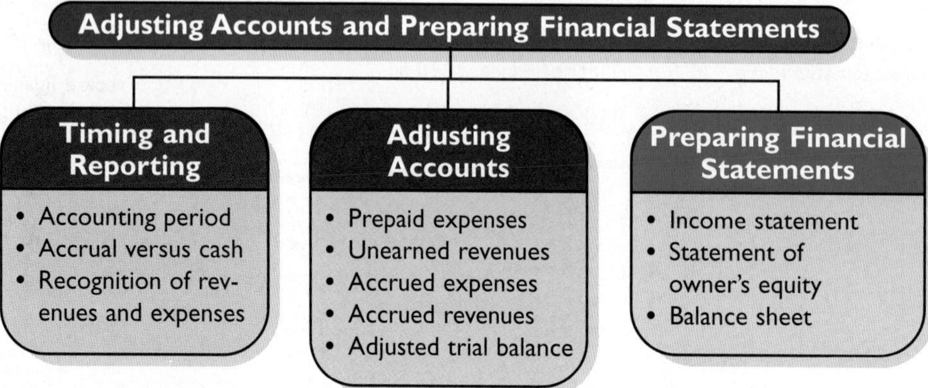

Timing and Reporting

Regular, or periodic, reporting is an important part of the accounting process. This section describes the impact on the accounting process of the point in time or the period of time that a report refers to.

The Accounting Period

C1 Explain the importance of periodic reporting and the time period principle.

"Krispy Kreme announces earnings per share of . . ."

The value of information is often linked to its timeliness. Useful information must reach decision makers frequently and promptly. To provide timely information, accounting systems prepare reports at regular intervals. This results in an accounting process impacted by the time period (or periodicity) principle. The **time period principle** assumes that an organization's activities can be divided into specific time periods such as a month, a three-month quarter, a six-month interval, or a year. Exhibit 3.1 shows various **accounting,** or *reporting,*

Exhibit 3.1

Accounting Periods

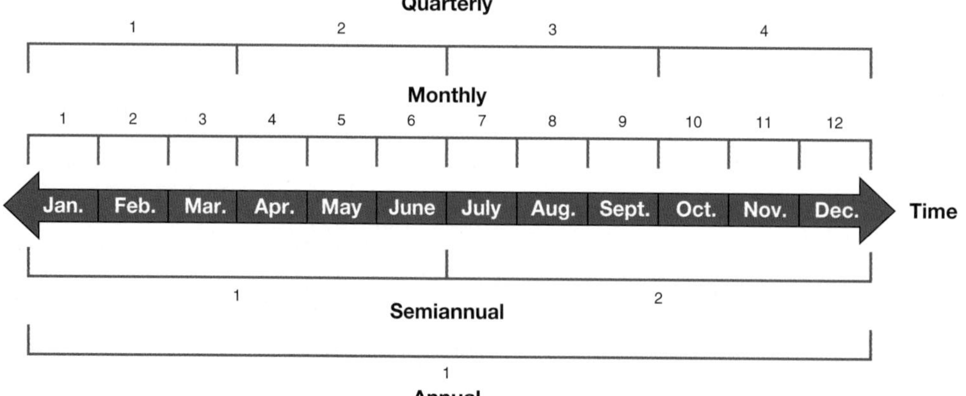

periods. Most organizations use a year as their primary accounting period. Reports covering a one-year period are known as **annual financial statements.** Many organizations also prepare **interim financial statements** covering one, three, or six months of activity.

The annual reporting period is not always a calendar year ending on December 31. An organization can adopt a **fiscal year** consisting of any 12 consecutive months. It is also acceptable to adopt an annual reporting period of 52 weeks. For example, **Gap**'s fiscal year consistently ends the final week of January or the first week of February each year.

Companies with little seasonal variation in sales often choose the calendar year as their fiscal year. For example, the financial statements of **Marvel Enterprises** reflect a fiscal year that ends on December 31. Companies experiencing seasonal variations in sales often choose a **natural business year** end, which is when sales activities are at their lowest level for the year. The natural business year for retailers such as **Wal-Mart**, **Dell**, and **FUBU** usually ends around January 31, after the holiday season.

Accrual Basis versus Cash Basis

After external transactions and events are recorded for an accounting period, several accounts still need adjustments before their balances appear in financial statements. This need arises because internal transactions and events remain unrecorded. **Accrual basis accounting** uses the adjusting process to recognize revenues when earned and to match expenses with revenues.

C2 Explain accrual accounting and how it makes financial statements more useful.

Cash basis accounting recognizes revenues when cash is received and records expenses when cash is paid. This means that cash basis net income for a period is the difference between cash receipts and cash payments. Cash basis accounting is not consistent with generally accepted accounting principles.

It is commonly held that accrual accounting better reflects business performance than information about cash receipts and payments. Accrual accounting also increases the *comparability* of financial statements from one period to another. Yet cash basis accounting is useful for several business decisions—which is the reason companies must report a statement of cash flows.

Topic Tackler 3-1

To see the difference between these two accounting systems, let's consider FastForward's Prepaid Insurance account. FastForward paid $2,400 for 24 months of insurance coverage beginning on December 1, 2004. Accrual accounting requires that $100 of insurance expense be reported on December's income statement. Another $1,200 of expense is reported in year 2005, and the remaining $1,100 is reported as expense in the first 11 months of 2006. Exhibit 3.2 illustrates this allocation of insurance cost across these three years. The accrual basis balance sheet reports any unexpired premium as a Prepaid Insurance asset.

Point: IBM's revenues from services to customers are recorded when services are performed. Its revenues from product sales are recorded when products are shipped.

A cash basis income statement for December 2004 reports insurance expense of $2,400, as shown in Exhibit 3.3. The cash basis income statements for years 2005 and 2006 report

Exhibit 3.2

Accrual Basis Accounting for Allocating Prepaid Insurance to Expense

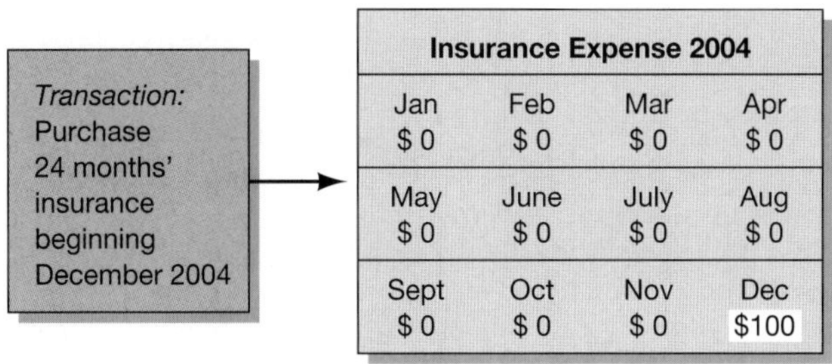

Insurance Expense 2004			
Jan $0	Feb $0	Mar $0	Apr $0
May $0	June $0	July $0	Aug $0
Sept $0	Oct $0	Nov $0	Dec $100

Insurance Expense 2005			
Jan $100	Feb $100	Mar $100	Apr $100
May $100	June $100	July $100	Aug $100
Sept $100	Oct $100	Nov $100	Dec $100

Insurance Expense 2006			
Jan $100	Feb $100	Mar $100	Apr $100
May $100	June $100	July $100	Aug $100
Sept $100	Oct $100	Nov $100	Dec $0

Exhibit 3.3

Cash Basis Accounting for Allocating Prepaid Insurance to Expense

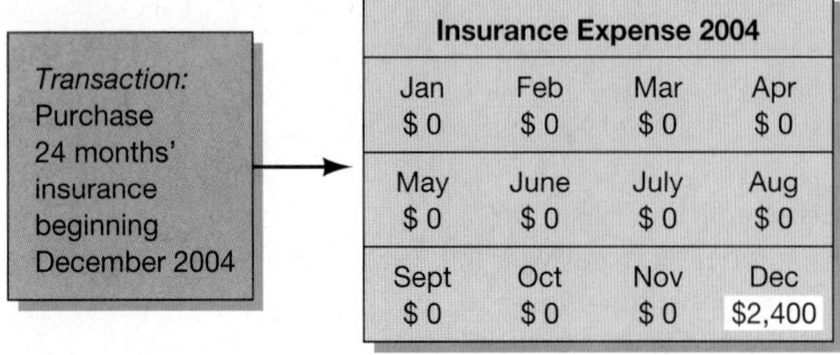

Insurance Expense 2004			
Jan $0	Feb $0	Mar $0	Apr $0
May $0	June $0	July $0	Aug $0
Sept $0	Oct $0	Nov $0	Dec $2,400

Insurance Expense 2005			
Jan $0	Feb $0	Mar $0	Apr $0
May $0	June $0	July $0	Aug $0
Sept $0	Oct $0	Nov $0	Dec $0

Insurance Expense 2006			
Jan $0	Feb $0	Mar $0	Apr $0
May $0	June $0	July $0	Aug $0
Sept $0	Oct $0	Nov $0	Dec $0

Point: Recording revenue early overstates current-period revenue and income; recording it late understates current-period revenue and income.

no insurance expense. The cash basis balance sheet never reports an insurance asset because it is immediately expensed. Note that reported income for 2004–2006 fails to match the cost of insurance with the insurance benefits received for those years and months.

Recognizing Revenues and Expenses

Decision Insight

Numbers Game **Ascential Software**, a software provider, recorded revenue when products were passed to distributors. It admits now that there were "errors in the way revenues had been recorded," and its CEO is in jail. **Centennial Technologies**, a computers manufacturer, recognized revenue when it shipped products. What is not common is that Centennial's CEO shipped products to the warehouses of friends and reported it as revenue. Risky or improper revenue recognition practices are often revealed by a large increase in the *Accounts Receivable to Sales* ratio.

We use the time period principle to divide a company's activities into specific time periods, but not all activities are complete when financial statements are prepared. Thus, adjustments often are required to get correct account balances.

We rely on two principles in the adjusting process: revenue recognition and matching. Chapter 1 explained that the *revenue recognition principle* requires that revenue be recorded when earned, not before and not after. Most companies earn revenue when they provide services and products to customers. A major goal of the adjusting process is to have revenue recognized (reported) in the time period when it is earned.

The **matching principle** aims to record expenses in the same accounting period as the revenues that are earned as a result of these expenses. This matching of expenses with the revenue benefits is a major part of the adjusting process.

Matching expenses with revenues often requires us to predict certain events. When we use financial statements, we must understand that they require estimates and therefore include measures that are not precise. **Walt Disney**'s annual report explains that its production costs from movies are matched to revenues based on a ratio of current revenues from the movie divided by its predicted total revenues.

Point: Recording expense early overstates current-period expense and understates current-period income; recording it late understates current-period expense and overstates current-period income.

Quick Check

Answers—p. 115

1. Describe a company's annual reporting period.
2. Why do companies prepare interim financial statements?
3. What two accounting principles most directly drive the adjusting process?
4. Is cash basis accounting consistent with the matching principle? Why or why not?
5. If your company pays a $4,800 premium on April 1, 2004, for two years' insurance coverage, how much insurance expense is reported in 2005 using cash basis accounting?

Adjusting Accounts

The process of adjusting accounts involves analyzing each account balance and the transactions and events that affect it to determine any needed adjustments. An **adjusting entry** is recorded to bring an asset or liability account balance to its proper amount. This entry also updates a related expense or revenue account.

C3 Identify the types of adjustments and their purpose.

Framework for Adjustments

Adjustments are necessary for transactions and events that extend over more than one period. It is helpful to group adjustments by the timing of cash receipt or cash payment in relation to the recognition of the related revenues or expenses. Exhibit 3.4 identifies four types of adjustments.

Topic Tackler 3-2

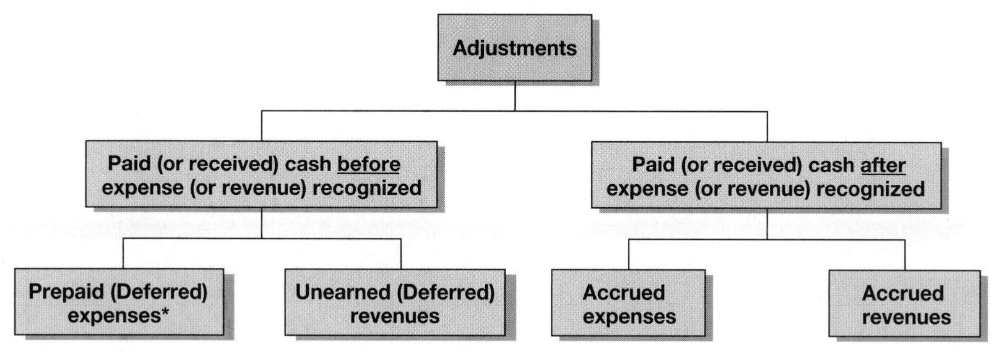

*Includes depreciation.

Exhibit 3.4

Types of Adjustments

The left side of this exhibit shows prepaid expenses (including depreciation) and unearned revenues, which reflect transactions when cash is paid or received *before* a related expense or revenue is recognized. They are also called *deferrals* because the recognition of an expense (or revenue) is *deferred* until after the related cash is paid (or received). The right side of this exhibit shows accrued expenses and accrued revenues, which reflect transactions when cash is paid or received *after* a related expense or revenue is recognized. Adjusting entries are necessary for each of these so that revenues, expenses, assets, and liabilities are correctly reported. It is helpful to remember that each adjusting entry affects one or more income statement accounts *and* one or more balance sheet accounts (but not the Cash account).

Point: Adjusting is a 3-step process: (1) Compute current account balance, (2) Compute what current account balance should be, and (3) Record entry to get from step *1* to step 2.

Prepaid (Deferred) Expenses

P1 Prepare and explain adjusting entries.

Prepaid expenses refer to items *paid for* in advance of receiving their benefits. Prepaid expenses are assets. When these assets are used, their costs become expenses. Adjusting entries for prepaids increase expenses and decrease assets as shown in the T-accounts of Exhibit 3.5. Such adjustments reflect transactions and events that use up prepaid expenses (including passage of time). To illustrate the accounting for prepaid expenses, this section focuses on prepaid insurance, supplies, and depreciation.

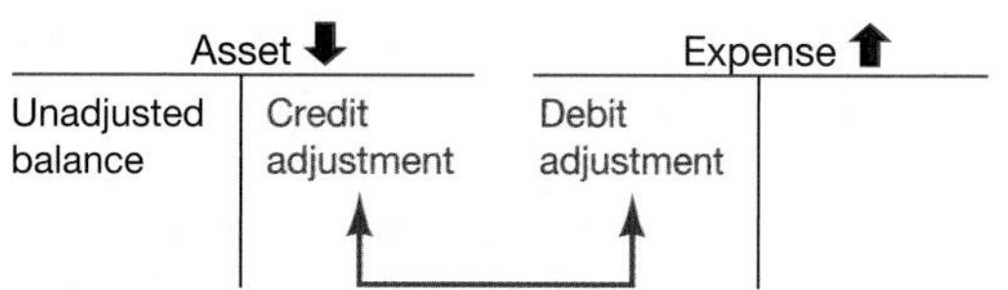

Exhibit 3.5

Adjusting for Prepaid Expenses

Prepaid Insurance We illustrate prepaid insurance using FastForward's payment of $2,400 for 24 months of insurance benefits beginning on December 1, 2004. With the passage of time, the benefits of the insurance gradually expire and a portion of the Prepaid

Insurance asset becomes expense. For instance, one month's insurance coverage expires by December 31, 2004. This expense is $100, or 1/24 of $2,400. The adjusting entry to record this expense and reduce the asset, along with T-account postings, follows:

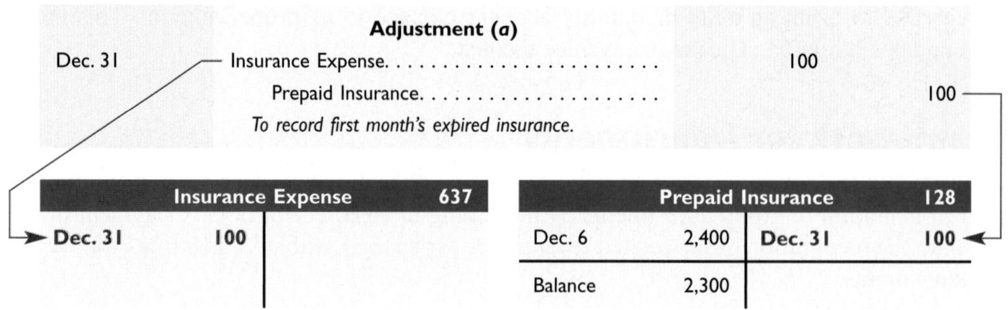

Point: Many companies record adjusting entries only at the end of each year because of the time and cost necessary.

Point: Source documents provide information for most daily transactions, and in many businesses the recordkeepers record them. Adjustments require more knowledge and are usually handled by senior accounting professionals.

After adjusting and posting, the $100 balance in Insurance Expense and the $2,300 balance in Prepaid Insurance are ready for reporting in financial statements. *Not* making the adjustment on or before December 31 would (1) understate expenses by $100 and overstate net income by $100 for the December income statement and (2) overstate both prepaid insurance (assets) and equity (because of net income) by $100 in the December 31 balance sheet. It is also evident from Exhibit 3.2 that 2005's adjustments must transfer a total of $1,200 from Prepaid Insurance to Insurance Expense, and 2006's adjustments must transfer the remaining $1,100 to Insurance Expense.

Supplies Supplies are a prepaid expense often requiring adjustment. To illustrate, FastForward purchased $9,720 of supplies in December and used some of them. When financial statements are prepared at December 31, the cost of supplies used during December must be recognized. When FastForward computes (takes inventory of) its remaining unused supplies at December 31, it finds $8,670 of supplies remaining of the $9,720 total supplies. The $1,050 difference between these two amounts is December's supplies expense. The adjusting entry to record this expense and reduce the Supplies asset account, along with T-account postings, follows:

Assets	=	Liabilities	+	Equity
−1,050				−1,050

Adjustment (*b*)

Dec. 31	Supplies Expense.	1,050	
	Supplies.		1,050
	To record supplies used.		

Supplies Expense 652			
Dec. 31	**1,050**		

Supplies 126			
Dec. 2	2,500	**Dec. 31**	**1,050**
6	7,100		
26	120		
Balance	8,670		

The balance of the Supplies account is $8,670 after posting—equaling the cost of the remaining supplies. *Not* making the adjustment on or before December 31 would (1) understate expenses by $1,050 and overstate net income by $1,050 for the December income statement and (2) overstate both supplies and equity (because of net income) by $1,050 in the December 31 balance sheet.

Point: An alternative method to record prepaids is to initially debit expense for the total amount. Appendix 3A discusses this alternative. The adjusted financial statement information is identical under either method.

Other Prepaid Expenses Other prepaid expenses, such as Prepaid Rent, are accounted for exactly as Insurance and Supplies are. We should also note that some prepaid expenses are both paid for and fully used up within a single accounting period. One example is when a company pays monthly rent on the first day of each month. This payment creates a prepaid expense on the first day of each month that fully expires by the end of the month. In these special cases, we can record the cash paid with a debit to an expense account instead of an asset account. This practice is described more completely later in the chapter.

Decision Maker

Investor A small publishing company signs a well-known athlete to write a book. The company pays the athlete $500,000 to sign plus future book royalties. A note to the company's financial statements says that "prepaid expenses include $500,000 in author signing fees to be matched against future expected sales." Is this accounting for the signing bonus acceptable? How does it affect your analysis?

Answer—p. 114

Depreciation A special category of prepaid expenses is **plant assets,** which refers to long-term tangible assets used to produce and sell products and services. Plant assets are expected to provide benefits for more than one period. Examples of plant assets are buildings, machines, vehicles, and fixtures. All plant assets, with a general exception for land, eventually wear out or decline in usefulness. The costs of these assets are deferred but are gradually reported as expenses in the income statement over the assets' useful lives (benefit periods). **Depreciation** is the process of allocating the costs of these assets over their expected useful lives. Depreciation expense is recorded with an adjusting entry similar to that for other prepaid expenses.

Point: Depreciation does not necessarily measure the decline in market value.

To illustrate, recall that FastForward purchased equipment for $26,000 in early December to use in earning revenue. This equipment's cost must be depreciated. The equipment is expected to have a useful life (benefit period) of four years and to be worth about $8,000 at the end of four years. This means the *net* cost of this equipment over its useful life is $18,000 ($26,000 − $8,000). We can use any of several methods to allocate this $18,000 net cost to expense. FastForward uses a method called **straight-line depreciation,** which allocates equal amounts of an asset's net cost to depreciation during its useful life. Dividing the $18,000 net cost by the 48 months in the asset's useful life gives a monthly cost of $375 ($18,000/48). The adjusting entry to record monthly depreciation expense, along with T-account postings, follows:

Point: An asset's expected value at the end of its useful life is called *salvage value.*

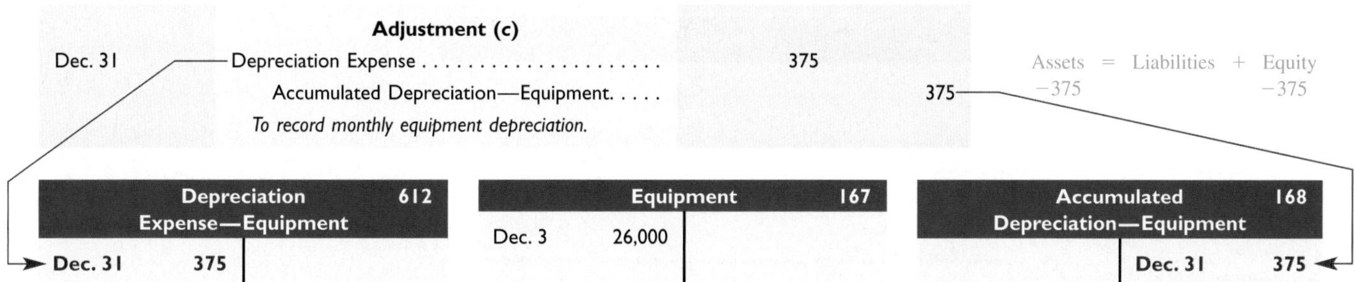

After posting the adjustment, the Equipment account ($26,000) less its Accumulated Depreciation ($375) account equals the $25,625 net cost of the 47 remaining months in the benefit period. The $375 balance in the Depreciation Expense account is reported in the December income statement. *Not* making the adjustment at December 31 would (1) understate expenses by $375 and overstate net income by $375 for the December income statement and (2) overstate both assets and equity (because of income) by $375 in the December 31 balance sheet.

The accumulated depreciation is kept in a separate contra account. A **contra account** is an account linked with another account, it has an opposite normal balance, and it is reported as a subtraction from that other account's balance. For instance, FastForward's contra account of Accumulated Depreciation—Equipment is subtracted from the Equipment account in the balance sheet (see Exhibit 3.7).

Point: The cost principle requires an asset to be initially recorded at acquisition cost. Depreciation causes the asset's book value (cost less accumulated depreciation) to decline over time.

Decision Maker

Entrepreneur You are preparing an offer to purchase a family-run restaurant. The depreciation schedule for the restaurant's building and equipment shows costs of $175,000 and accumulated depreciation of $155,000. This leaves a net for building and equipment of $20,000. Is this information useful in helping you decide on a purchase offer?

Answer—p. 115

A contra account allows balance sheet readers to know both the full costs of assets and the total amount of depreciation. By knowing both these amounts, decision makers can better assess a company's capacity and its need to replace assets. For example, FastForward's balance sheet shows both the $26,000 original cost of equipment and the $375 balance in the accumulated depreciation contra account. This information reveals that the equipment is close to new. If FastForward reports equipment only at its net amount of $25,625, users cannot assess the equipment's age or its need for replacement. The title of the contra account, *Accumulated Depreciation,* indicates that this account includes total depreciation expense for all prior periods for which the asset was used. To illustrate, the Equipment and the Accumulated Depreciation accounts appear as in Exhibit 3.6 on February 28, 2005, after three months of adjusting entries.

Exhibit 3.6

Accounts after Three Months of Depreciation Adjustments

Equipment			167
Dec. 3	26,000		

Accumulated Depreciation—Equipment			168
		Dec. 31	375
		Jan. 31	375
		Feb. 28	375
		Balance	**1,125**

The $1,125 balance in the accumulated depreciation account is subtracted from its related $26,000 asset cost. The difference ($24,875) between these two balances is the cost of the asset that has not yet been depreciated. This difference is called the **book value,** or *net amount,* which equals the asset's costs less its accumulated depreciation. These account balances are reported in the assets section of the February 28 balance sheet in Exhibit 3.7.

Point: The net cost of equipment is also called the *depreciable basis.*

Exhibit 3.7

Equipment and Accumulated Depreciation on February 28 Balance Sheet

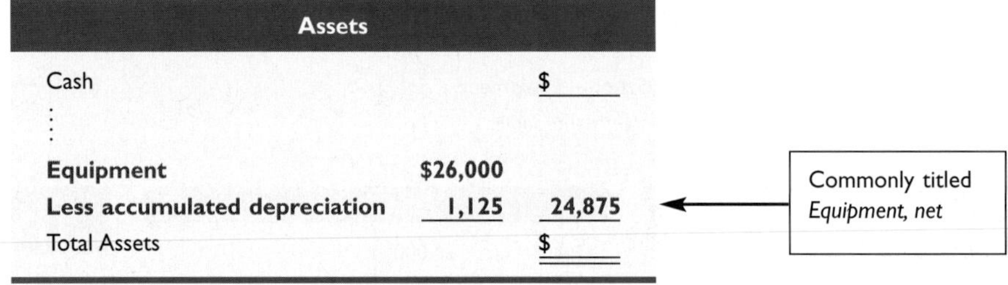

Assets		
Cash		$
⋮		
Equipment	**$26,000**	
Less accumulated depreciation	**1,125**	**24,875**
Total Assets		$

Unearned (Deferred) Revenues

The term **unearned revenues** refers to cash received in advance of providing products and services. Unearned revenues, also called *deferred revenues,* are liabilities. When cash is accepted, an obligation to provide products or services is accepted. As products or services are provided, the unearned revenues become *earned* revenues. Adjusting entries for unearned revenues involve increasing revenues and decreasing unearned revenues, as shown in Exhibit 3.8.

Exhibit 3.8

Adjusting for Unearned Revenues

Liability ⬇
Debit adjustment | Unadjusted balance

Revenue ⬆
Credit adjustment

An example of unearned revenues is from **The New York Times Company**, which reports unexpired (unearned) subscriptions of more than $60 million: "Proceeds from . . . subscriptions are deferred at the time of sale and are recognized in earnings on a pro rata basis over the terms of the subscriptions."

Point: To *defer* is to postpone. We postpone reporting amounts received as revenues until they are earned.

Unearned revenues are more than 10% of the current liabilities for the Times. Another example comes from the **Boston Celtics**. When the Celtics receive cash from advance ticket sales and broadcast fees, they record it in an unearned revenue account called *Deferred Game Revenues*. The Celtics recognize this unearned revenue with adjusting entries on a game-by-game basis. Since the NBA regular season begins in October and ends in April, revenue recognition is mainly limited to this period. For a recent season, the Celtics' quarterly revenues were $0 million for July–September; $34 million for October–December; $48 million for January–March; and $17 million for April–June.

FastForward has unearned revenues. It agreed on December 26 to provide consulting services to a client for a fixed fee of $3,000 for 60 days. On that same day, this client paid the 60-day fee in advance, covering the period December 27 to February 24. The entry to record the cash received in advance is

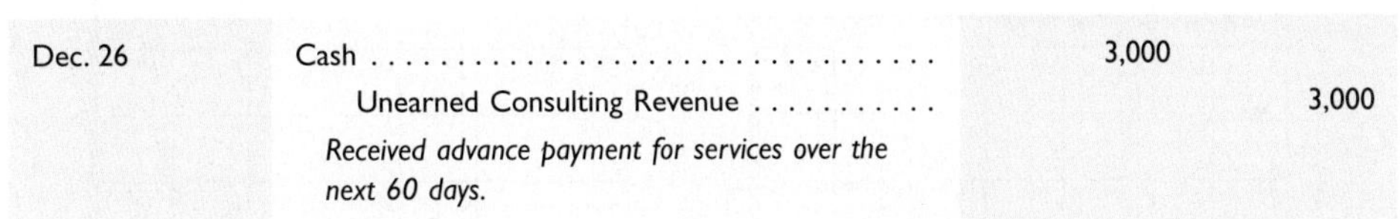

		Debit	Credit
Dec. 26	Cash	3,000	
	Unearned Consulting Revenue		3,000
	Received advance payment for services over the next 60 days.		

Assets = Liabilities + Equity
+3,000 +3,000

This advance payment increases cash and creates an obligation to do consulting work over the next 60 days. As time passes, FastForward will earn this payment through consulting. By December 31, it has provided five days' service and earned 5/60 of the $3,000 unearned revenue. This amounts to $250 ($3,000 × 5/60). The *revenue recognition principle* implies that $250 of unearned revenue must be reported as revenue on the December income statement. The adjusting entry to reduce the liability account and recognize earned revenue, along with T-account postings, follows:

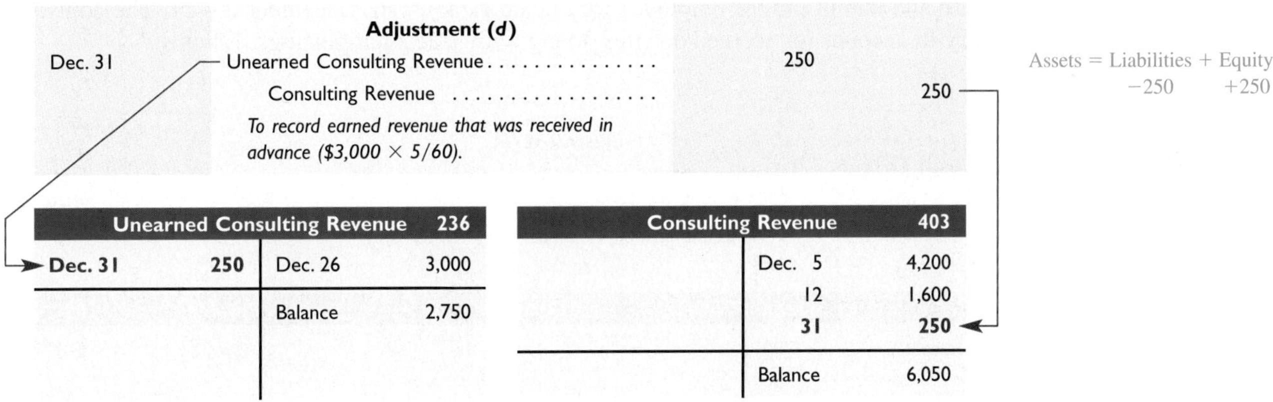

Adjustment (*d*)

		Debit	Credit
Dec. 31	Unearned Consulting Revenue	250	
	Consulting Revenue		250
	To record earned revenue that was received in advance ($3,000 × 5/60).		

Unearned Consulting Revenue 236

Dec. 31	250	Dec. 26	3,000
		Balance	2,750

Consulting Revenue 403

		Dec. 5	4,200
		12	1,600
		31	250
		Balance	6,050

Assets = Liabilities + Equity
−250 +250

The adjusting entry transfers $250 from unearned revenue (a liability account) to a revenue account. *Not* making the adjustment (1) understates revenue and net income by $250 in the December income statement and (2) overstates unearned revenue and understates equity by $250 on the December 31 balance sheet.

Accrued Expenses

Accrued expenses refer to costs that are incurred in a period but are both unpaid and unrecorded. Accrued expenses must be reported on the income statement of the period when incurred. Adjusting entries for recording accrued expenses involves increasing expenses and increasing liabilities as shown in Exhibit 3.9. This adjustment

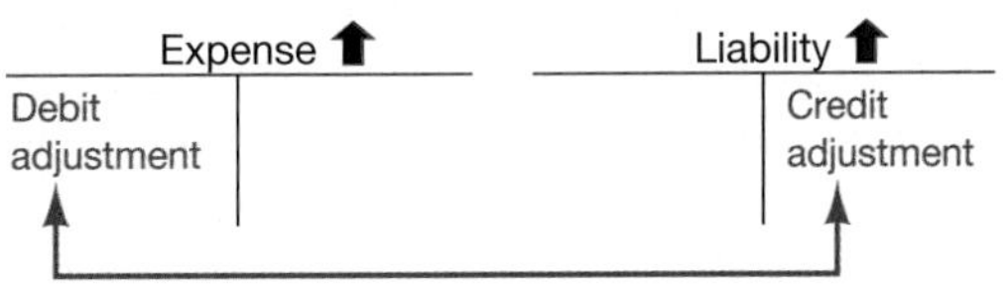

Exhibit 3.9

Adjusting for Accrued Expenses

Point: Accrued expenses are also called *accrued liabilities.*

recognizes expenses incurred in a period but not yet paid. Common examples of accrued expenses are salaries, interest, rent, and taxes. We use salaries and interest to show how to adjust accounts for accrued expenses.

Accrued Salaries Expense FastForward's employee earns $70 per day, or $350 for a five-day workweek beginning on Monday and ending on Friday. This employee is paid every two weeks on Friday. On December 12 and 26, the wages are paid, recorded in the journal, and posted to the ledger. The calendar in Exhibit 3.10 shows three working days after the December 26 payday (29, 30, and 31). This means the employee has earned three days' salary by the close of business on Wednesday, December 31, yet this salary cost is not paid or recorded.

Exhibit 3.10

Salary Accrual and Paydays

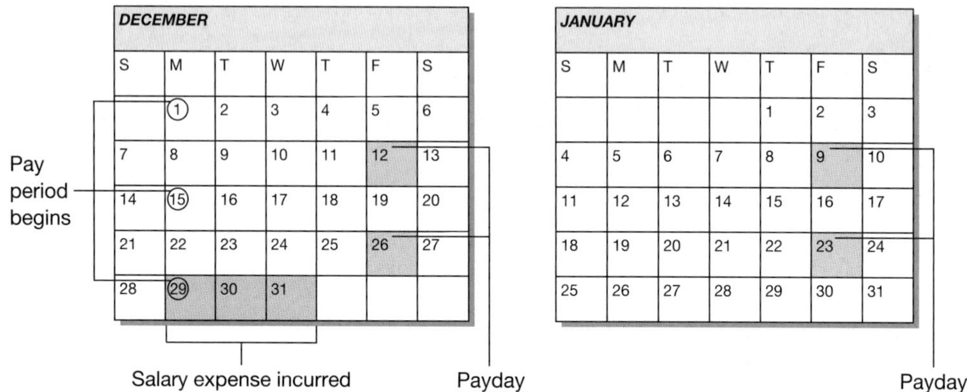

Point: Assume: (1) the last payday for the year is December 19, (2) the next payday is January 2, and (3) December 25 is a paid holiday. Record the December 31 adjusting entry.
Answer: We must accrue pay for eight working days (8 × $70):
Salaries Expense . . . 560
Salaries Payable 560

The financial statements would be incomplete if FastForward fails to report the added expense and liability to the employee for unpaid salary from December 29–31. The adjusting entry to account for accrued salaries, along with T-account postings, follows:

Adjustment (e)

Dec. 31	Salaries Expense	210	
	Salaries Payable		210
	To record three days' accrued salary (3 × $70).		

Salaries Expense		622
Dec. 12	700	
26	700	
31	**210**	
Balance	1,610	

Salaries Payable		209
	Dec. 31	**210**

Point: An employer records salaries expense and a vacation pay liability when employees earn vacation pay.

Salaries expense of $1,610 is reported on the December income statement and $210 of salaries payable (liability) is reported in the balance sheet. *Not* making the adjustment (1) understates salaries expense and overstates net income by $210 in the December income statement and (2) understates salaries payable (liabilities) and overstates equity by $210 on the December 31 balance sheet.

Accrued Interest Expense Companies commonly have accrued interest expense on notes payable and other long-term liabilities at the end of a period. Interest expense is incurred with the passage of time. Unless interest is paid on the last day of an accounting period, we need to adjust for interest expense incurred but not yet paid. This means we must accrue interest cost from the most recent payment date up to the end of the period. The formula for computing accrued interest is:

Principal amount owed × Annual interest rate × Fraction of year since last payment date.

To illustrate, if a company has a $6,000 loan from a bank at 6% annual interest, then 30 days' accrued interest expense is $30—computed as $6,000 × 0.06 × 30/360. The adjusting entry would be to debit Interest Expense for $30 and credit Interest Payable for $30.

Point: Interest computations assume a 360-day year.

Future Payment of Accrued Expenses Adjusting entries for accrued expenses foretell cash transactions in future periods. Specifically, accrued expenses at the end of one accounting period result in *cash payments* in a *future* period(s). To illustrate, recall that FastForward recorded accrued salaries of $210. On January 9, the first payday of the next period, the following entry settles the accrued liability (salaries payable) and records salaries expense for seven days of work in January:

Jan. 9	Salaries Payable (3 days at $70 per day)	210	
	Salaries Expense (7 days at $70 per day)	490	
	Cash		700
	Paid two weeks' salary including three days accrued in December.		

Assets	=	Liabilities	+	Equity
−700		−210		−490

The $210 debit reflects the payment of the liability for the three days' salary accrued on December 31. The $490 debit records the salary for January's first seven working days (including the New Year's Day holiday) as an expense of the new accounting period. The $700 credit records the total amount of cash paid to the employee.

Accrued Revenues

The term **accrued revenues** refers to revenues earned in a period that are both unrecorded and not yet received in cash (or other assets). An example is a technician who bills customers only when the job is done. If one-third of a job is complete by the end of a period, then the technician must record one-third of the expected billing as revenue in that period—even though there is no billing or collection. The adjusting entries for accrued revenues increase assets and increase revenues as shown in Exhibit 3.11. Accrued revenues commonly arise from services, products, interest, and rent. We use service fees and interest to show how to adjust for accrued revenues.

Point: Accrued revenues are also called *accrued assets*.

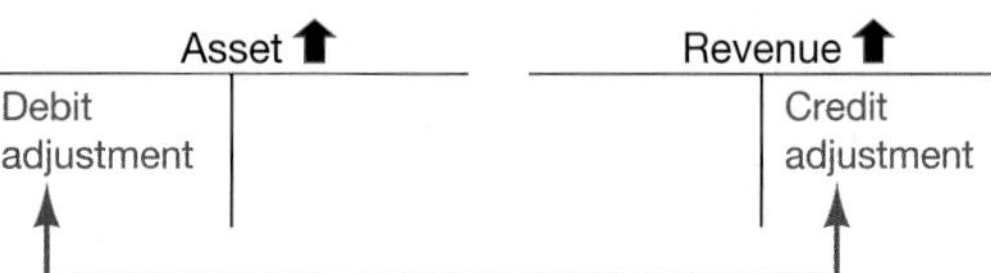

Exhibit 3.11
Adjusting for Accrued Revenues

Accrued Services Revenue Accrued revenues are not recorded until adjusting entries are made at the end of the accounting period. These accrued revenues are earned but unrecorded because either the buyer has not yet paid for them or the seller has not yet billed the buyer. FastForward provides an example. In the second week of December, it agreed to provide 30 days of consulting services to a local sports club for a fixed fee of $2,700. The terms of the initial agreement call for FastForward to provide services from December 12, 2004, through January 10, 2005, or 30 days of service. The club agrees to pay FastForward $2,700 on January 10, 2005, when the service period is complete. At December 31, 2004, 20 days of services have already been provided. Since the contracted services are not yet entirely provided, FastForward has neither billed the club nor recorded the services already provided. Still, FastForward has earned two-thirds of the 30-day fee, or $1,800 ($2,700 × 20/30). The *revenue recognition principle* implies that it must report the $1,800 on the December income statement. The balance sheet also must report that the club owes FastForward $1,800.

The year-end adjusting entry to account for accrued services revenue is

Assets	=	Liabilities	+	Equity
+1,800				+1,800

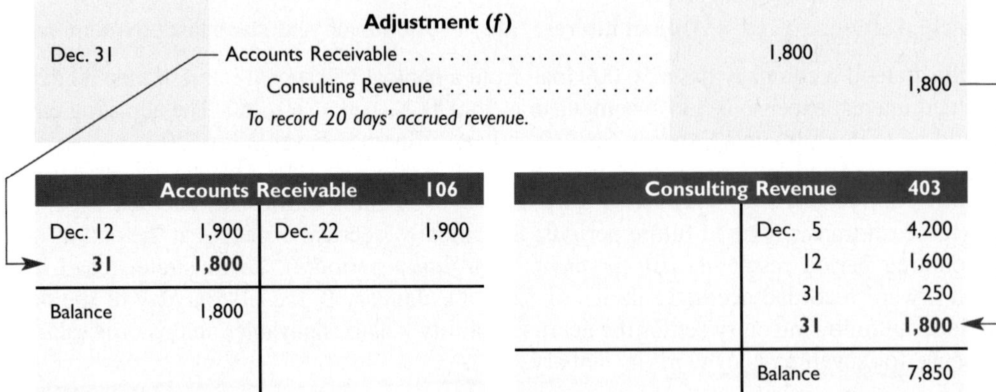

Adjustment (*f*)

Dec. 31	Accounts Receivable	1,800	
	Consulting Revenue		1,800
	To record 20 days' accrued revenue.		

Accounts Receivable			106
Dec. 12	1,900	Dec. 22	1,900
31	**1,800**		
Balance	1,800		

Consulting Revenue			403
		Dec. 5	4,200
		12	1,600
		31	250
		31	**1,800**
		Balance	7,850

Example: What is the adjusting entry if the 30-day consulting period began on December 22? *Answer:* One-third of the fee is earned:
Accounts Receivable . . . 900
Consulting Revenue . . . 900

Accounts receivable are reported on the balance sheet at $1,800, and the $7,850 of consulting revenue is reported on the income statement. *Not* making the adjustment would understate (1) both consulting revenue and net income by $1,800 in the December income statement and (2) both accounts receivable (assets) and equity by $1,800 on the December 31 balance sheet.

Decision Maker

Loan Officer The owner of an electronics store applies for a business loan. The store's financial statements reveal large increases in current-year revenues and income. Analysis shows that these increases are due to a promotion that let consumers buy now and pay nothing until January 1 of next year. The store recorded these sales as accrued revenue. Does your analysis raise any concerns?

Answer—p. 115

Accrued Interest Revenue In addition to the accrued interest expense we described earlier, interest can yield an accrued revenue when a debtor owes money (or other assets) to a company. If a company is holding notes or accounts receivable that produce interest revenue, we must adjust the accounts to record any earned and yet uncollected interest revenue. The adjusting entry is similar to the one for accruing services revenue. Specifically, we debit Interest Receivable (asset) and credit Interest Revenue.

Future Receipt of Accrued Revenues Accrued revenues at the end of one accounting period result in *cash receipts* in a *future* period(s). To illustrate, recall that FastForward made an adjusting entry for $1,800 to record 20 days' accrued revenue earned from its consulting contract. When FastForward receives $2,700 cash on January 10 for the entire contract amount, it makes the following entry to remove the accrued asset (accounts receivable) and recognize the revenue earned in January. The $2,700 debit reflects the cash received. The $1,800 credit reflects the removal of the receivable, and the $900 credit records the revenue earned in January.

Assets	=	Liabilities	+	Equity
+2,700				+900
−1,800				

Jan. 10	Cash	2,700	
	Accounts Receivable (20 days at $90 per day)		1,800
	Consulting Revenue (10 days at $90 per day)		900
	Received cash for the accrued asset and recorded earned consulting revenue.		

Links to Financial Statements

A1 Explain how accounting adjustments link to financial statements.

The process of adjusting accounts is intended to bring an asset or liability account balance to its correct amount. It also updates a related expense or revenue account. These adjustments are necessary for transactions and events that extend over more than one period. (Adjusting entries are posted like any other entry.)

Exhibit 3.12 summarizes the four types of transactions requiring adjustment. Understanding this exhibit is important to understanding the adjusting process and its

	Before Adjusting		
Category	Balance Sheet	Income Statement	Adjusting Entry
Prepaid expenses†	Asset overstated Equity overstated	Expense understated	Dr. Expense Cr. Asset*
Unearned revenues†	Liability overstated Equity understated	Revenue understated	Dr. Liability Cr. Revenue
Accrued expenses	Liability understated Equity overstated	Expense understated	Dr. Expense Cr. Liability
Accrued revenues	Asset understated Equity understated	Revenue understated	Dr. Asset Cr. Revenue

* For depreciation, the credit is to Accumulated Depreciation (contra asset).

† Exhibit assumes that Prepaid Expenses are initially recorded as assets and that Unearned Revenues are initially recorded as liabilities.

Exhibit 3.12

Summary of Adjustments and Financial Statement Links

importance to financial statements. Remember that each adjusting entry affects one or more income statement accounts *and* one or more balance sheet accounts (but not cash).

Information about some adjustments is not always available until several days or even weeks after the period-end. This means that some adjusting and closing entries are recorded later than, but dated as of, the last day of the period. One example is a company that receives a utility bill on January 10 for costs incurred for the month of December. When it receives the bill, the company records the expense and the payable as of December 31. Other examples include long-distance phone usage and costs of many Web billings. The December income statement reflects these additional expenses incurred, and the December 31 balance sheet includes these payables, although the amounts were not actually known on December 31.

Decision Ethics

Financial Officer At year-end, the president instructs you, the financial officer, not to record accrued expenses until next year because they will not be paid until then. The president also directs you to record in current-year sales a recent purchase order from a customer that requires merchandise to be delivered two weeks after the year-end. Your company would report a net income instead of a net loss if you carry out these instructions. What do you do?

Answer—p. 115

Quick Check

6. If an adjusting entry for accrued revenues of $200 at year-end is omitted, what is this error's effect on the year-end income statement and balance sheet?
7. What is a contra account? Explain its purpose.
8. What is an accrued expense? Give an example.
9. Describe how an unearned revenue arises. Give an example.

Answers—p. 115

Adjusted Trial Balance

P2 Explain and prepare an adjusted trial balance.

An **unadjusted trial balance** is a list of accounts and balances prepared *before* adjustments are recorded. An **adjusted trial balance** is a list of accounts and balances prepared *after* adjusting entries have been recorded and posted to the ledger.

Exhibit 3.13 shows both the unadjusted and the adjusted trial balances for FastForward at December 31, 2004. The order of accounts in the trial balance is usually set up to match the order in the chart of accounts. Notice that several new accounts arise from the adjusting entries. Each adjustment is identified by a letter in parentheses that links it to an adjusting entry explained earlier. Each amount in the Adjusted Trial Balance columns is computed by taking that account's amount from the Unadjusted Trial Balance columns and adding or subtracting any adjustment(s). To illustrate, Supplies has a $9,720 Dr. balance in the unadjusted columns. Subtracting the $1,050 Cr. amount shown in the adjustments

Exhibit 3.13

Unadjusted and Adjusted Trial Balances

FASTFORWARD
Trial Balances
December 31, 2004

Acct. No.	Account Title	Unadjusted Trial Balance Dr.	Unadjusted Trial Balance Cr.	Adjustments Dr.	Adjustments Cr.	Adjusted Trial Balance Dr.	Adjusted Trial Balance Cr.
101	Cash	$ 3,950				$ 3,950	
106	Accounts receivable	0		*(f)* $1,800		1,800	
126	Supplies	9,720			*(b)* $1,050	8,670	
128	Prepaid insurance	2,400			*(a)* 100	2,300	
167	Equipment	26,000				26,000	
168	Accumulated depreciation—Equip.		$ 0		*(c)* 375		$ 375
201	Accounts payable		6,200				6,200
209	Salaries payable		0		*(e)* 210		210
236	Unearned consulting revenue		3,000	*(d)* 250			2,750
301	C. Taylor, Capital		30,000				30,000
302	C. Taylor, Withdrawals	600				600	
403	Consulting revenue		5,800		*(d)* 250		7,850
					(f) 1,800		
406	Rental revenue		300				300
612	Depreciation expense—Equip.	0		*(c)* 375		375	
622	Salaries expense	1,400		*(e)* 210		1,610	
637	Insurance expense	0		*(a)* 100		100	
640	Rent expense	1,000				1,000	
652	Supplies expense	0		*(b)* 1,050		1,050	
690	Utilities expense	230				230	
	Totals	$45,300	$45,300	$3,785	$3,785	$47,685	$47,685

columns yields an adjusted $8,670 Dr. balance for Supplies. An account can have more than one adjustment, such as for Consulting Revenue. Also, some accounts might not require adjustment for this period, such as Accounts Payable.

Preparing Financial Statements

P3 Prepare financial statements from an adjusted trial balance.

We can prepare financial statements directly from information in the *adjusted* trial balance. An adjusted trial balance (see the right-most columns in Exhibit 3.13) includes all accounts and balances appearing in financial statements, and is easier to work from than the entire ledger when preparing financial statements.

Exhibit 3.14 shows how revenue and expense balances are transferred from the adjusted trial balance to the income statement (red lines). The net income and the withdrawals amount is then used to prepare the statement of owner's equity (black lines). Asset and liability balances on the adjusted trial balance are then transferred to the balance sheet (blue lines). The ending capital is determined on the statement of owner's equity and transferred to the balance sheet (green lines).

We usually prepare financial statements in the following order: income statement, statement of owner's equity, and balance sheet. This order makes sense since the balance sheet uses information from the statement of owner's equity, which in turn uses information from the income statement. The statement of cash flows is usually the final statement prepared.

Exhibit 3.14

Preparing the Financial Statements (Adjusted Trial Balance from Exhibit 3.13)

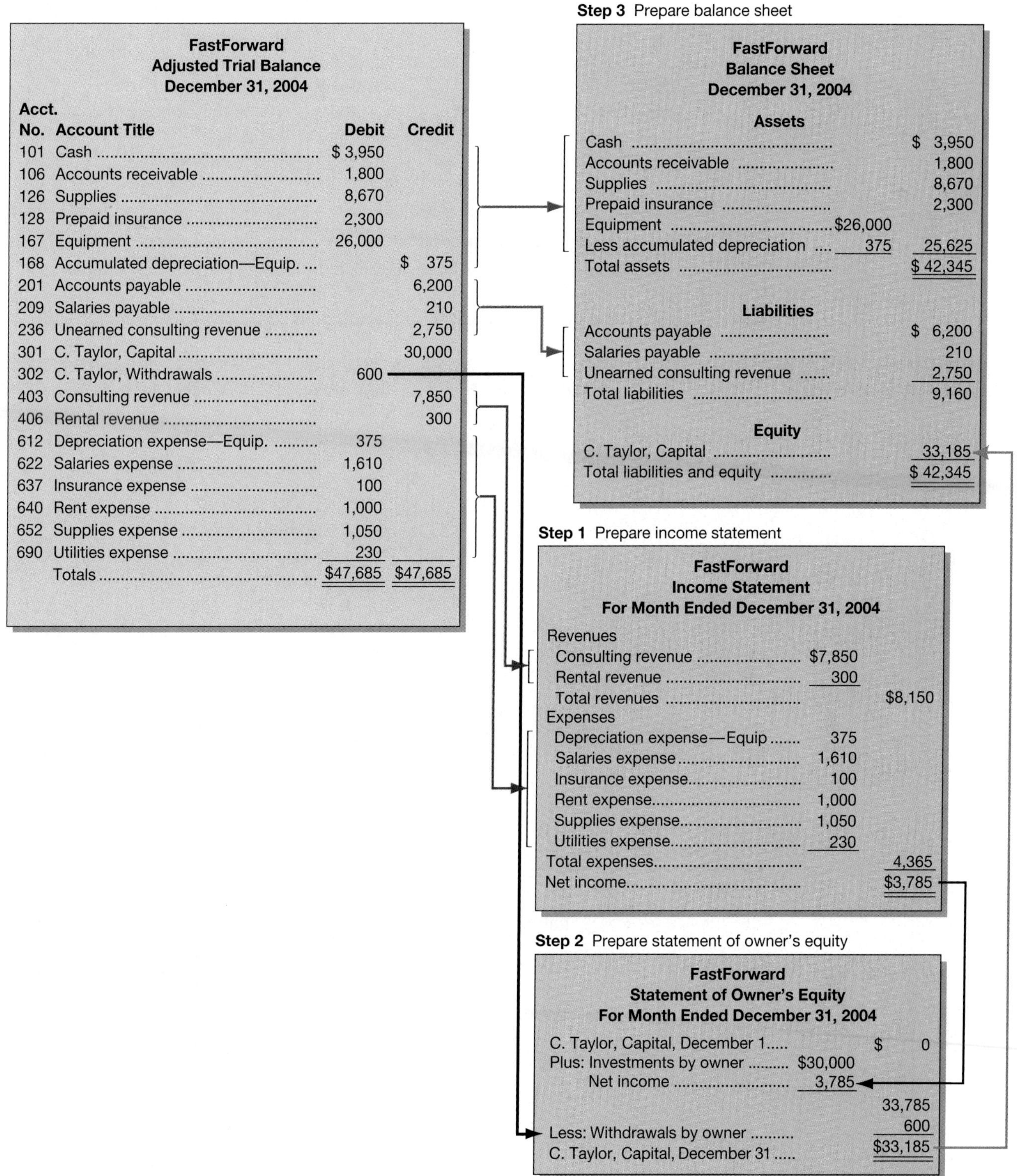

FastForward
Adjusted Trial Balance
December 31, 2004

Acct. No.	Account Title	Debit	Credit
101	Cash	$ 3,950	
106	Accounts receivable	1,800	
126	Supplies	8,670	
128	Prepaid insurance	2,300	
167	Equipment	26,000	
168	Accumulated depreciation—Equip.		$ 375
201	Accounts payable		6,200
209	Salaries payable		210
236	Unearned consulting revenue		2,750
301	C. Taylor, Capital		30,000
302	C. Taylor, Withdrawals	600	
403	Consulting revenue		7,850
406	Rental revenue		300
612	Depreciation expense—Equip.	375	
622	Salaries expense	1,610	
637	Insurance expense	100	
640	Rent expense	1,000	
652	Supplies expense	1,050	
690	Utilities expense	230	
	Totals	$47,685	$47,685

Step 3 Prepare balance sheet

FastForward
Balance Sheet
December 31, 2004

Assets		
Cash		$ 3,950
Accounts receivable		1,800
Supplies		8,670
Prepaid insurance		2,300
Equipment	$26,000	
Less accumulated depreciation	375	25,625
Total assets		$ 42,345
Liabilities		
Accounts payable		$ 6,200
Salaries payable		210
Unearned consulting revenue		2,750
Total liabilities		9,160
Equity		
C. Taylor, Capital		33,185
Total liabilities and equity		$ 42,345

Step 1 Prepare income statement

FastForward
Income Statement
For Month Ended December 31, 2004

Revenues		
Consulting revenue	$7,850	
Rental revenue	300	
Total revenues		$8,150
Expenses		
Depreciation expense—Equip	375	
Salaries expense	1,610	
Insurance expense	100	
Rent expense	1,000	
Supplies expense	1,050	
Utilities expense	230	
Total expenses		4,365
Net income		$3,785

Step 2 Prepare statement of owner's equity

FastForward
Statement of Owner's Equity
For Month Ended December 31, 2004

C. Taylor, Capital, December 1		$ 0
Plus: Investments by owner	$30,000	
Net income	3,785	
		33,785
Less: Withdrawals by owner		600
C. Taylor, Capital, December 31		$33,185

Quick Check

10. Music-Mart records $1,000 of accrued salaries on December 31. Five days later, on January 5 (the next payday), salaries of $7,000 are paid. What is the January 5 entry?

11. Jordan Air has the following information in its unadjusted and adjusted trial balances:

	Unadjusted		Adjusted	
	Debit	Credit	Debit	Credit
Prepaid insurance	$6,200		$5,900	
Salaries payable		$ 0		$1,400

What are the adjusting entries that Jordan Air likely recorded?

12. What accounts are taken from the adjusted trial balance to prepare an income statement?

13. In preparing financial statements from an adjusted trial balance, what statement is usually prepared second?

Answers—p. 115

Decision Analysis — Profit Margin

A2 Compute profit margin and describe its use in analyzing company performance.

A useful measure of a company's operating results is the ratio of its net income to net sales. This ratio is called **profit margin,** or *return on sales,* and is computed as in Exhibit 3.15.

Exhibit 3.15
Profit Margin

$$\textbf{Profit margin} = \frac{\textbf{Net income}}{\textbf{Net sales}}$$

This ratio is interpreted as reflecting the percent of profit in each dollar of sales. To illustrate how we compute and use profit margin, let's look at the results of **Limited Brands, Inc.,** in Exhibit 3.16 for the period 2000–2003.

Exhibit 3.16
Limited Brands's Profit Margin

	2003	2002	2001	2000
Net income (in mil.)	$ 502	$ 519	$ 428	$ 461
Net sales (in mil.)	$8,445	$8,423	$9,080	$8,765
Profit margin	**5.9%**	**6.2%**	**4.7%**	**5.3%**
Industry profit margin	**1.8%**	**1.5%**	**2.5%**	**2.9%**

The Limited's average profit margin is 5.5% during this period. This favorably compares to the average industry profit margin of 2.2%. Moreover, Limited's most recent two years' profit margins are markedly better than earlier years.

Thus, while 2001 was a difficult year for Limited in generating profits on its sales, Limited's performance has slightly improved in 2002–2003. Future success, of course, depends on Limited maintaining and preferably increasing its profit margin.

Demonstration Problem 1

The following information relates to Fanning's Electronics on December 31, 2005. The company, which uses the calendar year as its annual reporting period, initially records prepaid and unearned items in balance sheet accounts (assets and liabilities, respectively).

a. The company's weekly payroll is $8,750, paid each Friday for a five-day workweek. December 31, 2005, falls on a Monday, but the employees will not be paid their wages until Friday, January 4, 2006.

b. Eighteen months earlier, on July 1, 2004, the company purchased equipment that cost $20,000. Its useful life is predicted to be five years, at which time the equipment is expected to be worthless (zero salvage value).

c. On October 1, 2005, the company agreed to work on a new housing development. The company is paid $120,000 on October 1 in advance of future installation of similar alarm systems in 24 new homes. That amount was credited to the Unearned Services Revenue account. Between October 1 and December 31, work on 20 homes was completed.

d. On September 1, 2005, the company purchased a 12-month insurance policy for $1,800. The transaction was recorded with an $1,800 debit to Prepaid Insurance.

e. On December 29, 2005, the company performed a $7,000 service that has not been billed and not recorded as of December 31, 2005.

Required

1. Prepare any necessary adjusting entries on December 31, 2005, in relation to transactions and events *a* through *e*.
2. Prepare T-accounts for the accounts affected by adjusting entries, and post the adjusting entries. Determine the adjusted balances for the Unearned Revenue and the Prepaid Insurance accounts.
3. Complete the following table and determine the amounts and effects of your adjusting entries on the year 2005 income statement and the December 31, 2005, balance sheet. Use up (down) arrows to indicate an increase (decrease) in the Effect columns.

Entry	Amount in the Entry	Effect on Net Income	Effect on Total Assets	Effect on Total Liabilities	Effect on Total Equity

Planning the Solution

- Analyze each situation to determine which accounts need to be updated with an adjustment.
- Calculate the amount of each adjustment and prepare the necessary journal entries.
- Show the amount of each adjustment in the designated accounts, determine the adjusted balance, and identify the balance sheet classification of the account.
- Determine each entry's effect on net income for the year and on total assets, total liabilities, and total equity at the end of the year.

Solution to Demonstration Problem 1

1. Adjusting journal entries.

(*a*) Dec. 31	Wages Expense	1,750	
	Wages Payable		1,750
	To accrue wages for the last day of the year ($8,750 × 1/5).		
(*b*) Dec. 31	Depreciation Expense—Equipment	4,000	
	Accumulated Depreciation—Equipment.		4,000
	To record depreciation expense for the year ($20,000/5 years = $4,000 per year).		
(*c*) Dec. 31	Unearned Services Revenue.	100,000	
	Services Revenue		100,000
	To recognize services revenue earned ($120,000 × 20/24).		

[continued on next page]

[continued from previous page]

(*d*) Dec. 31	Insurance Expense.	600	
	Prepaid Insurance.		600
	To adjust for expired portion of insurance ($1,800 × 4/12).		
(e) Dec. 31	Accounts Receivable	7,000	
	Services Revenue.		7,000
	To record services revenue earned.		

2. T-accounts for adjusting journal entries *a* through *e*.

Wages Expense

(*a*) 1,750	

Wages Payable

	(*a*) 1,750

Depreciation Expense—Equipment

(*b*) 4,000	

Accumulated Depreciation—Equipment

	(*b*) 4,000

Unearned Revenue

	Unadj. Bal. 120,000
(*c*) 100,000	
	Adj. Bal. 20,000

Services Revenue

	(*c*) 100,000
	(*e*) 7,000
	Adj. Bal. 107,000

Insurance Expense

(*d*) 600	

Prepaid Insurance

Unadj. Bal. 1,800	
	(*d*) 600
Adj. Bal. 1,200	

Accounts Receivable

(*e*) 7,000	

3. Financial statement effects of adjusting journal entries.

Entry	Amount in the Entry	Effect on Net Income	Effect on Total Assets	Effect on Total Liabilities	Effect on Total Equity
a	$ 1,750	$ 1,750 ↓	No effect	$ 1,750 ↑	$ 1,750 ↓
b	4,000	4,000 ↓	$4,000 ↓	No effect	4,000 ↓
c	100,000	100,000 ↑	No effect	$100,000 ↓	100,000 ↑
d	600	600 ↓	$ 600 ↓	No effect	600 ↓
e	7,000	7,000 ↑	$7,000 ↑	No effect	7,000 ↑

Demonstration Problem 2

Use the following adjusted trial balance to answer questions 1–3.

CHOI COMPANY
Adjusted Trial Balance
December 31

	Debit	Credit
Cash	$ 3,050	
Accounts receivable	400	
Prepaid insurance	830	
Supplies	80	
Equipment	217,200	

[continued on next page]

[continued from previous page]

Accumulated depreciation—Equipment		$ 29,100
Wages payable		880
Interest payable		3,600
Unearned rent		460
Long-term notes payable		150,000
M. Choi, Capital		40,340
M. Choi, Withdrawals	21,000	
Rent earned		57,500
Wages expense	25,000	
Utilities expense	1,900	
Insurance expense	3,200	
Supplies expense	250	
Depreciation expense—Equipment	5,970	
Interest expense	3,000	
Totals	$281,880	$281,880

1. Prepare the annual income statement from the adjusted trial balance of Choi Company.

Answer:

CHOI COMPANY Income Statement For Year Ended December 31		
Revenues		
Rent earned		$57,500
Expenses		
Wages expense	$25,000	
Utilities expense	1,900	
Insurance expense	3,200	
Supplies expense	250	
Depreciation expense—Equipment	5,970	
Interest expense	3,000	
Total expenses		39,320
Net income		$18,180

2. Prepare a statement of owner's equity from the adjusted trial balance of Choi Company. Choi's capital account balance of $40,340 consists of a $30,340 beginning-year balance, plus a $10,000 owner investment during the current year.

Answer:

CHOI COMPANY Statement of Owner's Equity For Year Ended December 31		
M. Choi, Beginning-year Capital, December 31		$30,340
Plus: Owner investments	$10,000	
Net income	18,180	28,180
		58,520
Less: Withdrawals by owner		21,000
M. Choi, Year-end Capital, December 31		$37,520

3. Prepare a balance sheet from the adjusted trial balance of Choi Company.

Answer:

CHOI COMPANY Balance Sheet December 31		
Assets		
Cash		$ 3,050
Accounts receivable		400
Prepaid insurance		830
Supplies		80
Equipment	$217,200	
Less accumulated depreciation	29,100	188,100
Total assets		$192,460
Liabilities		
Wages payable		$ 880
Interest payable		3,600
Unearned rent		460
Long-term note payable		150,000
Total liabilities		154,940
Equity		
M. Choi, Capital		37,520
Total liabilities and equity		$192,460

APPENDIX

3A Alternative Accounting for Prepayments

This appendix explains an alternative in accounting for prepaid expenses and unearned revenues.

Recording the Prepayment of Expenses in Expense Accounts

P4 Identify and explain alternatives in accounting for prepaids.

An alternative method is to record *all* prepaid expenses with debits to expense accounts. If any prepaids remain unused or unexpired at the end of an accounting period, then adjusting entries must transfer the cost of the unused portions from expense accounts to prepaid expense (asset) accounts. This alternative method is acceptable. The financial statements are identical under either method, but the adjusting entries are different. To illustrate the differences between these two methods, let's look at FastForward's cash payment of December 6 for 24 months of insurance coverage beginning on December 1. FastForward recorded that payment with a debit to an asset account, but it could have recorded a debit to an expense account. These alternatives are shown in Exhibit 3A.1.

Exhibit 3A.1

Alternative Initial Entries for Prepaid Expenses

		Payment Recorded as Asset		Payment Recorded as Expense	
Dec. 6	Prepaid Insurance	2,400			
	Cash		2,400		
Dec. 6	Insurance Expense			2,400	
	Cash				2,400

At the end of its accounting period on December 31, insurance protection for one month has expired. This means $100 ($2,400/24) of insurance coverage expired and is an expense for December. The adjusting entry depends on how the original payment was recorded. This is shown in Exhibit 3A.2.

Exhibit 3A.2

Adjusting Entry for Prepaid Expenses for the Two Alternatives

		Payment Recorded as Asset		Payment Recorded as Expense	
Dec. 31	Insurance Expense	100			
	Prepaid Insurance		100		
Dec. 31	Prepaid Insurance			2,300	
	Insurance Expense				2,300

When these entries are posted to the accounts in the ledger, we can see that these two methods give identical results. The December 31 adjusted account balances in Exhibit 3A.3 show Prepaid Insurance of $2,300 and Insurance Expense of $100 for both methods.

Exhibit 3A.3

Account Balances under Two Alternatives for Recording Prepaid Expenses

Payment Recorded as Asset

Prepaid Insurance			128
Dec. 6	2,400	Dec. 31	100
Balance	**2,300**		

Insurance Expense			637
Dec. 31	**100**		

Payment Recorded as Expense

Prepaid Insurance			128
Dec. 31	**2,300**		

Insurance Expense			637
Dec. 6	2,400	Dec. 31	2,300
Balance	**100**		

Recording the Prepayment of Revenues in Revenue Accounts

As with prepaid expenses, an alternative method is to record *all* unearned revenues with credits to revenue accounts. If any revenues are unearned at the end of an accounting period, then adjusting entries must transfer the unearned portions from revenue accounts to unearned revenue (liability) accounts. This alternative method is acceptable. The adjusting entries are different for these two alternatives, but the financial statements are identical. To illustrate the accounting differences between these two methods, let's look at FastForward's December 26 receipt of $3,000 for consulting services covering the period December 27 to February 24. FastForward recorded this transaction with a credit to a liability account. The alternative is to record it with a credit to a revenue account, as shown in Exhibit 3A.4.

Exhibit 3A.4

Alternative Initial Entries for Unearned Revenues

		Receipt Recorded as Liability		Receipt Recorded as Revenue	
Dec. 26	Cash	3,000			
	Unearned Consulting Revenue		3,000		
Dec. 26	Cash			3,000	
	Consulting Revenue				3,000

By the end of its accounting period on December 31, FastForward has earned $250 of this revenue. This means $250 of the liability has been satisfied. Depending on how the initial receipt is recorded, the adjusting entry is as shown in Exhibit 3A.5.

Exhibit 3A.5

Adjusting Entry for Unearned Revenues for the Two Alternatives

		Receipt Recorded as Liability		Receipt Recorded as Revenue	
Dec. 31	Unearned Consulting Revenue	250			
	Consulting Revenue		250		
Dec. 31	Consulting Revenue			2,750	
	Unearned Consulting Revenue				2,750

After adjusting entries are posted, the two alternatives give identical results. The December 31 adjusted account balances in Exhibit 3A.6 show unearned consulting revenue of $2,750 and consulting revenue of $250 for both methods.

Exhibit 3A.6

Account Balances under Two Alternatives for Recording Unearned Revenues

Receipt Recorded as Liability

Unearned Consulting Revenue			236
Dec. 31	250	Dec. 26	3,000
		Balance	**2,750**

Consulting Revenue			403
		Dec. 31	**250**

Receipt Recorded as Revenue

Unearned Consulting Revenue			236
		Dec. 31	**2,750**

Consulting Revenue			403
Dec. 31	2,750	Dec. 26	3,000
		Balance	**250**

Summary

C1 Explain the importance of periodic reporting and the time period principle. The value of information is often linked to its timeliness. To provide timely information, accounting systems prepare periodic reports at regular intervals. The time period principle assumes that an organization's activities can be divided into specific time periods for periodic reporting.

C2 Explain accrual accounting and how it makes financial statements more useful. Accrual accounting recognizes revenue when earned and expenses when incurred—not necessarily when cash inflows and outflows occur. This information is valuable in assessing a company's financial position and performance.

C3 Identify the types of adjustments and their purpose. Adjustments can be grouped according to the timing of cash receipts and cash payments relative to when they are recognized as revenues or expenses as follows: prepaid expenses, unearned revenues, accrued expenses, and accrued revenues. Adjusting entries are necessary so that revenues, expenses, assets, and liabilities are correctly reported.

A1 Explain how accounting adjustments link to financial statements. Accounting adjustments bring an asset or liability account balance to its correct amount. They also update related expense or revenue accounts. Every adjusting entry affects one or more income statement accounts *and* one or more balance sheet accounts. An adjusting entry never affects cash.

A2 Compute profit margin and describe its use in analyzing company performance. *Profit margin* is defined as the reporting period's net income divided by its net sales. Profit margin reflects on a company's earnings activities by showing how much income is in each dollar of sales.

P1 Prepare and explain adjusting entries. *Prepaid expenses* refer to items paid for in advance of receiving their benefits. Prepaid expenses are assets. Adjusting entries for prepaids involve increasing (debiting) expenses and decreasing (crediting) assets. *Unearned* (or *prepaid*) *revenues* refer to cash received in advance of providing products and services. Unearned revenues are liabilities. Adjusting entries for unearned revenues involves increasing (crediting) revenues and decreasing (debiting) unearned revenues. *Accrued expenses* refer to costs incurred in a period that are both unpaid and unrecorded. Adjusting entries for recording accrued expenses involve increasing (debiting) expenses and increasing (crediting) liabilities. *Accrued revenues* refer to revenues earned in a period that are both unrecorded and not yet received in cash. Adjusting entries for recording accrued revenues involve increasing (debiting) assets and increasing (crediting) revenues.

P2 Explain and prepare an adjusted trial balance. An adjusted trial balance is a list of accounts and balances prepared after recording and posting adjusting entries. Financial statements are often prepared from the adjusted trial balance.

P3 Prepare financial statements from an adjusted trial balance. Revenue and expense balances are reported on the income statement. Asset, liability, and equity balances are reported on the balance sheet. We usually prepare statements in the following order: income statement, statement of owner's equity, balance sheet, and statement of cash flows.

P4^A Identify and explain alternatives in accounting for prepaids. Charging all prepaid expenses to expense accounts when they are purchased is acceptable. When this is done, adjusting entries must transfer any unexpired amounts from expense accounts to asset accounts. Crediting all unearned revenues to revenue accounts when cash is received is also acceptable. In this case, the adjusting entries must transfer any unearned amounts from revenue accounts to unearned revenue accounts.

Guidance Answers to **Decision Maker** and **Decision Ethics**

Investor Prepaid expenses are items paid for in advance of receiving their benefits. They are assets and are expensed as they are used up. The publishing company's treatment of the signing bonus is acceptable provided future book sales can at least match the $500,000 expense. As an investor, you are concerned about the risk of future book sales. The riskier the likelihood of future book sales is, the more likely your analysis is to treat the $500,000, or a portion of it, as an expense, not a prepaid expense (asset).

Entrepreneur Depreciation is a process of cost allocation, not asset valuation. Knowing the depreciation schedule is not especially useful in your estimation of what the building and equipment are currently worth. Your own assessment of the age, quality, and usefulness of the building and equipment is more important.

Loan Officer Your concern in lending to this store arises from analysis of current-year sales. While increased revenues and income are fine, your concern is with collectibility of these promotional sales. If the owner sold products to customers with poor records of paying bills, then collectibility of these sales is low. Your analysis must assess this possibility and recognize any expected losses.

Financial Officer Omitting accrued expenses and recognizing revenue early can mislead financial statement users. One action is to request a second meeting with the president so you can explain that accruing expenses when incurred and recognizing revenue when earned are required practices. If the president persists, you might discuss the situation with legal counsel and any auditors involved. Your ethical action might cost you this job, but the potential pitfalls for falsification of statements, reputation loss, personal integrity, and other costs are too great.

Guidance Answers to **Quick Checks**

1. An annual reporting (or accounting) period covers one year and refers to the preparation of annual financial statements. The annual reporting period is not always a calendar year that ends on December 31. An organization can adopt a fiscal year consisting of any consecutive 12 months or 52 weeks.
2. Interim financial statements (covering less than one year) are prepared to provide timely information to decision makers.
3. The revenue recognition principle and the matching principle lead most directly to the adjusting process.
4. No. Cash basis accounting is not consistent with the matching principle because it reports expenses when paid, not in the period when revenue is earned as a result of those expenses.
5. No expense is reported in 2005. Under cash basis accounting, the entire $4,800 is reported as an expense in April 2004 when the premium is paid.
6. If the accrued revenues adjustment of $200 is not made, then both revenues and net income are understated by $200 on the current year's income statement, and both assets and equity are understated by $200 on the balance sheet.
7. A contra account is an account that is subtracted from the balance of a related account. Use of a contra account provides more information than simply reporting a net amount.
8. An accrued expense is a cost incurred in a period that is both unpaid and unrecorded prior to adjusting entries. One example is salaries earned but not yet paid at period-end.
9. An unearned revenue arises when a firm receives cash (or other assets) from a customer before providing the services or products to the customer. A magazine subscription paid in advance is one example; season ticket sales is another.
10.

Salaries Payable	1,000	
Salaries Expense	6,000	
Cash		7,000
Paid salary including accrual from December.		

11. The probable adjusting entries of Jordan Air are:

Insurance Expense	300	
Prepaid Insurance		300
To record insurance expired.		
Salaries Expense	1,400	
Salaries Payable		1,400
To record accrued salaries.		

12. Revenue accounts and expense accounts.
13. Statement of owner's equity.

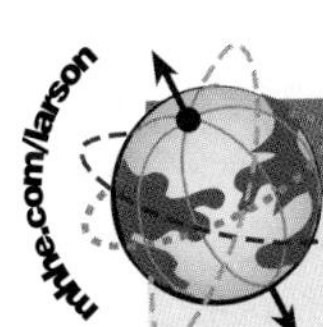

Key Terms

Key Terms are available at the book's Website for learning and testing in an online Flashcard Format.

Accounting period (p. 94)
Accrual basis accounting (p. 95)
Accrued expenses (p. 101)
Accrued revenues (p. 103)
Adjusted trial balance (p. 105)
Adjusting entry (p. 97)
Annual financial statements (p. 95)
Book value (p. 100)
Cash basis accounting (p. 95)
Contra account (p. 99)
Depreciation (p. 99)
Fiscal year (p. 95)
Interim financial statements (p. 95)
Matching principle (p. 96)
Natural business year (p. 95)
Plant assets (p. 99)
Prepaid expenses (p. 97)
Profit margin (p. 108)
Straight-line depreciation method (p. 99)
Time period principle (p. 94)
Unadjusted trial balance (p. 105)
Unearned revenues (p. 100)

Personal Interactive Quiz

Personal Interactive Quizzes A and B are available at the book's Website to reinforce and assess your learning.

Superscript letter A denotes assignments based on Appendix 3A.

Discussion Questions

1. What is the difference between the cash basis and the accrual basis of accounting?
2. Why is the accrual basis of accounting generally preferred over the cash basis?
3. What type of business is most likely to select a fiscal year that corresponds to its natural business year instead of the calendar year?
4. Where is a prepaid expense reported in the financial statements?
5. What type of asset(s) requires adjusting entries to record depreciation?
6. What contra account is used when recording and reporting the effects of depreciation? Why is it used?
7. Where is unearned revenue reported in financial statements?
8. What is an accrued revenue? Give an example.
9. [A] If a company initially records prepaid expenses with debits to expense accounts, what type of account is debited in the adjusting entries for those prepaid expenses?
10. Review the balance sheet of **Krispy Kreme** in Appendix A. Identify two asset accounts that require adjustment before annual financial statements can be prepared. What would be the effect on the income statement if these two asset accounts were not adjusted?
11. Review the balance sheet of **Tastykake** in Appendix A. In addition to Prepayments, identify two accounts (either assets or liabilities) requiring adjusting entries.
12. Refer to **Harley-Davidson**'s balance sheet in Appendix A. If it made an adjustment for unpaid wages at year-end, where would the Accrued Wages Expense be reported on its balance sheet?

Red numbers denote Discussion Questions that involve decision-making.

***Homework Manager** repeats all numerical Quick Study assignments on the book's Website with new numbers each time they are worked. It can be used in practice, homework, or exam mode.*

QUICK STUDY

QS 3-1
Identifying accounting adjustments
C3

Classify the following adjusting entries as involving prepaid expenses (PE), unearned revenues (UR), accrued expenses (AE), or accrued revenues (AR).

a. ______ To record revenue earned that was previously received as cash in advance.
b. ______ To record annual depreciation expense.
c. ______ To record wages expense incurred but not yet paid (nor recorded).
d. ______ To record revenue earned but not yet billed (nor recorded).
e. ______ To record expiration of prepaid insurance.

QS 3-2
Adjusting prepaid expenses
P1

a. On July 1, 2005, Beyonce Company paid $1,800 for six months of insurance coverage. No adjustments have been made to the Prepaid Insurance account, and it is now December 31, 2005. Prepare the journal entry to reflect expiration of the insurance as of December 31, 2005.

b. Tyrell Company has a Supplies account balance of $1,000 on January 1, 2005. During 2005, it purchased $3,000 of supplies. As of December 31, 2005, a supplies inventory shows $1,300 of supplies available. Prepare the adjusting journal entry to correctly report the balance of the Supplies account and the Supplies Expense account as of December 31, 2005.

QS 3-3
Adjusting for depreciation
P1

a. Carlos Company purchases $30,000 of equipment on January 1, 2005. The equipment is expected to last five years and be worth $5,000 at the end of that time. Prepare the entry to record one year's depreciation expense for the equipment as of December 31, 2005.

b. Chavez Company purchases $40,000 of land on January 1, 2005. The land is expected to last indefinitely. What depreciation adjustment, if any, should be made with respect to the Land account as of December 31, 2005?

QS 3-4
Adjusting for unearned revenues
A1 P1

a. Eager receives $20,000 cash in advance for 4 months of legal services on October 1, 2005, and records it by debiting Cash and crediting Unearned Revenue both for $20,000. It is now December 31, 2005, and Eager has provided legal services as planned. What adjusting entry should Eager make to account for the work performed from October 1 through December 31, 2005?

b. S. Morford started a new publication called *Contest News*. Her subscribers pay $48 to receive 12 issues. With every new subscriber, Morford debits Cash and credits Unearned Subscription Revenue for the amounts received. Morford has 100 new subscribers as of July 1, 2005. She sends *Contest News* to each of these subscribers every month from July through December. Assuming no changes in subscribers, prepare the journal entry that Morford must make as of December 31, 2005, to adjust the Subscription Revenue account and the Unearned Subscription Revenue account.

QS 3-5
Accruing salaries
A1 P1

Matia Mouder employs one college student every summer in her coffee shop. The student works the five weekdays and is paid on the following Monday. (For example, a student who works Monday through Friday, June 1 through June 5, is paid for that work on Monday, June 8.) Mouder adjusts her books monthly, if needed, to show salaries earned but unpaid at month-end. The student works the last week of July—Friday is August 1. If the student earns $100 per day, what adjusting entry must Mouder make on July 31 to correctly record accrued salaries expense for July?

QS 3-6
Recording and analyzing adjusting entries
A1

Adjusting entries affect at least one balance sheet account and at least one income statement account. For the following entries, identify the account to be debited and the account to be credited. Indicate which of the accounts is the income statement account and which is the balance sheet account.

a. Entry to record revenue earned that was previously received as cash in advance.
b. Entry to record annual depreciation expense.
c. Entry to record wage expenses incurred but not yet paid (nor recorded).
d. Entry to record revenue earned but not yet billed (nor recorded).
e. Entry to record expiration of prepaid insurance.

QS 3-7
Preparing adjusting entries
C3 P1

During the year, Lola Co. recorded prepayments of expenses in asset accounts, and cash receipts of unearned revenues in liability accounts. At the end of its annual accounting period, the company must make three adjusting entries: (1) accrue salaries expense, (2) adjust the Unearned Services Revenue account to recognize earned revenue, and (3) record services revenue earned for which cash will be received the following period. For each of these adjusting entries (1), (2), and (3), indicate the account from *a* through *g* to be debited and the account to be credited.

a. Accounts Receivable
b. Prepaid Salaries
c. Cash
d. Salaries Payable
e. Unearned Services Revenue
f. Salaries Expense
g. Services Revenue

QS 3-8
Interpreting adjusting entries
C2 P2

The following information is taken from Cruz Company's unadjusted and adjusted trial balances:

	Unadjusted		Adjusted	
	Debit	Credit	Debit	Credit
Prepaid insurance	$4,100		$3,700	
Interest payable		$ 0		$800

Given this information, which of the following is likely included among its adjusting entries?

a. A $400 credit to Prepaid Insurance and an $800 debit to Interest Payable.
b. A $400 debit to Insurance Expense and an $800 debit to Interest Payable.
c. A $400 debit to Insurance Expense and an $800 debit to Interest Expense.

QS 3-9
Computing accrual and cash income
C1 C2

In its first year of operations, Harden Co. earned $39,000 in revenues and received $33,000 cash from these customers. The company incurred expenses of $22,500 but had not paid $2,250 of them at year-end. Harden also prepaid $3,750 cash for expenses that would be incurred the next year. Calculate the first year's net income under both the cash basis and the accrual basis of accounting.

QS 3-10
Determining effects of adjusting entries
C3 A1 

In making adjusting entries at the end of its accounting period, Gomez Consulting failed to record $1,600 of insurance coverage that had expired. This $1,600 cost had been initially debited to the Prepaid Insurance account. The company also failed to record accrued salaries expense of $1,000. As a result of these two oversights, the financial statements for the reporting period will [choose one] (1) understate assets by $1,600; (2) understate expenses by $2,600; (3) understate net income by $1,000; or (4) overstate liabilities by $1,000.

QS 3-11
Analyzing profit margin
A2 

Yang Company reported net income of $37,925 and net sales of $390,000 for the current year. Calculate Yang's profit margin and interpret the result. Assume that Yang's competitors' average profit margin is 15%.

QS 3-12[A]
Preparing adjusting entries
C3 P4

Diego Consulting initially records prepaid and unearned items in income statement accounts. Given Diego Consulting's accounting practices, which of the following applies to the preparation of adjusting entries at the end of its first accounting period?

a. Earned but unbilled (and unrecorded) consulting fees are recorded with a debit to Unearned Consulting Fees and a credit to Consulting Fees Earned.

b. Unpaid salaries are recorded with a debit to Prepaid Salaries and a credit to Salaries Expense.

c. The cost of unused office supplies is recorded with a debit to Supplies Expense and a credit to Office Supplies.

d. Unearned fees (on which cash was received in advance earlier in the period) are recorded with a debit to Consulting Fees Earned and a credit to Unearned Consulting Fees.

Homework Manager *repeats all numerical Exercises on the book's Website with new numbers each time they are worked. It can be used in practice, homework, or exam mode.*

EXERCISES

Exercise 3-1
Classifying adjusting entries
C3

In the blank space beside each adjusting entry, enter the letter of the explanation *A* through *F* that most closely describes the entry:

A. To record this period's depreciation expense.

B. To record accrued salaries expense.

C. To record this period's use of a prepaid expense.

D. To record accrued interest revenue.

E. To record accrued interest expense.

F. To record the earning of previously unearned income.

		Account	Debit	Credit
_____	1.	Salaries Expense	13,280	
		Salaries Payable		13,280
_____	2.	Interest Expense	2,208	
		Interest Payable		2,208
_____	3.	Insurance Expense	3,180	
		Prepaid Insurance		3,180
_____	4.	Unearned Professional Fees	19,250	
		Professional Fees Earned		19,250
_____	5.	Interest Receivable	3,300	
		Interest Revenue		3,300
_____	6.	Depreciation Expense	38,217	
		Accumulated Depreciation		38,217

Exercise 3-2
Preparing adjusting entries
P1

For each of the following separate cases, prepare adjusting entries required for financial statements for the year ended (or date of) December 31, 2005. (Assume that prepaid expenses are initially recorded in asset accounts and that fees collected in advance of work are initially recorded as liabilities.)

a. One-third of the work related to $30,000 cash received in advance is performed this period.

b. Wages of $9,000 are earned by workers but not paid as of December 31, 2005.

c. Depreciation on the company's equipment for 2005 is $19,127.

d. The Office Supplies account had a $480 debit balance on December 31, 2004. During 2005, $5,349 of office supplies is purchased. A physical count of supplies at December 31, 2005, shows $587 of supplies available.

e. The Prepaid Insurance account had a $5,000 balance on December 31, 2004. An analysis of insurance policies shows that $2,200 of unexpired insurance benefits remain at December 31, 2005.

f. The company has earned (but not recorded) $750 of interest from investments in CDs for the year ended December 31, 2005. The interest revenue will be received on January 10, 2006.

g. The company has a bank loan and has incurred (but not recorded) interest expenses of $3,500 for the year ended December 31, 2005. The company must pay the interest on January 2, 2006.

Check (e) Dr. Insurance Expense, $2,800; (*f*) Cr. Interest Revenue, $750

Exercise 3-3
Preparing adjusting entries
P1

Prepare adjusting journal entries for the year ended (or date of) December 31, 2005, for each of these separate situations. Assume that prepaid expenses are initially recorded in asset accounts. Also assume that fees collected in advance of work are initially recorded as liabilities.

a. Depreciation on the company's equipment for 2005 is computed to be $16,000.

b. The Prepaid Insurance account had a $7,000 debit balance at December 31, 2005, before adjusting for the costs of any expired coverage. An analysis of the company's insurance policies showed that $1,040 of unexpired insurance coverage remains.

c. The Office Supplies account had a $300 debit balance on December 31, 2004; and $2,680 of office supplies was purchased during the year. The December 31, 2005, physical count showed $354 of supplies available.

d. One-half of the work related to $10,000 cash received in advance was performed this period.

e. The Prepaid Insurance account had a $5,600 debit balance at December 31, 2005, before adjusting for the costs of any expired coverage. An analysis of insurance policies showed that $4,600 of coverage had expired.

f. Wage expenses of $4,000 have been incurred but are not paid as of December 31, 2005.

Check (c) Dr. Office Supplies Expense, $2,626; (e) Dr. Insurance Expense, $4,600

Exercise 3-4
Adjusting and paying accrued wages
C1 P1

Pablo Management has five part-time employees, each of whom earns $100 per day. They are normally paid on Fridays for work completed Monday through Friday of the same week. They were paid in full on Friday, December 28, 2005. The next week, the five employees worked only four days because New Year's Day was an unpaid holiday. Show (*a*) the adjusting entry that would be recorded on Monday, December 31, 2005, and (*b*) the journal entry that would be made to record payment of the employees' wages on Friday, January 4, 2006.

Exercise 3-5
Determining cost flows through accounts
C1 A1 P1

Determine the missing amounts in each of these four separate situations *a* through *d*:

	a	b	c	d
Supplies available—prior year-end	$ 300	$1,600	$1,360	?
Supplies purchased during the current year	2,100	5,400	?	$6,000
Supplies available—current year-end	750	?	1,840	800
Supplies expense for the current year	?	1,300	9,600	6,575

Exercise 3-6
Adjusting and paying accrued expenses
A1 P1

The following three separate situations require adjusting journal entries to prepare financial statements as of April 30. For each situation, present both the April 30 adjusting entry and the subsequent entry during May to record the payment of the accrued expenses.

a. On April 1, the company retained an attorney at a flat monthly fee of $2,500. This amount is payable on the 12th of the following month.

b. A $780,000 note payable requires 9.6% annual interest, or $6,240 to be paid at the end of each 30 days. The interest was last paid on April 20 and the next payment is due on May 20. As of April 30, $2,080 of interest has accrued.

c. Total weekly salaries expense for all employees is $9,000. This amount is paid at the end of the day on Friday of each five-day workweek. April 30 falls on Tuesday of this year, which means that the employees had worked two days since the last payday. The next payday is May 3.

Check (*b*) May 20 Dr. Interest Expense, $4,160

Exercise 3-7
Determining assets and expenses for accrual and cash accounting
C2

On March 1, 2003, a company paid a $16,200 premium on a 36-month insurance policy for coverage beginning on that date. Refer to that policy and fill in the blanks in the following table:

Balance Sheet Insurance Asset Using			Insurance Expense Using		
	Accrual Basis	Cash Basis		Accrual Basis	Cash Basis
Dec. 31, 2003	$_____	$_____	2003	$_____	$_____
Dec. 31, 2004	_____	_____	2004	_____	_____
Dec. 31, 2005	_____	_____	2005	_____	_____
Dec. 31, 2006	_____	_____	2006	_____	_____
			Total	$_____	$_____

Check 2005 insurance expense: Accrual, $5,400; Cash, $0. Dec. 31, 2005, asset: Accrual, $900; Cash, $0.

Exercise 3-8
Analyzing and preparing adjusting entries
A1 P1 P3

Following are two income statements for Kendis Co. for the year ended December 31. The left column is prepared before any adjusting entries are recorded, and the right column includes the effects of adjusting entries. The company records cash receipts and payments related to unearned and prepaid items in balance sheet accounts. Analyze the statements and prepare the eight adjusting entries that likely were recorded. (*Note:* 30% of the $6,000 adjustment for Fees Earned has been earned but not billed, and the other 70% has been earned by performing services that were paid for in advance.)

KENDIS CO.
Income Statements
For Year Ended December 31

	Unadjusted	Adjusted
Revenues		
Fees earned	$24,000	$30,000
Commissions earned	42,500	42,500
Total revenues	66,500	72,500
Expenses		
Depreciation expense—Computers	0	1,500
Depreciation expense—Office furniture	0	1,750
Salaries expense	12,500	14,950
Insurance expense	0	1,300
Rent expense	4,500	4,500
Office supplies expense	0	480
Advertising expense	3,000	3,000
Utilities expense	1,250	1,320
Total expenses	21,250	28,800
Net income	$45,250	$43,700

Exercise 3-9
Computing and interpreting profit margin
A2 

Use the following information to compute profit margin for each separate company *a* through *e*:

	Net Income	Net Sales		Net Income	Net Sales
a.	$ 5,390	$ 44,830	**d.**	$55,234	$1,458,999
b.	87,644	398,954	**e.**	70,158	435,925
c.	93,385	257,082			

Which of the five companies is the most profitable according to the profit margin ratio? Interpret that company's profit margin ratio.

Exercise 3-10^A
Adjusting for prepaids recorded as expenses and unearned revenues recorded as revenues
P4

On-The-Mark Construction began operations on December 1. In setting up its accounting procedures, the company decided to debit expense accounts when it prepays its expenses and to credit revenue accounts when customers pay for services in advance. Prepare journal entries for items *a* through *d* and the adjusting entries as of its December 31 period-end for items *e* through *g*.

a. Supplies are purchased on December 1 for $3,000 cash.

b. The company prepaid its insurance premiums for $1,440 cash on December 2.

c. On December 15, the company receives an advance payment of $12,000 cash from a customer for remodeling work.

d. On December 28, the company receives $3,600 cash from another customer for remodeling work to be performed in January.

e. A physical count on December 31 indicates that On-The-Mark has $1,920 of supplies available.

f. An analysis of the insurance policies in effect on December 31 shows that $240 of insurance coverage had expired.

g. As of December 31, only one remodeling project has been worked on and completed. The $6,300 fee for this project had been received in advance.

Check (*f*) Cr. Insurance Expense, $1,200; (*g*) Dr. Remodeling Fees Earned, $9,300

Exercise 3-11A
Recording and reporting revenues received in advance
P4

Cosmo Company experienced the following events and transactions during July:

July	1	Received $2,000 cash in advance of performing work for Jill Dwyer.
	6	Received $8,400 cash in advance of performing work for Lisa Poe.
	12	Completed the job for Dwyer.
	18	Received $7,500 cash in advance of performing work for Vern Hillsman.
	27	Completed the job for Poe.
	31	None of the work for Hillsman has been performed.

a. Prepare journal entries (including any adjusting entries as of the end of the month) to record these events using the procedure of initially crediting the Unearned Fees account when payment is received from a customer in advance of performing services.

b. Prepare journal entries (including any adjusting entries as of the end of the month) to record these events using the procedure of initially crediting the Fees Earned account when payment is received from a customer in advance of performing services.

c. Under each method, determine the amount of earned fees reported on the income statement for July and the amount of unearned fees reported on the balance sheet as of July 31.

Check (c) Fees Earned, $10,400

PROBLEM SET A

Problem 3-1A
Identifying adjusting entries with explanations
C3 P1

For each of the following entries, enter the letter of the explanation that most closely describes it in the space beside each entry. (You can use letters more than once.)

A. To record receipt of unearned revenue.
B. To record this period's earning of prior unearned revenue.
C. To record payment of an accrued expense.
D. To record receipt of an accrued revenue.
E. To record an accrued expense.
F. To record an accrued revenue.
G. To record this period's use of a prepaid expense.
H. To record payment of a prepaid expense.
I. To record this period's depreciation expense.

______	1.	Rent Expense	2,000	
		Prepaid Rent		2,000
______	2.	Interest Expense	1,000	
		Interest Payable		1,000
______	3.	Depreciation Expense	4,000	
		Accumulated Depreciation		4,000
______	4.	Unearned Professional Fees	3,000	
		Professional Fees Earned		3,000
______	5.	Insurance Expense	4,200	
		Prepaid Insurance		4,200
______	6.	Salaries Payable	1,400	
		Cash		1,400
______	7.	Prepaid Rent	4,500	
		Cash		4,500
______	8.	Salaries Expense	6,000	
		Salaries Payable		6,000
______	9.	Interest Receivable	5,000	
		Interest Revenue		5,000
______	10.	Cash	9,000	
		Accounts Receivable (from consulting)		9,000
______	11.	Cash	7,500	
		Unearned Professional Fees		7,500
______	12.	Cash	2,000	
		Interest Receivable		2,000

Problem 3-2A
Preparing adjusting and subsequent journal entries

C1 A1 P1

Maja Co. follows the practice of recording prepaid expenses and unearned revenues in balance sheet accounts. Maja's annual accounting period ends on December 31, 2005. The following information concerns the adjusting entries to be recorded as of that date:

a. The Office Supplies account started the year with a $3,000 balance. During 2005, the company purchased supplies for $12,400, which was added to the Office Supplies account. The inventory of supplies available at December 31, 2005, totaled $2,640.

b. An analysis of the company's insurance policies provided these facts:

Policy	Date of Purchase	Months of Coverage	Cost
A	April 1, 2004	24	$15,840
B	April 1, 2005	36	13,068
C	August 1, 2005	12	2,700

The total premium for each policy was paid in full (for all months) at the purchase date, and the Prepaid Insurance account was debited for the full cost. (Note that year-end adjusting entries for Prepaid Insurance were properly recorded in all prior years.)

c. The company has 15 employees, who earn a total of $2,100 in salaries each working day. They are paid each Monday for their work in the five-day workweek ending on the previous Friday. Assume that December 31, 2005, is a Tuesday, and all 15 employees worked the first two days of that week. Because New Year's Day is a paid holiday, they will be paid salaries for five full days on Monday, January 6, 2006.

d. The company purchased a building on January 1, 2005. It cost $855,000 and is expected to have a $45,000 salvage value at the end of its predicted 30-year life.

e. Since the company is not large enough to occupy the entire building it owns, it rented space to a tenant at $2,400 per month, starting on November 1, 2005. The rent was paid on time on November 1, and the amount received was credited to the Rent Earned account. However, the tenant has not paid the December rent. The company has worked out an agreement with the tenant, who has promised to pay both December and January rent in full on January 15. The tenant has agreed not to fall behind again.

f. On November 1, the company rented space to another tenant for $2,175 per month. The tenant paid five months' rent in advance on that date. The payment was recorded with a credit to the Unearned Rent account.

Required

1. Use the information to prepare adjusting entries as of December 31, 2005.

2. Prepare journal entries to record the first subsequent cash transaction in 2006 for parts *c* and *e*.

Check (1*b*) Dr. Insurance Expense, $12,312 (1*d*) Dr. Depreciation Expense, $27,000

Problem 3-3A
Preparing adjusting entries, adjusted trial balance, and financial statements

A1 P1 P2 P3

mhhe.com/larson

Watson Technical Institute (WTI), a school owned by Tom Watson, provides training to individuals who pay tuition directly to the school. WTI also offers training to groups in off-site locations. Its unadjusted trial balance as of December 31, 2005, follows. WTI initially records prepaid expenses and unearned revenues in balance sheet accounts. Descriptions of items *a* through *h* that require adjusting entries on December 31, 2005, follow.

Additional Information Items

a. An analysis of the school's insurance policies shows that $3,000 of coverage has expired.

b. An inventory count shows that teaching supplies costing $2,600 are available at year-end 2005.

c. Annual depreciation on the equipment is $12,000.

d. Annual depreciation on the professional library is $6,000.

e. On November 1, the school agreed to do a special six-month course (starting immediately) for a client. The contract calls for a monthly fee of $2,200, and the client paid the first five months' fees in advance. When the cash was received, the Unearned Training Fees account was credited. The fee for the sixth month will be recorded when it is collected in 2006.

f. On October 15, the school agreed to teach a four-month class (beginning immediately) for an individual for $3,000 tuition per month payable at the end of the class. The services are being provided as agreed, and no payment has yet been received.

g. The school's two employees are paid weekly. As of the end of the year, two days' wages have accrued at the rate of $100 per day for each employee.

h. The balance in the Prepaid Rent account represents rent for December.

WATSON TECHNICAL INSTITUTE
Unadjusted Trial Balance
December 31, 2005

	Debit	Credit
Cash	$ 26,000	
Accounts receivable	0	
Teaching supplies	10,000	
Prepaid insurance	15,000	
Prepaid rent	2,000	
Professional library	30,000	
Accumulated depreciation—Professional library		$ 9,000
Equipment	70,000	
Accumulated depreciation—Equipment		16,000
Accounts payable		36,000
Salaries payable		0
Unearned training fees		11,000
T. Watson, Capital		63,600
T. Watson, Withdrawals	40,000	
Tuition fees earned		102,000
Training fees earned		38,000
Depreciation expense—Professional library	0	
Depreciation expense—Equipment	0	
Salaries expense	48,000	
Insurance expense	0	
Rent expense	22,000	
Teaching supplies expense	0	
Advertising expense	7,000	
Utilities expense	5,600	
Totals	$ 275,600	$ 275,600

Required

1. Prepare T-accounts (representing the ledger) with balances from the unadjusted trial balance.

2. Prepare the necessary adjusting journal entries for items *a* through *h* and post them to the T-accounts. Assume that adjusting entries are made only at year-end.

3. Update balances in the T-accounts for the adjusting entries and prepare an adjusted trial balance.

4. Prepare Watson Technical Institute's income statement and statement of owner's equity for the year 2005 and prepare its balance sheet as of December 31, 2005.

Check (2e) Cr. Training Fees Earned, $4,400; (2*f*) Cr. Tuition Fees Earned, $7,500; (3) Adj. Trial balance totals, $301,500; (4) Net income, $38,500; Ending T. Watson, Capital $62,100

Problem 3-4A
Interpreting unadjusted and adjusted trial balances, and preparing financial statements

A six-column table for JJW Company follows. The first two columns contain the unadjusted trial balance for the company as of July 31, 2005. The last two columns contain the adjusted trial balance as of the same date.

Required

Analysis Component

1. Analyze the differences between the unadjusted and adjusted trial balances to determine the eight adjustments that likely were made. Show the results of your analysis by inserting these adjustment amounts in the table's two middle columns. Label each adjustment with a letter *a* through *h* and provide a short description of it at the bottom of the table.

Check (2) Net income, $37,020; J. J. Winner, Capital (7/31/2005), $55,440; Total assets, $131,340

Preparation Component

2. Use the information in the adjusted trial balance to prepare the company's (*a*) income statement and its statement of owner's equity for the year ended July 31, 2005 (*note:* J. Winner, Capital at July 31, 2004, was $28,420, and the current-year withdrawals were $10,000), and (*b*) the balance sheet as of July 31, 2005.

	Unadjusted Trial Balance		Adjustments		Adjusted Trial Balance	
Cash	$ 27,000				$ 27,000	
Accounts receivable	12,000				22,460	
Office supplies	18,000				3,000	
Prepaid insurance	7,320				4,880	
Office equipment	92,000				92,000	
Accum. depreciation—Office equip.		$ 12,000				$ 18,000
Accounts payable		9,300				10,200
Interest payable		0				800
Salaries payable		0				6,600
Unearned consulting fees		16,000				14,300
Long-term notes payable		44,000				44,000
J. Winner, Capital		28,420				28,420
J. Winner, Withdrawals	10,000				10,000	
Consulting fees earned		156,000				168,160
Depreciation expense—Office equip.	0				6,000	
Salaries expense	71,000				77,600	
Interest expense	1,400				2,200	
Insurance expense	0				2,440	
Rent expense	13,200				13,200	
Office supplies expense	0				15,000	
Advertising expense	13,800				14,700	
Totals	$265,720	$265,720			$290,480	$290,480

Problem 3-5A
Preparing financial statements from the adjusted trial balance and calculating profit margin

P3 A1 A2

The adjusted trial balance for Callahay Company as of December 31, 2005, follows:

	Debit	Credit
Cash	$ 22,000	
Accounts receivable	44,000	
Interest receivable	10,000	
Notes receivable (due in 90 days)	160,000	
Office supplies	8,000	
Automobiles	160,000	
Accumulated depreciation—Automobiles		$ 42,000
Equipment	130,000	
Accumulated depreciation—Equipment		10,000
Land	70,000	
Accounts payable		88,000
Interest payable		12,000
Salaries payable		11,000
Unearned fees		22,000
Long-term notes payable		130,000
J. Callahay, Capital		247,800
J. Callahay, Withdrawals	38,000	

[continued on next page]

[continued from previous page]

Fees earned		420,000
Interest earned		16,000
Depreciation expense—Automobiles	18,000	
Depreciation expense—Equipment	10,000	
Salaries expense	180,000	
Wages expense	32,000	
Interest expense	24,000	
Office supplies expense	26,000	
Advertising expense	50,000	
Repairs expense—Automobiles	16,800	
Totals	$998,800	$998,800

Required

1. Use the information in the adjusted trial balance to prepare (*a*) the income statement for the year ended December 31, 2005; (*b*) the statement of owner's equity for the year ended December 31, 2005; and (*c*) the balance sheet as of December 31, 2005.

2. Calculate the profit margin for year 2005.

Check (1) Total assets, $552,000

Problem 3-6A[A]
Recording prepaid expenses and unearned revenues
P1 P4

Quisp Co. had the following transactions in the last two months of its year ended December 31:

Nov.	1	Paid $1,500 cash for future newspaper advertising.
	1	Paid $2,160 cash for 12 months of insurance through October 31 of the next year.
	30	Received $3,300 cash for future services to be provided to a customer.
Dec.	1	Paid $2,700 cash for a consultant's services to be received over the next three months.
	15	Received $7,650 cash for future services to be provided to a customer.
	31	Of the advertising paid for on November 1, $900 worth is not yet used.
	31	A portion of the insurance paid for on November 1 has expired. No adjustment was made in November to Prepaid Insurance.
	31	Services worth $1,200 are not yet provided to the customer who paid on November 30.
	31	One-third of the consulting services paid for on December 1 have been received.
	31	The company has performed $3,000 of services that the customer paid for on December 15.

Required

1. Prepare entries for these transactions under the method that records prepaid expenses as assets and records unearned revenues as liabilities. Also prepare adjusting entries at the end of the year.

2. Prepare entries for these transactions under the method that records prepaid expenses as expenses and records unearned revenues as revenues. Also prepare adjusting entries at the end of the year.

Analysis Component

3. Explain why the alternative sets of entries in requirements 1 and 2 do not result in different financial statement amounts.

PROBLEM SET B

Problem 3-1B
Identifying adjusting entries with explanations
C3 P1

For each of the following entries, enter the letter of the explanation that most closely describes it in the space beside each entry. (You can use letters more than once.)

A. To record payment of a prepaid expense.
B. To record this period's use of a prepaid expense.
C. To record this period's depreciation expense.
D. To record receipt of unearned revenue.
E. To record this period's earning of prior unearned revenue.
F. To record an accrued expense.
G. To record payment of an accrued expense.
H. To record an accrued revenue.
I. To record receipt of accrued revenue.

			Debit	Credit
______	1.	Unearned Professional Fees	6,000	
		Professional Fees Earned		6,000
______	2.	Interest Receivable	3,500	
		Interest Revenue		3,500
______	3.	Salaries Payable	9,000	
		Cash		9,000
______	4.	Depreciation Expense	8,000	
		Accumulated Depreciation		8,000
______	5.	Cash	9,000	
		Unearned Professional Fees		9,000
______	6.	Insurance Expense	4,000	
		Prepaid Insurance		4,000
______	7.	Interest Expense	5,000	
		Interest Payable		5,000
______	8.	Cash	1,500	
		Accounts Receivable (from services)		1,500
______	9.	Salaries Expense	7,000	
		Salaries Payable		7,000
______	10.	Cash	1,000	
		Interest Receivable		1,000
______	11.	Prepaid Rent	3,000	
		Cash		3,000
______	12.	Rent Expense	7,500	
		Prepaid Rent		7,500

Problem 3-2B
Preparing adjusting and subsequent journal entries

C1 A1 P1

Nomo Co. follows the practice of recording prepaid expenses and unearned revenues in balance sheet accounts. Nomo's annual accounting period ends on October 31, 2005. The following information concerns the adjusting entries that need to be recorded as of that date:

a. The Office Supplies account started the fiscal year with a $500 balance. During the fiscal year, the company purchased supplies for $3,650, which was added to the Office Supplies account. The supplies available at October 31, 2005, totaled $700.

b. An analysis of the company's insurance policies provided these facts:

Policy	Date of Purchase	Months of Coverage	Cost
A	April 1, 2004	24	$3,000
B	April 1, 2005	36	3,600
C	August 1, 2005	12	660

The total premium for each policy was paid in full (for all months) at the purchase date, and the Prepaid Insurance account was debited for the full cost. (Note that year-end adjusting entries for Prepaid Insurance were properly recorded in all prior fiscal years.)

c. The company has four employees, who earn a total of $800 for each workday. They are paid each Monday for their work in the five-day workweek ending on the previous Friday. Assume that October 31, 2005, is a Monday, and all five employees worked the first day of that week. They will be paid salaries for five full days on Monday, November 7, 2005.

d. The company purchased a building on November 1, 2004, that cost $155,000 and is expected to have a $20,000 salvage value at the end of its predicted 25-year life.

e. Since the company does not occupy the entire building it owns, it rented space to a tenant at $600 per month, starting on September 1, 2005. The rent was paid on time on September 1, and the amount received was credited to the Rent Earned account. However, the October rent has not been paid. The company has worked out an agreement with the tenant, who has promised to pay both October and November rent in full on November 15. The tenant has agreed not to fall behind again.

f. On September 1, the company rented space to another tenant for $525 per month. The tenant paid five months' rent in advance on that date. The payment was recorded with a credit to the Unearned Rent account.

Required

1. Use the information to prepare adjusting entries as of October 31, 2005.

2. Prepare journal entries to record the first subsequent cash transaction in 2006 for parts *c* and *e*.

Check (1*b*) Dr. Insurance Expense, $2,365; (1*d*) Dr. Depreciation Expense, $5,400.

Problem 3-3B
Preparing adjusting entries, adjusted trial balance, and financial statements

A1 P1 P2 P3

Following is the unadjusted trial balance for Alcorn Institute as of December 31, 2005, which initially records prepaid expenses and unearned revenues in balance sheet accounts. The Institute provides one-on-one training to individuals who pay tuition directly to the business and offers extension training to groups in off-site locations. Shown after the trial balance are items *a* through *h* that require adjusting entries as of December 31, 2005.

ALCORN INSTITUTE
Unadjusted Trial Balance
December 31, 2005

	Debit	Credit
Cash	$ 50,000	
Accounts receivable	0	
Teaching supplies	60,000	
Prepaid insurance	18,000	
Prepaid rent	2,600	
Professional library	10,000	
Accumulated depreciation—Professional library		$ 1,500
Equipment	30,000	
Accumulated depreciation—Equipment		16,000
Accounts payable		12,200
Salaries payable		0
Unearned training fees		27,600
M. Alcorn, Capital		68,500
M. Alcorn, Withdrawals	20,000	
Tuition fees earned		105,000
Training fees earned		62,000
Depreciation expense—Professional library	0	
Depreciation expense—Equipment	0	
Salaries expense	43,200	
Insurance expense	0	
Rent expense	28,600	
Teaching supplies expense	0	
Advertising expense	18,000	
Utilities expense	12,400	
Totals	$ 292,800	$292,800

Additional Information Items

a. An analysis of the Institute's insurance policies shows that $6,400 of coverage has expired.

b. An inventory count shows that teaching supplies costing $2,500 are available at year-end 2005.

c. Annual depreciation on the equipment is $4,000.

d. Annual depreciation on the professional library is $2,000.

e. On November 1, the Institute agreed to do a special four-month course (starting immediately) for a client. The contract calls for a $4,600 monthly fee, and the client paid the first two months' fees in advance. When the cash was received, the Unearned Training Fees account was credited. The last two months' fees will be recorded when collected in 2006.

f. On October 15, the Institute agreed to teach a four-month class (beginning immediately) to an individual for $2,200 tuition per month payable at the end of the class. The class started on October 15, but no payment has yet been received.

g. The Institute's only employee is paid weekly. As of the end of the year, three days' wages have accrued at the rate of $180 per day.

h. The balance in the Prepaid Rent account represents rent for December.

Check (2e) Cr. Training Fees Earned, $9,200; (2*f*) Cr. Tuition Fees Earned, $5,500; (3) Adj. trial balance totals, $304,840; (4) Net income, $6,460; Ending M. Alcorn, Capital, $54,960

Required

1. Prepare T-accounts (representing the ledger) with balances from the unadjusted trial balance.

2. Prepare the necessary adjusting journal entries for items *a* through *h*, and post them to the T-accounts. Assume that adjusting entries are made only at year-end.

3. Update balances in the T-accounts for the adjusting entries and prepare an adjusted trial balance.

4. Prepare Alcorn Institute's income statement and statement of owner's equity for the year 2005, and prepare its balance sheet as of December 31, 2005.

Problem 3-4B

Interpreting unadjusted and adjusted trial balances, and preparing financial statements

A six-column table for Daxu Consulting Company follows. The first two columns contain the unadjusted trial balance for the company as of December 31, 2005, and the last two columns contain the adjusted trial balance as of the same date.

	Unadjusted Trial Balance		Adjustments		Adjusted Trial Balance	
Cash	$ 48,000				$ 48,000	
Accounts receivable	70,000				76,660	
Office supplies	30,000				7,000	
Prepaid insurance	13,200				8,600	
Office equipment	150,000				150,000	
Accumulated depreciation—Office equip.		$ 30,000				$ 40,000
Accounts payable		36,000				42,000
Interest payable		0				1,600
Salaries payable		0				11,200
Unearned consulting fees		30,000				17,800
Long-term notes payable		80,000				80,000
D. Chen, Capital		70,200				70,200
D. Chen, Withdrawals	10,000				10,000	
Consulting fees earned		264,000				282,860
Depreciation expense—Office equip.	0				10,000	
Salaries expense	115,600				126,800	
Interest expense	6,400				8,000	
Insurance expense	0				4,600	
Rent expense	24,000				24,000	
Office supplies expense	0				23,000	
Advertising expense	43,000				49,000	
Totals	$510,200	$510,200			$545,660	$545,660

Required

Analysis Component

1. Analyze the differences between the unadjusted and adjusted trial balances to determine the eight adjustments that likely were made. Show the results of your analysis by inserting these adjustment amounts in the table's two middle columns. Label each adjustment with a letter *a* through *h* and provide a short description of it at the bottom of the table.

Preparation Component

Check (2) Net income, $37,460; D. Chen, Capital (12/31/05), $97,660; Total assets, $250,260

2. Use the information in the adjusted trial balance to prepare this company's (*a*) income statement and its statement of owner's equity for the year ended December 31, 2005 (*note:* D. Chen, Capital at December 31, 2004, was $70,200, and the current-year withdrawals were $10,000), and (*b*) the balance sheet as of December 31, 2005.

Problem 3-5B
Preparing financial statements from the adjusted trial balance and calculating profit margin
P3 A1 A2

The adjusted trial balance for Lightning Courier as of December 31, 2005, follows:

	Debit	Credit
Cash	$ 48,000	
Accounts receivable	110,000	
Interest receivable	6,000	
Notes receivable (due in 90 days)	200,000	
Office supplies	12,000	
Trucks	124,000	
Accumulated depreciation—Trucks		$ 48,000
Equipment	260,000	
Accumulated depreciation—Equipment		190,000
Land	90,000	
Accounts payable		124,000
Interest payable		22,000
Salaries payable		30,000
Unearned delivery fees		110,000
Long-term notes payable		190,000
J. Hallam, Capital		115,000
J. Hallam, Withdrawals	40,000	
Delivery fees earned		580,000
Interest earned		24,000
Depreciation expense—Trucks	24,000	
Depreciation expense—Equipment	46,000	
Salaries expense	64,000	
Wages expense	290,000	
Interest expense	25,000	
Office supplies expense	33,000	
Advertising expense	26,400	
Repairs expense—Trucks	34,600	
Totals	$1,433,000	$1,433,000

Required

1. Use the information in the adjusted trial balance to prepare (a) the income statement for the year ended December 31, 2005, (b) the statement of owner's equity for the year ended December 31, 2005, and (c) the balance sheet as of December 31, 2005.

2. Calculate the profit margin for year 2005.

Check (1) Total assets, $612,000

Problem 3-6B[A]
Recording prepaid expenses and unearned revenues
P1 P4

Quake Co. had the following transactions in the last two months of its fiscal year ended May 31:

Apr.	1	Paid $3,450 cash for future consulting services.
	1	Paid $2,700 cash for 12 months of insurance through March 31 of the next year.
	30	Received $7,500 cash for future services to be provided to a customer.
May	1	Paid $3,450 cash for future newspaper advertising.
	23	Received $9,450 cash for future services to be provided to a customer.
	31	Of the consulting services paid for on April 1, $1,500 worth has been received.
	31	A portion of the insurance paid for on April 1 has expired. No adjustment was made in April to Prepaid Insurance.
	31	Services worth $3,600 are not yet provided to the customer who paid on April 30.
	31	Of the advertising paid for on May 1, $1,050 worth is not yet used.
	31	The company has performed $4,500 of services that the customer paid for on May 23.

Required

1. Prepare entries for these transactions under the method that records prepaid expenses and unearned revenues in balance sheet accounts. Also prepare adjusting entries at the end of the year.
2. Prepare entries for these transactions under the method that records prepaid expenses and unearned revenues in income statement accounts. Also prepare adjusting entries at the end of the year.

Analysis Component

3. Explain why the alternative sets of entries in parts 1 and 2 do not result in different financial statement amounts.

PROBLEM SET C

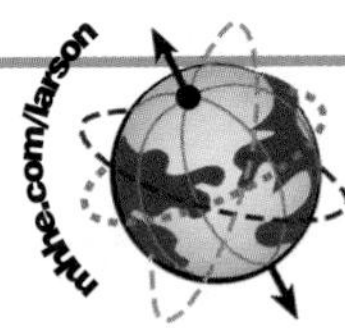

Problem Set C is available at the book's Website to further reinforce and assess your learning.

SERIAL PROBLEM

Success Systems

This serial problem began in Chapter 1 and continues through most of the book. If previous chapter segments were not completed, the serial problem can still begin at this point. It is helpful, but not necessary, that you use the Working Papers that accompany the book.

After the success of the company's first two months, Kay Breeze continues to operate Success Systems. (Transactions for the first two months are described in the serial problem of Chapter 2.) The November 30, 2004, unadjusted trial balance of Success Systems (reflecting its transactions for October and November of 2004) follows:

No.	Account Title	Debit	Credit
101	Cash	$ 48,052	
106	Accounts receivable	12,618	
126	Computer supplies	2,545	
128	Prepaid insurance	2,220	
131	Prepaid rent	3,300	
163	Office equipment	8,000	
164	Accumulated depreciation—Office equipment		$ 0
167	Computer equipment	20,000	
168	Accumulated depreciation—Computer equipment		0
201	Accounts payable		0
210	Wages payable		0
236	Unearned computer services revenue		0
301	K. Breeze, Capital		83,000
302	K. Breeze, Withdrawals	5,600	
403	Computer services revenue		25,659
612	Depreciation expense—Office equipment	0	
613	Depreciation expense—Computer equipment	0	
623	Wages expense	2,625	
637	Insurance expense	0	
640	Rent expense	0	
652	Computer supplies expense	0	
655	Advertising expense	1,940	
676	Mileage expense	704	
677	Miscellaneous expenses	250	
684	Repairs expense—Computer	805	
	Totals	$108,659	$108,659

Success Systems had the following transactions and events in December 2004:

Dec. 2 Paid $1,025 cash to Hilldale Mall for Success Systems' share of mall advertising costs.
3 Paid $500 cash for minor repairs to the company's computer.
4 Received $3,950 cash from Alex's Engineering Co. for the receivable from November.
10 Paid cash to Sherry Adams for six days of work at the rate of $125 per day.

14 Notified by Alex's Engineering Co. that Success's bid of $7,000 on a proposed project has been accepted. Alex's paid a $1,500 cash advance to Success Systems.
15 Purchased $1,100 of computer supplies on credit from Cain Office Products.
16 Sent a reminder to Gomez Co. to pay the fee for services recorded on November 8.
20 Completed a project for Chang Corporation and received $5,625 cash.
22–26 Took the week off for the holidays.
28 Received $3,000 cash from Gomez Co. on its receivable.
29 Reimbursed Breeze's business automobile mileage (600 miles at $0.32 per mile).
31 Breeze withdrew $1,500 cash for personal use.

The following additional facts are collected for use in making adjusting entries prior to preparing financial statements for the company's first three months:

a. The December 31 inventory count of computer supplies shows $580 still available.
b. Three months have expired since the 12-month insurance premium was paid in advance.
c. As of December 31, Sherry Adams has not been paid for four days of work at $125 per day.
d. The company's computer is expected to have a four-year life with no salvage value.
e. The office equipment is expected to have a five-year life with no salvage value.
f. Prepaid rent for three of the four months has expired.

Required

1. Prepare journal entries to record each of the December transactions and events for Success Systems. Post these entries to the accounts in the ledger.
2. Prepare adjusting entries to reflect *a* through *f*. Post these entries to the accounts in the ledger.
3. Prepare an adjusted trial balance as of December 31, 2004.
4. Prepare an income statement for the three months ended December 31, 2004.
5. Prepare a statement of owner's equity for the three months ended December 31, 2004.
6. Prepare a balance sheet as of December 31, 2004.

Check (3) Adjusted trial balance totals, $119,034

(6) Total assets, $93,248

BEYOND THE NUMBERS

REPORTING IN ACTION

C1 C2 A1 A2

BTN 3-1 Refer to **Krispy Kreme**'s financial statements in Appendix A to answer the following:

1. Identify and write down the revenue recognition principle as explained in the chapter.
2. Research Krispy Kreme's footnotes to discover how it applies the revenue recognition principle. Report what you discover.
3. What is Krispy Kreme's profit margin for 2003 and for 2002?

Roll On

4. Access Krispy Kreme's financial statements (10-K) for fiscal years ending after February 2, 2003, at its Website (KrispyKreme.com) or the SEC's EDGAR database (www.SEC.gov). Compare the February 2, 2003, fiscal year profit margin to any subsequent year's profit margin that you are able to calculate.

COMPARATIVE ANALYSIS

A2

BTN 3-2 Key figures for the recent two years of both **Krispy Kreme** and **Tastykake** follow:

Key Figures	Krispy Kreme		Tastykake	
($ thousands)	Current Year	Prior Year	Current Year	Prior Year
Net income	$ 33,478	$ 26,378	$ 2,000*	$ 8,048*
Net sales	491,549	394,354	162,263	166,245

* Net income without restructuring charges.

Required

1. Compute profit margins for (*a*) Krispy Kreme and (*b*) Tastykake for the two years of data shown.
2. Which company is more successful on the basis of profit margin? Explain.

ETHICS CHALLENGE

C1 C2 A1

BTN 3-3 Jackie Bergez works for Sea Biscuit Co. She and Bob Welch, her manager, are preparing adjusting entries for annual financial statements. Bergez computes depreciation and records it as

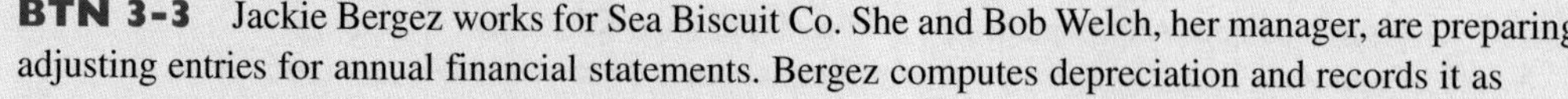

Depreciation Expense—Equipment	123,000	
Accumulated Depreciation—Equipment		123,000

Welch agrees with her computation but says the credit entry should be directly to the Equipment account. He argues that while accumulated depreciation is technically correct, "it is less hassle not to use a contra account and just credit the Equipment account directly. And besides, the balance sheet shows the same amount for total assets under either method."

Required

1. How should depreciation be recorded? Do you support Bergez or Welch?
2. Evaluate the strengths and weaknesses of Welch's reasons for preferring his method.
3. Indicate whether the situation Bergez faces is an ethical problem.

COMMUNICATING IN PRACTICE

C1 A2

BTN 3-4 The class should be divided into teams. Teams are to select an industry (such as automobile manufacturing, airlines, defense contractors), and each team member is to select a different company in that industry. Each team member is to acquire the annual report of the company selected. Annual reports can be downloaded from company Websites or from the SEC's EDGAR database at (www.SEC.gov).

Required

1. Use the annual report to compute the return on assets, debt ratio, and profit margin.
2. Communicate with team members via a meeting, e-mail, or telephone to discuss the meaning of the ratios, how different companies compare to each other, and the industry norm. The team must prepare a single memo reporting the ratios for each company and identifying the conclusions or consensus of opinion reached during the team's discussion. The memo is to be copied and distributed to the instructor and all classmates.

TAKING IT TO THE NET

C1 A2

mhhe.com/larson

BTN 3-5 Access the **Cannondale** promotional Website (Cannondale.com).

1. What is the primary product that Cannondale sells?
2. Review its form 10-K. You can access this from the EDGAR system (www.SEC.gov). You must scroll down the form to find the financial statements.
3. What is Cannondale's fiscal year-end?
4. What are Cannondale's net sales for the annual period ended June 29, 2002?
5. What is Cannondale's net income for the annual period ended June 29, 2002?
6. Compute Cannondale's profit margin ratio for the annual period ended June 29, 2002.
7. Do you think its decision to use a year-end of late June or early July relates to its natural business year?

TEAMWORK IN ACTION

C3 A1 P1

BTN 3-6 Four types of adjustments are described in the chapter: (1) prepaid expenses, (2) unearned revenues, (3) accrued expenses, and (4) accrued revenues.

Required

1. Form *learning teams* of four (or more) members. Each team member must select one of the four adjustments as an area of expertise (each team must have at least one expert in each area).
2. Form *expert teams* from the individuals who have selected the same area of expertise. Expert teams are to discuss and write a report that each expert will present to his or her learning team addressing the following:
   a. Description of the adjustment and why it's necessary.
   b. Example of a transaction or event, with dates and amounts, that requires adjustment.

c. Adjusting entry(ies) for the example in requirement *b*.
d. Status of the affected account(s) before and after the adjustment in requirement *c*.
e. Effects on financial statements of not making the adjustment.

3. Each expert should return to his or her learning team. In rotation, each member should present his or her expert team's report to the learning team. Team discussion is encouraged.

BUSINESS WEEK ACTIVITY

C2 

mhhe.com/larson

BTN 3-7 Read the article "It's Like When Someone Robs a Bank," in the August 19, 2002, issue of ***Business Week***. (Access the book's Website for a free link.)

Required

1. Describe the type of overall accounting reform that FASB Chairman Herz favors.
2. What does Herz assert as being at the core of most recent scandals in corporate America?
3. What is meant by "principles-based accounting"?
4. Why is "principles-based accounting" controversial?

ENTREPRENEURIAL DECISION

A2 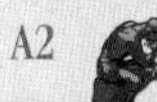 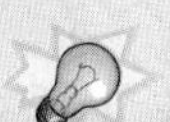

BTN 3-8 Melody Kulp of **Mellies** (see chapter's opening feature) is aware of Robin Drucker, who operates a collection agency. For a 50% commission, Drucker collects on accounts receivables for her clients' customers who are delinquent in their payments. For example, assume that a company turns over a $100 accounts receivable to Drucker. If she can collect the $100 from the customer, Drucker keeps $50 and remits the other $50 to her client. Kulp is negotiating with Drucker to offer her a discount from the normal 50% commission that Drucker charges. Kulp has proposed a fee of 40% on amounts collected by Drucker, and leaving 60% of the receivable for Mellies. Currently, Mellies uses a different collection agency that charges a 50% commission.

Required

1. Why would a company hire a collection agency to pursue its accounts receivable?
2. Assume that Mellies' profit margin is 8%. What is Mellies' net income on sales of $40 million?
3. Assume that Mellies currently pays 2% of its $40 million sales to collection agencies. What is the current amount of commission expense Mellies pays to collect delinquent accounts?
4. If Mellies is able to successfully negotiate with the Drucker agency for the reduced collection fee, how will its commission expense for collecting accounts change?
5. How would Mellies' profit margin change if it hires the Drucker collection agency at a 40% commission?

HITTING THE ROAD

C1

BTN 3-9 Visit the Website of a major company that interests you. Use the Investor Relations link at the Website to obtain the toll-free telephone number of the Investor Relations Department. Call the company, ask to speak to Investor Relations, and request a copy of the company's most recent annual report. You should receive the requested report within one to two weeks. Once you have received your report, consult it throughout the term to see the principles that you are learning in class are being applied in practice.

GLOBAL DECISION

A2 C1 C2 

BTN 3-10 **Grupo Bimbo** is a major producer and distributor of bakery products. Access its 2002 annual financial report at the company's Website (**GrupoBimbo.com**) to answer the following questions.

Required

1. Identify and report the revenue recognition policy applied by Grupo Bimbo?
2. What are the five types of assets depreciated by Grupo Bimbo? Which two assets classified as property, plant, and equipment are not depreciated?
3. What is Grupo Bimbo's profit margin for both fiscal years ended 2002 and 2001?

"Snowskates let you live out your skateboarding fantasies on the snow"—Andy Wolf

4 Completing the Accounting Cycle

A Look Back

Chapter 3 explained the timing of reports. We described why adjusting accounts is important for recognizing revenues and expenses in the proper period. We explained how to prepare an adjusted trial balance and use it in preparing financial statements.

A Look at This Chapter

This chapter emphasizes the final steps in the accounting process and reviews the entire accounting cycle. We explain the closing process, including accounting procedures and the use of a post-closing trial balance. We show how a work sheet aids in preparing financial statements. A classified balance sheet and its use in analyzing information are explained.

A Look Ahead

Chapter 5 looks at accounting for merchandising activities. We describe the sale and purchase of merchandise and their implications for preparing and analyzing financial statements.

CAP

Conceptual

C1 Explain why temporary accounts are closed each period. *(p. 140)*

C2 Identify steps in the accounting cycle. *(p. 143)*

C3 Explain and prepare a classified balance sheet. *(p. 146)*

Analytical

A1 Compute the current ratio and describe what it reveals about a company's financial condition. *(p. 148)*

Procedural

P1 Prepare a work sheet and explain its usefulness. *(p. 136)*

P2 Describe and prepare closing entries. *(p. 141)*

P3 Explain and prepare a post-closing trial balance. *(p. 143)*

Decision Feature

Snowskate on Upstart

PORTLAND—Andy Wolf was a frustrated skateboarder when he moved to Portland a few years ago because of its snow-covered surroundings for much of the year. Wolf toyed with the idea of making a skateboard for snow. His answer was the "snowskate"—similar in size and shape to a skateboard but ridden without bindings to allow *shove-its* and *flip tricks* that aren't possible with snowboards. He now heads the upstart **Premier Snowskate (PremierSnowsk8.com),** the maker of snowskates.

Wolf says his early business experiences were tough as people reacted to him as if "all he knows how to do is ride a snowboard and play Nintendo." People were wrong. One of Wolf's first goals was to control costs. "I wanted to keep the price under $100 retail," says Wolf; "that's how I sourced my materials." He also monitored revenues and kept track of financial performance. Closing procedures were important in helping identify the proper costs and revenues for specific periods. He also relied on classified balance sheets so that he would know what was due and when.

Still, it was tough. "It was still a job," says Wolf. "I had to handle my business, do my own deals, set up my traveling, and work with reps." Accounting work sheets helped Wolf identify temporary and permanent accounts, make crucial adjustments, and prepare and analyze financial reports. Yet the final business decisions were his to make.

Today, his decisions look good as forward-thinking resorts are building snowskate parks. "We're finding that resorts are totally into it," says Wolf. "Either embrace it or have it run them over."

Now for Wolf: How is he dealing with success? "I kind of hate to admit it," says Wolf, "but snowskates are going mainstream." From skateboarder to entrepreneur who uses accounting data—that must hurt. However, with annual sales projected to top $3 million this year, the hurt is tolerable. Admits Wolf, "I'm pretty damn lucky."

[Sources: *Premier Snowskates Website,* January 2004; *Entrepreneur Magazine,* May 2002; *Snowskates Underground,* May 2001; *USA Today,* January 2003; *Sports Guide,* December 2002; *Transworld Snowboarding,* February 2003.]

Many of the important steps leading to financial statements were explained in earlier chapters. We described how transactions and events are analyzed, journalized, and posted. This chapter describes important adjustments that are often necessary to properly reflect revenues when earned and expenses when incurred. This chapter also describes financial statement preparation. It explains the closing process that readies revenue, expense, and withdrawal accounts for the next reporting period and updates the capital account. A work sheet is shown to be a useful tool for these final steps and in preparing financial statements. It also explains how accounts are classified on a balance sheet to increase their usefulness to decision makers.

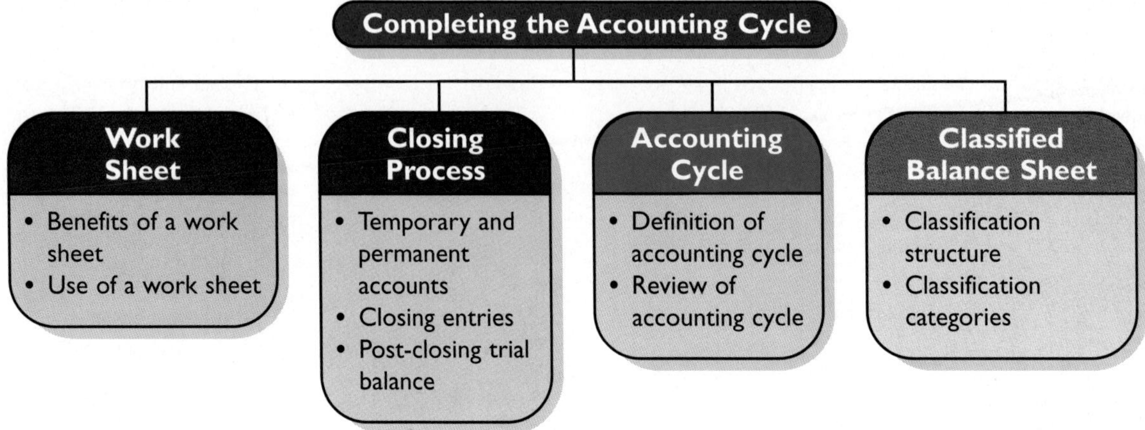

Work Sheet as a Tool

Information preparers use various analyses and internal documents when organizing information for internal and external decision makers. Internal documents are often called **working papers.** One widely used working paper is the **work sheet,** which is a useful tool for preparers in working with accounting information. It is usually not available to external decision makers.

Benefits of a Work Sheet

P1 Prepare a work sheet and explain its usefulness.

A work sheet is *not* a required report, yet using a manual or electronic work sheet has several potential benefits. Specifically, a work sheet:

- Aids the preparation of financial statements.
- Reduces the possibility of errors when working with many accounts and adjustments.
- Links accounts and adjustments to their impacts in financial statements.
- Assists in planning and organizing an audit of financial statements—as it can be used to reflect any adjustments necessary.
- Helps in preparing interim (monthly and quarterly) financial statements when the journalizing and posting of adjusting entries are postponed until the year-end.
- Shows the effects of proposed or "what if" transactions.

Point: Since a work sheet is *not* a required report or an accounting record, its format is flexible and can be modified by its user to fit his/her preferences.

Use of a Work Sheet

When a work sheet is used to prepare financial statements, it is constructed at the end of a period before the adjusting process. The complete work sheet includes a list of the accounts, their balances and adjustments, and their sorting into financial statement columns. It provides two columns each for the unadjusted trial balance,

Decision Insight

Accoun-tech An electronic work sheet using spreadsheet software such as Excel allows us to easily change numbers, assess the impact of alternative strategies, and quickly prepare financial statements at less cost. It can also increase the available time for analysis and interpretation.

the adjustments, the adjusted trial balance, the income statement, and the balance sheet (including the statement of owner's equity). To describe and interpret the work sheet, we use the information from FastForward. Preparing the work sheet has five important steps. Each step, 1 through 5, is color-coded and explained with reference to Exhibits 4.1 and 4.2.

1 Step 1. Enter Unadjusted Trial Balance

Refer to Exhibit 4.1. The first step in preparing a work sheet is to list the title of every account and its account number that is expected to appear on its financial statements. This includes all accounts in the ledger plus any new ones from adjusting entries. Most adjusting entries—including expenses from salaries, supplies, depreciation, and insurance—are predictable and recurring. The unadjusted balance for each account is then entered in the appropriate Debit or Credit column of the unadjusted trial balance columns. The totals of these two columns must be equal. Exhibit 4.1 shows FastForward's work sheet after completing this first step. Sometimes blank lines are left on the work sheet based on past experience to indicate where lines will be needed for adjustments to certain accounts. Exhibit 4.1 shows Consulting Revenue as one example. An alternative is to squeeze adjustments on one line or to combine the effects of two or more adjustments in one amount. In the unusual case when an account is not predicted, we can add a new line for such an account following the *Totals* line.

2 Step 2. Enter Adjustments

Refer to Exhibit 4.1a (turn over first transparency). The second step in preparing a work sheet is to enter adjustments in the Adjustments columns. The adjustments shown are the same ones shown in Exhibit 3.13. An identifying letter links the debit and credit of each adjusting entry. This is called *keying* the adjustments. After preparing a work sheet, adjusting entries must still be entered in the journal and posted to the ledger. The Adjustments columns provide the information for those entries.

Point: A recordkeeper often can complete the procedural task of journalizing and posting adjusting entries by using a work sheet and the guidance that *keying* provides.

3 Step 3. Prepare Adjusted Trial Balance

Refer to Exhibit 4.1b (turn over second transparency). The adjusted trial balance is prepared by combining the adjustments with the unadjusted balances for each account. As an example, the Prepaid Insurance account has a $2,400 debit balance in the Unadjusted Trial Balance columns. This $2,400 debit is combined with the $100 credit in the Adjustments columns to give Prepaid Insurance a $2,300 debit in the Adjusted Trial Balance columns. The totals of the Adjusted Trial Balance columns confirm the equality of debits and credits.

Point: To avoid omitting the transfer of an account balance, start with the first line (cash) and continue in account order.

4 Step 4. Sort Adjusted Trial Balance Amounts to Financial Statements

Refer to Exhibit 4.1c (turn over third transparency). This step involves sorting account balances from the adjusted trial balance to their proper financial statement columns. Expenses go to the Income Statement Debit column and revenues to the Income Statement Credit column. Assets and withdrawals go to the Balance Sheet & Statement of Owner's Equity Debit column. Liabilities and owner's capital go to the Balance Sheet & Statement of Owner's Equity Credit column.

5 Step 5. Total Statement Columns, Compute Income or Loss, and Balance Columns

Refer to Exhibit 4.1d (turn over fourth transparency). Each financial statement column (from Step 4) is totaled. The difference between the totals of the Income Statement columns is net income or net loss. This occurs because revenues are entered in the Credit column and expenses in the Debit column. If the Credit total exceeds the Debit total, there is net income. If the Debit total exceeds the Credit total, there is a net loss. For FastForward, the Credit total exceeds the Debit total, giving a $3,785 net income.

[continued on p. 140]

Exhibit 4.1

Work Sheet with Unadjusted Trial Balance

FastForward
Work Sheet
For Month Ended December 31, 2004

(1)

No.	Account	Unadjusted Trial Balance Dr.	Unadjusted Trial Balance Cr.	Adjustments Dr.	Adjustments Cr.	Adjusted Trial Balance Dr.	Adjusted Trial Balance Cr.	Income Statement Dr.	Income Statement Cr.	Balance Sheet & Statement of Owner's Equity Dr.	Balance Sheet & Statement of Owner's Equity Cr.
101	Cash	3,950									
106	Accounts receivable	0									
126	Supplies	9,720									
128	Prepaid insurance	2,400									
167	Equipment	26,000									
168	Accumulated depreciation—Equip.		0								
201	Accounts payable		6,200								
209	Salaries payable		0								
236	Unearned consulting revenue		3,000								
301	C. Taylor, Capital		30,000								
302	C. Taylor, Withdrawals	600									
403	Consulting revenue		5,800								
406	Rental revenue		300								
612	Depreciation expense—Equip.	0									
622	Salaries expense	1,400									
637	Insurance expense	0									
640	Rent expense	1,000									
652	Supplies expense	0									
690	Utilities expense	230									
	Totals	45,300	45,300								

List all accounts from the ledger and those expected to arise from adjusting entries.

Enter all amounts available from ledger accounts. Column totals must be equal.

A work sheet collects and summarizes information used to prepare adjusting entries, financial statements, and closing entries.

Exhibit 4.2

Financial Statements Prepared from the Work Sheet

FASTFORWARD Income Statement For Month Ended December 31, 2004		
Revenues		
Consulting revenue	$ 7,850	
Rental revenue	300	
Total revenues		$ 8,150
Expenses		
Depreciation expense—Equipment	375	
Salaries expense	1,610	
Insurance expense	100	
Rent expense	1,000	
Supplies expense	1,050	
Utilities expense	230	
Total expenses		4,365
Net income		$ 3,785

FASTFORWARD Statement of Owner's Equity For Month Ended December 31, 2004		
C. Taylor, Capital, December 1		$ 0
Add: Investment by owner	$30,000	
Net income	3,785	33,785
		33,785
Less: Withdrawals by owner		600
C. Taylor, Capital, December 31		$33,185

FASTFORWARD Balance Sheet December 31, 2004		
Assets		
Cash		$ 3,950
Accounts receivable		1,800
Supplies		8,670
Prepaid insurance		2,300
Equipment	$26,000	
Accumulated depreciation—Equipment	(375)	25,625
Total assets		$42,345
Liabilities		
Accounts payable		$ 6,200
Salaries payable		210
Unearned consulting revenue		2,750
Total liabilities		9,160
Equity		
C. Taylor, Capital		33,185
Total liabilities and equity		$42,345

Decision Maker

Entrepreneur You make a printout of the electronic work sheet used to prepare financial statements. There is no depreciation adjustment, yet you own a large amount of equipment. Does the absence of depreciation adjustment concern you?

Answer—p. 154

The net income from the Income Statement columns is then entered in the Balance Sheet & Statement of Owner's Equity Credit column. Adding net income to the last Credit column implies that it is to be added to owner's capital. If a loss occurs, it is added to the Debit column. This implies that it is to be subtracted from owner's capital. The ending balance of owner's capital does not appear in the last two columns as a single amount, but it is computed in the statement of owner's equity using these account balances. When net income or net loss is added to the proper Balance Sheet & Statement of Owner's Equity column, the totals of the last two columns must balance. If they do not, one or more errors have been made. The error can either be mathematical or involve sorting one or more amounts to incorrect columns.

Work Sheet Applications and Analysis

A work sheet does not substitute for financial statements. It is a tool we can use at the end of an accounting period to help organize data and prepare financial statements. FastForward's financial statements are shown in Exhibit 4.2. Its income statement amounts are taken from the Income Statement columns of the work sheet. Similarly, amounts for its balance sheet and its statement of owner's equity are taken from the Balance Sheet & Statement of Owner's Equity columns of the work sheet.

A work sheet is also useful to journalize adjusting entries as the information is in the Adjustments columns. It is important to remember that a work sheet is not a journal. This means that even when a work sheet is prepared, it is necessary to both journalize adjustments and post them to the ledger.

Work sheets are also useful in analyzing the effects of proposed, or what-if, transactions. This is done by entering financial statement amounts in the Unadjusted (what-if) columns. Proposed transactions are then entered in the Adjustments columns. We then compute "adjusted" amounts from these proposed transactions. The extended amounts in the financial statement columns show the effects of these proposed transactions. These financial statement columns yield **pro forma financial statements** because they show the statements *as if* the proposed transactions occurred.

Quick Check

1. Where do we get the amounts to enter in the Unadjusted Trial Balance columns of a work sheet?
2. What are the advantages of using a work sheet to help prepare adjusting entries?
3. What are the overall benefits of a work sheet?

Answers—p. 155

Closing Process

C1 Explain why temporary accounts are closed each period.

The **closing process** is an important step at the end of an accounting period *after* financial statements have been completed. It prepares accounts for recording the transactions and the events of the *next* period. In the closing process we must (1) identify accounts for closing, (2) record and post the closing entries, and (3) prepare a post-closing trial balance. The purpose of the closing process is twofold. First, it resets revenue, expense, and withdrawals account balances to zero at the end of each period. This is done so that these accounts can properly measure income and withdrawals for the next period. Second, it helps in summarizing a period's revenues and expenses. This section explains the closing process.

Temporary and Permanent Accounts

Temporary (or *nominal*) **accounts** accumulate data related to one accounting period. They include all income statement accounts, the withdrawals account, and the Income Summary account. They are temporary because the accounts are opened at the beginning of a period, used to record transactions and events for that period, and then closed at the end of the period. *The closing process applies only to temporary accounts.* **Permanent** (or *real*) **accounts** report on activities related to one or more future accounting periods. They carry their ending balances into the next period and generally consist of all balance sheet accounts. These asset, liability, and equity accounts are not closed.

Temporary Accounts

Revenues
Expenses
Owner Withdrawals
Income Summary

Permanent Accounts

Assets
Liabilities
Owner Capital

Recording Closing Entries

To record and post **closing entries** is to transfer the end-of-period balances in revenue, expense, and withdrawals accounts to the permanent capital account. Closing entries are necessary at the end of each period after financial statements are prepared because

- Revenue, expense, and withdrawals accounts must begin each period with zero balances.
- Owner's capital must reflect revenues, expenses, and withdrawals.

Topic Tackler 4-1

An income statement aims to report revenues and expenses for a *specific accounting period.* The statement of owner's equity reports similar information, including withdrawals. Since revenue, expense, and withdrawals accounts must accumulate information separately for each period, they must start each period with zero balances. To close these accounts, we transfer their balances first to an account called *Income Summary.* **Income Summary** is a temporary account (only used for the closing process) that contains a credit for the sum of all revenues (and gains) and a debit for the sum of all expenses (and losses). Its balance equals net income or net loss and it is transferred to the capital account. Next, the withdrawals account balance is transferred to the capital account. After these closing entries are posted, the revenue, expense, withdrawals, and Income Summary accounts have zero balances. These accounts are then said to be *closed* or *cleared.*

Point: To understand the closing process, focus on its *outcomes—updating* the capital account balance to its proper ending balance, and getting *temporary accounts* to show *zero balances* for purposes of accumulating data for the next period.

Exhibit 4.3 uses the adjusted account balances of FastForward (from the Adjusted Trial Balance columns of Exhibit 4.1 or from the left side of Exhibit 4.4) to show the four steps necessary to close its temporary accounts. We explain each step.

Step 1: Close Credit Balances in Revenue Accounts to Income Summary The first closing entry transfers credit balances in revenue (and gain) accounts to the Income Summary account. We bring accounts with credit balances to zero by debiting them. For FastForward, this journal entry is step 1 in Exhibit 4.4. This entry closes revenue accounts and leaves them with zero balances. The accounts are now ready to record revenues when they occur in the next period. The $8,150 credit entry to Income Summary equals total revenues for the period.

P2 Describe and prepare closing entries.

Step 2: Close Debit Balances in Expense Accounts to Income Summary The second closing entry transfers debit balances in expense (and loss) accounts to the Income Summary account. We bring expense accounts' debit balances to zero by crediting them. With a balance of zero, these accounts are ready to accumulate a record of expenses for the next period. This second closing entry for FastForward is step 2 in Exhibit 4.4. Exhibit 4.3 shows that posting this entry gives each expense account a zero balance.

Point: It is possible to close revenue and expense accounts directly to owner's capital. Computerized accounting systems do this.

Step 3: Close Income Summary to Owner's Capital After steps 1 and 2, the balance of Income Summary is equal to December's net income of $3,785. The third closing entry transfers the balance of the Income Summary account to the capital account. This entry closes the Income Summary account and is step 3 in Exhibit 4.4. The Income Summary account has a zero balance after posting this entry. It continues to have a zero balance until the closing process again occurs at the end of the next period. (If a net loss occurred because

Point: The Income Summary is used only for closing entries.

Exhibit 4.3

Four-Step Closing Process

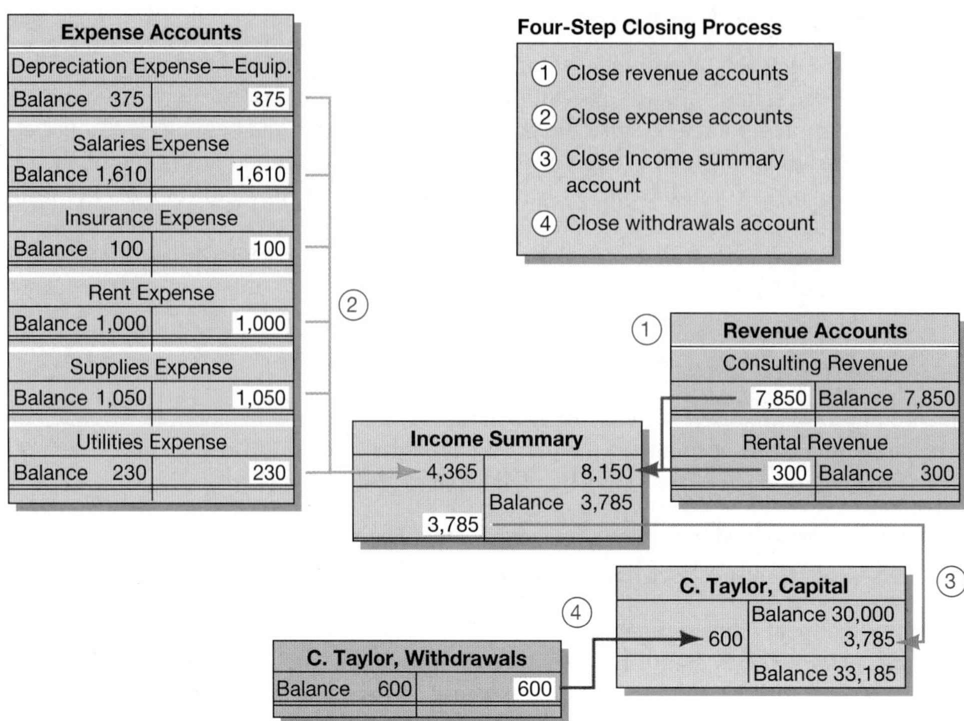

Exhibit 4.4

Preparing Closing Entries

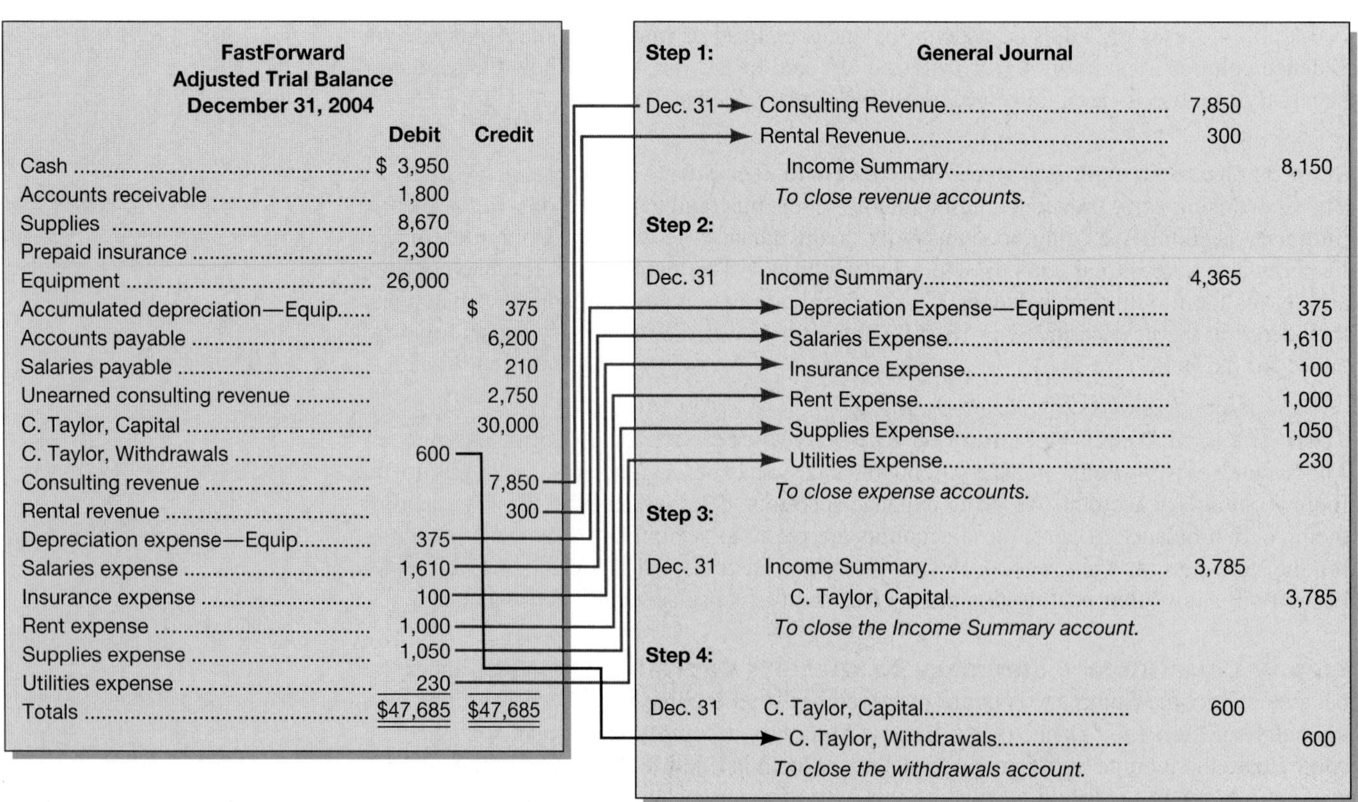

FastForward
Adjusted Trial Balance
December 31, 2004

	Debit	Credit
Cash	$ 3,950	
Accounts receivable	1,800	
Supplies	8,670	
Prepaid insurance	2,300	
Equipment	26,000	
Accumulated depreciation—Equip.		$ 375
Accounts payable		6,200
Salaries payable		210
Unearned consulting revenue		2,750
C. Taylor, Capital		30,000
C. Taylor, Withdrawals	600	
Consulting revenue		7,850
Rental revenue		300
Depreciation expense—Equip.	375	
Salaries expense	1,610	
Insurance expense	100	
Rent expense	1,000	
Supplies expense	1,050	
Utilities expense	230	
Totals	$47,685	$47,685

General Journal

Step 1:			
Dec. 31	Consulting Revenue	7,850	
	Rental Revenue	300	
	Income Summary		8,150
	To close revenue accounts.		
Step 2:			
Dec. 31	Income Summary	4,365	
	Depreciation Expense—Equipment		375
	Salaries Expense		1,610
	Insurance Expense		100
	Rent Expense		1,000
	Supplies Expense		1,050
	Utilities Expense		230
	To close expense accounts.		
Step 3:			
Dec. 31	Income Summary	3,785	
	C. Taylor, Capital		3,785
	To close the Income Summary account.		
Step 4:			
Dec. 31	C. Taylor, Capital	600	
	C. Taylor, Withdrawals		600
	To close the withdrawals account.		

expenses exceeded revenues, the third entry is reversed: debit Owner Capital and credit Income Summary.)

Step 4: Close Withdrawals Account to Owner's Capital The fourth closing entry transfers any debit balance in the withdrawals account to the owner's capital account—see step 4 in Exhibit 4.4. This entry gives the withdrawals account a zero balance, and the account is now ready to accumulate next period's withdrawals. This entry also reduces the capital account balance to the $33,185 amount reported on the balance sheet.

Notice that we can select the accounts and amounts needing to be closed by identifying individual revenue, expense, and withdrawals accounts in the ledger. This is illustrated in Exhibit 4.4 where we prepare closing entries using the adjusted trial balance.[1] (Information for closing entries is also in the financial statement columns of the work sheet.)

Decision Insight

Instant Numbers Quantum leaps in technology are increasing the importance of accounting analysis and interpretation. We are moving toward what some call the "virtual financial statement"—up-to-date financials with the click of a mouse. This reality increases the value of those individuals with the skills to use accounting data.

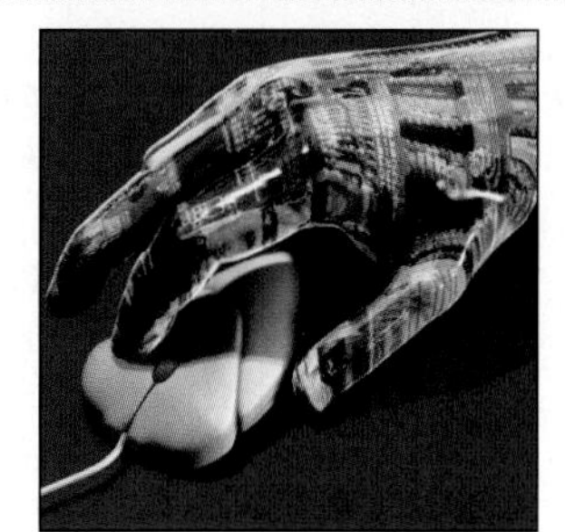

Post-Closing Trial Balance

P3 Explain and prepare a post-closing trial balance.

Exhibit 4.5 shows the entire ledger of FastForward as of December 31 after adjusting and closing entries are posted. (The transaction and adjusting entries are in Chapters 2 and 3.) Note that the temporary accounts (revenues, expenses, and withdrawals) have balances equal to zero.

A **post-closing trial balance** is a list of permanent accounts and their balances from the ledger after all closing entries have been journalized and posted. It lists the balances for all accounts not closed. These accounts comprise a company's assets, liabilities, and equity, which are identical to those in the balance sheet. The aim of a post-closing trial balance is to verify that (1) total debits equal total credits for permanent accounts and (2) all temporary accounts have zero balances. FastForward's post-closing trial balance is shown in Exhibit 4.6. The post-closing trial balance usually is the last step in the accounting process.

Accounting Cycle

C2 Identify steps in the accounting cycle.

The term **accounting cycle** refers to the steps in preparing financial statements. It is called a *cycle* because the steps are repeated each reporting period. Exhibit 4.7 shows the 10 steps in the cycle, beginning with analyzing transactions and ending with a post-closing trial balance or reversing entries. Steps 1 through 3 usually occur regularly as a company enters into transactions. Steps 4 through 9 are done at the end of a period. Reversing entries in step 10 are optional and are explained in Appendix 4A.

Decision Insight

Data Dash A few years ago **Sun Microsystems** took a month to prepare statements after its year-end. Today, it takes less than 24 hours to deliver preliminary figures to key decision makers. What is Sun's secret? Transactions are entered into a network of computerized systems.

[1] The closing process has focused on proprietorships. It is identical for partnerships with the exception that each owner has separate capital and withdrawals accounts (for steps 3 and 4). The closing process for a corporation is similar with the exception that it uses a Retained Earnings account instead of a Capital account, and a Dividend account instead of a Withdrawals account.

Exhibit 4.5

General Ledger after the Closing Process for FastForward

Asset Accounts

Cash Acct. No. 101

Date	Explan.	PR	Debit	Credit	Balance
2004					
Dec. 1		G1	30,000		30,000
2		G1		2,500	27,500
3		G1		26,000	1,500
5		G1	4,200		5,700
6		G1		2,400	3,300
12		G1		1,000	2,300
12		G1		700	1,600
22		G1	1,900		3,500
24		G1		900	2,600
24		G1		600	2,000
26		G1	3,000		5,000
26		G1		120	4,880
26		G1		230	4,650
26		G1		700	**3,950**

Accounts Receivable Acct. No. 106

Date	Explan.	PR	Debit	Credit	Balance
2004					
Dec. 12		G1	1,900		1,900
22		G1		1,900	0
31	Adj.	G1	1,800		**1,800**

Supplies Acct. No. 126

Date	Explan.	PR	Debit	Credit	Balance
2004					
Dec. 2		G1	2,500		2,500
6		G1	7,100		9,600
26		G1	120		9,720
31	Adj.	G1		1,050	**8,670**

Prepaid Insurance Acct. No. 128

Date	Explan.	PR	Debit	Credit	Balance
2004					
Dec. 6		G1	2,400		2,400
31	Adj.	G1		100	**2,300**

Equipment Acct. No. 167

Date	Explan.	PR	Debit	Credit	Balance
2004					
Dec. 3		G1	26,000		**26,000**

Accumulated Depreciation—Equipment Acct. No. 168

Date	Explan.	PR	Debit	Credit	Balance
2004					
Dec. 31	Adj.	G1		375	**375**

Liability and Equity Accounts

Accounts Payable Acct. No. 201

Date	Explan.	PR	Debit	Credit	Balance
2004					
Dec. 6		G1		7,100	7,100
24		G1	900		**6,200**

Salaries Payable Acct. No. 209

Date	Explan.	PR	Debit	Credit	Balance
2004					
Dec. 31	Adj	G1		210	**210**

Unearned Consulting Revenue Acct. No. 236

Date	Explan.	PR	Debit	Credit	Balance
2004					
Dec. 26		G1		3,000	3,000
31	Adj.	G1	250		**2,750**

C. Taylor, Capital Acct. No. 301

Date	Explan.	PR	Debit	Credit	Balance
2004					
Dec. 1		G1		30,000	30,000
31	**Closing**	**G1**		**3,785**	**33,785**
31	**Closing**	**G1**	**600**		**33,185**

C. Taylor, Withdrawals Acct. No. 302

Date	Explan.	PR	Debit	Credit	Balance
2004					
Dec. 24		G1	600		600
31	**Closing**	**G1**		**600**	**0**

Revenue and Expense Accounts (including Income Summary)

Consulting Revenue Acct. No. 403

Date	Explan.	PR	Debit	Credit	Balance
2004					
Dec. 5		G1		4,200	4,200
12		G1		1,600	5,800
31	Adj.	G1		250	6,050
31	Adj.	G1		1,800	7,850
31	**Closing**	**G1**	**7,850**		**0**

Rental Revenue Acct. No. 406

Date	Explan.	PR	Debit	Credit	Balance
2004					
Dec. 12		G1		300	300
31	**Closing**	**G1**	**300**		**0**

Depreciation Expense—Equipment Acct. No. 612

Date	Explan.	PR	Debit	Credit	Balance
2004					
Dec. 31	Adj.	G1	375		375
31	**Closing**	**G1**		**375**	**0**

Salaries Expense Acct. No. 622

Date	Explan.	PR	Debit	Credit	Balance
2004					
Dec. 12		G1	700		700
26		G1	700		1,400
31	Adj.	G1	210		1,610
31	**Closing**	**G1**		**1,610**	**0**

Insurance Expense Acct. No. 637

Date	Explan.	PR	Debit	Credit	Balance
2004					
Dec. 31	Adj.	G1	100		100
31	**Closing**	**G1**		**100**	**0**

Rent Expense Acct. No. 640

Date	Explan.	PR	Debit	Credit	Balance
2004					
Dec. 12		G1	1,000		1,000
31	**Closing**	**G1**		**1,000**	**0**

Supplies Expense Acct. No. 652

Date	Explan.	PR	Debit	Credit	Balance
2004					
Dec. 31	Adj.	G1	1,050		1,050
31	**Closing**	**G1**		**1,050**	**0**

Utilities Expense Acct. No. 690

Date	Explan.	PR	Debit	Credit	Balance
2004					
Dec. 26		G1	230		230
31	**Closing**	**G1**		**230**	**0**

Income Summary Acct. No. 901

Date	Explan.	PR	Debit	Credit	Balance
2004					
Dec. 31	**Closing**	**G1**		**8,150**	**8,150**
31	**Closing**	**G1**	**4,365**		**3,785**
31	**Closing**	**G1**	**3,785**		**0**

FASTFORWARD
Post-Closing Trial Balance
December 31, 2004

	Debit	Credit
Cash	$ 3,950	
Accounts receivable	1,800	
Supplies	8,670	
Prepaid insurance	2,300	
Equipment	26,000	
Accumulated depreciation—Equipment		$ 375
Accounts payable		6,200
Salaries payable		210
Unearned consulting revenue		2,750
C. Taylor, Capital		33,185
Totals	$42,720	$42,720

Exhibit 4.6

Post-Closing Trial Balance

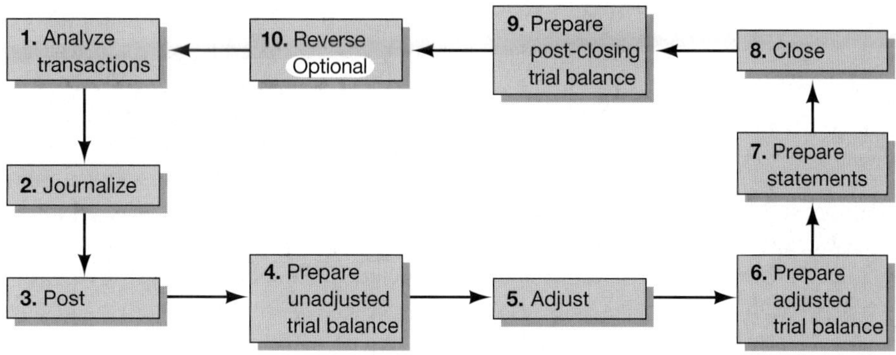

Exhibit 4.7

Steps in the Accounting Cycle*

Explanations

1. Analyze transactions	Analyze transactions to prepare for journalizing.
2. Journalize	Record accounts, including debits and credits, in a journal.
3. Post	Transfer debits and credits from the journal to the ledger.
4. Prepare unadjusted trial balance	Summarize unadjusted ledger accounts and amounts.
5. Adjust	Record adjustments to bring account balances up to date; journalize and post adjusting entries.
6. Prepare adjusted trial balance	Summarize adjusted ledger accounts and amounts.
7. Prepare statements	Use adjusted trial balance to prepare financial statements.
8. Close	Journalize and post entries to close temporary accounts.
9. Prepare post-closing trial balance	Test clerical accuracy of the closing procedures.
10. Reverse (optional)	Reverse certain adjustments in the next period—optional step; see Appendix 4A.

*Steps 4, 6, and 9 can be done on a work sheet. A work sheet is useful in planning adjustments, but adjustments (step 5) must always be journalized and posted. Steps 3, 4, 6, and 9 are automatic with a computerized system.

Quick Check

4. What are the major steps in preparing closing entries?
5. Why are revenue and expense accounts called *temporary?* Can you identify and list any other temporary accounts?
6. What accounts are listed on the post-closing trial balance?

Answers—p. 155

Classified Balance Sheet

C3 Explain and prepare a classified balance sheet.

Our discussion to this point has been limited to unclassified financial statements. This section describes a classified balance sheet. Chapter 5 describes a classified income statement. An **unclassified balance sheet** is one whose items are broadly grouped into assets, liabilities, and equity. One example is FastForward's balance sheet in Exhibit 4.2. A **classified balance sheet** organizes assets and liabilities into important subgroups that provide more information to decision makers.

Classification Structure

Topic Tackler 4-2

A classified balance sheet has no required layout, but it usually contains the categories in Exhibit 4.8. One of the more important classifications is the separation between current and noncurrent items for both assets and liabilities. Current items are those expected to come due (either collected or owed) within one year or the company's operating cycle, whichever is longer. The **operating cycle** is the time span from when *cash is used* to acquire goods and services until *cash is received* from the sale of those goods and services. "Operating" refers to company operations and "cycle" refers to the circular flow of cash used for company inputs and then cash received from its outputs. The length of a company's operating cycle depends on its activities. For a service company, the operating cycle is the time span between (1) paying employees who perform the services and (2) receiving cash from customers. For a merchandiser selling products, the operating cycle is the time span between (1) paying suppliers for merchandise and (2) receiving cash from customers.

Exhibit 4.8

Typical Categories in a Classified Balance Sheet

Assets	Liabilities and Equity
Current assets	Current liabilities
Noncurrent assets	Noncurrent liabilities
Long-term investments	Equity
Plant assets	
Intangible assets	

Point: Current is also called *short term*, and noncurrent is also called *long term*.

Most operating cycles are less than one year. This means most companies use a one-year period in deciding which assets and liabilities are current. A few companies have an operating cycle longer than one year. For instance, producers of certain beverages (wine) and products (ginseng) that require aging for several years have operating cycles longer than one year. A balance sheet lists current assets before noncurrent assets and current liabilities before noncurrent liabilities. This consistency in presentation allows users to quickly identify current assets that are most easily converted to cash and current liabilities that are shortly coming due. Items in current assets and current liabilities are listed in the order of how quickly they will be converted to, or paid in, cash.

Classification Categories

This section describes the most common categories in a classified balance sheet. The balance sheet for Snowboarding Components in Exhibit 4.9 shows these typical categories. Its assets are classified as either current or noncurrent. Its noncurrent assets include three main categories: long-term investments, plant assets, and intangible assets. Its liabilities are classified as either current or long term. Not all companies use the same categories of assets and liabilities for their balance sheets. **K2**'s balance sheet lists only three asset classes: current assets; property, plant and equipment; and other assets.

Point: Short-term investments maturing within three months are combined with cash on both the balance sheet and cash flow statement. This combination is called *cash and cash equivalents*.

Current Assets **Current assets** are cash and other resources that are expected to be sold, collected, or used within one year or the company's operating cycle, whichever is longer. Examples are cash, short-term investments, accounts receivable, short-term notes receivable, goods for sale (called *merchandise* or *inventory*), and prepaid expenses. The individual prepaid expenses of a company are usually small in amount compared to many other assets and are often combined and shown as a single item. The prepaid expenses in Exhibit 4.9 likely include items such as prepaid insurance, prepaid rent, office supplies,

SNOWBOARDING COMPONENTS Balance Sheet January 31, 2005			
Assets			
Current assets			
Cash		$ 6,500	
Short-term investments		2,100	
Accounts receivable		4,400	
Merchandise inventory		27,500	
Prepaid expenses		2,400	
Total current assets			$ 42,900
Long-term investments			
Notes receivable		1,500	
Investments in stocks and bonds		18,000	
Land held for future expansion		48,000	
Total long-term investments			67,500
Plant assets			
Store equipment	$ 33,200		
Less accumulated depreciation	8,000	25,200	
Buildings	170,000		
Less accumulated depreciation	45,000	125,000	
Land		73,200	
Total plant assets			223,400
Intangible assets			10,000
Total assets			$343,800
Liabilities			
Current liabilities			
Accounts payable		$15,300	
Wages payable		3,200	
Notes payable		3,000	
Current portion of long-term liabilities		7,500	
Total current liabilities			$ 29,000
Long-term liabilities (net of current portion)			150,000
Total liabilities			179,000
Equity			
T. Hawk, Capital			164,800
Total liabilities and equity			$343,800

Exhibit 4.9

Example of a Classified Balance Sheet

and store supplies. Prepaid expenses are usually listed last because they will not be converted to cash (instead, they are used).

Long-Term Investments A second major balance sheet classification is **long-term** (or *noncurrent*) **investments.** Notes receivable and investments in stocks and bonds are long-term assets when they are expected to be held for more than the longer of one year or the operating cycle. Land held for future expansion is a long-term investment because it is *not* used in operations.

Global: In the U.K. and many countries influenced by U.K. reporting, noncurrent assets are listed first and current assets are listed second.

Plant Assets Plant assets are tangible assets that are both *long lived* and *used to produce* or *sell products and services*. Examples are equipment, machinery, buildings, and land that are used to produce or sell products and services. The order listing for plant assets is usually from most liquid to least liquid such as equipment and machinery to buildings and land.

Point: Plant assets are also called **fixed assets; property, plant and equipment;** or **long-lived assets.**

Intangible Assets **Intangible assets** are long-term resources that benefit business operations. They usually lack physical form and have uncertain benefits. Examples are patents, trademarks, copyrights, franchises, and goodwill. Their value comes from the privileges or rights granted to or held by the owner. **Huffy Corporation** reports intangible assets of $48.1 million, which is more than 15 percent of its total assets. Its intangibles include trademarks, patents, and licensing agreements.

Current Liabilities **Current liabilities** are obligations due to be paid or settled within one year or the operating cycle, whichever is longer. They are usually settled by paying out current assets such as cash. Current liabilities often include accounts payable, notes payable, wages payable, taxes payable, interest payable, and unearned revenues. Also, any portion of a long-term liability due to be paid within one year or the operating cycle, whichever is longer, is a current liability. Unearned revenues are current liabilities when they will be settled by delivering products or services within one year or the operating cycle, whichever is longer. Current liabilities are reported in the order of those to be settled first.

Point: Many financial ratios are distorted if accounts are not classified correctly. We must be especially careful when analyzing accounts whose balances are separated into short and long term.

Long-Term Liabilities **Long-term liabilities** are obligations *not* due within one year or the operating cycle, whichever is longer. Notes payable, mortgages payable, bonds payable, and lease obligations are common long-term liabilities. If a company has both short- and long-term items in each of these categories, they are commonly separated into two accounts in the ledger.

Point: Many companies report two or more subgroups for long-term liabilities. See the balance sheets in Appendix A for examples.

Equity Equity is the owner's claim on assets. For a proprietorship, this claim is reported in the equity section with an owner's capital account. (For a partnership, the equity section reports a capital account for each partner. For a corporation, the equity section is divided into two main subsections, common stock and retained earnings.)

Quick Check

7. Identify which of the following assets are classified as (1) current assets or (2) plant assets: (*a*) land used in operations, (*b*) office supplies, (*c*) receivables from customers due in 10 months, (*d*) insurance protection for the next nine months, (e) trucks used to provide services to customers, (*f*) trademarks.
8. Cite two examples of assets classified as investments on the balance sheet.
9. Explain the operating cycle for a service company.

Answers—p. 155

Decision Analysis — Current Ratio

A1 Compute the current ratio and describe what it reveals about a company's financial condition.

An important use of financial statements is to help assess a company's ability to pay its debts in the near future. Such analysis affects decisions by suppliers when allowing a company to buy on credit. It also affects decisions by creditors when lending money to a company, including loan terms such as interest rate, due date, and collateral requirements. It can also affect a manager's decisions about using cash to pay existing debts when they come due. The **current ratio** is an important measure of a company's ability to pay its short-term obligations. It is defined in Exhibit 4.10 as current assets divided by current liabilities:

Exhibit 4.10 Current Ratio

$$\textbf{Current ratio} = \frac{\textbf{Current assets}}{\textbf{Current liabilities}}$$

Using financial information from **Limited Brands, Inc.**, we compute its current ratio for the recent four-year period. The results are in Exhibit 4.11.

Fiscal Year ($ Millions)	2003	2002	2001	2000
Current assets	$3,606	$2,784	$2,068	$2,285
Current liabilities	$1,259	$1,454	$1,000	$1,236
Current ratio	**2.9**	**1.9**	**2.1**	**1.8**
Industry current ratio	2.8	2.9	3.3	3.4

Exhibit 4.11

Limited Brands's Current Ratio

Limited Brands's current ratio rose to 2.9 in 2003 compared to lower ratios for prior years. Still, the current ratio for each of these years suggests that the company's short-term obligations can be covered with its short-term assets. However, if its ratio would approach 1.0, Limited would expect to face challenges in covering liabilities. If the ratio were *less* than 1.0, current liabilities would exceed current assets, and the company's ability to pay short-term obligations would be in doubt.

Decision Maker

Analyst You are analyzing the financial condition of a fitness club to assess its ability to meet upcoming loan payments. You compute its current ratio as 1.2. You also find that a major portion of accounts receivable is due from one client who has not made any payments in the past 12 months. Removing this receivable from current assets drops the current ratio to 0.7. What do you conclude?

Answer—p. 154

Demonstration Problem

The partial work sheet of Midtown Repair Company at December 31, 2005, follows:

	Adjusted Trial Balance		Income Statement		Balance Sheet and Statement of Owner's Equity	
	Debit	**Credit**	**Debit**	**Credit**	**Debit**	**Credit**
Cash	95,600					
Notes receivable (current)	50,000					
Prepaid insurance	16,000					
Prepaid rent	4,000					
Equipment	170,000					
Accumulated depreciation—Equipment		57,000				
Accounts payable		52,000				
Long-term notes payable		63,000				
C. Trout, Capital		178,500				
C. Trout, Withdrawals	30,000					
Repair services revenue		180,800				
Interest revenue		7,500				
Depreciation expense—Equipment	28,500					
Wages expense	85,000					
Rent expense	48,000					
Insurance expense	6,000					
Interest expense	5,700					
Totals	538,800	538,800				

Required

1. Complete the work sheet by extending the adjusted trial balance totals to the appropriate financial statement columns.
2. Prepare closing entries for Midtown Repair Company.

3. Set up the Income Summary and the C. Trout, Capital account in the general ledger (in balance column format) and post the closing entries to these accounts.
4. Determine the balance of the C. Trout, Capital account to be reported on the December 31, 2005, balance sheet.
5. Prepare an income statement, statement of owner's equity, and classified balance sheet (in report form) as of December 31, 2005.

Planning the Solution

- Extend the adjusted trial balance account balances to the appropriate financial statement columns.
- Prepare entries to close the revenue accounts to Income Summary, to close the expense accounts to Income Summary, to close Income Summary to the capital account, and to close the withdrawals account to the capital account.
- Post the first and second closing entries to the Income Summary account. Examine the balance of income summary and verify that it agrees with the net income shown on the work sheet.
- Post the third and fourth closing entries to the capital account.
- Use the work sheet's two right-most columns and your answer in part 4 to prepare the classified balance sheet.

Solution to Demonstration Problem

1. Completing the work sheet:

	Adjusted Trial Balance		Income Statement		Balance Sheet and Statement of Owner's Equity	
	Debit	**Credit**	**Debit**	**Credit**	**Debit**	**Credit**
Cash	95,600				95,600	
Notes receivable (current)	50,000				50,000	
Prepaid insurance	16,000				16,000	
Prepaid rent	4,000				4,000	
Equipment	170,000				170,000	
Accumulated depreciation—Equipment		57,000				57,000
Accounts payable		52,000				52,000
Long-term notes payable		63,000				63,000
C. Trout, Capital		178,500				178,500
C. Trout, Withdrawals	30,000				30,000	
Repair services revenue		180,800		180,800		
Interest revenue		7,500		7,500		
Depreciation expense—Equipment	28,500		28,500			
Wages expense	85,000		85,000			
Rent expense	48,000		48,000			
Insurance expense	6,000		6,000			
Interest expense	5,700		5,700			
Totals	538,800	538,800	173,200	188,300	365,600	350,500
Net Income			15,100			15,100
Totals			188,300	188,300	365,600	365,600

2. Closing entries:

Dec. 31	Repair Services Revenue	180,800	
	Interest Revenue	7,500	
	Income Summary		188,300
	To close revenue accounts.		

[continued on next page]

[continued from previous page]

Dec. 31	Income Summary	173,200	
	Depreciation Expense—Equipment		28,500
	Wages Expense		85,000
	Rent Expense		48,000
	Insurance Expense		6,000
	Interest Expense		5,700
	To close expense accounts.		
Dec. 31	Income Summary	15,100	
	C. Trout, Capital		15,100
	To close the Income Summary account.		
Dec. 31	C. Trout, Capital	30,000	
	C. Trout, Withdrawals		30,000
	To close the withdrawals account.		

3. Set up the Income Summary and the capital ledger accounts and post the closing entries.

Income Summary					Account No. 901
Date	**Explanation**	**PR**	**Debit**	**Credit**	**Balance**
2005					
Jan. 1	Beginning balance				0
Dec. 31	Close revenue accounts			188,300	188,300
31	Close expense accounts		173,200		15,100
31	Close income summary		15,100		0

C. Trout, Capital					Account No. 301
Date	**Explanation**	**PR**	**Debit**	**Credit**	**Balance**
2005					
Jan. 1	Beginning balance				178,500
Dec. 31	Close Income Summary			15,100	193,600
31	Close C. Trout, Withdrawals		30,000		163,600

4. The final capital balance of $163,600 (from part 3) will be reported on the December 31, 2005 balance sheet. The final capital balance reflects the increase due to the net income earned during the year and the decrease for the owner's withdrawals during the year.

5.

MIDTOWN REPAIR COMPANY
Income Statement
For Year Ended December 31, 2005

Revenues		
Repair services revenue	$180,800	
Interest revenue	7,500	
Total revenues		$188,300
Expenses		
Depreciation expense—Equipment	28,500	
Wages expense	85,000	
Rent expense	48,000	
Insurance expense	6,000	
Interest expense	5,700	
Total expenses		173,200
Net income		$ 15,100

MIDTOWN REPAIR COMPANY Statement of Owner's Equity For Year Ended December 31, 2005		
C. Trout, Capital, December 31, 2004		$178,500
Add: Investment by owner	$ 0	
Net income	15,100	15,100
		193,600
Less: Withdrawals by owner		30,000
C. Trout, Capital, December 31, 2005		$163,600

MIDTOWN REPAIR COMPANY Balance Sheet December 31, 2005		
Assets		
Current assets		
Cash		$ 95,600
Notes receivable		50,000
Prepaid insurance		16,000
Prepaid rent		4,000
Total current assets		165,600
Plant assets		
Equipment	$170,000	
Less: Accumulated depreciation—Equipment	(57,000)	
Total plant assets		113,000
Total assets		$278,600
Liabilities		
Current liabilities		
Accounts payable		$ 52,000
Long-term liabilities		
Long-term notes payable		63,000
Total liabilities		115,000
Equity		
C. Trout, Capital		163,600
Total liabilities and equity		$278,600

APPENDIX

Reversing Entries

Point: As a general rule, adjusting entries that create new asset or liability accounts are likely candidates for reversing.

Reversing entries are optional. They are recorded in response to accrued assets and accrued liabilities that were created by adjusting entries at the end of a reporting period. The purpose of reversing entries is to simplify a company's recordkeeping. Exhibit 4A.1 shows an example of FastForward's reversing entries. The top of the exhibit shows the adjusting entry FastForward recorded on December 31 for its employee's earned but unpaid salary. The entry recorded three days' salary of $210, which increased December's total salary expense to $1,610. The entry also recognized a liability of $210. The expense is reported on December's income statement. The expense account is then closed. The

Exhibit 4A.1

Reversing Entries for an Accrued Expense

Accrue salaries expense on December 31, 2004

Salaries Expense 210
    Salaries Payable 210

Salaries Expense

Date	Expl.	Debit	Credit	Balance
2004				
Dec. 12	(7)	700		700
26	(16)	700		1,400
31	*(e)*	210		1,610

Salaries Payable

Date	Expl.	Debit	Credit	Balance
2004				
Dec. 31	*(e)*		210	210

— OR —

No reversing entry recorded on January 1, 2005

NO ENTRY

Salaries Expense

Date	Expl.	Debit	Credit	Balance
2005				

Salaries Payable

Date	Expl.	Debit	Credit	Balance
2004				
Dec. 31	*(e)*		210	210
2005				

Reversing entry recorded on January 1, 2005

Salaries Payable 210
    Salaries Expense 210

Salaries Expense*

Date	Expl.	Debit	Credit	Balance
2005				
Jan. 1			210	(210)

Salaries Payable

Date	Expl.	Debit	Credit	Balance
2004				
Dec. 31	*(e)*		210	210
2004				
Jan. 1		210		0

Pay the accrued and current salaries on January 9, the first payday in 2005

Salaries Expense 490
Salaries Payable 210
    Cash 700

Salaries Expense

Date	Expl.	Debit	Credit	Balance
2005				
Jan. 9		490		**490**

Salaries Payable

Date	Expl.	Debit	Credit	Balance
2004				
Dec. 31	*(e)*		210	210
2005				
Jan. 9		210		**0**

Salaries Expense 700
    Cash 700

Salaries Expense*

Date	Expl.	Debit	Credit	Balance
2005				
Jan. 1			210	(210)
Jan. 9		700		**490**

Salaries Payable

Date	Expl.	Debit	Credit	Balance
2004				
Dec. 31	*(e)*		210	210
2005				
Jan. 1		210		**0**

Under both approaches, the expense and liability accounts have identical balances after the cash payment on January 9.

Salaries Expense $490
Salaries Payable .... $ 0

*Circled numbers in the *Balance* column indicate abnormal balances.

ledger on January 1, 2005, shows a $210 liability and a zero balance in the Salaries Expense account. At this point, the choice is made between using or not using reversing entries.

Accounting *without* Reversing Entries

The path down the left side of Exhibit 4A.1 is described in the chapter. To summarize here, when the next payday occurs on January 9, we record payment with a compound entry that debits both the expense and liability accounts and credits Cash. Posting that entry creates a $490 balance in the expense account and reduces the liability account balance to zero because the debt has been settled. The disadvantage of this approach is the slightly more complex entry required on January 9. Paying the accrued liability means that this entry differs from the routine entries made on all other paydays. To construct the proper entry on January 9, we must recall the effect of the December 31 adjusting entry. Reversing entries overcome this disadvantage.

Accounting *with* Reversing Entries

P4 Prepare reversing entries and explain their purpose.

The right side of Exhibit 4A.1 shows how a reversing entry on January 1 overcomes the disadvantage of the January 9 entry when not using reversing entries. A reversing entry is the exact opposite of an adjusting entry. For FastForward, the Salaries Payable liability account is debited for $210, meaning that this account now has a zero balance after the entry is posted. The Salaries Payable account temporarily understates the liability, but this is not a problem since financial statements are not prepared before the liability is settled on January 9. The credit to the Salaries Expense account is unusual because it gives the account an *abnormal credit balance*. We highlight an abnormal balance by circling it. Because of the reversing entry, the January 9 entry to record payment is straightforward. This entry debits the Salaries Expense account and credits Cash for the full $700 paid. It is the same as all other entries made to record 10 days' salary for the employee. Notice that after the payment entry is posted, the Salaries Expense account has a $490 balance that reflects seven days' salary of $70 per day (see the lower right side of Exhibit 4A.1). The zero balance in the Salaries Payable account is now correct. The lower section of Exhibit 4A.1 shows that the expense and liability accounts have exactly the same balances whether reversing entries are used or not. This means that both approaches yield identical results.

Summary

C1 **Explain why temporary accounts are closed each period.** Temporary accounts are closed at the end of each accounting period for two main reasons. First, the closing process updates the capital account to include the effects of all transactions and events recorded for the period. Second, it prepares revenue, expense, and withdrawals accounts for the next reporting period by giving them zero balances.

C2 **Identify steps in the accounting cycle.** The accounting cycle consists of 10 steps: (1) analyze transactions, (2) journalize, (3) post, (4) prepare an unadjusted trial balance, (5) adjust accounts, (6) prepare an adjusted trial balance, (7) prepare statements, (8) close, (9) prepare a post-closing trial balance, and (10) prepare (optional) reversing entries.

C3 **Explain and prepare a classified balance sheet.** Classified balance sheets report assets and liabilities in two categories: current and noncurrent. Noncurrent assets often include long-term investments, plant assets, and intangible assets. Owner's equity for proprietorships (and partnerships) report the capital account balance. A corporation separates equity into common stock and retained earnings.

A1 **Compute the current ratio and describe what it reveals about a company's financial condition.** A company's current ratio is defined as current assets divided by current liabilities. We use it to evaluate a company's ability to pay its current liabilities out of current assets.

P1 **Prepare a work sheet and explain its usefulness.** A work sheet can be a useful tool in preparing and analyzing financial statements. It is helpful at the end of a period in preparing adjusting entries, an adjusted trial balance, and financial statements. A work sheet usually contains five pairs of columns: Unadjusted Trial Balance, Adjustments, Adjusted Trial Balance, Income Statement, and Balance Sheet & Statement of Owner's Equity.

P2 **Describe and prepare closing entries.** Closing entries involve four steps: (1) close credit balances in revenue (and gain) accounts to Income Summary, (2) close debit balances in expense (and loss) accounts to Income Summary, (3) close Income Summary to the capital account, and (4) close withdrawals account to owner's capital.

P3 **Explain and prepare a post-closing trial balance.** A post-closing trial balance is a list of permanent accounts and their balances after all closing entries have been journalized and posted. Its purpose is to verify that (1) total debits equal total credits for permanent accounts and (2) all temporary accounts have zero balances.

P4[A] **Prepare reversing entries and explain their purpose.** Reversing entries are an optional step. They are applied to accrued expenses and revenues. The purpose of reversing entries is to simplify subsequent journal entries. Financial statements are unaffected by the choice to use or not use reversing entries.

Guidance Answers to **Decision Maker** and **Decision Ethics**

Entrepreneur Yes, you are concerned about the absence of a depreciation adjustment. Equipment does depreciate, and financial statements must recognize this occurrence. Its absence suggests an error or a misrepresentation.

Analyst A current ratio of 1.2 suggests that current assets are sufficient to cover current liabilities, but it implies a minimal buffer in case of errors in measuring current assets or current liabilities. Removing tardy receivables reduces the current ratio to 0.7. Your assessment is that the club will have some difficulty meeting its loan payments.

Guidance Answers to **Quick Checks**

1. Amounts in the Unadjusted Trial Balance columns are taken from current account balances in the ledger. The balances for new accounts expected to arise from adjusted entries can be left blank or set at zero.
2. A work sheet offers the advantage of listing on one page all necessary information to make adjusting entries.
3. A work sheet can help in (a) accounting efficiency and avoiding errors, (b) linking transactions and events to their effects in financial statements, (c) showing adjustments for audit purposes, (d) preparing interim financial statements, and (e) showing effects from proposed, or what-if, transactions.
4. The major steps in preparing closing entries are to close (1) credit balances in revenue accounts to Income Summary, (2) debit balances in expense accounts to Income Summary, (3) Income Summary to owner's capital, and (4) any withdrawals account to owner's capital.
5. Revenue (and gain) and expense (and loss) accounts are called *temporary* because they are opened and closed each period. The Income Summary and owner's withdrawals accounts are also temporary.
6. Permanent accounts make up the post-closing trial balance. These accounts are asset, liability, and equity accounts.
7. Current assets: (*b*), (*c*), (*d*). Plant assets: (*a*), (*e*). Item (*f*) is an intangible asset.
8. Investment in common stock, investment in bonds, and land held for future expansion.
9. For a service company, the operating cycle is the usual time between (1) paying employees who do the services and (2) receiving cash from customers for services provided.

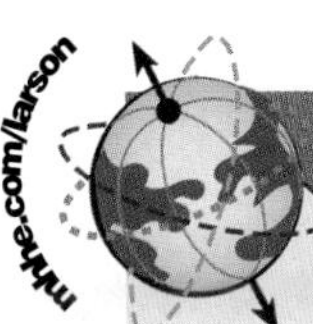

Key Terms

Key Terms are available at the book's Website for learning and testing in an online Flashcard Format.

Accounting cycle (p. 143)
Classified balance sheet (p. 146)
Closing entries (p. 141)
Closing process (p. 140)
Current assets (p. 146)
Current liabilities (p. 148)
Current ratio (p. 148)
Income Summary (p. 141)
Intangible assets (p. 148)
Long-term investments (p. 147)
Long-term liabilities (p. 148)
Operating cycle (p. 146)
Permanent accounts (p. 141)
Post-closing trial balance (p. 143)
Pro forma financial statements (p. 140)
Reversing entries (p. 152)
Temporary accounts (p. 141)
Unclassified balance sheet (p. 146)
Working papers (p. 136)
Work sheet (p. 136)

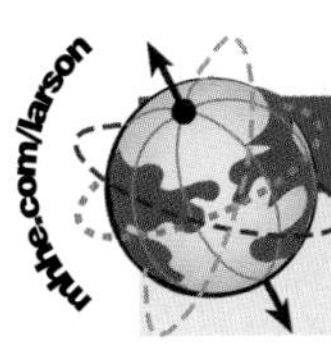

Personal Interactive Quiz

Personal Interactive Quizzes A and B are available at the book's Website to reinforce and assess your learning.

Superscript letter A denotes assignments based on Appendix 4A.

Discussion Questions

1. What accounts are affected by closing entries? What accounts are not affected?
2. What two purposes are accomplished by recording closing entries?
3. What are the steps in recording closing entries?
4. What is the purpose of the Income Summary account?
5. Explain whether an error has occurred if a post-closing trial balance includes a Depreciation Expense account.
6. What tasks are aided by a work sheet?
7. Why are the debit and credit entries in the Adjustments columns of the work sheet identified with letters?
8. What is a company's operating cycle?
9. What classes of assets and liabilities are shown on a typical classified balance sheet?
10. How is unearned revenue classified on the balance sheet?
11. What are the characteristics of plant assets?
12.[A] How do reversing entries simplify recordkeeping?
13.[A] If a company recorded accrued salaries expense of $500 at the end of its fiscal year, what reversing entry could be made? When would it be made?

14. Refer to the balance sheet for **Krispy Kreme** in Appendix A. What five noncurrent asset categories are used on its classified balance sheet?

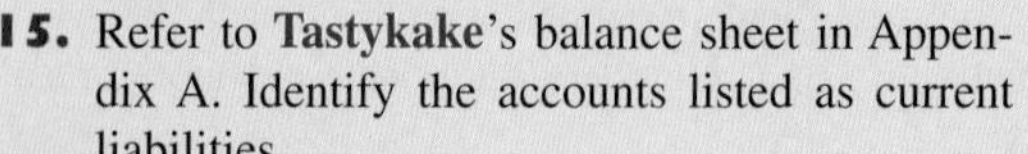

15. Refer to **Tastykake**'s balance sheet in Appendix A. Identify the accounts listed as current liabilities.

16. Refer to **Harley-Davidson**'s financial statements in Appendix A. What journal entry was likely recorded as of December 31, 2002, to close its Income Summary account?

Harley-Davidson

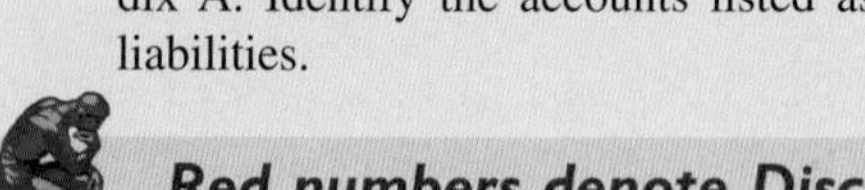

Red numbers denote Discussion Questions that involve decision-making.

Homework Manager  *repeats all numerical Quick Study assignments on the book's Website with new numbers.*

QUICK STUDY

QS 4-1
Determining effects of closing entries

C1 P2

Argosy Company began the current period with a $14,000 credit balance in the D. Argosy, Capital account. At the end of the period, the company's adjusted account balances include the following temporary accounts with normal balances:

Service fees earned	$35,000	Interest revenue	$3,500
Salaries expense	19,000	D. Argosy, Withdrawals	6,000
Depreciation expense	4,000	Utilities expense	2,300

After closing the revenue and expense accounts, what will be the balance of the Income Summary account? After all closing entries are journalized and posted, what will be the balance of the D. Argosy, Capital account?

QS 4-2
Identifying the accounting cycle

C2

List the following steps of the accounting cycle in their proper order:

a. Preparing the post-closing trial balance.
b. Posting the journal entries.
c. Journalizing and posting adjusting entries.
d. Preparing the adjusted trial balance.
e. Journalizing and posting closing entries.
f. Analyzing transactions and events.
g. Preparing the financial statements.
h. Preparing the unadjusted trial balance.
i. Journalizing transactions and events.

QS 4-3
Classifying balance sheet items

C3

The following are common categories on a classified balance sheet:

A. Current assets
B. Long-term investments
C. Plant assets
D. Intangible assets
E. Current liabilities
F. Long-term liabilities

For each of the following items, select the letter that identifies the balance sheet category where the item typically would appear.

_____ **1.** Trademarks
_____ **2.** Accounts receivable
_____ **3.** Land not currently used in operations
_____ **4.** Notes payable (due in three years)
_____ **5.** Cash
_____ **6.** Wages payable
_____ **7.** Store equipment
_____ **8.** Accounts payable

QS 4-4
Identifying current accounts and computing the current ratio

C3 A1

Compute Jamar Company's current ratio using the following information:

Accounts receivable	$15,000	Long-term notes payable	$20,000
Accounts payable	10,000	Office supplies	1,800
Buildings	42,000	Prepaid insurance	2,500
Cash	6,000	Unearned services revenue	4,000

QS 4-5
Interpreting a work sheet

P1

The following information is taken from the work sheet for Wayman Company as of December 31, 2005. Using this information, determine the amount for K. Wayman, Capital, that should be reported on its December 31, 2005, balance sheet.

	Income Statement		Balance Sheet and Statement of Owner's Equity	
	Dr.	Cr.	Dr.	Cr.
K.Wayman, Capital				65,000
K.Wayman, Withdrawals			32,000	
Totals	115,000	174,000		

QS 4-6
Applying a work sheet
P1

In preparing a work sheet, indicate the financial statement Debit column to which a normal balance in the following accounts should be extended. Use IS for the Income Statement Debit column and BS for the Balance Sheet and Statement of Owner's Equity Debit column.

_____ **a.** Insurance expense
_____ **b.** Equipment
_____ **c.** Owner, Withdrawals
_____ **d.** Depreciation expense—Equipment
_____ **e.** Prepaid rent
_____ **f.** Accounts receivable

QS 4-7
Ordering work sheet steps
P1

List the following steps in preparing a work sheet in their proper order by writing numbers 1–5 in the blank spaces provided.

a. _____ Prepare an adjusted trial balance on the work sheet.
b. _____ Prepare an unadjusted trial balance on the work sheet.
c. _____ Enter adjustments data on the work sheet.
d. _____ Extend adjusted balances to appropriate financial statement columns.
e. _____ Total the statement columns, compute net income (loss), and complete work sheet.

QS 4-8
Preparing a partial work sheet
P1 

The ledger of Terrel Company includes the following unadjusted normal balances: Prepaid Rent $800, Services Revenue $11,600, and Wages Expense $5,000. Adjusting entries are required for **(a)** accrued rent expense $240; **(b)** accrued services revenue $180; and **(c)** accrued wages expense $160. Enter these unadjusted balances and the necessary adjustments on a work sheet and complete the work sheet for these accounts. *Note:* You must include the following accounts: Accounts Receivable, Wages Payable, and Rent Expense.

QS 4-9
Prepare closing entries from the ledger P2

The ledger of Avril Company includes the following accounts with normal balances: L. Avril, Capital $6,000; L. Avril, Withdrawals $400; Services Revenue $10,000; Wages Expense $5,200; and Rent Expense $800. Prepare the necessary closing entries at December 31.

QS 4-10
Identify post-closing accounts P3

Identify the accounts listed in QS 4-9 that would be included in a post-closing trial balance.

QS 4-11[A]
Reversing entries
P4

On December 31, 2004, Yates Co. prepared an adjusting entry for $6,700 of earned but unrecorded management fees. On January 16, 2005, Yates received $15,500 cash in management fees, which included the accrued fees earned in 2004. Assuming the company uses reversing entries, prepare the January 1, 2005, reversing entry and the January 16, 2005, cash receipt entry.

Homework Manager *repeats all numerical Exercises on the book's Website with new numbers.*

EXERCISES

Exercise 4-1
Preparing and posting closing entries
P2

Use the March 31 fiscal year-end information from the following ledger accounts (assume that all accounts have normal balances) to prepare closing journal entries and then post those entries to the appropriate ledger accounts.

General Ledger

M. Mallon, Capital — Acct. No. 301

Date	PR	Debit	Credit	Balance
Mar. 31	G2			42,000

Salaries Expense — Acct. No. 622

Date	PR	Debit	Credit	Balance
Mar. 31	G2			21,000

[continued on next page]

[continued from previous page]

M. Mallon, Withdrawals Acct. No. 302

Date	PR	Debit	Credit	Balance
Mar. 31	G2			25,000

Insurance Expense Acct. No. 637

Date	PR	Debit	Credit	Balance
Mar. 31	G2			4,500

Check M. Mallon, Capital (ending balance), $38,900

Services Revenue Acct. No. 401

Date	PR	Debit	Credit	Balance
Mar. 31	G2			74,000

Rent Expense Acct. No. 640

Date	PR	Debit	Credit	Balance
Mar. 31	G2			9,600

Depreciation Expense Acct. No. 603

Date	PR	Debit	Credit	Balance
Mar. 31	G2			17,000

Income Summary Acct. No. 901

Date	PR	Debit	Credit	Balance

Exercise 4-2
Preparing closing entries and a post-closing trial balance

P2 P3

The adjusted trial balance for Schwepker Marketing Co. follows. Complete the four right-most columns of the table by first entering information for the four closing entries (keyed *1* through *4*) and second by completing the post-closing trial balance.

No.	Account Title	Adjusted Trial Balance		Closing Entry Information		Post-Closing Trial Balance	
		Dr.	Cr.	Dr.	Cr.	Dr.	Cr.
101	Cash	$ 8,200					
106	Accounts receivable	24,000					
153	Equipment	41,000					
154	Accumulated depreciation—Equipment		$ 16,500				
193	Franchise	30,000					
201	Accounts payable		14,000				
209	Salaries payable		3,200				
233	Unearned fees		2,600				
301	C. Schwepker, Capital		64,500				
302	C. Schwepker, Withdrawals	14,400					
401	Marketing fees earned		79,000				
611	Depreciation expense—Equipment	11,000					
622	Salaries expense	31,500					
640	Rent expense	12,000					
677	Miscellaneous expenses	7,700					
901	Income summary						
	Totals	$179,800	$179,800				

Exercise 4-3
Preparing closing entries and a post-closing trial balance

C1 P2 P3

The following adjusted trial balance contains the accounts and balances of Showers Company as of December 31, 2005, the end of its fiscal year. (1) Prepare the December 31, 2005, closing entries for Showers Company. (2) Prepare the December 31, 2005, post-closing trial balance for Showers Company.

No.	Account Title	Debit	Credit
101	Cash	$18,000	
126	Supplies	12,000	
128	Prepaid insurance	2,000	
167	Equipment	23,000	
168	Accumulated depreciation—Equipment		$ 6,500
301	R. Showers, Capital		46,600

[continued on next page]

[continued from previous page]

302	R. Showers, Withdrawals	6,000	
404	Services revenue		36,000
612	Depreciation expense—Equipment	2,000	
622	Salaries expense	21,000	
637	Insurance expense	1,500	
640	Rent expense	2,400	
652	Supplies expense	1,200	
	Totals	$89,100	$89,100

Check (2) R. Showers, Capital (ending), $48,500; Total debits, $55,000

Exercise 4-4
Preparing a classified balance sheet
C3

Use the following adjusted trial balance of Webb Trucking Company to prepare a classified balance sheet as of December 31, 2005.

Account Title	Debit	Credit
Cash	$ 7,000	
Accounts receivable	16,500	
Office supplies	2,000	
Trucks	170,000	
Accumulated depreciation—Trucks		$ 35,000
Land	75,000	
Accounts payable		11,000
Interest payable		3,000
Long-term notes payable		52,000
K. Webb, Capital		161,000
K. Webb, Withdrawals	19,000	
Trucking fees earned		128,000
Depreciation expense—Trucks	22,500	
Salaries expense	60,000	
Office supplies expense	7,000	
Repairs expense—Trucks	11,000	
Totals	$390,000	$390,000

Check Total assets, $235,500; K. Webb, Capital, $169,500

Exercise 4-5
Preparing the financial statements
C2

Use the information in the adjusted trial balance reported in Exercise 4-4 to prepare Webb Trucking Company's (1) income statement, and (2) statement of owner's equity. The K. Webb, Capital account balance is $161,000 at December 31, 2004.

Exercise 4-6
Computing the current ratio
A1 

Use the information in the adjusted trial balance reported in Exercise 4-4 to compute the current ratio as of the balance sheet date. Interpret the current ratio for this company. (Assume that the industry norm for the current ratio is 1.5.)

Exercise 4-7
Computing and analyzing the current ratio
A1 

Calculate the current ratio in each of the following separate cases. Identify the company case with the strongest liquidity position. (These cases represent competing companies in the same industry.)

	Current Assets	Current Liabilities
Case 1	$ 78,000	$31,000
Case 2	104,000	75,000
Case 3	44,000	48,000
Case 4	84,500	80,600
Case 5	60,000	99,000

Exercise 4-8
Preparing adjusting entries from a work sheet
P1

Use the following information from the Adjustments columns of a 10-column work sheet to prepare the necessary adjusting journal entries (*a*) through (*e*):

No.	Account Title	Adjustments Debit	Adjustments Credit
109	Interest receivable	(*d*) $ 580	
124	Office supplies		(*b*) $1,650
128	Prepaid insurance		(*a*) 900
164	Accumulated depreciation—Office equipment		(*c*) 3,300
209	Salaries payable		(*e*) 660
409	Interest revenue		(*d*) 580
612	Depreciation expense—Office equipment	(*c*) 3,300	
620	Office salaries expense	(*e*) 660	
636	Insurance expense—Office equipment	(*a*) 432	
637	Insurance expense—Store equipment	(*a*) 468	
650	Office supplies expense	(*b*) 1,650	
	Totals	$7,090	$7,090

Exercise 4-9
Extending adjusted account balances on a work sheet
P1

These 16 accounts are from the Adjusted Trial Balance columns of a company's 10-column work sheet. In the blank space beside each account, write the letter of the appropriate financial statement column (A, B, C, or D) to which a normal account balance is extended.

A. Debit column for the Income Statement columns.
B. Credit column for the Income Statement columns.
C. Debit column for the Balance Sheet and Statement of Owner's Equity columns.
D. Credit column for the Balance Sheet and Statement of Owner's Equity columns.

_____ **1.** Office Supplies
_____ **2.** Accounts Payable
_____ **3.** Owner, Capital
_____ **4.** Wages Payable
_____ **5.** Machinery
_____ **6.** Interest Receivable
_____ **7.** Interest Expense
_____ **8.** Owner, Withdrawals
_____ **9.** Service Fees Revenue
_____ **10.** Insurance Expense
_____ **11.** Accumulated Depreciation
_____ **12.** Interest Revenue
_____ **13.** Accounts Receivable
_____ **14.** Rent Expense
_____ **15.** Depreciation Expense
_____ **16.** Cash

Exercise 4-10
Extending accounts in a work sheet
P1

The Adjusted Trial Balance columns of a 10-column work sheet for Poppe Company follow. Complete the work sheet by extending the account balances into the appropriate financial statement columns and by entering the amount of net income for the reporting period.

No.	Account Title	Debit	Credit
101	Cash	$ 6,000	
106	Accounts receivable	26,200	
153	Trucks	41,000	
154	Accumulated depreciation—Trucks		$ 16,500
183	Land	30,000	
201	Accounts payable		14,000
209	Salaries payable		3,200
233	Unearned fees		2,600
301	J. Poppe, Capital		64,500
302	J. Poppe, Withdrawals	14,400	
401	Plumbing fees earned		79,000
611	Depreciation expense—Trucks	5,500	
622	Salaries expense	37,000	
640	Rent expense	12,000	
677	Miscellaneous expenses	7,700	
	Totals	$179,800	$179,800

Check Net income, $16,800

Exercise 4-11
Completing the income statement columns and preparing closing entries
P1 P2

These partially completed Income Statement columns from a 10-column work sheet are for Red Sail Rental Co. (1) Use the information to determine the amount that should be entered on the net income line of the work sheet. (2) Prepare Red Sail's closing entries. The owner, L. Welch, did not make any withdrawals this period.

Account Title	Debit	Credit
Rent earned		102,000
Salaries expense	45,300	
Insurance expense	6,400	
Dock rental expense	15,000	
Boat supplies expense	3,200	
Depreciation expense—Boats	19,500	
Totals		
Net income		
Totals		

Check Net income, $12,600

Exercise 4-12
Preparing a work sheet and recording closing entries
P1 P2

The following unadjusted trial balance contains the accounts and balances of Dalton Delivery Company as of December 31, 2005, its first year of operations. (1) Use the following information about the company's adjustments to complete a 10-column work sheet for Dalton.

a. Unrecorded depreciation on the trucks at the end of the year is $35,000.

b. The total amount of accrued interest expense at year-end is $8,000.

c. The cost of unused office supplies still available at year-end is $1,000.

(2) Prepare the year-end closing entries for Dalton, and determine the capital amount to be reported on the year-end balance sheet.

Microsoft Excel - Book1

	A	B	C
1	**Account Title**	**Debit**	**Credit**
2	Cash	$ 14,000	
3	Accounts receivable	33,000	
4	Office supplies	4,000	
5	Trucks	340,000	
6	Accumulated depreciation—Trucks		$ 70,000
7	Land	150,000	
8	Accounts payable		22,000
9	Interest payable		6,000
10	Long-term notes payable		104,000
11	V. Dalton, Capital		322,000
12	V. Dalton, Withdrawals	38,000	
13	Delivery fees earned		256,000
14	Depreciation expense—Truck	45,000	
15	Salaries expense	120,000	
16	Office supplies expense	14,000	
17	Interest expense	6,000	
18	Repairs expense—trucks	16,000	
19	Totals	$780,000	$780,000
20			

Check Adj. trial balance totals, $817,000; Net income, $15,000

Exercise 4-13[A]
Preparing reversing entries
P4

The following two events occurred for Totten Co. on October 31, 2005, the end of its fiscal year:

a. Totten rents a building from its owner for $3,200 per month. By a prearrangement, the company delayed paying October's rent until November 5. On this date, the company paid the rent for both October and November.

b. Totten rents space in a building it owns to a tenant for $750 per month. By prearrangement, the tenant delayed paying the October rent until November 8. On this date, the tenant paid the rent for both October and November.

Required

1. Prepare adjusting entries that Totten must record for these events as of October 31.

2. Assuming Totten does *not* use reversing entries, prepare journal entries to record Totten's payment of rent on November 5 and the collection of rent on November 8 from Totten's tenant.

3. Assuming that Totten uses reversing entries, prepare reversing entries on November 1 and the journal entries to record Totten's payment of rent on November 5 and the collection of rent on November 8 from Totten's tenant.

Exercise 4-14[A]
Preparing reversing entries
P4

Hinson Company records prepaid assets and unearned revenues in balance sheet accounts. The following information was used to prepare adjusting entries for Hinson Company as of August 31, the end of the company's fiscal year:

a. The company has earned $5,000 in unrecorded service fees.

b. The expired portion of prepaid insurance is $2,700.

c. The company has earned $1,900 of its Unearned Service Fees account balance.

d. Depreciation expense for office equipment is $2,300.

e. Employees have earned but have not been paid salaries of $2,400.

Prepare any necessary reversing entries for the accounting adjustments *a* through *e* assuming that Hinson uses reversing entries in its accounting system.

PROBLEM SET A

Problem 4-1A
Determining balance sheet classifications
C3

In the blank space beside each numbered balance sheet item, enter the letter of its balance sheet classification. If the item should not appear on the balance sheet, enter a *Z* in the blank.

A. Current assets
B. Long-term investments
C. Plant assets
D. Intangible assets
E. Current liabilities
F. Long-term liabilities
G. Equity

_____ **1.** Accumulated depreciation—Trucks
_____ **2.** Cash
_____ **3.** Buildings
_____ **4.** Store supplies
_____ **5.** Office equipment
_____ **6.** Land (used in operations)
_____ **7.** Repairs expense
_____ **8.** Office supplies
_____ **9.** Current portion of long-term note payable
_____ **10.** Long-term investment in stock
_____ **11.** Depreciation expense—Building
_____ **12.** Prepaid rent
_____ **13.** Interest receivable
_____ **14.** Taxes payable
_____ **15.** Automobiles
_____ **16.** Notes payable (due in 3 years)
_____ **17.** Accounts payable
_____ **18.** Prepaid insurance
_____ **19.** Owner, Capital
_____ **20.** Unearned services revenue

Problem 4-2A
Applying the accounting cycle
C1 C2 P2 P3

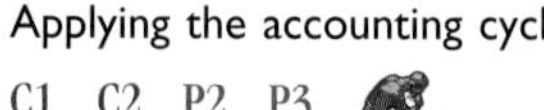

mhhe.com/larson

On April 1, 2005, Jennifer Stafford created a new travel agency, See-It-Now Travel. The following transactions occurred during the company's first month:

April	1	Stafford invested $20,000 cash and computer equipment worth $40,000 in the business.
	2	Rented furnished office space by paying $1,700 cash for the first month's (April) rent.
	3	Purchased $1,100 of office supplies for cash.
	10	Paid $3,600 cash for the premium on a 12-month insurance policy. Coverage begins on April 11.
	14	Paid $1,800 cash for two weeks' salaries earned by employees.
	24	Collected $7,900 cash on commissions from airlines on tickets obtained for customers.
	28	Paid another $1,800 cash for two weeks' salaries earned by employees.
	29	Paid $250 cash for minor repairs to the company's computer.
	30	Paid $650 cash for this month's telephone bill.
	30	Stafford withdrew $1,500 cash for personal use.

The company's chart of accounts follows:

101	Cash	405	Commissions Earned
106	Accounts Receivable	612	Depreciation Expense—Computer Equip.
124	Office Supplies	622	Salaries Expense
128	Prepaid Insurance	637	Insurance Expense
167	Computer Equipment	640	Rent Expense
168	Accumulated Depreciation—Computer Equip.	650	Office Supplies Expense
209	Salaries Payable	684	Repairs Expense
301	J. Stafford, Capital	688	Telephone Expense
302	J. Stafford, Withdrawals	901	Income Summary

Required

1. Use the balance column format to set up each ledger account listed in its chart of accounts.

2. Prepare journal entries to record the transactions for April and post them to the ledger accounts. The company records prepaid and unearned items in balance sheet accounts.

3. Prepare an unadjusted trial balance as of April 30.

Check (3) Unadj. trial balance totals, $67,900

4. Use the following information to journalize and post adjusting entries for the month:

a. Two-thirds of one month's insurance coverage has expired.

(4*a*) Dr. Insurance Expense, $200

b. At the end of the month, $700 of office supplies are still available.

c. This month's depreciation on the computer equipment is $600.

d. Employees earned $320 of unpaid and unrecorded salaries as of month-end.

e. The company earned $1,650 of commissions that are not yet billed at month-end.

5. Prepare the income statement and the statement of owner's equity for the month of April and the balance sheet at April 30, 2005.

(5) Net income, $1,830; Capital (4/30/2005), $60,330; Total assets, $60,650

6. Prepare journal entries to close the temporary accounts and post these entries to the ledger.

7. Prepare a post-closing trial balance.

(7) P-C trial balance totals, $61,250

Problem 4-3A
Preparing trial balances, closing entries, and financial statements

C3 P2 P3

mhhe.com/larson

The adjusted trial balance of Kobe Repairs on December 31, 2005, follows:

KOBE REPAIRS
Adjusted Trial Balance
December 31, 2005

No.	Account Title	Debit	Credit
101	Cash	$ 13,000	
124	Office supplies	1,200	
128	Prepaid insurance	1,950	
167	Equipment	48,000	
168	Accumulated depreciation—Equipment		$ 4,000
201	Accounts payable		12,000
210	Wages payable		500
301	S. Kobe, Capital		40,000
302	S. Kobe, Withdrawals	15,000	
401	Repair fees earned		77,750
612	Depreciation expense—Equipment	4,000	
623	Wages expense	36,500	
637	Insurance expense	700	
640	Rent expense	9,600	
650	Office supplies expense	2,600	
690	Utilities expense	1,700	
	Totals	$134,250	$134,250

Check (1) Ending capital balance, $47,650

(2) P-C trial balance totals, $64,150

Required

1. Prepare an income statement and a statement of owner's equity for the year 2005, and a classified balance sheet at December 31, 2005. There are no owner investments in 2005.

2. Enter the adjusted trial balance in the first two columns of a six-column table. Use columns three and four for closing entry information and the last two columns for a post-closing trial balance. Insert an Income Summary account as the last item in the trial balance.

3. Enter closing entry information in the six-column table and prepare journal entries for them.

Analysis Component

4. Assume for this part only that:

a. None of the $700 insurance expense had expired during the year. Instead, assume it is a prepayment of the next period's insurance protection.

b. There are no earned and unpaid wages at the end of the year. (*Hint:* Reverse the $500 wages payable accrual.)

Describe the financial statement changes that would result from these two assumptions.

Problem 4-4A
Preparing closing entries, financial statements, and ratios
C3 A1 P2

The adjusted trial balance for Sharp Construction as of December 31, 2005, follows:

SHARP CONSTRUCTION Adjusted Trial Balance December 31, 2005			
No.	**Account Title**	**Debit**	**Credit**
101	Cash	$ 4,000	
104	Short-term investments	22,000	
126	Supplies	7,100	
128	Prepaid insurance	6,000	
167	Equipment	39,000	
168	Accumulated depreciation—Equipment		$ 20,000
173	Building	130,000	
174	Accumulated depreciation—Building		55,000
183	Land	45,000	
201	Accounts payable		15,500
203	Interest payable		1,500
208	Rent payable		2,500
210	Wages payable		1,500
213	Property taxes payable		800
233	Unearned professional fees		6,500
251	Long-term notes payable		66,000
301	J. Sharp, Capital		82,700
302	J. Sharp, Withdrawals	12,000	
401	Professional fees earned		96,000
406	Rent earned		13,000
407	Dividends earned		1,900
409	Interest earned		1,000
606	Depreciation expense—Building	10,000	
612	Depreciation expense—Equipment	5,000	
623	Wages expense	31,000	
633	Interest expense	4,100	
637	Insurance expense	9,000	
640	Rent expense	12,400	
652	Supplies expense	6,400	
682	Postage expense	3,200	
683	Property taxes expense	4,000	
684	Repairs expense	7,900	
688	Telephone expense	2,200	
690	Utilities expense	3,600	
	Totals	$363,900	$363,900

J. Sharp invested $50,000 cash in the business during year 2005 (the December 31, 2004, credit balance of the J. Sharp, Capital account was $32,700). Sharp Construction is required to make a $6,600 payment on its long-term notes payable during 2006.

Required

1. Prepare the income statement and the statement of owner's equity for the calendar-year 2005, and the classified balance sheet at December 31, 2005.

2. Prepare the necessary closing entries at December 31, 2005.

3. Use the information in the financial statements to compute these ratios: (a) return on assets (total assets at December 31, 2004, was $200,000), (b) debt ratio, (c) profit margin ratio (use total revenues as the denominator), and (d) current ratio.

Check (1) Total assets (12/31/2005), $178,100; Net income, $13,100

Problem 4-5A
Preparing a work sheet, adjusting and closing entries, and financial statements

C3 P1 P2   

The following unadjusted trial balance is for Adams Construction Co. as of the end of its 2005 fiscal year. The June 30, 2004, credit balance of the owner's capital account was $52,660, and the owner invested $25,000 cash in the company during the 2005 fiscal year.

ADAMS CONSTRUCTION CO.
Unadjusted Trial Balance
June 30, 2005

No.	Account Title	Debit	Credit
101	Cash	$ 17,500	
126	Supplies	8,900	
128	Prepaid insurance	6,200	
167	Equipment	131,000	
168	Accumulated depreciation—Equipment		$ 25,250
201	Accounts payable		5,800
203	Interest payable		0
208	Rent payable		0
210	Wages payable		0
213	Property taxes payable		0
251	Long-term notes payable		24,000
301	S. Adams, Capital		77,660
302	S. Adams, Withdrawals	30,000	
401	Construction fees earned		134,000
612	Depreciation expense—Equipment	0	
623	Wages expense	45,860	
633	Interest expense	2,640	
637	Insurance expense	0	
640	Rent expense	13,200	
652	Supplies expense	0	
683	Property taxes expense	4,600	
684	Repairs expense	2,810	
690	Utilities expense	4,000	
	Totals	$ 266,710	$ 266,710

Required

1. Prepare a 10-column work sheet for fiscal year 2005, starting with the unadjusted trial balance and including adjustments based on these additional facts:

a. The supplies available at the end of fiscal year 2005 had a cost of $3,200.

b. The cost of expired insurance for the fiscal year is $3,900.

c. Annual depreciation on equipment is $8,500.

d. The June utilities expense of $550 is not included in the unadjusted trial balance because the bill arrived after the trial balance was prepared. The $550 amount owed needs to be recorded.

e. The company's employees have earned $1,600 of accrued wages at fiscal year-end.

f. The rent expense incurred and not yet paid or recorded at fiscal year-end is $200.

g. Additional property taxes of $900 have been assessed for this fiscal year but have not been paid or recorded in the accounts.

h. The long-term note payable bears interest at 1% per month. The unadjusted Interest Expense account equals the amount paid for the first 11 months of the 2005 fiscal year. The $240 accrued interest for June has not yet been paid or recorded. (Note that the company is required to make a $5,000 payment toward the note payable during the 2006 fiscal year.)

Check (3) Total assets, $120,250; current liabilities, $14,290; Net income, $39,300

2. Use the work sheet to enter the adjusting and closing entries; then journalize them.
3. Prepare the income statement and the statement of owner's equity for the year ended June 30 and the classified balance sheet at June 30, 2005.

Analysis Component

4. Analyze the following separate errors and describe how each would affect the 10-column work sheet. Explain whether the error is likely to be discovered in completing the work sheet and, if not, the effect of the error on the financial statements.
   a. Assume that the adjustment for supplies used consisted of a credit to Supplies for $3,200 and a debit for $3,200 to Supplies Expense.
   b. When the adjusted trial balance in the work sheet is completed, the $17,500 Cash balance is incorrectly entered in the Credit column.

Problem 4-6A[A]

Preparing adjusting, reversing, and next period entries

P4

The following six-column table for Bullseye Ranges includes the unadjusted trial balance as of December 31, 2005.

BULLSEYE RANGES
December 31, 2005

Account Title	Unadjusted Trial Balance		Adjustments		Adjusted Trial Balance	
	Dr.	Cr.	Dr.	Cr.	Dr.	Cr.
Cash	$ 13,000					
Accounts receivable	0					
Supplies	5,500					
Equipment	130,000					
Accumulated depreciation—Equipment		$ 25,000				
Interest payable		0				
Salaries payable		0				
Unearned member fees		14,000				
Notes payable		50,000				
T. Allen, Capital		58,250				
T. Allen, Withdrawals	20,000					
Member fees earned		53,000				
Depreciation expense—Equipment	0					
Salaries expense	28,000					
Interest expense	3,750					
Supplies expense	0					
Totals	$200,250	$200,250				

Required

1. Complete the six-column table by entering adjustments that reflect the following information:
   a. As of December 31, 2005, employees had earned $900 of unpaid and unrecorded salaries. The next payday is January 4, at which time $1,600 of salaries will be paid.
   b. The cost of supplies still available at December 31, 2005, is $2,700.
   c. The notes payable requires an interest payment to be made every three months. The amount of unrecorded accrued interest at December 31, 2005, is $1,250. The next interest payment, at an amount of $1,500, is due on January 15, 2006.
   d. Analysis of the unearned member fees account shows $5,600 remaining unearned at December 31, 2005.
   e. In addition to the member fees included in the revenue account balance, the company has earned another $9,100 in unrecorded fees that will be collected on January 31, 2006. The company is also expected to collect $8,000 on that same day for new fees earned in January 2006.
   f. Depreciation expense for the year is $12,500.

Check (1) Adjusted trial balance totals, $224,000

2. Prepare journal entries for the adjustments entered in the six-column table for part 1.

3. Prepare journal entries to reverse the effects of the adjusting entries that involve accruals.

4. Prepare journal entries to record the cash payments and cash collections described for January.

PROBLEM SET B

Problem 4-1B
Determining balance sheet classifications
C3

In the blank space beside each numbered balance sheet item, enter the letter of its balance sheet classification. If the item should not appear on the balance sheet, enter a *Z* in the blank.

A. Current assets
B. Long-term investments
C. Plant assets
D. Intangible assets
E. Current liabilities
F. Long-term liabilities
G. Equity

_____ **1.** Machinery
_____ **2.** Prepaid insurance
_____ **3.** Current portion of long-term note payable
_____ **4.** Interest receivable
_____ **5.** Rent receivable
_____ **6.** Land (used in operations)
_____ **7.** Copyrights
_____ **8.** Rent revenue
_____ **9.** Depreciation expense—Trucks
_____ **10.** Long-term investment in stock
_____ **11.** Office supplies
_____ **12.** Interest payable
_____ **13.** Owner, Capital
_____ **14.** Notes receivable (due in 120 days)
_____ **15.** Accumulated depreciation—Trucks
_____ **16.** Salaries payable
_____ **17.** Commissions earned
_____ **18.** Interest payable
_____ **19.** Office equipment
_____ **20.** Notes payable (due in 5 years)

Problem 4-2B
Applying the accounting cycle
C1 C2 P2 P3 

On July 1, 2005, Lucinda Fogle created a new self-storage business, KeepSafe Co. The following transactions occurred during the company's first month:

July 1 Fogle invested $20,000 cash and buildings worth $120,000 in the business.
2 Rented equipment by paying $1,800 cash for the first month's (July) rent.
5 Purchased $2,300 of office supplies for cash.
10 Paid $5,400 cash for the premium on a 12-month insurance policy. Coverage begins on July 11.
14 Paid an employee $900 cash for two weeks' salary earned.
24 Collected $8,800 cash for storage fees from customers.
28 Paid another $900 cash for two weeks' salary earned by an employee.
29 Paid $850 cash for minor repairs to a leaking roof.
30 Paid $300 cash for this month's telephone bill.
31 Fogle withdrew $1,600 cash for personal use.

The company's chart of accounts follows:

101	Cash	401	Storage Fees Earned
106	Accounts Receivable	606	Depreciation Expense—Buildings
124	Office Supplies	622	Salaries Expense
128	Prepaid Insurance	637	Insurance Expense
173	Buildings	640	Rent Expense
174	Accumulated Depreciation—Buildings	650	Office Supplies Expense
209	Salaries Payable	684	Repairs Expense
301	L. Fogle, Capital	688	Telephone Expense
302	L. Fogle, Withdrawals	901	Income Summary

Required

1. Use the balance column format to set up each ledger account listed in its chart of accounts.

2. Prepare journal entries to record the transactions for July and post them to the ledger accounts. Record prepaid and unearned items in balance sheet accounts.

Check (3) Unadj. trial balance totals, $148,800

(4a) Dr. Insurance Expense, $300

(5) Net income, $2,570; Capital (7/31/2005), $140,970; Total assets, $141,150

(7) P-C trial balance totals, $142,350

3. Prepare an unadjusted trial balance as of July 31.

4. Use the following information to journalize and post adjusting entries for the month:

a. Two-thirds of one month's insurance coverage has expired.

b. At the end of the month, $1,550 of office supplies are still available.

c. This month's depreciation on the buildings is $1,200.

d. An employee earned $180 of unpaid and unrecorded salary as of month-end.

e. The company earned $950 of storage fees that are not yet billed at month-end.

5. Prepare the income statement and the statement of owner's equity for the month of July and the balance sheet at July 31, 2005.

6. Prepare journal entries to close the temporary accounts and post these entries to the ledger.

7. Prepare a post-closing trial balance.

Problem 4-3B

Preparing trial balances, closing entries, and financial statements

C3 P2 P3 

Heel-To-Toe-Shoes' adjusted trial balance on December 31, 2005, follows:

HEEL-TO-TOE SHOES
Adjusted Trial Balance
December 31, 2005

No.	Account Title	Debit	Credit
101	Cash	$ 13,450	
125	Store supplies	4,140	
128	Prepaid insurance	2,200	
167	Equipment	33,000	
168	Accumulated depreciation—Equipment		$ 9,000
201	Accounts payable		1,000
210	Wages payable		3,200
301	P. Holt, Capital		31,650
302	P. Holt, Withdrawals	16,000	
401	Repair fees earned		62,000
612	Depreciation expense—Equipment	3,000	
623	Wages expense	28,400	
637	Insurance expense	1,100	
640	Rent expense	2,400	
651	Store supplies expense	1,300	
690	Utilities expense	1,860	
	Totals	$106,850	$106,850

Required

Check (1) Ending capital balance, $39,590

(2) P-C trial balance totals, $52,790

1. Prepare an income statement and a statement of owner's equity for the year 2005, and a classified balance sheet at December 31, 2005. There are no owner investments in 2005.

2. Enter the adjusted trial balance in the first two columns of a six-column table. Use the middle two columns for closing entry information and the last two columns for a post-closing trial balance. Insert an Income Summary account as the last item in the trial balance.

3. Enter closing entry information in the six-column table and prepare journal entries for them.

Analysis Component

4. Assume for this part only that:

a. None of the $1,100 insurance expense had expired during the year. Instead, assume it is a prepayment of the next period's insurance protection.

b. There are no earned and unpaid wages at the end of the year. (*Hint:* Reverse the $3,200 wages payable accrual.)

Describe the financial statement changes that would result from these two assumptions.

Problem 4-4B
Preparing closing entries, financial statements, and ratios

C3 A1 P2

The adjusted trial balance for Giovanni Co. as of December 31, 2005, follows:

GIOVANNI CO. Adjusted Trial Balance December 31, 2005			
No.	**Account Title**	**Debit**	**Credit**
101	Cash	$ 6,400	
104	Short-term investments	10,200	
126	Supplies	3,600	
128	Prepaid insurance	800	
167	Equipment	18,000	
168	Accumulated depreciation—Equipment		$ 3,000
173	Building	90,000	
174	Accumulated depreciation—Building		9,000
183	Land	28,500	
201	Accounts payable		2,500
203	Interest payable		1,400
208	Rent payable		200
210	Wages payable		1,180
213	Property taxes payable		2,330
233	Unearned professional fees		650
251	Long-term notes payable		32,000
301	J. Giovanni, Capital		91,800
302	J. Giovanni, Withdrawals	6,000	
401	Professional fees earned		47,000
406	Rent earned		3,600
407	Dividends earned		500
409	Interest earned		1,120
606	Depreciation expense—Building	2,000	
612	Depreciation expense—Equipment	1,000	
623	Wages expense	17,500	
633	Interest expense	1,200	
637	Insurance expense	1,425	
640	Rent expense	1,800	
652	Supplies expense	900	
682	Postage expense	310	
683	Property taxes expense	3,825	
684	Repairs expense	579	
688	Telephone expense	421	
690	Utilities expense	1,820	
	Totals	$196,280	$196,280

J. Giovanni invested $30,000 cash in the business during year 2005 (the December 31, 2004, credit balance of the J. Giovanni, Capital account was $61,800). Giovanni Company is required to make a $6,400 payment on its long-term notes payable during 2006.

Required

1. Prepare the income statement and the statement of owner's equity for the calendar year 2005 and the classified balance sheet at December 31, 2005.
2. Prepare the necessary closing entries at December 31, 2005.
3. Use the information in the financial statements to calculate these ratios: (a) return on assets (total assets at December 31, 2004, was $150,000), (b) debt ratio, (c) profit margin ratio (use total revenues as the denominator), and (d) current ratio.

Check (1) Total assets (12/31/2005), $145,500; Net income, $19,440

Problem 4-5B
Preparing a work sheet, adjusting and closing entries, and financial statements

C3 P1 P2 

The following unadjusted trial balance is for Crush Demolition Company as of the end of its April 30, 2005, fiscal year. The April 30, 2004, credit balance of the owner's capital account was $36,900, and the owner invested $30,000 cash in the company during the 2005 fiscal year.

No.	Account Title	Debit	Credit
	CRUSH DEMOLITION COMPANY **Unadjusted Trial Balance** **April 30, 2005**		
101	Cash	$ 9,000	
126	Supplies	18,000	
128	Prepaid insurance	14,600	
167	Equipment	140,000	
168	Accumulated depreciation—Equipment		$ 10,000
201	Accounts payable		16,000
203	Interest payable		0
208	Rent payable		0
210	Wages payable		0
213	Property taxes payable		0
251	Long-term notes payable		20,000
301	J. Bonair, Capital		66,900
302	J. Bonair, Withdrawals	24,000	
401	Demolition fees earned		177,000
612	Depreciation expense—Equipment	0	
623	Wages expense	51,400	
633	Interest expense	2,200	
637	Insurance expense	0	
640	Rent expense	8,800	
652	Supplies expense	0	
683	Property taxes expense	8,400	
684	Repairs expense	6,700	
690	Utilities expense	6,800	
	Totals	$ 289,900	$ 289,900

Required

1. Prepare a 10-column work sheet for fiscal year 2005, starting with the unadjusted trial balance and including adjustments based on these additional facts:

a. The supplies available at the end of fiscal year 2005 had a cost of $8,100.

b. The cost of expired insurance for the fiscal year is $11,500.

c. Annual depreciation on equipment is $18,000.

d. The April utilities expense of $700 is not included in the unadjusted trial balance because the bill arrived after the trial balance was prepared. The $700 amount owed needs to be recorded.

e. The company's employees have earned $2,200 of accrued wages at fiscal year-end.

f. The rent expense incurred and not yet paid or recorded at fiscal year-end is $5,360.

g. Additional property taxes of $450 have been assessed for this fiscal year but have not been paid or recorded in the accounts.

h. The long-term note payable bears interest at 1% per month. The unadjusted Interest Expense account equals the amount paid for the first 11 months of the 2005 fiscal year. The $200 accrued interest for April has not yet been paid or recorded. (Note that the company is required to make a $4,000 payment toward the note payable during the 2006 fiscal year.)

2. Use the work sheet to enter the adjusting and closing entries; then journalize them.

3. Prepare the income statement and the statement of owner's equity for the year ended April 30, and the classified balance sheet at April 30, 2005.

Check (3) Total assets, $132,200; current liabilities, $28,910; Net income, $44,390

Analysis Component

4. Analyze the following separate errors and describe how each would affect the 10-column work sheet. Explain whether the error is likely to be discovered in completing the work sheet and, if not, the effect of the error on the financial statements.

a. Assume the adjustment for expiration of the insurance coverage consisted of a credit to Prepaid Insurance for $3,100 and a debit for $3,100 to Insurance Expense.

b. When the adjusted trial balance in the work sheet is completed, the $6,700 Repairs Expense account balance is extended to the Debit column of the balance sheet columns.

Problem 4-6B[A]
Preparing adjusting, reversing, and next period entries
P4

The following six-column table for Solutions Co. includes the unadjusted trial balance as of December 31, 2005:

SOLUTIONS CO.
December 31, 2005

Account Title	Unadjusted Trial Balance		Adjustments		Adjusted Trial Balance	
	Dr.	Cr.	Dr.	Cr.	Dr.	Cr.
Cash	$ 9,000					
Accounts receivable	0					
Supplies	6,600					
Machinery	40,100					
Accumulated depreciation—Machinery		$15,800				
Interest payable		0				
Salaries payable		0				
Unearned rental fees		5,200				
Notes payable		20,000				
G. Clay, Capital		13,200				
G. Clay, Withdrawals	10,500					
Rental fees earned		37,000				
Depreciation expense—Machinery	0					
Salaries expense	23,500					
Interest expense	1,500					
Supplies expense	0					
Totals	$91,200	$91,200				

Required

1. Complete the six-column table by entering adjustments that reflect the following information:

a. As of December 31, 2005, employees had earned $420 of unpaid and unrecorded wages. The next payday is January 4, at which time $1,250 in wages will be paid.

b. The cost of supplies still available at December 31, 2005, is $2,450.

c. The notes payable requires an interest payment to be made every three months. The amount of unrecorded accrued interest at December 31, 2005, is $500. The next interest payment, at an amount of $600, is due on January 15, 2006.

d. Analysis of the unearned rental fees shows that $3,100 remains unearned at December 31, 2005.

e. In addition to the machinery rental fees included in the revenue account balance, the company has earned another $2,350 in unrecorded fees that will be collected on January 31, 2006. The company is also expected to collect $4,400 on that same day for new fees earned in January 2006.

f. Depreciation expense for the year is $3,800.

Check (1) Adjusted trial balance totals, $98,270

2. Prepare journal entries for the adjustments entered in the six-column table for part 1.

3. Prepare journal entries to reverse the effects of the adjusting entries that involve accruals.

4. Prepare journal entries to record the cash payments and cash collections described for January.

PROBLEM SET C

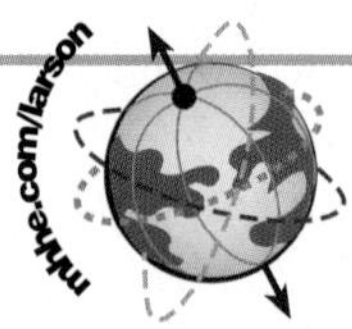

Problem Set C is available at the book's Website to further reinforce and assess your learning.

SERIAL PROBLEM

Success Systems P2 P3

(This serial problem began in Chapter 1 and continues through most of the book. If previous chapter segments were not completed, the serial problem can begin at this point. It is helpful, but not necessary, that you use the Working Papers that accompany the book.)

The December 31, 2004, adjusted trial balance of Success Systems (reflecting its transactions from October through December of 2004) follows:

No.	Account Title	Debit	Credit
101	Cash	$ 58,160	
106	Accounts receivable	5,668	
126	Computer supplies	580	
128	Prepaid insurance	1,665	
131	Prepaid rent	825	
163	Office equipment	8,000	
164	Accumulated depreciation—Office equipment		$ 400
167	Computer equipment	20,000	
168	Accumulated depreciation—Computer equipment		1,250
201	Accounts payable		1,100
210	Wages payable		500
236	Unearned computer services revenue		1,500
301	K. Breeze, Capital		83,000
302	K. Breeze, Withdrawals	7,100	
403	Computer services revenue		31,284
612	Depreciation expense—Office equipment	400	
613	Depreciation expense—Computer equipment	1,250	
623	Wages expense	3,875	
637	Insurance expense	555	
640	Rent expense	2,475	
652	Computer supplies expense	3,065	
655	Advertising expense	2,965	
676	Mileage expense	896	
677	Miscellaneous expenses	250	
684	Repairs expense—Computer	1,305	
901	Income summary		0
	Totals	$119,034	$119,034

Required

Check Post-closing trial balance totals, $94,898

1. Record and post the necessary closing entries for Success Systems.
2. Prepare a post-closing trial balance as of December 31, 2004.

BEYOND THE NUMBERS

REPORTING IN ACTION

C1 P2

BTN 4-1 Refer to **Krispy Kreme**'s financial statements in Appendix A to answer the following:

Required

1. For the fiscal year ended February 2, 2003, what amount will be credited to Income Summary to summarize its revenues earned?
2. For the fiscal year ended February 2, 2003, what amount will be debited to Income Summary to summarize its expenses incurred?

3. For the fiscal year ended February 2, 2003, what will be the balance of its Income Summary account before it is closed?
4. In its statement of cash flows for the year ended February 2, 2003, what amount of cash is paid in dividends to common stockholders?

Roll On

5. Access Krispy Kreme's annual report for fiscal years ending after February 2, 2003, at its Website (KrispyKreme.com) or the SEC's EDGAR database (www.SEC.gov). How has the amount of net income closed to Income Summary changed in the fiscal years ending after February 2, 2003? How has the amount of cash paid as dividends changed in the fiscal years ending after February 2, 2003?

COMPARATIVE ANALYSIS

A1 

BTN 4-2 Key figures ($ thousands) for the recent two years of both **Krispy Kreme** and **Tastykake** follow:

Key Figures	Krispy Kreme		Tastykake	
	Current Year	Prior Year	Current Year	Prior Year
Current assets	$141,128	$101,769	$36,095	$35,169
Current liabilities	59,687	52,533	19,307	16,885

Required

1. Compute the current ratio for both years and both companies.
2. Which has the better ability to pay short-term obligations according to the current ratio?
3. Analyze and comment on each company's current ratios for the past two years.
4. How do Krispy Kreme's and Tastykake's current ratios compare to their industry average ratio of about 1.0 to 1.2?

ETHICS CHALLENGE

C2 

BTN 4-3 On January 20, 2005, Jennifer Nelson, the accountant for Travon Enterprises, is feeling pressure to complete the annual financial statements. The company president has said he needs up-to-date financial statements to share with the bank on January 21 at a dinner meeting that has been called to discuss Travon's obtaining loan financing for a special building project. Jennifer knows that she will not be able to gather all the needed information in the next 24 hours to prepare the entire set of adjusting entries that must be posted before the financial statements accurately portray the company's performance and financial position for the fiscal period ended December 31, 2004. Jennifer ultimately decides to estimate several expense accruals at the last minute. When deciding on estimates for the expenses, she uses low estimates because she does not want to make the financial statements look worse than they are. Jennifer finishes the financial statements before the deadline and gives them to the president without mentioning that several accounts use estimated balances.

Required

1. Identify several courses of action that Jennifer could have taken instead of the one she took.
2. If you were in Jennifer's situation, what would you have done? Briefly justify your response.

COMMUNICATING IN PRACTICE

C1 P2

BTN 4-4 Assume that one of your classmates states that a company's books should be ongoing and therefore not closed until that business is terminated. Write a one-half page memo to this classmate explaining the concept of the closing process by drawing analogies between (1) a scoreboard for an athletic event and the revenue and expense accounts of a business or (2) a sports team's record book and the capital account. (*Hint:* Think about what would happen if the scoreboard is not cleared before the start of a new game.)

TAKING IT TO THE NET

A1

mhhe.com/larson

BTN 4-5 Access **Motley Fool**'s discussion of the current ratio at Fool.com/School/Valuation/CurrentAndQuickRatio.htm. (Note that if the page changed, search the site for the *current ratio*.)

Required

1. What level for the current ratio is generally regarded as sufficient to meet near-term operating needs?
2. Once you have calculated the current ratio for a company, what should you compare it against?
3. What are the implications for a company that has a current ratio that is too high?

TEAMWORK IN ACTION

P1 P2 P3

BTN 4-6 The unadjusted trial balance and information for the accounting adjustments of Noseworthy Investigators follow. Each team member involved in this project is to assume one of the four responsibilities listed. After completing each of these responsibilities, the team should work together to prove the accounting equation utilizing information from teammates (1 and 4). If your equation does not balance, you are to work as a team to resolve the error. The team's goal is to complete the task as quickly and accurately as possible.

Unadjusted Trial Balance

Account Title	Debit	Credit
Cash	$15,000	
Supplies	11,000	
Prepaid insurance	2,000	
Equipment	24,000	
Accumulated depreciation—Equipment		$ 6,000
Accounts payable		2,000
D. Noseworthy, Capital		31,000
D. Noseworthy, Withdrawals	5,000	
Investigation fees earned		32,000
Rent expense	14,000	
Totals	$71,000	$71,000

Additional Year-End Information

a. Insurance that expired in the current period amounts to $1,200.
b. Equipment depreciation for the period is $3,000.
c. Unused supplies total $4,000 at period-end.
d. Services in the amount of $500 have been provided but have not been billed or collected.

Responsibilities for Individual Team Members

1. Determine the accounts and adjusted balances to be extended to the balance sheet columns of the work sheet for Noseworthy. Also determine total assets and total liabilities.
2. Determine the adjusted revenue account balance and prepare the entry to close this account.
3. Determine the adjusted account balances for expenses and prepare the entry to close these accounts.
4. Prepare T-accounts for both D. Noseworthy, Capital (reflecting the unadjusted trial balance amount) and Income Summary. Prepare the third and fourth closing entries. Ask teammates assigned to parts 2 and 3 for the postings for Income Summary. Obtain amounts to complete the third closing entry and post both the third and fourth closing entries. Provide the team with the ending capital account balance.
5. The entire team should prove the accounting equation using post-closing balances.

HITTING THE ROAD

C2

BTN 4-7 Select a company that you can visit in person or interview on the telephone. Call ahead to the company to arrange a time when you can interview an employee (preferably an accountant) who helps prepare the annual financial statements. Inquire about the following aspects of its *accounting cycle:*

1. Does it prepare interim financial statements? What time period(s) is used for interim statements?
2. Does the company use the cash or accrual basis of accounting?

3. Does the company use a work sheet in preparing financial statements? Why or why not?
4. Does the company use a spreadsheet program? If so, which software program is used?
5. How long does it take after the end of its reporting period to complete annual statements?

BUSINESS WEEK ACTIVITY

A1 C3

mhhe.com/larson

BTN 4-8 Read the article "Weighing the Balance Sheet" in the April 1, 2002, issue of *Business Week*.

Required

1. This article explains how to evaluate whether a company has a financially strong balance sheet. What does the author of this article look for when evaluating the debt level carried by companies?
2. The article reports a table showing 12 companies that passed the test for strong balance sheets. Identify the range of the current ratio for these 12 companies and name the company with the highest and the company with the lowest current ratios.
3. What is the range of the return on assets ratio for the 12 companies with attractive numbers according to the article? Identify the company with the highest and the company with the lowest return on assets.
4. Some investors will not buy tobacco or asbestos-related companies even if they have a very strong balance sheet. What risk factor are these investors concerned with so that it is more important for these companies than the level of debt on their balance sheets?

ENTREPRENEURIAL DECISION

A1 C3 P2  

BTN 4-9 Review this chapter's opening feature involving Andy Wolf and his startup company, **Premier Snowskates**.

Required

1. What is a conservative estimate for the units of snowskates that will be sold if annual sales are $3 million and Andy Wolf meets his targeted retail price?
2. What ratios studied in Chapters 1 through 4 do you recommend that Andy use to monitor the financial performance of his company?
3. What portions of the classified balance sheet do you believe are most relevant in assisting Andy in discovering what obligations are due and when?
4. What objectives are met when Andy applies closing procedures each fiscal year?

GLOBAL DECISION

A1 

BTN 4-10 **Grupo Bimbo (GrupoBimbo.com)** is a leader in the baking and foods industry. Key financial information (millions of pesos) for Grupo Bimbo for its recent fiscal years follows:

Key Figures*	Current Year	Prior Year
Current assets	$7,155	$4,867
Current liabilities	5,409	4,026

*Key figures prepared in accordance with accounting principles generally accepted in Mexico.

Required

1. Compute the current ratio for Grupo Bimbo for both the current and prior years.
2. Comment on the level and the change in the current ratios computed in part 1.

"I felt we should go into something that we had some connection to"—Dwayne Lewis (standing; Michael Cherry sitting)

Accounting for Merchandising Operations

A Look Back

Chapter 4 focused on the final steps of the accounting process. We explained the importance of proper revenue and expense recognition and described the closing process. We also showed how to prepare financial statements from a work sheet.

A Look at This Chapter

This chapter emphasizes merchandising activities. We explain how reporting merchandising activities differs from reporting service activities. We also analyze and record merchandise purchases and sales transactions and explain the adjustments and closing process for merchandisers.

A Look Ahead

Chapter 6 extends our analysis of merchandising activities and focuses on the valuation of inventory. Topics include the items in inventory, costs assigned, costing methods used, and inventory estimation techniques.

Learning Objectives

CAP

Conceptual

C1 Describe merchandising activities and identify income components for a merchandising company. *(p. 178)*

C2 Identify and explain the inventory asset of a merchandising company. *(p. 179)*

C3 Describe both perpetual and periodic inventory systems. *(p. 179)*

C4 Analyze and interpret cost flows and operating activities of a merchandising company. *(p. 187)*

Analytical

A1 Compute the acid-test ratio and explain its use to assess liquidity. *(p. 193)*

A2 Compute the gross margin ratio and explain its use to assess profitability. *(p. 193)*

Procedural

P1 Analyze and record transactions for merchandise purchases using a perpetual system. *(p. 180)*

P2 Analyze and record transactions for merchandise sales using a perpetual system. *(p. 185)*

P3 Prepare adjustments and close accounts for a merchandising company. *(p. 188)*

P4 Define and prepare multiple-step and single-step income statements. *(p. 190)*

Decision Feature

Dada, Dada, Dada . . .

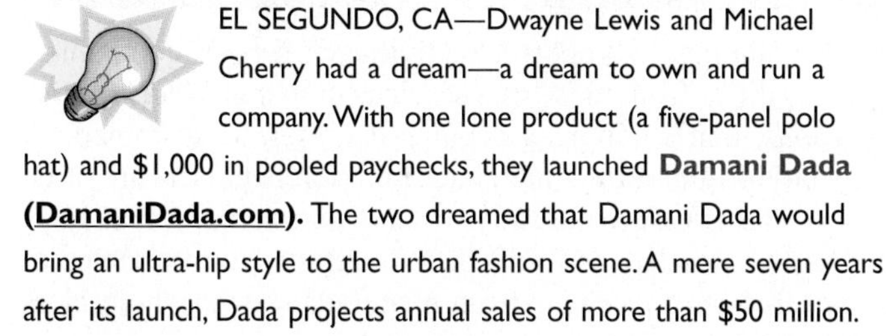

EL SEGUNDO, CA—Dwayne Lewis and Michael Cherry had a dream—a dream to own and run a company. With one lone product (a five-panel polo hat) and $1,000 in pooled paychecks, they launched **Damani Dada (DamaniDada.com).** The two dreamed that Damani Dada would bring an ultra-hip style to the urban fashion scene. A mere seven years after its launch, Dada projects annual sales of more than $50 million.

The early days, however, were far from easy as Lewis and Cherry struggled alone against long odds. "It was very tricky to try and learn the business without a mentor," recalls Lewis. "We always struggled with the task of maintaining a strong financial backing, and we had to learn a lot by making mistakes." Among those struggles was implementing and learning a merchandising system—one that could capture and communicate the costs and sales information so desperately needed by the young entrepreneurs.

A crucial part of their success was tracking merchandising activities. This was necessary for setting prices and making policies for everything from discounts and allowances to returns on both sales and purchases. Also, use of a perpetual inventory system enabled them to stock the right type and amount of merchandise and to avoid the costs of out-of-stock and excess inventory. This chapter describes how the accounting system captures merchandising information for these and other business decisions. It also introduces analysis tools for assessing the financial condition and performance of merchandisers.

Damani Dada successfully weathered the storm and now offers a full line of both men's and women's apparel and footwear. NBA star Chris Webber's chrome Dada shoes were the talk of the 2003 All-Star Game. But it's still a battle. "Business is war," says Lewis. "You have to be mentally strong, willing to sacrifice, and willing to accept delayed gratification."

[Sources: *Damani Dada Website,* January 2004; *Entrepreneur,* November 2000; *ESPN Sports Business,* February 2003.]

Merchandising activities are a major part of modern business. Consumers expect a wealth of products, discount prices, inventory on demand, and high quality. This chapter introduces the business and accounting practices used by companies engaged in merchandising activities. We show how financial statements reflect these merchandising activities and explain the new financial statement items created by merchandising activities. We also analyze and record merchandise purchases and sales, and explain the adjustments and the closing process for merchandising companies.

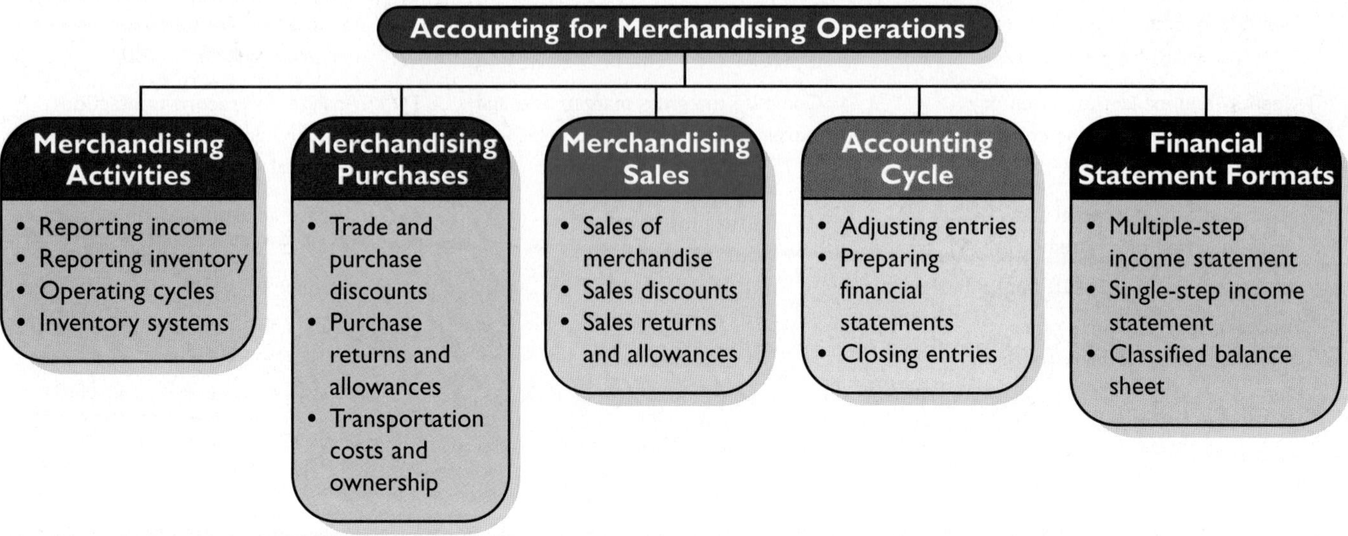

Merchandising Activities

C1 Describe merchandising activities and identify income components for a merchandising company.

Point: **Fleming, SuperValu,** and **SYSCO** are wholesalers. **Gap, Oakley,** and **Wal-Mart** are retailers.

Previous chapters emphasized the accounting and reporting activities of service companies. A merchandising company's activities differ from those of a service company. **Merchandise** consists of products, also called *goods,* that a company acquires to resell to customers. A **merchandiser** earns net income by buying and selling merchandise. Merchandisers are often identified as either wholesalers or retailers. A **wholesaler** is an *intermediary* that buys products from manufacturers or other wholesalers and sells them to retailers or other wholesalers. A **retailer** is an intermediary that buys products from manufacturers or wholesalers and sells them to consumers. Many retailers sell both products and services.

Reporting Income for a Merchandiser

Net income to a merchandiser equals revenues from selling merchandise minus both the cost of merchandise sold to customers and the cost of other expenses for the period (see Exhibit 5.1). The usual accounting term for revenues from selling merchandise is *sales,* and

Exhibit 5.1

Computing Income for a Merchandising Company versus a Service Company

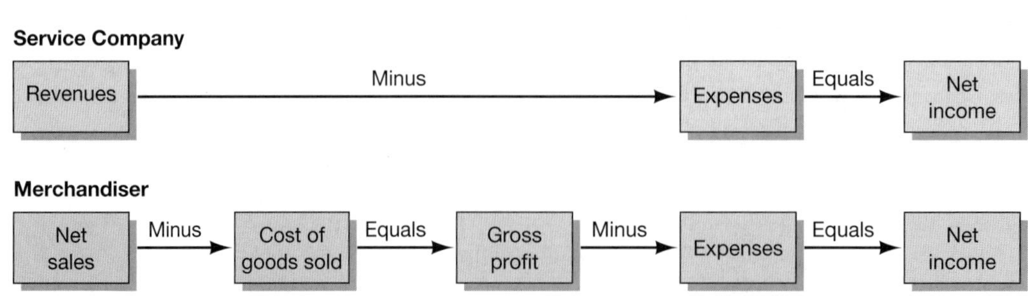

the term used for the expense of buying and preparing the merchandise is **cost of goods sold.** (Note that many service companies use the term *sales* instead of revenues, and cost of goods sold is also called *cost of sales.*)

The income statement for Z-Mart in Exhibit 5.2 illustrates these key components of a merchandiser's net income. The first two lines show that products are acquired at a cost of $230,400 and sold for $314,700. The third line shows an $84,300 **gross profit,** also called **gross margin,** which equals net sales less cost of goods sold. Finally, $71,400 of other expenses are reported, which leaves $12,900 in net income.

Exhibit 5.2

Merchandiser's Income Statement

Z-MART Income Statement For Year Ended December 31, 2005	
Net sales	$314,700
Cost of goods sold	**230,400**
Gross profit	**84,300**
Expenses	71,400
Net income	$ 12,900

Point: Analysis of gross profit is important to effective business decisions, and is described later in the chapter.

Reporting Inventory for a Merchandiser

A merchandiser's balance sheet includes a current asset called *merchandise inventory,* an item not on a service company's balance sheet. **Merchandise inventory,** or simply *inventory,* refers to products that a company owns and intends to sell. The cost of this asset includes the cost incurred to buy the goods, ship them to the store, and make them ready for sale.

C2 Identify and explain the inventory asset of a merchandising company.

Operating Cycle for a Merchandiser

A merchandising company's operating cycle begins by purchasing merchandise and ends by collecting cash from selling the merchandise. The length of an operating cycle differs across the types of businesses. Department stores often have operating cycles of two to five months. Operating cycles for grocery merchants usually range from two to eight weeks.

Exhibit 5.3 illustrates an operating cycle for a merchandiser with credit sales. The cycle moves from (*a*) cash purchases of merchandise to (*b*) inventory for sale to (*c*) credit sales to (*d*) accounts receivable to (*e*) cash. Companies try to keep their operating cycles short because assets tied up in inventory and receivables are not productive.

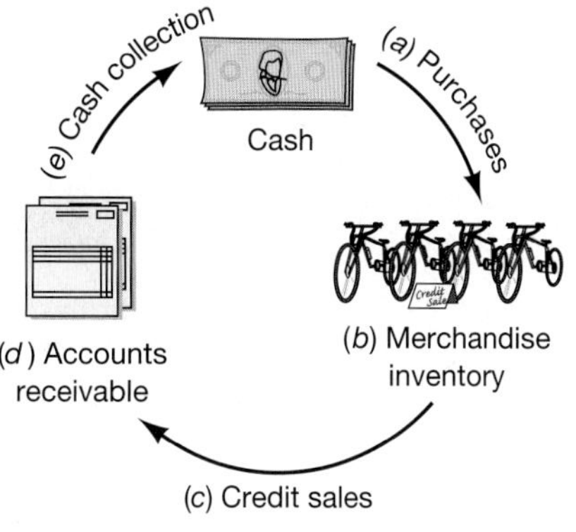

Exhibit 5.3

Merchandiser's Operating Cycle

Point: Cash sales shorten operating cycles. Credit purchases lengthen operating cycles.

Inventory Systems

Cost of goods sold is the cost of merchandise sold to customers during a period. It is often the largest single expense on a merchandiser's income statement. **Inventory** refers to products a company owns and expects to sell in its normal operations. Exhibit 5.4 shows that a company's merchandise available for sale consists of what it begins with (beginning inventory) and what it purchases (net cost of purchases). The merchandise available is either sold (cost of goods sold) or kept for future sales (ending inventory).

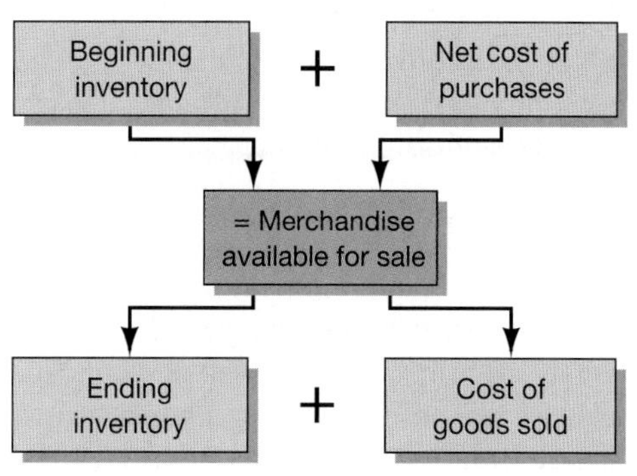

Exhibit 5.4

Merchandiser's Cost Flow for a Single Time Period

Two alternative inventory accounting systems can be used to collect information about cost of goods sold and cost of inventory: *perpetual system* or *periodic system*. The **perpetual**

C3 Describe both perpetual and periodic inventory systems.

Decision Insight

Technology and perpetual inventory systems are helping with purchasing activities, slashing inventory cycles, keeping popular items in stock, and cutting return rates. Technology has "totally changed the industry," says the chairman of **Western Merchandisers**, a supplier to more than 1,000 **Wal-Marts**.

inventory system continually updates accounting records for merchandising transactions—specifically, for those records of inventory available for sale and inventory sold. The **periodic inventory system** updates the accounting records for merchandise transactions only at the *end of a period*. Technological advances and competitive pressures have dramatically increased the use of the perpetual system.

Quick Check

1. Describe a merchandiser's cost of goods sold.
2. What is gross profit for a merchandising company?
3. Explain why use of the perpetual inventory system has dramatically increased.

Answers—p. 204

The following sections on purchasing, selling, and adjusting merchandise use the perpetual system. Appendix 5A uses the periodic system (with the perpetual results on the side). An instructor can choose to cover either one or both inventory systems.

Accounting for Merchandise Purchases

The cost of merchandise purchased for resale is recorded in the Merchandise Inventory asset account. To illustrate, Z-Mart records a $1,200 cash purchase of merchandise on November 2 as follows:

Assets = Liabilities + Equity
+1,200
−1,200

Nov. 2	Merchandise Inventory	1,200	
	Cash		1,200
	Purchased merchandise for cash.		

P1 Analyze and record transactions for merchandise purchases using a perpetual system.

The invoice for this merchandise is shown in Exhibit 5.5. The buyer usually receives the original invoice, and the seller keeps a copy. This *source document* serves as the purchase invoice of Z-Mart (buyer) and the sales invoice for Trex (seller). The amount recorded for merchandise inventory includes its purchase cost, shipping fees, taxes, and any other costs necessary to make it ready for sale. This section explains how we compute the recorded cost of merchandise purchases.

Topic Tackler 5-1

Trade Discounts

When a manufacturer or wholesaler prepares a catalog of items it has for sale, it usually gives each item a **list price,** also called a *catalog price.* However, an item's intended *selling price* equals list price minus a given percent called a **trade discount.** The amount of trade discount usually depends on whether a buyer is a wholesaler, retailer, or final consumer. A wholesaler buying in large quantities is often granted a larger discount than a retailer buying in smaller quantities. Note that a buyer records the net amount of list price minus trade discount. For example, in the November 2 purchase of merchandise by Z-Mart, the merchandise was listed in the seller's catalog at $2,000 and Z-Mart received a 40% trade discount. This meant that Z-Mart's purchase price was $1,200, computed as $2,000 − (40% × $2,000).

Point: The Merchandise Inventory account reflects the cost of goods available for resale.

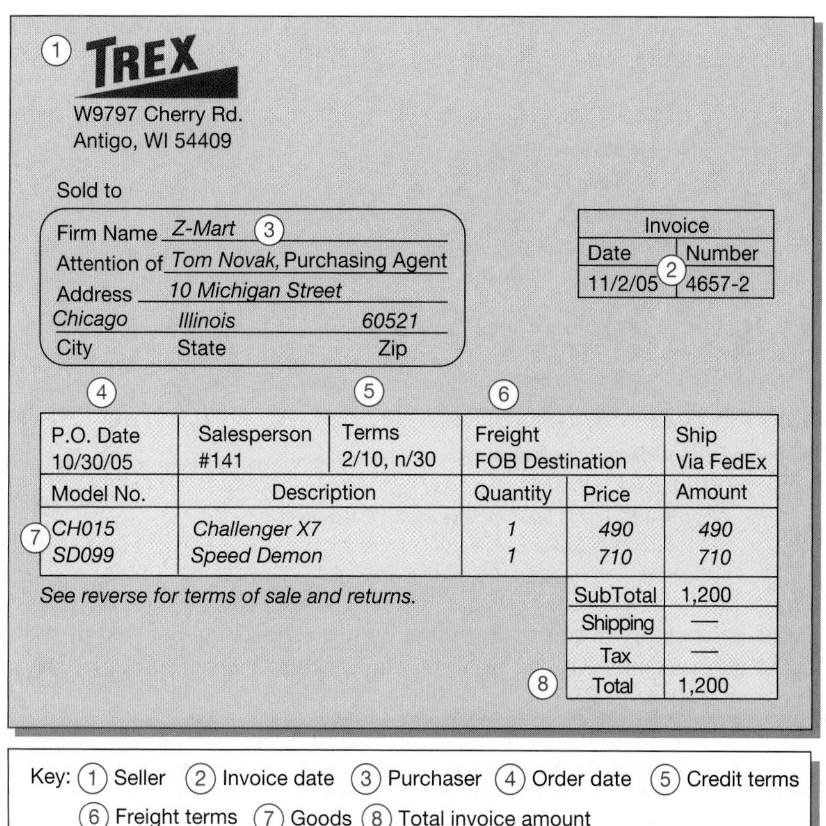

(1) TREX
W9797 Cherry Rd.
Antigo, WI 54409

Sold to
Firm Name Z-Mart (3)
Attention of Tom Novak, Purchasing Agent
Address 10 Michigan Street
Chicago Illinois 60521
City State Zip

Invoice	
Date	Number
11/2/05 (2)	4657-2

(4) (5) (6)

P.O. Date	Salesperson	Terms	Freight		Ship
10/30/05	#141	2/10, n/30	FOB Destination		Via FedEx
Model No.	Description		Quantity	Price	Amount
(7) CH015	Challenger X7		1	490	490
SD099	Speed Demon		1	710	710

See reverse for terms of sale and returns.

SubTotal	1,200
Shipping	—
Tax	—
(8) Total	1,200

Key: (1) Seller (2) Invoice date (3) Purchaser (4) Order date (5) Credit terms (6) Freight terms (7) Goods (8) Total invoice amount

Exhibit 5.5

Invoice

Purchase Discounts

The purchase of goods on credit requires a clear statement of expected future payments and dates to avoid misunderstandings. **Credit terms** for a purchase include the amounts and timing of payments from a buyer to a seller. Credit terms usually reflect an industry's practices. To illustrate, when sellers require payment within 10 days after the end of the month of the invoice date, the invoice will show credit terms as "n/10 EOM," which stands for net 10 days after end of month (**EOM**). When sellers require payment within 30 days after the invoice date, the invoice shows credit terms of "n/30," which stands for *net 30 days*.

Exhibit 5.6 portrays credit terms. The amount of time allowed before full payment is due is called the **credit period.** Sellers can grant a **cash discount** to encourage buyers to pay earlier. A buyer views a cash discount as a **purchase discount.** A seller views a cash discount as a **sales discount.** Any cash discounts are described in the credit terms on the invoice. For example, credit terms of "2/10, n/60" mean that full payment is due within a 60-day credit period, but the buyer can deduct 2% of the invoice amount if payment is made within 10 days of the invoice date. This reduced payment applies only for the **discount period.**

Point: Since both the buyer and seller know the invoice date, this date is used in determining the discount and credit periods.

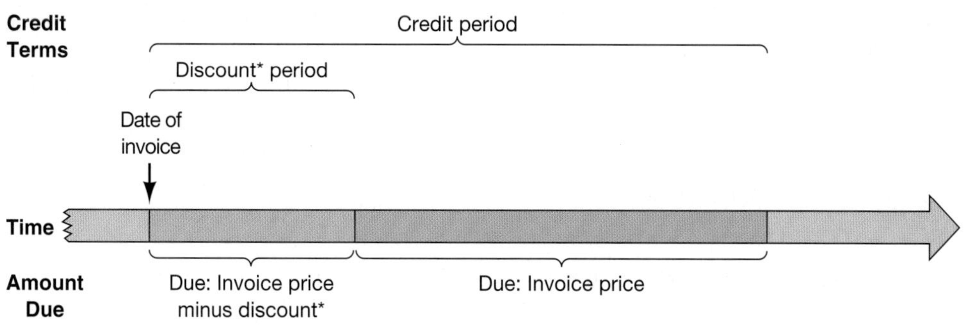

Exhibit 5.6

Credit Terms

Point: Appendix 5A repeats journal entries *a* through *f* using a periodic inventory system.

To illustrate how a buyer accounts for a purchase discount, assume that Z-Mart's $1,200 purchase of merchandise is on credit with terms of 2/10, n/30. Its entry is

Assets = Liabilities + Equity
+1,200 +1,200

(a) Nov. 2	Merchandise Inventory	1,200	
	Accounts Payable		1,200
	Purchased merchandise on credit, invoice dated Nov. 2, terms 2/10, n/30.		

If Z-Mart pays the amount due on (or before) November 12, the entry is

Assets = Liabilities + Equity
−24 −1,200
−1,176

(b) Nov. 12	Accounts Payable	1,200	
	Merchandise Inventory		24
	Cash		1,176
	Paid for the $1,200 purchase of Nov. 2 less the discount of $24 (2% × $1,200).		

Point: These entries illustrate what is called the *gross method* of accounting for purchases with discount terms.

The Merchandise Inventory account after these entries reflects the net cost of merchandise purchased, and the Accounts Payable account shows a zero balance. Both ledger accounts, in T-account form, follow:

Merchandise Inventory			
Nov. 2	1,200	Nov. 12	24
Balance	1,176		

Accounts Payable			
Nov. 12	1,200	Nov. 2	1,200
		Balance	0

Decision Maker

Entrepreneur You purchase a batch of products on terms of 3/10, n/90, but your company has limited cash and you must borrow funds at an 11% annual rate if you are to pay within the discount period. Do you take advantage of the purchase discount?

Answer—p. 203

A buyer's failure to pay within a discount period can be expensive. To illustrate, if Z-Mart does not pay within the 10-day 2% discount period, it can delay payment by 20 more days. This delay costs Z-Mart $24, computed as 2% × $1,200. Most buyers take advantage of a purchase discount because of the usually high interest rate implied from not taking it.[1] Also, good cash management means that no invoice is paid until the last day of the discount or credit period.

Purchase Returns and Allowances

Purchase returns refer to merchandise a buyer acquires but then returns to the seller. A *purchase allowance* is a reduction in the cost of defective or unacceptable merchandise that a buyer acquires. Buyers often keep defective but still marketable merchandise if the seller grants an acceptable allowance.

Point: The sender (maker) of a *debit memorandum* will debit the account of the memo's receiver. The memo's receiver will credit the account of the sender.

When a buyer returns or takes an allowance on merchandise, the buyer issues a **debit memorandum** to inform the seller of a debit made to the seller's account in the buyer's records. To illustrate, on November 15 Z-Mart (buyer) issues a $300 debit memorandum for

[1] The *implied annual interest rate* formula is:

(365 days ÷ [Credit period − Discount period]) × Cash discount rate.

For terms of 2/10, n/30, missing the 2% discount for an additional 20 days is equal to an annual interest rate of 36.5%, computed as (365 days/[30 days − 10 days]) × 2% discount rate. *Favorable purchase discounts* are those with implied annual interest rates that exceed the purchaser's annual rate for borrowing money.

an allowance from Trex for defective merchandise. Z-Mart's November 15 entry to update its Merchandise Inventory account to reflect the purchase allowance is

(c) Nov. 15	Accounts Payable	300	
	Merchandise Inventory		300
	Allowance for defective merchandise.		

Assets = Liabilities + Equity
−300 −300

If this had been a return, then the total *recorded cost* (all costs less any discounts) of the defective merchandise would be entered. The buyer's cost of returned and defective merchandise is usually offset against the buyer's current account payable balance to the seller. When cash is refunded, the Cash account is debited instead of Accounts Payable.

When goods are returned, a buyer can take a purchase discount on only the remaining balance of the invoice. For example, suppose Z-Mart purchases $1,000 of merchandise offered with a 2% cash discount. Two days later, Z-Mart returns $100 of goods before paying the invoice. When Z-Mart later pays within the discount period, it takes the 2% discount only on the $900 remaining balance. The discount is $18 (2% × $900) and the cash payment is $882 ($900 − $18).

Decision Ethics

Credit Manager As the new credit manager, you are being trained by the outgoing manager. She explains that the system prepares checks for amounts net of favorable cash discounts, and the checks are dated the last day of the discount period. She also tells you that checks are not mailed until five days later, adding that "the company gets free use of cash for an extra five days, and our department looks better. When a supplier complains, we blame the computer system and the mailroom." Do you continue this payment policy?

Answer—p. 203

Example: Z-Mart pays $980 cash for $1,000 of merchandise purchased within its 2% discount period. Later, Z-Mart returns $100 of the original $1,000 merchandise. The return entry is

Cash	98	
Merchandise Inventory . . .		98

Transportation Costs and Ownership Transfer

The buyer and seller must agree on who is responsible for paying any freight costs and who bears the risk of loss during transit for merchandising transactions. This is essentially the same as asking at what point ownership transfers from the seller to the buyer. The point of transfer is called the **FOB** (*free on board*) point, which determines who pays transportation costs (and often other incidental costs of transit such as insurance).

Exhibit 5.7 identifies two alternative points of transfer. (1) *FOB shipping point,* also called *FOB factory,* means the buyer accepts ownership when the goods depart the seller's place of business. The buyer is then responsible for paying shipping costs and bearing the risk of damage or loss when goods are in transit. The goods are part of the buyer's inventory when they are in transit since ownership has transferred to the buyer. **Cannondale**, a major bike manufacturer, uses FOB shipping point. (2) *FOB destination* means ownership of goods transfers to the buyer when the goods arrive at the buyer's place of business. The seller is responsible for paying shipping charges and bears the risk of damage or loss in transit. The

Exhibit 5.7

Ownership Transfer and Transportation Costs

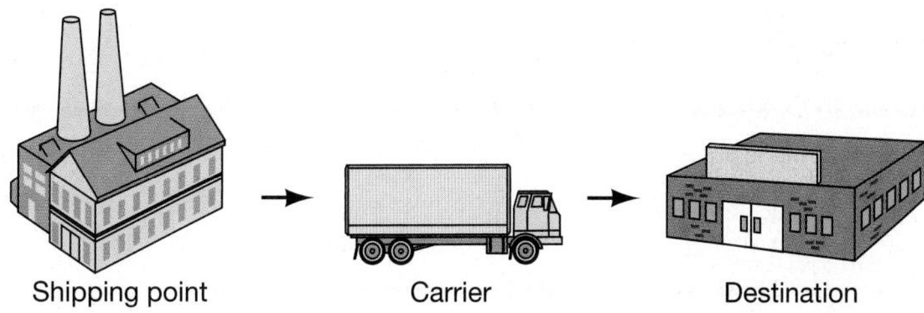

	Ownership Transfers when Goods Passed to	Transportation Costs Paid by
FOB shipping point	Carrier	Buyer
FOB destination	Buyer	Seller

Point: **Compaq Computer** at one time shipped its products FOB shipping point, but it found delivery companies unreliable. Compaq then changed its agreements to FOB destination, took control of shipping, and eliminated its problems.

Point: The party not responsible for shipping costs sometimes pays the carrier. In these cases, the party paying these costs either bills the party responsible or, more commonly, adjusts its account payable or account receivable with the other party. For example, a buyer paying a carrier when terms are FOB destination can decrease its account payable to the seller by the amount of shipping cost.

seller does not record revenue from this sale until the goods arrive at the destination because this transaction is not complete before that point.

Z-Mart's $1,200 purchase on November 2 is on terms of FOB destination. This means Z-Mart is not responsible for paying transportation costs. When a buyer is responsible for paying transportation costs, the payment is made to a carrier or directly to the seller depending on the agreement. The cost principle requires that any necessary transportation costs of a buyer (often called *transportation-in* or *freight-in*) be included as part of the cost of purchased merchandise. To illustrate, Z-Mart's entry to record a $75 freight charge from an independent carrier for merchandise purchased FOB shipping point is

Assets = Liabilities + Equity
+75
−75

(d) Nov. 24	Merchandise Inventory	75	
	Cash		75
	Paid freight costs on purchased merchandise.		

A seller records the costs of shipping goods to customers in a Delivery Expense account when the seller is responsible for these costs. Delivery Expense, also called *transportation-out* or *freight-out,* is reported as a selling expense in the seller's income statement.

In summary, purchases are recorded as debits to Merchandise Inventory. Any later purchase discounts, returns, and allowances are credited (decreases) to Merchandise Inventory. Transportation-in is debited (added) to Merchandise Inventory. Z-Mart's itemized costs of merchandise purchases for year 2005 are in Exhibit 5.8.

Exhibit 5.8

Itemized Costs of Merchandise Purchases

Z-MART Itemized Costs of Merchandise Purchases For Year Ended December 31, 2005	
Invoice cost of merchandise purchases	$235,800
Less: Purchase discounts received	(4,200)
Purchase returns and allowances	(1,500)
Add: Costs of transportation-in	2,300
Total cost of merchandise purchases	**$232,400**

Point: Some companies have separate accounts for purchase discounts, returns and allowances, and transportation-in. These accounts are then transferred to Merchandise Inventory at period-end. This is a *hybrid system* of perpetual and periodic. That is, Merchandise Inventory is updated on a perpetual basis but only for purchases and cost of goods sold.

The accounting system described here does not provide separate records (accounts) for total purchases, total purchase discounts, total purchase returns and allowances, and total transportation-in. Yet nearly all companies collect this information in supplementary records because managers need this information to evaluate and control each of these cost elements. **Supplementary records,** also called *supplemental records,* refer to information outside the usual general ledger accounts.

Quick Check

4. How long are the credit and discount periods when credit terms are 2/10, n/60?
5. Identify which items are subtracted from the *list* amount and not recorded when computing purchase price: (*a*) freight-in; (*b*) trade discount; (*c*) purchase discount; (*d*) purchase return.
6. What does *FOB* mean? What does *FOB destination* mean?

Answers—p. 204

Accounting for Merchandise Sales

Merchandising companies also must account for sales, sales discounts, sales returns and allowances, and cost of goods sold. A merchandising company such as Z-Mart reflects these items in its gross profit computation, as shown in Exhibit 5.9. This section explains how this information is derived from transactions.

Z-MART
Computation of Gross Profit
For Year Ended December 31, 2005

Sales		$321,000
Less: Sales discounts	$4,300	
Sales returns and allowances	2,000	6,300
Net sales		314,700
Cost of goods sold		230,400
Gross profit		**$ 84,300**

Exhibit 5.9

Gross Profit Computation

Sales of Merchandise

Each sales transaction for a seller of merchandise involves two parts. One part is the revenue received in the form of an asset from a customer. The second part is the recognition of the cost of merchandise sold to a customer. Accounting for a sales transaction under the perpetual system requires recording information about both parts. This means that each sales transaction for merchandisers, whether for cash or on credit, requires two entries: one for revenue and one for cost. To illustrate, Z-Mart sold $2,400 of merchandise on credit on November 3. The revenue part of this transaction is recorded as

P2 Analyze and record transactions for merchandise sales using a perpetual system.

Point: Growth of superstores such as **Price Club** and **Costco** is fed by the efficient use of perpetual inventory.

(e) Nov. 3	Accounts Receivable	2,400	
	Sales		2,400
	Sold merchandise on credit.		

Assets = Liabilities + Equity
+2,400 +2,400

This entry reflects an increase in Z-Mart's assets in the form of an accounts receivable. It also shows the increase in revenue (Sales). If the sale is for cash, the debit is to Cash instead of Accounts Receivable.

The cost part of each sales transaction ensures that the Merchandise Inventory account under a perpetual inventory system reflects the updated cost of the merchandise available for sale. For example, the cost of the merchandise Z-Mart sold on November 3 is $1,600, and the entry to record the cost part of this sales transaction is

Topic Tackler 5-2

(e) Nov. 3	Cost of Goods Sold	1,600	
	Merchandise Inventory		1,600
	To record the cost of Nov. 3 sale.		

Assets = Liabilities + Equity
−1,600 −1,600

Point: The Cost of Goods Sold account is only used in a perpetual system.

Sales Discounts

Sales discounts on credit sales can benefit a seller by decreasing the delay in receiving cash and reducing future collection efforts.

At the time of a credit sale, a seller does not know whether a customer will pay within the discount period and take advantage of a purchases discount. This means the seller usually does not record a sales discount until a customer actually pays within the discount period. To illustrate, Z-Mart completes a credit sale for $1,000 on November 12 with terms of 2/10, n/60. The entry to record the revenue part of this sale is

Decision Insight

Suppliers and Demands Merchandising companies often bombard suppliers with demands. These include special discounts for new stores, payment of fines for shipping errors, and free samples. Merchandisers' goals are to reduce inventories, shorten lead times, and eliminate errors.

Nov. 12	Accounts Receivable	1,000	
	Sales		1,000
	Sold merchandise under terms of 2/10, n/60.		

Assets = Liabilities + Equity
+1,000 +1,000

This entry records the receivable and the revenue as if the customer will pay the full amount. The customer has two options, however. One option is to wait 60 days until January 11 and pay the full $1,000. In this case, Z-Mart records that payment as

Assets = Liabilities + Equity
+1,000
−1,000

Jan. 11	Cash	1,000	
	Accounts Receivable		1,000
	Received payment for Nov. 12 sale.		

Point: Sales discounts is seldom reported on income statements distributed to external users.

The customer's second option is to pay $980 within a 10-day period ending November 22. If the customer pays on (or before) November 22, Z-Mart records the payment as

Assets = Liabilities + Equity
+980 −20
−1,000

Nov. 22	Cash	980	
	Sales Discounts	20	
	Accounts Receivable		1,000
	Received payment for Nov. 12 sale less discount.		

Decision Insight

Catalina Supermarkets uses bar codes, software, and the Web to help execs keep tabs on who buys what foods, how often, and at what price. Its high-profit customer rate is up because most discounts and services, such as coupons and free delivery, are given almost exclusively to its best customers.

Sales Discounts is a contra revenue account, meaning the Sales Discounts account is deducted from the Sales account when computing a company's net sales (see Exhibit 5.9). Management monitors Sales Discounts to assess the effectiveness and cost of its discount policy.

Sales Returns and Allowances

Sales returns refer to merchandise that customers return to the seller after a sale. Many companies allow customers to return merchandise for a full refund. *Sales allowances* refer to reductions in the selling price of merchandise sold to customers. This can occur with damaged or defective merchandise that a customer is willing to purchase with a decrease in selling price. Sales returns and allowances usually involve dissatisfied customers and the possibility of lost future sales, and managers need information about returns and allowances to monitor these problems.

Point: Published income statements rarely disclose Sales Returns and Allowances.

Decision Insight

Return to Sender Book merchandisers such as **Barnes & Noble** and **Borders Books** can return unsold books to publishers at purchase price. Publishers say returns of new hardcover books run between 35% and 50%.

To illustrate, recall Z-Mart's sale of merchandise on November 3 for $2,400 that had cost $1,600. Assume that the customer returns part of the merchandise on November 6, and the returned items sell for $800 and cost $600. The revenue part of this transaction must reflect the decrease in sales from the customer's return of merchandise as follows:

Assets = Liabilities + Equity
−800 −800

(f) Nov. 6	Sales Returns and Allowances	800	
	Accounts Receivable		800
	Customer returns merchandise of Nov. 3 sale.		

If the merchandise returned to Z-Mart is not defective and can be resold to another customer, Z-Mart returns these goods to its inventory. The entry to restore the cost of such goods to the Merchandise Inventory account is

Assets = Liabilities + Equity
+600 +600

Nov. 6	Merchandise Inventory	600	
	Cost of Goods Sold		600
	Returned goods added to inventory.[2]		

[2] This entry changes if the goods returned are defective—that is, the returned inventory is recorded at its estimated value, not its cost. To illustrate, if the goods (costing $600) returned to Z-Mart are defective and estimated to be worth $150, the following entry is made: Dr. Merchandise Inventory for $150, Dr. Loss from Defective Merchandise for $450, and Cr. Cost of Goods Sold for $600.

To illustrate sales allowances, assume that $800 of the merchandise Z-Mart sold on November 3 is defective but the buyer decides to keep it because Z-Mart offers a $100 price reduction. Z-Mart records the allowance and decreases expected assets as follows:

Nov. 6	Sales Returns and Allowances	100	
	Accounts Receivable		100
	To record sales allowance on Nov. 3 sale.		

Assets = Liabilities + Equity
−100 −100

The seller usually prepares a credit memorandum to confirm a buyer's return or allowance. A seller's **credit memorandum** informs a buyer of the seller's credit to the buyer's Account Receivable (on the seller's books).

Point: The sender (maker) of a credit memorandum will *credit* the account of the receiver. The receiver of a credit memorandum will *debit* the account of the sender.

Quick Check

7. Why are sales discounts and sales returns and allowances recorded in contra revenue accounts instead of directly in the Sales account?
8. Under what conditions are two entries necessary to record a sales return?
9. When merchandise is sold on credit and the seller notifies the buyer of a price allowance, does the seller create and send a credit memorandum or a debit memorandum?

Answers—p. 204

Completing the Accounting Cycle

C4 Analyze and interpret cost flows and operating activities of a merchandising company.

Exhibit 5.10 shows the flow of merchandising costs during a period and where these costs are reported at period-end. This chapter already discussed how a merchandiser's purchases and sales transactions during a period are analyzed, recorded, and reported. Specifically, beginning inventory plus the net cost of purchases is the merchandise available for sale. As inventory is sold, its cost is recorded in cost of goods sold on the income statement; what remains is ending inventory on the balance sheet. Note that a period's ending inventory is the next period's beginning inventory.

Each of the steps in the accounting cycle described in Chapter 4 for a service company applies to a merchandiser. This section extends that discussion to three remaining steps of the accounting cycle for a merchandiser—adjustments, statement preparation, and closing.

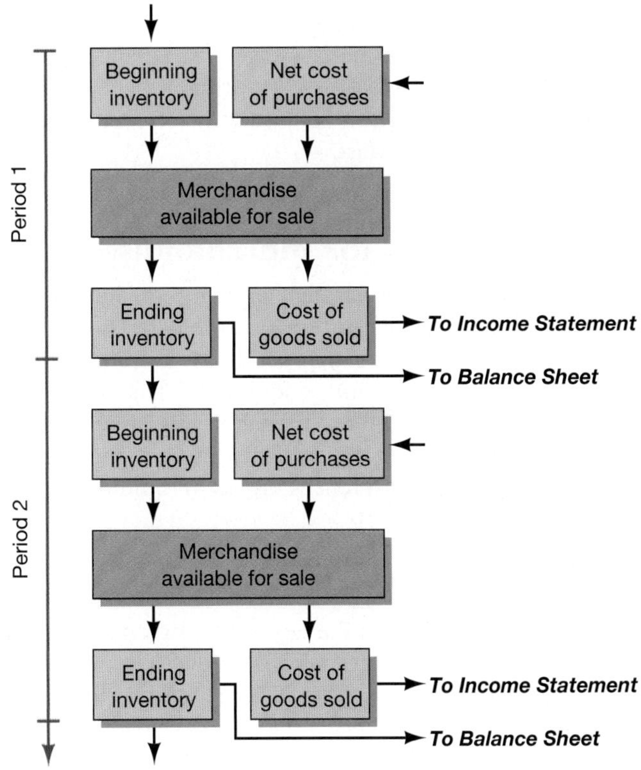

Exhibit 5.10

Merchandising Cost Flow in the Accounting Cycle

Adjusting Entries for Merchandisers

P3 Prepare adjustments and close accounts for a merchandising company.

Adjusting entries are generally the same for merchandising companies and service companies, including those for prepaid expenses (including depreciation), accrued expenses, unearned revenues, and accrued revenues. However, a merchandiser using a perpetual inventory system is usually required to make another adjustment to update the Merchandise Inventory account to reflect any loss of merchandise, including theft and deterioration. **Shrinkage** is the term used to refer to the loss of inventory and it is computed by comparing a physical count of inventory with recorded amounts. A physical count is usually performed at least once annually.

Decision Insight

Who Shrunk Inventory Shrinkage can be a sizable cost for many merchandisers. Recent annual losses due to shrinkage are

Musicland	$22 million
Sports Authority	9 million

Companies often invest considerable resources to reduce shrinkage.

Point: About two-thirds of shoplifting losses are thefts by employees.

To illustrate, Z-Mart's Merchandise Inventory account at the end of year 2005 has a balance of $21,250, but a physical count reveals that only $21,000 of inventory exists. The adjusting entry to record this $250 shrinkage is

Assets = Liabilities + Equity
−250 −250

Dec. 31	Cost of Goods Sold	250	
	Merchandise Inventory		250
	To adjust for $250 shrinkage revealed by a physical count of inventory.		

Preparing Financial Statements

The financial statements of a merchandiser, and their preparation, are similar to those for a service company described in Chapters 3 and 4. The income statement mainly differs by the inclusion of *cost of goods sold* and *gross profit.* Also, net sales is affected by discounts, returns, and allowances, and some additional expenses are possible such as delivery expense and loss from defective merchandise. The balance sheet mainly differs by the inclusion of *merchandise inventory* as part of current assets. The statement of owner's equity is unchanged. A work sheet can be used to help prepare these statements, and one is illustrated in Appendix 5B for Z-Mart.

Point: CompUSA's costs of shipping merchandise to its stores is included in the costs of its inventories as required by the cost principle.

Closing Entries for Merchandisers

Point: The Inventory account is not affected by the closing process under a perpetual system.

Closing entries are similar for service companies and merchandising companies using a perpetual system. The difference is that we must close some new temporary accounts that arise from merchandising activities. Z-Mart has several temporary accounts unique to merchandisers: Sales (of goods), Sales Discounts, Sales Returns and Allowances, and Cost of Goods Sold. Their existence in the ledger means that the first two closing entries for a merchandiser are slightly different from the ones described in Chapter 4 for a service company. These differences are set in boldface in the closing entries of Exhibit 5.11.

Summary of Merchandising Entries

Exhibit 5.12 summarizes the key adjusting and closing entries of a merchandiser (using a perpetual inventory system) that are different from those of a service company described in prior chapters (the Demonstration Problem 2 illustrates these merchandising entries).

Exhibit 5.11

Closing Entries for a Merchandiser

Step 1: Close Credit Balances in Temporary Accounts to Income Summary.

Z-Mart has one temporary account with a credit balance; it is closed with this entry:

Dec. 31	**Sales**	**321,000**	
	Income Summary		321,000
	To close credit balances in temporary accounts.		

Step 2: Close Debit Balances in Temporary Accounts to Income Summary.

The second entry closes temporary accounts having debit balances such as Cost of Goods Sold, Sales Discounts, and Sales Returns and Allowances and is shown here:

Dec. 31	Income Summary	308,100	
	Sales Discounts		**4,300**
	Sales Returns and Allowances		**2,000**
	Cost of Goods Sold		**230,400**
	Depreciation Expense—Store Equipment		3,000
	Depreciation Expense—Office Equipment		700
	Office Salaries Expense		25,300
	Sales Salaries Expense		18,500
	Insurance Expense		600
	Rent Expense—Office Space		900
	Rent Expense—Selling Space		8,100
	Office Supplies Expense		1,800
	Store Supplies Expense		1,200
	Advertising Expense		11,300
	To close debit balances in temporary accounts.		

Step 3: Close Income Summary to Owner's Capital.

The third closing entry is exactly the same for a merchandising company and a service company. It updates the owner's capital account for the net income or loss and is shown here:

Dec. 31	Income Summary	12,900	
	K. Marty, Capital		12,900
	To close the Income Summary account.		

The $12,900 amount in the entry is net income reported on the income statement in Exhibit 5.2.

Step 4: Close Withdrawals Account to Owner's Capital.

The fourth closing entry is exactly the same for a merchandising company and a service company. It closes the withdrawals account and adjusts the owner's capital account balance to the amount shown on the balance sheet. This entry for Z-Mart is

Dec. 31	K. Marty, Capital	4,000	
	K. Marty, Withdrawals		4,000
	To close the withdrawals accounts.		

When these entries are posted, all temporary accounts are set to zero and are ready to record events for the next period. The capital account is now updated to reflect all current and prior period transactions.

Exhibit 5.12

Summary of Merchandising Entries

	Merchandising Transactions	Merchandising Entries	Dr.	Cr.
Purchases	Purchasing merchandise for resale.	Merchandise Inventory	#	
		Cash or Accounts Payable		#
	Paying freight costs on purchases; FOB shipping point.	Merchandise Inventory	#	
		Cash		#
	Paying within discount period.	Accounts Payable	#	
		Merchandise Inventory		#
		Cash		#
	Recording purchase returns or allowances.	Cash or Accounts Payable	#	
		Merchandise Inventory		#
Sales	Selling merchandise.	Cash or Accounts Receivable	#	
		Sales		#
		Cost of Goods Sold	#	
		Merchandise Inventory		#
	Receiving payment within discount period.	Cash	#	
		Sales Discounts	#	
		Accounts Receivable		#
	Granting sales returns or allowances.	Sales Returns and Allowances	#	
		Cash or Accounts Receivable		#
		Merchandise Inventory	#	
		Cost of Goods Sold		#
	Paying freight costs on sales; FOB destination.	Delivery Expense	#	
		Cash		#

	Merchandising Events	Adjusting and Closing Entries	Dr.	Cr.
Adjusting	Adjusting due to shrinkage (recorded amount larger than physical inventory).	Cost of Goods Sold	#	
		Merchandise Inventory		#
Closing	Closing temporary accounts with credit balances.	Sales	#	
		Income Summary		#
	Closing temporary accounts with debit balances.	Income Summary	#	
		Sales Returns and Allowances		#
		Sales Discounts		#
		Cost of Goods Sold		#
		Delivery Expense		#
		"Other Expenses"		#

Quick Check

10. When a merchandiser uses a perpetual inventory system, why is it sometimes necessary to adjust the Merchandise Inventory balance with an adjusting entry?
11. What temporary accounts do you expect to find in a merchandising business but not in a service business?
12. Describe the closing entries normally made by a merchandising company.

Answers—p. 204

Financial Statement Formats

Generally accepted accounting principles do not require companies to use any one presentation format for financial statements so we see many different formats in practice. This section describes two common income statement formats: multiple-step and single-step. The classified balance sheet of a merchandiser is also explained.

P4 Define and prepare multiple-step and single-step income statements.

Multiple-Step Income Statement

A **multiple-step income statement** format shows detailed computations of net sales and other costs and expenses, and reports subtotals for various classes of items. Exhibit 5.13

Exhibit 5.13

Multiple-Step Income Statement

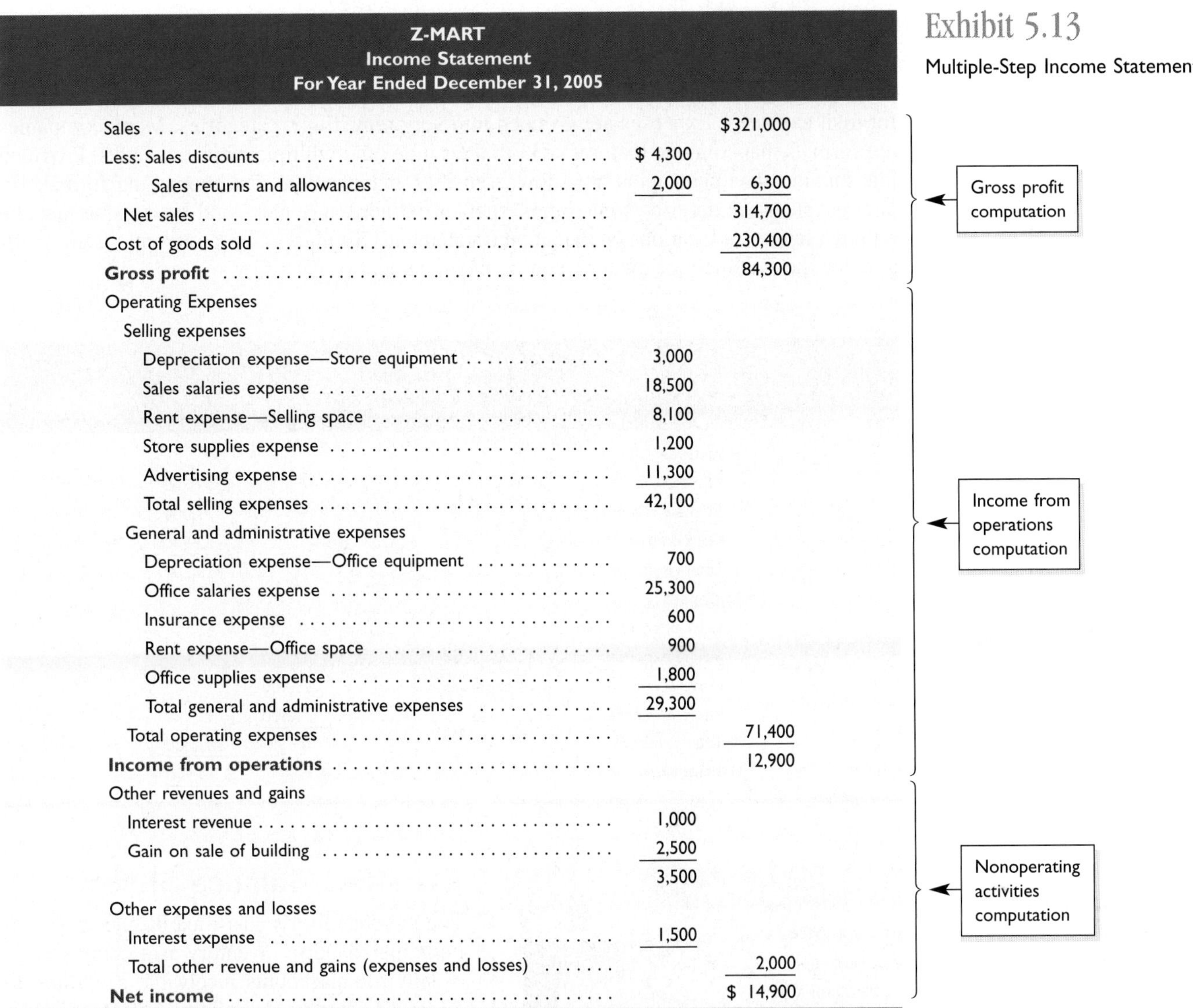

Z-MART
Income Statement
For Year Ended December 31, 2005

Sales		$321,000
Less: Sales discounts	$ 4,300	
Sales returns and allowances	2,000	6,300
Net sales		314,700
Cost of goods sold		230,400
Gross profit		84,300
Operating Expenses		
Selling expenses		
Depreciation expense—Store equipment	3,000	
Sales salaries expense	18,500	
Rent expense—Selling space	8,100	
Store supplies expense	1,200	
Advertising expense	11,300	
Total selling expenses	42,100	
General and administrative expenses		
Depreciation expense—Office equipment	700	
Office salaries expense	25,300	
Insurance expense	600	
Rent expense—Office space	900	
Office supplies expense	1,800	
Total general and administrative expenses	29,300	
Total operating expenses		71,400
Income from operations		12,900
Other revenues and gains		
Interest revenue	1,000	
Gain on sale of building	2,500	
	3,500	
Other expenses and losses		
Interest expense	1,500	
Total other revenue and gains (expenses and losses)		2,000
Net income		$ 14,900

shows a multiple-step income statement for Z-Mart. The statement has three main parts: (1) *gross profit,* determined by net sales less cost of goods sold, (2) *income from operations,* determined by gross profit less operating expenses, and (3) *net income,* determined by income from operations adjusted for nonoperating items.

Operating expenses are classified into two sections. **Selling expenses** include the expenses of promoting sales by displaying and advertising merchandise, making sales, and delivering goods to customers. **General and administrative expenses** support a company's overall operations and include expenses related to accounting, human resource management, and financial management. Note that expenses are allocated between sections when they contribute to more than one. Z-Mart allocates rent expense of $9,000 from its store building between two sections: $8,100 to selling expense and $900 to general and administrative expense.

Nonoperating activities consist of other expenses, revenues, losses, and gains that are unrelated to a company's operations. They are reported in two sections. (1) *Other revenues and gains,* which often include interest revenue, dividend revenue, rent revenue, and gains from asset disposals. (2) *Other expenses and losses,* which often include interest expense, losses from asset disposals, and casualty losses. When a company has no reportable nonoperating activities, its income from operations is simply labeled net income.

Point: Z-Mart did not have any nonoperating activities, however, Exhibit 5.13 includes some for illustrative purposes.

Single-Step Income Statement

A **single-step income statement** is another widely used format, and is shown in Exhibit 5.14 for Z-Mart. It lists cost of goods sold as another expense and shows only one subtotal for total expenses. Expenses are grouped into very few, if any, categories. Many companies use formats that combine features of both the single- and multiple-step statements. Provided that income statement items are shown sensibly, management can choose the format. (In later chapters, we describe some items, such as extraordinary gains and losses, that must be reported in certain locations on the income statement.) Similar presentation options are available for the statement of owner's equity and statement of cash flows.

Point: Many companies report interest expense and interest income in separate categories after income from operations and before subtracting income taxes expense. As one example, see Krispy Kreme's income statement in Appendix A.

Exhibit 5.14

Single-Step Income Statement

Z-MART
Income Statement
For Year Ended December 31, 2005

Revenues		
Net sales		$314,700
Interest revenue		1,000
Gain on sale of building		2,500
Total revenues		318,200
Expenses		
Cost of goods sold	$230,400	
Selling expenses	42,100	
General and administrative expenses	29,300	
Interest expense	1,500	
Total expenses		303,300
Net income		$ 14,900

Decision Insight

Head Start Incubators offer start-ups a space plus services such as management advice, office support, and financial, legal, and technical help. Studies show that nearly 90% of entrepreneurs that "hatch" from incubators (usually after two to three years) are still in business six years later—which is more than double the usual success rate.

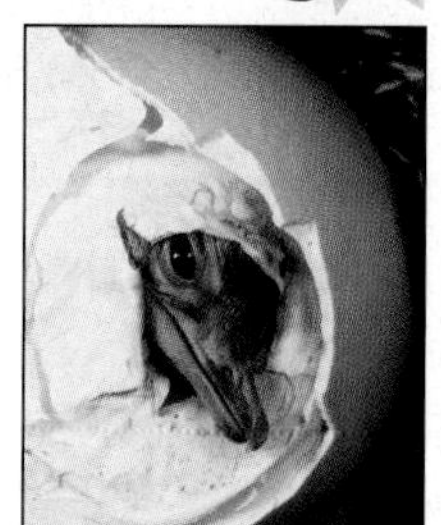

Classified Balance Sheet

The merchandiser's classified balance sheet reports merchandise inventory as a current asset, usually after accounts receivable according to an asset's nearness to liquidity. Inventory is usually less liquid than accounts receivable because receivables must first be sold before cash is received, but more liquid than supplies and prepaid expenses. Exhibit 5.15 shows the current asset section of Z-Mart's classified balance sheet (other sections are as shown in Chapter 4).

Exhibit 5.15

Classified Balance Sheet (partial) of a Merchandiser

Z-MART
Balance Sheet (partial)
December 31, 2005

Assets	
Current assets	
Cash	$ 8,200
Accounts receivable	11,200
Merchandise inventory	**21,000**
Office supplies	550
Store supplies	250
Prepaid insurance	300
Total current assets	$41,500

Acid-Test and Gross Margin Ratios

Decision Analysis

Acid-Test Ratio

For many merchandisers, inventory makes up a large portion of current assets. Inventory must be sold and any resulting accounts receivable must be collected before cash is available. Chapter 4 explained that the current ratio, defined as current assets divided by current liabilities, is useful in assessing a company's ability to pay current liabilities. Since it is sometimes unreasonable to assume that inventories are a source of payment for current liabilities, we look to other measures.

A1 Compute the acid-test ratio and explain its use to assess liquidity.

One measure of a merchandiser's ability to pay its current liabilities (its *liquidity*) is the acid-test ratio. It differs from the current ratio by excluding less liquid current assets such as inventory and prepaid expenses that take longer to be converted to cash. The **acid-test ratio,** also called *quick ratio,* is defined as *quick assets* (cash, short-term investments, and current receivables) divided by current liabilities—see Exhibit 5.16.

$$\textbf{Acid-test ratio} = \frac{\textbf{Cash and equivalents + Short-term investments + Current receivables}}{\textbf{Current liabilities}}$$

Exhibit 5.16

Acid-Test (Quick) Ratio

Exhibit 5.17 shows both the acid-test and current ratios of retailer **JCPenney** for fiscal years 1999 through 2003. JCPenney's acid-test ratio reveals a decline in 2000–2001 that exceeds the decline in the retailing industry. Still, JCPenney's current ratio (never less than 1.7) suggests that its short-term obligations can be covered with short-term assets.

An acid-test ratio less than 1.0 means that current liabilities exceed quick assets. A rule of thumb is that the acid-test ratio should have a value of, or higher than, 1.0 to conclude that a company is unlikely to face near-term liquidity problems. A value less than 1.0 raises liquidity concerns unless a company can generate enough cash from inventory sales or if much of its liabilities are not due until late in the next period. Similarly, a value greater than 1.0 can hide a liquidity problem if payables are due shortly and receivables are not collected until late in the next period. Analysis of JCPenney reveals a slight concern with its liquidity in 2000–2001, especially when benchmarked against the industry ratio. However, in 2002–2003 JCPenney raised its acid-test ratio to a reasonable level (and its inventory is fairly liquid).

Point: Successful use of a just-in-time inventory system can narrow the gap between the acid-test ratio and the current ratio.

Decision Maker

Supplier A retailer requests to purchase supplies on credit from your company. You have no prior experience with this retailer. The retailer's current ratio is 2.1, its acid-test ratio is 0.5, and inventory makes up most of its current assets. Do you extend credit?

Answer—p. 203

($ in millions)	2003	2002	2001	2000	1999
Total quick assets	$3,179	$3,538	$1,837	$2,076	$ 4,779
Total current assets	$8,353	$8,677	$7,257	$8,174	$11,007
Total current liabilities	$4,159	$4,499	$4,235	$4,272	$ 5,912
Acid-test ratio	**0.76**	**0.79**	**0.43**	**0.49**	**0.81**
Current ratio	**2.01**	**1.93**	**1.71**	**1.91**	**1.86**
Industry acid-test ratio	0.5	0.5	0.8	0.8	0.9
Industry current ratio	2.5	2.6	3.0	2.8	3.1

Exhibit 5.17

JCPenney's Acid-Test and Current Ratios

Gross Margin Ratio

The cost of goods sold makes up much of expenses for merchandisers. Without sufficient gross profit, a merchandiser will likely fail. Users often compute the gross margin ratio to help understand this relation. It differs from the profit margin ratio in that it excludes all costs except cost of goods sold. The **gross margin ratio** is defined as *gross margin* (net sales minus cost of goods sold) divided by net sales—see Exhibit 5.18.

A2 Compute the gross margin ratio and explain its use to assess profitability.

$$\textbf{Gross margin ratio} = \frac{\textbf{Net sales} - \textbf{Cost of goods sold}}{\textbf{Net sales}}$$

Exhibit 5.18

Gross Margin Ratio

Decision Maker

Financial Officer Your company has a 36% gross margin ratio and a 17% net profit margin ratio. Industry averages are 44% for gross margin and 16% for net profit margin. Do these comparative results concern you?

Answer—p. 204

Point: The power of a ratio is often its ability to identify areas for more detailed analysis.

Exhibit 5.19 shows the gross margin ratio of **JCPenney** for fiscal years 1999–2003. For JCPenney, each $1 of sales in 2003 yielded about 30¢ in gross margin to cover all other expenses and still produce a profit. This 30¢ margin is up from 29¢ in 2002 and from 28¢ in 2001. This rebound is an important (and positive) development. Success for merchandisers such as JCPenney depends on adequate gross margin. Overall, both the acid-test ratio and the gross margin ratio suggest that the financial condition and performance of JCPenney has markedly improved over the past two years.

Exhibit 5.19

JCPenney's Gross Margin Ratio

($ in millions)	2003	2002	2001	2000	1999
Gross margin	$ 9,774	$ 9,215	$ 8,815	$ 9,457	$ 9,140
Net sales	$32,347	$32,004	$31,846	$31,743	$29,761
Gross margin ratio	**30.2%**	**28.8%**	**27.7%**	**29.8%**	**30.7%**

Demonstration Problem 1

Use the following adjusted trial balance and additional information to complete the requirements:

KC ANTIQUES
Adjusted Trial Balance
December 31, 2005

	Debit	Credit
Cash	$ 20,000	
Merchandise inventory	60,000	
Store supplies	1,500	
Equipment	45,600	
Accumulated depreciation—Equipment		$ 16,600
Accounts payable		9,000
Salaries payable		2,000
K. Carter, Capital		79,000
K. Carter, Withdrawals	10,000	
Sales		343,250
Sales discounts	5,000	
Sales returns and allowances	6,000	
Cost of goods sold	159,900	
Depreciation expense—Store equipment	4,100	
Depreciation expense—Office equipment	1,600	
Sales salaries expense	30,000	
Office salaries expense	34,000	
Insurance expense	11,000	
Rent expense (70% is store, 30% is office)	24,000	
Store supplies expense	5,750	
Advertising expense	31,400	
Totals	$449,850	$449,850

KC Antiques' *supplementary records* for 2005 reveal the following itemized costs for merchandising activities:

Invoice cost of merchandise purchases	$150,000
Purchase discounts received	2,500
Purchase returns and allowances	2,700
Cost of transportation-in	5,000

Required

1. Use the supplementary records to compute the total cost of merchandise purchases for 2005.
2. Prepare a 2005 multiple-step income statement. (Inventory at December 31, 2004, is $70,100.)
3. Prepare a single-step income statement for 2005.
4. Prepare closing entries for KC Antiques at December 31, 2005.
5. Compute the acid-test ratio and the gross margin ratio. Explain the meaning of each ratio and interpret them for KC Antiques.

Planning the Solution

- Compute the total cost of merchandise purchases for 2005.
- To prepare the multiple-step statement, first compute net sales. Then, to compute cost of goods sold, add the net cost of merchandise purchases for the year to beginning inventory and subtract the cost of ending inventory. Subtract cost of goods sold from net sales to get gross profit. Then classify expenses as selling expenses or general and administrative expenses.
- To prepare the single-step income statement, begin with net sales. Then list and subtract the expenses.
- The first closing entry debits all temporary accounts with credit balances and opens the Income Summary account. The second closing entry credits all temporary accounts with debit balances. The third entry closes the Income Summary account to the owner's capital account, and the fourth entry closes the withdrawals account to the capital account.
- Identify the quick assets on the adjusted trial balance. Compute the acid-test ratio by dividing quick assets by current liabilities. Compute the gross margin ratio by dividing gross profit by net sales.

Solution to Demonstration Problem 1

1.

Invoice cost of merchandise purchases	$150,000
Less: Purchases discounts received	2,500
Purchase returns and allowances	2,700
Add: Cost of transportation-in	5,000
Total cost of merchandise purchases	$149,800

2. Multiple-step income statement

KC ANTIQUES
Income Statement
For Year Ended December 31, 2005

Sales		$343,250
Less: Sales discounts	$ 5,000	
Sales returns and allowances	6,000	11,000
Net sales		332,250
Cost of goods sold*		159,900
Gross profit		172,350
Expenses		
Selling expenses		
Depreciation expense—Store equipment	4,100	
Sales salaries expense	30,000	
Rent expense—Selling space	16,800	
Store supplies expense	5,750	
Advertising expense	31,400	
Total selling expenses	88,050	

[continued on next page]

[continued from previous page]

General and administrative expenses		
Depreciation expense—Office equipment	1,600	
Office salaries expense	34,000	
Insurance expense	11,000	
Rent expense—Office space	7,200	
Total general and administrative expenses	53,800	
Total operating expenses		141,850
Net income		$ 30,500

* Cost of goods sold can also be directly computed (applying concepts from Exhibit 5.4):

Merchandise inventory, December 31, 2004	$ 70,100
Total cost of merchandise purchases (from part 1)	149,800
Goods available for sale	219,900
Merchandise inventory, December 31, 2005	60,000
Cost of goods sold	$159,900

3. Single-step income statement

KC ANTIQUES
Income Statement
For Year Ended December 31, 2005

Net sales		$332,250
Expenses		
Cost of goods sold	$159,900	
Selling expenses	88,050	
General and administrative expenses	53,800	
Total expenses		301,750
Net income		$ 30,500

4.

Dec. 31	Sales	343,250	
	Income Summary		343,250
	To close credit balances in temporary accounts.		
Dec. 31	Income Summary	312,750	
	Sales Discounts		5,000
	Sales Returns and Allowances		6,000
	Cost of Goods Sold		159,900
	Depreciation Expense—Store Equipment		4,100
	Depreciation Expense—Office Equipment		1,600
	Sales Salaries Expense		30,000
	Office Salaries Expense		34,000
	Insurance Expense		11,000
	Rent Expense		24,000
	Store Supplies Expense		5,750
	Advertising Expense		31,400
	To close debit balances in temporary accounts.		
Dec. 31	Income Summary	30,500	
	K. Carter, Capital		30,500
	To close the Income Summary account.		
Dec. 31	K. Carter, Capital	10,000	
	K. Carter, Withdrawals		10,000
	To close the withdrawals account.		

5. Acid-test ratio = (Cash and equivalents + Short-term investments + Current receivables)/Current liabilities
= Cash/(Accounts payable + Salaries payable)
= $20,000/($9,000 + $2,000) = $20,000/$11,000 = 1.82

Gross margin ratio = Gross profit/Net sales = $172,350/$332,250 = 0.52 (or 52%)

KC Antiques has a healthy acid-test ratio of 1.82. This means it has more than $1.80 in liquid assets to satisfy each $1.00 in current liabilities. The gross margin of 0.52 shows that KC Antiques spends 48¢ ($1.00 − $0.52) of every dollar of net sales on the costs of acquiring the merchandise it sells. This leaves 52¢ of every dollar of net sales to cover other expenses incurred in the business and to provide a profit.

Demonstration Problem 2

Prepare journal entries to record the following merchandising transactions for both the seller (BMX) and buyer (Sanuk).

May 4 BMX sold $1,500 of merchandise on account to Sanuk, terms FOB shipping point, n/45, invoice dated May 4. The cost of the merchandise was $900.

May 6 Sanuk paid transportation charges of $30 on the May 4 purchase from BMX.

May 8 BMX sold $1,000 of merchandise on account to Sanuk, terms FOB destination, n/30, invoice dated May 8. The cost of the merchandise was $700.

May 10 BMX paid transportation costs of $50 for delivery of merchandise sold to Sanuk on May 8.

May 16 BMX issued Sanuk a $200 credit memorandum for merchandise returned. The merchandise was purchased by Sanuk on account on May 8. The cost of the merchandise returned was $140.

May 18 BMX received payment from Sanuk for purchase of May 8.

May 21 BMX sold $2,400 of merchandise on account to Sanuk, terms FOB shipping point, 2/10, n/EOM. BMX prepaid transportation costs of $100, which were added to the invoice. The cost of the merchandise was $1,440.

May 31 BMX received payment from Sanuk for purchase of May 21, less discount (2% × $2,400).

Solution to Demonstration Problem 2

Date	BMX (Seller)	Debit	Credit	Sanuk (Buyer)	Debit	Credit
May 4	Accounts Receivable—Sanuk	1,500		Merchandise Inventory	1,500	
	Sales		1,500	Accounts Payable—BMX		1,500
	Cost of Goods Sold	900				
	Merchandise Inventory		900			
6	No entry.			Merchandise Inventory	30	
				Cash		30
8	Accounts Receivable—Sanuk	1,000		Merchandise Inventory	1,000	
	Sales		1,000	Accounts Payable—BMX		1,000
	Cost of Goods Sold	700				
	Merchandise Inventory		700			
10	Delivery Expense	50		No entry.		
	Cash		50			
16	Sales Returns & Allowances	200		Accounts Payable—BMX	200	
	Accounts Receivable—Sanuk		200	Merchandise Inventory		200
	Merchandise Inventory	140				
	Cost of Goods Sold		140			
18	Cash	800		Accounts Payable—BMX	800	
	Accounts Receivable—Sanuk		800	Cash		800
21	Accounts Receivable—Sanuk	2,400		Merchandise Inventory	2,500	
	Sales		2,400	Accounts Payable—BMX		2,500
	Accounts Receivable—Sanuk	100				
	Cash		100			
	Cost of Goods Sold	1,440				
	Merchandise Inventory		1,440			
31	Cash	2,452		Accounts Payable—BMX	2,500	
	Sales Discounts	48		Merchandise Inventory		48
	Accounts Receivable—Sanuk		2,500	Cash		2,452

APPENDIX

Periodic (and Perpetual) Inventory System

A **periodic inventory system** requires updating the inventory account only at the *end of a period* to reflect the quantity and cost of both the goods available and the goods sold. Thus, during the period, the Merchandise Inventory balance remains unchanged. It reflects the beginning inventory balance until it is updated at the end of the period. During the period the cost of merchandise is recorded in a temporary *Purchases* account. When a company sells merchandise, it records revenue but not the cost of the goods sold. At the end of the period when a company prepares financial statements, it takes a *physical count of inventory* by counting the quantities and costs of merchandise available. The cost of goods sold is then computed by subtracting the ending inventory amount from the cost of merchandise available for sale.

Recording Merchandise Transactions

P5 Record and compare merchandising transactions using both periodic and perpetual inventory systems.

Under a periodic system, each purchase, purchase return and allowance, purchase discount, and transportation-in transaction is recorded in a separate temporary account. At period-end, each of these temporary accounts is closed and the Merchandise Inventory account is updated. To illustrate, journal entries under the periodic inventory system are shown for the most common transactions (codes ***a*** through ***f*** link these transactions to those in the chapter, and we drop explanations for simplicity). For comparison, perpetual system journal entries are shown to the right of each periodic entry.

Purchases The periodic system uses a temporary *Purchases* account that accumulates the cost of all purchase transactions during each period. Z-Mart's November 2 entry to record the purchase of merchandise for $1,200 on credit with terms of 2/10, n/30 is

(a)	*Periodic*			*Perpetual*		
	Purchases	1,200		Merchandise Inventory	1,200	
	Accounts Payable		1,200	Accounts Payable		1,200

Purchase Discounts The periodic system uses a temporary *Purchase Discounts* account that accumulates discounts taken on purchase transactions during the period. If payment in (*a*) is delayed until after the discount period expires, the entry is to debit Accounts Payable and credit Cash for $1,200 each. However, if Z-Mart pays the supplier for the previous purchase in (*a*) within the discount period, the required payment is $1,176 ($1,200 × 98%) and is recorded as

(b)	*Periodic*			*Perpetual*		
	Accounts Payable	1,200		Accounts Payable	1,200	
	Purchase Discounts . . .		24	Merchandise Inventory . . .		24
	Cash		1,176	Cash		1,176

Purchase Returns and Allowances Z-Mart returned merchandise purchased on November 2 because of defects. In the periodic system, the temporary *Purchase Returns and Allowances* account accumulates the cost of all returns and allowances during a period. The recorded cost (including discounts) of the defective merchandise is $300, and Z-Mart records the November 15 return with this entry:

(c)	*Periodic*			*Perpetual*		
	Accounts Payable	300		Accounts Payable	300	
	Purchase Returns and Allowances		300	Merchandise Inventory . . .		300

Transportation-In Z-Mart paid a $75 freight charge to transport merchandise to its store. In the periodic system, this cost is charged to a temporary *Transportation-In* account.

(d)

Periodic			*Perpetual*		
Transportation-In	75		Merchandise Inventory	75	
Cash		75	Cash		75

Sales Under the periodic system, the cost of goods sold is *not* recorded at the time of each sale. (We later show how to compute total cost of goods sold at the end of a period.) Z-Mart's November 3 entry to record sales of $2,400 in merchandise on credit (when its cost is $1,600) is:

(e)

Periodic			*Perpetual*		
Accounts Receivable	2,400		Accounts Receivable	2,400	
Sales		2,400	Sales		2,400
			Cost of Goods Sold	1,600	
			Merchandise Inventory		1,600

Sales Returns A customer returned part of the merchandise from the transaction in (*e*), where the returned items sell for $800 and cost $600. (*Recall:* The periodic system records only the revenue effect, not the cost effect, for sales transactions.) Z-Mart restores the merchandise to inventory and records the November 6 return as

(f)

Periodic			*Perpetual*		
Sales Returns and Allowances	800		Sales Returns and Allowances	800	
Accounts Receivable		800	Accounts Receivable		800
			Merchandise Inventory	600	
			Cost of Goods Sold		600

Adjusting and Closing Entries

The periodic and perpetual inventory systems have slight differences in adjusting and closing entries. The period-end Merchandise Inventory balance (unadjusted) is $19,000 under the periodic system and $21,250 under the perpetual system. Since the periodic system does not update the Merchandise Inventory balance during the period, the $19,000 amount is the beginning inventory. However, the $21,250 balance under the perpetual system is the recorded ending inventory before adjusting for any inventory shrinkage.

A physical count of inventory taken at the end of the period reveals $21,000 of merchandise available. The adjusting and closing entries for the two systems are shown in Exhibit 5A.1. The periodic

Exhibit 5A.1

Comparison of Adjusting and Closing Entries—Periodic and Perpetual

Periodic			**Perpetual**		
Adjusting Entry—Shrinkage			**Adjusting Entry—Shrinkage**		
None			Cost of Goods Sold	250	
			Merchandise Inventory		250
Closing Entries			**Closing Entries**		
(1) Sales	321,000		(1) Sales	321,000	
Merchandise Inventory	**21,000**		Income Summary		321,000
Purchase Discounts	**4,200**				
Purchase Returns and Allowances	**1,500**				
Income Summary		347,700			

[continued on next page]

[continued from previous page]

Periodic			Perpetual		
(2) Income Summary	334,800		(2) Income Summary	308,100	
Sales Discounts		4,300	Sales Discounts		4,300
Sales Returns and Allowances		2,000	Sales Returns and Allowances		2,000
Merchandise Inventory		**19,000**			
Purchases		**235,800**	**Cost of Goods Sold**		**230,400**
Transportation-In		**2,300**			
Depreciation Expense—Store eq.		3,000	Depreciation Expense—Store eq.		3,000
Depreciation Expense—Office eq.		700	Depreciation Expense—Office eq.		700
Office Salaries Expense		25,300	Office Salaries Expense		25,300
Sales Salaries Expense		18,500	Sales Salaries Expense		18,500
Insurance Expense		600	Insurance Expense		600
Rent Expense—Office space		900	Rent Expense—Office space		900
Rent Expense—Selling space		8,100	Rent Expense—Selling space		8,100
Office Supplies Expense		1,800	Office Supplies Expense		1,800
Store Supplies Expense		1,200	Store Supplies Expense		1,200
Advertising Expense		11,300	Advertising Expense		11,300
(3) Income Summary	12,900		(3) Income Summary	12,900	
K. Marty, Capital		12,900	K. Marty, Capital		12,900
(4) K. Marty, Capital	4,000		(4) K. Marty, Capital	4,000	
K. Marty, Withdrawals		4,000	K. Marty, Withdrawals		4,000

system records the ending inventory of $21,000 in the Merchandise Inventory account (which includes shrinkage) in the first closing entry and removes the $19,000 beginning inventory balance from the account in the second closing entry.*

By updating Merchandise Inventory and closing Purchases, Purchase Discounts, Purchase Returns and Allowances, and Transportation-In, the periodic system transfers the cost of goods sold amount to Income Summary. Review the periodic side of Exhibit 5A.1 and notice that the boldface items affect Income Summary as follows:

Credit to Income Summary in the first closing entry includes amounts from:	
Merchandise inventory (ending)	$ 21,000
Purchase discounts	4,200
Purchase returns and allowances	1,500
Debit to Income Summary in the second closing entry includes amounts from:	
Merchandise inventory (beginning)	(19,000)
Purchases	(235,800)
Transportation-in	(2,300)
Net effect on Income Summary	**$(230,400)**

This $230,400 effect on Income Summary is the cost of goods sold amount. The periodic system transfers cost of goods sold to the Income Summary account but without using a Cost of Goods Sold account. Also, the periodic system does not separately measure shrinkage. Instead, it computes cost of goods available for sale, subtracts the cost of ending inventory, and defines the difference as cost of goods sold, which includes shrinkage.

* (This approach is called the *closing entry method.* An alternative approach, referred to as the *adjusting entry method,* would not make any entries to Merchandise Inventory in the closing entries of Exhibit 5A.1, but instead would make two adjusting entries. Using Z-Mart data, the two adjusting entries would be: (1) Dr. Income Summary and Cr. Merchandise Inventory for $19,000 each, and (2) Dr. Merchandise Inventory and Cr. Income Summary for $21,000 each. The first entry removes the beginning balance of Merchandise Inventory, and the second entry records the actual ending balance.)

Preparing Financial Statements

The financial statements of a merchandiser using the periodic system are similar to those for a service company described in prior chapters. The income statement mainly differs by the inclusion of *cost of goods sold* and *gross profit*—of course, net sales is affected by discounts, returns, and allowances. The cost of goods sold section under the periodic system follows

Calculation of Cost of Goods Sold
For Year Ended December 31, 2005

Beginning inventory	$ 19,000
Cost of goods purchased	232,400
Cost of goods available for sale	251,400
Less ending inventory	21,000
Cost of goods sold	$230,400

The balance sheet mainly differs by the inclusion of *merchandise inventory* in current assets—see Exhibit 5.15. The statement of owner's equity is unchanged. Finally, a work sheet can be used to help prepare these statements. The only differences under the periodic system from the work sheet illustrated in Appendix 5B using the perpetual system follow:

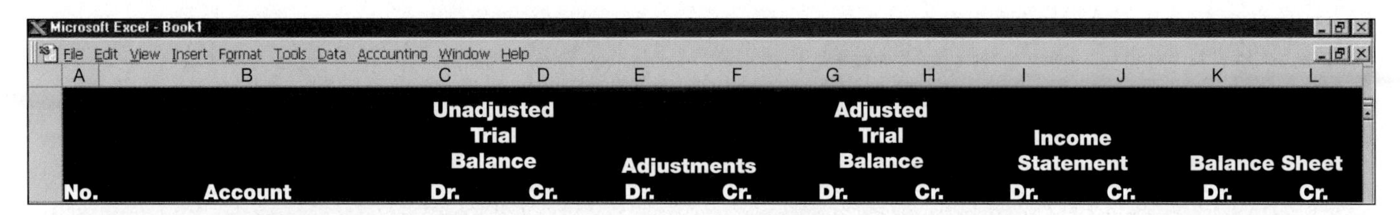

Microsoft Excel - Book1
File Edit View Insert Format Tools Data Accounting Window Help

	A	B	C	D	E	F	G	H	I	J	K	L
			Unadjusted Trial Balance		Adjustments		Adjusted Trial Balance		Income Statement		Balance Sheet	
	No.	Account	Dr.	Cr.	Dr.	Cr.	Dr.	Cr.	Dr.	Cr.	Dr.	Cr.

(1) Delete the following row for Merchandise Inventory

5	119	Merchandise Inventory	21,250			*(g)* 250	21,000				21,000	

and substitute the following row:

5	119	Merchandise Inventory	19,000				19,000		19,000	21,000	21,000	

(2) Delete the following cost of goods sold row

20	502	Cost of goods sold	230,150		*(g)* 250		230,400		230,400			

and substitute the following 4 rows:

20a	505	Purchases	235,800				235,800		235,800			
20b	506	Purchases returns & allow.		1,500				1,500		1,500		
20c	507	Purchases discounts		4,200				4,200		4,200		
20d	508	Transportation-In	2,300				2,300		2,300			

Of course, the worksheet column totals will slightly differ, but not the net income amount.

Quick Check

13. What account is used in a perpetual inventory system but not in a periodic system?

14. Which of the following accounts are temporary accounts under a periodic system? (*a*) Merchandise Inventory; (*b*) Purchases; (*c*) Transportation-In.

15. How is cost of goods sold computed under a periodic inventory system?

16. Do reported amounts of ending inventory and net income differ if the adjusting entry method of recording the change in inventory is used instead of the closing entry method?

Answer—p. 204

APPENDIX

5B Work Sheet—Perpetual System

Exhibit 5B.1 shows the work sheet for preparing financial statements of a merchandiser. It differs slightly from the work sheet layout in Chapter 4—the differences are in bold. Also, the adjustments in the work sheet reflect the following: (*a*) Expiration of $600 of prepaid insurance. (*b*) Use of $1,200 of store supplies. (*c*) Use of $1,800 of office supplies. (*d*) Depreciation of $3,000 for store equipment. (*e*) Depreciation of $700 for office equipment. (*f*) Accrual of $300 of unpaid office salaries and $500 of unpaid store salaries. (*g*) Inventory shrinkage of $250. Once the adjusted amounts are extended into the financial statement columns, the information is used to develop financial statements.

Exhibit 5B.1

Work Sheet for Merchandiser (using a perpetual system)

Microsoft Excel - Book1

	A	B	C	D	E	F	G	H	I	J	K	L
1			**Unadjusted Trial Balance**		**Adjustments**		**Adjusted Trial Balance**		**Income Statement**		**Balance Sheet and Statement of Owner's Equity**	
2	**No.**	**Account**	**Dr.**	**Cr.**	**Dr.**	**Cr.**	**Dr.**	**Cr.**	**Dr.**	**Cr.**	**Dr.**	**Cr.**
3	101	Cash	8,200				8,200				8,200	
4	106	Accounts receivable	11,200				11,200				11,200	
5	**119**	**Merchandise Inventory**	**21,250**			(*g*) 250	**21,000**				**21,000**	
6	124	Office supplies	2,350			(*c*) 1,800	550				550	
7	125	Store supplies	1,450			(*b*) 1,200	250				250	
8	128	Prepaid insurance	900			(*a*) 600	300				300	
9	163	Office equipment	4,200				4,200				4,200	
10	164	Accum. depr.—Office equip.		700		(*e*) 700		1,400				1,400
11	165	Store equipment	30,000				30,000				30,000	
12	166	Accum. depr.—Store equip.		3,000		(*d*) 3,000		6,000				6,000
13	201	Accounts payable		16,000				16,000				16,000
14	209	Salaries payable				(*f*) 800		800				800
15	301	K. Marty, Capital		42,600				42,600				42,600
16	302	K. Marty, Withdrawals	4,000				4,000				4,000	
17	**413**	**Sales**		**321,000**				**321,000**		**321,000**		
18	**414**	**Sales returns and allowances**	**2,000**				**2,000**		**2,000**			
19	**415**	**Sales discounts**	**4,300**				**4,300**		**4,300**			
20	**502**	**Cost of goods sold**	**230,150**		(*g*) 250		**230,400**		**230,400**			
21	612	Depr. expense—Store equip.			(*d*) 3,000		3,000		3,000			
22	613	Depr. expense—Office equip.			(*e*) 700		700		700			
23	620	Office salaries expense	25,000		(*f*) 300		25,300		25,300			
24	621	Sales salaries expense	18,000		(*f*) 500		18,500		18,500			
25	637	Insurance expense			(*a*) 600		600		600			
26	641	Rent expense—Office space	900				900		900			
27	642	Rent expense—Selling space	8,100				8,100		8,100			
28	650	Office supplies expense			(*c*) 1,800		1,800		1,800			
29	651	Store supplies expense			(*b*) 1,200		1,200		1,200			
30	655	Advertising expense	11,300				11,300		11,300			
31		Totals	383,300	383,300	8,350	8,350	387,800	387,800	308,100	321,000	79,700	66,800
32		Net income							12,900			12,900
33		Totals							321,000	321,000	79,700	79,700
34												

Sheet1 / Sheet2 / Sheet3

Summary

C1 Describe merchandising activities and identify income components for a merchandising company. Merchandisers buy products and resell them. Examples of merchandisers include Wal-Mart, Home Depot, The Limited, and Barnes & Noble. A merchandiser's costs on the income statement include an amount for cost of goods sold. Gross profit, or gross margin, equals sales minus cost of goods sold.

C2 Identify and explain the inventory asset of a merchandising company. The current asset section of a merchandising company's balance sheet includes *merchandise inventory,* which refers to the products a merchandiser sells and are available for sale at the balance sheet date.

C3 Describe both perpetual and periodic inventory systems. A perpetual inventory system continuously tracks the cost of goods available for sale and the cost of goods sold. A periodic system accumulates the cost of goods purchased during the period and does not compute the amount of inventory or the cost of goods sold until the end of a period.

C4 Analyze and interpret cost flows and operating activities of a merchandising company. Cost of merchandise purchases flows into Merchandise Inventory and from there to Cost of Goods Sold on the income statement. Any remaining inventory is reported as a current asset on the balance sheet.

A1 Compute the acid-test ratio and explain its use to assess liquidity. The acid-test ratio is computed as quick assets (cash, short-term investments, and current receivables) divided by current liabilities. It indicates a company's ability to pay its current liabilities with its existing quick assets. An acid-test ratio equal to or greater than 1.0 is often adequate.

A2 Compute the gross margin ratio and explain its use to assess profitability. The gross margin ratio is computed as gross margin (net sales minus cost of goods sold) divided by net sales. It indicates a company's profitability before considering other expenses.

P1 Analyze and record transactions for merchandise purchases using a perpetual system. For a perpetual inventory system, purchases of inventory (net of trade discounts) are added to the Merchandise Inventory account. Purchase discounts and purchase returns and allowances are subtracted from Merchandise Inventory, and transportation-in costs are added to Merchandise Inventory.

P2 Analyze and record transactions for merchandise sales using a perpetual system. A merchandiser records sales at list price less any trade discounts. The cost of items sold is transferred from Merchandise Inventory to Cost of Goods Sold. Refunds or credits given to customers for unsatisfactory merchandise are recorded in Sales Returns and Allowances, a contra account to Sales. If merchandise is returned and restored to inventory, the cost of this merchandise is removed from Cost of Goods Sold and transferred back to Merchandise Inventory. When cash discounts from the sales price are offered and customers pay within the discount period, the seller records Sales Discounts, a contra account to Sales.

P3 Prepare adjustments and close accounts for a merchandising company. With a perpetual system, it is often necessary to make an adjustment for inventory shrinkage. This is computed by comparing a physical count of inventory with the Merchandise Inventory balance. Shrinkage is normally charged to Cost of Goods Sold. Temporary accounts closed to Income Summary for a merchandiser include Sales, Sales Discounts, Sales Returns and Allowances, and Cost of Goods Sold.

P4 Define and prepare multiple-step and single-step income statements. Multiple-step income statements include greater detail for sales and expenses than do single-step income statements. They also show details of net sales and report expenses in categories reflecting different activities.

P5[A] Record and compare merchandising transactions using both periodic and perpetual inventory systems. Transactions involving the sale and purchase of merchandise are recorded and analyzed under both the periodic and perpetual inventory systems. Adjusting and closing entries for both inventory systems are illustrated and explained.

Guidance Answers to Decision Maker and Decision Ethics

Entrepreneur For terms of 3/10, n/90, missing the 3% discount for an additional 80 days equals an implied annual interest rate of 13.69% computed as (365 days ÷ 80 days) × 3%. Since you can borrow funds at 11% (assuming no other processing costs), it is better to borrow and pay within the discount period. You save 2.69% (13.69% − 11%) in interest costs by paying early.

Credit Manager Your decision is whether to comply with prior policy or to create a new policy and not abuse discounts offered by suppliers. Your first step should be to meet with your superior to find out if the late payment policy is the actual policy and, if so, its rationale. If it is the policy to pay late, you must apply your own sense of ethics. One point of view is that the late payment policy is unethical. A deliberate plan to make late payments means the company lies when it pretends to make payment within the discount period. Another view is that the late payment policy is acceptable. In some markets, attempts to take discounts through late payments are accepted as a continued phase of "price negotiation." Also, your company's suppliers can respond by billing your company for the discounts not accepted because of late payments. However, this is a dubious viewpoint, especially since the prior manager proposes that you explain late payments as computer or mail problems and since some suppliers have complained.

Supplier A current ratio of 2.1 suggests sufficient current assets to cover current liabilities. An acid-test ratio of 0.5 suggests, however, that quick assets can cover only about one-half of current liabilities. This implies that the retailer depends on money from sales of inventory to pay current liabilities. If sales of inventory decline or profit margins decrease, the likelihood that this retailer will default on its payments increases. Your decision is probably not to extend credit. If you do extend credit, you are likely to closely monitor the retailer's financial condition. (It is better to hold unsold inventory than uncollectible receivables.)

Financial Officer Your company's net profit margin is about equal to the industry average and suggests typical industry performance. However, gross margin reveals that your company is paying far more in cost of goods sold or receiving far less in sales price than competitors. Your attention must be directed to finding the problem with cost of goods sold, sales, or both. One positive note is that your company's expenses make up 19% of sales (36% − 17%). This favorably compares with competitors' expenses that make up 28% of sales (44% − 16%).

Guidance Answers to **Quick Checks**

1. Cost of goods sold is the cost of merchandise purchased from a supplier that is sold to customers during a specific period.
2. Gross profit (or gross margin) is the difference between net sales and cost of goods sold.
3. Widespread use of computing and related technology has dramatically increased the use of the perpetual inventory system.
4. Under credit terms of 2/10, n/60, the credit period is 60 days and the discount period is 10 days.
5. (*b*) trade discount.
6. *FOB* means "free on board." It is used in identifying the point when ownership transfers from seller to buyer. *FOB destination* means that the seller transfers ownership of goods to the buyer when they arrive at the buyer's place of business. It also means that the seller is responsible for paying shipping charges and bears the risk of damage or loss during shipment.
7. Recording sales discounts and sales returns and allowances separately from sales gives useful information to managers for internal monitoring and decision making.
8. When a customer returns merchandise *and* the seller restores the merchandise to inventory, two entries are necessary. One entry records the decrease in revenue and credits the customer's account. The second entry debits inventory and reduces cost of goods sold.
9. Credit memorandum—seller credits accounts receivable from buyer.
10. Merchandise Inventory may need adjusting to reflect shrinkage.
11. Sales (of goods), Sales Discounts, Sales Returns and Allowances, and Cost of Goods Sold (and maybe Delivery Expense).
12. Four closing entries: (1) close credit balances in temporary accounts to Income Summary, (2) close debit balances in temporary accounts to Income Summary, (3) close Income Summary to owner's capital, and (4) close withdrawals account to owner's capital.
13. Cost of Goods Sold.
14. (*b*) Purchases and (*c*) Transportation-In.
15. Under a periodic inventory system, the cost of goods sold is determined at the end of an accounting period by adding the net cost of goods purchased to the beginning inventory and subtracting the ending inventory.
16. Both methods report the same ending inventory and income.

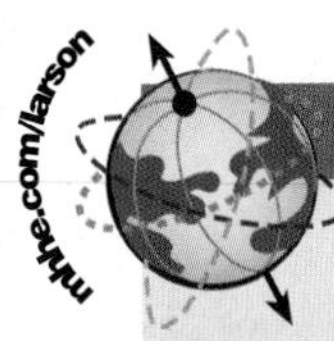

Key Terms

Key Terms are available at the book's Website for learning and testing in an online Flashcard Format.

Acid-test ratio (p. 193)
Cash discount (p. 181)
Cost of goods sold (p. 179)
Credit memorandum (p. 187)
Credit period (p. 181)
Credit terms (p. 181)
Debit memorandum (p. 182)
Discount period (p. 181)
EOM (p. 181)
FOB (p. 183)
General and administrative expenses (p. 191)
Gross margin (p. 179)
Gross margin ratio (p. 193)
Gross profit (p. 179)
Inventory (p. 179)
List price (p. 180)
Merchandise (p. 178)
Merchandise inventory (p. 179)
Merchandiser (p. 178)
Multiple-step income statement (p. 190)
Periodic inventory system (p. 180)
Perpetual inventory system (p. 179)
Purchase discount (p. 181)
Retailer (p. 178)
Sales discount (p. 181)
Selling expenses (p. 191)
Shrinkage (p. 188)
Single-step income statement (p. 192)
Supplementary records (p. 184)
Trade discount (p. 180)
Wholesaler (p. 178)

Personal Interactive Quiz

Personal Interactive Quizzes A and B are available at the book's Website to reinforce and assess your learning.

Superscript letter A (B) denotes assignments based on Appendix 5A (5B).

Discussion Questions

1. In comparing the accounts of a merchandising company with those of a service company, what additional accounts would the merchandising company likely use, assuming it employs a perpetual inventory system?
2. What items appear in financial statements of merchandising companies but not in the statements of service companies?
3. Explain how a business can earn a positive gross profit on its sales and still have a net loss.
4. Why do companies offer a cash discount?
5. How does a company that uses a perpetual inventory system determine the amount of inventory shrinkage?
6. Distinguish between cash discounts and trade discounts. Is the amount of a trade discount on purchased merchandise recorded in the accounts?
7. What is the difference between a sales discount and a purchase discount?
8. Why would a company's manager be concerned about the quantity of its purchase returns if its suppliers allow unlimited returns?
9. Does the sender (maker) of a debit memorandum record a debit or a credit in the recipient's account? What entry (debit or credit) does the recipient record?
10. What is the difference between the single-step and multiple-step income statement formats?
11. Refer to the income statement for **Krispy Kreme** in Appendix A. What term is used instead of cost of goods sold? Does the company present a detailed calculation of its cost of goods sold?
12. Refer to the balance sheet for **Tastykake** in Appendix A. What does Tastykake call its inventory account? What alternate name could it use?
13. Refer to the income statement of **Harley-Davidson** in Appendix A. Does its income statement report a gross profit figure? If yes, what is the amount?
14. Buyers negotiate purchase contracts with suppliers. What type of shipping terms should a buyer attempt to negotiate to minimize freight-in costs?

Red numbers denote Discussion Questions that involve decision-making.

***Homework Manager** repeats all numerical Quick Study assignments on the book's Website with new numbers.*

QUICK STUDY

QS 5-1
Recording purchases—perpetual system
P1

Prepare journal entries to record each of the following purchases transactions of a merchandising company. Show supporting calculations and assume a perpetual inventory system.

Mar. 5 Purchased 500 units of product with a list price of $5 per unit. The purchaser is granted a trade discount of 20%; terms of the sale are 2/10, n/60; invoice is dated March 5.
Mar. 7 Returned 50 defective units from the March 5 purchase and received full credit.
Mar. 15 Paid the amount due from the March 5 purchase, less the return on March 7.

QS 5-2
Recording sales—perpetual system
P2

Prepare journal entries to record each of the following sales transactions of a merchandising company. Show supporting calculations and assume a perpetual inventory system.

Apr. 1 Sold merchandise for $2,000, granting the customer terms of 2/10, EOM; invoice dated April 1. The cost of the merchandise is $1,400.
Apr. 4 The customer in the April 1 sale returned merchandise and received credit for $500. The merchandise, which had cost $350, is returned to inventory.
Apr. 11 Received payment for the amount due from the April 1 sale less the return on April 4.

QS 5-3
Computing and analyzing gross margin
C1 A2

Compute net sales, gross profit, and the gross margin ratio for each separate case *a* through *d*. Interpret the gross margin ratio for case *a*.

	a	b	c	d
Sales	$130,000	$512,000	$35,700	$245,700
Sales discounts	4,200	16,500	400	3,500
Sales returns and allowances	17,000	5,000	5,000	700
Cost of goods sold	76,600	326,700	21,300	125,900

QS 5-4
Accounting for shrinkage—perpetual system
P3

Nix'It Company's ledger on July 31, its fiscal year-end, includes the following accounts that have normal balances (Nix'It uses the perpetual inventory system):

Merchandise inventory	$ 34,800	Sales returns and allowances	$ 3,500
T. Nix, Capital	115,300	Cost of goods sold	102,000
T. Nix, Withdrawals	7,000	Depreciation expense	7,300
Sales	157,200	Salaries expense	29,500
Sales discounts	1,700	Miscellaneous expenses	2,000

A physical count of its July 31 year-end inventory discloses that the cost of the merchandise inventory still available is $32,900. Prepare the entry to record any inventory shrinkage.

QS 5-5
Closing entries P3

Refer to QS 5-4 and prepare journal entries to close the balances in temporary revenue and expense accounts. Remember to consider the entry for shrinkage that is made to solve QS 5-4.

QS 5-6
Computing and interpreting acid-test ratio
A1

Use the following information on current assets and current liabilities to compute and interpret the acid-test ratio. Explain what the acid-test ratio of a company measures.

Cash	$1,200	Prepaid expenses	$ 600
Accounts receivable	2,700	Accounts payable	4,750
Inventory	5,000	Other current liabilities	950

QS 5-7
Contrasting liquidity ratios A1

Identify similarities and differences between the acid-test ratio and the current ratio. Compare and describe how the two ratios reflect a company's ability to meet its current obligations.

QS 5-8[A]
Contrasting periodic and perpetual systems
C3

Identify whether each description best applies to a periodic or a perpetual inventory system.

a. Provides more timely information to managers.
b. Requires an adjusting entry to record inventory shrinkage.
c. Markedly increased in frequency and popularity in business within the past decade.
d. Records cost of goods sold each time a sales transaction occurs.

QS 5-9[A]
Recording purchases—periodic system P5

Refer to QS 5-1 and prepare journal entries to record each of the merchandising transactions assuming that the periodic inventory system is used.

QS 5-10[A]
Recording purchases—periodic system P5

Refer to QS 5-2 and prepare journal entries to record each of the merchandising transactions assuming that the periodic inventory system is used.

Homework Manager repeats all numerical Exercises on the book's Website with new numbers.

EXERCISES

Exercise 5-1
Recording entries for merchandise purchases
P1

Prepare journal entries to record the following transactions for a retail store. Assume a perpetual inventory system.

Apr. 2 Purchased merchandise from Blue Company under the following terms: $3,600 price, invoice dated April 2, credit terms of 2/15, n/60, and FOB shipping point.
3 Paid $200 for shipping charges on the April 2 purchase.
4 Returned to Blue Company unacceptable merchandise that had an invoice price of $600.
17 Sent a check to Blue Company for the April 2 purchase, net of the discount and the returned merchandise.
18 Purchased merchandise from Fox Corp. under the following terms: $7,500 price, invoice dated April 18, credit terms of 2/10, n/30, and FOB destination.
21 After negotiations, received from Fox a $2,100 allowance on the April 18 purchase.
28 Sent a check to Fox paying for the April 18 purchase, net of the discount and allowance.

Check April 28, Cr. Cash $5,292

Exercise 5-2
Analyzing and recording merchandise transactions—both buyer and seller
P1 P2 

Taos Company purchased merchandise for resale from Tucson Company with an invoice price of $22,000 and credit terms of 3/10, n/60. The merchandise had cost Tucson $15,000. Taos paid within the discount period. Assume that both buyer and seller use a perpetual inventory system.

1. Prepare entries that the buyer should record for the purchase and the cash payment.
2. Prepare entries that the seller should record for the sale and the cash collection.
3. Assume that the buyer borrowed enough cash to pay the balance on the last day of the discount period at an annual interest rate of 8% and paid it back on the last day of the credit period. Compute how much the buyer saved by following this strategy. (Assume a 365-day year and round dollar amounts to the nearest cent.)

Check (3) $426 savings

Exercise 5-3
Applying merchandising terms
C1

Insert the letter for each term in the blank space beside the definition that it most closely matches:

A. Cash discount
B. Credit period
C. Discount period
D. FOB destination
E. FOB shipping point
F. Gross profit
G. Merchandise inventory
H. Purchase discount
I. Sales discount
J. Trade discount

_____ **1.** Ownership of goods is transferred when delivered to the buyer's place of business.
_____ **2.** Time period in which a cash discount is available.
_____ **3.** Difference between net sales and the cost of goods sold.
_____ **4.** Reduction in a receivable or payable if it is paid within the discount period.
_____ **5.** Purchaser's description of a cash discount received from a supplier of goods.
_____ **6.** Ownership of goods is transferred when the seller delivers goods to the carrier.
_____ **7.** Reduction below list or catalog price that is negotiated in setting the price of goods.
_____ **8.** Seller's description of a cash discount granted to buyers in return for early payment.
_____ **9.** Time period that can pass before a customer's payment is due.
_____ **10.** Goods a company owns and expects to sell to its customers.

Exercise 5-4
Recording sales returns and allowances
P2

Spare Parts was organized on May 1, 2005, and made its first purchase of merchandise on May 3. The purchase was for 1,000 units at a price of $10 per unit. On May 5, Spare Parts sold 600 of the units for $14 per unit to DeSoto Co. Terms of the sale were 2/10, n/60. Prepare entries for Spare Parts to record the May 5 sale and each of the following separate transactions *a* through *c* using a perpetual inventory system.

a. On May 7, DeSoto returns 200 units because they did not fit the customer's needs. Spare Parts restores the units to its inventory.
b. On May 8, DeSoto discovers that 50 units are damaged but of some use and, therefore, keeps the units. Spare Parts sends DeSoto a credit memorandum for $300 to compensate for the damage.
c. On May 15, DeSoto returns 100 defective units and Spare Parts concludes that these units cannot be resold. As a result, Spare Parts discards them—it removes these units' cost from cost of good sold and records a loss from defective merchandise.

Check (c) Cr. Cost of Good Sold $1,000

Exercise 5-5
Recording purchase returns and allowances P1

Refer to Exercise 5-4 and prepare the appropriate journal entries for DeSoto Co. to record the May 5 purchase and each of the three separate transactions *a* through *c*. DeSoto is a retailer that uses a perpetual inventory system and purchases these units for resale.

Exercise 5-6
Analyzing and recording merchandise transactions—both buyer and seller
P1 P2

On May 11, Smythe Co. accepts delivery of $30,000 of merchandise it purchases for resale from Hope Corporation. With the merchandise is an invoice dated May 11, with terms of 3/10, n/90, FOB shipping point. The cost of the goods for Hope is $20,000. When the goods are delivered, Smythe pays $335 to Express Shipping for delivery charges on the merchandise. On May 12, Smythe returns $1,200 of goods to Hope, who receives them one day later and restores them to inventory. The returned goods had cost Hope $800. On May 20, Smythe mails a check to Hope Corporation for the amount owed. Hope receives it the following day. (Both Smythe and Hope use a perpetual inventory system)

Check (1) May 20, Cr. Cash $27,936

1. Prepare journal entries that Smythe Co. records for these transactions.
2. Prepare journal entries that Hope Corporation records for these transactions.

Exercise 5-7
Sales returns and allowances
C1 P2 

Explain why a company's manager wants the accounting system to record customers' returns of unsatisfactory goods in the Sales Returns and Allowances account instead of the Sales account. In addition, explain whether this information would be useful for external decision makers.

Exercise 5-8
Recording effects of merchandising activities
C4

The following supplementary records summarize Titus Company's merchandising activities for year 2005. Set up T-accounts for Merchandise Inventory and Cost of Goods Sold. Then record the summarized activities in those T-accounts and compute account balances.

Cost of merchandise sold to customers in sales transactions	$186,000
Merchandise inventory, December 31, 2004	27,000
Invoice cost of merchandise purchases	190,500
Shrinkage determined on December 31, 2005	700
Cost of transportation-in	1,900
Cost of merchandise returned by customers and restored to inventory	2,200
Purchase discounts received	1,600
Purchase returns and allowances	4,100

Check Merchandise Inventory (12/31/2005), $29,200

Exercise 5-9
Calculating revenues, expenses, and income
C1 C4

Fill in the blanks in the following separate income statements *a* through *e*. Identify any negative amount by putting it in parentheses.

	a	b	c	d	e
Sales	$60,000	$42,500	$36,000	$?	$23,600
Cost of goods sold					
Merchandise inventory (beginning)	6,000	17,050	7,500	7,000	2,560
Total cost of merchandise purchases	36,000	?	?	32,000	5,600
Merchandise inventory (ending)	?	(2,700)	(9,000)	(6,600)	?
Cost of goods sold	34,050	15,900	?	?	5,600
Gross profit	?	?	3,750	45,600	?
Expenses	9,000	10,650	12,150	2,600	6,000
Net income (loss)	$?	$15,950	$ (8,400)	$43,000	$?

Exercise 5-10
Preparing adjusting and closing entries for a merchandiser
P3

The following list includes some permanent accounts and all of the temporary accounts from the December 31, 2005, unadjusted trial balance of Deacon Co., a business owned by Julie Deacon. Use these account balances along with the additional information to journalize (*a*) adjusting entries and (*b*) closing entries. Deacon Co. uses a perpetual inventory system.

	Debit	Credit
Merchandise inventory	$ 28,000	
Prepaid selling expenses	5,000	
J. Deacon, Withdrawals	2,200	
Sales		$429,000
Sales returns and allowances	16,500	
Sales discounts	4,000	
Cost of goods sold	211,000	
Sales salaries expense	47,000	
Utilities expense	14,000	
Selling expenses	35,000	
Administrative expenses	95,000	

Additional Information

Accrued sales salaries amount to $1,600. Prepaid selling expenses of $2,000 have expired. A physical count of year-end merchandise inventory shows $27,450 of goods still available.

Check Entry to close Income Summary: Cr. J. Deacon, Capital $2,350

Exercise 5-11
Interpreting a physical count error as inventory shrinkage
A1 A2 P3 

A retail company recently completed a physical count of ending merchandise inventory to use in preparing adjusting entries. In determining the cost of the counted inventory, company employees failed to consider that $2,000 of incoming goods had been shipped by a supplier on December 31 under an FOB shipping point agreement. These goods had been recorded in Merchandise Inventory as a purchase, but they were not included in the physical count because they were in transit. Explain how this overlooked fact affects the company's financial statements and the following ratios: return on assets, debt ratio, current ratio, profit margin ratio, and acid-test ratio.

Exercise 5-12
Computing and analyzing acid-test and current ratios
A1 

Compute the current ratio and acid-test ratio for each of the following separate cases. Which company case is in the best position to meet short-term obligations? Explain.

	Case X	Case Y	Case Z
Cash	$ 800	$ 910	$1,100
Short-term investments	0	0	500
Current receivables	0	990	800
Inventory	2,000	1,000	4,000
Prepaid expenses	1,200	600	900
Total current assets	$4,000	$3,500	$7,300
Current liabilities	$2,200	$1,100	$3,650

Exercise 5-13[A]
Preparing journal entries for both the periodic and perpetual systems
P1 P2 P5

Journalize the following merchandising transactions for CSI Systems assuming it uses (*a*) a periodic inventory system and (*b*) a perpetual inventory system.

1. On November 1, CSI Systems purchases merchandise for $1,400 on credit with terms of 2/5, n/30, FOB shipping point; invoice dated November 1.
2. On November 5, CSI Systems pays cash for the November 1 purchase.
3. On November 7, CSI Systems discovers and returns $100 of defective merchandise purchased on November 1 for a cash refund.
4. On November 10, CSI Systems pays $80 cash for transportation costs with the November 1 purchase.
5. On November 13, CSI Systems sells merchandise for $1,500 on credit. The cost of the merchandise is $750.
6. On November 16, the customer returns merchandise from the November 13 transaction. The returned items sell for $200 and cost $100.

Exercise 5-14[A]
Recording purchases—periodic system P5

Refer to Exercise 5-1 and prepare journal entries to record each of the merchandising transactions assuming that the periodic inventory system is used.

Exercise 5-15[A]
Recording purchases and sales—periodic system P5

Refer to Exercise 5-2 and prepare journal entries to record each of the merchandising transactions assuming that the periodic inventory system is used by both the buyer and the seller. (Skip the part 3 requirement.)

Exercise 5-16[A]
Buyer and seller transactions—periodic system P5

Refer to Exercise 5-6 and prepare journal entries to record each of the merchandising transactions assuming that the periodic inventory system is used by both the buyer and the seller.

PROBLEM SET A

Problem 5-1A
Preparing journal entries for merchandising activities—perpetual system

P1 P2

Prepare journal entries to record the following merchandising transactions of Stone Company, which applies the perpetual inventory system. (*Hint:* It will help to identify each receivable and payable; for example, record the purchase on August 1 in Accounts Payable—Abilene.)

Aug. 1 Purchased merchandise from Abilene Company for $6,000 under credit terms of 1/10, n/30, FOB destination, invoice dated August 1.

4 At Abilene's request, Stone paid $100 cash for freight charges on the August 1 purchase, reducing the amount owed to Abilene.

5 Sold merchandise to Lux Corp. for $4,200 under credit terms of 2/10, n/60, FOB destination, invoice dated August 5. The merchandise had cost $3,000.

8 Purchased merchandise from Welch Corporation for $5,300 under credit terms of 1/10, n/45, FOB shipping point, invoice dated August 8. The invoice showed that at Stone's request, Welch paid the $240 shipping charges and added that amount to the bill.

9 Paid $120 cash for shipping charges related to the August 5 sale to Lux Corp.

Check Aug. 9, Dr. Delivery Expense, $120

10 Lux returned merchandise from the August 5 sale that had cost Stone $500 and been sold for $700. The merchandise was restored to inventory.

12 After negotiations with Welch Corporation concerning problems with the merchandise purchased on August 8, Stone received a credit memorandum from Welch granting a price reduction of $800.

15 Received balance due from Lux Corp. for the August 5 sale less the return on August 10.

18 Paid the amount due Welch Corporation for the August 8 purchase less the price reduction granted.

Aug. 18, Cr. Cash $4,695

19 Sold merchandise to Trax for $3,600 under credit terms of 1/10, n/30, FOB shipping point, invoice dated August 19. The merchandise had cost $2,500.

22 Trax requested a price reduction on the August 19 sale because the merchandise did not meet specifications. Stone sent Trax a $600 credit memorandum to resolve the issue.

29 Received Trax's cash payment for the amount due from the August 19 purchase.

Aug. 29, Dr. Cash $2,970

30 Paid Abilene Company the amount due from the August 1 purchase.

Problem 5-2A
Preparing journal entries for merchandising activities—perpetual system

P1 P2

Prepare journal entries to record the following merchandising transactions of Bask Company, which applies the perpetual inventory system. (*Hint:* It will help to identify each receivable and payable; for example, record the purchase on July 1 in Accounts Payable—Black.)

July 1 Purchased merchandise from Black Company for $6,000 under credit terms of 1/15, n/30, FOB shipping point, invoice dated July 1.

2 Sold merchandise to Coke Co. for $800 under credit terms of 2/10, n/60, FOB shipping point, invoice dated July 2. The merchandise had cost $500.

3 Paid $100 cash for freight charges on the purchase of July 1.

8 Sold merchandise that had cost $1,200 for $1,600 cash.

9 Purchased merchandise from Lane Co. for $2,300 under credit terms of 2/15, n/60, FOB destination, invoice dated July 9.

11 Received a $200 credit memorandum from Lane Co. for the return of part of the merchandise purchased on July 9.

12 Received the balance due from Coke Co. for the invoice dated July 2, net of the discount.
16 Paid the balance due to Black Company within the discount period.
19 Sold merchandise that cost $900 to AKP Co. for $1,250 under credit terms of 2/15, n/60, FOB shipping point, invoice dated July 19.
21 Issued a $150 credit memorandum to AKP Co. for an allowance on goods sold on July 19.
24 Paid Lane Co. the balance due after deducting the discount.
30 Received the balance due from AKP Co. for the invoice dated July 19, net of discount.
31 Sold merchandise that cost $3,200 to Coke Co. for $5,000 under credit terms of 2/10, n/60, FOB shipping point, invoice dated July 31.

Check July 12, Dr. Cash $784
July 16, Cr. Cash $5,940
July 24, Cr. Cash $2,058
July 30, Dr. Cash $1,078

Problem 5-3A
Preparing adjusting entries and income statements; and computing gross margin, acid-test, and current ratios

A1 A2 P3 P4

mhhe.com/larson

The following unadjusted trial balance is prepared at fiscal year-end for Rex Company:

REX COMPANY
Unadjusted Trial Balance
January 31, 2005

		Debit	Credit
2	Cash	$ 2,200	
3	Merchandise inventory	11,500	
4	Store supplies	4,800	
5	Prepaid insurance	2,300	
6	Store equipment	41,900	
7	Accumulated depreciation—Store equipment		$ 15,000
8	Accounts payable		9,000
9	T. Rex, Capital		32,000
10	T. Rex, Withdrawals	2,000	
11	Sales		104,000
12	Sales discounts	1,000	
13	Sales returns and allowances	2,000	
14	Cost of goods sold	37,400	
15	Depreciation expense—Store equipment	0	
16	Salaries expense	31,000	
17	Insurance expense	0	
18	Rent expense	14,000	
19	Store supplies expense	0	
20	Advertising expense	9,900	
21	Totals	$160,000	$160,000

Rent expense and salaries expense are equally divided between selling activities and the general and administrative activities. Rex Company uses a perpetual inventory system.

Required

1. Prepare adjusting journal entries to reflect each of the following:
 a. Store supplies still available at fiscal year-end amount to $1,650.
 b. Expired insurance, an administrative expense, for the fiscal year is $1,500.
 c. Depreciation expense on store equipment, a selling expense, is $1,400 for the fiscal year.
 d. To estimate shrinkage, a physical count of ending merchandise inventory is taken. It shows $11,100 of inventory is still available at fiscal year-end.

2. Prepare a multiple-step income statement for fiscal year 2005.

3. Prepare a single-step income statement for fiscal year 2005.

4. Compute the current ratio, acid-test ratio, and gross margin ratio as of January 31, 2005.

Check (2) Gross profit, $63,200; (3) Total expenses, $98,750; Net income, $2,250

Problem 5-4A
Computing merchandising amounts and formatting income statements
C4 P4

BizKid Company's adjusted trial balance on August 31, 2005, its fiscal year-end, follows:

	Debit	Credit
Merchandise inventory	$ 31,000	
Other (noninventory) assets	120,400	
Total liabilities		$ 35,000
N. Kidman, Capital		101,650
N. Kidman, Withdrawals	8,000	
Sales		212,000
Sales discounts	3,250	
Sales returns and allowances	14,000	
Cost of goods sold	82,600	
Sales salaries expense	29,000	
Rent expense—Selling space	10,000	
Store supplies expense	2,500	
Advertising expense	18,000	
Office salaries expense	26,500	
Rent expense—Office space	2,600	
Office supplies expense	800	
Totals	$348,650	$348,650

On August 31, 2004, merchandise inventory was $25,000. Supplementary records of merchandising activities for the year ended August 31, 2005, reveal the following itemized costs:

Invoice cost of merchandise purchases	$91,000
Purchase discounts received	1,900
Purchase returns and allowances	4,400
Costs of transportation-in	3,900

Required

1. Compute the company's net sales for the year.

2. Compute the company's total cost of merchandise purchased for the year.

3. Prepare a multiple-step income statement that includes separate categories for selling expenses and for general and administrative expenses.

4. Prepare a single-step income statement that includes these expense categories: cost of goods sold, selling expenses, and general and administrative expenses.

Check (2) $88,600; (3) Gross profit, $112,150; Net income, $22,750; (4) Total expenses, $172,000

Problem 5-5A
Preparing closing entries and interpreting information about discounts and returns
C4 P3

Use the data for BizKid Company in Problem 5-4A to complete the following requirements:

Required

1. Prepare closing entries as of August 31, 2005 (the perpetual inventory system is used).

Check (1) $22,750 Dr. to close Income Summary

Analysis Component

2. The company makes all purchases on credit, and its suppliers uniformly offer a 3% sales discount. Does it appear that the company's cash management system is accomplishing the goal of taking all available discounts? Explain.

3. In prior years, the company experienced a 5% returns and allowance rate on its sales, which means approximately 5% of its gross sales were eventually returned outright or caused the company to grant allowances to customers. How do this year's results compare to prior years' results?

(3) Current-year rate, 6.6%

Problem 5-6A[B]
Preparing a work sheet for a merchandiser

Refer to the data and information in Problem 5-3A.

Required

Prepare and complete the entire 10-column work sheet for Rex Company. Follow the structure of Exhibit 5B.1 in Appendix 5B.

PROBLEM SET B

Problem 5-1B
Preparing journal entries for merchandising activities—perpetual system

P1 P2

Prepare journal entries to record the following merchandising transactions of Wave Company, which applies the perpetual inventory system. (*Hint:* It will help to identify each receivable and payable; for example, record the purchase on July 3 in Accounts Payable—CAP.)

July 3 Purchased merchandise from CAP Corp. for $15,000 under credit terms of 1/10, n/30, FOB destination, invoice dated July 3.
4 At CAP's request, Wave paid $250 cash for freight charges on the July 3 purchase, reducing the amount owed to CAP.
7 Sold merchandise to Morris Co. for $10,500 under credit terms of 2/10, n/60, FOB destination, invoice dated July 7. The merchandise had cost $7,500.
10 Purchased merchandise from Murdock Corporation for $14,200 under credit terms of 1/10, n/45, FOB shipping point, invoice dated July 10. The invoice showed that at Wave's request, Murdock paid the $600 shipping charges and added that amount to the bill.
11 Paid $300 cash for shipping charges related to the July 7 sale to Morris Co.
12 Morris returned merchandise from the July 7 sale that had cost Wave $1,250 and been sold for $1,750. The merchandise was restored to inventory.
14 After negotiations with Murdock Corporation concerning problems with the merchandise purchased on July 10, Wave received a credit memorandum from Murdock granting a price reduction of $2,000.
17 Received balance due from Morris Co. for the July 7 sale less the return on July 12.
20 Paid the amount due Murdock Corporation for the July 10 purchase less the price reduction granted.
21 Sold merchandise to Ulsh for $9,000 under credit terms of 1/10, n/30, FOB shipping point, invoice dated July 21. The merchandise had cost $6,250.
24 Ulsh requested a price reduction on the July 21 sale because the merchandise did not meet specifications. Wave sent Ulsh a credit memorandum for $1,500 to resolve the issue.
30 Received Ulsh's cash payment for the amount due from the July 21 purchase.
31 Paid CAP Corp. the amount due from the July 3 purchase.

Check July 17, Dr. Cash $8,575
July 20, Cr. Cash $12,678
July 30, Dr. Cash $7,425

Problem 5-2B
Preparing journal entries for merchandising activities—perpetual system

P1 P2

Prepare journal entries to record the following merchandising transactions of Yang Company, which applies the perpetual inventory system. (*Hint:* It will help to identify each receivable and payable; for example, record the purchase on May 2 in Accounts Payable—Bots.)

May 2 Purchased merchandise from Bots Co. for $9,000 under credit terms of 1/15, n/30, FOB shipping point, invoice dated May 2.
4 Sold merchandise to Chase Co. for $1,200 under credit terms of 2/10, n/60, FOB shipping point, invoice dated May 4. The merchandise had cost $750.
5 Paid $150 cash for freight charges on the purchase of May 2.
9 Sold merchandise that had cost $1,800 for $2,400 cash.
10 Purchased merchandise from Snyder Co. for $3,450 under credit terms of 2/15, n/60, FOB destination, invoice dated May 10.
12 Received a $300 credit memorandum from Snyder Co. for the return of part of the merchandise purchased on May 10.
14 Received the balance due from Chase Co. for the invoice dated May 4, net of the discount.
17 Paid the balance due to Bots Co. within the discount period.
20 Sold merchandise that cost $1,450 to Tex Co. for $2,800 under credit terms of 2/15, n/60, FOB shipping point, invoice dated May 20.
22 Issued a $400 credit memorandum to Tex Co. for an allowance on goods sold from May 20.
25 Paid Snyder Co. the balance due after deducting the discount.
30 Received the balance due from Tex Co. for the invoice dated May 20, net of discount and allowance.
31 Sold merchandise that cost $4,800 to Chase Co. for $7,500 under credit terms of 2/10, n/60, FOB shipping point, invoice dated May 31.

Check May 14, Dr. Cash $1,176
May 17, Cr. Cash $8,910
May 30, Dr. Cash $2,352

Problem 5-3B
Preparing adjusting entries and income statements; and computing gross margin, acid-test, and current ratios
A1 A2 P3 P4

The following unadjusted trial balance is prepared at fiscal year-end for FAB Products Company:

	FAB PRODUCTS COMPANY Unadjusted Trial Balance October 31, 2005	Debit	Credit
2	Cash	$ 4,400	
3	Merchandise inventory	23,000	
4	Store supplies	9,600	
5	Prepaid insurance	4,600	
6	Store equipment	83,800	
7	Accumulated depreciation—Store equipment		$ 30,000
8	Accounts payable		16,000
9	A. Fab, Capital		64,000
10	A. Fab, Withdrawals	2,000	
11	Sales		208,000
12	Sales discounts	2,000	
13	Sales returns and allowances	4,000	
14	Cost of goods sold	74,800	
15	Depreciation expense—Store equipment	0	
16	Salaries expense	62,000	
17	Insurance expense	0	
18	Rent expense	28,000	
19	Store supplies expense	0	
20	Advertising expense	19,800	
21	Totals	$318,000	$318,000

Rent expense and salaries expense are equally divided between selling activities and the general and administrative activities. FAB Products Company uses a perpetual inventory system.

Required

1. Prepare adjusting journal entries to reflect each of the following:
   a. Store supplies still available at fiscal year-end amount to $3,300.
   b. Expired insurance, an administrative expense, for the fiscal year is $3,000.
   c. Depreciation expense on store equipment, a selling expense, is $2,800 for the fiscal year.
   d. To estimate shrinkage, a physical count of ending merchandise inventory is taken. It shows $22,200 of inventory is still available at fiscal year-end.

2. Prepare a multiple-step income statement for fiscal year 2005.

3. Prepare a single-step income statement for fiscal year 2005.

4. Compute the current ratio, acid-test ratio, and gross margin ratio as of October 31, 2005.

Check (2) Gross profit, $126,400; (3) Total expenses, $197,500; Net income, $4,500

Problem 5-4B
Computing merchandising amounts and formatting income statements
C1 C4 P4

Albin Company's adjusted trial balance on March 31, 2005, its fiscal year-end, follows:

	Debit	Credit
Merchandise inventory	$ 46,500	
Other (noninventory) assets	190,600	
Total liabilities		$ 52,500
R. Albin, Capital		152,475
R. Albin, Withdrawals	2,000	
Sales		318,000
Sales discounts	4,875	
Sales returns and allowances	21,000	
Cost of goods sold	123,900	
Sales salaries expense	43,500	
Rent expense—Selling space	15,000	

[continued on next page]

[continued from previous page]

Store supplies expense	3,750	
Advertising expense	27,000	
Office salaries expense	39,750	
Rent expense—Office space	3,900	
Office supplies expense	1,200	
Totals	$522,975	$522,975

On March 31, 2004, merchandise inventory was $37,500. Supplementary records of merchandising activities for the year ended March 31, 2005, reveal the following itemized costs:

Invoice cost of merchandise purchases	$136,500
Purchase discounts received	2,850
Purchase returns and allowances	6,600
Costs of transportation-in	5,850

Required

1. Calculate the company's net sales for the year.
2. Calculate the company's total cost of merchandise purchased for the year.
3. Prepare a multiple-step income statement that includes separate categories for selling expenses and for general and administrative expenses.
4. Prepare a single-step income statement that includes these expense categories: cost of goods sold, selling expenses, and general and administrative expenses.

Check (2) $132,900;
(3) Gross profit, $168,225; Net income, $34,125;
(4) Total expenses, $258,000

Problem 5-5B
Preparing closing entries and interpreting information about discounts and returns
C4 P3 

Use the data for Albin Company in Problem 5-4B to complete the following requirements:

Required

1. Prepare closing entries as of March 31, 2005 (the perpetual inventory system is used).

Analysis Component

2. The company makes all purchases on credit, and its suppliers uniformly offer a 3% sales discount. Does it appear that the company's cash management system is accomplishing the goal of taking all available discounts? Explain.
3. In prior years, the company experienced a 5% returns and allowance rate on its sales, which means approximately 5% of its gross sales were eventually returned outright or caused the company to grant allowances to customers. How do this year's results compare to prior years' results?

Check (1) $34,125 Dr. to close Income Summary

(3) Current-year rate, 6.6%

Problem 5-6B[B]
Preparing a work sheet for a merchandiser

Refer to the data and information in Problem 5-3B.

Required

Prepare and complete the entire 10-column work sheet for FAB Products Company. Follow the structure of Exhibit 5B.1 in Appendix 5B.

PROBLEM SET C

Problem Set C is available at the book's Website to further reinforce and assess your learning.

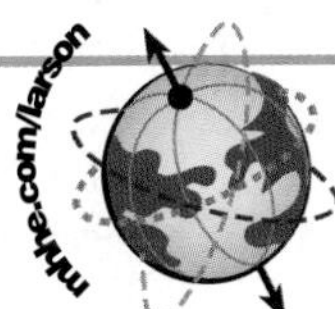

SERIAL PROBLEM

Success Systems

(This serial problem began in Chapter 1 and continues through most of the book. If previous chapter segments were not completed, the serial problem can begin at this point. It is helpful, but not necessary, that you use the Working Papers that accompany the book.)

Kay Breeze created Success Systems on October 1, 2004. The company has been successful, and its list of customers has grown. To accommodate the growth, the accounting system is modified to set up separate accounts for each customer. The following chart of accounts includes the account number used for each account and any balance as of December 31, 2004. Breeze decided to add a fourth digit with a decimal point to the 106 account number that had been used for the single Accounts Receivable account. This modification allows the company to continue using the existing chart of accounts.

No.	Account Title	Dr.	Cr.
101	Cash	58,160	
106.1	Alex's Engineering Co.	0	
106.2	Wildcat Services	0	
106.3	Easy Leasing	0	
106.4	Clark Co.	3,000	
106.5	Chang Corp.	0	
106.6	Gomez Co.	2,668	
106.7	Delta Co.	0	
106.8	KC, Inc.	0	
106.9	Dream, Inc.	0	
119	Merchandise inventory	0	
126	Computer supplies	580	
128	Prepaid insurance	1,665	
131	Prepaid rent	825	
163	Office equipment	8,000	
164	Accumulated depreciation—Office equipment		400
167	Computer equipment	20,000	
168	Accumulated depreciation—Computer equipment		1,250
201	Accounts payable		1,100

No.	Account Title	Dr.	Cr.
210	Wages payable		500
236	Unearned computer services revenue		1,500
301	K. Breeze, Capital		90,148
302	K. Breeze, Withdrawals	0	
403	Computer services revenue		0
413	Sales		0
414	Sales returns and allowances	0	
415	Sales discounts	0	
502	Cost of goods sold	0	
612	Depreciation expense—Office equipment	0	
613	Depreciation expense—Computer equipment	0	
623	Wages expense	0	
637	Insurance expense	0	
640	Rent expense	0	
652	Computer supplies expense	0	
655	Advertising expense	0	
676	Mileage expense	0	
677	Miscellaneous expenses	0	
684	Repairs expense—Computer	0	

In response to requests from customers, Breeze will begin selling computer software. The company will extend credit terms of 1/10, n/30, FOB shipping point, to all customers who purchase this merchandise. However, no cash discount is available on consulting fees. Note that additional accounts (Nos. 119, 413, 414, 415, and 502) are added to its general ledger to accommodate the company's new merchandising activities. Also, Success Systems does not use reversing entries and, therefore, all revenue and expense accounts have zero balances as of January 1, 2005. Its transactions for January through March follow:

Jan. 4 Paid cash to Sherry Adams for five days' work at the rate of $125 per day. Four of the five days relate to wages payable that were accrued in the prior year.

5 Kay Breeze invested an additional $25,000 cash in the business.

7 Purchased $5,800 of merchandise from Kansas Corp. with terms of 1/10, n/30, FOB shipping point, invoice dated January 7.

9 Received $2,668 cash from Gomez Co. as full payment on its account.

Check Jan. 11, Dr. Unearned Computer Services Revenue $1,500

11 Completed a five-day project for Alex's Engineering Co. and billed it $5,500, which is the total price of $7,000 less the advance payment of $1,500.

13 Sold merchandise with a retail value of $5,200 and a cost of $3,560 to Chang Corp., invoice dated January 13.

15 Paid $600 cash for freight charges on the merchandise purchased on January 7.

16 Received $4,000 cash from Delta Co. for computer services provided.

17 Paid Kansas Corp. for the invoice dated January 7, net of the discount.

Check Jan. 20, No entry to Cost of Goods Sold

20 Chang Corp. returned $500 of defective merchandise from its invoice dated January 13. The returned merchandise, which had a $320 cost, is discarded. (The policy of Success Systems is to leave the cost of defective products in cost of goods sold.)

22 Received the balance due from Chang Corp., net of both the discount and the credit for the returned merchandise.

24 Returned defective merchandise to Kansas Corp. and accepted a credit against future purchases. The defective merchandise invoice cost, net of the discount, was $496.

26 Purchased $9,000 of merchandise from Kansas Corp. with terms of 1/10, n/30, FOB destination, invoice dated January 26.

26 Sold merchandise with a $4,640 cost for $5,800 on credit to KC, Inc., invoice dated January 26.

29 Received a $496 credit memorandum from Kansas Corp. concerning the merchandise returned on January 24.

31 Paid cash to Sherry Adams for 10 days' work at $125 per day.

Feb. 1 Paid $2,475 cash to Summit Mall for another three months' rent in advance.

3 Paid Kansas Corp. for the balance due, net of the cash discount, less the $496 amount in the credit memorandum.

5 Paid $600 cash to the local newspaper for an advertising insert in today's paper.

11 Received the balance due from Alex's Engineering Co. for fees billed on January 11.

15 Kay Breeze withdrew $4,800 cash for personal use.

23 Sold merchandise with a $2,660 cost for $3,220 on credit to Delta Co., invoice dated February 23.
26 Paid cash to Sherry Adams for eight days' work at $125 per day.
27 Reimbursed Kay Breeze for business automobile mileage (600 miles at $0.32 per mile).
Mar. 8 Purchased $2,730 of computer supplies from Cain Office Products on credit, invoice dated March 8.
9 Received the balance due from Delta Co. for merchandise sold on February 23.
11 Paid $960 cash for minor repairs to the company's computer.
16 Received $5,260 cash from Dream, Inc., for computing services provided.
19 Paid the full amount due to Cain Office Products, including amounts created on December 15 and March 8.
24 Billed Easy Leasing for $8,900 of computing services provided.
25 Sold merchandise with a $2,002 cost for $2,800 on credit to Wildcat Services, invoice dated March 25.
30 Sold merchandise with a $1,100 cost for $2,220 on credit to Clark Company, invoice dated March 30.
31 Reimbursed Kay Breeze for business automobile mileage (400 miles at $0.32 per mile).

The following additional facts are available for preparing adjustments on March 31 prior to financial statement preparation:

a. The March 31 amount of computer supplies still available totals $2,005.
b. Three more months have expired since the company purchased its annual insurance policy at a $2,220 cost for 12 months of coverage.
c. Sherry Adams has not been paid for seven days of work at the rate of $125 per day.
d. Three months have passed since any prepaid rent has been transferred to expense. The monthly rent expense is $825.
e. Depreciation on the computer equipment for January 1 through March 31 is $1,250.
f. Depreciation on the office equipment for January 1 through March 31 is $400.
g. The March 31 amount of merchandise inventory still available totals $704.

Required

1. Prepare journal entries to record each of the January through March transactions.
2. Post the journal entries in part 1 to the accounts in the company's general ledger. (*Note:* Begin with the ledger's post-closing adjusted balances as of December 31, 2004.)
3. Prepare a partial work sheet consisting of the first six columns (similar to the one shown in Exhibit 5B.1) that includes the unadjusted trial balance, the March 31 adjustments (*a*) through (*g*), and the adjusted trial balance. Do not prepare closing entries and do not journalize the adjustments or post them to the ledger.
4. Prepare an income statement (from the adjusted trial balance in part 3) for the three months ended March 31, 2005. Use a single-step format. List all expenses without differentiating between selling expenses and general and administrative expenses.
5. Prepare a statement of owner's equity (from the adjusted trial balance in part 3) for the three months ended March 31, 2005.
6. Prepare a classified balance sheet (from the adjusted trial balance) as of March 31, 2005.

Check (2) Ending balances: Cash, $77,845; Sales, $19,240;
(3) Unadj. totals, $161,198; Adj. totals, $163,723;
(4) Net income, $18,686;
(5) K. Breeze, Capital (3/31/05), $129,034;
(6) Total assets, $129,909

BEYOND THE NUMBERS

REPORTING IN ACTION
C4 A1

BTN 5-1 Refer to **Krispy Kreme**'s financial statements in Appendix A to answer the following.

Required

1. Assume that the amounts reported for inventories and cost of sales reflect items purchased in a form ready for resale. Compute the net cost of goods purchased for the fiscal year ended February 2, 2003.
2. Compute the current ratio and acid-test ratio as of February 2, 2003, and February 3, 2002. Interpret and comment on the ratio results.

Roll On

3. Access Krispy Kreme's financial statements (form 10-K) for fiscal years ending after February 2, 2003, from its Website (**KrispyKreme.com**) or the SEC's EDGAR database (**www.SEC.gov**). Recompute and interpret the current ratio and acid-test ratio for these current fiscal years.

COMPARATIVE ANALYSIS

A2

BTN 5-2 Key comparative figures ($ thousands) for both **Krispy Kreme** and **Tastykake** follow:

	Krispy Kreme		Tastykake	
Key Figures	**Current Year**	**Prior Year**	**Current Year**	**Prior Year**
Revenues (net sales)	$491,549	$394,354	$162,263	$166,245
Cost of sales	381,489	316,946	111,187	103,297

Required

1. Compute the dollar amount of gross margin and the gross margin ratio for the two years shown for both companies.
2. Which company earns more in gross margin for each dollar of net sales?
3. Did the gross margin ratio improve or decline for these companies?

ETHICS CHALLENGE

C1 P2

BTN 5-3 Amy Martinez is a student who plans to attend approximately four professional events a year at her college. Each event necessitates a financial outlay of $100–$200 for a new suit and accessories. After incurring a major hit to her savings for the first event, Amy developed a different approach. She buys the suit on credit the week before the event, wears it to the event, and returns it the next week to the store for a full refund on her charge card.

Required

1. Comment on the ethics exhibited by Amy and possible consequences of her actions.
2. How does the merchandising company account for the suits that Amy returns?

COMMUNICATING IN PRACTICE

C3 C4 P3

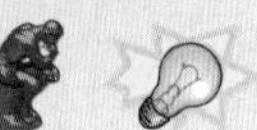

BTN 5-4 You are the financial officer for Music Plus, a retailer that sells goods for home entertainment needs. The business owner, Vic Velakturi, recently reviewed the annual financial statements you prepared and sent you an e-mail stating that he thinks you overstated net income. He explains that although he has invested a great deal in security, he is sure shoplifting and other forms of inventory shrinkage have occurred, but he does not see any deduction for shrinkage on the income statement. The store uses a perpetual inventory system.

Required

Prepare a brief memorandum that responds to the owner's concerns.

TAKING IT TO THE NET

A2 C1

mhhe.com/larson

BTN 5-5 Access the SEC's EDGAR database (www.SEC.gov) and obtain the April 22, 2003, filing of its fiscal 2003 10-K report (for the year ended February 1, 2003) for **J. Crew Group, Inc.**

Required

Prepare a table that reports the gross margin ratios for J. Crew using the revenues and cost of goods sold data from J. Crew's income statement for each of its most recent four years. Analyze and comment on the trend in its gross margin ratio.

TEAMWORK IN ACTION

C1 C4

BTN 5-6 Best Brands' general ledger and supplementary records at the end of its current period reveal the following:

Sales	$430,000	Merchandise inventory (beginning of period)	$ 49,000
Sales returns	18,000	Invoice cost of merchandise purchases	180,000
Sales discounts	6,600	Purchase discounts received	4,500
Cost of transportation-in	11,000	Purchase returns and allowances	5,500
Operating expenses	20,000	Merchandise inventory (end of period)	42,000

Required

1. *Each* member of the team is to assume responsibility for computing *one* of the following items. You are not to duplicate your teammates' work. Get any necessary amounts to compute your item from the appropriate teammate. Each member is to explain his or her computation to the team in preparation for reporting to the class.
   a. Net sales
   b. Total cost of merchandise purchases
   c. Cost of goods sold
   d. Gross profit
   e. Net income

Point: In teams of four, assign the same student *a* and *e*. Rotate teams for reporting on a different computation and the analysis in step 3.

2. Check your net income with the instructor. If correct, proceed to step 3.
3. Assume that a physical inventory count finds that actual ending inventory is $38,000. Discuss how this affects previously computed amounts in step 1.

BUSINESS WEEK ACTIVITY

C1 C4

BTN 5-7 Read the article, "The End of Fuzzy Math?" in the December 11, 2000, issue of *Business Week*. The book's Website provides free access to the article.

Required

1. How does the article define *fulfillment costs?*
2. Where does **Amazon.com** account for fulfillment costs on its income statement?
3. Where do similar companies, such as catalog companies and direct marketers, account for fulfillment costs on their income statements?
4. Does the FASB specify how to account for fulfillment costs? Explain.
5. Why is the issue of accounting for fulfillment costs important to investors?

ENTREPRENEURIAL DECISION

C1 C4 P4

BTN 5-8 Dwayne Lewis and Michael Cherry have earned well beyond the $1,000 they used to launch **Damani Dada** (see chapter's opening feature). Good entrepreneurs continually rethink and refine business strategies. Assume that Damani Dada's most recent income statement follows:

DAMANI DADA Income Statement ($ thousands) For Year Ended April 30, 2005	
Net sales	$50,000
Cost of sales	35,000
Expenses	4,000
Net income	$11,000

To increase income, Lewis and Cherry are proposing to offer sales discounts of 3/10, n/30, and to ship merchandise FOB shipping point. Assume that Damani Dada presently offers no discounts and ships merchandise FOB destination. The sales discounts are predicted to increase net sales by 14%, and the ratio of cost of sales divided by net sales is expected to remain unchanged. Since delivery expenses are zero under this proposal, the expenses are predicted to increase by only 10%.

Required

1. Prepare a forecasted income statement for the year ended April 30, 2006, based on this proposal.
2. Do you recommend that it implement the proposal given your analysis in part 1? Explain.
3. Identify any concerns you might express to Lewis and Cherry regarding their proposal.

HITTING THE ROAD

C1

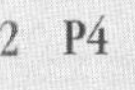

Point: This activity complements the Ethics Challenge assignment.

BTN 5-9 Arrange an interview (in person or by phone) with the manager of a retail shop in a mall or in the downtown area of your community. Explain to the manager that you are a student studying merchandising activities and the accounting for sales returns and sales allowances. Ask the manager what the store policy is regarding returns. Also find out if the sales allowances are ever negotiated with customers. Inquire whether management perceives that customers are abusing return policies and what actions management takes to counter potential abuses. Be prepared to discuss your findings in class.

GLOBAL DECISION

A2 P4

BTN 5-10 **Grupo Bimbo (GrupoBimbo.com), Krispy Kreme,** and **Tastykake** are all competitors in the global marketplace. Key comparative figures for each company follow:

	Net Sales	Cost of Sales
Grupo Bimbo*	41,373,269	19,155,865
Krispy Kreme**	$ 491,549	$ 381,489
Tastykake**	$ 162,263	$ 111,187

*Thousands of pesos (Grupo Bimbo).
**Thousands of dollars (Krispy Kreme and Tastykake).

Required

1. Rank the three companies (highest to lowest) based on the gross margin ratio.
2. Which of the companies uses a multiple-step income statement format? (Access their annual reports.)
3. Which company's income statement would likely be most easily interpreted by potential investors? Provide a brief justification for your choice.

"I am the COF—Chairman of Fun!"—Mike Becker

Inventories and Cost of Sales

A Look Back

Chapter 5 focused on merchandising activities and how they are reported and analyzed. We also analyzed and recorded merchandise purchases and sales and explained accounting adjustments and the closing process for merchandising companies.

A Look at This Chapter

This chapter emphasizes accounting for inventory. We describe the methods available for assigning costs to inventory and explain the items and costs making up merchandise inventory. We also analyze the effects of inventory on both financial and tax reporting, and we discuss other methods of estimating and measuring inventory.

A Look Ahead

Chapter 7 emphasizes accounting information systems. We describe fundamental system principles, the system's components, use of special journals and subsidiary ledgers, and technology-based systems. We also discuss segment data.

CAP

Conceptual

C1 Identify the items making up merchandise inventory. *(p. 222)*

C2 Identify the costs of merchandise inventory. *(p. 223)*

Analytical

A1 Analyze the effects of inventory methods for both financial and tax reporting. *(p. 229)*

A2 Analyze the effects of inventory errors on current and future financial statements. *(p. 232)*

A3 Assess inventory management using both inventory turnover and days' sales in inventory. *(p. 233)*

Procedural

P1 Compute inventory in a perpetual system using the methods of specific identification, FIFO, LIFO, and weighted average. *(p. 224)*

P2 Compute the lower of cost or market amount of inventory. *(p. 231)*

Decision Feature

Wacky Inventor of Wobblers

SNOHOMISH, WA—Mike Becker long collected nostalgia-based toys from his childhood. Becker imagined that "there's got to be people like me out there [who love such toys], where I could have a cool little business based on that love."

Drawing on his life savings of $35,000, Becker started **FunKo (Funko.com)** making Wacky Wobblers (bobbleheads) out of his garage. His Wobblers are based on characters and personalities from his youth. "It's about invoking a feeling," says Becker. "We want people to say, 'Oh, I remember that!'" Becker has now sold more than 600,000 of 50 different Wobblers (selling for about $15 each) in the past 5 years. He projects sales this year of more than $2 million.

Still, the road to the top was shaky. Becker struggled with purchases and sales and had to confront discounts, returns, and allowances. One of his biggest obstacles, and continuing challenges, is maintaining the right inventories and controlling costs of sales. "It was kind of by trial and error," says Becker. "I didn't understand what the heck I was doing. I didn't have any distribution networks, sales reps, employees, or even a place of business." Success is more than good products, says Becker; it depends on assigning and monitoring costs of inventory and applying sound inventory management procedures.

With business booming, he continues to keep watch over inventory turnover and days' sales in inventory. This chapter focuses on these issues, including measuring, monitoring and managing such inventories. Yet Becker keeps all in perspective. "I guess we totally underestimated the possibility that there were so many other weirdos like us out there."

[Sources: *FunKo Website,* January 2004; *Entrepreneur,* November 2002; *Puget Sound Business Journal,* June 8, 2001; *Tri-City Herald,* January 2002; *Seattle Times,* April 13, 2002.]

Merchandisers' activities include the purchasing and reselling of merchandise. We explained accounting for merchandisers in Chapter 5, including that for purchases and sales. In this chapter, we extend the study and analysis of inventory by explaining the methods used to assign costs to merchandise inventory *and* to cost of goods sold. Retailers, wholesalers, and other merchandising companies that purchase products for resale use the principles and methods described. Understanding inventory accounting helps in the analysis and interpretation of financial statements, and in helping people run their own businesses.

Inventories and Cost of Sales

Inventory Basics
- Determining inventory items
- Determining inventory costs
- Internal control of inventory and taking a physical count

Inventory Costing Under a Perpetual System
- Inventory cost flow assumptions
- Specific identification
- First-in, first-out
- Last-in, first-out
- Weighted average
- Financial statement effects
- Consistent use of methods

Inventory Valuation and Errors
- Inventory valuation at lower of cost or market
- Financial statement effects of inventory errors

Inventory Basics

This section identifies the items and costs making up merchandise inventory. It also describes the importance of internal controls in taking a physical count of inventory.

Determining Inventory Items

C1 Identify the items making up merchandise inventory.

Merchandise inventory includes all goods that a company owns and holds for sale. This rule holds regardless of where the goods are located when inventory is counted. Certain inventory items require special attention, including goods in transit, goods on consignment, and goods that are damaged or obsolete.

Goods in Transit Does a purchaser's inventory include goods in transit from a supplier? The answer is that if ownership has passed to the purchaser, the goods are included in the purchaser's inventory. We determine this by reviewing the shipping terms: *FOB destination* or *FOB shipping point.* If the purchaser is responsible for paying freight, ownership passes when goods are loaded on the transport vehicle. If the seller is responsible for paying freight, ownership passes when goods arrive at their destination.

Goods on Consignment Goods on consignment are goods shipped by the owner, called the **consignor,** to another party, the **consignee.** A consignee sells goods for the owner. The consignor continues to own the consigned goods and reports them in its inventory. **Upper Deck**, for instance, pays sports celebrities such as Tiger Woods to sign memorabilia, which are offered to shopping networks on consignment. Upper Deck, the consignor, must report these items in its inventory until sold.

Goods Damaged or Obsolete Damaged and obsolete (and deteriorated) goods are not counted in inventory if they cannot be sold. If these goods can be sold at a reduced price, they are included in inventory at a conservative estimate of their **net realizable value.** Net realizable value is sales price minus the cost of making the sale. The period when damage or obsolescence (or deterioration) occurs is the period when the loss in value is reported.

Decision Insight

A wireless portable computer with a two-way radio allows clerks to quickly record inventory by scanning bar codes and to instantly send and receive data. It gives managers access to up-to-date information on inventory and its location.

Determining Inventory Costs

C2 Identify the costs of merchandise inventory.

Merchandise inventory includes costs of expenditures necessary, directly or indirectly, to bring an item to a salable condition and location. This means that the cost of an inventory item includes its invoice cost minus any discount, and plus any added or incidental costs necessary to put it in a place and condition for sale. Added or incidental costs can include import duties, freight, storage, insurance, and costs incurred in an aging process (for example, aging wine or cheese).

Accounting principles prescribe that incidental costs be assigned to inventory. Also, the *matching principle* states that inventory costs should be recorded against revenue in the period when inventory is sold. However, some companies use the *materiality principle* (*cost-to-benefit constraint*) to avoid assigning incidental costs of acquiring merchandise to inventory. These companies argue either that incidental costs are immaterial or that the effort in assigning these costs to inventory outweighs the benefit.

Decision Insight

Some retailers are adding bar code readers on shopping carts for customers to swipe products over the reader, charging it to a credit card. There is no need to stand in a checkout line. Customers simply pass through a gate to verify that everything in the cart is scanned.

Internal Controls and Taking a Physical Count

The Inventory account under a perpetual system is updated for each purchase and sale, but events can cause the account balance to be different from the actual inventory available. Such events include theft, loss, damage, and errors. Thus, nearly all companies take a *physical count of inventory* at least once each year—informally called *taking an inventory.* This often occurs at the end of a fiscal year or when inventory amounts are low. This physical count is used to adjust the Inventory account balance to the actual inventory available.

A business must apply internal controls when taking a physical count of inventory that would usually include the following:

- *Prenumbered inventory tickets* are prepared and distributed to *counters*—each ticket must be accounted for.
- Counters of inventory are assigned that do not include those responsible for the inventory.
- Counters confirm the validity of inventory, including its existence, amounts, quality, and so forth.
- A second count should occur by a different counter.
- A manager confirms that all inventories are ticketed once, and only once.

Point: The Inventory account is a controlling account for the inventory subsidiary ledger. This *subsidiary ledger* contains a separate record (units and costs) for each separate product, and it can be in electronic or paper form. Subsidiary records assist managers in planning and monitoring inventory.

Quick Check

1. What accounting principle most guides the allocation of cost of goods available for sale between ending inventory and cost of goods sold?
2. If **Skechers** sells goods to **Target** with terms FOB shipping point, which company reports these goods in its inventory while they are in transit?
3. An art gallery purchases a painting for $11,400 on terms FOB shipping point. Additional costs in obtaining and offering the artwork for sale include $130 for transportation-in, $150 for import duties, $100 for insurance during shipment, $180 for advertising, $400 for framing, and $800 for office salaries. For computing inventory, what cost is assigned to the painting?

Answers—p. 245

Inventory Costing Under a Perpetual System

Accounting for inventory affects both the balance sheet and the income statement. A major goal in accounting for inventory is to properly match costs with sales. We use the *matching principle* to decide how much of the cost of the goods available for sale is deducted from sales and how much is carried forward as inventory and matched against future sales.

Management decisions in accounting for inventory involve the following

- Costing method (specific identification, FIFO, LIFO, or weighted average).
- Inventory system (perpetual or periodic).
- Items included in inventory and their costs.
- Use of market values or other estimates.

Decisions on these points affect the reported amounts for inventory, cost of goods sold, gross profit, income, current assets, and other accounts.

One of the most important issues in accounting for inventory is determining the per unit costs assigned to inventory items. When all units are purchased at the same unit cost, this process is simple. When identical items are purchased at different costs, however, a question arises as to which amounts to record in cost of goods sold and which amounts remain in inventory.

Four methods are commonly used to assign costs to inventory and to cost of goods sold: (1) specific identification; (2) first-in, first-out; (3) last-in, first-out; and (4) weighted average. Exhibit 6.1 shows the frequency in the use of these methods.

Exhibit 6.1

Frequency in Use of Inventory Methods

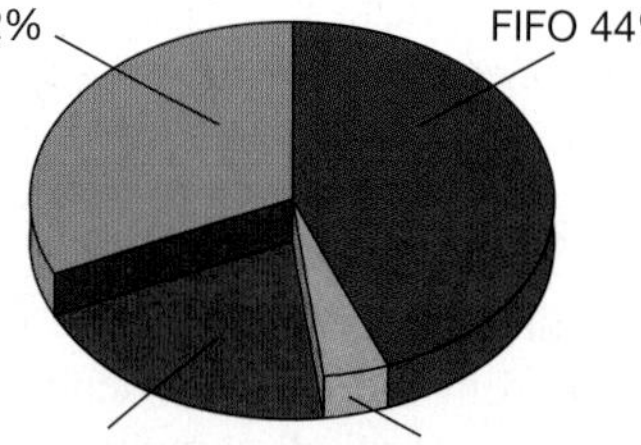

*Includes specific identification.

Each method assumes a particular pattern for how costs flow through inventory. Each of these four methods is acceptable whether or not the actual physical flow of goods follows the cost flow assumption. Physical flow of goods depends on the type of product and the way it is stored. (Perishable goods such as fresh fruit demand that a business attempt to sell them in a first-in, first-out physical flow. Other products such as crude oil and minerals such as coal, gold, decorative stone can be sold in a last-in, first-out physical flow.) **Physical flow and cost flow need not be the same.**

Inventory Cost Flow Assumptions

P1 Compute inventory in a perpetual system using the methods of specific identification, FIFO, LIFO, and weighted average.

This section introduces inventory cost flow assumptions. Assume that three identical units are purchased at the following three dates and costs: May 1 at $45, May 3 at $65, and May 6 at $70. One unit is then sold on May 7 for $100. Exhibit 6.2 gives a visual layout of the flow of costs to either the gross profit section of the income statement or the inventory reported on the balance sheet for FIFO, LIFO, and weighted average.

(1) *FIFO assumes costs flow in the order incurred.* The unit purchased on May 1 for $45 is the earliest cost incurred—it is sent to cost of goods sold on the income statement. The remaining two units ($65 and $70) are reported in inventory on the balance sheet.

(2) *LIFO assumes costs flow in the reverse order incurred.* The unit purchased on May 6 for $70 is the most recent cost incurred—it is sent to cost of goods sold on the income statement. The remaining two units ($45 and $65) are reported in inventory on the balance sheet.

(3) *Weighted average assumes costs flow at an average of the costs available.* The units available at the May 7 sale average $60 in cost, computed as ($45 + $65 + $70)/3. One unit's $60 average cost is sent to cost of goods sold on the income statement. The remaining two units' average costs are reported in inventory at $120 on the balance sheet.

Cost flow assumptions can markedly impact gross profit and inventory. Exhibit 6.2 shows that gross profit as a percent of net sales ranges from 30% to 55% due to nothing else but the cost flow assumption.

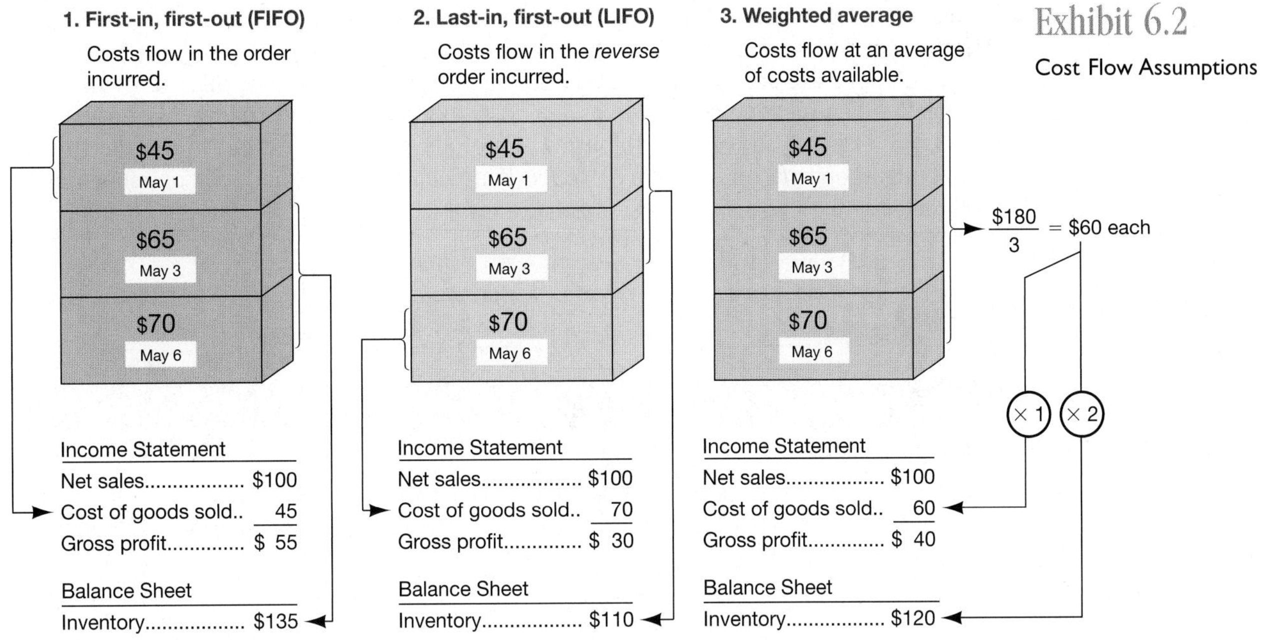

Exhibit 6.2

Cost Flow Assumptions

The following sections on inventory costing methods use the perpetual system. Appendix 6A uses the periodic system. An instructor can choose to cover either one or both inventory systems.

Inventory Costing Illustration

This section provides a comprehensive illustration of inventory costing methods. We use information from Trekking, a sporting goods store. Among its many products, Trekking carries one type of mountain bike whose sales are directed at resorts that provide inexpensive mountain bikes for complimentary guest use. Its customers usually purchase in amounts of 10 or more bikes. We use Trekking's data from August 2005. Its mountain bike (unit) inventory at the beginning of August and its purchases and sales during August are shown in Exhibit 6.3. It ends August with 12 bikes remaining in inventory.

Point: Inventories are a large portion of current assets for most wholesalers, retailers, and manufacturers. Accounting for inventories is key to determining cost of goods sold and gross profit.

Exhibit 6.3

Purchases and Sales of Goods

Date	Activity	Units Acquired at Cost	Units Sold at Retail	Unit Inventory
Aug. 1	Beginning inventory	10 units @ $ 91 = $ 910		10 units
Aug. 3	Purchases	15 units @ $106 = $ 1,590		25 units
Aug. 14	Sales		20 units @ $130	5 units
Aug. 17	Purchases	20 units @ $115 = $ 2,300		25 units
Aug. 28	Purchases	10 units @ $119 = $ 1,190		35 units
Aug. 31	Sales		23 units @ $150	12 units
	Totals	55 units $5,990	43 units	

Trekking uses the perpetual inventory system, which means that its merchandise inventory account is continually updated to reflect purchases and sales. **(Appendix 6A describes the assignment of costs to inventory using a periodic system.)** Regardless of what inventory method or system is used, cost of goods available for sale must be allocated between cost of goods sold and ending inventory.

Point: The perpetual inventory system is now the most dominant system across U.S. businesses.

Point: Cost of goods sold plus ending inventory equals cost of goods available for sale.

Specific Identification

When each item in inventory can be identified with a specific purchase and invoice, we can use **specific identification** (also called *specific invoice inventory pricing*) to assign costs.

Point: Three key variables determine the dollar value of ending inventory: (1) inventory quantity, (2) costs of inventory, and (3) cost flow assumption.

We also need sales records that identify exactly which items were sold and when. Trekking's internal documents reveal that 7 of the 12 unsold units in ending inventory were from the August 28 purchase and 5 were from the August 17 purchase. We use this information and the specific identification method to assign costs to the 12 units in ending inventory and to the 43 units sold as shown in Exhibit 6.4. Carefully study this exhibit to see the flow of costs both in and out of inventory. Notice that each unit, whether sold or remaining in inventory, has its own specific cost attached to it.

Exhibit 6.4

Specific Identification Computations

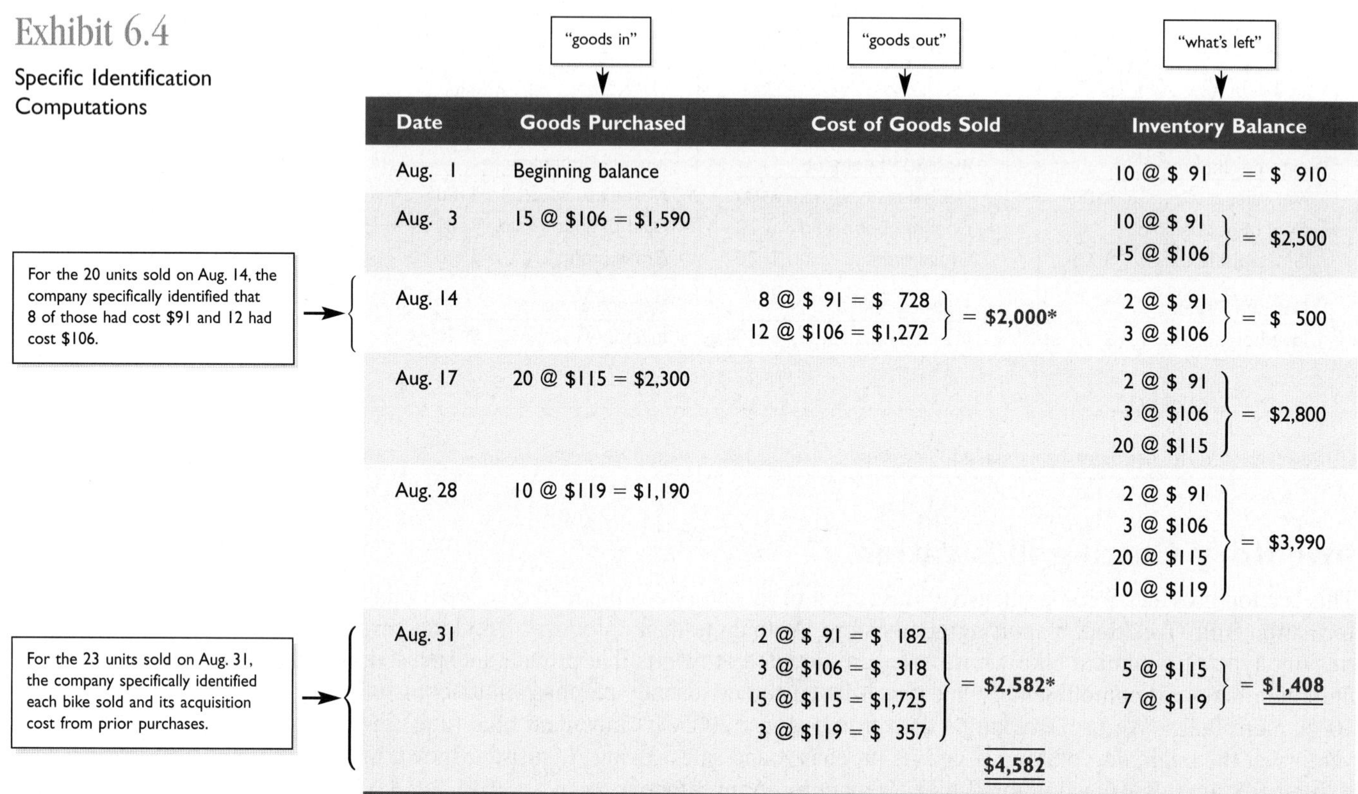

Date	Goods Purchased	Cost of Goods Sold	Inventory Balance
Aug. 1	Beginning balance		10 @ $ 91 = $ 910
Aug. 3	15 @ $106 = $1,590		10 @ $ 91 15 @ $106 } = $2,500
Aug. 14		8 @ $ 91 = $ 728 12 @ $106 = $1,272 } = $2,000*	2 @ $ 91 3 @ $106 } = $ 500
Aug. 17	20 @ $115 = $2,300		2 @ $ 91 3 @ $106 20 @ $115 } = $2,800
Aug. 28	10 @ $119 = $1,190		2 @ $ 91 3 @ $106 20 @ $115 10 @ $119 } = $3,990
Aug. 31		2 @ $ 91 = $ 182 3 @ $106 = $ 318 15 @ $115 = $1,725 3 @ $119 = $ 357 } = $2,582* $4,582	5 @ $115 7 @ $119 } = $1,408

* Identification of items sold (and their costs) is obtained from internal documents that track each unit from its purchase to its sale.

Point: Specific identification is usually only practical for companies with expensive, custom-made inventory.

When using specific identification, Trekking's cost of goods sold reported on the income statement totals $4,582, the sum of $2,000 and $2,582 from the third column of Exhibit 6.4. Trekking's ending inventory reported on the balance sheet is $1,408, which is the final inventory balance from the fourth column of Exhibit 6.4.

The purchases and sales entries for Exhibit 6.4 follow (the boldface numbers are those determined by the cost flow assumption):

Purchases

Date	Account	Debit	Credit
Aug. 3	Merchandise Inventory	1,590	
	Accounts Payable		1,590
17	Merchandise Inventory	2,300	
	Accounts Payable		2,300
28	Merchandise Inventory	1,190	
	Accounts Payable		1,190

Sales

Date	Account	Debit	Credit
Aug. 14	Accounts Receivable	2,600	
	Sales		2,600
14	Cost of Goods Sold	**2,000**	
	Merchandise Inventory		**2,000**
31	Accounts Receivable	3,450	
	Sales		3,450
31	Cost of Goods Sold	**2,582**	
	Merchandise Inventory		**2,582**

First-In, First-Out

The **first-in, first-out (FIFO)** method of assigning costs to both inventory and cost of goods sold assumes that inventory items are sold in the order acquired. When sales occur, the costs of the earliest units acquired are charged to cost of goods sold. This leaves the costs from the most recent purchases in ending inventory. Use of FIFO for computing the cost of inventory and cost of goods sold is shown in Exhibit 6.5.

Point: The "Goods Purchased" column is identical for all methods. Data are taken from Exhibit 6.3.

Exhibit 6.5

FIFO Computations—Perpetual System

Date	Goods Purchased	Cost of Goods Sold		Inventory Balance	
Aug. 1	Beginning balance			10 @ $ 91	= $ 910
Aug. 3	15 @ $106 = $1,590			10 @ $ 91 15 @ $106	= $2,500
Aug. 14		10 @ $ 91 = $ 910 10 @ $106 = $1,060	= **$1,970**	5 @ $106	= $ 530
Aug. 17	20 @ $115 = $2,300			5 @ $106 20 @ $115	= $2,830
Aug. 28	10 @ $119 = $1,190			5 @ $106 20 @ $115 10 @ $119	= $4,020
Aug. 31		5 @ $106 = $ 530 18 @ $115 = $2,070	= **$2,600**	2 @ $115 10 @ $119	= **$1,420**
			$4,570		

For the 20 units sold on Aug. 14, the first 10 sold are assigned the earliest cost of $91 (from beg. bal.). The next 10 sold are assigned the next earliest cost of $106.

For the 23 units sold on Aug. 31, the first 5 sold are assigned the earliest available cost of $106 (from Aug. 3 purchase). The next 18 sold are assigned the next earliest cost of $115 (from Aug. 17 purchase).

Trekking's FIFO cost of goods sold reported on its income statement (reflecting the 43 units sold) is **$4,570** ($1,970 + $2,600), and its ending inventory reported on the balance sheet (reflecting the 12 units unsold) is **$1,420**.

The purchases and sales entries for Exhibit 6.5 follow (the boldface numbers are those affected by the cost flow assumption):

Point: Under FIFO, a unit sold is assigned the earliest (oldest) cost from inventory. This leaves the most recent costs in ending inventory.

Purchases

Date	Account	Debit	Credit
Aug. 3	Merchandise Inventory.	1,590	
	Accounts Payable		1,590
17	Merchandise Inventory.	2,300	
	Accounts Payable		2,300
28	Merchandise Inventory.	1,190	
	Accounts Payable		1,190

Sales

Date	Account	Debit	Credit
Aug. 14	Accounts Receivable	2,600	
	Sales		2,600
14	Cost of Goods Sold.	**1,970**	
	Merchandise Inventory. . .		**1,970**
31	Accounts Receivable	3,450	
	Sales		3,450
31	Cost of Goods Sold.	**2,600**	
	Merchandise Inventory. . .		**2,600**

Last-In, First-Out

The **last-in, first-out (LIFO)** method of assigning costs assumes that the most recent purchases are sold first. These more recent costs are charged to the goods sold, and the costs of the earliest purchases are assigned to inventory. As with other methods, LIFO is acceptable even when the physical flow of goods does not follow a last-in, first-out pattern. One appeal of LIFO is that by assigning costs from the most recent purchases to cost of goods sold, LIFO comes closest to matching current costs of goods sold with revenues (compared to FIFO or weighted average). Exhibit 6.6 shows how LIFO assigns the costs of mountain bikes to the 12 units in ending inventory and to the 43 units sold.

Topic Tackler 6-1

Point: Under LIFO, a unit sold is assigned the most recent (latest) cost from inventory. This leaves the oldest costs in inventory.

Exhibit 6.6

LIFO Computations—Perpetual System

Date	Goods Purchased	Cost of Goods Sold		Inventory Balance	
Aug. 1	Beginning balance			10 @ $ 91	= $ 910
Aug. 3	15 @ $106 = $1,590			10 @ $ 91 15 @ $106	= $ 2,500
Aug. 14		15 @ $106 = $1,590 5 @ $ 91 = $ 455	= $2,045	5 @ $ 91	= $ 455
Aug. 17	20 @ $115 = $2,300			5 @ $ 91 20 @ $115	= $ 2,755
Aug. 28	10 @ $119 = $1,190			5 @ $ 91 20 @ $115 10 @ $119	= $ 3,945
Aug. 31		10 @ $119 = $1,190 13 @ $115 = $1,495	= $2,685	5 @ $ 91 7 @ $115	= $1,260
			$4,730		

For the 20 units sold on Aug. 14, the first 15 sold are assigned the most recent cost of $106. The next 5 sold are assigned the next most recent cost of $91.

For the 23 units sold on Aug. 31, the first 10 sold are assigned the most recent cost of $119. The next 13 sold are assigned the next most recent cost of $115.

Trekking's LIFO cost of goods sold reported on the income statement is **$4,730** ($2,045 + $2,685), and its ending inventory reported on the balance sheet is **$1,260**.

The purchases and sales entries for Exhibit 6.6 follow (the boldface numbers are those affected by the cost flow assumption):

Purchases

Aug. 3	Merchandise Inventory	1,590	
	Accounts Payable		1,590
17	Merchandise Inventory	2,300	
	Accounts Payable		2,300
28	Merchandise Inventory	1,190	
	Accounts Payable		1,190

Sales

Aug. 14	Accounts Receivable	2,600	
	Sales		2,600
14	Cost of Goods Sold	**2,045**	
	Merchandise Inventory		**2,045**
31	Accounts Receivable	3,450	
	Sales		3,450
31	Cost of Goods Sold	**2,685**	
	Merchandise Inventory		**2,685**

Weighted Average

The **weighted average** (also called **average cost**) method of assigning cost requires that we compute the weighted average cost per unit of inventory at the time of each sale. Weighted average cost per unit at the time of each sale equals the cost of goods available for sale divided by the units available. The results using weighted average for Trekking are shown in Exhibit 6.7.

Point: Under weighted average, a unit sold is assigned the average cost of all items currently available for sale at the date of each sale.

Trekking's cost of goods sold reported on the income statement (reflecting the 43 units sold) is **$4,622** ($2,000 + $2,622), and its ending inventory reported on the balance sheet (reflecting the 12 units unsold) is **$1,368**.

The purchases and sales entries for Exhibit 6.7 follow (the boldface numbers are those affected by the cost flow assumption):

Purchases

Aug. 3	Merchandise Inventory	1,590	
	Accounts Payable		1,590
17	Merchandise Inventory	2,300	
	Accounts Payable		2,300
28	Merchandise Inventory	1,190	
	Accounts Payable		1,190

Sales

Aug. 14	Accounts Receivable	2,600	
	Sales		2,600
14	Cost of Goods Sold	**2,000**	
	Merchandise Inventory		**2,000**
31	Accounts Receivable	3,450	
	Sales		3,450
31	Cost of Goods Sold	**2,622**	
	Merchandise Inventory		**2,622**

Date	Goods Purchased	Cost of Goods Sold	Inventory Balance	
Aug. 1	Beginning balance		10 @ $ 91	= $ 910
Aug. 3	15 @ $106 = $1,590		10 @ $ 91 15 @ $106	= $2,500 (or $100 per unit)[a]
Aug. 14		20 @ $100 = **$2,000**	5 @ $100	= $ 500 (or $100 per unit)[b]
Aug. 17	20 @ $115 = $2,300		5 @ $100 20 @ $115	= $2,800 (or $112 per unit)[c]
Aug. 28	10 @ $119 = $1,190		5 @ $100 20 @ $115 10 @ $119	= $3,990 (or $114 per unit)[d]
Aug. 31		23 @ $114 = **$2,622**	12 @ $114	= **$1,368** (or $114 per unit)[e]
		$4,622		

[a] $100 per unit = ($2,500 inventory balance ÷ 25 units in inventory).

[b] $100 per unit = ($500 inventory balance ÷ 5 units in inventory).

[c] $112 per unit = ($2,800 inventory balance ÷ 25 units in inventory).

[d] $114 per unit = ($3,990 inventory balance ÷ 35 units in inventory).

[e] $114 per unit = ($1,368 inventory balance ÷ 12 units in inventory).

Exhibit 6.7

Weighted Average Computations—Perpetual System

For the 20 units sold on Aug. 14, the cost assigned is the $100 *average cost* per unit from the inventory balance column at the time of sale.

For the 23 units sold on Aug. 31, the cost assigned is the $114 *average cost* per unit from the inventory balance column at the time of sale.

Advances in technology have greatly reduced the cost of a perpetual inventory system. Many companies are now asking whether they can afford *not* to have a perpetual inventory system because timely access to inventory information is a competitive advantage and it can help reduce the level of inventory, which reduces costs.

Decision Insight

Inventory War The Pentagon applies accounting tools to shrink inventories and speed deliveries. Use of bar codes, laser cards, radio tags, and perpetual accounting systems speeds delivery from factory to foxhole.

Financial Statement Effects of Costing Methods

A1 Analyze the effects of inventory methods for both financial and tax reporting.

When purchase prices do not change, each inventory costing method assigns the same cost amounts to inventory and to cost of goods sold. When purchase prices are different, however, the methods nearly always assign different cost amounts. We show these differences in Exhibit 6.8 using Trekking's data.

Exhibit 6.8

Financial Statement Effects of Inventory Costing Methods

TREKKING COMPANY
For Month Ended August 31

	Specific Identification	FIFO	LIFO	Weighted Average
Income Statement				
Sales	$6,050	$6,050	$6,050	$6,050
Cost of goods sold	4,582	4,570	4,730	4,622
Gross profit	1,468	1,480	1,320	1,428
Expenses	450	450	450	450
Income before taxes	1,018	1,030	870	978
Income tax expense (30%)	305	309	261	293
Net income	**$ 713**	**$ 721**	**$ 609**	**$ 685**
Balance Sheet				
Inventory	**$1,408**	**$1,420**	**$1,260**	**$1,368**

When purchase costs *regularly rise,* as in Trekking's case, note the following:

Point: FIFO is preferred when costs are rising and managers have incentives to report higher income for reasons such as bonus plans, job security, and reputation.

- FIFO assigns the lowest amount to cost of goods sold—yielding the highest gross profit and net income.
- LIFO assigns the highest amount to cost of goods sold—yielding the lowest gross profit and net income, which also yields a temporary tax advantage by postponing payment of some income tax.
- Weighted average yields results between FIFO and LIFO.
- Specific identification always yields results that depend on which units are sold.

Point: LIFO inventory is often less than the inventory's replacement cost because LIFO inventory is valued using the oldest inventory purchase costs.

When costs *regularly decline,* the reverse occurs for FIFO and LIFO.

All four inventory costing methods are acceptable. However, a company must disclose the inventory method it uses in its financial statements or notes. Each method offers certain advantages as follows:

- FIFO assigns an amount to inventory on the balance sheet that approximates its current cost; it also mimics the actual flow of goods for most businesses.
- LIFO assigns an amount to cost of goods sold on the income statement that approximates its current cost; it also better matches current costs with revenues in computing gross profit.
- Weighted average tends to smooth out erratic changes in costs.
- Specific identification exactly matches the costs of items with the revenues they generate.

Decision Maker

Financial Planner One of your clients asks if the inventory account of a company using FIFO needs any "adjustments" for analysis purposes in light of recent inflation. What is your advice? Does your advice depend on changes in the costs of these inventories?

Answer—p. 245

Decision Insight

Giving for Growth A recent survey found 76% of consumers saying they'd switch from their current product to one with a "good cause" if price and quality are equal. Many entrepreneurs combine their business ventures with their social passions for a win-win situation.

Tax Effects of Costing Methods Trekking's segment income statement in Exhibit 6.8 includes income tax expense (at a rate of 30%) because it was formed as a corporation. Since inventory costs affect net income, they have potential tax effects. Trekking gains a temporary tax advantage by using LIFO. Many companies use LIFO for this reason.

Companies can and often do use different costing methods for financial reporting and tax reporting. *The only exception is when LIFO is used for tax reporting; in this case, the IRS requires that it also be used in financial statements.*

Consistency in Using Costing Methods

Global: LIFO is acceptable under international accounting standards.

The **consistency principle** prescribes that a company use the same accounting methods period after period so that financial statements are comparable across periods—the only exception is when a change from one method to another will improve its financial reporting. The *full-disclosure principle* prescribes that the notes to the statements report this type of change, its justification, and its effect on net income.

The consistency principle does *not* require a company to use one method exclusively. For example, it can use different methods to value different categories of inventory.

Decision Ethics

Inventory Manager Your compensation as inventory manager includes a bonus plan based on gross profit. Your superior asks your opinion on changing the inventory costing method from FIFO to LIFO. Since costs are expected to continue to rise, your superior predicts that LIFO would match higher current costs against sales, thereby lowering taxable income (and gross profit). What do you recommend?

Answer—p. 245

Quick Check

4. Describe one advantage for each of the inventory costing methods: specific identification, FIFO, LIFO, and weighted average.
5. When costs are rising, which method reports higher net income—LIFO or FIFO?
6. When costs are rising, what effect does LIFO have on a balance sheet compared to FIFO?
7. A company takes a physical count of inventory at the end of 2005 and finds that ending inventory is understated by $10,000. Would this error cause cost of goods sold to be overstated or understated in 2005? In year 2006? If so, by how much?

Answers—p. 245

Valuing Inventory at LCM and the Effects of Inventory Errors

This section examines the role of market costs in determining inventory on the balance sheet and also the financial statement effects of inventory errors.

Lower of Cost or Market

P2 Compute the lower of cost or market amount of inventory.

We explained how to assign costs to ending inventory and cost of goods sold using one of four costing methods (FIFO, LIFO, weighted average, or specific identification). However, *accounting principles require that inventory be reported at the market value (cost) of replacing inventory when market value is lower than cost.* Merchandise inventory is then said to be reported on the balance sheet at the **lower of cost or market (LCM).**

Computing the Lower of Cost or Market *Market* in the term *LCM* is defined as the current replacement cost of purchasing the same inventory items in the usual manner. A decline in replacement cost reflects a loss of value in inventory. When the recorded cost of inventory is higher than the replacement cost, a loss is recognized. When the recorded cost is lower, no adjustment is made.

LCM is applied in one of three ways: (1) to each individual item separately, (2) to major categories of items, or (3) to the entire inventory. The less similar the items that make up inventory, the more likely companies are to apply LCM to individual items. To illustrate, we apply LCM to the ending inventory of a motorsports retailer in Exhibit 6.9.

Point: Advances in technology encourage the individual-item approach for LCM.

Exhibit 6.9

Lower of Cost or Market Computations

Inventory Items	Units	Per Unit Cost	Per Unit Market	Total Cost	Total Market	LCM Applied to Items	LCM Applied to Categories	LCM Applied to Whole
Cycles								
Roadster	20	$8,000	$7,000	$160,000	$140,000	$ 140,000		
Sprint	10	5,000	6,000	50,000	60,000	50,000		
Category subtotal				210,000	200,000		$ 200,000	
Off-Road								
Trax-4	8	5,000	6,500	40,000	52,000	40,000		
Blazer	5	9,000	7,000	45,000	35,000	35,000		
Category subtotal				85,000	87,000		85,000	
Totals				$295,000	$287,000	$265,000	$285,000	$287,000

When LCM is applied to the *entire* inventory, the market amount is $287,000. Since this market amount is $8,000 lower than the $295,000 recorded cost, the $287,000 amount is reported for inventory on the balance sheet. When LCM is applied to the major *categories* of inventory, the market is $285,000. When LCM is applied to individual *items* of inventory, the market is $265,000. Since market amounts for these cases are less than the $295,000 recorded cost, the market amount is reported for inventory. Any one of these three applications of LCM is acceptable. The retailer **Best Buy** applies LCM and reports that its "merchandise inventories are recorded at the lower of average cost or market."

Global: In Canada, the Netherlands, and the United Kingdom, the *market* in LCM is defined as "net realizable value" (selling price less costs to complete and sell).

Recording the Lower of Cost or Market Inventory must be adjusted downward when market is less than cost. To illustrate, if LCM is applied to the individual items of inventory in Exhibit 6.9, the Merchandise Inventory account must be adjusted from the $295,000 recorded cost down to the $265,000 market amount as follows

Cost of Goods Sold	30,000	
Merchandise Inventory		30,000
To adjust inventory cost to market.		

Accounting rules require that inventory be adjusted to market when market is less than cost, but inventory usually cannot be written up to market when market exceeds cost. If recording inventory down to market is acceptable, why are companies not allowed to record inventory up to market? One view is that a gain from a market increase should not be realized until a sales transaction verifies the gain. However, this problem also applies when market is less than cost. A second and primary reason is the **conservatism principle,** which prescribes the use of the less optimistic amount when more than one estimate of the amount to be received or paid exists and these estimates are about equally likely.

Financial Statement Effects of Inventory Errors

A2 Analyze the effects of inventory errors on current and future financial statements.

Companies must take care in both taking a physical count of inventory and in assigning a cost to it. An inventory error causes misstatements in cost of goods sold, gross profit, net income, current assets, and equity. It also causes misstatements in the next period's statements because ending inventory of one period is the beginning inventory of the next.

Topic Tackler 6-2

Income Statement Effects Exhibit 6.10 shows the effects of inventory errors on key amounts in the current period's income statement. Notice that inventory errors yield opposite effects in cost of goods sold and net income. Inventory errors also carry over to the next period, yielding reverse effects.

Exhibit 6.10

Effects of Inventory Errors on the Current Period's Income Statement

Inventory Error	Cost of Goods Sold	Net Income
Understate ending inventory	Overstated	Understated
Understate beginning inventory	Understated	Overstated
Overstate ending inventory*	Understated	Overstated
Overstate beginning inventory*	Overstated	Understated

* These errors are less likely under a perpetual system because they imply more inventory than is recorded (or less shrinkage than expected). Thus, management will normally follow up and discover and correct these errors before they impact any accounts.

To illustrate, consider an inventory error for a company with $100,000 in sales for each of the years 2004, 2005, and 2006. If this company maintains a steady $20,000 inventory level during this period and makes $60,000 in purchases in each of these years, its cost of goods sold is $60,000 and its gross profit is $40,000 each year. What if this company errs in computing its 2004 ending inventory and reports $16,000 instead of the correct amount of $20,000? The effects of this error are shown in Exhibit 6.11. The $4,000 understatement of the year 2004 ending inventory causes a $4,000 overstatement in year 2004 cost of goods sold and a $4,000 understatement in both gross profit and net income for year 2004. Since year 2004 ending inventory becomes year 2005 beginning inventory, this error causes an understatement in 2005 cost of goods sold and a $4,000 overstatement in both gross profit and net income for year 2005. Notice that an inventory error in period 1 (2004) does not affect the period 3, year 2006. An inventory error is said to be *self-correcting* because it always yields an offsetting error in the next period. This, however, does not make inventory errors less serious. Managers, lenders, owners, and other users make important decisions from analysis of changes in net income and cost of goods sold.

Point: A former internal auditor at Coca-Cola alleges that just before midnight at the 2002 period-end, fully loaded Coke trucks were ordered to drive about 2 feet away from the loading dock so that Coke could record millions of dollars in extra sales.

Income Statements	2004		2005		2006	
Sales		$100,000		$100,000		$100,000
Cost of goods sold						
Beginning inventory	$20,000		→$16,000*		→$20,000	
Cost of goods purchased	60,000		60,000		60,000	
Goods available for sale	80,000		76,000		80,000	
Ending inventory	16,000*		20,000		20,000	
Cost of goods sold		64,000†		56,000†		60,000
Gross profit		36,000		44,000		40,000
Expenses		10,000		10,000		10,000
Net income		$ 26,000		$ 34,000		$ 30,000

* Correct amount is $20,000. † Correct amount is $60,000.

Exhibit 6.11

Effects of Inventory Errors on Three Periods' Income Statements

Balance Sheet Effects Balance sheet effects of an inventory error can be seen by considering the components of the accounting equation: Assets = Liabilities + Equity. For example, understating ending inventory understates both current and total assets. An understatement in ending inventory also yields an understatement in equity because of the understatement in net income. Exhibit 6.12 shows the effects of inventory errors on the current period's balance sheet amounts. Errors in *beginning* inventory do not yield misstatements in the end-of-period balance sheet, but they do affect that current period's income statement.

Example: If year 2004 ending inventory in Exhibit 6.11 is overstated by $3,000, what is the effect on cost of goods sold, gross profit, assets, and equity? *Answer:* Cost of goods sold is understated by $3,000 in 2004 and overstated by $3,000 in 2005. Gross profit and net income are overstated in 2004 and understated in 2005. Assets and equity are overstated in 2004.

Inventory Error	Assets	Equity
Understate ending inventory	Understated	Understated
Overstate ending inventory	Overstated	Overstated

Exhibit 6.12

Effects of Inventory Errors on Current Period's Balance Sheet

Quick Check

8. Use LCM applied separately to individual items to compute ending inventory if the data are as follows:

Product	Units	Unit Recorded Cost	Unit Market Cost
A	20	$ 6	$ 5
B	40	9	8
C	10	12	15

Answer—p. 246

Inventory Turnover and Days' Sales in Inventory

Decision Analysis

Inventory Turnover

Earlier chapters described two important ratios useful in evaluating a company's short-term liquidity: current ratio and acid-test ratio. A merchandiser's ability to pay its short-term obligations also depends on how quickly it sells its merchandise inventory. **Inventory turnover,** also called *merchandise inventory turnover,* is one ratio used to assess this and is defined in Exhibit 6.13.

A3 Assess inventory management using both inventory turnover and days' sales in inventory.

$$\text{Inventory turnover} = \frac{\text{Cost of goods sold}}{\text{Average inventory}}$$

Exhibit 6.13

Inventory Turnover

Point: We must take care when comparing turnover ratios across companies that use different costing methods (such as FIFO and LIFO).

This ratio reveals how many *times* a company turns over (sells) its inventory during a period. If a company's inventory greatly varies within a year, average inventory amounts can be computed from interim periods such as quarters or months.

Users apply inventory turnover to help analyze short-term liquidity and to assess whether management is doing a good job controlling the amount of inventory available. A low ratio compared to that of competitors suggests inefficient use of assets. The company may be holding more inventory than it needs to support its sales volume. Similarly, a very high ratio compared to that of competitors suggests inventory might be too low. This can cause lost sales if customers must back order merchandise. Inventory turnover has no simple rule except to say *a high ratio is preferable provided inventory is adequate to meet demand.*

Decision Insight

Dell-ocity From its roots in a college dorm room, **Dell** now sells 50 million dollars' worth of computers each day from its Website. The speed of Web technology has allowed Dell to slash inventories. Dell's operating cycle is less than 15 hours and its days' sales in inventory is 3 days. Michael Dell asserts, "Speed is everything in this business."

Days' Sales in Inventory

Point: Inventory turnover is higher and days' sales in inventory is lower for industries such as foods and other perishable products. The reverse holds for nonperishable product industries.

To better interpret inventory turnover, many users measure the adequacy of inventory to meet sales demand. **Days' sales in inventory,** also called *days' stock on hand,* is a ratio that reveals how much inventory is available in terms of the number of days' sales. It can be interpreted as the number of days one can sell from inventory if no new items are purchased. This ratio is often viewed as a measure of the buffer against out-of-stock inventory and is useful in evaluating liquidity of inventory. It is defined in Exhibit 6.14.

Exhibit 6.14

Days' Sales in Inventory

$$\textbf{Days' sales in inventory} = \frac{\textbf{Ending inventory}}{\textbf{Cost of goods sold}} \times 365$$

Days' sales in inventory focuses on ending inventory and it estimates how many days it will take to convert inventory at the end of a period into accounts receivable or cash. Notice that days' sales in inventory focuses on *ending* inventory whereas inventory turnover focuses on *average* inventory.

Analysis of Inventory Management

Inventory management is a major emphasis for merchandisers. They must both plan and control inventory purchases and sales. **Toys "R" Us** is one of those merchandisers. Its inventory in fiscal year 2003 was $2,190 million. This inventory constituted 62% of its current assets and 23% of its total assets. We apply the analysis tools in this section to Toys "R" Us, as shown in Exhibit 6.15.

Its 2003 inventory turnover of 3.7 times means that Toys "R" Us turns over its inventory 3.7 times per year, or once every 99 days (365 days ÷ 3.7). We prefer inventory turnover to be high provided inventory is not out of stock and the company is not losing customers. The 2003 days' sales in inventory of 102 days reveals that it is carrying 102 days of sales in inventory. This inventory buffer seems more than adequate. Toys "R" Us would benefit from further management efforts to increase inventory turnover and reduce inventory levels.

Decision Maker

Entrepreneur Analysis of your retail store yields an inventory turnover of 5.0 and a days' sales in inventory of 73 days. The industry norm for inventory turnover is 4.4 and for days' sales in inventory is 74 days. What is your assessment of inventory management?

Answer—p. 245

Exhibit 6.15

Inventory Turnover and Days' Sales in Inventory for Toys "R" Us

($ in millions)	2003	2002	2001
Cost of goods sold	$7,799	$7,604	$7,815
Ending inventory	$2,190	$2,041	$2,307
Inventory turnover	**3.7** times	**3.5** times	**3.6** times
Industry inventory turnover	2.6 times	2.5 times	2.8 times
Days' sales in inventory	**102** days	**98** days	**108** days
Industry days' sales in inventory	139 days	146 days	130 days

Demonstration Problem

Craig Company uses a perpetual inventory system for its one product. Its beginning inventory, purchases, and sales during year 2005 follow:

Date	Activity	Units Acquired at Cost		Units Sold at Retail	Unit Inventory
Jan. 1	Beg. Inventory . .	400 units @ $14 =	$5,600		400 units
Jan. 15	Sale			200 units @ $30	200 units
March 10	Purchase	200 units @ $15 =	$3,000		400 units
April 1	Sale			200 units @ $30	200 units
May 9	Purchase	300 units @ $16 =	$4,800		500 units
Sept. 22	Purchase	250 units @ $20 =	$5,000		750 units
Nov. 1	Sale			300 units @ $35	450 units
Nov. 28	Purchase	100 units @ $21 =	$2,100		550 units
	Totals	1,250 units	$20,500	700 units	

Additional tracking data for applying specific identification: (1) January 15 sale—200 units @ $14, (2) April 1 sale—200 units @ $15, and (3) November 1 sale—200 units @ $14 and 100 units @ $20.

Required

1. Calculate the cost of goods available for sale.
2. Apply the four different methods of inventory costing (FIFO, LIFO, weighted average, and specific identification) to calculate ending inventory and cost of goods sold under each method.
3. In preparing financial statements for year 2005, the financial officer was instructed to use FIFO but failed to do so and instead computed cost of goods sold according to LIFO. Determine the impact on year 2005's income from the error. Also determine the effect of this error on year 2006's income. Assume no income taxes.
4. Management wants a report that shows how changing from FIFO to another method would change net income. Prepare a table showing (1) the cost of goods sold amount under each of the four methods, (2) the amount by which each cost of goods sold total is different from the FIFO cost of goods sold, and (3) the effect on net income if another method is used instead of FIFO.

Planning the Solution

- Compute cost of goods available for sale by multiplying the units of beginning inventory and each purchase by their unit costs to determine the total cost of goods available for sale.
- Prepare a perpetual FIFO table starting with beginning inventory and showing how inventory changes after each purchase and after each sale (see Exhibit 6.5).
- Prepare a perpetual LIFO table starting with beginning inventory and showing how inventory changes after each purchase and after each sale (see Exhibit 6.6).
- Make a table of purchases and sales recalculating the average cost of inventory prior to each sale to arrive at the weighted average cost of ending inventory. Total the average costs associated with each sale to determine cost of goods sold (see Exhibit 6.7).
- Prepare a table showing the computation of cost of goods sold and ending inventory using the specific identification method (see Exhibit 6.4).
- Compare the year-end 2005 inventory amounts under FIFO and LIFO to determine the misstatement of year 2005 income that results from using LIFO. The errors for year 2005 and 2006 are equal in amount but opposite in effect.
- Create a table showing cost of goods sold under each method and how net income would differ from FIFO net income if an alternate method is adopted.

Solution to Demonstration Problem

1. Cost of goods available for sale (this amount is the same for all methods):

Date		Units	Unit Cost	Total Cost
Jan. 1	Beg. Inventory	400	$14	$ 5,600
March 10	Purchase	200	15	3,000
May 9	Purchase	300	16	4,800
Sept. 22	Purchase	250	20	5,000
Nov. 28	Purchase	100	21	2,100
Total cost of goods available for sale				$20,500

2a. FIFO perpetual method:

Date	Goods Purchased	Cost of Goods Sold	Inventory Balance	
Jan. 1	Beginning balance		400 @ $14	= $ 5,600
Jan. 15		200 @ $14 = $2,800	200 @ $14	= $ 2,800
Mar. 10	200 @ $15 = $3,000		200 @ $14 200 @ $15	= $ 5,800
April 1		200 @ $14 = $2,800	200 @ $15	= $ 3,000
May 9	300 @ $16 = $4,800		200 @ $15 300 @ $16	= $ 7,800
Sept. 22	250 @ $20 = $5,000		200 @ $15 300 @ $16 250 @ $20	= $12,800
Nov. 1		200 @ $15 = $3,000 100 @ $16 = $1,600	200 @ $16 250 @ $20	= $ 8,200
Nov. 28	100 @ $21 = $2,100		200 @ $16 250 @ $20 100 @ $21	= **$10,300**
Total cost of goods sold		**$10,200**		

Note to students: **In a classroom situation,** once we compute cost of goods available for sale, we can compute the amount for either cost of goods sold or ending inventory—it is a matter of preference. **In practice,** the costs of items sold are identified as sales are made and immediately transferred from the inventory account to the cost of goods sold account. The previous solution showing the line-by-line approach illustrates actual application in practice. The following alternate solutions illustrate that, once the concepts are understood, other solution approaches are available—although this is only shown for FIFO, it could be shown for all methods.

Alternate Methods to Compute FIFO Perpetual Numbers

[FIFO Alternate No. 1: Computing cost of goods sold first]

Cost of goods available for sale (from part 1)		$ 20,500
Cost of goods sold		
Jan. 15 Sold (200 @ $14)	$2,800	
April 1 Sold (200 @ $14)	2,800	
Nov. 1 Sold (200 @ $15 and 100 @ $16)	4,600	**10,200**
Ending inventory		**$10,300**

[FIFO Alternate No. 2: Computing ending inventory first]

Cost of goods available for sale (from part 1)			$ 20,500
Ending inventory*			
Nov. 28	Purchase (100 @ $21)	$2,100	
Sept. 22	Purchase (250 @ $20)	5,000	
May 9	Purchase (200 @ $16)	3,200	
Ending inventory			10,300
Cost of goods sold			$10,200

* Since FIFO assumes that the earlier costs are the first to flow out, we determine ending inventory by assigning the most recent costs to the remaining items.

2b. LIFO perpetual method:

Date	Goods Purchased	Cost of Goods Sold	Inventory Balance	
Jan. 1	Beginning balance		400 @ $14	= $ 5,600
Jan. 15		200 @ $14 = $2,800	200 @ $14	= $ 2,800
Mar. 10	200 @ $15 = $3,000		200 @ $14 200 @ $15	= $ 5,800
April 1		200 @ $15 = $3,000	200 @ $14	= $ 2,800
May 9	300 @ $16 = $4,800		200 @ $14 300 @ $16	= $ 7,600
Sept. 22	250 @ $20 = $5,000		200 @ $14 300 @ $16 250 @ $20	= $12,600
Nov. 1		250 @ $20 = $5,000 50 @ $16 = $ 800	200 @ $14 250 @ $16	= $ 6,800
Nov. 28	100 @ $21 = $2,100		200 @ $14 250 @ $16 100 @ $21	= $ 8,900
Total cost of goods sold		$11,600		

2c. Weighted average perpetual method:

Date	Goods Purchased	Cost of Goods Sold	Inventory Balance	
Jan. 1	Beginning balance		400 @ $14	= $ 5,600
Jan. 15		200 @ $14 = $2,800	200 @ $14	= $ 2,800
Mar. 10	200 @ $15 = $3,000		200 @ $14 200 @ $15 (avg. cost is $14.5)	= $ 5,800
April 1		200 @ $14.5 = $2,900	200 @ $14.5	= $ 2,900
May 9	300 @ $16 = $4,800		200 @ $14.5 300 @ $16 (avg. cost is $15.4)	= $ 7,700

[continued on next page]

[continued from previous page]

Sept. 22	250 @ $20 = $5,000		200 @ $14.5 300 @ $16 250 @ $20 } = $ 12,700 (avg. cost is $16.93)
Nov. 1		300 @ $16.93 = $5,079	450 @ $16.93 = $ 7,618.5
Nov. 28	100 @ $21 = $2,100		450 @ $16.93 100 @ $21 } = $9,718.5
Total cost of goods sold*		**$10,779**	

* The cost of goods sold ($10,779) plus ending inventory ($9,718.5) is $2.5 less than the cost of goods available for sale ($20,500) due to rounding.

2d. Specific identification method:

Date	Goods Purchased	Cost of Goods Sold	Inventory Balance
Jan. 1	Beginning balance		400 @ $14 = $ 5,600
Jan. 15		200 @ $14 = $2,800	200 @ $14 = $ 2,800
Mar. 10	200 @ $15 = $3,000		200 @ $14 200 @ $15 } = $ 5,800
April 1		200 @ $15 = $3,000	200 @ $14 = $ 2,800
May 9	300 @ $16 = $4,800		200 @ $14 300 @ $16 } = $ 7,600
Sept. 22	250 @ $20 = $5,000		200 @ $14 300 @ $16 250 @ $20 } = $12,600
Nov. 1		200 @ $14 = $2,800 100 @ $20 = $2,000	300 @ $16 150 @ $20 } = $ 7,800
Nov. 28	100 @ $21 = $2,100		300 @ $16 150 @ $20 100 @ $21 } = $ 9,900
Total cost of goods sold		**$10,600**	

3. Mistakenly using LIFO when FIFO should have been used overstates cost of goods sold in year 2005 by $1,400, which is the difference between the FIFO and LIFO amounts of ending inventory. It understates income in 2005 by $1,400. In year 2006, income is overstated by $1,400 because of the understatement in beginning inventory.

4. Analysis of the effects of alternative inventory methods:

	Cost of Goods Sold	Difference from FIFO Cost of Goods Sold	Effect on Net Income if Adopted Instead of FIFO
FIFO	$10,200	—	—
LIFO	11,600	+$1,400	$1,400 lower
Weighted average	10,779	+ 579	579 lower
Specific identification	10,600	+ 400	400 lower

APPENDIX

Inventory Costing Under a Periodic System

The basic aim of the periodic system and the perpetual system is the same: to assign costs to inventory and cost of goods sold. The same four methods are used to assign costs under both systems: specific identification; first-in, first-out; last-in, first-out; and weighted average. We use information from Trekking to show how to assign costs using these four methods with a periodic system. Data for sales and purchases are reported in the chapter (see Exhibit 6.3). Recall that we explained the accounting under a periodic system in Appendix 5A.

P3 Compute inventory in a periodic system using the methods of specific identification, FIFO, LIFO, and weighted average.

Specific Identification

We use the information in Exhibit 6.3 and the specific identification method to assign costs to the 12 units in ending inventory and to the 43 units sold as shown in Exhibit 6A.1. Carefully study Exhibit 6A.1 to see the flow of costs both in and out of inventory. Notice that each unit, whether sold or remaining in inventory, has its own specific cost attached to it.

Exhibit 6A.1

Specific Identification Computations

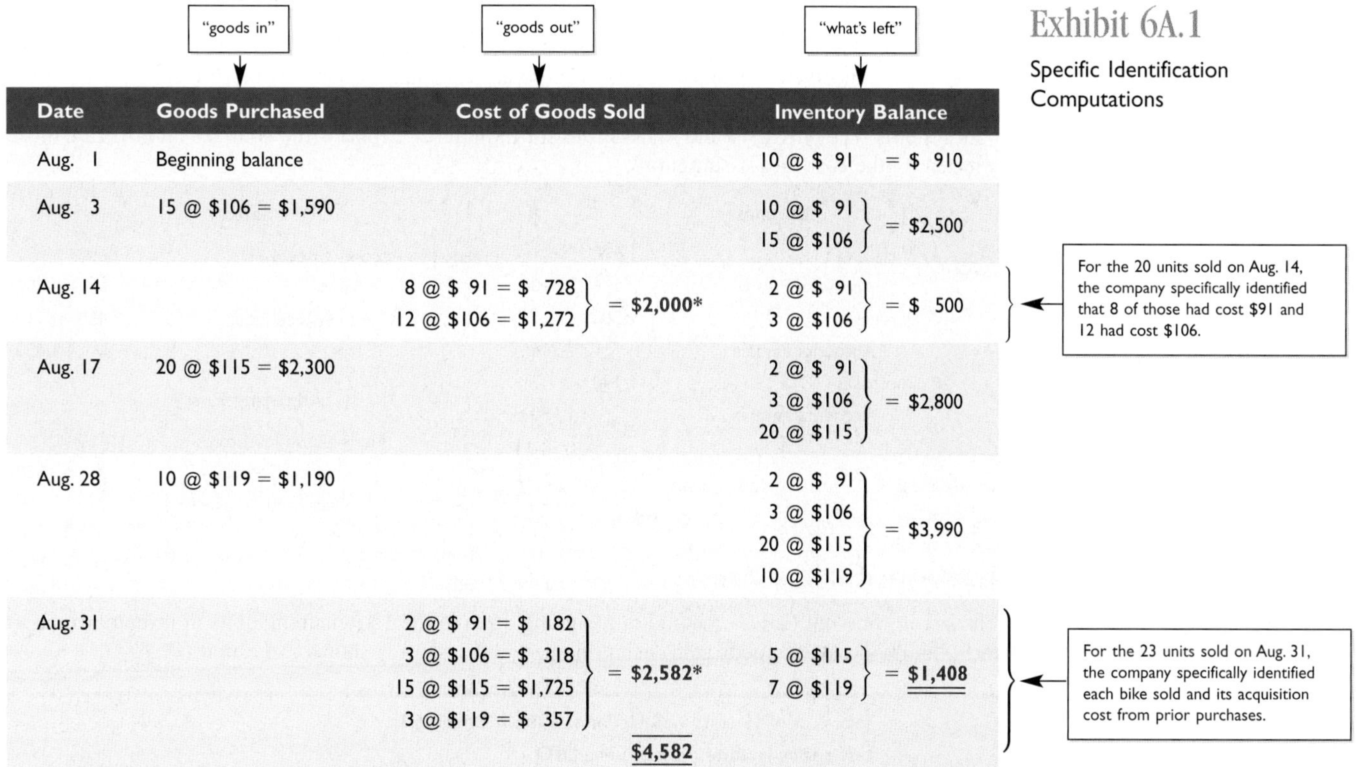

Date	Goods Purchased ("goods in")	Cost of Goods Sold ("goods out")	Inventory Balance ("what's left")
Aug. 1	Beginning balance		10 @ \$ 91 = \$ 910
Aug. 3	15 @ \$106 = \$1,590		10 @ \$ 91 15 @ \$106 } = \$2,500
Aug. 14		8 @ \$ 91 = \$ 728 12 @ \$106 = \$1,272 } = \$2,000*	2 @ \$ 91 3 @ \$106 } = \$ 500
Aug. 17	20 @ \$115 = \$2,300		2 @ \$ 91 3 @ \$106 20 @ \$115 } = \$2,800
Aug. 28	10 @ \$119 = \$1,190		2 @ \$ 91 3 @ \$106 20 @ \$115 10 @ \$119 } = \$3,990
Aug. 31		2 @ \$ 91 = \$ 182 3 @ \$106 = \$ 318 15 @ \$115 = \$1,725 3 @ \$119 = \$ 357 } = \$2,582*	5 @ \$115 7 @ \$119 } = \$1,408
		\$4,582	

For the 20 units sold on Aug. 14, the company specifically identified that 8 of those had cost \$91 and 12 had cost \$106.

For the 23 units sold on Aug. 31, the company specifically identified each bike sold and its acquisition cost from prior purchases.

* Identification of items sold (and their costs) is obtained from internal documents that track each unit from its purchase to its sale.

When using specific identification, Trekking's cost of goods sold reported on the income statement totals **\$4,582**, the sum of \$2,000 and \$2,582 from the third column of Exhibit 6A.1. Trekking's ending inventory reported on the balance sheet is **\$1,408**, which is the final inventory balance from the fourth column of Exhibit 6A.1. The purchases and sales entries for Exhibit 6A.1 follow (the

Point: The assignment of costs to the goods sold and to inventory using specific identification is the same for both the perpetual and periodic systems.

boldface numbers are those affected by the cost flow assumption):

Purchases

Aug. 3	Purchases	1,590	
	Accounts Payable		1,590
17	Purchases	2,300	
	Accounts Payable		2,300
28	Purchases	1,190	
	Accounts Payable		1,190

Sales

Aug. 14	Accounts Receivable	2,600	
	Sales		2,600
31	Accounts Receivable	3,450	
	Sales		3,450
	Adjusting Entry		
31	Merchandise Inventory	**1,408**	
	Income Summary		498
	Merchandise Inventory		**910**

First-In, First-Out

The first-in, first-out (FIFO) method of assigning cost to both inventory and cost of goods sold using the periodic system is shown in Exhibit 6A.2.

Exhibit 6A.2

FIFO Computations—Periodic System

Exhibit 6.3 shows that the 12 units in ending inventory consist of 10 units from the latest purchase on Aug. 28 and 2 units from the next latest purchase on Aug. 17.

Total cost of 55 units available for sale (from Exhibit 6.3)		$5,990
Less ending inventory priced using FIFO		
10 units from August 28 purchase at $119 each	$1,190	
2 units from August 17 purchase at $115 each	230	
Ending inventory		**1,420**
Cost of goods sold		**$4,570**

Point: The assignment of costs to the goods sold and to inventory using FIFO is the same for both the perpetual and periodic systems.

Trekking's ending inventory reported on the balance sheet is **$1,420**, and its cost of goods sold reported on the income statement is **$4,570**. These amounts are the same as those computed using the perpetual system. This always occurs because the most recent purchases are in ending inventory under both systems. The purchases and sales entries for Exhibit 6A.2 follow (the boldface numbers are those affected by the cost flow assumption):

Purchases

Aug. 3	Purchases	1,590	
	Accounts Payable		1,590
17	Purchases	2,300	
	Accounts Payable		2,300
28	Purchases	1,190	
	Accounts Payable		1,190

Sales

Aug. 14	Accounts Receivable	2,600	
	Sales		2,600
31	Accounts Receivable	3,450	
	Sales		3,450
	Adjusting Entry		
31	Merchandise Inventory	**1,420**	
	Income Summary		510
	Merchandise Inventory		**910**

Last-In, First-Out

The last-in, first-out (LIFO) method of assigning costs to the 12 remaining units in inventory (and to the 43 units in cost of goods sold) using the periodic system is shown in Exhibit 6A.3.

Exhibit 6A.3

LIFO Computations—Periodic System

Exhibit 6.3 shows that the 12 units in ending inventory consist of 10 units from the earliest purchase (beg. inv.) and 2 units from the next earliest purchase on Aug. 3.

Total cost of 55 units available for sale (from Exhibit 6.3)		$5,990
Less ending inventory priced using LIFO		
10 units in beginning inventory at $91 each	$910	
2 units from August 3 purchase at $106 each	212	
Ending inventory		**1,122**
Cost of goods sold		**$4,868**

Trekking's ending inventory reported on the balance sheet is **$1,122**, and its cost of goods sold reported on the income statement is **$4,868**. When LIFO is used with the periodic system, cost of goods sold is assigned costs from the most recent purchases for the period. With a perpetual system, cost of goods sold is assigned costs from the most recent purchases at the point of *each sale*. The purchases and sales entries for Exhibit 6A.3 follow (the boldface numbers are those affected by the cost flow assumption):

Purchases

Aug. 3	Purchases	1,590	
	Accounts Payable		1,590
17	Purchases	2,300	
	Accounts Payable		2,300
28	Purchases	1,190	
	Accounts Payable		1,190

Sales

Aug. 14	Accounts Receivable	2,600	
	Sales		2,600
31	Accounts Receivable	3,450	
	Sales		3,450
	Adjusting Entry		
31	Merchandise Inventory	**1,122**	
	Income Summary		212
	Merchandise Inventory		**910**

Weighted Average

The weighted average method of assigning cost involves three important steps. The first two steps are shown in Exhibit 6A.4. First, multiply the per unit cost for beginning inventory and each particular purchase by the corresponding number of units (from Exhibit 6.3). Second, add these amounts and divide by the total number of units available for sale to find the weighted average cost per unit.

Step 1:	10 units @ $ 91 =	$ 910
	15 units @ $106 =	1,590
	20 units @ $115 =	2,300
	10 units @ $119 =	1,190
	55	**$5,990**
Step 2:	$5,990/55 units = **$108.91** weighted average cost per unit	

Exhibit 6A.4

Weighted Average Cost per Unit

Example: In Exhibit 6A.4, if 5 more units had been purchased at $120 each, what would be the weighted average cost per unit?
Answer: $109.83 ($6,590/60)

The third step is to use the weighted average cost per unit to assign costs to inventory and to the units sold as shown in Exhibit 6A.5.

Step 3:	Total cost of 55 units available for sale (from Exhibit 6.3)	$5,990
	Less **ending inventory** priced on a weighted average cost basis: 12 units at $108.91 each (from Exhibit 6A.4)	**1,307**
	Cost of goods sold	**$4,683**

Exhibit 6A.5

Weighted Average Computations—Periodic

Trekking's ending inventory reported on the balance sheet is **$1,307**, and its cost of goods sold reported on the income statement is **$4,683** when using the weighted average (periodic) method. The purchases and sales entries for Exhibit 6A.5 follow (the boldface numbers are those affected by the cost flow assumption):

Point: Weighted average usually yields different results for the perpetual and the periodic systems because under a perpetual system it recomputes the per unit cost prior to each sale, whereas under a periodic system, the per unit cost is computed only at the end of a period.

Purchases

Aug. 3	Purchases	1,590	
	Accounts Payable		1,590
17	Purchases	2,300	
	Accounts Payable		2,300
28	Purchases	1,190	
	Accounts Payable		1,190

Sales

Aug. 14	Accounts Receivable	2,600	
	Sales		2,600
31	Accounts Receivable	3,450	
	Sales		3,450
	Adjusting Entry		
31	Merchandise Inventory	**1,307**	
	Income Summary		397
	Merchandise Inventory		**910**

Financial Statement Effects

When purchase prices do not change, each inventory costing method assigns the same cost amounts to inventory and to cost of goods sold. When purchase prices are different, however, the methods nearly always assign different cost amounts. We show these differences in Exhibit 6A.6 using Trekking's data. When purchase costs *regularly rise,* as in Trekking's case, note the following:

Point: LIFO inventory is often less than the inventory's replacement cost because LIFO inventory is valued using the oldest inventory purchase costs.

Exhibit 6A.6

Financial Statement Effects of Inventory Costing Methods

TREKKING COMPANY For Month Ended August 31	Specific Identification	FIFO	LIFO	Weighted Average
Income Statement				
Sales	$ 6,050	$ 6,050	$ 6,050	$ 6,050
Cost of goods sold	**4,582**	**4,570**	**4,868**	**4,683**
Gross profit	1,468	1,480	1,182	1,367
Expenses	450	450	450	450
Income before taxes	1,018	1,030	732	917
Income tax expense (30%)	305	309	220	275
Net income	**$ 713**	**$ 721**	**$ 512**	**$ 642**
Balance Sheet				
Inventory	**$1,408**	**$1,420**	**$1,122**	**$1,307**

- FIFO assigns the lowest amount to cost of goods sold—yielding the highest gross profit and net income.
- LIFO assigns the highest amount to cost of goods sold—yielding the lowest gross profit and net income, which also yields a temporary tax advantage by postponing payment of some income tax.
- Weighted average yields results between FIFO and LIFO.
- Specific identification always yields results that depend on which units are sold.

When costs *regularly decline,* the reverse occurs for FIFO and LIFO.

All four inventory costing methods are acceptable in practice. A company must disclose the inventory method it uses. Each method offers certain advantages as follows:

- FIFO assigns an amount to inventory on the balance sheet that approximates its current cost; it also mimics the actual flow of goods for most businesses.
- LIFO assigns an amount to cost of goods sold on the income statement that approximates its current cost; it also better matches current costs with revenues in computing gross profit.
- Weighted average tends to smooth out erratic changes in costs.
- Specific identification exactly matches the costs of items with the revenues they generate.

DILBERT reprinted by permission of United Feature Syndicate, Inc.

While Dilbert's suggestion may be easier said than done, it does reinforce the importance of inventory management. This includes attention to inventory turnover, days' sales in inventory, and other measures.

Quick Check

9. A company reports the following beginning inventory and purchases, and it ends the period with 30 units in inventory.

Beginning Inventory	100 units at $10 cost per unit
Purchase 1	40 units at $12 cost per unit
Purchase 2	20 units at $14 cost per unit

a. Compute ending inventory using the FIFO periodic system.

b. Compute cost of goods sold using the LIFO periodic system.

Answers—p. 246

APPENDIX

Inventory Estimation Methods

6B

P4 Apply both the retail inventory and gross profit methods to estimate inventory.

Inventory sometimes requires estimation for two reasons. First, companies may require **interim statements** (financial statements prepared for periods of less than one year), but they only annually take a physical count of inventory. Second, companies may require an inventory estimate if some casualty such as fire or flood makes taking a physical count impossible. Note that estimates are usually only required for companies that use the periodic system. Companies using a perpetual system would presumably have updated inventory data.

This appendix describes two methods to estimate inventory.

Retail Inventory Method

To avoid the time-consuming and expensive process of taking a physical inventory each month or quarter, some companies use the **retail inventory method** to estimate cost of goods sold and ending inventory. Some companies even use the retail inventory method to prepare the annual statements. **Home Depot**, for instance, says in its recent annual report: "Inventories are stated at the lower of cost (first-in, first-out) or market, as determined by the retail inventory method." A company may also estimate inventory for audit purposes or when inventory is damaged or destroyed.

Point: When a retailer takes a physical inventory, it can restate the retail value of inventory to a cost basis by applying the cost-to-retail ratio. It can also estimate the amount of shrinkage by comparing the inventory computed with the amount from a physical inventory.

The retail inventory method uses a three-step process to estimate ending inventory. We need to know the amount of inventory a company had at the beginning of the period in both *cost* and *retail* amounts. We already explained how to compute the cost of inventory. The *retail amount of inventory* refers to its dollar amount measured using selling prices of inventory items. We also need to know the net amount of goods purchased (minus returns, allowances, and discounts) in the period, both at cost and at retail. The amount of net sales at retail is also needed. The process is shown in Exhibit 6B.1.

The reasoning behind the retail inventory method is that if we can get a good estimate of the cost-to-retail ratio, we can multiply ending inventory at retail by this ratio to estimate ending inventory at cost. We show in Exhibit 6B.2 how these steps are applied to estimate ending inventory for

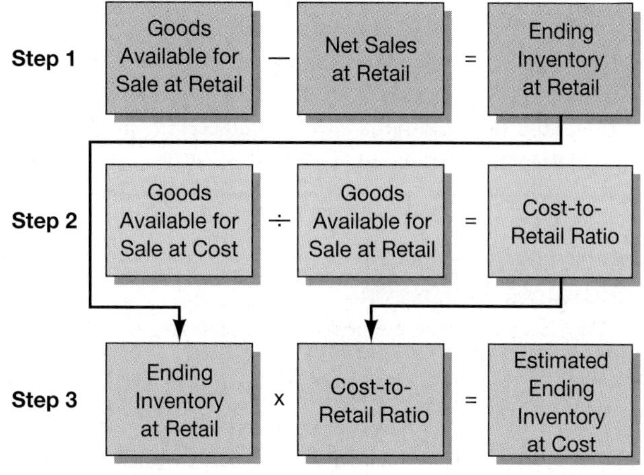

Exhibit 6B.1

Retail Inventory Method of Inventory Estimation

Exhibit 6B.2

Estimated Inventory Using the Retail Inventory Method

		At Cost	At Retail
	Goods available for sale		
	Beginning inventory	$ 20,500	$ 34,500
	Cost of goods purchased	39,500	65,500
Step 1:	Goods available for sale	60,000	100,000
	Deduct net sales at retail		**70,000**
	Ending inventory at retail		**$ 30,000**
Step 2:	**Cost-to-retail ratio: ($60,000 ÷ $100,000) = 60%**		
Step 3:	**Estimated ending inventory at cost ($30,000 × 60%)**	**$18,000**	

Example: What is the cost of ending inventory in Exhibit 6B.2 if the cost of beginning inventory is $22,500 and its retail value is $34,500? *Answer:* $30,000 × 62% = $18,600

a typical company. First, we find that $100,000 of goods (at retail selling prices) was available for sale. We see that $70,000 of these goods were sold, leaving $30,000 (retail value) of merchandise in ending inventory. Second, the cost of these goods is 60% of the $100,000 retail value. Third, since cost for these goods is 60% of retail, the estimated cost of ending inventory is $18,000.

Gross Profit Method

The **gross profit method** estimates the cost of ending inventory by applying the gross profit ratio to net sales (at retail). This type of estimate often is needed when inventory is destroyed, lost, or stolen. These cases require an inventory estimate so that a company can file a claim with its insurer. Users also apply this method to see whether inventory amounts from a physical count are reasonable. This method uses the historical relation between cost of goods sold and net sales to estimate the proportion of cost of goods sold making up current sales. This cost of goods sold estimate is then subtracted from cost of goods available for sale to estimate the ending inventory at cost. These two steps are shown in Exhibit 6B.3.

Exhibit 6B.3

Gross Profit Method of Inventory Estimation

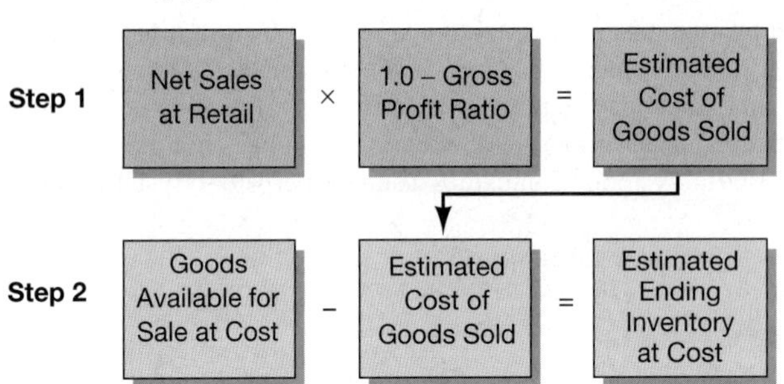

Point: A fire or other catastrophe can result in an insurance claim for lost inventory or income. Backup and off-site storage of data help ensure coverage for such losses.

Point: Reliability of the gross profit method depends on a good estimate of the gross profit ratio.

To illustrate, assume that a company's inventory is destroyed by fire in March 2005. When the fire occurs, the company's accounts show the following balances for January through March: sales, $31,500; sales returns, $1,500; inventory (January 1, 2005), $12,000; and cost of goods purchased, $20,500. If this company's gross profit ratio is 30%, then 30% of each net sales dollar is gross profit and 70% is cost of goods sold. We show in Exhibit 6B.4 how this 70% is used to estimate lost inventory of $11,500. To understand this exhibit, think of subtracting cost of goods sold from the goods available for sale to get ending inventory.

Exhibit 6B.4

Estimated Inventory Using the Gross Profit Method

	Goods available for sale		
	Inventory, January 1, 2005	$12,000	
	Cost of goods purchased	20,500	
	Goods available for sale (at cost)	32,500	
	Net sales at retail ($31,500 − $1,500)		$30,000
Step 1:	**Estimated cost of goods sold ($30,000 × 70%)**	**(21,000)**	× 0.70
Step 2:	**Estimated March inventory at cost**	**$11,500**	

Quick Check

10. Using the retail method and the following data, estimate the cost of ending inventory.

	Cost	Retail
Beginning inventory	$324,000	$530,000
Cost of goods purchased	195,000	335,000
Net sales		320,000

Answer—p. 246

Summary

C1 Identify the items making up merchandise inventory. Merchandise inventory refers to goods owned by a company and held for resale. Three special cases merit our attention. Goods in transit are reported in inventory of the company that holds ownership rights. Goods on consignment are reported in the consignor's inventory. Goods damaged or obsolete are reported in inventory at their net realizable value.

C2 Identify the costs of merchandise inventory. Costs of merchandise inventory include expenditures necessary to bring an item to a salable condition and location. This includes its invoice cost minus any discount plus any added or incidental costs necessary to put it in a place and condition for sale.

A1 Analyze the effects of inventory methods for both financial and tax reporting. When purchase costs are rising or falling, the inventory costing methods are likely to assign different costs to inventory. Specific identification exactly matches costs and revenues. Weighted average smooths out cost changes. FIFO assigns an amount to inventory closely approximating current replacement cost. LIFO assigns the most recent costs incurred to cost of goods sold and likely better matches current costs with revenues.

A2 Analyze the effects of inventory errors on current and future financial statements. An error in the amount of ending inventory affects assets (inventory), net income (cost of goods sold), and equity for that period. Since ending inventory is next period's beginning inventory, an error in ending inventory affects next period's cost of goods sold and net income. Inventory errors in one period are offset in the next period.

A3 Assess inventory management using both inventory turnover and days' sales in inventory. We prefer a high inventory turnover, provided that goods are not out of stock and customers are not turned away. We use days' sales in inventory to assess the likelihood of goods being out of stock. We prefer a small number of days' sales in inventory if we can serve customer needs and provide a buffer for uncertainties.

P1 Compute inventory in a perpetual system using the methods of specific identification, FIFO, LIFO, and weighted average. Costs are assigned to the cost of goods sold account *each time* a sale occurs in a perpetual system. Specific identification assigns a cost to each item sold by referring to its actual cost (for example, its net invoice cost). Weighted average assigns a cost to items sold by dividing the current balance in the inventory account by the total items available for sale to determine cost per unit. We then multiply the number of units sold by this cost per unit to get the cost of each sale. FIFO assigns cost to items sold assuming that the earliest units purchased are the first units sold. LIFO assigns cost to items sold assuming that the most recent units purchased are the first units sold.

P2 Compute the lower of cost or market amount of inventory. Inventory is reported at market cost when market is *lower* than recorded cost, called the *lower of cost or market (LCM) inventory.* Market is typically measured as replacement cost. Lower of cost or market can be applied separately to each item, to major categories of items, or to the entire inventory.

P3[A] Compute inventory in a periodic system using the methods of specific identification, FIFO, LIFO, and weighted average. Periodic inventory systems allocate the cost of goods available for sale between cost of goods sold and ending inventory *at the end of a period.* Specific identification and FIFO give identical results whether the periodic or perpetual system is used. LIFO assigns costs to cost of goods sold assuming the last units purchased for the period are the first units sold. The weighted average cost per unit is computed by dividing the total cost of beginning inventory and net purchases for the period by the total number of units available. Then, it multiplies cost per unit by the number of units sold to give cost of goods sold.

P4[B] Apply both the retail inventory and gross profit methods to estimate inventory. The retail inventory method involves three steps: (1) goods available at retail minus net sales at retail equals ending inventory at retail, (2) goods available at cost divided by goods available at retail equals the cost-to-retail ratio, and (3) ending inventory at retail multiplied by the cost-to-retail ratio equals estimated ending inventory at cost. The gross profit method involves two steps: (1) net sales at retail multiplied by 1 minus the gross profit ratio equals estimated cost of goods sold, and (2) goods available at cost minus estimated cost of goods sold equals estimated ending inventory at cost.

Guidance Answers to **Decision Maker** and **Decision Ethics**

Financial Planner The FIFO method implies that the oldest costs are the first ones assigned to cost of goods sold. This leaves the most recent costs in ending inventory. You report this to your client and note that in most cases, the ending inventory of a company using FIFO is reported at or near its replacement cost. This means that your client need not in most cases adjust the reported value of inventory. Your answer changes only if there are major increases in replacement cost compared to the cost of recent purchases reported in inventory. When major increases in costs occur, your client might wish to adjust inventory (for internal reports) for the difference between the reported cost of inventory and its replacement cost. (*Note:* Decreases in costs of purchases are recognized under the lower of cost or market adjustment.)

Inventory Manager It seems your company can save (or at least postpone) taxes by switching to LIFO, but the switch is likely to reduce bonus money that you think you have earned and deserve. Since the U.S. tax code requires companies that use LIFO for tax reporting also to use it for financial reporting, your options are further constrained. Your best decision is to tell your superior about the tax savings with LIFO. You also should discuss your bonus plan and how this is likely to hurt you unfairly. You might propose to compute inventory under the LIFO method for reporting purposes but use the FIFO method for your bonus calculations. Another solution is to revise the bonus plan to reflect the company's use of the LIFO method.

Entrepreneur Your inventory turnover is markedly higher than the norm, whereas days' sales in inventory approximates the norm. Since your turnover is already 14% better than average, you are probably best served by directing attention to days' sales in inventory. You should see whether you can reduce the level of inventory while maintaining service to customers. Given your higher turnover, you should be able to hold less inventory.

Guidance Answers to **Quick Checks**

1. The matching principle.
2. **Target** reports these goods in its inventory.
3. Total cost assigned to the painting is $12,180, computed as $11,400 + $130 + $150 + $100 + $400.
4. Specific identification exactly matches costs and revenues. Weighted average tends to smooth out cost changes. FIFO assigns an amount to inventory that closely approximates current replacement cost. LIFO assigns the most recent costs incurred

to cost of goods sold and likely better matches current costs with revenues.

5. FIFO—it gives a lower cost of goods sold, a higher gross profit, and a higher net income when costs are rising.

6. When costs are rising, LIFO gives a lower inventory figure on the balance sheet as compared to FIFO. FIFO's inventory amount approximates current replacement costs.

7. Cost of goods sold would be overstated by $10,000 in 2005 and understated by $10,000 in year 2006.

8. The reported LCM inventory amount (using items) is $540, computed as [(20 × $5) + (40 × $8) + (10 × $12)].

9.[A] a. FIFO periodic inventory = (20 × $14) + (10 × $12) = $400

b. LIFO periodic cost of goods sold = (20 × $14) + (40 × $12) + (70 × $10) = $1,460

10.[B] Estimated ending inventory (at cost) is $327,000. It is computed as follows:

Step 1: ($530,000 + $335,000) − $320,000 = $545,000

Step 2: $\frac{\$324{,}000 + \$195{,}000}{\$530{,}000 + \$335{,}000} = 60\%$

Step 3: $545,000 × 60% = $327,000

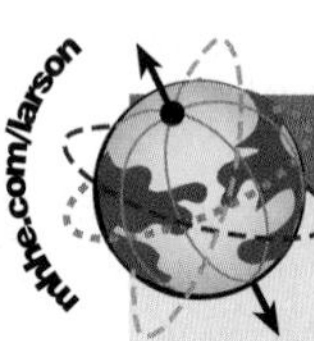

Key Terms

Key Terms are available at the book's Website for learning and testing in an online Flashcard Format.

Average cost (p. 228)
Conservatism principle (p. 232)
Consignee (p. 222)
Consignor (p. 222)
Consistency principle (p. 230)
Days' sales in inventory (p. 234)
First-in, first-out (FIFO) (p. 227)
Gross profit method (p. 244)
Interim statements (p. 243)
Inventory turnover (p. 233)
Last-in, first-out (LIFO) (p. 227)
Lower of cost or market (LCM) (p. 231)
Net realizable value (p. 223)
Retail inventory method (p. 243)
Specific identification (p. 225)
Weighted average (p. 228)

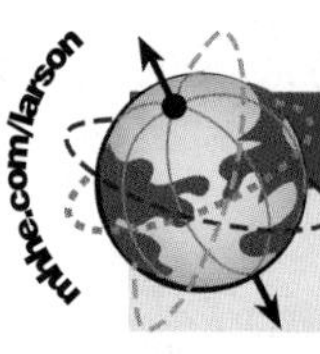

Personal Interactive Quiz

Personal Interactive Quizzes A and B are available at the book's Website to reinforce and assess your learning.

Superscript letter [A] ([B]) denotes assignments based on Appendix 6A (6B).

Discussion Questions

1. Describe the flow of costs from inventory to cost of goods sold for the following methods: (*a*) FIFO and (*b*) LIFO.

2. Where is the amount of merchandise inventory disclosed in the financial statements?

3. Why are incidental costs sometimes ignored in inventory costing? Under what principle is this permitted?

4. If costs are declining, will the LIFO or FIFO method of inventory valuation result in the lower cost of goods sold?

5. What does the full-disclosure principle prescribe if a company changes from one acceptable accounting method to another?

6. Can a company change its inventory method each accounting period? Explain.

7. Does the accounting principle of consistency preclude any changes from one accounting method to another?

8. If inventory errors are said to correct themselves, why are accounting users concerned when such errors are made?

9. Explain the following statement: "Inventory errors correct themselves."

10. What is the meaning of *market* as it is used in determining the lower of cost or market for inventory?

11. What guidance does the principle of conservatism offer?

12. What factors contribute to (or cause) inventory shrinkage?

13.[A] What accounts are used in a periodic inventory system but not in a perpetual inventory system?

14.[B] When preparing interim financial statements, what two methods can companies utilize to estimate cost of goods sold and ending inventory?

15. Refer to **Krispy Kreme**'s financial statements in Appendix A. On February 2, 2003, what percent of current assets are represented by inventory?

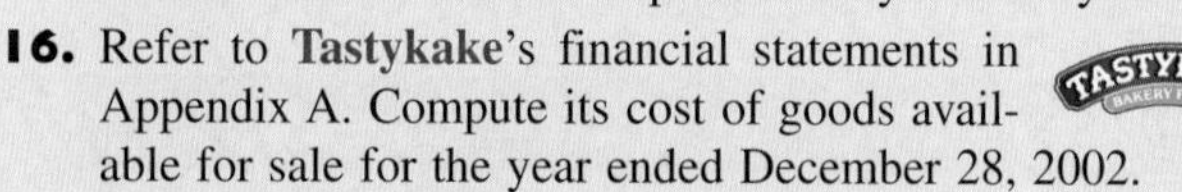

16. Refer to **Tastykake**'s financial statements in Appendix A. Compute its cost of goods available for sale for the year ended December 28, 2002.

17. What percent of **Harley-Davidson**'s current assets are inventory as of December 31, 2002, and as of December 31, 2001?

Harley-Davidson

Red numbers denote Discussion Questions that involve decision-making.

***Homework Manager** repeats all numerical Quick Study assignments on the book's Website with new numbers.*

QUICK STUDY

QS 6-1
Assigning costs to inventory—perpetual systems
P1

Tevin Trader starts a merchandising business on December 1 and enters into three inventory purchases:

December 7	10 units @ $ 6 cost
December 14	20 units @ $12 cost
December 21	15 units @ $14 cost

Trader sells 15 units for $25 each on December 15. Eight of the sold units are from the December 7 purchase and seven are from the December 14 purchase. Trader uses a perpetual inventory system. Determine the costs assigned to the December 31 ending inventory when costs are assigned based on (*a*) FIFO, (*b*) LIFO, (*c*) weighted average, and (*d*) specific identification.

Check (c) $360

QS 6-2
Computing goods available for sale
P1

Senona Company reports beginning inventory of 10 units at $50 each. Every week for four weeks it purchases an additional 10 units at respective costs of $51, $52, $55, and $60 per unit for weeks 1 through 4. Calculate the cost of goods available for sale and the units available for sale for this four-week period.

QS 6-3
Inventory costing methods
P1

A company reports the following beginning inventory and purchases for January. On January 26, 345 units were sold. What is the cost of the 140 units that remain in ending inventory, assuming costs are assigned based on (*a*) FIFO, (*b*) LIFO, and (*c*) weighted average? (Round unit costs to the nearest cent.)

	Units	Unit Cost
Beginning inventory on January 1	310	$3.00
Purchase on January 9	75	3.20
Purchase on January 25	100	3.35

QS 6-4
Contrasting inventory costing methods
A1 

Identify the inventory costing method best described by each of the following separate statements. Assume a period of increasing costs.

1. The preferred method when each unit of product has unique features that markedly affect cost.
2. Matches recent costs against net sales.
3. Provides a tax advantage (deferral) to a corporation.
4. Yields a balance sheet inventory amount often markedly less than its replacement cost.
5. Results in a balance sheet inventory amount approximating replacement cost.

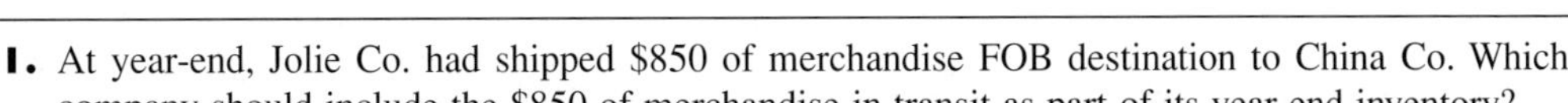

QS 6-5
Inventory ownership
C1

1. At year-end, Jolie Co. had shipped $850 of merchandise FOB destination to China Co. Which company should include the $850 of merchandise in transit as part of its year-end inventory?
2. Jolie Company has shipped $500 of goods to China Co., and China Co. has arranged to sell the goods for Jolie. Identify the consignor and the consignee. Which company should include any unsold goods as part of its inventory?

QS 6-6
Inventory ownership
C1

Crafts Galore, a distributor of handmade gifts, operates out of owner Jenny Finn's house. At the end of the current period, Jenny reports she has 1,500 units (products) in her basement, 30 of which were damaged by water and cannot be sold. She also has another 250 units in her van, ready to deliver per a customer order, terms FOB destination, and another 70 units out on consignment to a friend who owns a retail store. How many units should Jenny include in her company's period-end inventory?

QS 6-7
Inventory costs
C2

A car dealer acquires a used car for $3,000, terms FOB shipping point. Additional costs in obtaining and offering the car for sale include $150 for transportation-in, $200 for import duties, $50 for insurance during shipment, $25 for advertising, and $250 for sales staff salaries. For computing inventory, what cost is assigned to the used car?

QS 6-8
Inventory costs
C2

Duke & Son, antique dealers, purchased the contents of an estate for $37,500. Terms of the purchase were FOB shipping point, and the cost of transporting the goods to Duke & Son's warehouse was $1,200. Duke & Son insured the shipment at a cost of $150. Prior to putting the goods up for sale, they cleaned and refurbished them at a cost of $490. Determine the cost of the inventory acquired from the estate.

QS 6-9
Applying LCM to inventories
P2

Talisman Trading Co. has the following products in its ending inventory. Compute lower of cost or market for inventory (*a*) as a whole and (*b*) applied separately to each product.

Product	Quantity	Cost per Unit	Market per Unit
Mountain bikes	9	$360	$330
Skateboards	12	210	270
Gliders	25	480	420

QS 6-10
Inventory errors
A2 

In taking a physical inventory at the end of year 2005, Nadir Company erroneously forgot to count certain units. Explain how this error affects the following: (*a*) 2005 cost of goods sold, (*b*) 2005 gross profit, (*c*) 2005 net income, (*d*) 2006 net income, (*e*) the combined two-year income, and (*f*) income for years after 2006.

QS 6-11
Analyzing inventory A3

Market Company begins the year with $200,000 of goods in inventory. At year-end, the amount in inventory has increased to $230,000. Cost of goods sold for the year is $1,600,000. Compute Market's inventory turnover and days' sales in inventory. Assume that there are 365 days in the year.

QS 6-12[A]
Costing methods—periodic system P3

Refer to QS 6-1 and assume the periodic inventory system is used. Determine the costs assigned to the December 31 ending inventory when costs are assigned based on (*a*) FIFO, (*b*) LIFO, (*c*) weighted average, and (*d*) specific identification.

QS 6-13[A]
Costing methods—periodic system P3

Refer to QS 6-3 and assume the periodic inventory system is used. Determine the costs assigned to the ending inventory when costs are assigned based on (*a*) FIFO, (*b*) LIFO, and (*c*) weighted average. (Round unit costs to the nearest cent.)

QS 6-14[B]
Estimating inventories—gross profit method
P4

Dooling Store's inventory is destroyed by a fire on September 5, 2005. The following data for year 2005 are available from the accounting records. Estimate the cost of the inventory destroyed.

Jan. 1 inventory	$180,000
Jan. 1 through Sept. 5 purchases (net)	$342,000
Jan. 1 through Sept. 5 sales (net)	$675,000
Year 2005 estimated gross profit rate	42%

Homework Manager *repeats all numerical Exercises on the book's Website with new numbers.* 

EXERCISES

Exercise 6-1
Inventory costing methods—perpetual
P1

Lakia Corporation reported the following current-year purchases and sales data for its only product:

Date	Activities	Units Acquired at Cost		Units Sold at Retail
Jan. 1	Beginning inventory	120 units @ $6.00 =	$ 720	
Jan. 10	Sales			70 units @ $15
Mar. 7	Purchase	200 units @ $5.50 =	1,100	
Mar. 15	Sales			125 units @ $15
July 28	Purchase	500 units @ $5.00 =	2,500	
Oct. 3	Purchase	375 units @ $4.40 =	1,650	
Oct. 5	Sales			600 units @ $15
Dec. 19	Purchase	100 units @ $4.10 =	410	
	Totals	1,295 units	$6,380	795 units

Lakia uses a perpetual inventory system. Ending inventory consists of 500 units, 400 from the July 28 purchase and 100 from the December 19 purchase. Determine the cost assigned to ending inventory and to cost of goods sold using (*a*) specific identification, (*b*) weighted average, (*c*) FIFO, and (*d*) LIFO.

Check Ending inventory: LIFO, $2,498; WA, $2,350

Exercise 6-2
Income effects of inventory methods
A1

Use the data in Exercise 6-1 to prepare comparative income statements for Lakia Corporation (calendar year-end 2005) similar to those shown in Exhibit 6.8 for the four inventory methods. Assume expenses are $1,250. The applicable income tax rate is 30%.

1. Which method yields the highest net income?
2. Does net income using weighted average fall between that using FIFO and LIFO?
3. If costs are rising instead of declining, which method would yield the highest net income?

Exercise 6-3
Inventory costing methods (perpetual)—FIFO and LIFO
P1

Henin Co. reported the following current-year purchases and sales data for its only product:

Date	Activities	Units Acquired at Cost		Units Sold at Retail
Jan. 1	Beginning inventory	100 units @ $10 =	$ 1,000	
Jan. 10	Sales			90 units @ $40
Mar. 14	Purchase	250 units @ $15 =	3,750	
Mar. 15	Sales			140 units @ $40
July 30	Purchase	400 units @ $20 =	8,000	
Oct. 5	Sales			300 units @ $40
Oct. 26	Purchase	600 units @ $25 =	15,000	
	Totals	1,350 units	$27,750	530 units

Henin uses a perpetual inventory system. Determine the costs assigned to ending inventory and to cost of goods sold using (*a*) FIFO and (*b*) LIFO. Compute the gross margin for each method.

Check Ending inventory: LIFO, $18,750

Exercise 6-4
Specific Identification P1

Refer to the data in Exercise 6-3. Assume that ending inventory is made up of 200 units from the March 14 purchase, 20 units from the July 30 purchase, and all the units of the October 26 purchase. Using the specific identification method, calculate (*a*) the cost of goods sold and (*b*) the gross margin.

Exercise 6-5
Lower of cost or market
P2

Tanzy Company's ending inventory includes the following items. Compute the lower of cost or market for ending inventory (*a*) as a whole and (*b*) applied separately to each product.

		Per Unit	
Product	Units	Cost	Market
Helmets	22	$50	$54
Bats	15	78	72
Shoes	36	95	91
Uniforms	40	36	36

Check (*b*) $6,896

Exercise 6-6
Analysis of inventory errors
A2 

Ringo Company had $900,000 of sales in each of three consecutive years 2004–2006, and it purchased merchandise costing $500,000 in each of those years. It also maintained a $200,000 inventory from the beginning to the end of the three-year period. In accounting for inventory, it made an error at the end of year 2004 that caused its year-end 2004 inventory to appear on its statements as $180,000 rather than the correct $200,000.

1. Determine the correct amount of the company's gross profit in each of the years 2004–2006.
2. Prepare comparative income statements as in Exhibit 6.11 to show the effect of this error on the company's cost of goods sold and gross profit for each of the years 2004–2006.

Check 2004 gross profit, $380,000

Exercise 6-7
Inventory turnover and days' sales in inventory
A3  

Use the following information for Ryder Co. to compute inventory turnover for 2005 and 2004, and its days' sales in inventory at December 31, 2005 and 2004. (Round answers to the tenths place.) Comment on Ryder's efficiency in using its assets to increase sales from 2004 to 2005.

	2005	2004	2003
Cost of goods sold	$643,825	$426,650	$391,300
Inventory (Dec. 31)	96,400	86,750	91,500

Exercise 6-8
Comparing LIFO numbers to FIFO numbers; ratio analysis
A1 A3  

Checkers Company uses LIFO for inventory costing and reports the following financial data. It also recomputed inventory and cost of goods sold using FIFO for comparison purposes.

	2005	2004
LIFO inventory	$150	$100
LIFO cost of goods sold	730	670
FIFO inventory	220	125
FIFO cost of goods sold	685	—
Current assets (using LIFO)	210	180
Current liabilities	190	170

Check (1) FIFO: Current ratio, 1.5; Inventory turnover, 4.0 times

1. Compute its current ratio, inventory turnover, and days' sales in inventory for 2005 using (*a*) LIFO numbers and (*b*) FIFO numbers.
2. Comment on and interpret the results of part 1.

Exercise 6-9^A^
Inventory costing—periodic system P3

Refer to Exercise 6-1 and assume the periodic inventory system is used. Determine the costs assigned to ending inventory and to cost of goods sold using (*a*) specific identification, (*b*) weighted average, (*c*) FIFO, and (*d*) LIFO.

Exercise 6-10^A^
Inventory costing—periodic system P3

Refer to Exercise 6-3 and assume the periodic inventory system is used. Determine the costs assigned to ending inventory and to cost of goods sold using (*a*) FIFO, and (*b*) LIFO. Compute the gross margin for each method.

Exercise 6-11^A^
Alternative cost flow assumptions—periodic
P3

Rod & Roy Co. reported the following current-year data for its only product. The company uses a periodic inventory system, and its ending inventory consists of 300 units, 100 from each of the last three purchases. Determine the cost assigned to ending inventory and to cost of goods sold using (*a*) specific identification, (*b*) weighted average, (*c*) FIFO, and (*d*) LIFO. Which method yields the highest net income?

Jan. 1	Beginning inventory	200 units @ $2.00 =	$ 400
Mar. 7	Purchase	440 units @ $2.25 =	990
July 28	Purchase	1080 units @ $2.50 =	2,700
Oct. 3	Purchase	960 units @ $2.80 =	2,688
Dec. 19	Purchase	320 units @ $2.90 =	928
	Totals	3,000 units	$7,706

Check Inventory: LIFO, $625; FIFO, $870

Exercise 6-12^A^
Alternative cost flow assumptions—periodic
P3

Nyhus Gifts reported the following current-year data for its only product. The company uses a periodic inventory system, and its ending inventory consists of 300 units, 100 from each of the last three purchases. Determine the cost assigned to ending inventory and to cost of goods sold using (*a*) specific identification, (*b*) weighted average, (*c*) FIFO, and (*d*) LIFO. Which method yields the lowest net income?

Jan. 1	Beginning inventory	280 units @ $3.00 =	$ 840
Mar. 7	Purchase	600 units @ $2.80 =	1,680
July 28	Purchase	800 units @ $2.50 =	2,000
Oct. 3	Purchase	1,100 units @ $2.30 =	2,530
Dec. 19	Purchase	250 units @ $2.00 =	500
	Totals	3,030 units	$7,550

Check Inventory: LIFO, $896; FIFO, $615

Exercise 6-13[B]
Estimating ending inventory—retail method
P4

In 2005, Wichita Company had retail sales (net) of $130,000. The following additional information is available from its records at the end of 2005. Use the retail inventory method to estimate Wichita's 2005 ending inventory at cost.

	At Cost	At Retail
Beginning inventory	$31,900	$64,200
Cost of goods purchased	57,810	98,400

Check End. Inventory, $17,930

Exercise 6-14[B]
Estimating ending inventory—gross profit method
P4

On January 1, KB Store had $450,000 of inventory at cost. In the first quarter of the year, it purchased $1,590,000 of merchandise, returned $23,100, and paid freight charges of $37,600 on purchased merchandise, terms FOB shipping point. The store's gross profit averages 30%. The store had $2,000,000 of retail sales (net) in the first quarter of the year. Use the gross profit method to estimate its cost of inventory at the end of the first quarter.

PROBLEM SET A

Problem 6-1A
Alternative cost flows—perpetual
P1

Parker Company uses a perpetual inventory system. It entered into the following calendar-year 2005 purchases and sales transactions:

Date	Activities	Units Acquired at Cost	Units Sold at Retail
Jan. 1	Beginning inventory	600 units @ $44/unit	
Feb. 10	Purchase	200 units @ $40/unit	
Mar. 13	Purchase	100 units @ $20/unit	
Mar. 15	Sales		400 units @ $75/unit
Aug. 21	Purchase	160 units @ $60/unit	
Sept. 5	Purchase	280 units @ $48/unit	
Sept. 10	Sales		200 units @ $75/unit
	Totals	1,340 units	600 units

Required

1. Compute cost of goods available for sale and the number of units available for sale.

2. Compute the number of units in ending inventory.

3. Compute the cost assigned to ending inventory using (*a*) FIFO, (*b*) LIFO, (*c*) specific identification (*Note:* The units sold consist of 500 units from beginning inventory and 100 units from the March 13 purchase), and (*d*) weighted average.

Check (3) Ending inventory: FIFO, $33,040; LIFO, $35,440; WA, $34,055;

4. Compute the gross profit earned by the company for each of the four costing methods in part 3.

(4) LIFO gross profit, $21,000

Analysis Component

5. If the company's manager earns a bonus based on a percent of gross profit, which method of inventory costing will the manager likely prefer?

Problem 6-2A
Analysis of inventory errors
A2

mhhe.com/larson

Stover Company's financial statements report the following. Stover recently discovered that in making physical counts of inventory, it had made the following errors: Inventory on December 31, 2004, is understated by $66,000, and inventory on December 31, 2005, is overstated by $30,000.

Key Figures	For Year Ended December 31		
	2004	2005	2006
(*a*) Cost of goods sold	$ 715,000	$ 847,000	$ 770,000
(*b*) Net income	220,000	275,000	231,000
(*c*) Total current assets	1,155,000	1,265,000	1,100,000
(*d*) Total equity	1,287,000	1,430,000	1,232,000

Required

1. For each key financial statement figure—(*a*), (*b*), (*c*), and (*d*) above—prepare a table similar to the following to show the adjustments necessary to correct the reported amounts.

Figure: ________	2004	2005	2006
Reported amount			
Adjustments for: 12/31/2004 error			
12/31/2005 error			
Corrected amount			

Check (1) Corrected net income: 2004, $286,000; 2005, $179,000; 2006, $261,000

Analysis Component

2. What is the error in total net income for the combined three-year period resulting from the inventory errors? Explain.

3. Explain why the understatement of inventory by $66,000 at the end of 2004 results in an understatement of equity by the same amount in that year.

Problem 6-3A
Lower of cost or market
P2

A physical inventory of Ireland Unlimited taken at December 31 reveals the following:

Item	Units	Per Unit Cost	Per Unit Market
Audio equipment			
Receivers	335	$ 90	$ 98
CD players	250	111	100
DVD players	316	86	95
Speakers	194	52	41
Video equipment			
Televisions	470	150	125
VCRs	281	93	84
Video cameras	202	310	322
Car audio equipment			
DVD radios	175	70	84
CD radios	160	97	105

Required

Calculate the lower of cost or market for the inventory (*a*) as a whole, (*b*) by major category, and (*c*) applied separately to each item.

Check (*b*) $270,332; (*c*) $263,024

Problem 6-4A[A]
Alternative cost flows—periodic
P3

Viper Company began year 2005 with 20,000 units of product in its January 1 inventory costing $15 each. It made successive purchases of its product in year 2005 as follows:

Mar. 7	28,000 units @ $18 each
May 25	30,000 units @ $22 each
Aug. 1	20,000 units @ $24 each
Nov. 10	33,000 units @ $27 each

The company uses a periodic inventory system. On December 31, 2005, a physical count reveals that 35,000 units of its product remain in inventory.

Required

1. Compute the number and total cost of the units available for sale in year 2005.
2. Compute the amounts assigned to the 2005 ending inventory and the cost of goods sold using (*a*) FIFO, (*b*) LIFO, and (*c*) weighted average.

Check (2) Cost of goods sold: FIFO, $1,896,000; LIFO, $2,265,000; WA, $2,077,557

Problem 6-5A[A]
Income comparisons and cost flows—periodic
A1 P3

True Blue Corp. sold 5,500 units of its product at $45 per unit in year 2005 and incurred operating expenses of $6 per unit in selling the units. It began the year with 600 units in inventory and made successive purchases of its product as follows:

Jan. 1	Beginning inventory	600 units @ $18 per unit
Feb. 20	Purchase	1,500 units @ $19 per unit
May 16	Purchase	700 units @ $20 per unit
Oct. 3	Purchase	400 units @ $21 per unit
Dec. 11	Purchase	3,300 units @ $22 per unit
	Total	6,500 units

Required

1. Prepare comparative income statements similar to Exhibit 6.8 for the three inventory costing methods of FIFO, LIFO, and weighted average. Include a detailed cost of goods sold section as part of each statement. The company uses a periodic inventory system, and its income tax rate is 30%.
2. How would the financial results from using the three alternative inventory costing methods change if True Blue had been experiencing declining costs in its purchases of inventory?
3. What advantages and disadvantages are offered by using (*a*) LIFO and (*b*) FIFO? Assume the continuing trend of increasing costs.

Check (1) Net income: LIFO, $69,020; FIFO, $71,540; WA, $70,603

Problem 6-6A[B]
Retail inventory method
P4

mhhe.com/larson

The records of Nilson Company provide the following information for the year ended December 31:

	At Cost	At Retail
January 1 beginning inventory	$ 471,350	$ 927,150
Cost of goods purchased	3,276,030	6,279,350
Sales		5,495,700
Sales returns		44,600

Required

1. Use the retail inventory method to estimate the company's year-end inventory.
2. A year-end physical inventory at retail prices yields a total inventory of $1,675,800. Prepare a calculation showing the company's loss from shrinkage at cost and at retail.

Check (1) Inventory, $912,808 cost; (2) Inventory shortage at cost, $41,392

Problem 6-7A[B]
Gross profit method
P4

Wayman Company wants to prepare interim financial statements for the first quarter. The company wishes to avoid making a physical count of inventory. Wayman's gross profit rate averages 35%. The following information for the first quarter is available from its records:

January 1 beginning inventory	$ 300,260
Cost of goods purchased	939,050
Sales	1,191,150
Sales returns	9,450

Check Estimated ending inventory, $471,205

Required

Use the gross profit method to estimate the company's first-quarter ending inventory.

PROBLEM SET B

Problem 6-1B
Alternative cost flows—perpetual
P1 

Venus Company uses a perpetual inventory system. It entered into the following calendar-year 2005 purchases and sales transactions:

Date	Activities	Units Acquired at Cost	Units Sold at Retail
Jan. 1	Beginning inventory	600 units @ $55/unit	
Jan. 10	Purchase	450 units @ $56/unit	
Feb. 13	Purchase	200 units @ $57/unit	
Feb. 15	Sales		430 units @ $90/unit
July 21	Purchase	230 units @ $58/unit	
Aug. 5	Purchase	345 units @ $59/unit	
Aug. 10	Sales		335 units @ $90/unit
	Total	1,825 units	765 units

Required

1. Compute cost of goods available for sale and the number of units available for sale.

2. Compute the number of units in ending inventory.

Check (3) Ending inventory: FIFO, $61,055; LIFO, $59,250; WA, $60,293;

3. Compute the cost assigned to ending inventory using (*a*) FIFO, (*b*) LIFO, (*c*) specific identification (*Note:* The units sold consist of 600 units from beginning inventory and 165 units from the February 13 purchase), and (*d*) weighted average.

(4) LIFO gross profit, $24,805

4. Compute gross profit earned by the company for each of the four costing methods in part 3.

Analysis Component

5. If the company's manager earns a bonus based on a percent of gross profit, which method of inventory costing will the manager likely prefer?

Problem 6-2B
Analysis of inventory errors
A2 

Hector Company's financial statements report the following. Hector recently discovered that in making physical counts of inventory, it had made the following errors: Inventory on December 31, 2004, is overstated by $17,000, and inventory on December 31, 2005, is understated by $25,000.

	For Year Ended December 31		
Key Figures	2004	2005	2006
(*a*) Cost of goods sold	$205,200	$212,800	$196,030
(*b*) Net income	174,800	211,270	183,910
(*c*) Total current assets	266,000	276,500	262,950
(*d*) Total equity	304,000	316,000	336,000

Required

1. For each key financial statement figure—(*a*), (*b*), (*c*), and (*d*) above—prepare a table similar to the following to show the adjustments necessary to correct the reported amounts.

Figure: ________	2004	2005	2006
Reported amount	________	________	________
Adjustments for: 12/31/2004 error	________	________	________
12/31/2005 error	________	________	________
Corrected amount	========	========	========

Check (1) Corrected net income: 2004, $157,800; 2005, $253,270; 2006, $158,910

Analysis Component

2. What is the error in total net income for the combined three-year period resulting from the inventory errors? Explain.

3. Explain why the overstatement of inventory by $17,000 at the end of 2004 results in an overstatement of equity by the same amount in that year.

Problem 6-3B
Lower of cost or market

P2

A physical inventory of Office Deals taken at December 31 reveals the following:

	Item	Units	Per Unit Cost	Per Unit Market
3	Office furniture			
4	Desks	436	$261	$305
5	Credenzas	295	227	256
6	Chairs	587	49	43
7	Bookshelves	321	93	82
8	Filing cabinets			
9	Two-drawer	214	81	70
10	Four-drawer	398	135	122
11	Lateral	175	104	118
12	Office equipment			
13	Fax machines	430	168	200
14	Copiers	545	317	288
15	Telephones	352	125	117

Required

Calculate the lower of cost or market for the inventory (*a*) as a whole, (*b*) by major category, and (*c*) applied separately to each item.

Check (*b*) $607,707; (*c*) $584,444

Problem 6-4B[A]
Alternative cost flows—periodic

P3

Elfrink Co. began year 2005 with 6,300 units of product in its January 1 inventory costing $35 each. It made successive purchases of its product in year 2005 as follows:

Jan. 4	10,500 units @ $33 each
May 18	13,000 units @ $32 each
July 9	12,000 units @ $29 each
Nov. 21	15,500 units @ $26 each

The company uses a periodic inventory system. On December 31, 2005, a physical count reveals that 16,500 units of its product remain in inventory.

Required

1. Compute the number and total cost of the units available for sale in year 2005.

2. Compute the amounts assigned to the 2005 ending inventory and the cost of goods sold using (*a*) FIFO, (*b*) LIFO, and (*c*) weighted average.

Check (2) Cost of goods sold: FIFO, $1,302,000; LIFO, $1,176,900; WA, $1,234,681

Problem 6-5B[A]
Income comparisons and cost flows—periodic

A1 P3

Rikkers Corp. sold 2,500 units of its product at $98 per unit in year 2005 and incurred operating expenses of $14 per unit in selling the units. It began the year with 740 units in inventory and made successive purchases of its product as follows:

Jan. 1	Beginning inventory	740 units @ $58 per unit
April 2	Purchase	700 units @ $59 per unit
June 14	Purchase	600 units @ $61 per unit
Aug. 29	Purchase	500 units @ $64 per unit
Nov. 18	Purchase	800 units @ $65 per unit
	Total	3,340 units

Required

Check (1) Net income: LIFO, $40,500; FIFO, $44,805; WA, $42,519

1. Prepare comparative income statements similar to Exhibit 6.8 for the three inventory costing methods of FIFO, LIFO, and weighted average. Include a detailed cost of goods sold section as part of each statement. The company uses a periodic inventory system, and its income tax rate is 25%.
2. How would the financial results from using the three alternative inventory costing methods change if Rikkers had been experiencing decreasing prices in its purchases of inventory?
3. What advantages and disadvantages are offered by using (*a*) LIFO and (*b*) FIFO? Assume the continuing trend of increasing costs.

Problem 6-6B[B]
Retail inventory method
P4

The records of Alaina Co. provide the following information for the year ended December 31:

	At Cost	At Retail
January 1 beginning inventory	$ 81,670	$114,610
Cost of goods purchased	492,250	751,730
Sales		786,120
Sales returns		4,480

Required

Check (1) Inventory, $55,902 cost; (2) Inventory shortage at cost, $4,059

1. Use the retail inventory method to estimate the company's year-end inventory.
2. A year-end physical inventory at retail prices yields a total inventory of $78,550. Prepare a calculation showing the company's loss from shrinkage at cost and at retail.

Problem 6-7B[B]
Gross profit method
P4

Ernst Equipment Co. wants to prepare interim financial statements for the first quarter. The company wishes to avoid making a physical count of inventory. Ernst's gross profit rate averages 30%. The following information for the first quarter is available from its records:

January 1 beginning inventory	$ 752,880
Cost of goods purchased	2,159,630
Sales	3,710,250
Sales returns	74,200

Required

Check Estim. ending inventory, $367,275

Use the gross profit method to estimate the company's first quarter ending inventory.

PROBLEM SET C

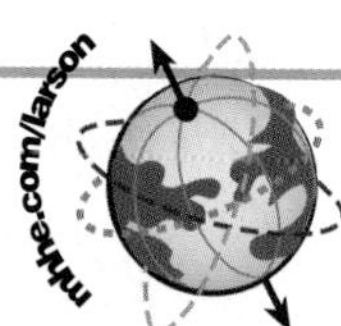

Problem Set C is available at the book's Website to further reinforce and assess your learning.

SERIAL PROBLEM

Success Systems 

(This serial problem began in Chapter 1 and continues through most of the book. If previous chapter segments were not completed, the serial problem can begin at this point.)

Selected accounts and balances for the three months ended March 31, 2005, for Success Systems follows:

January 1 beginning inventory	$ 0
Cost of goods sold	14,052
March 31 ending inventory	704

Required

1. Compute inventory turnover and days' sales in inventory for the three months ended March 31, 2005.
2. Assess its performance if competitors average 10 times for inventory turnover and 29 days for days' sales in inventory.

BEYOND THE NUMBERS

REPORTING IN ACTION

C2 A3 

BTN 6-1 Refer to **Krispy Kreme**'s financial statements in Appendix A to answer the following:

Required

1. What amount of inventories did Krispy Kreme hold as a current asset on February 2, 2003? On February 3, 2002?
2. Inventories represent what percent of total assets on February 2, 2003? On February 3, 2002?
3. Comment on the relative size of Krispy Kreme's inventories compared to its other types of assets.
4. What accounting method did Krispy Kreme use to compute inventory amounts on its balance sheet?
5. Compute inventory turnover for fiscal year ended February 2, 2003, and days' sales in inventory as of February 2, 2003. (*Note:* Cost of goods sold is titled operating expenses for Krispy Kreme.)

Roll On

6. Access Krispy Kreme's financial statements for fiscal years ended after February 2, 2003, from its Website (KrispyKreme.com) or the SEC's EDGAR database (www.SEC.gov). Answer questions 1 through 5 using the current Krispy Kreme information and compare results to those prior years.

COMPARATIVE ANALYSIS

A3 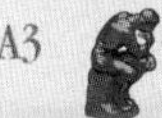

BTN 6-2 Key comparative figures ($ thousands) for both **Krispy Kreme** and **Tastykake** follow:

	Krispy Kreme			Tastykake		
Key Figures	Current Year	One Year Prior	Two Years Prior	Current Year	One Year Prior	Two Years Prior
Inventory	$ 24,365	$ 16,159	$ 12,031	$ 6,777	$ 8,412	$ 5,930
Cost of sales	381,489	316,946	250,690	111,187	103,297	105,036

Required

1. Calculate inventory turnover for both companies for the most recent two years shown.
2. Calculate days' sales in inventory for both companies for the three years shown.
3. Comment on and interpret your findings from parts 1 and 2.

ETHICS CHALLENGE

A1  

BTN 6-3 Golf Away Corp. is a retail sports store carrying golf apparel and equipment. The store is at the end of its second year of operation and is struggling. A major problem is that its cost of inventory has continually increased in the past two years. In the first year of operations, the store assigned inventory costs using LIFO. A loan agreement the store has with its bank, its prime source of financing, requires the store to maintain a certain profit margin and current ratio. The store's owner is currently looking over Golf Away's preliminary financial statements for its second year. The numbers are not favorable. The only way the store can meet the required financial ratios agreed on with the bank is to change from LIFO to FIFO. The store originally decided on LIFO because of its tax advantages. The owner recalculates ending inventory using FIFO and submits those numbers and statements to the loan officer at the bank for the required bank review. The owner thankfully reflects on the available latitude in choosing the inventory costing method.

Required

1. How does Golf Away's use of FIFO improve its net profit margin and current ratio?
2. Is the action by Golf Away's owner ethical? Explain.

COMMUNICATING IN PRACTICE

BTN 6-4 You are a financial adviser with a client in the wholesale produce business that just completed its first year of operations. Due to weather conditions, the cost of acquiring produce to resell has escalated during the later part of this period. Your client, Jariah Gish, mentions that because the business sells perishable goods, she has striven to maintain a FIFO flow of goods. Although sales are good, the increasing cost of inventory has put the business in a tight cash position. Gish has expressed concern regarding the ability of the business to meet income tax obligations.

Required

Prepare a memorandum that identifies, explains, and justifies the inventory method you recommend your client, Ms. Gish, adopt.

TAKING IT TO THE NET

A3 

mhhe.com/larson

BTN 6-5 Access the 2002 annual 10-K report for **Oakley, Inc.** (Ticker OO), filed on March 31, 2003, from the EDGAR filings at www.sec.gov.

Required

1. What product does Oakley sell that is especially popular with college students?
2. What inventory method does Oakley use? (*Hint:* See the notes to its financial statements.)
3. Compute Oakley's gross margin and gross margin ratio for the current year.
4. Compute Oakley's inventory turnover and days' sales in inventory for the current year.

TEAMWORK IN ACTION

Point: Step 1 allows four choices or areas for expertise. Larger teams will have some duplication of choice, but the specific identification method should not be duplicated.

BTN 6-6 Each team member has the responsibility to become an expert on an inventory method. This expertise will be used to facilitate teammates' understanding of the concepts relevant to that method.

1. Each learning team member should select an area for expertise by choosing one of the following inventory methods: specific identification, LIFO, FIFO, or weighted average.
2. Form expert teams made up of students who have selected the same area of expertise. The instructor will identify where each expert team will meet.
3. Using the following data, each expert team must collaborate to develop a presentation that illustrates the relevant concepts and procedures for its inventory method. Each team member must write the presentation in a format that can be shown to the learning team.

Data

Wiseman Corp. uses a perpetual inventory system. It had the following beginning inventory and current year purchases of its product:

Jan. 1	Beginning inventory	50 units @ $10 =	$ 500
Jan. 14	Purchase	150 units @ $12 =	1,800
Apr. 30	Purchase	200 units @ $15 =	3,000
Sept. 26	Purchase	300 units @ $20 =	6,000

Wiseman Corp. transacted sales on the following dates at a $35 per unit sales price:

Jan. 10	30 units	(specific cost: 30 @ $10)
Feb. 15	100 units	(specific cost: 100 @ $12)
Oct. 5	350 units	(specific cost: 100 @ $15 and 250 @ $20)

Concepts and Procedures to Illustrate in Expert Presentation

a. Identify and compute the costs to assign to the units sold.
b. Identify and compute the costs to assign to the units in ending inventory.
c. How likely is it that this inventory costing method will reflect the actual physical flow of goods? How relevant is that factor in determining whether this is an acceptable method to use?
d. What is the impact of this method versus others in determining net income and income taxes?
e. How closely does the ending inventory amount reflect replacement cost?

4. Re-form learning teams. In rotation, each expert is to present to the team the presentation developed in part 3. Experts are to encourage and respond to questions.

BUSINESS WEEK ACTIVITY

A3

mhhe.com/larson

BTN 6-7 Read the article "iPod: A Seed for Growth?" from the August 27, 2002, issue of ***Business Week***. (The book's Website provides a free link.)

Required

1. What percent of the U.S. market for digital music players does **Apple** have?
2. What firms are emerging with products to compete with the Apple iPod?
3. Why might the **Toshiba** product hold an inventory cost edge over the Apple iPod?
4. How does Apple expect its unit sales of the iPod to grow from 2002 to 2006?

ENTREPRENEURIAL DECISION

A3 

BTN 6-8 Review the chapter's opening feature highlighting Mike Becker and his company, **FunKo**. Assume that FunKo consistently maintains an inventory level of $500,000, meaning that its average and ending inventory levels are the same. Also assume its annual cost of sales is $1,050,000. To cut costs, Becker proposes to slash inventory to a constant level of $125,000 with no impact on cost of sales.

Required

1. Compute the company's inventory turnover and its days' sales in inventory under (*a*) current conditions and (*b*) proposed conditions.

2. Evaluate and comment on the merits of Becker's proposal given your analysis in part 1. Identify any concerns you would express about the proposal.

HITTING THE ROAD

C1 C2 

BTN 6-9 Visit four retail stores with another classmate. In each store, identify whether the store uses a bar-coding system to help manage its inventory. Try to find at least one store that does not use bar-coding. If a store does not use bar-coding, ask the store's manager or clerk whether he or she knows which type of inventory method the store employs. Create a table that shows columns for the name of store visited, type of merchandise sold, use or nonuse of bar-coding, and the inventory method used if bar-coding is not employed. You might also inquire as to what the store's inventory turnover is and how often physical inventory is taken.

GLOBAL DECISION

A3 

BTN 6-10 Key figures (pesos millions) for **Grupo Bimbo** (GrupoBimbo.com) follow:

Key Figures	Current Year	One Year Prior	Two Years Prior
Inventory	905	767	725
Cost of sales	19,156	15,708	13,939

Required

1. Use these data and those from BTN 6-2 to compute (*a*) inventory turnover and (*b*) days' sales in inventory for the most recent two years shown for **Grupo Bimbo**, **Krispy Kreme**, and **Tastykake**.

2. Comment on and interpret your findings from part 1.

"I still want to achieve something greater"—Devin Lazerine

7 Accounting Information Systems

A Look Back

Chapters 5 and 6 focused on merchandising activities and accounting for inventory. We explained both the perpetual and periodic inventory systems, accounting for inventory transactions, and methods for assigning costs to inventory.

A Look at This Chapter

This chapter emphasizes accounting information systems. We describe fundamental system principles, the system's components, use of special journals and subsidiary ledgers, and technology-based systems. We also briefly discuss segment reporting.

A Look Ahead

Chapter 8 focuses on internal controls and accounting for cash and cash equivalents. We explain good internal control procedures and their importance for accounting.

CAP

Conceptual

C1 Identify fundamental principles of accounting information systems. *(p. 262)*

C2 Identify components of accounting information systems. *(p. 263)*

C3 Explain the goals and uses of special journals. *(p. 265)*

C4 Describe the use of controlling accounts and subsidiary ledgers. *(p. 266)*

C5 Explain how technology-based information systems impact accounting. *(p. 276)*

Analytical

A1 Compute segment return on assets and use it to evaluate segment performance. *(p. 278)*

Procedural

P1 Journalize and post transactions using special journals. *(p. 267)*

P2 Prepare and prove the accuracy of subsidiary ledgers. *(p. 269)*

Decision Feature

Wrapping Up Rap Deals

CALABASAS, CA—Devin Lazerine's not your typical rap mogul, but then again, he is only 20. Devin is the founder of ***Rap-Up* (Rap-Up.com),** a nationwide hip-hop and R&B magazine that he launched four years ago.

Lazerine admits he has had to overcome many hurdles, including those of publishers. "They [publishers] don't know too much about hip-hop music. They think it's vulgar and something they don't want to touch at all." But overcome he has—today, *Rap-Up* has a circulation of more than 200,000. Lazerine did not reveal revenues, but his per monthly issues costs are about $120,000.

Lazerine says his path to success was rocky and with constant challenges. One of those challenges was implementing an accounting system. Controls had to be implemented, technology had to be purchased, and information had to be collected.

Interestingly, Lazerine's age was a barrier in the rap industry. He learned to avoid phone contact, afraid his youthful voice would hurt his credibility. "I was at school once when they [record publicists] called," admits Lazerine. "My mom picked up and said where I was, and they were like, 'What? I thought he was the editor-in-chief of a magazine?' "

Another hurdle for Lazerine was to address the need to track business transactions. He eventually set up several special journals for this purpose, including subsidiary ledgers to track subscribers and their balances owed.

What does the future hold for this rap mogul? When asked about his role models, Lazerine doesn't rattle off Ludacris or Ja Rule; instead, he mentions J Records head Clive Davis and Def Jam founder Russell Simmons. Thus, his interest in the business side of rap is natural. Lazerine adds that understanding and using accounting information systems help him direct and plan *Rap-Up* operations. "My ultimate goal," reveals Lazerine, "is to become a music mogul/entrepreneur." With his current record, he may well become hip-hop's business star.

[Sources: *Rap-Up Website,* January 2004; *Entrepreneur,* November 2002; *Folio Magazine,* May 1, 2002; *Entertainment,* July 19, 2001; *USA Weekend,* March 9, 2003.]

With increases in the number and complexity of business activities, the demands placed on accounting information systems increase. Accounting information systems must meet this challenge in an efficient and effective manner. In this chapter, we learn about fundamental principles guiding information systems, and we study components making up these systems. We also explain procedures that use special journals and subsidiary ledgers to make accounting information systems more efficient. An understanding of the details of accounting reports makes us better decision makers when using financial information, and it improves our ability to analyze and interpret financial statements.

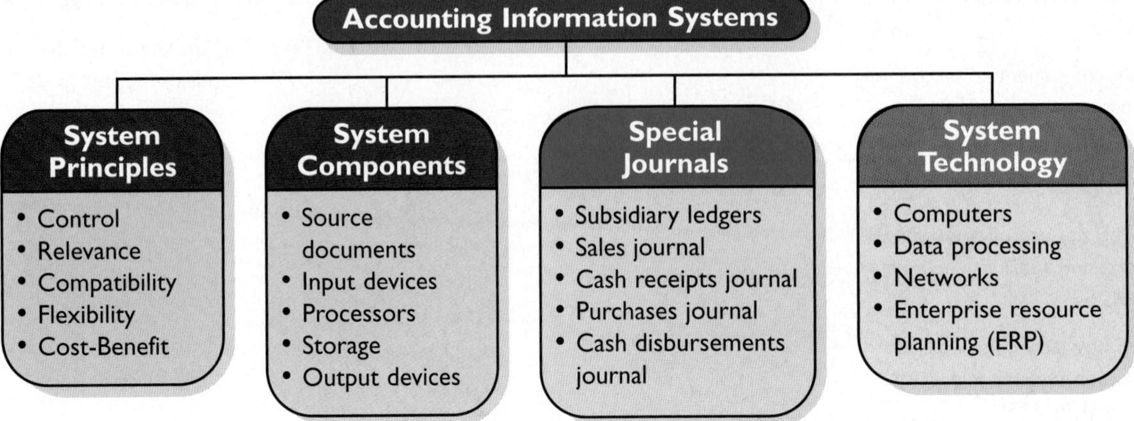

Fundamental System Principles

C1 Identify fundamental principles of accounting information systems.

Accounting information systems collect and process data from transactions and events, organize them in useful reports, and communicate results to decision makers. With the increasing complexity of business and the growing need for information, accounting information systems are more important than ever. All decision makers need to have a basic knowledge of how accounting information systems work. This knowledge gives decision makers a competitive edge as they gain a better understanding of information constraints, measurement limitations, and potential applications. It allows them to make more informed decisions and to better balance the risks and returns of different strategies. This section explains five basic principles of accounting information systems, shown in Exhibit 7.1.

Exhibit 7.1

System Principles

Control
Relevance
Compatibility
Flexibility
Cost-Benefit Principle
System Principles

Control Principle

Managers need to control and monitor business activities. The **control principle** prescribes that an accounting information system have internal controls. **Internal controls** are methods and procedures allowing managers to control and monitor business activities. They include policies to direct operations toward common goals, procedures to ensure reliable financial reports, safeguards to protect company assets, and methods to achieve compliance with laws and regulations. Chapter 8 describes detailed control procedures.

Point: A hacker stole 300,000 credit card numbers from online music retailer **CDUniverse** due to internal control failure.

Relevance Principle

Decision makers need relevant information to make informed decisions. The **relevance principle** prescribes that an accounting information system report useful, understandable, timely, and pertinent information for effective decision making. The system must be designed to capture data that make a difference in decisions. To ensure this, we must consider all decision makers when identifying relevant information for disclosure.

Compatibility Principle

Accounting information systems must be consistent with the aims of a company. The **compatibility principle** prescribes that an accounting information system conform with a company's activities, personnel, and structure. It also must adapt to a company's unique characteristics. The system must not be intrusive but must work in harmony with and be driven by company goals. Most start-up entrepreneurs require only a simple information system. **Harley-Davidson**, on the other hand, demands both a merchandising and a manufacturing information system able to assemble data from its global operations.

Flexibility Principle

Accounting information systems must be able to adjust to changes. The **flexibility principle** prescribes that an accounting information system be able to adapt to changes in the company, business environment, and needs of decisions makers. Technological advances, competitive pressures, consumer tastes, regulations, and company activities constantly evolve. A system must be designed to adapt to these changes.

Cost-Benefit Principle

The **cost-benefit principle** prescribes that the benefits from an activity in an accounting information system outweigh the costs of that activity. The costs and benefits of an activity such as producing a specific report will impact the decisions of both external and internal users. Decisions regarding other systems principles (control, relevance, compatibility, and flexibility) are also affected by the cost-benefit principle.

Components of Accounting Systems

Accounting information systems consist of people, records, methods, and equipment. The systems are designed to capture information about a company's transactions and to provide output including financial, managerial, and tax reports. All accounting information systems have these same goals, and thus share some basic components. These components apply whether or not a system is heavily computerized, yet the components of computerized systems usually provide more accuracy, speed, efficiency, and convenience than those of manual systems.

C2 Identify components of accounting information systems.

The five basic **components of accounting systems** are source documents, input devices, information processors, information storage, and output devices. Exhibit 7.2 shows these components as a series of steps, yet we know that much two-way communication occurs between many of these components. We briefly describe each of these key components in this section.

Exhibit 7.2

Accounting System Components

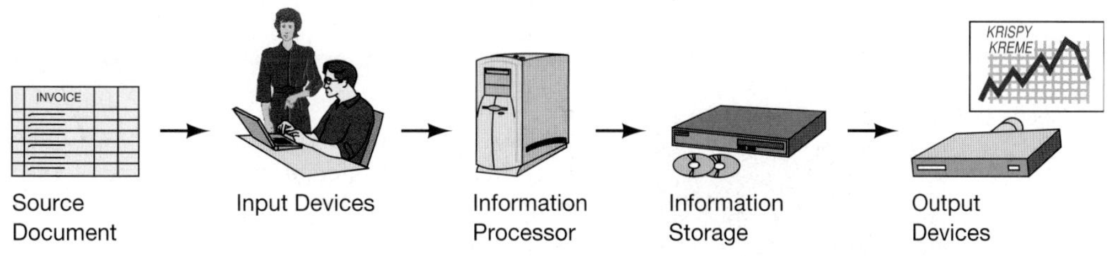

Source Documents

We introduced source documents in Chapters 1 and 2 and explained their importance for both business transactions and information collection. Source documents provide the basic information processed by an accounting system. Examples of source documents include bank statements and checks, invoices from suppliers, billings to customers, cash register files, and employee earnings records. Source documents can be paper, although they increasingly are taking the form of electronic files and Web communications. A growing number of companies are sending documents directly from their systems to their customers' and suppliers' systems. The Web is playing a major role in this transformation from paper-based to *paperless* systems.

Accurate source documents are crucial to accounting information systems. Input of faulty or incomplete information seriously impairs the reliability and relevance of the information system. We commonly refer to this as "garbage in, garbage out." Information systems are set up with attention on control procedures to limit the possibility of entering faulty data in the system.

Decision Insight

Remote Input Scanners are increasingly embedded in cell phones and other handheld devices to gain access to Websites equipped with bar code readers. The phones can scan the bar codes in and then the user gains access to sites that market products and services.

Input Devices

Input devices capture information from source documents and enable its transfer to the system's information processing component. These devices often involve converting data on source documents from written or electronic form to a form usable for the system. Journal entries, both electronic and paper based, are a type of input device. Keyboards, scanners, and modems are some of the most common input devices in practice today. For example, bar code readers capture code numbers and transfer them to the organization's computer for processing. Moreover, a scanner can capture writing samples and other input directly from source documents.

Point: Understanding a manual accounting system is useful in understanding an electronic system.

Controls are used to ensure that only authorized individuals input data to the system. Controls increase the system's reliability and allow information to be traced back to its source.

Information Processors

Information processors are systems that interpret, transform, and summarize information for use in analysis and reporting. An important part of an information processor in accounting systems is professional judgment. Accounting principles are never so structured that they limit the need for professional judgment. Other parts of an information processor include journals, ledgers, working papers, and posting procedures. Each assists in transforming raw data to useful information.

Increasingly, computer technology (both computing hardware and software) is assisting manual information processors. This assistance is freeing accounting professionals to take on increased analysis, interpretive, and managerial roles. Web-based application service providers (ASPs) offer another type of information processor.

Information Storage

Point: A financial accounting database can be designed to support a wide range of internal reports for management.

Information storage is the accounting system component that keeps data in a form accessible to information processors. After being input and processed, data are stored for use in future analyses and reports. The database must be accessible to preparers of periodic financial reports. Auditors rely on this database when they audit both financial statements and a company's controls. Companies also maintain files of source documents.

Older systems consisted almost exclusively of paper documents, but most modern systems depend on electronic storage devices. Advances in information storage enable accounting systems to increasingly store more detailed data. This means managers have more

Decision Insight

Geek Chic Cyberfashion pioneers are creating geek chic, a kind of wearable computer. Cyberfashion draws on digital cellular phones, lithium batteries, and miniature monitors. Special thread is woven into clothing to carry low-voltage signals from one part of the system to another, and fabric keyboards are sewn into clothes. These creations give new meaning to the term *software*.

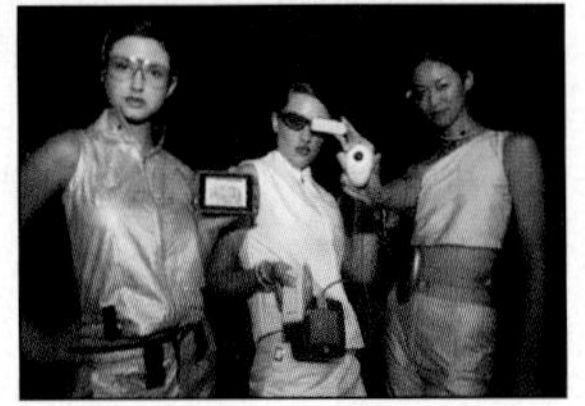

data to access and work with in planning and controlling business activities. Note that information storage can be online, meaning that data can be accessed whenever, and from wherever, it is needed. Off-line storage means access often requires assistance and authorization. Information storage is increasingly augmented by Web sources such as SEC databases, benchmarking services, and financial and product markets.

Decision Insight

Direct Output A screenless computer display, called *virtual retinal display* (VRD), scans rows of pixels directly onto the user's retina by means of a laser. VRDs can simulate three-dimensional virtual worlds, including 3D financial graphics.

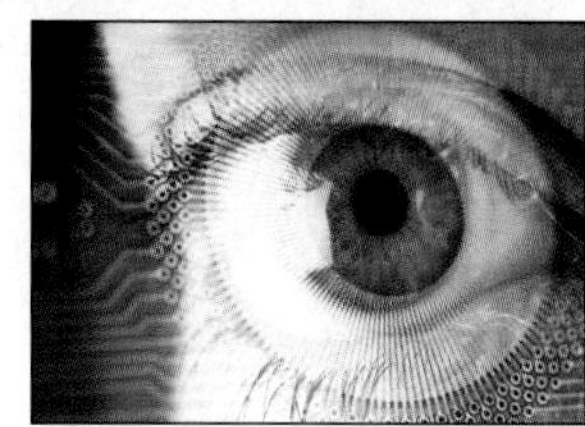

Output Devices

Output devices are the means to take information out of an accounting system and make it available to users. Common output devices are printers, monitors, LCD projectors, and Web communications. Output devices provide users a variety of items including graphics, analysis reports, bills to customers, checks to suppliers, employee paychecks, financial statements, and internal reports. When requests for output occur, an information processor takes the needed data from a database and prepares the necessary report, which is then sent to an output device. A special type of output is an electronic funds transfer (EFT). One example is the transfer of payroll from the company's bank account to its employees' bank accounts. This requires an interface to allow a company's accounting system to send payroll data directly to the bank's accounting system. This interface can involve a company recording its payroll data on CD and forwarding it to the bank. The bank then uses this output to transfer wages earned to employees' accounts.

Decision Ethics

Accountant Your client requests advice in purchasing software for its accounting system. You have been offered a 10% commission by a software company for each purchase of its system by one of your clients. Does this commission arrangement affect your evaluation of software? Do you tell your client about the commission arrangement?

Answer—p. 287

Quick Check

1. Identify the five primary components of an accounting information system.
2. What is the aim of information processors in an accounting system?
3. How are data in the information storage component of an accounting system used?

Answers—p. 288

Special Journals in Accounting

This section describes the underlying records of accounting information systems. Designed correctly, these records support efficiency in processing transactions and events. They are part of all systems in various forms and are increasingly electronic. Even in technologically advanced systems, a basic understanding of the records we describe in this section aids in using, interpreting, and applying accounting information. It also improves our knowledge of computer-based systems. Remember that all accounting systems have common purposes and internal workings whether or not they depend on technology.

C3 Explain the goals and uses of special journals.

This section focuses on special journals and subsidiary ledgers that are an important part of accounting systems. We describe how special journals are used to capture transactions, and we explain how subsidiary ledgers are set up to capture details of accounts. This section uses a *perpetual* inventory system, and the special journals are set up using this system. Appendix 7A describes the change in special journals required for a *periodic* system. We also include a note at the bottom of each of the special journals explaining the change required if a company uses a periodic system.

Basics of Special Journals

Point: Companies can use as many special journals as necessary given their unique business activities.

A **general journal** is an all-purpose journal in which we can record any transaction. Use of a general journal for all transactions is usually more costly for a business *and* is a less effective control procedure. Moreover, for less technologically advanced systems, use of a general journal requires that each debit and each credit entered be individually posted to its respective ledger account. To enhance internal control and reduce costs, transactions are organized into common groups. A **special journal** is used to record and post transactions of similar type. Most transactions of a merchandiser, for instance, can be categorized into the journals shown in Exhibit 7.3. This section assumes the use of these four special journals along with the general journal. The general journal continues to be used for transactions not covered by special journals and for adjusting, closing, and correcting entries. We show in the following discussion that special journals are *efficient tools in helping journalize and post transactions.* This is done, for instance, by accumulating debits and credits of similar transactions, which allows posting of amounts as column *totals* rather than as individual amounts. The advantage of this system increases as the number of transactions increases. Special journals allow an *efficient division of labor,* which is also an effective control procedure.

Point: A specific transaction is recorded in only *one* journal.

Exhibit 7.3

Using Special Journals with a General Journal

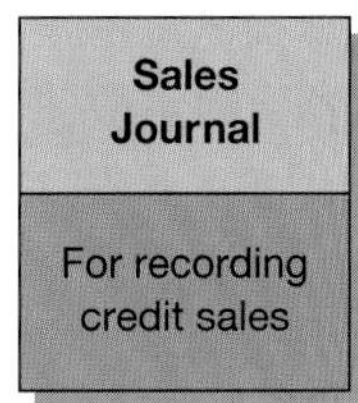

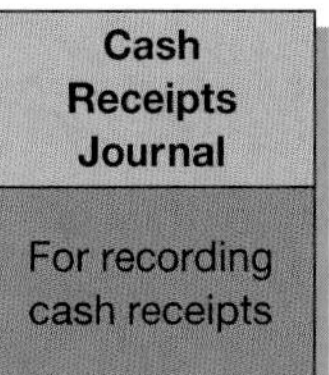

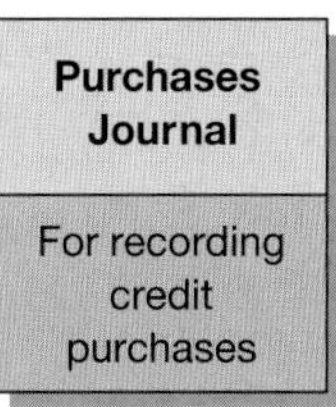

Cash Disbursement Journal

For recording cash payments

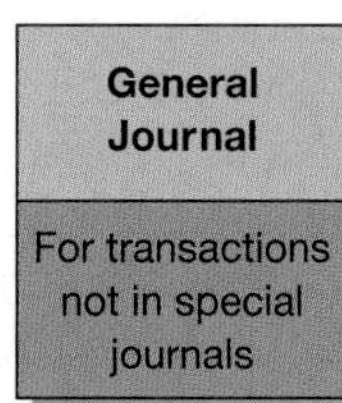

It is important to note that special journals and subsidiary ledgers *are designed in a manner that is best suited for each business.* The most likely candidates for special journal status are recurring transactions—for many businesses those are sales, cash receipts, purchases, and cash disbursements. However, good systems design for a business could involve collapsing sales and cash receipts in one journal, or purchases and cash disbursement in another. It could also involve adding more special journals or additional subsidiary ledgers for other recurring transactions. This design decision extends to journal and ledger format. That is, the selection on number of columns, column headings, and so forth is based on what is best suited for each business. Thus, you should read the following sections as one example of a common systems design, but not the only design.

Subsidiary Ledgers

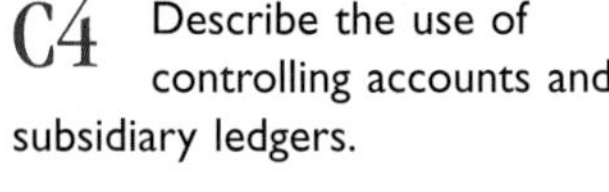

C4 Describe the use of controlling accounts and subsidiary ledgers.

To understand special journals, it is necessary to understand the workings of a **subsidiary ledger,** which is a list of individual accounts with a common characteristic. A subsidiary ledger contains detailed information on specific accounts in the general ledger. Information systems often include several subsidiary ledgers. Two of the most important are:

- *Accounts receivable ledger*—stores transaction data of individual customers.
- *Accounts payable ledger*—stores transaction data of individual suppliers.

Individual accounts in subsidiary ledgers are often arranged alphabetically, which is the approach taken here. We describe accounts receivable and accounts payable ledgers in this section. Our discussion of special journals uses these ledgers.

Topic Tackler 7-1

Accounts Receivable Ledger When we recorded credit sales in prior chapters, we debited (increased) Accounts Receivable. When a company has more than one credit customer, the accounts receivable records must show how much *each* customer purchased, paid, and has yet to pay. This information is collected by keeping a separate account receivable for each credit customer. A separate account for each customer *could* be kept in the general ledger with the other financial statement accounts, but this is uncommon. Instead, the general ledger usually has a single Accounts Receivable account, and a *subsidiary ledger* is set up to keep a separate account for each customer. This subsidiary ledger is called the **accounts receivable ledger** (also called *accounts receivable subsidiary ledger* or *customers ledger*), and it can exist in electronic or paper form.

Exhibit 7.4 shows the relation between the Accounts Receivable account and its individual accounts in the subsidiary ledger. After all items are posted, the balance in the Accounts Receivable account must equal the sum of all balances of its customers' accounts. The Accounts Receivable account is said to control the accounts receivable ledger and is called a **controlling account.** Since the accounts receivable ledger is a supplementary record controlled by an account in the general ledger, it is called a *subsidiary* ledger.

Point: When a general ledger account has a subsidiary ledger, any transaction that impacts one of them also impacts the other—some refer to this as *general and subsidiaries ledgers kept in tandem.*

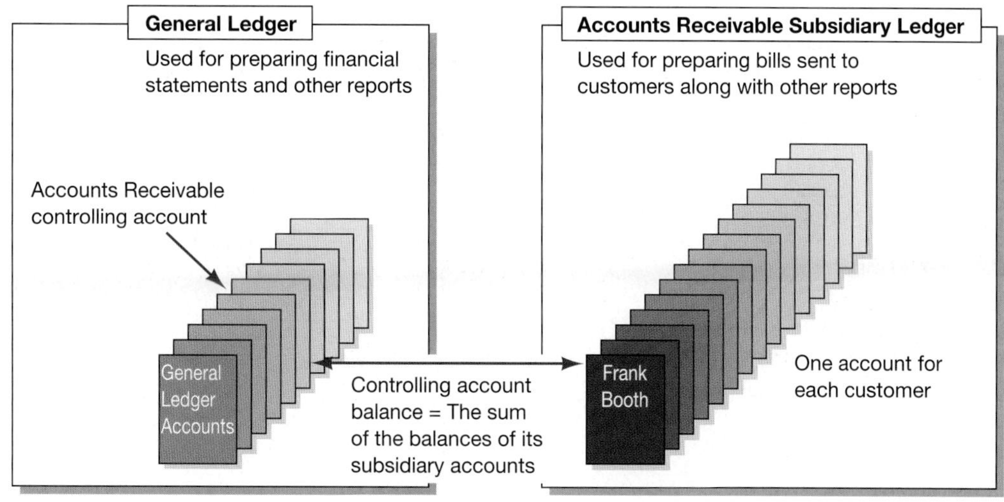

Exhibit 7.4

Accounts Receivable Controlling Account and Its Subsidiary Ledger

Accounts Payable Ledger There are other controlling accounts and subsidiary ledgers. We know, for example, that many companies buy on credit from several suppliers. This means that companies must keep a separate account for each supplier by keeping an Accounts Payable controlling account in the general ledger and a separate account for each supplier (creditor) in an **accounts payable ledger** (also called *accounts payable subsidiary ledger* or *creditors ledger*).

Point: Subsidiary ledgers: (1) remove excessive details from general ledger, (2) provide up-to-date info on customer or other specific account balances, (3) aid in error identification for individual accounts, and (4) help with division of labor (recordkeeping tasks).

Other Subsidiary Ledgers Subsidiary ledgers are common for several other accounts. A company with many classes of equipment, for example, might keep only one Equipment account in its general ledger, but its Equipment account would control a subsidiary ledger in which each class of equipment is recorded in a separate account. Similar treatment is common for investments, inventory, and any accounts needing separate detailed records. **Arctic Cat** reports sales information by product line in its annual report. Yet its accounting system keeps much more detailed sales records. Arctic Cat, for instance, sells hundreds of different products and must be able to analyze the sales performance of each. This detail can be captured by many different general ledger sales accounts but is instead captured by using supplementary records that function like subsidiary ledgers. Overall, subsidiary ledgers are applied in many different ways to ensure that the accounting system captures sufficient details to support analyses that decision makers need.

Sales Journal

A typical **sales journal** is used to record sales of inventory *on credit.* Sales of inventory for cash are not recorded in a sales journal but in a cash receipts journal. Sales of noninventory assets on credit are recorded in the general journal.

P1 Journalize and post transactions using special journals.

Topic Tackler 7-2

Journalizing Credit sale transactions are recorded with information about each sale entered separately in a sales journal. This information is often taken from a copy of the sales ticket or invoice prepared at the time of sale. The top portion of Exhibit 7.5 shows a typical sales journal from a merchandiser. It has columns for recording the date, customer's name, invoice number, posting reference, and the retail and cost amounts of each credit sale. The sales journal in this exhibit is called a **columnar journal,** which is any journal with more than one column.

Point: Each transaction in the sales journal includes a debit to accounts receivable and a credit to sales.

Each transaction recorded in the sales journal yields an entry in the "Accounts Receivable Dr., Sales Cr." column. We usually need only one column for these two accounts. (An exception is when managers need more information about taxes, returns, and other sales details.) Each transaction in the sales journal also yields an entry in the "Cost of Goods Sold Dr., Inventory Cr." column. This entry reflects the perpetual inventory system of tracking costs with each sale. To illustrate, on February 2, this company sold merchandise on account to Jason Henry for $450. The invoice number is 307, and the cost of this merchandise is

Exhibit 7.5

Sales Journal with Posting*

Accounting System: Exhibit 7-5

File Edit Maintain Tasks Analysis Options Reports Window Help

Sales Journal — Page 3

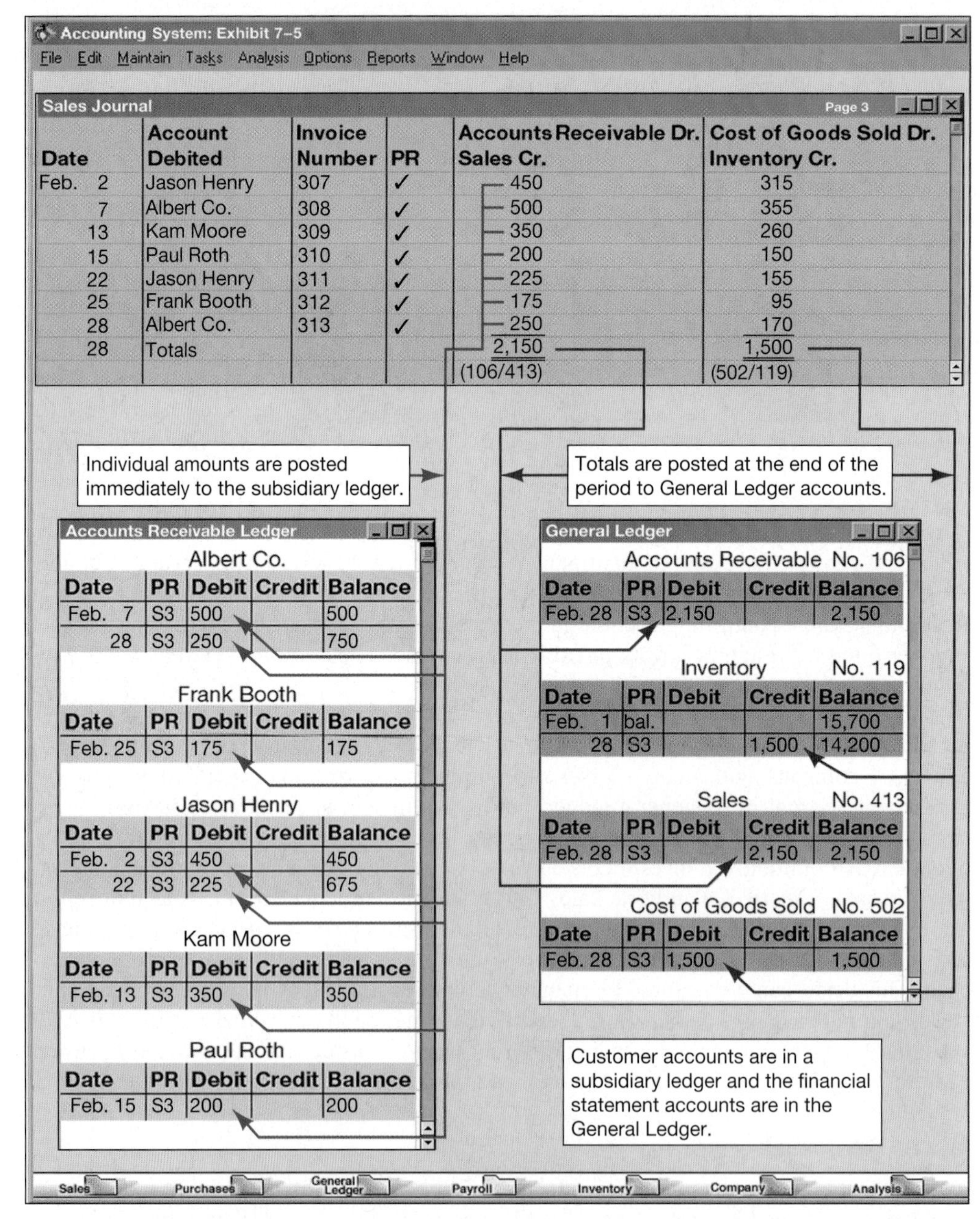

Date	Account Debited	Invoice Number	PR	Accounts Receivable Dr. Sales Cr.	Cost of Goods Sold Dr. Inventory Cr.
Feb. 2	Jason Henry	307	✓	450	315
7	Albert Co.	308	✓	500	355
13	Kam Moore	309	✓	350	260
15	Paul Roth	310	✓	200	150
22	Jason Henry	311	✓	225	155
25	Frank Booth	312	✓	175	95
28	Albert Co.	313	✓	250	170
28	Totals			2,150	1,500
				(106/413)	(502/119)

Individual amounts are posted immediately to the subsidiary ledger.

Totals are posted at the end of the period to General Ledger accounts.

Accounts Receivable Ledger

Albert Co.

Date	PR	Debit	Credit	Balance
Feb. 7	S3	500		500
28	S3	250		750

Frank Booth

Date	PR	Debit	Credit	Balance
Feb. 25	S3	175		175

Jason Henry

Date	PR	Debit	Credit	Balance
Feb. 2	S3	450		450
22	S3	225		675

Kam Moore

Date	PR	Debit	Credit	Balance
Feb. 13	S3	350		350

Paul Roth

Date	PR	Debit	Credit	Balance
Feb. 15	S3	200		200

General Ledger

Accounts Receivable No. 106

Date	PR	Debit	Credit	Balance
Feb. 28	S3	2,150		2,150

Inventory No. 119

Date	PR	Debit	Credit	Balance
Feb. 1	bal.			15,700
28	S3		1,500	14,200

Sales No. 413

Date	PR	Debit	Credit	Balance
Feb. 28	S3		2,150	2,150

Cost of Goods Sold No. 502

Date	PR	Debit	Credit	Balance
Feb. 28	S3	1,500		1,500

Customer accounts are in a subsidiary ledger and the financial statement accounts are in the General Ledger.

Sales Purchases General Ledger Payroll Inventory Company Analysis

*The Sales Journal in a *periodic* system would exclude the column on the far right titled "Cost of Goods Sold Dr., Inventory Cr." (see Exhibit 7A.1).

$315. This information is captured on one line in the sales journal. No further explanations or entries are necessary, saving time and effort. Moreover, this sales journal is consistent with most inventory systems that use bar codes to record both sales and costs with each sale transaction. Note that the Posting Reference (PR) column is not used when entering transactions but instead is used when posting.

Point: Continuously updated customer accounts provide timely information for customer inquiries on those accounts. Keeping creditor accounts updated provides timely information on current amounts owed.

Posting A sales journal is posted as reflected in the arrow lines of Exhibit 7.5. Two types of posting can be identified: (1) posting to the subsidiary ledger(s) and (2) posting to the general ledger.

Posting to subsidiary ledger. Individual transactions in the sales journal are posted regularly (typically concurrently) to customer accounts in the accounts receivable ledger. These postings keep customer accounts up-to-date, which is important for the person granting credit to customers. When sales recorded in the sales journal are individually posted to customer accounts in the accounts receivable ledger, check marks are entered in the sales journal's PR column. Check marks are used rather than account numbers because customer accounts usually are arranged alphabetically in the accounts receivable ledger. Note that posting debits to Accounts Receivable twice—once to Accounts Receivable and once to the customer's subsidiary account—does not violate the accounting equation of debits equal credits. The equality of debits and credits is always maintained in the general ledger.

Point: PR column is only checked *after* the amount(s) is posted.

Posting to general ledger. The sales journal's account columns are totaled at the end of each period (the month of February in this case). For the "sales" column, the $2,150 total is debited to Accounts Receivable and credited to Sales in the general ledger (see Exhibit 7.5). For the "cost" column, the $1,500 total is debited to Cost of Goods Sold and credited to Inventory in the general ledger. When totals are posted to accounts in the general ledger, the account numbers are entered below the column total in the sales journal for tracking. For example, we enter (106/413) below the total in the sales column after this amount is posted to account number 106 (Accounts Receivable) and account number 413 (Sales).

Point: Postings are automatic in a computerized system.

A company identifies in the PR column of its subsidiary ledgers the journal and page number from which an amount is taken. We identify a journal by using an initial. Items posted from the sales journal carry the initial ***S*** before their journal page numbers in a PR column. Likewise, items from the cash receipts journal carry the initial ***R***; items from the cash disbursements journal carry the initial ***D***; items from the purchases journal carry the initial ***P***; and items from the general journal carry the initial ***G***.

Proving the Ledgers Account balances in the general ledger and subsidiary ledgers are periodically proved (or reviewed) for accuracy after posting. To do this we first prepare a trial balance of the general ledger to confirm that debits equal credits. Second, we test a subsidiary ledger by preparing a *schedule* of individual accounts and amounts. A **schedule of accounts receivable** lists each customer and the balance owed. If this total equals the balance of the Accounts Receivable controlling account, the accounts in the accounts receivable ledger are assumed correct. Exhibit 7.6 shows a schedule of accounts receivable drawn from the accounts receivable ledger of Exhibit 7.5.

P2 Prepare and prove the accuracy of subsidiary ledgers.

Exhibit 7.6

Schedule of Accounts Receivable

Schedule of Accounts Receivable February 28	
Albert Co.	$ 750
Frank Booth	175
Jason Henry	675
Kam Moore	350
Paul Roth	200
Total accounts receivable	$2,150

Additional Issues We consider three additional issues with the sales journal: (1) recording sales taxes, (2) recording sales returns and allowances, and (3) using actual sales invoices as a journal.

Point: In accounting, the word *schedule* generally means a list.

Sales taxes. Governmental agencies such as cities and states often require sellers to collect sales taxes from customers and to periodically send these taxes to the appropriate agency.

When using a columnar sales journal, we can keep a record of taxes collected by adding a Sales Taxes Payable column as follows:

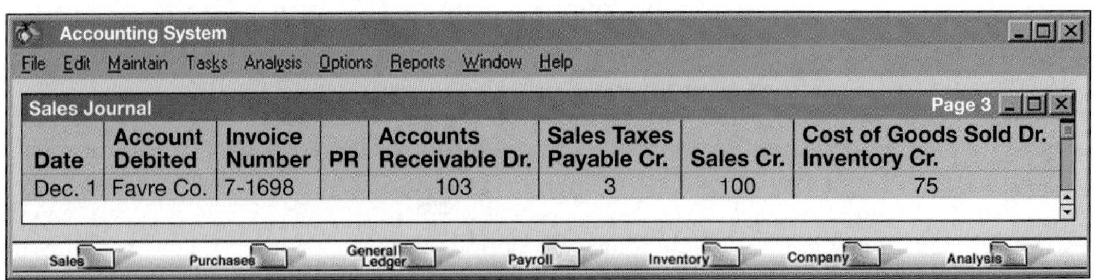

Date	Account Debited	Invoice Number	PR	Accounts Receivable Dr.	Sales Taxes Payable Cr.	Sales Cr.	Cost of Goods Sold Dr. Inventory Cr.
Dec. 1	Favre Co.	7-1698		103	3	100	75

Individual amounts in the Accounts Receivable column would continue to be posted immediately to customer accounts in the accounts receivable ledger. Individual amounts in the Sales Taxes Payable and Sales columns are not posted. Column totals would continue to be posted as usual. (A company that collects sales taxes on its cash sales can also use a Sales Taxes Payable column in its cash receipts journal.)

Sales returns and allowances. A company with only a few sales returns and allowances can record them in a general journal with an entry such as this:

Assets = Liabilities + Equity
−175 −175

May 17	Sales Returns and Allowances	414	175	
	Accounts Receivable—Ray Ball	106/✓		175
	Customer returned merchandise.			

The debit in this entry is posted to the Sales Returns and Allowances account (no. 414). The credit is posted to both the Accounts Receivable controlling account (no. 106) and to the customer's account. When we enter the account number and the check mark, 106/✓, in the PR column on the credit line, this means both the Accounts Receivable controlling account in the general ledger and the Ray Ball account in the accounts receivable ledger are credited for $175. [*Note:* If the returned goods can be resold to another customer, the company would debit (increase) the Inventory account and credit (decrease) the Cost of Goods Sold account. If the returned goods are defective (worthless), the company could simply leave their costs in the Cost of Goods Sold account (see Chapter 5).] A company with a large number of sales returns and allowances can save time by recording them in a separate sales returns and allowances journal.

Sales invoices as a sales journal. To save costs, some small companies avoid using a sales journal for credit sales and instead post each sales invoice amount directly to the customer's account in the accounts receivable ledger. They then put copies of invoices in a file. At the end of the period, they total all invoices for that period and make a general journal entry to debit Accounts Receivable and credit Sales for the total amount. The file of invoice copies act as a sales journal. This is called *direct posting of sales invoices*.

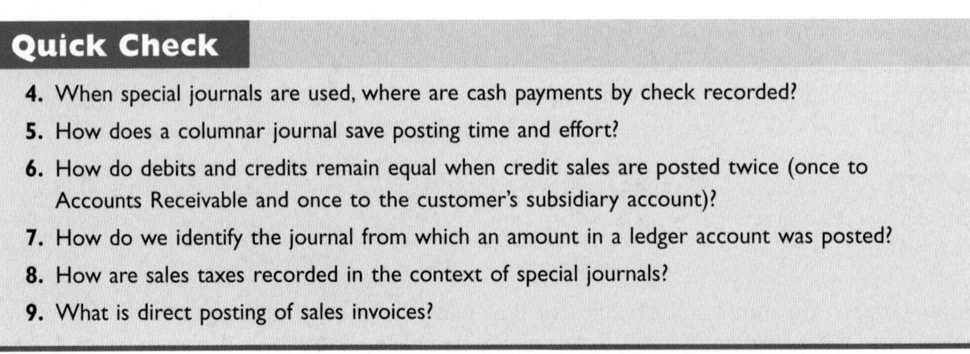

Quick Check

4. When special journals are used, where are cash payments by check recorded?
5. How does a columnar journal save posting time and effort?
6. How do debits and credits remain equal when credit sales are posted twice (once to Accounts Receivable and once to the customer's subsidiary account)?
7. How do we identify the journal from which an amount in a ledger account was posted?
8. How are sales taxes recorded in the context of special journals?
9. What is direct posting of sales invoices?

Answers—p. 288

Cash Receipts Journal

A **cash receipts journal** is typically used to record all receipts of cash. Exhibit 7.7 shows one common form of the cash receipts journal.

Exhibit 7.7

Cash Receipts Journal with Posting*

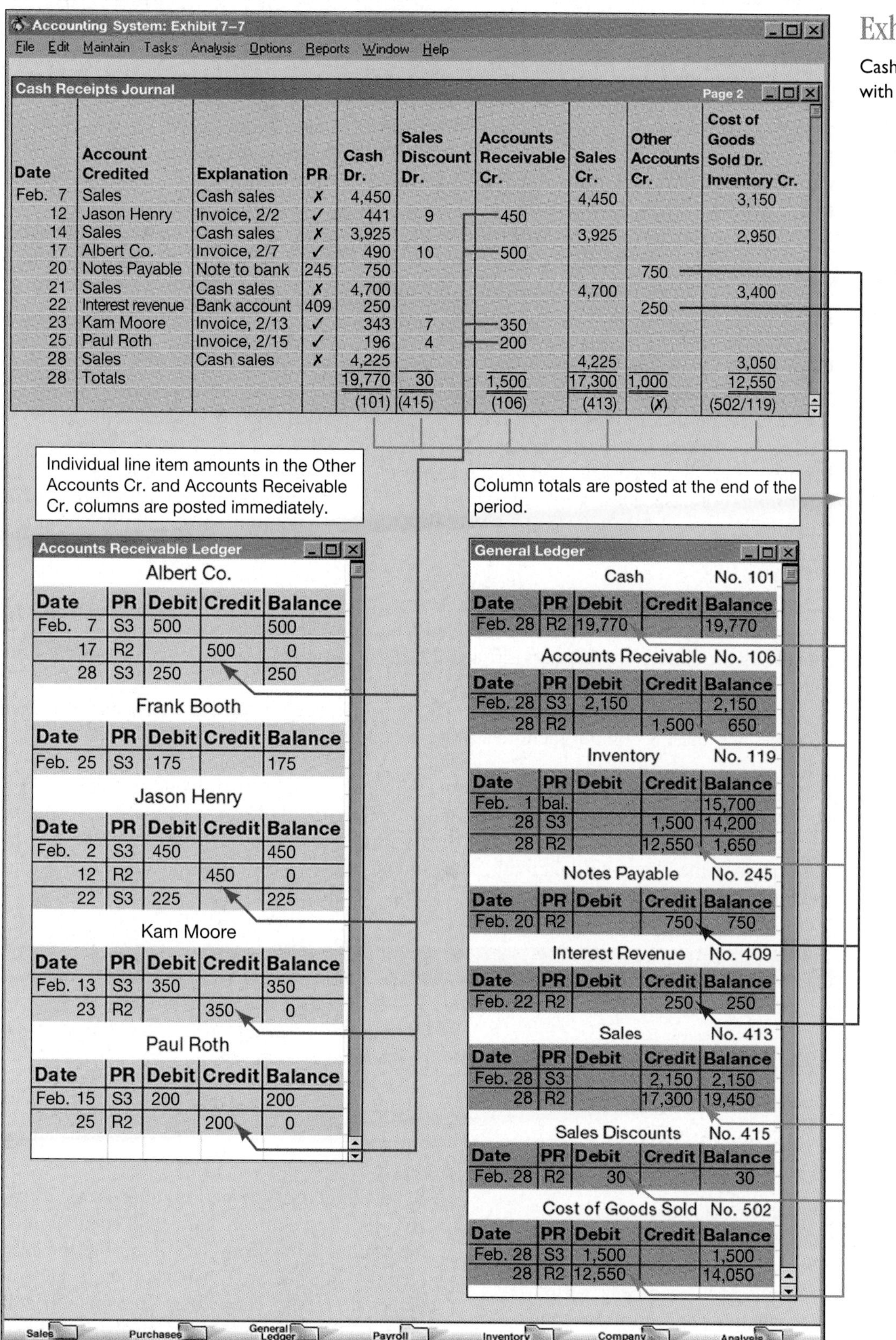

Accounting System: Exhibit 7–7

File Edit Maintain Tasks Analysis Options Reports Window Help

Cash Receipts Journal — Page 2

Date	Account Credited	Explanation	PR	Cash Dr.	Sales Discount Dr.	Accounts Receivable Cr.	Sales Cr.	Other Accounts Cr.	Cost of Goods Sold Dr. Inventory Cr.
Feb. 7	Sales	Cash sales	✗	4,450			4,450		3,150
12	Jason Henry	Invoice, 2/2	✓	441	9	450			
14	Sales	Cash sales	✗	3,925			3,925		2,950
17	Albert Co.	Invoice, 2/7	✓	490	10	500			
20	Notes Payable	Note to bank	245	750				750	
21	Sales	Cash sales	✗	4,700			4,700		3,400
22	Interest revenue	Bank account	409	250				250	
23	Kam Moore	Invoice, 2/13	✓	343	7	350			
25	Paul Roth	Invoice, 2/15	✓	196	4	200			
28	Sales	Cash sales	✗	4,225			4,225		3,050
28	Totals			19,770	30	1,500	17,300	1,000	12,550
				(101)	(415)	(106)	(413)	(✗)	(502/119)

Individual line item amounts in the Other Accounts Cr. and Accounts Receivable Cr. columns are posted immediately.

Column totals are posted at the end of the period.

Accounts Receivable Ledger

Albert Co.

Date	PR	Debit	Credit	Balance
Feb. 7	S3	500		500
17	R2		500	0
28	S3	250		250

Frank Booth

Date	PR	Debit	Credit	Balance
Feb. 25	S3	175		175

Jason Henry

Date	PR	Debit	Credit	Balance
Feb. 2	S3	450		450
12	R2		450	0
22	S3	225		225

Kam Moore

Date	PR	Debit	Credit	Balance
Feb. 13	S3	350		350
23	R2		350	0

Paul Roth

Date	PR	Debit	Credit	Balance
Feb. 15	S3	200		200
25	R2		200	0

General Ledger

Cash No. 101

Date	PR	Debit	Credit	Balance
Feb. 28	R2	19,770		19,770

Accounts Receivable No. 106

Date	PR	Debit	Credit	Balance
Feb. 28	S3	2,150		2,150
28	R2		1,500	650

Inventory No. 119

Date	PR	Debit	Credit	Balance
Feb. 1	bal.			15,700
28	S3		1,500	14,200
28	R2		12,550	1,650

Notes Payable No. 245

Date	PR	Debit	Credit	Balance
Feb. 20	R2		750	750

Interest Revenue No. 409

Date	PR	Debit	Credit	Balance
Feb. 22	R2		250	250

Sales No. 413

Date	PR	Debit	Credit	Balance
Feb. 28	S3		2,150	2,150
28	R2		17,300	19,450

Sales Discounts No. 415

Date	PR	Debit	Credit	Balance
Feb. 28	R2	30		30

Cost of Goods Sold No. 502

Date	PR	Debit	Credit	Balance
Feb. 28	S3	1,500		1,500
28	R2	12,550		14,050

Sales Purchases General Ledger Payroll Inventory Company Analysis

*The Cash Receipts Journal in a *periodic* system would exclude the column on the far right titled "Cost of Goods Sold Dr., Inventory Cr." (see Exhibit 7A.2).

Point: Each transaction in the cash receipts journal involves a debit to Cash. Credit accounts will vary.

Journalizing and Posting Cash receipts can be separated into one of three types: (1) cash from credit customers in payment of their accounts, (2) cash from cash sales, and (3) cash from other sources. The cash receipts journal in Exhibit 7.7 has a separate credit column for each of these three sources. We describe how to journalize transactions from each of these three sources. (An Explanation column is included in the cash receipts journal to identify the source.)

Cash from credit customers. *Journalizing.* To record cash received in payment of a customer's account, the customer's name is first entered in the Account Credited column—see transactions dated February 12, 17, 23, and 25. Then the amounts debited to both Cash and the Sales Discount (if any) are entered in their respective columns, and the amount credited to the customer's account is entered in the Accounts Receivable Cr. column.

Posting. Individual amounts in the Accounts Receivable Cr. column are posted immediately to customer accounts in the subsidiary accounts receivable ledger. The $1,500 column total is posted at the end of the period (month in this case) as a credit to the Accounts Receivable controlling account in the general ledger.

Cash sales. *Journalizing.* The amount for each cash sale is entered in the Cash Dr. column and the Sales Cr. column. The February 7, 14, 21, and 28 transactions are examples. (Cash sales are usually journalized daily or at point of sale, but are journalized weekly in Exhibit 7.7 for brevity.) Each cash sale also yields an entry to Cost of Goods Sold Dr. and Inventory Cr. for the cost of merchandise—see the far right column.

Point: Some software packages put cash sales in the sales journal.

Posting. For cash sales, we place an *x* in the PR column to indicate that its amount is not individually posted. We do post the $17,300 Sales Cr. total and the $12,550 total from the "cost" column.

Example: Record in the cash receipts journal a $700 cash sale of land when the land carries a $700 original cost. *Answer:* Debit the Cash column for $700, and credit the Other Accounts column for $700 (the account credited is Land).

Cash from other sources. *Journalizing.* Examples of cash from other sources are money borrowed from a bank, cash interest received on account, and cash sale of noninventory assets. The transactions of February 20 and 22 are illustrative. The Other Accounts Cr. column is used for these transactions.

Posting. Amounts from these transactions are immediately posted to their general ledger accounts and the PR column identifies those accounts.

Footing, Crossfooting, and Posting To be sure that total debits and credits in a columnar journal are equal, we often crossfoot column totals before posting them. To *foot* a column of numbers is to add it. To *crossfoot* in this case is to add the Debit column totals, then add the Credit column totals, and compare the two sums for equality. Footing and crossfooting of the numbers in Exhibit 7.7 results in the report in Exhibit 7.8.

Point: Subsidiary ledgers and their controlling accounts are *in balance* only after all posting is complete.

Exhibit 7.8
Footing and Crossfooting Journal Totals

Debit Columns		Credit Columns	
Cash Dr.	$19,770	Accounts Receivable Cr.	$ 1,500
Sales Discounts Dr.	30	Sales Cr.	17,300
Cost of Goods Sold Dr.	12,550	Other Accounts Cr.	1,000
		Inventory Cr.	12,550
Total	$32,350	Total	$32,350

Decision Maker

Entrepreneur You want to know how promptly customers are paying their bills. This information can help you decide whether to extend credit and to plan your cash payments. Where do you find this information?

Answer—p. 287

At the end of the period, after crossfooting the journal to confirm that debits equal credits, the total amounts from the columns of the cash receipts journal are posted to their general ledger accounts. The Other Accounts Cr. column total is not posted because the individual amounts are directly posted to their general ledger accounts. We place an *x* below the Other

Accounts Cr. column to indicate that this column total is not posted. The account numbers for the column totals that are posted are entered in parentheses below each column. (*Note:* Posting items immediately from the Other Accounts Cr. column with a delayed posting of their offsetting items in the Cash column total causes the general ledger to be out of balance during the period. Posting the Cash Dr. column total at the end of the period corrects this imbalance in the general ledger before the trial balance and financial statements are prepared.)

Purchases Journal

A **purchases journal** is typically used to record all credit purchases, including those for inventory. Purchases for cash are recorded in the Cash Disbursements Journal.

Journalizing Entries in the purchases journal in Exhibit 7.9 reflect purchase invoices or other source documents. We use the invoice date and terms to compute the date when payment

Point: The number of special journals and the design of each are based on a company's specific needs.

Exhibit 7.9

Purchases Journal with Posting*

Accounting System: Exhibit 7–9

File Edit Maintain Tasks Analysis Options Reports Window Help

Purchases Journal — Page 1

Date	Account	Date of Invoice	Terms	PR	Accounts Payable Cr.	Inventory Dr.	Office Supplies Dr.	Other Accounts Dr.
Feb. 3	Horning Supply Co.	2/2	n/30	✓	350	275	75	
5	Ace Mfg. Co.	2/5	2/10, n/30	✓	200	200		
13	Wynet & Co.	2/10	2/10, n/30	✓	150	150		
20	Smite Co.	2/18	2/10, n/30	✓	300	300		
25	Ace Mfg. Co.	2/24	2/10, n/30	✓	100	100		
28	Store Supplies/ITT Co.	2/28	n/30	125/✓	225	125	25	75
28	Totals				1,325	1,150	100	75
					(201)	(119)	(124)	(X)

Individual amounts in the Other Accounts Dr. and the Accounts Payable Cr. columns are posted immediately.

Column totals, except for Other Accounts Dr. column, are posted at the end of the period.

Accounts Payable Ledger

Ace Mfg. Company

Date	PR	Debit	Credit	Balance
Feb. 5	P1		200	200
25	P1		100	300

Horning Supply Company

Date	PR	Debit	Credit	Balance
Feb. 3	P1		350	350

ITT Company

Date	PR	Debit	Credit	Balance
Feb. 28	P1		225	225

Smite Company

Date	PR	Debit	Credit	Balance
Feb. 20	P1		300	300

Wynet and Company

Date	PR	Debit	Credit	Balance
Feb. 13	P1		150	150

General Ledger

Inventory No. 119

Date	PR	Debit	Credit	Balance
Feb. 1	bal.			15,700
28	S3		1,500	14,200
28	R2		12,550	1,650
28	P1	1,150		2,800

Office Supplies No. 124

Date	PR	Debit	Credit	Balance
Feb. 28	P1	100		100

Store Supplies No. 125

Date	PR	Debit	Credit	Balance
Feb. 28	P1	75		75

Accounts Payable No. 201

Date	PR	Debit	Credit	Balance
Feb. 28	P1		1,325	1,325

Sales Purchases General Ledger Payroll Inventory Company Analysis

*The Purchases Journal in a *periodic* system replaces "Inventory Dr." with "Purchases Dr." (see Exhibit 7A.3).

for each purchase is due. The Accounts Payable Cr. column is used to record the amounts owed to each creditor. Inventory purchases are recorded in the Inventory Dr. column.

To illustrate, inventory costing $200 is purchased from Ace Manufacturing on February 5. The creditor's name (Ace) is entered in the Account column, the invoice date is entered in the Date of Invoice column, the purchase terms are entered in the Terms column, and the $200 amount is entered in the Accounts Payable Cr. and the Inventory Dr. columns. When a purchase involves an amount recorded in the Other Accounts Dr. column, we use the Account column to identify the general ledger account debited. For example, the February 28 transaction involves purchases of inventory, office supplies, and store supplies from ITT. The journal has no column for store supplies, so the Other Accounts Dr. column is used. In this case, Store Supplies is entered in the Account column along with the creditor's name (ITT). This purchases journal also includes a separate column for credit purchases of office supplies. A separate column such as this is useful when several transactions involve debits to the same account. Each company uses its own judgment in deciding on the number of separate columns necessary.

Point: Each transaction in the purchases journal involves a credit to Accounts Payable. Debit accounts will vary.

Point: The Other Accounts Dr. column allows the purchases journal to be used for any purchase transaction on credit.

Posting The amounts in the Accounts Payable Cr. column are immediately posted to individual creditor accounts in the accounts payable subsidiary ledger. Individual amounts in the Other Accounts Dr. column are immediately posted to their general ledger accounts. At the end of the period, all column totals except the Other Accounts Dr. column are posted to their general ledger accounts.

Exhibit 7.10

Schedule of Accounts Payable

Schedule of Accounts Payable February 28	
Ace Mfg. Company	$ 300
Horning Supply Company	350
ITT Company	225
Smite Company	300
Wynet & Company	150
Total accounts payable	$1,325

Point: The balance in the Accounts Payable controlling account must equal the sum of the individual account balances in the accounts payable subsidiary ledger after posting.

Proving the Ledger Accounts payable balances in the subsidiary ledger are proved after posting the purchases journal. We prove the subsidiary ledger by preparing a **schedule of accounts payable,** which is a list of accounts from the accounts payable ledger with their balances and the total. If this total equals the balance of the Accounts Payable controlling account, the accounts in the accounts payable ledger are assumed correct. Exhibit 7.10 shows a schedule of accounts payable drawn from the accounts payable ledger of Exhibit 7.9.

Cash Disbursements Journal

A **cash disbursements journal,** also called a *cash payments journal,* is typically used to record all cash payments.

Journalizing The cash disbursements journal shown in Exhibit 7.11 illustrates repetitive entries to the Cash Cr. column of this journal (reflecting cash payments). Also note the frequent credits to Inventory (which reflect purchase discounts) and the debits to Accounts Payable. For example, on February 15, the company pays Ace on account (credit terms of 2/10, n/30—see February 5 transaction in Exhibit 7.9). Since payment occurs in the discount period, the company pays $196 ($200 invoice less $4 discount). The $4 discount is credited to Inventory. Note that when this company purchases inventory for cash, it is recorded using the Other Accounts Dr. column and the Cash Cr. column as illustrated in the February 3 and 12 transactions. Generally, the Other Accounts column is used to record cash payments on items for which no column exists. For example, on February 15, the company pays salaries expense of $250. The title of the account debited (Salaries Expense) is entered in the Account Debited column.

Point: Each transaction in the cash disbursements journal involves a credit to Cash. Debit accounts will vary.

The cash disbursements journal has a column titled Ck. No. (check number). For control over cash disbursements, all payments except for those of small amounts are made by check.

Decision Maker

Controller You wish to analyze your company's cash payments to suppliers and its purchases discounts. Where do you find this information?

Answer—p. 287

Exhibit 7.11

Cash Disbursements Journal with Posting*

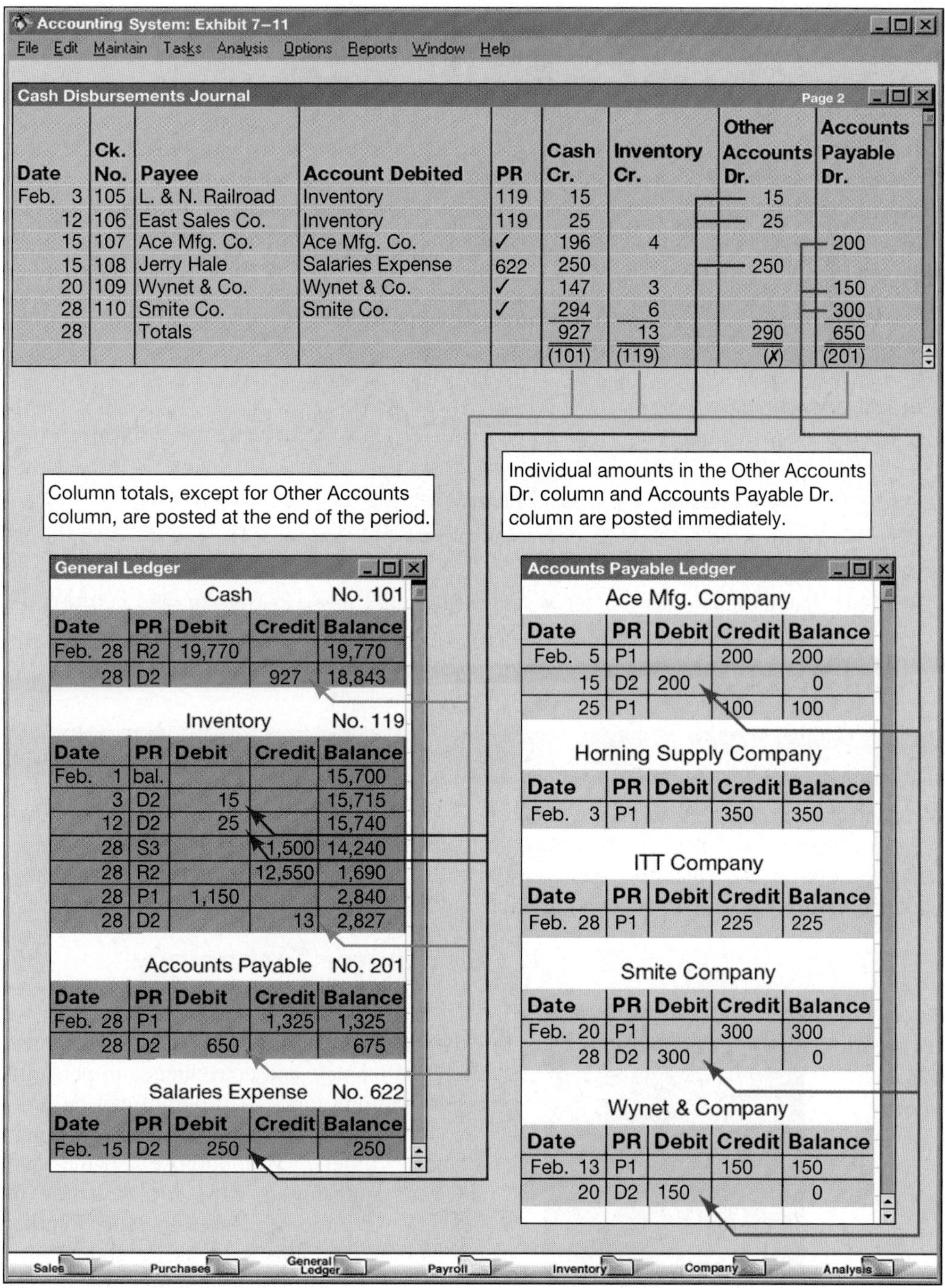

Cash Disbursements Journal

Date	Ck. No.	Payee	Account Debited	PR	Cash Cr.	Inventory Cr.	Other Accounts Dr.	Accounts Payable Dr.
Feb. 3	105	L. & N. Railroad	Inventory	119	15		15	
12	106	East Sales Co.	Inventory	119	25		25	
15	107	Ace Mfg. Co.	Ace Mfg. Co.	✓	196	4		200
15	108	Jerry Hale	Salaries Expense	622	250		250	
20	109	Wynet & Co.	Wynet & Co.	✓	147	3		150
28	110	Smite Co.	Smite Co.	✓	294	6		300
28		Totals			927	13	290	650
					(101)	(119)	(✗)	(201)

General Ledger

Cash — No. 101

Date	PR	Debit	Credit	Balance
Feb. 28	R2	19,770		19,770
28	D2		927	18,843

Inventory — No. 119

Date	PR	Debit	Credit	Balance
Feb. 1	bal.			15,700
3	D2	15		15,715
12	D2	25		15,740
28	S3		1,500	14,240
28	R2		12,550	1,690
28	P1	1,150		2,840
28	D2		13	2,827

Accounts Payable — No. 201

Date	PR	Debit	Credit	Balance
Feb. 28	P1		1,325	1,325
28	D2	650		675

Salaries Expense — No. 622

Date	PR	Debit	Credit	Balance
Feb. 15	D2	250		250

Accounts Payable Ledger

Ace Mfg. Company

Date	PR	Debit	Credit	Balance
Feb. 5	P1		200	200
15	D2	200		0
25	P1		100	100

Horning Supply Company

Date	PR	Debit	Credit	Balance
Feb. 3	P1		350	350

ITT Company

Date	PR	Debit	Credit	Balance
Feb. 28	P1		225	225

Smite Company

Date	PR	Debit	Credit	Balance
Feb. 20	P1		300	300
28	D2	300		0

Wynet & Company

Date	PR	Debit	Credit	Balance
Feb. 13	P1		150	150
20	D2	150		0

*The Cash Disbursements Journal in a *periodic* system replaces "Inventory Cr." with "Purchases Discounts Cr." (see Exhibit 7A.4).

Checks should be prenumbered and each check's number entered in the journal in numerical order in the column headed Ck. No. This makes it possible to scan the numbers in the column for omitted checks. When a cash disbursements journal has a column for check numbers, it is sometimes called a **check register.**

Posting Individual amounts in the Other Accounts Dr. column of a cash disbursements journal are immediately posted to their general ledger accounts. Individual amounts in the Accounts Payable Dr. column are also immediately posted to creditors' accounts in the subsidiary Accounts Payable ledger. At the end of the period, we crossfoot column totals and post the Accounts Payable Dr. column total to the Accounts Payable controlling account.

Also, the Inventory Cr. column total is posted to the Inventory account, and the Cash Cr. column total is posted to the Cash account.

General Journal Transactions

When special journals are used, we still need a general journal for adjusting, closing, and any other transactions for which no special journal has been set up. Examples of these other transactions might include purchases returns and allowances, purchases of plant assets by issuing a note payable, sales returns if a sales returns and allowances journal is not used, and receipt of a note receivable from a customer. We described the recording of transactions in a general journal in Chapters 2 and 3.

Quick Check

10. What are the normal recording and posting procedures when using special journals and controlling accounts with subsidiary ledgers?
11. What is the process for posting to a subsidiary ledger and its controlling account?
12. How do we prove the accuracy of account balances in the general ledger and subsidiary ledgers after posting?
13. Why does a company need a general journal when using special journals for sales, purchases, cash receipts, and cash disbursements?

Answers—p. 288

Technology-Based Accounting Systems

C5 Explain how technology-based information systems impact accounting.

Accounting information systems are supported with technology, which can range from simple calculators to advanced computerized systems. Since technology is increasingly important in accounting information systems, we discuss the impact of computer technology, how data processing works with accounting data, and the role of computer networks.

Decision Insight

Middleware is software allowing different computer programs in a company or across companies to work together. It allows transfer of purchase orders, invoices, and other electronic documents between accounting systems. For example, suppliers can monitor inventory levels of their buyers for production and shipping purposes.

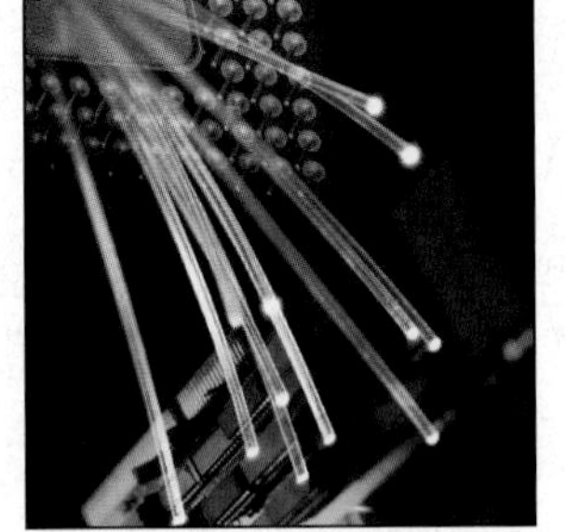

Computer Technology in Accounting

Computer technology provides accuracy, speed, efficiency, and convenience in performing accounting tasks. A program can be written, for instance, to process customers' merchandise orders. Multipurpose off-the-shelf software applications exist for a variety of business operations. These include familiar accounting programs such as Peachtree® and QuickBooks®. Off-the-shelf programs are designed to be user friendly and menu driven, and many operate more efficiently as *integrated* systems. In an integrated system, actions taken in one part of the system automatically affect related parts. When a credit sale is recorded in an integrated system, for instance, several parts of the system are automatically updated, such as posting.

Computer technology can dramatically reduce the time and effort devoted to recordkeeping. Less effort spent on recordkeeping means more time for accounting professionals to concentrate on analysis and managerial decision making. These advances have created a greater demand for accounting professionals who understand financial reports and can draw

Decision Insight

A new generation of Windows- and Web-based accounting support is available. With the touch of a key, users can create real-time inventory reports showing all payments, charges, and credit limits at any point in the accounting cycle. Many services also include "alert signals" notifying the company when, for example, a large order exceeds a customer's credit limit or when purchases need to be made.

insights and information from mountains of processed data. Accounting professionals have expertise in determining relevant and reliable information for decision making. They also can assess the effects of transactions and events on a company and its financial statements.

Data Processing in Accounting

Accounting systems differ with regard to how input is entered and processed. **Online processing** enters and processes data as soon as source documents are available. This means that databases are immediately updated. **Batch processing** accumulates source documents for a period of time and then processes them all at once such as daily, weekly, or monthly. The advantage of online processing is timeliness. This often requires additional costs related to both software and hardware requirements. Companies such as **NetLedger** (NetLedger.com) are making online processing of accounting data a reality for many businesses. The advantage of batch processing is that it requires only periodic updating of databases. Records used to send bills to customers, for instance, might require updating only once a month. The disadvantage of batch processing is the lack of updated databases for management to use when making business decisions.

Computer Networks in Accounting

Networking, or linking computers with each other, can create information advantages (and cost efficiencies). **Computer networks** are links among computers giving different users and different computers access to common databases, programs, and hardware. Many college computer labs, for instance, are networked. A small computer network is called a *local area network (LAN);* it links machines with *hard-wire* hookups. Large computer networks extending over long distances often rely on *modem* or *wireless* communication.

Demand for information sometimes requires advanced networks such as the systems **Federal Express** and **UPS** use to track packages and bill customers and the system **Wal-Mart** uses to monitor inventory levels in its stores. These networks include many computers and satellite communications to gather information and to provide ready access to its databases from all locations.

Enterprise Resource Planning Software

Enterprise resource planning (ERP) software includes the programs that manage a company's vital operations. They extend from order taking to manufacturing to accounting. When working properly, these integrated programs can speed decision making, identify costs for reduction, and give managers control over operations with the click of a mouse. For many managers, ERP software allows them to scrutinize business, identify where inventories are piling up, and see what plants are most efficient. The software is designed to link every part of a company's operations. This software allowed **Monsanto** to slash production planning from six weeks to three, trim its inventories, and increase its bargaining power with suppliers. Monsanto estimates that this software saves the company $200 million per year.

Total ERP Market: About $13 Billion

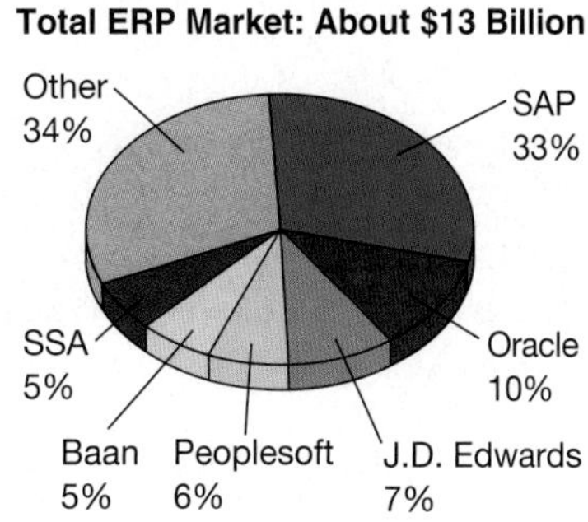

ERP has six major suppliers. **SAP** leads the market, with **Oracle** a distant second. SAP software is used by roughly half of the world's 500 largest companies. It links ordering, inventory, production, purchasing, planning, tracking, and human resources. A transaction or event triggers an immediate chain reaction of events throughout the enterprise. It is making companies more efficient and profitable.

ERP is pushing into cyberspace. Now companies can share data with customers and suppliers. Applesauce maker **Mott's** is using SAP so that distributors can check the status of orders and place them over the Net, and the **Coca-Cola Company** uses it to ship soda on time. ERP is also increasingly used by small business. For example, **NetLedger**'s accounting services to small and medium businesses are powered by Oracle's system.

Quick Check

14. Identify an advantage of an integrated computer-based accounting system.

15. What advantages do computer systems offer over manual systems?

16. Identify an advantage of computer networks.

17. Describe ERP software and its potential advantages to businesses.

Answers—p. 288

Decision Analysis — Segment Return on Assets

Good accounting information systems collect financial data for a company's various segments. A *segment* refers to a part of a company that is separately identified by its products or services, or by the geographic market it serves. **Harley-Davidson** reports that it operates in two business segments: (1) motorcycles and related and (2) financial services. Users of financial statements are especially interested in segment information to better understand a company's activities because segments often vary on profitability, risk, and growth.

Exhibit 7.12

Companies Reporting Operations by These Segments*

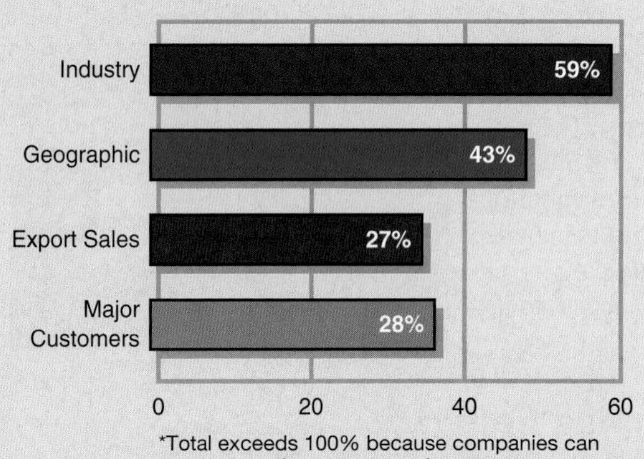

*Total exceeds 100% because companies can report more than one type of segment.

Full disclosure by segments is rare because managers are reluctant to release information that can harm its competitive position. Exhibit 7.12 shows survey results on the number of companies with different (reported) segments.

Point: Publicly traded companies must report segment information, including their sales, operating income, identifiable assets, capital expenditures, depreciation, depletion, and amortization.

One measure of success for business segments is the **segment return on assets** ratio defined as follows:

A1 Compute segment return on assets and use it to evaluate segment performance.

$$\textbf{Segment return on assets} = \frac{\textbf{Segment operating income}}{\textbf{Segment average assets}}$$

This ratio reflects on the profitability of a segment. Exhibit 7.13 shows the segment return on assets for Harley-Davidson from 2000 through 2002.

Exhibit 7.13

Harley-Davidson's Segment Return on Assets ($ millions)

	2002			2001			2000
Segment	Operating Income*	Average Assets	Return on Assets	Operating Income	Average Assets	Return on Assets	Return on Assets
Motorcycles and related	$791	$1,464	54%	$613	$1,272	48%	44%
Financial services	104	1,310	8	61	977	6	4

* A segment's operating income is usually measured as income before taxes, and assets is usually measured as identifiable assets.

The trend in Harley's segment return on assets is increasing for both segments, but its motorcycles segment is much more profitable (54%) than its financial services (8%) segment. Harley should consider further investment in its motorcycles segment if such returns can be sustained. Analysis can also be extended to geographical segments and any other segments that are reported.

Decision Maker

Banker A bicycle merchandiser requests a loan from you to expand operations. Its net income is $220,000, reflecting a 10% increase over the prior year. You ask about segment results. The owner reports that $160,000 of net income is from Cuban operations, reflecting a 60% increase over the prior year. The remaining $60,000 of net income is from U.S. operations, reflecting a 40% decrease. Does this segment information impact your loan decision?

Answer—p. 287

Demonstration Problem—Perpetual System

Pepper Company completed the following selected transactions and events during March of this year. (Terms of all credit sales for the company are 2/10, n/30.)

Mar. 4 Sold merchandise on credit to Jennifer Nelson, Invoice No. 954, for $16,800 (cost is $12,200).

6 Purchased $1,220 of office supplies on credit from Mack Company. Invoice dated March 3, terms n/30.

6 Sold merchandise on credit to Dennie Hoskins, Invoice No. 955, for $10,200 (cost is $8,100).

11 Purchased $52,600 of merchandise, invoice dated March 6, terms 2/10, n/30, from Defore Industries.

12 Borrowed $26,000 cash by giving Commerce Bank a long-term promissory note payable.

14 Received cash payment from Jennifer Nelson for the March 4 sale less the discount.

16 Received a $200 credit memorandum from Defore Industries for unsatisfactory merchandise Pepper purchased on March 11 and later returned.

16 Received cash payment from Dennie Hoskins for the March 6 sale less the discount.

18 Purchased $22,850 of store equipment on credit from Schmidt Supply, invoice dated March 15, terms n/30.

20 Sold merchandise on credit to Marjorie Allen, Invoice No. 956, for $5,600 (cost is $3,800).

21 Sent Defore Industries Check No. 516 in payment of its March 6 dated invoice less the return and the discount.

22 Purchased $41,625 of merchandise, invoice dated March 18, terms 2/10, n/30, from Welch Company.

26 Issued a $600 credit memorandum to Marjorie Allen for defective merchandise Pepper sold on March 20 and Allen later returned.

31 Issued Check No. 517, payable to Payroll, in payment of $15,900 sales salaries for the month. Cashed the check and paid the employees.

31 Cash sales for the month are $134,680 (cost is $67,340). (Cash sales are recorded daily but are recorded only once here to reduce repetitive entries.)

Required

1. Open the following selected general ledger accounts: Cash (101), Accounts Receivable (106) Inventory (119), Office Supplies (124), Store Equipment (165), Accounts Payable (201), Long-Term Notes Payable (251), Sales (413), Sales Returns and Allowances (414), Sales Discounts (415), Cost of Goods Sold (502), and Sales Salaries Expense (621). Open the following accounts receivable ledger accounts: Marjorie Allen, Dennie Hoskins, and Jennifer Nelson. Open the following accounts payable ledger accounts: Defore Industries, Mack Company, Schmidt Supply, and Welch Company.
2. Enter the transactions using a sales journal, a purchases journal, a cash receipts journal, a cash disbursements journal, and a general journal similar to the ones illustrated in the chapter. Regularly post to the individual customer and creditor accounts. Also, post any amounts that should be posted as individual amounts to general ledger accounts. Foot and crossfoot the journals and make the month-end postings. *Pepper Co. uses the perpetual inventory system.*
3. Prepare a trial balance for the selected general ledger accounts in part 1 and prove the accuracy of subsidiary ledgers by preparing schedules of accounts receivable and accounts payable.

Planning the Solution

- Set up the required general ledger, the subsidiary ledger accounts, and the five required journals as illustrated in the chapter.

- Read and analyze each transaction and decide in which special journal (or general journal) the transaction is recorded.
- Record each transaction in the proper journal (and post the appropriate individual amounts).
- Once you have recorded all transactions, total the journal columns. Post from each journal to the appropriate ledger accounts.
- Prepare a trial balance to prove the equality of the debit and credit balances in your general ledger.
- Prepare schedules of accounts receivable and accounts payable. Compare the totals of these schedules to the Accounts Receivable and Accounts Payable controlling account balances, making sure that they agree.

Solution to Demonstration Problem—Perpetual System

Sales Journal — Page 2

Date	Account Debited	Invoice Number	PR	Accounts Receivable Dr. Sales Cr.	Cost of Goods Sold Dr. Inventory Cr.
Mar. 4	Jennifer Nelson	954	✓	16,800	12,200
6	Dennie Hoskins	955	✓	10,200	8,100
20	Marjorie Allen	956	✓	5,600	3,800
31	Totals			32,600	24,100
				(106/413)	(502/119)

Cash Receipts Journal — Page 3

Date	Account Credited	Explanation	PR	Cash Dr.	Sales Discount Dr.	Accounts Receivable Cr.	Sales Cr.	Other Accounts Cr.	Cost of Goods Sold Dr. Inventory Cr.
Mar. 12	L.T. Notes Payable	Note to bank	251	26,000				26,000	
14	Jennifer Nelson	Invoice, 3/4	✓	16,464	336	16,800			
16	Dennie Hoskins	Invoice, 3/6	✓	9,996	204	10,200			
31	Sales	Cash sales	x	134,680			134,680		67,340
31	Totals			187,140	540	27,000	134,680	26,000	67,340
				(101)	(415)	(106)	(413)	(x)	(502/119)

Purchases Journal — Page 3

Date	Account	Date of Invoice	Terms	PR	Accounts Payable Cr.	Inventory Dr.	Office Supplies Dr.	Other Accounts Dr.
Mar. 6	Office Supplies/Mack Co	3/3	n/30	✓	1,220		1,220	
11	Defore Industries	3/6	2/10, n/30	✓	52,600	52,600		
18	Store Equipment/Schmidt Supp	3/15	n/30	165/✓	22,850			22,850
22	Welch Company	3/18	2/10, n/30	✓	41,625	41,625		
31	Totals				118,295	94,225	1,220	22,850
					(201)	(119)	(124)	(x)

Cash Disbursements Journal — Page 3

Date	Ck. No.	Payee	Account Debited	PR	Cash Cr.	Inventory Cr.	Other Accounts Dr.	Accounts Payable Dr.
Mar. 21	516	Defore Industries	Defore Industries	✓	51,352	1,048		52,400
31	517	Payroll	Sales Salaries Expense	621	15,900		15,900	
31		Totals			67,252	1,048	15,900	52,400
					(101)	(119)	(x)	(201)

General Journal — Page 2

Mar. 16	Accounts Payable—Defore Industries	201/✓	200	
	Inventory	119		200
	To record credit memorandum received.			
26	Sales Returns and Allowances	414	600	
	Accounts Receivable—Marjorie Allen	106/✓		600
	To record credit memorandum issued.			

Accounts Receivable Ledger

Marjorie Allen

Date	PR	Debit	Credit	Balance
Mar. 20	S2	5,600		5,600
26	G2		600	5,000

Dennie Hoskins

Date	PR	Debit	Credit	Balance
Mar. 6	S2	10,200		10,200
16	R3		10,200	0

Jennifer Nelson

Date	PR	Debit	Credit	Balance
Mar. 4	S2	16,800		16,800
14	R3		16,800	0

Accounts Payable Ledger

Defore Industries

Date	PR	Debit	Credit	Balance
Mar. 11	P3		52,600	52,600
16	G2	200		52,400
21	D3	52,400		0

Mack Company

Date	PR	Debit	Credit	Balance
Mar. 6	P3		1,220	1,220

Schmidt Supply

Date	PR	Debit	Credit	Balance
Mar. 18	P3		22,850	22,850

Welch Company

Date	PR	Debit	Credit	Balance
Mar. 22	P3		41,625	41,625

General Ledger (Partial Listing)

Cash Acct. No. 101

Date	PR	Debit	Credit	Balance
Mar. 31	R3	187,140		187,140
31	D3		67,252	119,888

Accounts Receivable Acct. No. 106

Date	PR	Debit	Credit	Balance
Mar. 26	G2		600	(600)
31	S2	32,600		32,000
31	R3		27,000	5,000

Inventory Acct. No. 119

Date	PR	Debit	Credit	Balance
Mar. 16	G2		200	(200)
21	D3		1,048	(1,248)
31	P3	94,225		92,977
31	S2		24,100	68,877
31	R3		67,340	1,537

Office Supplies Acct. No. 124

Date	PR	Debit	Credit	Balance
Mar. 31	P3	1,220		1,220

Store Equipment Acct. No. 165

Date	PR	Debit	Credit	Balance
Mar. 18	P3	22,850		22,850

Accounts Payable Acct. No. 201

Date	PR	Debit	Credit	Balance
Mar. 16	G2	200		(200)
31	P3		118,295	118,095
31	D3	52,400		65,695

Long-Term Notes Payable Acct. No. 251

Date	PR	Debit	Credit	Balance
Mar. 12	R3		26,000	26,000

Sales Acct. No. 413

Date	PR	Debit	Credit	Balance
Mar. 31	S2		32,600	32,600
31	R3		134,680	167,280

Sales Returns and Allowances Acct. No. 414

Date	PR	Debit	Credit	Balance
Mar. 26	G2	600		600

Sales Discounts Acct. No. 415

Date	PR	Debit	Credit	Balance
Mar. 31	R3	540		540

Cost of Goods Sold Acct. No. 502

Date	PR	Debit	Credit	Balance
Mar. 31	R3	67,340		67,340
31	S2	24,100		91,440

Sales Salaries Expense Acct. No. 621

Date	PR	Debit	Credit	Balance
Mar. 31	D3	15,900		15,900

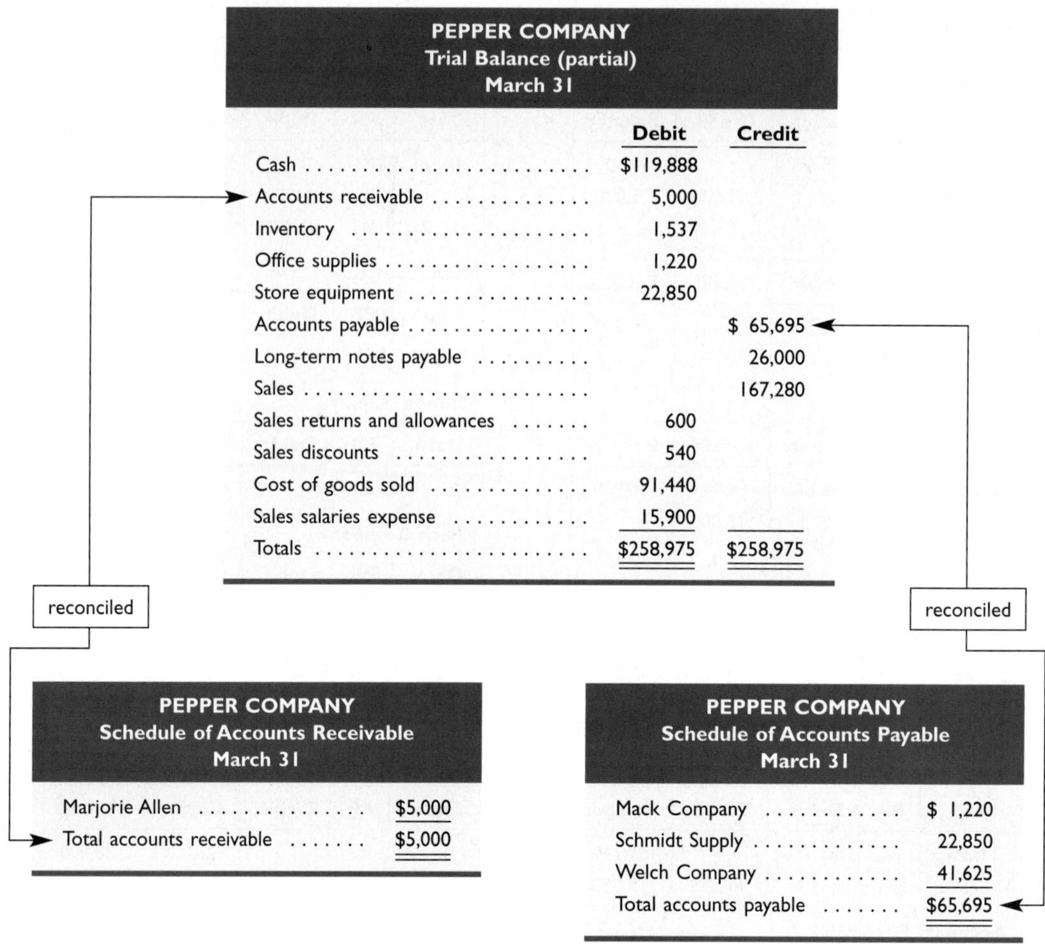

PEPPER COMPANY
Trial Balance (partial)
March 31

	Debit	Credit
Cash	$119,888	
Accounts receivable	5,000	
Inventory	1,537	
Office supplies	1,220	
Store equipment	22,850	
Accounts payable		$ 65,695
Long-term notes payable		26,000
Sales		167,280
Sales returns and allowances	600	
Sales discounts	540	
Cost of goods sold	91,440	
Sales salaries expense	15,900	
Totals	$258,975	$258,975

PEPPER COMPANY
Schedule of Accounts Receivable
March 31

Marjorie Allen	$5,000
Total accounts receivable	$5,000

PEPPER COMPANY
Schedule of Accounts Payable
March 31

Mack Company	$ 1,220
Schmidt Supply	22,850
Welch Company	41,625
Total accounts payable	$65,695

APPENDIX

7A Special Journals under a Periodic System

P3 Journalize and post transactions using special journals in a periodic inventory system.

This appendix describes special journals under a periodic inventory system. Each journal is slightly impacted. The sales journal and the cash receipts journal both require one less column (namely that of Cost of Goods Sold Dr., Inventory Cr.). The Purchases Journal replaces the Inventory Dr. column with a Purchases Dr. column in a periodic system. The cash disbursements journal replaces the Inventory Cr. column with a Purchases Discounts Cr. column in a periodic system. These changes are illustrated.

Sales Journal

The sales journal using the periodic inventory system is shown in Exhibit 7A.1. The difference in the sales journal between the perpetual and periodic system is the exclusion of the column to record cost of goods sold and inventory amounts for each sale. The periodic system does *not* record the increase in cost of goods sold and the decrease in inventory at the time of each sale.

Exhibit 7A.1

Sales Journal—Periodic System

Sales Journal — Page 3

Date	Account Debited	Invoice Number	PR	Accounts Receivable Dr. Sales Cr.
Feb. 2	Jason Henry	307	✓	450
7	Albert Co.	308	✓	500
13	Kam Moore	309	✓	350
15	Paul Roth	310	✓	200
22	Jason Henry	311	✓	225
25	Frank Booth	312	✓	175
28	Albert Co.	313	✓	250
28	Total			2,150
				(106/413)

Cash Receipts Journal

The cash receipts journal using the periodic system is shown in Exhibit 7A.2. Note the absence of the column on the far right side to record debits to Cost of Goods Sold and credits to Inventory for the cost of merchandise sold (seen under the perpetual system). Consistent with the cash receipts journal shown in Exhibit 7.7, we show only the weekly (summary) cash sale entries.

Exhibit 7A.2

Cash Receipts Journal—Periodic System

Cash Receipts Journal — Page 2

Date	Account Credited	Explanation	PR	Cash Dr.	Sales Discount Dr.	Accounts Receivable Cr.	Sales Cr.	Other Accounts Cr.
Feb. 7	Sales	Cash sales	x	4,450			4,450	
12	Jason Henry	Invoice, 2/2	✓	441	9	450		
14	Sales	Cash sales	x	3,925			3,925	
17	Albert Co.	Invoice, 2/7	✓	490	10	500		
20	Notes Payable	Note to bank	245	750				750
21	Sales	Cash sales	x	4,700			4,700	
22	Interest revenue	Bank account	409	250				250
23	Kam Moore	Invoice, 2/13	✓	343	7	350		
25	Paul Roth	Invoice, 2/15	✓	196	4	200		
28	Sales	Cash sales	x	4,225			4,225	
28	Totals			19,770	30	1,500	17,300	1,000
				(101)	(415)	(106)	(413)	(x)

Purchases Journal

The purchases journal using the periodic system is shown in Exhibit 7A.3. This journal under a perpetual system included an Inventory column where the periodic system now has a Purchases column.

Exhibit 7A.3

Purchases Journal—Periodic System

Purchases Journal — Page 1

Date	Account	Date of Invoice	Terms	PR	Accounts Payable Cr.	Purchases Dr.	Office Supplies Dr.	Other Accounts Dr.
Feb. 3	Horning Supply Co.	2/2	n/30	✓	350	275	75	
5	Ace Mfg. Co.	2/5	2/10, n/30	✓	200	200		
13	Wynet and Co.	2/10	2/10, n/30	✓	150	150		
20	Smite Co.	2/18	2/10, n/30	✓	300	300		
25	Ace Mfg. Co.	2/24	2/10, n/30	✓	100	100		
28	Store Supplies/ITT Co.	2/28	n/30	125/✓	225	125	25	75
28	Totals				1,325	1,150	100	75
					(201)	(505)	(124)	(x)

Cash Disbursements Journal

The cash disbursements journal using a periodic system is shown in Exhibit 7A.4. This journal under the perpetual system included an Inventory column where the periodic system now has the Purchases Discounts column.

Exhibit 7A.4

Cash Disbursements Journal—Periodic System

Cash Disbursements Journal — Page 2

Date	Ck. No.	Payee	Account Debited	PR	Cash Cr.	Purchases Discounts Cr.	Other Accounts Dr.	Accounts Payable Dr.
Feb. 3	105	L. and N. Railroad	Purchases	505	15		15	
12	106	East Sales Co.	Purchases	505	25		25	
15	107	Ace Mfg. Co.	Ace Mfg. Co.	✓	196	4		200
15	108	Jerry Hale	Salaries Expense	622	250		250	
20	109	Wynet and Co.	Wynet and Co.	✓	147	3		150
28	110	Smite Co.	Smite Co.	✓	294	6		300
28		Totals			927	13	290	650
					(101)	(507)	(x)	(201)

Demonstration Problem—Periodic System

Refer to Pepper Company's selected transactions described under the Demonstration Problem—Perpetual System to fulfill the following requirements.

Required

1. Open the following selected general ledger accounts: Cash (101), Accounts Receivable (106), Office Supplies (124), Store Equipment (165), Accounts Payable (201), Long-Term Notes Payable (251), Sales (413), Sales Returns and Allowances (414), Sales Discounts (415), Purchases (505), Purchases Returns and Allowances (506), Purchases Discounts (507), and Sales Salaries Expense (621). Open the following accounts receivable ledger accounts: Marjorie Allen, Dennie Hoskins, and Jennifer Nelson. Open the following accounts payable ledger accounts: Defore Industries, Mack Company, Schmidt Supply, and Welch Company.
2. Enter the transactions using a sales journal, a purchases journal, a cash receipts journal, a cash disbursements journal, and a general journal similar to the ones illustrated in Appendix 7A. Regularly post to the individual customer and creditor accounts. Also, post any amounts that should be posted as individual amounts to general ledger accounts. Foot and crossfoot the journals and make the month-end postings. *Pepper Co. uses the periodic inventory system in this problem.*
3. Prepare a trial balance for the selected general ledger accounts in part 1 and prove the accuracy of subsidiary ledgers by preparing schedules of accounts receivable and accounts payable.

Solution to Demonstration Problem—Periodic System

Sales Journal — Page 2

Date	Account Debited	Invoice Number	PR	Accounts Receivable Dr. Sales Cr.
Mar. 4	Jennifer Nelson	954	✓	16,800
6	Dennie Hoskins	955	✓	10,200
20	Marjorie Allen	956	✓	5,600
31	Totals			32,600
				(106/413)

Cash Receipts Journal — Page 3

Date	Account Credited	Explanation	PR	Cash Dr.	Sales Discount Dr.	Accounts Receivable Cr.	Sales Cr.	Other Accounts Cr.
Mar. 12	L.T. Notes Payable	Note to bank	251	26,000				26,000
14	Jennifer Nelson	Invoice, 3/4	✓	16,464	336	16,800		
16	Dennie Hoskins	Invoice, 3/6	✓	9,996	204	10,200		
31	Sales	Cash sales	x	134,680			134,680	
31	Totals			187,140	540	27,000	134,680	26,000
				(101)	(415)	(106)	(413)	(x)

Purchases Journal — Page 3

Date	Account	Date of Invoice	Terms	PR	Accounts Payable Cr.	Purchases Dr.	Office Supplies Dr.	Other Accounts Dr.
Mar. 6	Office Supplies/Mack Co	3/3	n/30	✓	1,220		1,220	
11	Defore Industries	3/6	2/10, n/30	✓	52,600	52,600		
18	Store Equipment/Schmidt Supp	3/15	n/30	165/✓	22,850			22,850
22	Welch Company	3/18	2/10, n/30	✓	41,625	41,625		
31	Totals				118,295	94,225	1,220	22,850
					(201)	(505)	(124)	(x)

Cash Disbursements Journal — Page 3

Date	Ck. No.	Payee	Account Debited	PR	Cash Cr.	Purch. Discount Cr.	Other Accounts Dr.	Accounts Payable Dr.
Mar. 21	516	Defore Industries	Defore Industries	✓	51,352	1,048		52,400
31	517	Payroll	Sales Salaries Expense	621	15,900		15,900	
31		Totals			67,252	1,048	15,900	52,400
					(101)	(507)	(x)	(201)

General Journal — Page 2

Date	Account	PR	Debit	Credit
Mar. 16	Accounts Payable—Defore Industries	201/✓	200	
	Purchases Returns and Allowances	506		200
	To record credit memorandum received.			
26	Sales Returns and Allowances	414	600	
	Accounts Receivable—Marjorie Allen	106/✓		600
	To record credit memorandum issued.			

Accounts Receivable Ledger

Marjorie Allen

Date	PR	Debit	Credit	Balance
Mar. 20	S2	5,600		5,600
26	G2		600	5,000

Dennie Hoskins

Date	PR	Debit	Credit	Balance
Mar. 6	S2	10,200		10,200
16	R3		10,200	0

Jennifer Nelson

Date	PR	Debit	Credit	Balance
Mar. 4	S2	16,800		16,800
14	R3		16,800	0

Accounts Payable Ledger

Defore Industries

Date	PR	Debit	Credit	Balance
Mar. 11	P3		52,600	52,600
16	G2	200		52,400
21	D3	52,400		0

Mack Company

Date	PR	Debit	Credit	Balance
Mar. 6	P3		1,220	1,220

Schmidt Supply

Date	PR	Debit	Credit	Balance
Mar. 18	P3		22,850	22,850

Welch Company

Date	PR	Debit	Credit	Balance
Mar. 22	P3		41,625	41,625

General Ledger (Partial Listing)

Cash — Acct. No. 101

Date	PR	Debit	Credit	Balance
Mar. 31	R3	187,140		187,140
31	D3		67,252	119,888

Accounts Receivable — Acct. No. 106

Date	PR	Debit	Credit	Balance
Mar. 26	G2		600	(600)
31	S2	32,600		32,000
31	R3		27,000	5,000

Office Supplies — Acct. No. 124

Date	PR	Debit	Credit	Balance
Mar. 31	P3	1,220		1,220

Store Equipment — Acct. No. 165

Date	PR	Debit	Credit	Balance
Mar. 18	P3	22,850		22,850

Accounts Payable — Acct. No. 201

Date	PR	Debit	Credit	Balance
Mar. 16	G2	200		(200)
31	P3		118,295	118,095
31	D3	52,400		65,695

Long-Term Notes Payable — Acct. No. 251

Date	PR	Debit	Credit	Balance
Mar. 12	R3		26,000	26,000

Sales — Acct. No. 413

Date	PR	Debit	Credit	Balance
Mar. 31	S2		32,600	32,600
31	R3		134,680	167,280

Sales Returns and Allowances — Acct. No. 414

Date	PR	Debit	Credit	Balance
Mar. 26	G2	600		600

Sales Discounts — Acct. No. 415

Date	PR	Debit	Credit	Balance
Mar. 31	R3	540		540

Purchases — Acct. No. 505

Date	PR	Debit	Credit	Balance
Mar. 31	P3	94,225		94,225

Purchases Returns and Allowances — Acct. No. 506

Date	PR	Debit	Credit	Balance
Mar. 16	G2		200	200

Purchases Discounts — Acct. No. 507

Date	PR	Debit	Credit	Balance
Mar. 31	D3		1,048	1,048

Sales Salaries Expense — Acct. No. 621

Date	PR	Debit	Credit	Balance
Mar. 31	D3	15,900		15,900

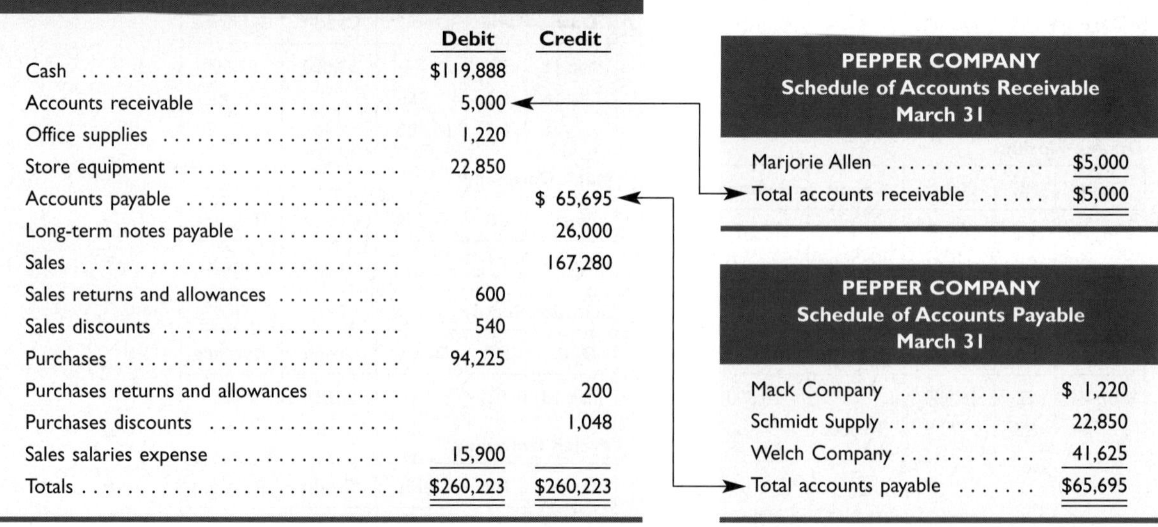

PEPPER COMPANY
Trial Balance (partial)
March 31

	Debit	Credit
Cash	$119,888	
Accounts receivable	5,000	
Office supplies	1,220	
Store equipment	22,850	
Accounts payable		$ 65,695
Long-term notes payable		26,000
Sales		167,280
Sales returns and allowances	600	
Sales discounts	540	
Purchases	94,225	
Purchases returns and allowances		200
Purchases discounts		1,048
Sales salaries expense	15,900	
Totals	$260,223	$260,223

PEPPER COMPANY
Schedule of Accounts Receivable
March 31

Marjorie Allen	$5,000
Total accounts receivable	$5,000

PEPPER COMPANY
Schedule of Accounts Payable
March 31

Mack Company	$ 1,220
Schmidt Supply	22,850
Welch Company	41,625
Total accounts payable	$65,695

Summary

C1 **Identify fundamental principles of accounting information systems.** Accounting information systems are governed by five fundamental principles: control, relevance, compatibility, flexibility, and cost-benefit.

C2 **Identify components of accounting information systems.** The five basic components of an accounting information system are source documents, input devices, information processors, information storage, and output devices.

C3 **Explain the goals and uses of special journals.** Special journals are used for recording transactions of similar type, each meant to cover one kind of transaction. Four of the most common special journals are the sales journal, cash receipts journal, purchases journal, and cash disbursements journal. Special journals are efficient and cost-effective tools in the journalizing and posting processes.

C4 **Describe the use of controlling accounts and subsidiary ledgers.** A general ledger keeps controlling accounts such as Accounts Receivable and Accounts Payable, but details on individual accounts making up the controlling account are kept in subsidiary ledgers (such as an accounts receivable ledger). The balance in a controlling account must equal the sum of its subsidiary account balances after posting is complete.

C5 **Explain how technology-based information systems impact accounting.** Technology-based information systems aim to increase the accuracy, speed, efficiency, and convenience of accounting procedures.

A1 **Compute segment return on assets and use it to evaluate segment performance.** A business segment is a part of a company that is separately identified by its products or services or by the geographic market it serves. Analysis of a company's segments is aided by the segment return on assets (segment operating income divided by segment average assets).

P1 **Journalize and post transactions using special journals.** Each special journal is devoted to similar kinds of transactions. Transactions are journalized on one line of a special journal, with columns devoted to specific accounts, dates, names, posting references, explanations, and other necessary information. Posting is threefold: (1) individual amounts in the Other Accounts column are posted to their general ledger accounts on a regular (daily) basis, (2) individual amounts in a column whose total is *not* posted to a controlling account at the end of a period (month) are posted regularly (daily) to their general ledger accounts, and (3) total amounts for all columns except the Other Accounts column are posted at the end of a period (month) to their column's account title in the general ledger. Most companies also maintain subsidiary ledgers for special accounts such as accounts receivable and accounts payable. Transactions that impact subsidiary ledgers are posted on a regular (daily) basis.

P2 **Prepare and prove the accuracy of subsidiary ledgers.** Account balances in the general ledger and its subsidiary ledgers are tested for accuracy after posting is complete. This procedure is twofold: (1) prepare a trial balance of the general ledger to confirm that debits equal credits and (2) prepare a schedule to confirm that the controlling account's balance equals the subsidiary ledger's balance.

P3[A] **Journalize and post transactions using special journals in a periodic inventory system.** Transactions are journalized and posted using special journals in a periodic system. The methods are similar to those in a perpetual system; the primary difference is that both cost of goods sold and inventory are not adjusted at the time of each sale. This usually results in the deletion (or renaming) of one or more columns devoted to these accounts in each special journal.

Guidance Answers to **Decision Maker** and **Decision Ethics**

Accountant The main issue is whether commissions have an actual or perceived impact on the integrity and objectivity of your advice. You probably should not accept a commission arrangement (the AICPA Code of Ethics prohibits it when you perform the audit or a review). In any event, you should tell the client of your commission arrangement. Also, you need to seriously examine the merits of agreeing to a commission arrangement when you are in a position to exploit it.

Entrepreneur The accounts receivable ledger has much of the information you need. It lists detailed information for each customer's account, including the amounts, dates for transactions, and dates of payments. It can be reorganized into an "aging schedule" to show how long customers wait before paying their bills.

Controller Much of the information you need is in the accounts payable ledger. It contains information for each supplier, the amounts due, and when payments are made. This subsidiary ledger along with information on credit terms should enable you to conduct your analyses.

Banker This merchandiser's segment information is likely to greatly impact your loan decision. The risks associated with the company's two sources of net income are quite different. While net income is up by 10%, U.S. operations are performing poorly and Cuban operations are subject to many uncertainties. These uncertainties depend on political events, legal issues, business relationships, Cuban economic conditions, and a host of other risks. Overall, net income results suggested a low-risk loan opportunity, but the segment information reveals a high-risk situation.

Guidance Answers to **Quick Checks**

1. The five components are source documents, input devices, information processors, information storage, and output devices.
2. Information processors interpret, transform, and summarize the recorded accounting information so that it can be used in analysis, interpretation, and decision making.

3. Data saved in information storage are used to prepare periodic financial reports and special-purpose internal reports as well as source documentation for auditors.
4. All cash payments by check are recorded in the cash disbursements journal.
5. Columnar journals allow us to accumulate repetitive debits and credits and post them as column totals rather than as individual amounts from each entry.
6. The equality of debits and credits is kept within the general ledger. The subsidiary ledger keeps the customer's individual account and is used only for supplementary information.
7. An initial and the page number of the journal from which the amount was posted are entered in the PR column next to the amount.
8. A separate column for Sales Taxes Payable can be included in both the cash receipts journal and the sales journal.
9. This refers to a procedure of using copies of sales invoices as a sales journal. Each invoice amount is posted directly to the customer's account. All invoices are totaled at period-end for posting to the general ledger accounts.
10. The normal recording and posting procedures are threefold. First, transactions are entered in a special journal if applicable. Second, individual amounts are posted to any subsidiary ledger accounts. Third, column totals are posted to general ledger accounts if not already individually posted.
11. Controlling accounts are debited periodically for an amount or amounts equal to the sum of their respective debits in the subsidiary ledgers (equals journal column totals), and they are credited periodically for an amount or amounts equal to the sum of their respective credits in the subsidiary ledgers (from journal column totals).
12. Tests for accuracy of account balances in the general ledger and subsidiary ledgers are twofold. First, we prepare a trial balance of the general ledger to confirm that debits equal credits. Second, we prove the subsidiary ledgers by preparing schedules of accounts receivable and accounts payable.
13. The general journal is still needed for adjusting, closing, and correcting entries and for special transactions such as sales returns, purchases returns, and certain asset purchases.
14. Integrated systems can save time and minimize errors. This is so because actions taken in one part of the system automatically affect and update related parts.
15. Computer systems offer increased accuracy, speed, efficiency, and convenience.
16. Computer networks can create advantages by linking computers, and giving different users and different computers access to common databases, programs, and hardware.
17. ERP software involves integrated programs, from order taking to manufacturing to accounting. It can speed decision-making, help identify costs for reduction, and aid managers in controlling operations.

Key Terms

Key Terms are available at the book's Website for learning and testing in an online Flashcard Format.

Accounting information systems (p. 262)
Accounts payable ledger (p. 267)
Accounts receivable ledger (p. 267)
Batch processing (p. 277)
Cash disbursements journal (p. 274)
Cash receipts journal (p. 271)
Check register (p. 275)
Columnar journal (p. 268)
Compatibility principle (p. 263)
Components of accounting systems (p. 263)
Computer networks (p. 277)
Controlling account (p. 267)
Control principle (p. 262)
Cost-benefit principle (p. 263)
Enterprise resource planning (ERP) software (p. 277)
Flexibility principle (p. 263)
General journal (p. 266)
Information processors (p. 264)
Information storage (p. 264)
Input devices (p. 264)
Internal controls (p. 262)
Online processing (p. 277)
Output devices (p. 265)
Purchases journal (p. 273)
Relevance principle (p. 262)
Sales journal (p. 267)
Schedule of accounts payable (p. 274)
Schedule of accounts receivable (p. 269)
Segment return on assets (p. 278)
Special journal (p. 266)
Subsidiary ledger (p. 266)

Personal Interactive Quiz

Personal Interactive Quizzes A and B are available at the book's Website to reinforce and assess your learning.

Superscript ^{A} denotes assignments based on Appendix 7A.

Discussion Questions

1. What are the five fundamental principles of accounting information systems?
2. What are five basic components of an accounting system?
3. What are source documents? Give two examples.

4. What is the purpose of an input device? Give examples of input devices for computer systems.

5. What is the difference between data that are stored off-line and data that are stored online?

6. What purpose is served by the output devices of an accounting system?

7. When special journals are used, they are usually used to record each of four different types of transactions. What are these four types of transactions?

8. What notations are entered into the Posting Reference column of a ledger account?

9. When a general journal entry is used to record sales returns, the credit of the entry must be posted twice. Does this cause the trial balance to be out of balance? Explain.

10. Describe the procedures involving the use of copies of a company's sales invoices as a sales journal.

11. Credits to customer accounts and credits to Other Accounts are individually posted from a cash receipts journal such as the one in Exhibit 7.7. Why not put both types of credits in the same column and save journal space?

12. Why should sales to and receipts of cash from credit customers be recorded and posted immediately?

13. Locate the note that discusses **Krispy Kreme**'s operations by segments in Appendix A. In what segment does it predominantly operate?

14. Does the income statement of **Tastykake** in Appendix A indicate the net income earned by its business segments? If so, list them.

15. Does the balance sheet of **Harley-Davidson** in Appendix A indicate the identifiable assets owned by its business segments? If so, list them.

Red numbers denote Discussion Questions that involve decision-making.

***Homework Manager** repeats all numerical Quick Studies on the book's Website with new numbers.*

QUICK STUDY

QS 7-1
Accounting information system principles
C1

Place the letter of each system principle in the blank next to its best description.

A. Control principle
B. Relevance principle
C. Compatibility principle
D. Flexibility principle
E. Cost-benefit principle

1. ______ The principle prescribes the accounting information system to change in response to technological advances and competitive pressures.

2. ______ The principle prescribes the accounting information system to help monitor activities.

3. ______ The principle prescribes the accounting information system to provide timely information for effective decision making.

4. ______ The principle prescribes the accounting information system to adapt to the unique characteristics of the company.

5. ______ The principle that affects all other accounting information system principles.

QS 7-2
Accounting information system
C2

Fill in the blanks to complete the following descriptions:

1. With ______ processing, source documents are accumulated for a period and then processed all at the same time, such as once a day, week, or month.

2. A computer ______ allows different computer users to share access to data and programs.

3. A ______ is an input device that captures writing and other input directly from source documents.

4. ______ ______ ______ software comprises programs that help manage a company's vital operations, from manufacturing to accounting.

QS 7-3
Accounting information system components
C2

Identify the most likely role in an accounting system played by each of the numbered items 1 through 12 by assigning a letter from the list A through E on the left:

A. Source documents
B. Input devices
C. Information processors
D. Information storage
E. Output devices

______ **1.** Bar code reader
______ **2.** Filing cabinet
______ **3.** Bank statement
______ **4.** Computer scanner
______ **5.** Computer keyboard
______ **6.** Zip drive
______ **7.** Computer monitor
______ **8.** Invoice from a supplier
______ **9.** Computer software
______ **10.** Computer printer
______ **11.** Digital camera
______ **12.** MP3 player

QS 7-4
Identifying the special journal of entry
C3 

Damron Electronics uses a sales journal, a purchases journal, a cash receipts journal, a cash disbursements journal, and a general journal as illustrated in this chapter. Damron recently completed the following transactions *a* through *h*. Identify the journal in which each transaction should be recorded.

a. Paid cash to a creditor.
b. Sold merchandise on credit.
c. Purchased shop supplies on credit.
d. Paid an employee's salary in cash.
e. Borrowed cash from the bank.
f. Sold merchandise for cash.
g. Purchased merchandise on credit.
h. Purchased inventory for cash.

QS 7-5
Entries in the general journal
C3

Lue Gifts uses a sales journal, a purchases journal, a cash receipts journal, a cash disbursements journal, and a general journal as illustrated in this chapter. Journalize its November transactions that should be recorded in the general journal. For those not recorded in the general journal, identify the special journal where each should be recorded.

Nov. 2 Purchased $2,900 of merchandise on credit from the Elko Co., terms 2/10, n/30.
12 The owner, T. Lue, contributed an automobile worth $15,000 to the business.
16 Sold $1,100 of merchandise (cost is $700) on credit to K. Gould, terms n/30.
19 K. Gould returned $150 of (worthless) merchandise originally purchased on November 16 (assume the cost of this merchandise is left in cost of goods sold).

QS 7-6
Required segment reporting
A1

Debray is a company with publicly traded securities and it operates in more than one industry. Which of the following items of information about each industry segment must the company report?

a. Operating income
b. Depreciation
c. Inventory
d. Sales
e. Cash flows
f. Capital expenditures
g. Identifiable assets
h. Amortization

Homework Manager *repeats all numerical Exercises on the book's Website with new numbers.* 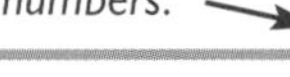

EXERCISES

Exercise 7-1
Sales journal—perpetual
P1

Hutton Company uses a sales journal, a purchases journal, a cash receipts journal, a cash disbursement journal, and a general journal. The following transactions occur in the month of March:

Mar. 2 Sold merchandise costing $300 to B. Fager for $450 cash, invoice no. 5703.
5 Purchased $2,300 of merchandise on credit from Marsh Corp.
7 Sold merchandise costing $800 to J. Dryer for $1,150, terms 2/10, n/30, invoice no. 5704.
8 Borrowed $8,000 cash by signing a note payable to the bank.
12 Sold merchandise costing $200 to R. Land for $320, terms n/30, invoice no. 5705.
16 Received $1,127 cash from J. Dryer to pay for the purchase of March 7.
19 Sold used store equipment for $900 cash to Malone, Inc.
25 Sold merchandise costing $350 to T. Burton for $550, terms n/30, invoice no. 5706.

Prepare headings for a sales journal like the one in Exhibit 7.5. Journalize the March transactions that should be recorded in this sales journal.

Exercise 7-2
Identifying journal of entry C3

Refer to Exercise 7-1 and for each of the March transactions identify the journal in which it would be recorded. Assume the company uses a sales journal, purchases journal, cash receipts journal, cash disbursements journal, and general journal as illustrated in this chapter.

Exercise 7-3[A]
Sales journal—periodic P3

Prepare headings for a sales journal like the one in Exhibit 7A.1. Journalize the March transactions shown in Exercise 7-1 that should be recorded in the sales journal assuming that the periodic inventory system is used.

Exercise 7-4
Cash receipts journal—perpetual
P1

Moeder Co. uses a sales journal, a purchases journal, a cash receipts journal, a cash disbursements journal, and a general journal. The following transactions occur in the month of November.

Nov. 3 Purchased $3,100 of merchandise on credit from Hargrave Co., terms n/20.
7 Sold merchandise costing $840 on credit to J. York for $900, subject to a $18 sales discount if paid by the end of the month.
9 Borrowed $2,750 cash by signing a note payable to the bank.
13 J. Emling, the owner, contributed $4,000 cash to the company.
18 Sold merchandise costing $130 to B. Box for $230 cash.
22 Paid Hargrave Co. $3,100 cash for the merchandise purchased on November 3.

27 Received $882 cash from J. York in payment of the November 7 purchase.
30 Paid salaries of $1,600 in cash.

Prepare headings for a cash receipts journal like the one in Exhibit 7.7. Journalize the November transactions that should be recorded in the cash receipts journal.

Exercise 7-5
Identifying journal of entry C3

Refer to Exercise 7-4 and for each of the November transactions identify the journal in which it would be recorded. Assume the company uses a sales journal, purchases journal, cash receipts journal, cash disbursements journal, and general journal as illustrated in this chapter.

Exercise 7-6[A]
Cash receipts journal—periodic P3

Prepare headings for a cash receipts journal like the one in Exhibit 7A.2. Journalize the November transactions shown in Exercise 7-4 that should be recorded in the cash receipts journal assuming that the periodic inventory system is used.

Exercise 7-7
Purchases journal—perpetual P1

Redmon Company uses a sales journal, a purchases journal, a cash receipts journal, a cash disbursements journal, and a general journal. The following transactions occur in the month of June.

June 1 Purchased $8,100 of merchandise on credit from Vick, Inc., terms n/30.
8 Sold merchandise costing $900 on credit to R. Panke for $1,500 subject to a $30 sales discount if paid by the end of the month.
14 Purchased $240 of store supplies from Poe Company on credit, terms n/30.
17 Purchased $260 of office supplies on credit from Rehmer Company, terms n/30.
24 Sold merchandise costing $400 to L. Barnett for $630 cash.
28 Purchased store supplies from Piburn's for $90 cash.
29 Paid Vick, Inc., $8,100 cash for the merchandise purchased on June 1.

Prepare headings for a purchases journal like the one in Exhibit 7.9. Journalize the June transactions that should be recorded in the purchases journal.

Exercise 7-8
Identifying journal of entry C3

Refer to Exercise 7-7 and for each of the June transactions identify the journal in which it would be recorded. Assume the company uses a sales journal, purchases journal, cash receipts journal, cash disbursements journal, and general journal as illustrated in this chapter.

Exercise 7-9[A]
Purchases journal—periodic P3

Prepare headings for a purchases journal like the one in Exhibit 7A.3. Journalize the June transactions from Exercise 7-7 that should be recorded in the purchases journal assuming the periodic inventory system is used.

Exercise 7-10
Cash disbursements journal—perpetual P1

Politte Supply uses a sales journal, a purchases journal, a cash receipts journal, a cash disbursements journal, and a general journal. The following transactions occur in the month of April.

Apr. 3 Purchased merchandise for $2,750 on credit from Scott, Inc., terms 2/10, n/30.
9 Issued check no. 210 to Kidman Corp. to buy store supplies for $450.
12 Sold merchandise costing $400 on credit to C. Myers for $670, terms n/30.
17 Issued check no. 211 for $1,500 to pay off a note payable to City Bank.
20 Purchased merchandise for $3,500 on credit from LeBron, terms 2/10, n/30.
29 Issued check no. 212 to LeBron to pay the amount due for the purchase of April 20, less the discount.
30 Paid salary of $1,700 to B. Decker by issuing check no. 213.
31 Issued check no. 214 to Scott, Inc., to pay the amount due for the purchase of April 3.

Prepare headings for a cash disbursements journal like the one in Exhibit 7.11. Journalize the April transactions that should be recorded in the cash disbursements journal.

Exercise 7-11
Identifying journal of entry C3

Refer to Exercise 7-10 and for each of the April transactions identify the journal in which it would be recorded. Assume the company uses a sales journal, purchases journal, cash receipts journal, cash disbursements journal, and general journal as illustrated in this chapter.

Exercise 7-12[A]
Cash disbursements journal—periodic P3

Prepare headings for a cash disbursements journal like the one in Exhibit 7A.4. Journalize the April transactions from Exercise 7-10 that should be recorded in the cash disbursements journal assuming that the periodic inventory system is used.

Exercise 7-13
Special journal transactions and error discovery
P1

Porter Pharmacy uses the following journals: sales journal, purchases journal, cash receipts journal, cash disbursements journal, and general journal. On June 5, Porter purchased merchandise priced at $12,000, subject to credit terms of 2/10, n/30. On June 14, the pharmacy paid the net amount due for the merchandise. In journalizing the payment, the pharmacy debited Accounts Payable for $12,000 but failed to record the cash discount on the purchases. Cash was properly credited for the actual $11,760 paid. (*a*) In what journals would the June 5 and the June 14 transactions be recorded? (*b*) What procedure is likely to discover the error in journalizing the June 14 transaction?

Exercise 7-14
Posting to subsidiary ledger accounts; preparing a schedule of accounts receivable
P1 P2

At the end of May, the sales journal of Clear View appears as follows:

Sales Journal

Date	Account Debited	Invoice Number	PR	Accounts Receivable Dr. Sales Cr.	Cost of Goods Sold Dr. Inventory Cr.
May 6	Aaron Reckers	190		2,880	2,200
10	Sara Reed	191		1,940	1,600
17	Anna Page	192		850	500
25	Sara Reed	193		340	200
31	Totals			6,010	4,500

Clear View also recorded the return of defective merchandise with the following entry:

May 20	Sales Returns and Allowances	250	
	Accounts Receivable—Anna Page		250
	Customer returned (worthless) merchandise.		

Required

1. Open an accounts receivable subsidiary ledger that has a T-account for each customer listed in the sales journal. Post to the customer accounts the entries in the sales journal and any portion of the general journal entry that affects a customer's account.

2. Open a general ledger that has T-accounts for Accounts Receivable, Inventory, Sales, Sales Returns and Allowances, and Cost of Goods Sold. Post the sales journal and any portion of the general journal entry that affects these accounts.

3. Prepare a schedule of accounts receivable and prove that its total equals the balance in the Accounts Receivable controlling account.

Check (3) Accounts Receivable, $5,760

Exercise 7-15
Accounts receivable ledger; posting from sales journal
P1 P2

Winslow Company posts its sales invoices directly and then binds them into a Sales Journal. Winslow had the following credit sales to these customers during June:

June 2	Joe Mack	$ 3,600
8	Eric Horner	6,100
10	Tess Cox	13,400
14	Hong Jiang	20,500
20	Tess Cox	11,200
29	Joe Mack	7,300
	Total credit sales	$62,100

Required

1. Open an accounts receivable subsidiary ledger having a T-account for each customer. Post the invoices to the subsidiary ledger.

2. Open an Accounts Receivable controlling T-account and a Sales T-account to reflect general ledger accounts. Post the end-of-month total from the sales journal to these accounts.

3. Prepare a schedule of accounts receivable and prove that its total equals the Accounts Receivable controlling account balance.

Exercise 7-16
Purchases journal and error identification

P1 

A company that records credit purchases in a purchases journal and records purchases returns in a general journal made the following errors. Indicate when each error should be discovered.

1. Posted a purchases return to the Accounts Payable account and to the creditor's subsidiary account but did not post the purchases return to the Inventory account.
2. Posted a purchases return to the Inventory account and to the Accounts Payable account but did not post to the creditor's subsidiary account.
3. Correctly recorded a $4,000 purchase in the purchases journal but posted it to the creditor's subsidiary account as a $400 purchase.
4. Made an addition error in determining the balance of a creditor's subsidiary account.
5. Made an addition error in totaling the Office Supplies column of the purchases journal.

Exercise 7-17
Computing and analyzing segment return on assets

A1 

Refer to Exhibit 7.13 and complete the segment return on assets table for Wolfe Company. Analyze your findings and identify the segment with the highest, and that with the lowest, segment return on assets.

	Segment Operating Income (in $ mil.)		Segment Assets (in $ mil.)		Segment Return on Assets
Segment	**2004**	**2003**	**2004**	**2003**	**2004**
Specialty					
Skiing Group	$ 62	$ 58	$ 581	$440	
Skating Group	9	6	53	42	
Specialty Footwear	22	19	155	136	
Other Specialty	11	4	37	24	
Subtotal	104	87	826	642	
General Merchandise					
South America	32	36	305	274	
United States	7	8	52	35	
Europe	5	3	14	12	
Subtotal	44	47	371	321	
Total	$148	$134	$1197	$963	

Check Europe segment return, 38.5%

PROBLEM SET A

Problem 7-1A
Special journals, subsidiary ledgers, and schedule of accounts receivable—perpetual

C4 P1 P2 

Wise Company completes these transactions during April of the current year (the terms of all its credit sales are 2/10, n/30):

Apr. 2 Purchased $13,300 of merchandise on credit from Negi Company, invoice dated April 2, terms 2/10, n/60.
3 Sold merchandise on credit to Brooke Sledd, Invoice No. 760, for $3,000 (cost is $2,000).
3 Purchased $1,380 of office supplies on credit from Madison, Inc. Invoice dated April 2, terms n/10 EOM.
4 Issued Check No. 587 to *U.S. View* for advertising expense, $999.
5 Sold merchandise on credit to Paul Kohr, Invoice No. 761, for $8,000 (cost is $6,500).
6 Received an $85 credit memorandum from Madison, Inc., for the return of some of the office supplies received on April 3.
9 Purchased $11,125 of store equipment on credit from Ned's Supply, invoice dated April 9, terms n/10 EOM.
11 Sold merchandise on credit to Amy Nilson, Invoice No. 762, for $9,500 (cost is $7,000).
12 Issued Check No. 588 to Negi Company in payment of its April 2 invoice, less the discount.
13 Received payment from Brooke Sledd for the April 3 sale, less the discount.
13 Sold $4,100 of merchandise on credit to Brooke Sledd (cost is $2,600), Invoice No. 763.
14 Received payment from Paul Kohr for the April 5 sale, less the discount.
16 Issued Check No. 589, payable to Payroll, in payment of sales salaries expense for the first half of the month, $9,750. Cashed the check and paid employees.

16 Cash sales for the first half of the month are $50,840 (cost is $33,880). (Cash sales are recorded daily from cash register data but are recorded only twice in this problem to reduce repetitive entries.)
17 Purchased $12,750 of merchandise on credit from Price Company, invoice dated April 17, terms 2/10, n/30.
18 Borrowed $50,000 cash from First State Bank by signing a long-term note payable.
20 Received payment from Amy Nilson for the April 11 sale, less the discount.
20 Purchased $730 of store supplies on credit from Ned's Supply, invoice dated April 19, terms n/10 EOM.
23 Received a $400 credit memorandum from Price Company for the return of defective merchandise received on April 17.
23 Received payment from Brooke Sledd for the April 13 sale, less the discount.
25 Purchased $10,375 of merchandise on credit from Negi Company, invoice dated April 24, terms 2/10, n/60.
26 Issued Check No. 590 to Price Company in payment of its April 17 invoice, less the return and the discount.
27 Sold $3,070 of merchandise on credit to Paul Kohr, Invoice No. 764 (cost is $2,420).
27 Sold $5,700 of merchandise on credit to Amy Nilson, Invoice No. 765 (cost is $3,305).
30 Issued Check No. 591, payable to Payroll, in payment of the sales salaries expense for the last half of the month, $9,750.
30 Cash sales for the last half of the month are $70,975 (cost is $55,900).

Required

1. Prepare a sales journal like that in Exhibit 7.5 and a cash receipts journal like that in Exhibit 7.7. Number both journal pages as page 3. Then review the transactions of Wise Company and enter those that should be journalized in the sales journal and those that should be journalized in the cash receipts journal. Ignore any transactions that should be journalized in a purchases journal, a cash disbursements journal, or a general journal.
2. Open the following general ledger accounts: Cash, Accounts Receivable, Inventory, Long-Term Notes Payable, Cost of Goods Sold, Sales, and Sales Discounts. Enter the March 31 balances for Cash ($85,000), Inventory ($125,000), and Long-Term Notes Payable ($210,000). Also open accounts receivable subsidiary ledger accounts for Paul Kohr, Brooke Sledd, and Amy Nilson.
3. Verify that amounts that should be posted as individual amounts from the journals have been posted. (Such items are immediately posted.) Foot and crossfoot the journals and make the month-end postings.
4. Prepare a trial balance of the general ledger and prove the accuracy of the subsidiary ledger by preparing a schedule of accounts receivable.

Check Trial balance totals, $415,185

Analysis Component

5. Assume that the total for the schedule of Accounts Receivable does not equal the balance of the controlling account in the general ledger. Describe steps you would take to discover the error(s).

Problem 7-2A[A]
Special journals, subsidiary ledgers, and schedule of accounts receivable—periodic
C4 P2 P3

Check Trial balance totals, $415,185

Assume that Wise Co. in Problem 7-1A uses the periodic inventory system.

Required

1. Prepare headings for a sales journal like the one in Exhibit 7A.1. Prepare headings for a cash receipts journal like the one in Exhibit 7A.2. Journalize the April transactions shown in Problem 7-1A that should be recorded in the sales journal and the cash receipts journal assuming the *periodic* inventory system is used.
2. Open the general ledger accounts with balances as shown in Problem 7-1A (do not open a Cost of Goods Sold ledger account). Under the periodic system, an Inventory account exists but is inactive until its balance is updated to the correct inventory balance at year-end. In this problem, the Inventory account remains inactive but must be included to correctly complete the trial balance.
3. Complete parts 3, 4, and 5 of Problem 7-1A using the results of parts 1 and 2 of this problem.

Problem 7-3A
Special journals, subsidiary ledgers, and schedule of accounts payable—perpetual
C4 P1 P2

The April transactions of Wise Company are described in Problem 7-1A.

Required

1. Prepare a general journal, a purchases journal like that in Exhibit 7.9, and a cash disbursements journal like that in Exhibit 7.11. Number all journal pages as page 3. Review the April transactions of Wise Company and enter those transactions that should be journalized in the general journal, the purchases journal, or the cash disbursements journal. Ignore any transactions that should be journalized in a sales journal or cash receipts journal.

2. Open the following general ledger accounts: Cash, Inventory, Office Supplies, Store Supplies, Store Equipment, Accounts Payable, Long-Term Notes Payable, Sales Salaries Expense, and Advertising Expense. Enter the March 31 balances of Cash ($85,000), Inventory ($125,000), and Long-Term Notes Payable ($210,000). Also open accounts payable subsidiary ledger accounts for Ned's Supply, Negi Company, Price Company, and Madison, Inc.

3. Verify that amounts that should be posted as individual amounts from the journals have been posted. (Such items are immediately posted.) Foot and crossfoot the journals and make the month-end postings.

4. Prepare a trial balance of the general ledger and a schedule of accounts payable.

Check Trial balance totals, $233,525

Problem 7-4A[A]
Special journals, subsidiary ledgers, and schedule of accounts payable—periodic
C4 P2 P3

Refer to Problem 7-1A and assume that Wise Co. uses the periodic inventory system.

Required

1. Prepare a general journal, a purchases journal like that in Exhibit 7A.3, and a cash disbursements journal like that in Exhibit 7A.4. Number all journal pages as page 3. Review the April transactions of Wise Company (Problem 7-1A) and enter those transactions that should be journalized in the general journal, the purchases journal, or the cash disbursements journal. Ignore any transaction that should be journalized in a sales journal or cash receipts journal.

2. Open the following general ledger accounts: Cash, Inventory, Office Supplies, Store Supplies, Store Equipment, Accounts Payable, Long-Term Notes Payable, Purchases, Purchases Returns and Allowances, Purchases Discounts, Sales Salaries Expense, and Advertising Expense. Enter the March 31 balances of Cash ($85,000), Inventory ($125,000), and Long-Term Notes Payable ($210,000). Also open accounts payable subsidiary ledger accounts for Ned's Supply, Negi Company, Price Company, and Madison, Inc.

3. Complete parts 3 and 4 of Problem 7-3A using the results of parts 1 and 2 of this problem.

Check Trial balance totals, $234,438

Problem 7-5A
Special journals, subsidiary ledgers, trial balance—perpetual
C4 P1 P2

mhhe.com/larson

(If the Working Papers that accompany this textbook are not being used, omit this problem.)
You have just taken over the accounting for Choi Enterprises, whose annual accounting period ends December 31. The company's previous accountant journalized its transactions through December 15 and posted all items that required posting as individual amounts (see the journals and ledgers in the Working Papers). The company's transactions beginning on December 16 follow (terms for all its credit sales are 2/10, n/30):

Dec. 16 Sold merchandise on credit to Hanna Seppa, Invoice No. 916, for $7,700 (cost is $4,600).
17 Received a $1,040 credit memorandum from Funk Company for the return of merchandise received on December 15.
17 Purchased $615 of office supplies on credit from KK's Supply Company, invoice dated December 16, terms n/10 EOM.
18 Received a $40 credit memorandum from KK's Supply Company for the return of office supplies received on December 17.
20 Issued a $500 credit memorandum to Bo Brown for defective (worthless) merchandise sold on December 15 and returned for credit.
21 Purchased $6,700 of store equipment on credit from KK's Supply Company, invoice dated December 21, terms n/10 EOM.
22 Received payment from Hanna Seppa for the December 12 sale less the discount.
23 Issued Check No. 623 to Crossland Company in payment of its December 15 invoice less the discount.
24 Sold merchandise on credit to Shilo Jones, Invoice No. 917, for $1,200 (cost is $600).
24 Issued Check No. 624 to Funk Company in payment of its December 15 invoice less the return and the discount.
25 Received payment from Bo Brown for the December 15 sale less the return and the discount.

26 Purchased $8,100 of merchandise from Crossland Company, invoice dated December 25, terms 2/10, n/60.
29 Sold a neighboring merchant five boxes of file folders (office supplies) at their cost of $50 cash.
30 Ken Choi, the sole owner of Choi Enterprises, used Check No. 625 to withdraw $2,500 in cash from the business for personal use.
31 Issued Check No. 626 to Jamie Inman, the company's only sales employee, in payment of her $2,020 salary for the last half of December.
31 Issued Check No. 627 to Access Electric Company in payment of its $710 December electric bill.
31 Cash sales for the last half of the month are $29,600 (cost is $11,200). (Cash sales are recorded daily but are recorded only twice in this problem to reduce repetitive entries.)

Required

1. Record these transactions in the journals provided in the working papers.
2. Verify that amounts that should be posted as individual amounts to the general ledger accounts have been posted, including posting to the customer and creditor accounts. (Such items are immediately posted.) Foot and crossfoot the journals and make the month-end postings.
3. Prepare a December 31 trial balance and prove the accuracy of the subsidiary ledgers by preparing schedules of both accounts receivable and accounts payable.

Check Trial balance totals, $219,408

Problem 7-6A
Special journals, subsidiary ledgers, trial balance—perpetual
C4 P1 P2

mhhe.com/larson

Bishop Company completes these transactions and events during March of the current year (terms for all its credit sales are 2/10, n/30):

Mar. 1 Purchased $42,600 of merchandise from Soy Industries, invoice dated March 1, terms 2/15, n/30.
2 Sold merchandise on credit to Min Cho, Invoice No. 854, for $15,800 (cost is $7,900).
3 Purchased $1,120 of office supplies on credit from Stacy Company, invoice dated March 3, terms n/10 EOM.
3 Sold merchandise on credit to Lance Snow, Invoice No. 855, for $9,200 (cost is $4,600).
6 Borrowed $72,000 cash from Federal Bank by signing a long-term note payable.
9 Purchased $20,850 of office equipment on credit from Tells Supply, invoice dated March 9, terms n/10 EOM.
10 Sold merchandise on credit to Taylor Few, Invoice No. 856, for $4,600 (cost is $2,300).
12 Received payment from Min Cho for the March 2 sale less the discount.
13 Sent Soy Industries Check No. 416 in payment of the March 1 invoice less the discount.
13 Received payment from Lance Snow for the March 3 sale less the discount.
14 Purchased $31,625 of merchandise from the JW Company, invoice dated March 13, terms 2/10, n/30.
15 Issued Check No. 417, payable to Payroll, in payment of sales salaries expense for the first half of the month, $15,900. Cashed the check and paid the employees.
15 Cash sales for the first half of the month are $164,680 (cost is $138,000). (Cash sales are recorded daily, but are recorded only twice here to reduce repetitive entries.)
16 Purchased $1,670 of store supplies on credit from Stacy Company, invoice dated March 16, terms n/10 EOM.
17 Received a $2,425 credit memorandum from JW Company for the return of unsatisfactory merchandise purchased on March 14.
19 Received a $630 credit memorandum from Tells Supply for office equipment received on March 9 and returned for credit.
20 Received payment from Taylor Few for the sale of March 10 less the discount.
23 Issued Check No. 418 to JW Company in payment of the invoice of March 13 less the return and the discount.
27 Sold merchandise on credit to Taylor Few, Invoice No. 857, for $13,910 (cost is $6,220).
28 Sold merchandise on credit to Lance Snow, Invoice No. 858, for $5,315 (cost is $2,280).
31 Issued Check No. 419, payable to Payroll, in payment of sales salaries expense for the last half of the month, $15,900. Cashed the check and paid the employees.
31 Cash sales for the last half of the month are $174,590 (cost is $143,000).
31 Verify that amounts impacting customer and creditor accounts were posted and that any amounts that should have been posted as individual amounts to the general ledger accounts were posted. Foot and crossfoot the journals and make the month-end postings.

Required

1. Open the following general ledger accounts: Cash; Accounts Receivable; Inventory (March 1 beg. bal. is $300,000); Office Supplies; Store Supplies; Office Equipment; Accounts Payable; Long-Term Notes Payable; M. Bishop, Capital (March 1 beg. bal. is $300,000); Sales; Sales Discounts; Cost of Goods Sold; and Sales Salaries Expense. Open the following accounts receivable subsidiary ledger accounts: Taylor Few, Min Cho, and Lance Snow. Open the following accounts payable subsidiary ledger accounts: Stacy Company, Soy Industries, Tells Supply, and JW Company.

2. Enter these transactions in a sales journal like Exhibit 7.5, a purchases journal like Exhibit 7.9, a cash receipts journal like Exhibit 7.7, a cash disbursements journal like Exhibit 7.11, or a general journal. Number all journal pages as page 2.

3. Prepare a trial balance of the general ledger and prove the accuracy of the subsidiary ledgers by preparing schedules of both accounts receivable and accounts payable.

Check Trial balance totals, $783,105

Problem 7-7A[A]
Special journals, subsidiary ledgers, trial balance—periodic
C4 P2 P3

Assume that Bishop Co. in Problem 7-6A uses the periodic inventory system.

Required

1. Open the following general ledger accounts: Cash; Accounts Receivable; Inventory (March 1 beg. bal. is $300,000); Office Supplies; Store Supplies; Office Equipment; Accounts Payable; Long-Term Notes Payable; M. Bishop, Capital (March 1 beg. bal. is $300,000); Sales; Sales Discounts; Purchases; Purchases Returns and Allowances; Purchases Discounts; and Sales Salaries Expense. Open the following accounts receivable subsidiary ledger accounts: Taylor Few, Min Cho, and Lance Snow. Open the following Accounts Payable subsidiary ledger accounts: Stacy Company, Soy Industries, Tells Supply, and JW Company.

2. Enter the transactions from Problem 7-6A in a sales journal like that in Exhibit 7A.1, a purchases journal like that in Exhibit 7A.3, a cash receipts journal like that in Exhibit 7A.2, a cash disbursements journal like that in Exhibit 7A.4, or a general journal. Number journal pages as page 2.

3. Prepare a trial balance of the general ledger and prove the accuracy of the subsidiary ledgers by preparing schedules of both accounts receivable and accounts payable.

Check Trial balance totals, $786,966

PROBLEM SET B

Problem 7-1B
Special journals, subsidiary ledgers, schedule of accounts receivable—perpetual
C4 P1 P2 

Alcorn Industries completes these transactions during July of the current year (the terms of all its credit sales are 2/10, n/30):

July 1 Purchased $6,300 of merchandise on credit from Tahoe Company, invoice dated June 30, terms 2/10, n/30.
3 Issued Check No. 300 to *The Weekly* for advertising expense, $575.
5 Sold merchandise on credit to Kim Newsom, Invoice No. 918, for $18,400 (cost is $9,700).
6 Sold merchandise on credit to Ruth Baker, Invoice No. 919, for $7,500 (cost is $4,300).
7 Purchased $1,050 of store supplies on credit from Pryor, Inc., invoice dated July 7, terms n/10 EOM.
8 Received a $150 credit memorandum from Pryor, Inc., for the return of store supplies received on July 7.
9 Purchased $37,710 of store equipment on credit from Caro's Supply, invoice dated July 8, terms n/10 EOM.
10 Issued Check No. 301 to Tahoe Company in payment of its June 30 invoice, less the discount.
13 Sold merchandise on credit to Stephanie Meyer, Invoice No. 920, for $8,350 (cost is $5,030).
14 Sold merchandise on credit to Kim Newsom, Invoice No. 921, for $4,100 (cost is $2,800).
15 Received payment from Kim Newsom for the July 5 sale, less the discount.
15 Issued Check No. 302, payable to Payroll, in payment of sales salaries expense for the first half of the month, $30,620. Cashed the check and paid employees.
15 Cash sales for the first half of the month are $121,370 (cost is $66,330). (Cash sales are recorded daily using data from the cash registers but are recorded only twice in this problem to reduce repetitive entries.)
16 Received payment from Ruth Baker for the July 6 sale, less the discount.
17 Purchased $8,200 of merchandise on credit from Dixon Company, invoice dated July 17, terms 2/10, n/30.
20 Purchased $750 of office supplies on credit from Caro's Supply, invoice dated July 19, terms n/10 EOM.
21 Borrowed $20,000 cash from College Bank by signing a long-term note payable.

23 Received payment from Stephanie Meyer for the July 13 sale, less the discount.
24 Received payment from Kim Newsom for the July 14 sale, less the discount.
24 Received a $2,400 credit memorandum from Dixon Company for the return of defective merchandise received on July 17.
26 Purchased $9,770 of merchandise on credit from Tahoe Company, invoice dated July 26, terms 2/10, n/30.
27 Issued Check No. 303 to Dixon Company in payment of its July 17 invoice, less the return and the discount.
29 Sold merchandise on credit to Ruth Baker, Invoice No. 922, for $28,090 (cost is $22,850).
30 Sold merchandise on credit to Stephanie Meyer, Invoice No. 923, for $15,750 (cost is $9,840).
31 Issued Check No. 304, payable to Payroll, in payment of the sales salaries expense for the last half of the month, $30,620.
31 Cash sales for the last half of the month are $79,020 (cost is $51,855).

Required

1. Prepare a sales journal like that in Exhibit 7.5 and a cash receipts journal like that in Exhibit 7.7. Number both journals as page 3. Then review the transactions of Alcorn Industries and enter those transactions that should be journalized in the sales journal and those that should be journalized in the cash receipts journal. Ignore any transactions that should be journalized in a purchases journal, a cash disbursements journal, or a general journal.

2. Open the following general ledger accounts: Cash, Accounts Receivable, Inventory, Long-Term Notes Payable, Cost of Goods Sold, Sales, and Sales Discounts. Enter the June 30 balances for Cash ($100,000), Inventory ($200,000), and Long-Term Notes Payable ($300,000). Also open accounts receivable subsidiary ledger accounts for Kim Newsom, Stephanie Meyer, and Ruth Baker.

3. Verify that amounts that should be posted as individual amounts from the journals have been posted. (Such items are immediately posted.) Foot and crossfoot the journals and make the month-end postings.

Check Trial balance totals, $602,580

4. Prepare a trial balance of the general ledger and prove the accuracy of the subsidiary ledger by preparing a schedule of accounts receivable.

Analysis Component

5. Assume that the total for the schedule of Accounts Receivable does not equal the balance of the controlling account in the general ledger. Describe steps you would take to discover the error(s).

Problem 7-2B[A]
Special journals, subsidiary ledgers, and schedule of accounts receivable—periodic
C4 P2 P3

Assume that Alcorn Industries in Problem 7-1B uses the periodic inventory system.

Required

1. Prepare headings for a sales journal like the one in Exhibit 7A.1. Prepare headings for a cash receipts journal like the one in Exhibit 7A.2. Journalize the July transactions shown in Problem 7-1B that should be recorded in the sales journal and the cash receipts journal assuming the periodic inventory system is used.

2. Open the general ledger accounts with balances as shown in Problem 7-1B (do not open a Cost of Goods Sold ledger account). Under the periodic system, an Inventory account exists but is inactive until its balance is updated to the correct inventory balance at year-end. In this problem, the Inventory account remains inactive but must be included to correctly complete the trial balance.

Check Trial balance totals, $602,580

3. Complete parts 3, 4, and 5 of Problem 7-1B using the results of parts 1 and 2 of this problem.

Problem 7-3B
Special journals, subsidiary ledgers, and schedule of accounts payable—perpetual
C4 P1 P2

The July transactions of Alcorn Industries are described in Problem 7-1B.

Required

1. Prepare a general journal, a purchases journal like that in Exhibit 7.9, and a cash disbursements journal like that in Exhibit 7.11. Number all journal pages as page 3. Review the July transactions of Alcorn Industries and enter those transactions that should be journalized in the general journal, the purchases journal, or the cash disbursements journal. Ignore any transactions that should be journalized in a sales journal or cash receipts journal.

2. Open the following general ledger accounts: Cash, Inventory, Office Supplies, Store Supplies, Store Equipment, Accounts Payable, Long-Term Notes Payable, Sales Salaries Expense, and Advertising Expense. Enter the June 30 balances of Cash ($100,000), Inventory ($200,000), and Long-Term Notes Payable ($300,000). Also open accounts payable subsidiary ledger accounts for Caro's Supply, Tahoe Company, Dixon Company, and Pryor, Inc.
3. Verify that amounts that should be posted as individual amounts from the journals have been posted. (Such items are immediately posted.) Foot and crossfoot the journals and make the month-end postings.
4. Prepare a trial balance of the general ledger and a schedule of accounts payable.

Check Trial balance totals, $349,130

Problem 7-4B^A
Special journals, subsidiary ledgers, and schedule of accounts payable—periodic
C4 P2 P3

Refer to Problem 7-1B and assume that Alcorn uses the periodic inventory system.

Required

1. Prepare a general journal, a purchases journal like that in Exhibit 7A.3, and a cash disbursements journal like that in Exhibit 7A.4. Number all journal pages as page 3. Review the July transactions of Alcorn Company (Problem 7-1B) and enter those transactions that should be journalized in the general journal, the purchases journal, or the cash disbursements journal. Ignore any transaction that should be journalized in a sales journal or cash receipts journal.
2. Open the following general ledger accounts: Cash, Inventory, Office Supplies, Store Supplies, Store Equipment, Accounts Payable, Long-Term Notes Payable, Purchases, Purchases Returns and Allowances, Purchases Discounts, Sales Salaries Expense, and Advertising Expense. Enter the June 30 balances of Cash ($100,000), Inventory ($200,000), and Long-Term Notes Payable ($300,000). Also open accounts payable subsidiary ledger accounts for Tahoe Company, Pryor, Inc., Caro's Supply, and Dixon Company.
3. Complete parts 3 and 4 of Problem 7-3B using the results of parts 1 and 2 of this problem.

Check Trial balance totals, $351,772

Problem 7-5B
Special journals, subsidiary ledgers, trial balance—perpetual
C4 P1 P2

(If the Working Papers that accompany this textbook are not being used, omit this problem.)
You have just taken over the accounting for YES Products, whose annual accounting period ends December 31. The company's previous accountant journalized its transactions through December 15 and posted all items that required posting as individual amounts (see the journals and ledgers in the working papers). The company's transactions beginning on December 16 follow (terms for all its credit sales are 2/10, n/30):

Dec. 16 Purchased $765 of office supplies on credit from Black Supply Company, invoice dated December 16, terms n/10 EOM.
16 Sold merchandise on credit to Brad Sills, Invoice No. 916, for $4,290 (cost is $2,821).
18 Issued a $200 credit memorandum to Leslie Wilson for defective (worthless) merchandise sold on December 15 and returned for credit.
19 Received a $640 credit memorandum from Chiefs Company for the return of merchandise received on December 15.
20 Received a $143 credit memorandum from Black Supply Company for the return of office supplies received on December 16.
20 Purchased $7,475 of store equipment on credit from Black Supply Company, invoice dated December 19, terms n/10 EOM.
21 Sold merchandise on credit to Mo Carp, Invoice No. 917, for $5,520 (cost is $3,210).
22 Received payment from Brad Sills for the December 12 sale less the discount.
25 Received payment from Leslie Wilson for the December 15 sale less the return and the discount.
25 Issued Check No. 623 to Chiefs Company in payment of its December 15 invoice less the return and the discount.
25 Issued Check No. 624 to Blue Company in payment of its December 15 invoice less a 2% discount.
28 Purchased $6,030 of merchandise from Blue Company, invoice dated December 28, terms 2/10, n/60.
28 Sold a neighboring merchant a carton of tape (store supplies) at its cost of $58 cash.
29 Sarah Morris, the sole owner of YES Products, used Check No. 625 to withdraw $4,000 in cash from the business for personal use.
30 Issued Check No. 626 to Bush Electric Company in payment of the $990 December electric bill.
30 Issued Check No. 627 to Sue Hart, the company's only sales employee, in payment of her $2,620 salary for the last half of December.
31 Cash sales for the last half of the month are $66,128 (cost is $33,850). (Cash sales are recorded daily but are recorded only twice here to reduce repetitive entries.)

Required

1. Record these transactions in the journals provided in the working papers.

2. Verify that amounts that should be posted as individual amounts to the general ledger accounts have been posted, including posting to the customer and creditor accounts. (These amounts are immediately posted.) Foot and crossfoot the journals and make the month-end postings.

Check Trial balance totals, $255,598

3. Prepare a December 31 trial balance and prove the accuracy of the subsidiary ledgers by preparing schedules of both accounts receivable and accounts payable.

Problem 7-6B
Special journals, subsidiary ledgers, trial balance—perpetual
C4 P1 P2

Suppan Company completes these transactions during November of the current year (terms for all its credit sales are 2/10, n/30):

Nov. 1 Purchased $5,062 of office equipment on credit from Blix Supply, invoice dated November 1, terms n/10 EOM.
2 Borrowed $86,250 cash from Kansas Bank by signing a long-term note payable.
4 Purchased $11,400 of merchandise from ATM Industries, invoice dated November 3, terms 2/10, n/30.
5 Purchased $1,020 of store supplies on credit from Globe Company, invoice dated November 5, terms n/10 EOM.
8 Sold merchandise on credit to Sid Ragan, Invoice No. 439, for $6,350 (cost is $3,710).
10 Sold merchandise on credit to Carlos Mane, Invoice No. 440, for $12,500 (cost is $7,500).
11 Purchased $2,887 of merchandise from Xu Company, invoice dated November 10, terms 2/10, n/30.
12 Sent ATM Industries Check No. 633 in payment of its November 3 invoice less the discount.
15 Issued Check No. 634, payable to Payroll, in payment of sales salaries expense for the first half of the month, $8,435. Cashed the check and paid the employees.
15 Cash sales for the first half of the month are $27,170 (cost is $17,000). (Cash sales are recorded daily but are recorded only twice in this problem to reduce repetitive entries.)
15 Sold merchandise on credit to Tony Timmons, Invoice No. 441, for $4,250 (cost is $1,450).
16 Purchased $559 of office supplies on credit from Globe Company, invoice dated November 16, terms n/10 EOM.
17 Received a $487 credit memorandum from Xu Company for the return of unsatisfactory merchandise purchased on November 11.
18 Received payment from Sid Ragan for the November 8 sale less the discount.
19 Received payment from Carlos Mane for the November 10 sale less the discount.
19 Issued Check No. 635 to Xu Company in payment of its invoice of November 10 less the return and the discount.
22 Sold merchandise on credit to Carlos Mane, Invoice No. 442, for $2,595 (cost is $1,060).
24 Sold merchandise on credit to Tony Timmons, Invoice No. 443, for $3,240 (cost is $1,090).
25 Received payment from Tony Timmons for the sale of November 15 less the discount.
26 Received a $922 credit memorandum from Blix Supply for the return of office equipment purchased on November 1.
30 Issued Check No. 636, payable to Payroll, in payment of sales salaries expense for the last half of the month, $8,435. Cashed the check and paid the employees.
30 Cash sales for the last half of the month are $35,703 (cost is $20,400).
30 Verify that amounts impacting customer and creditor accounts were posted and that any amounts that should have been posted as individual amounts to the general ledger accounts were posted. Foot and crossfoot the journals and make the month-end postings.

Required

1. Open the following general ledger accounts: Cash; Accounts Receivable; Inventory (November 1 beg. bal. is $40,000); Office Supplies; Store Supplies; Office Equipment; Accounts Payable; Long-Term Notes Payable; J. Suppan, Capital (November 1 beg. bal. is $40,000); Sales; Sales Discounts; Cost of Goods Sold; and Sales Salaries Expense. Open the following accounts receivable subsidiary ledger accounts: Carlos Mane, Tony Timmons, and Sid Ragan. Open the following accounts payable subsidiary ledger accounts: Globe Company, ATM Industries, Blix Supply, and Xu Company.

2. Enter these transactions in a sales journal like that in Exhibit 7.5, a purchases journal like that in Exhibit 7.9, a cash receipts journal like that in Exhibit 7.7, a cash disbursements journal like that in Exhibit 7.11, or a general journal. Number all journal pages as page 2.

Check Trial balance totals, $223,777

3. Prepare a trial balance of the general ledger and prove the accuracy of the subsidiary ledgers by preparing schedules of both accounts receivable and accounts payable.

Problem 7-7B^A
Special journals, subsidiary ledgers, trial balance—periodic
C4 P2 P3

Assume that Suppan Company in Problem 7-6B uses the periodic inventory system.

Required

1. Open the following general ledger accounts: Cash; Accounts Receivable; Inventory (November 1 beg. bal. is $40,000); Office Supplies; Store Supplies; Office Equipment; Accounts Payable; Long-Term Notes Payable; J. Suppan, Capital (November 1 beg. bal. is $40,000); Sales; Sales Discounts; Purchases; Purchases Returns and Allowances; Purchases Discounts; and Sales Salaries Expense. Open the following accounts receivable subsidiary ledger accounts: Carlos Mane, Tony Timmons, and Sid Ragan. Open the following accounts payable subsidiary ledger accounts: Globe Company, ATM Industries, Blix Supply, and Xu Company.
2. Enter the transactions from Problem 7-6B in a sales journal like that in Exhibit 7A.1, a purchases journal like that in Exhibit 7A.3, a cash receipts journal like that in Exhibit 7A.2, a cash disbursements journal like that in Exhibit 7A.4, or a general journal. Number journal pages as page 2.
3. Prepare a trial balance of the general ledger and prove the accuracy of the subsidiary ledgers by preparing schedules of both accounts receivable and accounts payable.

Check Trial balance totals, $224,540

PROBLEM SET C

Problem Set C is available at the book's Website to further reinforce and assess your learning.

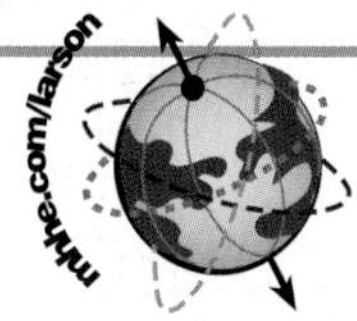

SERIAL PROBLEM

Success Systems

(This serial problem began in Chapter 1 and continues through most of the book. If previous chapter segments were not completed, the serial problem can begin at this point. It is helpful, but not necessary, that you use the Working Papers that accompany the book.)

Assume that Kay Breeze expands Success Systems' accounting system to include special journals.

Required

1. Locate the transactions related to January through March 2005 for Success Systems in Chapter 5.
2. Enter the Success Systems transactions for January through March in a sales journal like that in Exhibit 7.5 (insert "n/a" in the Invoice column), a cash receipts journal like that in Exhibit 7.7, a purchases journal like that in Exhibit 7.9 (use Computer Supplies heading instead of Office Supplies), and a cash disbursements journal like that in Exhibit 7.11 (insert "n/a" in the Check Number column), or a general journal. Number journal pages as page 2. If the transaction does not specify the name of the payee, state "not specified" in the Payee column of the cash disbursements journal.
3. The transactions on the following dates should be journalized in the general journal: January 5, 11, 20, 24, and 29 (no entry required) and March 24. Do not record and post the adjusting entries for the end of March.

COMPREHENSIVE PROBLEM—PERPETUAL

Colo Company

mhhe.com/larson

(If the Working Papers that accompany this book are not available, omit this comprehensive problem.) Assume it is Monday, May 1, the first business day of the month, and you have just been hired as the accountant for Colo Company, which operates with monthly accounting periods. All of the company's accounting work is completed through the end of April and its ledgers show April 30 balances. During your first month on the job, the company experiences the following transactions and events (terms for all its credit sales are 2/10, n/30 unless stated differently):

May 1 Issued Check No. 3410 to S&P Management Co. in payment of the May rent, $3,710. (Use two lines to record the transaction. Charge 80% of the rent to Rent Expense—Selling Space and the balance to Rent Expense—Office Space.)

2 Sold merchandise on credit to Hensel Company, Invoice No. 8785, for $6,100 (cost is $4,100).

2 Issued a $175 credit memorandum to Knox, Inc., for defective (worthless) merchandise sold on April 28 and returned for credit. The total selling price (gross) was $4,725.

3 Received a $798 credit memorandum from Peyton Products for the return of merchandise purchased on April 29.

4 Purchased the following on credit from Gear Supply Co.: merchandise, $37,072; store supplies, $574; and office supplies, $83. Invoice dated May 4, terms n/10 EOM.

5 Received payment from Knox, Inc., for the balance from the April 28 sale less the May 2 return and the discount.
8 Issued Check No. 3411 to Peyton Products to pay for the $7,098 of merchandise purchased on April 29 less the May 3 return and a 2% discount.
9 Sold store supplies to the merchant next door at their cost of $350 cash.
10 Purchased $4,074 of office equipment on credit from Gear Supply Co., invoice dated May 10, terms n/10 EOM.
11 Received payment from Hensel Company for the May 2 sale less the discount.
11 Purchased $8,800 of merchandise from Garcia, Inc., invoice dated May 10, terms 2/10, n/30.
12 Received an $854 credit memorandum from Gear Supply Co. for the return of defective office equipment received on May 10.
15 Issued Check No. 3412, payable to Payroll, in payment of sales salaries, $5,320, and office salaries, $3,150. Cashed the check and paid the employees.
15 Cash sales for the first half of the month are $59,220 (cost is $38,200). (Cash sales are recorded daily but are recorded only twice here to reduce repetitive entries.)
15 Post to the customer and creditor accounts. Also post individual items that are not included in column totals at the end of the month to the general ledger accounts. (Such items are posted daily but are posted only twice each month because they are few in number.)
16 Sold merchandise on credit to Hensel Company, Invoice No. 8786, for $3,990 (cost is $1,890).
17 Purchased $13,650 of merchandise from Fink Corp., invoice dated May 14, terms 2/10, n/60.
19 Issued Check No. 3413 to Garcia, Inc., in payment of its May 10 invoice less the discount.
22 Sold merchandise to Lee Services, Invoice No. 8787, for $6,850 (cost is $4,990), terms 2/10, n/60.
23 Issued Check No. 3414 to Fink Corp. in payment of its May 14 invoice less the discount.
24 Purchased the following on credit from Gear Supply Co.: merchandise, $8,120; store supplies, $630; and office supplies, $280. Invoice dated May 24, terms n/10 EOM.
25 Purchased $3,080 of merchandise from Peyton Products, invoice dated May 23, terms 2/10, n/30.
26 Sold merchandise on credit to Crane Corp., Invoice No. 8788, for $14,210 (cost is $8,230).
26 Issued Check No. 3415 to Perennial Power in payment of the May electric bill, $1,283.
29 The owner of Colo Company, Jenny Colo, used Check No. 3416 to withdraw $7,000 cash from the business for personal use.
30 Received payment from Lee Services for the May 22 sale less the discount.
30 Issued Check No. 3417, payable to Payroll, in payment of sales salaries, $5,320, and office salaries, $3,150. Cashed the check and paid the employees.
31 Cash sales for the last half of the month are $66,052 (cost is $42,500).
31 Post to the customer and creditor accounts. Also post individual items that are not included in column totals at the end of the month to the general ledger accounts. Foot and crossfoot the journals and make the month-end postings.

Required

1. Enter these transactions in a sales journal, a purchases journal, a cash receipts journal, a cash disbursements journal, or a general journal as illustrated in this chapter. Post when instructed to do so. Assume a perpetual inventory system.

Check (2) Unadjusted trial balance totals, $545,020; Adjustments column totals, $2,407

2. Prepare a trial balance in the Trial Balance columns of the work sheet form provided with the working papers. Complete the work sheet using the following information for accounting adjustments:

a. Expired insurance, $553.
b. Ending store supplies inventory, $2,632.
c. Ending office supplies inventory, $504.
d. Depreciation of store equipment, $567.
e. Depreciation of office equipment, $329.

Prepare and post adjusting and closing entries.

(3) Net income, $31,647; Total assets, $385,791

3. Prepare a May 2005 multiple-step income statement, a May 2005 statement of owner's equity, and a May 31, 2005, classified balance sheet.

4. Prepare a post-closing trial balance. Also prove the accuracy of subsidiary ledgers by preparing schedules of both accounts receivable and accounts payable.

BEYOND THE NUMBERS

REPORTING IN ACTION

A1  

BTN 7-1 Refer to **Krispy Kreme**'s financial statements in Appendix A to answer the following:

1. Identify the note disclosing Krispy Kreme's business segments.
2. Describe the nature and activities of each of Krispy Kreme's business segments.

Roll On

3. Access Krispy Kreme's annual report for fiscal years ending after February 2, 2003, from its Website (KrispyKreme.com) or the SEC's EDGAR database (www.SEC.gov). Has Krispy Kreme changed its reporting policy regarding segment information?

COMPARATIVE ANALYSIS

A1  

BTN 7-2 Key figures for **Krispy Kreme** follow ($ millions):

	Krispy Kreme		
Revenue by Segment	Current Year	One Year Prior	Two Years Prior
Company Store	$320	$266	$214
Franchise	19	14	9
KKM&D	348	269	201

Required

1. Compute the percent change in revenue (rounded to whole numbers) for each segment and for each of the most recent two years shown. Interpret and comment on your findings.
2. Identify the segment experiencing the largest growth in revenue for Krispy Kreme.

ETHICS CHALLENGE

C5  

BTN 7-3 Erica Gray, CPA, is a sole practitioner. She has been practicing as an auditor for 10 years. Recently a long-standing audit client asked Gray to design and implement an integrated computer-based accounting information system. The fees associated with this additional engagement with the client are very attractive. However, Gray wonders if she can remain objective on subsequent audits in her evaluation of the client's accounting system and its records if she was responsible for its design and implementation. Gray knows that professional auditing standards require her to remain independent in fact and appearance from her auditing clients.

Required

1. What do you believe auditing standards are mainly concerned with when they require independence in fact? In appearance?
2. Why is it important that auditors remain independent of their clients?
3. Do you think Gray can accept this engagement and remain independent? Justify your response.

COMMUNICATING IN PRACTICE

C3 C4  

BTN 7-4 Your friend, Wendy Geiger, owns a small retail store that sells candies and nuts. Geiger acquires her goods from a few select vendors. She generally makes purchase orders by phone and on credit. Sales are primarily for cash. Geiger keeps her own manual accounting system using a general journal and a general ledger. At the end of each business day, she records one summary entry for cash sales. Geiger recently began offering items in creative gift packages. This has increased sales substantially, and she is now receiving orders from corporate and other clients who order large quantities and prefer to buy on credit. As a result of increased credit transactions in both purchases and sales, keeping the accounting records has become extremely time consuming. Geiger wants to continue to maintain her own manual system and calls you for advice. Write a memo to her advising how she might modify her current manual accounting system to accommodate the expanded business activities. Geiger is accustomed to checking her ledger by using a trial balance. Your memo should explain the advantages of what you propose and of any other verification techniques you recommend.

TAKING IT TO THE NET

A1

mhhe.com/larson

BTN 7-5 Access the May 1, 2002, filing of the fiscal 2002 10-K report for **Dell Computer** (ticker DELL) at **www.SEC.gov**. Read the footnote that details Dell's segment information and answer the following:

1. Dell's operations are divided among which three geographic segments?

2. In fiscal year 2002, which geographic area had the largest dollar amount of operating income? Which had the largest amount of identifiable assets?

3. Compute the return on assets for each segment for fiscal year 2002. Use operating income and average total assets by segment for your calculation. Which segment has the highest return on assets?

4. For what product groups does Dell provide segment data? What percent of Dell's net revenue is earned by each product group?

TEAMWORK IN ACTION

C4 P1 P2

BTN 7-6 Each member of the team is to assume responsibility for one of the following tasks:

a. Journalizing in the purchases journal.

b. Journalizing in the cash disbursements journal.

c. Maintaining and verifying the Accounts Payable ledger.

d. Journalizing in the sales journal and the general journal.

e. Journalizing in the cash receipts journal.

f. Maintaining and verifying the Accounts Receivable ledger.

The team should abide by the following procedures in carrying out responsibilities.

Required

1. After tasks *a–f* are assigned, each team member is to quickly read the list of transactions in Problem 7-6A, identifying with initials the journal in which each transaction is to be recorded. Upon completion, the team leader is to read transaction dates, and the appropriate team member is to vocalize responsibility. Any disagreement between teammates must be resolved.

2. Journalize and continually update subsidiary ledgers. Journal recorders should alert teammates assigned to subsidiary ledgers when an entry must be posted to their subsidiary.

3. Team members responsible for tasks *a*, *b*, *d*, and *e* are to summarize and prove journals; members responsible for tasks *c* and *f* are to prepare both payables and receivables schedules.

4. The team leader is to take charge of the general ledger, rotating team members to obtain amounts to be posted. The person responsible for a journal must complete posting references in that journal. Other team members should verify the accuracy of account balance computations. To avoid any abnormal account balances, post in the following order: P, S, G, R, D. (*Note:* Posting any necessary individual general ledger amounts are also done at this time.)

5. The team leader is to read out general ledger account balances while another team member fills in the trial balance form. Concurrently, one member should keep a running balance of debit account balance totals and another credit account balance totals. Verify the final total of the trial balance and the schedules. If necessary, the team must resolve any errors. Turn in the trial balance and schedules to the instructor.

BUSINESS WEEK ACTIVITY

C1 C2

mhhe.com/larson

BTN 7-7 Read the article, "The Battle to Streamline Business Software" in the December 4, 2002, edition of ***Business Week***. (This book's Website provides a free link.)

Required

1. What functions are integrated by enterprise resource planning, or ERP, software?

2. How long does **Oregon Health and Sciences University** in Portland think it will take for it to earn a return on its $25 million dollar investment in **Oracle** software?

3. Which companies are identified in the article as the large (likely long-standing) names in the business software market?

4. In dollar terms, what is the current size of the ERP software market? What annual growth rate is predicted for this market through 2006?

ENTREPRENEURIAL DECISION

P1 

BTN 7-8 Refer to the chapter's opening feature about Devin Lazerine and his ***Rap-Up*** magazine.

Required

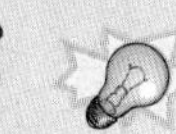

1. What is the current circulation (to the nearest one hundred thousand) of *Rap-Up* magazine?
2. Assume that Devin charges $2.40 per issue for subscribers and $3.60 per issue to newsstands that purchase copies of *Rap-Up*. Also assume that *Rap-Up*'s circulation (refer to your answer in part 1) is equally divided between newsstand and subscription sales.
   a. If Devin uses one mass mailing to ship magazines to newsstands each month, what journal entry would Devin make to record the sale upon shipment of the magazines? (You may ignore cost of goods sold and show only the revenue side of the transaction.)
   b. Assume that *Rap-Up* is a monthly publication. With the current level of subscribers, how much annual revenue will be earned from subscription sales?
   c. What journal entry does Devin record when an individual subscription order with payment is received? (*Note:* Subscribers pay $28.80 per year.)
   d. What journal entry does Devin record when an individual subscriber's magazine is mailed out each month?
   e. Construct a table to show annual revenue, cost of goods sold ($0.60 per issue), gross margin and gross margin percentage by each business segment (newsstand and subscription).
3. Devin is thinking of adding a sales subsidiary ledger to his accounting system. What information might the sales subsidiary ledger be designed to account for beyond each customer and the amount owed?

GLOBAL DECISION

A1 

BTN 7-9 Access and refer to the 2002 annual report for **Grupo Bimbo** at GrupoBimbo.com.

Required

1. Skim the management and discussion section until you find information relating to Grupo Bimbo's geographic segments. Identify those segments.
2. What three financial figures does it disclose for each geographic segment?
3. Does Grupo Bimbo have a dominant segment? Explain.
4. Does the total of sales by region match with the total amount of sales reported on Grupo Bimbo's consolidated statement of income?

"They [customers] love that it's very childhood, nostalgic"—Dylan Lauren (on right, Jeff Rubin on left)

Cash and Internal Controls

A Look Back

Chapter 7 focused on accounting information systems. We explained the fundamental principles and components of information systems, the use of special journals and subsidiary ledgers, and technology-based systems. We also discussed the analysis of segment data.

A Look at This Chapter

This chapter extends our study of accounting to the area of internal control and the analysis of cash. We describe procedures that are good for internal control. We also explain the control of and the accounting for cash, including control features of banking activities.

A Look Ahead

Chapter 9 focuses on receivables, which are some of the most liquid assets other than cash. We explain how to account and report on receivables and their related accounts. This includes estimating uncollectible receivables and computing interest earned.

Learning Objectives

CAP

Conceptual

C1 Define internal control and identify its purpose and principles. *(p. 308)*

C2 Define cash and cash equivalents and explain how to report them. *(p. 312)*

C3 Identify control features of banking activities. *(p. 319)*

Analytical

A1 Compute the days' sales uncollected ratio and use it to assess liquidity. *(p. 325)*

Procedural

P1 Apply internal control to cash receipts and disbursements. *(p. 313)*

P2 Explain and record petty cash fund transactions. *(p. 316)*

P3 Prepare a bank reconciliation. *(p. 322)*

Decision Feature

Sweet Success

NEW YORK—A 10-foot chocolate bunny named Jeffrey greets you as you enter the store—that should be warning enough! This elite designer candy store, christened **Dylan's Candy Bar (DylansCandyBar.com),** is the brainchild of co-founders Dylan Lauren and Jeff Rubin (the bunny is named for him). This sweet-lovers heaven offers more than 5,000 different choices of sweets from all over the world. In just under two years of operation, it has become a hip hangout for locals and tourists—and it has made candy cool. Says Lauren, "Park Avenue women come in, and the first thing they ask for is Gummi bears. They love that it's very childhood, nostalgic."

The New York store projects more than $5 million in sales this year. While marketing is an important part of its success, Lauren and Rubin's management of internal controls and cash is equally impressive. Several control procedures monitor its business activities and safeguard its assets. An example is the biometric time and attendance control system using fingerprint characteristics. Says Rubin, "There's no fooling the system! It is going to help us remotely manage our employees while eliminating human error and dishonesty. [It] is a cost effective and important business management tool." Similar controls are applied throughout the store. Rubin notes that such controls raise productivity and cut expenses.

The store's cash management practices are equally impressive, including controls over cash receipts, disbursements, and petty cash. The use of bank reconciliations further helps with the store's control and management of cash.

Internal controls are crucial when on a busy day its store brings in more than 8,000 customers, and their cash. Moreover, expansion is already underway in Orlando, Houston, Chicago, Toronto, and Las Vegas. Through it all, Lauren says it is "totally fun." And how is it that Lauren maintains her slim figure. "I work out a lot!" she exclaims.

[Sources: *Dylan's Candy Bar Website,* January 2004; *Entrepreneur,* December 2002; *USA Today,* October 26, 2001; *PR Newswire,* November 2001; ECommerce-Guide.com, June 2003.]

Chapter Preview

We all are aware of reports and experiences involving theft and fraud. These occurrences affect us in several ways: We lock doors, chain bikes, review sales receipts, and acquire alarm systems. A company also takes actions to safeguard, control, and manage what it owns. Experience tells us that small companies are most vulnerable, usually due to weak internal controls. It is management's responsibility to set up policies and procedures to safeguard a company's assets, especially cash. To do so, management *and* employees must understand and apply principles of internal control. This chapter describes these principles and how to apply them. It focuses special attention on cash because it is easily transferable and often at high risk of loss. An understanding of these controls and procedures makes us more secure in carrying out business activities and in assessing the activities of other companies.

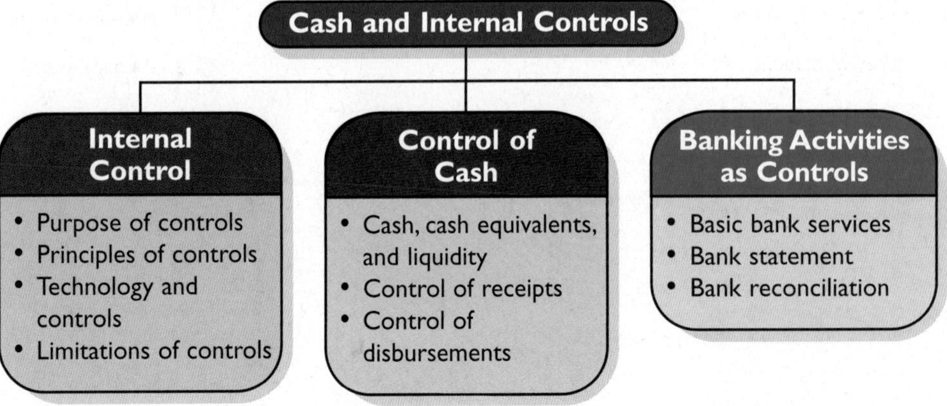

Internal Control

This section describes internal control and its fundamental principles. We also discuss the impact of technology on internal control and the limitations of control procedures.

Purpose of Internal Control

C1 Define internal control and identify its purpose and principles.

Managers (or owners) of small businesses often control the entire operation. These managers usually purchase all assets, hire and manage employees, negotiate all contracts, and sign all checks. They know from personal contact and observation whether the business is actually receiving the assets and services paid for. Most companies, however, cannot maintain this close personal supervision. They must delegate responsibilities and rely on formal procedures rather than personal contact in controlling business activities.

Point: With company growth comes increased reporting and controls to safeguard assets and manage operations.

Managers use an internal control system to monitor and control business activities. An **internal control system** consists of the policies and procedures managers use to

- Protect assets.
- Ensure reliable accounting.
- Promote efficient operations.
- Urge adherence to company policies.

A properly designed internal control system is a key part of systems design, analysis, and performance. Managers place a high priority on internal control systems because they can prevent avoidable losses, help managers plan operations, and monitor company and employee performance. Internal controls do not provide guarantees, but they lower the company's risk of loss.

Decision Insight

What's the Password? Good internal control prevents unauthorized access to assets and accounting records by requiring passwords. It takes a password, for instance, to boot up most office PCs, log onto a network, and access voice mail, e-mail, and online services—not to mention personal ID numbers on credit and cash cards.

Principles of Internal Control

Topic Tackler 8-1

Internal control policies and procedures vary from company to company according to such factors as the nature of the business and its size. Certain fundamental internal control principles apply to all companies. The **principles of internal control** are to

1. Establish responsibilities.
2. Maintain adequate records.
3. Insure assets and bond key employees.
4. Separate recordkeeping from custody of assets.
5. Divide responsibility for related transactions.
6. Apply technological controls.
7. Perform regular and independent reviews.

This section explains these seven principles and describes how internal control procedures minimize the risk of fraud and theft. These procedures also increase the reliability and accuracy of accounting records.

Establish Responsibilities Proper internal control means that responsibility for a task is clearly established and assigned to one person. When a problem occurs in a company where responsibility is not identified, determining who is at fault is difficult. For instance, if two salesclerks share the same cash register and there is a cash shortage, neither clerk can be held accountable. To prevent this problem, one clerk might be given responsibility for handling all cash sales. Alternately, a company can use a register with separate cash drawers for each clerk. Most of us have waited at a retail counter during a shift change while employees swap cash drawers.

Point: Many companies have a mandatory vacation policy for employees who handle cash. When another employee must cover for the one on vacation, it is more difficult to hide cash frauds.

Maintain Adequate Records Good recordkeeping is part of an internal control system. It helps protect assets and ensures that employees use prescribed procedures. Reliable records are also a source of information that managers use to monitor company activities. When detailed records of equipment are kept, for instance, items are unlikely to be lost or stolen without detection. Similarly, transactions are less likely to be entered in wrong accounts if a chart of accounts is set up and carefully used. Many preprinted forms and internal documents are also designed for use in a good internal control system. When sales slips are properly designed, for instance, sales personnel can record needed information efficiently with less chance of errors or delays to customers. When sales slips are prenumbered and controlled, each one issued is the responsibility of one salesperson, preventing the salesperson from pocketing cash by making a sale and destroying the sales slip. Computerized point-of-sale systems achieve the same control results.

Point: The Association of Certified Fraud Examiners **(cfenet.com)** estimates that employee fraud costs small companies an average of about $130,000 per incident.

Insure Assets and Bond Key Employees Good internal control means that assets are adequately insured against casualty and that employees handling large amounts of cash and easily transferable assets are bonded. An employee is *bonded* when a company purchases an insurance policy, or a bond, against losses from theft by that employee. Bonding reduces the risk of loss. It also discourages theft because bonded employees know an independent bonding company will be involved when theft is uncovered and is unlikely to be sympathetic with an employee involved in theft.

Decision Insight

Check It Out What lurks behind that spiffy résumé you just reviewed? The Association of Certified Fraud Examiners **(cfenet.com)** provides links to search engines to verify Social Security numbers, addresses, and phone numbers. Also, **KnowX.com** lets you check lawsuits and bankruptcies, and **EmployeeScreen.com** offers background searches, including employment verification.

Separate Recordkeeping from Custody of Assets A person who controls or has access to an asset must not keep that asset's accounting records. This principle reduces the risk of theft or waste of an asset because the person with control over it knows that another person keeps its records. Also, a recordkeeper who does not have access to the asset

Decision Insight

Tag Time A new technique exists for marking all physical assets. It involves embedding a less than one-inch-square tag of nylon fibers that creates a unique optical signature recordable by scanners. The manufacturer hopes to embed tags in everything from compact discs and credit cards to designer clothes.

has no reason to falsify records. This means that to steal an asset and hide the theft from the records, two or more people must *collude*—or agree in secret to commit the fraud.

Divide Responsibility for Related Transactions Good internal control divides responsibility for a transaction or a series of related transactions between two or more individuals or departments. This is to ensure that the work of one individual acts as a check on the other. This principle, often called *separation of duties,* is not a call for duplication of work. Each employee or department should perform unduplicated effort. Examples of transactions with divided responsibility are placing purchase orders, receiving merchandise, and paying vendors. These tasks should not be given to one individual or department. Assigning responsibility for two or more of these tasks to one party increases mistakes and perhaps fraud. Having an independent person, for example, check incoming goods for quality and quantity encourages more care and attention to detail than having the person who placed the order do the checking. Added protection can result from identifying a third person to approve payment of the invoice. A company can even designate a fourth person with authority to write checks as another protective measure.

Point: There's a new security device—a person's ECG (electrocardiogram) reading, which is as unique as a fingerprint and a lot harder to lose or steal than a PIN. An ECG also shows that a living person is actually there, whereas fingerprint and facial recognition software can be fooled. ECGs can be read through fingertip touches.

Apply Technological Controls Cash registers, check protectors, time clocks, and personal identification scanners are examples of devices that can improve internal control. Technology often improves the effectiveness of controls. A cash register with a locked-in tape or electronic file makes a record of each cash sale. A check protector perforates the amount of a check into its face and makes it difficult to alter the amount. A time clock registers the exact time an employee both arrives at and departs from the job. Mechanical change and currency counters quickly and accurately count amounts, and personal scanners limit access to only authorized individuals. Each of these and other technological controls are an effective part of many internal control systems.

Point: Evidence of any internal control failure for a company reduces user reliance on its financial statements.

Decision Insight

About Face Face-recognition software snaps a digital picture of the face and converts key facial features—say, the distance between the eyes—into a series of numerical values. These can be stored on an ID or ATM card as a simple bar code to prohibit unauthorized access.

Perform Regular and Independent Reviews Changes in personnel, stress of time pressures, and technological advances present opportunities for shortcuts and lapses. To counter these factors, regular reviews of internal control systems are needed to ensure that procedures are followed. These reviews are preferably done by internal auditors not directly involved in the activities. Their impartial perspective encourages an evaluation of the efficiency as well as the effectiveness of the internal control system. Many companies also pay for audits by independent, external auditors. These external auditors test the company's financial records to give an opinion as to whether its financial statements are presented fairly. Before external auditors decide on how much testing is needed, they evaluate the effectiveness of the internal control system. This evaluation is often helpful to a client.

Decision Maker

Entrepreneur As owner of a start-up information services company, you hire a systems analyst. One of her first recommendations is to require all employees to take at least one week of vacation per year. Why would she recommend a "forced vacation" policy?

Answer—p. 333

Technology and Internal Control

Point: Information on Internet fraud can be found at these Websites:
ftc.gov/ftc/consumer.htm
sec.gov/investor/pubs/cyberfraud.htm
www.fraud.org

The fundamental principles of internal control are relevant no matter what the technological state of the accounting system, from purely manual to fully automated systems. Technology impacts an internal control system in several important ways. Perhaps the most obvious is that technology allows us quicker access to databases and information. Used effectively, technology greatly improves managers' abilities to monitor and control business activities. This section describes some technological impacts we must be alert to.

Decision Insight

Undo Shredding? A Website that specializes in high-tech spy tools sold several $5,000 paper shredders fitted with scanners and wireless transmitters. When unsuspecting companies fed in confidential documents, the illegally obtained information was sent to the spy's e-mail address.

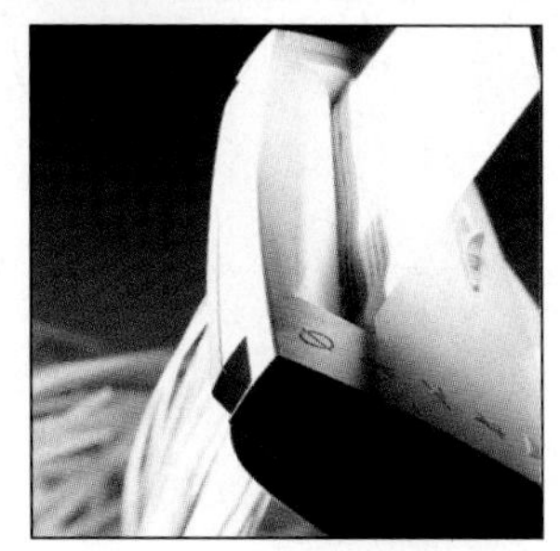

Reduced Processing Errors Technologically advanced systems reduce the number of errors in processing information. Provided the software and data entry are correct, the risk of mechanical and mathematical errors is nearly eliminated. However, we must remember that erroneous software or data entry does exist. Also, less human involvement in data processing can cause data entry errors to go undiscovered. Moreover, errors in software can produce consistent but erroneous processing of transactions. Continually checking and monitoring all types of systems are important.

More Extensive Testing of Records A company's review and audit of electronic records can include more extensive testing when information is easily and rapidly accessed. When accounting records are kept manually, auditors and others likely select only small samples of data to test. When data are accessible with computer technology, however, auditors can quickly analyze large samples or even the entire database.

Limited Evidence of Processing Many data processing steps are increasingly done by computer. Accordingly, fewer hard-copy items of documentary evidence are available for review. Yet technologically advanced systems can provide new evidence. They can, for instance, record who made the entries, the date and time, the source of the entry, and so on. Technology can also be designed to require the use of passwords or other identification before access to the system is granted. This means that internal control depends more on the design and operation of the information system and less on the analysis of its resulting documents.

Point: External decision makers look to several sources when assessing a company's internal controls. Sources include the auditor's report, management report on controls (if available), management discussion and analysis, and financial press.

Crucial Separation of Duties Technological advances in accounting information systems often yield some job eliminations or consolidations. While those who remain have the special skills necessary to operate advanced programs and equipment, a company with a reduced workforce risks losing its crucial separation of duties. The company must establish ways to control and monitor employees to minimize risk of error and fraud. For instance, the person who designs and programs the information system must not be the one who operates it. The company must also separate control over programs and files from the activities related to cash receipts and disbursements. For instance, a computer operator should not control check-writing activities. Achieving acceptable separation of duties can be especially difficult and costly in small companies with few employees.

Decision Insight

Hot Prospects A recent survey cites the shortage of accounting techies as one barrier to company growth. The most prized recruits are those adept at enterprise software, the Web, intranets, and accounting.

Limitations of Internal Control

All internal control policies and procedures have limitations which usually arise from either (1) the human element, or (2) the cost-benefit principle.

Internal control policies and procedures are applied by people. This human element creates several potential limitations that we can categorize as either (1) human error or (2) human fraud. *Human error* can occur from negligence, fatigue, misjudgment, or confusion. *Human fraud* involves intent by people to defeat internal controls, such as *management override,* for personal gain. Fraud also includes collusion to thwart the separation of duties. The human element highlights the importance of establishing an *internal control environment* to convey management's commitment to internal control policies and procedures.

Point: When the electronic manufacturer Casio (**Casio.com**) started an e-commerce site, it found 13% of its first-year customer purchases were fraudulent.

Point: Cybercrime.gov pursues computer and intellectual property crimes, including that of e-commerce.

The second major limitation on internal control is the *cost-benefit principle,* which dictates that the costs of internal controls must not exceed their benefits. Analysis of costs and benefits must consider all factors, including the impact on morale. Most companies, for instance, have a legal right to read employees' e-mails, yet companies seldom exercise that right unless they are confronted with evidence of potential harm to the company. The same holds for drug testing, phone tapping, and hidden cameras. The bottom line is that managers must establish internal control policies and procedures with a net benefit to the company.

Quick Check

1. Principles of internal control suggest that (choose one): (*a*) Responsibility for a series of related transactions (such as placing orders, receiving and paying for merchandise) should be assigned to one employee; (*b*) Responsibility for individual tasks should be shared by more than one employee so that one serves as a check on the other; or (*c*) Employees who handle considerable cash and easily transferable assets should be bonded.
2. What are some impacts of computing technology on internal control?

Answers—p. 333

Control of Cash

Cash is a necessary asset of every company. Most companies also own *cash equivalents* (defined below), which are assets similar to cash. Cash and cash equivalents are the most liquid of all assets and are easily hidden and moved. An effective system of internal controls protects these assets and it should meet three basic guidelines:

1. Handling cash is separate from recordkeeping of cash.
2. Cash receipts are promptly deposited in a bank.
3. Cash disbursements are made by check.

The first guideline applies separation of duties to minimize errors and fraud. When duties are separated, two or more people must collude to steal cash and conceal this action in the accounting records. The second guideline uses immediate (say, daily) deposits of all cash receipts to produce a timely independent record of the cash received. It also reduces the likelihood of cash theft (or loss) and the risk that an employee could personally use the money before depositing it. The third guideline uses payments by check to develop an independent bank record of cash disbursements. This guideline also reduces the risk of cash theft (or loss).

This section begins with definitions of cash and cash equivalents. Discussion then focuses on controls and accounting for both cash receipts and disbursements. The exact procedures used to achieve control over cash vary across companies. They depend on factors such as company size, number of employees, volume of cash transactions, and sources of cash.

Cash, Cash Equivalents, and Liquidity

C2 Define cash and cash equivalents and explain how to report them.

Good accounting systems help in managing the amount of cash and controlling who has access to it. Cash is the usual means of payment when paying for assets, services, or liabilities. **Liquidity** refers to a company's ability to pay for its near-term obligations. Cash and similar assets are called **liquid assets** because they can be readily used to settle such obligations. A company needs liquid assets to effectively operate.

Point: The most liquid assets are usually reported first on a balance sheet; the least liquid assets are reported last.

Cash includes currency and coins along with the amounts on deposit in bank accounts, checking accounts (called *demand deposits*), and many savings accounts (called *time deposits*). Cash also includes items that are acceptable for deposit in these accounts such as customer checks, cashier checks, certified checks, and money orders. **Cash equivalents** are short-term, highly liquid investment assets meeting two criteria: (1) readily convertible to a known cash amount and (2) sufficiently close to their due date so that their market value is not sensitive to interest rate changes. Only investments purchased within three months of their due date usually satisfy these criteria. Examples of cash equivalents are short-term investments in assets such as U.S. Treasury bills and money market funds. To increase their return, many companies invest idle cash in cash equivalents. Most companies combine cash equivalents with cash as a single item on the balance sheet.

Decision Insight

Days' Cash Expense Coverage The ratio of *cash (and cash equivalents)* to *average daily cash expenses* indicates the number of days a company can operate without additional cash inflows. It reflects on company liquidity.

Point: The e-commerce company i2 Technologies reports cash and cash equivalents of $538 million in its recent balance sheet. This amount makes up nearly one-third of its total assets.

Control of Cash Receipts

P1 Apply internal control to cash receipts and disbursements.

Internal control of cash receipts ensures that cash received is properly recorded and deposited. Cash receipts can arise from transactions such as cash sales, collections of customer accounts, receipts of interest earned, bank loans, sales of assets, and owner investments. This section explains internal control over two important types of cash receipts: over-the-counter and by mail.

Over-the-Counter Cash Receipts For purposes of internal control, over-the-counter cash receipts from sales should be recorded on a cash register at the time of each sale. To help ensure that correct amounts are entered, each register should be located so customers can read the amounts entered. Clerks also should be required to enter each sale before wrapping merchandise and to give the customer a receipt for each sale. The design of each cash register should provide a permanent, locked-in record of each transaction. In many systems, the register is directly linked with computing and accounting services. Less advanced registers simply print a record of each transaction on a paper tape or electronic file locked inside the register.

Decision Insight

Money Talk Projected cash receipts and cash disbursements are often summarized in a *cash budget.* Provided that sufficient cash exists for effective operations, managers wish to minimize the cash they hold because of its low return versus other investment opportunities.

Proper internal control prescribes that custody over cash should be separate from its recordkeeping. For over-the-counter cash receipts, this separation begins with the cash sale. The clerk who has access to cash in the register should not have access to its locked-in record. At the end of the clerk's work period, the clerk should count the cash in the register, record the amount, and turn over the cash and a record of its amount to the company cashier. The cashier, like the clerk, has access to the cash but should not have access to accounting records (or the register tape or file). A third employee compares the record of total register transactions (or the register tape or file) with the cash receipts reported by the cashier. This record is the basis for a journal entry recording over-the-counter cash receipts. The third employee has access to the records for cash but not to the actual cash. The clerk and the cashier have access to cash but not to the accounting records. None of them can make a mistake or divert cash without the difference being revealed.

Decision Insight

Link Time **Wal-Mart** uses a network of information links with its point-of-sale cash registers to coordinate sales, purchases, and distribution. Its supercenters, for instance, ring up to 15,000 separate sales on heavy days. By using cash register information, the company can fix pricing mistakes quickly and capitalize on sales trends.

Cash over and short. Sometimes errors in making change are discovered from differences between the cash in a cash register and the record of the amount of cash receipts. Although a clerk is careful, one or more customers can be given too much or too little change. This means that at the end of a work period, the cash in a cash register might not equal the record of cash receipts. This difference is reported in the **Cash Over and Short**

Point: Retailers often require cashiers to restrictively endorse checks immediately on receipt by stamping them "For deposit only."

account, also called *Cash Short and Over,* which is an income statement account recording the income effects of cash overages and cash shortages. To illustrate, if a cash register's record shows $550 but the count of cash in the register is $555, the entry to record cash sales and its overage is

Assets = Liabilities + Equity
+555 + 5
+550

Cash	555	
Cash Over and Short		5
Sales		550
To record cash sales and a cash overage.		

On the other hand, if a cash register's record shows $625 but the count of cash in the register is $621, the entry to record cash sales and its shortage is:

Assets = Liabilities + Equity
+621 − 4
+625

Cash	621	
Cash Over and Short	4	
Sales		625
To record cash sales and a cash shortage.		

Since customers are more likely to dispute being shortchanged than being given too much change, the Cash Over and Short account usually has a debit balance at the end of an accounting period. A debit balance reflects an expense. It can be shown on the income statement as part of general and administrative expenses. (Note that since the amount is usually small, it is often combined with other small expenses and reported as part of *miscellaneous expenses;* or as part of *miscellaneous revenues* if it has a credit balance.)

Point: Collusion implies that two or more individuals are knowledgeable or involved with the activities of the other(s).

Point: A complete set of financial statements includes a statement of cash flows, which provides useful information about a company's sources and uses of cash and cash equivalents during a period of time.

Cash Receipts by Mail Control of cash receipts that arrive through the mail starts with the person who opens the mail. Preferably, two people are assigned the task of, and are present for, opening the mail. In this case, theft of cash receipts by mail requires collusion between these two employees. Specifically, the person(s) opening the mail enters a list (in triplicate) of money received. This list should contain a record of each sender's name, the amount, and an explanation of why the money is sent. The first copy is sent with the money to the cashier. A second copy is sent to the recordkeeper in the accounting area. A third copy is kept by the clerks who opened the mail. The cashier deposits the money in a bank, and the recordkeeper records the amounts received in the accounting records.

This process reflects good internal control. That is, when the bank balance is reconciled by another person (explained later in the chapter), errors or acts of fraud by the mail clerks, the cashier, or the recordkeeper are revealed. They are revealed because the bank's record of cash deposited must agree with the records from each of the three. Moreover, if the mail clerks do not report all receipts correctly, customers will question their account balances. If the cashier does not deposit all receipts, the bank balance does not agree with the recordkeeper's cash balance. The recordkeeper and the person who reconciles the bank balance do not have access to cash and therefore have no opportunity to divert cash to themselves. This system makes errors and fraud highly unlikely. The exception is employee collusion.

Decision Insight

Look West In the annual Small Business Survival Index (**SBSC.org**), the first 4 of the top 5 states ranked as most entrepreneur friendly are west of the Mississippi: (1) South Dakota, (2) Nevada, (3) Wyoming, (4) Texas, and (5) Florida. Factors considered included taxes, regulations, costs, and crime.

Control of Cash Disbursements

Control of cash disbursements is especially important as most large thefts occur from payment of fictitious invoices. One key to controlling cash disbursements is to require all expenditures to be made by check. The only exception is small payments made from petty cash.

Another key is to deny access to the accounting records to anyone other than the owner who has the authority to sign checks. A small business owner often signs checks and knows from personal contact that the items being paid for are actually received. This arrangement is impossible in large businesses. Instead, internal control procedures must be substituted for personal contact. Such procedures are designed to assure the check signer that the obligations recorded are properly incurred and should be paid. This section describes these and other internal control procedures, including the voucher system and petty cash system. The management of cash disbursements for purchases is described in Appendix 8B.

Decision Insight

Hidden Risks The basic purposes of paper and electronic documents are similar. However, the internal control system must change to reflect different risks, including confidential and competitive-sensitive information that is at greater risk in electronic systems.

Voucher System of Control A **voucher system** is a set of procedures and approvals designed to control cash disbursements and the acceptance of obligations. The voucher system of control establishes procedures for

- Verifying, approving, and recording obligations for eventual cash disbursement.
- Issuing checks for payment of verified, approved, and recorded obligations.

A reliable voucher system follows standard procedures for every transaction. This applies even when multiple purchases are made from the same supplier.

A voucher system's control over cash disbursements begins when a company incurs an obligation that will result in payment of cash. A key factor in this system is that only approved departments and individuals are authorized to incur such obligations. The system often limits the type of obligations that a department or individual can incur. In a large retail store, for instance, only a purchasing department should be authorized to incur obligations for merchandise inventory. Another key factor is that procedures for purchasing, receiving, and paying for merchandise are divided among several departments (or individuals). These departments include the one requesting the purchase, the purchasing department, the receiving department, and the accounting department. To coordinate and control responsibilities of these departments, a company uses several different business documents. Exhibit 8.1 shows how documents are accumulated in a **voucher,** which is an internal document (or file) used to accumulate information to control cash

Decision Insight

Cyber Setup The FTC is on the cutting edge of cybersleuthing. Opportunists in search of easy money are lured to **WeMarket4U.net/netops.** Take the bait and you get warned—and possibly targeted. (The top 4 fraud complaints as compiled by the Internet Fraud Complaint Center are shown to the right.)

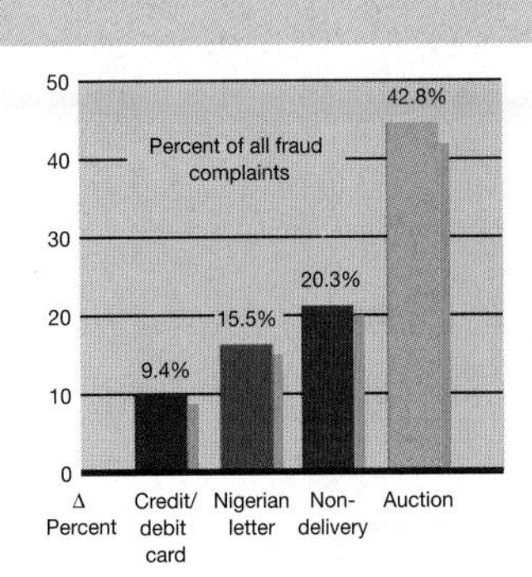

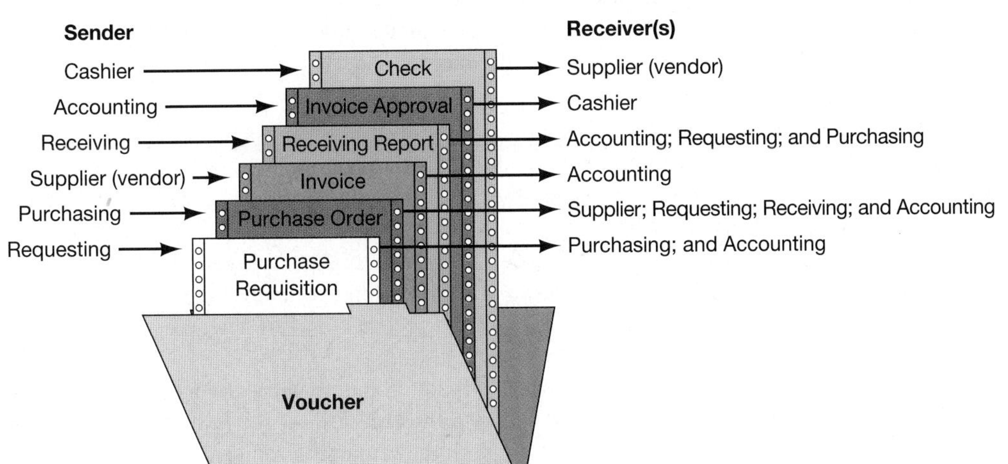

Exhibit 8.1

Document Flow in a Voucher System

Point: **MCI,** formerly WorldCom, paid a whopping $500 million in SEC fines for accounting fraud. Among the charges were that it inflated earnings by as much as $10 billion.

disbursements and to ensure that a transaction is properly recorded. This specific example begins with a *purchase requisition* and concludes with a *check* drawn against cash. Appendix 8A describes each document entering and leaving a voucher system. It also describes the internal control objective served by each document.

A voucher system should be applied not only to purchases of inventory but to all expenditures. To illustrate, when a company receives a monthly telephone bill, it should review and verify the charges, prepare a voucher (file), and insert the bill. This transaction is then recorded with a journal entry. If the amount is currently due, a check is issued. If not, the voucher is filed for payment on its due date. If no voucher is prepared, verifying the invoice and its amount after several days or weeks can be difficult. Also, without records, a dishonest employee could collude with a dishonest supplier to get more than one payment for an obligation, payment for excessive amounts, or payment for goods and services not received. An effective voucher system helps prevent such frauds.

Decision Insight

Hoodwinked Fictitious sales receipts and altered inventory tags deceived auditors, investors, and creditors of **Centennial Technologies.** Its CEO was eventually indicted on five counts of fraud. Many of these shenanigans could have been avoided with internal controls.

Point: A *voucher* is an internal document (or file).

Quick Check

3. Why must a company hold liquid assets?
4. Why does a company hold cash equivalent assets in addition to cash?
5. Identify at least two assets that are classified as cash equivalents.
6. Good internal control procedures for cash include which of the following? (*a*) All cash disbursements, other than those for very small amounts, are made by check; (*b*) One employee should count cash received from sales and promptly deposit cash receipts; or (*c*) Cash receipts by mail should be opened by one employee who is then responsible for recording and depositing receipts.
7. Should all companies require a voucher system? At what point in a company's growth would you recommend a voucher system?

Answers—p. 333

P2 Explain and record petty cash fund transactions.

Petty Cash System of Control A basic principle for controlling cash disbursements is that all payments must be made by check. An exception to this rule is made for *petty cash disbursements,* which are the small payments required for items such as postage, courier fees, minor repairs, and low-cost supplies. To avoid the time and cost of writing checks for small amounts, a company sets up a petty cash fund to make small payments. (**Petty cash** activities are part of an *imprest system,* which designates advance money to establish the fund, to withdraw from the fund, and to reimburse the fund.)

Operating a petty cash fund. Establishing a petty cash fund requires estimating the total amount of small payments likely to be made during a short period such as a week or month. A check is then drawn by the company cashier for an amount slightly in excess of this estimate. This check is recorded with a debit to the Petty Cash account (an asset) and a credit to Cash. The check is cashed, and the currency is given to an employee designated as the *petty cashier* or *petty cash custodian.* The petty cashier is responsible for keeping this cash safe, making payments from the fund, and keeping records of it in a secure place referred to as the *petty cashbox.*

For example, when each cash disbursement is made, the person receiving payment should sign a prenumbered *petty cash receipt,* also called *petty cash ticket*—see Exhibit 8.2. The petty cash receipt is then placed in the petty cashbox with the remaining money. Under this system, the sum of all receipts plus the remaining cash equals the total fund amount. A $100 petty cash fund, for instance, contains any combination of cash and petty cash receipts that totals

Point: A petty cash fund is used only for business expenses.

Petty Cash Receipt Z-Mart			No. 9
For	Freight charges	Date	11/5/05
Charge to	Merchandise Inventory	Amount	$6.75
Approved by	Jim Gibbs	Received by	Dick Fitch

Exhibit 8.2
Petty Cash Receipt

$100 (examples are $80 cash plus $20 in receipts, or $10 cash plus $90 in receipts). Each disbursement reduces cash and increases the amount of receipts in the petty cashbox.

The petty cash fund should be reimbursed when it is nearing zero and at the end of an accounting period when financial statements are prepared. For this purpose, the petty cashier sorts the paid receipts by the type of expense or account and then totals the receipts. The petty cashier presents all paid receipts to the company cashier, who stamps all receipts *paid* so they cannot be reused, files them for recordkeeping, and gives the petty cashier a check for their sum. When this check is cashed and the money placed in the cashbox, the total money in the cashbox is restored to its original amount. The fund is now ready for a new cycle of petty cash payments.

Point: Petty cash receipts with either no signature or a forged signature usually indicate misuse of petty cash. Companies respond with surprise petty cash counts for verification.

Illustrating a petty cash fund. To illustrate, assume Z-Mart establishes a petty cash fund on November 1 and designates one of its office employees as the petty cashier. A $75 check is drawn, cashed, and the proceeds given to the petty cashier. The entry to record the setup of this petty cash fund is

Nov. 1	Petty Cash	75	
	Cash.		75
	To establish a petty cash fund.		

Assets = Liabilities + Equity
+75
−75

After the petty cash fund is established, the *Petty Cash account is not debited or credited again unless the amount of the fund is changed.* (A fund probably should be increased if it requires reimbursement too frequently. On the other hand, if the fund is too large, some of its money should be redeposited in the Cash account.)

Next, assume that Z-Mart's petty cashier makes several November payments from petty cash. Each person who received payment is required to sign a receipt. On November 27, after making a $26.50 cash payment for tile cleaning, only $3.70 cash remains in the fund. The petty cashier then summarizes and totals the petty cash receipts as shown in Exhibit 8.3.

Point: Reducing or eliminating a petty cash fund would require a credit to Petty Cash.

Point: Although *individual* petty cash disbursements are not evidenced by a check, the initial petty cash fund is evidenced by a check, and later petty cash expenditures are evidenced by a check to replenish them *in total.*

Exhibit 8.3
Petty Cash Payments Report

Z-MART Petty Cash Payments Report			
Miscellaneous Expenses			
Nov. 2	Washing windows	$20.00	
Nov. 27	Tile cleaning	26.50	$ 46.50
Merchandise Inventory (transportation-in)			
Nov. 5	Transport of merchandise purchased	6.75	
Nov. 20	Transport of merchandise purchased	8.30	15.05
Delivery Expense			
Nov. 18	Customer's package delivered		5.00
Office Supplies Expense			
Nov. 15	Purchase of office supplies immediately used		4.75
Total			**$71.30**

Point: This report can also include receipt number and names of those who approved and received cash payment (see Demo Problem 2).

The petty cash payments report and all receipts are given to the company cashier in exchange for a $71.30 check to reimburse the fund. The petty cashier cashes the check and puts the $71.30 cash in the petty cashbox. The company records this reimbursement as follows:

Assets	= Liabilities	+ Equity
−71.30		−46.50
		−15.05
		− 5.00
		− 4.75

Nov. 27	Miscellaneous Expenses	46.50	
	Merchandise Inventory	15.05	
	Delivery Expense	5.00	
	Office Supplies Expense	4.75	
	Cash		71.30
	To reimburse petty cash.		

Point: To avoid errors in recording petty cash reimbursement, follow these steps: (1) prepare payments report, (2) compute cash needed by subtracting cash remaining from total fund amount, (3) record entry, and (4) check "Dr. = Cr." in entry—any difference is Cash Over and Short.

A petty cash fund is usually reimbursed at the end of an accounting period so that expenses are recorded in the proper period, even if the fund is not low on money. If the fund is not reimbursed at the end of a period, the financial statements would show both an overstated cash asset and understated expenses (or assets) that were paid out of petty cash. Some companies do not reimburse the petty cash fund at the end of each period under the principle that this amount is immaterial to users of financial statements.

Increasing or decreasing a petty cash fund. A decision to increase or decrease a petty cash fund is often made when reimbursing it. To illustrate, assume Z-Mart decides to *increase* its petty cash fund from $75 to $100 on November 27 when it reimburses the fund. The entries required are to (1) reimburse the fund as usual (see the preceding November 27 entry, and (2) increase the fund amount as follows:

Nov. 27	Petty Cash	25	
	Cash		25
	To increase the petty cash fund amount.		

Alternatively, if Z-Mart *decreases* the petty cash fund from $75 to $55 on November 27, the entry is to (1) credit Petty Cash for $20 (decreasing the fund from $75 to $55) and (2) debit Cash for $20 (reflecting the $20 transfer from Petty Cash to Cash).

Decision Ethics

Internal Auditor You make a surprise count of a $300 petty cash fund. You arrive at the petty cashier when she is on the telephone. She politely asks that you return after lunch so that she can finish her business on the telephone. You agree and return after lunch. In the petty cashbox, you find 14 new $20 bills with consecutive serial numbers plus receipts totaling $20. What is your evaluation?

Answer—p. 333

Cash over and short. Sometimes a petty cashier fails to get a receipt for payment or overpays for the amount due. When this occurs and the fund is later reimbursed, the petty cash payments report plus the cash remaining will not total to the fund balance. This mistake causes the fund to be *short*. This shortage is recorded as an expense in the reimbursing entry with a debit to the Cash Over and Short account. (An overage in the petty cash fund is recorded with a credit to Cash Over and Short in the reimbursing entry.) To illustrate, prepare the entry to reimburse a $200 petty cash fund when its payments report shows $178 in miscellaneous expenses and $15 cash remains.

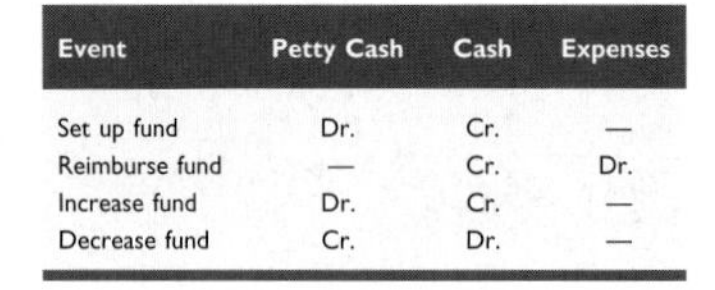

Event	Petty Cash	Cash	Expenses
Set up fund	Dr.	Cr.	—
Reimburse fund	—	Cr.	Dr.
Increase fund	Dr.	Cr.	—
Decrease fund	Cr.	Dr.	—

Miscellaneous Expenses	178	
Cash Over and Short	7	
Cash		185
To reimburse petty cash.		

Quick Check

8. Why are some cash payments made from a petty cash fund, and not by check?
9. Why should a petty cash fund be reimbursed at the end of an accounting period?
10. Identify at least two results of reimbursing a petty cash fund.

Answers—p. 333

Banking Activities as Controls

Banks (and other financial institutions) provide many services, including helping companies control cash. Banks safeguard cash, provide detailed and independent records of cash transactions, and are a source of cash financing. This section describes these services and the documents provided by banking activities that increase managers' control over cash.

Basic Bank Services

This section explains basic bank services—such as the bank account, the bank deposit, and checking—that contribute to the control of cash.

C3 Identify control features of banking activities.

Bank Account, Deposit, and Check A *bank account* is a record set up by a bank for a customer. It permits a customer to deposit money for safekeeping and helps control withdrawals. To limit access to a bank account, all persons authorized to write checks on the account must sign a **signature card,** which bank employees use to verify signatures on checks. Many companies have more than one bank account to serve different needs and to handle special transactions such as payroll.

Each bank deposit is supported by a **deposit ticket,** which lists items such as currency, coins, and checks deposited along with their corresponding dollar amounts. The bank gives the customer a copy of the deposit ticket or a deposit receipt as proof of the deposit. Exhibit 8.4 shows one type of deposit ticket.

Exhibit 8.4

Deposit Ticket

Front

Deposit Ticket

VideoBuster Company
901 Main Street
Hillcrest, NY 11749

Date October 2 20 05
Memo Deposit checks

99-DT/101

CASH	CURRENCY	36	50
	COIN		
LIST CHECKS SINGLY			
TOTAL FROM OTHER SIDE		203	50
TOTAL		240	00
NET DEPOSIT		240	00

USE OTHER SIDE FOR ADDITIONAL LISTINGS
BE SURE EACH ITEM IS PROPERLY ENDORSED

FN First National
Hillcrest, New York 11750

I:012410497 II: 457923 • 02 75

CHECKS AND OTHER ITEMS ARE RECEIVED FOR DEPOSIT SUBJECT TO THE PROVISIONS OF THE UNIFORM COMMERCIAL CODE OR ANY APPLICABLE COLLECTION AGREEMENT

Back

CHECKS	LIST SINGLY	DOLLARS	CENTS
1	14-287/939	90	50
2	82-759/339	82	80
3	76-907/919	30	20
4			
5			
6			
7			
8			
9			
10			
11			
12			
13			
14			
15			
16			
17			
18			
19			
20			
21			
22			
23			
24			
25			
26			
27			
28			
29			
30			
31			
32			
33			
34			
35			
TOTAL		203	50

ENTER TOTAL ON THE FRONT OF THIS TICKET

To withdraw money from an account, the depositor can use a **check,** which is a document signed by the depositor instructing the bank to pay a specified amount of money to a designated recipient. A check involves three parties: a *maker* who signs the check, a *payee* who is the recipient, and a *bank* (or *payer*) on which the check is drawn. The bank provides a depositor the checks

Decision Insight

Web-bank Many companies balance checkbooks and pay bills via the Web. Customers value the convenience and low cost of banking services anytime, anywhere. Services include the ability to stop payment on a check, move money between accounts, get up-to-date balances, and identify cleared checks and deposits.

that are serially numbered and imprinted with the name and address of both the depositor and bank. Both checks and deposit tickets are imprinted with identification codes in magnetic ink for computer processing. Exhibit 8.5 shows one type of check. It is accompanied with an optional *remittance advice* explaining the payment. When a remittance advice is unavailable, the *memo* line is often used for a brief explanation.

Exhibit 8.5

Check with Remittance Advice

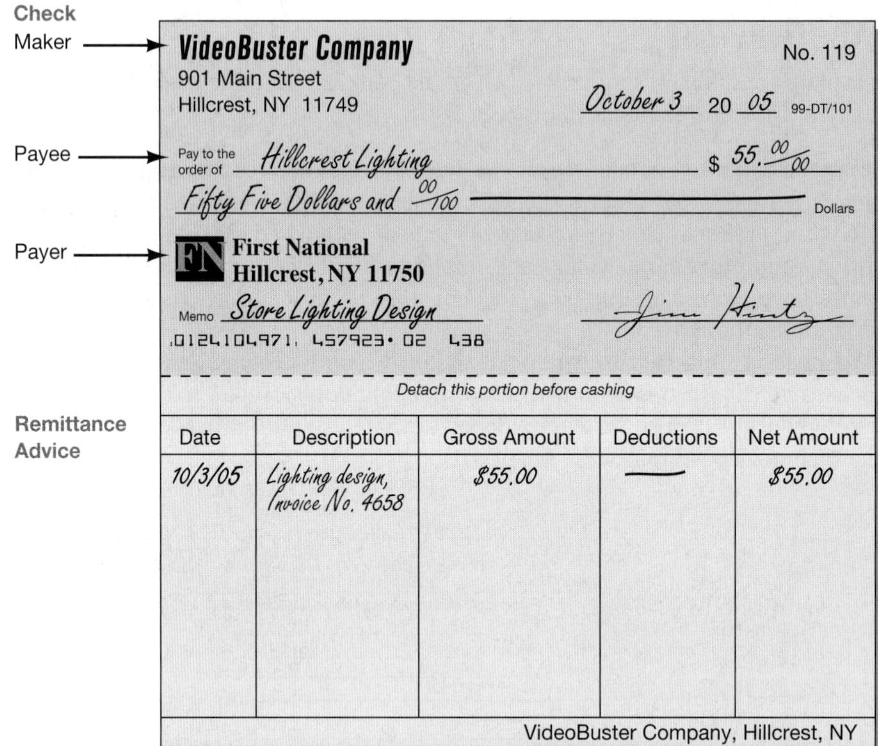

Check Maker
Payee
Payer
Remittance Advice
VideoBuster Company
901 Main Street
Hillcrest, NY 11749
No. 119
October 3 20 05 99-DT/101
Pay to the order of Hillcrest Lighting
$ 55.00/00
Fifty Five Dollars and 00/100
Dollars
First National
Hillcrest, NY 11750
Memo Store Lighting Design
Jim Hintz
Detach this portion before cashing
Date
Description
Gross Amount
Deductions
Net Amount
10/3/05
Lighting design, Invoice No. 4658
$55.00
—
$55.00
VideoBuster Company, Hillcrest, NY

Electronic Funds Transfer **Electronic funds transfer (EFT)** is the electronic communication transfer of cash from one party to another. No paper documents are necessary. Banks simply transfer cash from one account to another with a journal entry. Companies are increasingly using EFT because of its convenience and low cost. For instance, it can cost up to 50 cents to process a check through the banking system, whereas EFT cost is near zero. We now commonly see items such as payroll, rent, utilities, insurance, and interest payments being handled by EFT. The bank statement lists cash withdrawals by EFT with the checks and other deductions. Cash receipts by EFT are listed with deposits and other additions. A bank statement is sometimes a depositor's only notice of an EFT.

Bank Statement

Point: Good internal control is to deposit all cash receipts daily and make all payments for goods and services by check. This controls access to cash and creates an independent record of all cash activities.

Usually once a month, the bank sends each depositor a **bank statement** showing the activity in the account. Different banks use different formats for their bank statements, but all of them include the following items of information:

1. Beginning-of-period balance of the depositor's account.
2. Checks and other debits decreasing the account during the period.
3. Deposits and other credits increasing the account during the period.
4. End-of-period balance of the depositor's account.

This information reflects the bank's records. Exhibit 8.6 shows one type of bank statement. Identify each of these four items in that statement. Part Ⓐ of Exhibit 8.6 summarizes changes

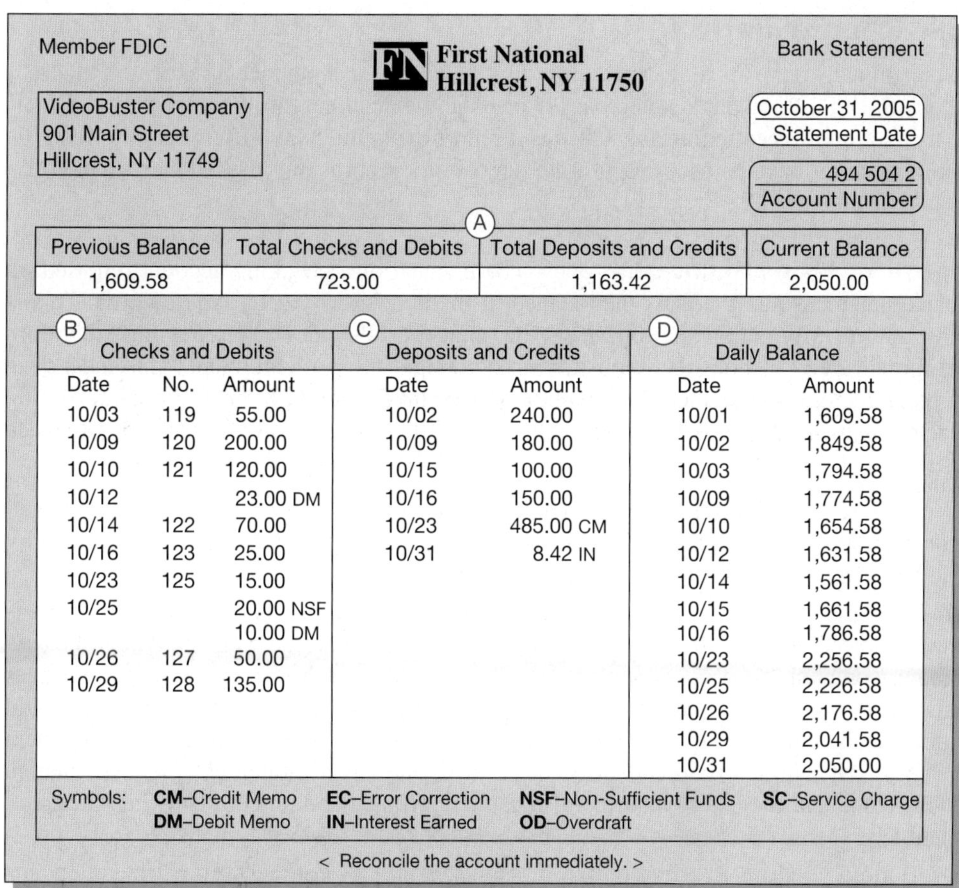

Member FDIC

FN First National
Hillcrest, NY 11750

Bank Statement

VideoBuster Company
901 Main Street
Hillcrest, NY 11749

October 31, 2005
Statement Date

494 504 2
Account Number

(A)

Previous Balance	Total Checks and Debits	Total Deposits and Credits	Current Balance
1,609.58	723.00	1,163.42	2,050.00

(B) Checks and Debits			(C) Deposits and Credits		(D) Daily Balance	
Date	No.	Amount	Date	Amount	Date	Amount
10/03	119	55.00	10/02	240.00	10/01	1,609.58
10/09	120	200.00	10/09	180.00	10/02	1,849.58
10/10	121	120.00	10/15	100.00	10/03	1,794.58
10/12		23.00 DM	10/16	150.00	10/09	1,774.58
10/14	122	70.00	10/23	485.00 CM	10/10	1,654.58
10/16	123	25.00	10/31	8.42 IN	10/12	1,631.58
10/23	125	15.00			10/14	1,561.58
10/25		20.00 NSF			10/15	1,661.58
		10.00 DM			10/16	1,786.58
10/26	127	50.00			10/23	2,256.58
10/29	128	135.00			10/25	2,226.58
					10/26	2,176.58
					10/29	2,041.58
					10/31	2,050.00

Symbols: **CM**–Credit Memo **EC**–Error Correction **NSF**–Non-Sufficient Funds **SC**–Service Charge **DM**–Debit Memo **IN**–Interest Earned **OD**–Overdraft

< Reconcile the account immediately. >

Exhibit 8.6

Bank Statement

in the account. Part (B) lists paid checks along with other debits. Part (C) lists deposits and credits to the account, and part (D) shows the daily account balances.

In reading a bank statement note that a depositor's account is a liability on the bank's records. This is so because the money belongs to the depositor, not the bank. When a depositor increases the account balance, the bank records it with a *credit* to that liability account. This means that debit memos from the bank produce *credits* on the depositor's books, and credit memos from the bank produce *debits* on the depositor's books.

Enclosed with a bank statement is a list of the depositor's canceled checks (or the actual canceled checks) along with any debit or credit memoranda affecting the account. **Canceled checks** are checks the bank has paid and deducted from the customer's account during the period. Other deductions that can appear on a bank statement include (1) service charges and fees assessed by the bank, (2) checks deposited that are uncollectible, (3) corrections of previous errors, (4) withdrawals through automated teller machines (ATMs), and (5) periodic payments arranged in advance by a depositor. (Most company checking accounts do not allow ATM withdrawals because of the company's desire to make all disbursements by check.) Except for service charges, the bank notifies the depositor of each deduction with a debit memorandum when the bank reduces the balance. A copy of each debit memorandum is usually sent with the statement.

Global: If cash is in more than one currency, a company usually translates these amounts into U.S. dollars using the exchange rate as of the balance sheet date.

Transactions that increase the depositor's account include amounts the bank collects on behalf of the depositor and the corrections of previous errors. Credit memoranda notify the depositor of all increases when they are recorded. A copy of each credit memorandum is often sent with the bank statement. Banks that pay interest on checking accounts often compute the amount of interest earned on the average cash balance and would credit it to the depositor's account each period. In Exhibit 8.6, the bank credits $8.42 of interest to the account.

Global: A company must disclose any restrictions on cash accounts located outside the United States.

Bank Reconciliation

P3 Prepare a bank reconciliation.

When a company deposits all cash receipts and makes all cash payments (except petty cash) by check, it can use the bank statement for proving the accuracy of its cash records. This is done using a **bank reconciliation,** which is a report explaining any differences between the checking account balance according to the depositor's records and the balance reported on the bank statement.

Topic Tackler 8-2

Purpose of Bank Reconciliation The balance of a checking account reported on the bank statement rarely equals the balance in the depositor's accounting records. This is usually due to information that one party has that the other does not. We must therefore prove the accuracy of both the depositor's records and those of the bank. This means we must *reconcile* the two balances and explain or account for any differences in them. Among the factors causing the bank statement balance to differ from the depositor's book balance are these:

- **Outstanding checks. Outstanding checks** are checks written (or drawn) by the depositor, deducted on the depositor's records, and sent to the payees but not yet received by the bank for payment at the bank statement date.
- **Deposits in transit** (also called **outstanding deposits**). **Deposits in transit** are deposits made and recorded by the depositor but not yet recorded on the bank statement. For example, companies can make deposits (in the night depository) at the end of a business day after the bank is closed. If such a deposit occurred on a bank statement date, it would not appear on this period's statement. The bank would record such a deposit on the next business day, and it would appear on the next period's bank statement. Deposits mailed to the bank near the end of a period also can be in transit and unrecorded when the statement is prepared.
- **Deductions for uncollectible items and for services.** A company sometimes deposits another party's check that is uncollectible (usually meaning the balance in such an account is not large enough to cover the check). This check is called a *non-sufficient funds (NSF)* check. The bank would have initially credited the depositor's account for the amount of the check. When the bank learns the check is uncollectible, it debits (reduces) the depositor's account for the amount of that check. The bank may also charge the depositor a fee for processing an uncollectible check and notify the depositor of the deduction by sending a debit memorandum. The depositor should record each deduction when a debit memorandum is received, but an entry is sometimes not made until the bank reconciliation is prepared. Other possible bank charges to a depositor's account that are first reported on a bank statement include printing new checks and service fees.
- **Additions for collections and for interest.** Banks sometimes act as collection agents for their depositors by collecting notes and other items. Banks can also receive electronic funds transfers to the depositor's account. When a bank collects an item, it is added to the depositor's account, less any service fee. The bank also sends a credit memorandum to notify the depositor of the transaction. When the memorandum is received, the depositor should record it; yet it sometimes remains unrecorded until the bank reconciliation is prepared. The bank statement also includes a credit for any interest earned.
- **Errors.** Both banks and depositors can make errors. Bank errors might not be discovered until the depositor prepares the bank reconciliation. Also, depositor errors are sometimes discovered when the bank balance is reconciled. Error testing includes: (a) comparing deposits on the bank statement with deposits in the accounting records and (b) comparing canceled checks on the bank statement with checks recorded in the accounting records.

Point: Small businesses with few employees often allow recordkeepers to both write checks and keep the general ledger. If this is done, it is essential that the owner do the bank reconciliation.

Point: The person preparing the bank reconciliation should not be responsible for processing cash receipts, managing checks, or maintaining cash records.

Illustration of a Bank Reconciliation We follow nine steps in preparing the bank reconciliation. It is helpful to refer to the bank reconciliation in Exhibit 8.7 when studying steps 1 through 9.

1. Identify the bank statement balance of the cash account (*balance per bank*). VideoBuster's bank balance is $2,050.
2. Identify and list any unrecorded deposits and any bank errors understating the bank balance. Add them to the bank balance. VideoBuster's $145 deposit placed in the bank's night depository on October 31 is not recorded on its bank statement.
3. Identify and list any outstanding checks and any bank errors overstating the bank balance. Deduct them from the bank balance. VideoBuster's comparison of canceled checks with its books shows two checks outstanding: No. 124 for $150 and No. 126 for $200.
4. Compute the *adjusted bank balance,* also called the *corrected* or *reconciled balance.*
5. Identify the company's book balance of the cash account (*balance per book*). VideoBuster's book balance is $1,404.58.
6. Identify and list any unrecorded credit memoranda from the bank, any interest earned, and errors understating the book balance. Add them to the book balance. Enclosed with VideoBuster's bank statement is a credit memorandum showing the bank collected a note receivable for the company on October 23. The note's proceeds of $500 (minus a $15 collection fee) are credited to the company's account. VideoBuster's bank statement also shows a credit of $8.42 for interest earned on the average cash balance. There was no prior notification of this item, and it is not yet recorded.
7. Identify and list any unrecorded debit memoranda from the bank, any service charges, and errors overstating the book balance. Deduct them from the book balance. Debits on VideoBuster's bank statement that are not yet recorded include (a) a $23 charge for check printing and (b) an NSF check for $20 plus a related $10 processing fee. (The NSF check is dated October 16 and was included in the book balance.)
8. Compute the *adjusted book balance,* also called *corrected* or *reconciled balance.*
9. Verify that the two adjusted balances from steps 4 and 8 are equal. If so, they are reconciled. If not, check for accuracy and missing data to achieve reconciliation.

Point: Outstanding checks are identified by comparing canceled checks on the bank statement with checks recorded. This includes identifying any outstanding checks listed on the *previous* period's bank reconciliation that are not included in the canceled checks on this period's bank statement.

Adjusting Entries from a Bank Reconciliation A bank reconciliation often identifies unrecorded items that need recording by the company. In VideoBuster's reconciliation, the adjusted balance of $1,845 is the correct balance as of October 31. But the company's accounting records show a $1,404.58 balance. We must prepare journal entries to adjust the book balance to the correct balance. *It is important to remember that only the items reconciling the book balance require adjustment.* A review of Exhibit 8.7 indicates that four entries are required for VideoBuster.

Point: The adjusting entries could be combined into one compound entry.

Exhibit 8.7

Bank Reconciliation

VIDEOBUSTER
Bank Reconciliation
October 31, 2005

①	Bank statement balance		$ 2,050.00	⑤	Book balance		$ 1,404.58
②	Add			⑥	Add		
	Deposit of Oct. 31 in transit		145.00		Collect $500 note less $15 fee	$485.00	
			2,195.00		Interest earned	8.42	493.42
③	Deduct						1,898.00
	Outstanding checks			⑦	Deduct		
	No. 124	$150.00			Check printing charge	23.00	
	No. 126	200.00	350.00		NSF check plus service fee	30.00	53.00
④	**Adjusted bank balance**		**$1,845.00**	⑧	**Adjusted book balance**		**$1,845.00**

⑨ Balances are equal (reconciled)

Collection of note. The first entry is to record the proceeds of its note receivable collected by the bank less the expense of having the bank perform that service.

Assets = Liabilities + Equity
+485 −15
−500

Oct. 31	Cash	485	
	Collection Expense	15	
	Notes Receivable		500
	To record the collection fee and proceeds for a note collected by the bank.		

Interest earned. The second entry records interest credited to its account by the bank.

Assets = Liabilities + Equity
+8.42 +8.42

Oct. 31	Cash	8.42	
	Interest Revenue		8.42
	To record interest earned on the cash balance in the checking account.		

Check printing. The third entry records expenses for the check printing charge.

Assets = Liabilities + Equity
−23 −23

Oct. 31	Miscellaneous Expenses	23	
	Cash		23
	Check printing charge.		

NSF check. The fourth entry records the NSF check that is returned as uncollectible. The $20 check was originally received from F. Heflin in payment of his account and then deposited. The bank charged $10 for handling the NSF check and deducted $30 total from VideoBuster's account. This means the entry must reverse the effects of the original entry made when the check was received and must record (add) the $10 bank fee.

Point: The company will try to collect the entire NSF amount of $30.

Assets = Liabilities + Equity
+30
−30

Oct. 31	Accounts Receivable—F. Heflin	30	
	Cash		30
	To charge Heflin's account for $20 NSF check and $10 bank fee.		

After these four entries are recorded, the book balance of cash is adjusted to the correct amount of $1,845 (computed as $1,404.58 + $485 + $8.42 − $23 − $30).

Point: The Demo Problem 1 shows an adjusting entry for an error correction.

Quick Check

11. What is a bank statement?
12. What is the meaning of the phrase *to reconcile a bank balance?*
13. Why do we reconcile the bank statement balance of cash and the depositor's book balance of cash?
14. List at least two items affecting the bank balance side of a bank reconciliation and indicate whether the items are added or subtracted.
15. List at least three items affecting the book balance side of a bank reconciliation and indicate whether the items are added or subtracted.

Answers—p. 333

Days' Sales Uncollected

Decision Analysis

A1 Compute the days' sales uncollected ratio and use it to assess liquidity.

Many companies attract customers by selling to them on credit. This means that cash receipts from customers are delayed until accounts receivable are collected. Users of accounting information often want to know how quickly a company can convert its accounts receivable into cash. This is important for evaluating a company's liquidity. One measure of the receivables' nearness to cash is the **days' sales uncollected,** also called *days' sales in receivables*. This measure is computed by dividing the current balance of receivables by net credit sales over the year just completed and then multiplying by 365 (number of days in a year). Since net credit sales usually are not reported to external users, the net sales (or revenues) figure is commonly used in the computation as in Exhibit 8.8.

$$\text{Days' sales uncollected} = \frac{\text{Accounts receivable}}{\text{Net sales}} \times 365$$

Exhibit 8.8

Days' Sales Uncollected

We use days' sales uncollected to estimate how much time is likely to pass before the current amount of accounts receivable is received in cash. For evaluation purposes, we need to compare this estimate to that for other companies in the same industry. We also make comparisons between current and prior periods.

To illustrate, we select data from the annual reports of two toy manufacturers, **Hasbro** and **Mattel**. Their days' sales uncollected figures are shown in Exhibit 8.9.

Exhibit 8.9

Analysis using Days' Sales Uncollected

Company	Figure ($ millions)	2002	2001	2000
Hasbro	Accounts receivable	$555	$572	$686
	Net sales	$2,816	$2,856	$3,787
	Days' sales uncollected	**72 days**	**73 days**	**66 days**
Mattel	Accounts receivable	$491	$666	$840
	Net sales	$4,885	$4,688	$4,565
	Days' sales uncollected	**37 days**	**52 days**	**67 days**

Days' sales uncollected for Hasbro in 2002 is computed as ($555/$2,816) × 365 days = 72 days. This means that it will take about 72 days to collect cash from ending accounts receivable. This number reflects one or more of the following factors: a company's ability to collect receivables, customer financial health, customer payment strategies, and discount terms. To further assess days' sales uncollected for Hasbro, we compare it to two prior years and to those of Mattel. We see that Hasbro's days' sales uncollected has slightly increased from 66 days in 2000 to 72 days in 2002, which is not good for its liquidity. In comparison, Mattel has improved on this factor. Specifically, Mattel's days' sales uncollected has declined from 67 days in 2000 to 37 days in 2002. The less time that money is tied up in receivables often translates into increased profitability.

Decision Maker

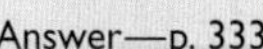

Sales Representative The sales staff is told to take action to help reduce days' sales uncollected. What can you, a salesperson, do to reduce days' sales uncollected?

Answer—p. 333

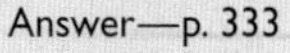

Demonstration Problem 1

Prepare a bank reconciliation for Jamboree Enterprises for the month ended November 30, 2005. The following information is available to reconcile Jamboree Enterprises' book balance of cash with its bank statement balance as of November 30, 2005:

a. After all posting is complete on November 30, the company's book balance of Cash has a $16,380 debit balance, but its bank statement shows a $38,520 balance.

b. Checks No. 2024 for $4,810 and No. 2036 for $5,000 are outstanding.

c. In comparing the canceled checks on the bank statement with the entries in the accounting records, it is found that Check No. 2025 in payment of rent is correctly drawn for $1,000 but is erroneously entered in the accounting records as $880.

d. The November 30 deposit of $17,150 was placed in the night depository after banking hours on that date, and this amount does not appear on the bank statement.

e. In reviewing the bank statement, a check written by Jumbo Enterprises in the amount of $160 was erroneously drawn against Jamboree's account.

f. A credit memorandum enclosed with the bank statement indicates that the bank collected a $30,000 note and $900 of related interest on Jamboree's behalf. This transaction was not recorded by Jamboree prior to receiving the statement.

g. A debit memorandum for $1,100 lists a $1,100 NSF check received from a customer, Marilyn Welch. Jamboree had not recorded the return of this check before receiving the statement.

h. Bank service charges for November total $40. These charges were not recorded by Jamboree before receiving the statement.

Planning the Solution

- Set up a bank reconciliation with a bank side and a book side (as in Exhibit 8.7). Leave room to both add and deduct items. Each column will result in a reconciled, equal balance.
- Examine each item *a* through *h* to determine whether it affects the book or the bank balance and whether it should be added or deducted from the bank or book balance.
- After all items are analyzed, complete the reconciliation and arrive at a reconciled balance between the bank side and the book side.
- For each reconciling item on the book side, prepare an adjusting entry. Additions to the book side require an adjusting entry that debits Cash. Deductions on the book side require an adjusting entry that credits Cash.

Solution to Demonstration Problem 1

JAMBOREE ENTERPRISES
Bank Reconciliation
November 30, 2005

Bank statement balance		$ 38,520	Book balance		$ 16,380
Add			Add		
Deposit of Nov. 30	$17,150		Collection of note	$30,000	
Bank error	160	17,310	Interest earned	900	30,900
		55,830			47,280
Deduct			Deduct		
Outstanding checks		9,810	NSF check	1,100	
			Recording error	120	
			Service charge	40	1,260
Adjusted bank balance		**$46,020**	**Adjusted book balance**		**$46,020**

Required Adjusting Entries for Jamboree

Nov. 30	Cash	30,900	
	Notes Receivable		30,000
	Interest Earned		900
	To record collection of note with interest.		
Nov. 30	Accounts Receivable—M. Welch	1,100	
	Cash		1,100
	To reinstate account due from an NSF check.		

[continued on next page]

[continued from previous page]

Nov. 30	Rent Expense	120	
	Cash		120
	To correct recording error on check no. 2025.		
Nov. 30	Bank Service Charges	40	
	Cash		40
	To record bank service charges.		

Demonstration Problem 2

Bacardi Company established a $150 petty cash fund with Dean Martin as the petty cashier. When the fund balance reached $19 cash, Martin prepared a petty cash payment report, which follows:

Petty Cash Payments Report

Receipt No.	Account Charged		Approved by	Received by
12	Delivery Expense	$ 29	Martin	A. Smirnoff
13	Merchandise Inventory	18	Martin	J. Daniels
15	(Omitted)	32	Martin	C. Carlsberg
16	Miscellaneous Expense	41	(Omitted)	J. Walker
	Total	$120		

Required

1. Identify four internal control weaknesses from the payment report.

2. Prepare general journal entries to record:

a. Establishment of the petty cash fund.

b. Reimbursement of the fund. (Assume for this part only that petty cash receipt no. 15 was issued for miscellaneous expenses.)

3. What is the Petty Cash account balance immediately before reimbursement? Immediately after reimbursement?

Solution to Demonstration Problem 2

1. Four internal control weaknesses are

a. Petty cash ticket no. 14 is missing. Its omission raises questions about the petty cashier's management of the fund.

b. The $19 cash balance means that $131 has been withdrawn ($150 − $19 = $131). However, the total amount of the petty cash receipts is only $120 ($29 + $18 + $32 + $41). The fund is $11 short of cash ($131 − $120 = $11). Was petty cash receipt no. 14 issued for $11? Management should investigate.

c. The petty cashier (Martin) did not sign petty cash receipt no. 16. This omission could have been an oversight on his part or he might not have authorized the payment. Management should investigate.

d. Petty cash receipt no. 15 does not indicate which account to charge. This omission could have been an oversight on the petty cashier's part. Management could check with C. Carlsberg and the petty cashier (Martin) about the transaction. Without further information, debit Miscellaneous Expense.

2. Petty cash general journal entries:

a. Entry to establish the petty cash fund:

Petty Cash	150	
Cash		150

b. Entry to reimburse the fund:

Delivery Expense	29	
Merchandise Inventory	18	
Miscellaneous Expense ($41 + $32)	73	
Cash Over and Short	11	
Cash		131

3. The Petty Cash account balance *always* equals its fund balance, in this case $150. This account balance does not change unless the fund is increased or decreased.

APPENDIX

8A Documents in a Voucher System

P4 Describe the voucher system to control cash disbursements.

This appendix describes the important business documents of a voucher system of control.

Purchase Requisition Department managers are usually not allowed to place orders directly with suppliers for control purposes. Instead, a department manager must inform the purchasing department of its needs by preparing and signing a **purchase requisition,** which lists the merchandise needed and requests that it be purchased—see Exhibit 8A.1. Two copies of the purchase requisition are sent to the purchasing department, which then sends one copy to the accounting department. When the accounting department receives a purchase requisition, it creates and maintains a voucher for this transaction. The requesting department keeps the third copy.

Exhibit 8A.1

Purchase Requisition

Purchase Requisition
Z-Mart
No. 917

From Sporting Goods Department
To Purchasing Department
Date October 28, 2005
Preferred Vendor Trex

Request purchase of the following item(s):

Model No.	Description	Quantity
CH 015	Challenger X7	1
SD 099	SpeedDemon	1

Reason for Request Replenish inventory
Approval for Request J.Z.

For Purchasing Department use only: Order Date 10/30/05 P.O. No. P98

Point: It is important to note that a voucher system is designed to uniquely meet the needs of a specific business. Thus, you should read this appendix as one example of a common voucher system design, but *not* the only design.

Purchase Order A **purchase order** is a document the purchasing department uses to place an order with a **vendor** (seller or supplier). A purchase order authorizes a vendor to ship ordered merchandise at the stated price and terms—see Exhibit 8A.2. When the purchasing department receives a purchase requisition, it prepares at least five copies of a purchase order. The copies are distributed as follows: *copy 1* to the vendor as a purchase request and as authority to ship merchandise; *copy 2,* along with a copy of the purchase requisition, to the accounting department, where it is entered in the voucher and used in approving payment of the invoice; *copy 3* to the requesting department to inform its manager that action is being taken; *copy 4* to the receiving department without order quantity so it can compare with goods received and provide independent count of goods received; and *copy 5* retained on file by the purchasing department.

Invoice An **invoice** is an itemized statement of goods prepared by the vendor listing the customer's name, items sold, sales prices, and terms of sale. An invoice is also a bill sent to the buyer from the supplier. From the vendor's point of view, it is a *sales invoice*. The buyer, or **vendee,** treats it as a *purchase invoice*. When receiving a purchase order, the vendor ships the ordered merchandise to the buyer and includes or mails a copy of the invoice covering the shipment to the buyer. The invoice is sent to the buyer's accounting department where it is placed in the voucher. (Refer back to Exhibit 5.5, which shows Z-Mart's purchase invoice.)

Purchase Order

No. P98

Z-Mart
10 Michigan Street
Chicago, Illinois 60521

To: Trex
W9797 Cherry Road
Antigo, Wisconsin 54409

Date 10/30/05
FOB Destination
Ship by As soon as possible
Terms 2/15, n/30

Request shipment of the following item(s):

Model No.	Description	Quantity	Price	Amount
CH 015	Challenger X7	1	490	490
SD 099	SpeedDemon	1	710	710

All shipments and invoices must include purchase order number

Ordered by J.W.

Exhibit 8A.2

Purchase Order

Receiving Report Many companies maintain a separate department to receive all merchandise and purchased assets. When each shipment arrives, this receiving department counts the goods and checks them for damage and agreement with the purchase order. It then prepares four or more copies of a **receiving report,** which is used within the company to notify the appropriate persons that ordered goods have been received and to describe the quantities and condition of the goods. One copy is sent to accounting and placed in the voucher. Copies are also sent to the requesting department and the purchasing department to notify them that the goods have arrived. The receiving department retains a copy in its files.

Invoice Approval When a receiving report arrives, the accounting department should have copies of the following documents in the voucher: purchase requisition, purchase order, and invoice. With the information in these documents, the accounting department can record the purchase and approve its payment. In approving an invoice for payment, it checks and compares information across all documents. To facilitate this checking and to ensure that no step is omitted, it often uses an **invoice approval,** also called *check authorization*—see Exhibit 8A.3. An invoice approval is a checklist of steps necessary for approving an invoice for recording and payment. It is a separate document either filed in the voucher or preprinted (or stamped) on the voucher.

Invoice Approval

Document		By	Date
Purchase requisition	917	TZ	10/28/05
Purchase order	P98	JW	10/30/05
Receiving report	R85	SK	11/3/05
Invoice:	4657		11/12/05
Price		JK	11/12/05
Calculations		JK	11/12/05
Terms		JK	11/12/05
Approved for payment		BC	

Exhibit 8A.3

Invoice Approval

As each step in the checklist is approved, the person initials the invoice approval and records the current date. Final approval implies the following steps have occurred:

1. **Requisition check:** Items on invoice are requested per purchase requisition.
2. **Purchase order check:** Items on invoice are ordered per purchase order.
3. **Receiving report check:** Items on invoice are received, per receiving report.
4. **Invoice check: Price:** Invoice prices are as agreed with the vendor.
   Calculations: Invoice has no mathematical errors.
   Terms: Terms are as agreed with the vendor.

Point: Recording a purchase is initiated by an invoice approval, not an invoice. An invoice approval verifies that the amount is consistent with that requested, ordered, and received. This controls and verifies purchases and related liabilities.

Voucher Once an invoice has been checked and approved, the voucher is complete. A complete voucher is a record summarizing a transaction. Once the voucher certifies a transaction, it authorizes recording an obligation. A voucher also contains approval for paying the obligation on an appropriate date. The physical form of a voucher varies across companies. Many are designed so that the invoice and other related source documents are placed inside the voucher, which can be a folder.

Completion of a voucher usually requires a person to enter certain information on both the inside and outside of the voucher. Typical information required on the inside of a voucher is shown in Exhibit 8A.4, and that for the outside is shown in Exhibit 8A.5. This information is taken from the invoice and the supporting documents filed in the voucher. A complete voucher is sent to an authorized individual (often called an *auditor*). This person performs a final review, approves the accounts and amounts for debiting (called the *accounting distribution*), and authorizes recording of the voucher.

Exhibit 8A.4

Inside of a Voucher

Z-Mart
Chicago, Illinois

Voucher No. 4657

Date Oct. 28, 2005
Pay to Trex
City Antigo State Wisconsin

For the following: (attach all invoices and supporting documents)

Date of Invoice	Terms	Invoice Number and Other Details	Terms
Nov. 2, 2005	2/15, n/30	Invoice No. 4657	1,200
		Less discount	24
		Net amount payable	1,176

Payment approved
N.O. Neal
Auditor

After a voucher is approved and recorded (in a journal called a **voucher register**), it is filed by its due date. A check is then sent on the payment date from the cashier, the voucher is marked "paid", and the voucher is sent to the accounting department and recorded (in a journal called the **check register**). The person issuing checks relies on the approved voucher and its signed supporting documents as proof that an obligation has been incurred and must be paid. The purchase requisition and purchase order confirm the purchase was authorized. The receiving report shows that items have been received, and the invoice approval form verifies that the invoice has been checked for errors. There is little chance for error and even less chance for fraud without collusion unless all the documents and signatures are forged.

Exhibit 8A.5

Outside of a Voucher

Voucher No. 4657

Accounting Distribution

Account Debited	Amount
Merch. Inventory	1,200
Store Supplies	
Office Supplies	
Sales Salaries	
Other	
Total Vouch. Pay. Cr.	1,200

Due Date November 12, 2005
Pay to Trex
City Antigo
State Wisconsin

Summary of charges:
Total charges 1,200
Discount 24
Net payment 1,176

Record of payment:
Paid
Check No.

APPENDIX

Control of Purchase Discounts 8B

This appendix explains how a company can better control its cash *disbursements* to take advantage of favorable purchases discounts. Chapter 5 described the entries to record the receipt and payment of an invoice for a merchandise purchase with and without discount terms. Those entries were prepared under what is called the **gross method** of recording purchases, which initially records the invoice at its *gross* amount ignoring any cash discount.

P5 Apply the net method to control purchase discounts.

The **net method** is another means of recording purchases, which initially records the invoice at its *net* amount of any cash discount. The net method gives management an advantage in controlling and monitoring cash payments involving purchase discounts.

To explain, when invoices are recorded at *gross* amounts, the amount of any discounts taken is deducted from the balance of the Merchandise Inventory account when cash payment is made. This means that the amount of any discounts lost is not reported in any account or on the income statement. Lost discounts recorded in this way are unlikely to come to the attention of management. When purchases are recorded at *net* amounts, a **Discounts Lost** expense account is recorded and brought to management's attention. Management can then seek to identify the reason for discounts lost such as oversight, carelessness, or unfavorable terms. (Chapter 5 explains how managers assess whether a discount is favorable or not.)

Perpetual Inventory System To illustrate, assume that a company purchases merchandise on November 2 at a $1,200 invoice price with terms of 2/10, n/30. Its November 2 entries under the gross and net methods are

Gross Method			Net Method		
Merchandise Inventory	1,200		Merchandise Inventory	1,176	
Accounts Payable		1,200	Accounts Payable		1,176

If the invoice is paid on November 12 within the discount period, it records the following

Gross Method			Net Method		
Accounts Payable	1,200		Accounts Payable	1,176	
Merchandise Inventory		24	Cash		1,176
Cash		1,176			

If the invoice is *not* paid within the discount period, it records the following November 12 entry (which is the date corresponding to the end of the discount period)

Gross Method			Net Method		
No entry			**Discounts Lost**	24	
			Accounts Payable		24

Then, when the invoice is later paid on December 2, outside the discount period, it records the following

Gross Method			Net Method		
Accounts Payable	1,200		Accounts Payable	1,200	
Cash		1,200	Cash		1,200

(Note that the discount lost can be recorded when the cash payment is made with a single entry. However, in this case, when financial statements are prepared after a discount is lost and before the cash payment is made, an adjusting entry is required to recognize any unrecorded discount lost in the period when incurred.)

Periodic Inventory System The preceding entries assume a perpetual inventory system. If a company is using a *periodic system*, its November 2 entries under the gross and net methods are

Gross Method—Periodic			Net Method—Periodic		
Purchases	1,200		Purchases	1,176	
Accounts Payable		1,200	Accounts Payable		1,176

If the invoice is paid on November 12 within the discount period, it records the following

Gross Method—Periodic			Net Method—Periodic		
Accounts Payable	1,200		Accounts Payable	1,176	
Purchases Discounts		24	Cash		1,176
Cash		1,176			

If the invoice is *not* paid within the discount period, it records the following November 12 entry

Gross Method—Periodic			Net Method—Periodic		
No entry			**Discounts Lost**	24	
			Accounts Payable		24

Then, when the invoice is later paid on December 2, outside the discount period, it records the following

Gross Method—Periodic			Net Method—Periodic		
Accounts Payable	1,200		Accounts Payable	1,200	
Cash		1,200	Cash		1,200

Summary

C1 **Define internal control and identify its purpose and principles.** An internal control system consists of the policies and procedures managers use to protect assets, ensure reliable accounting, promote efficient operations, and urge adherence to company policies. It can prevent avoidable losses and help managers both plan operations and monitor company and human performance. Principles of good internal control include establishing responsibilities, maintaining adequate records, insuring assets and bonding employees, separating recordkeeping from custody of assets, dividing responsibilities for related transactions, applying technological controls, and performing regular independent reviews.

C2 **Define cash and cash equivalents and explain how to report them.** Cash includes currency, coins, and amounts on (or acceptable for) deposit in checking and savings accounts. Cash equivalents are short-term, highly liquid investment assets readily convertible to a known cash amount and sufficiently close to their maturity date so that market value is not sensitive to interest rate changes. Cash and cash equivalents are liquid assets because they are readily converted into other assets or can be used to pay for goods, services, or liabilities.

C3 **Identify control features of banking activities.** Banks offer several services that promote the control and safeguarding of cash. A bank account is a record set up by a bank permitting a customer to deposit money for safekeeping and to draw checks on it. A bank deposit is money contributed to the account with a deposit ticket as proof. A check is a document signed by the depositor instructing the bank to pay a specified amount of money to a designated recipient.

A1 **Compute the days' sales uncollected ratio and use it to assess liquidity.** Many companies attract customers by selling to them on credit. This means that cash receipts from customers are delayed until accounts receivable are collected. Users want to know how quickly a company can convert its accounts receivable into cash. The days' sales uncollected ratio, one measure reflecting company liquidity, is computed by dividing the ending balance of receivables by annual net sales, and then multiplying by 365.

P1 **Apply internal control to cash receipts and disbursements.** Internal control of cash receipts ensures that all cash received is properly recorded and deposited. Attention focuses on two important types of cash receipts: over-the-counter and by mail. Good internal control for over-the-counter cash receipts includes use of a cash register, customer review, use of receipts, a permanent transaction record, and separation of the custody of cash from its recordkeeping. Good internal control for cash receipts by mail includes at least two people assigned to open mail and a listing of each sender's name, amount, and explanation.

P2 Explain and record petty cash fund transactions. Petty cash disbursements are payments of small amounts for items such as postage, courier fees, minor repairs, and supplies. A company usually sets up one or more petty cash funds. A petty fund cashier is responsible for safekeeping the cash, making payments from this fund, and keeping receipts and records. A Petty Cash account is debited only when the fund is established or increased in amount. When the fund is replenished, petty cash disbursements are recorded with debits to expense (or asset) accounts and a credit to cash.

P3 Prepare a bank reconciliation. A bank reconciliation proves the accuracy of the depositor's and the bank's records. The bank statement balance is adjusted for items such as outstanding checks and unrecorded deposits made on or before the bank statement date but not reflected on the statement. The book balance is adjusted for items such as service charges, bank collections for the depositor, and interest earned on the account.

P4[A] Describe the voucher system to control cash disbursements. A voucher system is a set of procedures and approvals designed to control cash disbursements and acceptance of obligations. The voucher system of control relies on several important documents, including the voucher and its supporting files. A key factor in this system is that only approved departments and individuals are authorized to incur certain obligations.

P5[B] Apply the net method to control purchase discounts. The net method aids management in monitoring and controlling purchase discounts. When invoices are recorded at gross amounts, the amount of discounts taken is deducted from the balance of the Inventory account. This means that the amount of any discounts lost is not reported in any account and is unlikely to come to the attention of management. When purchases are recorded at net amounts, a Discounts Lost account is brought to management's attention as an operating expense. Management can then seek to identify the reason for discounts lost, such as oversight, carelessness, or unfavorable terms.

Guidance Answers to **Decision Maker** and **Decision Ethics**

Entrepreneur A forced vacation policy is part of a good system of internal controls. When employees are forced to take vacations, their ability to hide any fraudulent behavior decreases because others must perform the vacationers' duties. A replacement employee potentially can uncover fraudulent behavior or falsified records. A forced vacation policy is especially important for employees in sensitive positions of handling money or in control of easily transferable assets.

Internal Auditor Since you were asked to postpone your count, along with the fact the fund consists of 14 new $20 bills, you have legitimate concerns about whether money is being used for personal use. It is possible the most recent reimbursement of the fund was for $280 (14 × $20) or more. In that case, this reimbursement can leave the fund with sequentially numbered $20 bills. But if the most recent reimbursement was for less than $280, the presence of 14 sequentially numbered $20 bills suggests that the new bills were obtained from a bank as replacement for bills that had been removed. Neither situation shows that the cashier is stealing money, but the second case indicates that the cashier "borrowed" the cash and later replaced it after the auditor showed up. In writing your report, you must not conclude that the cashier is unethical unless other evidence supports it. You should consider additional surprise counts of this petty cashier over the next few weeks.

Sales Representative A salesperson can take several steps to reduce days' sales uncollected. These include (1) decreasing the ratio of sales on account to total sales by encouraging more cash sales, (2) identifying customers most delayed in their payments and encouraging earlier payments or cash sales, and (3) applying stricter credit policies to eliminate credit sales to customers that never pay.

Guidance Answers to **Quick Checks**

1. (*c*)
2. Technology reduces processing errors. It also allows more extensive testing of records, limits the amount of hard evidence, and highlights the importance of separation of duties.
3. A company holds liquid assets so that it can purchase other assets, buy services, and pay obligations.
4. It owns cash equivalents because they yield a return greater than what cash earns (and are readily exchanged for cash).
5. Examples of cash equivalents are 90-day U.S. Treasury bills, money market funds, and commercial paper (notes).
6. (*a*)
7. A voucher system is used when an owner/manager can no longer control purchasing procedures through personal supervision and direct participation.
8. If all cash payments are made by check, numerous checks for small amounts must be written. Since this practice is expensive and time-consuming, a petty cash fund is often established for making small (immaterial) cash payments.
9. If the petty cash fund is not reimbursed at the end of an accounting period, the transactions involving petty cash are not yet recorded and the petty cash asset is overstated.
10. First, petty cash transactions are recorded when the petty cash fund is reimbursed. Second, reimbursement provides cash to allow the fund to continue being used. Third, reimbursement identifies any cash shortage or overage in the fund.
11. A bank statement is a report prepared by the bank describing the activities in a depositor's account.

12. To reconcile a bank balance means to explain the difference between the cash balance in the depositor's accounting records and the cash balance on the bank statement.

13. The purpose of the bank reconciliation is to determine whether the bank or the depositor has made any errors and whether the bank has entered any transactions affecting the account that the depositor has not recorded.

14. Outstanding checks—subtracted
Unrecorded deposits—added

15. Debit memos—subtracted
NSF checks—subtracted
Bank service charges—subtracted
Interest earned—added
Credit memos—added

Key Terms

Key Terms are available at the book's Website for learning and testing in an online Flashcard Format.

Bank reconciliation (p. 322)
Bank statement (p. 320)
Canceled checks (p. 321)
Cash (p. 312)
Cash equivalents (p. 312)
Cash Over and Short (p. 313)
Check (p. 319)
Check register (p. 330)
Days' sales uncollected (p. 325)
Deposits in transit (p. 322)
Deposit ticket (p. 319)
Discounts Lost (p. 331)
Electronic funds transfer (EFT) (p. 320)
Gross method (p. 331)
Internal control system (p. 308)
Invoice (p. 328)
Invoice approval (p. 329)
Liquid assets (p. 312)
Liquidity (p. 312)
Net method (p. 331)
Outstanding checks (p. 322)
Petty cash fund (p. 316)
Principles of internal control (p. 309)
Purchase order (p. 328)
Purchase requisition (p. 328)
Receiving report (p. 329)
Signature card (p. 319)
Vendee (p. 328)
Vendor (p. 328)
Voucher (p. 315)
Voucher register (p. 330)
Voucher system (p. 315)

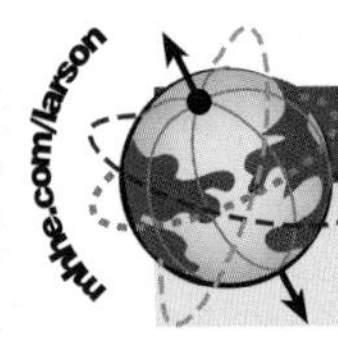

Personal Interactive Quiz

Personal Interactive Quizzes A and B are available at the book's Website to reinforce and assess your learning.

Superscript letter A (B) denotes assignments based on Appendix 8A (8B).

Discussion Questions

1. List the seven broad principles of internal control.
2. Why should responsibility for related transactions be divided among different departments or individuals?
3. Internal control procedures are important in every business, but at what stage in the development of a business do they become especially critical?
4. Which of the following assets is most liquid? Which is least liquid? Inventory, building, accounts receivable, or cash.
5. Why should the person who keeps the records of an asset not be the person responsible for its custody?
6. When a store purchases merchandise, why are individual departments not allowed to directly deal with suppliers?
7. What is a petty cash receipt? Who should sign it?
8. Why should cash receipts be deposited on the day of receipt?
9. **Krispy Kreme**'s statement of cash flows in Appendix A describes changes in cash and cash equivalents for the year ended February 2, 2003. What amount is provided (used) by investing activities? What amount is provided (used) by financing activities?
10. Refer to **Tastykake**'s balance sheet in Appendix A. Compare and discuss the amount of its cash with its other current assets (both in amount and percent) as of December 28, 2002. Compare and assess the cash amount at December 28, 2002, with its amount at December 29, 2001.
11. **Harley-Davidson**'s balance sheet in Appendix A reports that cash and equivalents decreased during the fiscal year ended December 31, 2002. Identify at least three major causes of this change in cash and equivalents.

Red numbers denote Discussion Questions that involve decision-making.

Homework Manager repeats all numerical Quick Studies on the book's Website with new numbers.

QUICK STUDY

QS 8-1
Internal control objectives
C1

An internal control system consists of all policies and procedures used to protect assets, ensure reliable accounting, promote efficient operations, and urge adherence to company policies.

1. What is the main objective of internal control procedures, and how is it achieved?

2. Why should recordkeeping for assets be separated from custody over the assets?

3. Why should the responsibility for a transaction be divided between two or more individuals or departments?

QS 8-2
Internal control for cash
P1

A good system of internal control for cash provides adequate procedures for protecting both cash receipts and cash disbursements.

1. What are three basic guidelines that help achieve this protection?

2. Identify two control systems or procedures for cash disbursements.

QS 8-3
Cash, liquidity, and return
C1 C2

Good accounting systems help with the management and control of cash and cash equivalents.

1. Define and contrast the terms *liquid asset* and *cash equivalent.*

2. Why would companies invest their idle cash in cash equivalents?

QS 8-4
Cash and equivalents
C2

Good accounting systems help in managing cash and controlling who has access to it.

1. What items are included in the category of cash?

2. What items are included in the category of cash equivalents?

3. What does the term *liquidity* refer to?

QS 8-5
Petty cash accounting
P2

1. The petty cash fund of the Rio Agency is established at $75. At the end of the current period, the fund contained $14 and had the following receipts: film rentals, $19, and refreshments for meetings, $23 (both expenditures to be classified as Entertainment Expense); postage, $6; and printing, $13. Prepare journal entries to record (*a*) establishment of the fund and (*b*) reimbursement of the fund at the end of the current period.

2. Identify the two events that cause a Petty Cash account to be credited in a journal entry.

QS 8-6
Bank reconciliation
P3

1. For each of the following items, indicate whether its amount (i) affects the bank or book side of a bank reconciliation and (ii) represents an addition or a subtraction in a bank reconciliation:

a. Outstanding checks	**d.** Unrecorded deposits	**g.** Bank service charges
b. Debit memos	**e.** Interest on cash balance	
c. NSF checks	**f.** Credit memos	

2. Which of the items in part 1 require an adjusting journal entry?

QS 8-7
Days' sales uncollected
A1

The following annual account balances are taken from Next Level Sports at December 31:

	2005	2004
Accounts receivable	$ 75,692	$ 70,484
Net sales	2,591,933	2,296,673

What is the change in the number of days' sales uncollected between years 2005 and 2004? According to this analysis, is the company's collection of receivables improving? Explain your answer.

QS 8-8[B]
Purchase discounts
P5

An important part of cash management is knowing when, and if, to take purchase discounts. (*a*) Which accounting method uses a Discounts Lost account? (*b*) What is the advantage of this method for management?

Homework Manager repeats all numerical Exercises on the book's Website with new numbers. 

EXERCISES

Exercise 8-1
Internal control recommendations
C1 

What internal control procedures would you recommend in each of the following situations?

1. A concession company has one employee who sells T-shirts and sunglasses at the beach. Each day, the employee is given enough shirts and sunglasses to last through the day and enough cash to make change. The money is kept in a box at the stand.
2. An antique store has one employee who is given cash and sent to garage sales each weekend. The employee pays cash for this merchandise that the antique store resells.

Exercise 8-2
Control of cash receipts by mail
P1 

Some of Castel Co.'s cash receipts from customers are sent to the company with the regular mail. Castel's recordkeeper opens these letters and deposits the cash received each day. (*a*) Identify any internal control problem(s) in this arrangement. (*b*) What changes do you recommend?

Exercise 8-3
Analyzing internal control
C1 

Bemis Company is a rapidly growing start-up business. Its recordkeeper, who was hired one year ago, left town after the company's manager discovered that a large sum of money had disappeared over the past six months. An audit disclosed that the recordkeeper had written and signed several checks made payable to her fiancé and then recorded the checks as salaries expense. The fiancé, who cashed the checks but never worked for the company, left town with the recordkeeper. As a result, the company incurred an uninsured loss of $84,000. Evaluate Bemis's internal control system and indicate which principles of internal control appear to have been ignored.

Exercise 8-4
Petty cash fund with a shortage
P2

Check (2) Cr. Cash $234 and Dr. Cash $100

Gannon Company establishes a $400 petty cash fund on September 9. On September 30, the fund shows $166 in cash along with receipts for the following expenditures: transportation-in, $32; postage expenses, $113; and miscellaneous expenses, $87. The petty cashier could not account for a $2 shortage in the fund. Gannon uses the perpetual system in accounting for merchandise inventory. Prepare (1) the September 9 entry to establish the fund and (2) the September 30 entry to both reimburse the fund and reduce it to $300.

Exercise 8-5
Petty cash fund accounting
P2

Check (3) Cr. Cash $472 (total)

Dane Co. establishes a $200 petty cash fund on January 1. One week later, the fund shows $28 in cash along with receipts for the following expenditures: postage, $64; transportation-in, $19; delivery expenses, $36; and miscellaneous expenses, $53. Dane uses the perpetual system in accounting for merchandise inventory. Prepare journal entries to (1) establish the fund on January 1, (2) reimburse it on January 8, and (3) both reimburse the fund and increase it to $500 on January 8, assuming no entry in part 2.

Exercise 8-6
Bank reconciliation and adjusting entries
P3

Prepare a table with the following headings for a monthly bank reconciliation dated September 30:

Bank Balance		Book Balance			Not Shown on the Reconciliation
Add	Deduct	Add	Deduct	Adjust	

For each item 1 through 12, place an *x* in the appropriate column to indicate whether the item should be added to or deducted from the book or bank balance, or whether it should not appear on the reconciliation. If the book balance is to be adjusted, place a *Dr.* or *Cr.* in the Adjust column to indicate whether the Cash balance should be debited or credited. At the left side of your table, number the items to correspond to the following list.

1. Bank service charge.
2. Checks written and mailed to payees on October 2.
3. Checks written by another depositor but charged against this company's account.
4. Principal and interest on a note collected by the bank but not yet recorded by the company.
5. Special bank charge for collection of note in part 4 on this company's behalf.
6. Check written against the company's account and cleared by the bank; erroneously not recorded by the company's recordkeeper.
7. Interest earned on the cash balance in the bank.
8. Night deposit made on September 30 after the bank closed.
9. Checks outstanding on August 31 that cleared the bank in September.
10. NSF check from customer returned on September 25 but not yet recorded by this company.
11. Checks written by the company and mailed to payees on September 30.
12. Deposit made on September 5 and processed by the bank on September 6.

Exercise 8-7
Voucher system
P1

The voucher system of control is designed to control cash disbursements and the acceptance of obligations.

1. The voucher system of control establishes procedures for what two processes?
2. What types of expenditures should be overseen by a voucher system of control?
3. When is the voucher initially prepared? Explain.

Exercise 8-8
Bank reconciliation
P3

Cruz Clinic deposits all cash receipts on the day when they are received and makes all cash payments by check. At the close of business on June 30, 2004, its Cash account shows an $11,352 debit balance. Cruz Clinic's June 30 bank statement shows $10,332 on deposit in the bank on that day. Prepare a bank reconciliation for Cruz Clinic using the following information:

a. Outstanding checks as of June 30 total $1,713.
b. The June 30 bank statement included an $18 debit memorandum for bank services.
c. Check No. 919, listed with the canceled checks, was correctly drawn for $489 in payment of a utility bill on June 15. Cruz Clinic mistakenly recorded it with a debit to Utilities Expense and a credit to Cash in the amount of $498.
d. The June 30 cash receipts of $2,724 were placed in the bank's night depository after banking hours and were not recorded on the June 30 bank statement.

Check Reconciled bal., $11,343

Exercise 8-9
Adjusting entries from bank reconciliation P3

Prepare the adjusting journal entries that Cruz Clinic must record as a result of preparing the bank reconciliation in Exercise 8-8.

Exercise 8-10
Liquid assets and accounts receivable
A1 

Deacon Co. reported annual net sales for 2004 and 2005 of $565,000 and $647,000, respectively. Its year-end balances of accounts receivable follow: December 31, 2004, $51,000; and December 31, 2005, $83,000. (*a*) Calculate its days' sales uncollected at the end of each year. (*b*) Evaluate and comment on any changes in the amount of liquid assets tied up in receivables.

Exercise 8-11[A]
Documents in a voucher system
P4

Management uses a voucher system to help control and monitor cash disbursements. Identify at least four key documents that are part of a voucher system of control. Explain each document's purpose, where it originates, and how it flows through the voucher system (including its copies).

Exercise 8-12[B]
Record invoices at gross or net amounts
P5

Trade Imports uses the perpetual system in accounting for merchandise inventory and had the following transactions during the month of October. Prepare entries to record these transactions assuming that Trade Imports records invoices (*a*) at gross amounts and (*b*) at net amounts.

Oct. 2 Purchased merchandise at a $4,000 price, invoice dated October 2, terms 2/10, n/30.
10 Received a $400 credit memorandum (at full invoice price) for the return of merchandise that it purchased on October 2.
17 Purchased merchandise at a $4,400 price, invoice dated October 16, terms 2/10, n/30.
26 Paid for the merchandise purchased on October 17, less the discount.
31 Paid for the merchandise purchased on October 2. Payment was delayed because the invoice was mistakenly filed for payment today. This error caused the discount to be lost.

PROBLEM SET A

Problem 8-1A
Analyzing internal control
C1 

For each of these five separate cases, identify the principle of internal control that is violated. Recommend what the business should do to ensure adherence to principles of internal control.

1. Heather Flatt records all incoming customer cash receipts for her employer and posts the customer payments to their respective accounts.
2. At Netco Company, Jeff and Jose alternate lunch hours. Jeff is the petty cash custodian, but if someone needs petty cash when he is at lunch, Jose fills in as custodian.
3. Nadine Cox posts all patient charges and payments at the P-Town Medical Clinic. Each night Nadine backs up the computerized accounting system to a tape and stores the tape in a locked file at her desk.
4. Barto Sayles prides himself on hiring quality workers who require little supervision. As office manager, Barto gives his employees full discretion over their tasks and for years has seen no reason to perform independent reviews of their work.
5. Desi West's manager has told her to reduce costs. Desi decides to raise the deductible on the plant's property insurance from $5,000 to $10,000. This cuts the property insurance premium in half. In a related move, she decides that bonding the plant's employees is a waste of money since the company has not experienced any losses due to employee theft. Desi saves the entire amount of the bonding insurance premium by dropping the bonding insurance.

Problem 8-2A
Establish, reimburse, and adjust petty cash
P2

Shawnee Co. set up a petty cash fund for payments of small amounts. The following transactions involving the petty cash fund occurred in May (the last month of the company's fiscal year):

May 1 Prepared a company check for $250 to establish the petty cash fund.
15 Prepared a company check both to replenish the fund for the following expenditures made since May 1 and to increase the fund to $450.
a. Paid $78 for janitorial services.
b. Paid $63.68 for miscellaneous expenses.
c. Paid postage expenses of $43.50.
d. Paid $57.15 to *The County Gazette* (the local newspaper) for an advertisement.
e. Counted $11.15 remaining in the petty cash box.
31 The petty cashier reports that $293.39 cash remains in the fund and decides that the May 15 increase in the fund was too large. A company check is drawn both to replenish the fund for the following expenditures made since May 15 and to reduce the fund to $400.
f. Paid postage expenses of $48.36.
g. Reimbursed the office manager for business mileage, $38.50.
h. Paid $39.75 to deliver merchandise to a customer, terms FOB destination.

Required

Check (1) Total Cr. to Cash: May 15, $438.85; May 31, $106.61

1. Prepare journal entries to establish the fund on May 1, to replenish it on May 15 and on May 31, and to reflect any increase or decrease in the fund balance on those dates.

Analysis Component

2. Explain how the company's financial statements are affected if the petty cash fund is not replenished and no entry is made on May 31.

Problem 8-3A
Establish, reimburse, and increase petty cash
P2

Inoke Gallery had the following petty cash transactions in February of the current year:

Feb. 2 Wrote a $300 check, cashed it, and gave the proceeds and the petty cashbox to Bo Brown, the petty cashier.
5 Purchased bond paper for the copier for $10.13 that is immediately used.
9 Paid $22.50 COD shipping charges on merchandise purchased for resale, terms FOB shipping point. Metro uses the perpetual system to account for merchandise inventory.
12 Paid $9.95 postage to express mail a contract to a client.
14 Reimbursed Alli Buck, the manager, $58 for business mileage on her car.
20 Purchased stationery for $77.76 that is immediately used.
23 Paid a courier $18 to deliver merchandise sold to a customer, terms FOB destination.
25 Paid $15.10 COD shipping charges on merchandise purchased for resale, terms FOB shipping point.
27 Paid $64 for postage expenses.
28 The fund had $21.23 remaining in the petty cash box. Sorted the petty cash receipts by accounts affected and exchanged them for a check to reimburse the fund for expenditures. The fund amount is also increased to $400.

Required

1. Prepare the journal entry to establish the petty cash fund.

2. Prepare a petty cash payments report for February with these categories: delivery expense, mileage expense, postage expense, merchandise inventory (for transportation-in), and office supplies expense. Sort the payments into the appropriate categories and total the expenditures in each category.

3. Prepare the journal entries for part 2 to both (*a*) reimburse and (*b*) increase the fund amount.

Check (3a & 3b) Cr. Cash $378.77

Problem 8-4A
Prepare a bank reconciliation and record adjustments
P3

mhhe.com/larson

The following information is available to reconcile Clark Company's book balance of cash with its bank statement cash balance as of July 31, 2005:

a. After all posting is complete on July 31, the company's Cash account has a $26,193 debit balance, but its July bank statement shows a $28,020 cash balance.

b. Check No. 3031 for $1,380 and Check No. 3040 for $552 were outstanding on the June 30 bank reconciliation. Check No. 3040 is listed with the July canceled checks, but Check No. 3031 is not. Also, Check No. 3065 for $336 and Check No. 3069 for $2,148, both written in July, are not among the canceled checks on the July 31 statement.

c. In comparing the canceled checks on the bank statement with the entries in the accounting records, it is found that Check No. 3056 for July rent was correctly written and drawn for $1,250 but was erroneously entered in the accounting records as $1,230.

d. A credit memorandum enclosed with the July bank statement indicates the bank collected $9,000 cash on a noninterest-bearing note for Clark, deducted a $45 collection fee, and credited the remainder to its account. Clark had not recorded this event before receiving the statement.

e. A debit memorandum for $805 lists a $795 NSF check plus a $10 NSF charge. The check had been received from a customer, Jim Shaw. Clark has not yet recorded this check as NSF.

f. Enclosed with the July statement is a $15 debit memorandum for bank services. It has not yet been recorded because no previous notification had been received.

g. Clark's July 31 daily cash receipts of $10,152 were placed in the bank's night depository on that date, but do not appear on the July 31 bank statement.

Required

1. Prepare the bank reconciliation for this company as of July 31, 2005.

2. Prepare the journal entries necessary to bring the company's book balance of cash into conformity with the reconciled cash balance as of July 31, 2005.

Check (1) Reconciled balance, $34,308; (2) Cr. Note Receivable $9,000

Analysis Component

3. Assume that the July 31, 2005, bank reconciliation for this company is prepared and some items are treated incorrectly. For each of the following errors, explain the effect of the error on (i) the adjusted bank statement cash balance and (ii) the adjusted cash account book balance.

a. The company's unadjusted cash account balance of $26,193 is listed on the reconciliation as $26,139.

b. The bank's collection of the $9,000 note less the $45 collection fee is added to the bank statement cash balance on the reconciliation.

Problem 8-5A
Prepare a bank reconciliation and record adjustments

P3

mhhe.com/larson

Els Company most recently reconciled its bank statement and book balances of cash on August 31 and it reported two checks outstanding, No. 5888 for $1,038.05 and No. 5893 for $484.25. The following information is available for its September 30, 2005, reconciliation:

From the September 30 Bank Statement

Previous Balance	Total Checks and Debits	Total Deposits and Credits	Current Balance
16,800.45	9,620.05	11,182.85	18,363.25

Checks and Debits			Deposits and Credits		Daily Balance	
Date	No.	Amount	Date	Amount	Date	Amount
09/03	5888	1,038.05	09/05	1,103.75	08/31	16,800.45
09/04	5902	731.90	09/12	2,226.90	09/03	15,762.40
09/07	5901	1,824.25	09/21	4,093.00	09/04	15,030.50
09/17		588.25 NSF	09/25	2,351.70	09/05	16,134.25
09/20	5905	937.00	09/30	22.50 IN	09/07	14,310.00
09/22	5903	399.10	09/30	1,385.00 CM	09/12	16,536.90
09/22	5904	2,080.00			09/17	15,948.65
09/28	5907	213.85			09/20	15,011.65
09/29	5909	1,807.65			09/21	19,104.65
					09/22	16,625.55
					09/25	18,977.25
					09/28	18,763.40
					09/29	16,955.75
					09/30	18,363.25

From Els Company's Accounting Records

Cash Receipts Deposited

Date			Cash Debit
Sept.	5		1,103.75
	12		2,226.90
	21		4,093.00
	25		2,351.70
	30		1,582.75
			11,358.10

Cash Disbursements

Check No.		Cash Credit
5901		1,824.25
5902		731.90
5903		399.10
5904		2,050.00
5905		937.00
5906		859.30
5907		213.85
5908		276.00
5909		1,807.65
		9,099.05

Cash — **Acct. No. 101**

Date		Explanation	PR	Debit	Credit	Balance
Aug.	31	Balance				15,278.15
Sept.	30	Total receipts	R12	11,358.10		26,636.25
	30	Total disbursements	D23		9,099.05	17,537.20

Additional Information

Check No. 5904 is correctly drawn for $2,080 to pay for computer equipment; however, the recordkeeper misread the amount and entered it in the accounting records with a debit to Computer Equipment and a credit to Cash of $2,050. The NSF check shown in the statement was originally received from a customer, S. Nilson, in payment of her account. Its return has not yet been recorded by the company. The credit memorandum is from the collection of a $1,400 note for Els Company by the bank. The bank deducted a $15 collection fee. The collection and fee are not yet recorded.

Required

1. Prepare the September 30, 2005, bank reconciliation for this company.
2. Prepare the journal entries to adjust the book balance of cash to the reconciled balance.

Check (1) Reconciled balance, $18,326.45 (2) Cr. Note Receivable $1,400

Analysis Component

3. The bank statement reveals that some of the prenumbered checks in the sequence are missing. Describe three situations that could explain this.

PROBLEM SET B

Problem 8-1B
Analyzing internal control
C1

For each of these five separate cases, identify the principle of internal control that is violated. Recommend what the business should do to ensure adherence to principles of internal control.

1. Latoya Tally is the company's computer specialist and oversees its computerized payroll system. Her boss recently asked her to put password protection on all office computers. Latoya has put a password in place that allows only the boss access to the file where pay rates are changed and personnel are added or deleted from the payroll.
2. Lake Theater has a computerized order-taking system for its tickets. The system is active all week and backed up every Friday night.
3. X2U Company has two employees handling acquisitions of inventory. One employee places purchase orders and pays vendors. The second employee receives the merchandise.
4. The owner of Super-Aid uses a check protector to perforate checks, making it difficult for anyone to alter the amount of the check. The check protector sits on the owner's desk in an office that contains company checks and is often unlocked.
5. LeAnn Company is a small business that has separated the duties of cash receipts and cash disbursements. The employee responsible for cash disbursements reconciles the bank account monthly.

Problem 8-2B
Establishing, reimbursing, and adjusting petty cash
P2

Pepco Co. establishes a petty cash fund for payments of small amounts. The following transactions involving the petty cash fund occurred in January (the last month of the company's fiscal year).

Jan. 3 A company check for $150 is written and made payable to the petty cashier to establish the petty cash fund.

14 A company check is written both to replenish the fund for the following expenditures made since January 3 and to increase the fund to $175.

- *a.* Purchased office supplies for $16.29 that are immediately used up.
- *b.* Paid $17.60 COD shipping charges on merchandise purchased for resale, terms FOB shipping point. Pepco uses the perpetual system to account for inventory.
- *c.* Paid $36.57 to All-Tech for minor repairs to a computer.
- *d.* Paid $14.82 for items classified as miscellaneous expenses.
- *e.* Counted $62.28 remaining in the petty cash box.

31 The petty cashier reports that $17.35 remains in the fund and decides that the February 14 increase in the fund was not large enough. A company check is written both to replenish the fund for the following expenditures made since January 14 and to increase it to $250.

- *f.* Paid $40 to *The Smart Shopper* for an advertisement in January's newsletter.
- *g.* Paid $38.19 for postage expenses.
- *h.* Paid $58 to Take-You-There for delivery of merchandise, terms FOB destination.

Required

Check (1) Total Cr. to Cash: Jan. 14, $112.72; Jan. 31, $232.65

1. Prepare journal entries to establish the fund on January 3, to replenish it on January 14 and January 31, and to reflect any increase or decrease in the fund balance on those dates.

Analysis Component

2. Explain how the company's financial statements are affected if the petty cash fund is not replenished and no entry is made on January 31.

Problem 8-3B
Establish, reimburse, and increase petty cash
P2

RPM Music Center had the following petty cash transactions in March of the current year:

March	5	Wrote a $200 check, cashed it, and gave the proceeds and the petty cashbox to Liz Buck, the petty cashier.
	6	Paid $14.50 COD shipping charges on merchandise purchased for resale, terms FOB shipping point. RPM uses the perpetual system to account for merchandise inventory.
	11	Paid $8.75 delivery charges on merchandise sold to a customer, terms FOB destination.
	12	Purchased file folders for $12.13 that are immediately used.
	14	Reimbursed Will Nelson, the manager, $9.65 for office supplies purchased and used.
	18	Purchased printer paper for $22.54 that is immediately used.
	27	Paid $47.10 COD shipping charges on merchandise purchased for resale, terms FOB shipping point.
	28	Paid postage expenses of $16.
	30	Reimbursed Nelson $58.80 for business car mileage.
	31	Cash of $11.53 remained in the fund. Sorted the petty cash receipts by accounts affected and exchanged them for a check to reimburse the fund for expenditures. The fund amount is also increased to $250.

Required

1. Prepare the journal entry to establish the petty cash fund.

Check (2) Total expenses $189.47

2. Prepare a petty cash payments report for March with these categories: delivery expense, mileage expense, postage expense, merchandise inventory (for transportation-in), and office supplies expense. Sort the payments into the appropriate categories and total the expenses in each category.

(3a & 3b) Cr. Cash $238.47

3. Prepare the journal entries for part 2 to both (*a*) reimburse and (*b*) increase the fund amount.

Problem 8-4B
Prepare a bank reconciliation and record adjustments

P3 

The following information is available to reconcile Style Co.'s book balance of cash with its bank statement cash balance as of December 31, 2005:

a. After posting is complete, the December 31 cash balance according to the accounting records is $31,743.70, and the bank statement cash balance for that date is $45,091.80.

b. Check No. 1273 for $1,084.20 and Check No. 1282 for $390.00, both written and entered in the accounting records in December, are not among the canceled checks. Two checks, No. 1231 for $2,289.00 and No. 1242 for $370.50, were outstanding on the most recent November 30 reconciliation. Check No. 1231 is listed with the December canceled checks, but Check No. 1242 is not.

c. When the December checks are compared with entries in the accounting records, it is found that Check No. 1267 had been correctly drawn for $2,435 to pay for office supplies but was erroneously entered in the accounting records as $2,453.

d. Two debit memoranda are enclosed with the statement and are unrecorded at the time of the reconciliation. One debit memorandum is for $749.50 and dealt with an NSF check for $732 received from a customer, Titus Industries, in payment of its account. The bank assessed a $17.50 fee for processing it. The second debit memorandum is a $79.00 charge for check printing. Style did not record these transactions before receiving the statement.

e. A credit memorandum indicates that the bank collected $20,000 cash on a note receivable for the company, deducted a $20 collection fee, and credited the balance to the company's Cash account. Style did not record this transaction before receiving the statement.

f. Style's December 31 daily cash receipts of $7,666.10 were placed in the bank's night depository on that date, but do not appear on the December 31 bank statement.

Required

1. Prepare the bank reconciliation for this company as of December 31, 2005.

2. Prepare the journal entries necessary to bring the company's book balance of cash into conformity with the reconciled cash balance as of December 31, 2005.

Check (1) Reconciled balance, $50,913.20; (2) Cr. Note Receivable $20,000

Analysis Component

3. Explain the nature of the communications conveyed by a bank when the bank sends the depositor (*a*) a debit memorandum and (*b*) a credit memorandum.

Problem 8-5B
Prepare a bank reconciliation and record adjustments
P3

Safe Systems Co. most recently reconciled its bank balance on April 30 and reported two checks outstanding at that time, No. 1771 for $781.00 and No. 1780 for $1,325.90. The following information is available for its May 31, 2005, reconciliation:

From the May 31 Bank Statement

Previous Balance	Total Checks and Debits	Total Deposits and Credits	Current Balance
18,290.70	12,898.90	16,416.80	21,808.60

Checks and Debits			Deposits and Credits		Daily Balance	
Date	No.	Amount	Date	Amount	Date	Amount
05/01	1771	781.00	05/04	2,438.00	04/30	18,290.70
05/02	1783	195.30	05/14	2,898.00	05/01	17,509.70
05/04	1782	1,285.50	05/22	1,801.80	05/02	17,314.40
05/11	1784	1,449.60	05/25	7,200.00 CM	05/04	18,466.90
05/18		431.80 NSF	05/26	2,079.00	05/11	17,017.30
05/25	1787	8,032.50			05/14	19,915.30
05/26	1785	157.20			05/18	19,483.50
05/29	1788	554.00			05/22	21,285.30
05/31		12.00 SC			05/25	20,452.80
					05/26	22,374.60
					05/29	21,820.60
					05/31	21,808.60

From Safe Systems' Accounting Records

Cash Receipts Deposited			
Date			Cash Debit
May	4		2,438.00
	14		2,898.00
	22		1,801.80
	26		2,079.00
	31		2,526.30
			11,743.10

Cash Disbursements		
Check No.		Cash Credit
1782		1,285.50
1783		195.30
1784		1,449.60
1785		157.20
1786		353.10
1787		8,032.50
1788		544.00
1789		639.50
		12,656.70

Cash					Acct. No. 101	
Date		Explanation	PR	Debit	Credit	Balance
Apr.	30	Balance				16,183.80
May	31	Total receipts	R7	11,743.10		27,926.90
	31	Total disbursements	D8		12,656.70	15,270.20

Additional Information

Check No. 1788 is correctly drawn for $554 to pay for May utilities; however, the recordkeeper misread the amount and entered it in the accounting records with a debit to Utilities Expense and a credit to Cash for $544. The bank paid and deducted the correct amount. The NSF check shown in the statement was originally received from a customer, S. Bax, in payment of her account. The company has not yet recorded its return. The credit memorandum is from a $7,300 note that the bank collected for the company. The bank deducted a $100 collection fee and deposited the remainder in the company's account. The collection and fee have not yet been recorded.

Required

Check (1) Reconciled balance, $22,016.40; (2) Cr. Note Receivable $7,300

1. Prepare the May 31, 2005, bank reconciliation for Safe Systems.
2. Prepare the journal entries to adjust the book balance of cash to the reconciled balance.

Analysis Component

3. The bank statement reveals that some of the prenumbered checks in the sequence are missing. Describe three possible situations to explain this.

PROBLEM SET C

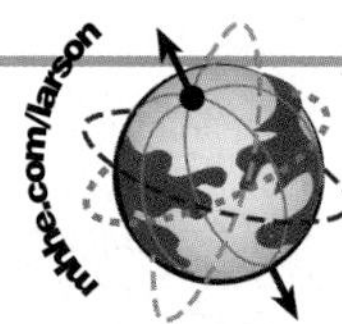

Problem Set C is available at the book's Website to further reinforce and assess your learning.

SERIAL PROBLEM

Success Systems

P3

(This serial problem began in Chapter 1 and continues through most of the book. If previous chapter segments were not completed, the serial problem can begin at this point. It is helpful, but not necessary, that you use the Working Papers that accompany the book.)

Kay Breeze receives the March bank statement for Success Systems on April 11, 2005. The March 31 bank statement shows an ending cash balance of $77,354. A comparison of the bank statement with the general ledger Cash account, No. 101, reveals the following:

a. Breeze notices that the bank erroneously cleared a $500 check against her account that she did not issue. The check documentation included with the bank statement shows that this check was actually issued by a company named Sierra Systems.
b. On March 25, the bank issues a $50 debit memorandum for the safety deposit box that Success Systems agreed to rent from the bank beginning March 25.
c. On March 26, the bank issues a $102 debit memorandum for printed checks that Success Systems ordered from the bank.
d. On March 31, the bank issues a credit memorandum for $33 interest earned on Success Systems' checking account for the month of March.
e. Breeze notices that the check she issued for $128 on March 31, 2005, has not yet cleared the bank.
f. Breeze verifies that all deposits made in March do appear on the March bank statement.
g. The general ledger Cash account, No. 101, shows an ending cash balance per books as $77,845 (prior to any reconciliation).

Required

1. Prepare a bank reconciliation in good form (refer to Exhibit 8.7) for Success Systems for the month ended March 31, 2005.
2. Prepare any necessary adjusting entries. Use Miscellaneous Expenses, No. 677, for any bank charges. Use Interest Revenue, No. 404, for any interest earned on the checking account for the month of March.

BEYOND THE NUMBERS

REPORTING IN ACTION

C2 A1

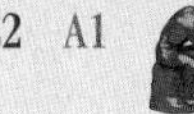

BTN 8-1 Refer to **Krispy Kreme**'s financial statements in Appendix A to answer the following:

1. For both fiscal year-end 2003 and 2002, identify the total amount of cash and cash equivalents. Determine the percent this amount represents of total current assets, total current liabilities, total shareholders' equity, and total assets for both years. Comment on any trends.

2. For both fiscal 2003 and 2002, use the information in the statement of cash flows to determine the percent change between the beginning and ending year amounts of cash and cash equivalents.

3. Compute the days' sales uncollected as of February 2, 2003, and February 3, 2002. Has the collection of receivables improved?

Roll On

4. Access Krispy Kreme's financial statements for fiscal years ending after February 2, 2003, from its Website (**KrispyKreme.com**) or the SEC's EDGAR database (**www.SEC.gov**). Recompute its days' sales uncollected for fiscal years ending after February 2, 2003. Compare this to the days' sales uncollected for 2003 and 2002.

COMPARATIVE ANALYSIS

A1

BTN 8-2 Key comparative figures ($ thousands) for both **Krispy Kreme** and **Tastykake** follow:

	Krispy Kreme		Tastykake	
Key Figures	**Current Year**	**Prior Year**	**Current Year**	**Prior Year**
Accounts receivable	$ 34,373	$ 26,894	$ 20,882	$ 22,233
Net sales	491,549	394,354	162,263	166,244

Required

Compute days' sales uncollected for both companies for each of the two years shown. Comment on any trends for both companies. Which company has the larger percent change in days' sales uncollected?

ETHICS CHALLENGE

C1

BTN 8-3 Carol Benton, Sue Knox, and Marcia Diamond work for a family physician, Dr. Gwen Conrad, who is in private practice. Dr. Conrad is knowledgeable about office management practices and has segregated the cash receipt duties as follows. Benton opens the mail and prepares a triplicate list of money received. She sends one copy of the list to Knox, the cashier, who deposits the receipts daily in the bank. Diamond, the recordkeeper, receives a copy of the list and posts payments to patients' accounts. About once a month the office clerks have an expensive lunch they pay for as follows. First, Knox endorses a patient's check in Dr. Conrad's name and cashes it at the bank. Benton then destroys the remittance advice accompanying the check. Finally, Diamond posts payment to the customer's account as a miscellaneous credit. The three justify their actions by their relatively low pay and knowledge that Dr. Conrad will likely never miss the money.

Required

1. Who is the best person in Dr. Conrad's office to reconcile the bank statement?

2. Would a bank reconciliation uncover this office fraud?

3. What are some ways to detect this type of fraud?

4. Suggest additional internal controls that Dr. Conrad could implement.

COMMUNICATING IN PRACTICE

P5

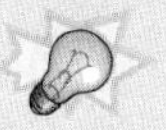

BTN 8-4[B] Assume you are a business consultant. The owner of a company sends you an e-mail expressing concern that the company is not taking advantage of its discounts offered by vendors. The company currently uses the gross method of recording purchases. The owner is considering a review of all invoices and payments from the previous period. Due to the volume of purchases, however, the owner recognizes this is time-consuming and costly. The owner seeks your advice about monitoring purchase discounts in the future. Provide a response in memorandum form.

TAKING IT TO THE NET

C1 P1 

mhhe.com/larson

BTN 8-5 Visit the Association of Certified Fraud Examiners Website at **cfenet.com**. Research the fraud facts (see media center—fraud statistics) presented at this site and fill in the blanks in the following statements.

1. It is estimated that ____% of revenues will be lost in 2002 as a result of occupational fraud and abuse. Applied to the U.S. gross domestic product, this translates to losses of approximately $____ billion, or about $____ per employee.
2. Organizations with fraud hotlines cut their fraud losses by approximately ____% per scheme. Internal audits, external audits, and background checks also significantly reduce fraud losses.
3. Small businesses are the most vulnerable to occupational fraud and abuse. The average scheme in a small business causes $____ in losses. The average scheme in the largest companies costs $____.
4. The most common method for detecting occupational fraud is through tips from ____, customers, vendors, and anonymous sources. The second most common method of discovery is ____.
5. The typical occupational fraud perpetrator is a first-time offender. Only ____% of occupational fraudsters in this study were known to have prior convictions for fraud-related offenses.
6. All occupational frauds fall into one of three categories: ____, corruption, or ____statements.
7. Over ____% of occupational frauds involve asset misappropriations. Cash is the targeted asset ____% of the time.
8. Corruption schemes account for ____% of all occupational frauds, and they cause over $____ in losses, on average.
9. Fraudulent statements are the most costly form of occupational fraud with median losses of $____ million per scheme.
10. Frauds committed by employees cause median losses of $____, while frauds committed by managers and executives cause median losses of $____. When managers and employees conspire in a fraud scheme, the median loss rises to $____.
11. Losses caused by perpetrators older than 60 are ____times higher than losses caused by employees 25 and younger.
12. The average fraud scheme lasted ____ months before it was detected.

TEAMWORK IN ACTION

C1

BTN 8-6 Organize the class into teams. Each team must prepare a list of 10 internal controls a consumer could observe in a typical retail department store. When called upon, the team's spokesperson must be prepared to share controls identified by the team that have not been shared by another team's spokesperson.

BUSINESS WEEK ACTIVITY

C1 P1 

mhhe.com/larson

BTN 8-7 Read the article "To Cure Fraud, Start at the Top" in the October 18, 2002, issue of *Business Week*. (The book's Website provides a free link.)

Required:

1. Which fraud case does Pergola (the interviewee) state was the most significant?
2. What are the character traits of individuals who might be more likely to commit fraud?
3. Which corporate structures make it easier for fraud to thrive?
4. How do corporate recruiters keep potential fraudsters from joining the company?
5. What role can co-workers play in stopping fraud?

ENTREPRENEURIAL DECISION

C1 P1  

BTN 8-8 Refer to the chapter's opening feature, "Sweet Success," describing the entrepreneurial efforts of Dylan Lauren and Jeff Rubin with **Dylan's Candy Bar**.

Required

List the seven principles of internal control. For each principle, identify how Lauren and Rubin could implement it in their candy store.

BTN 8-9 Visit a part of your college that serves the student community with either products or services. Some examples are food services, libraries, and book stores. Identify and describe between four and eight internal controls being implemented.

HITTING THE ROAD

C1

BTN 8-10 Review the consolidated statement of changes in financial position for **Grupo Bimbo** for the year ended December 31, 2002, at GrupoBimbo.com.

GLOBAL DECISION

C2 

Required

1. What item caused the largest change (excluding net income) in the Operations section of the statement?
2. What item caused the largest change in the Financing section of the statement?
3. What item caused the largest change in the Investing section of the statement?
4. Did the cash and marketable securities as of December 31, 2002, increase or decrease relative to December 31, 2001?
5. Calculate the percentage change in both the cash and the marketable securities balances between December 31, 2001 and December 31, 2002.
6. At December 31, 2002, what percentage of current assets is comprised of cash and marketable securities?

"My goal is to become the Oprah of raw materials"—Barbara Manzi

Accounting for Receivables

A Look Back

Chapter 8 focused on internal control and reporting for cash. We described procedures that are good for internal control, and we explained the accounting for and management of cash.

A Look at This Chapter

This chapter emphasizes receivables. We explain that they are liquid assets and describe how companies account for and report them. We also discuss the importance of estimating uncollectibles.

A Look Ahead

Chapter 10 focuses on plant assets, natural resources, and intangible assets. We explain how to account for, report, and analyze these long-term assets.

Learning Objectives

CAP

Conceptual

C1 Describe accounts receivable and how they occur and are recorded. *(p. 350)*

C2 Describe a note receivable and the computation of its maturity date and interest. *(p. 359)*

C3 Explain how receivables can be converted to cash before maturity. *(p. 363)*

Analytical

A1 Compute accounts receivable turnover and use it to help assess financial condition. *(p. 364)*

Procedural

P1 Apply the direct write-off and allowance methods to account for accounts receivable. *(p. 354)*

P2 Estimate uncollectibles using methods based on sales and accounts receivable. *(p. 356)*

P3 Record the receipt of a note receivable. *(p. 361)*

P4 Record the honoring and dishonoring of a note and adjustments for interest. *(p. 361)*

Decision Feature

Heavy into Metals

BROOKSVILLE, FL—"When you're an African-American entrepreneur, and a woman in a male-dominated industry, you learn some lessons very quickly, " says Barbara Manzi. Manzi launched **Manzi Metals** (**ManziMetals.com**) from her home eight years ago. Her lessons learned have translated into an annual $3 million in revenues as a distributor of aluminum, steel, titanium, brass, and other alloys.

Manzi, who runs Manzi Metals along with her son Louis, had to overcome long odds in achieving success. "There were 12 children in our family," she says. "But if I had listened to [those]... who told me I'd never do anything except get married, I would have gone astray." Instead, Manzi pursued her dreams.

Today, Manzi Metals is a major distributor of all types of metals in any shapes or sizes. Manzi strives for the highest quality service but maintains competitive prices. This includes special attention to customers and keeping control over receivables. Decisions such as selling on credit or not, and setting policies and criteria for extending credit, can make or break a startup.

Manzi, who has "a passion for people," never loses sight of the personal touch when making these business decisions. Recognizing economic downturns and adjusting past due accounts when appropriate are as much people decisions as accounting applications. Still, keeping an eye on accounts receivable turnover and uncollectible accounts is part of good business operations. This chapter focuses on these and related issues. Such factors, says Manzi, must be studied and carefully interpreted. "You have to get it right the first time," she says. "There's no room for mistakes!"

[Sources: *Manzi Metals Website,* January 2004; *Business Week,* January 2003; *Entre World,* February 2003.]

This chapter focuses on accounts receivable and short-term notes receivable. We describe each of these assets, their uses, and how they are accounted for and reported in financial statements. This knowledge helps us use accounting information to make better business decisions. It can also help in predicting future company performance and financial condition as well as in managing one's own business.

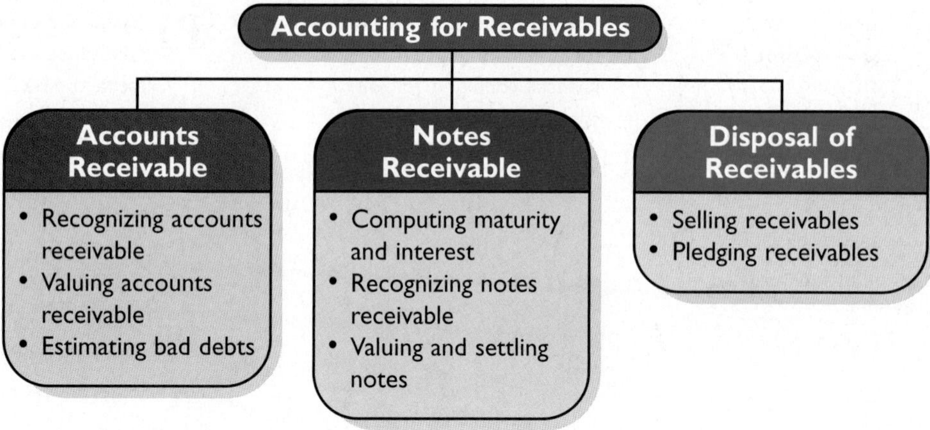

Accounts Receivable

A *receivable* is an amount due from another party. The two most common receivables are accounts receivable and notes receivable. Other receivables include interest receivable, rent receivable, tax refund receivable, and receivables from employees. **Accounts receivable** are amounts due from customers for credit sales. This section begins by describing how accounts receivable occur. It includes receivables that occur when customers use credit cards issued by third parties and when a company gives credit directly to customers. When a company does extend credit directly to customers, it must (1) maintain a separate account receivable for each customer and (2) account for bad debts from credit sales.

Recognizing Accounts Receivable

C1 Describe accounts receivable and how they occur and are recorded.

Accounts receivable occur from credit sales to customers. The amount of credit sales has increased in recent years, reflecting several factors including an efficient financial system. Retailers such as **Limited Brands** and **Best Buy** hold millions of dollars in accounts receivable. Similar amounts are held by wholesalers such as **SUPERVALU** and **SYSCO**. Exhibit 9.1 shows recent dollar amounts of accounts receivable and their percent of total assets for four well-known companies.

Sales on Credit Credit sales are recorded by increasing (debiting) Accounts Receivable. A company must also maintain a separate account for each customer that tracks how much that customer purchases, has already paid, and still owes. This information provides the basis for sending bills to customers and for other business analyses. To maintain this information, companies that extend credit directly to their customers keep a separate account receivable for each one of them. The general ledger continues to have a single Accounts Receivable account along with the other financial

Exhibit 9.1

Accounts Receivable for Selected Companies

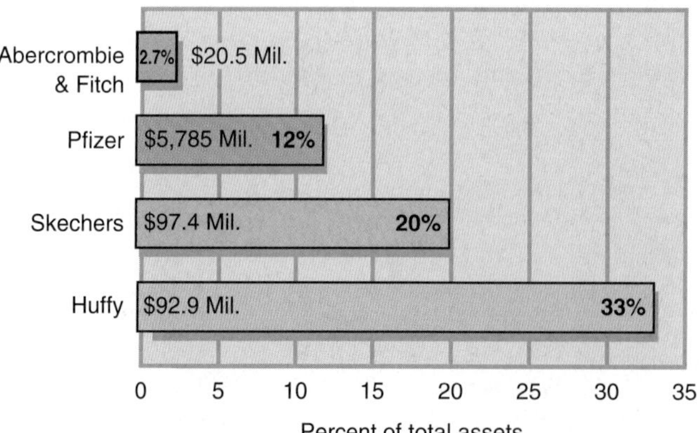

statement accounts, but a supplementary record is created to maintain a separate account for each customer. This supplementary record is called the *accounts receivable ledger.*

Point: Receivables, cash, cash equivalents, and short-term investments make up the most liquid assets of a company.

Exhibit 9.2 shows the relation between the Accounts Receivable account in the general ledger and its individual customer accounts in the accounts receivable ledger for TechCom, a small electronics wholesaler. This exhibit reports a $3,000 ending balance of TechCom's accounts receivable for June 30. TechCom's transactions are mainly in cash, but it has two major credit customers: CompStore and RDA Electronics. Its *schedule of accounts receivable* shows that the $3,000 balance of the Accounts Receivable account in the general ledger equals the total of its two customers' balances in the accounts receivable ledger.

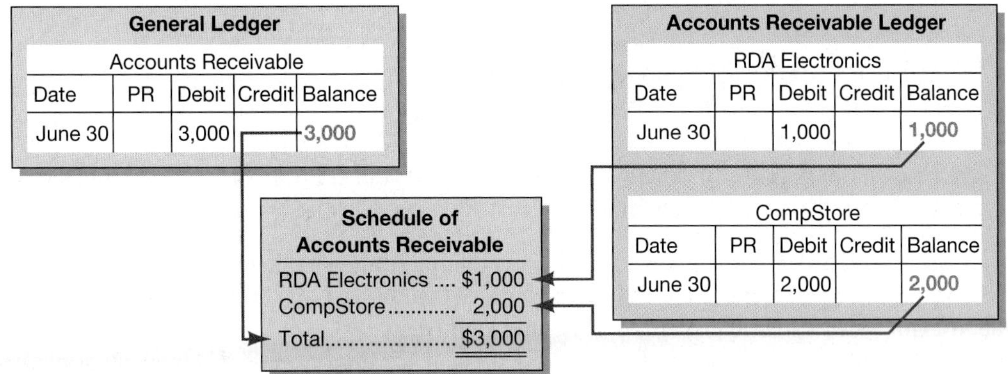

Exhibit 9.2

General Ledger and the Accounts Receivable Ledger (before July 1 transactions)

To see how accounts receivable from credit sales are recognized in the accounting records, we look at two transactions on July 1 between TechCom and its credit customers—see Exhibit 9.3. The first is a credit sale of $950 to CompStore. A credit sale is posted with both a debit to the Accounts Receivable account in the general ledger and a debit to the customer account in the accounts receivable ledger. The second transaction is a collection of $720 from RDA Electronics from a prior credit sale. Cash receipts from a credit customer are posted with a credit to both the Accounts Receivable account in the general ledger and to the customer account in the accounts receivable ledger. (Posting debits or credits to Accounts Receivable in two separate ledgers does not violate the requirement that debits equal credits. The equality of debits and credits is maintained in the general ledger. The accounts receivable ledger is a supplementary record providing information on each customer.)

July 1	Accounts Receivable—CompStore	950	
	Sales		950
	*To record credit sales**		
July 1	Cash	720	
	Accounts Receivable—RDA Electronics		720
	To record collection of credit sales.		

* We omit the entry to Dr. Cost of Sales and Cr. Merchandise Inventory to focus on sales and receivables.

Exhibit 9.3

Accounts Receivable Transactions

Assets = Liabilities + Equity
+950 +950
Assets = Liabilities + Equity
+720
−720

Exhibit 9.4 shows the general ledger and the accounts receivable ledger after recording the two July 1 transactions. The general ledger shows the effects of the sale, the collection, and the resulting balance of $3,230. These events are also reflected in the individual customer accounts: RDA Electronics has an ending balance of $280, and CompStore's ending balance is $2,950. The $3,230 sum of the individual accounts equals the debit balance of the Accounts Receivable account in the general ledger.

Point: Software helps merchants build Web storefronts quickly and easily. Merchants simply enter product details such as names and prices, and out comes a respectable-looking Website complete with order forms. They also offer security with credit card orders and can track sales and site visits.

Like TechCom, many large retailers such as **Sears** and **JCPenney** sell on credit. Many also maintain their own credit cards to grant credit to approved customers and to earn interest on any balance not paid within a specified period of time. This allows them to avoid the fee charged by credit card companies. The entries in this case are the same as those for TechCom

Exhibit 9.4

General Ledger and the Accounts Receivable Ledger (after July 1 transactions)

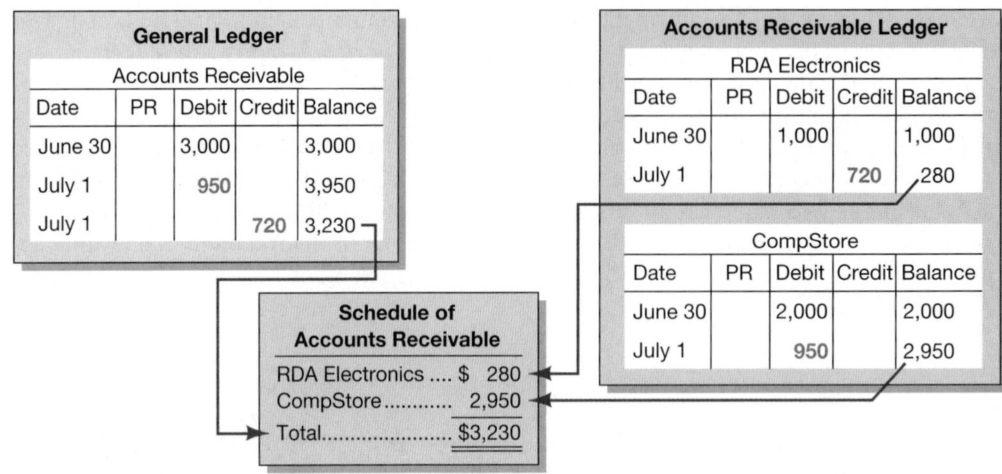

General Ledger

Accounts Receivable

Date	PR	Debit	Credit	Balance
June 30		3,000		3,000
July 1		950		3,950
July 1			720	3,230

Accounts Receivable Ledger

RDA Electronics

Date	PR	Debit	Credit	Balance
June 30		1,000		1,000
July 1			720	280

CompStore

Date	PR	Debit	Credit	Balance
June 30		2,000		2,000
July 1		950		2,950

Schedule of Accounts Receivable

RDA Electronics	$ 280
CompStore	2,950
Total.......................	$3,230

except for the possibility of added interest revenue. If a customer owes interest on a bill, we debit Interest Receivable and credit Interest Revenue for that amount.

Credit Card Sales Many companies allow their customers to pay for products and services using third-party credit cards such as **Visa**, **MasterCard**, or **American Express**, and debit cards (also called bankcards). This practice gives customers the ability to make purchases without cash or checks. Once credit is established with a credit card company or bank, the customer does not have to open an account with each store. Customers using these cards can make single monthly payments instead of several payments to different creditors and can defer their payments.

Sellers allow customers to use third-party credit cards and debit cards instead of granting credit directly for several reasons. First, the seller does not have to evaluate each customer's credit standing or make decisions about who gets credit and how much. Second, the seller avoids the risk of extending credit to customers who cannot or do not pay. This risk is transferred to the card company. Third, the seller typically receives cash from the card company sooner than had it granted credit directly to customers. Fourth, a variety of credit options for customers offers a potential increase in sales volume. **Sears** historically offered credit only to customers using a Sears card but later changed its policy to permit customers to charge purchases to third-party credit card companies in a desire to increase sales. It reported: "SearsCharge increased its share of Sears retail sales even as the company expanded the payment options available to its customers with the acceptance . . . of [Visa,] MasterCard, and American Express in addition to the Discover Card."

Decision Insight

Debit Card vs. Credit Card A buyer's debit card purchase reduces the buyer's cash account balance at the card company, which is often a bank. Since the buyer's cash account balance is a liability (with a credit balance) for the card company to the buyer, the card company would debit that account for a buyer's purchase—hence, the term *debit card.* A credit card reflects authorization by the card company of a line of credit for the buyer with predetermined interest rates and payment terms—hence, the term *credit card.* Most credit card companies waive interest charges on the line of credit if the buyer pays its balance in full each month.

There are guidelines in how companies account for credit card and debit card sales. Some credit cards, but mostly debit cards, credit a seller's Cash account immediately upon deposit. In this case the seller deposits a copy of each card sales receipt in its bank account just as it deposits a customer's check. Some other cards require the seller to remit a copy (often electronically) of each receipt to the card company. Until payment is received, the seller has an account receivable from the card company. In both cases, the seller pays a fee for services provided by the card company, often ranging

Decision Maker

Entrepreneur As a small retailer, you are considering allowing customers to purchase merchandise using credit cards. Until now, your store accepted only cash and checks. What form of analysis do you use to make this decision?

Answer—p. 367

from 1% to 5% of card sales. This charge is deducted from the credit to the seller's account or the cash payment to the seller.

The procedures used in accounting for credit card sales depend on whether cash is received immediately on deposit or cash receipt is delayed until the credit card company makes the payment. To illustrate, if TechCom has $100 of credit card sales with a 4% fee, and its $96 cash is received immediately on deposit, the entry is

Point: Web merchants pay twice as much in credit card association fees as other retailers because they suffer 10 times as much fraud.

July 15	Cash	96	
	Credit Card Expense	4	
	Sales		100
	*To record credit card sales less a 4% credit card expense.**		

Assets = Liabilities + Equity
+96 +100
−4

* We omit the entry to Dr. Cost of Sales and Cr. Merchandise Inventory to focus on credit card expense.

However, if instead TechCom must remit the credit card sales receipts to the credit card company and wait for the $96 cash payment, the entry on the date of sale is

July 15	**Accounts Receivable—Credit Card Co.**	96	
	Credit Card Expense	4	
	Sales		100
	*To record credit card sales less 4% credit card expense.**		

Assets = Liabilities + Equity
+96 +100
−4

* We omit the entry to Dr. Cost of Sales and Cr. Merchandise Inventory to focus on credit card expense.

When cash is later received from the credit card company, the entry is

July 25	Cash	96	
	Accounts Receivable—Credit Card Co.		96
	To record cash receipt.		

Assets = Liabilities + Equity
+96
−96

Point: Third-party credit card costs can be large. JCPenney recently reported sales exceeding $30,000 million along with third-party credit card costs of nearly $100 million.

Some firms report credit card expense in the income statement as a type of discount deducted from sales to get net sales. Other companies classify it as a selling expense or even as an administrative expense. Arguments can be made for each alternative.

Installment Sales and Receivables Many companies allow their credit customers to make periodic payments over several months. For example, **Harley-Davidson** holds more than $400 million in installment receivables. The seller refers to such assets as *installment accounts receivable,* which are amounts owed by customers from credit sales for which payment is required in periodic amounts over an extended time period. Source documents for installment accounts receivable include sales slips or invoices describing the sales transactions. The customer is usually charged interest. Although installment accounts receivable may have credit periods of more than one year, they are classified as current assets if the seller regularly offers customers such terms.

Quick Check

1. In recording credit card sales, when do you debit Accounts Receivable and when do you debit Cash?
2. A company accumulates sales receipts and remits them to the credit card company for payment. When are the credit card expenses recorded? When are these expenses incurred?

Answers—p. 368

Valuing Accounts Receivable

When a company directly grants credit to its customers, it expects that some customers will not pay what they promised. The accounts of these customers are *uncollectible accounts,* commonly called **bad debts.** The total amount of uncollectible accounts is an expense of selling on credit. Why do companies sell on credit if they expect some accounts

Decision Insight

Bad Debts Costs are rising for credit card issuers owing to default rates. Much of this is the fault of issuers who offer credit cards with low "teaser" rates. In response, credit card users have increased their debts, and many are unable to pay them.

Credit Card Default Rates	
Banc One	6.8%
First Chicago	6.7
Discover	6.1
Citicorp	5.5
Chase	5.1
Capital One	5.1
Advanta	5.1

to be uncollectible? The answer is that companies believe that granting credit will increase total sales and net income enough to offset bad debts. Companies use two methods to account for uncollectible accounts: (1) direct write-off method and (2) allowance method. We describe both.

P1 Apply the direct write-off and allowance methods to account for accounts receivable.

Direct Write-Off Method The **direct write-off method** of accounting for bad debts records the loss from an uncollectible account receivable when it is determined to be uncollectible. No attempt is made to predict bad debts expense. To illustrate, if TechCom determines on January 23 that it cannot collect $520 owed to it by its customer J. Kent, it recognizes the loss using the direct write-off method as follows:

Assets = Liabilities + Equity
−520 −520

Jan. 23	Bad Debts Expense	520	
	Accounts Receivable—J. Kent		520
	To write off an uncollectible account.		

The debit in this entry charges the uncollectible amount directly to the current period's Bad Debts Expense account. The credit removes its balance from the Accounts Receivable account in the general ledger (and its subsidiary ledger).

Point: Managers realize that some portion of credit sales will be uncollectible, but which credit sales are uncollectible is unknown.

Sometimes an account written off is later collected. This can be due to factors such as continual collection efforts or a customer's good fortune. If the account of J. Kent that was written off directly to Bad Debts Expense is later collected in full, the following two entries record this recovery:

Assets = Liabilities + Equity
+520 +520

Assets = Liabilities + Equity
+520
−520

Mar. 11	Accounts Receivable—J. Kent	520	
	Bad Debts Expense		520
	To reinstate account previously written off.		
Mar. 11	Cash	520	
	Accounts Receivable—J. Kent		520
	To record full payment of account.		

Point: If a customer fails to pay within the credit period, most companies send out repeated billings and make other efforts to collect.

Companies must weigh at least two accounting principles when considering the use of the direct write-off method: the (1) matching principle and (2) materiality principle.

Matching principle applied to bad debts. The **matching principle** requires expenses to be reported in the same accounting period as the sales they helped produce. This means that if extending credit to customers helped produce sales, the bad debts expense linked to those sales is matched and reported in the same period. The direct write-off method usually does not best match sales and expenses because bad debts expense is not recorded until an account becomes uncollectible, which often occurs in a period after that of the credit sale. To match bad debts expense with the sales it produces therefore requires a company to estimate future uncollectibles.

Point: Pier 1 Imports reports $7 million of bad debts expense matched against $413 million of credit sales in a recent fiscal year.

Materiality principle applied to bad debts. The **materiality principle** states that an amount can be ignored if its effect on the financial statements is unimportant to users' business decisions. The materiality principle permits the use of the direct write-off method when bad debts expenses are very small in relation to a company's other financial statement items such as sales and net income.

Point: Under the direct write-off method, expense is recorded each time an account is written off. Under the allowance method, expense is recorded with an adjusting entry equal to the total estimated uncollectibles for that period's sales.

Allowance Method The **allowance method** of accounting for bad debts matches the *estimated* loss from uncollectible accounts receivable against the sales they helped produce. We must use estimated losses because when sales occur, management does not know which customers will not pay their bills. This means that at the end of each period, the allowance method requires an estimate of the total bad debts expected to result from that period's sales. This method has two advantages over the direct write-off method: (1) it records estimated bad debts expense in the period when the related sales are recorded and (2) it reports accounts receivable on the balance sheet at the estimated amount of cash to be collected.

Topic Tackler 9-1

Recording bad debts expense. The allowance method estimates bad debts expense at the end of each accounting period and records it with an adjusting entry. TechCom, for instance, had credit sales of $300,000 during its first year of operations. At the end of the first year, $20,000 of credit sales remained uncollected. Based on the experience of similar businesses, TechCom estimated that $1,500 of its accounts receivable would be uncollectible. This estimated expense is recorded with the following adjusting entry:

Point: The Office of the Comptroller of the Currency reported that losses from bad debts are a major factor when banks fail.

Dec. 31	Bad Debts Expense	1,500	
	Allowance for Doubtful Accounts		1,500
	To record estimated bad debts.		

Assets	= Liabilities	+ Equity
−1,500		−1,500

The estimated Bad Debts Expense of $1,500 is reported on the income statement (as either a selling expense or an administrative expense) and offsets the $300,000 credit sales it helped produce. The **Allowance for Doubtful Accounts** is a contra asset account. A contra account is used instead of reducing accounts receivable directly because at the time of the adjusting entry, the company does not know which customers will not pay. After the bad debts adjusting entry is posted, TechCom's account balances for Accounts Receivable and its Allowance for Doubtful Accounts are as shown in Exhibit 9.5.

Point: Credit approval is usually not assigned to the selling department because its main goal is to increase sales, and it may approve customers at the expense of increased bad debts. Instead, approval is assigned to a separate credit-granting or administrative department.

Exhibit 9.5

General Ledger Balances after Bad Debts Adjusting Entry

Accounts Receivable			
Dec. 31	20,000		

Allowance for Doubtful Accounts			
		Dec. 31	1,500

The Allowance for Doubtful Accounts credit balance of $1,500 has the effect of reducing accounts receivable to its estimated realizable value. **Realizable value** refers to the expected proceeds from converting an asset into cash. Although credit customers owe $20,000 to TechCom, only $18,500 is expected to be realized in cash collections from these customers. In the balance sheet, the Allowance for Doubtful Accounts is subtracted from Accounts Receivable and is often reported as shown in Exhibit 9.6.

Point: Bad Debts Expense is also called *Uncollectible Accounts Expense*. The Allowance for Doubtful Accounts is also called *Allowance for Uncollectible Accounts*.

Exhibit 9.6

Balance Sheet Presentation of the Allowance for Doubtful Accounts

Current assets		
Accounts receivable	**$20,000**	
Less allowance for doubtful accounts	**1,500**	**$18,500**

Sometimes the Allowance for Doubtful Accounts is not reported separately. This alternative presentation is shown in Exhibit 9.7 (also see Appendix A).

Exhibit 9.7

Alternative Presentation of the Allowance for Doubtful Accounts

Current assets	
Accounts receivable (net of $1,500 doubtful accounts)	**$18,500**

Writing off a bad debt. When specific accounts are identified as uncollectible, they are written off against the Allowance for Doubtful Accounts. To illustrate, TechCom decides that J. Kent's $520 account is uncollectible and makes the following entry to write it off:

Jan. 23	Allowance for Doubtful Accounts	520	
	Accounts Receivable—J. Kent.		520
	To write off an uncollectible account.		

Assets	= Liabilities	+ Equity
+520		
−520		

Point: The Bad Debts Expense account is not debited in the write-off entry because it was recorded in the period when sales occurred.

Posting this write-off entry to the Accounts Receivable account removes the amount of the bad debt from the general ledger (it is also posted to the accounts receivable subsidiary ledger). The general ledger accounts now appear as in Exhibit 9.8 (assuming no other transactions affecting these accounts).

Exhibit 9.8

General Ledger Balances after Write-Off

Accounts Receivable			
Dec. 31	20,000		
		Jan. 23	520

Allowance for Doubtful Accounts			
		Dec. 31	1,500
Jan. 23	520		

Point: In posting a write-off, the ledger's Explanation column indicates the reason for this credit so it is not misinterpreted as payment in full.

The write-off does not affect the realizable value of accounts receivable as shown in Exhibit 9.9. Neither total assets nor net income is affected by the write-off of a specific account. Instead, both assets and net income are affected in the period when bad debts expense is predicted and then recorded with an adjusting entry.

Exhibit 9.9

Realizable Value before and after Write-Off of a Bad Debt

	Before Write-Off	After Write-Off
Accounts receivable	$ 20,000	$ 19,480
Less allowance for doubtful accounts	1,500	980
Estimated realizable accounts receivable	**$18,500**	**$18,500**

Recovering a bad debt. When a customer fails to pay and the account is written off as uncollectible, his or her credit standing is jeopardized. To help restore credit standing, a customer sometimes volunteers to pay all or part of the amount owed. A company makes two entries when collecting an account previously written off by the allowance method. The first is to reverse the write-off and reinstate the customer's account. The second entry records the collection of the reinstated account. To illustrate, if on March 11 Kent pays in full his account previously written off, the entries are

Assets = Liabilities + Equity
+520
−520

Assets = Liabilities + Equity
+520
−520

Date	Account	Debit	Credit
Mar. 11	Accounts Receivable—J. Kent	520	
	Allowance for Doubtful Accounts		520
	To reinstate account previously written off.		
Mar. 11	Cash	520	
	Accounts Receivable—J. Kent		520
	To record full payment of account.		

Example: If TechCom used a collection agency and paid a 35% commission on $520 collected from Kent, how is this recorded? *Answer:*
Cash 338
Collection Expense 182
Accts. Recble.—J. Kent 520

In this illustration, Kent paid the entire amount previously written off, but sometimes a customer pays only a portion of the amount owed. A question then arises as to whether the entire balance of the account or just the amount paid is returned to accounts receivable. This is a matter of judgment. If we believe this customer will later pay in full, we return the entire amount owed to accounts receivable, but if we expect no further collection, we return only the amount paid.

Estimating Bad Debts Expense

P2 Estimate uncollectibles using methods based on sales and accounts receivable.

Companies with direct credit sales must attempt to estimate bad debts expense to both manage their receivables and set credit policies. The allowance method also requires an estimate of bad debts expense to prepare an adjusting entry at the end of each accounting period. There are two common methods. One is based on the income statement relation between bad debts expense and sales. The second is based on the balance sheet relation between accounts receivable and the allowance for doubtful accounts.

Point: The focus is on *credit* sales because cash sales do not produce bad debts. If cash sales are a small or stable percent of credit sales, total sales can be used.

Percent of Sales Method The *percent of sales method* uses income statement relations to estimate bad debts. It is based on the idea that a given percent of a company's credit sales for the period are uncollectible. To illustrate, assume that Musicland has credit sales of $400,000 in year 2005. Based on past experience, Musicland estimates 0.6% of credit sales to be uncollectible. This implies that Musicland expects $2,400 of bad debts expense from its sales (computed as $400,000 \times 0.006 = \$2,400$). The adjusting entry to record this estimated expense is

Dec. 31	Bad Debts Expense	2,400	
	Allowance for Doubtful Accounts		2,400
	To record estimated bad debts.		

Assets = Liabilities + Equity
−2,400 −2,400

The allowance account ending balance on the balance sheet for this method would rarely equal the bad debts expense on the income statement. This is so because unless a company is in its first period of operations, its allowance account has a zero balance only if the prior amounts written off as uncollectible *exactly* equal the prior estimated bad debts expenses. (When computing bad debts expense as a percent of sales, managers monitor and adjust the percent so it is not too high or too low.)

Point: When using the *percent of sales method* for estimating uncollectibles, the estimate of bad debts is the number used in the adjusting entry.

Accounts Receivable Methods The *accounts receivable methods* use balance sheet relations to estimate bad debts—mainly the relation between accounts receivable and the allowance amount. The goal of the bad debts adjusting entry for these methods is to make the Allowance for Doubtful Accounts balance equal to the portion of accounts receivable that is estimated to be uncollectible. The estimated balance for the allowance account is obtained in one of two ways: (1) computing the percent uncollectible from the total accounts receivable or (2) aging accounts receivable.

Decision Insight

Bum Loans Want to pick up some cheap debt? **Sprint** recently put $145 million of its unpaid telephone bills up for sale on the Net, and **Bank One** listed $211 million of unpaid credit card receivables on **E-Debt.com.** Insiders say Sprint's $145 million portfolio fetched $2 million—better low margins than none.

Bum Loan Sources
E-Debt.com
DebtMarketplace.com
AssetExchange.com

Point: When using an accounts receivable method for estimating uncollectibles, the allowance account balance is adjusted to equal the estimate of uncollectibles.

Percent of accounts receivable method. The *percent of accounts receivable method* assumes that a given percent of a company's receivables is uncollectible. This percent is based on past experience and is impacted by current conditions such as economic trends and customer difficulties. The total dollar amount of all receivables is multiplied by this percent to get the estimated dollar amount of uncollectible accounts—reported in the balance sheet as the Allowance for Doubtful Accounts.

To illustrate, assume that Musicland has $50,000 of accounts receivable on December 31, 2005. Experience suggests 5% of its receivables are uncollectible. This means that after the adjusting entry is posted, we want the Allowance for Doubtful Accounts to show a $2,500 credit balance (5% of $50,000). (*Note:* Its beginning balance is $2,200, which is 5% of the $44,000 accounts receivable on December 31, 2004—see Exhibit 9.10.) Also, during 2005, accounts of customers are written off on February 6, July 10, and November 20. Thus, the account has a $200 credit balance prior to the December 31, 2005, adjustment. The adjusting entry to give the allowance account the estimated $2,500 balance is

Global: In China, government regulation constrains the *percents* used to estimate bad debts.

Dec. 31	Bad Debts Expense	2,300	
	Allowance for Doubtful Accounts		2,300
	To record estimated bad debts.		

Assets = Liabilities + Equity
−2,300 −2,300

Exhibit 9.10 shows the effects of these transactions and adjustments on the allowance account.

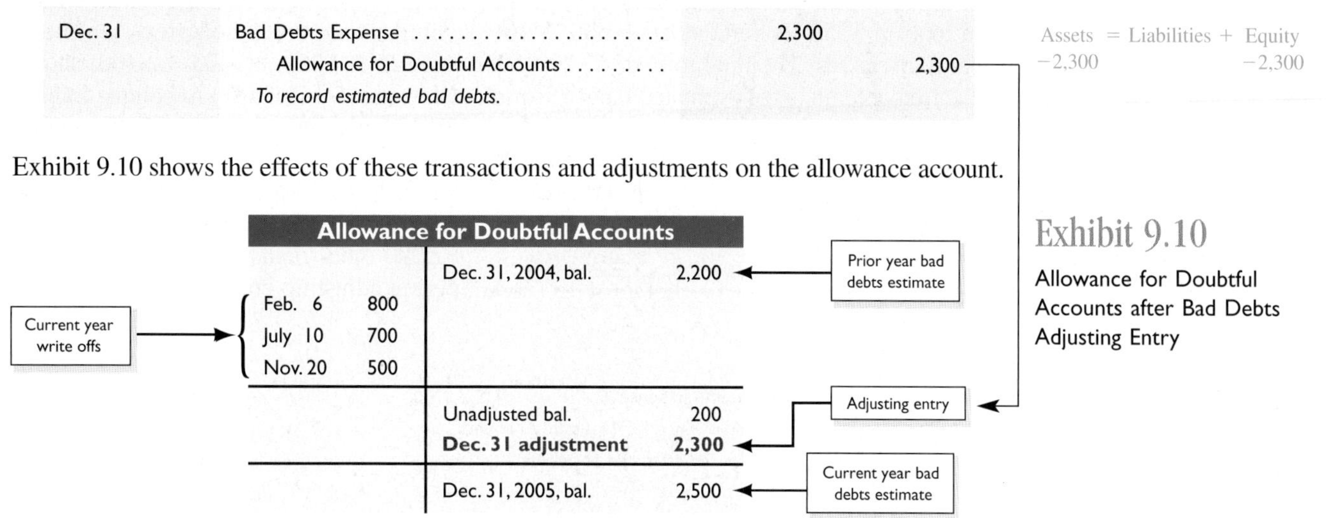

Exhibit 9.10

Allowance for Doubtful Accounts after Bad Debts Adjusting Entry

Aging of accounts receivable method. The **aging of accounts receivable** method uses both past and current receivables information to estimate the allowance amount. Specifically, each receivable is classified by how long it is past its due date. Then estimates of uncollectible amounts are made assuming that the longer an amount is past due, the more likely it is to be uncollectible. Classifications are often based on 30-day periods. After the amounts are classified (or aged), experience is used to estimate the percent of each uncollectible class. These percents are applied to the amounts in each class and then totaled to get the estimated balance of the Allowance for Doubtful Accounts. This computation is performed by setting up a schedule such as Exhibit 9.11.

Decision Insight

When you buy online with a credit card, you put your account number at risk. If, however, you slide a smart card into a reader on your PC and enter your password, the merchant never gets your account number but only a code authorizing the sale.

Exhibit 9.11

Aging of Accounts Receivable

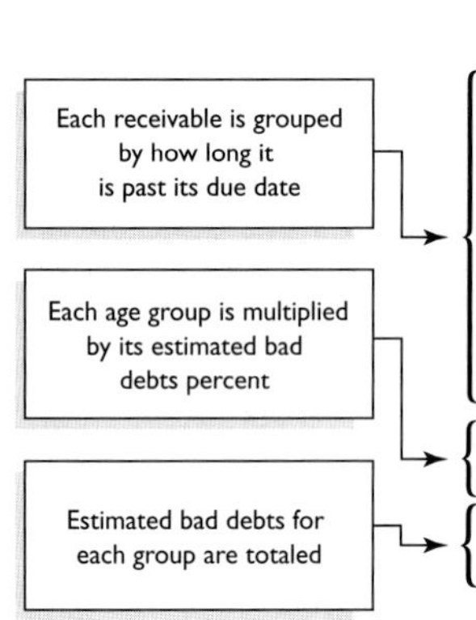

MUSICLAND
Schedule of Accounts Receivable by Age

Customer	Totals	Not Yet Due	1 to 30 Days Past Due	31 to 60 Days Past Due	61 to 90 Days Past Due	Over 90 Days Past Due
Carlos Abbot	$ 450	$ 450				
Jaime Allen	710			$ 710		
Chavez Andres	500	300	$ 200			
Belicia Co.	740				$ 100	$ 640
...						
Zamora Services	1,000	810	190			
Totals	$ 49,900	$ 37,000	$ 6,500	$ 3,500	$ 1,900	$ 1,000
Percent uncollectible		x 2%	x 5%	x 10%	x 25%	x 40%
Estimated uncollectible	$ 2,290	$ 740	$ 325	$ 350	$ 475	$ 400

Point: Experience shows the longer a receivable is past due, the lower is the likelihood of collection. An aging schedule exploits this relation.

Point: Spreadsheet software is especially useful for estimating bad debts. Using both current and past data, estimates of bad debts are obtained under different assumptions.

Exhibit 9.11 lists each customer's individual balances assigned to one of five classes based on its days past due. The amounts in each class are totaled and multiplied by the estimated percent of uncollectible accounts for each class. The percents used are regularly reviewed to reflect changes in the company and economy.

To explain, notice that Musicland has $3,500 in accounts receivable that are 31 to 60 days past due. Its management estimates 10% of the amounts in this age class are uncollectible, or a total of $350 (computed as $3,500 × 10%). Similar analysis is done for each of the other four classes. The final total of $2,290($740 + $325 + $350 + $475 + $400) shown in the first column is the estimated balance for the Allowance for Doubtful Accounts. Exhibit 9.12 shows that since the allowance account has an unadjusted credit balance of $200, the required adjustment to the Allowance for Doubtful Accounts is $2,090. This yields the following end-of-period adjusting entry:

Exhibit 9.12

Computation of the Required Adjustment for an Accounts Receivable Method

Unadjusted balance	$ 200 credit
Estimated balance	2,290 credit
Required adjustment	**$2,090 credit**

Assets = Liabilities + Equity
−2,090 −2,090

Dec. 31	Bad Debts Expense	2,090	
	Allowance for Doubtful Accounts		2,090
	To record estimated bad debts.		

Alternatively, if the allowance account had an unadjusted *debit* balance of $500 (instead of the $200 credit balance), its required adjustment would be computed as follows:

Global: International practices vary as to when receivables are written off. Some do not write off an account until it is 1 to 2 years past due.

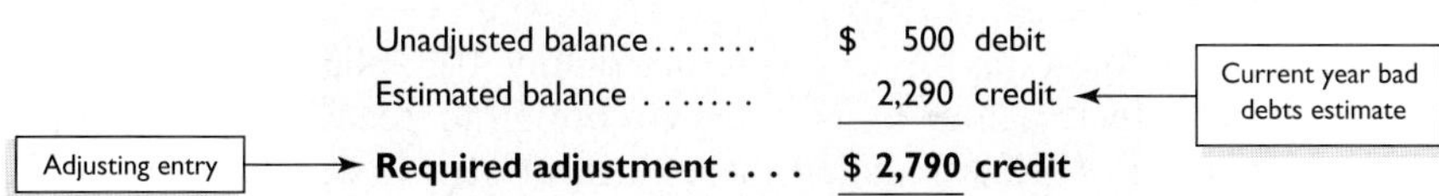

Unadjusted balance .... $ 500 debit
Estimated balance .... 2,290 credit
Current year bad debts estimate
Adjusting entry
Required adjustment .... $ 2,790 credit

The entry to record the end-of-period adjustment for this alternative case is

Dec. 31	Bad Debts Expense	2,790	
	Allowance for Doubtful Accounts		2,790
	To record estimated bad debts.		

Assets = Liabilities + Equity
−2,790 −2,790

The aging of accounts receivable method is a more detailed examination of specific accounts and is usually the most reliable of the estimation methods.

Exhibit 9.13 summarizes the principles guiding all three estimation methods and their focus of analysis.

Decision Maker

Labor Union Chief One week prior to labor contract negotiations, financial statements are released showing no income growth. A 10% growth was predicted. Your analysis finds that the company increased its allowance for uncollectibles from 1.5% to 4.5% of receivables. Without this change, income would show a 9% growth. Does this analysis impact negotiations?

Answer—p. 368

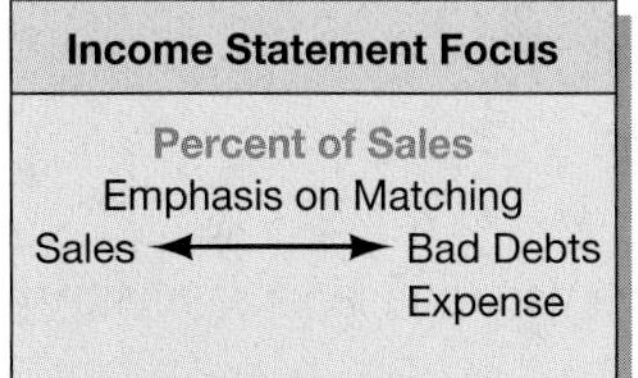

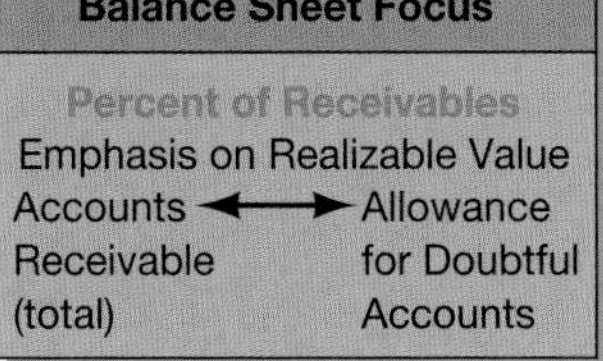

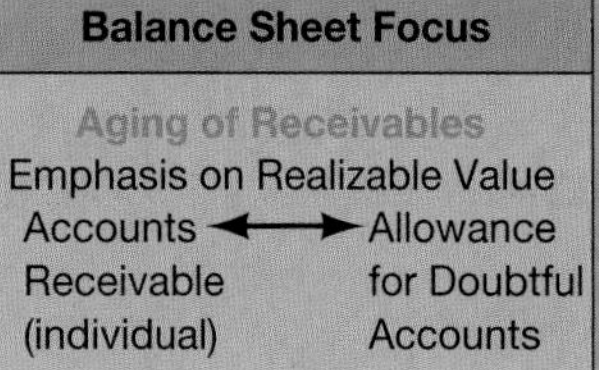

Exhibit 9.13

Methods to Estimate Bad Debts

Quick Check

3. Why must bad debts expense be estimated if such an estimate is possible?
4. What term describes the balance sheet valuation of Accounts Receivable less the Allowance for Doubtful Accounts?
5. Why is estimated bad debts expense credited to a contra account (Allowance for Doubtful Accounts) rather than to the Accounts Receivable account?
6. SnoBoard Company's year-end balance in its Allowance for Doubtful Accounts is a credit of $440. By aging accounts receivable, it estimates that $6,142 is uncollectible. Prepare SnoBoard's year-end adjusting entry for bad debts.
7. Record entries for these transactions assuming the allowance method is used:

   Jan. 10 The $300 account of customer Cool Jam is determined uncollectible.

   April 12 Cool Jam unexpectedly pays in full the account that was deemed uncollectible on January 10.

Answers—p. 368

Notes Receivable

C2 Describe a note receivable and the computation of its maturity date and interest.

A **promissory note** is a written promise to pay a specified amount of money, usually with interest, either on demand or at a definite future date. Promissory notes are used in many transactions, including paying for products and services, and lending and borrowing money. Sellers sometimes ask for a note to replace an account receivable when a customer requests additional time to pay a past-due account. For legal reasons, sellers generally prefer to receive notes when the credit period is long and when the receivable is for a large amount. If a lawsuit is needed to collect from a customer, a note is the buyer's written acknowledgment of the debt, its amount, and its terms.

Topic Tackler 9-2

Exhibit 9.14 shows a simple promissory note dated July 10, 2005. For this note, Julia Browne promises to pay TechCom or to its order (according to TechCom's instructions) a specified amount of money ($1,000), called the **principal of a note,** at a definite future date (October 8, 2005). As the one who signed the note and promised to pay it at maturity, Browne is the **maker of the note.** As the person to whom the note is payable, TechCom is the **payee of the note.** To Browne, the note is a liability called a *note payable*. To TechCom, the same note is an asset called a *note receivable*. This note bears interest at 12%, as written on the note. **Interest** is the charge for using (not paying) the money until a later date. To a borrower, interest is an expense. To a lender, it is revenue.

Exhibit 9.14

Promissory Note

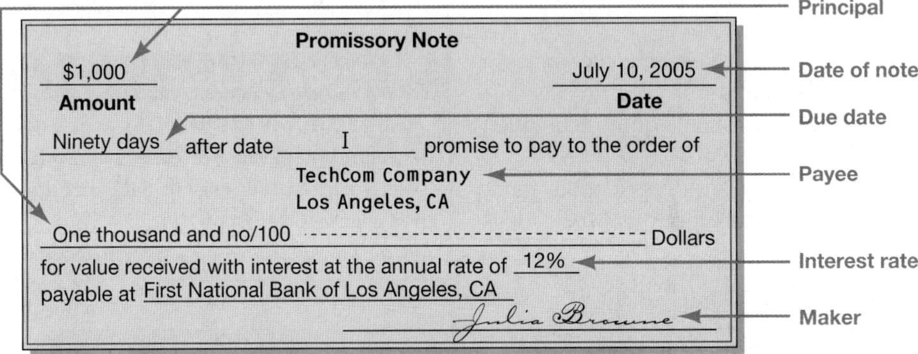

Principal
Promissory Note
$1,000
Amount
July 10, 2005
Date
Date of note
Due date
Ninety days after date I promise to pay to the order of
TechCom Company
Los Angeles, CA
Payee
One thousand and no/100 Dollars
for value received with interest at the annual rate of 12%
Interest rate
payable at First National Bank of Los Angeles, CA
Julia Browne
Maker

Computing Maturity and Interest

This section describes key computations for notes including the determination of maturity date, period covered, and interest computation.

Maturity Date and Period The **maturity date of a note** is the day the note (principal and interest) must be repaid. The *period* of a note is the time from the note's (contract) date to its maturity date. Many notes mature in less than a full year, and the period they cover is often expressed in days. When the time of a note is expressed in days, its maturity date is the specified number of days after the note's date. As an example, a five-day note dated June 15 matures and is due on June 20. A 90-day note dated July 10 matures on October 8. This October 8 due date is computed as shown in Exhibit 9.15. The period of a note is sometimes expressed in months or years. When months are used, the note matures and is payable in the month of its maturity on the *same day of the month* as its original date. A nine-month note dated July 10, for instance, is payable on April 10. The same analysis applies when years are used.

Exhibit 9.15

Maturity Date Computation

Days in July	31	
Minus the date of the note	10	
Days remaining in July		21
Add days in August		31
Add days in September		30
Days to equal 90 days, or **maturity date of October 8**		8
Period of the note in days		90

Interest Computation *Interest* is the cost of borrowing money for the borrower or, alternatively, the profit from lending money for the lender. Unless otherwise stated, the rate of interest on a note is the rate charged for the use of the principal for one year. The formula for computing interest on a note is shown in Exhibit 9.16.

$$\text{Principal of the note} \times \text{Annual interest rate} \times \text{Time expressed in years} = \text{Interest}$$

Exhibit 9.16

Computation of Interest Formula

To simplify interest computations, a year is commonly treated as having 360 days (called the *banker's rule*). **We treat a year as having 360 days for interest computations in the examples and assignments.** Using the promissory note in Exhibit 9.14 where we have a 90-day, 12%, $1,000 note, the total interest is computed as follows:

$$\$1{,}000 \times 12\% \times \frac{90}{360} = \$1{,}000 \times 0.12 \times 0.25 = \$30$$

Recognizing Notes Receivable

P3 Record the receipt of a note receivable.

Notes receivable are usually recorded in a single Notes Receivable account to simplify recordkeeping. The original notes are kept on file, including information on the maker, rate of interest, and due date. (When a company holds a large number of notes, it sometimes sets up a controlling account and a subsidiary ledger for notes. This is similar to the handling of accounts receivable.) To illustrate the recording for the receipt of a note, we use the $1,000, 90-day, 12% promissory note in Exhibit 9.14. TechCom received this note at the time of a product sale to Julia Browne. This transaction is recorded as follows:

July 10*	Notes Receivable	1,000	
	Sales		1,000
	Sold goods in exchange for a 90-day, 12% note.		

Assets	=	Liabilities	+	Equity
+1,000				+1,000

* We omit the entry to Dr. Cost of Sales and Cr. Merchandise Inventory to focus on sales and receivables.

When a seller accepts a note from an overdue customer as a way to grant a time extension on a past-due account receivable, it will often collect part of the past-due balance in cash. This partial payment forces a concession from the customer, reduces the customer's debt (and the seller's risk), and produces a note for a smaller amount. To illustrate, assume that TechCom agreed to accept $232 in cash along with a $600, 60-day, 15% note from Jo Cook to settle her $832 past-due account. TechCom made the following entry to record receipt of this cash and note:

Point: Notes receivable often are a major part of a company's assets. Likewise, notes payable often are a large part of a company's liabilities.

Oct. 5	Cash	232	
	Notes Receivable	600	
	Accounts Receivable—J. Cook		832
	Received cash and note to settle account.		

Assets	=	Liabilities	+	Equity
+232				
+600				
−832				

Valuing and Settling Notes

P4 Record the honoring and dishonoring of a note and adjustments for interest.

Recording an Honored Note The principal and interest of a note are due on its maturity date. The maker of the note usually *honors* the note and pays it in full. To illustrate, when J. Cook pays the note above on its due date, TechCom records it as follows:

Dec. 4	Cash	615	
	Notes Receivable		600
	Interest Revenue		15
	Collect note with interest of $600 × 15% × 60/360.		

Assets	=	Liabilities	+	Equity
+615				+15
−600				

Interest Revenue, also called *Interest Earned,* is reported on the income statement.

Recording a Dishonored Note When a note's maker is unable or refuses to pay at maturity, the note is *dishonored.* The act of dishonoring a note does not relieve the maker of the obligation to pay. The payee should use every legitimate means to collect. How do companies report this event? The balance of the Notes Receivable account should include only those notes that have not matured. Thus, when a note is dishonored, we remove the amount of this note from the Notes Receivable account and charge it back to an account receivable from its maker. To illustrate, TechCom holds an $800, 12%, 60-day note of Greg Hart. At maturity, Hart dishonors the note. TechCom records this dishonoring of the note as follows:

Point: When posting a dishonored note to a customer's account, an explanation is included so as not to misinterpret the debit as a sale on account.

Assets = Liabilities + Equity
+816 +16
−800

Oct. 14	Accounts Receivable—G. Hart	816	
	Interest Revenue		16
	Notes Receivable		800
	To charge account of G. Hart for a dishonored note and interest of $800 × 12% × 60/360.		

Point: Reporting the details of notes is consistent with the **full disclosure principle,** which requires financial statements (including footnotes) to report all relevant information.

Charging a dishonored note back to the account of its maker serves two purposes. First, it removes the amount of the note from the Notes Receivable account and records the dishonored note in the maker's account. Second, and more important, if the maker of the dishonored note applies for credit in the future, his or her account will reveal all past dealings, including the dishonored note. Restoring the account also reminds the company to continue collection efforts from Hart for both principal and interest. The entry records the full amount, including interest, to ensure that it is included in collection efforts.

Recording End-of-Period Interest Adjustment When notes receivable are outstanding at the end of a period, any accrued interest earned is computed and recorded. To illustrate, on December 16, TechCom accepts a $3,000, 60-day, 12% note from a customer in granting an extension on a past-due account. When TechCom's accounting period ends on December 31, $15 of interest has accrued on this note ($3,000 × 12% × 15/360). The following adjusting entry records this revenue:

Assets = Liabilities + Equity
+15 +15

Dec. 31	Interest Receivable	15	
	Interest Revenue		15
	To record accrued interest earned.		

Interest Revenue appears on the income statement, and Interest Receivable appears on the balance sheet as a current asset. When the December 16 note is collected on February 14, TechCom's entry to record the cash receipt is

Assets = Liabilities + Equity
+3,060 +45
−15
−3,000

Feb. 14	Cash	3,060	
	Interest Revenue		45
	Interest Receivable		15
	Notes Receivable		3,000
	Received payment of note and its interest.		

Total interest earned on the 60-day note is $60. The $15 credit to Interest Receivable on February 14 reflects the collection of the interest accrued from the December 31 adjusting entry. The $45 interest earned reflects TechCom's revenue from holding the note from January 1 to February 14 of the current period.

Quick Check

8. Irwin purchases $7,000 of merchandise from Stamford on December 16, 2005. Stamford accepts Irwin's $7,000, 90-day, 12% note as payment. Stamford's accounting period ends on December 31, and it does not make reversing entries. Prepare entries for Stamford on December 16, 2005, and December 31, 2005.
9. Using the information in Quick Check 8, prepare Stamford's March 16, 2006, entry if Irwin dishonors the note.

Answers—p. 368

Disposing of Receivables

Companies can convert receivables to cash before they are due. Reasons for this include the need for cash or the desire not to be involved in collection activities. Converting receivables is usually done either by (1) selling them or (2) using them as security for a loan. A recent survey shows that about 20% of companies obtain cash from either selling receivables or pledging them as security. In some industries such as textiles, apparel and furniture, this is common practice.

Selling Receivables

C3 Explain how receivables can be converted to cash before maturity.

A company can sell all or a portion of its receivables to a finance company or bank. The buyer, called a *factor*, charges the seller a *factoring fee* and then the buyer takes ownership of the receivables and receives cash when they come due. By incurring a factoring fee, the seller receives cash earlier and can pass the risk of bad debts to the factor. The seller can also choose to avoid costs of billing and accounting for the receivables. To illustrate, if TechCom sells $20,000 of its accounts receivable and is charged a 4% factoring fee, it records this sale as follows:

Global: Firms in export sales increasingly sell their receivables to factors.

Aug. 15	Cash	19,200	
	Factoring Fee Expense	800	
	Accounts Receivable		20,000
	Sold accounts receivable for cash, less 4% fee.		

Assets	= Liabilities	+ Equity
+19,200		−800
−20,000		

The accounting for sales of notes receivable is similar to that for accounts receivable. The detailed entries are covered in advanced courses.

Pledging Receivables

A company can raise cash by borrowing money and *pledging* its receivables as security for the loan. Pledging receivables does not transfer the risk of bad debts to the lender because the borrower retains ownership of the receivables. If the borrower defaults on the loan, the lender has a right to be paid from the cash receipts of the receivable when collected. To illustrate, when TechCom borrows $35,000 and pledges its receivables as security, it records this transaction as follows:

Point: When accounts receivable are sold, each subsidiary ledger account is credited along with the controlling account for the total.

Point: Chock Full O'Nuts reports, "Outstanding borrowings . . . are collateralized by, among other things, the trade accounts receivable."

Aug. 20	Cash	35,000	
	Notes Payable		35,000
	Borrowed money with a note secured by pledging receivables.		

Assets	= Liabilities	+ Equity
+35,000	+35,000	

Decision Insight

Money Source **Zenith** obtained a three-year, $60 million loan by pledging accounts receivable as collateral, and **Intel** converted accounts receivable to a note receivable for a major customer.

Since pledged receivables are committed as security for a specific loan, the borrower's financial statements disclose the pledging of them. TechCom, for instance, includes the following note with its statements: *Accounts receivable of $40,000 are pledged as security for a $35,000 note payable.*

Decision Analysis — Accounts Receivable Turnover

A1 Compute accounts receivable turnover and use it to help assess financial condition.

For a company selling on credit, we want to assess both the quality and liquidity of its accounts receivable. *Quality* of receivables refers to the likelihood of collection without loss. Experience shows that the longer receivables are outstanding beyond their due date, the lower the likelihood of collection. *Liquidity* of receivables refers to the speed of collection. **Accounts receivable turnover** is a measure of both the quality and liquidity of accounts receivable. It indicates how often, on average, receivables are received and collected during the period. The formula for this ratio is shown in Exhibit 9.17.

Exhibit 9.17

Accounts Receivable Turnover

$$\textbf{Accounts receivable turnover} = \frac{\textbf{Net sales}}{\textbf{Average accounts receivable}}$$

We prefer to use net *credit* sales in the numerator because cash sales do not create receivables. However, since financial statements rarely report net credit sales, our analysis uses net sales. The denominator is the *average* accounts receivable balance, computed as (Beginning balance + Ending balance) ÷ 2. TechCom has an accounts receivable turnover of 5.1. This indicates its average accounts receivable balance is converted into cash 5.1 times during the period. Exhibit 9.18 shows graphically this turnover activity for TechCom.

Exhibit 9.18

Rate of Accounts Receivable Turnover for TechCom

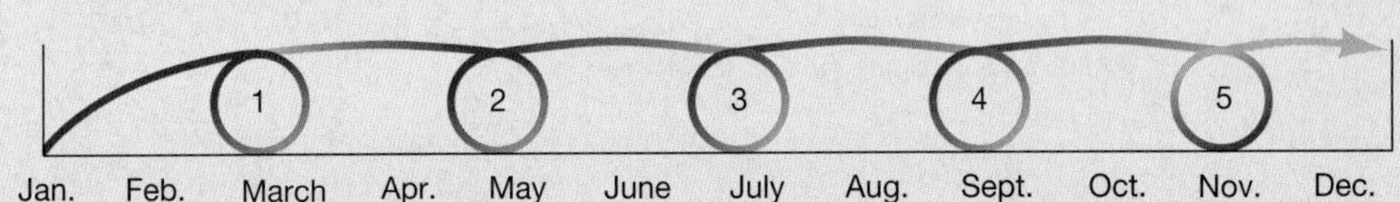

Accounts receivable turnover also reflects how well management is doing in granting credit to customers in a desire to increase sales. A high turnover in comparison with competitors suggests that management should consider using more liberal credit terms to increase sales. A low turnover suggests management should consider stricter credit terms and more aggressive collection efforts to avoid having its resources tied up in accounts receivable.

Point: **Credit risk ratio** is computed by dividing the Allowance for Doubtful Accounts by Accounts Receivable. The higher this ratio, the higher is credit risk.

To illustrate, we take data from two competitors: **Dell Computer** and **Apple Computer**. Exhibit 9.19 shows accounts receivable turnover for both companies.

Exhibit 9.19

Analysis Using Accounts Receivable Turnover

Company	Figure ($ millions)	2002	2001	2000
Dell	Net sales	$35,404	$31,168	$31,888
	Average accounts receivable	$ 2,428	$ 2,347	$ 2,752
	Accounts receivable turnover	**14.6**	**13.3**	**11.6**
Apple	Net sales	$ 5,742	$ 5,363	$ 7,983
	Average accounts receivable	$ 516	$ 710	$ 817
	Accounts receivable turnover	**11.1**	**7.6**	**9.8**

Dell's 2002 turnover is computed ($ millions) as $35,404/$2,428 = 14.6. This means that Dell's average accounts receivable balance was converted into cash 14.6 times in 2002. Also, its turnover improved in 2002 (versus its prior two years), and it is superior to that of Apple. Is Dell's turnover too high? Since sales are markedly growing over this time period, Dell's turnover does not appear to be too high. Instead, it seems to be doing well in managing receivables. Similarly, Apple has improved its management of receivables during this period. Turnover for competitors is generally in the range of 7 to 11 for this same period.[1]

Decision Maker

Family Physician Your practice is less profitable, so you hire a health care analyst. The analyst highlights several points including the following: *"Accounts receivable turnover is too low. Tighter credit policies are recommended along with discontinuing service to those most delayed in payments."* How do you interpret these recommendations? What actions do you take?

Answer—p. 368

Demonstration Problem

Clayco Company completes the following selected transactions during year 2005:

July 14	Writes off a $750 account receivable arising from a sale to Briggs Company that dates to 10 months ago. (Clayco Company uses the allowance method.)
30	Clayco Company receives a $1,000, 90-day, 10% note in exchange for merchandise sold to Sumrell Company (the merchandise cost $600).
Aug. 15	Receives $2,000 cash plus a $10,000 note from JT Co. in exchange for merchandise that sells for $12,000 (its cost is $8,000). The note is dated August 15, bears 12% interest, and matures in 120 days.
Nov. 1	Completed a $200 credit card sale with a 4% fee (the cost of sales is $150). The cash is received immediately from the credit card company.
3	Sumrell Company refuses to pay the note that was due to Clayco Company on October 28. Prepare the journal entry to charge the dishonored note plus accrued interest to Sumrell Company's accounts receivable.
5	Completed a $500 credit card sale with a 5% fee (the cost of sales is $300). The payment from the credit card company is received on Nov. 9.
15	Received the full amount of $750 from Briggs Company that was previously written off on July 14. Record the bad debts recovery.
Dec. 13	Received payment of principal plus interest from JT for the August 15 note.

Required

1. Prepare journal entries to record these transactions on Clayco Company's books.
2. Prepare an adjusting journal entry as of December 31, 2005, assuming the following:
   a. Bad debts expense is estimated to be $20,400 by aging accounts receivable. The unadjusted balance of the Allowance for Doubtful Accounts is $1,000 debit.
   b. Alternatively, assume that bad debts expense is estimated using the percent of sales method. The Allowance for Doubtful Accounts had a $1,000 debit balance before adjustment, and the company estimates bad debts to be 1% of its credit sales of $2,000,000.

Planning the Solution

- Examine each transaction to determine the accounts affected, and then record the entries.
- For the year-end adjustment, record the bad debts expense for the two approaches.

[1] As an estimate of *average days' sales uncollected,* we compute how many days (*on average*) it takes to collect receivables as follows: 365 days ÷ accounts receivable turnover. An increase in this *average collection period* can signal a decline in its customers' financial condition.

Solution to Demonstration Problem

1.

Date	Account	Debit	Credit
July 14	Allowance for Doubtful Accounts	750	
	Accounts Receivable—Briggs Co.		750
	Wrote off an uncollectible account.		
July 30	Notes Receivable—Sumrell Co.	1,000	
	Sales		1,000
	Sold merchandise for a 90-day, 10% note.		
July 30	Cost of Goods Sold	600	
	Merchandise Inventory		600
	To record the cost of July 30 sale.		
Aug. 15	Cash	2,000	
	Notes Receivable—JT Co.	10,000	
	Sales		12,000
	Sold merchandise to customer for $2,000 cash and $10,000 note.		
Aug. 15	Cost of Goods Sold	8,000	
	Merchandise Inventory		8,000
	To record the cost of Aug. 15 sale.		
Nov. 1	Cash	192	
	Credit Card Expense	8	
	Sales		200
	To record credit card sale less a 4% credit card expense.		
Nov. 1	Cost of Goods Sold	150	
	Merchandise Inventory		150
	To record the cost of Nov. 1 sale.		
Nov. 3	Accounts Receivable—Sumrell Co.	1,025	
	Interest Revenue		25
	Notes Receivable—Sumrell Co.		1,000
	To charge account of Sumrell Company for a $1,000 dishonored note and interest of $1,000 × 10% × 90/360.		
Nov. 5	Accounts Receivable—Credit Card Co.	475	
	Credit Card Expense	25	
	Sales		500
	To record credit card sale less a 5% credit card expense.		
Nov. 5	Cost of Goods Sold	300	
	Merchandise Inventory		300
	To record the cost of Nov. 5 sale.		
Nov. 9	Cash	475	
	Accounts Receivable—Credit Card Co.		475
	To record cash receipt from Nov. 5 sale.		
Nov. 15	Accounts Receivable—Briggs Co.	750	
	Allowance for Doubtful Accounts		750
	To reinstate the account of Briggs Company previously written off.		
Nov. 15	Cash	750	
	Accounts Receivable—Briggs Co.		750
	Cash received in full payment of account.		
Dec. 13	Cash	10,400	
	Interest Revenue		400
	Note Receivable—JT Co.		10,000
	Collect note with interest of $10,000 × 12% × 120/360.		

2a. Aging of accounts receivable method:

Dec. 31	Bad Debts Expense.	21,400	
	Allowance for Doubtful Accounts		21,400
	To adjust allowance account from a $1,000 debit balance to a $20,400 credit balance.		

2b. Percent of sales method:*

Dec. 31	Bad Debts Expense.	20,000	
	Allowance for Doubtful Accounts		20,000
	To provide for bad debts as 1% × $2,000,000 in credit sales.		

* For the income statement approach, which requires estimating bad debts as a percent of sales or credit sales, the Allowance account balance is *not* considered when making the adjusting entry.

Summary

C1 Describe accounts receivable and how they occur and are recorded. Accounts receivable are amounts due from customers for credit sales. A subsidiary ledger lists amounts owed by each customer. Credit sales arise from at least two sources: (1) sales on credit and (2) credit card sales. *Sales on credit* refers to a company's granting credit directly to customers. Credit card sales involve customers' use of third-party credit cards.

C2 Describe a note receivable and the computation of its maturity date and interest. A note receivable is a written promise to pay a specified amount of money at a definite future date. The maturity date is the day the note (principal and interest) must be repaid. Interest rates are normally stated in annual terms. The amount of interest on the note is computed by expressing time as a fraction of one year and multiplying the note's principal by this fraction and the annual interest rate.

C3 Explain how receivables can be converted to cash before maturity. Receivables can be converted to cash before maturity in three ways. First, a company can sell accounts receivable to a factor, who charges a factoring fee. Second, a company can borrow money by signing a note payable that is secured by pledging the accounts receivable. Third, notes receivable can be discounted at (sold to) a financial institution.

A1 Compute accounts receivable turnover and use it to help assess financial condition. Accounts receivable turnover is a measure of both the quality and liquidity of accounts receivable. The accounts receivable turnover measure indicates how often, on average, receivables are received and collected during the period. Accounts receivable turnover is computed as net sales divided by average accounts receivable.

P1 Apply the direct write-off and allowance methods to account for accounts receivable. The direct write-off method charges Bad Debts Expense when accounts are written off as uncollectible. This method is acceptable only when the amount of bad debts expense is immaterial. Under the allowance method, bad debts expense is recorded with an adjustment at the end of each accounting period that debits the Bad Debts Expense account and credits the Allowance for Doubtful Accounts. The uncollectible accounts are later written off with a debit to the Allowance for Doubtful Accounts.

P2 Estimate uncollectibles using methods based on sales and accounts receivable. Uncollectibles are estimated by focusing on either (1) the income statement relation between bad debts expense and credit sales or (2) the balance sheet relation between accounts receivable and the allowance for doubtful accounts. The first approach emphasizes the matching principle using the income statement. The second approach emphasizes realizable value of accounts receivable using the balance sheet.

P3 Record the receipt of a note receivable. A note received is recorded at its principal amount by debiting the Notes Receivable account. The credit amount is to the asset, product, or service provided in return for the note.

P4 Record the honoring and dishonoring of a note and adjustments for interest. When a note is honored, the payee debits the money received and credits both Notes Receivable and Interest Revenue. Dishonored notes are credited to Notes Receivable and debited to Accounts Receivable (to the account of the maker in an attempt to collect), and Interest Revenue is recorded for interest earned for the time the note is held.

Guidance Answers to Decision Maker and Decision Ethics

Entrepreneur Analysis of credit card sales should weigh the benefits against the costs. The primary benefit is the potential to increase sales by attracting customers who prefer the convenience of credit cards. The primary cost is the fee charged by the credit card company for providing this service. Analysis should therefore estimate the expected increase in dollar sales from allowing credit card sales and then subtract (1) the normal costs and expenses and (2) the credit card fees associated with this expected increase in dollar sales. If your analysis shows an increase in profit from allowing credit card sales, your store should probably accept them.

Labor Union Chief Yes, this information is likely to impact your negotiations. The obvious question is why the company markedly increased this allowance. The large increase in this allowance means a substantial increase in bad debts expense *and* a decrease in earnings. This change (coming immediately prior to labor contract discussions) also raises concerns since it reduces the union's bargaining power for increased compensation. You want to ask management for supporting documentation justifying this increase. You also want data for two or three prior years and similar data from competitors. These data should give you some sense of whether the change in the allowance for uncollectibles is justified.

Family Physician The recommendations are twofold. First, the analyst suggests more stringent screening of patients' credit standing. Second, the analyst suggests dropping patients who are most overdue in payments. You are likely bothered by both suggestions. They are probably financially wise recommendations, but you are troubled by eliminating services to those less able to pay. One alternative is to follow the recommendations while implementing a care program directed at patients less able to pay for services. This allows you to continue services to patients less able to pay and lets you discontinue services to patients able but unwilling to pay.

Guidance Answers to **Quick Checks**

1. If cash is immediately received when credit card sales receipts are deposited, the company debits Cash at the time of sale. If the company does not receive payment until after it submits receipts to the credit card company, it debits Accounts Receivable at the time of sale. (Cash is later debited when payment is received from the credit card company.)
2. Credit card expenses are usually *recorded* and *incurred* at the time of their related sales, not when cash is received from the credit card company.
3. If possible, bad debts expense must be matched with the sales that gave rise to the accounts receivable. This requires that companies estimate future bad debts at the end of each period before they learn which accounts are uncollectible.
4. Realizable value (also called *net realizable value*).
5. The estimated amount of bad debts expense cannot be credited to the Accounts Receivable account because the specific customer accounts that will prove uncollectible cannot yet be identified and removed from the accounts receivable subsidiary ledger. Moreover, if only the Accounts Receivable account is credited, its balance would not equal the sum of its subsidiary account balances.
6.

Dec. 31	Bad Debts Expense	5,702	
	Allowance for Doubtful Accounts		5,702

7.

Jan. 10	Allowance for Doubtful Accounts	300	
	Accounts Receivable—Cool Jam		300
Apr. 12	Accounts Receivable—Cool Jam	300	
	Allowance for Doubtful Accounts		300
Apr. 12	Cash	300	
	Accounts Receivable—Cool Jam		300

8.

Dec. 16	Note Receivable—Irwin	7,000	
	Sales		7,000
Dec. 31	Interest Receivable	35	
	Interest Revenue		35
	($7,000 × 12% × 15/360)		

9.

Mar. 16	Accounts Receivable—Irwin	7,210	
	Interest Revenue		175
	Interest Receivable		35
	Notes Receivable—Irwin		7,000

Key Terms

mhhe.com/larson

Key Terms are available at the book's Website for learning and testing in an online Flashcard Format.

Accounts receivable (p. 350)
Accounts receivable turnover (p. 364)
Aging of accounts receivable (p. 358)
Allowance for Doubtful Accounts (p. 355)
Allowance method (p. 354)
Bad debts (p. 353)
Direct write-off method (p. 354)
Interest (p. 360)
Maker of the note (p. 360)
Matching principle (p. 354)
Materiality principle (p. 354)
Maturity date of a note (p. 360)
Payee of the note (p. 360)
Principal of a note (p. 360)
Promissory note (or **note**) (p. 359)
Realizable value (p. 355)

Personal Interactive Quiz

Personal Interactive Quizzes A and B are available at the book's Website to reinforce and assess your learning.

Discussion Questions

1. How do sellers benefit from allowing their customers to use credit cards?
2. Why does the direct write-off method of accounting for bad debts usually fail to match revenues and expenses?
3. Explain the accounting principle of materiality.
4. Explain why writing off a bad debt against the Allowance for Doubtful Accounts does not reduce the estimated realizable value of a company's accounts receivable.
5. Why does the Bad Debts Expense account usually not have the same adjusted balance as the Allowance for Doubtful Accounts?
6. Why might a business prefer a note receivable to an account receivable?
7. Refer to **Krispy Kreme**'s balance sheet in Appendix A. What percent of accounts receivable at February 2, 2003, has been set aside as an allowance for doubtful accounts? How does this percent compare to the prior year?
8. Refer to the balance sheet of **Tastykake** in Appendix A. Does it use the direct write-off method or allowance method to account for doubtful accounts? What is the realizable value of its accounts receivable as of December 28, 2002? What is another name for the Allowance for Doubtful Accounts?
9. Refer to the balance sheet of **Harley-Davidson** in Appendix A. What two types of receivables does Harley show in its current asset section of the balance sheet?

Red numbers denote Discussion Questions that involve decision-making.

***Homework Manager** repeats all numerical Quick Studies on the book's Website with new numbers.*

QUICK STUDY

QS 9-1
Credit card sales
C1

Prepare journal entries for the following credit card sales transactions (the company uses the perpetual inventory system):

1. Sold $10,000 of merchandise, that cost $7,500, on MasterCard credit cards. The net cash receipts from sales are immediately deposited in the seller's bank account. MasterCard charges a 5% fee.
2. Sold $3,000 of merchandise, that cost $1,500, on an assortment of credit cards. Net cash receipts are received 7 days later, and a 4% fee is charged.

QS 9-2
Allowance method for bad debts
P1

Milner Corp. uses the allowance method to account for uncollectibles. On October 31, it wrote off a $1,000 account of a customer, C. Schaub. On December 9, it receives a $200 payment from Schaub.

1. Prepare the journal entry or entries for October 31.
2. Prepare the journal entry or entries for December 9; assume no additional money is expected from Schaub.

QS 9-3
Percent of accounts receivable and percent of sales methods
P1 P2

Wecker Company's year-end unadjusted trial balance shows accounts receivable of $89,000, allowance for doubtful accounts of $500 (credit), and sales of $270,000. Uncollectibles are estimated to be 1.5% of accounts receivable.

1. Prepare the December 31 year-end adjusting entry for uncollectibles.
2. What amount would have been used in the year-end adjusting entry if the allowance account had a year-end unadjusted debit balance of $200?
3. Assume the same facts as in part 1, except that Wecker estimates uncollectibles as 1.0% of sales. Prepare the December 31 year-end adjusting entry for uncollectibles.

QS 9-4
Note receivable
P3 P4

On August 2, 2005, JLK Co. receives a $5,500, 90-day, 12% note from customer Tom Menke as payment on his $5,500 account. Prepare JLK's journal entries for August 2 and for the note's maturity date assuming the note is honored by Menke.

QS 9-5
Note receivable
C2 P4

Dekon Company's December 31 year-end unadjusted trial balance shows an $8,000 balance in Notes Receivable. This balance is from one 6% note dated December 1, with a period of 45 days. Prepare journal entries for December 31 and for the note's maturity date assuming it is honored.

QS 9-6
Accounts receivable turnover
A1

The following data are taken from the comparative balance sheets of Fulton Company. Compute and interpret its accounts receivable turnover for year 2005 (competitors average a turnover of 7.5).

	2005	2004
Accounts receivable	$152,900	$133,700
Net sales	754,200	810,600

***Homework Manager** repeats all numerical Exercises on the book's Website with new numbers.*

EXERCISES

Exercise 9-1
Accounting for credit card sales
C1

Petri Company allows customers to use two credit cards in charging purchases. With the Omni Card, Petri receives an immediate credit to its account when it deposits sales receipts. Omni Card assesses a 4% service charge for credit card sales. The second credit card that Petri accepts is the Continental Bank Card. Petri sends its accumulated receipts to Continental Bank on a weekly basis and is paid by Continental about a week later. Continental Bank assesses a 2.5% charge on sales for using its card. Prepare journal entries to record the following selected credit card transactions of Petri Company:

Apr. 8 Sold merchandise for $9,200 (that had cost $6,800) and accepted the customer's Omni Card. The Omni receipts are immediately deposited in Petri's bank account.

12 Sold merchandise for $5,400 (that had cost $3,500) and accepted the customer's Continental Bank Card. Transferred $5,400 of credit card receipts to Continental Bank, requesting payment.

20 Received Continental Bank's check for the April 12 billing, less the service charge.

Exercise 9-2
Accounts receivable subsidiary ledger; schedule of accounts receivable
C1

Sami Company recorded the following selected transactions during November 2005:

Nov. 5	Accounts Receivable—Surf Shop	4,417	
	Sales		4,417
10	Accounts Receivable—Yum Enterprises	1,250	
	Sales		1,250
13	Accounts Receivable—Matt Albin.	733	
	Sales		733
21	Sales Returns and Allowances	189	
	Accounts Receivable—Matt Albin		189
30	Accounts Receivable—Surf Shop	2,606	
	Sales		2,606

1. Open a general ledger having T-accounts for Accounts Receivable, Sales, and Sales Returns and Allowances. Also open an accounts receivable subsidiary ledger having a T-account for each customer. Post these entries to both the general ledger and the accounts receivable ledger.
2. Prepare a schedule of accounts receivable (see Exhibit 9.4) and compare its total with the balance of the Accounts Receivable controlling account as of November 30.

Check Accounts Receivable ending balance, $8,817

Exercise 9-3
Percent of sales method; write-off
P1 P2

At year-end (December 31), Alvare Company estimates its bad debts as 0.5% of its annual credit sales of $875,000. Alvare records its Bad Debts Expense for that estimate. On the following February 1, Alvare decides that the $420 account of P. Coble is uncollectible and writes it off as a bad debt. On June 5, Coble unexpectedly pays the amount previously written off. Prepare the journal entries of Alvare to record these transactions and events of December 31, February 1, and June 5.

Exercise 9-4
Percent of accounts receivable method
P1 P2

At each calendar year-end, Cabool Supply Co. uses the percent of accounts receivable method to estimate bad debts. On December 31, 2005, it has outstanding accounts receivable of $53,000, and it estimates that 4% will be uncollectible. Prepare the adjusting entry to record bad debts expense for year 2005 under the assumption that the Allowance for Doubtful Accounts has (*a*) a $915 credit balance before the adjustment and (*b*) a $1,332 debit balance before the adjustment.

Exercise 9-5
Selling and pledging accounts receivable
C3

On June 30, Peña Co. has $125,900 of accounts receivable. Prepare journal entries to record the following selected July transactions. Also prepare any footnotes to the July 31 financial statements that result from these transactions. (The company uses the perpetual inventory system.)

July 4 Sold $6,295 of merchandise (that had cost $4,000) to customers on credit.
9 Sold $18,000 of accounts receivable to Center Bank. Center charges a 4% factoring fee.
17 Received $3,436 cash from customers in payment on their accounts.
27 Borrowed $10,000 cash from Center Bank, pledging $13,000 of accounts receivable as security for the loan.

Exercise 9-6
Honoring a note
P4

Prepare journal entries to record these selected transactions for Eduardo Company:

Nov. 1 Accepted a $5,000, 180-day, 6% note dated November 1 from Melosa Allen in granting a time extension on her past-due account receivable.
Dec. 31 Adjusted the year-end accounts for the accrued interest earned on the Allen note.
Apr. 30 Allen honors her note when presented for payment.

Exercise 9-7
Dishonoring a note
P4

Prepare journal entries to record the following selected transactions of Paloma Company:

Mar. 21 Accepted a $3,100, 180-day, 10% note dated March 21 from Salma Hernandez in granting a time extension on her past-due account receivable.
Sept. 17 Hernandez dishonors her note when it is presented for payment.
Dec. 31 After exhausting all legal means of collection, Paloma Company writes off Hernandez's account against the Allowance for Doubtful Accounts.

Exercise 9-8
Notes receivable transactions and entries
C2 P3 P4

Prepare journal entries for the following selected transactions of Deshawn Company:

2004

Dec. 13 Accepted a $10,000, 60-day, 8% note dated December 13 in granting Latisha Clark a time extension on her past-due account receivable.
31 Prepared an adjusting entry to record the accrued interest on the Clark note.

Check Dec. 31, Cr. Interest Revenue $40

2005

Feb. 11 Received Clark's payment for principal and interest on the note dated December 13.

Check Feb. 11, Dr. Cash $10,133

Mar. 3 Accepted a $4,000, 10%, 90-day note dated March 3 in granting a time extension on the past-due account receivable of Shandi Company.
17 Accepted a $2,000, 30-day, 9% note dated March 17 in granting Juan Torres a time extension on his past-due account receivable.
Apr. 16 Torres dishonors his note when presented for payment.
May 1 Wrote off the Torres account against the Allowance for Doubtful Accounts.
June 1 Received the Shandi payment for principal and interest on the note dated March 3.

Check June 1, Dr. Cash $4,100

Exercise 9-9
Accounts receivable turnover
A1

The following information is from the annual financial statements of Waseem Company. Compute its accounts receivable turnover for 2004 and 2005. Compare the two years results and give a possible explanation for any change (competitors average a turnover of 11).

	2005	2004	2003
Net sales	$305,000	$236,000	$288,000
Accounts receivable (December 31)	22,900	20,700	17,400

PROBLEM SET A

Problem 9-1A
Sales on account and credit card sales
C1

Atlas Co. allows select customers to make purchases on credit. Its other customers can use either of two credit cards: Zisa or Access. Zisa deducts a 3% service charge for sales on its credit card and credits the bank account of Atlas immediately when credit card receipts are deposited. Atlas deposits the Zisa credit card receipts each business day. When customers use Access credit cards, Atlas accumulates the receipts for several days before submitting them to Access for payment. Access deducts a 2% service charge and usually pays within one week of being billed. Atlas completes the following transactions in June. (The terms of all credit sales are 2/15, n/30, and all sales are recorded at the gross price.)

June 4 Sold $750 of merchandise (that had cost $500) on credit to Anne Cianci.
5 Sold merchandise for $5,900 (that had cost $3,200) to customers who used their Zisa credit cards.
6 Sold merchandise for $4,800 (that had cost $2,800) to customers who used their Access credit cards.
8 Sold merchandise for $3,200 (that had cost $1,900) to customers who used their Access credit cards.
10 Submitted Access card receipts accumulated since June 6 to the credit card company for payment.
13 Wrote off the account of Nakia Wells against the Allowance for Doubtful Accounts. The $329 balance in Wells' account stemmed from a credit sale in October of last year.
17 Received the amount due from Access.
18 Received Cianci's check paying for the purchase of June 4.

Check June 17, Dr. Cash $7,840

Required

Prepare journal entries to record the preceding transactions and events. (The company uses the perpetual inventory system.)

Problem 9-2A
Accounts receivable transactions and bad debts adjustments
C1 P1 P2

Lopez Company began operations on January 1, 2004. During its first two years, the company completed a number of transactions involving sales on credit, accounts receivable collections, and bad debts. These transactions are summarized as follows:

2004

a. Sold $1,803,750 of merchandise (that had cost $1,475,000) on credit, terms n/30.
b. Wrote off $20,300 of uncollectible accounts receivable.
c. Received $789,200 cash in payment of accounts receivable.
d. In adjusting the accounts on December 31, the company estimated that 1.5% of accounts receivable will be uncollectible.

Check (*d*) Dr. Bad Debts Expense $35,214

2005

e. Sold $1,825,700 of merchandise (that had cost $1,450,000) on credit, terms n/30.
f. Wrote off $28,800 of uncollectible accounts receivable.
g. Received $1,304,800 cash in payment of accounts receivable.
h. In adjusting the accounts on December 31, the company estimated that 1.5% of accounts receivable will be uncollectible.

Check (*h*) Dr. Bad Debts Expense $36,181

Required

Prepare journal entries to record Lopez's 2004 and 2005 summarized transactions and its year-end adjustments to record bad debts expense. (The company uses the perpetual inventory system.)

Problem 9-3A
Estimating and reporting bad debts
P1 P2 

On December 31, 2005, Ethan Co. records show the following results for the calendar-year:

Cash sales	$1,803,750
Credit sales	3,534,000

In addition, its unadjusted trial balance includes the following items:

Accounts receivable	$1,070,100 debit
Allowance for doubtful accounts	15,750 debit

Required

1. Prepare the adjusting entry for Ethan Co. to recognize bad debts under each of the following independent assumptions:
 a. Bad debts are estimated to be 2% of credit sales.
 b. Bad debts are estimated to be 1% of total sales.
 c. An aging analysis estimates that 5% of year-end accounts receivable are uncollectible.

Check Bad Debts Expense: (1*a*) $70,680, (1*c*) $69,255

2. Show how Accounts Receivable and the Allowance for Doubtful Accounts appear on the December 31, 2005, balance sheet given the facts in part 1*a*.
3. Show how Accounts Receivable and the Allowance for Doubtful Accounts appear on the December 31, 2005, balance sheet given the facts in part 1*c*.

Problem 9-4A
Aging accounts receivable and accounting for bad debts
P1 P2

Carmack Company has credit sales of $2.6 million for year 2005. On December 31, 2005, the company's Allowance for Doubtful Accounts has an unadjusted credit balance of $13,400. Carmack prepares a schedule of its December 31, 2005, accounts receivable by age. On the basis of past experience, it estimates the percent of receivables in each age category that will become uncollectible. This information is summarized here:

	A	B	C
1–2	**December 31, 2005 Accounts Receivable**	**Age of Accounts Receivable**	**Expected Percent Uncollectible**
3	$730,000	Not yet due	1.25%
4	354,000	1 to 30 days past due	2.00
5	76,000	31 to 60 days past due	6.50
6	48,000	61 to 90 days past due	32.75
7	12,000	Over 90 days past due	68.00
8			

Required

1. Estimate the required balance of the Allowance for Doubtful Accounts at December 31, 2005, using the aging of accounts receivable method.
2. Prepare the adjusting entry to record bad debts expense at December 31, 2005.

Check (2) Dr. Bad Debts Expense $31,625

Analysis Component

3. On June 30, 2006, Carmack Company concludes that a customer's $3,750 receivable (created in 2005) is uncollectible and that the account should be written off. What effect will this action have on Carmack's 2006 net income? Explain.

Problem 9-5A
Analyzing and journalizing notes receivable transactions
C2 C3 P3 P4

The following selected transactions are from Ohlde Company:

2004

Dec. 16 Accepted a $9,600, 60-day, 9% note dated this day in granting Todd Duke a time extension on his past-due account receivable.
31 Made an adjusting entry to record the accrued interest on the Duke note.

2005

Feb. 14 Received Duke's payment of principal and interest on the note dated December 16.

Check Feb. 14, Cr. Interest Revenue $108

Mar. 2 Accepted a $4,120, 8%, 90-day note dated this day in granting a time extension on the past-due account receivable from Mare Co.
17 Accepted a $2,400, 30-day, 7% note dated this day in granting Jolene Halaam a time extension on her past-due account receivable.
Apr. 16 Halaam dishonored her note when presented for payment.
June 2 Mare Co. refuses to pay the note that was due to Ohlde Co. on May 31. Prepare the journal entry to charge the dishonored note plus accrued interest to Mare Co.'s accounts receivable.

Check June 2, Cr. Interest Revenue $82

July 17 Received payment from Mare Co. for the maturity value of its dishonored note plus interest for 46 days beyond maturity at 8%.
Aug. 7 Accepted a $5,440, 90-day, 10% note dated this day in granting a time extension on the past-due account receivable of Birch and Byer Co.

Sept. 3 Accepted a $2,080, 60-day, 10% note dated this day in granting Kevin York a time extension on his past-due account receivable.

Check Nov. 2, Cr. Interest Revenue $35

Nov. 2 Received payment of principal plus interest from York for the September 3 note.

Nov. 5 Received payment of principal plus interest from Birch and Byer for the August 7 note.

Dec. 1 Wrote off the Jolene Halaam account against Allowance for Doubtful Accounts.

Required

1. Prepare journal entries to record these transactions and events.

Analysis Component

2. What reporting is necessary when a business pledges receivables as security for a loan and the loan is still outstanding at the end of the period? Explain the reason for this requirement and the accounting principle being satisfied.

PROBLEM SET B

Problem 9-1B

Sales on account and credit card sales

C1

Able Co. allows select customers to make purchases on credit. Its other customers can use either of two credit cards: Commerce Bank or Aztec. Commerce Bank deducts a 3% service charge for sales on its credit card and immediately credits the bank account of Able when credit card receipts are deposited. Able deposits the Commerce Bank credit card receipts each business day. When customers use the Aztec card, Able accumulates the receipts for several days and then submits them to Aztec for payment. Aztec deducts a 2% service charge and usually pays within one week of being billed. Able completed the following transactions in August (terms of all credit sales are 2/10, n/30; and all sales are recorded at the gross price).

Aug. 4 Sold $2,780 of merchandise (that had cost $1,750) on credit to Stacy Dalton.

10 Sold merchandise for $3,248 (that had cost $2,456) to customers who used their Commerce Bank credit cards.

11 Sold merchandise for $1,575 (that had cost $1,150) to customers who used their Aztec cards.

14 Received Dalton's check paying for the purchase of August 4.

15 Sold merchandise for $2,960 (that had cost $1,758) to customers who used their Aztec cards.

18 Submitted Aztec card receipts accumulated since August 11 to the credit card company for payment.

22 Wrote off the account of Ness City against the Allowance for Doubtful Accounts. The $398 balance in Ness City's account stemmed from a credit sale in November of last year.

Check Aug. 25, Dr. Cash $4,444

25 Received the amount due from Aztec.

Required

Prepare journal entries to record the preceding transactions and events. (The company uses the perpetual inventory system.)

Problem 9-2B

Accounts receivable transactions and bad debts adjustments

C1 P1 P2

Crist Co. began operations on January 1, 2004, and completed several transactions during 2004 and 2005 that involved sales on credit, accounts receivable collections, and bad debts. These transactions are summarized as follows:

2004

a. Sold $673,490 of merchandise (that had cost $500,000) on credit, terms n/30.

b. Received $437,250 cash in payment of accounts receivable.

c. Wrote off $8,330 of uncollectible accounts receivable.

Check (*d*) Dr. Bad Debts Expense $10,609

d. In adjusting the accounts on December 31, the company estimated that 1% of accounts receivable will be uncollectible.

2005

e. Sold $930,100 of merchandise (that had cost $650,000) on credit, terms n/30.

f. Received $890,220 cash in payment of accounts receivable.

g. Wrote off $10,090 of uncollectible accounts receivable.

Check (*h*) Dr. Bad Debts Expense $10,388

h. In adjusting the accounts on December 31, the company estimated that 1% of accounts receivable will be uncollectible.

Required

Prepare journal entries to record Crist's 2004 and 2005 summarized transactions and its year-end adjusting entry to record bad debts expense. (The company uses the perpetual inventory system.)

Problem 9-3B

Estimating and reporting bad debts

P1 P2 

On December 31, 2005, Klimek Co.'s records show the following results for the year:

Cash sales	$1,015,000
Credit sales	1,241,000

In addition, its unadjusted trial balance includes the following items:

Accounts receivable	$475,000 debit
Allowance for doubtful accounts	5,200 credit

Required

1. Prepare the adjusting entry for Klimek Co. to recognize bad debts under each of the following independent assumptions:

a. Bad debts are estimated to be 2.5% of credit sales.

b. Bad debts are estimated to be 1.5% of total sales.

c. An aging analysis estimates that 6% of year-end accounts receivable are uncollectible.

2. Show how Accounts Receivable and the Allowance for Doubtful Accounts appear on the December 31, 2005, balance sheet given the facts in part 1*a*.

3. Show how Accounts Receivable and the Allowance for Doubtful Accounts appear on the December 31, 2005, balance sheet given the facts in part 1*c*.

Check Bad debts expense: (1*b*) $33,840, (1*c*) $23,300

Problem 9-4B

Aging accounts receivable and accounting for bad debts

P1 P2 

Quisp Company has credit sales of $3.5 million for year 2005. On December 31, 2005, the company's Allowance for Doubtful Accounts has an unadjusted debit balance of $4,100. Quisp prepares a schedule of its December 31, 2005, accounts receivable by age. On the basis of past experience, it estimates the percent of receivables in each age category that will become uncollectible. This information is summarized here:

	A	B	C
1–2	**December 31, 2005 Accounts Receivable**	**Age of Accounts Receivable**	**Expected Percent Uncollectible**
3	$296,400	Not yet due	2.0%
4	177,800	1 to 30 days past due	4.0
5	58,000	31 to 60 days past due	8.5
6	7,600	61 to 90 days past due	39.0
7	3,700	Over 90 days past due	82.0
8			

Required

1. Compute the required balance of the Allowance for Doubtful Accounts at December 31, 2005, using the aging of accounts receivable method.

2. Prepare the adjusting entry to record bad debts expense at December 31, 2005.

Check (2) Dr. Bad Debts Expense $28,068

Analysis Component

3. On July 31, 2006, Quisp concludes that a customer's $2,345 receivable (created in 2005) is uncollectible and that the account should be written off. What effect will this action have on Quisp's 2006 net income? Explain.

Problem 9-5B
Analyzing and journalizing notes receivable transactions

C2 C3 P3 P4 

The following selected transactions are from Seeker Company:

2004

Nov.	1	Accepted a $4,800, 90-day, 8% note dated this day in granting Julie Stephens a time extension on her past-due account receivable.
Dec.	31	Made an adjusting entry to record the accrued interest on the Stephens note.

2005

Jan.	30	Received Stephens's payment for principal and interest on the note dated November 1.
Feb.	28	Accepted a $12,600, 6%, 30-day note dated this day in granting a time extension on the past-due account receivable from Kramer Co.
Mar.	1	Accepted a $6,200, 60-day, 8% note dated this day in granting Shelly Myers a time extension on her past-due account receivable.
	30	The Kramer Co. dishonored its note when presented for payment.
April	30	Received payment of principal plus interest from Myers for the March 1 note.
June	15	Accepted a $2,000, 60-day, 10% note dated this day in granting a time extension on the past-due account receivable of Rhonda Rye.
	21	Accepted a $9,500, 90-day, 12% note dated this day in granting Jack Striker a time extension on his past-due account receivable.
Aug.	14	Received payment of principal plus interest from R. Rye for the note of June 15.
Sep.	19	Received payment of principal plus interest from J. Striker for the June 21 note.
Nov.	30	Wrote off Kramer Co.'s account against Allowance for Doubtful Accounts.

Check Jan. 30, Cr. Interest Revenue $32

Check April 30, Cr. Interest Revenue $83

Check Sep. 19, Cr. Interest Revenue $285

Required

1. Prepare journal entries to record these transactions and events.

Analysis Component

2. What reporting is necessary when a business pledges receivables as security for a loan and the loan is still outstanding at the end of the period? Explain the reason for this requirement and the accounting principle being satisfied.

PROBLEM SET C

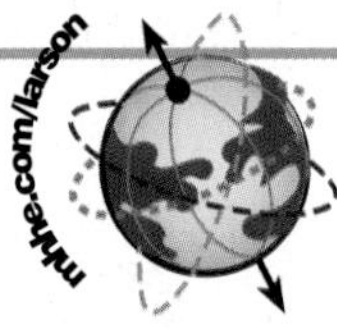

Problem Set C is available at the book's Website to further reinforce and assess your learning.

SERIAL PROBLEM

Success Systems

(This serial problem began in Chapter 1 and continues through most of the book. If previous chapter segments were not completed, the serial problem can begin at this point. It is helpful, but not necessary, that you use the Working Papers that accompany the book.)

Kay Breeze, owner of Success Systems, realizes that she needs to begin accounting for bad debts expense. Assume that Success Systems has total revenues of $43,853 during the first three months of 2005. The Accounts Receivable balance on March 31, 2005, is $22,720.

Required

1. Prepare the adjusting entry needed for Success Systems to recognize bad debts expense on March 31, 2005, under each of the following independent assumptions (assume a zero balance in the Allowance for Doubtful Accounts at March 31).

a. Bad debts are estimated to be 1% of total revenues.

b. Bad debts are estimated to be 2% of accounts receivable.

2. Assume that Success Systems' Accounts Receivable balance at June 30, 2005, is $20,250 and that one account of $100 has been written off against the Allowance for Doubtful Accounts since March 31, 2005. If Breeze uses the method prescribed in Part 1*b*, what adjusting journal entry must be made to recognize bad debts expense on June 30, 2005?

3. Should Breeze consider adopting the direct write-off method of accounting for bad debts expense rather than one of the allowance methods considered in part 1?

BEYOND THE NUMBERS

REPORTING IN ACTION

A1 

BTN 9-1 Refer to **Krispy Kreme**'s financial statements in Appendix A to answer the following:

1. What is the amount of its accounts receivable (net) on February 2, 2003?

2. Krispy Kreme's most liquid assets include (a) Cash and Cash Equivalents, (b) Short-Term Investments, (c) Accounts Receivable, (d) Accounts Receivable, Affiliates, and (e) Other Receivables. Compute the percent that liquid assets are of current liabilities as of February 2, 2003. Do the same for February 3, 2002. Comment on the company's ability to satisfy current liabilities at the end of the fiscal year 2003 as compared to the end of fiscal year 2002.

3. What criteria did Krispy Kreme's use to classify items as cash equivalents?

4. Compute Krispy Kreme's accounts receivable turnover as of February 2, 2003.

Roll On

5. Access Krispy Kreme's financial statements for fiscal years ending after February 2, 2003, at its Website (**KrispyKreme.com**) or the SEC's EDGAR database (**www.SEC.gov**). Recompute parts 2 and 4 and comment on any changes since February 2, 2003.

COMPARATIVE ANALYSIS

A1 P2 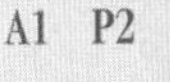

BTN 9-2 Key comparative figures ($ thousands) for both **Krispy Kreme** and **Tastykake** follow:

	Krispy Kreme			Tastykake		
Key Figures	Current Year	One-Year Prior	Two-Years Prior	Current Year	One-Year Prior	Two-Years Prior
Allowance for doubtful accounts	$ 1,453	$ 1,182	$ 1,302	$ 3,606	$ 3,752	$ 3,329
Accounts receivable, net	34,373	26,894	19,855	20,882	22,233	20,772
Net sales	491,549	394,354	300,715	162,263	166,245	162,877

Required

1. Compute the accounts receivable turnover for both Krispy Kreme and Tastykake for each of the two most recent years using the data shown.

2. Using results from part 1, compute how many days it takes each company, *on average,* to collect receivables.

Hint: Average collection period equals 365 divided by the accounts receivable turnover.

3. Which company is more efficient in collecting its accounts receivable?

4. Which company estimates a higher percent of uncollectible accounts receivable?

ETHICS CHALLENGE

P1 P2 

BTN 9-3 Kelly Steinman is the manager of a medium-size company. A few years ago, Steinman persuaded the owner to base a part of her compensation on the net income the company earns each year. Each December she estimates year-end financial figures in anticipation of the bonus she will receive. If the bonus is not as high as she would like, she offers several recommendations to the accountant for year-end adjustments. One of her favorite recommendations is for the controller to reduce the estimate of doubtful accounts.

Required

1. What effect does lowering the estimate for doubtful accounts have on the income statement and balance sheet?

2. Do you think Steinman's recommendation to adjust the allowance for doubtful accounts is within her right as manager, or do you think this action is an ethics violation? Justify your response.

3. What type of internal control(s) might be useful for this company in overseeing the manager's recommendations for accounting changes?

COMMUNICATING IN PRACTICE

P1 P2 

BTN 9-4 As the accountant for Pure-Air Distributing, you attend a sales managers' meeting devoted to a discussion of credit policies. At the meeting, you report that bad debts expense is estimated to be $59,000 and accounts receivable at year-end amount to $1,750,000 less a $43,000 allowance for doubtful accounts. Sid Omar, a sales manager, expresses confusion over why bad debts expense and the allowance for doubtful accounts are different amounts. Write a one-page memorandum to him explaining why a difference in bad debts expense and the allowance for doubtful accounts is not unusual. The company estimates bad debts expense as 2% of sales.

TAKING IT TO THE NET

C1

mhhe.com/larson

BTN 9-5 Access **Surg II, Inc.**'s, February 7, 2003, filing of its 10-KSB (small business 10-K) for the fiscal year-end of December 31, 2002 at www.SEC.gov.

Required

1. How does its accounts receivable balance for the fiscal year-end 2002 compare with its fiscal year-end 2001 balance?
2. What event accounts for its 2002 accounts receivable balance being zero?

TEAMWORK IN ACTION

P2

BTN 9-6 Each member of a team is to participate in estimating uncollectibles using the aging schedule and percents shown in Problem 9-4A. The division of labor is up to the team. Your goal is to accurately complete this task as soon as possible. After estimating uncollectibles, check your estimate with the instructor. If the estimate is correct, the team then should prepare the adjusting entry and the presentation of accounts receivable (net) for the December 31, 2005, balance sheet.

BUSINESS WEEK ACTIVITY

C1 P1

mhhe.com/larson

BTN 9-7 Read the article, "How Plastic Put **Sears** in a Pickle" in the October 30, 2002, issue of *Business Week*. (The book's Website provides a free link.)

Required

1. What two types of credit cards does Sears issue to its customers?
2. What is Sears' overall bad-debt charge-off rate as a percent of its receivables?
3. How many years does it usually take before a retailer's charge-off rates on new charge card programs peak?
4. What are the average balances carried by customers on the Sears MasterCard and on the Sears card? How do these balances compare to balances carried by consumers on general-purchase cards?

ENTREPRENEURIAL DECISION

BTN 9-8 The chapter's opening feature introduces Barbara Manzi and her business, **Manzi Metals**, a distributor of aluminum, steel, titanium, brass, and other alloys. Manzi Metals generates $3 million in annual sales. Assume that all sales are cash sales and that Manzi's net profit margin is 30%. Manzi's buyers would like to either use credit cards with their purchases or buy on credit. Therefore, Manzi has decided to pursue one of two plans (neither plan will impact cash sales nor alter current costs as a percent of sales):

Plan A. *Manzi accepts credit cards.* This plan is expected to yield new credit sales equal to 20% of current cash sales. Cost estimates of this plan as a percent of net credit sales are: credit card fee, 4.8%; recordkeeping, 1.2%.

Plan B. *Manzi grants credit directly to qualified buyers.* This plan is expected to yield new credit sales equal to 24% of current cash sales. Cost estimates of this plan as a percent of net credit sales are: uncollectibles, 6.7%; collection expenses, 1.3%; recordkeeping, 2.0%.

Required

Check (1b) Net income, $12,000

1. Compute the *added* monthly net income (loss) expected under (*a*) Plan A and (*b*) Plan B.
2. Should Manzi pursue either plan? Discuss the financial and nonfinancial factors relevant to this decision.

HITTING THE ROAD

C1 

BTN 9-9 Many commercials include comments similar to the following: "Bring your **VISA**" or "We do not accept **American Express**." Conduct your own research by contacting at least 5 companies via interviews, phone calls, or the Internet to determine the reason(s) companies discriminate in their use of credit cards. (The instructor may assign this as a team activity.)

GLOBAL DECISION

C1 P1

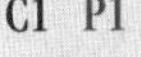

BTN 9-10 **Grupo Bimbo**, **Krispy Kreme**, and **Tastykake** are all competitors in the global marketplace. Review the Consolidated Balance Sheet for Grupo Bimbo for the year ended December 31, 2002, at GrupoBimbo.com.

Required

1. Contrast the presentation of the accounts receivable balance on the Grupo Bimbo balance sheet with that of both Krispy Kreme and Tastykake on their balance sheets in Appendix A.
2. As a potential investor in these companies, which presentation do you prefer: Grupo Bimbo's or that of Krispy Kreme and Tastykake? Explain.

"There are well over 2 million Hispanic owned businesses in the U.S. today"—Tina Cordova

10 Plant Assets, Natural Resources, and Intangibles

A Look Back

Chapters 8 and 9 focused on short-term assets: cash, cash equivalents, and receivables. We explained why they are known as liquid assets and described how companies account and report for them.

A Look at This Chapter

This chapter introduces us to long-term assets, including plant assets, natural resource assets, and intangible assets. We explain how to account for a long-term asset's cost, the allocation of an asset's cost to periods benefiting from it, the recording of additional costs after an asset is purchased, and the disposal of an asset.

A Look Ahead

Chapter 11 focuses on current liabilities. We explain how they are computed, recorded, and reported in financial statements. We also explain the accounting for payroll and contingencies.

Learning Objectives

CAP

Conceptual

C1 Describe plant assets and issues in accounting for them. *(p. 382)*

C2 Explain depreciation and the factors affecting its computation. *(p. 385)*

C3 Explain depreciation for partial years and changes in estimates. *(p. 390)*

Analytical

A1 Compare and analyze alternative depreciation methods. *(p. 389)*

A2 Compute total asset turnover and apply it to analyze a company's use of assets. *(p. 401)*

Procedural

P1 Apply the cost principle to compute the cost of plant assets. *(p. 383)*

P2 Compute and record depreciation using the straight-line, units-of-production, and declining-balance methods. *(p. 386)*

P3 Distinguish between revenue and capital expenditures, and account for them. *(p. 392)*

P4 Account for asset disposal through discarding, selling, and exchanging an asset. *(p. 394)*

P5 Account for natural resource assets and their depletion. *(p. 397)*

P6 Account for intangible assets. *(p. 398)*

Decision Feature

Climbing the Ladder

ALBUQUERQUE—Tina Cordova attended medical school and dreamed of being a doctor, but life had other plans. She found herself divorced with a child to support. Life became about survival. Cordova waited tables but something inside told her life had more to offer.

With her life savings of $5,000, she launched **Queston Construction**, a company devoted to roofing and commercial construction. When Cordova sat for the contractor's license exam, she was the only woman among more than 100 men. "Not one of them was particularly glad to see me," she laughs. Cordova soon found herself working with a crew of two men while removing old roofing, laying new roofing, and driving the dump truck. "I figured that the worst thing that could happen was that I'd have to go back to working for someone else," says Cordova. Her first-year sales of $50,000 was meager but enough to continue.

Today, Cordova oversees a crew of 28—swelling to 40 during high season—and reports annual sales of more than $3 million. One of her greatest challenges is maintaining the right kind, size, and amount of plant assets necessary to maintain her business. Cordova says that maintaining a strong sales to assets ratio is crucial. This includes monitoring and controlling asset costs ranging from expensive construction equipment and trucks to building and land costs. To be successful, Cordova's sales must cover these plant asset costs as well as yield a return adequate to pay other expenses and meet income goals. This chapter focuses on these and other crucial issues related to long-term assets. Cordova says that effective acquisition, use, and disposal of long-term assets are keys to business success.

Cordova doesn't look back at her dreams and what might have been. "Never in a million years," insists Cordova. "I have found my place." That place is at the top of the ladder.

[Sources: *Hispanic Magazine*, April 2003; *Small Business Association Website*, October 2002; *House of Representatives Committee on Small Business*, August 2001.]

This chapter focuses on long-term assets used to operate a company. These assets can be grouped into plant assets, natural resource assets, and intangible assets. Plant assets are a major investment for most companies. They make up a large part of assets on most balance sheets, and they yield depreciation, often one of the largest expenses on income statements. The acquisition or building of a plant asset is often referred to as a *capital expenditure.* Capital expenditures are important events because they impact both the short- and long-term success of a company. Natural resource assets and intangible assets have similar impacts. This chapter describes the purchase and use of these assets. We also explain what distinguishes these assets from other types of assets, how to determine their cost, how to allocate their costs to periods benefiting from their use, and how to dispose of them.

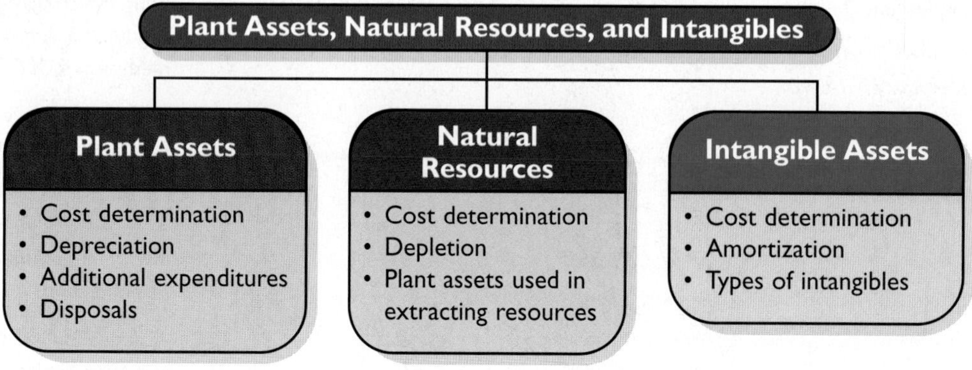

Section 1—Plant Assets

Plant assets are tangible assets used in a company's operations that have a useful life of more than one accounting period. Plant assets are also called *plant and equipment; property, plant, and equipment;* or *fixed assets.* For many companies, plant assets make up the single largest class of assets they own. Exhibit 10.1 shows plant assets as a percent of total assets for several companies. Not only do they make up a large percent of these companies' assets but also their dollar values are large. **McDonald's** plant assets, for instance, are reported at more than $18 billion, and **Wal-Mart** reports plant assets of more than $48 billion.

Exhibit 10.1

Plant Assets of Selected Companies

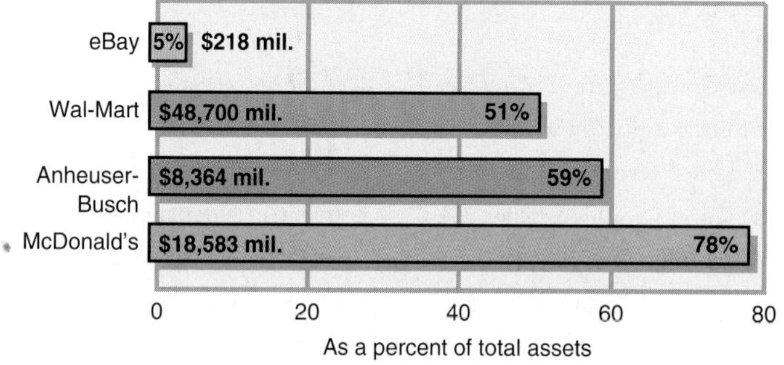

C1 Describe plant assets and issues in accounting for them.

Plant assets are set apart from other assets by two important features. First, *plant assets are used in operations.* This makes them different from, for instance, inventory that is held for sale and not used in operations. The distinctive feature here is use, not type of asset. A company that purchases a computer to resell it, reports it on the balance sheet as inventory. If the same company purchases this computer to use in operations, however, it is a plant asset. Another example is land held for future expansion, which is reported as a long-term investment. However, if this land holds a factory used in operations, the land is part of plant assets. Another example is equipment held for use in the event of a breakdown or for peak periods of production, which is reported in plant assets. If this same equipment is removed from use and held for sale, however, it is not reported in plant assets.

Point: Amazon.com's plant assets of $239 million make up 12% of its total assets.

The second important feature is that *plant assets have useful lives extending over more than one accounting period.* This makes plant assets different from current assets such as supplies that are normally consumed in a short time period after they are placed in use.

The accounting for plant assets reflects these two features. Since plant assets are used in operations, we try to match their costs against the revenues they generate. Also, since their useful lives extend over more than one period, our matching of costs and revenues must extend over several periods. Specifically, we value plant assets (balance sheet effect) and then allocate their costs to periods benefiting from their use (income statement effect).

Point: It can help to view plant assets as prepaid expenses that benefit several future accounting periods.

Exhibit 10.2 shows four main issues in accounting for plant assets: (1) computing the costs of plant assets, (2) allocating the costs of plant assets (less any salvage amounts) against revenues for the periods they benefit, (3) accounting for expenditures such as repairs and improvements to plant assets, and (4) recording the disposal of plant assets. The following sections discuss these issues.

Topic Tackler 10-1

Exhibit 10.2

Issues in Accounting for Plant Assets

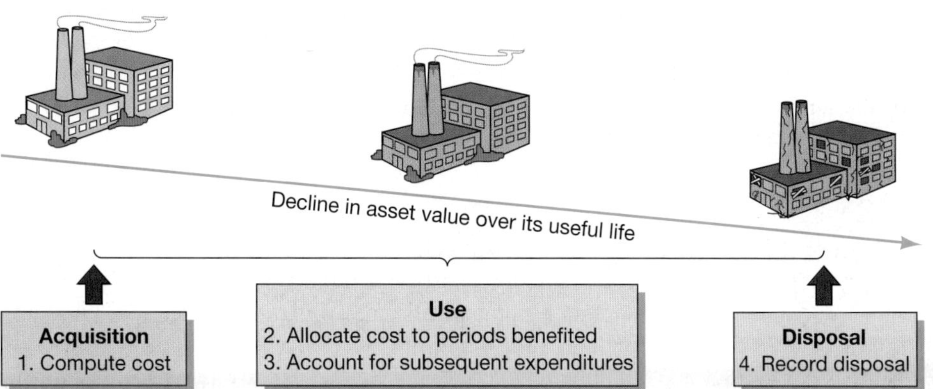

Cost Determination

Plant assets are recorded at cost when acquired. This is consistent with the *cost principle.* **Cost** includes all normal and reasonable expenditures necessary to get the asset in place and ready for its intended use. The cost of a factory machine, for instance, includes its invoice cost less any cash discount for early payment, plus any necessary freight, unpacking, assembling, installing, and testing costs. Examples are the costs of building a base or foundation for a machine, providing electrical hook-ups, and testing the asset before using it in operations.

To be recorded as part of the cost of a plant asset, an expenditure must be normal, reasonable, and necessary in preparing it for its intended use. If an asset is damaged during unpacking, the repairs are not added to its cost. Instead, they are charged to an expense account. Nor is a paid traffic fine for moving heavy machinery on city streets without a proper permit part of the machinery's cost; but payment for a proper permit is included in the cost of machinery. Charges are sometimes incurred to modify or customize a new plant asset. These charges are added to the asset's cost. We explain in this section how to determine the cost of plant assets for each of its four major classes.

Global: International accounting standards encourage use of the cost principle for plant assets. Plant asset revaluation is permitted if it is consistently applied across periods.

Land

P1 Apply the cost principle to compute the cost of plant assets.

When land is purchased for a building site, its cost includes the total amount paid for the land, including any real estate commissions, title insurance fees, legal fees, and any accrued property taxes paid by the purchaser. Payments for surveying, clearing, grading, and draining also are included in the cost of land. Other costs include government assessments, whether incurred at the time of purchase or later, for items such as public roadways, sewers, and sidewalks. These assessments are included because they permanently add to the land's value. Land purchased as a building site sometimes includes structures that must be removed. In such cases, the total purchase price is charged to the Land account as is the cost of removing the structures, less any amounts recovered through sale of salvaged materials. To illustrate, assume the **Hockey Co.** paid $167,000 cash to acquire land for a retail

Exhibit 10.3

Computing Cost of Land

Cash price of land	$ 167,000
Net cost of garage removal	13,000
Closing costs	10,000
Cost of land	**$190,000**

store. This land had an old service garage that was removed at a net cost of $13,000 ($15,000 in costs less $2,000 proceeds from salvaged materials). Additional closing costs total $10,000, consisting of brokerage fees ($8,000), legal fees ($1,500), and title costs ($500). The cost of this land to Hockey Co. is $190,000 and is computed as shown in Exhibit 10.3.

Land Improvements

Land has an unlimited life and is not usually used up over time. **Land improvements** such as parking lot surfaces, driveways, fences, shrubs, and lighting systems, however, have limited useful lives and are used up. While the costs of these improvements increase the usefulness of the land, they are charged to a separate Land Improvement account so that their costs can be allocated to the periods they benefit.

Buildings

A Building account is charged for the costs of purchasing or constructing a building that is used in operations. When purchased, a building's costs usually include its purchase price, brokerage fees, taxes, title fees, and attorney fees. Its costs also include all expenditures to ready it for its intended use, including any necessary repairs or renovations such as wiring, lighting, flooring, and wall coverings. When a company constructs a building or any plant asset for its own use, its costs include materials and labor plus a reasonable amount of indirect overhead cost. Overhead includes the costs of items such as heat, lighting, power, and depreciation on machinery used to construct the asset. Costs of construction also include design fees, building permits, and insurance during construction. However, costs such as insurance to cover the asset *after* it is placed in use are operating expenses.

Machinery and Equipment

The costs of machinery and equipment consist of all costs normal and necessary to purchase them and prepare them for their intended use. These include the purchase price, taxes, transportation charges, insurance while in transit, and the installing, assembling, and testing of the machinery and equipment.

Example: If appraised values in Exhibit 10.4 are land, $24,000; land improvements, $12,000; and building, $84,000, what cost is assigned to the building? *Answer:*
(1) $24,000 + $12,000 + $84,000 = $120,000 (total appraisal)
(2) $84,000/$120,000 = 70% (building's percent of total)
(3) 70% × $90,000 = $63,000 (building's apportioned cost)

Lump-Sum Purchase

Plant assets sometimes are purchased as a group in a single transaction for a lump-sum price. This transaction is called a *lump-sum purchase,* or *group, bulk,* or *basket purchase.* When this occurs, we allocate the cost of the purchase among the different types of assets acquired based on their *relative market values,* which can be estimated by appraisal or by using the tax-assessed valuations of the assets. To illustrate, Oakley paid $90,000 cash to acquire a group of items consisting of land appraised at $30,000, land improvements appraised at $10,000, and a building appraised at $60,000. The $90,000 cost is allocated on the basis of these appraised values as shown in Exhibit 10.4.

Exhibit 10.4

Computing Costs in a Lump-Sum Purchase

	Appraised Value	Percent of Total	Apportioned Cost
Land	$ 30,000	30% ($30,000/$100,000)	**$27,000** ($90,000 × 30%)
Land improvements	10,000	10 ($10,000/$100,000)	**9,000** ($90,000 × 10%)
Building	60,000	60 ($60,000/$100,000)	**54,000** ($90,000 × 60%)
Totals	$100,000	100%	$ 90,000

Quick Check

1. Identify the asset class for each of the following: (*a*) supplies, (*b*) office equipment, (*c*) inventory, (*d*) land for future expansion, and (*e*) trucks used in operations.
2. Identify the account charged for each of the following: (*a*) purchase price of a vacant lot to be used in operations and (*b*) cost of paving that same vacant lot.
3. Calculate the amount recorded as the cost of a new machine given the following payments related to its purchase: gross purchase price, $700,000; sales tax, $49,000; purchase discount taken, $21,000; freight cost—terms FOB shipping point, $3,500; normal assembly costs, $3,000; cost of necessary foundation for machine, $2,500; cost of parts used in maintaining the machine, $4,200.

Answers—p. 406

Depreciation

Depreciation is the process of allocating the cost of a plant asset to expense in the accounting periods benefiting from its use. Depreciation does not measure the decline in the asset's market value each period, nor does it measure the asset's physical deterioration. Since depreciation reflects the cost of using a plant asset, depreciation charges are only recorded when the asset is actually in service. This section describes the factors we must consider in computing depreciation, the depreciation methods used, revisions in depreciation, and depreciation for partial periods.

Topic Tackler 10-2

Factors in Computing Depreciation

Factors that determine depreciation are (1) cost, (2) salvage value, and (3) useful life.

C2 Explain depreciation and the factors affecting its computation.

Cost The **cost** of a plant asset consists of all necessary and reasonable expenditures to acquire it and to prepare it for its intended use.

Salvage Value The total amount of depreciation to be charged off over an asset's benefit period equals the asset's cost minus its salvage value. **Salvage value,** also called *residual value* or *scrap value,* is an estimate of the asset's value at the end of its benefit period. This is the amount the owner expects to receive from disposing the asset at the end of its benefit period. If the asset is expected to be traded in on a new asset, its salvage value is the expected trade-in value.

Point: If we expect additional costs in preparing a plant asset for disposal, the salvage value equals the expected amount from disposal less any disposal costs.

Useful Life The **useful life** of a plant asset is the length of time it is productively used in a company's operations. Useful life, also called *service life,* might not be as long as the asset's total productive life. For example, the productive life of a computer can be eight years or more. Some companies, however, trade in old computers for new ones every two years. In this case, these computers have a two-year useful life, meaning the cost of these computers (less their expected trade-in values) is charged to depreciation expense over a two-year period.

Point: Useful life and salvage value are estimates. Estimates require judgment based on consideration of all available information.

Several variables often make the useful life of a plant asset difficult to predict. A major variable is the wear and tear from use in operations. Two other variables, inadequacy and obsolescence, also demand consideration. **Inadequacy** refers to the insufficient capacity of a company's plant assets to meet its growing productive demands. **Obsolescence** refers to a plant asset that is no longer useful in producing goods or services with a competitive advantage because of new inventions and improvements. Both inadequacy and obsolescence

Decision Insight

Life Line Life expectancy of plant assets is often in the eye of the beholder. For instance, **Converse** and **Stride Rite** are competitors, yet their buildings' life expectancies are quite different. Converse depreciates buildings over 5 to 10 years, but Stride Rite depreciates them over 10 to 40 years. Such differences markedly impact financial statements.

Global: While U.S. accounting must consider inadequacy and obsolescence in estimating useful life, the accounting in many other countries does not.

are difficult to predict because of demand changes, new inventions, and improvements. A company usually disposes of an inadequate or obsolete asset before it wears out.

A company is often able to better predict a new asset's useful life when it has past experience with a similar asset. When it has no such experience, a company relies on the experience of others or on engineering studies and judgment. In note 1 of its annual report, **Brunswick**, a manufacturer of boats and motors, reports the following useful lives:

Estimated useful lives of buildings and equipment;	
Buildings	5–40 years
Equipment	2–20 years

Depreciation Methods

Depreciation methods are used to allocate a plant asset's cost over the accounting periods in its useful life. The most frequently used method of depreciation is the straight-line method. Another common depreciation method is the units-of-production method. We explain both of these methods in this section. This section also describes accelerated depreciation methods, with a focus on the declining-balance method.

The computations in this section use information about a machine that inspects athletic shoes before packaging. Manufacturers such as **Converse**, **Reebok**, **Adidas**, and **Fila** use this machine. Data for this machine are in Exhibit 10.5.

Exhibit 10.5

Data for Athletic Shoe-Inspecting Machine

Cost	$10,000
Salvage value	1,000
Depreciable cost	$ 9,000
Useful life	
Accounting periods	5 years
Units inspected	36,000 shoes

P2 Compute and record depreciation using the straight-line, units-of-production, and declining-balance methods.

Straight-Line Method **Straight-line depreciation** charges the same amount of expense to each period of the asset's useful life. A two-step process is used. We first compute the *depreciable cost* of the asset; this amount is also called the *cost to be depreciated.* It is computed by subtracting the asset's salvage value from its total cost. Second, depreciable cost is divided by the number of accounting periods in the asset's useful life. The formula for straight-line depreciation, along with its computation for the inspection machine described above, is shown in Exhibit 10.6.

Exhibit 10.6

Straight-Line Depreciation Formula and Example

$$\frac{\textbf{Cost} - \textbf{Salvage value}}{\textbf{Useful life in periods}} = \frac{\$10{,}000 - \$1{,}000}{5 \text{ years}} = \$1{,}800 \text{ per year}$$

If this machine is purchased on December 31, 2003, and used throughout its predicted useful life of five years, the straight-line method allocates an equal amount of depreciation to each of the years 2004 through 2008. We make the following adjusting entry at the end of each of the five years to record straight-line depreciation of this machine:

Dec. 31	Depreciation Expense	1,800	
	Accumulated Depreciation—Machinery.		1,800
	To record annual depreciation.		

Assets = Liabilities + Equity
−1,800 −1,800

Example: If salvage value of the machine is estimated to be $2,500, what is the annual depreciation expense? *Answer:* ($10,000 − $2,500)/5 years = $1,500

The $1,800 Depreciation Expense is reported on the income statement among operating expenses. The $1,800 Accumulated Depreciation is a contra asset account to the Machinery account in the balance sheet. The graph on the left in Exhibit 10.7 shows the $1,800 per year expenses reported in each of the five years. The graph on the right shows the amounts reported on each of the six December 31 balance sheets while the company owns the asset.

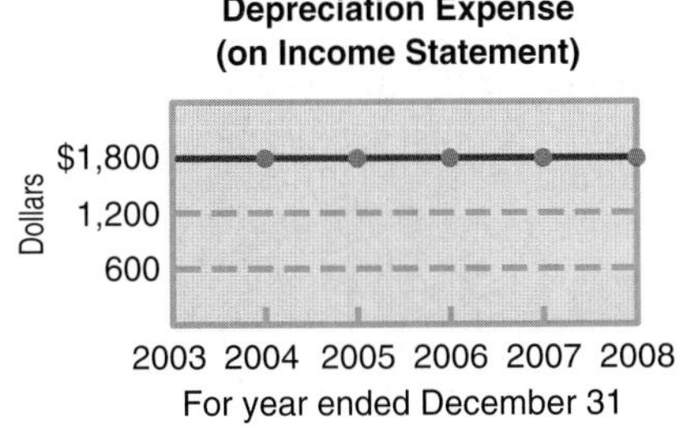

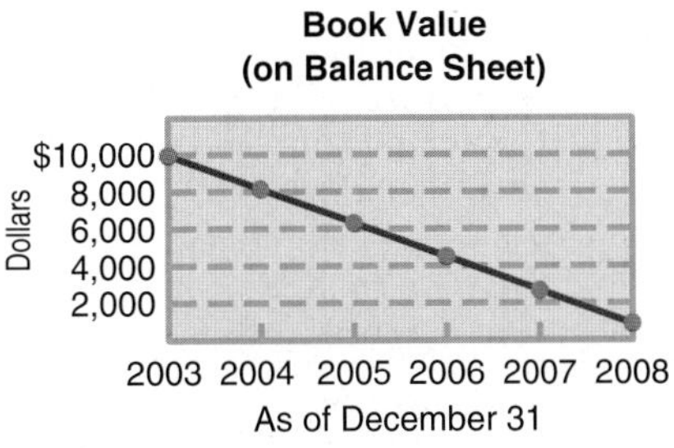

Exhibit 10.7

Financial Statement Effects of Straight-Line Depreciation

The net balance sheet amount is the asset's **book value** and is computed as the asset's total cost less its accumulated depreciation. For example, at the end of year 2 (December 31, 2005), its book value is $6,400 and is reported in the balance sheet as follows:

Machinery	$10,000	
Less accumulated depreciation	3,600	$6,400

The book value of this machine declines by $1,800 each year due to depreciation. From the graphs in Exhibit 10.7 we can see why this method is called straight line.

We also can compute the *straight-line depreciation rate,* defined as 100% divided by the number of periods in the asset's useful life. For the inspection machine, this rate is 20% (100% ÷ 5 years). We use this rate, along with other information, to compute the machine's *straight-line depreciation schedule* shown in Exhibit 10.8. Note three points in Exhibit 10.8. First, depreciation expense is the same each period. Second, accumulated depreciation is the sum of current and prior periods' depreciation expense. Third, book value declines each period until it equals salvage value at the end of the machine's useful life.

Point: Depreciation requires estimates for salvage value and useful life. Decision ethics are relevant when managers might be tempted to choose estimates to achieve desired results on financial statements.

Exhibit 10.8

Straight-Line Depreciation Schedule

	Depreciation for the Period			End of Period	
Annual Period	Depreciable Cost*	Depreciation Rate	Depreciation Expense	Accumulated Depreciation	Book Value†
2003	—	—	—	—	$10,000
2004	$9,000	20%	**$1,800**	$1,800	8,200
2005	9,000	20	**1,800**	3,600	6,400
2006	9,000	20	**1,800**	5,400	4,600
2007	9,000	20	**1,800**	7,200	2,800
2008	9,000	20	**1,800**	9,000	**1,000**

* $10,000 − $1,000. † Book value is total cost minus accumulated depreciation.

Units-of-Production Method The straight-line method charges an equal share of an asset's cost to each period. If plant assets are used up in about equal amounts each accounting period, this method produces a reasonable matching of expenses with revenues. However, the use of some plant assets varies greatly from one period to the next. A builder, for instance, might use a piece of construction equipment for a month and then not use it again for several months. When equipment use varies from period to period, the units-of-production depreciation method can better match expenses with revenues. **Units-of-production depreciation** charges a varying amount to expense for each period of an asset's useful life depending on its usage.

A two-step process is used to compute units-of-production depreciation. We first compute *depreciation per unit* by subtracting the asset's salvage value from its total cost and then dividing by the total number of units expected to be produced during its useful life. Units of production can be expressed in product or other units such as hours used or miles driven. The second step is to compute depreciation expense for the period by multiplying the units produced in the period by the depreciation per unit. The formula for units-of-production depreciation, along with its computation for the machine described in Exhibit 10.5, is shown in Exhibit 10.9. (*Note:* 7,000 shoes are inspected and sold in its first year.)

Exhibit 10.9

Units-of-Production Depreciation Formula and Example

Step 1

$$\textbf{Depreciation per unit} = \frac{\textbf{Cost} - \textbf{Salvage value}}{\textbf{Total units of production}} = \frac{\$10{,}000 - \$1{,}000}{36{,}000 \text{ shoes}} = \$0.25 \text{ per shoe}$$

Step 2

$$\textbf{Depreciation expense} = \textbf{Depreciation per unit} \times \textbf{Units produced in period}$$

$$\$0.25 \text{ per shoe} \times 7{,}000 \text{ shoes} = \$1{,}750$$

Using data on the number of shoes inspected by the machine, we can compute the *units-of-production depreciation schedule* shown in Exhibit 10.10. For example, depreciation for the first year is $1,750 (7,000 shoes at $0.25 per shoe). Depreciation for the second year is $2,000 (8,000 shoes at $0.25 per shoe). Other years are similarly computed. Notice in Exhibit 10.10 that (1) depreciation expense depends on unit output, (2) accumulated depreciation is the sum of current and prior periods' depreciation expense, and (3) book value declines each period until it equals salvage value at the end of the asset's useful life. **Boise Cascade** is one of many companies using the units-of-production depreciation method. It reports that most of its "paper and wood products manufacturing facilities determine depreciation by a units-of-production method."

Example: Refer to Exhibit 10.10. If the number of shoes inspected in 2008 is 5,500, what is depreciation expense for that year?
Answer: $1,250 (never depreciate below salvage value)

Exhibit 10.10

Units-of-Production Depreciation Schedule

	Depreciation for the Period			End of Period	
Annual Period	**Number of Units**	**Depreciation per Unit**	**Depreciation Expense**	**Accumulated Depreciation**	**Book Value**
2003	—	—	—	—	$10,000
2004	7,000	$0.25	**$1,750**	$1,750	8,250
2005	8,000	0.25	**2,000**	3,750	6,250
2006	9,000	0.25	**2,250**	6,000	4,000
2007	7,000	0.25	**1,750**	7,750	2,250
2008	5,000	0.25	**1,250**	9,000	**1,000**

Declining-Balance Method An **accelerated depreciation method** yields larger depreciation expenses in the early years of an asset's life and less depreciation in later years. Of several accelerated methods, the most common is the **declining-balance method** of depreciation, which uses a depreciation rate that is a multiple of the straight-line rate and applies it to the asset's beginning-of-period book value. The amount of depreciation declines each period because book value declines each period.

Global: German firms commonly apply accelerated depreciation of up to three times the straight-line rate.

Point: In the DDB method, *double* refers to the rate and *declining balance* refers to book value. The rate is applied to beginning book value each period.

A common depreciation rate for the declining-balance method is double the straight-line rate. This is called the *double-declining-balance* (*DDB*) method. This method is applied in three steps: (1) compute the asset's straight-line depreciation rate, (2) double the straight-line rate, and (3) compute depreciation expense by multiplying this rate by the asset's beginning-of-period book value. To illustrate, let's return to the machine in Exhibit 10.5 and apply the double-declining-balance method to compute depreciation expense. Exhibit 10.11 shows the first-year depreciation computation for the machine. The three-step process is to (1) divide 100% by five years to determine the straight-line rate of 20% per year, (2) double this 20% rate to get the declining-balance rate of 40% per year, and (3) compute depreciation expense as 40% multiplied by the beginning-of-period book value.

Exhibit 10.11

Double-Declining-Balance Depreciation Formula

Step 1

Straight-line rate = 100% ÷ Useful life = 100% ÷ 5 years = 20%

Step 2

Double-declining-balance rate = 2 × Straight-line rate = 2 × 20% = 40%

Step 3

Depreciation expense = Double-declining-balance rate × Beginning-period book value

40% × $10,000 = $4,000 (for 2004)

The *double-declining-balance depreciation schedule* is shown in Exhibit 10.12. The schedule follows the formula except for year 2008, when depreciation expense is $296. This $296 is not equal to 40% × $1,296, or $518.40. If we had used the $518.40 for depreciation expense in 2008, ending book value would equal $777.60, which is less than the $1,000 salvage value. Instead, the $296 is computed by subtracting the $1,000 salvage value from the $1,296 book value at the beginning of the fifth year (the year when DDB depreciation cuts into salvage value).

Example: What is DDB depreciation expense in year 2007 if the salvage value is $2,000?
Answer: $2,160 − $2,000 = $160

Exhibit 10.12

Double-Declining-Balance Depreciation Schedule

	Depreciation for the Period			End of Period	
Annual Period	Beginning of Period Book Value	Depreciation Rate	Depreciation Expense	Accumulated Depreciation	Book Value
2003	—	—	—	—	$10,000
2004	$10,000	40%	**$4,000**	$4,000	6,000
2005	6,000	40	**2,400**	6,400	3,600
2006	3,600	40	**1,440**	7,840	2,160
2007	2,160	40	**864**	8,704	1,296
2008	1,296	40	**296***	9,000	**1,000**

* Year 2008 depreciation is $1,296 − $1,000 = $296 (never depreciate book value below salvage value).

Comparing Depreciation Methods Exhibit 10.13 shows depreciation expense for each year of the machine's useful life under each of the three depreciation methods.

A1 Compare and analyze alternative depreciation methods.

Exhibit 10.13

Depreciation Expense for the Different Methods

Period	Straight-Line	Units-of-Production	Double-Declining-Balance
2004	$1,800	$1,750	$4,000
2005	1,800	2,000	2,400
2006	1,800	2,250	1,440
2007	1,800	1,750	864
2008	1,800	1,250	296
Totals	$9,000	$9,000	$9,000

While the amount of depreciation expense per period differs for different methods, total depreciation expense is the same over the machine's useful life. Each method starts with a total cost of $10,000 and ends with a salvage value of $1,000. The difference is the pattern

Global: Some Canadian companies use an "increasing charge" depreciation (the opposite of accelerated).

Decision Insight

Vogue About 83% of companies use straight-line depreciation for plant assets, 5% use units-of-production, and 4% use declining-balance. Another 8% use an unspecified accelerated method—most likely declining-balance.

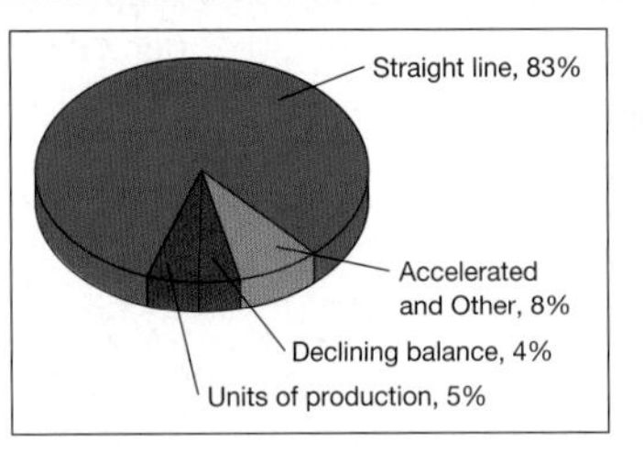

in depreciation expense over the useful life. The book value of the asset when using straight-line is always greater than the book value from using double-declining-balance, except at the beginning and end of the asset's useful life, when it is the same. Also, the straight-line method yields a steady pattern of depreciation expense while the units-of-production depreciation depends on the number of units produced. Each of these methods is acceptable because it allocates cost in a systematic and rational manner.

Depreciation for Tax Reporting The records a company keeps for financial accounting purposes are usually separate from the records it keeps for tax accounting purposes. This is so because financial accounting aims to report useful information on financial performance and position, whereas tax accounting reflects government objectives in raising revenues. Differences between these two accounting systems are normal and expected. Depreciation is a common example of how the records differ. For example, many companies use accelerated depreciation in computing taxable income. Reporting higher depreciation expense in the early years of an asset's life reduces the company's taxable income in those years and increases it in later years, when the depreciation expense is lower. The company's goal here is to *postpone* its tax payments. This means the company can use these resources now to earn additional income before payment is due.

Point: Understanding depreciation for financial accounting will help in learning MACRS for tax accounting. Rules for MACRS are available from www.IRS.com.

Global: A few countries require the depreciation method chosen for financial reporting to match the method chosen for tax reporting.

The U.S. federal income tax law has rules for depreciating assets. These rules include the **Modified Accelerated Cost Recovery System (MACRS),** which allows straight-line depreciation for some assets, but it requires accelerated depreciation for most kinds of assets. MACRS separates depreciable assets into different classes and defines the depreciable life and rate for each class. MACRS is not acceptable for financial reporting because it often allocates costs over an arbitrary period that is less than the asset's useful life. Details of MACRS are covered in tax accounting courses.

Decision Insight

Instant Numbers Computer technology greatly simplifies depreciation computations and revisions. Many inexpensive, off-the-shelf software packages and business calculators allow a user to choose from a variety of depreciation methods and quickly produce depreciation schedules.

Partial-Year Depreciation

C3 Explain depreciation for partial years and changes in estimates.

Plant assets are purchased and disposed of at various times. When an asset is purchased (or disposed of) at a time other than the beginning or end of an accounting period, depreciation is recorded for part of a year. This is done so that the year of purchase or the year of disposal is charged with its share of the asset's depreciation.

To illustrate, assume that the machine in Exhibit 10.5 is purchased and placed in service on October 8, 2003, and the annual accounting period ends on December 31. Since this machine is purchased and used for nearly three months in 2003, the calendar-year income statement should report depreciation expense on the machine for that part of the year. Normally, depreciation assumes that the asset is purchased on the first day of the month nearest the actual date of purchase. In this case, since the purchase occurred on October 8, we assume an October 1 purchase date. This means that three months' depreciation is recorded in 2003. Using straight-line depreciation, we compute three months' depreciation of $450 as follows:

$$\frac{\$10{,}000 - \$1{,}000}{5 \text{ years}} \times \frac{3}{12} = \$450$$

Example: If the machine's salvage value is zero and purchase occurs on Oct. 8, 2003, how much depreciation is recorded at Dec. 31, 2003?
Answer: $10,000/5 × 3/12 = $500

A similar computation is necessary when an asset disposal occurs during a period. To illustrate, assume that the machine is sold on June 24, 2008. Depreciation is recorded for the period January 1 through June 24 when it is disposed of. This partial year's depreciation, computed to the nearest whole month, is

$$\frac{\$10{,}000 - \$1{,}000}{5 \text{ years}} \times \frac{6}{12} = \$900$$

Change in Estimates for Depreciation

Depreciation is based on estimates of salvage value and useful life. During the useful life of an asset, new information may indicate that these estimates are inaccurate. If our estimate of an asset's useful life and/or salvage value changes, what should we do? The answer is to use the new estimate to compute depreciation for current and future periods. This means that we revise the depreciation expense computation by spreading the cost yet to be depreciated over the remaining useful life. This approach is used for all depreciation methods.

Point: Remaining depreciable cost equals book value less revised salvage value at the point of revision.

Let's return to the machine described in Exhibit 10.8 using straight-line depreciation. At the beginning of this asset's third year, its book value is $6,400, computed as $10,000 minus $3,600. Assume that at the beginning of its third year, the estimated number of years remaining in its useful life changes from three to four years *and* its estimate of salvage value changes from $1,000 to $400. Straight-line depreciation for each of the four remaining years is computed as shown in Exhibit 10.14.

Point: Income is overstated (and depreciation understated) when useful life is too high; a useful life that is too low yields opposite results.

Exhibit 10.14

Computing Revised Straight-Line Depreciation

$$\frac{\textbf{Book value} - \textbf{Revised salvage value}}{\textbf{Revised remaining useful life}} = \frac{\$6{,}400 - \$400}{4 \text{ years}} = \$1{,}500 \text{ per year}$$

Thus, $1,500 of depreciation expense is recorded for the machine at the end of the third through sixth years—each year of its remaining useful life. Since this asset was depreciated at $1,800 per year for the first two years, it is tempting to conclude that depreciation expense was overstated in the first two years. However, these expenses reflected the best information available at that time. We do not go back and restate prior years' financial statements for this type of new information. Instead, we adjust the current and future periods' statements to reflect this new information. Revising an estimate of the useful life or salvage value of a plant asset is referred to as a **change in an accounting estimate** and is reflected in current and future financial statements, not in prior statements.

Example: If at the beginning of its second year the machine's remaining useful life changes from four to three years and salvage value from $1,000 to $400, how much straight-line depreciation is recorded in remaining years? *Answer:* Revised depreciation = ($8,200 − $400)/3 = $2,600.

Reporting Depreciation

Both the cost and accumulated depreciation of plant assets are reported on the balance sheet or in its notes. **Titan Motorcycle**, for instance, reports the following:

Property and equipment:	
Land, building, and vehicles	$ 689,748
Machinery and equipment	1,116,318
Displays and leasehold improvements	837,414
Gross property and equipment	2,643,480
Less accumulated depreciation	629,575
Net property and equipment	$2,013,905

Many companies also show plant assets on one line with the net amount of cost less accumulated depreciation. When this is done, the amount of accumulated depreciation is disclosed in a note. **Krispy Kreme** reports only the net amount of its property and equipment in its balance sheet in Appendix A. To satisfy the full-disclosure principle, Krispy Kreme describes its depreciation methods in its Note 2 and the amounts comprising plant assets in its Note 5.

Point: A company usually keeps records for each asset showing its cost and depreciation to date. The combined records for individual assets are a type of *plant asset subsidiary ledger.*

Reporting both the cost and accumulated depreciation of plant assets helps users compare the assets of different companies. For example, a company holding assets costing $50,000 and accumulated depreciation of $40,000 is likely in a situation different from a company

Decision Ethics

Controller You are the controller for a struggling company. Its operations require regular investments in equipment, and depreciation is its largest expense. Its competitors frequently replace equipment—often depreciated over three years. The company president instructs you to revise useful lives of equipment from three to six years and to use a six-year life on all new equipment. What actions do you take?

Answer—p. 406

with new assets costing $10,000. While the net undepreciated cost of $10,000 is the same in both cases, the first company may have more productive capacity available but likely is facing the need to replace older assets. These insights are not provided if the two balance sheets report only the $10,000 book values.

Users must remember that plant assets are reported on a balance sheet at their undepreciated costs (book value), not at market values. This emphasis on costs rather than market values is based on the *going-concern principle* described in Chapter 1. This principle states that, unless there is evidence to the contrary, we assume that a company continues in business. This implies that plant assets are held and used long enough to recover their cost through the sale of products and services. Since plant assets are not for sale, their market values are not reported.

Point: Depreciation is higher and income lower in the short run when using accelerated versus straight-line methods.

Accumulated Depreciation is a contra asset account with a normal credit balance. It does *not* reflect funds accumulated to buy new assets when the assets currently owned are replaced. If a company has funds available to buy assets, the funds are shown on the balance sheet among liquid assets such as Cash or Investments.

Quick Check

4. On January 1, 2005, a company pays $77,000 to purchase office furniture with a zero salvage value. The furniture's useful life is somewhere between 7 and 10 years. What is the year 2005 straight-line depreciation on the furniture using (*a*) a 7-year useful life and (*b*) a 10-year useful life?
5. What does the term *depreciation* mean in accounting?
6. A company purchases a machine for $96,000 on January 1, 2005. Its useful life is five years or 100,000 units of product, and its salvage value is $8,000. During 2005, 10,000 units of product are produced. Compute the book value of this machine on December 31, 2005, assuming (*a*) straight-line depreciation and (*b*) units-of-production depreciation.
7. In early January 2005, a company acquires equipment for $3,800. The company estimates this equipment to have a useful life of three years and a salvage value of $200. Early in 2007, the company changes its estimates to a total four-year useful life and zero salvage value. Using the straight-line method, what is depreciation for the year ended 2007?

Answers—p. 406

Additional Expenditures

P3 Distinguish between revenue and capital expenditures, and account for them.

After a company acquires a plant asset and puts it into service, it often makes additional expenditures for that asset's operation, maintenance, repair, and improvement. In recording these expenditures, it must decide whether to capitalize or expense them (to capitalize an expenditure is to debit the asset account). The issue is whether more useful information is provided by reporting these expenditures as current period expenses or by adding them to the plant asset's cost and depreciating them over its remaining useful life.

Point: When an amount is said to be *capitalized* to an account, the amount is added to the account's normal balance.

Revenue expenditures, also called *income statement expenditures,* are additional costs of plant assets that do not materially increase the asset's life or productive capabilities. They are recorded as expenses and deducted from revenues in the current period's income statement. Examples of revenue expenditures are cleaning, repainting, adjustments, and lubricants. **Capital expenditures,** also called *balance sheet expenditures,* are additional costs of plant assets that provide benefits extending beyond the current period. They are debited to asset accounts and reported on the balance sheet. Capital expenditures increase or improve the type or amount of service an asset provides. Examples are roofing replacement, plant expansion, and major overhauls of machinery and equipment.

	Financial Statement Effect		
Cost Category	Accounting	Expense Timing	Current Income
Revenue expenditure	Income stmt. account debited	Expensed currently	Lower
Capital expenditure	Balance sheet account debited	Expensed in future	Higher

Financial statements are affected for several years by the accounting choice of recording costs as either revenue expenditures or capital expenditures. Managers must be careful in classifying them. This classification decision is based on whether these expenditures are identified as either ordinary repairs or as betterments and extraordinary repairs.

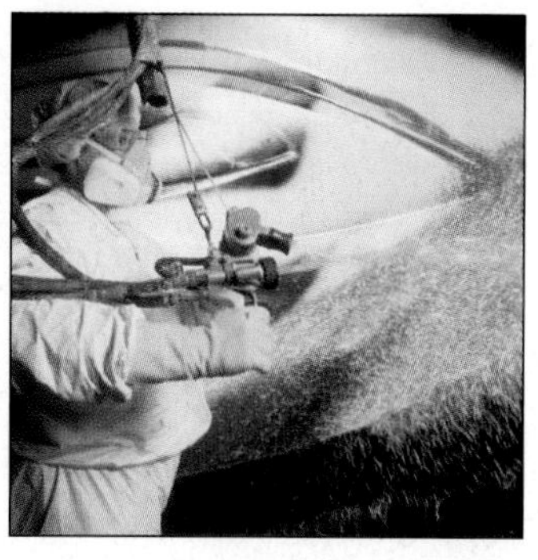

Ordinary Repairs

Ordinary repairs are expenditures to keep an asset in normal, good operating condition. They are necessary if an asset is to perform to expectations over its useful life. Ordinary repairs do not extend an asset's useful life beyond its original estimate or increase its productivity beyond original expectations. Examples are normal costs of cleaning, lubricating, adjusting, and replacing small parts of a machine. Ordinary repairs are treated as *revenue expenditures.* This means their costs are reported as expenses on the current period income statement. Following this rule, **Brunswick** reports that "maintenance and repair costs are expensed as incurred."

Point: Many companies apply the *materiality principle* to treat *low-cost plant assets* (say, less than $500) as revenue expenditures.

Betterments and Extraordinary Repairs

Accounting for betterments and extraordinary repairs is similar. **Betterments,** also called *improvements,* are expenditures that make a plant asset more efficient or productive. A betterment often involves adding a component to an asset or replacing one of its old components with a better one, and does not always increase an asset's useful life. An example is replacing manual controls on a machine with automatic controls. One special type of betterment is an *addition,* such as adding a new wing or dock to a warehouse. Since a betterment benefits future periods, it is debited to the asset account as a capital expenditure. The new book value (less salvage value) is then depreciated over the asset's remaining useful life. To illustrate, suppose a company pays $8,000 for a machine with an eight-year useful life and no salvage value. After three years and $3,000 of depreciation, it adds an automated control system to the machine at a cost of $1,800. This results in reduced labor costs in future periods. The cost of the betterment is added to the Machinery account with this entry:

Example: Assume a company owns a Web server. Identify each item as a revenue or capital expenditure: (1) purchase price, (2) necessary wiring, (3) platform for operation, (4) circuits to increase capacity, (5) cleaning after each three months of use, (6) repair of a faulty connection, and (7) replaced a worn cooling fan. *Answer:* Capital expenditures: 1, 2, 3, 4; Revenue expenditures: 5, 6, 7.

Jan. 2	Machinery	1,800	
	Cash		1,800
	To record installation of automated system.		

Assets = Liabilities + Equity
+1,800
−1,800

After the betterment, the remaining cost to be depreciated is $6,800, computed as $8,000 − $3,000 + $1,800. Depreciation expense for the remaining five years is $1,360 per year, computed as $6,800/5 years.

Point: Both extraordinary repairs and betterments demand revised depreciation schedules.

Extraordinary repairs are expenditures extending the asset's useful life beyond its original estimate. Extraordinary repairs are *capital expenditures* because they benefit future periods. Their costs are debited to the asset account. For example, **America West Airlines** reports: "the cost of major scheduled airframe, engine and certain component overhauls are capitalized (and expensed) . . . over the periods benefited."

Decision Maker

Entrepreneur Your start-up Internet services company needs cash, and you are preparing financial statements to apply for a short-term loan. A friend suggests that you treat as many expenses as possible as capital expenditures. What are the impacts on financial statements of this suggestion? What do you think is the aim of this suggestion?

Answer—p. 406

Disposals of Plant Assets

Plant assets are disposed of for several reasons. Some are discarded because they wear out or become obsolete. Others are sold because of changing business plans. Regardless of the reason, disposals of plant assets occur in one of three basic ways: discarding, sale, or exchange. The general steps in accounting for a disposal of plant assets is described in Exhibit 10.15.

Exhibit 10.15

Accounting for Disposals of Plant Assets

1. Record depreciation up to the date of disposal—this also updates Accumulated Depreciation.
2. Record the removal of the disposed asset's account balances—including its Accumulated Depreciation.
3. Record any cash (and/or other assets) received or paid in the disposal.
4. Record any gain or loss—computed by comparing the disposed asset's book value with the market value of any assets received.*

* One exception to step 4 is the case of a gain on a similar asset exchange—it is described later in this section.

Discarding Plant Assets

P4 Account for asset disposal through discarding, selling, and exchanging an asset.

A plant asset is *discarded* when it is no longer useful to the company and it has no market value. To illustrate, assume that a machine costing $9,000 with accumulated depreciation of $9,000 is discarded. When accumulated depreciation equals the asset's cost, it is said to be *fully depreciated* (zero book value). The entry to record the discarding of this asset is

Assets	= Liabilities	+ Equity
+9,000		
−9,000		

June 5	Accumulated Depreciation—Machinery	9,000	
	Machinery		9,000
	To discard fully depreciated machinery.		

This entry reflects all four steps of Exhibit 10.15. Step 1 is unnecessary since the machine is fully depreciated. Step 2 is reflected in the debit to Accumulated Depreciation and credit to Machinery. Since no other asset is involved, step 3 is irrelevant. Finally, since book value is zero and no other asset is involved, no gain or loss is recorded in step 4.

How do we account for discarding an asset that is not fully depreciated or one whose depreciation is not up-to-date? To answer this, consider equipment costing $8,000 with accumulated depreciation of $6,000 on December 31 of the prior fiscal year-end. This equipment is being depreciated using the straight-line method over eight years with zero salvage. On July 1 of the current year it is discarded. Step 1 is to bring depreciation up-to-date:

Point: Recording depreciation expense up-to-date gives an up-to-date book value for determining gain or loss.

Assets	= Liabilities	+ Equity
−500		−500

July 1	Depreciation Expense	500	
	Accumulated Depreciation—Equipment		500
	To record 6 months' depreciation ($1,000 × 6/12).		

Steps 2 through 4 of Exhibit 10.15 are reflected in the second (and final) entry:

Assets	= Liabilities	+ Equity
+6,500		−1,500
−8,000		

July 1	Accumulated Depreciation—Equipment	6,500	
	Loss on Disposal of Equipment	1,500	
	Equipment.		8,000
	To discard equipment with a $1,500 book value.		

Point: Gain or loss is determined by comparing "value given" (book value) to "value received."

The loss is computed by comparing the equipment's $1,500 book value ($8,000 − $6,000 − $500) with the zero net cash proceeds. This loss is reported in the Other Expenses and Losses section of the income statement. Discarding an asset can sometimes require a cash payment that would increase the loss. The income statement reports any loss from discarding an asset, and the balance sheet reflects the changes in the asset and accumulated depreciation accounts.

Selling Plant Assets

Companies often sell plant assets when they restructure or downsize operations. To illustrate the accounting for selling plant assets, we consider BTO's March 31 sale of equipment that cost $16,000 and has accumulated depreciation of $12,000 at December 31 of the prior calendar year-end. Annual depreciation on this equipment is $4,000 computed using straight-line depreciation. Step 1 of this sale is to record depreciation expense and update accumulated depreciation to March 31 of the current year:

March 31	Depreciation Expense	1,000	
	Accumulated Depreciation—Equipment.		1,000
	To record 3 months' depreciation ($4,000 × 3/12).		

Assets = Liabilities + Equity
−1,000 −1,000

Steps 2 through 4 of Exhibit 10.15 can be reflected in one final entry that depends on the amount received from the asset's sale. We consider three different possibilities.

Sale at Book Value If BTO receives $3,000, an amount equal to the equipment's book value as of March 31, no gain or loss occurs on disposal. The entry is

March 31	Cash	3,000	
	Accumulated Depreciation—Equipment	13,000	
	Equipment		16,000
	To record sale of equipment for no gain or loss.		

Assets = Liabilities + Equity
+3,000
+13,000
−16,000

Sale above Book Value If BTO receives $7,000, an amount that is $4,000 above the equipment's book value as of March 31, a gain on disposal occurs. The entry is

March 31	Cash	7,000	
	Accumulated Depreciation—Equipment	13,000	
	Gain on Disposal of Equipment.		4,000
	Equipment		16,000
	To record sale of equipment for a $4,000 gain.		

Assets = Liabilities + Equity
+7,000 +4,000
+13,000
−16,000

Sale below Book Value If BTO receives $2,500, an amount that is $500 below the equipment's book value as of March 31, a loss on disposal occurs. The entry is

March 31	Cash	2,500	
	Loss on Disposal of Equipment	500	
	Accumulated Depreciation—Equipment	13,000	
	Equipment.		16,000
	To record sale of equipment for a $500 loss.		

Assets = Liabilities + Equity
+2,500 −500
+13,000
−16,000

Exchanging Plant Assets

Many plant assets such as machinery, automobiles, and office equipment are disposed of by exchanging them for newer assets. In a typical exchange of plant assets, a *trade-in allowance* is received on the old asset and the balance is paid in cash. Accounting for the exchange of assets depends on whether the old and the new assets are similar or dissimilar in the functions they perform. Trading an old truck for a new truck is an exchange of similar assets, whereas trading a truck for a machine is an exchange of dissimilar assets. This section describes the accounting for the exchange of similar assets. Similar asset exchanges are common, whereas dissimilar asset exchanges are not (the latter are discussed in advanced courses).

Accounting for exchanges of similar assets depends on whether the book value of the asset given up is less or more than the market value of the asset received. When the market value of the asset received is less than the book value of the asset given up, the difference is recognized as a loss. However, when the value of the asset received is more than the asset's book value given up, the gain is *not* recognized.

Receiving Less in Exchange: A Loss Let's assume that a company exchanges both old equipment and $33,000 in cash for new equipment. The old equipment originally cost

Point: Trade-in allowance minus book value equals the gain (or loss if negative) on exchange.

$36,000 and has accumulated depreciation of $20,000 at the time of exchange. The new equipment has a market value of $42,000. These details are reflected in the middle (Loss) columns of Exhibit 10.16.

Exhibit 10.16

Computing Gain or Loss on *Similar* Asset Exchange

Similar Plant Asset Exchange	Loss		Gain	
Market value of assets received		$42,000		$52,000
Book value of assets given up:				
Equipment ($36,000 − $20,000)	$16,000		$16,000	
Cash	33,000	49,000	33,000	49,000
Gain (loss) on exchange		**$(7,000)**		**$ 3,000**

The entry to record this similar asset exchange is

Assets = Liabilities + Equity
+42,000 −7,000
+20,000
−36,000
−33,000

Jan. 3	Equipment (**new**)	42,000	
	Loss on Exchange of Assets.	7,000	
	Accumulated Depreciation—Equipment (**old**). . . .	20,000	
	Equipment (**old**)		36,000
	Cash.		33,000
	To record exchange of old equipment and cash for new equipment.		

Point: Parenthetical journal entry notes to "new" and "old" equipment are for illustration only. Both the debit and credit are to the same Equipment account in the general ledger.

The book value of the assets given up consists of the $33,000 cash and the $16,000 ($36,000 − $20,000) book value of the old equipment. The total $49,000 book value of assets given up is compared to the $42,000 market value of the new equipment received. This yields a loss of $7,000 ($42,000 − $49,000).

Receiving More in Exchange: A Gain Let's assume the same facts as in the preceding similar asset exchange *except* that the new equipment received has a market value of $52,000 instead of $42,000. The entry to record this similar asset exchange is

Assets = Liabilities + Equity
+49,000
+20,000
−36,000
−33,000

Jan. 3	Equipment (**new**)	49,000	
	Accumulated Depreciation—Equipment (**old**). . . .	20,000	
	Equipment (**old**)		36,000
	Cash.		33,000
	To record exchange of old equipment and cash for new equipment.		

Point: No gain is recognized for similar asset exchanges.

Exhibit 10.16 shows that there is a "gain" from this exchange in the far right (Gain) columns. This gain is *not* recognized in the entry because of a rule prohibiting recognizing a gain on similar asset exchanges.[1] The $49,000 recorded for the new equipment equals its cash price ($52,000) less the unrecognized gain ($3,000) on the exchange. The $49,000 cost recorded is called the *cost basis* of the new machine. This cost basis is the amount we use to compute depreciation and its book value. The cost basis of the new asset also can be computed by summing the book values of the assets given up as shown in Exhibit 10.17.

Exhibit 10.17

Cost Basis of New Asset when Gain Not Recognized

Cost of old equipment	$ 36,000
Less accumulated depreciation	20,000
Book value of old equipment	16,000
Cash paid in the exchange	33,000
Cost recorded for new equipment	**$49,000**

[1] The reason a gain from a similar asset exchange is not recognized is that the earnings process is not considered complete for the exchanged asset. The decision to recognize a loss from a similar asset exchange is an application of *accounting conservatism* in measuring and recording asset values.

Quick Check

8. Early in the fifth year of a machine's six-year useful life, it is overhauled, and its useful life is extended to nine years. This machine originally cost $108,000 and the overhaul cost is $12,000. Prepare the entry to record the overhaul cost.
9. Explain the difference between revenue expenditures and capital expenditures and how both are recorded.
10. What is a betterment? How is a betterment recorded?
11. A company acquires equipment on January 10, 2005, at a cost of $42,000. Straight-line depreciation is used with a five-year life and $7,000 salvage value. On June 27, 2006, the company sells this equipment for $32,000. Prepare the entry(ies) for June 27, 2006.
12. A company trades an old Web server for a new one. The cost of the old server is $30,000, and its accumulated depreciation at the time of the trade is $23,400. The new server has a cash price of $45,000. Prepare entries to record the trade under two different assumptions where the company receives a trade-in allowance of (*a*) $3,000 and (*b*) $7,000.

Example: Assume the old equipment in Exh. 10.17 is sold for $19,000 and, in a *separate* transaction, new equipment is bought for $52,000. Record both transactions. *Answer:*

Cash	19,000	
Accum. Depr — Eq. . . .	20,000	
Equipment (old)		36,000
Gain on Sale of Eq.		3,000
Equipment (new)	52,000	
Cash		52,000

Answers—p. 406

Section 2—Natural Resources

Natural resources are assets that are physically consumed when used. Examples are standing timber, mineral deposits, and oil and gas fields. Since they are consumed when used, they are often called *wasting assets*. These assets represent soon-to-be inventories of raw materials that will be converted into one or more products by cutting, mining, or pumping. Until that conversion takes place, they are noncurrent assets and are shown in a balance sheet using titles such as timberlands, mineral deposits, or oil reserves. Natural resources are reported under either plant assets or its own separate category. **Alcoa**, for instance, reports its natural resources under the balance sheet title *Properties, plants and equipment.* In a note to its financial statements, Alcoa reports a separate amount for *Land and land rights, including mines.* **Weyerhaeuser**, on the other hand, reports its timber holdings in a separate balance sheet category titled *Timber and timberlands.*

Cost Determination and Depletion

P5 Account for natural resource assets and their depletion.

Natural resources are recorded at cost, which includes all expenditures necessary to acquire the resource and prepare it for its intended use. **Depletion** is the process of allocating the cost of a natural resource to the period when it is consumed. Natural resources are reported on the balance sheet at cost less *accumulated depletion.* The depletion expense per period is usually based on units extracted from cutting, mining, or pumping. This is similar to units-of-production depreciation. **Exxon Mobil** uses this approach to amortize the costs of discovering and operating its oil wells.

To illustrate depletion of natural resources, let's consider a mineral deposit with an estimated 250,000 tons of available ore. It is purchased for $500,000, and we expect zero salvage value. The depletion charge per ton of ore mined is $2, computed as $500,000 ÷ 250,000 tons. If 85,000 tons are mined and sold in the first year, the depletion charge for that year is $170,000. These computations are detailed in Exhibit 10.18. Depletion expense for the first year is recorded as follows:

Dec. 31	Depletion Expense—Mineral Deposit.	170,000	
	Accumulated Depletion—Mineral Deposit. . .		170,000
	To record depletion of the mineral deposit.		

Assets	= Liabilities +	Equity
−170,000		−170,000

Exhibit 10.18

Depletion Formula and Example

Step 1

$$\textbf{Depletion per unit} = \frac{\textbf{Cost} - \textbf{Salvage value}}{\textbf{Total units of capacity}} = \frac{\$500{,}000 - \$0}{250{,}000 \text{ tons}} = \$2 \text{ per ton}$$

Step 2

$$\textbf{Depletion expense} = \textbf{Depletion per unit} \times \textbf{Units extracted and sold in period}$$
$$= \$2 \times 85{,}000 = \$170{,}000$$

The period-end balance sheet reports the mineral deposit as shown in Exhibit 10.19.

Exhibit 10.19

Balance Sheet Presentation of Natural Resources

Mineral deposit	$500,000	
Less accumulated depletion	**170,000**	$330,000

Since all 85,000 tons of the mined ore are sold during the year, the entire $170,000 of depletion is reported on the income statement. If some of the ore remains unsold at year-end, however, the depletion related to the unsold ore is carried forward on the balance sheet and reported as Ore Inventory, a current asset.

Plant Assets Used in Extracting Resources

The conversion of natural resources by mining, cutting, or pumping usually requires machinery, equipment, and buildings. When the usefulness of these plant assets is directly related to the depletion of a natural resource, their costs are depreciated using the units-of-production method in proportion to the depletion of the natural resource. For example, if a machine is permanently installed in a mine and 10% of the ore is mined and sold in the period, then 10% of the machine's cost (less any salvage value) is allocated to depreciation expense. The same procedure is used when a machine is abandoned once resources have been extracted. If, however, a machine will be moved to and used at another site when extraction is complete, the machine is depreciated over its own useful life.

Section 3—Intangible Assets

P6 Account for intangible assets.

Intangible assets are nonphysical assets (used in operations) that confer on their owners long-term rights, privileges, or competitive advantages. Examples are patents, copyrights, licenses, leaseholds, franchises, goodwill, and trademarks. Lack of physical substance does not necessarily make an asset intangible. Notes and accounts receivable, for instance, lack physical substance, but they are not intangibles. This section identifies the more common types of intangible assets and explains the accounting for them.

Cost Determination and Amortization

Point: Goodwill is not amortized; instead, it is annually tested for impairment.

Point: The cost to acquire a Website address is an intangible asset.

An intangible asset is recorded at cost when purchased. Its cost is systematically allocated to expense over its estimated useful life through the process of **amortization.** If an intangible asset has an **indefinite useful life**—meaning that no legal, regulatory, contractual, competitive, economic, or other factors limit its useful life—it should not be amortized. (If an intangible with an indefinite useful life is later judged to have a limited useful life, it is amortized over that limited useful life.) Amortization of intangible assets is similar to depreciation of plant assets and the depletion of natural resources in that it is a process of cost allocation. However, only the straight-line method is used for amortizing intangibles *unless* the company can show that another method is preferred. The effects of amortization are recorded in a contra account (Accumulated Amortization). The gross acquisition cost of intangible assets is disclosed in the balance sheet along with their accumulated amortization (these disclosures are new per *SFAS 142*). The eventual disposal of an intangible asset involves removing its book value, recording any other asset(s) received or given up, and recognizing any gain or loss for the difference.

Many intangibles have limited useful lives due to laws, contracts, or other asset characteristics. Examples are patents, copyrights, and leaseholds. Other intangibles such as goodwill, trademarks, and trade names have useful lives that cannot be easily determined. The cost of intangible assets is amortized over the periods expected to benefit by their use, but in no case can this period be longer than the asset's legal existence. The values of some intangible assets such as goodwill continue indefinitely into the future and are not amortized. (An intangible asset that is not amortized is tested annually for **impairment**—if necessary, an impairment loss is recorded. Details for this test are in advanced courses.)

Intangible assets are often shown in a separate section of the balance sheet immediately after plant assets. **Callaway Golf**, for instance, follows this approach in reporting more than $100 million of intangible assets in its recent balance sheet. Companies usually disclose their amortization periods for intangibles. The remainder of our discussion focuses on accounting for specific types of intangible assets.

Types of Intangibles

Patents The federal government grants patents to encourage the invention of new technology, mechanical devices, and production processes. A **patent** is an exclusive right granted to its owner to manufacture and sell a patented item or to use a process for 17 years. When patent rights are purchased, the cost to acquire the rights is debited to an account called Patents. If the owner engages in lawsuits to successfully defend a patent, the cost of lawsuits is debited to the Patents account. However, the costs of research and development leading to a new patent are expensed when incurred.

A patent's cost is amortized over its estimated useful life (not to exceed 17 years). If we purchase a patent costing $25,000 with a useful life of 10 years, we make the following adjusting entry at the end of each of the 10 years to amortize one-tenth of its cost:

Decision Insight

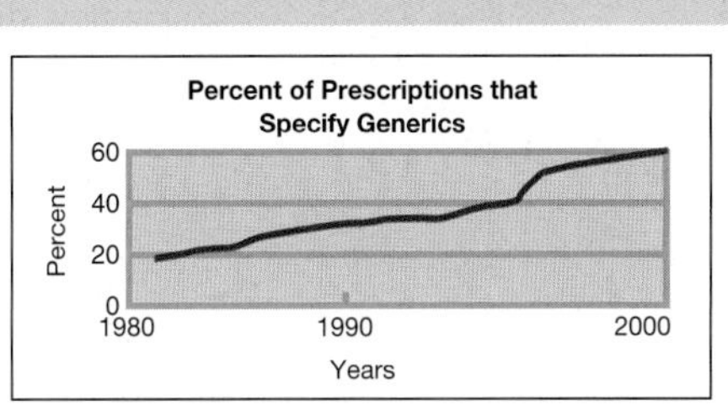

Mention "drug war" and most people think of fighting cocaine or heroin use. But another drug war is under way: Brand-name drugmakers are fighting to stop generic copies of their products from hitting the market once their patents expire. Successfully delaying a generic rival can mean hundreds of millions of dollars in extra sales.

Dec. 31	Amortization Expense—Patents	2,500	
	Accumulated Amortization—Patents		2,500
	To amortize patent costs over its useful life.		

Assets = Liabilities + Equity
−2,500 −2,500

The $2,500 debit to Amortization Expense appears on the income statement as a cost of the product or service provided under protection of the patent. The Accumulated Amortization—Patents account is a contra asset account to Patents.

Copyrights A **copyright** gives its owner the exclusive right to publish and sell a musical, literary, or artistic work during the life of the creator plus 70 years, although the useful life of most copyrights is much shorter. The costs of a copyright are amortized over its useful life. The only identifiable cost of many copyrights is the fee paid to the Copyright Office of the federal government or international agency granting the copyright. If this fee is immaterial, it is charged directly to an expense account, but if the identifiable costs of a copyright are material, they are capitalized (recorded in an asset account) and periodically amortized by debiting an account called Amortization Expense—Copyrights.

Leaseholds Property is rented under a contract called a **lease.** The property's owner, called the **lessor,** grants the lease. The one who secures the right to possess and use the property is called the **lessee.** A **leasehold** refers to the rights the lessor grants to the lessee under the terms of the lease. A leasehold is an intangible asset for the lessee.

Point: A leasehold account implies existence of future benefits that the lessee controls because of a prepayment. It also meets the definition of an asset.

Certain leases require no advance payment from the lessee but require monthly rent payments. In this case, we do not set up a Leasehold account. Instead, the monthly payments are debited to a Rent Expense account. If a long-term lease requires the lessee to pay the final period's rent in advance when the lease is signed, the lessee records this advance payment with a debit to the Leasehold account. Since the advance payment is not used until the final period, the Leasehold account balance remains intact until that final period when its balance is transferred to Rent Expense. (Some long-term leases give the lessee essentially the same rights as a purchaser. This results in a tangible asset and a liability reported by the lessee. Chapter 11 describes these so-called *capital leases.*)

A long-term lease can increase in value when current rental rates for similar property rise while the required payments under the lease remain constant. This increase in value of a lease is not reported on the lessee's balance sheet. However, if the property is subleased and the new tenant makes a cash payment to the original lessee for the rights under the old lease, the new tenant debits this payment to a Leasehold account, which is amortized to Rent Expense over the remaining life of the lease.

Leasehold Improvements A lessee sometimes pays for alterations or improvements to the leased property such as partitions, painting, and storefronts. These alterations and improvements are called **leasehold improvements,** and the lessee debits these costs to a Leasehold Improvements account. Since leasehold improvements become part of the property and revert to the lessor at the end of the lease, the lessee amortizes these costs over the life of the lease or the life of the improvements, whichever is shorter. The amortization entry debits Amortization Expense—Leasehold Improvements and credits Accumulated Amortization—Leasehold Improvements.

Franchises and Licenses **Franchises** and **licenses** are rights that a company or government grants an entity to deliver a product or service under specified conditions. Many organizations grant franchise and license rights—**McDonald's**, **Pizza Hut**, and **Major League Baseball** are just a few examples. The costs of franchises and licenses are debited to a Franchises and Licenses asset account and are amortized over the lives of the agreements.

Trademarks and Trade Names Companies often adopt unique symbols or select unique names and brands in marketing their products. A **trademark** or **trade (brand) name** is a symbol, name, phrase, or jingle identified with a company, product, or service. Examples are Nike swoosh, Marlboro Man, Big Mac, Coca-Cola, and Corvette. Ownership and exclusive right to use a trademark or trade name is often established by showing that one company used it before another. Ownership is best established by registering a trademark or trade name with the government's Patent Office. The cost of developing, maintaining, or enhancing the value of a trademark or trade name (such as advertising) is charged to expense when incurred. If a trademark or trade name is purchased, however, its cost is debited to an asset account and then amortized over its expected useful life.

Global: Some Australian and U.K. companies value brand names separately on their balance sheets.

Point: McDonald's "golden arches" is one of the world's most valuable trademarks, yet this asset is not shown on McDonald's balance sheet.

Goodwill **Goodwill** has a specific meaning in accounting. Goodwill is the amount by which a company's value exceeds the value of its individual assets and liabilities. This usually implies that the company as a whole has certain valuable attributes not measured among its individual assets and liabilities. These can include superior management, skilled workforce, good supplier or customer relations, quality products or services, good location, or other competitive advantages.

Point: IBM's balance sheet reports more than $4 billion of goodwill.

To keep accounting information from being too subjective, goodwill is not recorded unless an entire company or business segment is purchased. Purchased goodwill is measured by taking the purchase price of the company and subtracting the market value of its individual

Global: International accounting standards call for charging goodwill against income. The amortization period suggested is 20 or fewer years.

net assets (excluding goodwill). For instance, **Yahoo!** paid nearly $3.0 billion to acquire **GeoCities**; about $2.8 of the $3.0 billion was for goodwill and other intangibles.

Goodwill is measured as the excess of the cost of an acquired entity over the value of the acquired net assets. Goodwill is recorded as an asset, and it is *not* amortized. Instead, the FASB (*SFAS 142*) requires that goodwill be annually tested for impairment. If the book value of goodwill does not exceed its fair (market) value, goodwill is not impaired. However, if the book value of goodwill does exceed its fair value, an impairment loss is recorded equal to that excess. (Details of this test are in advanced courses.)

Point: Accounting for goodwill is different for financial accounting and tax accounting. The IRS requires the amortization of goodwill over a period not to exceed 15 years.

Quick Check

13. Give an example of a natural resource and of an intangible asset.
14. A company pays $650,000 for an ore deposit. The deposit is estimated to have 325,000 tons of ore that will be mined over the next 10 years. During the first year, it mined, processed, and sold 91,000 tons. What is that year's depletion expense?
15. On January 6, 2005, a company pays $120,000 for a patent with a 17-year legal life to produce a toy expected to be marketable for three years. Prepare entries to record its acquisition and the December 31, 2005, amortization entry.

Answers—p. 407

Total Asset Turnover

Decision Analysis

A2 Compute total asset turnover and apply it to analyze a company's use of assets.

A company's assets are important in determining its ability to generate sales and earn income. Managers devote much attention to deciding what assets a company acquires, how much it invests in assets, and how to use assets most efficiently and effectively. One important measure of a company's ability to use its assets is **total asset turnover,** defined in Exhibit 10.20.

Exhibit 10.20
Total Asset Turnover

$$\textbf{Total asset turnover} = \frac{\textbf{Net sales}}{\textbf{Average total assets}}$$

The numerator reflects the net amounts earned from the sale of products and services. The denominator reflects the average total resources devoted to operating the company and generating sales.

To illustrate, let's look at total asset turnover in Exhibit 10.21 for two competing companies: **Coors** and **Anheuser-Busch.**

Exhibit 10.21
Analysis Using Total Asset Turnover

Company	Figure ($ in millions)	2002	2001	2000	1999
Coors	Net sales	$ 3,776	$ 2,429	$ 2,414	$ 2,236
	Average total assets	$ 3,019	$ 1,684	$ 1,588	$ 1,503
	Total asset turnover	**1.25**	**1.44**	**1.52**	**1.49**
Anheuser-Busch	Net sales	$13,566	$12,912	$12,499	$11,895
	Average total assets	$14,032	$13,547	$12,914	$12,593
	Total asset turnover	**0.97**	**0.95**	**0.97**	**0.94**

To show how we use total asset turnover, let's look at Coors. We express Coors's use of assets in generating net sales by saying "it turned its assets over 1.25 times during 2002." This means that each $1.00 of assets produced $1.25 of net sales. Is a total asset turnover of 1.25 good or bad? It is safe to say that all companies desire a high total asset turnover. Like many ratio analyses, however, a company's total asset turnover must be interpreted in comparison with that of prior years and of its competitors. Interpreting the total asset turnover also requires an understanding of the company's operations. Some operations are capital intensive, meaning that a relatively large amount is invested in assets to generate sales. This suggests a relatively lower total asset turnover. Other companies' operations are labor intensive, meaning that they generate sales more by the efforts of people than the use of assets. In that case, we expect a higher total asset turnover. Companies with low total

Point: A measure of **plant asset useful life** equals the plant asset cost divided by depreciation expense.

Point: A measure of **plant asset age** is estimated by dividing accumulated depreciation by depreciation expense. Older plant assets can signal needed asset replacements; it may also signal use of less efficient assets.

Decision Maker

Environmentalist A paper manufacturer claims it cannot afford more environmental controls. It points to its low total asset turnover of 1.9 and argues that it cannot compete with companies whose total asset turnover is much higher. Examples cited are food stores (5.5) and auto dealers (3.8). How do you respond?

Answer—p. 406

asset turnover require higher profit margins (examples are hotels and real estate); companies with high total asset turnover can succeed with lower profit margins; examples are food stores and toy merchandisers. Coors's turnover recently declined, but it is superior to that for Anheuser-Busch. Total asset turnover for Coors's competitors, available in industry publications such as Dun & Bradstreet, is generally in the range of 1.0 to 1.2 over this same period. Overall, Coors appears to be competitive and doing slightly better than its competitors on total asset turnover.

Demonstration Problem

On July 14, 2004, Tulsa Company pays $600,000 to acquire a fully equipped factory. The purchase involves the following assets:

Asset	Appraised Value	Salvage Value	Useful Life	Depreciation Method
Land	$160,000			Not depreciated
Land improvements	80,000	$ 0	10 years	Straight-line
Building	320,000	100,000	10 years	Double-declining-balance
Machinery	240,000	20,000	10,000 units	Units-of-production*
Total	$800,000			

* The machinery is used to produce 700 units in 2004 and 1,800 units in 2005.

Required

1. Allocate the total $600,000 purchase cost among the separate assets.
2. Compute the 2004 (six months) and 2005 depreciation expense for each asset and compute total depreciation expense for both years.
3. On the first day of 2006, Tulsa exchanged the machinery that was acquired on July 14, 2004, and $5,000 cash for similar machinery with a $210,000 market value. Journalize the exchange of these similar assets.
4. On the last day of calendar year 2006, Tulsa discarded machinery that had been on its books for five years. The machinery's original cost was $12,000 (estimated life of five years) and its salvage value was $2,000. No depreciation had been recorded for the fifth year when the disposal occurred. Journalize the fifth year of depreciation (straight-line method) and the asset's disposal.
5. At the beginning of year 2006, Tulsa purchased a patent for $100,000 cash. The company estimated the patent's useful life to be 10 years. Journalize the patent acquisition and its amortization for the year 2006.
6. Late in the year 2006, Tulsa acquired an ore deposit for $600,000 cash. It added roads and built mine shafts for an additional cost of $80,000. Salvage value of the mine is estimated to be $20,000. The company estimated 330,000 tons of available ore. In year 2006, Tulsa mined and sold 10,000 tons of ore. Journalize the mine's acquisition and its first year's depletion.

Planning the Solution

- Complete a three-column table showing the following amounts for each asset: appraised value, percent of total value, and apportioned cost.
- Using allocated costs, compute depreciation for 2004 (only one-half year) and 2005 (full year) for each asset. Summarize those computations in a table showing total depreciation for each year.
- Remember that gains on exchanges of similar assets are not recognized. Make a journal entry to add the acquired machinery to the books and to remove the old machinery, along with its accumulated depreciation, and to record the cash given in the exchange.
- Remember that depreciation must be recorded up-to-date before discarding an asset. Calculate and record depreciation expense for the fifth year using the straight-line method. Since salvage value

is not received at the end of a discarded asset's life, the amount of any salvage value becomes a loss on disposal. Record the loss on the disposal as well as the removal of the discarded asset and its related accumulated depreciation.

- Record the patent (an intangible asset) at its purchase price. Use straight-line amortization over its useful life to calculate amortization expense.
- Record the ore deposit (a natural resource asset) at its cost, including any added costs to ready the mine for use. Calculate depletion per ton using the depletion formula. Multiply the depletion per ton by the amount of tons mined and sold to calculate depletion expense for the year.

Solution to Demonstration Problem

1. Allocation of the total cost of $600,000 among the separate assets:

Asset	Appraised Value	Percent of Total Value	Apportioned Cost
Land	$160,000	20%	**$120,000** ($600,000 × 20%)
Land improvements	80,000	10	**60,000** ($600,000 × 10%)
Building	320,000	40	**240,000** ($600,000 × 40%)
Machinery	240,000	30	**180,000** ($600,000 × 30%)
Total	$800,000	100%	$ 600,000

2. Depreciation for each asset. (*Note:* Land is not depreciated.)

Land Improvements	
Cost	$ 60,000
Salvage value	0
Depreciable cost	$ 60,000
Useful life	10 years
Annual depreciation expense ($60,000/10 years)	$ 6,000
2004 depreciation ($6,000 × 6/12)	**$ 3,000**
2005 depreciation	**$ 6,000**
Building	
Straight-line rate = 100%/10 years = 10%	
Double-declining-balance rate = 10% × 2 = 20%	
2004 depreciation ($240,000 × 20% × 6/12)	**$ 24,000**
2005 depreciation [($240,000 − $24,000) × 20%]	**$ 43,200**
Machinery	
Cost	$180,000
Salvage value	20,000
Depreciable cost	$160,000
Total expected units of production	10,000 units
Depreciation per unit ($160,000/10,000 units)	$ 16
2004 depreciation ($16 × 700 units)	**$ 11,200**
2005 depreciation ($16 × 1,800 units)	**$ 28,800**

Total depreciation expense:

	2004	2005
Land improvements	$ 3,000	$ 6,000
Building	24,000	43,200
Machinery	11,200	28,800
Total	$38,200	$78,000

3. Record the exchange of similar assets (machinery) with a gain on the exchange: The book value on the exchange date is $180,000 (cost) − $40,000 (accumulated depreciation). The book value of the machinery given up in the exchange ($140,000) plus the $5,000 cash paid is less than the $210,000 value of the machine acquired. The entry to record this exchange of similar assets does not recognize the $65,000 gain on exchange:

Machinery (new)	145,000*	
Accumulated Depreciation—Machinery (old)	40,000	
Machinery (old)		180,000
Cash		5,000
To record exchange of similar assets.		

* Market value of the acquired asset of $210,000 minus $65,000 gain.

4. Record the depreciation up to date on the discarded asset:

Depreciation Expense—Machinery	2,000	
Accumulated Depreciation—Machinery		2,000
To record depreciation on date of disposal: ($12,000 − $2,000)/5		

Record the removal of the discarded asset and its loss on disposal:

Accumulated Depreciation—Machinery	10,000	
Loss on Disposal of Machinery	2,000	
Machinery		12,000
To record the discarding of machinery with a $2,000 book value.		

5.

Patent	100,000	
Cash		100,000
To record patent acquisition.		

Amortization Expense—Patent	10,000	
Accumulated Amortization—Patent		10,000
To record amortization expense: $100,000/10 years = $10,000.		

6.

Ore Deposit	680,000	
Cash		680,000
To record ore deposit acquisition and its related costs.		

Depletion Expense—Ore Deposit	20,000	
Accumulated Depletion—Ore Deposit		20,000
To record depletion expense: ($680,000 − $20,000)/330,000 tons = $2 per ton. 10,000 tons mined and sold × $2 = $20,000 depletion.		

APPENDIX

10A Goodwill Estimation

A company has goodwill when its expected future income is greater than the normal income for its industry (competitors). To illustrate, consider the information in Exhibit 10A.1 for two competing companies, Z2 and Burton, of roughly equal size in the snowboard industry.

	Z2	Burton
Net assets* (excluding goodwill)	$190,000	$190,000
Normal return on net assets in the industry	10%	10%
Normal net income	19,000	19,000
Expected net income	24,000	19,000
Expected net income above normal	**$ 5,000**	**$ 0**

* Net assets (also called *equity*) equal total assets minus total liabilities.

Exhibit 10A.1

Data for Goodwill Illustration

The expected net income for Z2 is $24,000. This is $5,000 higher than the $19,000 industry norm based on the 10% return on net assets (equity) for its competitors. This implies that Z2 has goodwill that yields above normal net income. In contrast, Burton's expected income of $19,000 equals the norm for this industry. This implies zero goodwill for Burton. This means that Z2 buyers are willing to pay more than just the value of its net assets—specifically, to acquire its goodwill asset.

In accounting, goodwill is recorded when an entire company or business segment is purchased. The buyer and seller can estimate goodwill in more than one way. For instance, how do we value Z2's $5,000 per year above normal net income? One method is to value goodwill at some *multiple* of above normal net income. If we choose a multiple of 6, our goodwill estimate for Z2 is 6 × $5,000, or $30,000. Another method is to assume the $5,000 above normal net income continues indefinitely (often called *capitalizing*). This is like an *annuity*. For example, if we assume a 16% discount (interest) rate, the goodwill estimate is $5,000/16%, or $31,250. Whatever method we choose, the value of goodwill is confirmed only by the price the seller is willing to accept and the buyer is willing to pay.

Summary

C1 Describe plant assets and issues in accounting for them. Plant assets are tangible assets used in the operations of a company and have a useful life of more than one accounting period. Plant assets are set apart from other tangible assets by two important features: use in operations and useful lives longer than one period. The four main accounting issues with plant assets are (1) computing their costs, (2) allocating their costs to the periods they benefit, (3) accounting for subsequent expenditures, and (4) recording their disposal.

C2 Explain depreciation and the factors affecting its computation. *Depreciation* is the process of allocating to expense the cost of a plant asset over the accounting periods that benefit from its use. Depreciation does not measure the decline in a plant asset's market value or its physical deterioration. Three factors determine depreciation: cost, salvage value, and useful life. Salvage value is an estimate of the asset's value at the end of its benefit period. Useful (service) life is the length of time an asset is productively used.

C3 Explain depreciation for partial years and changes in estimates. Partial-year depreciation is often required because assets are bought and sold throughout the year. Depreciation is revised when changes in estimates such as salvage value and useful life occur. If the useful life of a plant asset changes, for instance, the remaining cost to be depreciated is spread over the remaining (revised) useful life of the asset.

A1 Compare and analyze alternative depreciation methods. The amount of depreciation expense per period is usually different for different methods, yet total depreciation expense over an asset's life is the same for all methods. Each method starts with the same total cost and ends with the same salvage value. The difference is in the pattern of depreciation expense over the asset's life. Common methods are straight-line, double-declining-balance, and units-of-production.

A2 Compute total asset turnover and apply it to analyze a company's use of assets. Total asset turnover measures a company's ability to use its assets to generate sales. It is defined as net sales divided by average total assets. While all companies desire a high total asset turnover, it must be interpreted in comparison with that for prior years and its competitors.

P1 Apply the cost principle to compute the cost of plant assets. Plant assets are recorded at cost when purchased. Cost includes all normal and reasonable expenditures necessary to get the asset in place and ready for its intended use. The cost of a lump-sum purchase is allocated among its individual assets.

P2 Compute and record depreciation using the straight-line, units-of-production, and declining-balance methods. The straight-line method divides cost less salvage value by the asset's useful life to determine depreciation expense per period. The units-of-production method divides cost less salvage value by the estimated number of units the asset will produce over its life to determine depreciation per unit. The declining-balance method multiplies the asset's beginning-of-period book value by a factor that is often double the straight-line rate.

P3 Distinguish between revenue and capital expenditures, and account for them. Revenue expenditures expire in the current period and are debited to expense accounts and matched with current revenues. Ordinary repairs are an example of revenue expenditures. Capital expenditures benefit future periods and are debited to asset accounts. Examples of capital expenditures are extraordinary repairs and betterments.

P4 Account for asset disposal through discarding, selling, or exchanging an asset. When a plant asset is discarded, sold, or exchanged, its cost and accumulated depreciation are removed from the accounts. Any cash proceeds from discarding or selling an asset are recorded and compared to the asset's book value to determine gain or loss. When similar assets are exchanged, losses are recognized but gains are not. When gains are not recognized, the new asset account is debited for the book value of the old asset plus any cash (assets) paid.

P5 Account for natural resource assets and their depletion. The cost of a natural resource is recorded in a noncurrent asset account. Depletion of a natural resource is recorded by allocating its cost to depletion expense using the units-of-production method. Depletion is credited to an Accumulated Depletion account.

P6 Account for intangible assets. An intangible asset is recorded at the cost incurred to purchase it. The cost of an intangible asset with a definite useful life is allocated to expense using the straight-line method, which is called *amortization.* Goodwill and intangible assets with an indefinite useful life are not amortized—they are annually tested for impairment. Intangible assets include patents, copyrights, leaseholds, goodwill, and trademarks.

Guidance Answers to Decision Maker and Decision Ethics

Controller The president's instructions may reflect an honest and reasonable prediction of the future. Since the company is struggling financially, the president may have concluded that the normal pattern of replacing assets every three years cannot continue. Perhaps the strategy is to avoid costs of frequent replacements and stretch use of equipment a few years longer until financial conditions improve. However, if you believe the president's decision is unprincipled, you might confront the president with your opinion that it is unethical to change the estimate to increase income. Another possibility is to wait and see whether the auditor will prohibit this change in estimate. In either case, you should insist that the statements be based on reasonable estimates.

Entrepreneur Treating an expense as a capital expenditure means that reported expenses will be lower and income higher in the short run. This is so because a capital expenditure is not expensed immediately but is spread over the asset's useful life. Treating an expense as a capital expenditure also means that asset and equity totals are reported at larger amounts in the short run. This continues until the asset is fully depreciated. Your friend is probably trying to help, but the suggestion is misguided. Only an expenditure benefiting future periods is a capital expenditure.

Environmentalist The paper manufacturer's comparison of its total asset turnover with food stores and auto dealers is misdirected. These other industries' turnovers are higher because their profit margins are lower (about 2%). Profit margins for the paper industry are usually 3% to 3.5%. You need to collect data from competitors in the paper industry to show that a 1.9 total asset turnover is about the norm for this industry. You might also want to collect data on this company's revenues and expenses, along with compensation data for its high-ranking officers and employees.

Guidance Answers to Quick Checks

1. a. Supplies—current assets
b. Office equipment—plant assets
c. Inventory—current assets
d. Land for future expansion—long-term investments
e. Trucks used in operations—plant assets

2. a. Land **b.** Land Improvements

3. $700,000 + $49,000 − $21,000 + $3,500 + $3,000 + $2,500 = $737,000

4. a. Straight-line with 7-year life: ($77,000/7) = $11,000
b. Straight-line with 10-year life: ($77,000/10) = $7,700

5. Depreciation is a process of allocating the cost of plant assets to the accounting periods that benefit from the assets' use.

6. a. Book value using straight-line depreciation: $96,000 − [($96,000 − $8,000)/5] = $78,400
b. Book value using units of production: $96,000 − [($96,000 − $8,000) × (10,000/100,000)] = $87,200

7. ($3,800 − $200)/3 = $1,200 (original depreciation per year)
$1,200 × 2 = $2,400 (accumulated depreciation)
($3,800 − $2,400)/2 = $700 (revised depreciation)

8.

Machinery	12,000	
Cash		12,000

9. A revenue expenditure benefits only the current period and should be charged to expense in the current period. A capital expenditure yields benefits that extend beyond the end of the current period and should be charged to an asset.

10. A betterment involves modifying an existing plant asset to make it more efficient, usually by replacing part of the asset with an improved or superior part. The cost of a betterment is debited to the asset account.

11.

Depreciation Expense	3,500	
Accumulated Depreciation		3,500
Cash	32,000	
Accumulated Depreciation	10,500	
Gain on Sale of Equipment		500
Equipment		42,000

12.

(*a*) Equipment	45,000	
Loss on Exchange of Assets	3,600	
Accumulated Depreciation—Equipment	23,400	
Equipment		30,000
Cash ($45,000 − $3,000)		42,000

(*b*) Equipment*	44,600	
Accumulated Depreciation—Equipment	23,400	
Equipment		30,000
Cash ($45,000 − $7,000)		38,000

* Includes $400 unrecognized gain.

13. Examples of natural resources are timberlands, mineral deposits, and oil reserves. Examples of intangible assets are patents, copyrights, leaseholds, leasehold improvements, goodwill, trademarks, and licenses.

14. ($650,000/325,000 tons) × 91,000 tons = $182,000

15.

Jan. 6	Patents	120,000	
	Cash		120,000
Dec. 31	Amortization Expense	40,000*	
	Accumulated Amortization—Patents		40,000

* $120,000/3 years = $40,000.

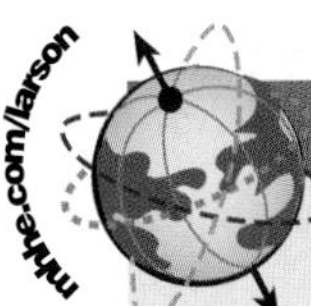

Key Terms

Key Terms are available at the book's Website for learning and testing in an online Flashcard Format.

Accelerated depreciation method (p. 388)
Amortization (p. 398)
Betterments (p. 393)
Book value (p. 387)
Capital expenditures (p. 392)
Change in an accounting estimate (p. 391)
Copyright (p. 399)
Cost (p. 383)
Declining-balance method (p. 388)
Depletion (p. 397)
Depreciation (p. 385)
Extraordinary repairs (p. 393)
Franchises (p. 400)
Goodwill (p. 400)
Impairment (p. 399)
Inadequacy (p. 385)
Indefinite useful life (p. 398)
Intangible assets (p. 398)
Land improvements (p. 384)
Lease (p. 400)
Leasehold (p. 400)
Leasehold improvements (p. 400)
Lessee (p. 400)
Lessor (p. 400)
Licenses (p. 400)
Modified Accelerated Cost Recovery System (MACRS) (p. 390)
Natural resources (p. 397)
Obsolescence (p. 385)
Ordinary repairs (p. 393)
Patent (p. 399)
Plant assets (p. 382)
Revenue expenditures (p. 392)
Salvage value (p. 385)
Straight-line depreciation (p. 386)
Total asset turnover (p. 401)
Trademark or trade (brand) name (p. 400)
Units-of-production depreciation (p. 387)
Useful life (p. 385)

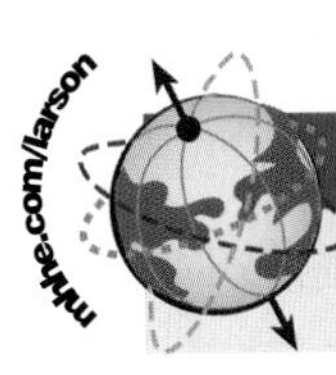

Personal Interactive Quiz

Personal Interactive Quizzes A and B are available at the book's Website to reinforce and assess your learning.

Superscript letter A denotes assignments based on Appendix 10A.

Discussion Questions

1. What is the general rule for costs included in a plant asset?
2. What characteristics of a plant asset make it different from other assets?
3. What is the balance sheet classification for land that is held for future expansion? Why is such land not classified as a plant asset?
4. What is different between land and land improvements?
5. Why is the Modified Accelerated Cost Recovery System not generally accepted for financial accounting purposes?
6. Does the balance in the Accumulated Depreciation—Machinery account represent funds to replace the machinery when it wears out? If not, what does it represent?
7. What accounting principle justifies charging low-cost plant asset purchases immediately to an expense account?

8. What is the difference between ordinary repairs and extraordinary repairs? How should each be recorded?
9. Identify events that might lead to disposal of a plant asset.
10. What is the process of allocating the cost of natural resources to expense as they are used?
11. What are the characteristics of an intangible asset?
12. Is the declining-balance method an acceptable way to compute depletion of natural resources? Explain.
13. What general procedures are applied in accounting for the acquisition and potential cost allocation of intangible assets?
14. When do we know that a company has goodwill? When can goodwill appear in a company's balance sheet?
15. Assume that a company buys another business and pays for its goodwill. If the company plans to incur costs each year to maintain the value of the goodwill, must it also amortize this goodwill?
16. How does accounting for long-term assets impact the statement of cash flows?
17. How is total asset turnover computed? Why would a financial statement user be interested in total asset turnover?
18. Refer to **Krispy Kreme**'s balance sheet in Appendix A. What title does Krispy Kreme use for its plant assets? What is its book value of plant assets as of February 2, 2003, and February 3, 2002?
19. Refer to **Tastykake**'s balance sheet in Appendix A. How are Tastykake's plant assets reported (with amounts) on its 2002 balance sheet?

20. Refer to the December 31, 2002, balance sheet of **Harley-Davidson** in Appendix A. What long-term assets discussed in this chapter are reported?

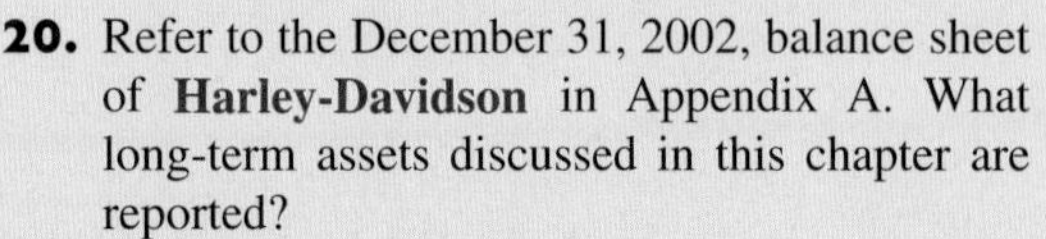

Harley-Davidson

Red numbers denote Discussion Questions that involve decision-making.

***Homework Manager** repeats all numerical Quick Studies on the book's Website with new numbers.*

QUICK STUDY

QS 10-1
Cost of plant assets
P1

Bowl-4-Fun installs automatic scorekeeping equipment with an invoice cost of $180,000. The electrical work required for the installation costs $18,000. Additional costs are $3,000 for delivery and $12,600 for sales tax. During the installation, a component of the equipment is carelessly left on a lane and hit by the automatic lane-cleaning machine. The cost of repairing the component is $2,250. What is the total recorded cost of the automatic scorekeeping equipment?

QS 10-2
Defining assets
C1

Identify the main difference between (1) plant assets and current assets, (2) plant assets and inventory, and (3) plant assets and long-term investments.

QS 10-3
Depreciation methods
P2

On January 2, 2005, the Crossover Band acquires sound equipment for concert performances at a cost of $55,900. The band estimates it will use this equipment for four years, during which time it anticipates performing about 120 concerts. It estimates that after four years it can sell the equipment for $1,900. During year 2005, the band performs 40 concerts. Compute the year 2005 depreciation using the (1) straight-line method and (2) units-of-production method.

QS 10-4
Computing revised depreciation
C3

Refer to the facts in QS 10-3. Assume that Crossover Band chose straight-line depreciation but realizes early in the second year that due to concert bookings beyond expectations, this equipment will last only a total of three years. The salvage value remains unchanged. Compute the revised depreciation for both the second and third years.

QS 10-5
Double-declining-balance method
P2

A fleet of refrigerated delivery trucks is acquired on January 5, 2005, at a cost of $930,000 with an estimated useful life of eight years and an estimated salvage value of $150,000. Compute the depreciation expense for the first three years using the double-declining-balance method.

QS 10-6
Revenue and capital expenditures
P3

1. Classify the following as either a revenue or a capital expenditure:
   a. Completed an addition to an office building for $250,000 cash.
   b. Paid $160 for the monthly cost of replacement filters on an air-conditioning system.
   c. Paid $300 cash per truck for the cost of their annual tune-ups.
   d. Paid $50,000 cash to replace a compressor on a refrigeration system that extends its useful life by four years.
2. Prepare the journal entries to record transactions *a* and *d* of part 1.

QS 10-7
Similar asset exchange
P4

Esteban Co. owns a machine that costs $38,400 with accumulated depreciation of $20,400. Esteban exchanges the machine for a similar but newer model that has a market value of $48,000. Record the exchange assuming Esteban also paid cash of (1) $32,000 and (2) $24,000.

QS 10-8
Natural resources and depletion
P5

Corazon Company acquires an ore mine at a cost of $1,300,000. It incurs additional costs of $200,000 to access the mine, which is estimated to hold 500,000 tons of ore. The estimated value of the land after the ore is removed is $150,000.

1. Prepare the entry(ies) to record the cost of the ore mine.
2. Prepare the year-end adjusting entry if 90,000 tons of ore are mined and sold the first year.

QS 10-9
Classify assets
P5 P6 

Which of the following assets are reported on the balance sheet as intangible assets? Which are reported as natural resources? (*a*) Oil well, (*b*) Trademark, (*c*) Leasehold, (*d*) Gold mine, (*e*) Building, (*f*) Copyright, (*g*) Franchise, (*h*) Timberland.

QS 10-10
Intangible assets and amortization
P6

On January 4 of this year, Best Boutique incurs a $95,000 cost to modernize its store. Improvements include new floors, ceilings, wiring, and wall coverings. These improvements are estimated to yield benefits for 10 years. Best leases its store and has eight years remaining on the lease. Prepare the entry to record (1) the cost of modernization and (2) amortization at the end of this current year.

QS 10-11
Computing total asset turnover
A2 

Eastman Company reports the following ($ millions): net sales of $13,557 for 2005 and $12,670 for 2004; end-of-year total assets of $14,968 for 2005 and $18,810 for 2004. Compute its total asset turnover for 2005 and assess its level if competitors average a total asset turnover of 2.0 times.

Homework Manager *repeats all numerical Exercises on the book's Website with new numbers.*

EXERCISES

Exercise 10-1
Cost of plant assets
P1

Farha Co. purchases a machine for $11,500, terms 2/10, n/60, FOB shipping point. The seller prepaid the $260 freight charges, adding the amount to the invoice and bringing its total to $11,760. The machine requires special steel mounting and power connections costing $795. Another $375 is paid to assemble the machine and get it into operation. In moving the machine to its steel mounting, $190 in damages occurred. Also, $30 of materials is used in adjusting the machine to produce a satisfactory product. The adjustments are normal for this machine and are not the result of the damages. Compute the cost recorded for this machine. (Farha pays for this machine within the cash discount period.)

Exercise 10-2
Recording costs of assets
C1 P1

Cerner Manufacturing purchases a large lot on which an old building is located as part of its plans to build a new plant. The negotiated purchase price is $225,000 for the lot plus $120,000 for the old building. The company pays $34,500 to tear down the old building and $51,000 to landscape the lot. It also pays a total of $1,440,000 in construction costs—this amount consists of $1,354,500 for the new building and $85,500 for lighting and paving a parking area next to the building. Prepare a single journal entry to record these costs incurred by Cerner, all of which are paid in cash.

Exercise 10-3
Lump-sum purchase of plant assets C1

Ming Yue Company pays $368,250 for real estate plus $19,600 in closing costs. The real estate consists of land appraised at $166,320; land improvements appraised at $55,440; and a building appraised at $174,240. Allocate the total cost among the three purchased assets and prepare the journal entry to record the purchase.

Exercise 10-4
Depreciation methods
P2

In early January 2004, LabTech purchases computer equipment for $147,000 to use in operating activities for the next four years. It estimates the equipment's salvage value at $30,000. Prepare tables showing depreciation and book value for each of the four years assuming (1) straight-line and (2) double-declining-balance depreciation.

Exercise 10-5
Depreciation methods
P2

Check (3) $6,768

Feng Company installs a computerized manufacturing machine in its factory at the beginning of the year at a cost of $42,300. The machine's useful life is estimated at 10 years, or 363,000 units of product, with a $6,000 salvage value. During its second year, the machine produces 35,000 units of product. Determine the machine's second-year depreciation under the (1) straight-line, (2) units-of-production, and (3) double-declining-balance methods.

Exercise 10-6
Depreciation methods; partial year depreciation C3

On April 1, 2004, Stone's Backhoe Co. purchases a trencher for $250,000. The machine is expected to last five years and have a salvage value of $25,000. Compute depreciation expense for year 2005 using the (1) straight-line and (2) double-declining-balance methods.

Exercise 10-7
Revising depreciation
C3

Check (2) $3,400

Summit Fitness Club uses straight-line depreciation for a machine costing $21,750, with an estimated four-year life and a $2,250 salvage value. At the beginning of the third year, Summit determines that the machine has three more years of remaining useful life, after which it will have an estimated $1,800 salvage value. Compute (1) the machine's book value at the end of its second year and (2) the amount of depreciation for each of the final three years given the revised estimates.

Exercise 10-8
Income effects of depreciation methods
A1 

Check (2) Year 3 NI, $53,328

Mulan Enterprises pays $235,200 for equipment that will last five years and have a $52,500 salvage value. By using the machine in its operations for five years, the company expects to earn $85,500 annually, after deducting all expenses except depreciation. Prepare a table showing income before depreciation, depreciation expense, and net (pretax) income for each year and for the total five-year period, assuming (1) straight-line depreciation and (2) double-declining-balance depreciation.

Exercise 10-9
Extraordinary repairs; plant asset age
P3 

Check (3) $207,450

Passat Company owns a building that appears on its prior year-end balance sheet at its original $561,000 cost less $420,750 accumulated depreciation. The building is depreciated on a straight-line basis assuming a 20-year life and no salvage value. During the first week in January of the current calendar year, major structural repairs are completed on the building at a $67,200 cost. The repairs extend its useful life for 7 years beyond the 20 years originally estimated.

1. Determine the building's age (plant asset age) as of the prior year-end balance sheet date.
2. Prepare the entry to record the cost of the structural repairs that are paid in cash.
3. Determine the book value of the building immediately after the repairs are recorded.
4. Prepare the entry to record the current calendar year's depreciation.

Exercise 10-10
Ordinary repairs, extraordinary repairs and betterments
P3

Patterson Company pays $262,500 for equipment expected to last four years and have a $30,000 salvage value. Prepare journal entries to record the following costs related to the equipment:

1. During the second year of the equipment's life, $21,000 cash is paid for a new component expected to increase the equipment's productivity by 10% a year.
2. During the third year, $5,250 cash is paid for normal repairs necessary to keep the equipment in good working order.
3. During the fourth year, $13,950 is paid for repairs expected to increase the useful life of the equipment from four to five years.

Exercise 10-11
Exchanging similar assets
P4 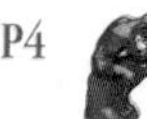

Check (2) $14,500

Jericho Construction trades in an old tractor for a new tractor, receiving a $28,000 trade-in allowance and paying the remaining $82,000 in cash. The old tractor had cost $95,000, and straight-line accumulated depreciation of $52,500 had been recorded to date under the assumption that it would last eight years and have a $11,000 salvage value. Answer the following questions:

1. What is the book value of the old tractor at the time of exchange?
2. What is the loss on this similar asset exchange?
3. What amount should be recorded (debited) in the asset account for the new tractor?

Exercise 10-12
Recording plant asset disposals
P4

On January 2, 2005, Atlantic Co. disposes of a machine costing $42,000 with accumulated depreciation of $22,625. Prepare the entries to record the disposal under each of the following separate assumptions:

1. Machine is sold for $16,250 cash.
2. Machine is traded in on a similar but newer machine having a $58,500 cash price. A $20,000 trade-in allowance is received, and the balance is paid in cash.
3. Machine is traded in on a similar but newer machine having a $58,500 cash price. A $15,000 trade-in allowance is received, and the balance is paid in cash.

Check (2) Dr. Machinery, $57,875

Exercise 10-13
Partial year depreciation; disposal of plant asset
P4

Finesse Co. purchases and installs a machine on January 1, 2004, at a total cost of $92,750. Straight-line depreciation is taken each year for four years assuming a seven-year life and no salvage value. The machine is disposed of on July 1, 2008, during its fifth year of service. Prepare entries to record the partial year's depreciation on July 1, 2008, and to record the disposal under the following separate assumptions: (1) the machine is sold for $35,000 cash and (2) Finesse receives an insurance settlement of $30,000 resulting from the total destruction of the machine in a fire.

Exercise 10-14
Depletion of natural resources
P2 P5

On April 2, 2005, Idaho Mining Co. pays $3,633,750 for an ore deposit containing 1,425,000 tons. The company installs machinery in the mine costing $171,000, with an estimated seven-year life and no salvage value. The machinery will be abandoned when the ore is completely mined. Idaho began mining on May 1, 2005, and mined and sold 156,200 tons of ore during the remaining eight months of 2005. Prepare the December 31, 2005, entries to record both the ore deposit depletion and the mining machinery depreciation. Mining machinery depreciation should be in proportion to the mine's depletion.

Exercise 10-15
Amortization of intangible assets
P6

Busch Gallery purchases the copyright on an oil painting for $236,700 on January 1, 2005. The copyright legally protects its owner for 19 more years. However, the company plans to market and sell prints of the original for only 12 years. Prepare entries to record the purchase of the copyright on January 1, 2005, and its annual amortization on December 31, 2005.

Exercise 10-16[A]
Goodwill estimation
P6 

Corey Alt has devoted years to developing a profitable business that earns an attractive return. Alt is now considering selling the business and is attempting to estimate its goodwill. The value of the business's net assets (excluding goodwill) is $437,000, and in a typical year net income is about $85,000. Most businesses of this type are expected to earn a return of about 10% on their net assets. Estimate the value of this business's goodwill for the following separate cases assuming it is (1) equal to 10 times the amount that net income is above normal and (2) computed by capitalizing at a rate of 8% the amount that net income is above normal.

Check (2) $516,250

Exercise 10-17
Cash flows related to assets
C1
Harley-Davidson

Refer to the statement of cash flows for **Harley-Davidson** in Appendix A for the fiscal year ended December 31, 2002, to answer the following:

1. What amount of cash is used to purchase property and equipment?
2. How much depreciation and amortization are recorded?
3. What total amount of net cash is used in investing activities?

Exercise 10-18
Evaluating efficient use of assets
A2 

Joy Co. reports net sales of $4,862,000 for 2004 and $7,542,000 for 2005. End-of-year balances for total assets are 2003, $1,586,000; 2004, $1,700,000; and 2005, $1,882,000. (*a*) Compute Joy's total asset turnover for 2004 and 2005. (*b*) Comment on Joy's efficiency in using its assets if its competitors average a total asset turnover of 3.0.

PROBLEM SET A

Problem 10-1A
Plant asset costs; depreciation methods

C1 C2 A1 P1 P2

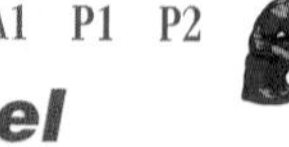

eXcel
mhhe.com/larson

Xavier Construction negotiates a lump-sum purchase of several assets from a company that is going out of business. The purchase is completed on January 1, 2005, at a total cash price of $787,500 for a building, land, land improvements, and six vehicles. The estimated market values of the assets are building, $408,000; land, $289,000; land improvements, $42,500; and four vehicles, $110,500. The company's fiscal year ends on December 31.

Required

1. Prepare a table to allocate the lump-sum purchase price to the separate assets purchased (round percents to the nearest 1%). Prepare the journal entry to record the purchase.

2. Compute the depreciation expense for year 2005 on the building using the straight-line method, assuming a 15-year life and a $25,650 salvage value.

3. Compute the depreciation expense for year 2005 on the land improvements assuming a five-year life and double-declining-balance depreciation.

Check (2) $23,490
(3) $15,750

Analysis Component

4. Defend or refute this statement: Accelerated depreciation results in payment of less taxes over the asset's life.

Problem 10-2A
Asset cost allocation; straight-line depreciation

C1 C2 P1 P2

eXcel
mhhe.com/larson

In January 2005, Keona Co. pays $2,800,000 for a tract of land with two buildings on it. It plans to demolish Building 1 and build a new store in its place. Building 2 will be a company office; it is appraised at $641,300, with a useful life of 20 years and an $80,000 salvage value. A lighted parking lot near Building 1 has improvements (Land Improvements 1) valued at $408,100 that are expected to last another 14 years with no salvage value. Without the buildings and improvements, the tract of land is valued at $1,865,600. Keona also incurs the following additional costs:

Cost to demolish Building 1	$ 422,600
Cost of additional land grading	167,200
Cost to construct new building (Building 3), having a useful life of 25 years and a $390,100 salvage value	2,019,000
Cost of new land improvements (Land Improvements 2) near Building 2 having a 20-year useful life and no salvage value	158,000

Required

1. Prepare a table with the following column headings: Land, Building 2, Building 3, Land Improvements 1, and Land Improvements 2. Allocate the costs incurred by Keona to the appropriate columns and total each column (round percents to the nearest 1%).

Check (1) Land costs, $2,381,800; Building 2 costs, $616,000

2. Prepare a single journal entry to record all the incurred costs assuming they are paid in cash on January 1, 2005.

3. Using the straight-line method, prepare the December 31 adjusting entries to record depreciation for the 12 months of 2005 when these assets were in use.

(3) Depr.—Land Improv. 1 and 2, $28,000 and $7,900

Problem 10-3A
Computing and revising depreciation; revenue and capital expenditures

C3 P1 P3

Clarion Contractors completed the following transactions and events involving the purchase and operation of equipment in its business:

2004

Jan. 1 Paid $255,440 cash plus $15,200 in sales tax and $2,500 in transportation (FOB shipping point) for a new loader. The loader is estimated to have a four-year life and a $34,740 salvage value. Loader costs are recorded in the Equipment account.

Jan. 3 Paid $3,660 to enclose the cab and install air conditioning in the loader to enable operations under harsher conditions. This increased the estimated salvage value of the loader by another $1,110.

Dec. 31 Recorded annual straight-line depreciation on the loader.

Check Dec. 31, 2004, Dr. Depr. Expense—Equip., $60,238

2005

Jan. 1 Paid $4,500 to overhaul the loader's engine, which increased the loader's estimated useful life by two years.

Feb. 17 Paid $920 to repair the loader after the operator backs it into a tree.

Dec. 31 Recorded annual straight-line depreciation on the loader.

Check Dec. 31, 2005, Dr. Depr. Expense—Equip., $37,042

Required

Prepare journal entries to record these transactions and events.

Problem 10-4A
Computing and revising depreciation; selling plant assets
C3 P2 P4

Chen Company completed the following transactions and events involving its delivery trucks:

2004

Jan. 1 Paid $19,415 cash plus $1,165 in sales tax for a new delivery truck estimated to have a five-year life and a $3,000 salvage value. Delivery truck costs are recorded in the Trucks account.

Dec. 31 Recorded annual straight-line depreciation on the truck.

2005

Dec. 31 Due to new information obtained earlier in the year, the truck's estimated useful life was changed from five to four years, and the estimated salvage value was increased to $3,500. Recorded annual straight-line depreciation on the truck.

Check Dec. 31, 2005, Dr. Depr. Expense—Trucks, $4,521

2006

Dec. 31 Recorded annual straight-line depreciation on the truck.

Dec. 31 Sold the truck for $6,200 cash.

Dec. 31, 2006, Dr. Loss on Disposal of Trucks, $1,822

Required

Prepare journal entries to record these transactions and events.

Problem 10-5A
Depreciation methods; disposal of plant asset
C3 P1 P2 P4

Part 1. A machine costing $210,000 with a four-year life and an estimated $20,000 salvage value is installed in Calhoon Company's factory on January 1. The factory manager estimates the machine will produce 475,000 units of product during its life. It actually produces the following units: year 1, 121,400; year 2, 122,400; year 3, 119,600; and year 4, 118,200. The total number of units produced by the end of year 4 exceeds the original estimate—this difference was not predicted. (The machine must not be depreciated below its estimated salvage value.)

Required

Prepare a table with the following column headings and compute depreciation for each year (and total depreciation of all years combined) for the machine under each depreciation method.

Year	Straight-Line	Units-of-Production	Double-Declining-Balance

Check Year 4: Units-of-Production Depreciation, $44,640; DDB Depreciation, $6,250

Part 2. Calhoon purchases a used machine for $167,000 cash on January 2 and readies it for use the next day at a $3,420 cost. On January 3, it is installed on a required operating platform costing $1,080, and it is readied for operations. The company predicts the machine will be used for six years and have a $14,600 salvage value. Depreciation is to be charged on a straight-line basis. On December 31, at the end of its fifth year in operations, it is disposed of.

Required

a. Prepare journal entries to record the machine's purchase and the costs to ready and install it. Cash is paid for all costs incurred.

b. Prepare journal entries to record depreciation of the machine at December 31 of its first year in operations and at December 31 in the year of its disposal.

(*b*) Depr. Exp., $26,150

c. Prepare journal entries to record the machine's disposal under each of the following separate assumptions: (i) it is sold for $13,500 cash; (ii) it is sold for $45,000 cash; and (iii) it is destroyed in a fire and the insurance company pays $24,000 cash to settle the loss claim.

(iii) Dr. Loss from Fire, $16,750

Problem 10-6A
Intangible assets and natural resources
A1 P5 P6 

Check Dr. Rent Expense for: (*d*) $9,250, (*f*) $35,000

Part 1. On July 1, 2000, Sweetman Company signed a contract to lease space in a building for 15 years. The lease contract calls for annual (prepaid) rental payments of $70,000 on each July 1 throughout the life of the lease and for the lessee to pay for all additions and improvements to the leased property. On June 25, 2005, Sweetman decides to sublease the space to Kirk & Associates for the remaining 10 years of the lease—Kirk pays $185,000 to Sweetman for the right to sublease and it agrees to assume the obligation to pay the $70,000 annual rent to the building owner beginning July 1, 2005. After taking possession of the leased space, Kirk pays for improving the office portion of the leased space at a $129,840 cost. The improvements are paid for on July 5, 2005, and are estimated to have a useful life equal to the 16 years remaining in the life of the building.

Required

Prepare entries for Kirk to record (*a*) its payment to Sweetman for the right to sublease the building space, (*b*) its payment of the 2005 annual rent to the building owner, and (*c*) its payment for the office improvements. Prepare Kirk's year-end adjusting entries required at December 31, 2005, to (*d*) amortize the $185,000 cost of the sublease, (*e*) amortize the office improvements, and (*f*) record rent expense.

Part 2. On July 23 of the current year, Dakota Mining Co. pays $4,836,000 for land estimated to contain 7,800,000 tons of recoverable ore. It installs machinery costing $390,000 that has a 10-year life and no salvage value and is capable of mining the ore deposit in eight years. The machinery is paid for on July 25, seven days before mining operations begin. The company removes and sells 400,000 tons of ore during its first five months of operations. Depreciation of the machinery is in proportion to the mine's depletion as the machinery will be abandoned after the ore is mined.

Required

Preparation Component

(*c*) Depletion, $248,000; (*d*) Depreciation, $20,000

Prepare entries to record (*a*) the purchase of the land, (*b*) the cost and installation of machinery, (*c*) the first five months' depletion assuming the land has a net salvage value of zero after the ore is mined, and (*d*) the first five months' depreciation on machinery.

Analysis Component

Describe both the similarities and differences in amortization, depletion, and depreciation.

Problem 10-7A[A]
Goodwill estimation and analysis
P6 

mhhe.com/larson

Rent-Center, an equipment rental business, has the following balance sheet on December 31, 2005:

Assets		
Cash		$ 93,930
Equipment	$678,800	
Accumulated depreciation—Equipment	271,500	407,300
Buildings	340,000	
Accumulated depreciation—Buildings	182,400	157,600
Land		93,000
Total assets		$751,830
Liabilities and Equity		
Accounts payable		$ 18,650
Long-term note payable		337,250
Total equity		395,930
Total liabilities and equity		$751,830

Normal annual net income averages 20% of equity in this industry. Rent-Center regularly expects to earn $100,000 annually. The balance sheet amounts are reasonable estimates of market values for both assets (except goodwill) and liabilities. In negotiations to sell the business, Rent-Center proposes to measure goodwill by capitalizing at a rate of 15% the amount of above-normal net income. The potential buyer thinks that goodwill should be valued at five times the amount of above-normal net income.

Required

Check (1) $138,760 (2) $104,070

1. Compute the amount of goodwill as proposed by Rent-Center.
2. Compute the amount of goodwill as proposed by the potential buyer.

3. The buyer purchases the business for the net asset amount (assets less liabilities) reported on the December 31, 2005, balance sheet plus the amount proposed by Rent-Center for goodwill. What is the buyer's purchase price?
4. If the buyer earns $100,225 of net income in its first year after acquiring the business under the terms in part 3, what rate of return does the buyer earn on this investment for the first year? Explain how goodwill impacts the buyer's net income computation.

Check (4) 18.7%

PROBLEM SET B

Problem 10-1B
Plant asset costs; depreciation methods
C1 C2 A1 P1 P2

Niemeyer Company negotiates a lump-sum purchase of several assets from a contractor who is relocating. The purchase is completed on January 1, 2005, at a total cash price of $1,610,000 for a building, land, land improvements, and six trucks. The estimated market values of the assets are building, $784,800; land, $540,640; land improvements, $226,720; and three trucks, $191,840. The company's fiscal year ends on December 31.

Required

1. Prepare a table to allocate the lump-sum purchase price to the separate assets purchased (round percents to the nearest 1%). Prepare the journal entry to record the purchase.
2. Compute the depreciation expense for year 2005 on the building using the straight-line method, assuming a 12-year life and a $100,500 salvage value.
3. Compute the depreciation expense for year 2005 on the land improvements assuming a 10-year life and double-declining-balance depreciation.

Check (2) $52,000

(3) $41,860

Analysis Component

4. Defend or refute this statement: Accelerated depreciation results in payment of more taxes over the asset's life.

Problem 10-2B
Asset cost allocation; straight-line depreciation
C1 C2 P1 P2

In January 2005, InTech pays $1,350,000 for a tract of land with two buildings. It plans to demolish Building A and build a new shop in its place. Building B will be a company office; it is appraised at $472,770, with a useful life of 15 years and a $90,000 salvage value. A lighted parking lot near Building B has improvements (Land Improvements B) valued at $125,145 that are expected to last another six years with no salvage value. Without the buildings and improvements, the tract of land is valued at $792,585. InTech also incurs the following additional costs:

Cost to demolish Building A	$ 117,000
Cost of additional land grading	172,500
Cost to construct new building (Building C), having a useful life of 20 years and a $295,500 salvage value	1,356,000
Cost of new land improvements (Land Improvements C) near building C, having a 10-year useful life and no salvage value	101,250

Required

1. Prepare a table with the following column headings: Land, Building B, Building C, Land Improvements B, and Land Improvements C. Allocate the costs incurred by InTech to the appropriate columns and total each column (round percents to the nearest 1%).
2. Prepare a single journal entry to record all incurred costs assuming they are paid in cash on January 1, 2005.
3. Using the straight-line method, prepare the December 31 adjusting entries to record depreciation for the 12 months of 2005 when these assets were in use.

Check (1) Land costs, $1,059,000; Building B costs, $459,000

(3) Depr.—Land Improv. B and C, $20,250 and $10,125

Problem 10-3B
Computing and revising depreciation; revenue and capital expenditures
C3 P1 P3

Xpress Delivery Service completed the following transactions and events involving the purchase and operation of equipment for its business:

2004

Jan. 1 Paid $24,950 cash plus $1,950 in sales tax for a new delivery van that was estimated to have a five-year life and a $3,400 salvage value. Van costs are recorded in the Equipment account.

Jan. 3 Paid $1,550 to install sorting racks in the van for more accurate and quicker delivery of packages. This increases the estimated salvage value of the van by another $200.

Dec. 31 Recorded annual straight-line depreciation on the van.

Check Dec. 31, 2004, Dr. Depr. Expense—Equip., $4,970

2005

Jan. 1 Paid $1,970 to overhaul the van's engine, which increased the van's estimated useful life by two years.

May 10 Paid $600 to repair the van after the driver backed it into a loading dock.

Dec. 31 Record annual straight-line depreciation on the van.

Check Dec. 31, 2005, Dr. Depr. Expense—Equip., $3,642

Required

Prepare journal entries to record these transactions and events.

Problem 10-4B
Computing and revising depreciation; selling plant assets
C3 P2 P4

Field Instruments completed the following transactions and events involving its machinery:

2004

Jan. 1 Paid $106,600 cash plus $6,400 in sales tax for a new machine. The machine is estimated to have a six-year life and a $9,800 salvage value.

Dec. 31 Recorded annual straight-line depreciation on the machinery.

2005

Dec. 31 Due to new information obtained earlier in the year, the machine's estimated useful life was changed from six to four years, and the estimated salvage value was increased to $13,050. Recorded annual straight-line depreciation on the machinery.

Check Dec. 31, 2005, Dr. Depr. Expense—Machinery, $27,583

2006

Dec. 31 Recorded annual straight-line depreciation on the machinery.

Dec. 31 Sold the machine for $25,240 cash.

Dec. 31, 2006, Dr. Loss on Disposal of Machine, $15,394

Required

Prepare journal entries to record these transactions and events.

Problem 10-5B
Depreciation methods; disposal of plant assets
C3 P1 P2 P4

Part 1. On January 2, Gannon Co. purchases and installs a new machine costing $312,000 with a five-year life and an estimated $28,000 salvage value. Management estimates the machine will produce 1,136,000 units of product during its life. Actual production of units is as follows: year 1, 245,600; year 2, 230,400; year 3, 227,000; year 4, 232,600; and year 5, 211,200. The total number of units produced by the end of year 5 exceeds the original estimate—this difference was not predicted. (The machine must not be depreciated below its estimated salvage value.)

Required

Prepare a table with the following column headings and compute depreciation for each year (and total depreciation of all years combined) for the machine under each depreciation method.

Check DDB depreciation, Year 3, $44,928; U-of-P depreciation, Year 4, $58,150

Year	Straight-Line	Units-of-Production	Double-Declining-Balance

Part 2. On January 1, Gannon purchases a used machine for $130,000 and readies it for use the next day at a cost of $3,390. On January 4, it is mounted on a required operating platform costing $4,800, and it is readied for operations. Management estimates the machine will be used for seven years and have an $18,000 salvage value. Depreciation is to be charged on a straight-line basis. On December 31, at the end of its sixth year of use, the machine is disposed of.

Required

a. Prepare journal entries to record the machine's purchase and the costs to ready and install it. Cash is paid for all costs incurred.

(*b*) Depr. Exp., $17,170

b. Prepare journal entries to record depreciation of the machine at December 31 of its first year in operations and at December 31 in the year of its disposal.

(iii) Dr. Loss from Fire, $15,170

c. Prepare journal entries to record the machine's disposal under each of the following separate assumptions: (i) it is sold for $30,000 cash; (ii) it is sold for $50,000 cash; and (iii) it is destroyed in a fire and the insurance company pays $20,000 cash to settle the loss claim.

Problem 10-6B
Intangible assets and natural resources
A1 P5 P6 

Part 1. On January 1, 2000, Liberty Co. entered into a 12-year lease on a building. The lease contract requires (1) annual (prepaid) rental payments of $26,400 each January 1 throughout the life of the lease and (2) for the lessee to pay for all additions and improvements to the leased property. On January 1, 2007, Liberty decides to sublease the space to Moberly Co. for the remaining five years of the lease—Moberly pays $30,000 to Liberty for the right to sublease and agrees to assume the obligation to pay the $26,400 annual rent to the building owner beginning January 1, 2007. After taking possession of the leased space, Moberly pays for improving the office portion of the leased space at an $18,000 cost. The improvements are paid for on January 3, 2007, and are estimated to have a useful life equal to the 13 years remaining in the life of the building.

Required

Prepare entries for Moberly to record (*a*) its payment to Liberty for the right to sublease the building space, (*b*) its payment of the 2007 annual rent to the building owner, and (*c*) its payment for the office improvements. Prepare Moberly's year-end adjusting entries required on December 31, 2007, to (*d*) amortize the $30,000 cost of the sublease, (*e*) amortize the office improvements, and (*f*) record rent expense.

Check Dr. Rent Expense: (*d*) $6,000, (*f*) $26,400

Part 2. On February 19 of the current year, Rock Chalk Co. pays $4,450,000 for land estimated to contain 5 million tons of recoverable ore. It installs machinery costing $200,000 that has a 16-year life and no salvage value and is capable of mining the ore deposit in 12 years. The machinery is paid for on March 21, eleven days before mining operations begin. The company removes and sells 352,000 tons of ore during its first nine months of operations. Depreciation of the machinery is in proportion to the mine's depletion as the machinery will be abandoned after the ore is mined.

Required

Preparation Component

Prepare entries to record (*a*) the purchase of the land, (*b*) the cost and installation of machinery, (*c*) the first nine months' depletion assuming the land has a net salvage value of zero after the ore is mined, and (*d*) the first nine months' depreciation on machinery.

(*c*) Depletion, $313,280; (*d*) Depreciation, $14,080

Analysis Component

Describe both the similarities and differences in amortization, depletion, and depreciation.

Problem 10-7B[A]
Goodwill estimation and analysis
P6  

Pack Casual Wear has the following balance sheet on December 31, 2005:

Assets		
Cash		$ 138,700
Merchandise inventory		607,950
Buildings	$451,500	
Accumulated depreciation—Buildings	210,800	240,700
Land		192,400
Total assets		$1,179,750
Liabilities and Equity		
Accounts payable		$ 98,325
Long-term note payable		414,050
Total equity		667,375
Total liabilities and equity		$1,179,750

Normal annual net income averages 32% of equity in this industry. Pack regularly expects to earn $230,000 annually. The balance sheet amounts are reasonable estimates of market values for both assets (except goodwill) and liabilities. In negotiations to sell the business, Pack proposes to measure goodwill by capitalizing at a rate of 10% the amount of above-normal net income. The potential buyer believes that goodwill should be valued at eight times the amount of above-normal net income.

Required

Check (1) $164,400
(2) $131,520

1. Compute the amount of goodwill as proposed by Pack.
2. Compute the amount of goodwill as proposed by the potential buyer.
3. The buyer purchases the business for the net asset amount (assets less liabilities) reported on the December 31, 2005, balance sheet plus the amount proposed by Pack for goodwill. What is the buyer's purchase price?

(4) 24.1%

4. If the buyer earns $200,175 of net income in its first year after acquiring the business under the terms in part 3, what rate of return does the buyer earn on this investment for the first year? Is the goodwill asset amortized or not? Explain.

PROBLEM SET C

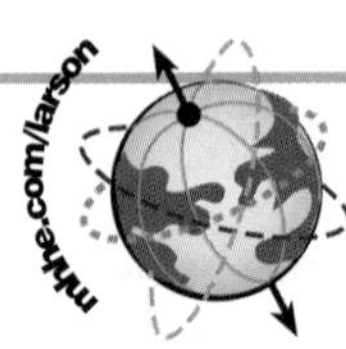

Problem Set C is available at the book's Website to further reinforce and assess your learning.

SERIAL PROBLEM

Success Systems

(This serial problem began in Chapter 1 and continues through most of the book. If previous chapter segments were not completed, the serial problem can begin at this point. It is helpful, but not necessary, for you to use the Working Papers that accompany the book.)

Selected ledger account balances for Success Systems follow.

	For the Three Months Ended December 31, 2004	For the Three Months Ended March 31, 2005
Office equipment	$ 8,000	$ 8,000
Accumulated depreciation—Office equipment	400	800
Computer equipment	20,000	20,000
Accumulated depreciation—Computer equipment	1,250	2,500
Total revenue	31,284	43,853
Total assets	93,248	129,909

Required

1. Assume that Success Systems does not acquire additional office equipment or computer equipment in 2005. Compute the amounts for the year ended December 31, 2005, for Depreciation Expense—Office Equipment and for Depreciation Expense—Computer Equipment (assume use of the straight-line method).
2. What is the book value of both the Office Equipment account and the Computer Equipment account as of December 31, 2005?
3. Compute the 3-month total asset turnover for Success Systems as of March 31, 2005. Use total revenue for the numerator and average the December 31, 2004, total assets and the March 31, 2005, total assets for the denominator. Interpret its total asset turnover if competitors average 2.5 for annual periods.

BEYOND THE NUMBERS

REPORTING IN ACTION

A1 A2

BTN 10-1 Refer to the financial statements of **Krispy Kreme** in Appendix A to answer the following:

1. What percent of the original cost of Krispy Kreme's property, plant, and equipment remains to be depreciated as of February 2, 2003, and February 3, 2002? Assume these assets have no salvage value.
2. Over what length(s) of time is Krispy Kreme amortizing its intangible assets?
3. What is the change in total property and equipment (before accumulated depreciation) for the year ended February 2, 2003? What is the amount of cash provided (used) by investing activities for property and equipment for the year ended February 2, 2003? What is one possible explanation for the difference between these two amounts?
4. Compute its total asset turnover for the year ended February 2, 2003.

Roll On

5. Access Krispy Kreme's financial statements for fiscal years ending after February 2, 2003, at its Website (KrispyKreme.com) or the SEC's EDGAR database (www.SEC.gov). Recompute Krispy's total asset turnover for the additional years' data you collect. Comment on any differences relative to the turnover computed in part 4.

BTN 10-2 Key comparative figures ($ thousands) for **Krispy Kreme** and **Tastykake** follow:

COMPARATIVE ANALYSIS

A2

Key Figures	Krispy Kreme Current Year	Krispy Kreme One Year Prior	Krispy Kreme Two Years Prior	Tastykake Current Year	Tastykake One Year Prior	Tastykake Two Years Prior
Total assets	$410,487	$255,376	$171,493	$116,560	$116,137	$112,192
Net sales	491,549	394,354	300,715	162,263	166,245	162,877

Required

1. Compute total asset turnover for the most recent two years for both Krispy Kreme and Tastykake using the data shown.

2. Which company is more efficient in generating net sales given the total assets it employs?

BTN 10-3 Flo Choi owns a small business and manages its accounting. Her company just finished a year in which a large amount of borrowed funds was invested in a new building addition as well as in equipment and fixture additions. Choi's banker requires her to submit semiannual financial statements so he can monitor the financial health of her business. He has warned her that if profit margins erode, he might raise the interest rate on the borrowed funds to reflect the increased loan risk from the bank's point of view. Choi knows profit margin is likely to decline this year. As she prepares year-end adjusting entries, she decides to apply the following depreciation rule: All asset additions are considered to be in use on the first day of the following month. (The previous rule assumed assets are in use on the first day of the month nearest to the purchase date.)

ETHICS CHALLENGE

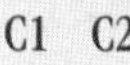

C1 C2

Required

1. Identify decisions that managers like Choi must make in applying depreciation methods.

2. Is Choi's rule an ethical violation, or is it a legitimate decision in computing depreciation?

3. How will Choi's depreciation rule affect the profit margin of her business?

BTN 10-4 Teams are to select an industry, and each team member is to select a different company in that industry. Each team member is to acquire the financial statements (form 10-K) of the company selected—see the company's Website or the SEC's EDGAR database (www.SEC.gov). Use the financial statements to compute total asset turnover. Communicate with teammates via a meeting, e-mail, or telephone to discuss the meaning of this ratio, how different companies compare to each other, and the industry norm. The team must prepare a one-page report that describes the ratios for each company and identifies the conclusions reached during the team's discussion.

COMMUNICATING IN PRACTICE

A2

BTN 10-5 Access **Adaptec**'s (ticker: ADPT) 10-K report for its fiscal year ended March 31, 2002, filed on June 24, 2002, at www.SEC.gov to answer the following.

TAKING IT TO THE NET

C1 P6

mhhe.com/larson

Required

1. Read the overview of Adaptec's business and briefly describe the types of products it produces.

2. On page 12 of its 10-K, what information is provided regarding the company's patents?

3. Does Adaptec show any patent-related revenue or expense on its consolidated statement of operations (income statement)?

TEAMWORK IN ACTION

C2 A1 P2

Point: This activity can follow an overview of each method. Step 1 allows for three areas of expertise. Larger teams will have some duplication of areas, but the straight-line choice should not be duplicated. Expert teams can use the book and consult with the instructor.

BTN 10-6 Each team member is to become an expert on one depreciation method to facilitate teammates' understanding of that method. Follow these procedures:

a. Each team member is to select an area for expertise from one of the following depreciation methods: straight-line, units-of-production, or double-declining-balance.

b. Expert teams are to be formed from those who have selected the same area of expertise. The instructor will identify the location where each expert team meets.

c. Using the following data, expert teams are to collaborate and develop a presentation answering the requirements. Expert team members must write the presentation in a format they can show to their learning teams.

Data and Requirements On January 8, 2004, Whitewater Riders purchases a van to transport rafters back to the point of departure at the conclusion of the rafting adventures they operate. The cost of the van is $44,000. It has an estimated salvage value of $2,000 and is expected to be used for four years and driven 60,000 miles. The van is expected to be driven 12,000 miles in 2004, 18,000 miles in 2005, 21,000 in 2006, and 10,000 in 2007.

1. Compute annual depreciation expense for each year of the van's estimated useful life.
2. Explain when and how annual depreciation is recorded.
3. Explain the impact on income of this depreciation method versus others over the van's life.
4. Identify the van's book value for each year of its life and illustrate the reporting of this amount for any one year.

d. Re-form original learning teams. In rotation, experts are to present to their teams the results from part *c*. Experts are to encourage and respond to questions.

BUSINESS WEEK ACTIVITY

C1 P6

mhhe.com/larson

BTN 10-7 Read the article "How Much Is the Goodwill Worth?" in the September 16, 2002, issue of ***Business Week***. (The book's Website provides a free link.)

Required

1. Explain how goodwill is calculated in accounting terms.
2. Before the accounting rules changed, how was goodwill accounted for?
3. How have the accounting rules governing goodwill recently changed?
4. Why is it a good idea to become familiar with accounting for goodwill?

ENTREPRENEURIAL DECISION

A2

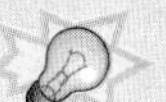

BTN 10-8 Review the chapter's opening feature involving **Queston Construction**. Assume that it generates annual sales of $3 million on an average total asset base of $1,000,000. To increase sales, Cordova proposes to expand her construction company, which would increase average total assets by $500,000. This expansion is expected to increase net sales by $2,500,000.

Required

1. Compute the company's total asset turnover under (*a*) current conditions and (*b*) proposed conditions.
2. Evaluate and comment on the merits of Cordova's proposal given your analysis in part 1. Identify any concerns you would express about the proposal.

HITTING THE ROAD

C1 P5 P6

BTN 10-9 Team up with one or more classmates for this activity. Identify companies in your community or area that must account for at least one of the following assets: natural resource; patent; lease; leasehold improvement; copyright; trademark; or goodwill. You might find a company having more than one type of asset. Once you identify a company with a specific asset, describe the accounting this company uses to allocate the cost of that asset to the periods benefited from its use.

GLOBAL DECISION

A2

BTN 10-10 **Grupo Bimbo**, **Krispy Kreme**, and **Tastykake** are all competitors in the global marketplace. Key comparative figures (in millions) for these companies' recent annual accounting periods follow.

	Grupo Bimbo (millions of pesos)			Krispy Kreme		Tastykake	
Key Figures	Current Year	Prior Year	Two Years Prior	Current Year	Prior Year	Current Year	Prior Year
Total assets	31,719	23,781	25,035	$410	$255	$117	$116
Net sales	41,373	34,968	32,008	$492	$394	$162	$166
Total asset turnover	?	?	—	1.48	1.85	1.39	1.46

Required

1. Compute total asset turnover for the most recent two years for Grupo Bimbo using the data shown.

2. Which company of the three is most efficient in generating net sales given the total assets it employs?

"I like to be independent and to be able to control my own destiny"—André Downey

11 Current Liabilities and Payroll Accounting

A Look Back

Chapter 10 focused on long-term assets including plant assets, natural resources, and intangibles. We showed how to record their costs, allocate their costs to periods benefiting from their use, record their disposal, and assess their turnover.

A Look at This Chapter

This chapter emphasizes current liabilities. We explain how to identify, compute, record, and report current liabilities in financial statements. We also analyze and interpret these liabilities, including those related to employee payroll.

A Look Ahead

Chapter 12 explains the partnership form of organization. It also describes the accounting concepts and procedures for the basic transactions of partnerships.

CAP

Conceptual

C1 Describe current and long-term liabilities and their characteristics. *(p. 424)*

C2 Identify and describe known current liabilities. *(p. 426)*

C3 Explain how to account for contingent liabilities. *(p. 436)*

Analytical

A1 Compute the times interest earned ratio and use it to analyze liabilities. *(p. 437)*

Procedural

P1 Prepare entries to account for short-term notes payable. *(p. 427)*

P2 Compute and record *employee* payroll deductions and liabilities. *(p. 429)*

P3 Compute and record *employer* payroll expenses and liabilities. *(p. 431)*

P4 Account for estimated liabilities, including warranties and bonuses. *(p. 433)*

Decision Feature

Cleaning Up in Business

LANDOVER, MD—26-year-old André Downey saw opportunity in environmental cleanup. Downey, however, faced obstacles in funding his business because banks did not share his enthusiasm. Convinced of his eventual success, Downey obtained 10 credit cards that, in sum, provided him $100,000 for his start-up called **Environmental, Engineering & Construction, Inc. (EECinc.com).** That was 1993. Today, Downey's company projects annual revenues of more than $3 million.

"There is a lot of risk involved," admits Downey. "But if you're successful, the benefits definitely outweigh the risks." His company focuses on cleanup of environmental hazards such as black toxic mold, asbestos, and lead.

Downey's service-oriented business demands good employees and he is devoted to them. "Luckily, I have good people working for me," says Downey. "So I can go to the next level." This next level requires Downey to attend to many aspects of business, including the crucial task of managing liabilities for payroll, supplies, employee benefits, vacations, training, and taxes. Without his effective management of liabilities, especially payroll and employee benefits, his company would not be where it is today. Adds Downey, if you want your business to be successful, monitoring and controlling liabilities is a must.

This chapter focuses on measuring and analyzing current liabilities like those Downey insists must be dealt with by good business owners. To ignore them, especially those requiring payments to government agencies and to key employees, is too risky. "This way," says Downey, "if I fail, it's on me." Given his revenue projections, Downey is cleaning up with more than the environment.

[Sources: *Environmental, Engineering & Construction Website,* January 2004; *Black Enterprise,* November 2002; *Gazette Community News,* December 2002.]

Previous chapters introduced liabilities such as accounts payable, notes payable, wages payable, and unearned revenues. This chapter further explains these liabilities and additional ones such as warranties, taxes, payroll, vacation pay, and bonuses. It also describes contingent liabilities and introduces some basic long-term liabilities. The focus is on how to define, classify, measure, report, and analyze these liabilities so that this information is useful to business decision makers.

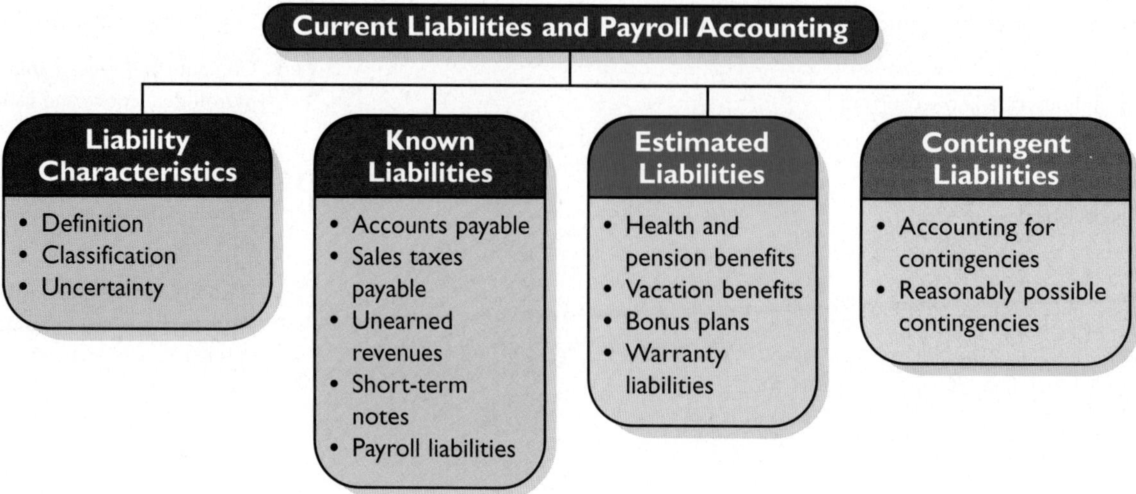

Characteristics of Liabilities

This section discusses important characteristics of liabilities and how liabilities are classified and reported.

Defining Liabilities

C1 Describe current and long-term liabilities and their characteristics.

A *liability* is a probable future payment of assets or services that a company is presently obligated to make as a result of past transactions or events. This definition includes three crucial factors:

- A past transaction or event.
- A present obligation.
- A future payment of assets or services.

Exhibit 11.1

Characteristics of a Liability

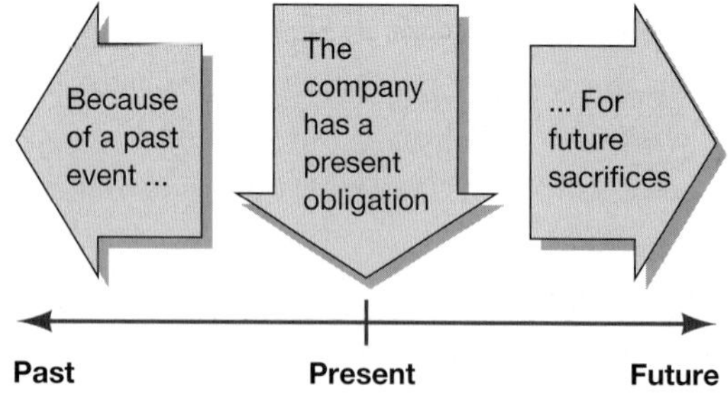

These three important elements are portrayed visually in Exhibit 11.1. Liabilities do not include all expected future payments. For example, most companies expect to pay wages to their employees in upcoming months and years, but these future payments are not liabilities because no past event such as employee work resulted in a present obligation. Instead, such liabilities arise when employees perform their work and earn the wages.

Classifying Liabilities

Information about liabilities is more useful when the balance sheet identifies them as either current or long term. Decision makers need to know when obligations are due so they can plan for them and take appropriate action.

Current Liabilities **Current liabilities,** also called *short-term liabilities,* are obligations due within one year or the company's operating cycle, whichever is longer. They are expected to be paid using current assets or by creating other current liabilities. Common examples of current liabilities are accounts payable, short-term notes payable, wages payable, warranty liabilities, lease liabilities, taxes payable, and unearned revenues.

Point: Improper classification of liabilities can distort key ratios used in financial statement analysis and decision making.

Current liabilities differ across companies because they depend on the type of company operations. **Univision Communications**, for instance, reported the following current liabilities related to its Spanish-language media operations ($000s):

Music copyright and artist royalties	$25,611
Deferred advertising revenues	4,250

Harley-Davidson reports a much different set of current liabilities. It discloses current liabilities made up of items such as warranty, recall, and dealer incentive liabilities.

Long-Term Liabilities A company's obligations not expected to be paid within the longer of one year or the company's operating cycle are reported as **long-term liabilities.** They can include long-term notes payable, warranty liabilities, lease liabilities, and bonds payable. They are sometimes reported on the balance sheet in a single long-term liabilities total or in multiple categories. **Domino's Pizza**, for instance, reports long-term liabilities of $641 million. They are reported after current liabilities. A single liability also can be divided between the current and noncurrent sections if a company expects to make payments toward it in both the short and long term. Domino's reports ($ millions) long-term debt, $599; and current portion of long-term debt, $3. The second item is reported in current liabilities. We sometimes see liabilities that do not have a fixed due date but instead are payable on the creditor's demand. These are reported as current liabilities because of the possibility of payment in the near term. Exhibit 11.2 shows amounts of current liabilities and as a percent of total liabilities for selected companies.

Global: In some countries such as France, the balance sheet does not separate current liabilities into their own category.

Point: The current ratio will be overstated if a company fails to classify any portion of long-term debt due next period as a current liability.

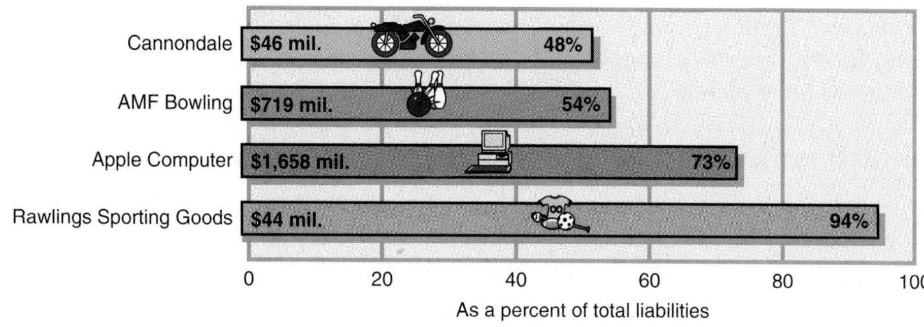

Exhibit 11.2

Current Liabilities of Selected Companies

Uncertainty in Liabilities

Accounting for liabilities involves addressing three important questions: Whom to pay? When to pay? How much to pay? Answers to these questions are often decided when a liability is incurred. For example, if a company has a $100 account payable to a specific individual, payable on March 15, the answers are clear. The company knows whom to pay, when to pay, and how much to pay. However, the answers to one or more of these questions are uncertain for some liabilities.

Uncertainty in Whom to Pay Liabilities can involve uncertainty in whom to pay. For instance, a company can create a liability with a known amount when issuing a note that is payable to its holder. In this case, a specific amount is payable to the note's holder at a specified date, but the company does not know who the holder is until that date. Despite this uncertainty, the company reports this liability on its balance sheet.

Point: An *accrued expense* is an unpaid expense that is also a liability. This is the reason accrued expenses are also called *accrued liabilities.*

Uncertainty in When to Pay A company can have an obligation of a known amount to a known creditor but not know when it must be paid. For example, a legal services firm can accept fees in advance from a client who plans to use the firm's services in the future. This means that the firm has a liability that it settles by providing services at an unknown future date. Although this uncertainty exists, the legal firm's balance sheet must report this liability. These types of obligations are reported as current liabilities because they are likely to be settled in the short term.

Uncertainty in How Much to Pay A company can be aware of an obligation but not know how much will be required to settle it. For example, a company using electrical power is billed only after the meter has been read. This cost is incurred and the liability created before a bill is received. A liability to the power company is reported as an estimated amount if the balance sheet is prepared before a bill arrives.

Quick Check

1. What is a liability? Identify its crucial characteristics.
2. Is every expected future payment a liability?
3. If a liability is payable in 15 months, is it classified as current or long term?

Answers—p. 448

Known (Determinable) Liabilities

Most liabilities arise from situations with little uncertainty. They are set by agreements, contracts, or laws and are measurable. These liabilities are **known liabilities,** also called *definitely determinable liabilities.* Known liabilities include accounts payable, notes payable, payroll, sales taxes, unearned revenues, and leases. We describe how to account for these known liabilities in this section.

Accounts Payable

C2 Identify and describe known current liabilities.

Accounts payable, or trade accounts payable, are amounts owed to suppliers for products or services purchased on credit. Accounting for accounts payable is primarily explained and illustrated in our discussion of merchandising activities in Chapters 5 and 6.

Sales Taxes Payable

Nearly all states and many cities levy taxes on retail sales. Sales taxes are stated as a percent of selling prices. The seller collects sales taxes from customers when sales occur and remits these collections (often monthly) to the proper government agency. Since sellers currently owe these collections to the government, this amount is a current liability. **Home Depot**, for instance, reports sales taxes payable of $307 million in its recent annual report. To illustrate, if Home Depot sells materials on August 31 for $6,000 cash that are subject to a 5% sales tax, the revenue portion of this transaction is recorded as follows:

Assets	=	Liabilities	+	Equity
+6,300		+300		+6,000

Aug. 31	Cash	6,300	
	Sales		6,000
	Sales Taxes Payable ($6,000 × 0.05)		300
	To record cash sales and 5% sales tax.		

Sales Taxes Payable is debited and Cash credited when it remits these collections to the government. Sales Taxes Payable is not an expense. It arises because laws require sellers to collect this cash from customers for the government.[1]

Unearned Revenues

Unearned revenues (also called *deferred revenues, collections in advance,* and *prepayments*) are amounts received in advance from customers for future products or services. Advance ticket sales for sporting events or music concerts are examples. The **New York Jets**, for instance, report "deferred game revenues" from advance ticket sales in its balance sheet. To illustrate, assume the Jets sell $5 million of season tickets for 8 home games; its entry is

Point: To *defer* a revenue means to postpone recognition of a revenue collected in advance until it is earned. Sport teams must defer recognition of ticket sales until games are played.

June 30	Cash	5,000,000	
	Unearned Season Ticket Revenue		5,000,000
	To record sale of season tickets.		

Assets = Liabilities + Equity
+5,000,000 +5,000,000

When a home game is played, the Jets record revenue for that portion earned:

Oct. 31	Unearned Season Ticket Revenue	625,000	
	Season Ticket Revenue		625,000
	To record season ticket revenues earned.		

Assets = Liabilities + Equity
−625,000 +625,000

Unearned Season Ticket Revenue is an unearned revenue account and is reported as a current liability. Unearned revenues also arise with airline ticket sales, magazine subscriptions, construction projects, hotel reservations, and custom orders.

Short-Term Notes Payable

P1 Prepare entries to account for short-term notes payable.

A **short-term note payable** is a written promise to pay a specified amount on a definite future date within one year or the company's operating cycle, whichever is longer. These promissory notes are negotiable (as are checks), meaning they can be transferred from party to party by endorsement. The written documentation provided by notes is helpful in resolving disputes and for pursuing legal actions involving these liabilities. Most notes payable bear interest to compensate for use of the money until payment is made. Short-term notes payable can arise from many transactions. A company that purchases merchandise on credit can sometimes extend the credit period by signing a note to replace an account payable. Such notes also can arise when money is borrowed from a bank. We describe both of these cases.

Point: Required characteristics for negotiability of a note: (1) unconditional promise, (2) in writing, (3) specific amount, and (4) definite due date.

Note Given to Extend Credit Period A company can replace an account payable with a note payable. A common example is a creditor that requires the substitution of an interest-bearing note for an overdue account payable that does not bear interest. A less common situation occurs when a debtor's weak financial condition motivates the creditor to accept a note, sometimes for a lesser amount, and to close the account to ensure that this customer makes no additional credit purchases.

---

[1] Sales taxes can be computed from total sales receipts when sales taxes are not separately identified on the register. To illustrate, assume a 5% sales tax and $420 in total sales receipts (which includes sales taxes). Sales are computed as follows:

$$\text{Sales} = \text{Total sales receipts}/(1 + \text{Sales tax percentage}) = \$420/1.05 = \$400$$

Thus, the sales tax amount equals total sales receipts minus sales, or $420 − $400 = $20.

To illustrate, let's assume that on August 23, Irwin asks to extend its past-due $600 account payable to McGraw. After some negotiations, McGraw agrees to accept $100 cash and a 60-day, 12%, $500 note payable to replace the account payable. Irwin records the transaction with this entry:

Assets = Liabilities + Equity
−100 −600
+500

Aug. 23	Accounts Payable—McGraw	600	
	Cash		100
	Notes Payable—McGraw		500
	Gave $100 cash and a 60-day, 12% note for payment on account.		

Point: Accounts payable are detailed in a subsidiary ledger, but notes payable are sometimes not. A file with copies of notes often serves as a subsidiary ledger.

Signing the note does not resolve Irwin's debt. Instead, the form of debt is changed from an account payable to a note payable. McGraw prefers the note payable over the account payable because it earns interest and it is written documentation of the debt's existence, term, and amount. When the note comes due, Irwin pays the note and interest by giving McGraw a check for $510. Irwin records that payment with this entry:

Assets = Liabilities + Equity
−510 −500 −10

Oct. 22	Notes Payable—McGraw	500	
	Interest Expense	10	
	Cash		510
	Paid note with interest ($500 × 12% × 60/360).		

Point: Companies commonly compute interest using a 360-day year. This is known as the *banker's rule.*

Interest expense is computed by multiplying the principal of the note ($500) by the annual interest rate (12%) for the fraction of the year the note is outstanding (60 days/360 days).

Point: Cash received from long-term borrowing is reported on the statement of cash flows as a source of financing Cash from short-term borrowing is part of operating activities. Interest incurred on a note is reported on the income statement as an expense.

Point: When money is borrowed from a bank, the loan is reported as an asset (receivable) on the bank's balance sheet.

Note Given to Borrow from Bank A bank nearly always requires a borrower to sign a promissory note when making a loan. When the note matures, the borrower repays the note with an amount larger than the amount borrowed. The difference between the amount borrowed and the amount repaid is *interest.* This section considers a type of note whose signer promises to pay *principal* (the amount borrowed) plus interest. In this case, the *face value* of the note equals principal. Face value is the value shown on the face (front) of the note. To illustrate, assume that a company needs $2,000 for a project and borrows this money from a bank at 12% annual interest. The loan is made on September 30, 2005, and is due in 60 days. Specifically, the borrowing company signs a note with a face value equal to the amount borrowed. The note includes a statement similar to this: *"I promise to pay $2,000 plus interest at 12% within 60 days after September 30."* This simple note is shown in Exhibit 11.3.

Exhibit 11.3

Note with Face Value Equal to Amount Borrowed

Promissory Note

$2,000 — **Face Value** Sept. 30, 2005 — **Date**

Sixty days **after date,** I **promise to pay to the order of**

National Bank
Boston, MA

Two thousand and no/100 ---------- **Dollars**

plus interest at the annual rate of 12% .

Janet Lee

The borrower records its receipt of cash and the new liability with this entry:

Assets = Liabilities + Equity
+2,000 +2,000

Sept. 30	Cash	2,000	
	Notes Payable		2,000
	Borrowed $2,000 cash with a 60-day, 12%, $2,000 note.		

When principal and interest are paid, the borrower records payment with this entry:

Nov. 29	Notes Payable	2,000	
	Interest Expense	40	
	Cash		2,040
	Paid note with interest ($2,000 × 12% × 60/360).		

Assets = Liabilities + Equity
−2,040 −2,000 −40

End-of-period interest adjustment. When the end of an accounting period occurs between the signing of a note payable and its maturity date, the *matching principle* requires us to record the accrued but unpaid interest on the note. To illustrate, let's return to the note in Exhibit 11.3, but assume that the company borrows $2,000 cash on December 16, 2005, instead of September 30. This 60-day note matures on February 14, 2006, and the company's fiscal year ends on December 31. Thus, we need to record interest expense for the final 15 days in December.

Decision Insight

Many franchisors such as **Curves for Women** use notes to help entrepreneurs acquire their franchises. Many allow the franchise fee and equipment to be paid with notes. Payments on these notes are collected monthly and are secured by the franchisees' assets.

Specifically, we know that 15 days of the 60-day loan period for the $2,000, 12% note have elapsed by December 31. This means that one-fourth (15 days/60 days) of the $40 total interest is an expense of year 2005. The borrower records this expense with the following adjusting entry:

2005			
Dec. 31	Interest Expense	10	
	Interest Payable		10
	To record accrued interest on note ($2,000 × 12% × 15/360).		

Assets = Liabilities + Equity
+10 −10

Example: If this note is dated December 1 instead of December 16, how much expense is recorded on December 31? *Answer:* $2,000 × 12% × 30/360 = $20

When this note matures on February 14, the borrower must recognize 45 days of interest expense for year 2006 and remove the balances of the two liability accounts:

2006			
Feb. 14	Interest Expense*	30	
	Interest Payable	10	
	Notes Payable	2,000	
	Cash		2,040
	*Paid note with interest. *($2,000 × 12% × 45/360)*		

Assets = Liabilities + Equity
−2,040 −10 −30
−2,000

Payroll Liabilities

P2 Compute and record *employee* payroll deductions and liabilities.

An employer incurs several expenses and liabilities from having employees. These expenses and liabilities are often large and arise from salaries and wages earned, from employee benefits, and from payroll taxes levied on the employer. **Anheuser-Busch**, for instance, reports payroll-related current liabilities of more than $280 million from "accrued salaries, wages and benefits." We discuss payroll liabilities and related accounts in this section. The appendix to this chapter describes details about payroll reports, records, and procedures.

Point: Internal control is important for payroll accounting. Managers must monitor (1) employee hiring, (2) timekeeping, (3) payroll listings, and (4) payroll payments. Poor controls led the U.S. Army to pay nearly $10 million to deserters, fictitious soldiers, and other unauthorized entities.

***Employee* Payroll Deductions** **Gross pay** is the total compensation an employee earns including wages, salaries, commissions, bonuses, and any compensation earned before deductions such as taxes. (*Wages* usually refer to payments to employees at an hourly

Decision Insight

Delay or failure to pay withholding taxes to the government has severe consequences. For example, a 100% penalty can be levied, with interest, on the unpaid balance. The government can even close a company, take its assets, and pursue legal actions against those involved.

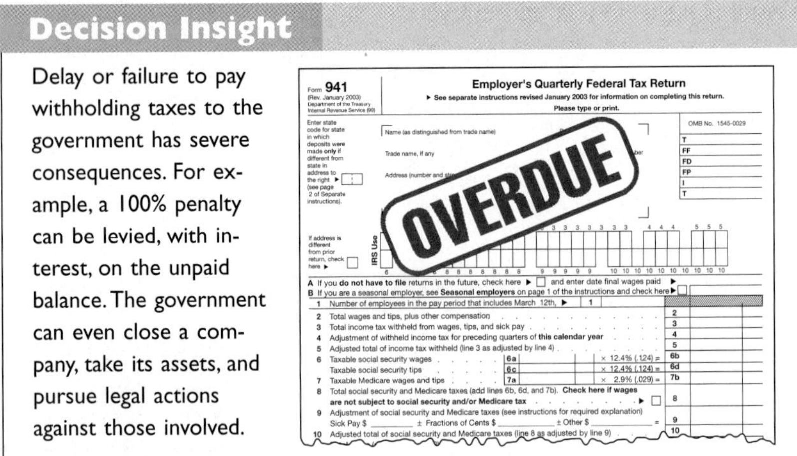

Form 941 (Rev. January 2003) Department of the Treasury Internal Revenue Service (99)

Employer's Quarterly Federal Tax Return

▶ See separate instructions revised January 2003 for information on completing this return.

Please type or print.

OMB No. 1545-0029

Name (as distinguished from trade name)

Trade name, if any

Address (number and street)

OVERDUE

A If you do not have to file returns in the future, check here ▶ ☐ and enter date final wages paid ▶

B If you are a seasonal employer, see Seasonal employers on page 1 of the instructions and check here ▶ ☐

1 Number of employees in the pay period that includes March 12th. ▶ 1

2 Total wages and tips, plus other compensation . . . 2

3 Total income tax withheld from wages, tips, and sick pay . . . 3

4 Adjustment of withheld income tax for preceding quarters of this calendar year . . . 4

5 Adjusted total of income tax withheld (line 3 as adjusted by line 4) . . . 5

6 Taxable social security wages . . . 6a × 12.4% (.124) = 6b

Taxable social security tips . . . 6c × 12.4% (.124) = 6d

7 Taxable Medicare wages and tips . . . 7a × 2.9% (.029) = 7b

8 Total social security and Medicare taxes (add lines 6b, 6d, and 7b). Check here if wages are not subject to social security and/or Medicare tax . . . ▶ ☐ 8

9 Adjustment of social security and Medicare taxes (see instructions for required explanation) Sick Pay $ ± Fractions of Cents $ ± Other $ = 9

10 Adjusted total of social security and Medicare taxes (line 8 as adjusted by line 9) 10

rate. *Salaries* usually refer to payments to employees at a monthly or yearly rate.) **Net pay,** also called *take-home pay,* is gross pay less all deductions. **Payroll deductions,** commonly called *withholdings,* are amounts withheld from an employee's gross pay, either required or voluntary. Required deductions result from laws and include income taxes and Social Security taxes. Voluntary deductions, at an employee's option, include pension and health contributions, union dues, and charitable giving. Exhibit 11.4 shows the typical payroll deductions of an employee. The employer withholds payroll deductions from employees' pay and is obligated to transmit this money to the designated organization. The employer records payroll deductions as current liabilities until these amounts are transmitted. This section discusses the major payroll deductions.

Exhibit 11.4

Payroll Deductions

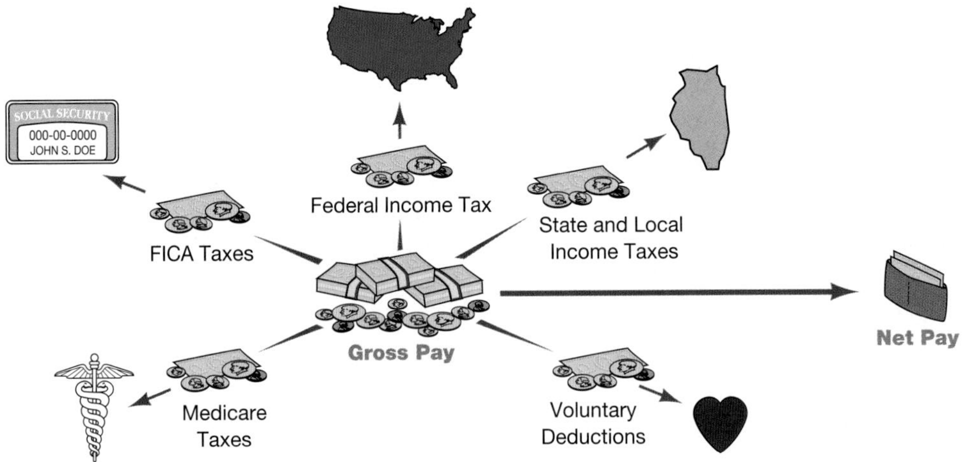

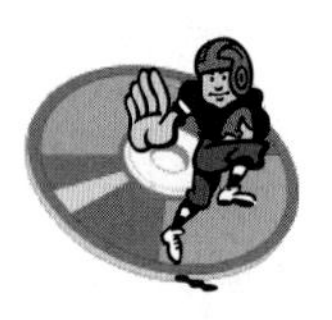

Topic Tackler 11-1

Employee FICA taxes. The federal Social Security system provides retirement, disability, survivorship, and medical benefits to qualified workers. Laws *require* employers to withhold **Federal Insurance Contributions Act (FICA) taxes** from employees' pay to cover costs of the system. Employers usually separate FICA taxes into two groups: (1) retirement, disability, and survivorship and (2) medical. For the first group, the Social Security system provides monthly cash payments to qualified retired workers for the rest of their lives. These payments are often called *Social Security benefits.* Taxes related to this group are often called *Social Security taxes.* For the second group, the system provides monthly payments to deceased workers' surviving families and to disabled workers who qualify for assistance. These payments are commonly called *Medicare benefits;* like those in the first group, they are paid with *Medicare taxes* (part of FICA taxes).

Law requires employers to withhold FICA taxes from each employee's salary or wages on each payday. The taxes for Social Security and Medicare are computed separately. For example, for the year 2003, the amount withheld from each employee's pay for Social Security tax was 6.2% of the first $87,000 the employee earns in the calendar year, or a maximum of $5,394. The Medicare tax was 1.45% of *all* amounts the employee earns; there is no maximum limit to Medicare tax.

Employers must pay withheld taxes to the Internal Revenue Service (IRS) on specific filing dates during the year. Employers who fail to send the withheld taxes to the IRS on time can be assessed substantial penalties. Until all the taxes are sent to the IRS, they are included

Point: The sources of U.S. tax receipts are roughly as follows:

10%	Corporate income tax
50	Personal income tax
35	FICA and FUTA taxes
5	Other taxes

in employers' current liabilities. For any changes in rates or with the maximum earnings level, check the IRS Website at www.IRS.gov.

Employee income tax. Most employers are required to withhold federal income tax from each employee's paycheck. The amount withheld is computed using tables published by the IRS. The amount depends on the employee's annual earnings rate and the number of *withholding allowances* the employee claims. Allowances reduce the amount of taxes one owes the government. The more allowances one claims, the less tax the employer will withhold. Employees can claim allowances for themselves and their dependents. They also can claim additional allowances if they expect major declines in their taxable income for medical expenses. (An employee who claims more allowances than appropriate is subject to a fine.) Most states and many local governments require employers to withhold income taxes from employees' pay and to remit them promptly to the proper government agency. Until they are paid, withholdings are reported as a current liability on the employer's balance sheet.

Point: Part-time employees may claim "exempt from withholding" if they did not have any income tax liability in the prior year and do not expect any in the current year.

Point: IRS withholding tables are based on projecting weekly (or other period) pay into an annual figure.

Employee voluntary deductions. Beyond Social Security, Medicare, and income taxes, employers often withhold other amounts from employees' earnings. These withholdings arise from employee requests, contracts, unions, or other agreements. They can include amounts for charitable giving, medical insurance premiums, pension contributions, and union dues. Until they are paid, such withholdings are reported as part of employers' current liabilities.

Recording employee payroll deductions. Employers must accrue payroll expenses and liabilities at the end of each pay period. To illustrate, assume that an employee earns a salary of $2,000 per month. At the end of January, the employer's entry to accrue payroll expenses and liabilities for this employee is

Jan. 31	Salaries Expense	2,000	
	FICA—Social Security Taxes Payable (6.2%) . .		124
	FICA—Medicare Taxes Payable (1.45%)		29
	Employee Federal Income Taxes Payable*		213
	Employee Medical Insurance Payable*		85
	Employee Union Dues Payable*		25
	Accrued Payroll Payable		1,524
	To record accrued payroll for January.		

Assets	=	Liabilities	+	Equity
		+124		−2,000
		+29		
		+213		
		+85		
		+25		
		+1,524		

*Amounts taken from employer's accounting records.

Salaries Expense (debit) shows that the employee earns a gross salary of $2,000. The first five payables (credits) show the liabilities the employer owes on behalf of this employee to cover FICA taxes, income taxes, medical insurance, and union dues. The Accrued Payroll Payable account (credit) records the $1,524 net pay the employee receives from the $2,000 gross pay earned. When the employee is paid, another entry (or a series of entries) is required to record the check written and distributed (or funds transferred). The entry to record cash payment to this employee is to debit Accrued Payroll Payable and credit Cash for $1,524.

Decision Insight

Check List Millions are lost annually to check schemes. Companies are fighting back with an internal control method called *positive pay*. Here's how it works: A company regularly (daily) sends the bank a "positive file" listing all checks written. When a check reaches the bank for payment, the bank compares the check against the positive file. This flags any forged checks and altered authentic checks.

Employer Payroll Taxes

Employers must pay payroll taxes in addition to those required of employees. Employer taxes include FICA and unemployment taxes.

P3 Compute and record *employer* payroll expenses and liabilities.

Employer FICA tax. Employers must pay FICA taxes *equal in amount to* the FICA taxes withheld from their employees. An employer's tax is credited to the same FICA Taxes Payable accounts used to record the Social Security and Medicare taxes withheld from employees. (A self-employed person must pay both the employee and employer FICA taxes.)

Federal and state unemployment taxes. The federal government participates with states in a joint federal and state unemployment insurance program. Each state administers its program. These programs provide unemployment benefits to qualified workers. The federal government approves state programs and pays a portion of their administrative expenses.

Federal Unemployment Taxes (FUTA). Employers are subject to a federal unemployment tax on wages and salaries paid to their employees. For the year 2003, employers were required to pay FUTA taxes of as much as 6.2% of the first $7,000 earned by each employee. This federal tax can be reduced by a credit of up to 5.4% for taxes paid to a state program. As a result, the net federal unemployment tax is often only 0.8%.

Decision Insight

eTax Technology helps reduce errors and increase speed in computing taxes as compared with manual computation of taxes. Also, tax tables and forms can be downloaded off the Web (**www.IRS.gov**) and then used to accurately and quickly compute payroll taxes.

State Unemployment Taxes (SUTA). All states support their unemployment insurance programs by placing a payroll tax on employers. (A few states require employees to make a contribution. In the book's assignments, we assume that this tax is only on the employer.) In most states, the base rate for SUTA taxes is 5.4% of the first $7,000 paid each employee. This base rate is adjusted according to an employer's merit rating. The state assigns a **merit rating** that reflects a company's stability or instability in employing workers. A good rating reflects stability in employment and means an employer can pay less than the 5.4% base rate. A low rating reflects high turnover or seasonal hirings and layoffs. To illustrate, an employer with 50 employees each of whom earns $7,000 or more per year saves $15,400 annually if it has a merit rating of 1.0% versus 5.4%. This is computed by comparing taxes of $18,900 at the 5.4% rate to only $3,500 at the 1.0% rate.

Decision Ethics

Web Designer You take a summer job working for a family friend who runs a small IT service. On your first payday, the owner slaps you on the back, gives you full payment in cash, winks, and adds: "No need to pay those high taxes, eh." What action do you take?

Answer—p. 448

Recording employer payroll taxes. Employer payroll taxes are an added expense beyond the wages and salaries earned by employees. These taxes are often recorded in an entry separate from the one recording payroll expenses and deductions. To illustrate, assume that the $2,000 recorded salaries expense from the previous example is earned by an employee whose earnings have not yet reached $5,000 for the year. Also assume that the federal unemployment tax rate is 0.8% and the state unemployment tax rate is 5.4%. Consequently, the FICA portion of the employer's tax is $153, computed by multiplying both the 6.2% and 1.45% by the $2,000 gross pay. Moreover, state unemployment (SUTA) taxes are $108 (5.4% of the $2,000 gross pay), and federal unemployment (FUTA) taxes are $16 (0.8% of $2,000). The entry to record the employer's payroll tax expense and related liabilities is

Example: If the employer's merit rating in this example reduces its SUTA rate to 2.9%, what is its SUTA liability? *Answer:* SUTA payable = $2,000 × 2.9% = $58

Assets	=	Liabilities	+	Equity
		+124		−277
		+29		
		+108		
		+16		

Jan. 31	Payroll Taxes Expense	277	
	FICA—Social Security Taxes Payable (6.2%) . .		124
	FICA—Medicare Taxes Payable (1.45%)		29
	State Unemployment Taxes Payable		108
	Federal Unemployment Taxes Payable		16
	To record employer payroll taxes.		

Multi-Period Known Liabilities

Many known liabilities extend over multiple periods. These often include unearned revenues and notes payable. For example, if **Sports Illustrated** sells a four-year magazine subscription, it records amounts received for this subscription in an Unearned Subscription Revenues account. Amounts in this account are liabilities, but are they current or long term? They are *both.* The portion of the Unearned Subscription Revenues account that will be fulfilled in the next year is reported as a current liability. The remaining portion is reported as a long-term liability.

Decision Insight

Small is Big The Small Business Administration (**SBA.gov**) publishes a yearly report of likely sources of small business loans. It shows that small businesses number more than 25 million, employ 53% of the private workforce, make 47% of all sales, create most new jobs, and produce 55% of innovations.

The same analysis applies to notes payable. For example, a borrower reports a three-year note payable as a long-term liability in the first two years it is outstanding. In the third year, the borrower reclassifies this note as a current liability since it is due within one year or the operating cycle, whichever is longer. The **current portion of long-term debt** refers to that part of long-term debt due within one year or the operating cycle, whichever is longer. Long-term debt is reported under long-term liabilities, but the *current portion due* is reported under current liabilities. To illustrate, assume that a $7,500 debt is paid in installments of $1,500 per year for five years. The $1,500 due within the year is reported as a current liability. No journal entry is necessary for this reclassification. Instead, we simply classify the amounts for debt as either current or long term when the balance sheet is prepared.

Some known liabilities are rarely reported in long-term liabilities. These include accounts payable, sales taxes, and wages and salaries.

Quick Check

4. Why does a creditor prefer a note payable to a past-due account payable?
5. A company pays its one employee $3,000 per month. This company's FUTA rate is 0.8% on the first $7,000 earned; its SUTA rate is 4.0% on the first $7,000; its Social Security tax rate is 6.2% of the first $87,000; and its Medicare tax rate is 1.45% of all amounts earned. The entry to record this company's March payroll includes what amount for total payroll taxes expense?
6. Identify whether the employer or employee or both incurs each of the following: (*a*) FICA taxes, (*b*) FUTA taxes, (*c*) SUTA taxes, and (*d*) withheld income taxes.

Answers—p. 448

Estimated Liabilities

P4 Account for estimated liabilities, including warranties and bonuses.

An **estimated liability** is a known obligation that is of an uncertain amount but that can be reasonably estimated. Common examples are employee benefits such as pensions, health care and vacation pay, and warranties offered by a seller. We discuss each of these in this section. Other examples of estimated liabilities include property taxes and certain contracts to provide future services.

Health and Pension Benefits

Many companies provide **employee benefits** beyond salaries and wages. An employer often pays all or part of medical, dental, life, and disability insurance. Many employers also contribute to *pension plans,* which are agreements by employers to provide benefits (payments) to employees after retirement. Many companies also provide medical care and insurance benefits to their retirees. When payroll taxes and charges for employee benefits are totaled, payroll cost often exceeds employees' gross earnings by 25% or more.

Decision Insight

Postgame Gripes Several ex-players sued **Major League Baseball** over a pension system they say unfairly excludes them and fails to reward them for their contributions. Gripes include a failure to extend pensions to players whose careers ended years ago or were interrupted by war. A full pension exceeds $120,000 per year.

To illustrate, assume that an employer agrees to (1) pay an amount for medical insurance equal to $8,000 and (2) contribute an additional 10% of the employees' $120,000 gross salary to a retirement program. The entry to record these accrued benefits is

Assets = Liabilities + Equity
+8,000 −20,000
+12,000

Jan. 31	Employee Benefits Expense	20,000	
	Employee Medical Insurance Payable		8,000
	Employee Retirement Program Payable		12,000
	To record costs of employee benefits.		

Vacation Benefits

Many employers offer paid vacation benefits, also called *paid absences*. To illustrate, assume that salaried employees earn 2 weeks' vacation per year. This benefit increases employers' payroll expenses because employees are paid for 52 weeks but work for only 50 weeks. Total annual salary is the same, but the cost per week worked is greater than the amount paid per week. For example, if an employee is paid $20,800 for 52 weeks but works only 50 weeks, the total weekly expense to the employer is $416 ($20,800/50 weeks) instead of the $400 cash paid weekly to the employee ($20,800/52 weeks). The $16 difference between these two amounts is recorded weekly as follows:

Assets = Liabilities + Equity
+16 −16

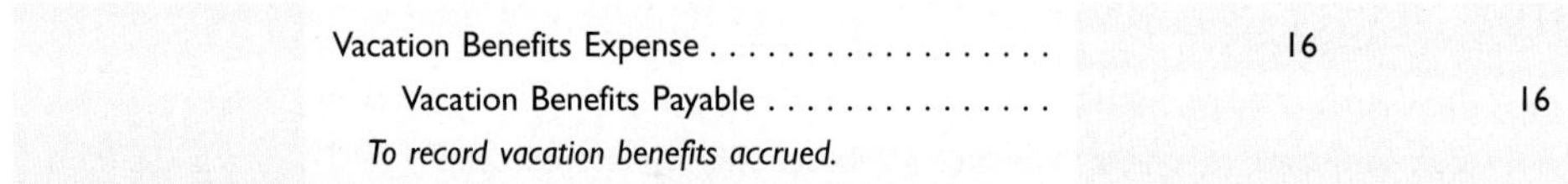

Vacation Benefits Expense	16	
Vacation Benefits Payable		16
To record vacation benefits accrued.		

Vacation Benefits Expense is an operating expense, and Vacation Benefits Payable is a current liability. When the employee takes a vacation, the employer reduces (debits) the Vacation Benefits Payable and credits Cash (no additional expense is recorded).

Global: Bonuses are considered part of salary expense in most countries. In Japan, bonuses to members of the board of directors and to external auditors are directly charged against equity rather than treated as an expense.

Bonus Plans

Many companies offer bonuses to employees, and many of the bonuses depend on net income. To illustrate, assume that an employer offers a bonus to its employees equal to 5% of the company's annual net income (to be equally shared by all). The company's expected annual net income is $210,000. The year-end adjusting entry to record this benefit is

Assets = Liabilities + Equity
+10,000 −10,000

Dec. 31	Employee Bonus Expense*.	10,000	
	Bonus Payable		10,000
	To record expected bonus costs.		

* Bonus Expense (B) equals 5% of the quantity $210,000 minus the bonus—computed as:

$$B = 0.05\ (\$210{,}000 - B)$$
$$B = \$10{,}500 - 0.05B$$
$$1.05B = \$10{,}500$$
$$\mathbf{B = \$10{,}500/1.05 = \$10{,}000}$$

When the bonus is paid, Bonus Payable is debited and Cash is credited for $10,000.

Warranty Liabilities

A **warranty** is a seller's obligation to replace or correct a product (or service) that fails to perform as expected within a specified period. Most new cars, for instance, are sold with a warranty covering parts for a specified period of time. **Ford Motor Company** reported more than $14 billion in "dealer and customer allowances and claims" in its recent annual report. To comply with the *full disclosure* and *matching principles,* the seller reports the expected warranty expense in the period when revenue from the sale of the product or service is reported. The seller reports this warranty obligation as a liability, although the existence,

Point: Zenith recently reported $32.1 million on its balance sheet for warranties.

amount, payee, and date of future sacrifices are uncertain. This is because such warranty costs are probable and the amount can be estimated using, for instance, past experience with warranties.

To illustrate, a dealer sells a used car for $16,000 on December 1, 2005, with a maximum one-year or 12,000-mile warranty covering parts. This dealer's experience shows that warranty expense averages about 4% of a car's selling price, or $640 in this case ($16,000 × 4%). The dealer records the estimated expense and liability related to this sale with this entry:

2005			
Dec. 1	Warranty Expense	640	
	Estimated Warranty Liability		640
	To record estimated warranty expense.		

Assets = Liabilities − Equity
+640 −640

This entry alternatively could be made as part of end-of-period adjustments. Either way, the estimated warranty expense is reported on the 2005 income statement and the warranty liability on the 2005 balance sheet. To further extend this example, suppose the customer returns the car for warranty repairs on January 9, 2006. The dealer performs this work by replacing parts costing $200. The entry to record partial settlement of the estimated warranty liability is

Point: Recognition of expected warranty liabilities is necessary to comply with the matching and full disclosure principles.

2006			
Jan. 9	Estimated Warranty Liability	200	
	Auto Parts Inventory		200
	To record costs of warranty repairs.		

Assets = Liabilities + Equity
−200 −200

This entry reduces the balance of the estimated warranty liability. Warranty expense was previously recorded in 2005, the year the car was sold with the warranty. Finally, what happens if total warranty expenses are more or less than the estimated 4%, or $640? The answer is that management should monitor actual warranty expenses to see whether the 4% rate is accurate. If experience reveals a large difference from the estimate, the rate for current and future sales should be changed. Differences are expected, but they should be small.

Multi-Period Estimated Liabilities

Estimated liabilities can be both current and long term. For example, pension liabilities to employees are long term to workers who will not retire within the next period. For employees who are retired or will retire within the next period, a portion of pension liabilities is current. Other examples include employee health benefits and warranties. Specifically, many warranties are for 30 or 60 days in length. Estimated costs under these warranties are properly reported in current liabilities. Many other automobile warranties are for three years or 36,000 miles. A portion of these warranties is reported as long term.

Quick Check

7. Estimated liabilities involve an obligation to pay which of these? (*a*) An uncertain but reasonably estimated amount owed on a known obligation or (*b*) A known amount to a specific entity on an uncertain due date.
8. A car is sold for $15,000 on June 1, 2005, with a one-year warranty on parts. Warranty expense is estimated at 1.5% of selling price at each calendar year-end. On March 1, 2006, the car is returned for warranty repairs costing $135. The amount recorded as warranty expense on March 1 is (*a*) $0; (*b*) $60; (*c*) $75; (*d*) $135; (*e*) $225.

Answers—p. 449

Contingent Liabilities

C3 Explain how to account for contingent liabilities.

A **contingent liability** is a potential obligation that depends on a future event arising from a past transaction or event. An example is a pending lawsuit. Here, a past transaction or event leads to a lawsuit whose result depends on the outcome of the suit. Future payment of a contingent liability depends on whether an uncertain future event occurs.

Accounting for Contingent Liabilities

Accounting for contingent liabilities depends on the likelihood that a future event will occur and the ability to estimate the future amount owed if this event occurs. Three categories are identified (see the table in the margin)

	Probable	Reasonably Possible	Remote
Amount estimable	Record contingent liability	Disclose liability in notes	No action
Amount not estimable	Disclose liability in notes	Disclose liability in notes	No action

(1) The future event is *probable* (likely) and the amount owed can be *reasonably estimated.* We record this amount as a liability. Examples are the estimated liabilities described earlier such as warranties, vacation pay, and income taxes.
(2) The future event is *remote* (unlikely). We do not record or disclose information on remote contingent liabilities.
(3) Likelihood of the future event is between these two extremes. That is, if the future event is *reasonably possible* (could occur), we disclose information about the contingent liability in notes to the financial statements.

This section identifies contingent liabilities that often fall in the third category—when the future event is reasonably possible. Disclosing information about contingencies in this third category is motivated by the *full-disclosure principle,* which requires information relevant to decision makers be reported.

Point: A contingency is an *if.* Namely, if a future event occurs, then financial consequences are likely for the entity.

Reasonably Possible Contingent Liabilities

This section discusses common examples of reasonably possible contingent liabilities.

Point: A sale of a note receivable is often a contingent liability. It becomes a liability if the original signer of the note fails to pay it at maturity.

Potential Legal Claims Many companies are sued or at risk of being sued. The accounting issue is whether the defendant should recognize a liability on its balance sheet or disclose a contingent liability in its notes while a lawsuit is outstanding and not yet settled. The answer is that a potential claim is recorded in the accounts *only* if payment for damages is probable and the amount can be reasonably estimated. If the potential claim cannot be reasonably estimated or is less than probable but reasonably possible, it is disclosed. **Ford Motor Company**, for example, includes the following note in its recent annual report: "Various legal actions, governmental investigations and proceedings and claims are pending . . . arising out of alleged defects in our products."

Decision Insight

Hot Claims Remember the infamous lawsuit against **McDonald's** that awarded an 81-year-old New Mexico woman $2.9 million—later reduced to $640,000—after she spilled hot coffee in her lap? Well, copycat litigation is booming. Companies from **Burger King** to **Starbucks** now print cautions on coffee cups, chili bowls, and so forth.

Debt Guarantees Sometimes a company guarantees the payment of debt owed by a supplier, customer, or another company. The guarantor usually discloses the guarantee in its financial statement notes as a contingent liability. If it is probable that the debtor will default, the guarantor needs to record and report the guarantee in its financial statements as a liability. The **Boston Celtics** report a unique guarantee when it comes to coaches and players: "Certain of the contracts provide for guaranteed payments which must be paid even if the employee [player] is injured or terminated."

Decision Insight

Pricing Priceless What's it worth to see from one side of the Grand Canyon to the other? What's the cost when beaches are closed due to pollution? One method to measure these environmental liabilities is **contingent valuation,** by which people are asked to answer such questions. Regulators use their answers to levy fines and assess punitive damages.

Other Contingencies Other examples of contingencies include environmental damages, possible tax assessments, insurance losses, and government investigations. **Sunoco,** for instance, reports that "federal, state and local laws . . . result in liabilities and loss contingencies. Sunoco accrues . . . cleanup costs [that] are probable and reasonably estimable. [Sunoco also] believes it is reasonably possible (i.e., less than probable but greater than remote) that additional . . . losses will be incurred." Many of Sunoco's contingencies are revealed only in notes.

Point: Auditors and managers often have different views about whether a contingency is recorded, disclosed, or omitted.

Uncertainties All organizations face uncertainties from future events such as natural disasters and the development of new competing products or services. These uncertainties are not contingent liabilities because they are future events *not* arising from past transactions. Accordingly, they are not disclosed.

Topic Tackler 11-2

Global: Accounting for contingencies varies across countries. International accounting standards require disclosure only for contingent liabilities that are reasonably possible or probable.

Quick Check

9. A future payment is reported as a liability on the balance sheet if payment is contingent on a future event that (*a*) is reasonably possible but the payment cannot be reasonably estimated; (*b*) is probable and the payment can be reasonably estimated; or (*c*) is not probable but the payment is known.
10. Under what circumstances is a future payment reported in the notes to the financial statements as a contingent liability?

Answers—p. 449

Times Interest Earned Ratio

Decision Analysis

A company incurs interest expense on many of its current and long-term liabilities. Examples extend from its short-term notes and the current portion of long-term liabilities to its long-term notes and bonds. Interest expense is often viewed as a *fixed expense* because the amount of these liabilities is likely to remain in one form or another for a substantial period of time. This means that the amount of interest is unlikely to vary due to changes in sales or other operating activities. While fixed expenses can be advantageous when a company is growing, they create risk. This risk stems from the possibility that a company might be unable to pay fixed expenses if sales decline. To illustrate, consider X-Caliber's results for year 2005 and two possible outcomes for year 2006 in Exhibit 11.5.

A1 Compute the times interest earned ratio and use it to analyze liabilities.

Exhibit 11.5
Actual and Projected Results

		Year 2006 Projections	
($ thousands)	**Year 2005**	**Sales Increase**	**Sales Decrease**
Sales	$600	$900	$300
Expenses (75% of sales)	450	675	225
Income before interest	150	225	75
Interest expense (fixed)	60	60	60
Net income	$ 90	$165	$ 15

Expenses excluding interest are at, and expected to remain at, 75% of sales. Expenses such as these that change with sales volume are called *variable expenses.* However, interest expense is at, and expected to remain at, $60,000 per year due to its fixed nature.

The middle numerical column of Exhibit 11.5 shows that X-Caliber's income nearly doubles to $165,000 if sales increase by 50% to $900,000. In contrast, the far right column shows that income falls sharply if sales decline by 50%. These results reveal that the amount of fixed interest expense affects a company's risk of its ability to pay interest, which is numerically reflected in the **times interest earned** ratio in Exhibit 11.6.

Exhibit 11.6
Times Interest Earned

$$\textbf{Times interest earned} = \frac{\textbf{Income before interest expense and income taxes}}{\textbf{Interest expense}}$$

For 2005, X-Caliber's times interest earned is computed as $150,000/$60,000, or 2.5 times. This ratio suggests that X-Caliber faces low to moderate risk because its sales must decline sharply before it would be unable to cover its interest expenses. (X-Caliber is an LLC and does not pay income taxes.)

Experience shows that when times interest earned falls below 1.5 to 2.0 and remains at that level or lower for several periods, the default rate on liabilities increases sharply. This reflects increased risk for companies and their creditors. We also must interpret the times interest earned ratio in light of information about the variability of a company's income before interest. If income is stable from year to year or if it is growing, the company can afford to take on added risk by borrowing. If its income greatly varies from year to year, fixed interest expense can increase the risk that it will not earn enough income to pay interest.

Decision Maker

Entrepreneur You wish to invest in a franchise for either one of two national chains. Each franchise has an expected annual net income *after* interest and taxes of $100,000. Net income for the first franchise includes a regular fixed interest charge of $200,000. The fixed interest charge for the second franchise is $40,000. Which franchise is riskier to you if sales forecasts are not met? Does your decision change if the first franchise has more variability in its income stream?

Answer—p. 448

Demonstration Problem

The following transactions and events took place at Kern Company during its recent calendar-year reporting period (Kern does not use reversing entries):

a. In September 2005, Kern sold $140,000 of merchandise covered by a 180-day warranty. Prior experience shows that costs of the warranty equal 5% of sales. Compute September's warranty expense and prepare the adjusting journal entry for the warranty liability as recorded at September 30. Also prepare the journal entry on October 8 to record a $300 cash expenditure to provide warranty service on an item sold in September.

b. On October 12, 2005, Kern arranged with a supplier to replace Kern's overdue $10,000 account payable by paying $2,500 cash and signing a note for the remainder. The note matures in 90 days and has a 12% interest rate. Prepare the entries recorded on October 12, December 31, and January 10, 2006, related to this transaction.

c. In late December, Kern learns it is facing a product liability suit filed by an unhappy customer. Kern's lawyer advises that although it will probably suffer a loss from the lawsuit, it is not possible to estimate the amount of damages at this time.

d. Sally Kline works for Kern. For the pay period ended November 30, her gross earnings are $3,000. Kline has $800 deducted for federal income taxes and $200 for state income taxes from each paycheck. Additionally, a $35 premium for her health care insurance and a $10 donation for the United Way are deducted. Kline pays FICA Social Security taxes at a rate of 6.2% and FICA Medicare taxes at a rate of 1.45%. She has not earned enough this year to be exempt from any FICA taxes. Journalize the payment of Kline's wages by Kern.

e. On November 1, Kern borrows $5,000 cash from a bank in return for a 60-day, 12%, $5,000 note. Record the note's issuance on November 1 and its repayment with interest on December 31.

f.[B] Kern has estimated and recorded its quarterly income tax payments. In reviewing its year-end tax adjustments, it identifies an additional $5,000 of income tax expense that should be recorded. A portion of this additional expense, $1,000, is deferrable to future years. Record this year-end income taxes expense adjusting entry.

g. For this calendar-year, Kern's net income is $1,000,000, its interest expense is $275,000, and its income taxes expense is $225,000. Calculate Kern's times interest earned ratio.

Planning the Solution

- For *a*, compute the warranty expense for September and record it with an estimated liability. Record the October expenditure as a decrease in the liability.
- For *b*, eliminate the liability for the account payable and create the liability for the note payable. Compute interest expense for the 80 days that the note is outstanding in 2005 and record it as an

additional liability. Record the payment of the note, being sure to include the interest for the 10 days in 2006.

- For *c,* decide whether the company's contingent liability needs to be disclosed or accrued (recorded) according to the two necessary criteria: probable loss and reasonably estimable.
- For *d,* set up payable accounts for all items in Kline's paycheck that require deductions. After deducting all necessary items, credit the remaining amount to Accrued Payroll Payable.
- For *e,* record the issuance of the note. Calculate 60 days' interest due using the 360-day convention in the interest formula.
- For *f,* determine how much of the income taxes expense is payable in the current year and how much needs to be deferred.
- For *g,* apply and compute times interest earned.

Solution to Demonstration Problem

a. Warranty expense = 5% × $140,000 = $7,000

Sept. 30	Warranty Expense	7,000	
	Estimated Warranty Liability		7,000
	To record warranty expense for the month.		
Oct. 8	Estimated Warranty Liability.	300	
	Cash		300
	To record the cost of the warranty service.		

b. Interest expense for 2005 = 12% × $7,500 × 80/360 = $200
Interest expense for 2006 = 12% × $7,500 × 10/360 = $25

Oct. 12	Accounts Payable	10,000	
	Notes Payable		7,500
	Cash.		2,500
	Paid $2,500 cash and gave a 90-day, 12% note to extend the due date on the account.		
Dec. 31	Interest Expense.	200	
	Interest Payable		200
	To accrue interest on note payable.		
Jan. 10	Interest Expense.	25	
	Interest Payable	200	
	Notes Payable.	7,500	
	Cash		7,725
	Paid note with interest, including the accrued interest payable.		

c. Disclose the pending lawsuit in the financial statement notes. Although the loss is probable, no liability can be accrued since the loss cannot be reasonably estimated.

d.

Nov. 30	Salaries Expense	3,000.00	
	FICA—Social Security Taxes Payable (6.2%) . .		186.00
	FICA—Medicare Taxes Payable (1.45%)		43.50
	Employee Federal Income Taxes Payable.		800.00
	Employee State Income Taxes Payable		200.00
	Employee Medical Insurance Payable		35.00
	Employee United Way Payable.		10.00
	Accrued Payroll Payable		1,725.50
	To record Kline's accrued payroll.		

e.

Nov. 1	Cash	5,000	
	Notes Payable		5,000
	Borrowed cash with a 60-day, 12% note.		

When the note and interest are paid 60 days later, Kern Company records this entry:

Dec. 31	Notes Payable	5,000	
	Interest Expense	100	
	Cash		5,100
	Paid note with interest ($5,000 × 12% × 60/360).		

f.

Dec. 31	Income Taxes Expense	5,000	
	Income Taxes Payable		4,000
	Deferred Income Tax Liability		1,000
	To record added income taxes expense and the deferred tax liability.		

g. $\text{Times interest earned} = \dfrac{\$1{,}000{,}000 + \$275{,}000 + \$225{,}000}{\$275{,}000} = \underline{\underline{5.45 \text{ times}}}$

APPENDIX

11A Payroll Reports, Records, and Procedures

Understanding payroll procedures and keeping adequate payroll reports and records are essential to a company's success. This appendix focuses on payroll accounting and its reports, records, and procedures.

Payroll Reports

Most employees and employers are required to pay local, state, and federal payroll taxes. Payroll expenses involve liabilities to individual employees, to federal and state governments, and to other organizations such as insurance companies. Beyond paying these liabilities, employers are required to prepare and submit reports explaining how they computed these payments.

C4 Identify and describe payroll reporting.

Reporting FICA Taxes and Income Taxes The Federal Insurance Contributions Act (FICA) requires each employer to file an Internal Revenue Service (IRS) **Form 941,** the *Employer's Quarterly Federal Tax Return,* within one month after the end of each calendar quarter. A sample Form 941 is shown in Exhibit 11A.1 for Phoenix Sales & Service, a landscape design company. Accounting information and software are helpful in tracking payroll transactions and reporting the accumulated information on Form 941. Specifically, the employer reports total wages subject to income

Exhibit 11A.1
Form 941

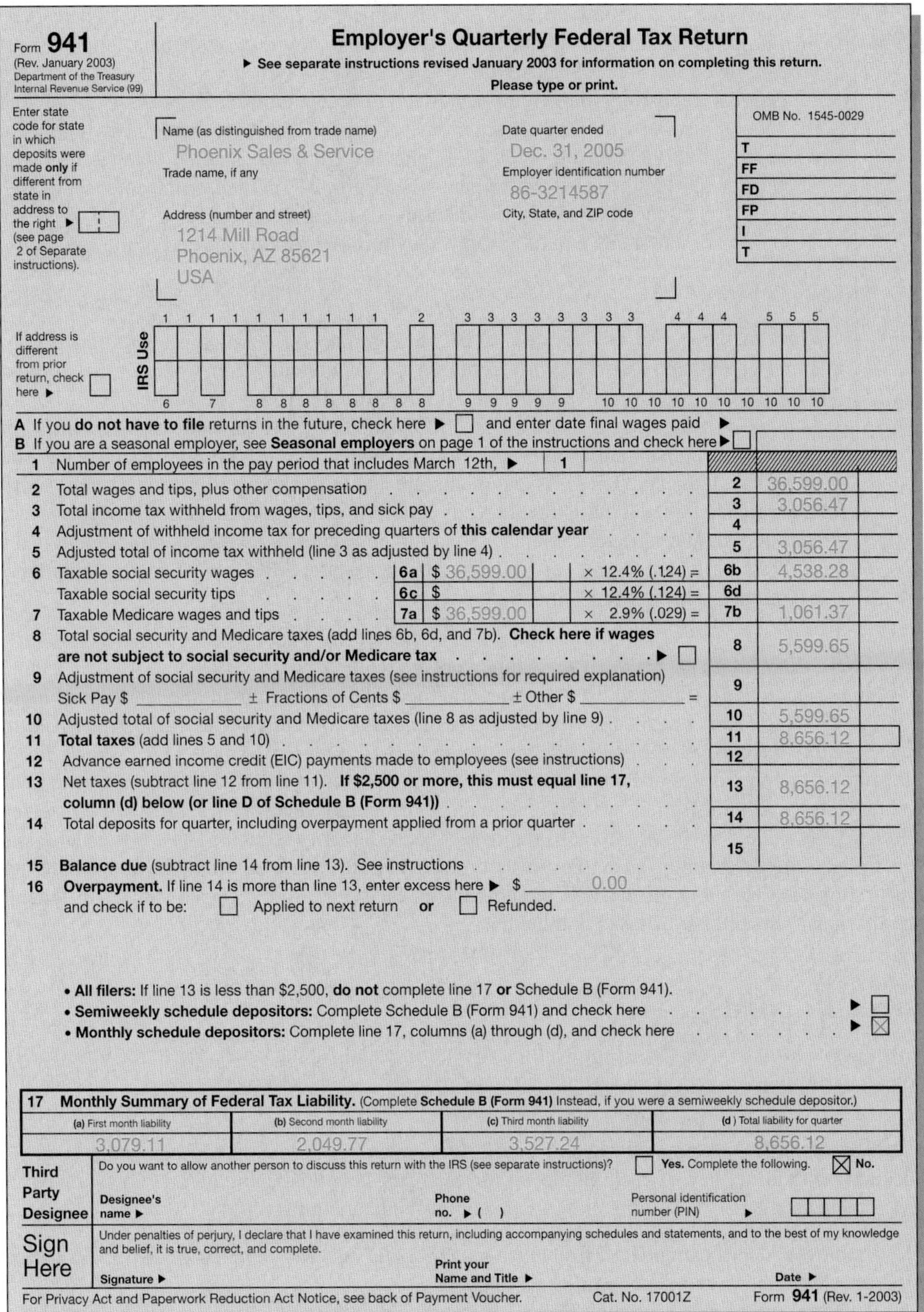

Form **941** (Rev. January 2003) Department of the Treasury Internal Revenue Service (99)

Employer's Quarterly Federal Tax Return

▶ See separate instructions revised January 2003 for information on completing this return.

Please type or print.

Enter state code for state in which deposits were made **only** if different from state in address to the right ▶ (see page 2 of Separate instructions).

Name (as distinguished from trade name): Phoenix Sales & Service
Date quarter ended: Dec. 31, 2005
Trade name, if any
Employer identification number: 86-3214587
Address (number and street): 1214 Mill Road, Phoenix, AZ 85621, USA
City, State, and ZIP code

OMB No. 1545-0029
T
FF
FD
FP
I
T

If address is different from prior return, check here ▶ ☐ IRS Use

A If you **do not have to file** returns in the future, check here ▶ ☐ and enter date final wages paid ▶
B If you are a seasonal employer, see **Seasonal employers** on page 1 of the instructions and check here ▶ ☐

1	Number of employees in the pay period that includes March 12th, ▶ 1		
2	Total wages and tips, plus other compensation	2	36,599.00
3	Total income tax withheld from wages, tips, and sick pay	3	3,056.47
4	Adjustment of withheld income tax for preceding quarters of **this calendar year**	4	
5	Adjusted total of income tax withheld (line 3 as adjusted by line 4)	5	3,056.47
6	Taxable social security wages 6a $ 36,599.00 × 12.4% (.124) =	6b	4,538.28
	Taxable social security tips 6c $ × 12.4% (.124) =	6d	
7	Taxable Medicare wages and tips 7a $ 36,599.00 × 2.9% (.029) =	7b	1,061.37
8	Total social security and Medicare taxes (add lines 6b, 6d, and 7b). **Check here if wages are not subject to social security and/or Medicare tax** ▶ ☐	8	5,599.65
9	Adjustment of social security and Medicare taxes (see instructions for required explanation) Sick Pay $ ± Fractions of Cents $ ± Other $ =	9	
10	Adjusted total of social security and Medicare taxes (line 8 as adjusted by line 9)	10	5,599.65
11	**Total taxes** (add lines 5 and 10)	11	8,656.12
12	Advance earned income credit (EIC) payments made to employees (see instructions)	12	
13	Net taxes (subtract line 12 from line 11). **If $2,500 or more, this must equal line 17, column (d) below (or line D of Schedule B (Form 941))**	13	8,656.12
14	Total deposits for quarter, including overpayment applied from a prior quarter	14	8,656.12
15	**Balance due** (subtract line 14 from line 13). See instructions	15	
16	**Overpayment.** If line 14 is more than line 13, enter excess here ▶ $ 0.00 and check if to be: ☐ Applied to next return **or** ☐ Refunded.		

- **All filers:** If line 13 is less than $2,500, **do not** complete line 17 **or** Schedule B (Form 941).
- **Semiweekly schedule depositors:** Complete Schedule B (Form 941) and check here ▶ ☐
- **Monthly schedule depositors:** Complete line 17, columns (a) through (d), and check here ▶ ☒

17 Monthly Summary of Federal Tax Liability. (Complete **Schedule B (Form 941)** instead, if you were a semiweekly schedule depositor.)

(a) First month liability	(b) Second month liability	(c) Third month liability	(d) Total liability for quarter
3,079.11	2,049.77	3,527.24	8,656.12

Third Party Designee Do you want to allow another person to discuss this return with the IRS (see separate instructions)? ☐ **Yes.** Complete the following. ☒ **No.**
Designee's name ▶ Phone no. ▶ ( ) Personal identification number (PIN) ▶

Sign Here Under penalties of perjury, I declare that I have examined this return, including accompanying schedules and statements, and to the best of my knowledge and belief, it is true, correct, and complete.
Signature ▶ Print your Name and Title ▶ Date ▶

For Privacy Act and Paperwork Reduction Act Notice, see back of Payment Voucher. Cat. No. 17001Z Form **941** (Rev. 1-2003)

tax withholding on line 2 of Form 941. (For simplicity, this appendix uses *wages* to refer to both wages and salaries.) The income tax withheld is reported on lines 3 and 5. The combined amount of employee and employer FICA (Social Security) taxes for Phoenix Sales & Service is reported on line 6a (taxable Social Security wages, $36,599 × 12.4% = $4,538.28). The 12.4% is the sum of the Social Security tax withheld, computed as 6.2% tax withheld from the employee wages for the quarter plus the 6.2% tax levied on the employer. The combined amount of employee Medicare wages is reported on line 7. The 2.9% is the sum of 1.45% withheld from employee wages for the quarter plus 1.45% tax levied on the employer. Total FICA taxes are reported on lines 8 and 10 and are added to the total income taxes withheld of $3,056.47 to yield a total of $8,656.12. For this

COPYRIGHT JOHN S. PRITCHETT WWW.PRITCHETTCARTOONS.COM

Although the IRS may not be at the end of the rainbow, this cartoon reinforces the importance of taxation in all business activities and management decisions.

year, assume that income up to $87,000 is subject to Social Security tax. There is no income limit on amounts subject to Medicare tax. Congress sets annual limits on the amount owed for Social Security tax.

Federal depository banks are authorized to accept deposits of amounts payable to the federal government. Deposit requirements depend on the amount of tax owed. For example, when the sum of FICA taxes plus the employee income taxes is less than $500 for a quarter, the taxes can be paid when Form 941 is filed. Companies with large payrolls are often required to pay monthly or even semiweekly. If taxes owed are $100,000 or more at the end of any day, they must be paid by the end of the next banking day.

Reporting FUTA Taxes and SUTA Taxes An employer's federal unemployment taxes (FUTA) are reported on an annual basis by filing an *Annual Federal Unemployment Tax Return,* IRS **Form 940.** It must be mailed on or before January 31 following the end of each tax year. Ten more days are allowed if all required tax deposits are filed on a timely basis and the full amount of tax is paid on or before January 31. FUTA payments are made quarterly to a federal depository bank if the total amount due exceeds $100. If $100 or less is due, the taxes are remitted annually. Requirements for paying and reporting state unemployment taxes (SUTA) vary depending on the laws of each state. Most states require quarterly payments and reports.

Reporting Wages and Salaries Employers are required to give each employee an annual report of his or her wages subject to FICA and federal income taxes along with the amounts of these taxes withheld. This report is called a *Wage and Tax Statement,* or **Form W-2.** It must be given to employees before January 31 following the year covered by the report. Exhibit 11A.2 shows Form W-2 for one of the employees at Phoenix Sales & Service. Copies of the W-2 Form must be sent to the Social Security Administration, where the amount of the employee's wages subject to FICA taxes and FICA taxes withheld are posted to each employee's Social Security account. These posted amounts become the basis for determining an employee's retirement and survivors' benefits. The Social Security Administration also transmits to the IRS the amount of each employee's wages subject to federal income taxes and the amount of taxes withheld.

Payroll Records

Employers must keep payroll records in addition to reporting and paying taxes. These records usually include a payroll register and an individual earnings report for each employee.

C5 Identify and describe payroll records.

Payroll Register A **payroll register** usually shows the pay period dates, hours worked, gross pay, deductions, and net pay of each employee for each pay period. Exhibit 11A.3 shows a payroll register for Phoenix Sales & Service. It is organized into nine columns:

Col. 1 Employee identification (ID); Employee name; Social Security number (SS No.); Reference (check number); and Date (date check issued)
Col. 2 Pay Type (regular and overtime)
Col. 3 Pay Hours (number of hours worked as regular and overtime)
Col. 4 Gross Pay (amount of gross pay)[2]
Col. 5 FIT (federal income taxes withheld); FUTA (federal unemployment taxes)
Col. 6 SIT (state income taxes withheld); SUTA (state unemployment taxes)
Col. 7 FICA-SS_EE (social security taxes withheld, employee); FICA-SS_ER (social security taxes, employer)
Col. 8 FICA-Med_EE (medicare tax withheld, employee); FICA-Med_ER (medicare tax, employer)
Col. 9 Net pay (Gross pay less amounts withheld from employees)

[2] The Gross Pay column shows regular hours worked on the first line multiplied by the regular pay rate—this equals regular pay. Overtime hours multiplied by the overtime premium rate equals overtime premium pay reported on the second line. If employers are engaged in interstate commerce, federal law sets a minimum overtime rate of pay to employees. For this company, workers earn 150% of their regular rate for hours in excess of 40 per week.

Exhibit 11A.2

Form W-2

a Control number AR101		OMB No. 1545-0008	
b Employer identification number 86-3214587		1 Wages, tips, other compensation 4910.00	2 Federal income tax withheld 333.37
c Employer's name, address, and ZIP code Phoenix Sales & Service 1214 Mill Road Phoenix, AZ 85621 USA		3 Social security wages 4910.00	4 Social security tax withheld 304.42
		5 Medicare wages and tips 4910.00	6 Medicare tax withheld 71.20
		7 Social security tips	8 Allocated tips
d Employee's social security number 333-22-9999		9 Advance EIC payment	10 Dependent care benefits
e Employee's first name and initial / Last name Robert Austin 18 Roosevelt Blvd., Apt C Tempe, AZ 86322		11 Nonqualified plans	12a
		13 Statutory employee ☐ Retirement plan ☐ Third-party sick pay ☐	12b
		14 Other	12c
			12d
f Employee's address and ZIP code			

15 State Employer's state ID number	16 State wages, tips, etc.	17 State income tax	18 Local wages, tips, etc.	19 Local income tax	20 Locality name
AZ 13-902319	4910.00	26.68			

Form **W-2** Wage and Tax Statement **2003** Department of the Treasury—Internal Revenue Service

Copy 1 For State, City, or Local Tax Department

Exhibit 11A.3

Payroll Register

Accounting System: Exhibit 11A.3

File Edit Maintain Tasks Analysis Options Reports Window Help

Phoenix Sales & Service
Payroll Register
For Week Ended Oct. 8, 2005

Employee ID / Employee / SS No. / Refer., Date	Pay Type	Pay Hours	Gross Pay	FIT / FUTA	SIT / SUTA	FICA-SS_EE / FICA-SS_ER	FICA-Med_EE / FICA-Med_ER	Net Pay
AR101	Regular	40.00	400.00	−28.99	−2.32	−24.80	−5.80	338.09
Robert Austin	Overtime		–					
333-22-9999			400.00	−3.20	−10.80	−24.80	−5.80	
9001, 10/8/05								
CJ102	Regular	40.00	560.00	−52.97	−4.24	−36.02	−8.42	479.35
Judy Cross	Overtime	1.00	21.00					
299-11-9201			581.00	−4.65	−15.69	−36.02	−8.42	
9002, 10/8/05								
DJ103	Regular	40.00	560.00	−48.33	−3.87	−37.32	−8.73	503.75
John Diaz	Overtime	2.00	42.00					
444-11-9090			602.00	−4.82	−16.25	−37.32	−8.73	
9003, 10/8/05								
KK104	Regular	40.00	560.00	−68.57	−5.49	−34.72	−8.12	443.10
Kay Keife	Overtime		–					
909-11-3344			560.00	−4.48	−15.12	−34.72	−8.12	
9004, 10/8/05								
ML105	Regular	40.00	560.00	−34.24	−2.74	−34.72	−8.12	480.18
Lee Miller	Overtime		–					
444-56-3211			560.00	−4.48	−15.12	−34.72	−8.12	
9005, 10/8/05								
SD106	Regular	40.00	560.00	−68.57	−5.49	−34.72	−8.12	443.10
Dale Sears	Overtime		–					
909-33-1234			560.00	−4.48	−15.12	−34.72	−8.12	
9006, 10/8/05								
Totals	Regular	240.00	3,200.00	−301.67	−24.15	−202.30	−47.31	2,687.57
	Overtime	3.00	63.00					
			3,263.00	−26.11	−88.10	−202.30	−47.31	

Sales Purchases General Ledger Payroll Inventory Company Analysis

Net pay for each employee is computed as gross pay minus the items on the first line of columns 5–8. The employer's payroll tax for each employee is computed as the sum of items on the third line of columns 5–8. A payroll register includes all data necessary to record payroll. In some software programs the entries to record payroll are made in a special *payroll journal.*

Payroll Check Payment of payroll is usually done by check or electronic funds transfer. Exhibit 11A.4 shows a *payroll check* for a Phoenix employee. This check is accompanied with a detachable *statement of earnings* (at top) showing gross pay, deductions, and net pay.

Exhibit 11A.4

Check and Statement of Earnings

EMPLOYEE NO.	EMPLOYEE NAME	SOCIAL SECURITY NO.	PAY PERIOD END	CHECK DATE
AR101	Robert Austin	333-22-9999	10/8/05	10/8/05

ITEM	RATE	HOURS	TOTAL	ITEM	THIS CHECK	YEAR TO DATE
Regular	10.00	40.00	400.00	Gross	400.00	400.00
Overtime	15.00			Fed. Income tax	-28.99	-28.99
				FICA-Soc. Sec.	-24.80	-24.80
				FICA-Medicare	-5.80	-5.80
				State Income tax	-2.32	-2.32

HOURS WORKED	GROSS THIS PERIOD	GROSS YEAR TO DATE	NET CHECK	CHECK No.
40.00	400.00	400.00	$338.09	9001

(Detach and retain for your records)

PHOENIX SALES & SERVICE
1214 Mill Road
Phoenix, AZ 85621
602-555-8900

Phoenix Bank and Trust
Phoenix, AZ 85621
3312-87044

9001

CHECK NO.	DATE	AMOUNT
9001	Oct 8, 2005	**************$338.09*

Three Hundred Thirty-Eight and 9/100 Dollars

PAY TO THE ORDER OF
Robert Austin
18 Roosevelt Blvd., Apt C
Tempe, AZ 86322

Mary Wills
AUTHORIZED SIGNATURE

Decision Insight

Virtual Reports Off-the-shelf and Web-based programs can produce payroll reports including the (1) payroll register, (2) payroll checks, and (3) employee earnings report.

Employee Earnings Report An **employee earnings report** is a cumulative record of an employee's hours worked, gross earnings, deductions, and net pay. Payroll information on this report is taken from the payroll register. The employee earnings report for R. Austin at Phoenix Sales & Service is shown in Exhibit 11A.5.

An employee earnings report accumulates information that can show when an employee's earnings reach the tax-exempt points for FICA, FUTA, and SUTA taxes. It also gives data an employer needs to prepare Form W-2.

Payroll Procedures

Employers must be able to compute federal income tax for payroll purposes. This section explains how we compute this tax and how to use a payroll bank account.

P5 Compute payroll taxes.

Computing Federal Income Taxes To compute the amount of taxes withheld from each employee's wages, we need to determine both the employee's wages earned and the employee's number of *withholding allowances.* Each employee records the number of withholding allowances claimed on a withholding allowance certificate, **Form W-4,** filed with the employer. When the number of withholding allowances increases, the amount of income taxes withheld decreases.

Employers often use a **wage bracket withholding table** similar to the one shown in Exhibit 11A.6 to compute the federal income taxes withheld from each employee's gross pay. The table in

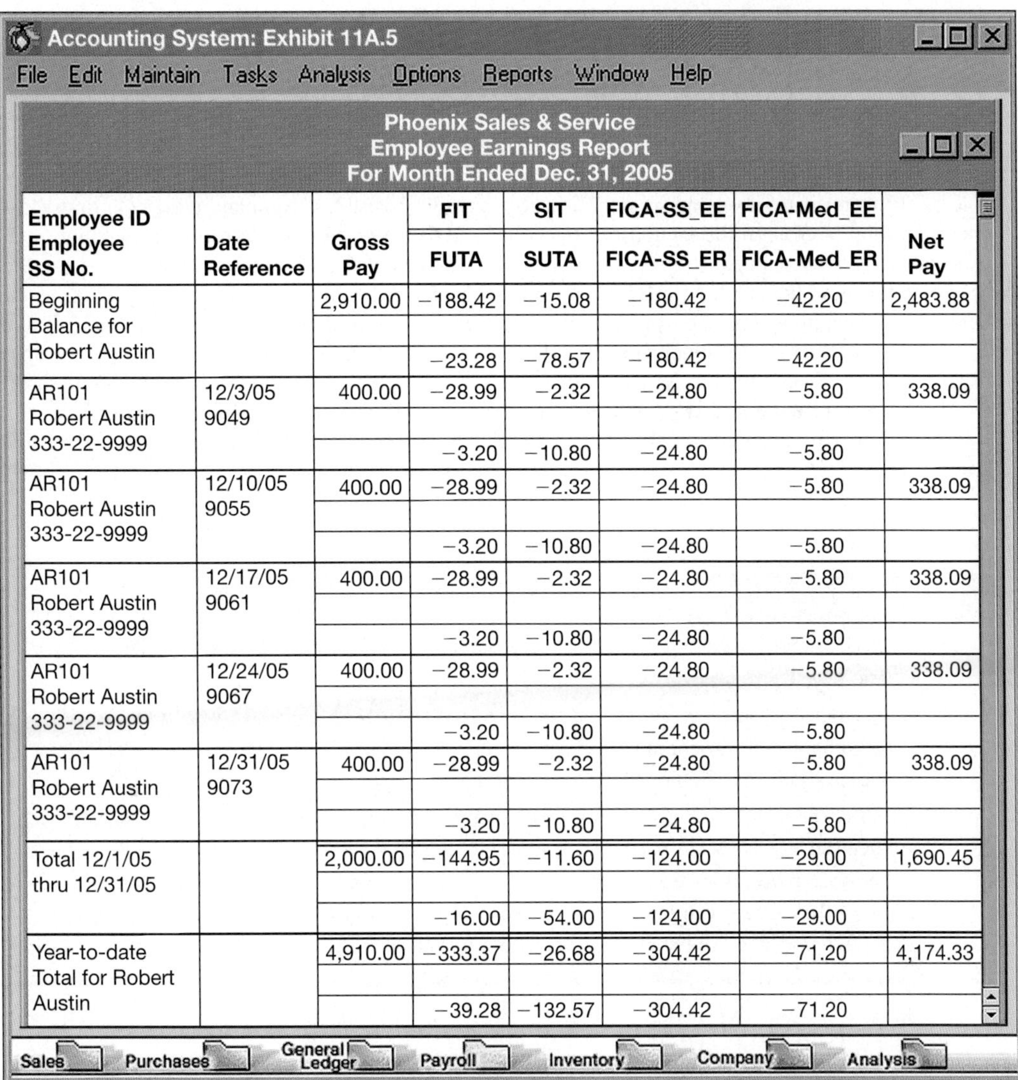

Accounting System: Exhibit 11A.5

File Edit Maintain Tasks Analysis Options Reports Window Help

Phoenix Sales & Service
Employee Earnings Report
For Month Ended Dec. 31, 2005

Employee ID Employee SS No.	Date Reference	Gross Pay	FIT / FUTA	SIT / SUTA	FICA-SS_EE / FICA-SS_ER	FICA-Med_EE / FICA-Med_ER	Net Pay
Beginning Balance for Robert Austin		2,910.00	−188.42	−15.08	−180.42	−42.20	2,483.88
			−23.28	−78.57	−180.42	−42.20	
AR101 Robert Austin 333-22-9999	12/3/05 9049	400.00	−28.99	−2.32	−24.80	−5.80	338.09
			−3.20	−10.80	−24.80	−5.80	
AR101 Robert Austin 333-22-9999	12/10/05 9055	400.00	−28.99	−2.32	−24.80	−5.80	338.09
			−3.20	−10.80	−24.80	−5.80	
AR101 Robert Austin 333-22-9999	12/17/05 9061	400.00	−28.99	−2.32	−24.80	−5.80	338.09
			−3.20	−10.80	−24.80	−5.80	
AR101 Robert Austin 333-22-9999	12/24/05 9067	400.00	−28.99	−2.32	−24.80	−5.80	338.09
			−3.20	−10.80	−24.80	−5.80	
AR101 Robert Austin 333-22-9999	12/31/05 9073	400.00	−28.99	−2.32	−24.80	−5.80	338.09
			−3.20	−10.80	−24.80	−5.80	
Total 12/1/05 thru 12/31/05		2,000.00	−144.95	−11.60	−124.00	−29.00	1,690.45
			−16.00	−54.00	−124.00	−29.00	
Year-to-date Total for Robert Austin		4,910.00	−333.37	−26.68	−304.42	−71.20	4,174.33
			−39.28	−132.57	−304.42	−71.20	

Sales Purchases General Ledger Payroll Inventory Company Analysis

Exhibit 11A.5

Employee Earnings Report

Exhibit 11A.6

Wage Bracket Withholding Table

SINGLE Persons—**WEEKLY** Payroll Period

(For Wages Paid in 2003)

If the wages are –		And the number of withholding allowances claimed is —										
At least	But less than	0	1	2	3	4	5	6	7	8	9	10
		The amount of income tax to be withheld is —										
$600	**$610**	$81	$69	$60	$51	$42	$33	$25	$16	$8	$3	$0
610	**620**	83	70	61	53	44	35	26	17	9	4	0
620	**630**	86	72	63	54	45	36	28	19	10	5	0
630	**640**	89	73	64	55	47	38	29	20	12	6	0
640	**650**	91	76	65	57	48	39	31	22	13	7	1
650	**660**	94	78	67	59	60	41	32	23	15	8	2
660	**670**	97	81	69	60	61	42	34	25	16	9	3
670	**680**	99	84	70	62	63	44	35	26	18	10	4
680	**690**	102	85	72	63	64	45	37	28	19	11	5
690	**700**	103	89	73	65	65	47	38	29	21	12	6
700	**710**	108	92	70	66	67	48	40	31	22	13	7
710	**720**	110	94	79	69	69	60	41	32	24	15	8
720	**730**	113	97	81	69	60	61	43	34	25	16	9
730	**740**	116	100	84	71	62	63	44	35	27	18	10
740	**750**	118	103	87	72	63	64	45	37	28	19	11

Exhibit 11A.6 is for a single employee paid weekly. Tables are also provided for married employees and for biweekly, semimonthly, and monthly pay periods (most payroll software includes these tables). When using a wage bracket withholding table to compute federal income tax withheld from an employee's gross wages, we need to locate an employee's wage bracket within the first two columns. We then find the amount withheld by looking in the withholding allowance column for that employee.

P6 Record payment of payroll.

Payroll Bank Account Companies with few employees often pay them with checks drawn on the company's regular bank account. Companies with many employees often use a special **payroll bank account** to pay employees. When this account is used, a company either (1) draws one check for total payroll on the regular bank account and deposits it in the payroll bank account or (2) executes an *electronic funds transfer* to the payroll bank account. Individual payroll checks are then drawn on this payroll bank account. Since only one check for the total payroll is drawn on the regular bank account each payday, use of a special payroll bank account helps with internal control. It also helps in reconciling the regular bank account. When companies use a payroll bank account, they usually include check numbers in the payroll register. The payroll register in Exhibit 11A.3 shows check numbers in column 1. For instance, Check No. 9001 is issued to Robert Austin. With this information, the payroll register serves as a supplementary record of wages earned by and paid to employees.

Quick Check

11. What two items determine the amount deducted from an employee's wages for federal income taxes?
12. What amount of income tax is withheld from the salary of an employee who is single with three withholding allowances and earnings of $675 in a week? (*Hint:* Use the wage bracket withholding table in Exhibit 11A.6.)
13. Which of the following steps are executed when a company draws one check for total payroll and deposits it in a special payroll bank account? (*a*) Write a check to the payroll bank account for the total payroll and record it with a debit to Accrued Payroll Payable and a credit to Cash. (*b*) Deposit a check (or transfer funds) for the total payroll in the payroll bank account. (*c*) Issue individual payroll checks drawn on the payroll bank account. (*d*) All of the above.

Answers—p. 449

APPENDIX 11B Income Taxes

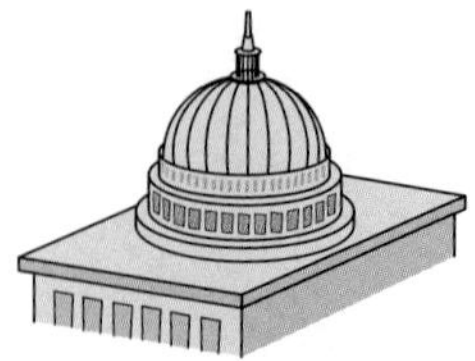

This appendix explains current liabilities involving income taxes for corporations.

Income Tax Liabilities Corporations are subject to income taxes and must estimate their income tax liability when preparing financial statements. Since income tax expense is created by earning income, a liability is incurred when income is earned. This tax must be paid quarterly under federal regulations. To illustrate, consider a corporation that prepares monthly financial statements. Based on its income in January 2005, this corporation estimates that it owes income taxes of $12,100. The following adjusting entry records this estimate:

Assets	=	Liabilities	+	Equity
		+12,100		−12,100

Jan. 31	Income Taxes Expense	12,100	
	Income Taxes Payable		12,100
	To accrue January income taxes.		

The tax liability is recorded each month until the first quarterly payment is made. If the company's estimated taxes for this first quarter total $30,000, the entry to record its payment is

Apr. 10	Income Taxes Payable	30,000	
	Cash		30,000
	Paid estimated quarterly income taxes based on first quarter income.		

Assets	=	Liabilities	+	Equity
−30,000		−30,000		

This process of accruing and then paying estimated income taxes continues through the year. When annual financial statements are prepared at year-end, the corporation knows its actual total income and the actual amount of income taxes it must pay. This information allows it to properly record income taxes expense for the fourth quarter so that the total of the four quarters' expense amounts equals the actual taxes paid to the government.

Deferred Income Tax Liabilities An income tax liability for corporations can arise when the amount of income before taxes that the corporation reports on its income statement is not the same as the amount of income reported on its income tax return. This difference occurs because income tax laws and GAAP measure income differently. (Differences between tax laws and GAAP arise because Congress uses tax laws to generate receipts, stimulate the economy, and influence behavior, whereas GAAP are intended to provide financial information useful for decision making. Also, tax accounting often follows the cash basis, whereas GAAP follows the accrual basis.)

Some differences between tax laws and GAAP are temporary. *Temporary differences* arise when the tax return and the income statement report a revenue or expense in different years. As an example, companies are often able to deduct higher amounts of depreciation in the early years of an asset's life and smaller amounts in later years for tax reporting in comparison to GAAP. This means that in the early years, depreciation for tax reporting is often more than depreciation on the income statement. In later years, depreciation for tax reporting is often less than depreciation on the income statement. When temporary differences exist between taxable income on the tax return and the income before taxes on the income statement, corporations compute income taxes expense based on the income reported on the income statement. The result is that income taxes expense reported in the income statement is often different from the amount of income taxes payable to the government. This difference is the **deferred income tax liability.**

To illustrate, assume that in recording its usual quarterly income tax payments, a corporation computes $25,000 of income taxes expense. It also determines that only $21,000 is currently due and $4,000 is deferred to future years (a timing difference). The entry to record this end-of-period adjustment is

Dec. 31	Income Taxes Expense	25,000	
	Income Taxes Payable		21,000
	Deferred Income Tax Liability		4,000
	To record tax expense and deferred tax liability.		

Assets	=	Liabilities	+	Equity
		+21,000		−25,000
		+4,000		

The credit to Income Taxes Payable reflects the amount currently due to be paid. The credit to Deferred Income Tax Liability reflects tax payments deferred until future years when the temporary difference reverses.

Temporary differences also can cause a company to pay income taxes *before* they are reported on the income statement as expense. If so, the company reports a *Deferred Income Tax Asset* on its balance sheet.

Summary

C1 **Describe current and long-term liabilities and their characteristics.** Liabilities are probable future payments of assets or services that past transactions or events obligate an entity to make. Current liabilities are due within one year or the operating cycle, whichever is longer. All other liabilities are long term.

C2 **Identify and describe known current liabilities.** Known (determinable) current liabilities are set by agreements or laws and are measurable with little uncertainty. They include accounts payable, sales taxes payable, unearned revenues, notes payable, payroll liabilities, and the current portion of long-term debt.

C3 Explain how to account for contingent liabilities. If an uncertain future payment depends on a probable future event and the amount can be reasonably estimated, the payment is recorded as a liability. The uncertain future payment is reported as a contingent liability (in the notes) if (*a*) the future event is reasonably possible but not probable or (*b*) the event is probable but the payment amount cannot be reasonably estimated.

C4[A] Identify and describe payroll reporting. Employers report FICA taxes and federal income tax withholdings using Form 941. FUTA taxes are reported on Form 940. Earnings and deductions are reported to each employee and the federal government on Form W-2.

C5[A] Identify and describe payroll records. An employer's payroll records include a payroll register for each pay period, payroll checks and statements of earnings, and individual employee earnings reports.

A1 Compute the times interest earned ratio and use it to analyze liabilities. Times interest earned is computed by dividing a company's net income before interest expense and income taxes by the amount of interest expense. The times interest earned ratio reflects a company's ability to pay interest obligations.

P1 Prepare entries to account for short-term notes payable. Short-term notes payable are current liabilities; most bear interest. When a short-term note's face value equals the amount borrowed, it identifies a rate of interest to be paid at maturity.

P2 Compute and record *employee* payroll deductions and liabilities. Employee payroll deductions include FICA taxes, income taxes, and voluntary deductions such as for pensions and charities. They make up the difference between gross and net pay.

P3 Compute and record *employer* payroll expenses and liabilities. An employer's payroll expenses include employees' gross earnings, any employee benefits, and the payroll taxes levied on the employer. Payroll liabilities include employees' net pay amounts, withholdings from employee wages, any employer-promised benefits, and the employer's payroll taxes.

P4 Account for estimated liabilities, including warranties and bonuses. Liabilities for health and pension benefits, warranties, and bonuses are recorded with estimated amounts. These items are recognized as expenses when incurred and matched with revenues generated.

P5[A] Compute payroll taxes. Federal income tax deductions depend on the employee's earnings and the number of withholding allowances claimed. Wage bracket withholding tables are available for different pay periods and employee classes.

P6[A] Record payment of payroll. Employers with a large number of employees often use a separate payroll bank account. When this is done, the payment of employees is recorded with a transfer of cash from the regular bank account to the payroll bank account.

Guidance Answers to **Decision Maker** and **Decision Ethics**

Web Designer You need to be concerned about being an accomplice to unlawful payroll activities. Not paying federal and state taxes on wages earned is illegal and unethical. Such payments also will not provide the employee with Social Security and some Medicare credits. The best course of action is to request payment by check. If this fails to change the owner's payment practices, you must consider quitting this job.

Entrepreneur Risk is partly reflected by the times interest earned ratio. This ratio for the first franchise is 1.5 [($100,000 + $200,000)/$200,000], whereas the ratio for the second franchise is 3.5 [($100,000 + $40,000)/$40,000]. This analysis shows that the first franchise is more at risk of incurring a loss if its sales decline. The second question asks about variability of income. If income greatly varies, this increases the risk an owner will not earn sufficient income to cover interest. Since the first franchise has the greater variability, it is a riskier investment.

Guidance Answers to **Quick Checks**

1. A liability involves a probable future payment of assets or services that an entity is presently obligated to make as a result of past transactions or events.
2. No, an expected future payment is not a liability unless an existing obligation was created by a past event or transaction.
3. In most cases, a liability due in 15 months is classified as long term. It is classified as a current liability if the company's operating cycle is 15 months or longer.
4. A creditor prefers a note payable instead of a past-due account payable so as to (*a*) charge interest and/or (*b*) have evidence of the debt and its terms for potential litigation or disputes.
5. $1,000(.008) + $1,000(.04) + $3,000(.062) + $3,000(.0145) = $277.50
6. (*a*) FICA taxes are incurred by both employee and employer.
   (*b*) FUTA taxes are incurred by the employer.
   (*c*) SUTA taxes are incurred by the employer.
   (*d*) Withheld income taxes are incurred by the employee.

7. (*a*)
8. (*a*) Warranty expense was previously estimated and recorded.
9. (*b*)
10. A future payment is reported in the notes as a contingent liability if (*a*) the uncertain future event is probable but the amount of payment cannot be reasonably estimated or (*b*) the uncertain future event is not probable but has a reasonable possibility of occurring.
11. An employee's gross earnings and number of withholding allowances determine the deduction for federal income taxes.
12. $62
13. (*d*)

Key Terms

Key Terms are available at the book's Website for learning and testing in an online Flashcard Format.

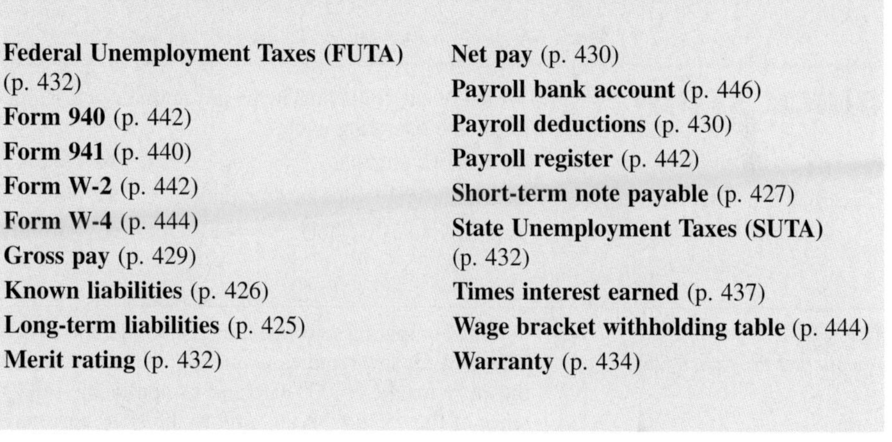

Contingent liability (p. 436)
Current liabilities (p. 425)
Current portion of long-term debt (p. 433)
Deferred income tax liability (p. 447)
Employee benefits (p. 433)
Employee earnings report (p. 444)
Estimated liability (p. 433)
Federal depository bank (p. 442)
Federal Insurance Contributions Act (FICA) Taxes (p. 430)
Federal Unemployment Taxes (FUTA) (p. 432)
Form 940 (p. 442)
Form 941 (p. 440)
Form W-2 (p. 442)
Form W-4 (p. 444)
Gross pay (p. 429)
Known liabilities (p. 426)
Long-term liabilities (p. 425)
Merit rating (p. 432)

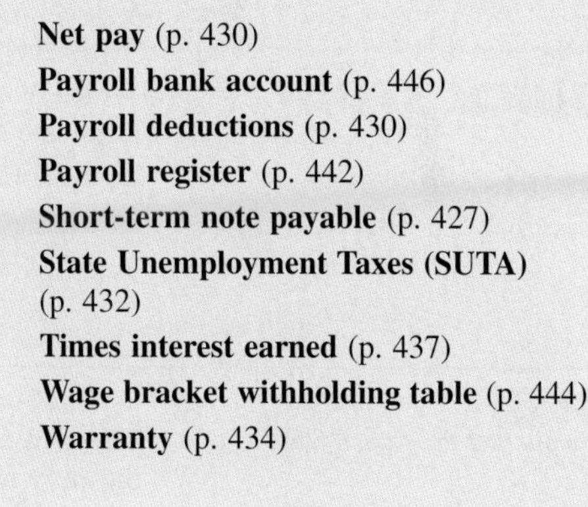

Net pay (p. 430)
Payroll bank account (p. 446)
Payroll deductions (p. 430)
Payroll register (p. 442)
Short-term note payable (p. 427)
State Unemployment Taxes (SUTA) (p. 432)
Times interest earned (p. 437)
Wage bracket withholding table (p. 444)
Warranty (p. 434)

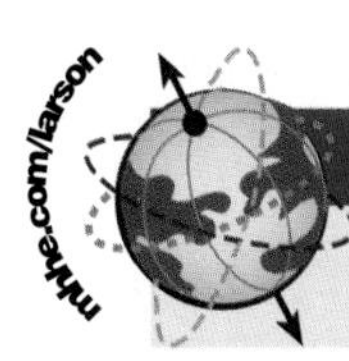

Personal Interactive Quiz

Personal Interactive Quizzes A and B are available at the book's Website to reinforce and assess your learning.

Superscript letter A (B) denotes assignments based on Appendix 11A (11B).

Discussion Questions

1. What are the three important questions concerning the uncertainty of liabilities?
2. What is the difference between a current and a long-term liability?
3. What is an estimated liability?
4. If $894.40 is the total of a sale that includes its sales tax of 4%, what is the selling price of the item only?
5. What is the combined amount (in percent) of the employee and employer Social Security tax rate?
6. What is the current Medicare tax rate? This rate is applied to what maximum level of salary and wages?
7. What determines the amount deducted from an employee's wages for federal income taxes?
8. Which payroll taxes are the employee's responsibility and which are the employer's responsibility?
9. What is an employer's unemployment merit rating? How are these ratings assigned to employers?
10. Why are warranty liabilities usually recognized on the balance sheet as liabilities even when they are uncertain?
11. Suppose that a company has a facility located where disastrous weather conditions often occur. Should it report a probable loss from a future disaster as a liability on its balance sheet? Explain.
12.[A] What is a wage bracket withholding table?

13.[A] What amount of income tax is withheld from the salary of an employee who is single with two withholding allowances and earning $725 per week? What if the employee earned $625 and has no withholding allowances? (Use Exhibit 11A.6.)

14. Refer to **Krispy Kreme**'s financial statements in Appendix A. As an alternative to short-term notes, Krispy Kreme meets short-term borrowing needs through revolving lines of credit. Briefly explain how a line of credit differs from a short-term note payable.

15. Refer to **Tastykake**'s balance sheet in Appendix A. What accounts related to income taxes are on its balance sheet? Explain the meaning of each income tax account you identify.

16. Refer to **Harley-Davidson**'s balance sheet in Appendix A. Which current liability account reports its payroll-related liabilities (if any) as of December 31, 2002?

Red numbers denote Discussion Questions that involve decision-making.

Homework Manager *repeats all numerical Quick Studies on the book's Website with new numbers.*

QUICK STUDY

QS 11-1
Classifying liabilities C1

Which of the following items are normally classified as a current liability for a company that has a 15-month operating cycle?

1. Salaries payable.
2. Note payable due in 18 months.
3. FICA taxes payable.
4. Note payable maturing in 2 years.
5. Note payable due in 11 months.
6. Portion of long-term note due in 15 months.

QS 11-2
Accounting for sales taxes
C2

Gomez Computing sells merchandise for $5,000 cash on September 30 (cost of merchandise is $2,900). The sales tax law requires Gomez to collect 4% sales tax on every dollar of merchandise sold. Record the entry for the $5,000 sale and its applicable sales tax. Also record the entry that shows the remittance of the 4% tax on this sale to the state government on October 15.

QS 11-3
Unearned revenue C2

Ticketmaster receives $4,000,000 in advance ticket sales for a four-date tour of the Rolling Stones. Record the advance ticket sales on October 31. Record the revenue earned for the first concert date of November 5, assuming it represents one-fourth of the advance ticket sales.

QS 11-4
Interest-bearing note transactions
P1

On November 7, 2005, Ortez Company borrows $150,000 cash by signing a 90-day, 8% note payable with a face value of $150,000. (1) Compute the accrued interest payable on December 31, 2005, (2) prepare the journal entry to record the accrued interest expense at December 31, 2005, and (3) prepare the journal entry to record payment of the note at maturity.

QS 11-5
Record employer payroll taxes
P2 P3

Meredith Co. has five employees, each of whom earns $2,600 per month and has been employed since January 1. FICA Social Security taxes are 6.2% of gross pay and FICA Medicare taxes are 1.45% of gross pay. FUTA taxes are 0.8% and SUTA taxes are 2.8% of the first $7,000 paid to each employee. Prepare the March 31 journal entry to record the March payroll taxes expense.

QS 11-6
Recording warranty repairs
P4

On September 11, 2004, Home Store sells a mower for $400 with a one-year warranty that covers parts. Warranty expense is estimated at 5% of sales. On July 24, 2005, the mower is brought in for repairs covered under the warranty requiring $35 in materials taken from the Repair Parts Inventory. Prepare the July 24, 2005, entry to record the warranty repairs.

QS 11-7
Accounting for bonuses P4

Paris Company offers an annual bonus to employees if the company meets certain net income goals. Prepare the journal entry to record a $10,000 bonus owed to its workers (to be shared equally) at calendar year-end.

QS 11-8
Accounting for contingent liabilities
C3 

The following legal claims exist for Kalamazoo Co. Identify the accounting treatment for each claim as either (*a*) a liability that is recorded or (*b*) an item described in notes to its financial statements.

1. Kalamazoo (defendant) estimates that a pending lawsuit could result in damages of $1,000,000; it is reasonably possible that the plaintiff will win the case.
2. Kalamazoo faces a probable loss on a pending lawsuit; the amount is not reasonably estimable.
3. Kalamazoo estimates damages in a case at $2,500,000 with a high probability of losing the case.

QS 11-9
Times interest earned
A1 

Compute the times interest earned for Dechow Company, which reports income before interest expense and income taxes of $1,575,000 and interest expense of $137,000. Interpret its times interest earned—assume that its competitors average a times interest earned of 4.0.

QS 11-10[B]
Record deferred income tax liability
P4

Cather Corporation has made and recorded its quarterly income tax payments. After a final review of taxes for the year, the company identifies an additional $30,000 of income tax expense that should be recorded. A portion of this additional expense, $8,000, is deferred for payment in future years. Record Cather's year-end adjusting entry for income tax expense.

***Homework Manager** repeats all numerical Exercises on the book's Website with new numbers.*

EXERCISES

Exercise 11-1
Classifying liabilities
C1 

The following items appear on the balance sheet of a company with a two-month operating cycle. Identify the proper classification of each item as follows: *C* if it is a current liability, *L* if it is a long-term liability, or *N* if it is not a liability.

_____	**1.** Sales taxes payable.	_____	**6.** Notes payable (due in 6 to 12 months).
_____	**2.** FUTA taxes payable.	_____	**7.** Notes payable (due in 120 days).
_____	**3.** Accounts receivable.	_____	**8.** Current portion of long-term debt.
_____	**4.** Accrued payroll payable.	_____	**9.** Notes payable (mature in five years).
_____	**5.** Wages payable.	_____	**10.** Notes payable (due in 13 to 24 months).

Exercise 11-2
Adjusting entries for liabilities
C2 C3 P4

Prepare any necessary adjusting entries at December 31, 2005, for Yacht Company's year-end financial statements for each of the following separate transactions and events:

1. During December, Yacht Company sold 3,000 units of a product that carries a 60-day warranty. December sales for this product total $120,000. The company expects 8% of the units to need warranty repairs, and it estimates the average repair cost per unit will be $15.
2. A disgruntled employee is suing Yacht Company. Legal advisers believe that the company will probably need to pay damages, but the amount cannot be reasonably estimated.
3. Employees earn vacation pay at a rate of one day per month. During December, 20 employees qualify for one vacation day each. Their average daily wage is $120 per employee.
4. Yacht Company guarantees the $5,000 debt of a supplier. The supplier will probably not default on the debt.
5. Yacht Company records an adjusting entry for $2,000,000 of previously unrecorded cash sales (costing $1,000,000) and its sales taxes at a rate of 5%.
6. The company earned $40,000 of $100,000 previously received in advance for services.

Exercise 11-3
Computing and recording bonuses C2

Check (1) $29,126

For the year ended December 31, 2005, Winter Company has implemented an employee bonus program equal to 3% of Winter's net income, which employees will share equally. Winter's net income (prebonus) is expected to be $1,000,000, and bonus expense is deducted in computing net income.

1. Compute the amount of the bonus payable to the employees at year-end (use the method described in the chapter and round to the nearest dollar).
2. Prepare the journal entry at December 31, 2005, to record the bonus due the employees.
3. Prepare the journal entry at January 19, 2006, to record payment of the bonus to employees.

Exercise 11-4
Accounting for note payable
P1

Check (2b) Interest expense, $1,880

Perfect Systems borrows $94,000 cash on May 15, 2005, by signing a 60-day, 12% note.

1. On what date does this note mature?

2. Suppose the face value of the note equals $94,000, the principal of the loan. Prepare the journal entries to record (*a*) issuance of the note and (*b*) payment of the note at maturity.

Exercise 11-5
Interest-bearing notes payable with year-end adjustments
P1

Check (2) $2,250
(3) $1,125

Kwon Co. borrows $150,000 cash on November 1, 2005, by signing a 90-day, 9% note with a face value of $150,000.

1. On what date does this note mature?

2. How much interest expense results from this note in 2005? (Assume a 360-day year.)

3. How much interest expense results from this note in 2006? (Assume a 360-day year.)

4. Prepare journal entries to record (*a*) issuance of the note, (*b*) accrual of interest at the end of 2005, and (*c*) payment of the note at maturity.

Exercise 11-6
Computing payroll taxes
P2 P3

MRI Co. has one employee, and the company is subject to the following taxes:

Tax	Rate	Applied To
FICA—Social Security	6.20%	First $87,000
FICA—Medicare	1.45	All gross pay
FUTA	0.80	First $7,000
SUTA	2.90	First $7,000

Compute MRI's amounts for each of these four taxes as applied to the employee's gross earnings for September under each of three separate situations (*a*), (*b*), and (*c*):

Check (*a*) FUTA, $4.80; SUTA, $17.40

	Gross Pay through August	Gross Pay for September
a.	$ 6,400	$ 800
b.	18,200	2,100
c.	82,000	8,000

Exercise 11-7
Payroll-related journal entries
P2 P3

Using the data in situation *a* of Exercise 11-6, prepare the employer's September 30 journal entries to record (1) salary expense and its related payroll liabilities for this employee and (2) the employer's payroll taxes expense and its related liabilities. The employee's federal income taxes withheld by the employer are $135 for this pay period.

Exercise 11-8
Warranty expense and liability computations and entries
P4

Check (1) $220
(4) $21

Chang Co. sold a copier costing $3,800 with a two-year parts warranty to a customer on August 16, 2005, for $5,500 cash. Chang uses the perpetual inventory system. On November 22, 2006, the copier requires on-site repairs that are completed the same day. The repairs cost $199 for materials taken from the Repair Parts Inventory. These are the only repairs required in 2006 for this copier. Based on experience, Chang expects to incur warranty costs equal to 4% of dollar sales. It records warranty expense with an adjusting entry at the end of each year.

1. How much warranty expense does the company report in 2005 for this copier?

2. How much is the estimated warranty liability for this copier as of December 31, 2005?

3. How much warranty expense does the company report in 2006 for this copier?

4. How much is the estimated warranty liability for this copier as of December 31, 2006?

5. Prepare journal entries to record (*a*) the copier's sale; (*b*) the adjustment on December 31, 2005, to recognize the warranty expense; and (*c*) the repairs that occur in November 2006.

Exercise 11-9
Computing and interpreting times interest earned
A1

Use the following information from separate companies *a* through *f* to compute times interest earned. Which company indicates the strongest ability to pay interest expense as it comes due?

	Net Income (Loss)	Interest Expense	Income Taxes
a.	$140,000	$48,000	$ 35,000
b.	140,000	15,000	50,000
c.	140,000	8,000	70,000
d.	265,000	12,000	130,000
e.	79,000	12,000	30,000
f.	(4,000)	12,000	0

Check (b) 13.67

Exercise 11-10^A
Net pay and tax computations
P5

The payroll records of Clix Software show the following information about Trish Farqua, an employee, for the weekly pay period ending September 30, 2005. Farqua is single and claims one allowance. Compute her Social Security tax (6.2%), Medicare tax (1.45%), federal income tax withholding, state income tax (0.5%), and net pay for the current pay period. The state income tax is 0.5 percent on the first $9,000 earned. (Use the withholding table in Exhibit 11A.6.)

Total (gross) earnings for current pay period	$ 735
Cumulative earnings of previous pay periods	9,700

Check Net pay, 578.77

Exercise 11-11^A
Gross and net pay computation
P5 P6

LaShonda Blake, an unmarried employee, works 48 hours in the week ended January 12. Her pay rate is $12 per hour, and her wages are subject to no deductions other than FICA—Social Security, FICA— Medicare, and federal income taxes. She claims two withholding allowances. Compute her regular pay, overtime pay (overtime premium is 50% of the regular rate for hours in excess of 40 per week), and gross pay. Then compute her FICA tax deduction (use 6.2% for the Social Security portion and 1.45% for the Medicare portion), income tax deduction (use the wage bracket withholding table of Exhibit 11A.6), total deductions, and net pay.

Check Net pay, $513.26

Exercise 11-12^B
Accounting for income taxes
P4

Ming Corporation prepares financial statements for each month-end. As part of its accounting process, estimated income taxes are accrued each month for 30% of the current month's net income. The income taxes are paid in the first month of each quarter for the amount accrued for the prior quarter. The following information is available for the fourth quarter of year 2005. When tax computations are completed on January 20, 2006, Ming determines that the quarter's Income Taxes Payable account balance should be $29,100 on December 31, 2005 (its unadjusted balance is $23,640).

October 2005 net income	$27,900
November 2005 net income	18,200
December 2005 net income	32,700

1. Determine the amount of the accounting adjustment (dated as of December 31, 2005) to produce the proper ending balance in the Income Taxes Payable account.

Check (1) $5,460

2. Prepare journal entries to record (*a*) the December 31, 2005, adjustment to the Income Taxes Payable account and (*b*) the January 20, 2006, payment of the fourth-quarter taxes.

PROBLEM SET A

Problem 11-1A
Short-term notes payable transactions and entries
P1

Tytus Co. entered into the following transactions involving short-term liabilities in 2004 and 2005.

2004

Apr. 20 Purchased $38,500 of merchandise on credit from Frier, terms are 1/10, n/30. Tytus uses the perpetual inventory system.

May 19 Replaced the April 20 account payable to Frier with a 90-day, $30,000 note bearing 9% annual interest along with paying $8,500 in cash.

mhhe.com/larson

July 8	Borrowed $60,000 cash from Community Bank by signing a 120-day, 10% interest-bearing note with a face value of $60,000.
?	Paid the amount due on the note to Frier at the maturity date.
?	Paid the amount due on the note to Community Bank at the maturity date.
Nov. 28	Borrowed $21,000 cash from UMB Bank by signing a 60-day, 8% interest-bearing note with a face value of $21,000.
Dec. 31	Recorded an adjusting entry for accrued interest on the note to UMB Bank.

2005

?	Paid the amount due on the note to UMB Bank at the maturity date.

Required

1. Determine the maturity date for each of the three notes described.

2. Determine the interest due at maturity for each of the three notes. (Assume a 360-day year.)

3. Determine the interest expense to be recorded in the adjusting entry at the end of 2004.

4. Determine the interest expense to be recorded in 2005.

5. Prepare journal entries for all the preceding transactions and events for years 2004–2005.

Check (2) Frier, $675
(3) $154
(4) $126

Problem 11-2A
Warranty expense and liability estimation
P4 

On October 29, 2004, Lue Co. began operations by purchasing razors for resale. Lue uses the perpetual inventory method. The razors have a 90-day warranty that requires the company to replace any nonworking razor. When a razor is returned, the company discards it and mails a new one from Merchandise Inventory to the customer. The company's cost per new razor is $18 and its retail selling price is $80 in both 2004 and 2005. The manufacturer has advised the company to expect warranty costs to equal 7% of dollar sales. The following transactions and events occurred:

2004

Nov. 11	Sold 75 razors for $6,000 cash.
30	Recognized warranty expense related to November sales with an adjusting entry.
Dec. 9	Replaced 15 razors that were returned under the warranty.
16	Sold 210 razors for $16,800 cash.
29	Replaced 30 razors that were returned under the warranty.
31	Recognized warranty expense related to December sales with an adjusting entry.

2005

Jan. 5	Sold 130 razors for $10,400 cash.
17	Replaced 50 razors that were returned under the warranty.
31	Recognized warranty expense related to January sales with an adjusting entry.

Required

1. Prepare journal entries to record these transactions and adjustments for 2004 and 2005.

2. How much warranty expense is reported for November 2004 and for December 2004?

3. How much warranty expense is reported for January 2005?

4. What is the balance of the Estimated Warranty Liability account as of December 31, 2004?

5. What is the balance of the Estimated Warranty Liability account as of January 31, 2005?

Check (3) $728
(4) $786 Cr.
(5) $614 Cr.

Problem 11-3A
Computing and analyzing times interest earned
A1  

Shown here are condensed income statements for two different companies (both are organized as LLCs and pay no income taxes):

Ace Co.	
Sales	$500,000
Variable expenses (80%)	400,000
Income before interest	100,000
Interest expense (fixed)	30,000
Net income	$ 70,000

Deuce Co.	
Sales	$500,000
Variable expenses (60%)	300,000
Income before interest	200,000
Interest expense (fixed)	130,000
Net income	$ 70,000

Required

1. Compute times interest earned for Ace Co.
2. Compute times interest earned for Deuce Co.
3. What happens to each company's net income if sales increase by 30%?
4. What happens to each company's net income if sales increase by 50%?
5. What happens to each company's net income if sales increase by 80%?
6. What happens to each company's net income if sales decrease by 10%?
7. What happens to each company's net income if sales decrease by 20%?
8. What happens to each company's net income if sales decrease by 40%?

Check (3) Ace net income, $100,000 (43% increase)

(6) Deuce net income, $50,000 (29% decrease)

Analysis Component

9. Comment on the results from parts 3 through 8 in relation to the fixed-cost strategies of the two companies and the ratio values you computed in parts 1 and 2.

Problem 11-4A
Payroll expenses, withholdings, and taxes
P2 P3

mhhe.com/larson

Legal Stars pays its employees each week. Its employees' gross pay is subject to these taxes:

Tax	Rate	Applied To
FICA—Social Security	6.20%	First $87,000
FICA—Medicare	1.45	All gross pay
FUTA	0.80	First $7,000
SUTA	2.15	First $7,000

The company is preparing its payroll calculations for the week ended August 25. Payroll records show the following information for the company's four employees:

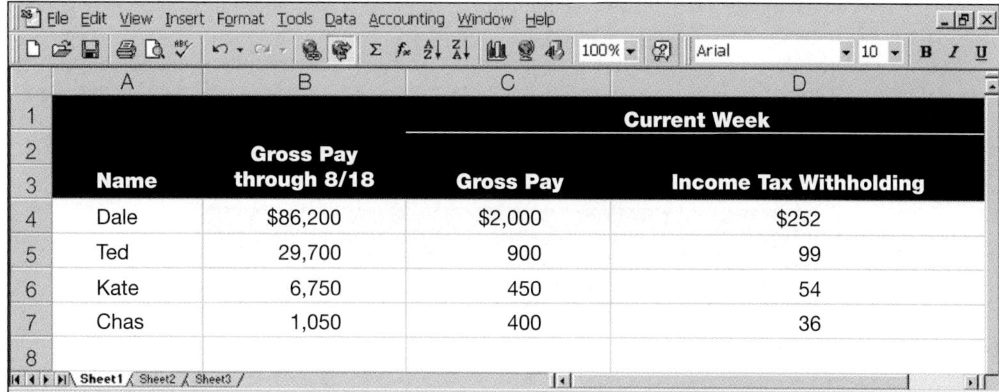

Name	Gross Pay through 8/18	Current Week Gross Pay	Current Week Income Tax Withholding
Dale	$86,200	$2,000	$252
Ted	29,700	900	99
Kate	6,750	450	54
Chas	1,050	400	36

In addition to gross pay, the company must pay one-half of the $32 per employee weekly health insurance; each employee pays the remaining one-half. The company also contributes an extra 8% of each employee's gross pay (at no cost to employees) to a pension fund.

Required

Compute the following for the week ended August 25 (round amounts to the nearest cent):

1. Each employee's FICA withholdings for Social Security.
2. Each employee's FICA withholdings for Medicare.
3. Employer's FICA taxes for Social Security.
4. Employer's FICA taxes for Medicare.
5. Employer's FUTA taxes.
6. Employer's SUTA taxes.
7. Each employee's net (take-home) pay.
8. Employer's total payroll-related expense for each employee.

Check (3) $158.10
(4) $54.38
(5) $5.20

(7) Total net pay, $3,032.52

Problem 11-5A
Entries for payroll transactions
P2 P3

On January 8, the end of the first weekly pay period of the year, Royal Company's payroll register showed that its employees earned $11,380 of office salaries and $32,920 of sales salaries. Withholdings from the employees' salaries include FICA Social Security taxes at the rate of 6.2%, FICA Medicare taxes at the rate of 1.45%, $6,340 of federal income taxes, $670 of medical insurance deductions, and $420 of union dues. No employee earned more than $7,000 in this first period.

Required

Check (1) Cr. Accrued Payroll Payable, $33,481.05

(2) Dr. Payroll Taxes Expense, $5,515.35

1. Calculate FICA Social Security taxes payable and FICA Medicare taxes payable. Prepare the journal entry to record Royal Company's January 8 (employee) payroll expenses and liabilities.

2. Prepare the journal entry to record Royal's (employer) payroll taxes resulting from the January 8 payroll. Royal's merit rating reduces its state unemployment tax rate to 4.0% of the first $7,000 paid each employee. The federal unemployment tax rate is 0.8%.

Problem 11-6A[A]
Entries for payroll transactions
P2 P3 P5 P6

Polo Company has 10 employees, each of whom earns $2,600 per month and is paid on the last day of each month. All 10 have been employed continuously at this amount since January 1. Polo uses a payroll bank account and special payroll checks to pay its employees. On March 1, the following accounts and balances exist in its general ledger:

a. FICA—Social Security Taxes Payable, $3,224; FICA—Medicare Taxes Payable, $754. (The balances of these accounts represent total liabilities for *both* the employer's and employees' FICA taxes for the February payroll only.)

b. Employees' Federal Income Taxes Payable, $3,900 (liability for February only).

c. Federal Unemployment Taxes Payable, $416 (liability for January and February together).

d. State Unemployment Taxes Payable, $2,080 (liability for January and February together).

During March and April, the company had the following payroll transactions:

Mar. 15 Issued check payable to Fleet Bank, a federal depository bank authorized to accept employers' payments of FICA taxes and employee income tax withholdings. The $7,878 check is in payment of the February FICA and employee income taxes.

Check March 31: Cr. Accrued Payroll Payable, $20,111

31 Recorded the March payroll and transferred funds from the regular bank account to the payroll bank account. Issued checks payable to each employee in payment of the March payroll. The payroll register shows the following summary totals for the March pay period:

Salaries and Wages					
Office Salaries	Shop Wages	Gross Pay	FICA Taxes*	Federal Income Taxes	Net Pay
$10,400	$15,600	$26,000	$1,612 $ 377	$3,900	$20,111

* FICA taxes are Social Security and Medicare, respectively.

March 31: Dr. Payroll Taxes Expenses, $2,853

April 15: Cr. Cash, $7,878 (Fleet)

31 Recorded the employer's payroll taxes resulting from the March payroll. The company has a merit rating that reduces its state unemployment tax rate to 4.0% of the first $7,000 paid each employee. The federal rate is 0.8%.

Apr. 15 Issued check to Fleet Bank in payment of the March FICA and employee income taxes.

15 Issued check to the State Tax Commission for the January, February, and March state unemployment taxes. Mailed the check and the first quarter tax return to the Commission.

30 Issued check payable to Fleet Bank in payment of the employer's FUTA taxes for the first quarter of the year.

30 Mailed Form 941 to the IRS, reporting the FICA taxes and the employees' federal income tax withholdings for the first quarter.

Required

Prepare journal entries to record the transactions and events for both March and April.

PROBLEM SET B

Problem 11-1B
Short-term notes payable transactions and entries

P1

Bargen Co. entered into the following transactions involving short-term liabilities in 2004 and 2005.

2004

Apr. 22	Purchased $4,000 of merchandise on credit from Quinn Products, terms are 1/10, n/30. Bargen uses the perpetual inventory system.
May 23	Replaced the April 22 account payable to Quinn Products with a 60-day, $3,600 note bearing 15% annual interest along with paying $400 in cash.
July 15	Borrowed $9,000 cash from Blackhawk Bank by signing a 120-day, 10% interest-bearing note with a face value of $9,000.
?	Paid the amount due on the note to Quinn Products at maturity.
?	Paid the amount due on the note to Blackhawk Bank at maturity.
Dec. 6	Borrowed $16,000 cash from City Bank by signing a 45-day, 9% interest-bearing note with a face value of $16,000.
31	Recorded an adjusting entry for accrued interest on the note to City Bank.

2005

?	Paid the amount due on the note to City Bank at maturity.

Required

1. Determine the maturity date for each of the three notes described.

2. Determine the interest due at maturity for each of the three notes. (Assume a 360-day year.)

3. Determine the interest expense to be recorded in the adjusting entry at the end of 2004.

4. Determine the interest expense to be recorded in 2005.

5. Prepare journal entries for all the preceding transactions and events for years 2004–2005.

Check (2) Quinn, $90
(3) $100
(4) $80

Problem 11-2B
Warranty expense and liability estimation

P4

On November 10, 2004, Byung Co. began operations by purchasing coffee grinders for resale. Byung uses the perpetual inventory method. The grinders have a 60-day warranty that requires the company to replace any nonworking grinder. When a grinder is returned, the company discards it and mails a new one from Merchandise Inventory to the customer. The company's cost per new grinder is $14 and its retail selling price is $35 in both 2004 and 2005. The manufacturer has advised the company to expect warranty costs to equal 10% of dollar sales. The following transactions and events occurred.

2004

Nov. 16	Sold 50 grinders for $1,750 cash.
30	Recognized warranty expense related to November sales with an adjusting entry.
Dec. 12	Replaced six grinders that were returned under the warranty.
18	Sold 150 grinders for $5,250 cash.
28	Replaced 17 grinders that were returned under the warranty.
31	Recognized warranty expense related to December sales with an adjusting entry.

2005

Jan. 7	Sold 60 grinders for $2,100 cash.
21	Replaced 38 grinders that were returned under the warranty.
31	Recognized warranty expense related to January sales with an adjusting entry.

Required

1. Prepare journal entries to record these transactions and adjustments for 2004 and 2005.

2. How much warranty expense is reported for November 2004 and for December 2004?

3. How much warranty expense is reported for January 2005?

4. What is the balance of the Estimated Warranty Liability account as of December 31, 2004?

5. What is the balance of the Estimated Warranty Liability account as of January 31, 2005?

Check (3) $210
(4) $378 Cr.
(5) $56 Cr.

Problem 11-3B
Computing and analyzing times interest earned

Shown here are condensed income statements for two different companies (both are organized as LLCs and pay no income taxes):

Virgo Co.	
Sales	$120,000
Variable expenses (50%)	60,000
Income before interest	$ 60,000
Interest expense (fixed)	45,000
Net income	$ 15,000

Zodiac Co.	
Sales	$120,000
Variable expenses (75%)	90,000
Income before interest	$ 30,000
Interest expense (fixed)	15,000
Net income	$ 15,000

Required

1. Compute times interest earned for Virgo.
2. Compute times interest earned for Zodiac.
3. What happens to each company's net income if sales increase by 10%?
4. What happens to each company's net income if sales increase by 40%?
5. What happens to each company's net income if sales increase by 90%?
6. What happens to each company's net income if sales decrease by 20%?
7. What happens to each company's net income if sales decrease by 50%?
8. What happens to each company's net income if sales decrease by 80%?

Check (4) Virgo net income, $39,000 (160% increase)

(6) Zodiac net income, $9,000 (40% decrease)

Analysis Component

9. Comment on the results from parts 3 through 8 in relation to the fixed cost strategies of the two companies and the ratio values you computed in parts 1 and 2.

Problem 11-4B
Payroll expenses, withholdings, and taxes

P2 P3

Sea Biz Company pays its employees each week. Employees' gross pay is subject to these taxes:

Tax	Rate	Applied To
FICA—Social Security	6.20%	First $87,000
FICA—Medicare	1.45	All gross pay
FUTA	0.80	First $7,000
SUTA	1.75	First $7,000

The company is preparing its payroll calculations for the week ended September 30. Payroll records show the following information for the company's four employees:

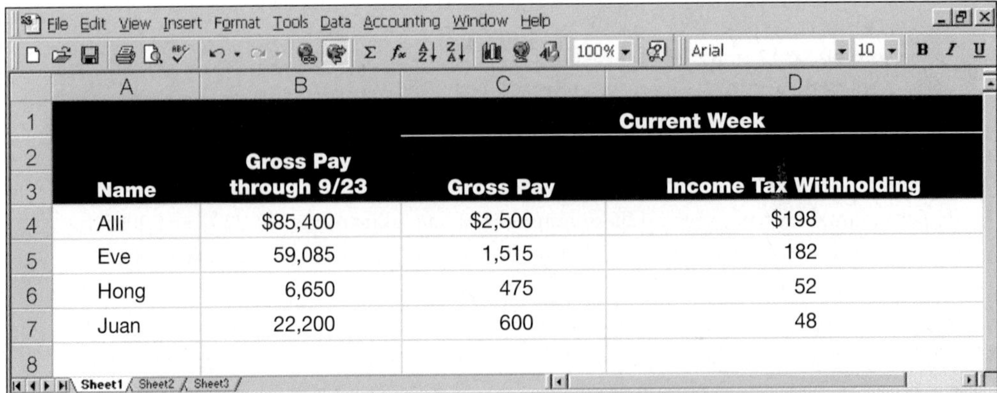

Name	Gross Pay through 9/23	Current Week Gross Pay	Current Week Income Tax Withholding
Alli	$85,400	$2,500	$198
Eve	59,085	1,515	182
Hong	6,650	475	52
Juan	22,200	600	48

In addition to gross pay, the company must pay one-half of the $44 per employee weekly health insurance; each employee pays the remaining one-half. The company also contributes an extra 5% of each employee's gross pay (at no cost to employees) to a pension fund.

Required

Compute the following for the week ended September 30 (round amounts to the nearest cent):

1. Each employee's FICA withholdings for Social Security.
2. Each employee's FICA withholdings for Medicare.
3. Employer's FICA taxes for Social Security.
4. Employer's FICA taxes for Medicare.
5. Employer's FUTA taxes.
6. Employer's SUTA taxes.
7. Each employee's net (take-home) pay.
8. Employer's total payroll-related expense for each employee.

Check (3) $259.78
(4) $73.81
(5) $2.80

(7) Total net pay, $4,188.41

Problem 11-5B
Entries for payroll transactions
P2 P3

Palmer Company's first weekly pay period of the year ends on January 8. On that date, the column totals in Palmer's payroll register indicate its sales employees earned $69,490, its office employees earned $42,450, and its delivery employees earned $2,060. The employees are to have withheld from their wages FICA Social Security taxes at the rate of 6.2%, FICA Medicare taxes at the rate of 1.45%, $17,250 of federal income taxes, $2,320 of medical insurance deductions, and $275 of union dues. No employee earned more than $7,000 in the first pay period.

Required

1. Calculate FICA Social Security taxes payable and FICA Medicare taxes payable. Prepare the journal entry to record Palmer Company's January 8 (employee) payroll expenses and liabilities.
2. Prepare the journal entry to record Palmer's (employer) payroll taxes resulting from the January 8 payroll. Palmer's merit rating reduces its state unemployment tax rate to 3.4% of the first $7,000 paid each employee. The federal unemployment tax rate is 0.8%.

Check (1) Cr. Accrued Payroll Payable, $85,434
(2) Dr. Payroll Taxes Expense, $13,509

Problem 11-6B[A]
Entries for payroll transactions
P2 P3 P5 P6

JLK Company has five employees, each of whom earns $1,200 per month and is paid on the last day of each month. All five have been employed continuously at this amount since January 1. JLK uses a payroll bank account and special payroll checks to pay its employees. On June 1, the following accounts and balances exist in its general ledger:

a. FICA—Social Security Taxes Payable, $744; FICA—Medicare Taxes Payable, $174. (The balances of these accounts represent total liabilities for *both* the employer's and employees' FICA taxes for the May payroll only.)

b. Employees' Federal Income Taxes Payable, $900 (liability for May only).

c. Federal Unemployment Taxes Payable, $96 (liability for April and May together).

d. State Unemployment Taxes Payable, $480 (liability for April and May together).

During June and July, the company had the following payroll transactions:

June 15 Issued check payable to Security Bank, a federal depository bank authorized to accept employers' payments of FICA taxes and employee income tax withholdings. The $1,818 check is in payment of the May FICA and employee income taxes.

30 Recorded the June payroll and transferred funds from the regular bank account to the payroll bank account. Issued checks payable to each employee in payment of the June payroll. The payroll register shows the following summary totals for the June pay period:

Check June 30: Cr. Accrued Payroll Payable, $4,641

Salaries and Wages					
Office Salaries	Shop Wages	Gross Pay	FICA Taxes*	Federal Income Taxes	Net Pay
$2,000	$4,000	$6,000	$372 $ 87	$900	$4,641

* FICA taxes are Social Security and Medicare, respectively.

Check June 30: Dr. Payroll Taxes Expenses, $699

July 15: Cr. Cash $1,818 (Security Bank)

30 Recorded the employer's payroll taxes resulting from the June payroll. The company has a merit rating that reduces its state unemployment tax rate to 4.0% of the first $7,000 paid each employee. The federal rate is 0.8%.

July 15 Issued check payable to Security Bank in payment of the June FICA and employee income taxes.

15 Issued check to the State Tax Commission for the April, May, and June state unemployment taxes. Mailed the check and the second quarter tax return to the State Tax Commission.

31 Issued check payable to Security Bank in payment of the employer's FUTA taxes for the second quarter of the year.

31 Mailed Form 941 to the IRS, reporting the FICA taxes and the employees' federal income tax withholdings for the second quarter.

Required

Prepare journal entries to record the transactions and events for both June and July.

PROBLEM SET C

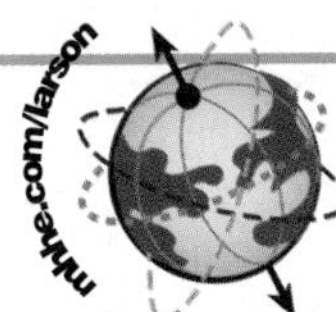

Problem Set C is available at the book's Website to further reinforce and assess your learning.

SERIAL PROBLEM

Success Systems

(This serial problem began in Chapter 1 and continues through most of the book. If previous chapter segments were not completed, the serial problem can begin at this point. It is helpful, but not necessary, for you to use the Working Papers that accompany the book.)

Review the February 26 and March 25 transactions for Success Systems found in Chapter 5.

Required

1.[A] Assume that Sherry Adams is an unmarried employee. Her wages are subject to no deductions other than FICA Social Security taxes, FICA Medicare taxes, and federal income taxes. Her federal income taxes for this pay period total $189. Compute her net pay for the eight days' work paid on February 26.

2. Make the required journal entry to record the payroll payment to Sherry Adams as calculated in part 1.

3. Make the required journal entry to record the (employer) payroll tax expenses for the February 26 payroll. Assume Sherry Adams has not met earnings limits for FUTA and SUTA—the FUTA rate is 0.8% and the SUTA rate is 4%.

4. Record the entry(ies) for the merchandise sold on March 25 if a 4% sales tax rate applies.

COMPREHENSIVE PROBLEM

Bug-Off Exterminators (Review of Chapters 1–11)

Bug-Off Exterminators provides pest control services and sells extermination products manufactured by other companies. The following six-column table contains the company's unadjusted trial balance as of December 31, 2005.

BUG-OFF EXTERMINATORS
December 31, 2005

	Unadjusted Trial Balance		Adjustments		Adjusted Trial Balance	
Cash	$ 17,000					
Accounts receivable	4,000					
Allowance for doubtful accounts		$ 828				
Merchandise inventory	11,700					
Trucks	32,000					
Accum. depreciation—Trucks		0				
Equipment	45,000					
Accum. depreciation—Equipment		12,200				
Accounts payable		5,000				

[continued on next page]

[continued from previous page]

Estimated warranty liability		1,400					
Unearned services revenue		0					
Long-term notes payable		15,000					
Interest payable		0					
T. Newman, Capital		59,700					
T. Newman, Withdrawals	10,000						
Extermination services revenue		60,000					
Interest revenue		872					
Sales (of merchandise)		71,026					
Cost of goods sold	46,300						
Depreciation expense—Trucks	0						
Depreciation expense—Equipment	0						
Wages expense	35,000						
Interest expense	0						
Rent expense	9,000						
Bad debts expense	0						
Miscellaneous expense	1,226						
Repairs expense	8,000						
Utilities expense	6,800						
Warranty expense	0						
Totals	$226,026	$226,026					

The following information applies to the company at the end of the current year:

a. The bank reconciliation as of December 31, 2005, includes these facts:

Balance per bank	$15,100
Balance per books	17,000
Outstanding checks	1,800
Deposit in transit	2,450
Interest earned (on bank account)	52
Bank service charges (miscellaneous expense)	15

Reported on the bank statement is a canceled check that the company failed to record. (Information from the bank reconciliation allows you to determine the amount of this check, which is a payment on an account payable.)

b. An examination of customers' accounts shows that accounts totaling $679 should be written off as uncollectible. Using an aging of receivables, the company determines that the ending balance of the Allowance for Doubtful Accounts should be $700.

c. A truck is purchased and placed in service on January 1, 2005. Its cost is being depreciated with the straight-line method using these facts and estimates:

Original cost	$32,000
Expected salvage value	8,000
Useful life (years)	4

d. Two items of equipment (a sprayer and an injector) were purchased and put into service in early January 2003. They are being depreciated with the straight-line method using these facts and estimates:

	Sprayer	Injector
Original cost	$27,000	$18,000
Expected salvage value	3,000	2,500
Useful life (years)	8	5

e. On August 1, 2005, the company is paid $3,840 in advance to provide monthly service for an apartment complex for one year. The company began providing the services in August. When the cash was received, the full amount was credited to the Extermination Services Revenue account.

f. The company offers a warranty for the services it sells. The expected cost of providing warranty service is 2.5% of the extermination services revenue of $57,760 for 2005. No warranty expense has been recorded for 2005. All costs of servicing warranties in 2005 were properly debited to the Estimated Warranty Liability account.

g. The $15,000 long-term note is a 8%, five-year, interest-bearing note with interest payable annually on December 31. The note was signed with First National Bank on December 31, 2005.

h. The ending inventory of merchandise is counted and determined to have a cost of $11,700. Bug-Off uses a perpetual inventory system.

Required

1. Use the preceding information to determine amounts for the following items:

Check (1*a*) Cash, $15,750
(1*b*) $551 credit

a. Correct (reconciled) ending balance of Cash, and the amount of the omitted check.

b. Adjustment needed to obtain the correct ending balance of the Allowance for Doubtful Accounts.

c. Depreciation expense for the truck used during year 2005.

d. Depreciation expense for the two items of equipment used during year 2005.

e. The adjusted 2005 ending balances of the Extermination Services Revenue and Unearned Services Revenue accounts.

(1*f*) Estim. warranty liability, $2,844 Cr.

f. The adjusted 2005 ending balances of the accounts for Warranty Expense and Estimated Warranty Liability.

g. The adjusted 2005 ending balances of the accounts for Interest Expense and Interest Payable. (Round amounts to nearest whole dollar.)

(2) Adjusted trial balance totals, $238,207

2. Use the results of part 1 to complete the six-column table by first entering the appropriate adjustments for items *a* through *g* and then completing the adjusted trial balance columns. (*Hint:* Item *b* requires two adjustments.)

3. Prepare journal entries to record the adjustments entered on the six-column table. Assume Bug-Off's adjusted balance for Merchandise Inventory matches the year-end physical count.

(4) Net income, $9,274; Total assets, $82,771

4. Prepare a single-step income statement, a statement of owner's equity (withdrawals during 2005 were $10,000), and a classified balance sheet.

BEYOND THE NUMBERS

REPORTING IN ACTION

A1 P4

BTN 11-1 Refer to the financial statements of **Krispy Kreme** in Appendix A to answer the following:

1. Compute times interest earned for the fiscal years ended 2003, 2002, and 2001. Comment on Krispy Kreme's ability to cover its interest expense for this period.

2. What evidence can you identify as an indication that Krispy Kreme has temporary differences between income reported on its income statement and income reported on its tax return?

Roll On

3. Access Krispy Kreme's financial statements for fiscal years ending after February 2, 2003, at its Website (**KrispyKreme.com**) or the SEC's EDGAR database (**www.sec.gov**). Compute its times interest earned for years ending after February 2, 2003, and compare your results to those in part 1.

COMPARATIVE ANALYSIS

A1

BTN 11-2 Key comparative figures ($ thousands) for both **Krispy Kreme** and **Tastykake** follow:

	Krispy Kreme			Tastykake		
Key Figures	Current Year	One Year Prior	Two Years Prior	Current Year	One Year Prior	Two Years Prior
Net income	$33,478	$26,378	$14,725	$2,000*	$8,048*	$8,144
Income taxes	21,295	16,168	9,058	0	3,775	4,609
Interest expense	1,781	337	607	1,066	1,103	1,540

* Net income without restructuring charges.

Required

1. Compute times interest earned for the three years' data shown for each company.
2. Comment on which company appears stronger in its ability to pay interest obligations if income should decline.

ETHICS CHALLENGE

P4

BTN 11-3 Cannon Bly is a sales manager for an automobile dealership. He earns a bonus each year based on revenue from the number of autos sold in the year less related warranty expenses. Actual warranty expenses have varied over the prior 10 years from a low of 3% of an automobile's selling price to a high of 10%. In the past, Bly has tended to estimate warranty expenses on the high end to be conservative. He must work with the dealership's accountant at year-end to arrive at the warranty expense accrual for cars sold each year.

1. Does the warranty accrual decision create any ethical dilemma for Bly?
2. Since warranty expenses vary, what percent do you think Bly should choose for the current year? Justify your response.

COMMUNICATING IN PRACTICE

C3

BTN 11-4 Dustin Clemens is the accounting and finance manager for a manufacturer. At year-end, he must determine how to account for the company's contingencies. His manager, Tom Pretti, objects to Clemens's proposal to recognize an expense and a liability for warranty service on units of a new product introduced in the fourth quarter. Pretti comments, "There's no way we can estimate this warranty cost. We don't owe anyone anything until a product fails and it is returned. Let's report an expense if and when we do any warranty work."

Required

Prepare a one-page memorandum for Clemens to send to Pretti defending his proposal.

TAKING IT TO THE NET

C1 A1

mhhe.com/larson

BTN 11-5 Access the March 12, 2003, filing of the December 31, 2002, annual 10-K report of **McDonald's Corporation** (Ticker: MCD), which is available from **www.SEC.gov**.

Required

1. Identify the current liabilities on McDonald's balance sheet as of December 31, 2002.
2. What portion (in percent) of McDonald's long-term debt matures within the next 12 months?
3. Use the consolidated statement of income for the year ended December 31, 2002, to compute McDonald's times interest earned ratio. Comment on the result.

TEAMWORK IN ACTION

C2 P1

BTN 11-6 Assume that your team is in business and you must borrow $6,000 cash for short-term needs. You have been shopping banks for a loan, and you have the following two options:

A. Sign a $6,000, 90-day, 10% interest-bearing note dated June 1.

B. Sign a $6,000, 120-day, 8% interest-bearing note dated June 1.

Required

1. Discuss these two options and determine the best choice. Ensure that all teammates concur with the decision and understand the rationale.
2. Each member of the team is to prepare *one* of the following journal entries:
   - **a.** Option A—at date of issuance.
   - **b.** Option B—at date of issuance.
   - **c.** Option A—at maturity date.
   - **d.** Option B—at maturity date.
3. In rotation, each member is to explain the entry he or she prepared in part 2 to the team. Ensure that all team members concur with and understand the entries.

4. Assume that the funds are borrowed on December 1 (instead of June 1) and your business operates on a calendar-year reporting period. Each member of the team is to prepare *one* of the following entries:

a. Option A—the year-end adjustment.

b. Option B—the year-end adjustment.

c. Option A—at maturity date.

d. Option B—at maturity date.

5. In rotation, each member is to explain the entry he or she prepared in part 4 to the team. Ensure that all team members concur with and understand the entries.

BUSINESS WEEK ACTIVITY

P4

mhhe.com/larson

BTN 11-7 Read the article "Bed, Board—and Big Trouble" in the October 23, 2002, online issue of ***Business Week***. (This book's Website provides a free link.)

Required

1. What arrangement does the motel owner have with the long-term resident?

2. What risks is the motel operator exposed to by this arrangement?

3. How will the state of New York probably classify the tenant, and what should the motel owner do to respond to New York's probable action? Are there payroll tax implications?

ENTREPRENEURIAL DECISION

A1  

BTN 11-8 Review the chapter's opening feature involving André Downey and **Environmental, Engineering & Construction**. EEC is considering a major technological investment in a plant asset to improve its environmental cleanup process. Assume that this investment would cut variable costs from 60% of sales to 45% of sales. However, fixed interest expense would increase from $540,000 per year to $1,140,000 per year to fund the $4,800,000 plant asset investment (with zero salvage, 50-year life, and depreciated using the straight-line method). Also assume that its recent income statement (absent this potential investment) appears as follows (assume zero income taxes):

EEC Income Statement For Year Ended January 31, 2005	
Sales	$3,000,000
Depreciation	60,000
Variable expenses (60%)	1,800,000
Income before interest	1,140,000
Interest expense (fixed)	540,000
Net income	$ 600,000

Required

1. Compute EEC's times interest earned ratio at January 31, 2005.

2. If EEC expects sales to remain at $3,000,000, what would net income and times interest earned equal if it makes the investment?

3. What would net income and times interest earned equal if sales increase to $3,600,000 and the investment is (*a*) not made and (*b*) made?

4. What would net income and times interest earned equal if sales increase to $4,639,998 and the investment is (*a*) not made and (*b*) made?

5. What would net income and times interest earned equal if sales increase to $5,400,000 and the investment is (*a*) not made and (*b*) made?

6. Comment on the results from parts 1 through 5 and their relation to the times interest earned ratio.

HITTING THE ROAD

P2

BTN 11-9 Check your phone book or the Social Security Administration Website (**www.SSA.gov**) to locate the Social Security office near you. Visit the office to request a personal earnings and estimate form. Fill out the form and mail according to the instructions. You will receive a statement from the Social Security Administration regarding your earnings history and future Social Security benefits you can receive. (*Note:* Formerly the request could be made online. The online service has been discontinued and is now under review by the Social Security Administration due to security concerns.) It is good to request an earnings and benefit statement every 5 to 10 years to make sure you have received credit for all wages earned and for which you and your employer have paid taxes into the system.

BTN 11-10 **Grupo Bimbo**, **Krispy Kreme**, and **Tastykake** are all competitors in the global marketplace. Key comparative figures for Grupo Bimbo **(GrupoBimbo.com)** for the year ended December 31, 2002 (along with selected figures from Krispy Kreme and Tastykake) follow:

GLOBAL DECISION

A1

	Grupo Bimbo (millions of pesos)		Krispy Kreme		Tastykake	
Key Figures	Current Year	Prior Year	Current Year	Prior Year	Current Year	Prior Year
Net income	$1,003	$1,682	—	—	—	—
Income taxes	575	805	—	—	—	—
Interest expense	703	193	—	—	—	—
Times interest earned	?	?	31.8	127.2	2.9	10.2

Required

1. Compute the times interest earned ratio for the most recent two years for Grupo Bimbo using the data shown.
2. Which company of the three presented provides the best coverage of interest expense?

"I started everything from nothing and figured it out along the way"—Michael Koch

Accounting for Partnerships

A Look Back

Chapter 11 focused on current liabilities. We explained how liabilities are identified, computed, recorded, and reported in financial statements. Attention was directed at notes, payroll, sales taxes, warranties, employee benefits, and contingencies.

A Look at This Chapter

This chapter explains the partnership form of organization. Important characteristics of this form of organization are described along with the accounting concepts and procedures for its most fundamental transactions.

A Look Ahead

Chapter 13 extends our discussion to the corporate form of organization. We describe the accounting for stock issuances, dividends, and other equity transactions. We also explain how income, earnings per share, and retained earnings are reported.

CAP

Conceptual

C1 Identify characteristics of partnerships and similar organizations. *(p. 468)*

Analytical

A1 Compute partner return on equity and use it to evaluate partnership performance. *(p. 480)*

Procedural

P1 Prepare entries for partnership formation. *(p. 471)*

P2 Allocate and record income and loss among partners. *(p. 471)*

P3 Account for the admission and withdrawal of partners. *(p. 474)*

P4 Prepare entries for partnership liquidation. *(p. 478)*

Decision Feature

Sound of Success

PORT WASHINGTON, NY—Michael Koch knows the value of a good idea and a partnership. Koch was 24, having just moved to the United States from Innsbruck, and had a job pressing CDs. "I quickly realized I'd better get something else going, because pressing CDs . . . was kind of hard," says Koch. "So I had to look around for something else to do." Koch soon found his niche. He partnered with a friend, and says Koch, "We started importing classical CDs." Koch soon expanded from classical music to rap, jazz, rock, punk, country, and Broadway. He set up **Koch Entertainment LLC** **(www.KochEnt.com)** to focus those efforts.

Koch believes the knowledge of partnerships and their financial implications is important to successful operation. By partnering with others, Koch was able to make serious inroads in the music industry in a relatively short time. His partnering approach extends to the artists. "We don't dictate their creative process as much as larger labels," says Koch. "We focus more on the artist and the relationship."

That partnership philosophy pervades his company, which Koch chose to set up as an LLC (an organizational form with partnership characteristics). He emphasizes the importance of attending to partnership formation, agreements, and financial statements to stay afloat. He points to his own LLC's success as supportive evidence. "Obviously we're doing something right," say Koch.

Koch is not finished with partnerships. He recently signed an agreement to partner with the BBC to market its CDs. First on the list: *Bob the Builder*. If that isn't diversity, nothing is. Koch has also done well by partnering with WWF and Pokémon. He also has partnerships with Dwight Yoakam, Ani DeFranco, Jody Watley, Rancid, and Nick Cave. Koch points to this diversity in artists as a strength: "Let the music speak for itself," he says.

Knowledge of partnerships has set Koch on the road to success. Not bad for someone who started with nothing!

[Sources: *Koch Entertainment Website,* January 2004; *Entrepreneur,* May 2003; *Newsday,* April 2003; *Billboard,* June 2002.]

The three basic types of business organizations are proprietorships, partnerships, and corporations. Partnerships are similar to proprietorships, except they have more than one owner. This chapter explains partnerships and looks at several variations of them such as limited partnerships, limited liability partnerships, S corporations, and limited liability companies. Understanding the advantages and disadvantages of the partnership form of business organization is important for making informed business decisions.

Accounting for Partnerships

Partnership Organization
- Characteristics
- Organizations with partnership characteristics
- Choice of a business form

Basic Partnership Accounting
- Organizing a partnership
- Dividing income or loss
- Partnership financial statements

Partner Admission and Withdrawal
- Admission of partner
- Withdrawal of partner
- Death of partner

Partnership Liquidation
- No capital deficiency
- Capital deficiency

Partnership Form of Organization

C1 Identify characteristics of partnerships and similar organizations.

A **partnership** is an unincorporated association of two or more people to pursue a business for profit as co-owners. Many businesses are organized as partnerships. They are especially common in small retail and service businesses. Many professional practitioners, including physicians, lawyers, investors, and accountants, also organize their practices as partnerships.

Characteristics of Partnerships

Partnerships are an important type of organization because they offer certain advantages with their unique characteristics. We describe these characteristics in this section.

Voluntary Association A partnership is a voluntary association between partners. Joining a partnership increases the risk to one's personal financial position. Some courts have ruled that partnerships are created by the actions of individuals even when there is no expressed agreement to form one.

Partnership Agreement Forming a partnership requires that two or more legally competent people (who are of age and of sound mental capacity) agree to be partners. Their agreement becomes a **partnership contract,** also called *articles of copartnership.* Although it should be in writing, the contract is binding even if it is only expressed verbally. Partnership agreements normally include details of the partners' (1) names and contributions, (2) rights and duties, (3) sharing of income and losses, (4) withdrawal arrangement, (5) dispute procedures, (6) admission and withdrawal of partners, and (7) rights and duties in the event a partner dies.

Point: When a new partner is admitted, all parties usually must agree to the admission.

Limited Life The life of a partnership is limited. Death, bankruptcy, or any event taking away the ability of a partner to enter into or fulfill a contract ends a partnership. Any one of the partners can also terminate a partnership at will.

Point: The end of a partnership is referred to as its *dissolution.*

Taxation A partnership has the same tax status as a proprietorship and is not subject to taxes on its income. The income or loss of a partnership is allocated to the partners according to the partnership agreement, and it is included in determining the taxable income for each partner's tax return. Partnership income or loss is allocated each year whether or not cash is distributed to partners.

Point: Partners are taxed on their share of partnership income, not on their withdrawals.

Mutual Agency **Mutual agency** implies that each partner is a fully authorized agent of the partnership. As its agent, a partner can commit or bind the partnership to any contract within the scope of the partnership business. For instance, a partner in a merchandising business can sign contracts binding the partnership to buy merchandise, lease a store building, borrow money, or hire employees. These activities are all within the scope of a merchandising firm. A partner in a law firm, acting alone, however, cannot bind the other partners to a contract to buy snowboards for resale or rent an apartment for parties. These actions are outside the normal scope of a law firm's business. Partners also can agree to limit the power of any one or more of the partners to negotiate contracts for the partnership. This agreement is binding on the partners and on outsiders who know it exists. It is not binding on outsiders who do not know it exists. Outsiders unaware of the agreement have the right to assume each partner has normal agency powers for the partnership. Mutual agency exposes partners to the risk of unwise actions by any one partner.

Point: The majority of states adhere to the Uniform Partnership Act for the basic rules of partnership formation, operation, and dissolution.

Unlimited Liability **Unlimited liability** implies that each partner can be called on to pay a partnership's debts. When a partnership cannot pay its debts, creditors usually can apply their claims to partners' *personal* assets. If a partner does not have enough assets to meet his or her share of the partnership debt, the creditors can apply their claims to the assets of the other partners. A partnership in which all partners have *mutual agency* and *unlimited liability* is called a **general partnership.** Mutual agency and unlimited liability are two main reasons that most general partnerships have only a few members.

Point: Limited life, mutual agency, and unlimited liability are disadvantages of a partnership.

Co-Ownership of Property Partnership assets are owned jointly by all partners. Any investment by a partner becomes the joint property of all partners. Partners have a claim on partnership assets based on their capital account and the partnership contract.

Organizations with Partnership Characteristics

Organizations exist that combine certain characteristics of partnerships with other forms of organizations. We discuss several of these forms in this section.

Limited Partnerships Some individuals who want to invest in a partnership are unwilling to accept the risk of unlimited liability. Their needs can be met with a **limited partnership.** This type of organization is identified in its name with the words "Limited Partnership," or "Ltd.," or "LP." A limited partnership has two classes of partners, general and limited. At least one partner must be a **general partner,** who assumes management duties and unlimited liability for the debts of the partnership. The **limited partners** have no personal liability beyond the amounts they invest in the partnership. Limited partners have no active role except as specified in the partnership agreement. A limited partnership agreement often specifies unique procedures for allocating income and losses between general and limited partners. The accounting procedures are similar for both limited and general partnerships.

Decision Insight

Team Up The **Boston Celtics** is organized as a limited partnership. It owns and operates the Boston Celtics NBA team. The general partner of the Boston Celtics is Paul E. Gaston.

Limited Liability Partnerships Most states allow individuals to form a **limited liability partnership.** This is identified in its name with the words "Limited Liability Partnership" or by "LLP." This type of partnership is designed to protect innocent partners from malpractice or negligence claims resulting from the acts of another partner. When a partner provides service resulting in a malpractice claim, that partner has personal liability for the claim. The remaining partners who were not responsible for the actions resulting in the claim are not personally liable for it. However, most states hold all partners personally liable for other partnership debts. Accounting for a limited liability partnership is the same as for a general partnership.

Point: Many accounting services firms are set up as LLPs.

S Corporations Certain corporations with 75 or fewer stockholders can elect to be treated as a partnership for income tax purposes. These corporations are called *Sub-Chapter S* or simply **S corporations.** This distinguishes them from other corporations, called *Sub-Chapter C* or simply **C corporations.** S corporations provide stockholders the same limited liability feature that C corporations do. The advantage of an S corporation is that it does not pay income taxes. If stockholders work for an S corporation, their salaries are treated as expenses of the corporation. The remaining income or loss of the corporation is allocated to stockholders for inclusion on their personal tax returns. Except for C corporations having to account for income tax expenses and liabilities, the accounting procedures are the same for both S and C corporations.

Point: The majority of proprietorships and partnerships that are being organized today are being set up as an LLC.

Limited Liability Companies A relatively new form of business organization is the **limited liability company.** The names of these businesses usually include the words "Limited Liability Company" or an abbreviation such as "LLC" or "LC." This form of business has certain features similar to a corporation and others similar to a limited partnership. The owners, who are called *members,* are protected with the same limited liability feature as owners of corporations. While limited partners cannot actively participate in the management of a limited partnership, the members of a limited liability company can assume an active management role. A limited liability company usually has a limited life. For income tax purposes, a limited liability company is typically treated as a partnership. This treatment depends on factors such as whether the members' equity interests are freely transferable and whether the company has continuity of life. A limited liability company's accounting system is designed to help management comply with the dictates of the articles of organization and company regulations adopted by its members. The accounting system also must provide information to support the company's compliance with state and federal laws, including taxation.

Point: Accounting for LLCs is similar to that for partnerships (and proprietorships). One difference is that Owner (Partner), Capital is usually called *Members, Capital* for LLCs.

Choosing a Business Form

Choosing the proper business form is crucial. Many factors should be considered, including taxes, liability risk, tax and fiscal year-end, ownership structure, estate planning, business risks, and earnings and property distributions. The following table summarizes several important characteristics of business organizations:

	Proprietorship	Partnership	LLP	LLC	S Corp.	Corporation
Business entity	yes	yes	yes	yes	yes	yes
Legal entity	no	no	no	yes	yes	yes
Limited liability	no	no	limited*	yes	yes	yes
Business taxed	no	no	no	no	no	yes
One owner allowed . .	yes	no	no	yes	yes	yes

* A partner's personal liability for LLP debts is limited. Most LLPs carry insurance to protect against malpractice.

Point: Small Business Administration provides suggestions and information on setting up the proper form for your organization—see **SBA.gov**.

We must remember that this table is a summary, not a detailed list. Many details underlie each of these business forms, and several details differ across states. Also, state and federal laws change, and a body of law is still developing around LLCs. Business owners should look at these details and consider unique business arrangements such as organizing various parts of their businesses in different forms.

Quick Check

1. A partnership is terminated in the event (*a*) a partnership agreement is not in writing, (*b*) a partner dies, (*c*) a partner exercises mutual agency.
2. What does the term *unlimited liability* mean when applied to a general partnership?
3. Which of the following forms of organization do not provide limited liability to *all* of its owners: (*a*) S corporation, (*b*) limited liability company, (*c*) limited partnership?

Answers—p. 483

Basic Partnership Accounting

Since ownership rights in a partnership are divided among partners, partnership accounting

- Uses a capital account for each partner.
- Uses a withdrawals account for each partner.
- Allocates net income or loss to partners according to the partnership agreement.

This section describes partnership accounting for organizing a partnership, distributing income and loss, and preparing financial statements.

Organizing a Partnership

P1 Prepare entries for partnership formation.

When partners invest in a partnership, their capital accounts are credited for the invested amounts. Partners can invest both assets and liabilities. Each partner's investment is recorded at an agreed-on value, normally the market values of the contributed assets and liabilities at the date of contribution. To illustrate, Kayla Zayn and Hector Perez organize a partnership called BOARDS that offers year-round facilities for skateboarding and snowboarding. Zayn's initial net investment in BOARDS is $30,000, made up of cash ($7,000), boarding facilities ($33,000), and a note payable reflecting a bank loan for the new business ($10,000). Perez's initial investment is cash of $10,000. These amounts are the values agreed on by both partners. The entries to record these investments follow:

Zayn's Investment

Jan. 11	Cash	7,000	
	Boarding facilities	33,000	
	Note payable		10,000
	K. Zayn, Capital		30,000
	To record the investment of Zayn.		

Assets = Liabilities + Equity
+7,000 +10,000 +30,000
+33,000

Perez's Investment

Jan. 11	Cash	10,000	
	H. Perez, Capital		10,000
	To record the investment of Perez.		

Assets = Liabilities + Equity
+10,000 +10,000

Note that in accounting for a partnership, the following additional relations hold true: (1) Partners' withdrawals are debited to their own separate withdrawals accounts. (2) Partners' capital accounts are credited (or debited) for their shares of net income (or net loss) when closing the accounts at the end of a period. (3) Each partner's withdrawals account is closed to that partner's capital account. Note, too, that separate capital and withdrawals accounts are kept for each partner.

Point: Both equity and cash are reduced when a partner withdraws cash from a partnership.

Decision Insight

Nutty Partners The Hawaii-based **ML Macadamia Orchards LP** is one of the world's largest growers of macadamia nuts. It reported the following partners' capital balances ($ thousands) in its recent balance sheet:

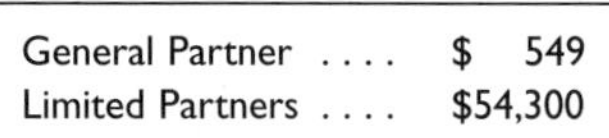

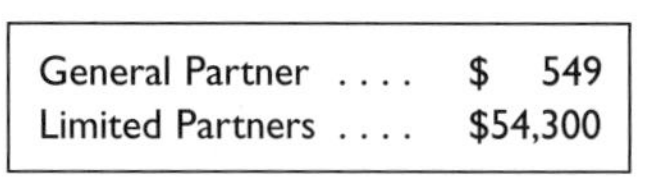

General Partner	$ 549
Limited Partners	$54,300

Dividing Income or Loss

P2 Allocate and record income and loss among partners.

Partners are not employees of the partnership but are its owners. If partners devote their time and services to their partnership, they are understood to do so for profit, not for salary. This means there are no salaries to partners that are reported as expenses on the partnership income statement. However, when net income or loss of a partnership is allocated among partners, the partners can agree to allocate "salary allowances" reflecting the relative value of services provided. Partners also can agree to allocate "interest allowances" based on the amount invested. For instance, since Zayn contributes three times the investment of Perez, it is only fair that this be considered when allocating income between them. Like salary allowances, these interest allowances are not expenses on the income statement.

Partners can agree to any method of dividing income or loss. In the absence of an agreement, the law says that the partners share income or loss of a partnership equally. If partners agree on how to share income but say nothing about losses, they share losses the same way they share income. Three common methods to divide income or loss use (1) a stated ratio basis, (2) the ratio of capital balances, or (3) salary and interest allowances and any remainder according to a fixed ratio. We explain each of these methods in this section.

Point: Partners can agree on one ratio to divide income and another ratio to divide a loss.

Allocation on Stated Ratios The *stated ratio* (also called the *income-and-loss-sharing ratio,* the *profit and loss ratio,* or the *P&L ratio*) method of allocating partnership income or loss gives each partner a fraction of the total. Partners must agree on the fractional share each receives. To illustrate, assume the partnership agreement of K. Zayn and H. Perez says Zayn receives two-thirds and Perez one-third of partnership income and loss. If their partnership's net income is $60,000, it is allocated to the partners when the Income Summary account is closed as follows:

Point: The fractional basis can be stated as a proportion, ratio, or percent. For example, a 3:2 basis is the same as 3/5 and 2/5, or 60% and 40%.

Dec. 31	Income Summary	60,000	
	K. Zayn, Capital		40,000
	H. Perez, Capital		20,000
	To allocate income and close Income Summary.		

Assets = Liabilities + Equity
−60,000
+40,000
+20,000

Allocation on Capital Balances The *capital balances* method of allocating partnership income or loss assigns an amount based on the ratio of each partner's relative capital balance. If Zayn and Perez agree to share income and loss on the ratio of their beginning capital balances—Zayn's $30,000 and Perez's $10,000—Zayn receives three-fourths of any income or loss ($30,000/$40,000) and Perez receives one-fourth ($10,000/$40,000). The journal entry follows the same format as that using stated ratios (see preceding entries).

Point: To determine the percent of income received by each partner, divide an individual partner's share by total net income.

Topic Tackler 12-1

Allocation on Services, Capital, and Stated Ratios The *services, capital, and stated ratio* method of allocating partnership income or loss recognizes that service and capital contributions of partners often are not equal. Salary allowances can make up for differences in service contributions. Interest allowances can make up for unequal capital contributions. Also, the allocation of income and loss can include *both* salary and interest allowances. To illustrate, assume that the partnership agreement of K. Zayn and H. Perez reflects differences in service and capital contributions as follows: (1) annual salary allowances of $36,000 to Zayn and $24,000 to Perez, (2) annual interest allowances of 10% of a partner's beginning-year capital balance, and (3) equal share of any remaining balance of income or loss. These salaries and interest allowances are *not* reported as expenses on the income statement. They are simply a means of dividing partnership income or loss. The remainder of this section provides two illustrations using this three-point allocation agreement.

Illustration when income exceeds allowance. If BOARDS has first-year net income of $70,000, and Zayn and Perez apply the three-point partnership agreement described in the prior paragraph, income is allocated as shown in Exhibit 12.1. Zayn gets $42,000 and Perez gets $28,000 of the $70,000 total.

Illustration when allowances exceed income. The sharing agreement between Zayn and Perez must be followed even if net income is less than the total of the allowances. For example, if BOARDS' first-year net income is $50,000 instead of $70,000, it is allocated to the partners as shown in Exhibit 12.2. Computations for salaries and interest are identical to those in Exhibit 12.1. However, when we apply the total allowances against income, the balance of income is negative. This $(14,000) negative balance is allocated equally to the partners per their sharing agreement. This means that a negative $(7,000) is allocated to each partner. In this case, Zayn ends up with $32,000 and Perez with $18,000. If BOARDS had experienced a net loss, Zayn and Perez would share it in the same manner as the $50,000 income. The only difference is that they would have begun with a negative amount because of the loss. Specifically, the partners would still have been allocated their salary and interest

Point: When allowances exceed income, the amount of this negative balance often is referred to as a *sharing agreement loss* or *deficit.*

Point: Check to make sure the sum of the dollar amounts allocated to each partner equals net income or loss.

	Zayn	Perez	Total
Net income			$70,000
Salary allowances			
Zayn	$ 36,000		
Perez		$ 24,000	
Interest allowances			
Zayn (10% × $30,000)	3,000		
Perez (10% × $10,000)		1,000	
Total salaries and interest	39,000	25,000	64,000
Balance of income			**6,000**
Balance allocated equally			
Zayn	3,000 ←		
Perez		3,000 ←	
Total allocated			6,000
Balance of income			**$ 0**
Income of each partner	$42,000	$28,000	

Exhibit 12.1

Dividing Income When Income Exceeds Allowances

	Zayn	Perez	Total
Net income			$50,000
Salary allowances			
Zayn	$ 36,000		
Perez		$ 24,000	
Interest allowances			
Zayn (10% × $30,000)	3,000		
Perez (10% × $10,000)		1,000	
Total salaries and interest	39,000	25,000	64,000
Balance of income			**(14,000)**
Balance allocated equally			
Zayn	(7,000) ←		
Perez		(7,000) ←	
Total allocated			(14,000)
Balance of income			**$ 0**
Income of each partner	$32,000	$18,000	

Exhibit 12.2

Dividing Income When Allowances Exceed Income

allowances, further adding to the negative balance of the loss. This *total* negative balance *after* salary and interest allowances would have been allocated equally between the partners. These allocations would have been applied against the positive numbers from any allowances to determine each partner's share of the loss.

Point: When a loss occurs, it is possible for a specific partner's capital to increase (when closing income summary) if that partner's allowance is in excess of his or her share of the negative balance. This implies that decreases to the capital balances of other partners exceed the partnership's loss amount.

Quick Check

4. Denzel and Shantell form a partnership by contributing $70,000 and $35,000, respectively. They agree to an interest allowance equal to 10% of each partner's capital balance at the beginning of the year, with the remaining income shared equally. Allocate first-year income of $40,000 to each partner.

Answers—p. 483

Partnership Financial Statements

Partnership financial statements are similar to those of other organizations. The **statement of partners' equity,** also called *statement of partners' capital,* is one exception. It shows *each* partner's beginning capital balance, additional investments, allocated income or loss, withdrawals, and ending capital balance. To illustrate, Exhibit 12.3 shows the statement of

Decision Insight

Beach Buddies The **Casa Munras Hotel Partners LP** operates the Casa Munras Garden Hotel and several leased retail stores in Monterey, California. Its recent statement of partners' equity reports that total partners' withdrawals equal $135,000, of which $1,350 is distributed to the general partner and the remainder of $133,650 to limited partners.

partners' equity for BOARDS prepared using the sharing agreement of Exhibit 12.1. Recall that BOARDS' income was $70,000; also, assume that Zayn withdrew $20,000 and Perez $12,000 at year-end.

The equity section of the balance sheet of a partnership usually shows the separate capital account balance of each partner. In the case of BOARDS, both K. Zayn, Capital, and H. Perez, Capital, are listed in the equity section along with their balances of $52,000 and $26,000, respectively.

Exhibit 12.3

Statement of Partners' Equity

BOARDS
Statement of Partners' Equity
For Year Ended December 31, 2005

	Zayn		Perez		Total
Beginning capital balances		$ 0		$ 0	$ 0
Plus					
Investments by owners		30,000		10,000	40,000
Net income					
Salary allowances	$36,000		$24,000		
Interest allowances	3,000		1,000		
Balance allocated	3,000		3,000		
Total net income		42,000		28,000	70,000
		72,000		38,000	110,000
Less partners' withdrawals		(20,000)		(12,000)	(32,000)
Ending capital balances		**$52,000**		**$26,000**	**$78,000**

Admission and Withdrawal of Partners

P3 Account for the admission and withdrawal of partners.

A partnership is based on a contract between individuals. When a partner is admitted or withdraws, the present partnership ends. Still, the business can continue to operate as a new partnership consisting of the remaining partners. This section considers how to account for the admission and withdrawal of partners.

Admission of a Partner

A new partner is admitted in one of two ways: by purchasing an interest from one or more current partners or by investing cash or other assets in the partnership.

Topic Tackler 12-2

Purchase of Partnership Interest The purchase of partnership interest is a *personal transaction between one or more current partners and the new partner.* To become a partner, the current partners must accept the purchaser. Accounting for the purchase of partnership interest involves reallocating current partners' capital to reflect the transaction. To illustrate, at the end of BOARDS' first year, H. Perez sells one-half of his partnership interest to Tyrell Rasheed for $18,000. This means that Perez gives up a $13,000 recorded interest ($26,000 × 1/2) in the partnership (see the ending capital balance in Exhibit 12.3). The partnership records this as follows:

Assets = Liabilities + Equity
−13,000
+13,000

Jan. 4	H. Perez, Capital	13,000	
	T. Rasheed, Capital		13,000
	To record admission of Rasheed by purchase.		

After this entry is posted, BOARDS' equity shows K. Zayn, Capital; H. Perez, Capital; and T. Rasheed, Capital, and their respective balances of $52,000, $13,000, and $13,000.

Two aspects of this transaction are important. First, the partnership, does *not* record the $18,000 Rasheed paid Perez. The partnership's assets, liabilities, and *total equity* are unaffected by this transaction among partners. Second, Zayn and Perez must agree that Rasheed is to become a partner. If they agree to accept Rasheed, a new partnership is formed and a new contract with a new income-and-loss-sharing agreement is prepared. If Zayn or Perez refuses to accept Rasheed as a partner, then (under the Uniform Partnership Act) Rasheed gets Perez's sold share of partnership income and loss. If the partnership is liquidated, Rasheed gets Perez's sold share of partnership assets. Rasheed gets no voice in managing the company unless Rasheed is admitted as a partner.

Point: Partners' withdrawals are not constrained by the partnership's annual income or loss.

Investing Assets in a Partnership Admitting a partner by accepting assets is a *transaction between the new partner and the partnership.* The invested assets become partnership property. To illustrate, if Zayn (with a $52,000 interest) and Perez (with a $26,000 interest) agree to accept Rasheed as a partner in BOARDS after an investment of $22,000 cash, this is recorded as follows:

Jan. 4	Cash	22,000	
	T. Rasheed, Capital		22,000
	To record admission of Rasheed by investment.		

Assets = Liabilities + Equity
+22,000 +22,000

After this entry is posted, both assets (cash) and equity (T. Rasheed, Capital) increase by $22,000. Rasheed now has a 22% equity in the assets of the business, computed as $22,000 divided by the entire partnership equity ($52,000 + $26,000 + $22,000). Rasheed does not necessarily have a right to 22% of income. Dividing income and loss is a separate matter on which partners must agree.

Bonus to old partners. When the current value of a partnership is greater than the recorded amounts of equity, the partners usually require a new partner to pay a bonus for the privilege of joining. To illustrate, assume that Zayn and Perez agree to accept Rasheed as a partner with a 25% interest in BOARDS if Rasheed invests $42,000. Recall the partnership's accounting records show Zayn's recorded equity in the business is $52,000 and Perez's recorded equity is $26,000 (see Exhibit 12.3). Rasheed's equity is determined as follows:

Equities of existing partners ($52,000 + $26,000)	$ 78,000
Investment of new partner	42,000
Total partnership equity	$120,000
Equity of Rasheed (25% × $120,000)	$ 30,000

Although Rasheed invests $42,000, the equity attributed to Rasheed in the new partnership is only $30,000. The $12,000 difference is called a *bonus* and is allocated to existing partners (Zayn and Perez) according to their income-and-loss-sharing agreement. A bonus is shared in this way because it is viewed as reflecting a higher value of the partnership that is not yet reflected in income. The entry to record this transaction follows:

Jan. 4	Cash	42,000	
	T. Rasheed, Capital		30,000
	K. Zayn, Capital ($12,000 × ½)		6,000
	H. Perez, Capital ($12,000 × ½)		6,000
	To record admission of Rasheed and bonus.		

Assets = Liabilities + Equity
+42,000 +30,000
+6,000
+6,000

Bonus to new partner. Alternatively, existing partners can grant a bonus to a new partner. This usually occurs when they need additional cash or the new partner has exceptional talents. The bonus to the new partner is in the form of a larger share of equity than the amount invested. To illustrate, assume that Zayn and Perez agree to accept Rasheed as a partner with a 25% interest in the partnership, but they require Rasheed to invest only $18,000. Rasheed's equity is determined as follows:

Equities of existing partners ($52,000 + $26,000)	$78,000
Investment of new partner	18,000
Total partnership equity	$96,000
Equity of Rasheed (25% × $96,000)	$24,000

The old partners contribute the $6,000 bonus (computed as $24,000 minus $18,000) to Rasheed according to their income-and-loss-sharing ratio. Moreover, Rasheed's 25% equity does not necessarily entitle Rasheed to 25% of future income or loss. This is a separate matter for agreement by the partners. The entry to record the admission and investment of Rasheed is

Assets	= Liabilities +	Equity
+18,000		−3,000
		−3,000
		+24,000

Date	Account	Debit	Credit
Jan. 4	Cash	18,000	
	K. Zayn, Capital ($6,000 × ½)	3,000	
	H. Perez, Capital ($6,000 × ½)...............	3,000	
	T. Rasheed, Capital....................		24,000
	To record Rasheed's admission and bonus.		

Withdrawal of a Partner

A partner generally withdraws from a partnership in one of two ways. (1) First, the withdrawing partner can sell his or her interest to another person who pays for it in cash or other assets. For this, we need only debit the withdrawing partner's capital account and credit the new partner's capital account. (2) The second case is when cash or other assets of the partnership are distributed to the withdrawing partner in settlement of his or her interest. To illustrate these cases, assume that Perez withdraws from the partnership of BOARDS in some future period. The partnership shows the following capital balances at the date of Perez's withdrawal: K. Zayn, $84,000; H. Perez, $38,000; and T. Rasheed, $38,000. The partners (Zayn, Perez, and Rasheed) share income and loss equally. Accounting for Perez's withdrawal depends on whether a bonus is paid. We describe three possibilities.

No Bonus If Perez withdraws and takes cash equal to Perez's capital balance, the entry is

Assets	= Liabilities +	Equity
−38,000		−38,000

Date	Account	Debit	Credit
Oct. 31	H. Perez, Capital	38,000	
	Cash..............................		38,000
	To record withdrawal of Perez from partnership with no bonus.		

Perez can take any combination of assets to which the partners agree to settle Perez's equity. Perez's withdrawal creates a new partnership between the remaining partners. A new partnership contract and a new income-and-loss-sharing agreement are required.

Bonus to Remaining Partners A withdrawing partner is sometimes willing to take less than the recorded value of his or her equity to get out of the partnership or because the recorded value is overstated. Whatever the reason, when this occurs, the withdrawing partner in effect gives the remaining partners a bonus equal to the equity left behind. The remaining partners share this unwithdrawn equity according to their income-and-loss-sharing ratio. To illustrate, if Perez withdraws and agrees to take $34,000 cash in settlement of

Perez's capital balance, the entry is

Oct. 31	H. Perez, Capital	38,000	
	Cash		34,000
	K. Zayn, Capital		2,000
	T. Rasheed, Capital		2,000
	To record withdrawal of Perez and bonus to remaining partners.		

Assets	= Liabilities +	Equity
−34,000		−38,000
		+2,000
		+2,000

Perez withdrew $4,000 less than Perez's recorded equity of $38,000. This $4,000 is divided between Zayn and Rasheed according to their income-and-loss-sharing ratio.

Bonus to Withdrawing Partner A withdrawing partner may be able to receive more than his or her recorded equity for at least two reasons. First, the recorded equity may be understated. Second, the remaining partners may agree to remove this partner by giving assets of greater value than this partner's recorded equity. In either case, the withdrawing partner receives a bonus. The remaining partners reduce their equity by the amount of this bonus according to their income-and-loss-sharing ratio. To illustrate, if Perez withdraws and receives $40,000 cash in settlement of Perez's capital balance, the entry is

Oct. 31	H. Perez, Capital	38,000	
	K. Zayn, Capital	1,000	
	T. Rasheed, Capital	1,000	
	Cash		40,000
	To record Perez's withdrawal from partnership with a bonus to Perez.		

Assets	= Liabilities +	Equity
−40,000		−38,000
		−1,000
		−1,000

Falcon Cable Communications LLC has a partnership withdrawal agreement. Falcon owns and operates cable television systems and has two managing general partners. The partnership agreement states that either partner "can offer to sell to the other partner the offering partner's entire partnership interest . . . for a negotiated price. If the partner receiving such an offer rejects it, the offering partner may elect to cause [the partnership] . . . to be liquidated and dissolved."

Death of a Partner

A partner's death dissolves a partnership. A deceased partner's estate is entitled to receive his or her equity. The partnership contract should contain provisions for settlement in this case. These provisions usually require (1) closing the books to determine income or loss since the end of the previous period and (2) determining and recording current market values for both assets and liabilities. The remaining partners and the deceased partner's estate then must agree to a settlement of the deceased partner's equity. This can involve selling the equity to remaining partners or to an outsider, or it can involve withdrawing assets.

Decision Ethics

Financial Planner You are hired by the two remaining partners of a three-member partnership after the third partner's death. The partnership agreement states that a deceased partner's estate is entitled to a "share of partnership assets equal to the partner's relative equity balance" (partners' equity balances are equal). The estate argues it is entitled to one-third of the current value of partnership assets. The remaining partners say the distribution should use asset book values, which are 75% of current value. They also point to partnership liabilities, which equal 40% of total asset book value and 30% of current value. How would you resolve this situation?

Answer—p. 483

Liquidation of a Partnership

When a partnership is liquidated, its business ends and four concluding steps are required:

1. Record the sale of noncash assets for cash and any gain or loss from their liquidation.
2. Allocate any gain or loss from liquidation of the assets in step 1 to the partners using their income-and-loss-sharing ratio.

3. Pay or settle all partner liabilities.
4. Distribute any remaining cash to partners based on their capital balances.

Partnership liquidation usually falls into one of two cases, as described in this section.

No Capital Deficiency

P4 Prepare entries for partnership liquidation.

No capital deficiency means that all partners have a zero or credit balance in their capital accounts for final distribution of cash. To illustrate, assume that Zayn, Perez, and Rasheed operate their partnership in BOARDS for several years, sharing income and loss equally. The partners then decide to liquidate. On the liquidation date, the current period's income or loss is transferred to the partners' capital accounts according to the sharing agreement. After that transfer, assume the partners' recorded equity balances (immediately prior to liquidation) are Zayn, $70,000; Perez, $66,000; and Rasheed, $62,000.

Next, assume that BOARDS sells its noncash assets for a net gain of $6,000. In a liquidation, gains or losses usually result from the sale of noncash assets, which are called *losses and gains from liquidation.* Partners share losses and gains from liquidation according to their income-and-loss-sharing agreement (equal for these partners) yielding the partners' revised equity balances of Zayn, $72,000; Perez, $68,000; and Rasheed, $64,000.[1] Then, after partnership assets are sold and any gain or loss is allocated, the liabilities must be paid. After creditors are paid, any remaining cash is divided among the partners according to their capital account balances. BOARDS' only liability at liquidation is $20,000 in accounts payable. The entries to record the payment to creditors and the final distribution of cash to partners follow:

Assets	= Liabilities	+ Equity
−20,000	−20,000	

Date	Account	Debit	Credit
Jan. 15	Accounts Payable	20,000	
	Cash		20,000
	To pay claims of creditors.		
Jan. 15	K. Zayn, Capital	72,000	
	H. Perez, Capital	68,000	
	T. Rasheed, Capital	64,000	
	Cash		204,000
	To distribute remaining cash to partners.		

Assets	= Liabilities	+ Equity
−204,000		−72,000
		−68,000
		−64,000

It is important to remember that the final cash payment is distributed to partners according to their capital account balances, whereas gains and losses from liquidation are allocated according to the income-and-loss-sharing ratio.

[1] The concepts behind these entries are not new. For example, assume that BOARDS has two noncash assets recorded as boarding facilities, $15,000, and land, $25,000. The entry to sell these assets for $46,000 is

Date	Account	Debit	Credit
Jan. 15	Cash	46,000	
	Boarding facilities		15,000
	Land		25,000
	Gain from Liquidation		6,000
	Sold noncash assets at a gain.		

We then record the allocation of any loss or gain (a gain in this case) from liquidation according to the partners' income-and-loss-sharing agreement as follows:

Date	Account	Debit	Credit
Jan. 15	Gain from Liquidation	6,000	
	K. Zayn, Capital		2,000
	H. Perez, Capital		2,000
	T. Rasheed, Capital		2,000
	To allocate liquidation gain to partners.		

Capital Deficiency

Capital deficiency means that at least one partner has a debit balance in his or her capital account at the point of final cash distribution. This can arise from liquidation losses, excessive withdrawals before liquidation, or recurring losses in prior periods. A partner with a capital deficiency must, if possible, cover the deficit by paying cash into the partnership.

To illustrate, assume that Zayn, Perez, and Rasheed operate their partnership in BOARDS for several years, sharing income and losses equally. The partners then decide to liquidate. Immediately prior to the final distribution of cash, the partners' recorded capital balances are Zayn, $19,000; Perez, $8,000; and Rasheed, $(3,000). Rasheed's capital deficiency means that Rasheed owes the partnership $3,000. Both Zayn and Perez have a legal claim against Rasheed's personal assets. The final distribution of cash in this case depends on how this capital deficiency is handled. Two possibilities exist.

Partner Pays Deficiency Rasheed is obligated to pay $3,000 into the partnership to cover the deficiency. If Rasheed is willing and able to pay, the entry to record receipt of payment from Rasheed follows:

Jan. 15	Cash	3,000	
	T. Rasheed, Capital		3,000
	To record payment of deficiency by Rasheed.		

Assets	= Liabilities +	Equity
+3,000		+3,000

After the $3,000 payment, the partners' capital balances are Zayn, $19,000; Perez, $8,000; and Rasheed, $0. The entry to record the final cash distributions to partners is

Jan. 15	K. Zayn, Capital	19,000	
	H. Perez, Capital	8,000	
	Cash		27,000
	To distribute remaining cash to partners.		

Assets	= Liabilities +	Equity
−27,000		−19,000
		−8,000

Partner Cannot Pay Deficiency The remaining partners with credit balances absorb any partner's unpaid deficiency according to their income-and-loss-sharing ratio. To illustrate, if Rasheed is unable to pay the $3,000 deficiency, Zayn and Perez absorb it. Since they share income and loss equally, Zayn and Perez each absorb $1,500 of the deficiency. This is recorded as follows:

Jan. 15	K. Zayn, Capital	1,500	
	H. Perez, Capital	1,500	
	T. Rasheed, Capital		3,000
	To transfer Rasheed deficiency to Zayn and Perez.		

Assets	= Liabilities +	Equity
		−1,500
		−1,500
		+3,000

After Zayn and Perez absorb Rasheed's deficiency, the capital accounts of the partners are Zayn, $17,500; Perez, $6,500; and Rasheed, $0. The entry to record the final cash distribution to the partners is

Jan. 15	K. Zayn, Capital	17,500	
	H. Perez, Capital	6,500	
	Cash		24,000
	To distribute remaining cash to partners.		

Assets	= Liabilities +	Equity
−24,000		−17,500
		−6,500

Rasheed's inability to cover this deficiency does not relieve Rasheed of the liability. If Rasheed becomes able to pay at a future date, Zayn and Perez can each collect $1,500 from Rasheed.

Decision Analysis

Partner Return on Equity

A1 Compute partner return on equity and use it to evaluate partnership performance.

An important role of partnership financial statements is to aid current and potential partners in evaluating partnership success compared with other opportunities. One measure of this success is the **partner return on equity** ratio:

$$\textbf{Partner return on equity} = \frac{\textbf{Partner net income}}{\textbf{Average partner equity}}$$

This measure is separately computed for each partner. To illustrate, Exhibit 12.4 reports selected data from the **Boston Celtics LP**. The return on equity for the *total* partnership is computed as \$216/[(\$84 + \$252)/2] = 128.6%. However, return on equity is quite different across the partners. For example, the **Boston Celtics LP I** partner return on equity is computed as \$44/[(\$122 + \$166)/2] = 30.6%, whereas the **Celtics LP** partner return on equity is computed as \$111/[(\$270 + \$333)/2] = 36.8%. Partner return on equity provides *each* partner an assessment of its return on its equity invested in the partnership. A specific partner often uses this return to decide whether additional investment or withdrawal of resources is best for that partner. Exhibit 12.4 reveals that year 2002 produced good returns for all partners (the Boston Celtics LP II return is not computed because its average equity is negative due to an unusual and large distribution in the prior year).

Exhibit 12.4

Selected Data from Boston Celtics LP

($ thousands)	Total	Boston Celtics LP I	Boston Celtics LP II	Celtics LP
Balance at June 30, 2001	$ 84	$122	$(307)	$270
Net income (loss) for year	216	44	61	111
Cash distribution	(48)	—	—	(48)
Balance at June 30, 2002	$252	$166	$(246)	$333
Partner return on equity	**128.6%**	**30.6%**	**n.a.**	**36.8%**

Demonstration Problem

The following transactions and events affect the partners' capital accounts in several successive partnerships. Prepare a table with six columns, one for each of the five partners along with a total column to show the effects of the following events on the five partners' capital accounts.

Part 1

4/13/2004 Ries and Bax create R&B Company. Each invests \$10,000, and they agree to share income and losses equally.

12/31/2004 R&B Co. earns \$15,000 in income for its first year. Ries withdraws \$4,000 from the partnership, and Bax withdraws \$7,000.

1/1/2005 Royce is made a partner in RB&R Company after contributing \$12,000 cash. The partners agree that a 10% interest allowance will be given on each partner's beginning-year capital balance. In addition, Bax and Royce are to receive \$5,000 salary allowances. The remainder of the income or loss is to be divided evenly.

12/31/2005 The partnership's income for the year is \$40,000, and withdrawals at year-end are Ries, \$5,000; Bax, \$12,500; and Royce, \$11,000.

1/1/2006 Ries sells her interest for \$20,000 to Murdock, whom Bax and Royce accept as a partner in the new BR&M Co. Income or loss is to be shared equally after Bax and Royce each receives \$25,000 salary allowances.

12/31/2006 The partnership's income for the year is \$35,000, and year-end withdrawals are Bax, \$2,500, and Royce, \$2,000.

1/1/2007 Elway is admitted as a partner after investing \$60,000 cash in the new Elway & Associates partnership. He is given a 50% interest in capital after the other partners transfer \$3,000 to his account from each of theirs. A 20% interest allowance (on the beginning-year capital balances) will be used in sharing any income or loss, there will be no salary allowances, and Elway will receive 40% of the remaining balance—the other three partners will each get 20%.

12/31/2007 Elway & Associates earns $127,600 in income for the year, and year-end withdrawals are Bax, $25,000; Royce, $27,000; Murdock, $15,000; and Elway, $40,000.

1/1/2008 Elway buys out Bax and Royce for the balances of their capital accounts after a revaluation of the partnership assets. The revaluation gain is $50,000, which is divided in using a 1:1:1:2 ratio (Bax:Royce:Murdock:Elway). Elway pays the others from personal funds. Murdock and Elway will share income on a 1:9 ratio.

2/29/2008 The partnership earns $10,000 of income since the beginning of the year. Murdock retires and receives partnership cash equal to her capital balance. Elway takes possession of the partnership assets in his own name, and the company is dissolved.

Part 2

Journalize the events affecting the partnership for the year ended December 31, 2005.

Planning the Solution

- Evaluate each transaction's effects on the capital accounts of the partners.
- Each time a new partner is admitted or a partner withdraws, allocate any bonus based on the income-or-loss-sharing agreement.
- Each time a new partner is admitted or a partner withdraws, allocate subsequent net income or loss in accordance with the new partnership agreement.
- Prepare entries to (1) record Royce's initial investment; (2) record the allocation of interest, salaries, and remainder; (3) show the cash withdrawals from the partnership; and (4) close the withdrawal accounts on December 31, 2005.

Solution to Demonstration Problem

Part I

Event	Ries	Bax	Royce	Murdock	Elway	Total
4/13/2004						
Initial Investment	$10,000	$10,000				$ 20,000
12/31/2004						
Income (equal)	7,500	7,500				15,000
Withdrawals	(4,000)	(7,000)				(11,000)
Ending balance	$13,500	$10,500				$ 24,000
1/1/2005						
New investment			$12,000			$ 12,000
12/31/2005						
10% interest	1,350	1,050	1,200			3,600
Salaries		5,000	5,000			10,000
Remainder (equal)	8,800	8,800	8,800			26,400
Withdrawals	(5,000)	(12,500)	(11,000)			(28,500)
Ending balance	$18,650	$12,850	$16,000			$ 47,500
1/1/2006						
Transfer interest	(18,650)			$18,650		$ 0
12/31/2006						
Salaries		25,000	25,000			50,000
Remainder (equal)		(5,000)	(5,000)	(5,000)		(15,000)
Withdrawals		(2,500)	(2,000)			(4,500)
Ending balance	$ 0	$30,350	$34,000	$13,650		$ 78,000
1/1/2007						
New investment					$ 60,000	60,000
Bonuses to Elway		(3,000)	(3,000)	(3,000)	9,000	0
Adjusted balance		$27,350	$31,000	$10,650	$ 69,000	$138,000

[continued on next page]

[continued from previous page]

12/31/2007					
20% interest	5,470	6,200	2,130	13,800	27,600
Remainder (1:1:1:2)	20,000	20,000	20,000	40,000	100,000
Withdrawals	(25,000)	(27,000)	(15,000)	(40,000)	(107,000)
Ending Balance	$27,820	$30,200	$17,780	$ 82,800	$158,600
1/1/2008					
Gain (1:1:1:2)	10,000	10,000	10,000	20,000	50,000
Adjusted balance	$37,820	$40,200	$27,780	$102,800	$208,600
Transfer interests	(37,820)	(40,200)		78,020	0
Adjusted balance	$ 0	$ 0	$27,780	$180,820	$208,600
2/29/2008					
Income (1:9)			1,000	9,000	10,000
Adjusted balance			$28,780	$189,820	$218,600
Settlements			(28,780)	(189,820)	(218,600)
Final balance			$ 0	$ 0	$ 0

Part 2

Date	Account	Debit	Credit
2005			
Jan. 1	Cash	12,000	
	Royce, Capital		12,000
	To record investment of Royce.		
Dec. 31	Income Summary	40,000	
	Ries, Capital		10,150
	Bax, Capital		14,850
	Royce, Capital		15,000
	To allocate interest, salaries, and remainders.		
Dec. 31	Ries, Withdrawals	5,000	
	Bax, Withdrawals	12,500	
	Royce, Withdrawals	11,000	
	Cash		28,500
	To record cash withdrawals by partners.		
Dec. 31	Ries, Capital	5,000	
	Bax, Capital	12,500	
	Royce, Capital	11,000	
	Ries, Withdrawals		5,000
	Bax, Withdrawals		12,500
	Royce, Withdrawals		11,000
	To close withdrawal accounts.		

Summary

C1 Identify characteristics of partnerships and similar organizations. Partnerships are voluntary associations, involve partnership agreements, have limited life, are not subject to income tax, include mutual agency, and have unlimited liability. Organizations that combine selected characteristics of partnerships and corporations include limited partnerships, limited liability partnerships, S corporations, and limited liability companies.

A1 Compute partner return on equity and use it to evaluate partnership performance. Partner return on equity provides each partner an assessment of his or her return on equity invested in the partnership.

P1 Prepare entries for partnership formation. A partner's initial investment is recorded at the market value of the assets contributed to the partnership.

P2 Allocate and record income and loss among partners. A partnership agreement should specify how to allocate partnership income or loss among partners. Allocation can be based on a stated ratio, capital balances, or salary and interest allowances to compensate partners for differences in their service and capital contributions.

P3 Account for the admission and withdrawal of partners. When a new partner buys a partnership interest directly from one or more existing partners, the amount of cash paid from one partner to another does not affect the partnership total recorded equity. When a new partner purchases equity by investing additional assets in the partnership, the new partner's investment can yield a bonus either to existing partners or to the new partner. The entry to record a withdrawal can involve payment from either (1) the existing partners' personal assets or (2) partnership assets. The latter can yield a bonus to either the withdrawing or remaining partners.

P4 Prepare entries for partnership liquidation. When a partnership is liquidated, losses and gains from selling partnership assets are allocated to the partners according to their income-and-loss-sharing ratio. If a partner's capital account has a deficiency that the partner cannot pay, the other partners share the deficit according to their relative income-and-loss-sharing ratio.

Guidance Answer to **Decision Ethics**

Financial Planner The partnership agreement apparently fails to mention liabilities or use the term *net assets.* To give the estate one-third of total assets is not fair to the remaining partners because if the partner had lived and the partners had decided to liquidate, the liabilities would need to be paid out of assets before any liquidation. Also, a settlement based on the deceased partner's recorded equity would fail to recognize excess of current value over book value. This value increase would be realized if the partnership were liquidated. A fair settlement would seem to be a payment to the estate for the balance of the deceased partner's equity based on the *current value of net assets.*

Guidance Answers to **Quick Checks**

1. (*b*)
2. *Unlimited liability* means that the creditors of a partnership require each partner to be personally responsible for all partnership debts.
3. (*c*)
4.

	Denzel	Shantell	Total
Net Income			$40,000
Interest allowance (10%)	$ 7,000	$ 3,500	10,500
Balance of income	↓	↓	**$29,500**
Balance allocated equally	14,750	14,750	29,500
Balance of income			$ 0
Income of partners	**$21,750**	**$18,250**	

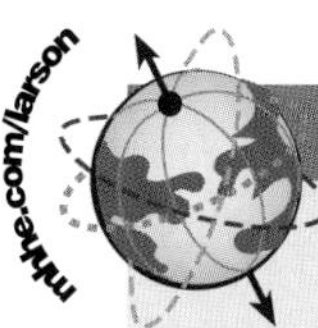

Key Terms

Key Terms are available at the book's Website for learning and testing in an online Flashcard Format.

C corporation (p. 470)
General partner (p. 469)
General partnership (p. 469)
Limited liability company (LLC) (p. 470)
Limited liability partnership (p. 469)
Limited partners (p. 469)
Limited partnership (p. 469)
Mutual agency (p. 469)
Partner return on equity (p. 480)
Partnership (p. 468)
Partnership contract (p. 468)
Partnership liquidation (p. 478)
S corporation (p. 470)
Statement of partners' equity (p. 473)
Unlimited liability (p. 469)

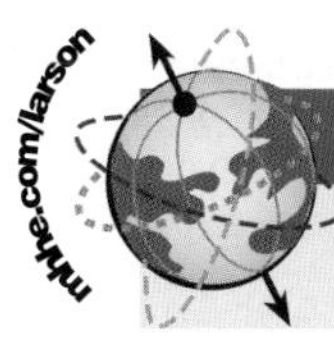

Personal Interactive Quiz

Personal Interactive Quizzes A and B are available at the book's Website to reinforce and assess your learning.

Discussion Questions

1. If a partnership contract does not state the period of time the partnership is to exist, when does the partnership end?
2. What does the term *mutual agency* mean when applied to a partnership?
3. Can partners limit the right of a partner to commit their partnership to contracts? Would such an agreement be binding (*a*) on the partners and (*b*) on outsiders?

4. Assume that Amey and Lacey are partners. Lacey dies, and her son claims the right to take his mother's place in the partnership. Does he have this right? Why or why not?
5. Assume that the Barnes and Ardmore partnership agreement provides for a two-third/one-third sharing of income but says nothing about losses. The first year of partnership operation resulted in a loss, and Barnes argues that the loss should be shared equally because the partnership agreement said nothing about sharing losses. Is Barnes correct? Explain.
6. Allocation of partnership income among the partners appears on what financial statement?
7. What does the term *unlimited liability* mean when it is applied to partnership members?
8. How does a general partnership differ from a limited partnership?
9. George, Burton, and Dillman have been partners for three years. The partnership is being dissolved. George is leaving the firm, but Burton and Dillman plan to carry on the business. In the final settlement, George places a $75,000 salary claim against the partnership. He contends that he has a claim for a salary of $25,000 for each year because he devoted all of his time for three years to the affairs of the partnership. Is his claim valid? Why or why not?
10. Kay, Kat, and Kim are partners. In a liquidation, Kay's share of partnership losses exceeds her capital account balance. Moreover, she is unable to meet the deficit from her personal assets, and her partners shared the excess losses. Does this relieve Kay of liability?
11. After all partnership assets have been converted to cash and all liabilities paid, the remaining cash should equal the sum of the balances of the partners' capital accounts. Why?
12. Assume a partner withdraws from a partnership and receives assets of greater value than the book value of his equity. Should the remaining partners share the resulting reduction in their equities in the ratio of their relative capital balances or according to their income-and-loss-sharing ratio?

Red numbers denote Discussion Questions that involve decision-making.

Homework Manager *repeats all numerical Quick Studies on the book's Website with new numbers.*

QUICK STUDY

QS 12-1
Partnership liability
C1

Kent and Davis are partners in operating a store. Without consulting Kent, Davis enters into a contract to purchase merchandise for the store. Kent contends that he did not authorize the order and refuses to pay for it. The vendor sues the partners for the contract price of the merchandise. (*a*) Must the partnership pay for the merchandise? Why? (*b*) Does your answer differ if Kent and Davis are partners in a public accounting firm?

QS 12-2
Partnership income allocation
P2

Ann Keeley and Susie Norton are partners in a business they started two years ago. The partnership agreement states that Keeley should receive a salary allowance of $30,000 and that Norton should receive a $40,000 salary allowance. Any remaining income or loss is to be shared equally. Determine each partner's share of the current year's net income of $104,000.

QS 12-3
Partnership income allocation
P2

Jakes and Ness are partners who agree that Jakes will receive a $50,000 salary allowance and that any remaining income or loss will be shared equally. If Ness's capital account is credited for $1,000 as his share of the net income in a given period, how much net income did the partnership earn in that period?

QS 12-4
Liability in limited partnerships
P1

Lamb organized a limited partnership and is the only general partner. Maxi invested $20,000 in the partnership and was admitted as a limited partner with the understanding that he would receive 10% of the profits. After two unprofitable years, the partnership ceased doing business. At that point, partnership liabilities were $85,000 larger than partnership assets. How much money can the partnership's creditors obtain from Maxi's personal assets to satisfy the unpaid partnership debts?

QS 12-5
Partner admission through purchase of interest P3

Mintz agrees to pay Bogg and Meyer $10,000 each for a one-third (33⅓%) interest in the Bogg and Meyer partnership. Immediately prior to Mintz's admission, each partner had a $30,000 capital balance. Make the journal entry to record Mintz's purchase of the partners' interest.

QS 12-6
Admission of a partner P3

Jones and Jordan are partners, each with $30,000 in their partnership capital accounts. Holly is admitted to the partnership by investing $30,000 cash. Make the entry to show Holly's admission to the partnership.

QS 12-7
Partner return on equity
A1

Gilson and Lott's company is organized as a partnership. At the prior year-end, partnership equity totaled $300,000 ($200,000 from Gilson and $100,000 from Lott). For the current year, partnership net income is $50,000 ($40,000 allocated to Gilson and $10,000 allocated to Lott), and year-end total partnership equity is $400,000 ($280,000 from Gilson and $120,000 from Lott). Compute the total partnership return on equity *and* the individual partner return on equity ratios.

***Homework Manager** repeats all numerical Exercises on the book's Website with new numbers.*

EXERCISES

Exercise 12-1
Characteristics of partnerships
C1

Next to the following list of eight characteristics of business organizations, write a brief description of how each characteristic applies to general partnerships.

Characteristic	Application to General Partnerships
1. Life	
2. Owners' liability	
3. Legal status	
4. Tax status of income	
5. Owners' authority	
6. Ease of formation	
7. Transferability of ownership	
8. Ability to raise large amounts of capital	

Exercise 12-2
Forms of organization
C1

For each of the following separate cases, recommend a form of business organization. With each recommendation, explain how business income would be taxed if the owners adopt the form of organization recommended. Also list several advantages that the owners will enjoy from the form of business organization that you recommend.

a. Ross, Jenks, and Keim are recent college graduates in computer science. They want to start a Website development company. They all have college debts and currently do not own any substantial computer equipment needed to get the company started.

b. Dr. Langholz and Dr. Clark are recent graduates from medical residency programs. Both are family practice physicians and would like to open a clinic in an underserved rural area. Although neither has any funds to bring to the new venture, a banker has expressed interest in making a loan to provide start-up funds for their practice.

c. Milan has been out of school for about five years and has become quite knowledgeable about the commercial real estate market. He would like to organize a company that buys and sells real estate. Milan believes he has the expertise to manage the company but needs funds to invest in commercial property.

Exercise 12-3
Journalizing partnership transactions
P2

On March 1, 2005, Abbey and Adams formed a partnership. Abbey contributed $88,000 cash and Adams contributed land valued at $70,000 and a building valued at $100,000. The partnership also assumed responsibility for Adams's $80,000 long-term note payable associated with the land and building. The partners agreed to share income as follows: Abbey is to receive an annual salary allowance of $30,000, both are to receive an annual interest allowance of 10% of their beginning-year capital investment, and any remaining income or loss is to be shared equally. On October 20, 2005, Abbey withdrew $32,000 cash and Adams withdrew $25,000 cash. After the adjusting and closing entries are made to the revenue and expense accounts at December 31, 2005, the Income Summary account had a credit balance of $79,000.

1. Prepare journal entries to record (*a*) the partners' initial capital investments, (*b*) their cash withdrawals, and (*c*) the December 31 closing of both the Withdrawals and Income Summary accounts.

2. Determine the balances of the partners' capital accounts as of December 31, 2005.

Check (2) Adams, $89,600

Exercise 12-4
Income allocation in a partnership
P2

Cosmo and Ellis began a partnership by investing $50,000 and $75,000, respectively. During its first year, the partnership earned $165,000. Prepare calculations showing how the $165,000 income should be allocated to the partners under each of the following three separate plans for sharing income and loss: (1) the partners failed to agree on a method to share income; (2) the partners agreed to share income and loss in proportion to their initial investments (round proportions to the nearest hundredth);

and (3) the partners agreed to share income by granting a $55,000 per year salary allowance to Cosmo, a $45,000 per year salary allowance to Ellis, 10% interest on their initial capital investments, and the remaining balance shared equally.

Check Plan 3, Cosmo, $86,250

Exercise 12-5
Income allocation in a partnership
P2

Assume that the partners of Exercise 12-4 agreed to share net income and loss by granting annual salary allowances of $55,000 to Cosmo and $45,000 to Ellis, 10% interest allowances on their investments, and any remaining balance shared equally.

1. Determine the partners' shares of Cosmo and Ellis given a first-year net income of $94,400.
2. Determine the partners' shares of Cosmo and Ellis given a first-year net loss of $15,700.

Check (2) Cosmo, $(4,100)

Exercise 12-6
Sale of partnership interest P3

The partners in the Biz Partnership have agreed that partner Madonna may sell her $90,000 equity in the partnership to Streisand, for which Streisand will pay Madonna $75,000. Present the partnership's journal entry to record the sale of Madonna's interest to Streisand on September 30.

Exercise 12-7
Admission of new partner
P3

The Treed Partnership has total partners' equity of $510,000, which is made up of Elm, Capital, $400,000, and Oak, Capital, $110,000. The partners share net income and loss in a ratio of 80% to Elm and 20% to Oak. On November 1, Ash is admitted to the partnership and given a 15% interest in equity and a 15% share in any income and loss. Prepare the journal entry to record the admission of Ash under each of the following separate assumptions: Ash invests cash of (1) $90,000; (2) $125,000; and (3) $60,000.

Exercise 12-8
Retirement of partner
P3

Holland, Flowers, and Tulip have been partners while sharing net income and loss in a 5:3:2 ratio. On January 31, the date Tulip retires from the partnership, the equities of the partners are Holland, $350,000; Flowers, $240,000; and Tulip, $180,000. Present journal entries to record Tulip's retirement under each of the following separate assumptions: Tulip is paid for her equity using partnership cash of (1) $180,000; (2) $200,000; and (3) $150,000.

Exercise 12-9
Liquidation of partnership
P4

The Red, White & Blue partnership was begun with investments by the partners as follows: Red, $175,000; White, $220,000; and Blue, $205,000. The operations did not go well, and the partners eventually decided to liquidate the partnership, sharing all losses equally. On August 31, after all assets were converted to cash and all creditors were paid, only $60,000 in partnership cash remained.

1. Compute the capital account balance of each partner after the liquidation of assets and the payment of creditors.
2. Assume that any partner with a deficit agrees to pay cash to the partnership to cover the deficit. Present the journal entries on August 31 to record (*a*) the cash receipt from the deficient partner(s) and (*b*) the final disbursement of cash to the partners.
3. Assume that any partner with a deficit is not able to reimburse the partnership. Present journal entries (*a*) to transfer the deficit of any deficient partners to the other partners and (*b*) to record the final disbursement of cash to the partners.

Check (1) Red, $(5,000)

Exercise 12-10
Liquidation of partnership P4

Tuttle, Ritter, and Lee are partners who share income and loss in a 1:4:5 ratio. After lengthy disagreements among the partners and several unprofitable periods, the partners decided to liquidate the partnership. Immediately before liquidation, the partnership balance sheet shows: total assets, $116,000; total liabilities, $88,000; Tuttle, Capital, $1,200; Ritter, Capital, $11,700; and Lee, Capital, $15,100. The cash proceeds from selling the assets were sufficient to repay all but $24,000 to the creditors. (*a*) Calculate the loss from selling the assets. (*b*) Allocate the loss to the partners. (*c*) Determine how much of the remaining liability should be paid by each partner.

Check (b) Lee, Capital after allocation, $(10,900)

Exercise 12-11
Liquidation of limited partnership
P4

Assume that the Tuttle, Ritter, and Lee partnership of Exercise 12-10 is a limited partnership. Tuttle and Ritter are general partners and Lee is a limited partner. How much of the remaining $24,000 liability should be paid by each partner?

Exercise 12-12
Partner return on equity
A1

Hunt Sports Enterprises LP is organized as a limited partnership consisting of two individual partners: Soccer LP and Football LP. Both partners separately operate a minor league soccer team and a semipro football team. Compute partner return on equity for each limited partnership (and the total) for the year ended June 30, 2005, using the following selected data on partner capital balances from Hunt Sports Enterprises LP:

	Soccer LP	Football LP	Total
Balance at 6/30/04	$378,000	$1,516,000	$1,894,000
Annual net income	44,268	891,796	936,064
Cash distribution	—	(100,000)	(100,000)
Balance at 6/30/05	$422,268	$2,307,796	$2,730,064

PROBLEM SET A

Problem 12-1A
Allocating partnership income
P2

Kim Ries, Tere Bax, and Josh Thomas invested $40,000, $56,000, and $64,000, respectively, in a partnership. During its first calendar-year, the firm earned $124,500.

Required

Prepare the entry to close the firm's Income Summary account as of its December 31 year-end and to allocate the $124,500 net income to the partners under each of the following separate assumptions: The partners (1) have no agreement on the method of sharing income and loss; (2) agreed to share income and loss in the ratio of their beginning capital investments; and (3) agreed to share income and loss by providing annual salary allowances of $33,000 to Ries, $28,000 to Bax, and $40,000 to Thomas; granting 10% interest on the partners' beginning capital investments; and sharing the remainder equally.

Check (3) Thomas, Capital, $48,900

Problem 12-2A
Allocating partnership income and loss; sequential years
P2

mhhe.com/larson

Rex Baker and Ty Farney are forming a partnership to which Baker will devote one-half time and Farney will devote full time. They have discussed the following alternative plans for sharing income and loss: (*a*) in the ratio of their initial capital investments, which they have agreed will be $21,000 for Baker and $31,500 for Farney; (*b*) in proportion to the time devoted to the business; (*c*) a salary allowance of $3,000 per month to Farney and the balance in accordance with the ratio of their initial capital investments; or (*d*) a salary allowance of $3,000 per month to Farney, 10% interest on their initial capital investments, and the balance shared equally. The partners expect the business to perform as follows: Year 1, $18,000 net loss; Year 2, $45,000 net income; and Year 3, $75,000 net income.

Required

Prepare three tables with the following column headings:

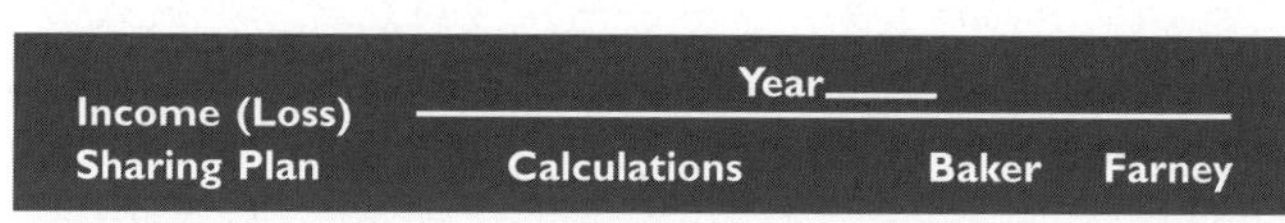

Income (Loss) Sharing Plan	Year____ Calculations	Baker	Farney

Complete the tables, one for each of the first three years, by showing how to allocate partnership income or loss to the partners under each of the four plans being considered. (Round answers to the nearest whole dollar.)

Check Plan d, Year 1, Farney's share, $9,525

Problem 12-3A
Partnership income allocation, statement of partners' equity, and closing entries
P2

mhhe.com/larson

Bill Beck, Ron Beck, and Barb Beck formed the BRB Partnership by making capital contributions of $183,750, $131,250, and $210,000, respectively. They predict annual partnership net income of $225,000 and are considering the following alternative plans of sharing income and loss: (*a*) equally; (*b*) in the ratio of their initial capital investments; or (*c*) salary allowances of $40,000 to Bill, $30,000 to Ron, and $45,000 to Barb; interest allowances of 10% on their initial capital investments; and the balance shared equally.

Required

1. Prepare a table with the following column headings:

Income (Loss) Sharing Plan	Calculations	Bill	Ron	Barb	Total

Use the table to show how to distribute net income of $225,000 for the calendar year under each of the alternative plans being considered. (Round answers to the nearest whole dollar.)

Check (2) Barb, Ending Capital, $223,000

2. Prepare a statement of partners' equity showing the allocation of income to the partners assuming they agree to use plan (*c*), that income earned is $104,500, and that Bill, Ron, and Barb withdraw $17,000, $24,000, and $32,000, respectively, at year-end.

3. Prepare the December 31 journal entry to close Income Summary assuming they agree to use plan (*c*) and that net income is $104,500. Also close the withdrawals accounts.

Problem 12-4A
Partner withdrawal and admission
P3

Part 1. Goering, Gore, and Schmit are partners and share income and loss in a 3:2:5 ratio. The partnership's capital balances are as follows: Goering, $84,000; Gore, $69,000; and Schmit, $147,000. Gore decides to withdraw from the partnership, and the partners agree to not have the assets revalued upon Gore's retirement. Prepare journal entries to record Gore's February 1 withdrawal from the partnership under each of the following separate assumptions: Gore (*a*) sells his interest to Getz for $80,000 after Goering and Schmit approve the entry of Getz as a partner; (*b*) gives his interest to a son-in-law, Swanson, and thereafter Goering and Schmit accept Swanson as a partner; (*c*) is paid $69,000 in partnership cash for his equity; (*d*) is paid $107,000 in partnership cash for his equity; and (*e*) is paid $15,000 in partnership cash plus equipment recorded on the partnership books at $35,000 less its accumulated depreciation of $11,600.

Check (1e) Cr. Schmit, Capital, $19,125

(2c) Cr. Gore, Capital, $4,650

Part 2. Assume that Gore does not retire from the partnership described in Part 1. Instead, Ford is admitted to the partnership on February 1 with a 25% equity. Prepare journal entries to record Ford's entry into the partnership under each of the following separate assumptions: Ford invests (*a*) $100,000; (*b*) $72,500; and (*c*) $131,000.

Problem 12-5A
Liquidation of a partnership
P4

Quick, Drake, and Sage share income and loss in a 3:2:1 ratio. The partners have decided to liquidate their partnership. On the day of liquidation their balance sheet appears as follows:

QUICK, DRAKE, AND SAGE
Balance Sheet
May 31

Assets		Liabilities and Equity	
Cash	$ 90,400	Accounts payable	$122,750
Inventory	268,600	Quick, Capital	46,500
		Drake, Capital	106,250
		Sage, Capital	83,500
Total assets	$359,000	Total liabilities and equity	$359,000

Required

Prepare journal entries for (*a*) the sale of inventory, (*b*) the allocation of its gain or loss, (*c*) the payment of liabilities at book value, and (*d*) the distribution of cash in each of the following four separate cases: Inventory is sold for (1) $300,000; (2) $250,000; (3) $160,000 and any partners with capital deficits pay in the amount of their deficits; and (4) $125,000 and the partners have no assets other than those invested in the partnership. (Round to the nearest dollar.)

Check (4) Cash distribution, Sage, $51,134

PROBLEM SET B

Problem 12-1B
Allocating partnership income
P2

Matt Albin, Ryan Peters, and Seth Ramsey invested $82,000, $49,200, and $32,800, respectively, in a partnership. During its first calendar-year, the firm earned $135,000.

Required

Prepare the entry to close the firm's Income Summary account as of its December 31 year-end and to allocate the $135,000 net income to the partners under each of the following separate assumptions. (Round answers to whole dollars.) The partners (1) have no agreement on the method of sharing income and loss; (2) agreed to share income and loss in the ratio of their beginning capital investments; and (3) agreed to share income and loss by providing annual salary allowances of $48,000 to Albin, $36,000 to Peters, and $25,000 to Ramsey; granting 10% interest on the partners' beginning capital investments; and sharing the remainder equally.

Check (3) Ramsey, Capital, $31,480

Problem 12-2B
Allocating partnership income and loss; sequential years
P2

Maria Barto and J. R. Black are forming a partnership to which Barto will devote one-third time and Black will devote full time. They have discussed the following alternative plans for sharing income and loss: (*a*) in the ratio of their initial capital investments, which they have agreed will be $52,000 for Barto and $78,000 for Black; (*b*) in proportion to the time devoted to the business; (*c*) a salary allowance of $2,000 per month to Black and the balance in accordance with the ratio of their initial capital investments; or (*d*) a salary allowance of $2,000 per month to Black, 10% interest on their initial capital investments, and the balance shared equally. The partners expect the business to perform as follows: Year 1, $18,000 net loss; Year 2, $38,000 net income; and Year 3, $94,000 net income.

Required

Prepare three tables with the following column headings:

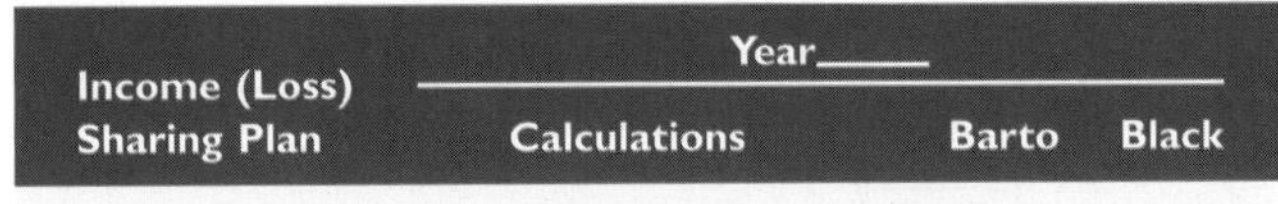

Income (Loss) Sharing Plan	Year____ Calculations	Barto	Black

Complete the tables, one for each of the first three years, by showing how to allocate partnership income or loss to the partners under each of the four plans being considered. (Round answers to the nearest whole dollar.)

Check Plan d, Year 1, Black's share, $4,300

Problem 12-3B
Partnership income allocation, statement of partners' equity, and closing entries
P2

Staci Cook, Lin Xi, and Kevin Schwartz formed the CXS Partnership by making capital contributions of $72,000, $108,000, and $60,000, respectively. They predict annual partnership net income of $120,000 and are considering the following alternative plans of sharing income and loss: (*a*) equally; (*b*) in the ratio of their initial capital investments; or (*c*) salary allowances of $20,000 to Cook, $15,000 to Xi, and $40,000 to Schwartz; interest allowances of 12% on their initial capital investments; and the balance shared equally.

Required

1. Prepare a table with the following column headings:

Income (Loss) Sharing Plan	Calculations	Cook	Xi	Schwartz	Total

   Use the table to show how to distribute net income of $120,000 for the calendar year under each of the alternative plans being considered. (Round answers to the nearest whole dollar.)

2. Prepare a statement of partners' equity showing the allocation of income to the partners assuming they agree to use plan (*c*), that income earned is $43,800, and that Cook, Xi, and Schwartz withdraw $9,000, $19,000, and $12,000, respectively, at year-end.

   Check (2) Schwartz, Ending Capital, $75,200

3. Prepare the December 31 journal entry to close Income Summary assuming they agree to use plan (*c*) and that net income is $43,800. Also close the withdrawals accounts.

Problem 12-4B
Partner withdrawal and admission
P3

Part 1. Gibbs, Gier, and Gill are partners and share income and loss in a 5:1:4 ratio. The partnership's capital balances are as follows: Gibbs, $303,000; Gier, $74,000; and Gill, $223,000. Gibbs decides to withdraw from the partnership, and the partners agree not to have the assets revalued upon Gibbs's retirement. Prepare journal entries to record Gibbs's April 30 withdrawal from the partnership under each of the following separate assumptions: Gibbs (*a*) sells her interest to Grady for $250,000 after Gier and Gill approve the entry of Grady as a partner; (*b*) gives her interest to a daughter-in-law, Gannon, and thereafter Gier and Gill accept Gannon as a partner; (*c*) is paid $303,000 in partnership cash for her equity; (*d*) is paid $175,000 in partnership cash for her equity; and (*e*) is paid $100,000 in partnership cash plus manufacturing equipment recorded on the partnership books at $269,000 less its accumulated depreciation of $168,000.

Check (1e) Cr. Gill, Capital, $81,600

Part 2. Assume that Gibbs does not retire from the partnership described in Part 1. Instead, Grise is admitted to the partnership on April 30 with a 20% equity. Prepare journal entries to record the entry of Grise under each of the following separate assumptions: Grise invests (*a*) $150,000; (*b*) $98,000; and (*c*) $213,000.

(2c) Cr. Gier, Capital, $5,040

Problem 12-5B
Liquidation of a partnership
P4

Rasure, Ramirez, and Roney, who share income and loss in a 2:1:2 ratio, plan to liquidate their partnership. At liquidation, their balance sheet appears as follows:

RASURE, RAMIREZ, AND RONEY
Balance Sheet
January 18

Assets		**Liabilities and Equity**	
Cash	$174,300	Accounts payable	$171,300
Equipment	308,600	Rasure, Capital	150,200
		Ramirez, Capital	97,900
		Roney, Capital	63,500
Total assets	$482,900	Total liabilities and equity	$482,900

Required

Prepare journal entries for (*a*) the sale of equipment, (*b*) the allocation of its gain or loss, (*c*) the payment of liabilities at book value, and (*d*) the distribution of cash in each of the following four separate cases: Equipment is sold for (1) $325,000; (2) $265,000; (3) $100,000 and any partners with capital deficits pay in the amount of their deficits; and (4) $75,000 and the partners have no assets other than those invested in the partnership.

Check (4) Cash distribution, Rasure, $36,800

PROBLEM SET C

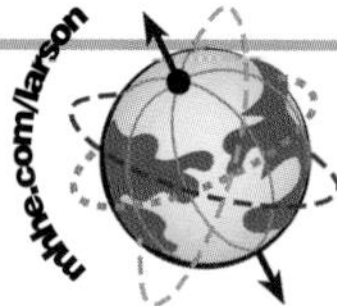

Problem Set C is available at the book's Website to further reinforce and assess your learning.

SERIAL PROBLEM

Success Systems

At the start of 2005, Kay Breeze is considering adding a partner to her business. She envisions the new partner taking the lead in generating sales of both services and merchandise for Success Systems. Kay Breeze's equity in Success Systems as of January 1, 2005, is reflected in the following capital balance:

K. Breeze, Capital $90,148

Required

1. Breeze is evaluating whether the prospective partner should be an equal partner with respect to capital investment and profit sharing (1:1) or whether the agreement should be 3:1 with Breeze retaining three-fourths interest with rights to three-fourths of the profits. What factors should she consider in deciding which partnership agreement to offer?

2. Prepare the January 1, 2005, journal entry(ies) necessary to admit a new partner to Success Systems through the purchase of a partnership interest for each of the following two separate cases (*a*) 1:1 sharing agreement and (*b*) 3:1 sharing agreement.
3. Prepare the January 1, 2005, journal entry(ies) required to admit a new partner if the new partner invests cash of $30,050.
4. After posting the entry in part 3, what would be the new partner's equity percentage?

BEYOND THE NUMBERS

REPORTING IN ACTION

C1 

BTN 12-1 Take a step back in time and imagine **Krispy Kreme** in its infancy as a company. The year is 1937.

Required

1. Read the history of Krispy Kreme at KrispyKreme.com/history.html. Can you determine from its history whether it was originally organized as a sole proprietorship, partnership, or corporation?
2. Assume that Krispy Kreme was originally organized as a partnership. Krispy Kreme's income statement in Appendix A varies in several key ways from what it would look like for a partnership. Explain how a corporate income statement differs from a partnership income statement.
3. Compare the Krispy Kreme balance sheet in Appendix A to what a partnership balance sheet would have shown in 1937. Identify and explain any account differences you would anticipate.

COMPARATIVE ANALYSIS

C1 

BTN 12-2 Over the years **Krispy Kreme** and **Tastykake** have evolved into large corporations. Today it is difficult to imagine them as fledgling start-ups. Research each company's history online.

Required

1. Which company is older?
2. Which company was named by the founder's wife after tasting the first bakery samples?
3. Which company first sold its cakes for $0.10 each and had $28 in sales on the first day of business?
4. Which company has developed more of a global presence?
5. Which company had its first initial public offering of stock in April 2000?

ETHICS CHALLENGE

P2 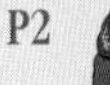 

BTN 12-3 Doctors Maben, Orlando, and Clark have been in a group practice for several years. Maben and Orlando are family practice physicians, and Clark is a general surgeon. Clark receives many referrals for surgery from his family practice partners. Upon the partnership's original formation, the three doctors agreed to a two-part formula to share income. Every month each doctor receives a salary allowance of $3,000. Additional income is divided according to a percent of patient charges the doctors generate for the month. In the current month, Maben generated 10% of the billings, Orlando 30%, and Clark 60%. The group's income for this month is $50,000. Clark has expressed dissatisfaction with the income-sharing formula and asks that income be split entirely on patient charge percents.

Required

1. Compute the income allocation for the current month using the original agreement.
2. Compute the income allocation for the current month using Clark's proposed agreement.
3. Identify the ethical components of this partnership decision for the doctors.

COMMUNICATING IN PRACTICE

C1

BTN 12-4 Assume that you are studying for an upcoming accounting exam with a good friend. Your friend says that she has a solid understanding of general partnerships but is less sure that she understands organizations that combine certain characteristics of partnerships with other forms of business organization. You offer to make some study notes for your friend to help her learn about limited partnerships, limited liability partnerships, S Corporations, and limited liability companies. Prepare a one-page set of well-organized, complete study notes on these four forms of business organization.

TAKING IT TO THE NET

P1 P2

BTN 12-5 Access the September 27, 2002, filing of the June 30, 2002, 10-K report for **Henley Limited Partnership** (formerly the Boston Celtics Limited Partnership) at www.SEC.gov.

Required

1. Locate the June 30, 2002, balance sheet for the Boston Celtics Limited Partnership. List the account titles used in the equity section of this balance sheet.
2. How many units of limited partnership interest are authorized, issued, and outstanding as of June 30, 2002?
3. What are the equity balances of the general partners and limited partners as of June 30, 2002?
4. What is the partnership's largest asset and its amount as of June 30, 2002?

TEAMWORK IN ACTION

P2

BTN 12-6 This activity requires teamwork to reinforce understanding of accounting for partnerships.

Required

1. Assume that Baker, Warner, and Rice form the BWR Partnership by making capital contributions of $200,000, $300,000, and $500,000, respectively. BWR predicts annual partnership net income of $600,000. The partners are considering various plans for sharing income and loss. Assign a different team member to compute how the projected $600,000 income would be shared under each of the following separate plans:
   a. Shared equally.
   b. In the ratio of the partners' initial capital investments.
   c. Salary allowances of $50,000 to Baker, $60,000 to Warner, and $70,000 to Rice, with the remaining balance shared equally.
   d. Interest allowances of 10% on the partners' initial capital investments, with the remaining balance shared equally.
2. In sequence, each member is to present his or her income-sharing calculations with the team.
3. As a team, identify and discuss at least one other possible way that income could be shared.

BUSINESS WEEK ACTIVITY

C1

BTN 12-7 Read the article "Take Me Online to the Ball Game," in the April 9, 2001, issue of *Business Week*. (This book's Website provides a free link.)

Required

1. What is the business relation between **Major League Baseball** (MLB) and **MLB.com**?
2. Based on your reading of the article, who are the limited partners of MLB.com?
3. What does the media analyst quoted in the article think of MLB.com's self-sufficient strategy?
4. Why do MLB.com executives think they can be successful?
5. Does the article lend any insight into the profit-sharing formula for MLB.com? Explain.

ENTREPRENEURIAL DECISION

C1  

BTN 12-8 Revisit the chapter's opening feature involving Michael Koch and his company **Koch Entertainment LLC**. Assume that Koch has decided to organize all future business endeavors with artists as general partnerships.

Required

1. What details should Koch and his future partners specify in their general partnership agreements?
2. What advantages should Koch and his future partners be aware of with respect to organizing as general partnerships?
3. What disadvantages should Koch and his future partners be aware of with respect to organizing as general partnerships?

BTN 12-9 Access **Grupo Bimbo**'s Website at GrupoBimbo.com. Research the history, philosophy, and commitments of the company using the "about Grupo Bimbo" link.

GLOBAL DECISION

C1

Required

1. Grupo Bimbo was founded when and where?
2. Can you determine its original form of business organization from reading its company history?
3. What commitment does Grupo Bimbo have toward social responsibility?
4. When was Grupo Bimbo first listed on the Mexican Stock Exchange (Bolsa Mexica Valores)? (*Hint:* See company FAQs under the "about Grupo Bimbo" link.)
5. Why doesn't Grupo Bimbo trade its stock abroad?

Financial Statement Information

This appendix includes financial information for (1) **Krispy Kreme**, (2) **Tastykake**, and (3) **Harley-Davidson**. This information is taken from their annual reports. An **annual report** is a summary of a company's financial results for the year along with its current financial condition and future plans. This report is directed to external users of financial information, but it also affects the actions and decisions of internal users.

A company uses an annual report to showcase itself and its products. Many annual reports include attractive photos, diagrams, and illustrations related to the company. The primary objective of annual reports, however, is the *financial section,* which communicates much information about a company, with most data drawn from the accounting information system. The layout of an annual report's financial section is fairly established and typically includes the following:

- Letter to Shareholders
- Financial History and Highlights
- Management Discussion and Analysis
- Management's Report
- Report of Independent Accountants (Auditor's Report)
- Financial Statements
- Notes to Financial Statements
- List of Directors and Officers

This appendix provides the financial statements for Krispy Kreme (plus selected notes), Tastykake, and Harley-Davidson. The appendix is organized as follows:

- **Krispy Kreme A-2** through **A-17**
- **Tastykake A-18** through **A-24**
- **Harley-Davidson A-25** through **A-30**

Many assignments at the end of each chapter refer to information in this appendix. We encourage readers to spend time with these assignments; they are especially useful in showing the relevance and diversity of financial accounting and reporting.

Special note: The SEC maintains the EDGAR (**E**lectronic **D**ata **G**athering, **A**nalysis, and **R**etrieval) database at **www.sec.gov.** The **Form 10-K** is the annual report form for most companies. It provides electronically accessible information. The **Form 10-KSB** is the annual report form filed by "small businesses." It requires slightly less information than the Form 10-K. One of these forms must be filed within 90 days after the company's fiscal year-end. (Forms 10-K405, 10-KT, 10-KT405, and 10-KSB405 are slight variations of the usual form due to certain regulations or rules.)

KRISPY KREME
2003 ANNUAL REPORT

SELECTED FINANCIAL DATA

The following table shows selected financial data for Krispy Kreme. The selected historical statement of operations data for each of the years ended, and the selected historical balance sheet data as of January 31, 1999, January 30, 2000, January 28, 2001, February 3, 2002 and February 2, 2003 have been derived from our audited consolidated financial statements. Please note that our fiscal year ended February 3, 2002 contained 53 weeks.

Systemwide sales include the sales by both our company and franchised stores and exclude the sales by our KKM&D business segment and the royalties and fees received from our franchised stores. Our consolidated financial statements appearing elsewhere in this annual report exclude franchised store sales and include royalties and fees received from our franchisees. The consolidated financial statements also include the results of Freedom Rings, LLC, the area developer in Philadelphia, and Golden Gate Doughnuts, LLC, the area developer in Northern California, in which Krispy Kreme has a majority ownership interest, as well as the results of Glazed Investments, LLC, the area developer in Colorado, Minnesota and Wisconsin, for periods subsequent to August 22, 2002, the date the Company acquired a controlling interest in this area developer.

You should read the following selected financial data in conjunction with "Management's Discussion and Analysis of Financial Condition and Results of Operations," the consolidated financial statements and accompanying notes and the other financial data included elsewhere herein. All references to per share amounts and any other reference to shares in "Selected Financial Data," unless otherwise noted, have been adjusted to reflect a two-for-one stock split paid on March 19, 2001 to shareholders of record as of March 5, 2001 and a two-for-one stock split paid on June 14, 2001 to shareholders of record as of May 29, 2001. Unless otherwise specified, references in this annual report to "Krispy Kreme," the "Company," "we," "us" or "our" refer to Krispy Kreme Doughnuts, Inc. and its subsidiaries.

IN THOUSANDS, EXCEPT PER SHARE DATA AND STORE NUMBERS

YEAR ENDED	Jan. 31, 1999	Jan. 30, 2000	Jan. 28, 2001	Feb. 3, 2002	Feb. 2, 2003
Statement of Operations Data:					
Total revenues	$180,880	$220,243	$300,715	$394,354	$491,549
Operating expenses	159,941	190,003	250,690	316,946	381,489
General and administrative expenses	10,897	14,856	20,061	27,562	28,897
Depreciation and amortization expenses	4,278	4,546	6,457	7,959	12,271
Arbitration award	—	—	—	—	9,075
Provision for restructuring	9,466	—	—	—	—
Income (loss) from operations	(3,702)	10,838	23,507	41,887	59,817
Interest expense (income), net, and other	1,577	1,232	(1,698)	(2,408)	749
Equity loss in joint ventures	—	—	706	602	2,008
Minority interest	—	—	716	1,147	2,287
Income (loss) before income taxes	(5,279)	9,606	23,783	42,546	54,773
Provision (benefit) for income taxes	(2,112)	3,650	9,058	16,168	21,295
Net income (loss)	$ (3,167)	$ 5,956	$ 14,725	$ 26,378	$ 33,478
Net income (loss) per share:					
Basic	$ (.09)	$ .16	$ .30	$ .49	$ .61
Diluted	(.09)	.15	.27	.45	.56
Shares used in calculation of net income (loss) per share:					
Basic	32,996	37,360	49,184	53,703	55,093
Diluted	32,996	39,280	53,656	58,443	59,492
Cash dividends declared per common share	$ .04	$ —	$ —	$ —	$ —
Operating Data (Unaudited):					
Systemwide sales	$240,316	$318,854	$448,129	$621,665	$778,573
Number of stores at end of period:					
Company	61	58	63	75	99
Franchised	70	86	111	143	177
Systemwide	131	144	174	218	276
Average weekly sales per store:					
Company	$ 47	$ 54	$ 69	$ 72	$ 76
Franchised	28	38	43	53	58
Balance Sheet Data (at end of period):					
Working capital	$ 8,387	$ 11,452	$ 29,443	$ 49,236	$ 81,441
Total assets	93,312	104,958	171,493	255,376	410,487
Long-term debt, including current maturities	21,020	22,902	—	4,643	60,489
Total shareholders' equity	42,247	47,755	125,679	187,667	273,352

KRISPY KREME DOUGHNUTS, INC.
REPORT OF INDEPENDENT ACCOUNTANTS

To the Board of Directors and Shareholders of Krispy Kreme Doughnuts, Inc.

In our opinion, the accompanying consolidated balance sheets and the related consolidated statements of operations, of shareholders' equity and of cash flows present fairly, in all material respects, the financial position of Krispy Kreme Doughnuts, Inc. and its subsidiaries (the Company) at February 3, 2002 and February 2, 2003, and the results of their operations and their cash flows for each of the three years in the period ended February 2, 2003, in conformity with accounting principles generally accepted in the United States of America. These financial statements are the responsibility of the Company's management; our responsibility is to express an opinion on these financial statements based on our audits. We conducted our audits of these statements in accordance with auditing standards generally accepted in the United States of America, which require that we plan and perform the audit to obtain reasonable assurance about whether the financial statements are free of material misstatement. An audit includes examining, on a test basis, evidence supporting the amounts and disclosures in the financial statements, assessing the accounting principles used and significant estimates made by management, and evaluating the overall financial statement presentation. We believe that our audits provide a reasonable basis for the opinion expressed above.

As discussed in Note 2 to the consolidated financial statements, effective February 4, 2002, the Company changed its method of accounting for goodwill and other intangible assets to conform to Statement of Financial Accounting Standards No. 142, "Goodwill and Other Intangible Assets."

Greensboro, North Carolina
March 13, 2003

KRISPY KREME DOUGHNUTS, INC.
CONSOLIDATED STATEMENTS OF OPERATIONS

IN THOUSANDS, EXCEPT PER SHARE AMOUNTS

YEAR ENDED	Jan. 28, 2001	Feb. 3, 2002	Feb. 2, 2003
Total revenues	$300,715	$394,354	$491,549
Operating expenses*	250,690	316,946	381,489
General and administrative expenses	20,061	27,562	28,897
Depreciation and amortization expenses	6,457	7,959	12,271
Arbitration award (Note 18)	—	—	9,075
Income from operations	23,507	41,887	59,817
Interest income	2,325	2,980	1,966
Interest expense	(607)	(337)	(1,781)
Equity loss in joint ventures	(706)	(602)	(2,008)
Minority interest	(716)	(1,147)	(2,287)
Loss on sale of property and equipment	(20)	(235)	(934)
Income before income taxes	23,783	42,546	54,773
Provision for income taxes	9,058	16,168	21,295
Net income	$ 14,725	$ 26,378	$ 33,478
Basic earnings per share	$ 0.30	$ 0.49	$ 0.61
Diluted earnings per share	$ 0.27	$ 0.45	$ 0.56

* Operating expenses consist entirely of cost of goods sold.

The accompanying notes are an integral part of these consolidated financial statements.

KRISPY KREME DOUGHNUTS, INC.
CONSOLIDATED BALANCE SHEETS

		In Thousands
	Feb. 3, 2002	**Feb. 2, 2003**
ASSETS		
Current Assets:		
Cash and cash equivalents	$ 21,904	$ 32,203
Short-term investments	15,292	22,976
Accounts receivable, less allowance for doubtful accounts of $1,182 (2002) and $1,453 (2003)	26,894	34,373
Accounts receivable, affiliates	9,017	11,062
Other receivables	2,771	884
Inventories	16,159	24,365
Prepaid expenses	2,591	3,478
Income taxes refundable	2,534	1,963
Deferred income taxes	4,607	9,824
Total current assets	101,769	141,128
Property and equipment, net	112,577	202,558
Long-term investments	12,700	4,344
Investments in unconsolidated joint ventures	3,400	6,871
Intangible assets	16,621	48,703
Other assets	8,309	6,883
Total assets	$255,376	$410,487
LIABILITIES AND SHAREHOLDERS' EQUITY		
Current Liabilities:		
Accounts payable	$ 12,095	$ 14,055
Book overdraft	9,107	11,375
Accrued expenses	26,729	20,981
Arbitration award	—	9,075
Revolving line of credit	3,871	—
Current maturities of long-term debt	731	3,301
Short-term debt — related party	—	900
Total current liabilities	52,533	59,687
Deferred income taxes	3,930	9,849
Long-term debt, net of current portion	3,912	49,900
Revolving lines of credit	—	7,288
Other long-term obligations	4,843	5,218
Total long-term liabilities	12,685	72,255
Commitments and contingencies		
Minority interest	2,491	5,193
Shareholders' Equity:		
Preferred stock, no par value, 10,000 shares authorized; none issued and outstanding	—	—
Common stock, no par value, shares authorized — 100,000 (2002) and 300,000 (2003); issued and outstanding — 54,271 (2002) and 56,295 (2003)	121,052	173,112
Unearned compensation	(186)	(119)
Notes receivable, employees	(2,580)	(558)
Nonqualified employee benefit plan assets	(138)	(339)
Nonqualified employee benefit plan liability	138	339
Accumulated other comprehensive income (loss)	456	(1,486)
Retained earnings	68,925	102,403
Total shareholders' equity	187,667	273,352
Total liabilities and shareholders' equity	$255,376	$410,487

The accompanying notes are an integral part of these consolidated financial statements.

KRISPY KREME DOUGHNUTS, INC.
CONSOLIDATED STATEMENTS OF SHAREHOLDERS' EQUITY

	KRISPY KREME DOUGHNUT CORPORATION			KRISPY KREME DOUGHNUTS, INC.			
	Common Shares	**Common Stock**	**Additional Paid-In Capital**	**Preferred Shares**	**Preferred Stock**	**Common Shares**	**Common Stock**
Balance at January 30, 2000	467	$ 4,670	$ 10,805	—	$ —	—	$ —
Comprehensive income:							
Net income for the year ended January 28, 2001							
Unrealized holding gain, net							
Total comprehensive income							
Proceeds from public offering						13,800	65,637
Conversion of Krispy Kreme Doughnut Corporation shares to Krispy Kreme Doughnuts, Inc. shares	(467)	(4,670)	(10,805)			37,360	15,475
Cash dividend to shareholders							
Issuance of shares to employee stock ownership plan						580	3,039
Contribution to the nonqualified employee benefit plan							
Liability under the nonqualified employee benefit plan							
Issuance of restricted common shares						12	210
Exercise of stock options, including tax benefit of $595						80	699
Amortization of restricted common shares							
Collection of notes receivable							
Balance at January 28, 2001	—	$ —	$ —	—	$ —	51,832	$ 85,060
Comprehensive income:							
Net income for the year ended February 3, 2002							
Unrealized holding loss, net							
Foreign currency translation adjustment, net							
Total comprehensive income							
Proceeds from public offering						1,086	17,202
Exercise of stock options, including tax benefit of $9,772						1,183	13,678
Issuance of shares in conjunction with acquisition of franchise market						115	4,183
Adjustment of nonqualified employee benefit plan investments							
Issuance of restricted common shares						1	50
Amortization of restricted common shares							
Issuance of stock for notes receivable						54	879
Collection of notes receivable							
Balance at February 3, 2002	—	$ —	$ —	—	$ —	54,271	$121,052
Comprehensive income:							
Net income for the year ended February 2, 2003							
Unrealized holding loss, net of tax benefit of $241							
Foreign currency translation adjustment, net of tax expense of $7							
Unrealized loss from cash flow hedge, net of tax benefit of $982							
Total comprehensive income							
Exercise of stock options, including tax benefit of $13,795						1,187	20,935
Issuance of shares in conjunction with acquisition of franchise markets						837	30,975
Adjustment of nonqualified employee benefit plan investments							
Amortization of restricted common shares							
Issuance of stock options in exchange for services							150
Collection of notes receivable							
Balance at February 2, 2003	—	$ —	$ —	—	$ —	56,295	$173,112

The accompanying notes are an integral part of these consolidated financial statements.

IN THOUSANDS

Unearned Compensation	Notes Receivable, Employees	Nonqualified Employee Benefit Plan Assets	Nonqualified Employee Benefit Plan Liability	Accumulated Other Comprehensive Income (Loss)	Retained Earnings	Total
$ —	$(2,547)	$ —	$ —	$ —	$ 34,827	$ 47,755
					14,725	14,725
				609		609
						15,334
						65,637
						—
					(7,005)	(7,005)
						3,039
		(126)				(126)
			126			126
(210)						—
						699
22						22
	198					198
$(188)	$(2,349)	$(126)	$126	$ 609	$ 42,547	$125,679
					26,378	26,378
				(111)		(111)
				(42)		(42)
						26,225
						17,202
						13,678
						4,183
		(12)	12			—
(50)						—
52						52
	(879)					—
	648					648
$(186)	$(2,580)	$(138)	$138	$ 456	$ 68,925	$187,667
					33,478	33,478
				(385)		(385)
				11		11
				(1,568)		(1,568)
						31,536
						20,935
						30,975
		(201)	201			—
67						67
						150
	2,022					2,022
$(119)	$ (558)	$(339)	$339	$ (1,486)	$102,403	$273,352

KRISPY KREME

KRISPY KREME DOUGHNUTS, INC.
CONSOLIDATED STATEMENTS OF CASH FLOWS

IN THOUSANDS

YEAR ENDED	Jan. 28, 2001	Feb. 3, 2002	Feb. 2, 2003
Cash Flow From Operating Activities:			
Net income	$ 14,725	$ 26,378	$ 33,478
Items not requiring cash:			
Depreciation and amortization	6,457	7,959	12,271
Deferred income taxes	1,668	2,553	1,632
Loss on disposal of property and equipment, net	20	235	934
Compensation expense related to restricted stock awards	22	52	67
Tax benefit from exercise of nonqualified stock options	595	9,772	13,795
Provision for store closings and impairment	318	—	—
Minority interest	716	1,147	2,287
Equity loss in joint ventures	706	602	2,008
Change in assets and liabilities:			
Receivables	(3,434)	(13,317)	(7,390)
Inventories	(2,052)	(3,977)	(7,866)
Prepaid expenses	1,239	(682)	(331)
Income taxes, net	902	(2,575)	571
Accounts payable	2,279	3,884	(33)
Accrued expenses	7,966	4,096	(9,296)
Arbitration award	—	—	9,075
Other long-term obligations	(15)	83	(166)
Net cash provided by operating activities	32,112	36,210	51,036
Cash Flow From Investing Activities:			
Purchase of property and equipment	(25,655)	(37,310)	(83,196)
Proceeds from disposal of property and equipment	1,419	3,196	701
Proceeds from disposal of assets held for sale	—	—	1,435
Acquisition of franchise markets, net of cash acquired	—	(20,571)	(4,965)
Investments in unconsolidated joint ventures	(4,465)	(1,218)	(7,869)
Purchases of investments	(41,375)	(10,128)	(32,739)
Proceeds from investments	6,004	18,005	33,097
Increase in other assets	(3,216)	(4,237)	(1,038)
Net cash used for investing activities	(67,288)	(52,263)	(94,574)
Cash Flow From Financing Activities:			
Borrowings of long-term debt	—	4,643	44,234
Repayment of long-term debt	(3,600)	—	(2,170)
Net (repayments) borrowings from revolving line of credit	(15,775)	345	(121)
Repayment of short-term debt — related party	—	—	(500)
Debt issue costs	—	—	(194)
Proceeds from exercise of stock options	104	3,906	7,140
Proceeds from stock offering	65,637	17,202	—
Book overdraft	(941)	3,960	2,268
Collection of notes receivable	198	648	3,612
Minority interest	401	227	(432)
Cash dividends paid	(7,005)	—	—
Net cash provided by financing activities	39,019	30,931	53,837
Net increase in cash and cash equivalents	3,843	14,878	10,299
Cash and cash equivalents at beginning of year	3,183	7,026	21,904
Cash and cash equivalents at end of year	$ 7,026	$ 21,904	$ 32,203
Supplemental schedule of non-cash investing and financing activities:			
Issuance of stock in conjunction with acquisition of franchise markets	$ —	$ 4,183	$ 8,727
Issuance of stock in conjunction with acquisition of additional interest in area developer franchisee	—	—	22,248
Unrealized gain (loss) on investments	609	(111)	(385)
Issuance of stock options in exchange for services	—	—	150
Issuance of stock to Krispy Kreme Profit-Sharing Stock Ownership Plan	3,039	—	—
Issuance of restricted common shares	210	50	—
Issuance of stock in exchange for employee notes receivable	—	879	—

The accompanying notes are an integral part of these consolidated financial statements.

KRISPY KREME DOUGHNUTS, INC.
SELECTED NOTES TO CONSOLIDATED FINANCIAL STATEMENTS

1. ORGANIZATION AND PURPOSE

Krispy Kreme Doughnuts, Inc. was incorporated in North Carolina on December 2, 1999 as a wholly-owned subsidiary of Krispy Kreme Doughnut Corporation ("KKDC"). Pursuant to a plan of merger approved by shareholders on November 10, 1999, the shareholders of KKDC became shareholders of Krispy Kreme Doughnuts, Inc. on April 4, 2000. Each shareholder received 80 shares of Krispy Kreme Doughnuts, Inc. common stock and $15 in cash for each share of KKDC common stock they held. As a result of the merger, KKDC became a wholly-owned subsidiary of Krispy Kreme Doughnuts, Inc. Krispy Kreme Doughnuts, Inc. closed a public offering of its common stock on April 10, 2000.

All consolidated financial statements prior to the merger are those of KKDC and all consolidated financial statements after the merger are those of Krispy Kreme Doughnuts, Inc.

2. NATURE OF BUSINESS AND SIGNIFICANT ACCOUNTING POLICIES

Nature of Business. Krispy Kreme Doughnuts, Inc. and its subsidiaries (the "Company") are engaged principally in the sale of doughnuts and related items through Company-owned stores. The Company also derives revenue from franchise and development fees and the collection of royalties from franchisees. Additionally, the Company sells doughnut-making equipment, mix, coffee and other ingredients and supplies used in operating a doughnut store to Company-owned and franchised stores.

The significant accounting policies followed by the Company in preparing the accompanying consolidated financial statements are as follows:

Basis of Consolidation. The consolidated financial statements include the accounts of the Company and its wholly-owned subsidiaries. All significant intercompany accounts and transactions are eliminated in consolidation. Generally, investments greater than 50 percent in affiliates for which the Company maintains control are also consolidated and the portion not owned by the Company is shown as a minority interest. As of February 2, 2003, the Company consolidated the accounts of three joint ventures which the Company controlled: Freedom Rings, LLC ("Freedom Rings"), the joint venture with the rights to develop stores in the Philadelphia market; Glazed Investments, LLC ("Glazed Investments"), the joint venture with the rights to develop stores in Colorado, Minnesota and Wisconsin; and Golden Gate Doughnuts, LLC ("Golden Gate"), the joint venture with the rights to develop stores in Northern California. Generally, investments in 20- to 50-percent owned affiliates for which the Company has the ability to exercise significant influence over operating and financial policies are accounted for by the equity method of accounting, whereby the investment is carried at the cost of acquisition, plus the Company's equity in undistributed earnings or losses since acquisition, less any distributions received by the Company. Accordingly, the Company's share of the net earnings of these companies is included in consolidated net income. Investments in less than 20-percent owned affiliates are accounted for by the cost method of accounting.

Fiscal Year. The Company's fiscal year is based on a fifty-two/fifty-three week year. The fiscal year ends on the Sunday closest to the last day in January. The years ended January 28, 2001, February 3, 2002 and February 2, 2003 contained 52, 53 and 52 weeks, respectively.

Cash and Cash Equivalents. The Company considers cash on hand, deposits in banks, and all highly liquid debt instruments with a maturity of three months or less at date of acquisition to be cash and cash equivalents.

Inventories. Inventories are recorded at the lower of average cost (first-in, first-out) or market.

Investments. Investments consist of United States Treasury notes, mortgage-backed government securities, corporate debt securities, municipal securities and certificates of deposit and are included in short-term and long-term investments in the accompanying consolidated balance sheets. Certificates of deposit are carried at cost which approximates fair value. All other marketable securities are stated at market value as determined by the most recently traded price of each security at the balance sheet date.

Management determines the appropriate classification of its investments in marketable securities at the time of the purchase and reevaluates such determination at each balance sheet date. At February 2, 2003, all marketable securities are classified as available-for-sale. Available-for-sale securities are carried at fair value with the unrealized gains and losses reported as a separate component of shareholders' equity in accumulated other comprehensive income (loss). The cost of investments sold is determined on the specific identification or the first-in, first-out method.

Property and Equipment. Property and equipment are stated at cost less accumulated depreciation. Major renewals and betterments are charged to the property accounts while replacements, maintenance and repairs which do not improve or extend the lives of the respective assets are expensed currently. Interest is capitalized on major capital expenditures during the period of construction.

Depreciation of property and equipment is provided on the straight-line method over the estimated useful lives: Buildings — 15 to 35 years; Machinery and equipment — 3 to 15 years; Leasehold improvements — lesser of useful lives of assets or lease term.

Intangible Assets. In July 2001, the Financial Accounting Standards Board ("FASB") issued Statement of Financial Accounting Standards ("SFAS") No. 141, "Business Combinations," and SFAS No. 142, "Goodwill and Other Intangible Assets." These pronouncements provide guidance on accounting for the acquisition of businesses and other intangible assets, including goodwill, which arise from such activities. SFAS No. 141 affirms that only the purchase method of accounting may be applied to a business combination and provides guidance on the allocation of purchase price to the assets acquired. SFAS No. 141 applies to all business combinations initiated after June 30, 2001. Under SFAS No. 142, goodwill and intangible assets that have indefinite useful lives are no longer amortized but are reviewed at least annually for impairment. SFAS No. 142 is effective for the Company's fiscal 2003, although goodwill and intangible assets acquired after June 30, 2001 were subject immediately to the non-amortization provisions of SFAS No. 142. The Company has evaluated its intangible assets, which at February 2, 2003 consist of goodwill recorded in connection with a business acquisition ($201,000) and the value assigned to reacquired franchise rights in connection with the acquisition of rights to certain markets from franchisees ($48,502,000), and determined that all such assets have indefinite lives and, as a result, are not subject to amortization provisions. For the fiscal year ended February 3, 2002, the Company recorded an expense of $100,000 to amortize intangible assets related to an acquisition completed prior to June 30, 2001. The Company completed impairment analyses of its intangible assets in fiscal 2003 and found no instances of impairment.

Use of Estimates in Preparation of Financial Statements. The preparation of financial statements in conformity with generally accepted accounting principles requires management to make estimates and assumptions that affect the reported amounts of assets and liabilities and disclosure of contingent assets and liabilities at the date of the financial statements and the reported amounts of revenues and expenses during the reporting period. Actual results could differ from those estimates.

Revenue Recognition. A summary of the revenue recognition policies for each segment of the Company (see Note 14) is as follows:

- Company Store Operations revenue is derived from the sale of doughnuts and related items to on-premises and off-premises customers. Revenue is recognized at the time of sale for on-premises sales. For off-premises sales, revenue is recognized at the time of delivery.

- Franchise Operations revenue is derived from: (1) development and franchise fees from the opening of new stores; and (2) royalties charged to franchisees based on sales. Development and franchise fees are charged for certain new stores and are deferred until the store is opened and the Company has performed substantially all of the initial services it is required to provide. The royalties recognized in each period are based on the sales in that period.

- KKM&D revenue is derived from the sale of doughnut-making equipment, mix, coffee and other supplies needed to operate a doughnut store to Company-owned and franchised stores. Revenue is recognized at the time the title and the risk of loss pass to the customer, generally upon delivery of the goods. Revenue from Company-owned stores and consolidated joint venture stores is eliminated in consolidation.

Income Taxes. The Company uses the asset and liability method to account for income taxes, which requires the recognition of deferred tax assets and liabilities for the expected future tax consequences of temporary differences between tax bases and financial reporting bases for assets and liabilities.

Fair Value Of Financial Instruments. Cash, accounts receivable, accounts payable, accrued liabilities and debt are reflected in the financial statements at carrying amounts which approximate fair value.

Advertising Costs. All costs associated with advertising and promoting products are expensed in the period incurred.

Store Opening Costs. All costs, both direct and indirect, incurred to open either Company or franchise stores are expensed in the period incurred. Direct costs to open stores amounted to $464,000, $551,000 and $845,000 in fiscal 2001, 2002 and 2003, respectively.

Asset Impairment. When a store is identified as underperforming or when a decision is made to close a store, the Company makes an assessment of the potential impairment of the related assets. The assessment is based upon a comparison of the carrying amount of the assets, primarily property and equipment, to the estimated undiscounted cash flows expected to be generated from those assets. To estimate cash flows, management projects the net cash flows anticipated from continuing operation of the store until its closing as well as cash flows anticipated from disposal of the related assets, if any. If the carrying amount of the assets exceeds the sum of the undiscounted cash flows, the Company records an impairment charge measured as the excess of the carrying value over the fair value of the assets. The resulting net book value of the assets less estimated net realizable value at disposition, is depreciated over the remaining term that the store will continue in operation.

Comprehensive Income. SFAS No. 130, "Reporting Comprehensive Income," requires that certain items such as foreign currency translation adjustments, unrealized gains and losses on certain investments in debt and equity securities and minimum pension liability adjustments be presented as separate components of shareholders' equity. SFAS No. 130 defines these as items of other comprehensive income which must be reported in a financial statement displayed with the same prominence as other financial statements. Accumulated other comprehensive income (loss), as reflected in the consolidated statements of shareholders' equity, was comprised of net unrealized holding gains on marketable securities of $498,000 at February 3, 2002 and $113,000 at February 2, 2003 and foreign currency translation adjustment, net, of $42,000 at February 3, 2002 and $31,000 at February 2, 2003. At February 2, 2003, accumulated other comprehensive income (loss) also included the unrealized loss from a cash flow hedge, net of related tax benefits, of $1,568,000. Total comprehensive income for fiscal 2001, 2002 and 2003 was $15,334,000, $26,225,000 and $31,536,000, respectively.

Foreign Currency Translation. For all non-U.S. joint ventures, the functional currency is the local currency. Assets and liabilities of those operations are translated into U.S. dollars using exchange rates at the balance sheet date. Revenue and expenses are translated using the average exchange rates for the reporting period. Translation adjustments are deferred in accumulated other comprehensive income (loss), a separate component of shareholders' equity.

3. INVESTMENTS

The following table provides certain information about investments at February 3, 2002 and February 2, 2003.

IN THOUSANDS

	Amortized Cost	Gross Unrealized Holding Gains	Gross Unrealized Holding Losses	Fair Value
February 3, 2002				
U.S. government notes	$ 9,049	$ —	$ (17)	$ 9,032
Federal government agencies	10,959	442	(166)	11,235
Corporate debt securities	6,475	317	(88)	6,704
Other bonds	1,043	—	(22)	1,021
Total	$27,526	$759	$(293)	$27,992
February 2, 2003				
U.S. government notes	$16,657	$152	$ (97)	$16,712
Federal government agencies	7,485	289	(197)	7,577
Corporate debt securities	1,000	76	(45)	1,031
Certificate of deposit	2,000	—	—	2,000
Total	$27,142	$517	$(339)	$27,320

Maturities of investments were as follows at February 2, 2003:

IN THOUSANDS

	Amortized Cost	Fair Value
Due within one year	$22,844	$22,976
Due after one year through five years	4,298	4,344
Total	$27,142	$27,320

4. INVENTORIES

The components of inventories are as follows:

IN THOUSANDS

	Distribution Center	Equipment Department	Mix Department	Company Stores	Total
February 3, 2002					
Raw materials	$ —	$3,060	$ 788	$1,826	$ 5,674
Work in progress	—	28	—	—	28
Finished goods	1,318	2,867	95	—	4,280
Purchased merchandise	5,503	—	—	613	6,116
Manufacturing supplies	—	—	61	—	61
Totals	$ 6,821	$5,955	$ 944	$2,439	$16,159
February 2, 2003					
Raw materials	$ —	$3,828	$1,069	$1,922	$ 6,819
Work in progress	—	234	—	—	234
Finished goods	2,222	3,616	172	—	6,010
Purchased merchandise	10,191	—	—	966	11,157
Manufacturing supplies	—	—	145	—	145
Totals	$12,413	$7,678	$1,386	$2,888	$24,365

5. PROPERTY AND EQUIPMENT

Property and equipment consists of the following:

IN THOUSANDS

	Feb. 3, 2002	Feb. 2, 2003
Land	$ 14,823	$ 24,741
Buildings	39,566	88,641
Machinery and equipment	86,683	118,332
Leasehold improvements	13,463	19,522
Construction in progress	1,949	1,534
	156,484	252,770
Less: accumulated depreciation	43,907	50,212
Property and equipment, net	$112,577	$202,558

Depreciation expense was $6,141,000, $7,398,000 and $11,570,000 for fiscal 2001, fiscal 2002 and fiscal 2003, respectively.

6. ACCRUED EXPENSES

Accrued expenses consist of the following:

IN THOUSANDS

	Feb. 3, 2002	Feb. 2, 2003
Insurance	$ 4,891	$ 6,150
Salaries, wages and incentive compensation	11,686	6,034
Deferred revenue	2,082	1,485
Taxes, other than income	1,632	1,865
Other	6,438	5,447
Total	$ 26,729	$ 20,981

7. DEBT

The Company's debt, including debt of consolidated joint ventures, consists of the following:

	In Thousands	
	Feb. 3, 2002	**Feb. 2, 2003**
Krispy Kreme Doughnut Corporation:		
$40 million revolving line of credit	$ —	$ —
Golden Gate:		
$6.75 million revolving line of credit	3,871	4,750
Freedom Rings:		
$5 million revolving line of credit	—	2,538
Revolving lines of credit	$ 3,871	$ 7,288
Glazed Investments:		
Short-term debt — related party	$ —	$ 900
Krispy Kreme Doughnut Corporation:		
$33 million term loan	$ —	$ 31,763
Golden Gate:		
$4.5 million term loan	4,418	3,926
$3 million term loan	—	2,976
Glazed Investments:		
Real Estate and Equipment loans	—	14,400
Subordinated notes	—	136
Freedom Rings:		
Other debt	225	—
	4,643	53,201
Current maturities of long-term debt	(731)	(3,301)
Long-term debt, net of current portion	$ 3,912	$ 49,900

$40 Million Revolving Line of Credit

On December 29, 1999, the Company entered into an unsecured loan agreement ("Agreement") with a bank to increase borrowing availability and extend the maturity of its revolving line of credit. The Agreement provides a $40 million revolving line of credit and expires on June 30, 2004.

Under the terms of the Agreement, interest on the revolving line of credit is charged, at the Company's option, at either the lender's prime rate less 110 basis points or at the one-month LIBOR plus 100 basis points. There was no interest, fee or other charge for the unadvanced portion of the line of credit until July 1, 2002 at which time the Company began paying a fee of 0.10% on the unadvanced portion. No amounts were outstanding on the revolving line of credit at February 3, 2002 or February 2, 2003. The amount available under the revolving line of credit is reduced by letters of credit, amounts outstanding under certain loans made by the bank to franchisees which are guaranteed by the Company and certain amounts available or outstanding in connection with credit cards issued by the lender on behalf of the Company and was $31,695,000 at February 2, 2003. Outstanding letters of credit, primarily for insurance purposes, totaled $6,626,000, amounts outstanding under the loans guaranteed by the Company totaled $152,000 and amounts available in connection with credit cards issued by the lender totaled $1,527,000 at February 2, 2003.

The Agreement contains provisions that, among other requirements, restrict capital expenditures, require the maintenance of certain financial ratios, place various restrictions on the sale of properties, restrict the Company's ability to enter into collateral repurchase agreements and guarantees, restrict the payment of dividends and require compliance with other customary financial and nonfinancial covenants. At February 2, 2003, the Company was in compliance with each of these covenants.

8. LEASE COMMITMENTS

The Company conducts some of its operations from leased facilities and, additionally, leases certain equipment under operating leases. Generally, these leases have initial terms of 5 to 18 years and contain provisions for renewal options of 5 to 10 years.

At February 2, 2003, future minimum annual rental commitments, gross, under noncancelable operating leases, including lease commitments of consolidated joint ventures, are as follows:

IN THOUSANDS

FISCAL YEAR ENDING IN	Amount
2004	$10,969
2005	9,187
2006	6,707
2007	5,018
2008	5,433
Thereafter	32,397
	$69,711

Rental expense, net of rental income, totaled $8,540,000 in fiscal 2001, $10,576,000 in fiscal 2002 and $13,169,000 in fiscal 2003.

9. INCOME TAXES

The components of the provision for federal and state income taxes are summarized as follows:

IN THOUSANDS

YEAR ENDED	Jan. 28, 2001	Feb. 3, 2002	Feb. 2, 2003
Currently payable	$7,390	$13,615	$19,663
Deferred	1,668	2,553	1,632
	$9,058	$16,168	$21,295

A reconciliation of the statutory federal income tax rate with the company's effective rate is as follows:

IN THOUSANDS

YEAR ENDED	Jan. 28, 2001	Feb. 3, 2002	Feb. 2, 2003
Federal taxes at statutory rate	$8,321	$14,891	$19,170
State taxes, net of federal benefit	673	1,158	1,405
Other	64	119	720
	$9,058	$16,168	$21,295

Income tax payments, net of refunds, were $5,894,000 in fiscal 2001, $6,616,000 in fiscal 2002 and $5,298,000 in fiscal 2003. The income tax payments in fiscal 2002 and fiscal 2003 were lower than the current provision due to the income tax benefit of stock option exercises of $9,772,000 and $13,795,000 during fiscal 2002 and fiscal 2003, respectively.

The net current and non-current components of deferred income taxes recognized in the balance sheet are as follows:

IN THOUSANDS

	Feb. 3, 2002	Feb. 2, 2003
Net current assets	$ 4,607	$ 9,824
Net non-current liabilities	(3,930)	(9,849)
	$ 677	$ (25)

The tax effects of the significant temporary differences which comprise the deferred tax assets and liabilities are as follows:

IN THOUSANDS	Feb. 3, 2002	Feb. 2, 2003
ASSETS		
Compensation deferred (unpaid)	$ 676	$ 663
Insurance	1,859	2,368
Other long-term obligations	659	395
Accrued restructuring expenses	1,183	501
Deferred revenue	791	1,165
Accounts receivable	449	556
Inventory	436	278
Charitable contributions carryforward	—	714
Gain/loss on hedging transactions	—	982
Accrued litigation	—	3,494
Accrued payroll	—	1,018
State tax credit carryforwards	—	179
State NOL carryforwards	2,524	2,463
Other	676	687
Gross deferred tax assets	9,253	15,463
LIABILITIES		
Property and equipment	5,589	11,628
Goodwill	198	1,037
Prepaid expenses	265	360
Gross deferred tax liabilities	6,052	13,025
Valuation allowance — State NOL carryforwards	(2,524)	(2,463)
Net asset/(liability)	$ 677	$ (25)

At February 2, 2003, the Company has recorded a valuation allowance against the state NOL carryforwards of $2,463,000. If these carryforwards are realized in the future, $2,232,000 of the tax benefit would be recorded as an addition to common stock as this portion of the carryforwards were a result of the tax benefits of stock option exercises in fiscal 2002 and 2003.

The Company records deferred tax assets reflecting the benefit of future deductible amounts. Realization of these assets is dependent on generating sufficient future taxable income and the ability to carryback losses to previous years in which there was taxable income. Although realization is not assured, management believes it is more likely than not that all of the deferred tax assets, for which a valuation allowance has not been established, will be realized. The amount of the deferred tax assets considered realizable, however, could be reduced in the near term if estimates of future taxable income are reduced.

10. EARNINGS PER SHARE

The computation of basic earnings per share is based on the weighted average number of common shares outstanding during the period. The computation of diluted earnings per share reflects the potential dilution that would occur if stock options were exercised and the dilution from the issuance of restricted shares. The treasury stock method is used to calculate dilutive shares. This reduces the gross number of dilutive shares by the number of shares purchasable from the proceeds of the options assumed to be exercised, the proceeds of the tax benefits recognized by the Company in conjunction with nonqualified stock plans and from the amounts of unearned compensation associated with the restricted shares.

The following table sets forth the computation of basic and diluted earnings per share:

IN THOUSANDS, EXCEPT SHARE AMOUNTS

YEAR ENDED	Jan. 28, 2001	Feb. 3, 2002	Feb. 2, 2003
Numerator:			
Net income	$ 14,725	$ 26,378	$ 33,478
Denominator:			
Basic earnings per share — weighted average shares	49,183,916	53,702,916	55,092,542
Effect of dilutive securities:			
Stock options	4,471,576	4,734,371	4,395,864
Restricted stock	—	5,698	3,967
Diluted earnings per share — adjusted weighted average shares	53,655,492	58,442,985	59,492,373

KRISPY KREME

14. BUSINESS SEGMENT INFORMATION

The Company has three reportable business segments. The Company Store Operations segment is comprised of the operating activities of the stores owned by the Company and those in consolidated joint ventures. These stores sell doughnuts and complementary products through both on-premises and off-premises sales. The majority of the ingredients and materials used by Company Store Operations is purchased from the KKM&D business segment.

The Franchise Operations segment represents the results of the Company's franchise program. Under the terms of the franchise agreements, the licensed operators pay royalties and fees to the Company in return for the use of the Krispy Kreme name. Expenses for this business segment include costs incurred to recruit new franchisees and to open, monitor and aid in the performance of these stores and direct general and administrative expenses.

The KKM&D segment supplies mix, equipment, coffee and other items to both Company and franchisee-owned stores. All intercompany transactions between the KKM&D business segment and Company stores and consolidated joint venture stores are eliminated in consolidation.

Segment information for total assets and capital expenditures is not presented as such information is not used in measuring segment performance or allocating resources among segments.

Segment operating income is income before general corporate expenses and income taxes.

Information about the Company's operations by business segment is as follows:

IN THOUSANDS

YEAR ENDED	Jan. 28, 2001	Feb. 3, 2002	Feb. 2, 2003
Revenues:			
Company Store Operations	$ 213,677	$ 266,209	$ 319,592
Franchise Operations	9,445	14,008	19,304
KKM&D	201,406	269,396	347,642
Intercompany sales eliminations	(123,813)	(155,259)	(194,989)
Total revenues	$ 300,715	$ 394,354	$ 491,549
Operating income:			
Company Store Operations	$ 27,370	$ 42,932	$ 58,214
Franchise Operations	5,730	9,040	14,319
KKM&D	11,712	18,999	26,843
Unallocated general and administrative expenses	(21,305)	(29,084)	(30,484)
Arbitration award	—	—	(9,075)
Total operating income	$ 23,507	$ 41,887	$ 59,817
Depreciation and Amortization Expenses:			
Company Store Operations	$ 4,838	$ 5,859	$ 8,854
Franchise Operations	72	72	108
KKM&D	303	507	1,723
Corporate administration	1,244	1,521	1,586
Total depreciation and amortization expenses	$ 6,457	$ 7,959	$ 12,271

16. COMMITMENTS AND CONTINGENCIES

In order to assist certain associate and franchise operators in obtaining third-party financing, the Company from time-to-time enters into collateral repurchase agreements involving both Company stock and doughnut-making equipment. The Company's contingent liability related to these agreements was approximately $70,000 at February 3, 2002. The Company was not contingently liable under any such agreements at February 2, 2003. Additionally, primarily for the purpose of providing financing guarantees in a percentage equivalent to the Company's ownership percentage in various joint venture investments, the Company has guaranteed certain leases and loans from third-party financial institutions on behalf of franchise operators. The Company's contingent liability related to these guarantees was approximately $3,805,000 at February 3, 2002 and $7,652,000 at February 2, 2003. Of the total guaranteed amount of $7,652,000 at February 2, 2003, $6,450,000 are for franchisees in which we have an ownership interest and $1,202,000 are for franchisees in which we have no ownership interest. The expirations of these guarantees for the five fiscal years ending after February 2, 2003 are $2,903,000, $498,000, $517,000, $357,000 and $355,000, respectively.

Because the Company enters into long-term contracts with its suppliers, in the event that any of these relationships terminate unexpectedly, even where it has multiple suppliers for the same ingredient, the Company's ability to obtain adequate quantities of the same high quality ingredient at the same competitive price could be negatively impacted.

COMPANY PROFILE

Krispy Kreme is a leading branded specialty retailer of premium quality doughnuts which are made throughout the day in our stores. We opened our first store in 1937, and there were 276 Krispy Kreme stores, consisting of 99 company-owned and 177 franchised stores, as of February 2, 2003. Our principal business is the high volume production and sale of over 20 varieties of premium quality doughnuts, including our signature Hot Original Glazed. We have established Krispy Kreme as a leading consumer brand with a loyal customer base through our longstanding commitment to quality and consistency. Our place in American society was recognized in 1997 with the induction of Krispy Kreme artifacts into the Smithsonian Institution's National Museum of American History. We differentiate ourselves by combining quality ingredients, vertical integration and a unique retail experience featuring our stores' fully displayed production process, or doughnut-making theater.

Krispy Kreme has been a publicly held company since April 5, 2000. Our stock is listed on the New York Stock Exchange with shares trading under the ticker symbol KKD.

Tasty Baking Company 2002 Annual Report

FIVE YEAR SELECTED FINANCIAL DATA

All amounts presented are in thousands except for per share amounts.

	2002(a)	2001(b)	2000	1999(c)	1998
Operating Results					
Gross sales	$ $255,504	$ 255,336	$ 249,691	$ 226,350	$ 228,453
Net sales **(d)**	162,263	166,245	162,877	148,830	149,054
Net income (loss)	(4,341)	6,320	8,144	4,703	5,729
Per Share Amounts					
Net income:					
Basic	$ (.54)	$ .79	$ 1.04	$ .60	$ .73
Diluted	(.54)	.78	1.04	.60	.72
Cash dividends	.48	.48	.48	.48	.48
Shareholders' equity	5.86	6.84	6.40	5.81	5.67
Financial Position					
Working capital	$ 16,788	$ 18,284	$ 15,474	$ 14,406	$ 15,830
Total assets	116,560	116,137	112,192	111,753	101,744
Long-term obligations	12,486	14,603	16,843	21,060	13,761
Shareholders' equity	47,525	55,065	50,174	45,422	44,357
Shares of common stock					
Outstanding	8,104	8,052	7,845	7,823	7,822
Statistical Information					
Capital expenditures	$ 5,359	$ 7,314	$ 8,116	$ 14,038	$ 11,328
Depreciation	6,807	7,204	7,759	7,016	6,650
Average common shares					
Outstanding:					
Basic	8,075	7,998	7,837	7,824	7,808
Diluted	8,159	8,140	7,861	7,865	7,953

(a) During the second quarter of 2002, the company incurred a $1,405 restructure charge related to its decision to close six thrift stores and to eliminate certain manufacturing and administrative positions.

During the fourth quarter of 2002, the company incurred a $4,936 restructure charge related to the closing of the remaining twelve thrift stores and the specific arrangements made with senior executives who departed the company in the fourth quarter of 2002.

Also, during the fourth quarter of 2002, the company recorded additional pension expense in the amount of $4,656 in connection with the company's method of immediately recognizing gains and losses that fall outside the pension corridor.

(b) During the fourth quarter of 2001, the company incurred a $1,728 restructure charge related to its decision to close its Dutch Mill Baking Company production facility and two company thrift stores.

(c) During 1999 the company incurred a route restructure charge of $950. Also included is an after-tax charge of $205 that is the cumulative effect of an accounting change that required the write-off of start-up costs. Long-term obligations reflect the renewal of a capital lease with the trustees of the company pension plan.

(d) For comparative purposes net sales for 2001, 2000, 1999 and 1998 have been reclassified to reflect changes in accounting for thrift stores and cooperative advertising. The change was an increase of $1,637 for 2001 and a decrease of $1,406, $1,832 and $1,675, for 2000, 1999 and 1998 respectively.

CONSOLIDATED FINANCIAL STATEMENTS
Tasty Baking Company and Subsidiaries

Consolidated Statements of Operations and Retained Earnings

	52 Weeks Ended Dec. 28, 2002	52 Weeks Ended Dec. 29, 2001(a)	53 Weeks Ended Dec. 30, 2000(a)
Operations			
Gross sales	$ 255,503,818	$ 255,335,587	$ 249,690,639
Less discounts and allowances	(93,240,612)	(89,090,607)	(86,813,226)
Net sales	162,263,206	166,244,980	162,877,413
Costs and expenses:			
Cost of sales	111,187,357	103,297,040	105,036,081
Depreciation	6,807,369	7,203,688	7,759,345
Selling, general and administrative	44,982,205	43,236,117	35,959,008
Restructure charges	6,340,810	1,727,844	–
Interest expense	1,066,250	1,102,777	1,540,242
Provision for doubtful accounts	958,365	772,372	1,250,385
Other income, net	(1,165,548)	(1,189,606)	(1,420,557)
	170,176,808	156,150,232	150,124,504
Income (loss) before provision for income taxes	(7,913,602)	10,094,748	12,752,909
Provision for (benefit from) income taxes:			
Federal	(11,432)	3,284,796	2,562,171
State	(315,262)	(89,526)	(269,625)
Deferred	(3,246,179)	579,276	2,316,823
	(3,572,873)	3,774,546	4,609,369
Net income (loss)	(4,340,729)	6,320,202	8,143,540
Retained Earnings			
Balance, beginning of year	34,838,636	32,351,894	27,968,811
Cash dividends paid on common shares ($.48 per share in 2002, 2001 and 2000)	(3,875,855)	(3,833,460)	(3,760,457)
Balance, end of year	$ 26,622,052	$ 34,838,636	$ 32,351,894
Per share of common stock:			
Net income:			
Basic	$ (.54)	$ .79	$ 1.04
Diluted	$ (.54)	$ .78	$ 1.04

(a) 2001 and 2000 have been reclassified for comparative purposes to reflect the changes in accounting for thrift stores and cooperative advertising.

See accompanying notes to consolidated financial statements.

Consolidated Statements of Cash Flows

	52 Weeks Ended Dec. 28, 2002	52 Weeks Ended Dec. 29, 2001	53 Weeks Ended Dec. 30, 2000
Cash flows from (used for) operating activities			
Net income (loss)	$ (4,340,729)	$ 6,320,202	$ 8,143,540
Adjustments to reconcile net income to net cash provided by operating activities:			
Depreciation	6,807,369	7,203,688	7,759,345
Restructure charges, net of cash expenditures	5,133,794	850,879	–
Conditional stock grant	–	804,759	319,016
Provision for doubtful accounts	958,365	772,372	1,250,385
Pension expense	5,456,000	(216,770)	(2,318,000)
Deferred taxes	(3,246,179)	579,276	2,316,823
Other	(547,841)	(420,277)	(154,683)
Changes in assets and liabilities:			
Decrease (increase) in receivables	393,451	(2,233,932)	(2,339,505)
Decrease (increase) in inventories	1,634,632	(2,481,235)	(1,424,770)
Increase in prepayments and other	(1,839,688)	(197,658)	(948,500)
Increase (decrease) in accrued payroll, accrued income taxes, accounts payable and other current liabilities	(294,575)	(76,690)	594,924
Net cash from operating activities	10,114,599	10,904,614	13,198,575
Cash flows from (used for) investing activities			
Proceeds from owner/operator loan repayments	3,987,420	3,494,763	4,065,144
Purchase of property, plant and equipment	(5,359,051)	(7,313,982)	(8,116,213)
Loans to owner/operators	(3,881,472)	(4,043,379)	(3,038,759)
Other	(46,359)	46,131	40,402
Net cash used for investing activities	(5,299,462)	(7,816,467)	(7,049,426)
Cash flows from (used for) financing activities			
Dividends paid	(3,875,855)	(3,833,460)	(3,760,457)
Payment of long-term debt	(2,117,092)	(3,216,821)	(10,196,240)
Net increase in short-term debt	600,000	1,700,000	1,450,000
Additional long-term debt	–	1,000,000	6,000,000
Net proceeds from sale of common stock	492,275	1,318,112	(36,704)
Net cash used for financing activities	(4,900,672)	(3,032,169)	(6,543,401)
Net increase (decrease) in cash	(85,535)	55,978	(394,252)
Cash, beginning of year	367,220	311,242	705,494
Cash, end of year	$ 281,685	$ 367,220	$ 311,242
Supplemental cash flow information			
Cash paid during the year for:			
Interest	$ 1,084,322	$ 1,231,521	$ 1,750,990
Income taxes	$ 1,011,650	$ 3,065,069	$ 4,819,057

See accompanying notes to consolidated financial statements.

Consolidated Balance Sheets

	Dec. 28, 2002	Dec. 29, 2001
Assets		
Current Assets:		
Cash	$ 281,685	$ 367,220
Receivables, less allowance of $3,606,117 and $3,751,854, respectively	20,881,597	22,233,413
Inventories	6,777,152	8,411,784
Deferred income taxes	5,213,847	3,055,410
Prepayments and other	2,941,033	1,101,345
Total current assets	36,095,314	35,169,172
Property, plant and equipment:		
Land	1,097,987	1,097,987
Buildings and improvements	37,831,789	37,103,226
Machinery and equipment	148,990,425	146,023,373
	187,920,021	184,224,586
Less accumulated depreciation and amortization	129,528,979	124,522,610
	58,391,222	59,701,976
Other assets:		
Long-term receivables from owner/operators	10,095,101	10,201,049
Deferred income taxes	8,229,612	7,381,934
Spare parts inventory	3,698,780	3,632,687
Miscellaneous	50,001	50,001
	22,073,494	21,265,671
	$ 116,560,030	$ 116,136,819

See accompanying notes to consolidated financial statements.

	Dec. 28, 2002	Dec. 29, 2001
Liabilities		
Current Liabilities:		
Current obligations under capital leases	$ 175,715	$ 239,593
Notes payable, banks	4,500,000	3,900,000
Accounts payable	6,074,193	5,306,976
Accrued payroll and employee benefits	5,158,820	6,208,889
Reserve for restructures	2,417,178	850,879
Other	981,459	378,982
Total current liabilities	19,307,365	16,885,319
Long-term debt	9,000,000	11,000,000
Long-term obligations under capital leases, less current portion	3,486,218	3,603,310
Reserve for restructures-less current portion	3,567,495	–
Accrued pensions and other liabilities	15,923,020	11,506,969
Postretirement benefits other than pensions	17,750,696	18,076,719
Total liabilities	69,034,794	61,072,317
Shareholders' Equity		
Common stock, par value $.50 per share, and entitled to one vote per share: Authorized 15,000,000 shares, issued 9,116,483 shares	4,558,243	4,558,243
Capital in excess of par value of stock	29,432,917	29,388,567
Retained earnings	26,622,052	34,838,636
	60,613,212	68,785,446
Less:		
Treasury stock, at cost: 1,012,798 shares and 1,064,539 shares, respectively	12,538,632	13,167,082
Management Stock Purchase Plan receivables and deferrals	549,344	553,862
	47,525,236	55,064,502
	$ 116,560,030	$ 116,136,819

See accompanying notes to consolidated financial statements.

TASTYKAKE

Consolidated Statements of Changes in Capital Accounts

	Dec. 28, 2002		Dec. 29, 2001		Dec. 30, 2000	
	Shares	**Amount**	**Shares**	**Amount**	**Shares**	**Amount**
Common Stock:						
Balance, beginning of year	9,116,483	$ 4,558,243	9,116,483	$ 4,558,243	9,116,483	$ 4,558,243
Balance, end of year	9,116,483	$ 4,558,243	9,116,483	$ 4,558,243	9,116,483	$ 4,558,243
Capital in Excess of Par Value of Stock:						
Balance, beginning of year		$ 29,388,567		$ 29,742,434		$ 29,778,768
Issuances:						
Management Stock Purchase Plan		16,975		53,766		(4,211)
Stock Option Plan		(24,777)		(599,642)		–
Conditional Stock Grant		–		(11,535)		(35,573)
Tax benefits related to Management Stock Purchase Plan and Stock Option Plan		52,152		203,544		3,450
Balance, end of year		$ 29,432,917		$ 29,388,567		$ 29,742,434
Treasury Stock:						
Balance, beginning of year	1,064,539	$ 13,167,082	1,271,171	$ 16,106,361	1,293,135	$ 16,408,808
Management Stock Purchase Plan:						
Reissued	(11,900)	(159,117)	(20,345)	(270,021)	(1,400)	(20,048)
Reacquired	7,634	128,490	5,775	64,790	2,365	35,488
Net shares reissued in connection with:						
Stock Option Plan	(47,475)	(597,823)	(155,820)	(2,141,247)	–	–
Conditional Stock Grant	–	–	(36,242)	(592,801)	(22,929)	(317,887)
Balance, end of year	1,012,798	$ 12,538,632	1,064,539	$ 13,167,082	1,271,171	$ 16,106,361
Management Stock Purchase Plan Receivables and Deferrals:						
Balance, beginning of year		$ 553,862		$ 372,532		$ 475,470
Common stock issued		176,092		323,787		15,837
Common stock repurchased		(98,861)		(60,083)		(29,904)
Note payments and amortization of deferred compensation		(81,749)		(82,374)		(88,871)
Balance, end of year		$ 549,344		$ 553,862		$ 372,532

See accompanying notes to consolidated financial statements.

Harley-Davidson

CONSOLIDATED STATEMENTS *of* INCOME

(In thousands, except per share amounts) Years ended December 31,	**2002**	2001	2000
Net revenue	**$4,090,970**	$3,406,786	$2,943,346
Cost of goods sold	**2,673,129**	2,253,815	1,979,572
Gross profit	**1,417,841**	1,152,971	963,774
Financial services income	**211,500**	181,545	140,135
Financial services expense	**107,273**	120,272	102,957
Operating income from financial services	**104,227**	61,273	37,178
Selling, administrative and engineering expense	**(639,366)**	(551,743)	(485,980)
Income from operations	**882,702**	662,501	514,972
Gain on sale of credit card business	—	—	18,915
Interest income, net	**16,541**	17,478	17,583
Other, net	**(13,416)**	(6,524)	(2,914)
Income before provision for income taxes	**885,827**	673,455	548,556
Provision for income taxes	**305,610**	235,709	200,843
Net income	**$ 580,217**	$ 437,746	$ 347,713
Basic earnings per common share	**$1.92**	$1.45	$ 1.15
Diluted earnings per common share	**$1.90**	$1.43	$ 1.13
Cash dividends per common share	**$ .14**	$ .12	$ .10

The accompanying notes are an integral part of the consolidated financial statements.

REPORT *of* ERNST & YOUNG LLP, INDEPENDENT AUDITORS

We have audited the accompanying consolidated balance sheets of Harley-Davidson, Inc. as of December 31, 2002 and 2001, and the related consolidated statements of income, shareholders' equity and cash flows for each of the three years in the period ended December 31, 2002. These financial statements are the responsibility of the Company's management. Our responsibility is to express an opinion on these financial statements based on our audits.

We conducted our audits in accordance with auditing standards generally accepted in the United States. Those standards require that we plan and perform the audit to obtain reasonable assurance about whether the financial statements are free of material misstatement. An audit includes examining, on a test basis, evidence supporting the amounts and disclosures in the financial statements. An audit also includes assessing the accounting principles used and significant estimates made by management, as well as evaluating the overall financial statement presentation. We believe that our audits provide a reasonable basis for our opinion.

In our opinion, the consolidated financial statements referred to above present fairly, in all material respects, the consolidated financial position of Harley-Davidson, Inc. at December 31, 2002 and 2001, and the consolidated results of its operations and its cash flows for each of the three years in the period ended December 31, 2002, in conformity with accounting principles generally accepted in the United States.

As discussed in Note 1 to the consolidated financial statements, on January 1, 2002, the Company changed its method of accounting for goodwill.

Ernst & Young LLP

Milwaukee, Wisconsin
January 16, 2003

HARLEY-DAVIDSON

CONSOLIDATED BALANCE SHEETS

(In thousands, except share amounts) December 31,	**2002**	2001
ASSETS		
Current assets:		
Cash and cash equivalents	**$ 280,928**	$ 439,438
Marketable securities	**514,800**	196,011
Accounts receivable, net	**108,694**	118,843
Current portion of finance receivables, net	**855,771**	656,421
Inventories	**218,156**	181,115
Deferred income taxes	**41,430**	38,993
Prepaid expenses & other current assets	**46,807**	34,443
Total current assets	**2,066,586**	1,665,264
Finance receivables, net	**589,809**	379,335
Property, plant, and equipment, net	**1,032,596**	891,820
Goodwill, net	**49,930**	49,711
Other assets	**122,296**	132,365
	$3,861,217	$3,118,495
LIABILITIES *and* SHAREHOLDERS' EQUITY		
Current liabilities:		
Accounts payable	**$ 226,977**	$ 194,683
Accrued expenses and other liabilities	**380,496**	304,376
Current portion of finance debt	**382,579**	217,051
Total current liabilities	**990,052**	716,110
Finance debt	**380,000**	380,000
Other long-term liabilities	**123,353**	158,374
Postretirement health care benefits	**105,419**	89,912
Deferred income taxes	**29,478**	17,816
Commitments and contingencies (Note 7)		
Shareholders' equity:		
Series A Junior participating preferred stock, none issued	**—**	—
Common stock, 325,298,404 and 324,340,432 shares issued in 2002 and 2001, respectively	**3,254**	3,242
Additional paid-in capital	**386,284**	359,165
Retained earnings	**2,372,095**	1,833,335
Accumulated other comprehensive loss	**(46,266)**	(13,728)
	2,715,367	2,182,014
Less:		
Treasury stock (22,636,295 and 21,550,923 shares in 2002 and 2001, respectively), at cost	**(482,360)**	(425,546)
Unearned compensation	**(92)**	(185)
Total shareholders' equity	**2,232,915**	1,756,283
	$3,861,217	$3,118,495

The accompanying notes are an integral part of the consolidated financial statements.

CONSOLIDATED STATEMENTS *of* SHAREHOLDERS' EQUITY

(In thousands, except share amounts)

	Common Stock	
	Issued Shares	Balance
BALANCE DECEMBER 31, 1999	**318,586,144**	**$3,184**
Comprehensive income:		
Net income	—	—
Other comprehensive income (loss):		
Foreign currency translation adjustment	—	—
Change in net unrealized gains on investment in retained securitization interests, net of taxes of $(3,759)	—	—
Minimum pension liability adjustment, net of tax benefit of $120	—	—
Comprehensive income		
Dividends	—	—
Repurchase of common stock	—	—
Amortization of unearned compensation	—	—
Exercise of stock options	2,599,423	26
Tax benefit of stock options	—	—
BALANCE DECEMBER 31, 2000	**321,185,567**	**$3,210**
Comprehensive income:		
Net income	—	—
Other comprehensive income (loss):		
Foreign currency translation adjustment	—	—
Change in net unrealized gains on investment in retained securitization interests, net of taxes of $(6,117)	—	—
Change in net unrealized gains on derivative financial instruments, net of taxes of $(407)	—	—
Minimum pension liability adjustment, net of tax benefit of $11,515	—	—
Comprehensive income		
Dividends	—	—
Repurchase of common stock	—	—
Amortization of unearned compensation	—	—
Exercise of stock options	3,154,865	32
Tax benefit of stock options	—	—
BALANCE DECEMBER 31, 2001	**324,340,432**	**$3,242**
Comprehensive income:		
Net income	—	—
Other comprehensive income (loss):		
Foreign currency translation adjustment	—	—
Change in net unrealized gains on investment in retained securitization interests, net of taxes of $(6,113)	—	—
Change in net unrealized losses on derivative financial instruments, net of tax benefit of $5,929	—	—
Change in net unrealized gains on marketable securities, net of taxes of $(377)	—	—
Minimum pension liability adjustment, net of tax benefit of $29,896	—	—
Comprehensive income		
Dividends	—	—
Repurchase of common stock	—	—
Amortization of unearned compensation	—	—
Exercise of stock options	957,972	12
Tax benefit of stock options	—	—
BALANCE DECEMBER 31, 2002	**325,298,404**	**$3,254**

The accompanying notes are an integral part of the consolidated financial statements.

CONSOLIDATED STATEMENTS *of* SHAREHOLDERS' EQUITY

Additional Paid-In Capital	Retained Earnings	Other Comprehensive Income (Loss)	Treasury Balance	Unearned Compensation	Total
$234,948	**$ 1,113,376**	**$ (2,067)**	**$ (187,992)**	**$(369)**	**$ 1,161,080**
—	347,713	—	—	—	347,713
—	—	(4,383)	—	—	(4,383)
—	—	6,981	—	—	6,981
—	—	(223)	—	—	(223)
					350,088
—	(30,072)	—	—	—	(30,072)
—	—	—	(126,002)	—	(126,002)
—	—	—	—	93	93
14,566	—	—	—	—	14,592
35,876	—	—	—	—	35,876
$285,390	**$ 1,431,017**	**$ 308**	**$ (313,994)**	**$(276)**	**$1,405,655**
—	437,746	—	—	—	437,746
—	—	(6,143)	—	—	(6,143)
—	—	11,115	—	—	11,115
—	—	668	—	—	668
—	—	(19,676)	—	—	(19,676)
					423,710
—	(35,428)	—	—	—	(35,428)
—	—	—	(111,552)	—	(111,552)
—	—	—	—	91	91
28,807	—	—	—	—	28,839
44,968	—	—	—	—	44,968
$ 359,165	**$ 1,833,335**	**$ (13,728)**	**$(425,546)**	**$ (185)**	**$1,756,283**
—	580,217	—	—	—	580,217
—	—	14,545	—	—	14,545
—	—	11,108	—	—	11,108
—	—	(9,824)	—	—	(9,824)
—	—	618	—	—	618
—	—	(48,985)	—	—	(48,985)
					547,679
—	(41,457)	—	—	—	(41,457)
—	—	—	(56,814)	—	(56,814)
—	—	—	—	93	93
12,667	—	—	—	—	12,679
14,452	—	—	—	—	14,452
$386,284	**$2,372,095**	**$(46,266)**	**$(482,360)**	**$ (92)**	**$2,232,915**

HARLEY-DAVIDSON

CONSOLIDATED STATEMENTS *of* CASH FLOWS

(In thousands) Years ended December 31,	**2002**	2001	2000
Cash flows from operating activities:			
Net income	**$ 580,217**	$ 437,746	$ 347,713
Adjustments to reconcile net income to net cash provided by operating activities:			
Depreciation and amortization	**175,778**	153,061	133,348
Gain on sale of credit card business	**—**	—	(18,915)
Tax benefit from the exercise of stock options	**14,452**	44,968	35,876
Provision for finance credit losses	**6,167**	22,178	9,919
Deferred income taxes	**38,560**	(3,539)	1,363
Long-term employee benefits	**57,124**	40,882	17,433
Contributions to pension plans	**(153,636)**	(19,294)	(12,802)
Other	**7,057**	3,045	1,800
Net changes in current assets and current liabilities	**53,827**	77,761	49,609
Total adjustments	**199,329**	319,062	217,631
Net cash provided by operating activities	**779,546**	756,808	565,344
Cash flows from investing activities:			
Capital expenditures	**(323,866)**	(290,381)	(203,611)
Finance receivables acquired or originated	**(5,611,217)**	(4,387,371)	(3,556,195)
Finance receivables collected	**3,933,125**	3,123,941	2,727,746
Finance receivables sold	**1,279,324**	987,676	723,928
Net proceeds from sale of credit card business	**—**	—	170,146
Purchase of marketable securities	**(1,508,285)**	(247,989)	—
Sales and redemptions of marketable securities	**1,190,114**	51,978	—
Purchase of Italian distributor	**—**	(1,873)	(18,777)
Other, net	**22,813**	(7,488)	(14,124)
Net cash used in investing activities	**(1,017,992)**	(771,507)	(170,887)
Cash flows from financing activities:			
Net increase (decrease) in finance debt	**165,528**	152,542	(16,654)
Dividends paid	**(41,457)**	(35,428)	(30,072)
Purchase of common stock for treasury	**(56,814)**	(111,552)	(126,002)
Issuance of common stock under employee stock option plans	**12,679**	28,839	14,592
Net cash provided by (used in) financing activities	**79,936**	34,401	(158,136)
Net (decrease) increase in cash and cash equivalents	**(158,510)**	19,702	236,321
Cash and cash equivalents:			
At beginning of year	**439,438**	419,736	183,415
At end of year	**$ 280,928**	$ 439,438	$ 419,736

The accompanying notes are an integral part of the consolidated financial statements.

HARLEY-DAVIDSON

Appendix

Present and Future Values in Accounting

Learning Objectives

CAP

Conceptual

C1 Describe the earning of interest and the concepts of present and future values. *(p. B-2)*

Procedural

P1 Apply present value concepts to a single amount by using interest tables. *(p. B-3)*

P2 Apply future value concepts to a single amount by using interest tables. *(p. B-5)*

P3 Apply present value concepts to an annuity by using interest tables. *(p. B-6)*

P4 Apply future value concepts to an annuity by using interest tables. *(p. B-7)*

The concepts of present and future values are important to modern business activity. The purpose of this appendix is to explain, illustrate, and compute present and future values. This appendix applies these concepts with reference to both business and everyday activities.

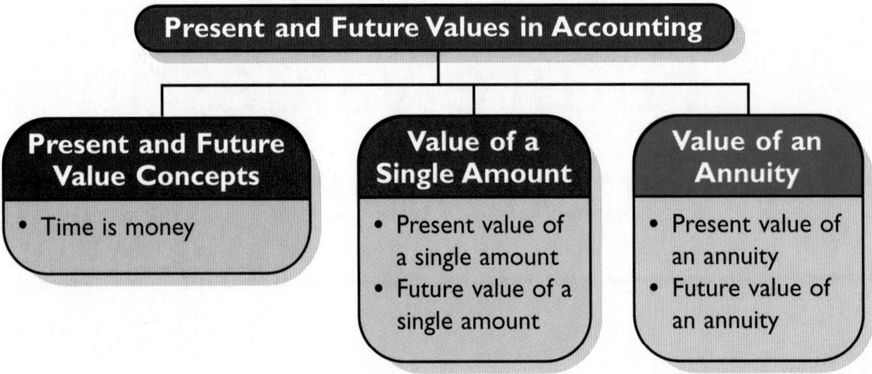

Present and Future Value Concepts

The old saying "Time is money" reflects the notion that as time passes, the values of our assets and liabilities change. This change is due to *interest,* which is a borrower's payment to the owner of an asset for its use. The most common example of interest is a savings account asset. As we keep a balance of cash in the account, it earns interest that the financial institution pays us. An example of a liability is a car loan. As we carry the balance of the loan, we accumulate interest costs on it. We must ultimately repay this loan with interest.

C1 Describe the earning of interest and the concepts of present and future values.

Present and future value computations enable us to measure or estimate the interest component of holding assets or liabilities over time. The present value computation is important when we want to know the value of future-day assets *today.* The future value computation is important when we want to know the value of present-day assets *at a future date.* The first section focuses on the present value of a single amount. The second section focuses on the future value of a single amount. Then both the present and future values of a series of amounts (called an *annuity*) are defined and explained.

Present Value of a Single Amount

We graphically express the present value, called p, of a single future amount, called f, that is received or paid at a future date in Exhibit B.1.

Exhibit B.1

Present Value of a Single Amount Diagram

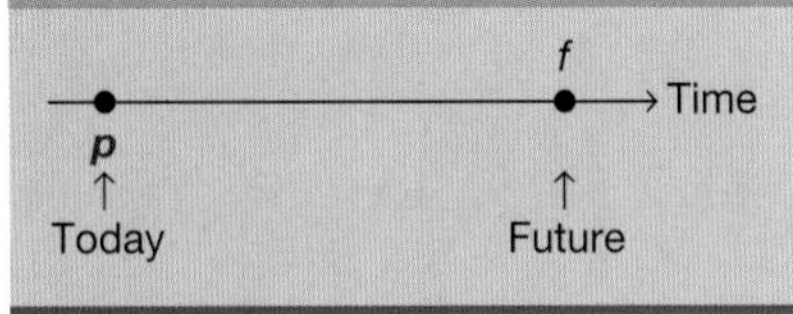

The formula to compute the present value of a single amount is shown in Exhibit B.2, where p = present value; f = future value; i = rate of interest per period; and n = number of periods. (Interest is also called the *discount,* and an interest rate is also called the *discount rate.*)

Exhibit B.2

Present Value of a Single Amount Formula

$$p = \frac{f}{(1 + i)^n}$$

To illustrate present value concepts, assume that we need \$220 one period from today. We want to know how much we must invest now, for one period, at an interest rate of 10% to provide for this \$220. For this illustration, the p, or present value, is the unknown amount—the specifics are shown graphically as follows:

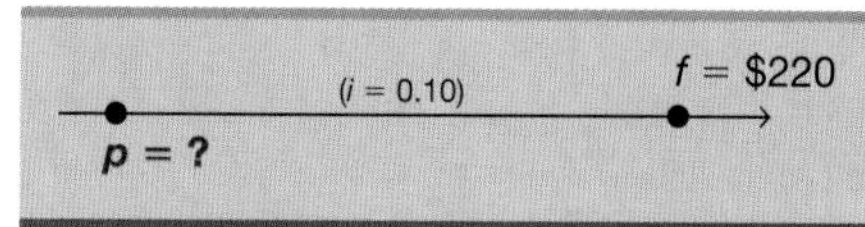

Conceptually, we know p must be less than \$220. This is obvious from the answer to this question: Would we rather have \$220 today or \$220 at some future date? If we had \$220 today, we could invest it and see it grow to something more than \$220 in the future. Therefore, we would prefer the \$220 today. This means that if we were promised \$220 in the future, we would take less than \$220 today. But how much less? To answer that question, we compute an estimate of the present value of the \$220 to be received one period from now using the formula in Exhibit B.2 as follows:

$$p = \frac{f}{(1 + i)^n} = \frac{\$220}{(1 + 0.10)^1} = \$200$$

We interpret this result to say that given an interest rate of 10%, we are indifferent between \$200 today or \$220 at the end of one period.

We can also use this formula to compute the present value for *any number of periods.* To illustrate, consider a payment of \$242 at the end of two periods at 10% interest. The present value of this \$242 to be received two periods from now is computed as follows:

$$p = \frac{f}{(1 + i)^n} = \frac{\$242}{(1 + 0.10)^2} = \$200$$

Together, these results tell us we are indifferent between \$200 today, or \$220 one period from today, or \$242 two periods from today given a 10% interest rate per period.

I will pay your allowance at the end of the month. Do you want to wait or receive its present value today?

The number of periods (n) in the present value formula does not have to be expressed in years. Any period of time such as a day, a month, a quarter, or a year can be used. Whatever period is used, the interest rate (i) must be compounded for the same period. This means that if a situation expresses n in months and i equals 12% per year, then i is transformed into interest earned per month (or 1%). In this case, interest is said to be *compounded monthly.*

A present value table helps us with present value computations. It gives us present values (factors) for a variety of both interest rates (i) and periods (n). Each present value in a present value table assumes that the future value (f) equals 1. When the future value (f) is different from 1, we simply multiply the present value (p) from the table by that future value to give us the estimate. The formula used to construct a table of present values for a single future amount of 1 is shown in Exhibit B.3.

$$p = \frac{1}{(1 + i)^n}$$

Exhibit B.3

Present Value of 1 Formula

This formula is identical to that in Exhibit B.2 except that f equals 1. Table B.1 at the end of this appendix is such a present value table. It is often called a **present value of 1 table.** A present value table involves three factors: p, i, and n. Knowing two of these three factors allows us to compute the third. (A fourth is f, but as already explained, we need only multiply the 1 used in the formula by f.) To illustrate the use of a present value table, consider three cases.

P1 Apply present value concepts to a single amount by using interest tables.

Case 1 (solve for p when knowing i and n). To show how we use a present value table, let's look again at how we estimate the present value of \$220 (the f value) at the end of one period ($n = 1$) where the interest rate (i) is 10%. To solve this case, we go to the present value table (Table B.1) and look in the row for 1 period and in the column for 10% interest. Here we find a present value (p) of 0.9091 based on a future value of 1. This means, for instance, that \$1 to be received one period from today at 10% interest is worth \$0.9091 today. Since the future value in this case is not \$1 but \$220, we multiply the 0.9091 by \$220 to get an answer of \$200.

Case 2 (solve for n when knowing p and i). To illustrate, assume a \$100,000 future value (f) that is worth \$13,000 today (p) using an interest rate of 12% (i) but where n is unknown. In particular, we want to know how many periods (n) there are between the present value and the future value. To put this in context, it would fit a situation in which we want to retire with \$100,000 but currently have only \$13,000 that is earning a 12% return. How long will it be before we can retire? To answer this, we go to Table B.1 and look in the 12% interest column. Here we find a column of present values (p) based on a future value of 1. To use the present value table for this solution, we must divide \$13,000 (p) by \$100,000 (f), which equals 0.1300. This is necessary because *a present value table defines* f *equal to 1, and* p *as a fraction of 1*. We look for a value nearest to 0.1300 (p), which we find in the row for 18 periods (n). This means that the present value of \$100,000 at the end of 18 periods at 12% interest is \$13,000 or, alternatively stated, we must work 18 more years.

Decision Insight

Keep That Job Lottery winners often never work again. Kenny Dukes, a recent Georgia lottery winner, doesn't have that option. He is serving parole for burglary charges, and Georgia requires its parolees to be employed (or in school). Dukes had to choose between \$31 million in 30 annual payments or \$16 million in one lump sum (\$10.6 million after-tax); he chose the latter.

Case 3 (solve for i when knowing p and n). In this case, we have, say, a \$120,000 future value (f) worth \$60,000 today (p) when there are nine periods (n) between the present and future values, but the interest rate is unknown. As an example, suppose we want to retire with \$120,000, but we have only \$60,000 and hope to retire in nine years. What interest rate must we earn to retire with \$120,000 in nine years? To answer this, we go to the present value table (Table B.1) and look in the row for nine periods. To use the present value table, we must divide \$60,000 (p) by \$120,000 (f), which equals 0.5000. Recall that this step is necessary because a present value table defines f equal to 1 and p as a fraction of 1. We look for a value in the row for nine periods that is nearest to 0.5000 (p), which we find in the column for 8% interest (i). This means that the present value of \$120,000 at the end of nine periods at 8% interest is \$60,000 or, in our example, we must earn 8% annual interest to retire in nine years.

Quick Check

1. A company is considering an investment expected to yield \$70,000 after six years. If this company demands an 8% return, how much is it willing to pay for this investment?

Answer—p. B-8

Future Value of a Single Amount

We must modify the formula for the present value of a single amount to obtain the formula for the future value of a single amount. In particular, we multiply both sides of the equation in Exhibit B.2 by $(1 + i)^n$ to get the result shown in Exhibit B.4.

Exhibit B.4

Future Value of a Single Amount Formula

$$f = p \times (1 + i)^n$$

The future value (f) is defined in terms of p, i, and n. We can use this formula to determine that \$200 (p) invested for 1 (n) period at an interest rate of 10% (i) yields a future value of \$220 as follows:

$$
\begin{aligned}
f &= p \times (1 + i)^n \\
&= \$200 \times (1 + 0.10)^1 \\
&= \$220
\end{aligned}
$$

This formula can also be used to compute the future value of an amount for *any number of periods* into the future. To illustrate, assume that \$200 is invested for three periods at 10%. The future value of this \$200 is \$266.20, computed as follows:

$$
\begin{aligned}
f &= p \times (1 + i)^n \\
&= \$200 \times (1 + 0.10)^3 \\
&= \$266.20
\end{aligned}
$$

A future value table makes it easier for us to compute future values (f) for many different combinations of interest rates (i) and time periods (n). Each future value in a future value table assumes the present value (p) is 1. As with a present value table, if the future amount is something other than 1, we simply multiply our answer by that amount. The formula used to construct a table of future values (factors) for a single amount of 1 is in Exhibit B.5.

P2 Apply future value concepts to a single amount by using interest tables.

Exhibit B.5

Future Value of 1 Formula

$$f = (1 + i)^n$$

Table B.2 at the end of this appendix shows a table of future values for a current amount of 1. This type of table is called a **future value of 1 table**.

There are some important relations between Tables B.1 and B.2. In Table B.2, for the row where $n = 0$, the future value is 1 for each interest rate. This is so because no interest is earned when time does not pass. Also notice that Tables B.1 and B.2 report the same information but in a different manner. In particular, one table is simply the *inverse* of the other. To illustrate this inverse relation, let's say we invest \$100 annually for a period of five years at 12% per year. How much do we expect to have after five years? We can answer this question using Table B.2 by finding the future value (f) of 1, for five periods from now, compounded at 12%. From that table we find $f = 1.7623$. If we start with \$100, the amount it accumulates to after five years is \$176.23 (\$100 × 1.7623). We can alternatively use Table B.1. Here we find that the present value (p) of 1, discounted five periods at 12%, is 0.5674. Recall the inverse relation between present value and future value. This means that $p = 1/f$ (or equivalently, $f = 1/p$). We can compute the future value of \$100 invested for five periods at 12% as follows: $f = \$100 \times (1/0.5674) = \$176.24$.

A future value table involves three factors: f, i, and n. Knowing two of these three factors allows us to compute the third. To illustrate, consider these three possible cases.

Case 1 (solve for f when knowing i and n). Our preceding example fits this case. We found that \$100 invested for five periods at 12% interest accumulates to \$176.24.

Case 2 (solve for n when knowing f and i). In this case, we have, say, \$2,000 (p) and we want to know how many periods (n) it will take to accumulate to \$3,000 (f) at 7% (i) interest. To answer this, we go to the future value table (Table B.2) and look in the 7% interest column. Here we find a column of future values (f) based on a present value of 1. To use a future value table, we must divide \$3,000 (f) by \$2,000 (p), which equals 1.500. This is necessary because *a future value table defines* p *equal to 1, and* f *as a multiple of 1*. We look for a value nearest to 1.50 (f), which we find in the row for six periods (n). This means that \$2,000 invested for six periods at 7% interest accumulates to \$3,000.

Case 3 (solve for i when knowing f and n). In this case, we have, say, \$2,001 (p) and in nine years (n), we want to have \$4,000 (f). What rate of interest must we earn to accomplish this? To answer that, we go to Table B.2 and search in the row for nine periods. To use a future value table, we must divide \$4,000 (f) by \$2,001 (p), which equals 1.9990. Recall that this is necessary because a future value table defines p equal to 1 and f as a multiple of 1. We look for a value nearest to 1.9990 (f), which we find in the column for 8% interest (i). This means that \$2,001 invested for nine periods at 8% interest accumulates to \$4,000.

Quick Check

2. Assume that you win a $150,000 cash sweepstakes. You decide to deposit this cash in an account earning 8% annual interest, and you plan to quit your job when the account equals $555,000. How many years will it be before you can quit working?

Answer—p. B-8

Present Value of an Annuity

An *annuity* is a series of equal payments occurring at equal intervals. One example is a series of three annual payments of $100 each. An *ordinary annuity* is defined as equal end-of-period payments at equal intervals. An ordinary annuity of $100 for 3 periods and its present value (p) are illustrated in Exhibit B.6.

Exhibit B.6

Present Value of an Ordinary Annuity Diagram

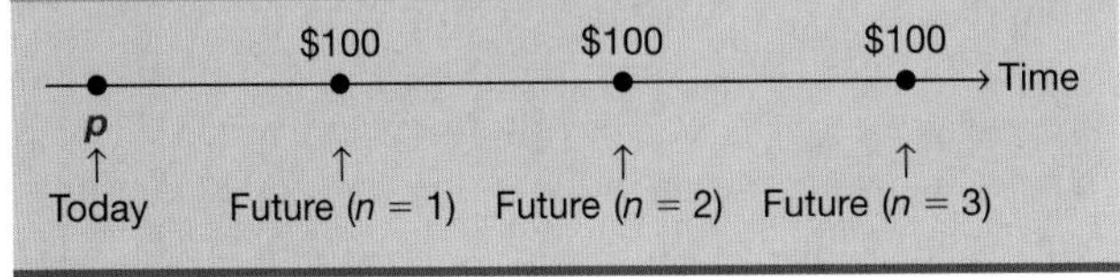

P3 Apply present value concepts to an annuity by using interest tables.

One way to compute the present value of an ordinary annuity is to find the present value of each payment using our present value formula from Exhibit B.3. We then add each of the three present values. To illustrate, let's look at three $100 payments at the end of each of the next three periods with an interest rate of 15%. Our present value computations are

$$p = \frac{\$100}{(1 + 0.15)^1} + \frac{\$100}{(1 + 0.15)^2} + \frac{\$100}{(1 + 0.15)^3} = \$228.32$$

This computation is identical to computing the present value of each payment (from Table B.1) and taking their sum or, alternatively, adding the values from Table B.1 for each of the three payments and multiplying their sum by the $100 annuity payment.

A more direct way is to use a present value of annuity table. Table B.3 at the end of this appendix is one such table. This table is called a **present value of an annuity of 1 table.** If we look at Table B.3 where $n = 3$ and $i = 15\%$, we see the present value is 2.2832. This means that the present value of an annuity of 1 for three periods, with a 15% interest rate, equals 2.2832.

Decision Insight

Aw-Shucks "I don't have good luck—I'm blessed," proclaimed Andrew "Jack" Whittaker, 55, a sewage treatment contractor, after winning the largest-ever, undivided jackpot in a U.S. lottery. Whittaker had to choose between $315 million in 30 annual installments or $170 million in one lump sum ($112 million after-tax). Says Whittaker, "My biggest problem is to keep my daughter and granddaughter from spending all their money in one week."

A present value of an annuity formula is used to construct Table B.3. It can also be constructed by adding the amounts in a present value of 1 table. To illustrate, we use Table B.1 and B.3 to confirm this relation for the prior example:

From Table B.1		From Table B.3	
i = 15%, n = 1	0.8696		
i = 15%, n = 2	0.7561		
i = 15%, n = 3	0.6575		
Total	2.2832	i = 15%, n = 3	2.2832

We can also use business calculators or spreadsheet programs to find the present value of an annuity.

Quick Check

3. A company is considering an investment paying $10,000 every six months for three years. The first payment would be received in six months. If this company requires an 8% annual return, what is the maximum amount it is willing to pay for this investment?

Answer—p. B-8

Future Value of an Annuity

The future value of an *ordinary annuity* is the accumulated value of each annuity payment with interest as of the date of the final payment. To illustrate, let's consider the earlier annuity of three annual payments of $100. Exhibit B.7 shows the point in time for the future value (f). The first payment is made two periods prior to the point when future value is determined, and the final payment occurs on the future value date.

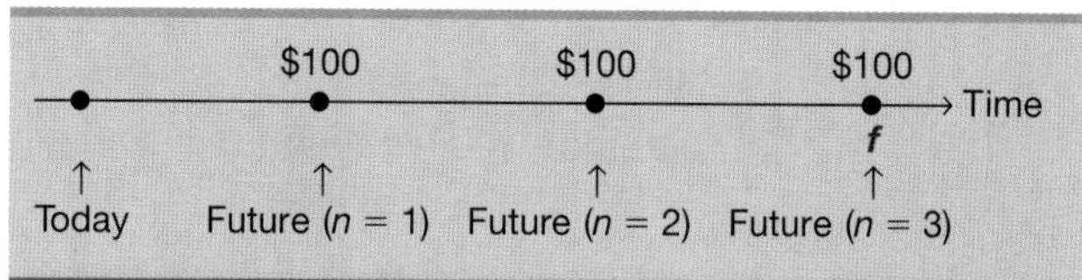

Exhibit B.7

Future Value of an Ordinary Annuity Diagram

One way to compute the future value of an annuity is to use the formula to find the future value of *each* payment and add them. If we assume an interest rate of 15%, our calculation is

$$f = \$100 \times (1 + 0.15)^2 + \$100 \times (1 + 0.15)^1 + \$100 \times (1 + 0.15)^0 = \$347.25$$

This is identical to using Table B.2 and summing the future values of each payment, or by adding the future values of the three payments of 1 and multiplying the sum by $100.

A more direct way is to use a table showing future values of annuities. Such a table is called a **future value of an annuity of 1 table**. Table B.4 at the end of this appendix is one such table. Note that in Table B.4 when $n = 1$, the future values equal 1 ($f = 1$) for all rates of interest. This is so because such an annuity consists of only one payment and the future value is determined on the date of that payment—no time passes between the payment and its future value. The future value of an annuity formula is used to construct Table B.4. We can also construct it by adding the amounts from a future value of 1 table. To illustrate, we use Tables B.2 and B.4 to confirm this relation for the prior example:

P4 Apply future value concepts to an annuity by using interest tables.

From Table B.2		From Table B.4	
i = 15%, n = 0	1.0000		
i = 15%, n = 1	1.1500		
i = 15%, n = 2	1.3225		
Total	3.4725	i = 15%, n = 3	3.4725

Note that the future value in Table B.2 is 1.0000 when $n = 0$, but the future value in Table B.4 is 1.0000 when $n = 1$. Is this a contradiction? No. When $n = 0$ in Table B.2, the future value is determined on the date when a single payment occurs. This means that no interest is earned because no time has passed, and the future value equals the payment. Table B.4 describes annuities with equal payments occurring at the end of each period. When $n = 1$, the annuity has one payment, and its future value equals 1 on the date of its final and only payment. Again, no time passes from the payment and its future value date.

Quick Check

4. A company invests $45,000 per year for five years at 12% annual interest. Compute the value of this annuity investment at the end of five years.

Answer—p. B-8

Summary

C1 Describe the earning of interest and the concepts of present and future values. Interest is payment by a borrower to the owner of an asset for its use. Present and future value computations are a way for us to estimate the interest component of holding assets or liabilities over a period of time.

P1 Apply present value concepts to a single amount by using interest tables. The present value of a single amount received at a future date is the amount that can be invested now at the specified interest rate to yield that future value.

P2 Apply future value concepts to a single amount by using interest tables. The future value of a single amount invested at a specified rate of interest is the amount that would accumulate by the future date.

P3 Apply present value concepts to an annuity by using interest tables. The present value of an annuity is the amount that can be invested now at the specified interest rate to yield that series of equal periodic payments.

P4 Apply future value concepts to an annuity by using interest tables. The future value of an annuity invested at a specific rate of interest is the amount that would accumulate by the date of the final payment.

Guidance Answers to Quick Checks

1. $70,000 × 0.6302 = $44,114 (use Table B.1, $i = 8\%$, $n = 6$).
2. $555,000/$150,000 = 3.7000; Table B.2 shows this value is not achieved until after 17 years at 8% interest.
3. $10,000 × 5.2421 = $52,421 (use Table B.3, $i = 4\%$, $n = 6$).
4. $45,000 × 6.3528 = $285,876 (use Table B.4, $i = 12\%$, $n = 5$).

Homework Manager *repeats all numerical Quick Studies on the book's Website with new numbers.*

QS B-1
Identifying interest rates in tables
C1

Assume that you must make future value estimates using the *future value of 1 table* (Table B.2). Which interest rate column do you use when working with the following rates?

1. 8% compounded quarterly
2. 12% compounded annually
3. 6% compounded semiannually
4. 12% compounded monthly

QS B-2
Interest rate on an investment P1

Ken Francis is offered the possibility of investing $2,745 today and in return to receive $10,000 after 15 years. What is the annual rate of interest for this investment? (Use Table B.1.)

QS B-3
Number of periods of an investment P1

Megan Brink is offered the possibility of investing $6,651 today at 6% interest per year in a desire to accumulate $10,000. How many years must Brink wait to accumulate $10,000? (Use Table B.1.)

QS B-4
Present value of an amount P1

Flaherty is considering an investment that, if paid for immediately, is expected to return $140,000 five years from now. If Flaherty demands a 9% return, how much is she willing to pay for this investment?

CII, Inc., invests $630,000 in a project expected to earn a 12% annual rate of return. The earnings will be reinvested in the project each year until the entire investment is liquidated 10 years later. What will the cash proceeds be when the project is liquidated?

QS B-5
Future value of an amount P2

Beene Distributing is considering a project that will return $150,000 annually at the end of each year for six years. If Beene demands an annual return of 7% and pays for the project immediately, how much is it willing to pay for the project?

QS B-6
Present value of an annuity P3

Claire Fitch is planning to begin an individual retirement program in which she will invest $1,500 at the end of each year. Fitch plans to retire after making 30 annual investments in the program earning a return of 10%. What is the value of the program on the date of the last payment?

QS B-7
Future value of an annuity P4

Homework Manager *repeats all numerical Exercises on the book's Website with new numbers.*

EXERCISES

Bill Thompson expects to invest $10,000 at 12% and, at the end of a certain period, receive $96,463. How many years will it be before Thompson receives the payment? (Use Table B.2.)

Exercise B-1
Number of periods of an investment P2

Ed Summers expects to invest $10,000 for 25 years, after which he wants to receive $108,347. What rate of interest must Summers earn? (Use Table B.2.)

Exercise B-2
Interest rate on an investment P2

Jones expects an immediate investment of $57,466 to return $10,000 annually for eight years, with the first payment to be received one year from now. What rate of interest must Jones earn? (Use Table B.3.)

Exercise B-3
Interest rate on an investment P3

Keith Riggins expects an investment of $82,014 to return $10,000 annually for several years. If Riggins earns a return of 10%, how many annual payments will he receive? (Use Table B.3.)

Exercise B-4
Number of periods of an investment P3

Algoe expects to invest $1,000 annually for 40 years to yield an accumulated value of $154,762 on the date of the last investment. For this to occur, what rate of interest must Algoe earn? (Use Table B.4.)

Exercise B-5
Interest rate on an investment P4

Kate Beckwith expects to invest $10,000 annually that will earn 8%. How many annual investments must Beckwith make to accumulate $303,243 on the date of the last investment? (Use Table B.4.)

Exercise B-6
Number of periods of an investment P4

Sam Weber finances a new automobile by paying $6,500 cash and agreeing to make 40 monthly payments of $500 each, the first payment to be made one month after the purchase. The loan bears interest at an annual rate of 12%. What is the cost of the automobile?

Exercise B-7
Present value of an annuity P3

Spiller Corp. plans to issue 10%, 15-year, $500,000 par value bonds payable that pay interest semiannually on June 30 and December 31. The bonds are dated December 31, 2005, and are issued on that date. If the market rate of interest for the bonds is 8% on the date of issue, what will be the total cash proceeds from the bond issue?

Exercise B-8
Present value of bonds
P1 P3

McAdams Company expects to earn 10% per year on an investment that will pay $606,773 six years from now. Use Table B.1 to compute the present value of this investment.

Exercise B-9
Present value of an amount P1

Exercise B-10
Present value of an amount and of an annuity P1 P3

Compute the amount that can be borrowed under each of the following circumstances:

1. A promise to repay $90,000 seven years from now at an interest rate of 6%.

2. An agreement made on February 1, 2005, to make three separate payments of $20,000 on February 1 of 2006, 2007, and 2008. The annual interest rate is 10%.

Exercise B-11
Present value of an amount P1

On January 1, 2005, a company agrees to pay $20,000 in three years. If the annual interest rate is 10%, determine how much cash the company can borrow with this agreement.

Exercise B-12
Present value of an amount P1

Find the amount of money that can be borrowed today with each of the following separate debt agreements *a* through *f*:

Case	Single Future Payment	Number of Periods	Interest Rate
a.	$40,000	3	4%
b.	75,000	7	8
c.	52,000	9	10
d.	18,000	2	4
e.	63,000	8	6
f.	89,000	5	2

Exercise B-13
Present values of annuities
P3

C&H Ski Club recently borrowed money and agrees to pay it back with a series of six annual payments of $5,000 each. C&H subsequently borrows more money and agrees to pay it back with a series of four annual payments of $7,500 each. The annual interest rate for both loans is 6%.

1. Use Table B.1 to find the present value of these two separate annuities. (Round amounts to the nearest dollar.)

2. Use Table B.3 to find the present value of these two separate annuities.

Exercise B-14
Present value with semiannual compounding
C1 P3

Otto Co. borrows money on April 30, 2005, by promising to make four payments of $13,000 each on November 1, 2005; May 1, 2006; November 1, 2006; and May 1, 2007.

1. How much money is Otto able to borrow if the interest rate is 8%, compounded semiannually?

2. How much money is Otto able to borrow if the interest rate is 12%, compounded semiannually?

3. How much money is Otto able to borrow if the interest rate is 16%, compounded semiannually?

Exercise B-15
Future value of an amount P2

Mark Welsch deposits $7,200 in an account that earns interest at an annual rate of 8%, compounded quarterly. The $7,200 plus earned interest must remain in the account 10 years before it can be withdrawn. How much money will be in the account at the end of 10 years?

Exercise B-16
Future value of an annuity P4

Kelly Malone plans to have $50 withheld from her monthly paycheck and deposited in a savings account that earns 12% annually, compounded monthly. If Malone continues with her plan for two and one-half years, how much will be accumulated in the account on the date of the last deposit?

Exercise B-17
Future value of an amount plus an annuity P2 P4

Starr Company decides to establish a fund that it will use 10 years from now to replace an aging production facility. The company will make a $100,000 initial contribution to the fund and plans to make quarterly contributions of $50,000 beginning in three months. The fund earns 12%, compounded quarterly. What will be the value of the fund 10 years from now?

Exercise B-18
Future value of an amount P2

Catten, Inc., invests $163,170 today earning 7% per year for nine years. Use Table B.2 to compute the future value of the investment nine years from now.

Exercise B-19
Using present and future value tables
C1 P1 P2 P3 P4

For each of the following situations, identify (1) the case as either (*a*) a present or a future value and (*b*) a single amount or an annuity, (2) the table you would use in your computations (but do not solve the problem), and (3) the interest rate and time periods you would use.

a. You need to accumulate $10,000 for a trip you wish to take in four years. You are able to earn 8% compounded semiannually on your savings. You plan to make only one deposit and let the money accumulate for four years. How would you determine the amount of the one-time deposit?

b. Assume the same facts as in part (*a*) except that you will make semiannual deposits to your savings account.

c. You want to retire after working 40 years with savings in excess of $1,000,000. You expect to save $4,000 a year for 40 years and earn an annual rate of interest of 8%. Will you be able to retire with more than $1,000,000 in 40 years? Explain.

d. A sweepstakes agency names you a grand prize winner. You can take $225,000 immediately or elect to receive annual installments of $30,000 for 20 years. You can earn 10% annually on any investments you make. Which prize do you choose to receive?

Table B.1

Present Value of 1

$$p = 1/(1 + i)^n$$

Periods	Rate 1%	2%	3%	4%	5%	6%	7%	8%	9%	10%	12%	15%
1	0.9901	0.9804	0.9709	0.9615	0.9524	0.9434	0.9346	0.9259	0.9174	0.9091	0.8929	0.8696
2	0.9803	0.9612	0.9426	0.9246	0.9070	0.8900	0.8734	0.8573	0.8417	0.8264	0.7972	0.7561
3	0.9706	0.9423	0.9151	0.8890	0.8638	0.8396	0.8163	0.7938	0.7722	0.7513	0.7118	0.6575
4	0.9610	0.9238	0.8885	0.8548	0.8227	0.7921	0.7629	0.7350	0.7084	0.6830	0.6355	0.5718
5	0.9515	0.9057	0.8626	0.8219	0.7835	0.7473	0.7130	0.6806	0.6499	0.6209	0.5674	0.4972
6	0.9420	0.8880	0.8375	0.7903	0.7462	0.7050	0.6663	0.6302	0.5963	0.5645	0.5066	0.4323
7	0.9327	0.8706	0.8131	0.7599	0.7107	0.6651	0.6227	0.5835	0.5470	0.5132	0.4523	0.3759
8	0.9235	0.8535	0.7894	0.7307	0.6768	0.6274	0.5820	0.5403	0.5019	0.4665	0.4039	0.3269
9	0.9143	0.8368	0.7664	0.7026	0.6446	0.5919	0.5439	0.5002	0.4604	0.4241	0.3606	0.2843
10	0.9053	0.8203	0.7441	0.6756	0.6139	0.5584	0.5083	0.4632	0.4224	0.3855	0.3220	0.2472
11	0.8963	0.8043	0.7224	0.6496	0.5847	0.5268	0.4751	0.4289	0.3875	0.3505	0.2875	0.2149
12	0.8874	0.7885	0.7014	0.6246	0.5568	0.4970	0.4440	0.3971	0.3555	0.3186	0.2567	0.1869
13	0.8787	0.7730	0.6810	0.6006	0.5303	0.4688	0.4150	0.3677	0.3262	0.2897	0.2292	0.1625
14	0.8700	0.7579	0.6611	0.5775	0.5051	0.4423	0.3878	0.3405	0.2992	0.2633	0.2046	0.1413
15	0.8613	0.7430	0.6419	0.5553	0.4810	0.4173	0.3624	0.3152	0.2745	0.2394	0.1827	0.1229
16	0.8528	0.7284	0.6232	0.5339	0.4581	0.3936	0.3387	0.2919	0.2519	0.2176	0.1631	0.1069
17	0.8444	0.7142	0.6050	0.5134	0.4363	0.3714	0.3166	0.2703	0.2311	0.1978	0.1456	0.0929
18	0.8360	0.7002	0.5874	0.4936	0.4155	0.3503	0.2959	0.2502	0.2120	0.1799	0.1300	0.0808
19	0.8277	0.6864	0.5703	0.4746	0.3957	0.3305	0.2765	0.2317	0.1945	0.1635	0.1161	0.0703
20	0.8195	0.6730	0.5537	0.4564	0.3769	0.3118	0.2584	0.2145	0.1784	0.1486	0.1037	0.0611
25	0.7798	0.6095	0.4776	0.3751	0.2953	0.2330	0.1842	0.1460	0.1160	0.0923	0.0588	0.0304
30	0.7419	0.5521	0.4120	0.3083	0.2314	0.1741	0.1314	0.0994	0.0754	0.0573	0.0334	0.0151
35	0.7059	0.5000	0.3554	0.2534	0.1813	0.1301	0.0937	0.0676	0.0490	0.0356	0.0189	0.0075
40	0.6717	0.4529	0.3066	0.2083	0.1420	0.0972	0.0668	0.0460	0.0318	0.0221	0.0107	0.0037

Table B.2

Future Value of 1

$$f = (1 + i)^n$$

Periods	Rate 1%	2%	3%	4%	5%	6%	7%	8%	9%	10%	12%	15%
0	1.0000	1.0000	1.0000	1.0000	1.0000	1.0000	1.0000	1.0000	1.0000	1.0000	1.0000	1.0000
1	1.0100	1.0200	1.0300	1.0400	1.0500	1.0600	1.0700	1.0800	1.0900	1.1000	1.1200	1.1500
2	1.0201	1.0404	1.0609	1.0816	1.1025	1.1236	1.1449	1.1664	1.1881	1.2100	1.2544	1.3225
3	1.0303	1.0612	1.0927	1.1249	1.1576	1.1910	1.2250	1.2597	1.2950	1.3310	1.4049	1.5209
4	1.0406	1.0824	1.1255	1.1699	1.2155	1.2625	1.3108	1.3605	1.4116	1.4641	1.5735	1.7490
5	1.0510	1.1041	1.1593	1.2167	1.2763	1.3382	1.4026	1.4693	1.5386	1.6105	1.7623	2.0114
6	1.0615	1.1262	1.1941	1.2653	1.3401	1.4185	1.5007	1.5869	1.6771	1.7716	1.9738	2.3131
7	1.0721	1.1487	1.2299	1.3159	1.4071	1.5036	1.6058	1.7138	1.8280	1.9487	2.2107	2.6600
8	1.0829	1.1717	1.2668	1.3686	1.4775	1.5938	1.7182	1.8509	1.9926	2.1436	2.4760	3.0590
9	1.0937	1.1951	1.3048	1.4233	1.5513	1.6895	1.8385	1.9990	2.1719	2.3579	2.7731	3.5179
10	1.1046	1.2190	1.3439	1.4802	1.6289	1.7908	1.9672	2.1589	2.3674	2.5937	3.1058	4.0456
11	1.1157	1.2434	1.3842	1.5395	1.7103	1.8983	2.1049	2.3316	2.5804	2.8531	3.4785	4.6524
12	1.1268	1.2682	1.4258	1.6010	1.7959	2.0122	2.2522	2.5182	2.8127	3.1384	3.8960	5.3503
13	1.1381	1.2936	1.4685	1.6651	1.8856	2.1329	2.4098	2.7196	3.0658	3.4523	4.3635	6.1528
14	1.1495	1.3195	1.5126	1.7317	1.9799	2.2609	2.5785	2.9372	3.3417	3.7975	4.8871	7.0757
15	1.1610	1.3459	1.5580	1.8009	2.0789	2.3966	2.7590	3.1722	3.6425	4.1772	5.4736	8.1371
16	1.1726	1.3728	1.6047	1.8730	2.1829	2.5404	2.9522	3.4259	3.9703	4.5950	6.1304	9.3576
17	1.1843	1.4002	1.6528	1.9479	2.2920	2.6928	3.1588	3.7000	4.3276	5.0545	6.8660	10.7613
18	1.1961	1.4282	1.7024	2.0258	2.4066	2.8543	3.3799	3.9960	4.7171	5.5599	7.6900	12.3755
19	1.2081	1.4568	1.7535	2.1068	2.5270	3.0256	3.6165	4.3157	5.1417	6.1159	8.6128	14.2318
20	1.2202	1.4859	1.8061	2.1911	2.6533	3.2071	3.8697	4.6610	5.6044	6.7275	9.6463	16.3665
25	1.2824	1.6406	2.0938	2.6658	3.3864	4.2919	5.4274	6.8485	8.6231	10.8347	17.0001	32.9190
30	1.3478	1.8114	2.4273	3.2434	4.3219	5.7435	7.6123	10.0627	13.2677	17.4494	29.9599	66.2118
35	1.4166	1.9999	2.8139	3.9461	5.5160	7.6861	10.6766	14.7853	20.4140	28.1024	52.7996	133.176
40	1.4889	2.2080	3.2620	4.8010	7.0400	10.2857	14.9745	21.7245	31.4094	45.2593	93.0510	267.864

$$p = \left[1 - \frac{1}{(1+i)^n}\right]/i$$

Table B.3

Present Value of an Annuity of 1

Periods	Rate 1%	2%	3%	4%	5%	6%	7%	8%	9%	10%	12%	15%
1	0.9901	0.9804	0.9709	0.9615	0.9524	0.9434	0.9346	0.9259	0.9174	0.9091	0.8929	0.8696
2	1.9704	1.9416	1.9135	1.8861	1.8594	1.8334	1.8080	1.7833	1.7591	1.7355	1.6901	1.6257
3	2.9410	2.8839	2.8286	2.7751	2.7232	2.6730	2.6243	2.5771	2.5313	2.4869	2.4018	2.2832
4	3.9020	3.8077	3.7171	3.6299	3.5460	3.4651	3.3872	3.3121	3.2397	3.1699	3.0373	2.8550
5	4.8534	4.7135	4.5797	4.4518	4.3295	4.2124	4.1002	3.9927	3.8897	3.7908	3.6048	3.3522
6	5.7955	5.6014	5.4172	5.2421	5.0757	4.9173	4.7665	4.6229	4.4859	4.3553	4.1114	3.7845
7	6.7282	6.4720	6.2303	6.0021	5.7864	5.5824	5.3893	5.2064	5.0330	4.8684	4.5638	4.1604
8	7.6517	7.3255	7.0197	6.7327	6.4632	6.2098	5.9713	5.7466	5.5348	5.3349	4.9676	4.4873
9	8.5660	8.1622	7.7861	7.4353	7.1078	6.8017	6.5152	6.2469	5.9952	5.7590	5.3282	4.7716
10	9.4713	8.9826	8.5302	8.1109	7.7217	7.3601	7.0236	6.7101	6.4177	6.1446	5.6502	5.0188
11	10.3676	9.7868	9.2526	8.7605	8.3064	7.8869	7.4987	7.1390	6.8052	6.4951	5.9377	5.2337
12	11.2551	10.5753	9.9540	9.3851	8.8633	8.3838	7.9427	7.5361	7.1607	6.8137	6.1944	5.4206
13	12.1337	11.3484	10.6350	9.9856	9.3936	8.8527	8.3577	7.9038	7.4869	7.1034	6.4235	5.5831
14	13.0037	12.1062	11.2961	10.5631	9.8986	9.2950	8.7455	8.2442	7.7862	7.3667	6.6282	5.7245
15	13.8651	12.8493	11.9379	11.1184	10.3797	9.7122	9.1079	8.5595	8.0607	7.6061	6.8109	5.8474
16	14.7179	13.5777	12.5611	11.6523	10.8378	10.1059	9.4466	8.8514	8.3126	7.8237	6.9740	5.9542
17	15.5623	14.2919	13.1661	12.1657	11.2741	10.4773	9.7632	9.1216	8.5436	8.0216	7.1196	6.0472
18	16.3983	14.9920	13.7535	12.6593	11.6896	10.8276	10.0591	9.3719	8.7556	8.2014	7.2497	6.1280
19	17.2260	15.6785	14.3238	13.1339	12.0853	11.1581	10.3356	9.6036	8.9501	8.3649	7.3658	6.1982
20	18.0456	16.3514	14.8775	13.5903	12.4622	11.4699	10.5940	9.8181	9.1285	8.5136	7.4694	6.2593
25	22.0232	19.5235	17.4131	15.6221	14.0939	12.7834	11.6536	10.6748	9.8226	9.0770	7.8431	6.4641
30	25.8077	22.3965	19.6004	17.2920	15.3725	13.7648	12.4090	11.2578	10.2737	9.4269	8.0552	6.5660
35	29.4086	24.9986	21.4872	18.6646	16.3742	14.4982	12.9477	11.6546	10.5668	9.6442	8.1755	6.6166
40	32.8347	27.3555	23.1148	19.7928	17.1591	15.0463	13.3317	11.9246	10.7574	9.7791	8.2438	6.6418

$$f = [(1+i)^n - 1]/i$$

Table B.4

Future Value of an Annuity of 1

Periods	Rate 1%	2%	3%	4%	5%	6%	7%	8%	9%	10%	12%	15%
1	1.0000	1.0000	1.0000	1.0000	1.0000	1.0000	1.0000	1.0000	1.0000	1.0000	1.0000	1.0000
2	2.0100	2.0200	2.0300	2.0400	2.0500	2.0600	2.0700	2.0800	2.0900	2.1000	2.1200	2.1500
3	3.0301	3.0604	3.0909	3.1216	3.1525	3.1836	3.2149	3.2464	3.2781	3.3100	3.3744	3.4725
4	4.0604	4.1216	4.1836	4.2465	4.3101	4.3746	4.4399	4.5061	4.5731	4.6410	4.7793	4.9934
5	5.1010	5.2040	5.3091	5.4163	5.5256	5.6371	5.7507	5.8666	5.9847	6.1051	6.3528	6.7424
6	6.1520	6.3081	6.4684	6.6330	6.8019	6.9753	7.1533	7.3359	7.5233	7.7156	8.1152	8.7537
7	7.2135	7.4343	7.6625	7.8983	8.1420	8.3938	8.6540	8.9228	9.2004	9.4872	10.0890	11.0668
8	8.2857	8.5830	8.8923	9.2142	9.5491	9.8975	10.2598	10.6366	11.0285	11.4359	12.2997	13.7268
9	9.3685	9.7546	10.1591	10.5828	11.0266	11.4913	11.9780	12.4876	13.0210	13.5795	14.7757	16.7858
10	10.4622	10.9497	11.4639	12.0061	12.5779	13.1808	13.8164	14.4866	15.1929	15.9374	17.5487	20.3037
11	11.5668	12.1687	12.8078	13.4864	14.2068	14.9716	15.7836	16.6455	17.5603	18.5312	20.6546	24.3493
12	12.6825	13.4121	14.1920	15.0258	15.9171	16.8699	17.8885	18.9771	20.1407	21.3843	24.1331	29.0017
13	13.8093	14.6803	15.6178	16.6268	17.7130	18.8821	20.1406	21.4953	22.9534	24.5227	28.0291	34.3519
14	14.9474	15.9739	17.0863	18.2919	19.5986	21.0151	22.5505	24.2149	26.0192	27.9750	32.3926	40.5047
15	16.0969	17.2934	18.5989	20.0236	21.5786	23.2760	25.1290	27.1521	29.3609	31.7725	37.2797	47.5804
16	17.2579	18.6393	20.1569	21.8245	23.6575	25.6725	27.8881	30.3243	33.0034	35.9497	42.7533	55.7175
17	18.4304	20.0121	21.7616	23.6975	25.8404	28.2129	30.8402	33.7502	36.9737	40.5447	48.8837	65.0751
18	19.6147	21.4123	23.4144	25.6454	28.1324	30.9057	33.9990	37.4502	41.3013	45.5992	55.7497	75.8364
19	20.8109	22.8406	25.1169	27.6712	30.5390	33.7600	37.3790	41.4463	46.0185	51.1591	63.4397	88.2118
20	22.0190	24.2974	26.8704	29.7781	33.0660	36.7856	40.9955	45.7620	51.1601	57.2750	72.0524	102.444
25	28.2432	32.0303	36.4593	41.6459	47.7271	54.8645	63.2490	73.1059	84.7009	98.3471	133.334	212.793
30	34.7849	40.5681	47.5754	56.0849	66.4388	79.0582	94.4608	113.283	136.308	164.494	241.333	434.745
35	41.6603	49.9945	60.4621	73.6522	90.3203	111.435	138.237	172.317	215.711	271.024	431.663	881.170
40	48.8864	60.4020	75.4013	95.0255	120.800	154.762	199.635	259.057	337.882	442.593	767.091	1,779.09

Glossary

Accelerated depreciation method Method that produces larger depreciation charges in the early years of an asset's life and smaller charges in its later years. *(p. 388)*

Account Record within an accounting system in which increases and decreases are entered and stored in a specific asset, liability, equity, revenue, or expense. *(p. 49)*

Account balance Difference between total debits and total credits (including the beginning balance) for an account. *(p. 53)*

Account form balance sheet Balance sheet that lists assets on the left side and liabilities and equity on the right. *(p. 18)*

Account payable Liability created by buying goods or services on credit; backed by the buyer's general credit standing. *(p. 50)*

Accounting Information and measurement system that identifies, records, and communicates relevant information about a company's business activities. *(p. 4)*

Accounting cycle Recurring steps performed each accounting period, starting with analyzing transactions and continuing through the post-closing trial balance (or reversing entries). *(p. 143)*

Accounting equation Equality involving a company's assets, liabilities, and equity; Assets = Liabilities + Equity; also called *balance sheet equation. (p. 12)*

Accounting information system People, records, and methods that collect and process data from transactions and events, organize them in useful forms, and communicate results to decision makers. *(p. 262)*

Accounting period Length of time covered by financial statements; also called *reporting period. (p. 94)*

Accounts payable ledger Subsidiary ledger listing individual creditor (supplier) accounts. *(p. 267)*

Accounts receivable Amounts due from customers for credit sales; backed by the customer's general credit standing. *(p. 350)*

Accounts receivable ledger Subsidiary ledger listing individual customer accounts. *(p. 267)*

Accounts receivable turnover Measure of both the quality and liquidity of accounts receivable; indicates how often receivables are received and collected during the period; computed by dividing net sales by average accounts receivable. *(p. 364)*

Accrual basis accounting Accounting system that recognizes revenues when earned and expenses when incurred; the basis for GAAP. *(p. 95)*

Accrued expenses Costs incurred in a period that are both unpaid and unrecorded; adjusting entries for recording accrued expenses involve increasing expenses and increasing liabilities. *(p. 101)*

Accrued revenues Revenues earned in a period that are both unrecorded and not yet received in cash (or other assets); adjusting entries for recording accrued revenues involve increasing assets and increasing revenues. *(p. 103)*

Accumulated depreciation Cumulative sum of all depreciation expense recorded for an asset. *(p. 99)*

Acid-test ratio Ratio used to assess a company's ability to settle its current debts with its most liquid assets; defined as quick assets (cash, short-term investments, and current receivables) divided by current liabilities. *(p. 193)*

Adjusted trial balance List of accounts and balances prepared after period-end adjustments are recorded and posted. *(p. 105)*

Adjusting entry Journal entry at the end of an accounting period to bring an asset or liability account to its proper amount and update the related expense or revenue account. *(p. 97)*

Aging of accounts receivable Process of classifying accounts receivable by how long they are past due for purposes of estimating uncollectible accounts. *(p. 358)*

Allowance for Doubtful Accounts Contra asset account with a balance approximating uncollectible accounts receivable; also called *Allowance for Uncollectible Accounts. (p. 355)*

Allowance method Procedure that (a) estimates and matches bad debts expense with its sales for the period and/or (b) reports accounts receivable at estimated realizable value. *(p. 354)*

Amortization Process of allocating the cost of an intangible asset to expense over its estimated useful life. *(p. 398)*

Annual financial statements Financial statements covering a one-year period; often based on a calendar year, but any consecutive 12-month (or 52-week) period is acceptable. *(p. 95)*

Annual report Summary of a company's financial results for the year with its current financial condition and future planes; directed to external users of financial information. *(p. A-1)*

Annuity Series of equal payments at equal intervals. *(p. 570)*

Assets Resources a business owns or controls that are expected to provide current and future benefits to the business. *(p. 12)*

Average cost See *weighted average. (p. 228)*

Bad debts Accounts of customers who do not pay what they have promised to pay; an expense of selling on credit; also called *uncollectible accounts. (p. 353)*

Balance column account Account with debit and credit columns for recording entries and another column for showing the balance of the account after each entry. *(p. 56)*

Balance sheet Financial statement that lists types and dollar amounts of assets, liabilities, and equity at a specific date. *(p. 17)*

Balance sheet equation (See *accounting equation.*) *(p. 12)*

Bank reconciliation Report that explains the difference between the book (company) balance of cash and the cash balance reported on the bank statement. *(p. 322)*

Bank statement Bank report on the depositor's beginning and ending cash balances, and a listing of its changes, for a period. *(p. 320)*

Batch processing Accumulating source documents for a period of time and then processing them all at once such as once a day, week, or month. *(p. 277)*

Betterments Expenditures to make a plant asset more efficient or productive; also called *improvements. (p. 393)*

Bookkeeping (See *recordkeeping.*) *(p. 5)*

Book value Asset's acquisition costs less its accumulated depreciation (or depletion, or amortization); also sometimes used synonymously as the *carrying value* of an account. *(p. 387)*

Business An organization of one or more individuals selling products and/or services for profit. *(p. 10)*

Business entity principle Principle that requires a business to be accounted for separately from its owner(s) and from any other entity. *(p. 10)*

C corporation Corporation that does not qualify for nor elect to be treated as a partnership for income tax purposes and therefore is subject to income taxes; also called *C corp. (p. 470)*

Canceled checks Checks that the bank has paid and deducted from the depositor's account. *(p. 321)*

Capital expenditures Additional costs of plant assets that provide material benefits extending beyond the current period; also called *balance sheet expenditures. (p. 392)*

Capitalize Record the cost as part of a permanent account and allocate it over later periods. *(p. 392)*

Cash Includes currency, coins, and amounts on deposit in bank checking or savings accounts. *(p. 312)*

Cash basis accounting Accounting system that recognizes revenues when cash is received and records expenses when cash is paid. *(p. 95)*

Cash disbursements journal Special journal normally used to record all payments of cash; also called *cash payments journal. (p. 274)*

Cash discount Reduction in the price of merchandise granted by a seller to a buyer when payment is made within the discount period. *(p. 181)*

Cash equivalents Short-term, investment assets that are readily convertible to a known cash amount or sufficiently close to their maturity date (usually within 90 days) so that market value is not sensitive to interest rate changes. *(p. 312)*

Cash Over and Short Income statement account used to record cash overages and cash shortages arising from errors in cash receipts or payments. *(p. 313)*

Cash receipts journal Special journal normally used to record all receipts of cash. *(p. 271)*

Change in an accounting estimate Change in an accounting estimate that results from new information, subsequent developments, or improved judgment that impacts current and future periods. *(p. 391)*

Chart of accounts List of accounts used by a company; includes an identification number for each account. *(p. 52)*

Check Document signed by a depositor instructing the bank to pay a specified amount to a designated recipient. *(p. 319)*

Check register Another name for a cash disbursements journal when the journal has a column for check numbers. *(p. 275 & 330)*

Classified balance sheet Balance sheet that presents assets and liabilities in relevant subgroups, including current and noncurrent classifications. *(p. 146)*

Closing entries Entries recorded at the end of each accounting period to transfer end-of-period balances in revenue, gain, expense, loss, and withdrawal (dividend for a corporation) accounts to the capital account (to retained earnings for a corporation). *(p. 141)*

Closing process Necessary end-of-period steps to prepare the accounts for recording the transactions of the next period. *(p. 140)*

Columnar journal Journal with more than one column. *(p. 268)*

Common stock Corporation's basic ownership share; also generically called *capital stock. (p. 11)*

Compatibility principle Information system principle that requires an accounting system to conform with a company's activities, personnel, and structure. *(p. 263)*

Compound journal entry Journal entry that affects at least three accounts. *(p. 59)*

Computer hardware Physical equipment in a computerized accounting information system. *(p. 277)*

Computer network Linkage giving different users and different computers access to common databases and programs. *(p. 277)*

Computer software Programs that direct operations of computer hardware. *(p. 276)*

Conservatism principle Principle that prescribes the less optimistic estimate when two estimates are about equally likely. *(p. 232)*

Consignee Receiver of goods owned by another who holds them for purposes of selling them for the owner. *(p. 222)*

Consignor Owner of goods who ships them to another party who will sell them for the owner. *(p. 222)*

Consistency principle Principle encouraging use of the same accounting method(s) over time so that financial statements are comparable across periods. *(p. 230)*

Contingent liability Obligation to make a future payment if, and only if, an uncertain future event occurs. *(p. 436)*

Contra account Account linked with another account and having an opposite normal balance; reported as a subtraction from the other account's balance. *(p. 99)*

Control principle Information system principle that requires an accounting system to aid managers in controlling and monitoring business activities. *(p. 262)*

Controlling account General ledger account, the balance of which (after posting) equals the sum of the balances in its related subsidiary ledger. *(p. 267)*

Copyright Right giving the owner the exclusive privilege to publish and sell musical, literary, or artistic work during the creator's life plus 70 years. *(p. 399)*

Corporation Business that is a separate legal entity under state or federal laws with owners called *shareholders* or *stockholders*. *(p. 11)*

Cost All normal and reasonable expenditures necessary to get an asset in place and ready for its intended use. *(p. 383)*

Cost-benefit principle Information system principle that requires the benefits from an activity in an accounting system to outweigh the costs of that activity. *(p. 263)*

Cost of goods available for sale Consists of beginning inventory plus net purchases of a period. *(p. 179)*

Cost of goods sold Cost of inventory sold to customers during a period; also called *cost of sales*. *(p. 179)*

Cost principle Accounting principle that requires financial statement information to be based on actual costs incurred in business transactions. *(p. 9)*

Credit Recorded on the right side; an entry that decreases asset and expense accounts, and increases liability, revenue, and most equity accounts; abbreviated Cr. *(p. 53)*

Credit memorandum Notification that the sender has credited the recipient's account in the sender's records. *(p. 187)*

Credit period Time period that can pass before a customer's payment is due. *(p. 181)*

Credit terms Description of the amounts and timing of payments that a buyer (debtor) agrees to make in the future. *(p. 181)*

Creditors Individuals or organizations entitled to receive payments. *(p. 50)*

Current assets Cash and other assets expected to be sold, collected, or used within one year or the company's operating cycle, whichever is longer. *(p. 146)*

Current liabilities Obligations due to be paid or settled within one year or the company's operating cycle, whichever is longer. *(p. 148 & 425)*

Current portion of long-term debt Portion of long-term debt due within one year or the operating cycle, whichever is longer; reported under current liabilities. *(p. 433)*

Current ratio Ratio used to evaluate a company's ability to pay its short-term obligations, calculated by dividing current assets by current liabilities. *(p. 148)*

Date of declaration Date the directors vote to pay a dividend. *(p. 506)*

Date of payment Date the corporation makes the dividend payment. *(p. 506)*

Days' sales in inventory Estimate of number of days needed to convert inventory into receivables or cash; equals ending inventory divided by cost of goods sold and then multiplied by 365; also called *days' stock on hand*. *(p. 234)*

Days' sales uncollected Measure of the liquidity of receivables computed by dividing the current balance of receivables by the annual credit (or net) sales and then multiplying by 365; also called *days' sales in receivables*. *(p. 325)*

Debit Recorded on the left side; an entry that increases asset and expense accounts, and decreases liability, revenue, and most equity accounts; abbreviated Dr. *(p. 53)*

Debit memorandum Notification that the sender has debited the recipient's account in the sender's records. *(p. 182)*

Debt ratio Ratio of total liabilities to total assets; used to reflect risk associated with a company's debts. *(p. 67)*

Debtors Individuals or organizations that owe money. *(p. 49)*

Declining-balance method Method that determines depreciation charge for the period by multiplying a depreciation rate (often twice the straight-line rate) by the asset's beginning-period book value. *(p. 388)*

Deferred income tax liability Corporation income taxes that are deferred until future years because of temporary differences between GAAP and tax rules. *(p. 447)*

Depletion Process of allocating the cost of natural resources to periods when they are consumed and sold. *(p. 397)*

Deposit ticket Lists items such as currency, coins, and checks deposited and their corresponding dollar amounts. *(p. 319)*

Deposits in transit Deposits recorded by the company but not yet by its bank. *(p. 322)*

Depreciable cost Cost of a plant asset less its salvage value. *(p. 386)*

Depreciation Expense created by allocating the cost of plant and equipment to periods in which they are used; represents the expense of using the asset. *(p. 385)*

Direct write-off method Method that records the loss from an uncollectible account receivable at the time it is determined to be uncollectible; no attempt is made to estimate bad debts. *(p. 354)*

Discount on note payable Difference between the face value of a note payable and the (lesser) amount borrowed; reflects the added interest to be paid on the note over its life.

Discount period Time period in which a cash discount is available and the buyer can make a reduced payment. *(p. 181)*

Discount rate Expected rate of return on investments; also called *cost of capital, hurdle rate,* or *required rate of return*. *(p. B-2)*

Discounts lost Expenses resulting from not taking advantage of cash discounts on purchases. *(p. 331)*

Double-declining-balance (DDB) depreciation Depreciation equals beginning book value multiplied by 2 times the straight-line rate. *(p. 388)*

Double-entry accounting Accounting system in which each transaction affects at least two accounts and has at least one debit and one credit. *(p. 53)*

Double taxation Corporate income is taxed and then its later distribution through dividends is normally taxed again for shareholders. *(p. 11)*

Earnings (See *net income*.) *(p. 13)*

Electronic funds transfer (EFT) Use of electronic communication to transfer cash from one party to another. *(p. 320)*

Employee benefits Additional compensation paid to or on behalf of employees, such as premiums for medical, dental, life, and disability insurance, and contributions to pension plans. *(p. 433)*

Employee earnings report Record of an employee's net pay, gross pay, deductions, and year-to-date payroll information. *(p. 444)*

Enterprise resource planning (ERP) software Programs that manage a company's vital operations, which range from order taking to production to accounting. *(p. 277)*

Entity Organization that, for accounting purposes, is separate from other organizations and individuals. *(p. 10)*

EOM Abbreviation for *end of month;* used to describe credit terms for credit transactions. *(p. 181)*

Equity Owner's claim on the assets of a business; equals the residual interest in an entity's assets after deducting liabilities; also called *net assets. (p. 12)*

Estimated liability Obligation of an uncertain amount that can be reasonably estimated. *(p. 433)*

Ethics Codes of conduct by which actions are judged as right or wrong, fair or unfair, honest or dishonest. *(p. 8)*

Events Happenings that both affect an organization's financial position and can be reliably measured. *(p. 13)*

Expanded accounting equation Assets = Liabilities + Equity; Equity equals [Owner capital − Owner withdrawals + Revenues − Expenses] for a noncorporation; Equity equals [Contributed capital + Retained earnings + Revenues − Expenses] for a corporation where dividends are subtracted from retained earnings. *(p. 13)*

Expenses Outflows or using up of assets as part of operations of a business to generate sales. *(p. 13)*

External transactions Exchanges of economic value between one entity and another entity. *(p. 13)*

External users Persons using accounting information who are not directly involved in running the organization. *(p. 5)*

Extraordinary repairs Major repairs that extend the useful life of a plant asset beyond prior expectations; treated as a capital expenditure. *(p. 393)*

Federal depository bank Bank authorized to accept deposits of amounts payable to the federal government. *(p. 442)*

Federal Insurance Contributions Act (FICA) Taxes Taxes assessed on both employers and employees; for Social Security and Medicare programs. *(p. 430)*

Federal Unemployment Taxes (FUTA) Payroll taxes on employers assessed by the federal government to support its unemployment insurance program. *(p. 432)*

Financial accounting Area of accounting mainly aimed at serving external users. *(p. 5)*

Financial Accounting Standards Board (FASB) Independent group of full-time members responsible for setting accounting rules. *(p. 9)*

Financial statements Includes the balance sheet, income statement, statement of owner's (or stockholder's) equity, and statement of cash flows. *(p. 17)*

First-in, first-out (FIFO) Method to assign cost to inventory that assumes items are sold in the order acquired; earliest items purchased are the first sold. *(p. 227)*

Fiscal year Consecutive 12-month (or 52-week) period chosen as the organization's annual accounting period. *(p. 95)*

Flexibility principle Information system principle that requires an accounting system be able to adapt to changes in the company, its operations, and needs of decision makers. *(p. 263)*

FOB Abbreviation for *free on board;* the point when ownership of goods passes to the buyer; *FOB shipping point* (or *factory*) means the buyer pays shipping costs and accepts ownership of goods when the seller transfers goods to carrier; *FOB destination* means the seller pays shipping costs and buyer accepts ownership of goods at the buyer's place of business. *(p. 183)*

Form 940 IRS form used to report an employer's federal unemployment taxes (FUTA) on an annual filing basis. *(p. 442)*

Form 941 IRS form filed to report FICA taxes owed and remitted. *(p. 440)*

Form 10-K (or 10-KSB) Annual report form filed with SEC by businesses (small businesses) with publicly-traded securities. *(p. A-1)*

Form W-2 Annual report by an employer to each employee showing the employee's wages subject to FICA and federal income taxes along with amounts withheld. *(p. 442)*

Form W-4 Withholding allowance certificate, filed with the employer, identifying the number of withholding allowances claimed. *(p. 444)*

Franchises Privileges granted by a company or government to sell a product or service under specified conditions. *(p. 400)*

Full-disclosure principle Principle that prescribes financial statements (including notes) to report all relevant information about an entity's operations and financial condition. *(p. 362)*

GAPP (See *generally accepted accounting principles.*) *(p. 9)*

General and administrative expenses Expenses that support the operating activities of a business. *(p. 191)*

General journal All-purpose journal for recording the debits and credits of transactions and events. *(p. 55 & 266)*

General ledger (See *ledger.*) *(p. 49)*

General partner Partner who assumes unlimited liability for the debts of the partnership; responsible for partnership management. *(p. 469)*

General partnership Partnership in which all partners have mutual agency and unlimited liability for partnership debts. *(p. 469)*

Generally accepted accounting principles (GAAP) Rules that specify acceptable accounting practices. *(p. 9)*

Generally accepted auditing standards (GAAS) Rules that specify acceptable auditing practices. *(p. 5 & 9)*

Going-concern principle Principle that requires financial statements to reflect the assumption that the business will continue operating. *(p. 10)*

Goodwill Amount by which a company's (or a segment's) value exceeds the value of its individual assets less its liabilities. *(p. 400)*

Gross margin (See *gross profit.*) *(p. 179)*

Gross margin ratio Gross margin (net sales minus cost of goods sold) divided by net sales; also called *gross profit ratio. (p. 193)*

Gross method Method of recording purchases at the full invoice price without deducting any cash discounts. *(p. 331)*

Gross pay Total compensation earned by an employee. *(p. 429)*

Gross profit Net sales minus cost of goods sold; also called *gross margin. (p. 179)*

Gross profit method Procedure to estimate inventory when the past gross profit rate is used to estimate cost of goods sold, which is then subtracted from the cost of goods available for sale. *(p. 244)*

Impairment Diminishment of an asset value. *(p. 399)*

Imprest system Method to account for petty cash; maintains a constant balance in the fund, which equals cash plus petty cash receipts. *(p. 316)*

Inadequacy Condition in which the capacity of plant assets is too small to meet the company's production demands. *(p. 385)*

Income (See *net income.*) *(p. 13)*

Income statement Financial statement that subtracts expenses from revenues to yield a net income or loss over a specified period of time; also includes any gains or losses. *(p. 17)*

Income Summary Temporary account used only in the closing process to which the balances of revenue and expense accounts (including any gains or losses) are transferred; its balance is transferred to the capital account (or retained earnings for a corporation). *(p. 141)*

Indefinite useful life Asset life that is not limited by legal, regulatory, contractural, competitive, economic, or other factors. *(p. 398)*

Information processor Component of an accounting system that interprets, transforms, and summarizes information for use in analysis and reporting. *(p. 264)*

Information storage Component of an accounting system that keeps data in a form accessible to information processors. *(p. 264)*

Input device Means of capturing information from source documents that enables its transfer to information processors. *(p. 264)*

Intangible assets Long-term assets (resources) used to produce or sell products or services; usually lack physical form and have uncertain benefits. *(p. 148 & 398)*

Interest Charge for using money (or other assets) loaned from one entity to another. *(p. 360)*

Interim financial statements Financial statements covering periods of less than one year; usually based on one-, three-, or six-month periods. *(p. 95 & 243)*

Internal control system All policies and procedures used to protect assets, ensure reliable accounting, promote efficient operations, and urge adherence to company policies. *(p. 262 & 308)*

Internal transactions Activities within an organization that can affect the accounting equation. *(p. 13)*

Internal users Persons using accounting information who are directly involved in managing the organization. *(p. 6)*

International Accounting Standards Board (IASB) Group that identifies preferred accounting practices and encourages global acceptance; issues International Financial Reporting Standards (IFRS). *(p. 9)*

Inventory Goods a company owns and expects to sell in its normal operations. *(p. 179)*

Inventory turnover Number of times a company's average inventory is sold during a period; computed by dividing cost of goods sold by average inventory; also called *merchandise turnover. (p. 233)*

Invoice Itemized record of goods prepared by the vendor that lists the customer's name, items sold, sales prices, and terms of sale. *(p. 328)*

Invoice approval Document containing a checklist of steps necessary for approving the recording and payment of an invoice; also called *check authorization. (p. 329)*

Journal Record in which transactions are entered before they are posted to ledger accounts; also called *book of original entry. (p. 55)*

Journalizing Process of recording transactions in a journal. *(p. 55)*

Known liabilities Obligations of a company with little uncertainty; set by agreements, contracts, or laws; also called *definitely determinable liabilities. (p. 426)*

Land improvements Assets that increase the benefits of land, have a limited useful life, and are depreciated. *(p. 384)*

Last-in, first-out (LIFO) Method to assign cost to inventory that assumes costs for the most recent items purchased are sold first and charged to cost of goods sold. *(p. 227)*

Lease Contract specifying the rental of property. *(p. 400)*

Leasehold Rights the lessor grants to the lessee under the terms of a lease. *(p. 400)*

Leasehold improvements Alterations or improvements to leased property such as partitions and storefronts. *(p. 400)*

Ledger Record containing all accounts (with amounts) for a business; also called *general ledger. (p. 49)*

Lessee Party to a lease who secures the right to possess and use the property from another party (the lessor). *(p. 400)*

Lessor Party to a lease who grants another party (the lessee) the right to possess and use its property. *(p. 400)*

Liabilities Creditors' claims on an organization's assets; involves a probable future payment of assets, products, or services that a company is obligated to make due to past transactions or events. *(p. 12)*

Licenses (See *franchises.*) *(p. 400)*

Limited liability Owner can lose no more than the amount invested. *(p. 11)*

Limited liability company Organization form that combines select features of a corporation and a limited partnership; provides limited liability to its members (owners), is free of business tax, and allows members to actively participate in management. *(p. 470)*

Limited liability partnership Partnership in which a partner is not personally liable for malpractice or negligence unless that partner is responsible for providing the service that resulted in the claim. *(p. 469)*

Limited partners Partners who have no personal liability for partnership debts beyond the amounts they invested in the partnership. *(p. 469)*

Limited partnership Partnership that has two classes of partners, limited partners and general partners. *(p. 469)*

Liquid assets Resources such as cash that are easily converted into other assets or used to pay for goods, services, or liabilities. *(p. 312)*

List price Catalog (full) price of an item before any trade discount is deducted. *(p. 180)*

Long-term investments Long-term assets not used in operating activities such as notes receivable and investments in stocks and bonds. *(p. 147)*

Long-term liabilities Obligations not due to be paid within one year or the operating cycle, whichever is longer. *(p. 148 & 425)*

Lower of cost or market (LCM) Required method to report inventory at market replacement cost when that market cost is lower than recorded cost. *(p. 231)*

Maker of the note Entity who signs a note and promises to pay it at maturity. *(p. 360)*

Managerial accounting Area of accounting mainly aimed at serving the decision-making needs of internal users; also called *management accounting. (p. 6)*

Manufacturer Company that uses labor and operating assets to convert raw materials to finished goods. *(p. 13)*

Matching principle Prescribes expenses to be reported in the same period as the revenues that were earned as a result of the expenses. *(p. 96 & 354)*

Materiality Prescribes that accounting for items that significantly impact financial statement and any inferences from them adhere strictly to GAAP. *(p. 354)*

Maturity date of a note Date when a note's principal and interest are due. *(p. 360)*

Merchandise (See *merchandise inventory.*) *(p. 178)*

Merchandise inventory Goods that a company owns and expects to sell to customers; also called *merchandise* or *inventory. (p. 179)*

Merchandiser Entity that earns net income by buying and selling merchandise. *(p. 178)*

Merit rating Rating assigned to an employer by a state based on the employer's record of employment. *(p. 432)*

Monetary unit principle Principle that assumes transactions and events can be expressed in money units. *(p. 10)*

Multiple-step income statement Income statement format that shows subtotals between sales and net income, categorizes expenses, and often reports the details of net sales and expenses. *(p. 190)*

Mutual agency Legal relationship among partners whereby each partner is an agent of the partnership and is able to bind the partnership to contracts within the scope of the partnership's business. *(p. 469)*

Natural business year Twelve-month period that ends when a company's sales activities are at their lowest point. *(p. 95)*

Natural resources Assets physically consumed when used; examples are timber, mineral deposits, and oil and gas fields; also called *wasting assets. (p. 397)*

Net assets (See *equity.*) *(p. 12)*

Net income Amount earned after subtracting all expenses necessary for and matched with sales for a period; also called *income, profit,* or *earnings. (p. 13)*

Net loss Excess of expenses over revenues for a period. *(p. 13)*

Net method Method of recording purchases at the full invoice price less any cash discounts. *(p. 331)*

Net pay Gross pay less all deductions; also called *take-home pay. (p. 430)*

Net realizable value Expected selling price (value) of an item minus the cost of making the sale. *(p. 223)*

Noninterest-bearing note Note with no stated (contract) rate of interest; interest is implicitly included in the note's face value.

Nonsufficient funds (NSF) check Maker's bank account has insufficient money to pay the check; also called *hot check. (p. 322)*

Note (See promissory note.) *(p. 359)*

Note payable Lability expressed by a written promise to pay a definite sum of money on demand or on a specific future date(s). *(p. 360)*

Note receivable Asset consisting of a written promise to receive a definite sum of money on demand or on a specific future date(s). *(p. 49)*

Objectivity principle Principle that prescribes independent, unbiased evidence to support financial statement information. *(p. 9)*

Obsolescence Condition in which, because of new inventions and improvements, a plant asset can no longer be used to produce goods or services with a competitive advantage. *(p. 385)*

Online processing Approach to inputting data from source documents as soon as the information is available. *(p. 277)*

Operating cycle Normal time between paying cash for merchandise or employee services and receiving cash from customers. *(p. 146)*

Ordinary repairs Repairs to keep a plant asset in normal, good operating condition; treated as a revenue expenditure and immediately expensed. *(p. 393)*

Output devices Means by which information is taken out of the accounting system and made available for use. *(p. 265)*

Outstanding checks Checks written and recorded by the depositor but not yet paid by the bank at the bank statement date. *(p. 322)*

Owner, capital Account showing the owner's claim on company assets; equals owner investments plus net income (or less net losses) minus owner withdrawals since the company's inception; also referred to as *equity. (p. 51)*

Owner investment Assets put into the business by the owner. *(p. 13)*

Owner's equity (See *equity.*) *(p. 12)*

Owner withdrawals (See *withdrawals.*) *(p. 13)*

Partner return on equity Partner net income divided by average partner equity for the period. *(p. 480)*

Partnership Unincorporated association of two or more persons to pursue a business for profit as co-owners. *(p. 10 & 468)*

Partnership contract Agreement among partners that sets terms under which the affairs of the partnership are conducted; also called *articles of partnership. (p. 468)*

Partnership liquidation Dissolution of a partnership by (1) selling noncash assets and allocating any gain or loss according to partners' income-and-loss ratio, (2) paying liabilities, and (3) distributing any remaining cash according to partners' capital balances. *(p. 478)*

Patent Exclusive right granted to its owner to produce and sell an item or to use a process for 17 years. *(p. 399)*

Payee of the note Entity to whom a note is made payable. *(p. 360)*

Payroll bank account Bank account used solely for paying employees; each pay period an amount equal to the total employees' net pay is deposited in it and the payroll checks are drawn on it. *(p. 446)*

Payroll deductions Amounts withheld from an employee's gross pay; also called *withholdings. (p. 430)*

Payroll register Record for a pay period that shows the pay period dates, regular and overtime hours worked, gross pay, net pay, and deductions. *(p. 442)*

Periodic inventory system Method that records the cost of inventory purchased but does not continuously track the quantity available or sold to customers; records are updated at the end of each period to reflect the physical count and costs of goods available. *(p. 180)*

Permanent accounts Accounts that reflect activities related to one or more future periods; balance sheet accounts whose balances are not closed; also called *real accounts. (p. 141)*

Perpetual inventory system Method that maintains continuous records of the cost of inventory available and the cost of goods sold. *(p. 179)*

Petty cash Small amount of cash in a fund to pay minor expenses; accounted for using an imprest system. *(p. 316)*

Plant assets Tangible long-lived assets used to produce or sell products and services; also called *property, plant and equipment (PP&E)* or *fixed assets. (p. 99 & 382)*

Post-closing trial balance List of permanent accounts and their balances from the ledger after all closing entries are journalized and posted. *(p. 143)*

Posting Process of transferring journal entry information to the ledger; computerized systems automate this process. *(p. 55)*

Posting reference (PR) column A column in journals in which individual ledger account numbers are entered when entries are posted to those ledger accounts. *(p. 56)*

Prepaid expenses Items paid for in advance of receiving their benefits; classified as assets. *(p. 97)*

Principal of a note Amount that the signer of a note agrees to pay back when it matures, not including interest. *(p. 360)*

Principles of internal control Principles prescribing management to establish responsibility, maintain records, insure assets, separate recordkeeping from custody of assets, divide responsibility for related transactions, apply technological controls, and perform reviews. *(p. 309)*

Pro forma financial statements Statements that show the effects of proposed transactions and events as if they had occurred. *(p. 140)*

Profit (See *net income.*) *(p. 13)*

Profit margin Ratio of a company's net income to its net sales; the percent of income in each dollar of revenue; also called *net profit margin. (p. 108)*

Promissory note (or **note**) Written promise to pay a specified amount either on demand or at a definite future date; is a *note receivable* for the lender but a *note payable* for the lendee. *(p. 359)*

Proprietorship (See *sole proprietorship.*) *(p. 10)*

Purchase discount Term used by a purchaser to describe a cash discount granted to the purchaser for paying within the discount period. *(p. 181)*

Purchase order Document used by the purchasing department to place an order with a seller (vendor). *(p. 328)*

Purchase requisition Document listing merchandise needed by a department and requesting it be purchased. *(p. 328)*

Purchases journal Journal normally used to record all purchases on credit. *(p. 273)*

Realizable value Expected proceeds from converting an asset into cash. *(p. 355)*

Receiving report Form used to report that ordered goods are received and to describe their quantity and condition. *(p. 329)*

Recordkeeping Part of accounting that involves recording transactions and events, either manually or electronically; also called *bookkeeping. (p. 5)*

Relevance principle Information system principle prescribing that its reports be useful, understandable, timely, and pertinent for decision making. *(p. 262)*

Report form balance sheet Balance sheet that lists accounts vertically in the order of assets, liabilities, and equity. *(p. 18)*

Retail inventory method Method to estimate ending inventory based on the ratio of the amount of goods for sale at cost to the amount of goods for sale at retail. *(p. 243)*

Retailer Intermediary that buys products from manufacturers or wholesalers and sells them to consumers. *(p. 178)*

Return Monies received from an investment; often in percent form. *(p. 23)*

Return on assets (See *return on total assets*) *(p. 20)*

Revenue expenditures Expenditures reported on the current income statement as an expense because they do not provide benefits in future periods. *(p. 392)*

Revenue recognition principle The principle prescribing that revenue is recognized when earned. *(p. 10)*

Revenues Gross increase in equity from a company's business activities that earn income; also called *sales. (p. 13)*

Reversing entries Optional entries recorded at the beginning of a period that prepare the accounts for the usual journal entries as if adjusting entries had not occurred in the prior period. *(p. 152)*

Risk Uncertainty about an expected return. *(p. 24)*

S corporation Corporation that meets special tax qualifications so as to be treated like a partnership for income tax purposes. *(p. 470)*

Sales (See *revenues.*) *(p. 13)*

Sales discount Term used by a seller to describe a cash discount granted to buyers who pay within the discount period. *(p. 181)*

Sales journal Journal normally used to record sales of goods on credit. *(p. 267)*

Salvage value Estimate of amount to be recovered at the end of an asset's useful life; also called *residual value* or *scrap value. (p. 385)*

Schedule of accounts payable List of the balances of all accounts in the accounts payable ledger and their total. *(p. 274)*

Schedule of accounts receivable List of balances for all accounts in the accounts receivable ledger and their total. *(p. 269)*

Securities and Exchange Commission (SEC) Federal agency Congress has charged to set reporting rules for organizations that sell ownership shares to the public. *(p. 9)*

Segment return on assets Segment operating income divided by segment average (identifiable) assets for the period. *(p. 278)*

Selling expenses Expenses of promoting sales, such as displaying and advertising merchandise, making sales, and delivering goods to customers. *(p. 191)*

Service company Organization that provides services instead of tangible products. *(p. 178)*

Shareholders Owners of a corporation; also called *stockholders. (p. 11)*

Shares Equity of a corporation divided into units; also called *stock. (p. 11)*

Short-term note payable Current obligation in the form of a written promissory note. *(p. 427)*

Shrinkage Inventory losses that occur as a result of theft or deterioration. *(p. 188)*

Signature card Includes the signatures of each person authorized to sign checks on the bank account. *(p. 319)*

Single-step income statement Income statement format that includes cost of goods sold as an expense and shows only one subtotal for total expenses. *(p. 192)*

Social responsibility Being accountable for the impact that one's actions might have on society. *(p. 8)*

Sole proprietorship Business owned by one person that is not organized as a corporation; also called *proprietorship. (p. 10)*

Source documents Source of information for accounting entries that can be in either paper or electronic form; also called *business papers. (p. 49)*

Special journal Any journal used for recording and posting transactions of a similar type. *(p. 266)*

Specific identification Method to assign cost to inventory when the purchase cost of each item in inventory is identified and used to compute cost of inventory. *(p. 225)*

Spreadsheet Computer program that organizes data by means of formulas and format; also called *electronic work sheet. (p. 136)*

State Unemployment Taxes (SUTA) State payroll taxes on employers to support its unemployment programs. *(p. 432)*

Statement of cash flows A financial statement that lists cash inflows (receipts) and cash outflows (payments) during a period; arranged by operating, investing, and financing. *(p. 17)*

Statement of owner's equity Report of changes in equity over a period; adjusted for increases (owner investment and net income) and for decreases (withdrawals and net loss). *(p. 17)*

Statement of partners' equity Financial statement that shows total capital balances at the beginning of the period, any additional investment by partners, the income or loss of the period, the partners' withdrawals, and the partners' ending capital balances; also called *statement of partners' capital. (p. 473)*

Statements of Financial Accounting Standards (SFAS) FASB publications that establish U.S. GAAP. *(p. 9)*

Stock (See *shares.*) *(p. 11)*

Stockholders (See *shareholders.*) *(p. 11)*

Straight-line depreciation Method that allocates an equal portion of the depreciable cost of plant asset (cost minus salvage) to each accounting period in its useful life. *(p. 99 & 386)*

Subsidiary ledger List of individual sub-accounts and amounts with a common characteristic; linked to a controlling account in the general ledger. *(p. 266)*

Supplementary records Information outside the usual accounting records; also called *supplemental records. (p. 184)*

T-account Tool used to show the effects of transactions and events on individual accounts. *(p. 53)*

Temporary accounts Accounts used to record revenues, expenses, and withdrawals (dividends for a corporation); they are closed at the end of each period; also called *nominal accounts. (p. 141)*

Time period principle Assumption that an organization's activities can be divided into specific time periods such as months, quarters, or years. *(p. 94)*

Times interest earned Ratio of income before interest expense (and any income taxes) divided by interest expense; reflects risk of covering interest commitments when income varies. *(p. 437)*

Total asset turnover Measure of a company's ability to use its assets to generate sales; computed by dividing net sales by average total assets. *(p. 401)*

Trade discount Reduction from a list or catalog price that can vary for wholesalers, retailers, and consumers. *(p. 180)*

Trademark or **Trade (Brand) name** Symbol, name, phrase, or jingle identified with a company, product, or service. *(p. 400)*

Transaction Exchange of economic consideration affecting an entity's financial position that can be reliably measured. *(p. 13)*

Trial balance List of accounts and their balances at a point in time; total debit balances equal total credit balances. *(p. 63)*

Unadjusted trial balance List of accounts and balances prepared before accounting adjustments are recorded and posted. *(p. 105)*

Unclassified balance sheet Balance sheet that broadly groups assets, liabilities, and equity accounts. *(p. 146)*

Unearned revenue Liability created when customers pay in advance for products or services; earned when the products or services are later delivered. *(p. 51 & 100)*

Units-of-production depreciation Method that charges a varying amount to depreciation expense for each period of an asset's useful life depending on its usage. *(p. 387)*

Unlimited liability Legal relationship among general partners that makes each of them responsible for partnership debts if the other partners are unable to pay their shares. *(p. 469)*

Useful life Length of time an asset will be productively used in the operations of a business; also called *service life. (p. 385)*

Vendee Buyer of goods or services. *(p. 328)*

Vendor Seller of goods or services. *(p. 328)*

Voucher Internal file used to store documents and information to control cash disbursements and to ensure that a transaction is properly authorized and recorded. *(p. 315)*

Voucher system Procedures and approvals designed to control cash disbursements and acceptance of obligations. *(p. 315)*

Wage bracket withholding table Table of the amounts of income tax withheld from employees' wages. *(p. 444)*

Warranty Agreement that obligates the seller to correct or replace a product or service when it fails to perform properly within a specified period. *(p. 434)*

Weighted average Method to assign inventory cost to sales; the cost of available-for-sale units is divided by the number of units available to determine per unit cost prior to each sale that is then multiplied by the units sold to yield the cost of that sale. *(p. 228)*

Wholesaler Intermediary that buys products from manufacturers or other wholesalers and sells them to retailers or other wholesalers. *(p. 178)*

Withdrawals Payment of cash or other assets from a proprietorship or partnership to its owner or owners. *(p. 13)*

Work sheet Spreadsheet used to draft an unadjusted trial balance, adjusting entries, adjusted trial balance, and financial statements. *(p. 136)*

Working papers Analyses and other informal reports prepared by accountants and managers when organizing information for formal reports and financial statements. *(p. 136)*

Credits

Page 2 © Neal Stafford/The Chocolate Farm, LLC
Page 6 © Reuters/New Media CORBIS
Page 10 top AP/Wide World Photos
Page 10 bottom AP/Wide World Photos
Page 11 AP/Wide World Photos

Page 46 Courtesy of York Entertainment, Inc.
Page 51 AP/Wide World Photos
Page 64 © David Young-Wolff/PhotoEdit

Page 92 left and right Courtesy of Mellies
Page 95 AP/Wide World Photos
Page 96 © Getty Images
Page 108 © ASHBY DON/CORBIS SYGMA

Page 134 Courtesy of Premier Snowskates
Page 143 © Firefly Productions/CORBIS
Page 146 © Peter Barrett/CORBIS

Page 176 Courtesy of Damani Dada
Page 180 © Flip Chalfant/Getty Images/The Image Bank
Page 183 © David Woods/CORBIS
Page 186 top © David Young-Wolff/PhotoEdit
Page 186 bottom © Robert Ginn/Index Stock Imagery, Inc.
Page 192 © Martin Harvey; Gallo Images/CORBIS

Page 220 Courtesy of FunKo, Inc.
Page 223 ©Kwame Zikomo/SuperStock
Page 229 AP/Wide World Photos
Page 230 AP/Wide World Photos

Page 260 left and right Zach Cordner/Courtesy of Rap-Up
Page 264 top AP/Wide World Photos
Page 264 bottom AP/Wide World Photos
Page 265 © Benjamin Shearn/Getty Images/Taxi
Page 267 © Duomo/CORBIS
Page 272 PhotoDisc Blue/Getty Images
Page 276 (c) Ralph Mercer/Getty Images/Stone
Page 277 © 1997–1998 Federal Express Corporation. All Rights Reserved.

Page 306 left Courtesy of Dylan's Candy Bar
Page 306 right Courtesy of Dylan's Candy Bar
Page 310 © Lawrence Manning/CORBIS
Page 311 PhotoDisc Green/Getty Images
Page 313 © Bob Rowan/CORBIS
Page 314 © Darrell Gulin/CORBIS

Page 348 left Courtesy of Manzi Metals Inc.
Page 348 right © James L. Amos/CORBIS
Page 352 © Topham/The Image Works
Page 353 © David McNew/Getty Images
Page 358 ©Thierry Dosogne/Getty Images/The Image Bank
Page 364 © Royalty Free/Corbis

Page 380 left © Cable Risdon Photography/Courtesy of Queston Construction
Page 380 right © photolibrary.com pty. ltd../Index Stock Photography
Page 383 AP/Wide World Photos
Page 384 © Michael J. Doolittle/The Image Works
Page 386 © Neil Rabinowitz/Corbis
Page 391 AP/Wide World Photos
Page 393 © DOUG KNUTSON/Time Life Pictures/Getty Images
Page 397 © Jan Stromme/PhotoEdit
Page 399 AP/Wide World Photos

Page 422 © Doby Photography
Page 427 AP/Wide World Photos
Page 429 © Michael Keller/Corbis
Page 433 AP/Wide World Photos
Page 436 © David Muench/Getty Images/Stone

Page 466 Courtesy of KOCH Entertainment
Page 469 AP/Wide World Photos
Page 471 © James L. Amos/Corbis
Page 474 © Rick Doyle/Corbis
Page 477 © Chuck Keeler, Jr./Corbis

Index

Note: Page numbers followed by *n* indicate material found in footnotes. Items in **boldface** type indicate defined terms; underlined items are URLs.

Chart of Accounts

Following is a typical chart of accounts. Each company has its own unique accounts and numbering system.

Assets

Current Assets

101 Cash
102 Petty cash
103 Cash equivalents
104 Short-term investments
105 Market adjustment, _______ securities (S-T)
106 Accounts receivable
107 Allowance for doubtful accounts
108 Legal fees receivable
109 Interest receivable
110 Rent receivable
111 Notes receivable
119 Merchandise inventory
120 __________ inventory
121 __________ inventory
124 Office supplies
125 Store supplies
126 _______ supplies
128 Prepaid insurance
129 Prepaid interest
131 Prepaid rent
132 Raw materials inventory
133 Goods in process inventory, _______
134 Goods in process inventory, _______
135 Finished goods inventory

Long-Term Investments

141 Long-term investments
142 Market adjustment, _______ securities (L-T)
144 Investment in _______
145 Bond sinking fund

Plant Assets

151 Automobiles
152 Accumulated depreciation—Automobiles
153 Trucks
154 Accumulated depreciation—Trucks
155 Boats
156 Accumulated depreciation—Boats
157 Professional library
158 Accumulated depreciation—Professional library
159 Law library
160 Accumulated depreciation—Law library
161 Furniture
162 Accumulated depreciation—Furniture
163 Office equipment
164 Accumulated depreciation—Office equipment
165 Store equipment
166 Accumulated depreciation—Store equipment
167 _______ equipment
168 Accumulated depreciation—_______ equipment
169 Machinery
170 Accumulated depreciation—Machinery
173 Building _______
174 Accumulated depreciation—Building _______
175 Building _______
176 Accumulated depreciation—Building _______
179 Land improvements _______
180 Accumulated depreciation—Land improvements _______
181 Land improvements _______
182 Accumulated depreciation—Land improvements _______
183 Land

Natural Resources

185 Mineral deposit
186 Accumulated depletion—Mineral deposit

Intangible Assets

191 Patents
192 Leasehold
193 Franchise
194 Copyrights
195 Leasehold improvements
196 Licenses
197 Accumulated amortization—_______

Liabilities

Current Liabilities

201 Accounts payable
202 Insurance payable
203 Interest payable
204 Legal fees payable
207 Office salaries payable
208 Rent payable
209 Salaries payable
210 Wages payable
211 Accrued payroll payable
214 Estimated warranty liability
215 Income taxes payable
216 Common dividend payable
217 Preferred dividend payable
218 State unemployment taxes payable
219 Employee federal income taxes payable
221 Employee medical insurance payable
222 Employee retirement program payable
223 Employee union dues payable
224 Federal unemployment taxes payable
225 FICA taxes payable
226 Estimated vacation pay liability

Unearned Revenues

230 Unearned consulting fees
231 Unearned legal fees
232 Unearned property management fees
233 Unearned _______ fees
234 Unearned _______ fees
235 Unearned janitorial revenue
236 Unearned _______ revenue
238 Unearned rent

Notes Payable

240 Short-term notes payable
241 Discount on short-term notes payable
245 Notes payable
251 Long-term notes payable
252 Discount on long-term notes payable

Long-Term Liabilities

253 Long-term lease liability
255 Bonds payable
256 Discount on bonds payable
257 Premium on bonds payable
258 Deferred income tax liability

Equity

Owner's Equity

301 _____________, Capital
302 _____________, Withdrawals
303 _____________, Capital
304 _____________, Withdrawals
305 _____________, Capital
306 _____________, Withdrawals

Contributed Capital

307 Common stock, $ _______ par value
308 Common stock, no-par value
309 Common stock, $ _______ stated value
310 Common stock dividend distributable
311 Contributed capital in excess of par value, Common stock
312 Contributed capital in excess of stated value, No-par common stock
313 Contributed capital from retirement of common stock
314 Contributed capital, Treasury stock
315 Preferred stock
316 Contributed capital in excess of par value, Preferred stock

Retained Earnings

318 Retained earnings
319 Cash dividends (or Dividends)
320 Stock dividends

Other Equity Accounts

321 Treasury stock, Common
322 Unrealized gain—Equity
323 Unrealized loss—Equity

Revenues

401 ____________ fees earned
402 ____________ fees earned
403 ____________ services revenue
404 ____________ services revenue
405 Commissions earned
406 Rent revenue (or Rent earned)
407 Dividends revenue (or Dividend earned)
408 Earnings from investment in ______
409 Interest revenue (or Interest earned)
410 Sinking fund earnings
413 Sales
414 Sales returns and allowances
415 Sales discounts

Cost of Sales

Cost of Goods Sold

502 Cost of goods sold
505 Purchases
506 Purchases returns and allowances
507 Purchases discounts
508 Transportation-in

Manufacturing

520 Raw materials purchases
521 Freight-in on raw materials
530 Factory payroll
531 Direct labor
540 Factory overhead
541 Indirect materials
542 Indirect labor
543 Factory insurance expired
544 Factory supervision
545 Factory supplies used
546 Factory utilities
547 Miscellaneous production costs
548 Property taxes on factory building
549 Property taxes on factory equipment
550 Rent on factory building
551 Repairs, factory equipment
552 Small tools written off
560 Depreciation of factory equipment
561 Depreciation of factory building

Standard Cost Variance

580 Direct material quantity variance
581 Direct material price variance
582 Direct labor quantity variance
583 Direct labor price variance
584 Factory overhead volume variance
585 Factory overhead controllable variance

Expenses

Amortization, Depletion, and Depreciation

601 Amortization expense—______
602 Amortization expense—______
603 Depletion expense—______
604 Depreciation expense—Boats
605 Depreciation expense—Automobiles
606 Depreciation expense—Building ______
607 Depreciation expense—Building ______
608 Depreciation expense—Land improvements ______
609 Depreciation expense—Land improvements ______
610 Depreciation expense—Law library
611 Depreciation expense—Trucks
612 Depreciation expense—______ equipment
613 Depreciation expense—______ equipment
614 Depreciation expense—______
615 Depreciation expense—______

Employee-Related Expenses

620 Office salaries expense
621 Sales salaries expense
622 Salaries expense
623 ______ wages expense
624 Employees' benefits expense
625 Payroll taxes expense

Financial Expenses

630 Cash over and short
631 Discounts lost
632 Factoring fee expense
633 Interest expense

Insurance Expenses

635 Insurance expense—Delivery equipment
636 Insurance expense—Office equipment
637 Insurance expense—______

Rental Expenses

640 Rent expense
641 Rent expense—Office space
642 Rent expense—Selling space
643 Press rental expense
644 Truck rental expense
645 ______ rental expense

Supplies Expenses

650 Office supplies expense
651 Store supplies expense
652 ______ supplies expense
653 ______ supplies expense

Miscellaneous Expenses

655 Advertising expense
656 Bad debts expense
657 Blueprinting expense
658 Boat expense
659 Collection expense
661 Concessions expense
662 Credit card expense
663 Delivery expense
664 Dumping expense
667 Equipment expense
668 Food and drinks expense
671 Gas and oil expense
672 General and administrative expense
673 Janitorial expense
674 Legal fees expense
676 Mileage expense
677 Miscellaneous expenses
678 Mower and tools expense
679 Operating expense
680 Organization expense
681 Permits expense
682 Postage expense
683 Property taxes expense
684 Repairs expense—______
685 Repairs expense—______
687 Selling expense
688 Telephone expense
689 Travel and entertainment expense
690 Utilities expense
691 Warranty expense
695 Income taxes expense

Gains and Losses

701 Gain on retirement of bonds
702 Gain on sale of machinery
703 Gain on sale of investments
704 Gain on sale of trucks
705 Gain on ______
706 Foreign exchange gain or loss
801 Loss on disposal of machinery
802 Loss on exchange of equipment
803 Loss on exchange of ______
804 Loss on sale of notes
805 Loss on retirement of bonds
806 Loss on sale of investments
807 Loss on sale of machinery
808 Loss on ______
809 Unrealized gain—Income
810 Unrealized loss—Income

Clearing Accounts

901 Income summary
902 Manufacturing summary

A Rose by Any Other Name

The same financial statement sometimes receives different titles. Below are some of the more common aliases.†

Balance Sheet	Statement of Financial Position Statement of Financial Condition
Income Statement	Statement of Income Operating Statement Statement of Operations Statement of Operating Activity Earnings Statement Statement of Earnings Profit and Loss (P&L) Statement
Statement of Cash Flows	Statement of Cash Flow Cash Flows Statement Statement of Changes in Cash Position Statement of Changes in Financial Position
Statement of Owner's Equity	Statement of Changes in Owner's Equity Statement of Changes in Owner's Capital Statement of Shareholders' Equity* Statement of Changes in Shareholders' Equity* Statement of Changes in Capital Accounts*

† The term "**Consolidated**" often precedes or follows these statement titles to reflect the combination of different entities, such as a parent company and its subsidiaries.
* Corporation only.

We thank Dr. Louella Moore from Arkansas State University for suggesting this listing.